T0189286

Lecture Notes in Computer Science   12364

More information about this series at http://www.springer.com/series/7412

Andrea Vedaldi · Horst Bischof ·
Thomas Brox · Jan-Michael Frahm (Eds.)

Computer Vision – ECCV 2020

16th European Conference
Glasgow, UK, August 23–28, 2020
Proceedings, Part XIX

Springer

Editors
Andrea Vedaldi ⓘ
University of Oxford
Oxford, UK

Horst Bischof ⓘ
Graz University of Technology
Graz, Austria

Thomas Brox ⓘ
University of Freiburg
Freiburg im Breisgau, Germany

Jan-Michael Frahm
University of North Carolina at Chapel Hill
Chapel Hill, NC, USA

ISSN 0302-9743   ISSN 1611-3349 (electronic)
Lecture Notes in Computer Science
ISBN 978-3-030-58528-0   ISBN 978-3-030-58529-7 (eBook)
https://doi.org/10.1007/978-3-030-58529-7

LNCS Sublibrary: SL6 – Image Processing, Computer Vision, Pattern Recognition, and Graphics

This Springer imprint is published by the registered company Springer Nature Switzerland AG
The registered company address is: Gewerbestrasse 11, 6330 Cham, Switzerland

Foreword

Hosting the European Conference on Computer Vision (ECCV 2020) was certainly an exciting journey. From the 2016 plan to hold it at the Edinburgh International Conference Centre (hosting 1,800 delegates) to the 2018 plan to hold it at Glasgow's Scottish Exhibition Centre (up to 6,000 delegates), we finally ended with moving online because of the COVID-19 outbreak. While possibly having fewer delegates than expected because of the online format, ECCV 2020 still had over 3,100 registered participants.

Although online, the conference delivered most of the activities expected at a face-to-face conference: peer-reviewed papers, industrial exhibitors, demonstrations, and messaging between delegates. In addition to the main technical sessions, the conference included a strong program of satellite events with 16 tutorials and 44 workshops.

Furthermore, the online conference format enabled new conference features. Every paper had an associated teaser video and a longer full presentation video. Along with the papers and slides from the videos, all these materials were available the week before the conference. This allowed delegates to become familiar with the paper content and be ready for the live interaction with the authors during the conference week. The live event consisted of brief presentations by the oral and spotlight authors and industrial sponsors. Question and answer sessions for all papers were timed to occur twice so delegates from around the world had convenient access to the authors.

As with ECCV 2018, authors' draft versions of the papers appeared online with open access, now on both the Computer Vision Foundation (CVF) and the European Computer Vision Association (ECVA) websites. An archival publication arrangement was put in place with the cooperation of Springer. SpringerLink hosts the final version of the papers with further improvements, such as activating reference links and supplementary materials. These two approaches benefit all potential readers: a version available freely for all researchers, and an authoritative and citable version with additional benefits for SpringerLink subscribers. We thank Alfred Hofmann and Aliaksandr Birukou from Springer for helping to negotiate this agreement, which we expect will continue for future versions of ECCV.

August 2020

Vittorio Ferrari
Bob Fisher
Cordelia Schmid
Emanuele Trucco

Preface

Welcome to the proceedings of the European Conference on Computer Vision (ECCV 2020). This is a unique edition of ECCV in many ways. Due to the COVID-19 pandemic, this is the first time the conference was held online, in a virtual format. This was also the first time the conference relied exclusively on the Open Review platform to manage the review process. Despite these challenges ECCV is thriving. The conference received 5,150 valid paper submissions, of which 1,360 were accepted for publication (27%) and, of those, 160 were presented as spotlights (3%) and 104 as orals (2%). This amounts to more than twice the number of submissions to ECCV 2018 (2,439). Furthermore, CVPR, the largest conference on computer vision, received 5,850 submissions this year, meaning that ECCV is now 87% the size of CVPR in terms of submissions. By comparison, in 2018 the size of ECCV was only 73% of CVPR.

The review model was similar to previous editions of ECCV; in particular, it was double blind in the sense that the authors did not know the name of the reviewers and vice versa. Furthermore, each conference submission was held confidentially, and was only publicly revealed if and once accepted for publication. Each paper received at least three reviews, totalling more than 15,000 reviews. Handling the review process at this scale was a significant challenge. In order to ensure that each submission received as fair and high-quality reviews as possible, we recruited 2,830 reviewers (a 130% increase with reference to 2018) and 207 area chairs (a 60% increase). The area chairs were selected based on their technical expertise and reputation, largely among people that served as area chair in previous top computer vision and machine learning conferences (ECCV, ICCV, CVPR, NeurIPS, etc.). Reviewers were similarly invited from previous conferences. We also encouraged experienced area chairs to suggest additional chairs and reviewers in the initial phase of recruiting.

Despite doubling the number of submissions, the reviewer load was slightly reduced from 2018, from a maximum of 8 papers down to 7 (with some reviewers offering to handle 6 papers plus an emergency review). The area chair load increased slightly, from 18 papers on average to 22 papers on average.

Conflicts of interest between authors, area chairs, and reviewers were handled largely automatically by the Open Review platform via their curated list of user profiles. Many authors submitting to ECCV already had a profile in Open Review. We set a paper registration deadline one week before the paper submission deadline in order to encourage all missing authors to register and create their Open Review profiles well on time (in practice, we allowed authors to create/change papers arbitrarily until the submission deadline). Except for minor issues with users creating duplicate profiles, this allowed us to easily and quickly identify institutional conflicts, and avoid them, while matching papers to area chairs and reviewers.

Papers were matched to area chairs based on: an affinity score computed by the Open Review platform, which is based on paper titles and abstracts, and an affinity score computed by the Toronto Paper Matching System (TPMS), which is based on the paper's full text, the area chair bids for individual papers, load balancing, and conflict avoidance. Open Review provides the program chairs a convenient web interface to experiment with different configurations of the matching algorithm. The chosen configuration resulted in about 50% of the assigned papers to be highly ranked by the area chair bids, and 50% to be ranked in the middle, with very few low bids assigned.

Assignments to reviewers were similar, with two differences. First, there was a maximum of 7 papers assigned to each reviewer. Second, area chairs recommended up to seven reviewers per paper, providing another highly-weighed term to the affinity scores used for matching.

The assignment of papers to area chairs was smooth. However, it was more difficult to find suitable reviewers for all papers. Having a ratio of 5.6 papers per reviewer with a maximum load of 7 (due to emergency reviewer commitment), which did not allow for much wiggle room in order to also satisfy conflict and expertise constraints. We received some complaints from reviewers who did not feel qualified to review specific papers and we reassigned them wherever possible. However, the large scale of the conference, the many constraints, and the fact that a large fraction of such complaints arrived very late in the review process made this process very difficult and not all complaints could be addressed.

Reviewers had six weeks to complete their assignments. Possibly due to COVID-19 or the fact that the NeurIPS deadline was moved closer to the review deadline, a record 30% of the reviews were still missing after the deadline. By comparison, ECCV 2018 experienced only 10% missing reviews at this stage of the process. In the subsequent week, area chairs chased the missing reviews intensely, found replacement reviewers in their own team, and managed to reach 10% missing reviews. Eventually, we could provide almost all reviews (more than 99.9%) with a delay of only a couple of days on the initial schedule by a significant use of emergency reviews. If this trend is confirmed, it might be a major challenge to run a smooth review process in future editions of ECCV. The community must reconsider prioritization of the time spent on paper writing (the number of submissions increased a lot despite COVID-19) and time spent on paper reviewing (the number of reviews delivered in time decreased a lot presumably due to COVID-19 or NeurIPS deadline). With this imbalance the peer-review system that ensures the quality of our top conferences may break soon.

Reviewers submitted their reviews independently. In the reviews, they had the opportunity to ask questions to the authors to be addressed in the rebuttal. However, reviewers were told not to request any significant new experiment. Using the Open Review interface, authors could provide an answer to each individual review, but were also allowed to cross-reference reviews and responses in their answers. Rather than PDF files, we allowed the use of formatted text for the rebuttal. The rebuttal and initial reviews were then made visible to all reviewers and the primary area chair for a given paper. The area chair encouraged and moderated the reviewer discussion. During the discussions, reviewers were invited to reach a consensus and possibly adjust their ratings as a result of the discussion and of the evidence in the rebuttal.

After the discussion period ended, most reviewers entered a final rating and recommendation, although in many cases this did not differ from their initial recommendation. Based on the updated reviews and discussion, the primary area chair then made a preliminary decision to accept or reject the paper and wrote a justification for it (meta-review). Except for cases where the outcome of this process was absolutely clear (as indicated by the three reviewers and primary area chairs all recommending clear rejection), the decision was then examined and potentially challenged by a secondary area chair. This led to further discussion and overturning a small number of preliminary decisions. Needless to say, there was no in-person area chair meeting, which would have been impossible due to COVID-19.

Area chairs were invited to observe the consensus of the reviewers whenever possible and use extreme caution in overturning a clear consensus to accept or reject a paper. If an area chair still decided to do so, she/he was asked to clearly justify it in the meta-review and to explicitly obtain the agreement of the secondary area chair. In practice, very few papers were rejected after being confidently accepted by the reviewers.

This was the first time Open Review was used as the main platform to run ECCV. In 2018, the program chairs used CMT3 for the user-facing interface and Open Review internally, for matching and conflict resolution. Since it is clearly preferable to only use a single platform, this year we switched to using Open Review in full. The experience was largely positive. The platform is highly-configurable, scalable, and open source. Being written in Python, it is easy to write scripts to extract data programmatically. The paper matching and conflict resolution algorithms and interfaces are top-notch, also due to the excellent author profiles in the platform. Naturally, there were a few kinks along the way due to the fact that the ECCV Open Review configuration was created from scratch for this event and it differs in substantial ways from many other Open Review conferences. However, the Open Review development and support team did a fantastic job in helping us to get the configuration right and to address issues in a timely manner as they unavoidably occurred. We cannot thank them enough for the tremendous effort they put into this project.

Finally, we would like to thank everyone involved in making ECCV 2020 possible in these very strange and difficult times. This starts with our authors, followed by the area chairs and reviewers, who ran the review process at an unprecedented scale. The whole Open Review team (and in particular Melisa Bok, Mohit Unyal, Carlos Mondragon Chapa, and Celeste Martinez Gomez) worked incredibly hard for the entire duration of the process. We would also like to thank René Vidal for contributing to the adoption of Open Review. Our thanks also go to Laurent Charling for TPMS and to the program chairs of ICML, ICLR, and NeurIPS for cross checking double submissions. We thank the website chair, Giovanni Farinella, and the CPI team (in particular Ashley Cook, Miriam Verdon, Nicola McGrane, and Sharon Kerr) for promptly adding material to the website as needed in the various phases of the process. Finally, we thank the publication chairs, Albert Ali Salah, Hamdi Dibeklioglu, Metehan Doyran, Henry Howard-Jenkins, Victor Prisacariu, Siyu Tang, and Gul Varol, who managed to compile these substantial proceedings in an exceedingly compressed schedule. We express our thanks to the ECVA team, in particular Kristina Scherbaum for allowing open access of the proceedings. We thank Alfred Hofmann from Springer who again serve as the publisher. Finally, we thank the other chairs of ECCV 2020, including in particular the general chairs for very useful feedback with the handling of the program.

August 2020   Andrea Vedaldi
                                                               Horst Bischof
                                                               Thomas Brox
                                                          Jan-Michael Frahm

Organization

General Chairs

Vittorio Ferrari   Google Research, Switzerland
Bob Fisher   University of Edinburgh, UK
Cordelia Schmid   Google and Inria, France
Emanuele Trucco   University of Dundee, UK

Program Chairs

Andrea Vedaldi   University of Oxford, UK
Horst Bischof   Graz University of Technology, Austria
Thomas Brox   University of Freiburg, Germany
Jan-Michael Frahm   University of North Carolina, USA

Industrial Liaison Chairs

Jim Ashe   University of Edinburgh, UK
Helmut Grabner   Zurich University of Applied Sciences, Switzerland
Diane Larlus   NAVER LABS Europe, France
Cristian Novotny   University of Edinburgh, UK

Local Arrangement Chairs

Yvan Petillot   Heriot-Watt University, UK
Paul Siebert   University of Glasgow, UK

Academic Demonstration Chair

Thomas Mensink   Google Research and University of Amsterdam, The Netherlands

Poster Chair

Stephen Mckenna   University of Dundee, UK

Technology Chair

Gerardo Aragon Camarasa   University of Glasgow, UK

Tutorial Chairs

Carlo Colombo	University of Florence, Italy
Sotirios Tsaftaris	University of Edinburgh, UK

Publication Chairs

Albert Ali Salah	Utrecht University, The Netherlands
Hamdi Dibeklioglu	Bilkent University, Turkey
Metehan Doyran	Utrecht University, The Netherlands
Henry Howard-Jenkins	University of Oxford, UK
Victor Adrian Prisacariu	University of Oxford, UK
Siyu Tang	ETH Zurich, Switzerland
Gul Varol	University of Oxford, UK

Website Chair

Giovanni Maria Farinella	University of Catania, Italy

Workshops Chairs

Adrien Bartoli	University of Clermont Auvergne, France
Andrea Fusiello	University of Udine, Italy

Area Chairs

Lourdes Agapito	University College London, UK
Zeynep Akata	University of Tübingen, Germany
Karteek Alahari	Inria, France
Antonis Argyros	University of Crete, Greece
Hossein Azizpour	KTH Royal Institute of Technology, Sweden
Joao P. Barreto	Universidade de Coimbra, Portugal
Alexander C. Berg	University of North Carolina at Chapel Hill, USA
Matthew B. Blaschko	KU Leuven, Belgium
Lubomir D. Bourdev	WaveOne, Inc., USA
Edmond Boyer	Inria, France
Yuri Boykov	University of Waterloo, Canada
Gabriel Brostow	University College London, UK
Michael S. Brown	National University of Singapore, Singapore
Jianfei Cai	Monash University, Australia
Barbara Caputo	Politecnico di Torino, Italy
Ayan Chakrabarti	Washington University, St. Louis, USA
Tat-Jen Cham	Nanyang Technological University, Singapore
Manmohan Chandraker	University of California, San Diego, USA
Rama Chellappa	Johns Hopkins University, USA
Liang-Chieh Chen	Google, USA

Yung-Yu Chuang	National Taiwan University, Taiwan
Ondrej Chum	Czech Technical University in Prague, Czech Republic
Brian Clipp	Kitware, USA
John Collomosse	University of Surrey and Adobe Research, UK
Jason J. Corso	University of Michigan, USA
David J. Crandall	Indiana University, USA
Daniel Cremers	University of California, Los Angeles, USA
Fabio Cuzzolin	Oxford Brookes University, UK
Jifeng Dai	SenseTime, SAR China
Kostas Daniilidis	University of Pennsylvania, USA
Andrew Davison	Imperial College London, UK
Alessio Del Bue	Fondazione Istituto Italiano di Tecnologia, Italy
Jia Deng	Princeton University, USA
Alexey Dosovitskiy	Google, Germany
Matthijs Douze	Facebook, France
Enrique Dunn	Stevens Institute of Technology, USA
Irfan Essa	Georgia Institute of Technology and Google, USA
Giovanni Maria Farinella	University of Catania, Italy
Ryan Farrell	Brigham Young University, USA
Paolo Favaro	University of Bern, Switzerland
Rogerio Feris	International Business Machines, USA
Cornelia Fermuller	University of Maryland, College Park, USA
David J. Fleet	Vector Institute, Canada
Friedrich Fraundorfer	DLR, Austria
Mario Fritz	CISPA Helmholtz Center for Information Security, Germany
Pascal Fua	EPFL (Swiss Federal Institute of Technology Lausanne), Switzerland
Yasutaka Furukawa	Simon Fraser University, Canada
Li Fuxin	Oregon State University, USA
Efstratios Gavves	University of Amsterdam, The Netherlands
Peter Vincent Gehler	Amazon, USA
Theo Gevers	University of Amsterdam, The Netherlands
Ross Girshick	Facebook AI Research, USA
Boqing Gong	Google, USA
Stephen Gould	Australian National University, Australia
Jinwei Gu	SenseTime Research, USA
Abhinav Gupta	Facebook, USA
Bohyung Han	Seoul National University, South Korea
Bharath Hariharan	Cornell University, USA
Tal Hassner	Facebook AI Research, USA
Xuming He	Australian National University, Australia
Joao F. Henriques	University of Oxford, UK
Adrian Hilton	University of Surrey, UK
Minh Hoai	Stony Brooks, State University of New York, USA
Derek Hoiem	University of Illinois Urbana-Champaign, USA

Timothy Hospedales	University of Edinburgh and Samsung, UK
Gang Hua	Wormpex AI Research, USA
Slobodan Ilic	Siemens AG, Germany
Hiroshi Ishikawa	Waseda University, Japan
Jiaya Jia	The Chinese University of Hong Kong, SAR China
Hailin Jin	Adobe Research, USA
Justin Johnson	University of Michigan, USA
Frederic Jurie	University of Caen Normandie, France
Fredrik Kahl	Chalmers University, Sweden
Sing Bing Kang	Zillow, USA
Gunhee Kim	Seoul National University, South Korea
Junmo Kim	Korea Advanced Institute of Science and Technology, South Korea
Tae-Kyun Kim	Imperial College London, UK
Ron Kimmel	Technion-Israel Institute of Technology, Israel
Alexander Kirillov	Facebook AI Research, USA
Kris Kitani	Carnegie Mellon University, USA
Iasonas Kokkinos	Ariel AI, UK
Vladlen Koltun	Intel Labs, USA
Nikos Komodakis	Ecole des Ponts ParisTech, France
Piotr Koniusz	Australian National University, Australia
M. Pawan Kumar	University of Oxford, UK
Kyros Kutulakos	University of Toronto, Canada
Christoph Lampert	IST Austria, Austria
Ivan Laptev	Inria, France
Diane Larlus	NAVER LABS Europe, France
Laura Leal-Taixe	Technical University Munich, Germany
Honglak Lee	Google and University of Michigan, USA
Joon-Young Lee	Adobe Research, USA
Kyoung Mu Lee	Seoul National University, South Korea
Seungyong Lee	POSTECH, South Korea
Yong Jae Lee	University of California, Davis, USA
Bastian Leibe	RWTH Aachen University, Germany
Victor Lempitsky	Samsung, Russia
Ales Leonardis	University of Birmingham, UK
Marius Leordeanu	Institute of Mathematics of the Romanian Academy, Romania
Vincent Lepetit	ENPC ParisTech, France
Hongdong Li	The Australian National University, Australia
Xi Li	Zhejiang University, China
Yin Li	University of Wisconsin-Madison, USA
Zicheng Liao	Zhejiang University, China
Jongwoo Lim	Hanyang University, South Korea
Stephen Lin	Microsoft Research Asia, China
Yen-Yu Lin	National Chiao Tung University, Taiwan, China
Zhe Lin	Adobe Research, USA

Haibin Ling	Stony Brooks, State University of New York, USA
Jiaying Liu	Peking University, China
Ming-Yu Liu	NVIDIA, USA
Si Liu	Beihang University, China
Xiaoming Liu	Michigan State University, USA
Huchuan Lu	Dalian University of Technology, China
Simon Lucey	Carnegie Mellon University, USA
Jiebo Luo	University of Rochester, USA
Julien Mairal	Inria, France
Michael Maire	University of Chicago, USA
Subhransu Maji	University of Massachusetts, Amherst, USA
Yasushi Makihara	Osaka University, Japan
Jiri Matas	Czech Technical University in Prague, Czech Republic
Yasuyuki Matsushita	Osaka University, Japan
Philippos Mordohai	Stevens Institute of Technology, USA
Vittorio Murino	University of Verona, Italy
Naila Murray	NAVER LABS Europe, France
Hajime Nagahara	Osaka University, Japan
P. J. Narayanan	International Institute of Information Technology (IIIT), Hyderabad, India
Nassir Navab	Technical University of Munich, Germany
Natalia Neverova	Facebook AI Research, France
Matthias Niessner	Technical University of Munich, Germany
Jean-Marc Odobez	Idiap Research Institute and Swiss Federal Institute of Technology Lausanne, Switzerland
Francesca Odone	Università di Genova, Italy
Takeshi Oishi	The University of Tokyo, Tokyo Institute of Technology, Japan
Vicente Ordonez	University of Virginia, USA
Manohar Paluri	Facebook AI Research, USA
Maja Pantic	Imperial College London, UK
In Kyu Park	Inha University, South Korea
Ioannis Patras	Queen Mary University of London, UK
Patrick Perez	Valeo, France
Bryan A. Plummer	Boston University, USA
Thomas Pock	Graz University of Technology, Austria
Marc Pollefeys	ETH Zurich and Microsoft MR & AI Zurich Lab, Switzerland
Jean Ponce	Inria, France
Gerard Pons-Moll	MPII, Saarland Informatics Campus, Germany
Jordi Pont-Tuset	Google, Switzerland
James Matthew Rehg	Georgia Institute of Technology, USA
Ian Reid	University of Adelaide, Australia
Olaf Ronneberger	DeepMind London, UK
Stefan Roth	TU Darmstadt, Germany
Bryan Russell	Adobe Research, USA

Mathieu Salzmann	EPFL, Switzerland
Dimitris Samaras	Stony Brook University, USA
Imari Sato	National Institute of Informatics (NII), Japan
Yoichi Sato	The University of Tokyo, Japan
Torsten Sattler	Czech Technical University in Prague, Czech Republic
Daniel Scharstein	Middlebury College, USA
Bernt Schiele	MPII, Saarland Informatics Campus, Germany
Julia A. Schnabel	King's College London, UK
Nicu Sebe	University of Trento, Italy
Greg Shakhnarovich	Toyota Technological Institute at Chicago, USA
Humphrey Shi	University of Oregon, USA
Jianbo Shi	University of Pennsylvania, USA
Jianping Shi	SenseTime, China
Leonid Sigal	University of British Columbia, Canada
Cees Snoek	University of Amsterdam, The Netherlands
Richard Souvenir	Temple University, USA
Hao Su	University of California, San Diego, USA
Akihiro Sugimoto	National Institute of Informatics (NII), Japan
Jian Sun	Megvii Technology, China
Jian Sun	Xi'an Jiaotong University, China
Chris Sweeney	Facebook Reality Labs, USA
Yu-wing Tai	Kuaishou Technology, China
Chi-Keung Tang	The Hong Kong University of Science and Technology, SAR China
Radu Timofte	ETH Zurich, Switzerland
Sinisa Todorovic	Oregon State University, USA
Giorgos Tolias	Czech Technical University in Prague, Czech Republic
Carlo Tomasi	Duke University, USA
Tatiana Tommasi	Politecnico di Torino, Italy
Lorenzo Torresani	Facebook AI Research and Dartmouth College, USA
Alexander Toshev	Google, USA
Zhuowen Tu	University of California, San Diego, USA
Tinne Tuytelaars	KU Leuven, Belgium
Jasper Uijlings	Google, Switzerland
Nuno Vasconcelos	University of California, San Diego, USA
Olga Veksler	University of Waterloo, Canada
Rene Vidal	Johns Hopkins University, USA
Gang Wang	Alibaba Group, China
Jingdong Wang	Microsoft Research Asia, China
Yizhou Wang	Peking University, China
Lior Wolf	Facebook AI Research and Tel Aviv University, Israel
Jianxin Wu	Nanjing University, China
Tao Xiang	University of Surrey, UK
Saining Xie	Facebook AI Research, USA
Ming-Hsuan Yang	University of California at Merced and Google, USA
Ruigang Yang	University of Kentucky, USA

Kwang Moo Yi	University of Victoria, Canada
Zhaozheng Yin	Stony Brook, State University of New York, USA
Chang D. Yoo	Korea Advanced Institute of Science and Technology, South Korea
Shaodi You	University of Amsterdam, The Netherlands
Jingyi Yu	ShanghaiTech University, China
Stella Yu	University of California, Berkeley, and ICSI, USA
Stefanos Zafeiriou	Imperial College London, UK
Hongbin Zha	Peking University, China
Tianzhu Zhang	University of Science and Technology of China, China
Liang Zheng	Australian National University, Australia
Todd E. Zickler	Harvard University, USA
Andrew Zisserman	University of Oxford, UK

Technical Program Committee

Sathyanarayanan
N. Aakur
Wael Abd Almgaeed
Abdelrahman
Abdelhamed
Abdullah Abuolaim
Supreeth Achar
Hanno Ackermann
Ehsan Adeli
Triantafyllos Afouras
Sameer Agarwal
Aishwarya Agrawal
Harsh Agrawal
Pulkit Agrawal
Antonio Agudo
Eirikur Agustsson
Karim Ahmed
Byeongjoo Ahn
Unaiza Ahsan
Thalaiyasingam Ajanthan
Kenan E. Ak
Emre Akbas
Naveed Akhtar
Derya Akkaynak
Yagiz Aksoy
Ziad Al-Halah
Xavier Alameda-Pineda
Jean-Baptiste Alayrac

Samuel Albanie
Shadi Albarqouni
Cenek Albl
Hassan Abu Alhaija
Daniel Aliaga
Mohammad
S. Aliakbarian
Rahaf Aljundi
Thiemo Alldieck
Jon Almazan
Jose M. Alvarez
Senjian An
Saket Anand
Codruta Ancuti
Cosmin Ancuti
Peter Anderson
Juan Andrade-Cetto
Alexander Andreopoulos
Misha Andriluka
Dragomir Anguelov
Rushil Anirudh
Michel Antunes
Oisin Mac Aodha
Srikar Appalaraju
Relja Arandjelovic
Nikita Araslanov
Andre Araujo
Helder Araujo

Pablo Arbelaez
Shervin Ardeshir
Sercan O. Arik
Anil Armagan
Anurag Arnab
Chetan Arora
Federica Arrigoni
Mathieu Aubry
Shai Avidan
Angelica I. Aviles-Rivero
Yannis Avrithis
Ismail Ben Ayed
Shekoofeh Azizi
Ioan Andrei Bârsan
Artem Babenko
Deepak Babu Sam
Seung-Hwan Baek
Seungryul Baek
Andrew D. Bagdanov
Shai Bagon
Yuval Bahat
Junjie Bai
Song Bai
Xiang Bai
Yalong Bai
Yancheng Bai
Peter Bajcsy
Slawomir Bak

Mahsa Baktashmotlagh
Kavita Bala
Yogesh Balaji
Guha Balakrishnan
V. N. Balasubramanian
Federico Baldassarre
Vassileios Balntas
Shurjo Banerjee
Aayush Bansal
Ankan Bansal
Jianmin Bao
Linchao Bao
Wenbo Bao
Yingze Bao
Akash Bapat
Md Jawadul Hasan Bappy
Fabien Baradel
Lorenzo Baraldi
Daniel Barath
Adrian Barbu
Kobus Barnard
Nick Barnes
Francisco Barranco
Jonathan T. Barron
Arslan Basharat
Chaim Baskin
Anil S. Baslamisli
Jorge Batista
Kayhan Batmanghelich
Konstantinos Batsos
David Bau
Luis Baumela
Christoph Baur
Eduardo
  Bayro-Corrochano
Paul Beardsley
Jan Bednavr'ik
Oscar Beijbom
Philippe Bekaert
Esube Bekele
Vasileios Belagiannis
Ohad Ben-Shahar
Abhijit Bendale
Róger Bermúdez-Chacón
Maxim Berman
Jesus Bermudez-cameo

Florian Bernard
Stefano Berretti
Marcelo Bertalmio
Gedas Bertasius
Cigdem Beyan
Lucas Beyer
Vijayakumar Bhagavatula
Arjun Nitin Bhagoji
Apratim Bhattacharyya
Binod Bhattarai
Sai Bi
Jia-Wang Bian
Simone Bianco
Adel Bibi
Tolga Birdal
Tom Bishop
Soma Biswas
Mårten Björkman
Volker Blanz
Vishnu Boddeti
Navaneeth Bodla
Simion-Vlad Bogolin
Xavier Boix
Piotr Bojanowski
Timo Bolkart
Guido Borghi
Larbi Boubchir
Guillaume Bourmaud
Adrien Bousseau
Thierry Bouwmans
Richard Bowden
Hakan Boyraz
Mathieu Brédif
Samarth Brahmbhatt
Steve Branson
Nikolas Brasch
Biagio Brattoli
Ernesto Brau
Toby P. Breckon
Francois Bremond
Jesus Briales
Sofia Broomé
Marcus A. Brubaker
Luc Brun
Silvia Bucci
Shyamal Buch

Pradeep Buddharaju
Uta Buechler
Mai Bui
Tu Bui
Adrian Bulat
Giedrius T. Burachas
Elena Burceanu
Xavier P. Burgos-Artizzu
Kaylee Burns
Andrei Bursuc
Benjamin Busam
Wonmin Byeon
Zoya Bylinskii
Sergi Caelles
Jianrui Cai
Minjie Cai
Yujun Cai
Zhaowei Cai
Zhipeng Cai
Juan C. Caicedo
Simone Calderara
Necati Cihan Camgoz
Dylan Campbell
Octavia Camps
Jiale Cao
Kaidi Cao
Liangliang Cao
Xiangyong Cao
Xiaochun Cao
Yang Cao
Yu Cao
Yue Cao
Zhangjie Cao
Luca Carlone
Mathilde Caron
Dan Casas
Thomas J. Cashman
Umberto Castellani
Lluis Castrejon
Jacopo Cavazza
Fabio Cermelli
Hakan Cevikalp
Menglei Chai
Ishani Chakraborty
Rudrasis Chakraborty
Antoni B. Chan

Kwok-Ping Chan
Siddhartha Chandra
Sharat Chandran
Arjun Chandrasekaran
Angel X. Chang
Che-Han Chang
Hong Chang
Hyun Sung Chang
Hyung Jin Chang
Jianlong Chang
Ju Yong Chang
Ming-Ching Chang
Simyung Chang
Xiaojun Chang
Yu-Wei Chao
Devendra S. Chaplot
Arslan Chaudhry
Rizwan A. Chaudhry
Can Chen
Chang Chen
Chao Chen
Chen Chen
Chu-Song Chen
Dapeng Chen
Dong Chen
Dongdong Chen
Guanying Chen
Hongge Chen
Hsin-yi Chen
Huaijin Chen
Hwann-Tzong Chen
Jianbo Chen
Jianhui Chen
Jiansheng Chen
Jiaxin Chen
Jie Chen
Jun-Cheng Chen
Kan Chen
Kevin Chen
Lin Chen
Long Chen
Min-Hung Chen
Qifeng Chen
Shi Chen
Shixing Chen
Tianshui Chen

Weifeng Chen
Weikai Chen
Xi Chen
Xiaohan Chen
Xiaozhi Chen
Xilin Chen
Xingyu Chen
Xinlei Chen
Xinyun Chen
Yi-Ting Chen
Yilun Chen
Ying-Cong Chen
Yinpeng Chen
Yiran Chen
Yu Chen
Yu-Sheng Chen
Yuhua Chen
Yun-Chun Chen
Yunpeng Chen
Yuntao Chen
Zhuoyuan Chen
Zitian Chen
Anchieh Cheng
Bowen Cheng
Erkang Cheng
Gong Cheng
Guangliang Cheng
Jingchun Cheng
Jun Cheng
Li Cheng
Ming-Ming Cheng
Yu Cheng
Ziang Cheng
Anoop Cherian
Dmitry Chetverikov
Ngai-man Cheung
William Cheung
Ajad Chhatkuli
Naoki Chiba
Benjamin Chidester
Han-pang Chiu
Mang Tik Chiu
Wei-Chen Chiu
Donghyeon Cho
Hojin Cho
Minsu Cho

Nam Ik Cho
Tim Cho
Tae Eun Choe
Chiho Choi
Edward Choi
Inchang Choi
Jinsoo Choi
Jonghyun Choi
Jongwon Choi
Yukyung Choi
Hisham Cholakkal
Eunji Chong
Jaegul Choo
Christopher Choy
Hang Chu
Peng Chu
Wen-Sheng Chu
Albert Chung
Joon Son Chung
Hai Ci
Safa Cicek
Ramazan G. Cinbis
Arridhana Ciptadi
Javier Civera
James J. Clark
Ronald Clark
Felipe Codevilla
Michael Cogswell
Andrea Cohen
Maxwell D. Collins
Carlo Colombo
Yang Cong
Adria R. Continente
Marcella Cornia
John Richard Corring
Darren Cosker
Dragos Costea
Garrison W. Cottrell
Florent Couzinie-Devy
Marco Cristani
Ioana Croitoru
James L. Crowley
Jiequan Cui
Zhaopeng Cui
Ross Cutler
Antonio D'Innocente

Rozenn Dahyot
Bo Dai
Dengxin Dai
Hang Dai
Longquan Dai
Shuyang Dai
Xiyang Dai
Yuchao Dai
Adrian V. Dalca
Dima Damen
Bharath B. Damodaran
Kristin Dana
Martin Danelljan
Zheng Dang
Zachary Alan Daniels
Donald G. Dansereau
Abhishek Das
Samyak Datta
Achal Dave
Titas De
Rodrigo de Bem
Teo de Campos
Raoul de Charette
Shalini De Mello
Joseph DeGol
Herve Delingette
Haowen Deng
Jiankang Deng
Weijian Deng
Zhiwei Deng
Joachim Denzler
Konstantinos G. Derpanis
Aditya Deshpande
Frederic Devernay
Somdip Dey
Arturo Deza
Abhinav Dhall
Helisa Dhamo
Vikas Dhiman
Fillipe Dias Moreira
   de Souza
Ali Diba
Ferran Diego
Guiguang Ding
Henghui Ding
Jian Ding

Mingyu Ding
Xinghao Ding
Zhengming Ding
Robert DiPietro
Cosimo Distante
Ajay Divakaran
Mandar Dixit
Abdelaziz Djelouah
Thanh-Toan Do
Jose Dolz
Bo Dong
Chao Dong
Jiangxin Dong
Weiming Dong
Weisheng Dong
Xingping Dong
Xuanyi Dong
Yinpeng Dong
Gianfranco Doretto
Hazel Doughty
Hassen Drira
Bertram Drost
Dawei Du
Ye Duan
Yueqi Duan
Abhimanyu Dubey
Anastasia Dubrovina
Stefan Duffner
Chi Nhan Duong
Thibaut Durand
Zoran Duric
Iulia Duta
Debidatta Dwibedi
Benjamin Eckart
Marc Eder
Marzieh Edraki
Alexei A. Efros
Kiana Ehsani
Hazm Kemal Ekenel
James H. Elder
Mohamed Elgharib
Shireen Elhabian
Ehsan Elhamifar
Mohamed Elhoseiny
Ian Endres
N. Benjamin Erichson

Jan Ernst
Sergio Escalera
Francisco Escolano
Victor Escorcia
Carlos Esteves
Francisco J. Estrada
Bin Fan
Chenyou Fan
Deng-Ping Fan
Haoqi Fan
Hehe Fan
Heng Fan
Kai Fan
Lijie Fan
Linxi Fan
Quanfu Fan
Shaojing Fan
Xiaochuan Fan
Xin Fan
Yuchen Fan
Sean Fanello
Hao-Shu Fang
Haoyang Fang
Kuan Fang
Yi Fang
Yuming Fang
Azade Farshad
Alireza Fathi
Raanan Fattal
Joao Fayad
Xiaohan Fei
Christoph Feichtenhofer
Michael Felsberg
Chen Feng
Jiashi Feng
Junyi Feng
Mengyang Feng
Qianli Feng
Zhenhua Feng
Michele Fenzi
Andras Ferencz
Martin Fergie
Basura Fernando
Ethan Fetaya
Michael Firman
John W. Fisher

Matthew Fisher
Boris Flach
Corneliu Florea
Wolfgang Foerstner
David Fofi
Gian Luca Foresti
Per-Erik Forssen
David Fouhey
Katerina Fragkiadaki
Victor Fragoso
Jean-Sébastien Franco
Ohad Fried
Iuri Frosio
Cheng-Yang Fu
Huazhu Fu
Jianlong Fu
Jingjing Fu
Xueyang Fu
Yanwei Fu
Ying Fu
Yun Fu
Olac Fuentes
Kent Fujiwara
Takuya Funatomi
Christopher Funk
Thomas Funkhouser
Antonino Furnari
Ryo Furukawa
Erik Gärtner
Raghudeep Gadde
Matheus Gadelha
Vandit Gajjar
Trevor Gale
Juergen Gall
Mathias Gallardo
Guillermo Gallego
Orazio Gallo
Chuang Gan
Zhe Gan
Madan Ravi Ganesh
Aditya Ganeshan
Siddha Ganju
Bin-Bin Gao
Changxin Gao
Feng Gao
Hongchang Gao

Jin Gao
Jiyang Gao
Junbin Gao
Katelyn Gao
Lin Gao
Mingfei Gao
Ruiqi Gao
Ruohan Gao
Shenghua Gao
Yuan Gao
Yue Gao
Noa Garcia
Alberto Garcia-Garcia
Guillermo
    Garcia-Hernando
Jacob R. Gardner
Animesh Garg
Kshitiz Garg
Rahul Garg
Ravi Garg
Philip N. Garner
Kirill Gavrilyuk
Paul Gay
Shiming Ge
Weifeng Ge
Baris Gecer
Xin Geng
Kyle Genova
Stamatios Georgoulis
Bernard Ghanem
Michael Gharbi
Kamran Ghasedi
Golnaz Ghiasi
Arnab Ghosh
Partha Ghosh
Silvio Giancola
Andrew Gilbert
Rohit Girdhar
Xavier Giro-i-Nieto
Thomas Gittings
Ioannis Gkioulekas
Clement Godard
Vaibhava Goel
Bastian Goldluecke
Lluis Gomez
Nuno Gonçalves

Dong Gong
Ke Gong
Mingming Gong
Abel Gonzalez-Garcia
Ariel Gordon
Daniel Gordon
Paulo Gotardo
Venu Madhav Govindu
Ankit Goyal
Priya Goyal
Raghav Goyal
Benjamin Graham
Douglas Gray
Brent A. Griffin
Etienne Grossmann
David Gu
Jiayuan Gu
Jiuxiang Gu
Lin Gu
Qiao Gu
Shuhang Gu
Jose J. Guerrero
Paul Guerrero
Jie Gui
Jean-Yves Guillemaut
Riza Alp Guler
Erhan Gundogdu
Fatma Guney
Guodong Guo
Kaiwen Guo
Qi Guo
Sheng Guo
Shi Guo
Tiantong Guo
Xiaojie Guo
Yijie Guo
Yiluan Guo
Yuanfang Guo
Yulan Guo
Agrim Gupta
Ankush Gupta
Mohit Gupta
Saurabh Gupta
Tanmay Gupta
Danna Gurari
Abner Guzman-Rivera

JunYoung Gwak
Michael Gygli
Jung-Woo Ha
Simon Hadfield
Isma Hadji
Bjoern Haefner
Taeyoung Hahn
Levente Hajder
Peter Hall
Emanuela Haller
Stefan Haller
Bumsub Ham
Abdullah Hamdi
Dongyoon Han
Hu Han
Jungong Han
Junwei Han
Kai Han
Tian Han
Xiaoguang Han
Xintong Han
Yahong Han
Ankur Handa
Zekun Hao
Albert Haque
Tatsuya Harada
Mehrtash Harandi
Adam W. Harley
Mahmudul Hasan
Atsushi Hashimoto
Ali Hatamizadeh
Munawar Hayat
Dongliang He
Jingrui He
Junfeng He
Kaiming He
Kun He
Lei He
Pan He
Ran He
Shengfeng He
Tong He
Weipeng He
Xuming He
Yang He
Yihui He

Zhihai He
Chinmay Hegde
Janne Heikkila
Mattias P. Heinrich
Stéphane Herbin
Alexander Hermans
Luis Herranz
John R. Hershey
Aaron Hertzmann
Roei Herzig
Anders Heyden
Steven Hickson
Otmar Hilliges
Tomas Hodan
Judy Hoffman
Michael Hofmann
Yannick Hold-Geoffroy
Namdar Homayounfar
Sina Honari
Richang Hong
Seunghoon Hong
Xiaopeng Hong
Yi Hong
Hidekata Hontani
Anthony Hoogs
Yedid Hoshen
Mir Rayat Imtiaz Hossain
Junhui Hou
Le Hou
Lu Hou
Tingbo Hou
Wei-Lin Hsiao
Cheng-Chun Hsu
Gee-Sern Jison Hsu
Kuang-jui Hsu
Changbo Hu
Di Hu
Guosheng Hu
Han Hu
Hao Hu
Hexiang Hu
Hou-Ning Hu
Jie Hu
Junlin Hu
Nan Hu
Ping Hu

Ronghang Hu
Xiaowei Hu
Yinlin Hu
Yuan-Ting Hu
Zhe Hu
Binh-Son Hua
Yang Hua
Bingyao Huang
Di Huang
Dong Huang
Fay Huang
Haibin Huang
Haozhi Huang
Heng Huang
Huaibo Huang
Jia-Bin Huang
Jing Huang
Jingwei Huang
Kaizhu Huang
Lei Huang
Qiangui Huang
Qiaoying Huang
Qingqiu Huang
Qixing Huang
Shaoli Huang
Sheng Huang
Siyuan Huang
Weilin Huang
Wenbing Huang
Xiangru Huang
Xun Huang
Yan Huang
Yifei Huang
Yue Huang
Zhiwu Huang
Zilong Huang
Minyoung Huh
Zhuo Hui
Matthias B. Hullin
Martin Humenberger
Wei-Chih Hung
Zhouyuan Huo
Junhwa Hur
Noureldien Hussein
Jyh-Jing Hwang
Seong Jae Hwang

Sung Ju Hwang
Ichiro Ide
Ivo Ihrke
Daiki Ikami
Satoshi Ikehata
Nazli Ikizler-Cinbis
Sunghoon Im
Yani Ioannou
Radu Tudor Ionescu
Umar Iqbal
Go Irie
Ahmet Iscen
Md Amirul Islam
Vamsi Ithapu
Nathan Jacobs
Arpit Jain
Himalaya Jain
Suyog Jain
Stuart James
Won-Dong Jang
Yunseok Jang
Ronnachai Jaroensri
Dinesh Jayaraman
Sadeep Jayasumana
Suren Jayasuriya
Herve Jegou
Simon Jenni
Hae-Gon Jeon
Yunho Jeon
Koteswar R. Jerripothula
Hueihan Jhuang
I-hong Jhuo
Dinghuang Ji
Hui Ji
Jingwei Ji
Pan Ji
Yanli Ji
Baoxiong Jia
Kui Jia
Xu Jia
Chiyu Max Jiang
Haiyong Jiang
Hao Jiang
Huaizu Jiang
Huajie Jiang
Ke Jiang

Lai Jiang
Li Jiang
Lu Jiang
Ming Jiang
Peng Jiang
Shuqiang Jiang
Wei Jiang
Xudong Jiang
Zhuolin Jiang
Jianbo Jiao
Zequn Jie
Dakai Jin
Kyong Hwan Jin
Lianwen Jin
SouYoung Jin
Xiaojie Jin
Xin Jin
Nebojsa Jojic
Alexis Joly
Michael Jeffrey Jones
Hanbyul Joo
Jungseock Joo
Kyungdon Joo
Ajjen Joshi
Shantanu H. Joshi
Da-Cheng Juan
Marco Körner
Kevin Köser
Asim Kadav
Christine Kaeser-Chen
Kushal Kafle
Dagmar Kainmueller
Ioannis A. Kakadiaris
Zdenek Kalal
Nima Kalantari
Yannis Kalantidis
Mahdi M. Kalayeh
Anmol Kalia
Sinan Kalkan
Vicky Kalogeiton
Ashwin Kalyan
Joni-kristian Kamarainen
Gerda Kamberova
Chandra Kambhamettu
Martin Kampel
Meina Kan

Christopher Kanan
Kenichi Kanatani
Angjoo Kanazawa
Atsushi Kanehira
Takuhiro Kaneko
Asako Kanezaki
Bingyi Kang
Di Kang
Sunghun Kang
Zhao Kang
Vadim Kantorov
Abhishek Kar
Amlan Kar
Theofanis Karaletsos
Leonid Karlinsky
Kevin Karsch
Angelos Katharopoulos
Isinsu Katircioglu
Hiroharu Kato
Zoltan Kato
Dotan Kaufman
Jan Kautz
Rei Kawakami
Qiuhong Ke
Wadim Kehl
Petr Kellnhofer
Aniruddha Kembhavi
Cem Keskin
Margret Keuper
Daniel Keysers
Ashkan Khakzar
Fahad Khan
Naeemullah Khan
Salman Khan
Siddhesh Khandelwal
Rawal Khirodkar
Anna Khoreva
Tejas Khot
Parmeshwar Khurd
Hadi Kiapour
Joe Kileel
Chanho Kim
Dahun Kim
Edward Kim
Eunwoo Kim
Han-ul Kim

Hansung Kim
Heewon Kim
Hyo Jin Kim
Hyunwoo J. Kim
Jinkyu Kim
Jiwon Kim
Jongmin Kim
Junsik Kim
Junyeong Kim
Min H. Kim
Namil Kim
Pyojin Kim
Seon Joo Kim
Seong Tae Kim
Seungryong Kim
Sungwoong Kim
Tae Hyun Kim
Vladimir Kim
Won Hwa Kim
Yonghyun Kim
Benjamin Kimia
Akisato Kimura
Pieter-Jan Kindermans
Zsolt Kira
Itaru Kitahara
Hedvig Kjellstrom
Jan Knopp
Takumi Kobayashi
Erich Kobler
Parker Koch
Reinhard Koch
Elyor Kodirov
Amir Kolaman
Nicholas Kolkin
Dimitrios Kollias
Stefanos Kollias
Soheil Kolouri
Adams Wai-Kin Kong
Naejin Kong
Shu Kong
Tao Kong
Yu Kong
Yoshinori Konishi
Daniil Kononenko
Theodora Kontogianni
Simon Korman

Adam Kortylewski
Jana Kosecka
Jean Kossaifi
Satwik Kottur
Rigas Kouskouridas
Adriana Kovashka
Rama Kovvuri
Adarsh Kowdle
Jedrzej Kozerawski
Mateusz Kozinski
Philipp Kraehenbuehl
Gregory Kramida
Josip Krapac
Dmitry Kravchenko
Ranjay Krishna
Pavel Krsek
Alexander Krull
Jakob Kruse
Hiroyuki Kubo
Hilde Kuehne
Jason Kuen
Andreas Kuhn
Arjan Kuijper
Zuzana Kukelova
Ajay Kumar
Amit Kumar
Avinash Kumar
Suryansh Kumar
Vijay Kumar
Kaustav Kundu
Weicheng Kuo
Nojun Kwak
Suha Kwak
Junseok Kwon
Nikolaos Kyriazis
Zorah Lähner
Ankit Laddha
Florent Lafarge
Jean Lahoud
Kevin Lai
Shang-Hong Lai
Wei-Sheng Lai
Yu-Kun Lai
Iro Laina
Antony Lam
John Wheatley Lambert

Xiangyuan lan
Xu Lan
Charis Lanaras
Georg Langs
Oswald Lanz
Dong Lao
Yizhen Lao
Agata Lapedriza
Gustav Larsson
Viktor Larsson
Katrin Lasinger
Christoph Lassner
Longin Jan Latecki
Stéphane Lathuilière
Rynson Lau
Hei Law
Justin Lazarow
Svetlana Lazebnik
Hieu Le
Huu Le
Ngan Hoang Le
Trung-Nghia Le
Vuong Le
Colin Lea
Erik Learned-Miller
Chen-Yu Lee
Gim Hee Lee
Hsin-Ying Lee
Hyungtae Lee
Jae-Han Lee
Jimmy Addison Lee
Joonseok Lee
Kibok Lee
Kuang-Huei Lee
Kwonjoon Lee
Minsik Lee
Sang-chul Lee
Seungkyu Lee
Soochan Lee
Stefan Lee
Taehee Lee
Andreas Lehrmann
Jie Lei
Peng Lei
Matthew Joseph Leotta
Wee Kheng Leow

Gil Levi
Evgeny Levinkov
Aviad Levis
Jose Lezama
Ang Li
Bin Li
Bing Li
Boyi Li
Changsheng Li
Chao Li
Chen Li
Cheng Li
Chenglong Li
Chi Li
Chun-Guang Li
Chun-Liang Li
Chunyuan Li
Dong Li
Guanbin Li
Hao Li
Haoxiang Li
Hongsheng Li
Hongyang Li
Houqiang Li
Huibin Li
Jia Li
Jianan Li
Jianguo Li
Junnan Li
Junxuan Li
Kai Li
Ke Li
Kejie Li
Kunpeng Li
Lerenhan Li
Li Erran Li
Mengtian Li
Mu Li
Peihua Li
Peiyi Li
Ping Li
Qi Li
Qing Li
Ruiyu Li
Ruoteng Li
Shaozi Li

Sheng Li
Shiwei Li
Shuang Li
Siyang Li
Stan Z. Li
Tianye Li
Wei Li
Weixin Li
Wen Li
Wenbo Li
Xiaomeng Li
Xin Li
Xiu Li
Xuelong Li
Xueting Li
Yan Li
Yandong Li
Yanghao Li
Yehao Li
Yi Li
Yijun Li
Yikang LI
Yining Li
Yongjie Li
Yu Li
Yu-Jhe Li
Yunpeng Li
Yunsheng Li
Yunzhu Li
Zhe Li
Zhen Li
Zhengqi Li
Zhenyang Li
Zhuwen Li
Dongze Lian
Xiaochen Lian
Zhouhui Lian
Chen Liang
Jie Liang
Ming Liang
Paul Pu Liang
Pengpeng Liang
Shu Liang
Wei Liang
Jing Liao
Minghui Liao

Renjie Liao
Shengcai Liao
Shuai Liao
Yiyi Liao
Ser-Nam Lim
Chen-Hsuan Lin
Chung-Ching Lin
Dahua Lin
Ji Lin
Kevin Lin
Tianwei Lin
Tsung-Yi Lin
Tsung-Yu Lin
Wei-An Lin
Weiyao Lin
Yen-Chen Lin
Yuewei Lin
David B. Lindell
Drew Linsley
Krzysztof Lis
Roee Litman
Jim Little
An-An Liu
Bo Liu
Buyu Liu
Chao Liu
Chen Liu
Cheng-lin Liu
Chenxi Liu
Dong Liu
Feng Liu
Guilin Liu
Haomiao Liu
Heshan Liu
Hong Liu
Ji Liu
Jingen Liu
Jun Liu
Lanlan Liu
Li Liu
Liu Liu
Mengyuan Liu
Miaomiao Liu
Nian Liu
Ping Liu
Risheng Liu

Sheng Liu
Shu Liu
Shuaicheng Liu
Sifei Liu
Siqi Liu
Siying Liu
Songtao Liu
Ting Liu
Tongliang Liu
Tyng-Luh Liu
Wanquan Liu
Wei Liu
Weiyang Liu
Weizhe Liu
Wenyu Liu
Wu Liu
Xialei Liu
Xianglong Liu
Xiaodong Liu
Xiaofeng Liu
Xihui Liu
Xingyu Liu
Xinwang Liu
Xuanqing Liu
Xuebo Liu
Yang Liu
Yaojie Liu
Yebin Liu
Yen-Cheng Liu
Yiming Liu
Yu Liu
Yu-Shen Liu
Yufan Liu
Yun Liu
Zheng Liu
Zhijian Liu
Zhuang Liu
Zichuan Liu
Ziwei Liu
Zongyi Liu
Stephan Liwicki
Liliana Lo Presti
Chengjiang Long
Fuchen Long
Mingsheng Long
Xiang Long

Yang Long
Charles T. Loop
Antonio Lopez
Roberto J. Lopez-Sastre
Javier Lorenzo-Navarro
Manolis Lourakis
Boyu Lu
Canyi Lu
Feng Lu
Guoyu Lu
Hongtao Lu
Jiajun Lu
Jiasen Lu
Jiwen Lu
Kaiyue Lu
Le Lu
Shao-Ping Lu
Shijian Lu
Xiankai Lu
Xin Lu
Yao Lu
Yiping Lu
Yongxi Lu
Yongyi Lu
Zhiwu Lu
Fujun Luan
Benjamin E. Lundell
Hao Luo
Jian-Hao Luo
Ruotian Luo
Weixin Luo
Wenhan Luo
Wenjie Luo
Yan Luo
Zelun Luo
Zixin Luo
Khoa Luu
Zhaoyang Lv
Pengyuan Lyu
Thomas Möllenhoff
Matthias Müller
Bingpeng Ma
Chih-Yao Ma
Chongyang Ma
Huimin Ma
Jiayi Ma

K. T. Ma
Ke Ma
Lin Ma
Liqian Ma
Shugao Ma
Wei-Chiu Ma
Xiaojian Ma
Xingjun Ma
Zhanyu Ma
Zheng Ma
Radek Jakob Mackowiak
Ludovic Magerand
Shweta Mahajan
Siddharth Mahendran
Long Mai
Ameesh Makadia
Oscar Mendez Maldonado
Mateusz Malinowski
Yury Malkov
Arun Mallya
Dipu Manandhar
Massimiliano Mancini
Fabian Manhardt
Kevis-kokitsi Maninis
Varun Manjunatha
Junhua Mao
Xudong Mao
Alina Marcu
Edgar Margffoy-Tuay
Dmitrii Marin
Manuel J. Marin-Jimenez
Kenneth Marino
Niki Martinel
Julieta Martinez
Jonathan Masci
Tomohiro Mashita
Iacopo Masi
David Masip
Daniela Massiceti
Stefan Mathe
Yusuke Matsui
Tetsu Matsukawa
Iain A. Matthews
Kevin James Matzen
Bruce Allen Maxwell
Stephen Maybank

Helmut Mayer
Amir Mazaheri
David McAllester
Steven McDonagh
Stephen J. Mckenna
Roey Mechrez
Prakhar Mehrotra
Christopher Mei
Xue Mei
Paulo R. S. Mendonca
Lili Meng
Zibo Meng
Thomas Mensink
Bjoern Menze
Michele Merler
Kourosh Meshgi
Pascal Mettes
Christopher Metzler
Liang Mi
Qiguang Miao
Xin Miao
Tomer Michaeli
Frank Michel
Antoine Miech
Krystian Mikolajczyk
Peyman Milanfar
Ben Mildenhall
Gregor Miller
Fausto Milletari
Dongbo Min
Kyle Min
Pedro Miraldo
Dmytro Mishkin
Anand Mishra
Ashish Mishra
Ishan Misra
Niluthpol C. Mithun
Kaushik Mitra
Niloy Mitra
Anton Mitrokhin
Ikuhisa Mitsugami
Anurag Mittal
Kaichun Mo
Zhipeng Mo
Davide Modolo
Michael Moeller

Pritish Mohapatra
Pavlo Molchanov
Davide Moltisanti
Pascal Monasse
Mathew Monfort
Aron Monszpart
Sean Moran
Vlad I. Morariu
Francesc Moreno-Noguer
Pietro Morerio
Stylianos Moschoglou
Yael Moses
Roozbeh Mottaghi
Pierre Moulon
Arsalan Mousavian
Yadong Mu
Yasuhiro Mukaigawa
Lopamudra Mukherjee
Yusuke Mukuta
Ravi Teja Mullapudi
Mario Enrique Munich
Zachary Murez
Ana C. Murillo
J. Krishna Murthy
Damien Muselet
Armin Mustafa
Siva Karthik Mustikovela
Carlo Dal Mutto
Moin Nabi
Varun K. Nagaraja
Tushar Nagarajan
Arsha Nagrani
Seungjun Nah
Nikhil Naik
Yoshikatsu Nakajima
Yuta Nakashima
Atsushi Nakazawa
Seonghyeon Nam
Vinay P. Namboodiri
Medhini Narasimhan
Srinivasa Narasimhan
Sanath Narayan
Erickson Rangel
  Nascimento
Jacinto Nascimento
Tayyab Naseer

Lakshmanan Nataraj
Neda Nategh
Nelson Isao Nauata
Fernando Navarro
Shah Nawaz
Lukas Neumann
Ram Nevatia
Alejandro Newell
Shawn Newsam
Joe Yue-Hei Ng
Trung Thanh Ngo
Duc Thanh Nguyen
Lam M. Nguyen
Phuc Xuan Nguyen
Thuong Nguyen Canh
Mihalis Nicolaou
Andrei Liviu Nicolicioiu
Xuecheng Nie
Michael Niemeyer
Simon Niklaus
Christophoros Nikou
David Nilsson
Jifeng Ning
Yuval Nirkin
Li Niu
Yuzhen Niu
Zhenxing Niu
Shohei Nobuhara
Nicoletta Noceti
Hyeonwoo Noh
Junhyug Noh
Mehdi Noroozi
Sotiris Nousias
Valsamis Ntouskos
Matthew O'Toole
Peter Ochs
Ferda Ofli
Seong Joon Oh
Seoung Wug Oh
Iason Oikonomidis
Utkarsh Ojha
Takahiro Okabe
Takayuki Okatani
Fumio Okura
Aude Oliva
Kyle Olszewski

William Robson Schwartz
Alex Schwing
Sinisa Segvic
Lorenzo Seidenari
Pradeep Sen
Ozan Sener
Soumyadip Sengupta
Arda Senocak
Mojtaba Seyedhosseini
Shishir Shah
Shital Shah
Sohil Atul Shah
Tamar Rott Shaham
Huasong Shan
Qi Shan
Shiguang Shan
Jing Shao
Roman Shapovalov
Gaurav Sharma
Vivek Sharma
Viktoriia Sharmanska
Dongyu She
Sumit Shekhar
Evan Shelhamer
Chengyao Shen
Chunhua Shen
Falong Shen
Jie Shen
Li Shen
Liyue Shen
Shuhan Shen
Tianwei Shen
Wei Shen
William B. Shen
Yantao Shen
Ying Shen
Yiru Shen
Yujun Shen
Yuming Shen
Zhiqiang Shen
Ziyi Shen
Lu Sheng
Yu Sheng
Rakshith Shetty
Baoguang Shi
Guangming Shi

Hailin Shi
Miaojing Shi
Yemin Shi
Zhenmei Shi
Zhiyuan Shi
Kevin Jonathan Shih
Shiliang Shiliang
Hyunjung Shim
Atsushi Shimada
Nobutaka Shimada
Daeyun Shin
Young Min Shin
Koichi Shinoda
Konstantin Shmelkov
Michael Zheng Shou
Abhinav Shrivastava
Tianmin Shu
Zhixin Shu
Hong-Han Shuai
Pushkar Shukla
Christian Siagian
Mennatullah M. Siam
Kaleem Siddiqi
Karan Sikka
Jae-Young Sim
Christian Simon
Martin Simonovsky
Dheeraj Singaraju
Bharat Singh
Gurkirt Singh
Krishna Kumar Singh
Maneesh Kumar Singh
Richa Singh
Saurabh Singh
Suriya Singh
Vikas Singh
Sudipta N. Sinha
Vincent Sitzmann
Josef Sivic
Gregory Slabaugh
Miroslava Slavcheva
Ron Slossberg
Brandon Smith
Kevin Smith
Vladimir Smutny
Noah Snavely

Roger
    D. Soberanis-Mukul
Kihyuk Sohn
Francesco Solera
Eric Sommerlade
Sanghyun Son
Byung Cheol Song
Chunfeng Song
Dongjin Song
Jiaming Song
Jie Song
Jifei Song
Jingkuan Song
Mingli Song
Shiyu Song
Shuran Song
Xiao Song
Yafei Song
Yale Song
Yang Song
Yi-Zhe Song
Yibing Song
Humberto Sossa
Cesar de Souza
Adrian Spurr
Srinath Sridhar
Suraj Srinivas
Pratul P. Srinivasan
Anuj Srivastava
Tania Stathaki
Christopher Stauffer
Simon Stent
Rainer Stiefelhagen
Pierre Stock
Julian Straub
Jonathan C. Stroud
Joerg Stueckler
Jan Stuehmer
David Stutz
Chi Su
Hang Su
Jong-Chyi Su
Shuochen Su
Yu-Chuan Su
Ramanathan Subramanian
Yusuke Sugano

Masanori Suganuma
Yumin Suh
Mohammed Suhail
Yao Sui
Heung-Il Suk
Josephine Sullivan
Baochen Sun
Chen Sun
Chong Sun
Deqing Sun
Jin Sun
Liang Sun
Lin Sun
Qianru Sun
Shao-Hua Sun
Shuyang Sun
Weiwei Sun
Wenxiu Sun
Xiaoshuai Sun
Xiaoxiao Sun
Xingyuan Sun
Yifan Sun
Zhun Sun
Sabine Susstrunk
David Suter
Supasorn Suwajanakorn
Tomas Svoboda
Eran Swears
Paul Swoboda
Attila Szabo
Richard Szeliski
Duy-Nguyen Ta
Andrea Tagliasacchi
Yuichi Taguchi
Ying Tai
Keita Takahashi
Kouske Takahashi
Jun Takamatsu
Hugues Talbot
Toru Tamaki
Chaowei Tan
Fuwen Tan
Mingkui Tan
Mingxing Tan
Qingyang Tan
Robby T. Tan

Xiaoyang Tan
Kenichiro Tanaka
Masayuki Tanaka
Chang Tang
Chengzhou Tang
Danhang Tang
Ming Tang
Peng Tang
Qingming Tang
Wei Tang
Xu Tang
Yansong Tang
Youbao Tang
Yuxing Tang
Zhiqiang Tang
Tatsunori Taniai
Junli Tao
Xin Tao
Makarand Tapaswi
Jean-Philippe Tarel
Lyne Tchapmi
Zachary Teed
Bugra Tekin
Damien Teney
Ayush Tewari
Christian Theobalt
Christopher Thomas
Diego Thomas
Jim Thomas
Rajat Mani Thomas
Xinmei Tian
Yapeng Tian
Yingli Tian
Yonglong Tian
Zhi Tian
Zhuotao Tian
Kinh Tieu
Joseph Tighe
Massimo Tistarelli
Matthew Toews
Carl Toft
Pavel Tokmakov
Federico Tombari
Chetan Tonde
Yan Tong
Alessio Tonioni

Andrea Torsello
Fabio Tosi
Du Tran
Luan Tran
Ngoc-Trung Tran
Quan Hung Tran
Truyen Tran
Rudolph Triebel
Martin Trimmel
Shashank Tripathi
Subarna Tripathi
Leonardo Trujillo
Eduard Trulls
Tomasz Trzcinski
Sam Tsai
Yi-Hsuan Tsai
Hung-Yu Tseng
Stavros Tsogkas
Aggeliki Tsoli
Devis Tuia
Shubham Tulsiani
Sergey Tulyakov
Frederick Tung
Tony Tung
Daniyar Turmukhambetov
Ambrish Tyagi
Radim Tylecek
Christos Tzelepis
Georgios Tzimiropoulos
Dimitrios Tzionas
Seiichi Uchida
Norimichi Ukita
Dmitry Ulyanov
Martin Urschler
Yoshitaka Ushiku
Ben Usman
Alexander Vakhitov
Julien P. C. Valentin
Jack Valmadre
Ernest Valveny
Joost van de Weijer
Jan van Gemert
Koen Van Leemput
Gul Varol
Sebastiano Vascon
M. Alex O. Vasilescu

Subeesh Vasu
Mayank Vatsa
David Vazquez
Javier Vazquez-Corral
Ashok Veeraraghavan
Erik Velasco-Salido
Raviteja Vemulapalli
Jonathan Ventura
Manisha Verma
Roberto Vezzani
Ruben Villegas
Minh Vo
MinhDuc Vo
Nam Vo
Michele Volpi
Riccardo Volpi
Carl Vondrick
Konstantinos Vougioukas
Tuan-Hung Vu
Sven Wachsmuth
Neal Wadhwa
Catherine Wah
Jacob C. Walker
Thomas S. A. Wallis
Chengde Wan
Jun Wan
Liang Wan
Renjie Wan
Baoyuan Wang
Boyu Wang
Cheng Wang
Chu Wang
Chuan Wang
Chunyu Wang
Dequan Wang
Di Wang
Dilin Wang
Dong Wang
Fang Wang
Guanzhi Wang
Guoyin Wang
Hanzi Wang
Hao Wang
He Wang
Heng Wang
Hongcheng Wang

Hongxing Wang
Hua Wang
Jian Wang
Jingbo Wang
Jinglu Wang
Jingya Wang
Jinjun Wang
Jinqiao Wang
Jue Wang
Ke Wang
Keze Wang
Le Wang
Lei Wang
Lezi Wang
Li Wang
Liang Wang
Lijun Wang
Limin Wang
Linwei Wang
Lizhi Wang
Mengjiao Wang
Mingzhe Wang
Minsi Wang
Naiyan Wang
Nannan Wang
Ning Wang
Oliver Wang
Pei Wang
Peng Wang
Pichao Wang
Qi Wang
Qian Wang
Qiaosong Wang
Qifei Wang
Qilong Wang
Qing Wang
Qingzhong Wang
Quan Wang
Rui Wang
Ruiping Wang
Ruixing Wang
Shangfei Wang
Shenlong Wang
Shiyao Wang
Shuhui Wang
Song Wang

Tao Wang
Tianlu Wang
Tiantian Wang
Ting-chun Wang
Tingwu Wang
Wei Wang
Weiyue Wang
Wenguan Wang
Wenlin Wang
Wenqi Wang
Xiang Wang
Xiaobo Wang
Xiaofang Wang
Xiaoling Wang
Xiaolong Wang
Xiaosong Wang
Xiaoyu Wang
Xin Eric Wang
Xinchao Wang
Xinggang Wang
Xintao Wang
Yali Wang
Yan Wang
Yang Wang
Yangang Wang
Yaxing Wang
Yi Wang
Yida Wang
Yilin Wang
Yiming Wang
Yisen Wang
Yongtao Wang
Yu-Xiong Wang
Yue Wang
Yujiang Wang
Yunbo Wang
Yunhe Wang
Zengmao Wang
Zhangyang Wang
Zhaowen Wang
Zhe Wang
Zhecan Wang
Zheng Wang
Zhixiang Wang
Zilei Wang
Jianqiao Wangni

Anne S. Wannenwetsch
Jan Dirk Wegner
Scott Wehrwein
Donglai Wei
Kaixuan Wei
Longhui Wei
Pengxu Wei
Ping Wei
Qi Wei
Shih-En Wei
Xing Wei
Yunchao Wei
Zijun Wei
Jerod Weinman
Michael Weinmann
Philippe Weinzaepfel
Yair Weiss
Bihan Wen
Longyin Wen
Wei Wen
Junwu Weng
Tsui-Wei Weng
Xinshuo Weng
Eric Wengrowski
Tomas Werner
Gordon Wetzstein
Tobias Weyand
Patrick Wieschollek
Maggie Wigness
Erik Wijmans
Richard Wildes
Olivia Wiles
Chris Williams
Williem Williem
Kyle Wilson
Calden Wloka
Nicolai Wojke
Christian Wolf
Yongkang Wong
Sanghyun Woo
Scott Workman
Baoyuan Wu
Bichen Wu
Chao-Yuan Wu
Huikai Wu
Jiajun Wu

Jialin Wu
Jiaxiang Wu
Jiqing Wu
Jonathan Wu
Lifang Wu
Qi Wu
Qiang Wu
Ruizheng Wu
Shangzhe Wu
Shun-Cheng Wu
Tianfu Wu
Wayne Wu
Wenxuan Wu
Xiao Wu
Xiaohe Wu
Xinxiao Wu
Yang Wu
Yi Wu
Yiming Wu
Ying Nian Wu
Yue Wu
Zheng Wu
Zhenyu Wu
Zhirong Wu
Zuxuan Wu
Stefanie Wuhrer
Jonas Wulff
Changqun Xia
Fangting Xia
Fei Xia
Gui-Song Xia
Lu Xia
Xide Xia
Yin Xia
Yingce Xia
Yongqin Xian
Lei Xiang
Shiming Xiang
Bin Xiao
Fanyi Xiao
Guobao Xiao
Huaxin Xiao
Taihong Xiao
Tete Xiao
Tong Xiao
Wang Xiao

Yang Xiao
Cihang Xie
Guosen Xie
Jianwen Xie
Lingxi Xie
Sirui Xie
Weidi Xie
Wenxuan Xie
Xiaohua Xie
Fuyong Xing
Jun Xing
Junliang Xing
Bo Xiong
Peixi Xiong
Yu Xiong
Yuanjun Xiong
Zhiwei Xiong
Chang Xu
Chenliang Xu
Dan Xu
Danfei Xu
Hang Xu
Hongteng Xu
Huijuan Xu
Jingwei Xu
Jun Xu
Kai Xu
Mengmeng Xu
Mingze Xu
Qianqian Xu
Ran Xu
Weijian Xu
Xiangyu Xu
Xiaogang Xu
Xing Xu
Xun Xu
Yanyu Xu
Yichao Xu
Yong Xu
Yongchao Xu
Yuanlu Xu
Zenglin Xu
Zheng Xu
Chuhui Xue
Jia Xue
Nan Xue

Tianfan Xue
Xiangyang Xue
Abhay Yadav
Yasushi Yagi
I. Zeki Yalniz
Kota Yamaguchi
Toshihiko Yamasaki
Takayoshi Yamashita
Junchi Yan
Ke Yan
Qingan Yan
Sijie Yan
Xinchen Yan
Yan Yan
Yichao Yan
Zhicheng Yan
Keiji Yanai
Bin Yang
Ceyuan Yang
Dawei Yang
Dong Yang
Fan Yang
Guandao Yang
Guorun Yang
Haichuan Yang
Hao Yang
Jianwei Yang
Jiaolong Yang
Jie Yang
Jing Yang
Kaiyu Yang
Linjie Yang
Meng Yang
Michael Ying Yang
Nan Yang
Shuai Yang
Shuo Yang
Tianyu Yang
Tien-Ju Yang
Tsun-Yi Yang
Wei Yang
Wenhan Yang
Xiao Yang
Xiaodong Yang
Xin Yang
Yan Yang

Yanchao Yang
Yee Hong Yang
Yezhou Yang
Zhenheng Yang
Anbang Yao
Angela Yao
Cong Yao
Jian Yao
Li Yao
Ting Yao
Yao Yao
Zhewei Yao
Chengxi Ye
Jianbo Ye
Keren Ye
Linwei Ye
Mang Ye
Mao Ye
Qi Ye
Qixiang Ye
Mei-Chen Yeh
Raymond Yeh
Yu-Ying Yeh
Sai-Kit Yeung
Serena Yeung
Kwang Moo Yi
Li Yi
Renjiao Yi
Alper Yilmaz
Junho Yim
Lijun Yin
Weidong Yin
Xi Yin
Zhichao Yin
Tatsuya Yokota
Ryo Yonetani
Donggeun Yoo
Jae Shin Yoon
Ju Hong Yoon
Sung-eui Yoon
Laurent Younes
Changqian Yu
Fisher Yu
Gang Yu
Jiahui Yu
Kaicheng Yu

Ke Yu
Lequan Yu
Ning Yu
Qian Yu
Ronald Yu
Ruichi Yu
Shoou-I Yu
Tao Yu
Tianshu Yu
Xiang Yu
Xin Yu
Xiyu Yu
Youngjae Yu
Yu Yu
Zhiding Yu
Chunfeng Yuan
Ganzhao Yuan
Jinwei Yuan
Lu Yuan
Quan Yuan
Shanxin Yuan
Tongtong Yuan
Wenjia Yuan
Ye Yuan
Yuan Yuan
Yuhui Yuan
Huanjing Yue
Xiangyu Yue
Ersin Yumer
Sergey Zagoruyko
Egor Zakharov
Amir Zamir
Andrei Zanfir
Mihai Zanfir
Pablo Zegers
Bernhard Zeisl
John S. Zelek
Niclas Zeller
Huayi Zeng
Jiabei Zeng
Wenjun Zeng
Yu Zeng
Xiaohua Zhai
Fangneng Zhan
Huangying Zhan
Kun Zhan

Xiaohang Zhan
Baochang Zhang
Bowen Zhang
Cecilia Zhang
Changqing Zhang
Chao Zhang
Chengquan Zhang
Chi Zhang
Chongyang Zhang
Dingwen Zhang
Dong Zhang
Feihu Zhang
Hang Zhang
Hanwang Zhang
Hao Zhang
He Zhang
Hongguang Zhang
Hua Zhang
Ji Zhang
Jianguo Zhang
Jianming Zhang
Jiawei Zhang
Jie Zhang
Jing Zhang
Juyong Zhang
Kai Zhang
Kaipeng Zhang
Ke Zhang
Le Zhang
Lei Zhang
Li Zhang
Lihe Zhang
Linguang Zhang
Lu Zhang
Mi Zhang
Mingda Zhang
Peng Zhang
Pingping Zhang
Qian Zhang
Qilin Zhang
Quanshi Zhang
Richard Zhang
Rui Zhang
Runze Zhang
Shengping Zhang
Shifeng Zhang

Shuai Zhang
Songyang Zhang
Tao Zhang
Ting Zhang
Tong Zhang
Wayne Zhang
Wei Zhang
Weizhong Zhang
Wenwei Zhang
Xiangyu Zhang
Xiaolin Zhang
Xiaopeng Zhang
Xiaoqin Zhang
Xiuming Zhang
Ya Zhang
Yang Zhang
Yimin Zhang
Yinda Zhang
Ying Zhang
Yongfei Zhang
Yu Zhang
Yulun Zhang
Yunhua Zhang
Yuting Zhang
Zhanpeng Zhang
Zhao Zhang
Zhaoxiang Zhang
Zhen Zhang
Zheng Zhang
Zhifei Zhang
Zhijin Zhang
Zhishuai Zhang
Ziming Zhang
Bo Zhao
Chen Zhao
Fang Zhao
Haiyu Zhao
Han Zhao
Hang Zhao
Hengshuang Zhao
Jian Zhao
Kai Zhao
Liang Zhao
Long Zhao
Qian Zhao
Qibin Zhao

Qijun Zhao
Rui Zhao
Shenglin Zhao
Sicheng Zhao
Tianyi Zhao
Wenda Zhao
Xiangyun Zhao
Xin Zhao
Yang Zhao
Yue Zhao
Zhichen Zhao
Zijing Zhao
Xiantong Zhen
Chuanxia Zheng
Feng Zheng
Haiyong Zheng
Jia Zheng
Kang Zheng
Shuai Kyle Zheng
Wei-Shi Zheng
Yinqiang Zheng
Zerong Zheng
Zhedong Zheng
Zilong Zheng
Bineng Zhong
Fangwei Zhong
Guangyu Zhong
Yiran Zhong
Yujie Zhong
Zhun Zhong
Chunluan Zhou
Huiyu Zhou
Jiahuan Zhou
Jun Zhou
Lei Zhou
Luowei Zhou
Luping Zhou
Mo Zhou
Ning Zhou
Pan Zhou
Peng Zhou
Qianyi Zhou
S. Kevin Zhou
Sanping Zhou
Wengang Zhou
Xingyi Zhou

Yanzhao Zhou
Yi Zhou
Yin Zhou
Yipin Zhou
Yuyin Zhou
Zihan Zhou
Alex Zihao Zhu
Chenchen Zhu
Feng Zhu
Guangming Zhu
Ji Zhu
Jun-Yan Zhu
Lei Zhu
Linchao Zhu
Rui Zhu
Shizhan Zhu
Tyler Lixuan Zhu

Wei Zhu
Xiangyu Zhu
Xinge Zhu
Xizhou Zhu
Yanjun Zhu
Yi Zhu
Yixin Zhu
Yizhe Zhu
Yousong Zhu
Zhe Zhu
Zhen Zhu
Zheng Zhu
Zhenyao Zhu
Zhihui Zhu
Zhuotun Zhu
Bingbing Zhuang
Wei Zhuo

Christian Zimmermann
Karel Zimmermann
Larry Zitnick
Mohammadreza
    Zolfaghari
Maria Zontak
Daniel Zoran
Changqing Zou
Chuhang Zou
Danping Zou
Qi Zou
Yang Zou
Yuliang Zou
Georgios Zoumpourlis
Wangmeng Zuo
Xinxin Zuo

Additional Reviewers

Victoria Fernandez
    Abrevaya
Maya Aghaei
Allam Allam
Christine
    Allen-Blanchette
Nicolas Aziere
Assia Benbihi
Neha Bhargava
Bharat Lal Bhatnagar
Joanna Bitton
Judy Borowski
Amine Bourki
Romain Brégier
Tali Brayer
Sebastian Bujwid
Andrea Burns
Yun-Hao Cao
Yuning Chai
Xiaojun Chang
Bo Chen
Shuo Chen
Zhixiang Chen
Junsuk Choe
Hung-Kuo Chu

Jonathan P. Crall
Kenan Dai
Lucas Deecke
Karan Desai
Prithviraj Dhar
Jing Dong
Wei Dong
Turan Kaan Elgin
Francis Engelmann
Erik Englesson
Fartash Faghri
Zicong Fan
Yang Fu
Risheek Garrepalli
Yifan Ge
Marco Godi
Helmut Grabner
Shuxuan Guo
Jianfeng He
Zhezhi He
Samitha Herath
Chih-Hui Ho
Yicong Hong
Vincent Tao Hu
Julio Hurtado

Jaedong Hwang
Andrey Ignatov
Muhammad
    Abdullah Jamal
Saumya Jetley
Meiguang Jin
Jeff Johnson
Minsoo Kang
Saeed Khorram
Mohammad Rami Koujan
Nilesh Kulkarni
Sudhakar Kumawat
Abdelhak Lemkhenter
Alexander Levine
Jiachen Li
Jing Li
Jun Li
Yi Li
Liang Liao
Ruochen Liao
Tzu-Heng Lin
Phillip Lippe
Bao-di Liu
Bo Liu
Fangchen Liu

Hanxiao Liu
Hongyu Liu
Huidong Liu
Miao Liu
Xinxin Liu
Yongfei Liu
Yu-Lun Liu
Amir Livne
Tiange Luo
Wei Ma
Xiaoxuan Ma
Ioannis Marras
Georg Martius
Effrosyni Mavroudi
Tim Meinhardt
Givi Meishvili
Meng Meng
Zihang Meng
Zhongqi Miao
Gyeongsik Moon
Khoi Nguyen
Yung-Kyun Noh
Antonio Norelli
Jaeyoo Park
Alexander Pashevich
Mandela Patrick
Mary Phuong
Bingqiao Qian
Yu Qiao
Zhen Qiao
Sai Saketh Rambhatla
Aniket Roy
Amelie Royer
Parikshit Vishwas
    Sakurikar
Mark Sandler
Mert Bülent Sarıyıldız
Tanner Schmidt
Anshul B. Shah

Ketul Shah
Rajvi Shah
Hengcan Shi
Xiangxi Shi
Yujiao Shi
William A. P. Smith
Guoxian Song
Robin Strudel
Abby Stylianou
Xinwei Sun
Reuben Tan
Qingyi Tao
Kedar S. Tatwawadi
Anh Tuan Tran
Son Dinh Tran
Eleni Triantafillou
Aristeidis Tsitiridis
Md Zasim Uddin
Andrea Vedaldi
Evangelos Ververas
Vidit Vidit
Paul Voigtlaender
Bo Wan
Huanyu Wang
Huiyu Wang
Junqiu Wang
Pengxiao Wang
Tai Wang
Xinyao Wang
Tomoki Watanabe
Mark Weber
Xi Wei
Botong Wu
James Wu
Jiamin Wu
Rujie Wu
Yu Wu
Rongchang Xie
Wei Xiong

Yunyang Xiong
An Xu
Chi Xu
Yinghao Xu
Fei Xue
Tingyun Yan
Zike Yan
Chao Yang
Heran Yang
Ren Yang
Wenfei Yang
Xu Yang
Rajeev Yasarla
Shaokai Ye
Yufei Ye
Kun Yi
Haichao Yu
Hanchao Yu
Ruixuan Yu
Liangzhe Yuan
Chen-Lin Zhang
Fandong Zhang
Tianyi Zhang
Yang Zhang
Yiyi Zhang
Yongshun Zhang
Yu Zhang
Zhiwei Zhang
Jiaojiao Zhao
Yipu Zhao
Xingjian Zhen
Haizhong Zheng
Tiancheng Zhi
Chengju Zhou
Hao Zhou
Hao Zhu
Alexander Zimin

Contents – Part XIX

High-Resolution Image Inpainting with Iterative Confidence Feedback and Guided Upsampling

Yu Zeng[1], Zhe Lin[2], Jimei Yang[2], Jianming Zhang[2], Eli Shechtman[2], and Huchuan Lu[1(✉)]

[1] Dalian University of Technology, Dalian, China
`zengxianyu18@qq.com,lhchuan@dlut.edu.cn`
[2] Adobe Research, San Jose, USA
`{zlin,jimyang,jianmzha,elishe}@adobe.com`

Abstract. Existing image inpainting methods often produce artifacts when dealing with large holes in real applications. To address this challenge, we propose an iterative inpainting method with a feedback mechanism. Specifically, we introduce a deep generative model which not only outputs an inpainting result but also a corresponding confidence map. Using this map as feedback, it progressively fills the hole by trusting only high-confidence pixels inside the hole at each iteration and focuses on the remaining pixels in the next iteration. As it reuses partial predictions from the previous iterations as known pixels, this process gradually improves the result. In addition, we propose a guided upsampling network to enable generation of high-resolution inpainting results. We achieve this by extending the Contextual Attention module [39] to borrow high-resolution feature patches in the input image. Furthermore, to mimic real object removal scenarios, we collect a large object mask dataset and synthesize more realistic training data that better simulates user inputs. Experiments show that our method significantly outperforms existing methods in both quantitative and qualitative evaluations. More results and Web APP are available at https://zengxianyu.github.io/iic.

1 Introduction

Image inpainting is a task of reconstructing missing regions in an image. It is an important problem in computer vision and an essential functionality in many imaging and graphics applications, *e.g.* object removal, image restoration, manipulation, re-targeting, compositing, and image-based rendering [9,26,33]

Classical inpainting methods such as [9,17,25] typically rely on the principle of borrowing example patches from known regions or external database images and pasting them into the holes. These methods are quite effective for easy cases

---

Electronic supplementary material The online version of this chapter (https://doi.org/10.1007/978-3-030-58529-7_1) contains supplementary material, which is available to authorized users.

© Springer Nature Switzerland AG 2020
A. Vedaldi et al. (Eds.): ECCV 2020, LNCS 12364, pp. 1–17, 2020.
https://doi.org/10.1007/978-3-030-58529-7_1

Input   EdgeConnect   PConv   PatchMatch   GConv   Global&Local   Ours

Fig. 1. Results of state-of-the-art methods on real object removal requests [4,7].

with small holes or uniform textured background. They can also handle high-resolution images efficiently. However, due to the lack of high-level structural understanding and ability to generate novel contents, they often fail to produce realistic results when the hole is large.

Deep learning has achieved great success on various dense prediction problems [12–15,36,42–45]. Recent research effort on inpainting has shifted towards a data-driven learning-based approach [22,29,34,39,40]. These methods train a deep neural network to directly predict the inpainting result given a corrupted image and hole channel as input. The original images before corruption are used as the ground truth to train the network. To generate visually realistic results with sufficient texture details, they often use an adversarial loss based on GANs [20] in addition to a reconstruction loss. These deep generative models show significant improvements on filling holes in complex images but often produce visual artifacts, especially when the hole is large. For large holes, the reconstruction loss is less effective due to the increased ambiguity, leading to undesired predictions during testing as shown in Fig. 1.

In this paper, we aim to address the challenge of filling large holes in high resolution images for real image editing applications, *e.g.*, object removal. We observe that in the failure cases of existing approaches, despite the artifacts, there often exist sub-regions with good predictions. If we trust the good part and treat the remaining region as a new hole and run the model again, then the hole become progressively smaller and the model can produce better results. Inspired by this observation, we propose a novel iterative inpainting method with a feedback mechanism. Our method is based on a deep generative model which not only outputs an inpainting result but also a corresponding confidence map.

The model is encouraged to generate a confidence map that highlights pixels where the prediction error is likely small and can help overcome the prediction ambiguity. Using this confidence map as feedback, our model is trained to progressively fill the hole by trusting only high-confidence pixels inside the hole at each iteration and update the remaining pixels in the next iteration. By predicting what portion of the hole was filled successfully in the previous iteration and using those pixels as "known", our model can gradually improve the result when filling large holes. The proposed confidence prediction scheme is general and can be potentially attached to any deep generative inpainting model.

To generate high-quality inpainting results at high-resolution, we propose a guided inpainting upsampling network as a post-processing method. We achieve this by extending the Contextual Attention module [39] to borrow known high-resolution feature patches in the input image based on the patch similarities computed on the result for down-sampled input. The motivation is that it is easier to train a deep network to generate globally coherent structures for down-sampled inputs as effective receptive fields of neurons are larger; while the surrounding regions of the high-resolution input can be used to enhance fine-grained texture details inside the hole. In this way, our method decouples high-level structural understanding and low-level texture reconstruction, and can produce results that are both semantically plausible and visually realistic at high resolution.

On the data side, previous methods construct training data by synthesizing square [22,34,39] or irregular holes [29,40]. However, in real applications for removing undesirable objects or scene segments, the hole-filling regions are more likely to be object-shaped. In this work, we collect a large set of object masks and propose to use the object shapes as holes to mimic real use cases.

In summary, our contributions are three-fold:

- We address the challenge of completing large missing regions in images by proposing an iterative inpainting method with a confidence feedback loop.
- We propose a guided up-sampling network as a post processing step to enable generation of high-resolution inpainting results.
- We introduce a new procedure to synthesize training data for building deep generative models for real object removal applications.

2   Related Work

Earlier image inpainting methods rely on existing content to fill the holes. Diffusion-based methods [8,10] propagate neighboring appearances to the target holes, but they often generate significant artifacts when the holes are large or texture variation is severe. Patch-based methods [9,17,25] search for most similar patches from valid regions to complete missing regions. Drori *et al.* [16] propose to iteratively fill missing regions from high to low confidence with similar patches. Although they also use a map to determine the region to fill in each iteration, the map is predefined based on spatial distances from unknown pixels to their closest valid pixels. The above methods use real image patches sampled from the input to fill the holes and can often generate high-quality results. However, they lack high-level structural understanding and cannot generate entirely new content that does not exist in the input image. Thus, their results may not be semantically consistent to regions surrounding the holes.

By learning from a large corpus of data, deep learning based inpainting methods can understand the semantic structure of the input image and hence can handle more difficult cases. To produce sharper results, these methods typically adopt adversarial training inspired by GANs [20]. Pathak *et al.* [34] made a first attempt to use a convolutional neural network (CNN) for hole filling. Iizuka *et al.* [22] use two discriminators for adversarial training to make the inpainted content both locally and globally consistent. Yu *et al.* [39] propose a deep generative model with contextual attention to explicitly utilize surrounding image features as references in the latent feature space. Zeng *et al.* [41] propose to use region affinity from a high-level feature map to guide the completion of missing regions in the previous low-level feature map of a single input. Our upsampling network is similar in spirit of using coarse scale information to guide the generation of fine-grained details but different in architecture and functionality; it upsamples a low-resoluiotn results by filling the fine-grained details from the high-resolution input. Yang *et al.* [38] upsamples the results of a similar network with a neural patch search and vote approach followed by an optimization. Our method uses a related neural patch-vote approach but avoids the slow optimization. The above methods use square holes in their training data, which causes a bias to rectangular holes. To address this, Liu *et al.* [29] collect estimated occlusion/dis-occlusion masks between two consecutive frames of videos and use them to generate holes for training. The resulting masks are highly irregular and do not represent well holes typical to an image inpainting task. They also propose partial convolution layers to infer missing pixels conditioned only on valid pixels. Yu *et al.* [40] introduce free-form masks by simulating random strokes and generalizes partial convolution to gated convolution that learns to select features for each channel at each spatial location across all layers. Although these irregular holes lead to more diverse samples, they do not represent well real inpainting use-cases.

Most recently, a few works have been introduced to study progressive inpainting models. Zhang *et al.* [46] adopt a UNet generator with an LSTM in the bottleneck. It takes a sequence of inputs with large to small holes in the image center and generates a sequence of corresponding outputs. Guo *et al.* [21] propose to gradually fill a hole using consecutive residual blocks. They use partial convolutions in these blocks and update the hole mask according to the invalid pixels selected by partial convolutions. Oh *et al.* [32] propose an onion-peel network that progressively fills the hole from the hole boundary for video hole filling. All of the above methods fill the holes from the boundary to inner regions in a *predefined* sequence. Different from them, our proposed method jointly predicts a confidence map when generating an inpainting result. Using the confidence map from the previous iteration as feedback, it can automatically detect regions with bad fill to revise in following iterations. To our best knowledge, it is the first attempt to model confidence of predictions in inpainting and the first iterative inpainting method to fill holes with a confidence-driven feedback loop.

3   Approach

Our inpainting method consists of two models: an iterative inpainting model (Fig. 3(a)) with confidence feedback and a guided upsampling network ((Fig. 3(b)) that upsamples a low-resolution result by factor of 2 using the high resolution (HR) input as guidance. In this section, we first describe how we prepare data for building and evaluating our model, and then introduce the details of our iterative inpainting model and guided upsampling network.

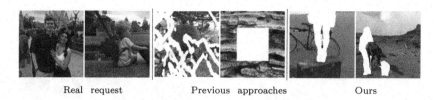

Real request   Previous approaches   Ours

Fig. 2. Comparison of input with holes. The first two columns are real object removal requests on the Web [2,5]. The second two are from PConv [29] and ContextAttention [39], respectively. The right two are our samples with object-shaped holes.

3.1 Data Generation

Previous approaches to image inpainting typically construct their training and testing data pairs by corrupting the original images with square-shaped [22,34, 39] or highly irregular holes [29,40], as shown in the first two columns in Fig. 2. Images with holes are the input and the original images are the corresponding ground-truth. However, in real-world inpainting use cases such as distracting region removal, the regions users typically want to remove are objects or scene segments, which are rarely of square or highly irregular shapes, as shown in the middle two columns of Fig. 2.

To mimic a more typical image editing scenario, in this work, we synthesize training samples with realistic holes. We collect 82,020 object masks from densely annotated segmentation datasets [11,18,19,27,28,35] to use as holes. We use a mix of random strokes [40] and the object masks as holes to create a more diverse training dataset and overcome a bias towards object shaped holes. The images for synthesizing training samples are from two sources: the Places2 [47] dataset and salient object segmentation dataset [37]. We use 1,000 images with salient objects as testing samples and the other 60,525 are merged with Places2 for training and validation. For images in Places2, we sample randomly the location of the holes so they can appear in any region and may overlap with the main object. For images originating from salient object segmentation datasets, we subtract from the holes the intersection area with the salient objects. This is to simulate the case of removing distracting regions occluded by salient objects. As shown in the last two columns of Fig. 2, such generated samples with holes are more similar to real cases than those of previous approaches.

3.2 Inpainting Model

We adopt a generative approach based on generative adversarial networks (GANs) [20]. Thus our model has a generator and a discriminator. Figure 3(a) illustrates an overall structure of the generator. It is a cascade of a coarse and a fine networks, similar to [39]. The coarse network takes an incomplete image and the corresponding hole mask as input to produce a coarse completed image. Then, the coarse result is passed to the fine network to generate a final completed image and a confidence map. The fine network has one encoder and two

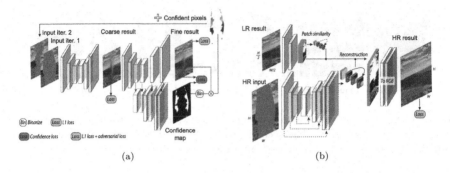

Fig. 3. The overall structure. (a) Iterative inpainting with confidence feedback. (b) Guided upsampling.

decoders: an image decoder that predicts the inpainting image result, and a confidence decoder that returns a corresponding confidence map of the predicted image. To make confidence prediction aware of the full generation process, we let the confidence decoder take as input all the feature layers up to the bottleneck of the image decoder, as illustrated by the dashed blocks in Fig. 3(a).

We use a PatchGAN discriminator [23] with spectral normalization as in [40] for adversarial training. It takes as input either the inpainted image or the ground-truth image and classifies each patch of the input image as real or fake. Its output is a score map rather than a single score, where each element corresponds to a local region of the input image covered by its receptive field.

Generative Inpainting Loss. We train our model on the realistic hole dataset described in Sect. 3.1. We use L1 reconstruction loss on the coarse level. On the fine level, we use both L1 and a hinge adversarial loss with spectral normalization [30] applied on the discriminator. The loss for the discriminator D is:

$$\mathcal{L}_D = \mathbb{E}_{x \sim p_{data}(x)}[\text{ReLU}(\mathbb{1} - D(x))] + \mathbb{E}_{z \sim p_z(z)}[\text{ReLU}(\mathbb{1} + D(G(z) \circ m + z))], \quad (1)$$

where x denotes the real (ground truth) image and z represents the incomplete image of which the pixels inside the hole are set to zero; m represents the hole mask, in which the pixels having value one belong to the hole; $G(\cdot)$ represents the image decoder; $\circ$ denotes element-wise multiplication; the inpainting result $G(z) \circ m + z$ is composed by the generated content $G(z)$ inside the hole and the original content z outside the hole. Let y denote the output of the image decoder, i.e. $y = G(z)$, then the loss for the inpainting result is:

$$\mathcal{L}_G = \mathbb{E}_{z,x \sim p(z,x)}[L(y)], \text{where } L(y) = \text{ReLU}(\mathbb{1} - D(y \circ m + z)) + \|y - x\|_1. \quad (2)$$

Confidence Prediction Loss. We make the confidence decoder detect good regions by using its output map as spatial attention on the predicted image when calculating the loss. Let c denote the confidence map, i.e., output of the

Fig. 4. Results and confidence maps. Blue masks indicate holes. Brighter pixels in confidence maps are of higher confidence. We use solid blue masks for synthetic samples and transparent ones for real object removal cases. (Color figure online)

confidence decoder of which each element is constrained to $[0, 1]$ by a sigmoid function, we define the following loss for the confidence decoder:

$$\mathcal{L}_C = \mathbb{E}_{z,x \sim p(z,x)}[L(y \circ c + x \circ (1-c)) + \lambda(\|(\mathbb{1}-c) \circ m\|_1 + \|(\mathbb{1}-c) \circ m\|_2)], \quad (3)$$

where λ is a hyperparameter controlling the size of the confident area. We set it to 0.1 in all evaluations but also provide sensitivity analysis of it in the experiments.

To minimize $\mathcal{L}_C$, the map c should highlight confidence regions, i.e. pixels contributing less to the overall loss. To prove this, we assume that: (1) $L(y)$ can be written as the summation over local pixel-wise losses, i.e. $L(y) = \sum_{i \in \mathcal{H}} l(y_i)$ where $l(y_i) \geq 0$ is an unknown local loss function, $\mathcal{H}$ is the index set of pixels inside the holes and y_i is a pixel of the generator output y, and (2) $l(x_i) = 0$ for every ground-truth pixel x_i. For simplification, we consider c as binary and let $\mathcal{C}$ to be the index set of non-zero elements of c, then $\mathcal{L}_C$ can be re-written as:

$$\begin{aligned} \mathcal{L}_C &= \mathbb{E}_{z,x \sim p(z,x)}[L(y \circ c + x \circ (1-c)) - \lambda\|c\|] \\ &= \mathbb{E}_{z,x \sim p(z,x)}[\sum_{i \in \mathcal{C}} l(y_i) + \sum_{i \in (\mathcal{H}-\mathcal{C})} l(x_i) - \lambda|\mathcal{C}|] \\ &= \mathbb{E}_{z,x \sim p(z,x)}[\sum_{i \in \mathcal{C}} l(y_i) - \lambda|\mathcal{C}|]; \end{aligned} \quad (4)$$

for a single sample y, the loss is the summation of local loss over $\mathcal{C}$. Therefore, the minimum is achieved when $\mathcal{C}$ covers the set of pixels with the smallest local loss values. Intuitively, the first term in Eq. 3 encourages the confidence map to have high response where the loss $L(y)$ is small, as $\mathcal{L}_C$ is expected to be smaller by choosing low-loss area from the generator output $y \circ c$ and replacing high-loss are with ground-truth $x \circ (1-c)$; the second term penalizes a trivial solution of all-zero confidence maps by encouraging the confident region to cover as much of the missing region as possible.

Figure 4 shows examples of inpainting results and the corresponding confidence maps. We can see that the confidence maps tend to highlight good regions of the result. As one may expect, confident regions are often located close to the hole boundaries. However, there are also other cases: 1) in easy cases like filling a hole in the sky, all generated pixels can have high confidence; 2) flat regions tend to be more confident than highly-textured regions; 3) artifacts have low confidence.

Algorithm 1: $G(\cdot)$: generator; $C(\cdot)$: confidence decoder

---

Input : Incomplete image z_1, hole mask m_1, the number of iterations T
Output: Completed image y_T

1 Set initial confidence map $c_0 = 0.5m_1$
2 **for** $t \in \{1, ..., T\}$ **do**
3 $\quad$ Get confidence map $c_t = C(z_t) \circ m_t$
4 $\quad$ Get mask of regions to update $u_t = \mathrm{Binarize}(c_t - c_{t-1} \circ m_t)$
5 $\quad$ Update mask $m_{t+1} = m_t - u_t$
6 $\quad$ **if** $t = 1$ **then**
7 $\quad\quad$ | Initialize completed image $y_1 = z_1 + G(z_1) \circ m_t$
8 $\quad$ **else**
9 $\quad\quad$ | Update competed image $y_t = G(z_t) \circ u_t + y_{t-1} \circ (1 - u_t)$
10 $\quad$ **end**
11 $\quad$ Update incomplete image $z_{t+1} = y_t \circ m_{t+1}$
12 **end**

Fig. 5. Inpainting results as iterations increase.

Iterative Inpainting. We can use the confidence decoder output to identify confident sub-regions in the inpainting result and run the inpainting model again and repeat the process. In each iteration, we set the confident pixels as "valid" pixels in the new input and set the remaining low-confidence regions as new holes for the next iteration to process. Overall, holes are shrinking as the iteration goes so that the network should be more certain about the generated result.

Algorithm 1 describes the iterative inpainting process in details. In the first iteration, we initialize the completed image by filling the whole missing region with the generated content and set the pixels of which confidence is below 0.5 as the missing regions for the second iteration. From the second iteration, a pixel is replaced by new generated one if its confidence increases over the previous iteration. When training, we iterate twice. We also fix the number of iterations during the testing. There is no convergence issue because our algorithm always keep the current-best complete prediction inside the hole at every iteration. Figure 5 shows inpainting results in three consecutive iterations. As iteration goes, lines are connected and distorted area or artifacts are corrected.

Input   (a)   (b)   Input   (a)   (b)

Fig. 6. Effect of guided upsampling network. (a) results obtained by the iterative inpainting model on original size; (b) running the iterative model on half size and using guided upsampling network to upsample to the original size.

3.3 Guided Upsampling

Our iterative inpainting model is trained on low-resolution (LR) (256×256) so it is not ideal to directly apply it to high-resolution (HR) inputs. To solve this issue, we propose a guided inpainting upsampling network to generate a HR inpainting result given a LR inpainting result. We propose a new architecture extending the contextual attention module [39] which can match and use feature patches from valid surrounding areas to help synthesize the hole pixels.

As illustrated in Fig. 3(b), the proposed guided upsampling network consists of two shallow networks, one for learning patch similarity and the other for image reconstruction. Their feature maps are of different sizes, but we can split them into an equal number of patches using different patch sizes so that patches of the similarity network feature map have 1:1 correspondence to patches of the reconstruction network feature map which allows us to use shared indices to represent patches. Let $\mathcal{H}$ and $\mathcal{V}$ to be the index set of patches inside the holes and the valid patches, respectively. Valid patches are those with at least one pixel outside the holes, and others are taken as patches inside the hole. The patch similarity network calculates the cosine similarity s_{ij} between a pair of patch i, j. The reconstruction network is a shallow encoder-decoder network with skip connections from each layer of the encoder to the mirrored layer of the decoder. Before converting an HR feature map (of the HR input size) into an HR inpainting result, each feature patch inside the holes is replaced with a weighted sum of valid patches. Let ϕ_i to be an HR feature patch. The patch replacement in the HR feature maps can be summarized as $\phi_i = \sum_{j \in \mathcal{V}} s'_{ij} \phi_j, \quad i \in \mathcal{H}$, where s'_{ij} is the softmax of s_{ij}. Then the HR feature maps are transformed to an output image by two convolution layers ("ToRGB" in Fig. 3(b)). The loss on the HR output is a combined L1 and adversarial loss, the same as in Eq. 2. As mentioned earlier, we take the patches with at least one valid pixel as valid patches. For missing regions reconstructed by these partially valid patches, we simply take them as holes and run the previously described iterative inpainting model one more time. By separating high-level similarity learning and low-level texture reconstruction, the proposed guided upsampling network can generate inpainting results that are both semantically reasonable and visually realistic, as shown in Fig. 6. Furthermore, by specifying patches in $\mathcal{V}$, the users can control over the results, as we show in the supplementary material.

4   Experiments

4.1   Implementation Details

We implement our method using Python and Pytorch. Detailed network architectures can be found in the supplementary material[1]. We train the models with Adam [24] optimizer; the learning rate set to 0.0001. The training batch size is 64. As the Places2 is much larger than the saliency dataset, we sample an equal number of images from Places2 dataset and saliency dataset to constitute each batch to prevent the model from ignoring the scarce samples. We use 256×256 patches for training the iterative inpainting model and train the guided upsampling network to upsample 256×256 results to 512×512. We randomly take 400 images from the training split of Places2 and the saliency dataset as validation samples and generate holes on them as described in Sect. 3.1. The model is trained until the PSNR on this validation set does not increase. The 1,000 testing images are kept unseen during training. When testing, the number of iterations for iterative inpainting is set to 4.

4.2   Comparison with State-of-the-Art Methods

We evaluate quantitative scores and visual quality of two variants of our method: *i.e.* **Ours***: the iterative inpainting model running on original input without guided upsampling and **Ours**: the iterative inpainting model running on 2× downsampled input and then using the guided upsample model to obtain the results of original size. We compare our methods with four state-of-the-art methods: Global&Local [22], PatchMatch [9], GConv [40] and EdgeConnect [31]. Comparison with more methods can be found in supplementary material.

Quantitative Evaluation. We evaluate two variants of our method and state-of-the-art methods on the test set of 1,000 images with object shaped holes. These images are of various size, from short side 256 to long side 1024. For random 500 images of them, we exclude salient objects from holes to simulate the case of distracting objects behind the main objects. For the rest 500 images the holes are placed randomly. For fair comparisons with previous methods, we also evaluate on the standard Places2 validation set resized to 256×256 with 128×128 center square holes as in most previous methods *e.g.* [22,39,41], and irregular holes as in [37,40]. We use L1 loss, PSNR, and SSIM as they are most commonly used metrics in image inpainting. Table 1 shows quantitative comparisons of our method with state-of-the-art methods. Both variants of our method compare favourably against previous methods. Without guided upsampling and running on original resolution, **Ours*** model tends to generate smoother results, which are favored by these scores at per-pixel basis. To validate superiority of our method on filling large holes, we show scores measured on images with holes of different sizes in Fig. 7. The X-axis represents the range of hole-to-image area

---

[1] https://zengxianyu.github.io/iic.

Table 1. Quantitative evaluation and user preference of various methods. P.c.: preference count in user study.

Method	Object shaped holes			Irregular holes (Places2)			Square holes (Places2)			User study
	L1 Loss	PSNR	SSIM	L1 Loss	PSNR	SSIM	L1 Loss	PSNR	SSIM	P. c.
[9]	.0273	25.64	.8780	.0288	22.87	.8549	.0432	19.19	.7922	13
[22]	.0292	24.23	.8653	.0385	20.95	.8185	.0386	20.16	.7950	2
[40]	.0243	26.07	.8803	.0245	24.31	.8718	.0430	19.08	.7984	8
[31]	.0246	26.24	.8871	.0221	24.78	.8701	.0368	20.30	.8017	10
Ours*	.0194	28.20	.8985	.0203	25.43	.8828	.0361	20.21	.8130	62
Ours	.0205	27.67	.8949	0220	24.70	.8744	.0384	19.69	.8063	80

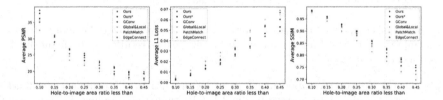

Fig. 7. Quantitative comparisons when hole size varies.

ratio and Y-axis represents average L1 loss, SSIM and PSNR over all samples of which the hole-to-image area ratio are in the corresponding range. For example, the first column is averaged over samples whose hole-to-image ratio is less than 0.1 and the second column is averaged over those greater than 0.1 but less than 0.15. For small holes, all methods perform almost equally well. It is increasingly more difficult to fill holes when their size grow. So the SSIM, PSNR of all methods decrease and L1 loss increases as the hole-to-image ratio increases. When it comes to larger holes, our method performs better.

Visual Quality. Figure 8 shows visual comparisons of two variants of our method and state-of-the-art methods on real object removal tasks [1,3,6]. As shown in the figure, existing deep learning based methods do not work well in real requests. They often generate artifacts removing a large object. Patch-Match can generate clear texture, however, since it does not have a semantic understanding of input images, its results are not semantically reasonable. Both **Ours*** and **Ours** can provide reasonable alternatives for the region to remove. **Ours*** tends to generate smoother results. In comparison, by reconstructing LR results using patches from HR inputs, **Ours** method is better at keeping fine-grained details. Its results are similar to PatchMatch in terms of texture but more reasonable in terms of structure.

To evaluate visual quality of our method, we conduct a user study on 25 real object removal cases collected from object removal requests on the Web. All images are resized to make the short side equal to 512. Each input image with a marked region to remove and the results of different methods are shown in

Input   EdgeConnect   Global&Local   PatchMatch   GConv   Ours*   Ours

Fig. 8. Visual comparison on mid-resolution images. Zoom-in to see the details. Images are compressed due to limited submission file size. More results can be found in the supplementary material.

Table 2. Effect of each component. IT: iterative inpainting; CF: confidence feedback; RT: realistic training data as described in 3.1; GU: guided upsampling. PC represents preference counts in user study. Time is measured in seconds on 512×512 input.

IT	CF	RT	GU	L1 Loss	PSNR	SSIM	PC	Time
				.0205	27.79	.8903	–	.064
√				.0204	27.57	.8925	–	.301
√	√			.0200	28.06	.8952	–	.323
√	√	√		.0194	28.20	.8985	62	.323
√	√	√	√	.0205	27.67	.8949	80	.182
Confidence > 0.5				.0033	36.38	.981	–	–
Confidence ≤ 0.5				.0165	30.00	.923	–	–

random order to 11 users and we ask them to select a single best result. Each combination of input and results are shown twice, and a valid vote is counted only when a user selects the same result twice. Finally we collect 175 valid votes. The user study results are shown in Table 1. Both variants of our method are preferred more than previous methods. **Ours** model with guided upsampling tends to generate results that are less smooth and with more clear texture, which are often favored by users.

4.3   Ablation Study

First, to validate the proposed confidence prediction mechanism, we separately evaluate the results of high-confidence (> 0.5) and low-confidence (≤ 0.5) regions inside the hole. The results are in the bottom two rows of Table 2, which indicates that the prediction in high-confidence regions are significantly better than

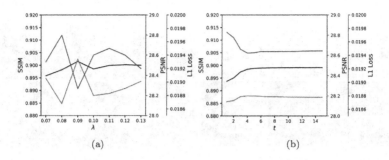

(a)   (b)

Fig. 9. (a) Sensitivity analysis of λ. (b) Effect of increasing test iterations.

low-confidence regions. We show the effect of realistic training data, iterative inpainting, and guided upsample model in the first to the third rows of Table 2. The first row corresponds to our baseline model without confidence decoder trained on the Places2 dataset using irregular and square holes. The second row shows the effect of conducting progressive inpainting (IT) in a predefined boundary-to-center manner. For this setting, we evenly split each hole into four parts based on distance transformation and run the baseline model four times for each input. Each time we fill the part closest to the hole boundaries and update the hole mask accordingly. The third row shows the iterative inpainting method with confidence feedback (CF) trained on Places2 using irregular and square holes. By predicting confidence map, it can automatically correct wrong inpainted pixels and gradually improve the results, which yields better performance than predefined progressive inpainting in terms of quantitative scores. The sixth row corresponds to **Ours*** model described in previous sections. The comparison between the third and the fourth row shows the effect of including realistic training (RT) samples. All the variants discussed above output results of the same size as the input. So when evaluating these models, we give them the original input and do not apply post processing on their results. To analyze the effect of guide upsampling, we first run the proposed iterative inpainting method on 2× downsampled input images, and then upsample the results to the original resolution using guided upsampling. This corresponds to **Ours** described previously, and the effect is shown in the fifth row of Table 2. By running the iterative process on the downsampled input, it significantly cuts down the overall run-time.s

The sensitivity analysis of λ (Eq. 3) is shown in Fig. 9(a). The performance is not very sensitive to λ when it changes in a small range. For example, for $\lambda \in [0.7, 0.13]$, PSNR is in $[28.1, 28.5]$. Figure 9(b) shows the effect of increasing test iterations. More test iterations generally lead to better scores, especially in the first four iterations. We fix the number of iterations to 4 during testing.

| Input | Ours* | Ours | Input | Ours* | Ours |

Fig. 10. Inpainting results on 1024 × 1024 images. Zoom-in to see the details. Images are compressed due to limited submission file size.

Figure 10 shows inpainting results of **Ours*** and **Ours** on input images of size 1024 × 1024. As the guided upsampling network lifts the LR result to HR by utilizing features from a HR input, it brings the details from existing contents to generated contents, resulting in a more visually pleasant HR output. It also can be reflected from the user study, in which **Ours** is preferred by users more frequently. However, reconstructing with existing patches is a constraint on generation, making it less free and difficult to restore exactly the original content in the missing region. As a result, **Ours** has lower quantitative scores than **Ours*** as shown in the last row of Table 2.

5   Conclusion

We propose a high-resolution image inpainting method for large object removal. Our model predicts the inpainting result as well as its confidence map, which is used to revise unsatisfactory regions in an iterative manner. To improve visual quality for high-res inputs, we first obtain a low-res result and then reconstruct it using high-res neural patches. Furthermore, we collect a large object masks dataset and synthesize realistic training samples that simulate realistic user inputs. Experiments show that our method outperforms existing methods and achieves better visual quality.

Acknowledgements. The paper is supported in part by National Key R&D Program of China under Grant No. 2018AAA0102001, National Natural Science Foundation of China under grant No. 61725202, U1903215, 61829102, 91538201, 61771088,61751212, Fundamental Research Funds for the Central Universities under Grant No. DUT19GJ201, Dalian Innovation leader's support Plan under Grant No. 2018RD07.

References

1. can someone please remove my co-worker on the right and just leave the rhino and my friend on the left? https://www.reddit.com/r/PhotoshopRequest/comments/82v6x1/specific_can_someone_please_remove_my_coworker_on/

2. Can someone please remove the backpack and 'lead' from my sons back? would love to have this picture of my kids without it! https://www.reddit.com/r/PhotoshopRequest/comments/6szh1i/specific_can_someone_please_remove_the_backpack/

3. can someone please remove the people holding the balloons and their shadows from this engagement photo? https://www.reddit.com/r/PhotoshopRequest/comments/8d12tw/specific_can_someone_please_remove_the_people/

4. Can someone remove the woman in purple please? will give reddit gold! https://www.reddit.com/r/PhotoshopRequest/comments/6ddjg3/paid_specific_can_someone_remove_the_woman_in/

5. Could someone help me remove background people - especially the guys head? will venmo $5. https://www.reddit.com/r/PhotoshopRequest/comments/b2y0o5/specific_paid_could_someone_help_me_remove/

6. Could someone please remove the people in the background if at all possible! https://www.reddit.com/r/PhotoshopRequest/comments/6f0g4k/specific_could_someone_please_remove_the_people/

7. If possible, can anyone help me remove the people on the side, esp the people facing towards the camera :) thank you. https://www.reddit.com/r/PhotoshopRequest/comments/anizco/specific_if_possible_can_anyone_help_me_remove/

8. Ballester, C., Bertalmio, M., Caselles, V., Sapiro, G., Verdera, J.: Filling-in by joint interpolation of vector fields and gray levels. IEEE Trans. Image Process. **10**(8), 1200–1211 (2001)

9. Barnes, C., Shechtman, E., Finkelstein, A., Goldman, D.B.: Patchmatch: a randomized correspondence algorithm for structural image editing. ACM Trans. Graph. **28**(3), 24 (2009)

10. Bertalmio, M., Sapiro, G., Caselles, V., Ballester, C.: Image inpainting. In: The 27th Annual Conference on Computer Graphics and Interactive Techniques (2000)

11. Caelles, S., Pont-Tuset, J., Perazzi, F., Montes, A., Maninis, K.K., Van Gool, L.: The 2019 davis challenge on vos: Unsupervised multi-object segmentation. arXiv:1905.00737 (2019)

12. Ding, H., Cohen, S., Price, B., Jiang, X.: Phraseclick: toward achieving flexible interactive segmentation by phrase and click. In: European Conference on Computer Vision. Springer, Heidelberg (2020)

13. Ding, H., Jiang, X., Liu, A.Q., Thalmann, N.M., Wang, G.: Boundary-aware feature propagation for scene segmentation. In: IEEE International Conference on Computer Vision (2019)

14. Ding, H., Jiang, X., Shuai, B., Liu, A.Q., Wang, G.: Context contrasted feature and gated multi-scale aggregation for scene segmentation. In: IEEE Conference on Computer Vision and Pattern Recognition (2018)

15. Ding, H., Jiang, X., Shuai, B., Liu, A.Q., Wang, G.: Semantic correlation promoted shape-variant context for segmentation. In: IEEE Conference on Computer Vision and Pattern Recognition (2019)

16. Drori, I., Cohen-Or, D., Yeshurun, H.: Fragment-based image completion. In: ACM SIGGRAPH 2003 Papers, vol. 22, no. 3, pp. 303–312 (2003)

17. Efros, A.A., Freeman, W.T.: Image quilting for texture synthesis and transfer. In: The 28th Annual Conference on Computer Graphics and Interactive Techniques, pp. 341–346. ACM (2001)
18. Everingham, M., Van Gool, L., Williams, C.K., Winn, J., Zisserman, A.: The pascal visual object classes (voc) challenge. Int. J. Comput. Vis. **88**(2), 303–338 (2010)
19. Fan, D.P., Cheng, M.M., Liu, J.J., Gao, S.H., Hou, Q., Borji, A.: Salient objects in clutter: bringing salient object detection to the foreground. In: European Conference on Computer Vision (2018)
20. Goodfellow, I., et al.: Generative adversarial nets. In: Advances in Neural Information Processing Systems (2014)
21. Guo, Z., Chen, Z., Yu, T., Chen, J., Liu, S.: Progressive image inpainting with full-resolution residual network. In: Proceedings of the 27th ACM International Conference on Multimedia. ACM (2019)
22. Iizuka, S., Simo-Serra, E., Ishikawa, H.: Globally and locally consistent image completion. ACM Trans. Graph. (ToG) **36**(4), 107 (2017)
23. Isola, P., Zhu, J.Y., Zhou, T., Efros, A.A.: Image-to-image translation with conditional adversarial networks. In: IEEE Conference on Computer Vision and Pattern Recognition, pp. 1125–1134 (2017)
24. Kingma, D.P., Ba, J.: Adam: A method for stochastic optimization. arXiv preprint arXiv:1412.6980 (2014)
25. Kwatra, V., Essa, I., Bobick, A., Kwatra, N.: Texture optimization for example-based synthesis. In: ACM SIGGRAPH 2005 Papers, vol. 24, no. 3, pp. 795–802 (2005)
26. Levin, A., Zomet, A., Peleg, S., Weiss, Y.: Seamless image stitching in the gradient domain. In: Pajdla, T., Matas, J. (eds.) ECCV 2004. LNCS, vol. 3024, pp. 377–389. Springer, Heidelberg (2004). https://doi.org/10.1007/978-3-540-24673-2_31
27. Li, G., Yu, Y.: Deep contrast learning for salient object detection. In: IEEE Conference on Computer Vision and Pattern Recognition (2016)
28. Liang, X., et al.: Deep human parsing with active template regression. IEEE Trans. Pattern Anal. Mach. Intell. **37**(12), 2402–2414 (2015)
29. Liu, G., Reda, F.A., Shih, K.J., Wang, T.C., Tao, A., Catanzaro, B.: Image inpainting for irregular holes using partial convolutions. In: European Conference on Computer Vision (2018)
30. Miyato, T., Kataoka, T., Koyama, M., Yoshida, Y.: Spectral normalization for generative adversarial networks. arXiv preprint arXiv:1802.05957 (2018)
31. Nazeri, K., Ng, E., Joseph, T., Qureshi, F., Ebrahimi, M.: Edgeconnect: Generative image inpainting with adversarial edge learning. arXiv preprint arXiv:1901.00212 (2019)
32. Oh, S.W., Lee, S., Lee, J.Y., Kim, S.J.: Onion-peel networks for deep video completion. In: IEEE International Conference on Computer Vision (2019)
33. Park, E., Yang, J., Yumer, E., Ceylan, D., Berg, A.C.: Transformation-grounded image generation network for novel 3D view synthesis. In: IEEE Conference on Computer Vision and Pattern Recognition, pp. 3500–3509 (2017)
34. Pathak, D., Krahenbuhl, P., Donahue, J., Darrell, T., Efros, A.A.: Context encoders: feature learning by inpainting. In: IEEE Conference on Computer Vision and Pattern Recognition (2016)
35. Wang, J., Jiang, H., Yuan, Z., Cheng, M.M., Hu, X., Zheng, N.: Salient object detection: a discriminative regional feature integration approach. Int. J. Comput. Vision **123**(2), 251–268 (2017)

36. Wang, L., Zhang, J., Wang, O., Lin, Z., Lu, H.: SDC-depth: semantic divide-and-conquer network for monocular depth estimation. In: IEEE Conference on Computer Vision and Pattern Recognition (2020)
37. Xiong, W., et al.: Foreground-aware image inpainting. In: IEEE Conference on Computer Vision and Pattern Recognition (2019)
38. Yang, C., Lu, X., Lin, Z., Shechtman, E., Wang, O., Li, H.: High-resolution image inpainting using multi-scale neural patch synthesis. In: The IEEE Conference on Computer Vision and Pattern Recognition (CVPR) (2017)
39. Yu, J., Lin, Z., Yang, J., Shen, X., Lu, X., Huang, T.S.: Generative image inpainting with contextual attention. In: IEEE Conference on Computer Vision and Pattern Recognition, pp. 5505–5514 (2018)
40. Yu, J., Lin, Z., Yang, J., Shen, X., Lu, X., Huang, T.S.: Free-form image inpainting with gated convolution. In: IEEE International Conference on Computer Vision (2019)
41. Zeng, Y., Fu, J., Chao, H., Guo, B.: Learning pyramid-context encoder network for high-quality image inpainting. In: IEEE Conference on Computer Vision and Pattern Recognition, pp. 1486–1494 (2019)
42. Zeng, Y., Lin, Z., Yang, J., Zhang, J., Shechtman, E., Lu, H.: High-resolution image inpainting with iterative confidence feedback and guided upsampling. In: European Conference on Computer Vision. Springer, Heidelberg (2020)
43. Zeng, Y., Lu, H., Zhang, L., Feng, M., Borji, A.: Learning to promote saliency detectors. In: IEEE Conference on Computer Vision and Pattern Recognition (2018)
44. Zeng, Y., Zhuge, Y., Lu, H., Zhang, L.: Joint learning of saliency detection and weakly supervised semantic segmentation. In: IEEE International Conference on Computer Vision (2019)
45. Zeng, Y., Zhuge, Y., Lu, H., Zhang, L., Qian, M., Yu, Y.: Multi-source weak supervision for saliency detection. In: IEEE Conference on Computer Vision and Pattern Recognition (2019)
46. Zhang, H., Hu, Z., Luo, C., Zuo, W., Wang, M.: Semantic image inpainting with progressive generative networks. In: 2018 ACM Multimedia Conference on Multimedia Conference, pp. 1939–1947. ACM (2018)
47. Zhou, B., Lapedriza, A., Khosla, A., Oliva, A., Torralba, A.: Places: a 10 million image database for scene recognition. IEEE Trans. Pattern Anal. Mach. Intell. **40**(6), 1452–1464 (2017)

Online Ensemble Model Compression Using Knowledge Distillation

Devesh Walawalkar$^{(\boxtimes)}$, Zhiqiang Shen, and Marios Savvides

Carnegie Mellon University, Pittsburgh, PA 15213, USA
devwalkar64@gmail.com, {zhiqians,marioss}@andrew.cmu.edu

Abstract. This paper presents a novel knowledge distillation based model compression framework consisting of a student ensemble. It enables distillation of simultaneously learnt ensemble knowledge onto each of the compressed student models. Each model learns unique representations from the data distribution due to its distinct architecture. This helps the ensemble generalize better by combining every model's knowledge. The distilled students and ensemble teacher are trained simultaneously without requiring any pretrained weights. Moreover, our proposed method can deliver multi-compressed students with single training, which is efficient and flexible for different scenarios. We provide comprehensive experiments using state-of-the-art classification models to validate our framework's effectiveness. Notably, using our framework a 97% compressed ResNet110 student model managed to produce a 10.64% relative accuracy gain over its individual baseline training on CIFAR100 dataset. Similarly a 95% compressed DenseNet-BC (k = 12) model managed a 8.17% relative accuracy gain.

Keywords: Deep model compression · Image classification · Knowledge distillation · Ensemble deep model training

1 Introduction

Deep Learning based neural networks have provided tremendous improvements over the past decade in various domains of Computer Vision. These include Image Classification [17,20,24,40], Object Detection [3,12,26,30,31], Semantic Segmentation [4,5,16,44,45] among others. The drawbacks of these methods however include the fact that a large amount of computational resources are required to achieve state-of-the-art accuracy. A trend started setting in where constructing deeper and wider models provided better accuracy at the cost of considerable resource utilization [27,35,38]. The difference in resource utilization is considerable compared to traditional computer vision techniques. To alleviate this gap, model compression techniques started being developed to reduce these large computational requirements. These techniques can broadly be classified into four types [7] i.e. Parameter Pruning [6,14,15,37], Low Rank Factorization [8,29,36], Transferred Convolutional Filters [9,11,25,33] and Knowledge Distillation methods [1,13,18,21,22,46]. Each of these types was able to provide

© Springer Nature Switzerland AG 2020
A. Vedaldi et al. (Eds.): ECCV 2020, LNCS 12364, pp. 18–35, 2020.
https://doi.org/10.1007/978-3-030-58529-7_2

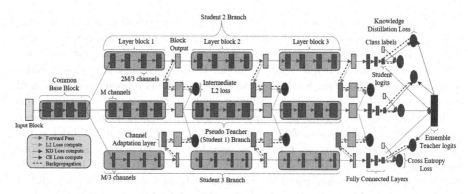

Fig. 1. Overview of our *model compression framework* for a *3 student ensemble*. Each student is composed of the base block and one of the network branches on top of it. The original model is the first student in the ensemble, termed as *pseudo teacher* due to its simultaneous knowledge transfer capability and training from scratch properties. The *ensemble teacher* is a weighted combination of all student's output logits. Each student is divided into four blocks such that each block incorporates approximately the same number of layers. The layer channels for the compressed student branches are reduced by a specific ratio with respect to the original model. For a 3 student ensemble, the layer channels assigned are M, 2M/3 and M/3, where M is the original layer channel count. *Channel adaptation layers* help map the compressed student's block output channels to the pseudo teacher's output channels in order to compute an intermediate feature representation loss

impressive computational reductions while simultaneously managing to keep the accuracy degradation to a minimum.

Knowledge Distillation (KD) in particular has provided great model compression capabilities using a novel teacher-student model concept [18]. Here a teacher, the original model trained for a specific task is used to teach a compressed or replicated version of itself referred to as student. The student is encouraged to mimic the teacher output distribution, which helps the student generalize much better and in certain cases leads to the student performing better than the teacher itself. Drawbacks of these methods include the fact that a pre-trained model is required to distill knowledge onto a student model. To solve this, simultaneous distillation methods [2,46] were developed wherein multiple students were being trained with an ensemble teacher learning on the fly with the students itself in an ensemble training scheme. These methods however primarily focused on replicating the teacher multiple times, causing the ensemble to gain sub-optimal generalized knowledge due to model architecture redundancy. Also in parallel, methods [1,22,34] were developed which focused on distilling not only the output knowledge but also the intermediate representations of teacher onto the student to have more effective knowledge transfer. These techniques are efficient, however still suffering from the drawback of requiring teacher model pre-training in addition to the student training.

In this paper, we present a novel model compression and ensemble training framework which improves on all aforementioned drawbacks and provides a new perspective for ensemble model compression techniques. We present a framework which enables multiple student model training using knowledge transfer from an *ensemble teacher*. Each of these student models represents a version of the original model compressed to different degrees. Knowledge is distilled onto each of the compressed student through the ensemble teacher and also through intermediate representations from a *pseudo teacher*. The original model is the first student in our ensemble, termed as pseudo teacher due to its simultaneous knowledge transfer capability and training from scratch property. Moreover this framework simultaneously provides multiple compressed models having different computational budget with each having benefited from every other model's training. Our framework facilitates the choice of selecting a student that fits the resource budget for a particular use case with the knowledge that every student provides decent comparable performance to the original model. Also, the ensemble training significantly reduces the training time of all student combined, compared to when they are trained individually. We specifically focus on image classification task while providing extensive experimentation on popular image classification models and bench-marked datasets.

Our contributions from this paper can be thus summarized as follows:

1. We present a novel ensemble model compression framework based on knowledge distillation that can generate multiple compressed networks simultaneously with a single training run and is completely model agnostic.
2. We provide extensive experiments on popular classification models on standard datasets with corresponding baseline comparisons of each individual student training to provide evidence of our framework's effectiveness.
3. We provide hyper parameter ablation studies which help provide insights into the effective ensemble knowledge distillation provided by our framework.

2   Related Works

2.1   Model Compression Using Knowledge Distillation

Hinton et al. [18] introduced the concept of distilling knowledge from a larger teacher model onto a smaller compressed student model. Mathematically this meant training the student on softened teacher output distribution in addition to the traditional cross entropy with dataset labels. The paper argued that the teacher distribution provided much richer information about an image compared to just one hot labels. For e.g. consider a classification task of differentiating between various breeds of dogs. The output distribution of a higher capability teacher provides the student with the information of how alike one breed of dogs looks to the other. This helps the student learn more generalized features of each dog breed compared to providing just one hot labels which fails to provide any comparative knowledge. Also, in process of trying to mimic the distribution of a much deeper teacher model the student tries to find a compact series of transformation that tries to mimic the teacher's larger series of transformations. This inherently helps the student negate the accuracy loss due to compression. Impressively, in certain cases the student manages to outperform its teacher due to this superior generalization training. Further works extended this concept by using internal feature representations [1], adversarial learning [34] and inner product between feature maps [42].

2.2   Online Knowledge Distillation

The single practical drawback of Knowledge Distillation is the fact that a pre-trained model is required to play the role of a teacher. This entails multiple sequential training runs on the same dataset. Anil et al. [2] came up with a method to train the student in parallel with the teacher termed as codistillation. Here the student is an exact replica of the teacher and roles of teacher and student were continuously interchanged between the models during training with one training the other iteratively. The primary distinguishing property between the models was their distinct parameter initialization. This enabled each model to learn unique features which were then distilled from one to the other as training progressed.

Zhang et al. [43] employed a unique KD loss, by using KL divergence loss between two model output distributions to penalize the differences between them. Each model's training involved a combination loss of KL divergence loss with other model's distribution and traditional cross entropy loss. Both models acting as teacher and student simultaneously were trained jointly in an online fashion.

Lan et al. [46] extended this online KD concept by having multiple replicas of a given model in a multi branch architecture fashion. Multi branch architecture designs became popular with the image classification models like Resnet [17], Inception [38,39] and ResNext [41]. In this paper, the multiple replicated models have a common base of block of layers with each model represented as a branch on top of this base with subsequent layer blocks from the original model architecture right until the final fully connected layers. The teacher in this concept was the combined output of all the student models in the ensemble. Each student model learnt from the ensemble joint knowledge represented by the teacher outputs. Our paper builds on this core concept however is fundamentally different as we incorporate compressed student branches, more efficient training procedure, incorporate intermediate representation distillation in addition to the final output distillation among others.

2.3   Intermediate Representation Knowledge Distillation

A separate branch of Knowledge Distillation focuses on training the student to mimic the intermediate representations obtained in form of feature maps from certain intermediate layer blocks within the teacher. This provides a more stricter learning regime for the student who has to focus not only on the final teacher output distribution but also on its intermediate layer feature maps. Romero et al. [1] provide one of the preliminary works in this direction by distilling a single intermediate layer's knowledge onto the student which they term as providing hint to the student. Mathematically, hint training involves minimizing a combination of L2 loss between the features maps at an immediate layer of the two models and the regular KD (KL divergence loss) between the output distributions.

Koratana et al. [22] extend this concept by comparing feature maps at not just one but multiple intermediate locations within the model which can be related to as multiple hint training. This method however again requires a pre-trained teacher model which might be time consuming and compute expensive for certain real world scenarios. Our method incorporates multiple hint training for all student models with respect to pseudo teacher, which is also the first student in the ensemble. A network's depth measures its function modeling capacity in general. Koratana et al. [22] compress the model by removing blocks of layers from the network which severely affects the network depth. Our work incorporates a more robust compression logic where the number of channels in every student layer are simply reduced by a certain percent, thus preserving the model depth.

3   Methodology

An overview of our ensemble compression framework is presented in Fig. 1, which can be split up into three major sections for the ease of understanding. We would be going into their details in the following sections.

3.1   Ensemble Student Model Compression

First, the entire architecture of a given neural network is broken down into a series of layer blocks, ideally into four blocks. The first block is designated as a common base block and the rest of the blocks are replicated in parallel to create branches as shown in Fig. 1. A single student model can be viewed as a series of base block and one of the branches on top of it. As previously mentioned, the original network is designated as the first student model, also termed as pseudo teacher. For every successive student branch the number of channels in each layer of its blocks is reduced by a certain ratio with respect to the pseudo teacher. This ratio becomes higher for every new student branch created. For example, for a four student ensemble and C being number of channels in pseudo teacher, the channels in other three students are assigned to be $0.75C$, $0.5C$ and $0.25C$. The students are compressed versions of the original model to varying degrees, which still manage to maintain the original network depth. The channels in the common base block are kept the same as original whose main purpose is to provide constant low level features to all the student branches.

The output logits from all the student models are averaged together to create the ensemble teacher logits. This ensemble teacher output distribution represents the joint knowledge of the ensemble. During inference stage, any of the individual

Table 1. Model size and test set accuracy comparison of every student in a five student ensemble, with their percent relative size in respect to the original model and their CIFAR10 test accuracies achieved using our ensemble framework.

Classification model	Student Model size and accuracy (%)									
	First		Second		Third		Fourth		Fifth	
	Size	Accuracy	Size	Accuracy	Size	Accuracy	Size	Accuracy	Size	Accuracy
ResNet20 [17]	100.0	92.13	62.95	92.18	35.61	91.78	15.50	91.45	3.95	91.03
ResNet33 [17]	100.0	92.25	62.87	92.76	35.43	92.45	15.33	92.11	3.8	91.78
ResNet44 [17]	100.0	93.45	62.84	93.29	35.36	93.11	15.25	92.89	3.74	92.56
ResNet110 [17]	100.0	94.24	62.79	94.18	35.26	93.98	15.15	93.57	3.64	93.28
DenseNet (k = 12) [20]	100.0	94.76	58.01	94.51	36.34	94.29	13.31	94.08	4.29	93.57
ResNext50 (32 × 4d) [41]	100.0	96.03	62.10	95.95	35.60	95.84	16.09	95.69	4.76	95.47
EfficientNet-B0 [40]	100.0	98.20	64.11	98.13	35.94	98.01	18.88	97.84	5.43	97.57
EfficientNet-B2 [40]	100.0	98.41	65.16	98.35	37.87	98.23	18.13	98.02	4.69	97.88
EfficientNet-B4 [40]	100.0	98.70	64.43	98.59	36.27	98.47	16.40	98.23	4.91	98.14

student models can be selected from the ensemble depending on the computational hardware constraints. In case of lenient constraints, the entire ensemble can be used with the ensemble teacher providing inference based on the learnt ensemble knowledge. From our studies we find that having 5 students (inclusive of pseudo teacher) provides an optimal trade off between training time and effective model compression. Table 1 provides an overview of compressed student model sizes and their CIFAR10 [23] trained accuracies for a five student ensemble based on various classification model architectures.

3.2 Intermediate Knowledge Distillation

The intermediate block knowledge (feature map representation) is additionally distilled onto every compressed student from the pseudo teacher. This provides a more stricter training and distillation regime for all the compressed students. The loss in every student's representational capacity due to compression is countered, by making each student block try and learn the intermediate feature map of its corresponding pseudo teacher block. The feature map pairs are compared using traditional Mean Squared Error loss, on which the network is trained to reduce any differences between them. Since the number of feature map channels varies across every corresponding student and pseudo teacher block, an adaptation layer consisting of pointwise convolution (1×1 kernel) is used to map compressed student block channels to its pseudo teacher counterpart. Figure 2(a) presents this idea in detail for an EfficientNet-B0 [40] based ensemble. The intermediate knowledge is transferred at three locations corresponding to the three blocks in every student branch as shown in Fig. 1.

3.3 Knowledge Distillation Based Training

The overall ensemble is trained using a combination of three separate losses which are described in detail as follows:

Cross-Entropy Loss. Each student model is trained individually on classical cross entropy loss [Eq. 1, 2] with one hot vector of labels and student output logits. This loss helps each student directly train on a given dataset. This loss procedure makes the pseudo teacher learn alongside the compressed students as the framework doesn't use pretrained weights of any sort. It also helps the ensemble teacher gain richer knowledge of the dataset as it incorporates combination of every student's learnt knowledge. It additionally enables the framework to avoid training the ensemble teacher separately and is trained implicitly through the students. The output softmax distribution and combined normal loss can be expressed as follows,

$$X_{ijk} = \frac{exp(x_{ijk})}{\sum_{k=1}^{C} exp(x_{ijk})} \tag{1}$$

$$L^{Normal} = \sum_{i=1}^{S} \sum_{j=1}^{N} \sum_{k=1}^{C} -\mathbb{1}_{jk} \log(X_{ijk}) \tag{2}$$

where i, j, k represents student, batch sample and class number indices respectively. $\mathbb{1}_{jk}$ is an one hot label indicator function for j^{th} sample and k^{th} class. Similarly, x_{ijk} is a single output logit from i^{th} student model for j^{th} batch sample and k^{th} class and X_{ijk} is its corresponding softmax output.

Intermediate Loss. For every pseudo teacher and compressed student pair, the output feature maps from every pseudo teacher block are compared to the ones at its corresponding compressed student block. In order to facilitate an effective knowledge distillation between these respective map pairs, the compressed student maps are first passed through an adaptation layer which as mentioned earlier is a simple 1×1 convolution, mapping the student map channels to the pseudo teacher map channels. A Mean Squared Error loss is used to compare each single element of a given pseudo teacher-student feature map pair. This loss is averaged across the batch. The loss for a single block across all students can be expressed as follows,

$$l_{block}^{intermediate} = \sum_{l=2}^{S} \left(\sum_{m=1}^{N} (|x_m^{PT} - x_m^l|)^2 \right) \tag{3}$$

where x_m^l is a feature map of size $H \times W \times C$ corresponding to m^{th} batch sample of the lth student model. $|.|^2$ represents element wise squared L2 norm. $l = 1$ represents the pseudo teacher, also designated as PT in x_m^{PT} which is the corresponding pseudo teacher feature map. The overall intermediate loss can be expressed as:

$$L^{intermediate} = \sum_{b=1}^{B} l_b^{intermediate} \tag{4}$$

This loss is used to update only the compressed student model parameters in order to have the compressed student learn from the pseudo teacher and not the other way round. In our experiments we observed that the mean of adaptation layer weights is on average lower for larger student models. This in turn propagates a smaller model response term in the intermediate loss equation, thus increasing their losses slightly compared to thinner students. This helps balance this loss term across all students.

Knowledge Distillation Loss. To facilitate global knowledge transfer from the ensemble teacher to each of the students, a KD loss in form of Kullback-Leibler Divergence Loss is incorporated between the ensemble teacher and student outputs. The outputs of the ensemble teacher and each respective student are softened using a certain temperature T to help students learn efficiently from highly confident ensemble teacher predictions where the wrong class outputs are almost zero. The softened softmax and overall KD loss can be expressed as follows,

$$X_{ijk} = \frac{exp(\frac{x_{ijk}}{T})}{\sum_{k=1}^{C} exp(\frac{x_{ijk}}{T})} \tag{5}$$

$$L^{KD} = \sum_{i=1}^{S}\sum_{j=1}^{N}\sum_{k=1}^{C} X_{jk}^{T} \log\left(\frac{X_{jk}^{T}}{X_{ijk}}\right) \tag{6}$$

where X_{ijk} is the softened softmax output of the ith student for j^{th} batch sample and k^{th} class. Similarly X_{jk}^{T} represents the ensemble teacher softened softmax output for j^{th} batch sample and k^{th} class.

Combined Loss. The above presented three losses are combined using a weighted combination, on which the entire framework is trained to reduce this overall loss. This can be mathematically expressed as,

$$L = \alpha L^{Normal} + \beta L^{intermediate} + \gamma L^{KD} \tag{7}$$

The optimal weight value combination which was found out to be $\alpha = 0.7$, $\beta = 0.15$, $\gamma = 0.15$ is discussed in detail in an ablation study presented in later sections.

4 Experiments

Datasets. We incorporate four major academic datasets: (1) CIFAR10 dataset [23] which contains 50,000/10,000 training/test samples drawn from 10 classes. Each class has 6,000 images included in both training and test set sized at 32×32 pixels. (2) CIFAR100 dataset [23] which contains 50,000/10,000 training/test samples drawn from 100 classes. Each class has 600 images included in both training and test set sized at 32×32 pixels. (3) SVHN dataset [28] which contains 73,257/26,032 training/test samples drawn from 10 classes. Each class represents a digit from 0 to 9. Each image is sized at 32×32 pixels. (4) ImageNet dataset [10] is a comprehensive database containing around 1.2 million images, specifically 1,281,184/50,000 training/testing images drawn from 1000 classes.

Table 2. Individual Test Set performance comparison for five compressed students trained using our ensemble and using baseline training on CIFAR10 dataset. Reported results are averaged over five individual experimental runs.

Classification model	Student test accuracy (%)									
	First		Second		Third		Fourth		Fifth	
	Baseline	Ensemble	Baseline	Ensemble	Baseline	Ensemble	Baseline	Ensemble	Baseline	Ensemble
Resnet20 [17]	91.34	**92.13**	91.12	**92.18**	90.89	**91.78**	90.16	**91.45**	89.67	**91.03**
Resnet32 [17]	92.12	**92.95**	91.94	**92.76**	91.56	**92.45**	91.07	**92.11**	90.47	**91.78**
Resnet44 [17]	92.94	**93.45**	92.67	**93.29**	92.24	**93.11**	91.97	**92.89**	91.23	**92.56**
Resnet110 [17]	93.51	**94.24**	93.25	**94.18**	93.11	**93.98**	92.86	**93.57**	92.27	**93.28**
Densenet-BC (k = 12) [20]	94.02	**94.76**	93.78	**94.51**	93.52	**94.29**	93.24	**94.08**	92.85	**93.57**
ResNext50 (32 × 4d) [41]	95.78	**96.03**	95.56	**95.95**	95.27	**95.84**	95.09	**95.69**	94.97	**95.47**
EfficientNet-B0 [40]	97.82	**98.20**	97.58	**98.13**	97.28	**98.01**	97.04	**97.84**	96.73	**97.57**
EfficientNet-B2 [40]	98.21	**98.41**	98.13	**98.35**	97.99	**98.23**	97.77	**98.02**	97.41	**97.88**
EfficientNet-B4 [40]	98.56	**98.70**	98.36	**98.59**	98.21	**98.47**	98.04	**98.23**	97.92	**98.14**

Table 3. Individual Test Set performance comparison for five compressed students trained using our ensemble and using baseline training on CIFAR100. Reported results are averaged over five individual experimental runs.

Classification model	Student test accuracy (%)									
	First		Second		Third		Fourth		Fifth	
	Baseline	Ensemble	Baseline	Ensemble	Baseline	Ensemble	Baseline	Ensemble	Baseline	Ensemble
Resnet32 [17]	70.21	**70.97**	67.87	**68.24**	64.17	**65.67**	61.85	61.17	39.12	**42.17**
Resnet44 [17]	71.12	**71.76**	68.42	**69.12**	65.69	**67.04**	62.31	**62.87**	40.82	**43.11**
Resnet56 [17]	71.59	**72.16**	**68.45**	68.39	65.37	**66.21**	62.42	62.21	41.19	**43.27**
Resnet110 [17]	72.64	**72.81**	69.53	**70.14**	67.12	**67.73**	64.58	**65.08**	42.26	**46.76**
Densenet-BC (k = 12) [20]	75.79	**75.96**	71.97	**72.39**	70.23	70.09	67.13	**68.14**	45.41	**49.12**
ResNeXt50 (32 × 4d) [41]	72.37	**72.59**	70.19	**70.32**	67.02	**67.81**	65.19	**65.72**	42.82	**45.29**
EfficientNet-B0 [40]	87.17	**88.12**	85.78	**86.94**	83.25	**85.14**	80.24	**83.21**	76.35	**78.45**
EfficientNet-B2 [40]	89.05	**89.31**	87.34	**88.78**	85.23	**87.58**	82.14	**84.13**	79.34	**81.12**
EfficientNet-B4 [40]	90.26	**90.81**	88.59	**89.78**	86.34	**88.04**	84.32	**86.78**	81.34	**84.10**

Experimental Hypothesis. Experiments are conducted in order to: (1) compare every compressed student's test set performance trained using our ensemble framework versus simply training each one of them individually without any knowledge distillation component. These experiments help validate the advantages of using an ensemble teacher and intermediate knowledge transfer for every compressed student compared to using only the traditional individual cross entropy loss based training. (2) Compare the test set accuracy of our ensemble teacher to other notable ensemble knowledge distillation based techniques in

Table 4. Comparison of notable knowledge distillation and ensemble based techniques with our ensemble teacher reported test accuracy performance (Error rate %). The best performing model accuracy is chosen for DML.

Ensemble technique	Dataset							
	CIFAR10		CIFAR100		SVHN		ImageNet	
	ResNet-32	ResNet-110	ResNet-32	ResNet-110	ResNet-32	ResNet-110	Resnet-18	ResNeXt-50
KD-ONE [46]	5.99	5.17	26.61	21.62	**1.83**	1.76	29.45	21.85
DML [43]	–	–	29.03	24.10	–	–	–	–
Snopshot Ensemble [19]	–	5.32	27.12	24.19	–	1.63	–	–
Ours	**5.73**	**4.85**	**26.09**	**21.14**	1.97	**1.61**	**29.34**	**21.17**

Table 5. Individual Test Set performance comparison for five compressed students trained using our ensemble and using baseline training on SVHN. Reported results are averaged over five individual experimental runs.

Classification model	Student test accuracy (%)									
	First		Second		Third		Fourth		Fifth	
	Baseline	Ensemble	Baseline	Ensemble	Baseline	Ensemble	Baseline	Ensemble	Baseline	Ensemble
Resnet20 [17]	96.64	**97.10**	95.03	**96.92**	94.45	**95.53**	**92.12**	92.03	89.58	**92.67**
Resnet32 [17]	96.78	**96.92**	95.67	**96.31**	**94.85**	94.61	92.78	**95.03**	90.75	**92.89**
Resnet44 [17]	97.23	**97.46**	**96.38**	96.26	95.35	**96.32**	93.26	**95.76**	91.24	**93.47**
Resnet110 [17]	97.64	**97.87**	96.61	**97.84**	95.83	**96.81**	93.73	**95.90**	91.77	**93.78**
Densenet-BC (k = 12) [20]	97.92	**98.03**	97.31	**98.02**	96.12	**97.59**	**94.58**	94.25	92.15	**94.17**
ResNext50 (32 × 4d) [41]	97.65	**97.88**	**96.84**	96.69	95.72	**96.64**	**94.79**	94.23	91.73	**93.80**
EfficientNet-B0 [40]	97.53	**97.72**	97.07	**97.79**	95.52	**96.71**	**94.44**	94.26	91.12	**93.34**
EfficientNet-B2 [40]	97.75	**97.92**	**97.76**	97.63	95.87	**96.92**	93.37	**96.24**	**91.42**	91.29
EfficientNet-B4 [40]	98.16	**98.56**	97.79	**98.03**	**96.71**	96.48	93.64	**96.83**	91.75	**94.17**

literature on all four mentioned datasets to prove our framework's overall superiority and effectiveness, which are presented in Table 4. (3) Compare the time taken for training our five student based ensemble versus the combined time taken for training each of those students individually. This comparison helps substantiate the training time benefits of our hybrid multi-student architecture compared to training each student alone either sequentially or in parallel. These are presented in Fig. 2(b).

Performance Metrics. We compare the test set accuracy (Top-1) of each of our student models within the ensemble, trained using our framework and as an individual baseline model with only the traditional cross entropy loss. For each of our ensemble students, this test set accuracy is computed as an average of the best student test accuracies achieved during each of five conducted runs.

Table 6. Individual Test Set performance comparison for five compressed students trained using our ensemble and using baseline training on ImageNet (Top-1 accuracy). Reported results are averaged over five individual experimental runs.

Classification model	Student test accuracy (Top-1 accuracy %)									
	First		Second		Third		Fourth		Fifth	
	Baseline	Ensemble	Baseline	Ensemble	Baseline	Ensemble	Baseline	Ensemble	Baseline	Ensemble
Resnet18 [17]	69.73	**70.47**	67.27	**67.61**	62.98	**64.88**	59.47	**61.17**	55.23	**58.52**
Resnet34 [17]	73.22	**74.13**	71.95	**73.64**	67.62	**69.32**	63.07	**64.19**	60.76	**61.29**
Resnet50 [17]	76.18	**76.52**	75.43	75.32	70.16	**71.93**	66.89	**69.46**	62.24	**66.78**
Resnet101 [17]	77.31	**77.97**	76.27	**76.71**	73.49	**74.04**	69.47	**71.10**	65.79	**68.57**
Densenet-121 [20]	74.96	**75.82**	73.94	**74.17**	68.53	68.44	66.64	**67.83**	63.42	**66.09**
ResNext50 (32 × 4d) [41]	77.58	**78.19**	76.62	**77.85**	73.45	73.37	69.73	**70.89**	65.82	**68.48**

Experimental Setup. For fair comparison, we keep the training schedule the same for both our ensemble framework and baseline training. Specifically, for ResNet, DenseNet and ResNeXt models SGD is used with Nesterov momentum set to 0.9, following a standard learning rate schedule that drops from 0.1 to 0.01 at 50% training and to 0.001 at 75%. For EfficientNet models RMSProp optimizer is implemented with decay 0.9 and momentum 0.9 and initial learning rate of 0.256 that decays by 0.97 every 3 epochs. The models are trained for 350/450/50/100 epochs each for the CIFAR10/CIFAR100/SVHN/ImageNet datasets respectively.

4.1   Evaluation of Our Online Model Compression Framework

Results on CIFAR10 and CIFAR100. Tables 2, 3 present our experimental results for CIFAR10 and CIFAR100 dataset respectively. Each compressed student's test set performance is on an average 1% better using our ensemble framework as compared to the simple baseline training for both the datasets. Our ensemble teacher also provides the best Test set accuracy when compared to the teacher accuracies of three other ensemble knowledge distillation techniques for ResNet32 and ResNet110 models as presented in Table 4. Our framework provides substantial training time benefits for all models tested with CIFAR10 and CIFAR100 datasets as presented in Fig. 2(b). For fair comparison the ensemble and each of the baseline students are trained for the same number epochs on both datasets. Notably, training a five student ensemble of an EfficientNet-B4 architecture is roughly 7.5K GPU minutes quicker as compared to their combined individual baseline training.

Results on SVHN and ImageNet. Tables 5, 6 present our experimental results for SVHN and ImageNet datasets respectively. Again, each compressed student test set performance is on an average 1% better using our ensemble framework as compared to the simple baseline training for both the datasets.

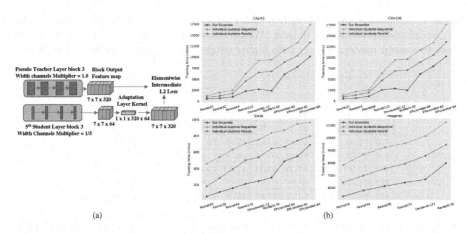

(a)   (b)

Fig. 2. (a) *Channel Adaptation Logic* for mapping output channels of an *EfficientNet-B0* model based ensemble, depicting Block 3 outputs of the pseudo Teacher and 5th student in the ensemble. (b) Comparison of our ensemble framework training time (Blue) to the combined training time of individual baseline students performed sequentially (Orange) and in parallel (Green). Timings recorded for training carried out on a GPU cluster of Nvidia GTX 1080Ti. (Color figure online)

Notably for both datasets, the heavily compressed fourth and fifth students perform around 3% on average better than their baseline counterparts. This provide an excellent evidence of our framework's efficient knowledge transfer capabilities for the heavily compressed student cases. Similar to the aforementioned datasets, our ensemble teacher provides the best Test set accuracy when compared to the ensemble teacher accuracy of three other ensemble knowledge distillation based techniques for ResNet32 and ResNet110 models as presented in Table 4.

5   Ablation Studies

Loss Contribution Ratios. A selective grid search was conducted for the optimal values of loss contribution ratios, specifically α, β, γ referenced in Eq. 7. The grid search was conducted with the constraint that the ratio should sum to one which would represent the overall loss factor. The study was carried out using ResNet110 [17] model on the CIFAR100 [23] dataset. Firstly, a grid search was conducted for α which is the normal loss contribution ratio. The other two contribution ratio namely β, γ were kept equal to half the fraction left from subtracting the grid search α from 1. This study is presented in Table 7. All accuracies are averaged over five runs to reduce any weight initialization effect. The value of 0.7 provided the best weighted average accuracy across all the students. Weights of $\frac{1}{5}, \frac{2}{5}, \frac{3}{5}, \frac{4}{5}, 1$ were assigned to the students, with higher importance given to accuracy achieved by more compressed student.

With the value of α set as 0.7, a grid search was then conducted for the value of β and γ. This study is presented in Table 8. Here also the same weighted average technique was used to find the effective student test accuracy. $\beta = 0.15$ and

Table 7. Ablation Study for α contribution ratio grid search conducted with ResNet110 [17] model on CIFAR100 [23] dataset. Weighted average technique used for calculating effective student model accuracy with higher weight given to more compressed students.

α	Student test accuracy (%)					Ensemble teacher test accuracy (%)	Weighted average
	1	2	3	4	5		
0.3	69.58	64.47	63.21	55.64	39.57	69.08	161.71
0.4	68.27	65.36	62.35	57.54	40.14	68.81	163.38
0.5	71.32	69.58	67.92	62.69	45.16	72.15	178.16
0.6	72.11	67.82	65.55	60.93	43.19	71.64	172.81
0.7	**71.25**	**69.32**	**67.29**	**62.16**	**47.23**	**72.51**	**179.31**
0.8	71.05	70.21	68.01	62.61	45.10	71.85	178.29
0.9	69.21	66.56	63.12	58.85	45.76	71.86	171.18

Table 8. Ablation Study for β, γ contribution ratios grid search conducted with ResNet110 [17] model on CIFAR100 [23] dataset. Weighted average technique used for calculating combined student model test accuracy with higher weight given to more compressed students. α is set at optimal value of 0.7 referred from Table 7.

β	γ	Student test accuracy (%)					Ensemble teacher test accuracy (%)	Weighted average
		1	2	3	4	5		
0.05	0.25	68.57	66.69	64.34	59.92	47.26	71.97	174.19
0.1	0.2	68.72	68.19	65.94	62.09	44.88	71.73	175.14
0.15	**0.15**	**69.37**	**68.39**	**66.44**	**62.17**	**46.82**	**72.28**	**177.65**
0.2	0.1	66.79	64.92	62.46	57.78	41.34	69.64	164.37
0.25	0.05	67.97	67.22	65.37	61.08	46.69	71.12	175.26

$\gamma = 0.15$ gave the optimal performance and were thus selected as the final contribution ratios for our framework. These final ratios seem to indicate the major importance of cross entropy loss with $\alpha = 0.7$ in individual student's training and equal importance of intermediate and output distribution knowledge transfer with $\beta = \gamma = 0.15$ for the knowledge distillation process.

Knowledge Distillation Temperature. A temperature variable T is used to soften the student and ensemble teacher model logits before computing its respective softmax distribution as referenced in Eq. 5. A grid search was conducted for its optimal value, which would facilitate optimum knowledge transfer from the ensemble teacher to each student model. Similar to the previous study, we incorporate a ResNet110 [17] model to train on CIFAR100 [23] dataset. This study is presented in Table 9. The resulting optimal value of 2 is used for all of our conducted experiments. The study results provide evidence to the fact that higher temperature values tend to over-soften the output logits leading to sub optimal knowledge transfer and test accuracy gains.

Table 9. Ablation Study for softmax temperature (T) grid search conducted with ResNet110 [17] model on CIFAR100 [23] dataset. Mean accuracy computed using only student test accuracies.

Temperature T	Student test accuracy (%)					Ensemble teacher test accuracy (%)	Mean accuracy (%)
	1	2	3	4	5		
1	70.29	67.16	64.22	62.46	44.75	71.57	61.78
2	**71.89**	**69.56**	**68.43**	**59.48**	**47.26**	**71.02**	**63.32**
3	69.14	68.18	65.33	57.52	46.33	69.36	61.3
4	68.35	66.77	64.36	56.41	46.45	69.37	60.49
5	66.58	66.95	65.67	56.1	42.62	69.27	59.58
6	66.92	66.28	65.33	55.97	43.06	69.34	59.51

6   Discussion

The performed experiments provide a strong evidence of the efficient compression and generalization capabilities of our framework over individual baseline training for every compressed student model. In most of the experiments the ensemble teacher's test accuracy is much better than any of its ensemble students and their baseline counterparts. This additional test accuracy gain can be attributed to the joint ensemble knowledge learnt by the framework.

The intermediate knowledge transfer from the pseudo teacher onto each one of the compressed students helps guide every student compressed block to reproduce the same transformations its respective higher capacity pseudo teacher block is learning. Enabling the low capacity compressed block to try and imitate the higher capacity pseudo teacher block helps reduce any redundant (sub-optimal) transformations inside the student block that would generally be present during baseline training. This is substantiated by the fact that the test accuracy gains of heavily compressed students, specifically the fourth and fifth students in the ensemble are substantial over their baseline counterparts. Figure 3 presents a comparison of the gradient based class activation mapping (Grad-CAM) [32] of the last block of an EfficientNet-B4 framework pseudo teacher and one of its compressed students. These are compared to the Grad-CAM of the same compressed student with baseline training. The smaller differences between the Grad-CAMs of pseudo teacher and its ensemble student compared to those between the pseudo teacher and the baseline student provide evidence of how our efficient knowledge distillation helps the student imitate the pseudo teacher and learn better as compared to the baseline student.

Pseudo Teacher Grad CAM   Baseline Student Grad CAM   Ensemble Student Grad CAM

Fig. 3. Gradient Class Activation Mapping (Grad CAM) [32] comparison of a EfficientNet-B4 based ensemble pseudo teacher and one of its compressed students with that of its respective individually trained student. The ensemble student's CAM is more accurate compared to that of baseline student. Also the former follows the pseudo teacher more closely as compared to the latter, which provides evidence of the effective knowledge distillation taking place in our ensemble framework.

7   Conclusion

We present a novel model compression technique using an ensemble knowledge distillation learning procedure without requiring the need of any pretrained weights. The framework manages to provide multiple compressed versions of a given base (pseudo teacher) model simultaneously, providing gains in each of the participating model's test performance and in overall framework's training time compared to each model's individual baseline training. Comprehensive experiments conducted using a variety of current state-of-the-art image classification based models and benchmarked academic datasets provide substantial evidence of the framework's effectiveness. It also provides an account of the highly modular nature of the framework which makes it easier to incorporate any existing classification model into the framework without any major modifications. It manages to provide multiple efficient versions of the same, compressed to varying degree without making any major manual architecture changes on the user's part.

References

1. Adriana, R., Nicolas, B., Ebrahimi, K.S., Antoine, C., Carlo, G., Yoshua, B.: Fitnets: hints for thin deep nets. In: Proceedings of International Conference on Learning Representations (2015)
2. Anil, R., Pereyra, G., Passos, A., Ormandi, R., Dahl, G.E., Hinton, G.E.: Large scale distributed neural network training through online distillation. In: International Conference on Learning Representations (2018)
3. Cai, Z., Vasconcelos, N.: Cascade r-cnn: delving into high quality object detection. In: Proceedings of the IEEE Conference on Computer Vision and Pattern Recognition, pp. 6154–6162 (2018)
4. Chen, L.C., Papandreou, G., Schroff, F., Adam, H.: Rethinking atrous convolution for semantic image segmentation. arXiv preprint arXiv:1706.05587 (2017)

5. Chen, L.C., Zhu, Y., Papandreou, G., Schroff, F., Adam, H.: Encoder-decoder with atrous separable convolution for semantic image segmentation. In: Proceedings of the European Conference on Computer Vision (ECCV), pp. 801–818 (2018)
6. Chen, W., Wilson, J., Tyree, S., Weinberger, K., Chen, Y.: Compressing neural networks with the hashing trick. In: International Conference on Machine Learning, pp. 2285–2294 (2015)
7. Cheng, Y., Wang, D., Zhou, P., Zhang, T.: A survey of model compression and acceleration for deep neural networks. arXiv preprint arXiv:1710.09282 (2017)
8. Cheng, Y., Yu, F.X., Feris, R.S., Kumar, S., Choudhary, A., Chang, S.F.: An exploration of parameter redundancy in deep networks with circulant projections. In: Proceedings of the IEEE International Conference on Computer Vision, pp. 2857–2865 (2015)
9. Cohen, T., Welling, M.: Group equivariant convolutional networks. In: International Conference on Machine Learning, pp. 2990–2999 (2016)
10. Deng, J., Dong, W., Socher, R., Li, L.J., Li, K., Fei-Fei, L.: Imagenet: a large-scale hierarchical image database. In: Proceedings of the IEEE Conference on Computer Vision and Pattern Recognition, pp. 248–255 (2009)
11. Dieleman, S., De Fauw, J., Kavukcuoglu, K.: Exploiting cyclic symmetry in convolutional neural networks. In: Proceedings of the 33rd International Conference on International Conference on Machine Learning, vol. 48, pp. 1889–1898 (2016)
12. Duan, K., Bai, S., Xie, L., Qi, H., Huang, Q., Tian, Q.: Centernet: keypoint triplets for object detection. In: Proceedings of the IEEE International Conference on Computer Vision, pp. 6569–6578 (2019)
13. Furlanello, T., Lipton, Z.C., Tschannen, M., Itti, L., Anandkumar, A.: Born again neural networks. arXiv preprint arXiv:1805.04770 (2018)
14. Han, S., Pool, J., Tran, J., Dally, W.: Learning both weights and connections for efficient neural network. In: Advances in Neural Information Processing Systems, pp. 1135–1143 (2015)
15. Hanson, S.J., Pratt, L.Y.: Comparing biases for minimal network construction with back-propagation. In: Advances in Neural Information Processing Systems, pp. 177–185 (1989)
16. He, K., Gkioxari, G., Dollár, P., Girshick, R.: Mask r-cnn. In: Proceedings of the IEEE International Conference on Computer Vision, pp. 2961–2969 (2017)
17. He, K., Zhang, X., Ren, S., Sun, J.: Deep residual learning for image recognition. In: Proceedings of the IEEE Conference on Computer Vision and Pattern Recognition, pp. 770–778 (2016)
18. Hinton, G., Vinyals, O., Dean, J.: Distilling the knowledge in a neural network. arXiv preprint arXiv:1503.02531 (2015)
19. Huang, G., Li, Y., Pleiss, G., Liu, Z., Hopcroft, J.E., Weinberger, K.Q.: Snapshot ensembles: Train 1, get m for free. arXiv preprint arXiv:1704.00109 (2017)
20. Huang, G., Liu, Z., Van Der Maaten, L., Weinberger, K.Q.: Densely connected convolutional networks. In: Proceedings of the IEEE Conference on Computer Vision and Pattern Recognition, pp. 4700–4708 (2017)
21. Kim, Y., Rush, A.M.: Sequence-level knowledge distillation. arXiv preprint arXiv:1606.07947 (2016)
22. Koratana, A., Kang, D., Bailis, P., Zaharia, M.: Lit: learned intermediate representation training for model compression. In: International Conference on Machine Learning, pp. 3509–3518 (2019)
23. Krizhevsky, A., Hinton, G., et al.: Learning multiple layers of features from tiny images (2009). https://www.cs.toronto.edu/~kriz/learning-features-2009-TR.pdf

24. Krizhevsky, A., Sutskever, I., Hinton, G.E.: Imagenet classification with deep convolutional neural networks. In: Advances in Neural Information Processing Systems, pp. 1097–1105 (2012)
25. Li, H., Ouyang, W., Wang, X.: Multi-bias non-linear activation in deep neural networks. In: International Conference on Machine Learning, pp. 221–229 (2016)
26. Liu, W., et al.: SSD: single shot multibox detector. In: Leibe, B., Matas, J., Sebe, N., Welling, M. (eds.) ECCV 2016. LNCS, vol. 9905, pp. 21–37. Springer, Cham (2016). https://doi.org/10.1007/978-3-319-46448-0_2
27. Liu, Y., et al.: Cbnet: a novel composite backbone network architecture for object detection. arXiv preprint arXiv:1909.03625 (2019)
28. Netzer, Y., Wang, T., Coates, A., Bissacco, A., Wu, B., Ng, A.Y.: Reading digits in natural images with unsupervised feature learning. In: NIPS Workshop on Deep Learning and Unsupervised Feature Learning (2011)
29. Rakhuba, M., Oseledets, I.V.: Fast multidimensional convolution in low-rank tensor formats via cross approximation. SIAM J. Sci. Comput. **37**(2), A565–A582 (2015)
30. Redmon, J., Divvala, S., Girshick, R., Farhadi, A.: You only look once: unified, real-time object detection. In: Proceedings of the IEEE Conference on Computer Vision and Pattern Recognition, pp. 779–788 (2016)
31. Ren, S., He, K., Girshick, R., Sun, J.: Faster r-cnn: towards real-time object detection with region proposal networks. In: Advances in Neural Information Processing Systems, pp. 91–99 (2015)
32. Selvaraju, R.R., Cogswell, M., Das, A., Vedantam, R., Parikh, D., Batra, D.: Gradcam: Visual explanations from deep networks via gradient-based localization. In: Proceedings of the IEEE International Conference on Computer Vision, pp. 618–626 (2017)
33. Shang, W., Sohn, K., Almeida, D., Lee, H.: Understanding and improving convolutional neural networks via concatenated rectified linear units. In: International Conference on Machine Learning, pp. 2217–2225 (2016)
34. Shen, Z., He, Z., Xue, X.: Meal: multi-model ensemble via adversarial learning. In: Proceedings of the AAAI Conference on Artificial Intelligence, vol. 33, pp. 4886–4893 (2019)
35. Simonyan, K., Zisserman, A.: Very deep convolutional networks for large-scale image recognition. arXiv preprint arXiv:1409.1556 (2014)
36. Sindhwani, V., Sainath, T., Kumar, S.: Structured transforms for small-footprint deep learning. In: Advances in Neural Information Processing Systems, pp. 3088–3096 (2015)
37. Srinivas, S., Babu, R.V.: Data-free parameter pruning for deep neural networks. arXiv preprint arXiv:1507.06149 (2015)
38. Szegedy, C., et al.: Going deeper with convolutions. In: Proceedings of the IEEE Conference on Computer Vision and Pattern Recognition, pp. 1–9 (2015)
39. Szegedy, C., Vanhoucke, V., Ioffe, S., Shlens, J., Wojna, Z.: Rethinking the inception architecture for computer vision. In: Proceedings of the IEEE Conference on Computer Vision and Pattern Recognition, pp. 2818–2826 (2016)
40. Tan, M., Le, Q.V.: Efficientnet: rethinking model scaling for convolutional neural networks. arXiv preprint arXiv:1905.11946 (2019)
41. Xie, S., Girshick, R., Dollár, P., Tu, Z., He, K.: Aggregated residual transformations for deep neural networks. In: Proceedings of the IEEE Conference on Computer Vision and Pattern Recognition, pp. 1492–1500 (2017)
42. Yim, J., Joo, D., Bae, J., Kim, J.: A gift from knowledge distillation: fast optimization, network minimization and transfer learning. In: Proceedings of the IEEE Conference on Computer Vision and Pattern Recognition, pp. 4133–4141 (2017)

43. Zhang, Y., Xiang, T., Hospedales, T.M., Lu, H.: Deep mutual learning. In: Proceedings of the IEEE Conference on Computer Vision and Pattern Recognition, pp. 4320–4328 (2018)
44. Zhang, Z., Zhang, X., Peng, C., Xue, X., Sun, J.: Exfuse: enhancing feature fusion for semantic segmentation. In: Proceedings of the European Conference on Computer Vision (ECCV), pp. 269–284 (2018)
45. Zhong, Z., Lin, Z.Q., Bidart, R., Hu, X., Daya, I.B., Li, J., Wong, A.: Squeeze-and-attention networks for semantic segmentation. arXiv preprint arXiv:1909.03402 (2019)
46. Zhu, X., Gong, S., et al.: Knowledge distillation by on-the-fly native ensemble. In: Advances in Neural Information Processing Systems, pp. 7517–7527 (2018)

Deep Learning-Based Pupil Center Detection for Fast and Accurate Eye Tracking System

Kang Il Lee, Jung Ho Jeon, and Byung Cheol Song[(⊠)]

Department of Electrical Engineering, Inha University, Incheon, Korea
{kangil-lee,jungho-jeon}@inha.edu, bcsong@inha.ac.kr

Abstract. In augmented reality (AR) or virtual reality (VR) systems, eye tracking is a key technology and requires significant accuracy as well as real-time operation. Many techniques for detecting pupil centers with error range of iris radius have been developed, but few techniques have precise performance with error range of pupil radius. In addition, the conventional methods rarely guarantee real-time pupil center detection in a general-purpose computer environment due to high complexity. Thus, we propose more accurate pupil center detection by improving the representation quality of the network in charge of pupil center detection. This is realized by representation learning based on mutual information. Also, the latency of the entire system is greatly reduced by using non-local block and self-attention block with large receptive field, which makes it accomplish real-time operation. The proposed system not only shows real-time performance of 52 FPS in a general-purpose computer environment but also provides state-of-the-art accuracy in terms of fine level index of 96.71%, 99.84% and 96.38% for BioID, GI4E and Talking Face Video datasets, respectively.

Keywords: Remote eye tracking · Mobile applications

1 Introduction

In general, the performance of computer vision applications such as AR and VR highly depend on gaze estimation and eye tracking techniques. The pupil center detection plays a crucial role in those applications. As a result, the real-time operation and high accuracy of pupil center detection make the AR/VR system more practical. Pupil center detection or tracking (PCT) methods are divided into two categories, i.e., model-based and appearance-based approaches. Model-based methods are limitedly used in equipments such as head-mounted goggles. For example, user-specific calibrations were performed using eye geometry models and coordinate systems for accurate pupil center detection at a close distance [1].

Electronic supplementary material The online version of this chapter (https://doi.org/10.1007/978-3-030-58529-7_3) contains supplementary material, which is available to authorized users.

On the other hand, appearance-based methods [2–12] detect the pupil center using a remote camera without head-mount goggles or user-specific calibrations.In general, appearance-based methods consist of two steps: the eye region extraction and the pupil center detection. The eye region extraction step is again composed of a face detection and an eye region extraction using features such as landmarks. The pupil center detection methods can be prior knowledge-based approach or context-based approach. Prior knowledge-based approaches adopt a regression model designed based on generic eye appearance information [2,4–11]. The context-based techniques separate a given eye region image into a pupil center and a background using specific segmentation networks [12,13]. Alternatively, [3] improved the performance of the regression model with the hand-crafted features extracted from the pupil area.

Most of the latest PCT methods provide high accuracy in the error range of iris radius, whereas their accuracy in the error range of pupil radius, a more precise level, is not satisfactory yet. In addition, many previous techniques seldom guarantee real-time PCT in a general purpose computer environment due to high latency of eye region extraction modules [4,10,11].

This paper proposes a new appearance-based PCT to secure real-time operation as well as high accuracy even at the precise level. We propose the PCT system to enable pupil center detection robust against glasses wearing, inspired by [13]. First, representation learning using mutual information (MI) is applied to the pupil center detection network so that the network can extract features which have rich location information. Note that as the representation of the network improves, the pupil center detection accuracy increases together. Next, in order to realize consistent real-time processing of the PCT system, nonlocal block (NLB) and self-attention block (SAB) are applied to face detection network and glasses removal network, which are bottlenecks in terms of latency. Using NLB and SAB, each network can obtain a low latency because large receptive field effect is produced even with only a few layers. On the other hand, glasses removal network tends to blur the eye region during erasing glasses. Therefore, we propose a method to mitigate blur phenomenon by employing perceptual loss, resulting in improvement of detection performance.

The main contribution points of the proposed PCT system are as follows.

- Overall pupil detection accuracy was increased by improving representation quality of pupil detection network through representation learning using MI.
- The latency of the entire system was greatly reduced by the face detection network and the glasses removal network which utilize the large receptive field features of NLB and SAB. That is, it guarantees real-time operation.
- The spatial loss or blur due to the structural lightweighting of the glasses removal network is compensated by employing perceptual loss.
- In terms of fine-level index [4], i.e., most precise accuracy level, the proposed PCT system shows state-of-the-art(SOTA) performance of 96.71%, 99.84%, and 96.38% for BioID, GI4E, and Talking Face Video datasets, respectively.

2   Related Works

Appearance-Based Methods. [2], which is a representative appearance-based method using prior knowledge, first detects a face from an input image through the face detector of [14]. The eye area is then cropped using biometric statistics from the face. Next, the radial gradients for all the points on the iris contour are computed. Finally, a pupil center is detected by using the prior knowledge that the origin of the displacement vector with the maximum radial gradient is the pupil center. One of the latest techniques using prior knowledge is based on cascade regression model and circle fitting [4]. This algorithm trains three cascade regression models: two regression models for eye corners and eye centers, and a regression model for circle fitting.

On the other hand, appearance-based techniques considering the context have been reported [12,13]. For instance, [13] detects a face using [15], and then determines whether there is glasses in the face. If glasses exist, an eye region is detected after removing the glasses using CycleGAN [16]. Otherwise, the eye region detection module is activated immediately. Finally, a pupil center is detected by applying the semantic segmentation network to the detected eye region so as to separate the pupil center from the background. [12] detects the eye center by directly inputting the face image to the semantic segmentation network. Note that [12] does not include any separate module for dealing with glasses.

Non-local Neural Networks. The most popular convolutional neural network (CNN) is based on convolutional operations for local neighborhood. Therefore, a deep network is required to secure a large receptive field. However, this approach causes a gradient vanishing problem, making learning difficult and inefficient. In order to solve this fundamental limitation, NLB was born in [17]. If NLB receives an embedded feature map, it measures point-to-point graphical relations for all points in the feature map. The measured graphical relation can produce a self-attention effect similar to [18]. This helps to solve a given task efficiently. In addition, since the receptive field size of NLB is the same as that of the input data, NLB generally has an effect of enlarging a receptive field. Therefore, if NLB is applied to a network, the network can achieve a large receptive field effect without stacking deep convolutional layers.

Thus, we apply NLB to the face detection network that is a bottleneck in terms of latency so that overall latency can be decreased. In addition, SAB, which has a structure similar to NLB, is applied to another bottleneck, i.e., the glasses removal network, to maximize operational speed.

Perceptual Loss. In typical image processing tasks such as noise reduction, super-resolution, and colorization, traditional pixel loss does not reflect perceptual characteristics well. With this in mind, [19] defines a loss in feature level, i.e., perceptual loss. Then high level features are extracted by VGG-16 [20] that is pre-trained with ImageNet [21]. The extracted features are used to induce perceptual loss. Inspired by the image super resolution technique proposed in [19], we add perceptual loss to the cycle consistency loss [16] defined for learning the lightweight glasses removal network.

Mutual Information Maximization. In information theory, the mutual information (MI) of two random variables indicates the mutual dependence between the two random variables. More specifically, MI quantifies the amount of information of one random variable through observing the other random variable. Representation learning aimed at maximizing MI between target representation and features or intermediate features has been studied for a long time [22–24]. Most recent studies focus on variational approach [24,25]. This is because it is very difficult to estimate the MI of continuous random variables in high dimensional space. So the variational approach derives the tight lower bound of MI. Recently, a few methods have proposed tight lower bounds of MI estimation by using neural network [22,23]. For example, [22] achieved high performance in downstream tasks through representation learning using MI maximization. Inspired by [22], we apply MI-based representation learning to the segmentation network. This greatly improves the pupil center detection accuracy.

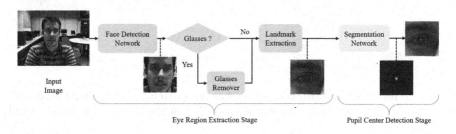

Fig. 1. The proposed pupil center tracking system.

3   Method

Figure 1 is the overview of the proposed PCT system (Sect. 3.1). We designed the entire system, inspired by [13], which combines glasses removal module with the structure of a universal pupil center detection scheme. Even though we follow the basic structure of [13], we propose a few novel methods for dramatically improving the speed and accuracy of the PCT system. First, we present a low latency face detection network using NLB (Sect. 3.2). Next, we propose a structure applying SAB for the low latency of the glasses removal module that is the critical latency bottleneck of the entire PCT system in [13]. Plus, perceptual loss is introduced to mitigate the blur phenomenon (Sect. 3.3). Finally, we propose a representation learning using MI maximization to improve the representation quality of the segmentation network which has an absolute influence on the overall accuracy of the PCT system (Sect. 3.4).

3.1   Overview

This section describes the purpose and operation of each module of the proposed PCT system. As shown in Fig. 1, the proposed PCT system consists of an eye region extraction stage and a pupil center detection stage. The face detection network, the first step of the eye region extraction stage, is responsible for cropping the face from an input image. Next, the glasses classifier determines whether glasses exist in the face image. If it is determined that the glasses are worn, the glasses removal network removes the glasses. Next, the landmarks are extracted from the face image, while glasses are removed selectively. The final step of the eye region extraction stage is to extract the eye region in the face image using landmark information. Subsequent pupil center detection stage is performed by a segmentation network. Given an eye region image, the heat map is calculated as shown in the lower right corner of Fig. 1. The glasses classifier and landmark extractor of the proposed PCT system follow the methods of [13].

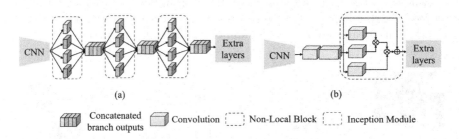

Fig. 2. (a) FaceBoxes [26] (b) the modified face detection network. CNN is the encoder network and extra layers are convolution layers designed to address multi-scale in [26]

3.2   Face Detection Network

The face detection networks used in conventional PCT methods can have a high accuracy, but requires a long latency to guarantee high precision. So we choose a high-performance face detection network [26], and apply NLB to the network to reduce the latency while maintaining reasonable accuracy.

Faceboxes of [26] effectively used context information through an inception module [27] while properly coping with multi-scale like SSD [15]. So [26] is robust for scale and occlusion. However, since the inception module is basically a concatenation structure, it can be a bottleneck when operating on GPU. To remedy this problem, we introduce NLB that can apply context information, which secures a large receptive field with only a few layers. In detail, the inception module is replaced with the NLB having two convolutional layers, as shown in Fig. 2(b). As a result, the modified FaceBoxes network provides high face detection performance with low latency (see the results in Sect. 4).

3.3   Glasses Removal Network

This section describes how to lighten the glasses removal network, which was proposed in [13]. Also, how to mitigate the blur phenomenon during light-weighting is given.

The CycleGAN [16] was used to refine landmark information as the glasses removal network [13]. But the CycleGAN generator used in [13] has a structural problem. Since the encoder has only two down-sampling layers as shown in Fig. 3(a), it faces with a critical problem that the computational cost varies depending on the resolution of an input image. In addition, constructing a network by just stacking nine residual blocks in a high level layer is an inefficient configuration [18]. To address the computational cost problem caused by the above-mentioned structural factor of the existing glasses removal network, we attempt the following approach. First, add a down-sampling layer and an up-sampling layer to the encoder and decoder as shown in Fig. 3(b) to reduce the spatial size of the feature map for the transformation stage to 1/4. Also, the transformation stage is configured to have a comparable receptive field to the generator of CycleGAN by using one self-attention block [28] and two residual blocks.

However, this structural approach causes additional spatial loss in encoding process. So, we address the spatial loss problem by utilizing the method proposed in [19]. Since CycleGAN basically learns using unpaired datasets, there is no high resolution (HR) reference for the domain translated image. Thus, we propose the cycle consistency loss in feature-level as shown in Fig. 3(c). We call this perceptual cycle consistency loss (PCCL), which is defined as Eq. (1).

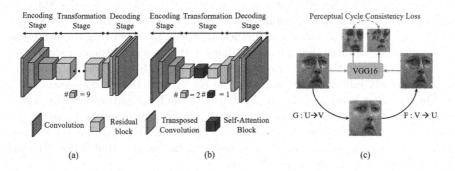

Fig. 3. (a) The glasses removal network in [13] (b) the proposed glasses removal network (c) the illustration of how to calculate perceptual cycle consistency loss.

$$L_{PCCL} = E_{u \sim P_{data(U)}} \left[\sum_{i=1}^{5} |\phi_i(F(G(u))) - \phi_i(u)|_1 \right] +$$
$$E_{v \sim P_{data(V)}} \left[\sum_{i=1}^{5} |\phi_i(G(F(v))) - \phi_i(v)|_1 \right]$$

(1)

where U and V mean different domains. G and F denote a generator for removing the glasses and a generator for restoring glasses, respectively. In addition, $\phi_i(\cdot)$ stands for the feature map of the last layer per unit of five convolution blocks of VGG-16 [20]. By integrating GAN loss L_{GAN} of [16] and L_{PCCL}, total GAN loss L_{GAN}^{Total} is defined as Eq. (2).

$$L_{GAN}^{Total} = L_{GAN} + L_{PCCL}$$

(2)

As a result, we construct the glasses removal network with significantly lower computational cost than [13] through the proposed light-weighting strategy. Since PCCL compensates for the spatial loss due to the light-weighting, we can keep the performance comparable to the glasses removal network of [13].

3.4   Segmentation Network

This section proposes a method to improve the accuracy of the proposed PCT system. We enhance the representation quality of the pupil center detection network, i.e., the segmentation network, through representation learning using MI maximization. [13] showed that low-level feature transfer to decoder through skip connection can improve pupil center detection performance. Also, the pupil center detection performance was further improved by enhancing the representation of latent features through an auxiliary network of auto-encoder structure. Therefore, we found that the representation quality of the pupil center detection network greatly influences the overall pupil center detection performance.

On the other hand, in [22], the MI between the local feature and the representation of the auto-encoder was measured, and then unsupervised representation learning was conducted by maximizing the MI. [22] showed that the learned encoder provides high performance in classification, that is a kind of downstream task such as semantic segmentation task.

Based on the results of [13] and [22], in order to maximize the pupil center detection performance of the segmentation network, we propose a method of enhancing the representation quality through MI maximization only during training. First, the low-level feature X_1 and latent feature X_2 of the segmentation network and the feature map Y of the decoder are extracted, as shown in Fig. 4. We define X_1 and X_2 as local features and Y as the representation of segmentation network. Then, to calculate the MI regardless of the spatial dimensions of X_1 and X_2, we transform Y into a feature vector $\tilde{Y}$ through the vectorization network. $\tilde{Y}$ is input to the shuffle and concatenation module together with X_1 and X_2. Next, the concatenated feature maps are produced for computing the conditional entropy (CE) and marginal entropy (ME) estimates. If the CE and ME estimates enter two discriminators D_1 and D_2, the MI is calculated according to Eq. (3).

$$I(X_k; \tilde{Y}) = E_{\mathbb{P} \otimes \mathbb{P}'}[sp(D_k(C(X_k')))] - E_{\mathbb{P}}[-sp(D_k(C(X_k, \tilde{Y})))] \qquad (3)$$

where sp indicates the softplus operator and C means the concatenation operation. And $\mathbb{P}$ is the distribution of an input local feature X_k. X_k' is the local feature processed by batch-wise shuffle as in Fig. 4, and $\mathbb{P}'$ is the distribution of X_k' (k = 1,2). Finally, by adding MI to the segmentation loss L_{Seg} [13] based on pixel-wise mean squared error, the total loss function L_{total} of the segmentation network is defined by Eq. (4).

$$L_{total} = L_{seg} - (I_1(X_1; \tilde{Y}) + I_2(X_2; \tilde{Y})) \qquad (4)$$

The operation of the proposed segmentation network is summarized as follows:

- Define local features(X_1, X_2) and representation(Y) suitable for segmentation network.
- In order to compute MI irrespective of the spatial dimensions of X_1 and X_2 transform Y into $\tilde{Y}$ through the vectorization network.
- Based on the loss function using the computed MI, learn the segmentation network.

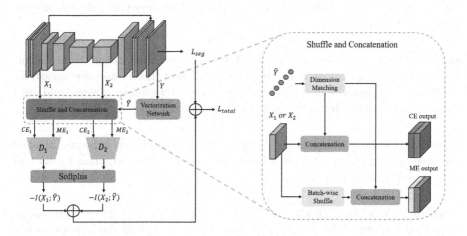

Fig. 4. The representation learning framework for semantic segmentation network.

4   Experiments

We performed three experiments to verify the proposed system. First, we evaluated the accuracy of pupil center detection by the proposed method. The quantitative evaluation metric of accuracy is defined by Eq. (5).

$$e = \frac{max(d_l, d_r)}{d} \tag{5}$$

where d_r, d_l denote Euclidean distance between the detected pupil center and Ground Truth (GT) in the right and left eyes, respectively, and d denotes Euclidean distance between the GT centers of two eyes calculated. In addition, FLoating point Operations Per second(FLOPs), the number of parameters, and latency were measured to evaluate the light-weighting level of the face detection network and glasses removal network. Second, the qualitative test was performed. Third, an ablation study was conducted using the fine level index to evaluate each module's contribution in performance. In order to make a fair comparison, we compared the proposed method with some prior knowledge-based methods and other context-based methods, respectively.

Except landmark extractor and VGG-16, we trained other models from scratch. We used five-point landmark extractor provided by dlib [29] and VGG-16 pretrained on ImageNet.

4.1   Datasets and Experimental Environment

We used four public datasets: WIDER FACE [30] BioID [31], GI4E [32], Talking Face Video [33]. Also, we collected a dataset to train the glasses classifier and glasses removal network through web crawling. More detail information of each dataset is as follows.

BioID. This is a dataset consisting of 1,521 low-resolution images from various subjects. The image resolution is 384×286. Images in this dataset are negatively affected by varying illumination, head-poses and occlusion by glasses, and even include eyes closed. That is, a very challenging dataset.

GI4E. It is a dataset consisting of 1,236 images from various subjects. Most of the images in this dataset have a larger resolution (800×600) than BioID and consist of frontal face images.

Talking Face Video(TFV). It is a dataset consisting of a total of 5000 images of just one subject. The image resolution is 720×576. This dataset was taken while the subject was talking, including various head poses and eyes closed.

WIDER FACE. It is a dataset with annotated face location information of people in various event images. The dataset consists of 393,703 face images with various scales, head poses and occlusions.

Customized Dataset. We collected 1,700 images of glasses wearers and 1,700 images of non-wearers through web crawling and annotated them.

We composed whole training datasets and evaluation datasets as follows. We composed a training dataset for the proposed face detection network by randomly selecting 12,880 images from 60 event classes in WIDER FACE dataset. And color distortion, random cropping, scale transformation, and horizontal flipping were used as data augmentations for face detection network training. In case of glasses classifier and glasses removal network, we used 3,224 images of the customized dataset as a training dataset and 176 images as a validation dataset. For the segmentation network, we constructed the training datasets by cropping the eye region (R_i) that satisfies Eq.(6) using the label data of each image.

$$R_i = \{z \mid \parallel z - o^i \parallel_1 \leq 3l\}, i \in \{Right, Left\}, z \in \mathbb{R}^2 \qquad (6)$$

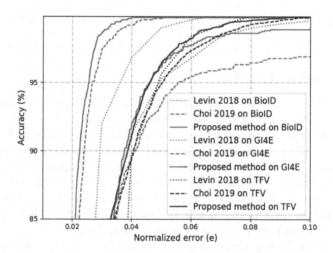

Fig. 5. Accuracy vs. the normalized error (e) for BioID, GI4E and TFV datasets.

where o_i is the midpoint between the two ends of eye, and l is $1/2$ of the distance between the two ends of the eye. Meanwhile, we employed two different dataset compositions for the segmentation network. Firstly, due to lack of dataset, we integrated BioID and GI4E dataset. And we equally split the integrated dataset into five-folds. In other words, we used 80% data of the integrated dataset as a training dataset and evaluated the proposed method by using the other data for each fold. Secondly, we entirely used the integrated dataset for training dataset and evaluated the segmentation network on TFV dataset. Color jittering was used as data augmentation for training of the segmentation network. Note that the TFV is only used for evaluation. The more details of implementation can be found in the supplementary material.

Meanwhile, each module in the PCT system was learned individually. A hardware environment consisting of one NVIDA GTX 1070 Ti GPU and one Intel i7-8700 CPU was used.

Fig. 6. Qualitative comparison between [13] (left) and ours (right) for BioID dataset.

4.2   Quantitative Results

The proposed method and the SOTA methods were compared in terms of three accuracy levels for BioID, GI4E and Talking Face Video datasets. All quantitative results in Table 1 and Table 2 were acquired by five-times experiments and the figures in Tables are the average values. The first accuracy level of $e \leq 0.05$ means that the estimated pupil center position is within pupil radius, which is also called the fine level because it reflects the highest precision of pupil center detection. The middle level of $e \leq 0.1$ indicates that the estimated pupil center position is within iris radius. Finally, the coarsest level of $e \leq 0.25$ means that the estimated pupil center position is within eye radius.

Table 1 shows the experimental results for the BioID dataset. In terms of fine level ($e \leq 0.05$), the proposed method showed outstanding accuracy of 96.71% ($\pm0.05\%$). This is 1.44% higher than the best SOTA method [4]. However, we could see the proposed method gives a little bit lower performance in case of $e \leq 0.1$. This is because other SOTA methods were evaluated by using clean face image through annotated data. However, unlike [3,4,12], the proposed method is evaluated with a face image predicted by the proposed face detector. In other words, the inaccuracy of the face detection is included in the result of the proposed method. For the GI4E dataset, the proposed method showed the SOTA performance of 99.84%($\pm0.00\%$) in terms of fine level (see Table 2). Even for TFV dataset, the proposed method showed the best performance for fine level by 0.76% ($\pm0.12\%$). Figure 5 shows accuracy curves of the proposed method, [4] and [13] for BioID, GI4E and TFV datasets. Figure 5 illustrates that the proposed method is more accurate than other methods under the fine level range ($e \leq 0.05$).

Table 1. Comparison results for BioID dataset.

Method	Category	$e \leq 0.05$	$e \leq 0.1$	$e \leq 0.25$
Tian2016 [5]	Prior	93.93%	98.22%	NA
Vater2016 [6]	Prior	89.48%	94.85%	NA
Zhang2016 [7]	Prior	85.66%	93.68%	99.21%
Kacete2016 [8]	Prior	91.30%	97.90%	99.6%
Ahuja2016 [9]	Prior	92.06%	97.96%	100%
Cai2018 [10]	Prior	92.80%	NA	NA
Xiao2018 [11]	Prior	94.35%	98.75%	99.80%
Levin2018 [4]	Prior	95.27%	99.52%	100%
Gou2017 [3]	Context	91.20%	99.40%	99.80%
Choi2019 [13]	Context	93.30%	96.91%	100%
Xia2019 [12]	Context	94.40%	**99.90%**	100%
Ours	Context	**96.71%**	98.95%	**100%**

Table 2. Comparison results for GI4E and TFV datasets.

GI4E dataset				
Method	Category	$e \leq 0.05$	$e \leq 0.1$	$e \leq 0.25$
Zhang2016 [7]	Prior	97.90%	99.60%	NA
Cai2018 [10]	Prior	99.50%	NA	NA
Xiao2018 [11]	Prior	97.90%	100%	100%
Levin2018 [4]	Prior	99.03%	99.92%	100%
Gou2017 [3]	Context	98.30%	99.80%	NA
Xia2019 [12]	Context	99.10%	**100%**	100%
Choi2019 [13]	Context	99.60%	99.84%	100%
Ours	Context	**99.84%**	99.84%	**100%**
TFV dataset				
Ahuja2016 [9]	Prior	94.78%	99.00%	99.42%
Xiao2018 [11]	Prior	91.24%	97.56%	99.96%
Levin2018 [4]	Prior	95.62%	99.88%	99.98%
Choi2019 [13]	Context	95.18%	99.72%	100%
Ours	Context	**96.38%**	**100%**	**100%**

On the other hand, in order to quantitatively verify the complexity of the proposed PCT system, the FLOPs, the number of parameters, and the latency of the face detection network and the glasses removal network were measured. And the measured values were compared with those of [13] and [26]. In Table 3, the number of FLOPs and parameters of the proposed face detection network increased, but its latency was lower than that of [26]. This phenomenon can

Table 3. Complexity comparision in terms of FLOPs, the number of parameters and latency

	Face detection network			Glasses removal network	
Method	Choi2019 [13]	Faceboxes [26]	Ours	Choi2019 [13]	Ours
FLOPs	2.39 G	0.09 G	0.15 G	245 G	59 G
Parameters	2.6 M	1 M	1.74 M	11 M	3.2 M
Latency	13 ms	10 ms	7 ms	10 ms	4 ms

be attributed to the bottleneck of the concatenation structure of the inception module. Note that the FLOPs and parameters of the proposed glasses removal network decreased to only 24.1% and 29.1% of [13]. The latency of the proposed glasses removal network also decreased significantly to around 40% of [13]. As a result, the total latency of the proposed PCT system amounts to about 19 ms, which is enough for real-time operation on general purpose computers.

4.3   Qualitative Results

This section qualitatively compared the proposed method and [13] (see Fig. 6). For this experiment, the BioID dataset was used. We could observe that the proposed method provides closer result to the actual pupil center. We also qualitatively verified the validity of the PCCL proposed in Sect. 3.3. Figure 7 shows the results of the glasses removal network. The customized dataset was used for this experiment. Looking at the second and third rows, we could see that the PCCL significantly mitigates the blur problem. Also, in rows 3 and 4 of Fig. 7, in spite that the proposed glasses removal network is lighter than [13], the details are better preserved than [13].

4.4   Ablation Study

This section further analyzes the effects of the proposed techniques on pupil center detection performance. BioID dataset was used for this experiment, and the fine level of $e \leq 0.05$ was evaluated. Since we used the five-point landmark extractor provided by dlib [29] to ensure low latency, we increased the size of the bounding box horizontally by about 10 pixels to extract the exact landmarks. For fair comparison, the size of the bounding box obtained from the face detection network of [13] was also increased by 10 pixels.

The experiment identifies the effects of the proposed techniques by replacing each module of [13] with the proposed technique. Table 4 shows the experimental results. The fine level accuracy of [13] was 95.39%. We used this accuracy as a baseline in the following experiment. When the face detection network of [13] is replaced with the proposed network (FD), the performance increases to 95.59% (+0.2%). In case of changing the glasses removal network to the proposed method (GR), the overall performance was 95.79% (+0.4%). If both face detection and

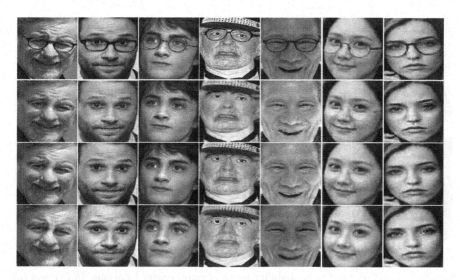

Fig. 7. Qualitative comparison with [13]'s glasses remover and ours for the customized dataset. First row is input images. Second and third rows are the proposed glasses remover's outputs without/with PCCL. Lastly, fourth row is [13]'s glasses remover's outputs.

Table 4. The effect of each module on the overall performance.

Face detection (FD)	Glasses removal (GR)	Mutual information (MI)	$e \leq 0.05$
			95.39%
✓			95.59%
	✓		95.79%
✓	✓		95.99%
✓	✓	✓	96.71%

glasses removal networks of [13] were modified with the proposed techniques (FD + GR), the detection accuracy became 95.99% (+0.6%). Finally, when all the modules including the segmentation network were replaced with the proposed methods (FD + GR + MI), that is, the proposed PCT system itself showed the detection accuracy of 96.71% (+1.32%). Meanwhile, we investigated practical effect of the proposed representation learning on the segmentation network (see Fig. 8). As shown in Fig. 8(b) and (d), the proposed representation learning using MI did not practically affect on output shapes. However, as shown in Fig. 8(a) and (c), we can observe that the proposed representation learning provides the segmentation network with additional location information for accurate pupil center detection. To sum up with, all of the proposed modules provide significant performance improvements, and the segmentation network combined with the proposed representation learning has the greatest effect on pupil center detection performance without additional cost during inference.

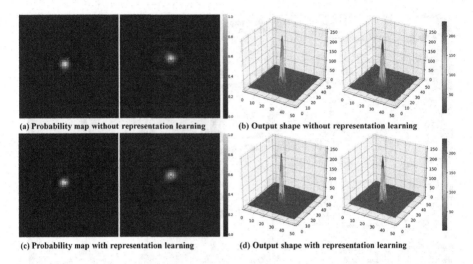

(a) Probability map without representation learning   (b) Output shape without representation learning

(c) Probability map with representation learning   (d) Output shape with representation learning

Fig. 8. (a) and (c) are the probability maps of pupil center locations. In (a) and (c), Red 'x' marks are ground truth locations.(b) and (d) are the shapes of segmentation network outputs. Here, BioID dataset was used.

5 Conclusions

This paper proposes pupil center detection methods for high accuracy and light weight methods to secure real-time operation. The proposed representation learning can provide an additional information into the segmentation network for accurate pupil center detection by using mutual information. Also, we designed a low latency face detection network using a non-local block and a lightweight glasses removal network that provides good image quality by using self-attention block and perceptual loss. Experimental results show that the proposed scheme has a low latency of 19 ms per frame with state-of-the-art accuracy in fine level index. The proposed real-time PCT system is expected to be effectively used in systems such as AR, VR, and hologram.

Acknowledgements. This work was supported by 'The Cross-Ministry Giga KOREA Project' grant funded by the Korea government (MSIT) [1711093798, Development of full-3D mobile display terminal and its contents] and Institute of Information & communications Technology Planning & Evaluation (IITP) grant funded by the Korea government (MSIT) [2020-0-01389, Artificial Intelligence Convergence Research Center (Inha University)].

References

1. Li, J., Li, S.: Eye-model-based gaze estimation by RGB-d camera. In: The IEEE Conference on Computer Vision and Pattern Recognition (CVPR) Workshops (2014)
2. Timm, F., Barth, E.: Accurate eye centre localisation by means of gradients (2011)

3. Gou, C., Yue, W., Wang, K., Wang, K., Wang, F.-Y., Ji, Q.: A joint cascaded framework for simultaneous eye detection and eye state estimation. Pattern Recogn. **67**, 23–31 (2017)

4. Levinshtein, A., Phung, E., Aarabi, P.: Hybrid eye center localization using cascaded regression and hand-crafted model fitting. Image Vision Comput. **71**, 17–24 (2018)

5. Tian, D., He, G., Wu, J., Chen, H., Jiang, Y.: An accurate eye pupil localization approach based on adaptive gradient boosting decision tree. In: 2016 Visual Communications and Image Processing (VCIP), pp. 1–4. IEEE (2016)

6. Vater, S., Puente León, F.: Combining isophote and cascade classifier information for precise pupil localization. In: 2016 IEEE International Conference on Image Processing (ICIP), pp. 589–593. IEEE (2016)

7. Zhang, W., Smith, M.L., Smith, L.N., Farooq, A.: Eye center localization and gaze gesture recognition for human-computer interaction. JOSA A **33**(3), 314–325 (2016)

8. Kacete, A., Royan, J.,Seguier, R., Collobert, M., Soladie, C.: Real-time eye pupil localization using hough regression forest. In: 2016 IEEE Winter Conference on Applications of Computer Vision (WACV), pp. 1–8. IEEE (2016)

9. Ahuja, K., Banerjee, R., Nagar, S., Dey, K., Barbhuiya, F.: Eye center localization and detection using radial mapping. In: 2016 IEEE International Conference on image processing (ICIP), pp. 3121–3125. IEEE (2016)

10. Cai, H., et al.: Accurate eye center localization via hierarchical adaptive convolution. In: BMVC, p. 284 (2018)

11. Xiao, F., Huang, K., Qiu, Y., Shen, H.: Accurate iris center localization method using facial landmark, snakuscule, circle fitting and binary connected component. Multimedia Tools Appl. **77**(19), 25333–25353 (2018)

12. Xia, Y., Hui, Yu., Wang, F.-Y.: Accurate and robust eye center localization via fully convolutional networks. IEEE/CAA J. Automatica Sinica **6**(5), 1127–1138 (2019)

13. Choi, J.H., Lee, K.I., Kim, Y.C., Song, B.C.: Accurate eye pupil localization using heterogeneous CNN models. In: 2019 IEEE International Conference on Image Processing (ICIP), pp. 2179–2183. IEEE (2019)

14. Viola, P., Jones, M.J.: Robust real-time face detection. Int. J. Comput. Vis. **57**(2), 137–154 (2004)

15. Liu, W., et al.: SSD: single shot multibox detector. In: Leibe, B., Matas, J., Sebe, N., Welling, M. (eds.) ECCV 2016. LNCS, vol. 9905, pp. 21–37. Springer, Cham (2016). https://doi.org/10.1007/978-3-319-46448-0_2

16. Zhu, J.Y., Park, T., Isola, P., Efros, A.A.: Unpaired image-to-image translation using cycle-consistent adversarial networks. In: Proceedings of the IEEE International Conference on Computer Vision, pp. 2223–2232 (2017)

17. Wang, X., Girshick, R., Gupta, A., He, K.: Non-local neural networks. In: Proceedings of the IEEE Conference on Computer Vision and Pattern Recognition, pp. 7794–7803 (2018)

18. Vaswani, A., et al.: Attention is all you need. In: Advances in Neural Information Processing Systems, pp. 5998–6008 (2017)

19. Johnson, J., Alahi, A., Fei-Fei, L.: Perceptual losses for real-time style transfer and super-resolution. In: Leibe, B., Matas, J., Sebe, N., Welling, M. (eds.) ECCV 2016. LNCS, vol. 9906, pp. 694–711. Springer, Cham (2016). https://doi.org/10.1007/978-3-319-46475-6_43

20. Simonyan, K., Zisserman, A.: Very deep convolutional networks for large-scale image recognition. arXiv preprint arXiv:1409.1556 (2014)

21. Deng, J., Dong, W., Socher, R., Li, L.J., Li, K., Fei-Fei, L.: Imagenet: a large-scale hierarchical image database. In 2009 IEEE Conference on Computer Vision and Pattern Recognition, pp. 248–255. IEEE (2009)

22. Hjelm, R.D., et al.: Learning deep representations by mutual information estimation and maximization. arXiv preprint arXiv:1808.06670 (2018)

23. Belghazi, M.I., et al.: Mine: mutual information neural estimation. arXiv preprint arXiv:1801.04062 (2018)

24. Kingma, D.P., Welling, M.: Auto-encoding variational bayes. arXiv preprint arXiv:1312.6114 (2013)

25. Chen, X., Duan, Y., Houthooft, R., Schulman, J., Sutskever, I., Abbeel, P.: Infogan: interpretable representation learning by information maximizing generative adversarial nets. In Advances in Neural Information Processing Systems, pp. 2172–2180 (2016)

26. Zhang, S., Zhu, X., Lei, Z., Shi, H., Wang, X., Li, S.Z.: Faceboxes: a cpu real-time face detector with high accuracy. In 2017 IEEE International Joint Conference on Biometrics (IJCB), pp. 1–9. IEEE (2017)

27. Szegedy, C., et al.: Going deeper with convolutions. In Proceedings of the IEEE Conference on Computer Vision and Pattern Recognition, pp. 1–9 (2015)

28. Zhang, H., Goodfellow, I., Metaxas, D., Odena, A.: Self-attention generative adversarial networks (2018). arXiv preprint arXiv:1805.08318

29. King, D.E.: Dlib-ml: a machine learning toolkit. J. Mach. Learn. Res. **10**, 1755–1758 (2009)

30. Yang, S., Luo, P., Loy, C.C., Tang, X.: Wider face: a face detection benchmark. In: Proceedings of the IEEE Conference on Computer Vision and Pattern Recognition, pp. 5525–5533 (2016)

31. Jesorsky, O., Kirchberg, K.J., Frischholz, R.W.: Robust face detection using the hausdorff distance. In: Bigun, J., Smeraldi, F. (eds.) AVBPA 2001. LNCS, vol. 2091, pp. 90–95. Springer, Heidelberg (2001). https://doi.org/10.1007/3-540-45344-X_14

32. Villanueva, A., Ponz, V., Sesma-Sanchez, L., Ariz, M., Porta, S., Cabeza, R.: Hybrid method based on topography for robust detection of iris center and eye corners. ACM Trans. Multimedia Comput. Commun. Appl. **9**(4), 1–20 (2013)

33. Petrovska-Delacrétaz, D., et al.: The IV 2 multimodal biometric database (including iris, 2d, 3d, stereoscopic, and talking face data), and the IV 2–2007 evaluation campaign. In: 2008 IEEE Second International Conference on Biometrics: Theory, Applications and Systems, pp. 1–7. IEEE (2008)

Efficient Residue Number System Based Winograd Convolution

Zhi-Gang Liu$^{(\boxtimes)}$ and Matthew Mattina

Arm ML Research Lab, Boston, MA, USA
{Zhi-Gang.Liu,Matthew.Mattina}@arm.com

Abstract. Prior research has shown that Winograd algorithm can reduce the computational complexity of convolutional neural networks (CNN) with weights and activations represented in floating point. However it is difficult to apply the scheme to the inference of low-precision quantized (e.g. INT8) networks. Our work extends the Winograd algorithm to Residue Number System (RNS). The minimal complexity convolution is computed precisely over large transformation tile (e.g. 10×10 to 16×16) of filters and activation patches using the Winograd transformation and low cost (e.g. 8-bit) arithmetic without degrading the prediction accuracy of the networks during inference. The arithmetic complexity reduction is up to $7.03\times$ while the performance improvement is up to $2.30\times$ to $4.69\times$ for 3×3 and 5×5 filters respectively.

1 Introduction

Machine learning has achieved great success in the past decade on a variety of applications including computer vision, natural language processing, and automatic speech recognition. In particular, deep convolutional neural networks (CNNs) have achieved better than human-level accuracy on image classification. The learning capability of CNNs improves with increasing depth and number of channels in the network layers. However this improvement comes at the expense of growing computation cost, particularly the expensive matrix or tensor multiplication and convolution. Thus reducing the computational complexity, especially the cost of the convolution operations, is critical for the deployment of these models on mobile and embedded devices with limited processing power.

Most recent CNN architectures [6] for image classification use low dimensional filters, typically 3×3, 5×5 or 7×7. The conventional Fast Fourier Transform (FFT) based convolution in the complex domain is inefficient with small filter dimensions. Faster algorithms for CNN inference based on Winograd minimal filters [14] can speed up the convolution by a factor of 2 to 4. The downside of the Winograd approach is that numerical problems and accuracy loss can occur unless high precision floating-point values are used.

Electronic supplementary material The online version of this chapter (https:// doi.org/10.1007/978-3-030-58529-7_4) contains supplementary material, which is available to authorized users.

© Springer Nature Switzerland AG 2020
A. Vedaldi et al. (Eds.): ECCV 2020, LNCS 12364, pp. 53–68, 2020.
https://doi.org/10.1007/978-3-030-58529-7_4

Research on the quantization of neural network [2,9] has shown that using reduced-precision representation (e.g. INT8) for the storage and computation of CNNs has significant benefits such as decreased memory bandwidth, lower memory foot-print, lower power consumption and higher throughput, while only having a negligible prediction accuracy degradation. The predominant numerical format used for training neural networks is IEEE floating-point format (FP32). There is a potential 4× reduction in memory bandwidth and storage achieved by quantizing FP32 weights and activations to INT8 values. The corresponding energy and area saving are 13.5× and 27.3× [3] respectively. But, both Winograd and FFT methods [7] [10] require high precision arithmetic to avoid prediction accuracy degradation and are therefore non-ideal for improving low-precision integer e.g. INT8 convolution efficiently.

In this paper, we extend the Winograd minimal convolution [14] to Residue Number System (RNS) [12] targeting the inference of low-precision e.g. INT8 quantized convolutional neural networks. The key contributions are summarized here:

- We formulate the Winograd minimal complexity integer convolution over Residue Number System (RNS). The use of the RNS enables our algorithm to operate on quantized, low-precision e.g. INT8 CNNs with low cost, low precision integer arithmetic, without computational instability issues and without impacting the accuracy of the networks.
- Our RNS-based formulation enables the use of much larger Winograd transformation tiles, e.g. from 8x8 to 16x16. The theoretical arithmetic reduction is up to 2.3× and 4.69× for 3×3 and 5×5 filters respectively over 3-residue power efficient 8-bit RNS; 3.45× and 7.03× for 2-residue 16-bit RNS.
- We analyzed the performance with 8-bit quantized VGG16 models and show 2.02× to 2.2× improvement of inference latency on Arm Cortex-A73 CPU.

2   Related Work

Earlier work applied the classical FFT to speedup convolutional layers by reducing the arithmetic complexity [10]. This approach requires float arithmetic in the complex number C, and multiplication involves the real and imaginary parts of complex value. A product of two complex values needs 3 or 4 floating multiplications, which is inefficient, especially for the small size filters commonly defined in popular CNNs.

The Winograd minimal filtering algorithm [14], first applied to CNNs by Lavin and Gray [7], can reduce arithmetic complexity from 2.25× to 4× for typical 3×3 CNN filters. However, the algorithm requires high precision arithmetic and hits computational instability issues when applied to large transform tile sizes [1]. An efficient sparse implementation of Winograd convolution have also been proposed [8]. The conventional Winograd convolution algorithm, including the latest enhancements, requires high precision floating point arithmetic.

Meanwhile, some researchers have tried to extend the Winograd algorithm to reduced-precision integer arithmetic by choosing complex interpolation points

[11] with a 17.37% throughput improvement claimed, however it depends on a lossy precision scaling scheme, which would cause predication accuracy drop.

3 Residue Number System (RNS)

A Residue Number System, $\text{RNS}(m_0, m_1, .., m_{n-1})$ [12], is number system to represent an integer by its value modulo n pairwise coprime moduli $m_0, m_1, ..,$ and m_{n-1}.

$$x_0 = x \quad (\text{mod } m_0)$$
$$x_1 = x \quad (\text{mod } m_1)$$
$$...$$
$$x_{n-1} = x \quad (\text{mod } m_{n-1})$$

For example, to represent $x = 48$ in $\text{RNS}(m_0 = 7, m_1 = 9)$

$$\{x \quad (\text{mod } m_0), x \quad (\text{mod } m_1)\} = \{6, 3\}$$

We can construct the value of x from its RNS representation as long as $x < M$, where $M = \prod_{i=1}^{n-1} m_i$ is the dynamic range of the $\text{RNS}(m_0, m_1, .., m_{n-1})$. For example, to convert $\{6, 3\}$ from RNS(7,9) back to standard form using Mixed Radix Conversion(MRC) [13] or Chinese Remainder Theorem (CRT) [5].

$$x = \left[6 + 7 * \left[\frac{3-6}{7} \quad (\text{mod } 9)\right]\right] \quad (\text{mod } 7 * 9) = 6 + 7 * 6 = 48$$

For addition($+$), subtraction($-$) and multiplication($*$) of two RNS values $x = \{x_0, x_1, .., x_{n-1}\}$ and $y = \{y_0, y_1, .., y_{n-1}\}$, it's sufficient to perform the operation on corresponding pair of residues. For example, $x = \{6, 3\}, y = \{5, 10\} \in$ RNS(7,9)

$$x + y = \{6 + 5 \quad (\text{mod } 7), 3 + 10 \quad (\text{mod } 9)\} = \{4, 4\}$$
$$x - y = \{6 - 5 \quad (\text{mod } 7), 3 - 10 \quad (\text{mod } 9)\} = \{1, 2\}$$
$$x * y = \{6 * 5 \quad (\text{mod } 7), 3 * 10 \quad (\text{mod } 9)\} = \{2, 3\}$$

3.1 Convolution in RNS

Equivalently, we could calculate the convolution y of N-element vector $d = (d_0, d_1, d_2, .., d_{N-1})$ and R-element filter $g = (g_0, g_1, g_2, .., g_{R-1})$ over $\text{RNS}(m_0, m_1, .., m_{n-1})$.

$$y = (y_0, y_1, y_2, .., y_{N-R}) = d \circledast g$$

and $y_k = \{y_k^{(0)}, y_k^{(1)}, .., y_k^{(n-1)}\} \in \text{RNS}(m_0, m_1, .., m_{n-1})$, where

$$y_k^{(i)} = \left(\sum_{j=0}^{R-1} d_{k+j} * g_j\right) \quad (\text{mod } m_i)$$

4 Winograd Convolution

The Winograd convolution [14] is an optimal algorithm to compute short convolution over real numbers, outperforming conventional Discrete Fourier Transform (DFT). $F(M, R)$ denotes the convolution computation of M-tuple output y of a R-tuple filter g and N-tuple input d where $N = M + R - 1$. The Winograd algorithm calculates the $F(M, R)$ in a bilinear form as

$$y = A^T \left[(Gg) \odot (B^T d) \right]$$

where $\odot$ acts as element-wise production and B^T, G and A^T are $N \times N$, $N \times R$ and $M \times N$ transform matrices respectively.

Specifically, A^T, G and B^T are derived from the Vandermonde matrix[1] V generated from N distinct Lagrange interpolation points $S_0, S_1, S_2, ..S_{N-1}$ (Note: Require a special handling if $S_{N-1} = \infty$).

$$V = \begin{pmatrix} 1 & S_0 & S_0^2 & \cdots & S_0^{N-1} \\ 1 & S_1 & S_1^2 & \cdots & S_1^{N-1} \\ 1 & S_2 & S_2^2 & \cdots & S_2^{N-1} \\ .. & .. & .. & \cdots & .. \\ 1 & S_{N-1} & S_{N-1}^2 & \cdots & S_{N-1}^{N-1} \end{pmatrix}_{N \times N} \tag{1}$$

and

$$A^T = V^T_{[0:M-1;0:N-1]}$$
$$G = V_{[0:N-1;0:R-1]}$$
$$B^T = V^{-T}$$

For 2-D convolution, similar fast algorithm $F(M \times M, R \times R)$ can be represented as

$$y = A^T \left[(GgG^T) \odot (B^T dB) \right] A \tag{2}$$

We call GgG^T and $B^T dB$ the *forward transform* and $A^T[\cdot]A$ the *backward transform*.

Assuming the computation cost of transformation GgG^T and $B^T dB$ was amortized completely due to reuse, the fast algorithm requires $N^2 = (M + R - 1)^2$ multiplications while the standard method uses $M^2 R^2$. The arithmetic complexity reduction is $\frac{M^2 R^2}{(M+R-1)^2}$. For example:

$F(2 \times 2, 3 \times 3)$ with interpolation points $\{0, \pm 1, \infty\}$. The fractions in B^T are arranged into matrix G. The arithmetic complexity reduction is $2.25\times$.

$$A^T = \begin{pmatrix} 1 & 1 & 1 & 0 \\ 0 & 1 & -1 & 1 \end{pmatrix}; \quad B^T = \begin{pmatrix} 1 & 0 & -1 & 0 \\ 0 & 1 & 1 & 0 \\ 0 & -1 & 1 & 0 \\ 0 & -1 & 0 & 1 \end{pmatrix}; \quad G = \begin{pmatrix} 1 & 0 & 0 \\ \frac{1}{2} & \frac{1}{2} & \frac{1}{2} \\ \frac{1}{2} & \frac{-1}{2} & \frac{1}{2} \\ 0 & 0 & 1 \end{pmatrix} = \frac{1}{2} G'; \quad G' = \begin{pmatrix} 2 & 0 & 0 \\ 1 & 1 & 1 \\ 1 & -1 & 1 \\ 0 & 0 & 2 \end{pmatrix}$$

---

[1] https://en.wikipedia.org/wiki/Vandermonde_matrix.

Table 1. The required data width of transformation and the corresponding arithmetic reduction for integer (INT8) Wingograd convolution algorithms. *DW* is transformation data width in bit. *Arithmetic Reduction* is the reduction of operation in *DW* bits.

Algorithm	DW (bit)	Arithmetic reduction
$F(2 \times 2, 3 \times 3)$	12	2.25×
$F(4 \times 4, 3 \times 3)$	18	4.00×
$F(6 \times 6, 3 \times 3)$	24	5.06×
$F(8 \times 8, 3 \times 3)$	36	5.76×
$F(8 \times 8, 5 \times 5)$	43	11.1×
$F(10 \times 10, 3 \times 3)$	50	6.26×
$F(10 \times 10, 5 \times 5)$	60	12.7×

$F(4 \times 4, 3 \times 3)$ with interpolation points $\{0, \pm 1, \pm 2, \infty\}$. The arithmetic complexity reduction is 4×.

$$A^T = \begin{pmatrix} 1 & 1 & 1 & 1 & 1 & 0 \\ 0 & 1 & -1 & 2 & -2 & 0 \\ 0 & 1 & 1 & 4 & 4 & 0 \\ 0 & 1 & -1 & 8 & -8 & 1 \end{pmatrix}; \quad B^T = \begin{pmatrix} 4 & 0 & -5 & 0 & 1 & 0 \\ 0 & 4 & 4 & -1 & -1 & 0 \\ 0 & -4 & 4 & 1 & -1 & 0 \\ 0 & -2 & -1 & 2 & 1 & 0 \\ 0 & 2 & -1 & -2 & 1 & 0 \\ 0 & 4 & 0 & -5 & 0 & 1 \end{pmatrix}; \quad G = \begin{pmatrix} \frac{1}{4} & 0 & 0 \\ \frac{1}{6} & \frac{1}{6} & \frac{1}{6} \\ \frac{1}{6} & \frac{-1}{6} & \frac{1}{6} \\ \frac{1}{24} & \frac{1}{12} & \frac{1}{6} \\ \frac{1}{24} & \frac{-1}{12} & \frac{1}{6} \\ 0 & 0 & 1 \end{pmatrix} = \frac{1}{24} G'; \quad G' = \begin{pmatrix} 6 & 0 & 0 \\ 4 & 4 & 4 \\ 4 & -4 & 4 \\ 1 & 2 & 4 \\ 1 & -2 & 4 \\ 0 & 0 & 24 \end{pmatrix}$$

where matrices A^T, G and B^T are derived from Vandermonde matrix of the roots to construct the transform.

$F(2 \times 2, 3 \times 3)$ and $F(4 \times 4, 3 \times 3)$ have theoretical arithmetic complexity reduction of 2.25× and 4× respectively. We can achieve the expected speedup using floating-point operation i.e. FP32. However, it's a challenge to implement the Winograd convolution using low-precision integral arithmetic for quantized CNN. To calculate exact convolution using integer arithmetic, we can obtain matrix G' by factoring out the common fraction α, e.g. $\alpha = \frac{1}{2}$ for $F(2 \times 2, 3 \times 3)$ and $\alpha = \frac{1}{24}$ for $F(4 \times 4, 3 \times 3)$, from corresponding matrix G. Then Eq. 2 becomes

$$y = \alpha^2 A^T \left[(G' g G'^T) \odot (B^T d B) \right].$$

The magnitude of element in transformation $G' g G'^T$ and $B^T d B$ would be $\frac{trace(G' G'^T)}{N}$ and $\frac{trace(B^T B)}{N}$ times as large as the quantity of filter g and input d on average. Particularly, the magnification are 3.5× and 2× for $F(2 \times 2, 3 \times 3)$ and 125× and 28.7× for $F(4 \times 4, 3 \times 3)$. Moreover, the magnifications we calculated correspond to the standard deviation statistically, the outliers could have much larger magnitudes. Practically, we need 12 bits to hold each element of transformation and INT16 arithmetic for element-wise multiply for $F(2 \times 2, 3 \times 3)$. $F(4 \times 4, 4 \times 3)$ demands 18 bits for transformation and INT32 arithmetic operations. We summarized the data width of transformation and arithmetic reduction of integer Winograd algorithms in Table 1. Although the Winograd algorithms enable complexity reduction, they require higher precision arithmetic than INT8. Considering INT8 multipliers cost about $\frac{1}{4}$ power and area of INT16 case; $\frac{1}{15}$ and $\frac{1}{12}$ of INT32; $\frac{1}{18}$ and $\frac{1}{27}$ of FP32 respectively [3], there will be advantage in implementing the Winograd algorithm using INT8 arithmetic. For this reason, a lossy precision scaling scheme was proposed [11], which scales down the transformation in the range of the desired low-precision arithmetic operation. However the scaling method introduces errors to the convolution output and would cause predication accuracy degradation.

The fundamental difficulty with performing the standard Winograd algorithm using low cost integral arithmetic is due to the ill-conditioned Vandermonde (and its inverse) matrix V in Eq. 1 with real interpolation points especially for large transformation (e.g. M > 6). We propose a different approach to implement the Winograd algorithm over Residue Number System (RNS) via low-precision integer arithmetic (e.g. INT8 or INT16) in the next section.

5 Winograd Convolution over Residue Number System

We extend the Winograd convolution algorithm described in Sect. 4 to Residue Number System (RNS) in Sect. 3 to formulate a new implementation. This new approach solves the numerical stability issue of the conventional Winograd algorithm for large transformation, i.e. $M \in [8, 16]$, moreover the new method is compatible with low precision 8-bit multiply and accumulation.

To simplify the description, without loss of generality, we take $F(10 \times 10, 3 \times 3)$ with interpolation points $\{0, \pm 1, \pm 2, \pm 3, \pm 4, \pm 5, \infty\}$ as a running example with the following transform matrices A^T, B^T and G.

$$
A^T = \begin{pmatrix}
1 & 1 & 1 & 1 & 1 & 1 & 1 & 1 & 1 & 1 & 1 & 0 \\
0 & 1 & -1 & 2 & -2 & 3 & -3 & 4 & -4 & 5 & -5 & 0 \\
0 & 1 & 1 & 4 & 4 & 9 & 9 & 16 & 16 & 25 & 25 & 0 \\
0 & 1 & -1 & 8 & -8 & 27 & -27 & 64 & -64 & 125 & -125 & 0 \\
0 & 1 & 1 & 16 & 16 & 81 & 81 & 256 & 256 & 625 & 625 & 0 \\
0 & 1 & -1 & 32 & -32 & 243 & -243 & 1024 & -1024 & 3125 & -3125 & 0 \\
0 & 1 & 1 & 64 & 64 & 729 & 729 & 4096 & 4096 & 15625 & 15625 & 0 \\
0 & 1 & -1 & 128 & -128 & 2187 & -2187 & 16384 & -16384 & 78125 & -78125 & 0 \\
0 & 1 & 1 & 256 & 256 & 6561 & 6561 & 65536 & 65536 & 390625 & 390625 & 0 \\
0 & 1 & -1 & 512 & -512 & 19683 & -19683 & 262144 & -262144 & 1953125 & -1953125 & 1
\end{pmatrix}
$$

$$
B^T = \begin{pmatrix}
14400 & 0 & -21076 & 0 & 7645 & 0 & -1023 & 0 & 55 & 0 & -1 & 0 \\
0 & 14400 & 14400 & -6676 & -6676 & 969 & 969 & -54 & -54 & 1 & 1 & 0 \\
0 & -14400 & 14400 & 6676 & -6676 & -969 & 969 & 54 & -54 & -1 & 1 & 0 \\
0 & -7200 & -3600 & 8738 & 4369 & -1638 & -819 & 102 & 51 & -2 & -1 & 0 \\
0 & 7200 & -3600 & -8738 & 4369 & 1638 & -819 & -102 & 51 & 2 & -1 & 0 \\
0 & 4800 & 1600 & -6492 & -2164 & 1827 & 609 & -138 & -46 & 3 & 1 & 0 \\
0 & -4800 & 1600 & 6492 & -2164 & -1827 & 609 & 138 & -46 & -3 & 1 & 0 \\
0 & -3600 & -900 & 5044 & 1261 & -1596 & -399 & 156 & 39 & -4 & -1 & 0 \\
0 & 3600 & -900 & -5044 & 1261 & 1596 & -399 & -156 & 39 & 4 & -1 & 0 \\
0 & 2880 & 576 & -4100 & -820 & 1365 & 273 & -150 & -30 & 5 & 1 & 0 \\
0 & -2880 & 576 & 4100 & -820 & -1365 & 273 & 150 & -30 & -5 & 1 & 0 \\
0 & -14400 & 0 & 21076 & 0 & -7645 & 0 & 1023 & 0 & -55 & 0 & 1
\end{pmatrix}
$$

$$G = \begin{pmatrix} \frac{1}{14400} & 0 & 0 \\ \frac{1}{17280} & \frac{1}{17280} & \frac{1}{17280} \\ \frac{1}{17280} & \frac{-1}{17280} & \frac{1}{17280} \\ \frac{1}{30240} & \frac{1}{15120} & \frac{1}{7560} \\ \frac{1}{30240} & \frac{-1}{15120} & \frac{1}{7560} \\ \frac{1}{80640} & \frac{1}{26880} & \frac{1}{8960} \\ \frac{1}{80640} & \frac{-1}{26880} & \frac{1}{8960} \\ \frac{1}{362880} & \frac{1}{90720} & \frac{1}{22680} \\ \frac{1}{362880} & \frac{-1}{90720} & \frac{1}{22680} \\ \frac{1}{3628800} & \frac{1}{725760} & \frac{1}{145152} \\ \frac{1}{3628800} & \frac{-1}{725760} & \frac{1}{145152} \\ 0 & 0 & 1 \end{pmatrix} = \frac{1}{3628800} G' ; \quad G' = \begin{pmatrix} 252 & 0 & 0 \\ 210 & 210 & 210 \\ 210 & -210 & 210 \\ 120 & 240 & 480 \\ 120 & -240 & 480 \\ 45 & 135 & 405 \\ 45 & -135 & 405 \\ 10 & 40 & 160 \\ 10 & -40 & 160 \\ 1 & 5 & 25 \\ 1 & -5 & 25 \\ 0 & 0 & 3628800 \end{pmatrix}$$

These transforms are derived from the 12×12 Vandermonde matrix and its inverse matrix[2], which are not computationally friendly in standard number systems, including FP32 due to its numerical instability. However, we could mitigate the instability by carrying out the computation of Eq. 2 over $\mathrm{RNS}(m_0, m_1, .., m_{n-1})$.

To represent the transform matrix G in RNS, the modulus $m_0, m_1, ..,$ and m_{n-1} need be coprime to $\frac{1}{\alpha}$, e.g. $\frac{1}{\alpha} = 3628800 = 2^8 \cdot 3^4 \cdot 5^2 \cdot 7$ for the $F(10 \times 10, 3 \times 3)$ example.

Generically, the inverse of $N \times N$ Vandermonde matrix V in Eq. 1 [4], $V^{-1} = \{V_{i,j}^{-1}\}$, and $i, j \in [0, N-1]$ and $V_{i,j}^{-1}$ is given in Eq. 3.

$$V_{i,j}^{-1} = \begin{cases} \dfrac{1}{\prod\limits_{m=0, \ m\neq j}^{N-1} (S_j - S_m)} & for \ j = N - 1 \\[2em] (-1)^{N-1-i} \dfrac{\sum\limits_{0 \leq j_0 < j_1 < ... < j_{N-1-i} < N, \ j_k \neq j} S_{j_0} S_{j_1} ... S_{j_{N-1-i}}}{\prod\limits_{m=0, m\neq j}^{N-1} (S_j - S_m)} & otherwise \end{cases}$$

$$(3)$$

where $S_0, S_1, S_2, ..., S_{N-1}$ are the interpolation points we choose to construct the Winograd transform. To obtain the multiplicative inverse of the denominator of $V_{i,j}^{-1}$ in Eq. 3, each modulus m_i need be coprime to the denominator $\prod\limits_{m=0, \ m\neq j}^{N-1} (S_j - S_m)$.

---

[2] https://proofwiki.org/wiki/Inverse_of_Vandermonde_Matrix.

For our example, the denominators in G are $14400 = 2^6 \cdot 3^2 \cdot 5^2$, $17280 = 2^7 \cdot 3^3 \cdot 5$, $30240 = 2^5 \cdot 3^5 \cdot 5 \cdot 7$, $80640 = 2^8 \cdot 3^2 \cdot 5 \cdot 7$, $362880 = 2^7 \cdot 3^4 \cdot 5 \cdot 7$ and $3628800 = 2^8 \cdot 3^4 \cdot 5^2 \cdot 7$. We chose moduli $m_0 = 11 \times 23 = 253$, $m_1 = 251$ and $m_2 = 13 \times 19 = 247$, which are all coprime to the denominators in G. Therefore the fractions in matrix G are all well-defined for modular division, for instance $\frac{1}{14400}$ (mod 253) $= 12$ as a result of multiplicative inverse of denominator, e.g. 14400×12 (mod 253) $= 1$. Similarly, $\frac{1}{14400}$ (mod 251) $= 27$ and $\frac{1}{14400}$ (mod 247) $= -10$. Moreover, moduli $(253, 251, 247)$ are the largest suitable 8-bit values for the interpolation points we chose. Given that we can convert matrix A^T, G and B^T to corresponding modular format, e.g. $A^T_{m_i} = A^T$ (mod m_i), $G_{m_i} = G$ (mod m_i) and $B^T_{m_i} = B^T$ (mod m_i), where $m_i \in (253, 251, 247)$. The RNS representation of Eq. 2 is

$$y = (A^T_{253}\left[[G_{253} g G^T_{253}] \odot [B^T_{253} d B_{253}]\right]A_{253},$$
$$A^T_{251}\left[[G_{251} g G^T_{251}] \odot [B^T_{251} d B_{251}]\right]A_{251},$$
$$A^T_{247}\left[[G_{247} g G^T_{247}] \odot [B^T_{247} d B_{247}]\right]A_{247}) \tag{4}$$

For modulo 253, the corresponding transform matrices are

$$A^T_{253} = \begin{pmatrix} 1 & 1 & 1 & 1 & 1 & 1 & 1 & 1 & 1 & 1 & 1 & 0 \\ 0 & 1 & -1 & 2 & -2 & 3 & -3 & 4 & -4 & 5 & -5 & 0 \\ 0 & 1 & 1 & 4 & 4 & 9 & 9 & 16 & 16 & 25 & 25 & 0 \\ 0 & 1 & -1 & 8 & -8 & 27 & -27 & 64 & -64 & 125 & -125 & 0 \\ 0 & 1 & 1 & 16 & 16 & 81 & 81 & 3 & 3 & 119 & 119 & 0 \\ 0 & 1 & -1 & 32 & -32 & -10 & 10 & 12 & -12 & 89 & -89 & 0 \\ 0 & 1 & 1 & 64 & 64 & -30 & -30 & 48 & 48 & -61 & -61 & 0 \\ 0 & 1 & -1 & -125 & 125 & -90 & 90 & -61 & 61 & -52 & 52 & 0 \\ 0 & 1 & 1 & 3 & 3 & -17 & -17 & 9 & 9 & -7 & -7 & 0 \\ 0 & 1 & -1 & 6 & -6 & -51 & 51 & 36 & -36 & -35 & 35 & 1 \end{pmatrix}; \; G_{253} = \begin{pmatrix} 12 & 0 & 0 \\ 10 & 10 & 10 \\ 10 & -10 & 10 \\ 78 & -97 & 59 \\ 78 & 97 & 59 \\ -34 & -102 & -53 \\ -34 & 102 & -53 \\ -120 & 26 & 104 \\ -120 & -26 & 104 \\ -12 & -60 & -47 \\ -12 & 60 & -47 \\ 0 & 0 & 1 \end{pmatrix}$$

$$B^T_{253} = \begin{pmatrix} -21 & 0 & -77 & 0 & 55 & 0 & -11 & 0 & 55 & 0 & -1 & 0 \\ 0 & -21 & -21 & -98 & -98 & -43 & -43 & -54 & -54 & 1 & 1 & 0 \\ 0 & 21 & -21 & 98 & -98 & 43 & -43 & 54 & -54 & -1 & 1 & 0 \\ 0 & -116 & -58 & -117 & 68 & -120 & -60 & 102 & 51 & -2 & -1 & 0 \\ 0 & 116 & -58 & 117 & 68 & 120 & -60 & -102 & 51 & 2 & -1 & 0 \\ 0 & -7 & 82 & 86 & 113 & 56 & 103 & 115 & -46 & 3 & 1 & 0 \\ 0 & 7 & 82 & -86 & 113 & -56 & 103 & -115 & -46 & -3 & 1 & 0 \\ 0 & -58 & 112 & -16 & -4 & -78 & 107 & -97 & 39 & -4 & -1 & 0 \\ 0 & 58 & 112 & 16 & -4 & 78 & 107 & 97 & 39 & 4 & -1 & 0 \\ 0 & 97 & 70 & -52 & -61 & 100 & 20 & 103 & -30 & 5 & 1 & 0 \\ 0 & -97 & 70 & 52 & -61 & -100 & 20 & -103 & -30 & -5 & 1 & 0 \\ 0 & 21 & 0 & 77 & 0 & -55 & 0 & 11 & 0 & -55 & 0 & 1 \end{pmatrix}$$

All elements in these matrices are in the range of $[-\frac{253-1}{2}, \frac{253-1}{2}]$. The computation of the fast convolution over (mod 253) can be performed with 8-bit low cost arithmetic operation without numerical concerns. Similarly, we can get the transforms for 251 and 247.

$$A_{251}^T = \begin{pmatrix}
1 & 1 & 1 & 1 & 1 & 1 & 1 & 1 & 1 & 1 & 1 & 0 \\
0 & 1 & -1 & 2 & -2 & 3 & -3 & 4 & -4 & 5 & -5 & 0 \\
0 & 1 & 1 & 4 & 4 & 9 & 9 & 16 & 16 & 25 & 25 & 0 \\
0 & 1 & -1 & 8 & -8 & 27 & -27 & 64 & -64 & 125 & -125 & 0 \\
0 & 1 & 1 & 16 & 16 & 81 & 81 & 5 & 5 & 123 & 123 & 0 \\
0 & 1 & -1 & 32 & -32 & -8 & 8 & 20 & -20 & 113 & -113 & 0 \\
0 & 1 & 1 & 64 & 64 & -24 & -24 & 80 & 80 & 63 & 63 & 0 \\
0 & 1 & -1 & -123 & 123 & -72 & 72 & 69 & -69 & 64 & -64 & 0 \\
0 & 1 & 1 & 5 & 5 & 35 & 35 & 25 & 25 & 69 & 69 & 0 \\
0 & 1 & -1 & 10 & -10 & 105 & -105 & 100 & -100 & 94 & -94 & 1
\end{pmatrix} \; ; \; G_{251} = \begin{pmatrix}
27 & 0 & 0 \\
-103 & -103 & -103 \\
-103 & 103 & -103 \\
-23 & -46 & -92 \\
-23 & 46 & -92 \\
-40 & -120 & -109 \\
-40 & 120 & -109 \\
19 & 76 & 53 \\
19 & -76 & 53 \\
27 & -116 & -78 \\
27 & 116 & -78 \\
0 & 0 & 1
\end{pmatrix}$$

$$B_{251}^T = \begin{pmatrix}
93 & 0 & 8 & 0 & 115 & 0 & -19 & 0 & 55 & 0 & -1 & 0 \\
0 & 93 & 93 & 101 & 101 & -35 & -35 & -54 & -54 & 1 & 1 & 0 \\
0 & -93 & 93 & -101 & 101 & 35 & -35 & 54 & -54 & -1 & 1 & 0 \\
0 & 79 & -86 & -47 & 102 & 119 & -66 & 102 & 51 & -2 & -1 & 0 \\
0 & -79 & -86 & 47 & 102 & -119 & -66 & 102 & 51 & 2 & -1 & 0 \\
0 & 31 & 94 & 34 & 95 & 70 & 107 & 113 & -46 & 3 & 1 & 0 \\
0 & -31 & 94 & -34 & 95 & -70 & 107 & -113 & -46 & -3 & 1 & 0 \\
0 & -86 & 104 & 24 & 6 & -90 & 103 & -95 & 39 & -4 & -1 & 0 \\
0 & 86 & 104 & -24 & 6 & 90 & 103 & 95 & 39 & 4 & -1 & 0 \\
0 & 119 & 74 & -84 & -67 & 110 & 22 & 101 & -30 & 5 & 1 & 0 \\
0 & -119 & 74 & 84 & -67 & -110 & 22 & -101 & -30 & -5 & 1 & 0 \\
0 & -93 & 0 & -8 & 0 & -115 & 0 & 19 & 0 & -55 & 0 & 1
\end{pmatrix}$$

$$A_{247}^T = \begin{pmatrix}
1 & 1 & 1 & 1 & 1 & 1 & 1 & 1 & 1 & 1 & 1 & 0 \\
0 & 1 & -1 & 2 & -2 & 3 & -3 & 4 & -4 & 5 & -5 & 0 \\
0 & 1 & 1 & 4 & 4 & 9 & 9 & 16 & 16 & 25 & 25 & 0 \\
0 & 1 & 1 & 8 & -8 & 27 & -27 & 64 & -64 & -122 & 122 & 0 \\
0 & 1 & 1 & 16 & 16 & 81 & 81 & 9 & 9 & -116 & -116 & 0 \\
0 & 1 & -1 & 32 & -32 & -4 & 4 & 36 & -36 & -86 & 86 & 0 \\
0 & 1 & 1 & 64 & 64 & -12 & -12 & -103 & -103 & 64 & 64 & 0 \\
0 & 1 & -1 & -119 & 119 & -36 & 36 & 82 & -82 & 73 & -73 & 0 \\
0 & 1 & 1 & 9 & 9 & -108 & -108 & 81 & 81 & 118 & 118 & 0 \\
0 & 1 & -1 & 18 & -18 & -77 & 77 & 77 & -77 & 96 & -96 & 1
\end{pmatrix} \; ; \; G_{247} = \begin{pmatrix}
-10 & 0 & 0 \\
74 & 74 & 74 \\
74 & -74 & 74 \\
7 & 14 & 28 \\
7 & -14 & 28 \\
-90 & -23 & -69 \\
-90 & 23 & -69 \\
-20 & -80 & -73 \\
-20 & 80 & -73 \\
-2 & -10 & -50 \\
-2 & 10 & -50 \\
0 & 0 & 1
\end{pmatrix}$$

$$B_{247}^T = \begin{pmatrix}
74 & 0 & -81 & 0 & -12 & 0 & -35 & 0 & 55 & 0 & -1 & 0 \\
0 & 74 & 74 & -7 & -7 & -19 & -19 & -54 & -54 & 1 & 1 & 0 \\
0 & -74 & 74 & 7 & -7 & 19 & -19 & 54 & -54 & -1 & 1 & 0 \\
0 & -37 & 105 & 93 & -77 & 91 & -78 & 102 & 51 & -2 & -1 & 0 \\
0 & 37 & 105 & -93 & -77 & -91 & -78 & -102 & 51 & 2 & -1 & 0 \\
0 & 107 & 118 & -70 & 59 & 98 & 115 & 109 & -46 & 3 & 1 & 0 \\
0 & -107 & 118 & 70 & 59 & -98 & 115 & -109 & -46 & -3 & 1 & 0 \\
0 & 105 & 88 & 104 & 26 & -114 & 95 & -91 & 39 & -4 & -1 & 0 \\
0 & -105 & 88 & -104 & 26 & 114 & 95 & 91 & 39 & 4 & -1 & 0 \\
0 & -84 & 82 & 99 & -79 & -117 & 26 & 97 & -30 & 5 & 1 & 0 \\
0 & 84 & 82 & -99 & -79 & 117 & 26 & -97 & -30 & -5 & 1 & 0 \\
0 & -74 & 0 & 81 & 0 & 12 & 0 & 35 & 0 & -55 & 0 & 1
\end{pmatrix}$$

RNS(253, 251, 247) has the dynamic range of $[-7842620, +7842620]$ being large enough for 8-bit quantized CNN models. The algorithm $F(10 \times 10, 3 \times 3)$ over RNS(253, 251, 247) need 3 element-wise multiplications in 8-bit (accumulation is 32-bit). The implementation can yield up to $2.08\times$ throughput improvement (or Speed-up).

Alternatively, we can compute the Winograd convolution $F(10 \times 10, 3 \times 3)$ over 16-bit RNS(4001, 4331) for instance.

$$g \circledast d = (A_{4001}^T \left[[G_{4001} g G_{4001}^T] \odot [B_{4001}^T d B_{4001}] \right] A_{4001},$$
$$A_{4331}^T \left[[G_{4331} g G_{4331}^T] \odot [B_{4331}^T d B_{4331}] \right] A_{4331}) \tag{5}$$

where the transform matrices are

$$A^T_{4001} = \begin{pmatrix}
1 & 1 & 1 & 1 & 1 & 1 & 1 & 1 & 1 & 1 & 1 & 0 \\
0 & 1 & -1 & 2 & -2 & 3 & -3 & 4 & -4 & 5 & -5 & 0 \\
0 & 1 & 1 & 4 & 4 & 9 & 9 & 16 & 16 & 25 & 25 & 0 \\
0 & 1 & -1 & 8 & -8 & 27 & -27 & 64 & -64 & 125 & -125 & 0 \\
0 & 1 & 1 & 16 & 16 & 81 & 81 & 256 & 256 & 625 & 625 & 0 \\
0 & 1 & -1 & 32 & -32 & 243 & -243 & 1024 & -1024 & -876 & 876 & 0 \\
0 & 1 & 1 & 64 & 64 & 729 & 729 & 95 & 95 & -379 & -379 & 0 \\
0 & 1 & -1 & 128 & -128 & -1814 & 1814 & 380 & -380 & -1895 & 1895 & 0 \\
0 & 1 & 1 & 256 & 256 & -1441 & -1441 & 1520 & 1520 & -1473 & -1473 & 0 \\
0 & 1 & -1 & 512 & -512 & -322 & 322 & -1922 & 1922 & 637 & -637 & 1
\end{pmatrix} ; \quad G_{4001} = \begin{pmatrix}
222 & 0 & 0 \\
185 & 185 & 185 \\
185 & -185 & 185 \\
-1609 & 783 & 1566 \\
-1609 & -783 & 1566 \\
897 & -1310 & 71 \\
897 & 1310 & 71 \\
1533 & -1870 & 522 \\
1533 & 1870 & 522 \\
-1047 & -1234 & 1832 \\
-1047 & 1234 & 1832 \\
0 & 0 & 1
\end{pmatrix}$$

$$B^T_{4001} = \begin{pmatrix}
-1604 & 0 & -1071 & 0 & -357 & 0 & -1023 & 0 & 55 & 0 & -1 & 0 \\
0 & -1604 & -1604 & 1326 & 1326 & 969 & 969 & -54 & -54 & 1 & 1 & 0 \\
0 & 1604 & -1604 & -1326 & 1326 & -969 & 969 & 54 & -54 & -1 & 1 & 0 \\
0 & 802 & 401 & 736 & 368 & -1638 & -819 & 102 & 51 & -2 & -1 & 0 \\
0 & -802 & 401 & -736 & 368 & 1638 & -819 & -102 & 51 & 2 & -1 & 0 \\
0 & 799 & 1600 & 1510 & 1837 & 1827 & 609 & -138 & -46 & 3 & 1 & 0 \\
0 & -799 & 1600 & -1510 & 1837 & -1827 & 609 & 138 & -46 & -3 & 1 & 0 \\
0 & 401 & -900 & 1043 & 1261 & -1596 & -399 & 156 & 39 & -4 & -1 & 0 \\
0 & -401 & -900 & -1043 & 1261 & 1596 & -399 & -156 & 39 & 4 & -1 & 0 \\
0 & -1121 & 576 & -99 & -820 & 1365 & 273 & -150 & -30 & 5 & 1 & 0 \\
0 & 1121 & 576 & 99 & -820 & -1365 & 273 & 150 & -30 & -5 & 1 & 0 \\
0 & 1604 & 0 & 1071 & 0 & 357 & 0 & 1023 & 0 & -55 & 0 & 1
\end{pmatrix}$$

$$A^T_{4331} = \begin{pmatrix}
1 & 1 & 1 & 1 & 1 & 1 & 1 & 1 & 1 & 1 & 1 & 0 \\
0 & 1 & -1 & 2 & -2 & 3 & -3 & 4 & -4 & 5 & -5 & 0 \\
0 & 1 & 1 & 4 & 4 & 9 & 9 & 16 & 16 & 25 & 25 & 0 \\
0 & 1 & -1 & 8 & -8 & 27 & -27 & 64 & -64 & 125 & -125 & 0 \\
0 & 1 & 1 & 16 & 16 & 81 & 81 & 256 & 256 & 625 & 625 & 0 \\
0 & 1 & -1 & 32 & -32 & 243 & -243 & 1024 & -1024 & -1206 & 1206 & 0 \\
0 & 1 & 1 & 64 & 64 & 729 & 729 & -235 & -235 & -1699 & -1699 & 0 \\
0 & 1 & -1 & 128 & -128 & -2144 & 2144 & -940 & 940 & 167 & -167 & 0 \\
0 & 1 & 1 & 256 & 256 & -2101 & -2101 & 571 & 571 & 835 & 835 & 0 \\
0 & 1 & -1 & 512 & -512 & -1972 & 1972 & -2047 & 2047 & -156 & 156 & 1
\end{pmatrix} ; \quad G_{4331} = \begin{pmatrix}
1693 & 0 & 0 \\
689 & 689 & 689 \\
689 & -689 & 689 \\
-225 & -450 & -900 \\
-225 & 450 & -900 \\
457 & 1371 & -218 \\
457 & -1371 & -218 \\
1064 & -75 & -300 \\
1064 & 75 & -300 \\
-1626 & 532 & -1671 \\
-1626 & -532 & -1671 \\
0 & 0 & 1
\end{pmatrix}$$

$$B^T_{4331} = \begin{pmatrix}
1407 & 0 & 579 & 0 & -1017 & 0 & -1023 & 0 & 55 & 0 & -1 & 0 \\
0 & 1407 & 1407 & 1986 & 1986 & 969 & 969 & -54 & -54 & 1 & 1 & 0 \\
0 & -1407 & 1407 & -1986 & 1986 & -969 & 969 & 54 & -54 & -1 & 1 & 0 \\
0 & 1462 & 731 & 76 & 38 & -1638 & -819 & 102 & 51 & -2 & -1 & 0 \\
0 & -1462 & 731 & -76 & 38 & 1638 & -819 & -102 & 51 & 2 & -1 & 0 \\
0 & 469 & 1600 & -2161 & -2164 & 1827 & 609 & -138 & -46 & 3 & 1 & 0 \\
0 & -469 & 1600 & 2161 & -2164 & -1827 & 609 & 138 & -46 & -3 & 1 & 0 \\
0 & 731 & -900 & 713 & 1261 & -1596 & -399 & 156 & 39 & -4 & -1 & 0 \\
0 & -731 & -900 & -713 & 1261 & 1596 & -399 & -156 & 39 & 4 & -1 & 0 \\
0 & -1451 & 576 & 231 & -820 & 1365 & 273 & -150 & -30 & 5 & 1 & 0 \\
0 & 1451 & 576 & -231 & -820 & -1365 & 273 & 150 & -30 & -5 & 1 & 0 \\
0 & -1407 & 0 & -579 & 0 & 1017 & 0 & 1023 & 0 & -55 & 0 & 1
\end{pmatrix}$$

The modulus 4001 and 4331 are both coprime to $\frac{1}{\alpha} = 3628800$. The 16-bit RNS has dynamic range $4001 \times 4331 = 17328331$, which allows the convolution output having the maximum magnitude of $\frac{17328331-1}{2} = 8664165$. The 16-bit RNS(4001,4331) requires two element-wise multiply, therefore it has arithmetic reduction 3.13×, which is better than the 2.08× of 8-bit RNS(253,251,247). But, each element-wise multiplication is of 16-bit op.

6 Fast Convolution via Integral Arithmetic for Convolutional Neural Networks (CNN)

Unlike the conventional Winograd algorithm, which could benefit to CNN for both network training and inference, the integer version can only apply to inference of the low-precision (e.g. INT8) quantized CNN models. For a qunatized CNN layer, its major computation is the 2D convolution, $g \circledast x$, between $(R \times R \times C \times K)$ weight tensor g and $(B \times W \times H \times C)$ input feature maps x, where $R \times R$ is the filter size, C is the depth, K is the filter count (or output channels), B is the batch number and $W \times H$ is the dimension of the 2D input plane. All elements of g and x are signed integers, e.g. from -128 to 127. Then we can utilize the complexity reduced algorithm, Eq. 4 or 5 described in Sect. 5 to compute the integer convolution.

We can decompose input x into $M \times M$ patches $\{d_i\}$ i.e. $x = \bigoplus_i d_i$, and apply Winograd algorithm $F(M \times M, R \times R)$ over $\text{RNS}(m_0, m_1, .., m_{n-1})$ to each corresponding weight g and patch d_i to compute $g \circledast x$ with the reduced arithmetic as Eq. 6.

$$
g \circledast x = \bigoplus_{B,K,i} \{ \sum_C A_{m_0}^T ((G_{m_0} g^{(C)(K)} G_{m_0}^T) \odot (B_{m_0}^T d_i^{(C)(B)} B_{m_0})) A_{m_0}, \tag{6}
$$

$$
\sum_C A_{m_1}^T ((G_{m_1} g^{(C)(K)} G_{m_1}^T) \odot (B_{m_1}^T d_i^{(C)(B)} B_{m_1})) A_{m_1}, ..,
$$

$$
\sum_C A_{m_{n-1}}^T ((G_{m_{n-1}} g^{(C)(K)} G_{m_{n-1}}^T) \odot (B_{m_{n-1}}^T d_i^{(C)(B)} B_{m_{n-1}})) A_{m_{n-1}} \}
$$

$$
= \{ A_{m_0}^T (\bigoplus_{B,K,i} (\sum_C ((G_{m_0} g^{(C)(K)} G_{m_0}^T) \odot (B_{m_0}^T d_i^{(C)(B)} B_{m_0})))) A_{m_0}, \tag{7}
$$

$$
A_{m_1}^T (\bigoplus_{B,K,i} (\sum_C ((G_{m_1} g^{(C)(K)} G_{m_1}^T) \odot (B_{m_1}^T d_i^{(C)(B)} B_{m_1})))) A_{m_1},
$$

$$
... ,
$$

$$
A_{m_{n-1}}^T (\bigoplus_{B,K,i} (\sum_C ((G_{m_{n-1}} g^{(C)(K)} G_{m_{n-1}}^T) \odot (B_{m_{n-1}}^T d_i^{(C)(B)} B_{m_{n-1}})))) A_{m_{n-1}} \}
$$

In Eq. 7, the forward Winograd Transform of filter e.g. $G_{m_0} w^{(C)(K)} G_{m_0}^T$ can be pre-calculated. The forward transform of input e.g. $B_{m_0}^T x_i^{(C)(B)} B_{m_0}$ is shared or reused across K filters, therefore their computation cost got amortized by factor K. The backward transform was performed after the reduction across depth C due to linearity of transform, so the backward transform was amortized by factor of C.

The point-wise multiply terms in Eq. 7, for instance,

$$
\bigoplus_{B,K,i} (\sum_C ((G_{m_0} g^{(C)(K)} G_{m_0}^T) \odot (B_{m_0}^T d_i^{(C)(B)} B_{m_0}))) \quad (\text{mod } m_0) \tag{8}
$$

(Equation 8) is a matrix multiply (GEMM) function essentially followed by a modulo operation, which can be executed by existing highly optimized GEMM library, such as gemmlowp[3] or accelerator. Notably, we can perform the modulo operation after the GEMM to reduce its overhead. In the final step after the backward transform, we convert the $g \circledast x$ from the RNS presentation to the standard format using MRC or CRT.

7 Performance Analysis

The performance of RNS based Winograd convolution depends on the transformation and filter size i.e. $N = M + R - 1$ and R respectively. When computation

---

[3] https://github.com/google/gemmlowp.

is carried out in RNS and the cost of Winograd transformation and MRC are amortized due to reuse, the theoretical arithmetic reduction is given by

$$\frac{M^2 R^2}{N^2} \times \frac{1}{n}$$

where n is the modulus number of the RNS. Table 2 contains the complexity reduction for different algorithms, $F(M \times M, R \times R)$. The Winograd algorithm has better complexity reduction for large values of M and achieves more benefit for 5×5 filters than the 3×3. Moreover, 2-residue RNS, such as RNS(4001,4331), has more arithmetic reduction than 3-residue case. For example, $F(12 \times 12, 5 \times 5)$ over RNS(4001,4331) generates $7.03\times$ reduction vs $4.69\times$ over RNS(251,241,239). However, 2-residue RNS(4001,4331) requires 16-bit GEMM operation, which will be less efficient than the 8-bit case regarding throughput and power consumption.

Table 2. Complexity reduction of Winograd convolution in RNS.

Algorithms $F(M \times M, R \times R)$	Arithmetic complexity reduction	
	RNS(4001,4331)	RNS(251,241,239)
$F(2 \times 2, 3 \times 3)$	$1.125\times$	~~$0.75\times$~~
$F(4 \times 4, 3 \times 3)$	$2.00\times$	$1.33\times$
$F(6 \times 6, 3 \times 3)$	$2.53\times$	$1.69\times$
$F(8 \times 8, 3 \times 3)$	$2.88\times$	$1.92\times$
$F(8 \times 8, 5 \times 5)$	$5.56\times$	$3.70\times$
$F(9 \times 9, 3 \times 3)$	$3.01\times$	$2.01\times$
$F(9 \times 9, 5 \times 5)$	$5.99\times$	$3.99\times$
$F(10 \times 10, 3 \times 3)$	$3.13\times$	$2.08\times$
$F(10 \times 10, 5 \times 5)$	$6.38\times$	$4.25\times$
$F(11 \times 11, 3 \times 3)$	$3.22\times$	$2.14\times$
$F(11 \times 11, 5 \times 5)$	$6.72\times$	$4.48\times$
$F(12 \times 12, 3 \times 3)$	$3.31\times$	$2.20\times$
$F(12 \times 12, 5 \times 5)$	$7.03\times$	$4.69\times$
$F(14 \times 14, 3 \times 3)$	$3.45\times$	$2.30\times$

Our RNS approach is in favor of large transformation, such as 10×10 to 16×16 etc. since the numerical issue is mitigated by using RNS. However, the computation cost of Winograd transform, both forward and backward ones, will be higher than using small transformation.

The critical path of the computation is the element-wise multiplication, which is low-precision GEMM operations. Table 3 shows the throughput in GOPS(Giga (10^9) Operations Per-Second) of 8-bit and 16-bit GEMM measured on a single core of Arm Cortex-A73 CPU for variety of size and shape.

Table 3. Throughput (GOPS) of 8-bit, 16-bit and 32-bit GEMM (32-bit output) on 1 CPU of Arm Cortex-A73. e.g. $1024 \times 64 \times 1024$ GEMM indicates the matrix multiply of 1024×64 by 64×1024.

GEMM	8-bit GOPS	16-bit GOPS
$1024 \times 64 \times 1024$	11.1	8.46
$1024 \times 128 \times 1024$	13.3	10.1
$1024 \times 256 \times 1024$	14.8	10.9
$256 \times 256 \times 256$	14.5	11.1
$512 \times 512 \times 512$	15.4	11.2
$1024 \times 1024 \times 1024$	14.6	9.58
$2048 \times 2048 \times 2048$	14.2	11.2
$4096 \times 4906 \times 4096$	14.5	9.83

For a given hardware e.g. CPU, GPU or accelerator we can determine the optimal implementation based on Table 2 and the corresponding GEMM performance. For example, targeting Arm Cortex-A73 CPU used in the benchmark, if we choose RNS(4001,4331) to compute the convolution using $F(12 \times 12, 5 \times 5)$ with $1024 \times 1024 \times 1024$ GEMM, it will have a theoretical speed-up up to $\frac{7.03 \times 9.58}{14.6} = 4.6\times$ to the Im2col+INT16GEMM baseline, while the improvement of RNS(253,251,247) is about $\frac{4.69 \times 14.6}{14.6} = 4.69\times$ over Im2col+INT8GEMM. So, RNS(251,241,239) and RNS(4001,4331) happen to deliver roughly the same improvement with the benchmark program on the Cortex-A73 CPU specifically, but in general 8-bit implementation RNS(251, 241, 239) will consume less power since it uses 8-bit arithmetic. Other hardware, for example Nvidia's RTX2020Ti GPU with up to 215 TOPS of INT8 ops[4], could potentially gain up to a factor of $2.30\times$ or $4.69\times$ performance boost for 3×3 or 5×5 filters respectively through 16×16 RNS-Winograd transformation.

8 Experiments

To validate the proposal, the RNS based Winograd convolution algorithm was implemented in a highly optimized kernel in C on Ubuntu Linux. The program takes advantage of ILP (vector units) to boost the throughput of Winograd transforms, MRC and GEMM functions.

The 2D convolution of 8-bit quantized (for both weight and activation) VGG16 network was benchmarked using the RNS based Winograd algorithm implemented on Arm Cortex-A73 CPU. The convolution output of all CNN layers are within the range of $[-3.0 \times 10^5, 3.0 \times 10^5]$ measured from validation images of ImageNet dataset. We used RNS(251,241,239) and RNS(4001,4331), which have the large enough dynamic ranges, $[-7228674, 7228674]$ and

---

[4] https://devblogs.nvidia.com/nvidia-turing-architecture-in-depth/.

Table 4. Inference performance of 8-bit activation and 8-bit weight quantized CNN layers of VGG16 with Winograd algorithm $F(14 \times 14, 3 \times 3)$ over RNS(251,241,239) and RNS(4001,4331) on Arm Cortex-A73, having 71.4% top-1 prediction accuracy with ImageNet dataset. The corresponding transforms are in the supplementary materials. The speed-up of RNS(251,241,239) and RNS(4001,4331) are the runtime improvement relative to the standard INT8 and INT16 Im2col+GEMM convolution baselines respectively.

VGG16 model	conv2d op (int8) x (int8)	Winograd algorithm	Speed-up	
			RNS(251,241,239)	RNS(4001,4331)
conv1_1	$(224, 224, 3) \times (3, 3, 3, 64)$	$-^\dagger$	1×	1×
conv1_2	$(224, 224, 3) \times (3, 3, 3, 64)$	$F(14 \times 14, 3 \times 3)$	1.86×	2.05×
conv2_1	$(112, 224, 64) \times (3, 3, 64, 64)$	$F(14 \times 14, 3 \times 3)$	1.97×	2.13×
conv2_2	$(112, 112, 64) \times (3, 3, 64, 128)$	$F(14 \times 14, 3 \times 3)$	2.07×	2.25×
conv3_1	$(56, 56, 128) \times (3, 3, 128, 128)$	$F(14 \times 14, 3 \times 3)$	2.14×	2.33×
conv3_2	$(56, 56, 128) \times (3, 3, 128, 256)$	$F(14 \times 14, 3 \times 3)$	2.15×	2.37×
conv3_3	$(56, 56, 256) \times (3, 3, 256, 256)$	$F(14 \times 14, 3 \times 3)$	2.16×	2.35×
conv4_1	$(28, 28, 256) \times (3, 3, 256, 512)$	$F(14 \times 14, 3 \times 3)$	2.21×	2.40×
conv4_2	$(28, 28, 512) \times (3, 3, 512, 512)$	$F(14 \times 14, 3 \times 3)$	2.25×	2.37×
conv4_3	$(28, 28, 512) \times (3, 3, 512, 512)$	$F(14 \times 14, 3 \times 3)$	2.27×	2.39×
conv5_1	$(14, 14, 512) \times (3, 3, 512, 512)$	$F(14 \times 14, 3 \times 3)$	2.21×	2.44×
conv5_2	$(14, 14, 512) \times (3, 3, 512, 512)$	$F(14 \times 14, 3 \times 3)$	2.24×	2.39×
conv5_3	$(14, 14, 512) \times (3, 3, 512, 512)$	$F(14 \times 14, 3 \times 3)$	2.22×	2.43×
Average			2.02×	2.20×

†Fallback to the baseline.

$[-8664165, 8664165]$ respectively to guarantee the correctness of the computation.

Using algorithm $F(14 \times 14, 3 \times 3)$, the performance improvement or speed-up over the Im2col+INT8/16 GEMM baselines for both 8-bit and 16-bit RNS are listed in Table 4. The overall convolution computation latency reduction is **2.02×** for 8-bit RNS(251,241,239) or **2.20×** for 16-bit RNS(4001,4331). On average, the execution overheads, measured in time, of the 8-bit RNS(251, 241, 239) are 7.9% for the forward Winograd Transform of input feature maps, 9.2% for the backward Winograd transform of output, and 1.1% for MRC while for the 16-bit RNS(4001, 4331), the corresponding overheads are 9.4%, 10.2%, and 1.3% respectively. Table 5 provides extra experimental results for 8-bit ResNet50-v1 and Inception v1 and v3 models using INT8 arithmetic ops. Notably, the Inception-v3 contains three 5×5 convolutional layers, (1) Mixed_5/Branch_1/ Conv2d_0b_5x5, (2) Mixed_5c/Branch_1/Conv_1_0c_5x5 and (3) Mixed_ 5d/Branch_1/Conv2d_0b_5x5 with $(5 \times 5 \times 48 \times 64)$ kernels. The average speed-up for the 5×5 layers are 2.31× with 8-bit 3-residue RNS.

9   Conclusions

We proposed a Residue Number System (RNS) based fast integral Winograd convolution that overcomes the computational instability of the conventional Winograd algorithm. The method enables the execution of the Winograd algorithm

Table 5. Inference performance improvement over the Im2col+INT8GEMM base-line of CNN layers for 8-bit quantized ResNet50-v1, Inception v1 and v3 models with ImageNet dataset, using 8-bit RNS(251,241,239).

Models	Bits of weight/input	Top-1 Acc.(%)	Speed-up of CNN layers[†]
ResNet50-v1	8/8	75.1	1.76×
Inception-v1	8/8	70.1	1.82×
Inception-v3	8/8	77.5	1.35×

[†]Not include the CNN layers with the stride ≥ 2.

using low cost, low precision arithmetic operations (e.g. INT8 MAC) for infer-ence of existing quantized CNN networks. The convolution outputs are precise, which means there is no prediction accuracy degradation with the RNS-based Winograd convolution scheme we have presented.

Our RNS-based approach can benefit the common hardware platforms, including CPU, GPU, and hardware accelerators, which can deliver high throughput, low cost integer MAC operations. The theoretical performance improvement of 8-bit quantized CNN layers can be up to 2.3× and 4.6× over 8-bit 3-residue RNS for 3×3 and 5×5 CNN layers respectively using up to 16×16 transformation.

The experiment showed, on average, the new proposal improved the runtime performance of 3×3 INT8 CNN layers by 2.02× using power efficient 8-bit arithmetic and 2.20× for 16-bit arithmetic over the standard Im2col + INT8 and INT16 GEMM baseline performances respectively measured on an Arm Cortex-A73 mobile CPU using the 8-bit quantized VGG16 model, including the computation overheads such as Winograd transforms over RNS, modulo, and MRC operations etc. The new proposal achieved higher improvement e.g. 2.31× for the CNN layers with larger filter size i.e. 5×5 in Inception-v3.

Although it is possible to increase the transformation size (i.e. $> 16 \times 16$), to further boost arithmetic reduction, the transformation cost increases roughly linearly, therefore it is a reasonable trade-off to choose transformation size from 8 to 16.

References

1. Barabasz, B., Anderson, A., Soodhalter, K.M., Gregg, D.: Error Analysis and Improving the Accuracy of Winograd Convolution for Deep Neural Networks. arXiv e-prints arXiv:1803.10986 (2018)
2. Courbariaux, M., Bengio, Y.: Binarynet: Training deep neural networks with weights and activations constrained to +1 or −1. CoRR abs/1602.02830 (2016)
3. Dally, W.: Nips tutorial 2015 (2015). https://media.nips.cc/Conferences/2015/tutorialslides/Dally-NIPS-Tutorial-2015.pdf
4. Knuth, D.E.: The Art of Computer Programming, vol. 1: Fundamental Algorithms. §1.2.3: Sums and Products: Exercise 40, 3rd ed. (1997)

5. Knuth, D.E.: The Art of Computer Programming, vol. 2: Seminumerical Algorithms. Section 4.3.2, 3rd ed., pp. 286–291, exercise 4.6.2-3, p. 456. Addison-Wesley (2001)
6. Krizhevsky, A., Sutskever, I., Hinton, G.E.: Imagenet classification with deepconvolutional neural networks. Commun. ACM **60**(6), 84–90 (2017). https://doi.org/10.1145/3065386, http://doi.acm.org/10.1145/3065386
7. Lavin, A., Gray, S.: Fast algorithms for convolutional neural networks. In: 2016 IEEE Conference on Computer Vision and Pattern Recognition (CVPR) (2016)
8. Liu, X., Pool, J., Han, S., Dally, W.J.: Efficient sparse-winograd convolutional neural networks. In: International Conference on Learning Representations (2018). https://openreview.net/forum?id=HJzgZ3JCW
9. Liu, Z.G., Mattina, M.: Learning low-precision neural networks without straight-through estimator (ste). In: Proceedings of the Twenty-Eighth International Joint Conference on Artificial Intelligence, IJCAI-19, pp. 3066–3072. International Joint Conferences on Artificial Intelligence Organization (2019). https://doi.org/10.24963/ijcai.2019/425
10. Mathieu, M., Henaff, M., LeCun, Y.: Fast training of convolutional networks through ffts. In: Bengio, Y., LeCun, Y. (eds.) 2nd International Conference on Learning Representations, ICLR 2014, Banff, AB, Canada, 14–16 April 2014. Conference Track Proceedings (2014)
11. Meng, L., Brothers, J.: Efficient Winograd Convolution via Integer Arithmetic. arXiv e-prints arXiv:1901.01965 (2019)
12. Mohan, P.V.: Residue Number Systems: Algorithms and Architectures. Kluwer Academic Publishers, New York (2002)
13. Schonheim, J.: Conversion of modular numbers to their mixed radix representation by matrix formula. Math. Comput. **21**, 253–257 (1967)
14. Winograd, S.: Arithmetic Complexity of Computations, vol. 33. SIAM, Philadelphia (1980)

Robust Tracking Against Adversarial Attacks

Shuai Jia[1], Chao Ma[1($\boxtimes$)], Yibing Song[2], and Xiaokang Yang[1]

[1] MoE Key Lab of Artificial Intelligence, AI Institute,
Shanghai Jiao Tong University, Shanghai, China
{jiashuai,chaoma,xkyang}@sjtu.edu.cn
[2] Tencent AI Lab, Bellevue, USA
yibingsong.cv@gmail.com

Abstract. While deep convolutional neural networks (CNNs) are vulnerable to adversarial attacks, considerably few efforts have been paid to construct robust deep tracking algorithms against adversarial attacks. Current studies on adversarial attack and defense mainly reside in a single image. In this work, we first attempt to generate adversarial examples on top of video sequences to improve the tracking robustness against adversarial attacks. To this end, we take temporal motion into consideration when generating lightweight perturbations over the estimated tracking results frame-by-frame. On one hand, we add the temporal perturbations into the original video sequences as adversarial examples to greatly degrade the tracking performance. On the other hand, we sequentially estimate the perturbations from input sequences and learn to eliminate their effect for performance restoration. We apply the proposed adversarial attack and defense approaches to state-of-the-art deep tracking algorithms. Extensive evaluations on the benchmark datasets demonstrate that our defense method not only eliminates the large performance drops caused by adversarial attacks, but also achieves additional performance gains when deep trackers are not under adversarial attacks. The source code is available at https://github.com/joshuajss/RTAA.

Keywords: Visual tracking · Adversarial attack

1 Introduction

Recent years have witnessed the success of CNNs for numerous computer vision tasks. Along with the success, the problem of attacking CNN models using adversarial examples emerges recently. That is, small perturbations on input images can lead the pretrained CNN models to complete failures. A number of adversarial attack methods inject perturbations into input images to degrade the performance of CNNs on a wide range of vision tasks, such as image classification [35], object detection [43], semantic segmentation [42], and face recognition [6]. In view of the vulnerability of CNNs, the defense approaches [33,44] aim to improve the robustness of CNNs against adversarial attacks. Despite the

© Springer Nature Switzerland AG 2020
A. Vedaldi et al. (Eds.): ECCV 2020, LNCS 12364, pp. 69–84, 2020.
https://doi.org/10.1007/978-3-030-58529-7_5

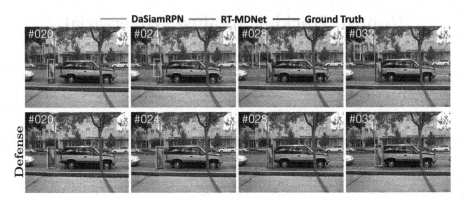

Fig. 1. Adversarial attack and defense for visual tracking. On top of the two state-of-the-art deep trackers DaSiamRPN [47] and RT-MDNet [13], we learn to generate adversarial examples to attack and defend them on the *David3* sequence [41].

significant progress, current studies on adversarial attack and defense mainly rest in static images. Considerably less attention has been paid to generating adversarial examples on top of video sequences for robust deep tracking, where motion consistency between frames involves more challenges.

In this work, we start by investigating the vulnerability of the state-of-the-art deep trackers [18,27], which pose object tracking as a sequential detection problem to distinguish between the target and background. The CNN classifiers are often updated online with positive and negative examples, which are collected according to the previously estimated tracking results. In our investigation, we do not modify existing deep trackers and keep their sampling schemes unchanged. For adversarial attack, we learn perturbations and inject them into input frames, yielding indistinguishable binary samples (i.e., a portion of the samples are incorrect). We use these binary adversarial examples to retrain CNN classifiers to degrade their performance. Specifically, we minimize the classification loss difference between the correct and incorrect binary samples. When taking the temporal consistency between frames into consideration, we use the learned perturbations in the current frame to initialize the perturbation learning in the next frame. Applying the temporally generated perturbations for every frame further degrades the performance of deep trackers. In addition to the CNN classifiers, existing deep trackers widely use a regression network to refine bounding boxes. We first attempt to randomly shift and rescale ground truth boxes to attack the regression network. Note that attacking the bounding box locations significantly differs from existing adversarial attack approaches on object detection [43], where perturbations are generated via considering mis-classifications. Figure 1 shows such an example that the state-of-the-art deep trackers under adversarial attacks drift rapidly (see the first row).

We step further to improve the robustness of deep trackers against adversarial attacks. Note that the adversarial perturbations are assumed to be unknown at this moment. Our motivation is to estimate the unknown perturbations in the input videos and learn to eliminate their effects during tracking. The estimation process is similar to the attack but the involved samples are different. As an example shown in Fig. 1, we perform the proposed adversarial attack and defense approaches on two state-of-the-art deep tracking methods [13,47]. Extensive evaluations on large-scale benchmark datasets indicate the proposed defense approach is effective in improving the tracking robustness against adversarial attacks. When the trackers are not under adversarial attacks, the proposed defense scheme helps to achieve additional performance gains. This is because our defense is able to estimate the naturally existing adversarial perturbations during the image formation process.

The main contributions of this work are summarized as follows:

- We propose to generate adversarial examples to investigate the robustness of existing deep tracking algorithms. We inject dense adversarial perturbations into input video sequences in the spatiotemporal domain to degrade the tracking accuracy.
- We propose to defend deep trackers against adversarial attacks. We estimate the adversarial perturbations and eliminate their effect to alleviate performance drops caused by the adversarial attack.
- We perform adversarial attack and defense on state-of-the-art deep trackers. The extensive evaluations on the benchmark datasets demonstrate the effectiveness of both attack and defense. Our defense can further advance the state-of-the-art deep trackers not under adversarial attacks.

2 Related Works

2.1 Deep Visual Tracking

Existing object tracking approaches can be generally categorized as one-stage regression based methods and two-stage detection based methods. Deep learning advances both categories of tracking methods significantly. The regression based methods typically learn correlation filters over CNN features to locate target objects as in [23]. Since that, numerous methods are proposed to improve tracking performance in different aspects, including feature hedging [29], continuous convolution [5], particle filter integration [45], efficient convolution [4], spatiotemporal regularization [19], and roi pooling [34]. Meanwhile, there are end-to-end learnable regression networks aiming to directly predict response maps [11,21,31,36–39] for localizing the target object.

On the other hand, two-stage tracking-by-detection approaches first generate multiple proposals and then classify each as either the target or the background. The representative deep tracking-by-detection methods include multi-domain learning [13,27], ensemble learning [10], adversarial learning [32], reciprocative learning [28] and overlap maximization [3]. Recently, Siamese trackers [1,2,17, 18,22,46,47] are prevalent due to their efficiency in online inference. The main difference between the Siamese trackers and other tracking-by-detection methods is that Siamese trackers typically do not online update CNN models while other methods do. In this work, we deploy the proposed adversarial attack and defense schemes on two representative state-of-the-art trackers including one Siamese tracker [47] without online update and one detector based tracker [27] with online update. Our goal is to illustrate the general effectiveness of adversarial attack and defense on deep trackers with or without online update.

2.2   Adversarial Attacks and Defense

Recent studies [8,35] have shown that CNNs are vulnerable to adversarial examples. Despite the favorable performance on natural input images, the pretrained CNNs perform poorly given intentionally generated adversarial examples. Existing adversarial attack methods mainly fall into two categories: white-box and black-box attacks. The CNN models are assumed to be known in white-box attacks [8,24,25], whereas they are unknown in black-box attack [6,12]. In addition to algorithmic attacks, physical attack methods generate real world objects to lead CNNs models to misclassifications. These are typically useful to examine the robustness of automotive driving in the road sign scenarios [7,16,40].

Defending CNNs against adversarial attacks can be regarded as robustly learning CNNs with adversarial examples. Attempts have been made to formulate defense as a denoising problem. From this perspective, the adversarial examples produce noise on CNN features to distract the network inference process. In [20,44], denoising algorithms are proposed to eliminate the effect of noise. In addition, images are transformed to be non-differentiable in [9] to resist adversarial attacks. Different from existing attack and defense methods, we attack both the classification and regression modules of deep trackers to decrease accuracy. Then, we gradually estimate adversarial perturbations and eliminate their effect on the input images without modifying existing deep trackers.

3   Proposed Algorithm

This section illustrates how to perform adversarial attack and defense for visual tracking. Given an input video sequence and a labeled bounding box in the initial frame, we generate adversarial examples spatiotemporally to decrease tracking accuracy. On the other hand, our defense learns to estimate unknown adversarial perturbations and eliminate their effect from input sequences. We deploy the proposed attack and defense algorithms on the tracking-by-detection framework. The details are presented in the following.

3.1   Adversarial Example Generation

We generate adversarial perturbations based on the input frame and the output response of deep trackers, i.e., classification scores or regression maps. These perturbations are then added to the input frame for adversarial example generation. In the tracking-by-detection framework, deep trackers usually employ a CNN architecture containing two branches. The sampled proposals are classified as either the target or background in the first branch, while the proposal axis is regressed in another branch for precise localization. A detailed illustration is referred to [18]. We denote an input frame by I, the proposal number by N, the binary classification loss by L_c, the bounding box regression loss by L_r, the correct classification label and regression label by p_c and p_r, respectively. Both labels p_c and p_r are predicted by the tracking results S^{t-1} from the last frame, while S^1 is the ground-truth annotation in the initial frame. The original loss function of the tracking-by-detection network can be written as:

$$\mathcal{L}(I, N, \theta) = \sum_{n=1}^{N} [L_c(I_n, p_c, \theta) + \lambda \cdot L_r(I_n, p_r, \theta)] \tag{1}$$

where I_n is one proposal in the image, λ is a fixed weight parameter, and θ denotes the CNN parameters to be optimized during the training process.

When generating adversarial perturbations, we expect CNNs to make inaccurate inference. We create a pseudo classification label $p_c^\star$ and a pseudo regression label $p_r^\star$. The adversarial loss is set to make L_c and L_r the same when we use correct and pseudo labels. The adversarial loss can be written as follows:

$$\mathcal{L}_{adv}(I, N, \theta) = \sum_{n=1}^{N} \{[L_c(I_n, p_c, \theta) - L_c(I_n, p_c^\star, \theta)] \\ + \lambda \cdot [L_r(I_n, p_r, \theta) - L_r(I_n, p_r^\star, \theta)]\} \tag{2}$$

where θ is fixed because the CNN is in the inference stage. The adversarial loss $\mathcal{L}_{adv}$ reflects the loss similarity between using correct and pseudo labels. When minimizing $\mathcal{L}_{adv}$, the CNN predictions will be close to pseudo labels and the performance will degrade rapidly.

We set pseudo labels specifically for each branch. In $p_c^\star$, there are two elements (i.e., 0 and 1) which indicate the probabilities of the input belonging to the target and background. We set $p_c^\star$ by reversing the elements of p_c to confuse the classification branch. On the other hand, p_r consists of four elements (x_r, y_r, w_r, h_r) representing the target location. We set $p_r^\star$ by adding a random distance offset and a random scale variation to p_r. Each element of $p_r^\star$ can be written as:

$$x_r^\star = x_r + \delta_{\text{offset}}$$
$$y_r^\star = y_r + \delta_{\text{offset}}$$
$$w_r^\star = w_r * \delta_{\text{scale}}$$
$$h_r^\star = h_r * \delta_{\text{scale}} \tag{3}$$

where δ_{offset} and δ_{scale} indicate the random distance offset and random scale variation, respectively.

After computing the adversarial loss in Eq. 2, we take partial derivatives of the adversarial loss with respect to the input I. Formally, the partial derivative r is computed as:

$$r = \frac{\partial \mathcal{L}_{adv}}{\partial I}. \tag{4}$$

Algorithm 1: Adversarial Example Generation

   Input: input video V with T frames; target location S^1;

   Output: adversarial examples of T frames;

1 **for** $t = 2$ **to** T **do**

2   Get current frame I_1^t;

3   **if** $t \neq 2$ **then**

4 | Update I_1^t via Eq. 6;

5   **end**

6   **for** $m = 1$ **to** M **do**

7   Create p_c and p_r via IoU ratios between proposals and target location S^{t-1};

8   Create $p_c^\star$ by reversing elements of p_c;

9   Create $p_r^\star$ via Eq. 3;

10   Generate adversarial loss via Eq. 2;

11   Update I_m^t via Eq. 5;

12   **end**

13   **return** I_M^t;

14 **end**

We pass r into a sign function to reduce outlier effects. Given an input frame I, we take M iterations to produce the final adversarial perturbations. The output of the last iteration is added into the input frame, which can be written as follows:

$$I_{m+1} = I_m + \alpha \cdot sign(r_m) \tag{5}$$

where $\alpha = \frac{\epsilon}{M}$ is a constant weight, ϵ is the maximum value of the perturbations, m indicates the iteration index, I_m is the input frame for the m-th iteration, $\alpha \cdot sign(r_m)$ is the perturbations generated during the m-th iteration. The final adversarial example is I_M.

As video frames are temporally coherent, we consider the adversarial attacks in the spatiotemporal domain. When there are T frames in an input video sequence, we use the learned perturbations in the last frame as initialization for the current frame. Specifically, for the t-th frame, we use perturbations from the last frame to initialize I^t, which can be written as:

$$I_1^t = I_1^t + (I_M^{t-1} - I_1^{t-1}) \tag{6}$$

where $I_M^{t-1} - I_1^{t-1}$ is the perturbation from the last frame. Then we gradually update I^t by using Eq. 5 to generate the final perturbations for the t-th frame. The pseudo code is shown in Algorithm 1. Note that we use the IoU metric [30] to assign proposal labels.

3.2 Adversarial Defense

We propose an adversarial defense method to recover tracking accuracy that is deteriorated via adversarial attacks. Our motivation comes from the adversarial

---

Algorithm 2: Adversarial Example Defense

Input: input video V with T adversarial examples; target location S^1;
Output: adversarial examples of T frames;

1 **for** $t = 2$ **to** T **do**
2   Get current frame I_1^t;
3   **if** $t \neq 2$ **then**
4 | Update I_1^t via Eq. 8;
5   **end**
6   **for** $m = 1$ **to** M **do**
7   Create p_c and p_r via IoU ratios between proposals and target location S^{t-1};
8   Create $p_c^\star$ by reversing elements of p_c;
9   Create $p_r^\star$ via Eq. 3;
10   Generate adversarial loss via Eq. 2;
11   Update I_m^t via Eq. 7;
12   **end**
13   **return** I_M^t;
14 **end**

---

perturbations which are accumulated during the iterations in each frame. From Eq. 4, we observe that perturbations originate from partial derivatives. Instead of adding perturbations to the input frame to decrease tracking accuracy, we estimate the perturbations and subtract them from the input frame gradually. As a result, the effect of perturbations will be eliminated to help CNNs to make the correct inference. We defend adversarial examples without updating CNNs.

Given an input frame I with unknown adversarial perturbations, we first generate correct and pseudo labels according to the predicted location S^{t-1} from the previous frame. The label generation process is similar to that in Sect. 3.1 except that the utilized proposals during defense are resampled. Then, we estimate the adversarial loss by using Eq. 2 and compute the partial derivatives via Eq. 4. We apply partial derivatives r on the input frame I via the following operation:

$$I_{m+1} = I_m - \underset{\beta \cdot r \in [-\hat{\alpha}, \hat{\alpha}]}{\text{Trunc}} (\beta \cdot r) \qquad (7)$$

where β is a constant weight, Trunc$(\cdot)$ is a truncation function to constrain the values of $\beta \cdot r$ within the range between $-\hat{\alpha}$ and $\hat{\alpha}$. The parameter $\hat{\alpha}$ resembles the parameter α in Eq. 5. Since the perturbation is unknown during defense, we empirically set different values for these two parameters. When the input videos contain T frames, we still transfer the perturbations from the last frame to the current frame as initialization. For the t-th frame, we update it initially as:

$$I_1^t = I_1^t - \gamma \cdot (I_1^{t-1} - I_M^{t-1}) \qquad (8)$$

where γ is a constant weight. The pseudo code of adversarial defense is shown in Algorithm 2.

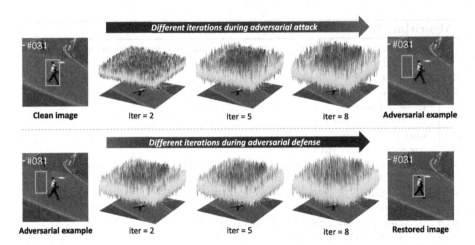

Fig. 2. Variations of adversarial perturbations during attack and defense. The 3D response map above the image represents the difference between the clean image and the adversarial example at the current iteration. In adversarial attack, the perturbations increase along with training iterations. In adversarial defense, the perturbations decrease when training iteration increases.

3.3 Deployment of Deep Trackers

From the perspective of online update, existing tracking-by-detection methods involves two main stages. In the first stage, trackers do not update online while utilizing an offline pretrained CNN model. In the second stage, trackers collect samples online from previous frames to update the model. Note that trackers with online update tend to improve model adaption by collecting samples incrementally, which may help defend adversarial perturbations. We deploy the proposed adversarial attack and defense on two state-of-the-art trackers, DaSiamRPN [47] and RT-MDNet [13]. Details are presented in the following:

DaSiamRPN. There are two output branches in DaSiamRPN to classify and regress proposals. During tracking, DaSiamRPN does not perform online update. When processing each frame, we follow Algorithm 1 and Algorithm 2 to generate and defend adversarial examples, respectively. As the inputs contain a template and search patch, we take partial derivatives with respect to the search patch when computing Eq. 4 for both attack and defense.

RT-MDNet. The CNN model of RT-MDNet only performs classification. During tracking, RT-MDNet online updates its model by collecting samples from previous frames. When processing each frame, we first generate adversarial examples and then perform prediction and model update. This configuration aims to analyze whether online update is effective to defend adversarial examples. We generate and defend adversarial examples using Algorithm 1 and Algorithm 2, except that we remove the regression terms when computing Eq. 2.

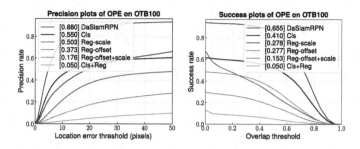

Fig. 3. Ablation studies of DaSiamRPN on the OTB100 dataset [41]. We denote Cls as the attack on the classification branch, Reg as the attack on the regression branch where there are offset and scale attacks.

Visualizations. We show how adversarial perturbations vary during different training iterations in Fig. 2. DaSiamRPN is our baseline tracker to be attacked and defended. Given an input frame, we visualize the perturbations during adversarial attack. Along with the training iterations, the variation of perturbations increases as well. The adversarial examples lead DaSiamRPN to drift rapidly. When defending this adversarial example, we observe that the variation of the perturbations decreases when training iteration increases. This indicates that our defense method is effective to estimate and exclude the adversarial perturbations, which helps to alleviate performance drops caused by adversarial attack.

4   Experiments

In this section, we evaluate the proposed attack and defense methods on benchmark datasets. We develop our methods on top of DaSiamRPN and RT-MDNet for all the experiments. The maximum variation value of each pixel in the perturbations is set to 10 (i.e., $\epsilon = 10$) for attack and set to 5 for (i.e., $\epsilon = 5$) defense, respectively. When computing IoU ratios between proposals and the target location S_{t-1}, we follow the threshold setting of DaSiamRPN and RT-MDNet to draw training samples. The parameters of deep trackers are kept fixed during both adversarial attack and defense.

4.1   Ablation Studies

We analyze the effectiveness of each component of the proposed method. We take the DaSiamRPN tracker as a baseline as it contains both the classification and regression branches. We first evaluate the baseline performance on the OTB100 dataset. Then, we separately apply our attack method on the classification and regression branches. When we attack the regression branch, we analyze the offset and scale variation effects. Meanwhile, we combine both classification and regression attacks. Figure 3 shows the evaluation results where the attack on the

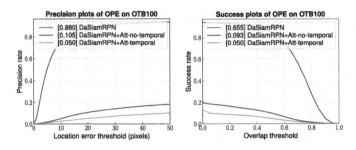

Fig. 4. Temporal consistency validation of DaSiamRPN on the OTB100 dataset [41].

regression branch degrades the performance more than the attack on the classification branch. Combining attacks on both branches leads to more degraded tracking performance.

In addition to analyzing the attack in single frames, we show performance degradation via temporally consistent attack. We transfer the perturbation of the last frame to the current frame as initialization. Figure 4 shows that our temporally consistent attack decreases tracking accuracies more than the static image attack.

4.2   Benchmark Performance

We deploy the proposed attack and defense methods on DaSiamRPN and RT-MDNet on four standard benchmark datasets (OTB100 [41], VOT-2016 [15], VOT-2018 [14] and UAV123 [26]). The results are presented as follows:

OTB100. There are 100 video sequences in this dataset with substantial target variations. We apply the one-pass evaluation (OPE) with success and precision plots. The precision metric evaluates the ratio of frames whose center location error is within a certain threshold among all frames. The success plot measures the IoU scores between the tracking results and ground truth at different thresholds. The area under the curve (AUC) success scores are also reported.

In order to evaluate our adversarial attack and defense methods, we first show the results of the baseline trackers. Second, we attack the baseline trackers by adding adversarial perturbations to input video sequences. In addition, we show the attack performance by adding random perturbations containing the same variations to those of adversarial perturbations. Figure 5 shows that our attack method reduces the AUC scores of DaSiamRPN from 0.655 to 0.050, and the AUC scores of RT-MDnet from 0.643 to 0.131. The baseline trackers under adversarial attacks perform much worse than that under random perturbations. This indicates the effectiveness of our adversarial attack method on baseline trackers. On the other hand, our defense method is able to suppress the maximal value of adversarial perturbations to restore the tracking performance. It recovers the AUC score of DaSiamRPN to 0.721 and RT-MDNet to 0.653. This demonstrates that our defense method can effectively remove the perturbations to restore tracking performance. In addition, we apply our defense method

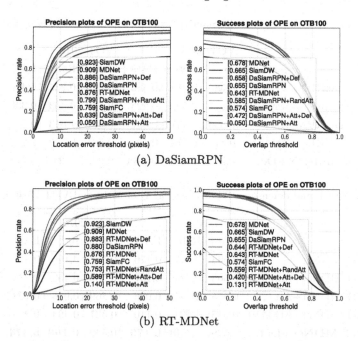

(a) DaSiamRPN

(b) RT-MDNet

Fig. 5. Tracking performance of the adversarial attack and defense methods on the OTB100 dataset. We denote Att and Def as the adversarial attack and defense, respectively, and denote Rand as random perturbations.

on original tracking sequences and improves AUC score from 0.880 to 0.886 for DaSiamRPN and from 0.876 to 0.883 for RT-MDNet. This indicates that perturbations (e.g., noise) exist in real world scenarios during image formation process (e.g., camera sensor noise, transformation from optical perception to digital storage). Our defense method is effective to estimate these naturally existing perturbations and eliminate their effects.

VOT-2018. There are 60 sequences on the VOT-2018 dataset. The VOT toolkit will reinitialize the tracker if it loses the target object during 5 consecutive frames. The evaluation metrics of VOT are expected average overlap (EAO), accuracy (Acc) and robustness (Rob). The accuracy represents the average overlap ratio and the robustness is measured by the number of reinitialization. EAO measures the overall performance of trackers.

Table 1 and Table 2 show the experimental results of DaSiamRPN and RT-MDnet. The failure number increases rapidly after attacking the original sequences. The EAO drops dramatically from 0.380 to 0.097 (i.e., a 74.5% decrease) for DaSiamRPN and from 0.176 to 0.076 (i.e., a 56.8% decrease) for RT-MDNet. By integrating our adversarial defense method, the EAO scores of DaSiamRPN and RT-MDNet are restored to 0.195 and 0.110, respectively. The performance decrease and restoration indicate the effectiveness of our adversarial attack and defense method. In addition, our defense method also improves

Table 1. Attack and defense on DaSiamRPN on VOT-2018 and VOT-2016 datasets.

	VOT-2018			VOT-2016		
	Acc ↑	Rob ↓	EAO ↑	Acc ↑	Rob ↓	EAO ↑
DaSiamRPN	0.585	0.272	0.380	0.625	0.224	0.439
DaSiamRPN+RandAtt	0.571	0.529	0.223	0.606	0.303	0.336
DaSiamRPN+Att	0.536	1.447	0.097	0.521	1.613	0.078
DaSiamRPN+Att+Def	0.579	0.674	0.195	0.581	0.722	0.211
DaSiamRPN+Def	0.584	**0.253**	**0.384**	0.622	**0.214**	0.418

Table 2. Attack and defense on RT-MDNet on VOT-2018 and VOT-2016 datasets.

	VOT-2018			VOT-2016		
	Acc ↑	Rob ↓	EAO ↑	Acc ↑	Rob ↓	EAO ↑
RT-MDNet	0.533	0.567	0.176	0.567	0.196	0.370
RT-MDNet+RandAtt	0.503	0.871	0.137	0.550	0.452	0.235
RT-MDNet+Att	0.475	1.611	0.076	0.469	0.928	0.128
RT-MDNet+Att+Def	0.515	1.021	0.110	0.531	0.494	0.225
RT-MDNet+Def	0.529	**0.538**	**0.179**	0.540	**0.168**	**0.374**

the performance slightly when the baseline trackers are not under adversarial attacks.

VOT-2016. The VOT-2016 dataset consists of 60 sequences. The evaluation metrics are the same as those used in the VOT-2018 dataset. Table 1 and Table 2 illustrate the performance of our attack and defense methods on DaSiamRPN and RT-MDNet. Our adversarial attack algorithm reduces the EAO scores by 82.2% for DaSiamRPN and 65.4% for RT-MDNet. With the use of the defense method on the adversarial examples, the accuracy of EAO is restored by 48.1% for DaSiamRPN and 60.8% for RT-MDNet. It indicates the effectiveness of both adversarial attack and defense methods. In addition, when applying our defense method to the attack-free deep trackers, the robustness gets largely improved. Due to the reinitialization scheme in VOT, we observe that EAO and robustness values decrease dramatically during attacks but accuracy value does not vary much.

UAV123. The UAV123 dataset contains 123 sequences with more 110 K frames, which are captured from low-altitude unmanned aerial vehicles. We adopt the success and precision plots to evaluate the performance. Figure 6 illustrates the precision and success plots of DaSiamRPN and RT-MDNet. Under attacks, the AUC scores drop by 95.6% for DaSiamRPN and 84.6% for RT-MDNet. The precision rate at 20 pixels is reduced by 94.3% and 83.0% for DaSiamRPN and RT-MDNet. The AUC scores are restored by 80.8% and 82.2% respectively

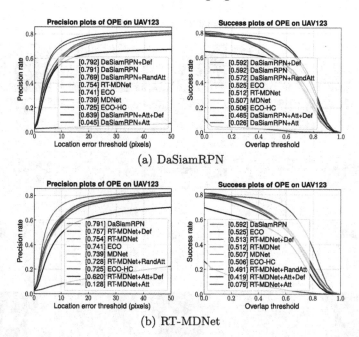

Fig. 6. Results of the adversarial attack and defense methods on UAV123 dataset.

after defending the adversarial examples since the target objects on the UAV123 dataset mostly undergo large shape changes.

4.3 Qualitative Evaluations

Figure 7 qualitatively shows the tracking results of our adversarial attack and defense methods for DaSiamPRN [47] and RT-MDNet [13] on 5 challenging sequences. We visualize the attack and defense perturbations in (b) and (d). In the original sequences shown in (a), both DaSiamRPN and RT-MDNet locate the target objects and estimate the scale changes accurately. After injecting adversarial perturbations in (b), DaSiamRPN fails to track the target and RT-MDNet estimates the target scale inaccurately as shown in (c). The tracking accuracy of RT-MDNet does not degrade severely compared to DaSiamRPN because RT-MDNet only contains the classification branch while DaSiamRPN contains both classification and regression branches. When we perform defense, the adversarial perturbations are estimated and shown in (d). By subtracting the estimated perturbations from the adversarial examples, DaSiamRPN and RT-MDNet are able to locate target objects correctly in the video sequences shown in (e).

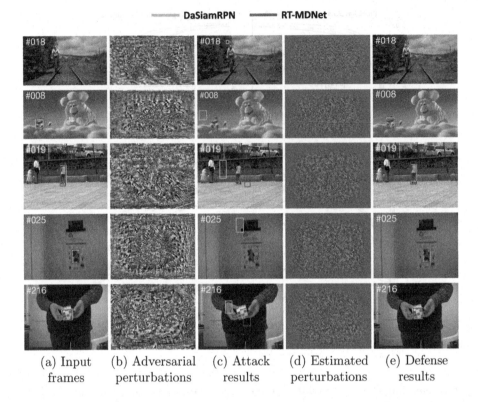

(a) Input   (b) Adversarial   (c) Attack   (d) Estimated   (e) Defense
    frames   perturbations   results   perturbations   results

Fig. 7. Qualitative evaluation of adversarial attack and defense on video sequences.

5   Concluding Remarks

In this paper, we propose the adversarial attack and defense methods by generating lightweight perturbations within the deep tracking framework. When generating adversarial examples, we integrate the temporal perturbations into frames by perplexing trackers with indistinguishable correct and incorrect inferences. When defending adversarial examples, we suppress the maximum of adversarial perturbation to restore the tracking accuracy. Extensive experiments on four standard benchmarks demonstrate that the proposed methods perform favorably both in adversarial attack and defense. In addition, our defense method is capable of reducing interference from perturbations in the real world scenarios to robustify deep trackers.

Acknowledgements. This work was supported by National Key Research and Development Program of China (2016YFB1001003), NSFC (U19B2035, 61527804, 60906119), STCSM (18DZ1112300). C. Ma was sponsored by Shanghai Pujiang Program.

References

1. Bertinetto, L., Valmadre, J., Henriques, J.F., Vedaldi, A., Torr, P.H.: Fully-convolutional siamese networks for object tracking. In: ECCV Workshop (2016)
2. Bhat, G., Danelljan, M., Van Gool, L., Timofte, R.: Learning discriminative model prediction for tracking. In: ICCV (2019)
3. Danelljan, M., Bhat, G., Khan, F.S., Felsberg, M.: Atom: accurate tracking by overlap maximization. In: CVPR (2019)
4. Danelljan, M., Bhat, G., Shahbaz Khan, F., Felsberg, M.: ECO: efficient convolution operators for tracking. In: CVPR (2017)
5. Danelljan, M., Robinson, A., Shahbaz Khan, F., Felsberg, M.: Beyond correlation filters: learning continuous convolution operators for visual tracking. In: Leibe, B., Matas, J., Sebe, N., Welling, M. (eds.) ECCV 2016. LNCS, vol. 9909, pp. 472–488. Springer, Cham (2016). https://doi.org/10.1007/978-3-319-46454-1_29
6. Dong, Y., et al.: Efficient decision-based black-box adversarial attacks on face recognition. In: CVPR (2019)
7. Eykholt, K., et al.: Robust physical-world attacks on deep learning models. In: CVPR (2018)
8. Goodfellow, I.J., Shlens, J., Szegedy, C.: Explaining and harnessing adversarial examples. In: ICLR (2015)
9. Guo, C., Rana, M., Cisse, M., Van Der Maaten, L.: Countering adversarial images using input transformations. In: ICLR (2018)
10. Han, B., Sim, J., Adam, H.: Branchout: regularization for online ensemble tracking with convolutional neural networks. In: CVPR (2017)
11. Held, D., Thrun, S., Savarese, S.: Learning to track at 100 FPS with deep regression networks. In: Leibe, B., Matas, J., Sebe, N., Welling, M. (eds.) ECCV 2016. LNCS, vol. 9905, pp. 749–765. Springer, Cham (2016). https://doi.org/10.1007/978-3-319-46448-0_45
12. Ilyas, A., Engstrom, L., Athalye, A., Lin, J.: Black-box adversarial attacks with limited queries and information. arXiv preprint: 1804.08598 (2018)
13. Jung, I., Son, J., Baek, M., Han, B.: Real-time mdnet. In: ECCV (2018)
14. Kristan, M., et al.: The sixth visual object tracking vot2018 challenge results. In: ECCV Workshop (2018)
15. Kristan, M., et al.: The visual object tracking vot2016 challenge results. In: ECCV Workshop (2016)
16. Kurakin, A., Goodfellow, I., Bengio, S.: Adversarial examples in the physical world. In: ICLR (2017)
17. Li, B., Wu, W., Wang, Q., Zhang, F., Xing, J., Yan, J.: Siamrpn++: evolution of siamese visual tracking with very deep networks. In: CVPR (2019)
18. Li, B., Yan, J., Wu, W., Zhu, Z., Hu, X.: High performance visual tracking with siamese region proposal network. In: CVPR (2018)
19. Li, F., Tian, C., Zuo, W., Zhang, L., Yang, M.H.: Learning spatial-temporal regularized correlation filters for visual tracking. In: CVPR (2018)
20. Liao, F., Liang, M., Dong, Y., Pang, T., Hu, X., Zhu, J.: Defense against adversarial attacks using high-level representation guided denoiser. In: CVPR (2018)
21. Lu, X., Ma, C., Ni, B., Yang, X., Reid, I., Yang, M.H.: Deep regression tracking with shrinkage loss. In: ECCV (2018)
22. Lu, X., Wang, W., Ma, C., Shen, J., Shao, L., Porikli, F.: See more, know more: unsupervised video object segmentation with co-attention siamese networks. In: CVPR (2019)

23. Ma, C., Huang, J.B., Yang, X., Yang, M.H.: Hierarchical convolutional features for visual tracking. In: ICCV (2015)
24. Moosavi-Dezfooli, S.M., Fawzi, A., Fawzi, O., Frossard, P.: Universal adversarial perturbations. In: CVPR (2017)
25. Moosavi-Dezfooli, S.M., Fawzi, A., Frossard, P.: Deepfool: a simple and accurate method to fool deep neural networks. In: CVPR (2016)
26. Mueller, M., Smith, N., Ghanem, B.: A benchmark and simulator for UAV tracking. In: Leibe, B., Matas, J., Sebe, N., Welling, M. (eds.) ECCV 2016. LNCS, vol. 9905, pp. 445–461. Springer, Cham (2016). https://doi.org/10.1007/978-3-319-46448-0_27
27. Nam, H., Han, B.: Learning multi-domain convolutional neural networks for visual tracking. In: CVPR (2016)
28. Pu, S., Song, Y., Ma, C., Zhang, H., Yang, M.H.: Deep attentive tracking via reciprocative learning. In: NeurIPS (2018)
29. Qi, Y., et al.: Hedged deep tracking. In: CVPR (2016)
30. Ren, S., He, K., Girshick, R., Sun, J.: Faster r-cnn: towards real-time object detection with region proposal networks. TPAMI (2016)
31. Song, Y., Ma, C., Gong, L., Zhang, J., Lau, R.W., Yang, M.H.: CREST: convolutional residual learning for visual tracking. In: ICCV (2017)
32. Song, Y., et al.: VITAL: visual tracking via adversarial learning. In: CVPR (2018)
33. Sun, B., Tsai, N.H., Liu, F., Yu, R., Su, H.: Adversarial defense by stratified convolutional sparse coding. In: CVPR (2019)
34. Sun, Y., Sun, C., Wang, D., He, Y., Lu, H.: Roi pooled correlation filters for visual tracking. In: CVPR (2019)
35. Szegedy, C., et al.: Intriguing properties of neural networks. In: ICLR (2014)
36. Valmadre, J., Bertinetto, L., Henriques, J., Vedaldi, A., Torr, P.H.: End-to-end representation learning for correlation filter based tracking. In: CVPR (2017)
37. Wang, L., Ouyang, W., Wang, X., Lu, H.: Visual tracking with fully convolutional networks. In: ICCV (2015)
38. Wang, N., Song, Y., Ma, C., Zhou, W., Liu, W., Li, H.: Unsupervised deep tracking. In: CVPR (2019)
39. Wang, N., Zhou, W., Song, Y., Ma, C., Liu, W., Li, H.: Unsupervised deep representation learning for real-time tracking. IJCV (2020). https://doi.org/10.1007/s11263-020-01357-4
40. Wiyatno, R.R., Xu, A.: Physical adversarial textures that fool visual object tracking. In: ICCV (2019)
41. Wu, Y., Lim, J., Yang, M.H.: Object tracking benchmark. TPAMI (2015)
42. Xiao, C., Deng, R., Li, B., Yu, F., Liu, M., Song, D.: Characterizing adversarial examples based on spatial consistency information for semantic segmentation. In: ECCV (2018)
43. Xie, C., Wang, J., Zhang, Z., Zhou, Y., Xie, L., Yuille, A.: Adversarial examples for semantic segmentation and object detection. In: ICCV (2017)
44. Xie, C., Wu, Y., Maaten, L.V.d., Yuille, A.L., He, K.: Feature denoising for improving adversarial robustness. In: CVPR (2019)
45. Zhang, T., Xu, C., Yang, M.H.: Multi-task correlation particle filter for robust object tracking. In: CVPR (2017)
46. Zhang, Z., Peng, H.: Deeper and wider siamese networks for real-time visual tracking. In: CVPR (2019)
47. Zhu, Z., Wang, Q., Li, B., Wu, W., Yan, J., Hu, W.: Distractor-aware siamese networks for visual object tracking. In: ECCV (2018)

Single-Shot Neural Relighting
and SVBRDF Estimation

Shen Sang[1,2(✉)] and Manmohan Chandraker[1]

[1] University of California, San Diego, La Jolla, USA
ssang@eng.ucsd.edu
[2] ByteDance Research, Mountain View, USA

Abstract. We present a novel physically-motivated deep network for joint shape and material estimation, as well as relighting under novel illumination conditions, using a single image captured by a mobile phone camera. Our physically-based modeling leverages a deep cascaded architecture trained on a large-scale synthetic dataset that consists of complex shapes with microfacet SVBRDF. In contrast to prior works that train rendering layers subsequent to inverse rendering, we propose deep feature sharing and joint training that transfer insights across both tasks, to achieve significant improvements in both reconstruction and relighting. We demonstrate in extensive qualitative and quantitative experiments that our network generalizes very well to real images, achieving high-quality shape and material estimation, as well as image-based relighting. Code, models and data will be publicly released.

Keywords: Single-image relighting · SVBRDF estimation · Physically-based networks

1 Introduction

Single-image relighting is a canonical ill-posed challenge in computer vision, due to the complexity of image formation where spatially-varying material and shape interact with light in myriad ways. Inverse rendering methods have typically recovered shape and material properties, while forward rendering acts on those components for relighting. In this paper, we propose a novel deep network that estimates object shape and material, while jointly learning to relight it under novel illumination conditions, in order to achieve mutual benefits for both tasks. At test time, we use a single image acquired using a flash-enabled commodity mobile phone camera, with possibly unknown environment lighting, to demonstrate recovery of arbitrary object shape and spatially-varying material of complex reflectance, as well as relighting under novel conditions, in a single forward pass.

Electronic supplementary material The online version of this chapter (https://doi.org/10.1007/978-3-030-58529-7_6) contains supplementary material, which is available to authorized users.

© Springer Nature Switzerland AG 2020
A. Vedaldi et al. (Eds.): ECCV 2020, LNCS 12364, pp. 85–101, 2020.
https://doi.org/10.1007/978-3-030-58529-7_6

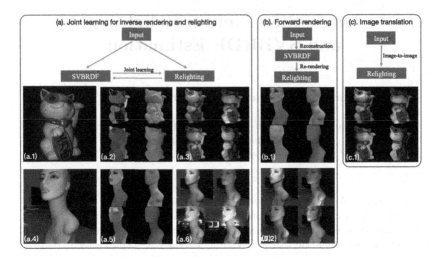

Fig. 1. Three approaches for image relighting with single input images (a.1) and (a.4). **(a)** Our proposed joint inverse rendering and relighting method achieves significant improvements for both tasks, shown in (a.2), (a.3), (a.5) and (a.6). In addition point lights, our method also edits the environment illumination (a.6) **(b)** Forward rendering [19] on recovered shape and material parameters may introduce artifacts (the neck in (b.2)) in the reconstruction stage. **(c)** Image-to-image translation such as [13] lacks physically-motivated modeling and cannot create realistic specularities in (c.1) compared to ours (a.3). More comparisons with forward rendering are shown in Fig. 8.

We achieve this through a physically-motivated modeling and network design. We train a cascaded convolutional neural network (CNN) to estimate shape (depth and surface normals), a spatially-varying bidirectional reflectance distribution function (SVBRDF) consisting of diffuse albedo and specular roughness, as well as synthesize images under different lighting conditions. Unlike prior works that use a shared encoder but separate decoders for various SVBRDF components [18,19], we encourage coherence among them through a shared decoder. More importantly, while prior works have considered relighting as a separate forward problem or used "thin" in-network rendering layers that operate at image resolution, we use a deep network that accepts a lighting and decodes the latent shape and SVBRDF codes to an image under novel illumination. This allows us to propose a novel feature sharing mechanism between the inverse rendering and relighting decoders to simulate a physically-based rendering process. Our novel network design, feature sharing and joint training of the inverse and forward tasks allow significant performance improvements in both reconstruction and relighting.

Our reconstruction contrasts with previous works that assume Lambertian or homogeneous material [14], or assume near-planar surfaces as input [7,17,18]. It shares insights such as cascaded design with recent works that recover shape and SVBRDF from a single image [19], but goes beyond them in introducing new learning pathways through neural lighting with a shared feature space. For relighting, prior works use multiple images for an exhaustive acquisition [6], or interpolate from sparse samples [20,25,26]. The recent method of [35] learns to interpolate using five samples captured under pre-defined directional lights. All these methods produce good relighting results, however, they rely on a large number of images or specialized hardware for acquisition. In contrast, we produce high-quality relighting using a single image captured with a flash-enabled mobile-phone camera under unknown environment lighting, in a single forward pass of a network, which is cheaper in terms of cost and runtime. Examples are shown in Fig. 1. All code, models and data are publicly available.[1]

To summarize, we make the following contributions:

- Joint shape and SVBRDF reconstruction, as well as image relighting, from a single mobile phone image, under point light or environment illumination.
- Physically-based network and feature sharing to jointly learn inverse reconstruction and forward relighting tasks.
- Demonstration of mutual benefits on real images through improved reconstruction and relighting with respect to prior state-of-the-art.

2   Related Works

Shape and Reflectance Reconstruction. Shape from shading has been explored with calibrated illumination and Lambertian assumption [14], as also with arbitrary shape and reflectance under natural illumination [23]. A few recent methods reconstruct SVBRDF based on near-planar assumption under unknown illumination [17] or collocated flash lighting [1,7,18]. Barron and Malik [3] pose the reconstruction problem as one of statistical inference and optimize for the most likely explanation of a single image. Recently, Li et al. [19] propose a deep network to recover shape and SVBRDF from a single image with data-driven priors. In contrast, we reconstruct high-quality shape and reflectance properties from a single image jointly with relighting constraints, to improve both tasks.

Deep Learning for Inverse Rendering. In recent years, deep learning-based methods have shown promising results for inverse rendering problems including illumination estimation [9–11], material recognition [4] and estimation [21], reflectance maps extraction [27], surface appearance recovery [17], normal estimation [2] and depth estimation [8]. For shape and reflectance estimation, near-planar assumption is held in some works for simplicity. To reduce the amount of required labeled training data, Li et al. [17] propose to leverage the appearance information embedded in unlabeled images of spatially varying materials to self-augment the training process. Deschaintre et al. [7] and Li et al. [18] train CNNs to regress SVBRDF and surface normal of a near-planar surface from a single image using in-network rendering to provide additional supervision during training. In contrast, our approach learns to reconstruct shape and

---

[1] http://cseweb.ucsd.edu/~viscomp/projects/ECCV20NeuralRelighting/.

BRDF parameters and synthesize relighted images jointly, where the relighting constraint can improve the reconstruction by a large margin compared to the in-network rendering layer.

Image-Based Relighting. Image-based relighting methods offer realistic rendering of images under novel illumination without modeling the scene by directly reconstructing the light transport function and the reflectance field. Previous methods on light transport acquisition use either brute-force [6] or sparse sampling [20,25,26]. Debevec et al. [6] proposes a dense fixed-pattern sampling method to render faces under arbitrary changes in lighting and viewing direction based on recorded imagery. The complete 8D reflectance field, which describes the light transport from the incident light field to the outgoing light field, can be simplified to a 4D function with a fixed viewpoint and 2D incident illumination [25,26]. Recently, neural network-based method [28] leverages a neural network to exploit the non-linear local coherence in the light transport matrix using sparse image samples. Xu et al. [35] do relighting with five image samples captured under pre-defined directional lights using a deep neural network trained on a large, synthetically rendered dataset. These works demonstrate high-quality results by modeling the complex light transport, but require multiple images to achieve this. In contrast, our method can relight images based on a single input image under a collocated light source, without explicitly learning the light transport. In addition to the relighting constraint, our method also leverages BRDF reconstruction for auxiliary learning. This allows our work to pose the two problems as a joint learning problem in a single network, leading to significant improvements.

Cascaded Network Architecture. Cascaded models have been effective in different tasks such as human pose estimation [22,34], face detection [16] and object detection [5]. For example, Newell et al. [22] propose eight-stacked hourglass networks to do repeated bottom-up, top-down processing with intermediate supervision to produce more accurate part detection. For shape and SVBRDF estimation, Li et al. [19] use a cascade model to refine the estimation, taking rendering error as input to the following stage. Similarly, our model consists of several cascades, whose effectiveness is shown for both SVBRDF estimation and image relighting in our experiments, for example, in Tables 1 and 2.

3 Method

Given a single image of a complex shape captured under a flash light and environment illumination, our method can reconstruct the shape and spatially-varying BRDF, while simultaneously synthesizing new images under novel lighting. We solve this problem by training a cascaded CNN that derives intuitions from a physically-based rendering process. The framework is illustrated in Fig. 2.

Preliminaries and Notation. Our microfacet BRDF model follows [15]. Let A, N, R, D be the diffuse albedo, normal, roughness and depth, respectively.

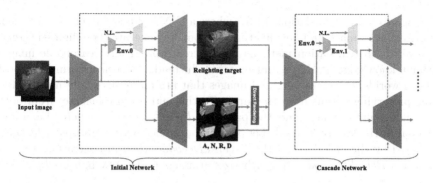

Fig. 2. Overview of the proposed network architecture. We use different colors to visualize various functional components (blue for encoder, green for *InverseDecoder* used for BRDF estimation, and red for *RelightDecoder* used for relighting). Our design consists of an initial model and several cascade stages for iterative refinement. **Left:** The initial model has one encoder for feature extraction and two decoders for BRDF estimation and relighting. The input has either four (without environment lighting) or seven channels (with environment lighting). Besides using skip connections between the encoder and the two decoders, we also feed the features from *InverseDecoder* to *RelightDecoder* to simulate a physically-based rendering process (shown as red dotted arrows). **Right:** The cascade stage is similar to the initial model. It takes the outputs from the first stage and the original inputs as input, leading to a fifteen-channel input. **Abbreviations:** N.L: new light. Env.X: the estimated environment map in the X-th cascade. A, N, R, D: albedo, normal, roughness and depth. (Color figure online)

Let l and v be light and view directions and h be the half-vector. Our BRDF model is:

$$f(A, N, R, l) = \frac{A}{\pi} + \frac{\hat{D}(h, R)\hat{F}(V, h)\hat{G}(l, v, h, R)}{4(N \cdot l)(N \cdot v)} \tag{1}$$

where $\hat{D}(h, R)$, $\hat{F}(v, h)$ and $\hat{G}(l, v, h, R)$ are the distribution, Fresnel and geometric terms, respectively. Since we may use point lights for rendering, depth maps are used for computing the attenuation according to the distance from the light source to the surface. Given (1), an intuitive approach to single-image relighting is to re-render the image with estimated BRDF parameters. Given estimated parameters $\tilde{A}$, $\tilde{N}$, $\tilde{R}$, with a novel lighting l_{new}, the relighted image I_{new} is:

$$I_{new} = f(\tilde{A}, \tilde{N}, \tilde{R}, l_{new}). \tag{2}$$

3.1 Motivation for Our Design

Although there exist reconstruction methods such as [19] that can produce high-quality estimations, relighting by directly rendering the estimated parameters does not take advantage of any details from the original image. Such image details are removed in the reconstruction step, which results in a loss of detail that might also be useful for new image synthesis. Another intuitive way for relighting can be image-to-image translation [13,37] where a U-Net [30] architecture is trained, taking a single image and new lighting as input, to generate the relighted target. However, such translation methods fail to create physically reasonable images without knowledge of shape and material. Instead, we seek to bring the best of both worlds, to create relighted images that are more physically meaningful, while preserving details from the input. To this end, we use features from both the original input image and the proposed $InverseDecoder$ where shape and material intrinsics are learned. Let f_{enc} and f_{inv} be the two groups of features extracted by the encoder and the $InverseDecoder$, then in contrast to (2), we propose a $RelightDecoder$ to synthesize an image under new lighting l_{new}:

$$I_{new} = RelightDecoder(f_{enc}, f_{inv}, l_{new}) \tag{3}$$

Jointly training for the forward and inverse tasks has the advantage that our reconstruction effectively benefits from training under different relighting directions, allowing learning of complex relationships between appearance and lighting directions for an object with arbitrary SVBRDF. This arguably allows higher accuracy and better generalization.

3.2   Joint SVBRDF Estimation and Relighting

Our model is built upon an encoder-decoder architecture, which consists of a single shared encoder and two decoders for reconstruction and relighting. Among the three components, there are skip connections used for feature sharing. The input to our encoder consists of a single image, I_{src}, captured under a collocated point light and a mask, M, stacked with the source image. While our formulation is more general, we choose this setup for convenience since a light source collocated with the camera can minimize cast shadows and high-frequency specularities, allowing better observation of the details of shape and material [12,29].

SVBRDF Estimation. Unlike [18,19], which use multiple decoders to reconstruct different parameters, we use only a single decoder, called $InverseDecoder$, to reconstruct the different shape and BRDF parameters: diffuse albedo (A), specular roughness (R), surface normal (N) and depth (D). Since all the parameters correspond to the properties of a particular shape and material, there are internal correlations among them, so we use a single decoder to learn the internal correlations and predict the parameters jointly rather than independently. Compared to [19], we observe that the design for ours not only has faster runtime speed and fewer parameters, but also can achieve higher quality estimations.

Relighting. For relighting, we introduce $RelightDecoder$ which takes as input a new lighting vector as well as the feature maps from the encoder and $InverseDecoder$. Instead of being fed into the $RelightDecoder$ directly, the target lighting position, l_{new}, is encoded by a light mapping block that contains three fully connected layers. After concatenating the encoder feature with the lighting vector, we feed it to the $RelightDecoder$, which then creates a new image for the shape and material under a novel light source.

Feature Sharing. As shown in Fig. 2, in addition to using skip connections to transfer the encoder features to the two decoders for retaining spatial details, we also build skip connections between the *InverseDecoder* and the *RelightDecoder*. This design is inspired by the physically-based rendering where a realistic image is formed by the interaction of shape and BRDF with incident illumination. This allows joint training of the two different but related tasks: reconstruction and relighting, allowing the latent space to encode how appearances vary with light source positions for various shape and SVBRDF configurations. This bidirectional connection provides physical hints for image relighting to produce photorealistic results, as well as introducing additional supervision for SVBRDF estimation, while most other works tend to use non-learnable in-network rendering layers to achieve this. Thus, this skip connection between leads to significant improvements in relighting and SVBRDF reconstruction compared with previous works.

Standard encoder-decoder methods such as [33,36] do well on relighting faces with environment lighting, but not for complex shapes with arbitrary SVBRDF under point lights. Qualitatively, we show in Fig. 1 that an image translation method does not handle specularities, while our method produces photorealistic outputs since it is physically-motivated. Indeed, the joint learning of relighting and SVBRDF requires new design choices. In Table 1, we quantitatively show that our architecture does better than a single encoder-decoder by ablation study.

Environment Map. In practice, environment illumination is always present outside of darkroom settings, which has a significant effect on the appearance. In addition to relighting under only a point light, our method can also be generalized to relighting under a point light with an arbitrary unknown environment map. To make our model environment-aware, we append a new branch to our encoder to predict environment maps modeled by spherical harmonics (SH). For each color channel, our network estimates the first nine SH coefficients. Following [19], we add an image with the background to our input which can provide more context information for SH coefficient estimation. Thus, the input to our network with environment map estimation has seven channels.

Cascade Refinement. The level of detail required for SVBRDF reconstruction and relighting for complex shape is often too high for a single encoder-decoder architecture. Similar to [19], we use a cascaded network to refine our estimation. Let $\tilde{A}_n, \tilde{N}_n, \tilde{R}_n, \tilde{D}_n, I_n^{ren}$ be the SVBRDF estimates and direct rendered image of the n-th cascade. Let *InitialNet* and *CascadeNet* be our basic model and cascade models, then our entire model is:

$$I_0^{new}, \tilde{A}_0, \tilde{N}_0, \tilde{R}_0, \tilde{D}_0 = InitialNet(I_{src}, M)$$
$$I_n^{new}, \tilde{A}_n, \tilde{N}_n, \tilde{R}_n, \tilde{D}_n = CascadeNet(I_{src}, M, \tilde{A_{n-1}}, \tag{4}$$
$$\tilde{N_{n-1}}, \tilde{R_{n-1}}, \tilde{D_{n-1}}, I_{n-1}^{new}, I_{n-1}^{ren})$$

The effectiveness of our cascade is quantitatively demonstrated in Table 1 and Table 2. With two cascade stages, both reconstruction and relighting are significantly improved qualitatively and quantitatively.

3.3   Training Details

Training Data. To our best understanding, there is no such large-scale dataset that includes both BRDF parameters and various images illuminated under different light sources. Thus, we adopt the shapes and BRDF parameters of the synthetic dataset from [19] and render a new dataset. We implement a rendering layer using the BRDF model defined by Eq. 1 with PyTorch [24] deep learning framework and CUDA acceleration. Instead of pre-rendering all the training set, we render images in an online manner. For each iteration, we render relighting target image under random point light sources as the supervision. In this way, our model can see more varied samples as our ground-truth are rendered with a larger set of lights compared with an offline rendering method. We define the position of the point light as the hemisphere in front of the shape.

Network Design. We implement the *InitialNet* with large receptive fields to capture the appearance. Our encoder has six convolutional layers with strides of 2. Except for the first layer whose kernel size is 6, all following layers have a kernel size of 4. For *InverseDecoder* and *RelightDecoder*, we use transposed convolutions for decoding and skip links to retain details, with a kernel size of 4 and stride of 2. Instead of feeding the feature from the encoder to *RelightDecoder* directly, we first map the input light to a lighting code using three fully connected layers. The encoded lighting vector is concatenated with the encoder features and then passed to the *RelightDecoder*. We concatenate both the feature from the encoder and *InverseDecoder* to the *RelightDecoder*. For environment estimation, we pass the highest-level feature from the encoder through two fully connected layers to regress the 3×9 coefficients. For *CascadeNet*, it has the same structure and feature sharing mechanism as the *InitialNet* but has fewer network layers.

Loss Function. We use L2 loss as supervision for BRDF estimation and image relighting. We use the inverse transformation in [19] to project it into a fixed range. Given an estimation $\tilde{I}$ and its ground truth I, the L2 loss $\mathcal{L}$ is given by

$$\mathcal{L} = \frac{1}{\Sigma_{i,j} M_{i,j}} \cdot \|(I - \tilde{I}) \cdot M\|_2^2 \tag{5}$$

Let $\mathcal{L}_a$, $\mathcal{L}_n$, $\mathcal{L}_r$, $\mathcal{L}_d$, $\mathcal{L}_{env}$, $\mathcal{L}_{relit}$ be the L2 losses for albedo, normal, roughness, depth, environment map and relighting, the final loss function for our network is:

$$\mathcal{L} = \lambda_a \mathcal{L}_a + \lambda_n \mathcal{L}_n + \lambda_r \mathcal{L}_r + \lambda_d \mathcal{L}_d + \lambda_{env} \mathcal{L}_{env} + \lambda_{relit} \mathcal{L}_{relit} \tag{6}$$

where $\lambda_a = \lambda_n = \lambda_{relit} = 1$, $\lambda_r = \lambda_d = 0.5$ and $\lambda_{env} = 0.01$.

Training Strategy. We train the networks stage-by-stage. We use a batch size of 16. We use Adam optimizer, with an initial learning rate of 10^{-4} for encoder and 2×10^{-4} for decoders and decrease it by half after every two epochs. We train the initial stage and the two cascade stages for 14, 10 and 9 epochs, respectively.

4   Experiments

We validate the effectiveness of our method with evaluations on synthetic and real data, with comparisons on both relighting and SVBRDF estimation. Please see the supplementary material for several further examples.

4.1   Ablation Study

Feature Sharing. When training our *RelightDecoder*, we feed the features from the encoder, as well as the features from *InverseDecoder* to simulate a physics-based rendering process, which gives a better performance compared with that without feature sharing. According to the first three experiments— Inv, Relit, Inv-Relit-C0 in Table 1, it turns out that both the relighting and the reconstruction performance get improved by feature sharing. For relighting, the skip connections between the encoder and *RelightDecoder* give our model the ability to retain details from the original image, while the features from *InverseDecoder* help the *RelightDecoder* to learn a physics-based rendering process. Thus, the relighting performance exceeds both the reconstruction-based method and image-to-image translation method with a large gap. For BRDF reconstruction, a re-rendering loss is proven to be useful in reconstruction tasks [7,18,19]. For the *InverseRender*, we apply L2 loss to all the estimated parameters explicitly, as well as an implicit supervision from the relighting branch, which plays a role similar to the re-rendering loss in aforementioned works. In forward phase of training, features from the *InverseDecoder* are passed to the *RelightDecoder*. Then, the gradients from the *RelightDecoder* will be back-propagated to the *InverseDecoder* in backward phase, acting as an implicit supervision. Thus, a joint training of the two tasks gives a significant improvement for both tasks.

Environment Map. For the relighting task under an environment mapping as well as a point light, a possible concern can be whether the environment background helps. We train two variants of our *InitialNet* – one with only a masked image as input and the other with both masked and original images as input. Quantitative comparison between the first two columns of Table 2 show that both relighting and BRDF estimation are improved with a context input.

Cascade Design. We show the effectiveness of our cascade design by the quantitative result in Table 1 and 2. By adding two cascades after the *InitialNet*, both of the two tasks are improved significantly. In our experiment, we find that more cascade stages do not provide very significant improvement, and are expensive to train and hard to fit in memory in inference. Thus, two cascade stage suffices.

Table 1. Quantitative results of different architecture choices for both SVBRDF reconstruction and relighting under only a point light source. Inv means a *InverseDecoder* is trained. Relit means training a *RelightDecoder*. Inv-Relit means we train the *RelightDecoder* with feature sharing from *InverseDecoder*. The *Render* column in right hand of the table means relighting using the reconstructed BRDF and the novel lighting. Cn means cascade stage n and C0 is the initial stage. By default, we use MSE and the magnitude is 10^{-2}. In addition to MSE, we compute the multi-scale structural similarity (MS-SSIM) between our relighting results and its targets.

	A	N	R	D	Render	Relight	MS-SSIM
Inv	1.64	4.02	4.65	1.80	1.42	-	-
Relit	-	-	-	-	-	1.18	0.867
Inv-Relit-C0	1.57	3.67	4.31	1.74	1.31	1.07	0.888
Inv-Relit-C1	1.43	3.42	4.18	1.55	1.20	1.02	0.889
Inv-Relit-C2	**1.39**	**3.32**	**4.18**	**1.44**	**1.14**	**0.99**	**0.893**

Table 2. Quantitative comparison results for our design choices under environment illumination. I_p^e means an image illuminated by both point light and environment map, -bg means a background image is taken as input.

	I_p^e	I_p^e-bg-C0	I_p^e-bg-C1	I_p^e-bg-C2
Albedo (10^{-2})	1.386	1.324	1.166	**1.157**
Normal (10^{-2})	3.741	3.608	3.344	**3.340**
Roughness (10^{-2})	4.486	4.447	4.305	**4.289**
Depth (10^{-2})	1.802	1.747	1.467	**1.455**
Relight (10^{-3})	9.194	9.062	8.630	**8.626**
Relight (MS-SSIM)	0.892	0.902	0.907	**0.908**

Table 3. Quantitative comparison with [19] on shape and SVBRDF reconstruction, using their proposed test set. (MSE, 10^{-2})

	Li et al.	Ours
Albedo	1.215	**1.157**
Normal	3.822	**3.340**
Rough	4.858	**4.289**
Depth	1.505	**1.455**

4.2   Generalization to Real Data

We use real images to demonstrate that our method can generalize to real data in Fig. 3 and 4. Real images are captured using an iPhone with the flash enabled. For relighting under a single point light, images are captured in a darkroom. It is evident that our method produces accurate SVBRDF estimations and relighting outputs, with high-quality shadows and specular highlights under various lights.

We provide ground-truth comparison using two examples in DiLiGenT dataset [31], as well as our own captured images. For DiLiGenT dataset, note that the images are captured under directional lights, so the images are not exactly matched to our relighting task. We demonstrate our approach by using its ground-truth as reference. We take as input the images acquired under a directional light that is approximately collocated to the camera. For each light direction, our method uses a point light source to approximate it. Example results in Fig. 5 show that our network is robust enough to yield plausible results on real inputs which do not correspond to the training assumptions. In Fig. 6, we show

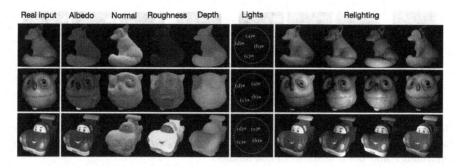

Fig. 3. Reconstruction and relighting results on real data illuminated by the flash light of mobile phone in a darkroom. The input images are shown on the first column, and the following four columns show the BRDF reconstructions. The remaining columns show the light sources and relighting images illuminated under the corresponding lights. The new lights are shown as orange points in a unit circle projected from a hemisphere. (Color figure online)

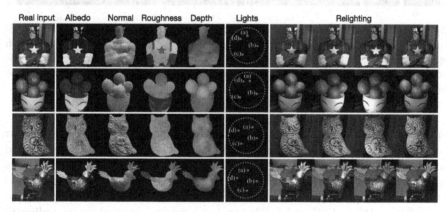

Fig. 4. Results on real images illuminated by a flash light and indoor environment.

two groups of ground-truth comparison with real images, as well as the results from [19]. Images are captured using a gantry, where we bind a cellphone flash to simulate a point light. The results demonstrate that our method can produce realistic relighting images while also reducing the artifacts.

4.3 Comparative Study

We do comparisons study in two aspects, image relighting and SVBRDF estimation. First, we compare our proposed method with previous works for shape and material estimation and intrinsic image decomposition. Then, we include a comprehensive comparison with [19] to show our superior in both tasks.

Comparisons on SVBRDF Estimation with Previous Works. For SVBRDF estimation, we compare our work with [3,19,32]. The diffuse albedo

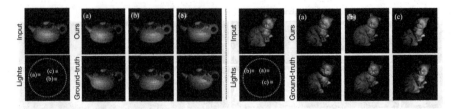

Fig. 5. Relighting results on DiLiGenT dataset consisting of real images. We use the images illuminated by directional lights as reference to demonstrate our relighting performance and the robustness of our method.

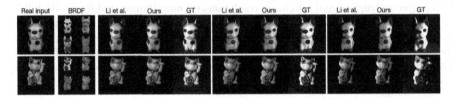

Fig. 6. Comparison between our relighting results with [19], as well as the ground-truth. We capture these ground-truth images using a gantry with a cellphone flash light bound to it. Note that our method can produce realistic results compared to the ground-truth. Limitation: in some cases, cast shadows cannot be produced (e.g. the third of the cat).

estimation with [19,32] is shown in Fig. 7. By comparison, we observe that our SVBRDF estimation is comparable with the state-of-the-art method [19] and outperforms [32] significantly. The result of [32] is smooth and lots of details lost in reconstruction. By contrast, our methods can produce a more detailed estimation. We provide normal estimation comparison in Fig. 7. Our method outperforms [19] and [3] and produce more accurate estimations according to the visual quality. Obviously, for the owl shape which is full of bumps, Li et al. [19] fail to recover a high-quality normal, while our method produces a superior result.

Quantitative Comparison with [19] for SVBRDF Estimation. We provide a quantitative comparison with [19] using their test set, in Table 3. We obtain significantly improvements for all components of shape and SVBRDF. This shows that our joint learning allows insights from the forward problem to benefit the inverse problem, in comparison to [19] which focuses only on the inverse problem.

Qualitative Comparisons with [19] on Real Data. We also compare with [19] for reconstruction and relighting on real images acquired by a mobile phone camera. To relight in the case of [19], we apply forward rendering using the estimated SVBRDF, while our relighting output is predicted by the network. In Fig. 8, green rectangles show artifacts introduced by [19] due to inaccuracy in the estimation of surface normal and roughness, while the visual quality of

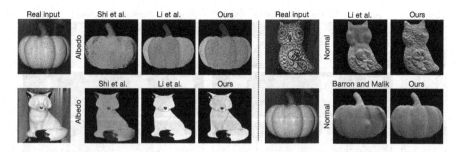

Fig. 7. Comparison on shape and material reconstruction with previous works on real data. **Left:** We compare the diffuse albedo estimation with [19,32]. Our method outperforms [32] significantly in visual quality and is also comparable with the state-of-the-art method [19]. **Right:** We use two real images to compare the normal estimation with [3,19]. For a shape full of bumps (the owl), our method produces a more accurate and superior result than [19]. For the pumpkin shape, the accuracy and visual quality of our normal is significantly higher compared with that of [3].

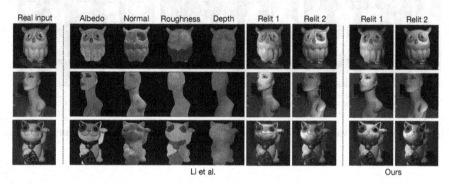

Fig. 8. Comparison with [19] on relighting a real image. Since we learn to jointly relight, our relighting results are less susceptible to errors in shape or SVBRDF estimation. (Color figure online)

ours is better. Figure 9 shows that our SVBRDF estimation is also qualitatively better. The video in our supplementary material shows further comparisons.

4.4 Environment Illumination Editing

In addition to relighting under a new light source, our model may also be fine-tuned to allow relighting with a novel environment map. For the new environment map, we compute the SH coefficients. Then, we replace the estimated environment coefficients with the new ones as input to the *RelightDecoder*. The environment editing model is fine-tuned on the pre-trained model without any cascade stages involved. Example results are shown in Fig. 11. Note that the

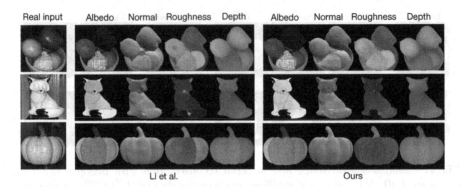

Fig. 9. Comparison with [19] on SVBRDF estimation on real images. While both methods produce high-quality estimates, some factors such as roughness are better estimated by our method.

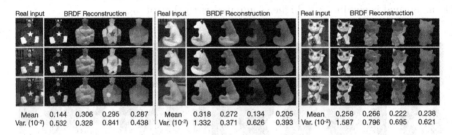

Mean	0.144	0.306	0.295	0.287	Mean	0.318	0.272	0.134	0.205	Mean	0.258	0.266	0.222	0.238
Var. (10⁻²)	0.532	0.328	0.841	0.438	Var. (10⁻²)	1.332	0.371	0.626	0.393	Var. (10⁻²)	1.587	0.796	0.695	0.621

Fig. 10. Mean and variance of SVBRDF estimation under various environment maps.

edited images display realistic shading variations, shadows and specularities. We also include examples of environment illumination editing in the supplementary video.

4.5   Variance Under Different Environment Maps

It is non-trivial to obtain ground-truth shape and material measurements aligned with input images. So, we report variance in estimation outputs with different environment maps as an indirect indicator of the accuracy. Using a turntable setup, we acquire images of the same object when illuminated by different parts of an indoor environment. In Fig. 10, we show the average across all pixels of the mean and variance of SVBRDF estimates. While some qualitative differences in roughness are understandable for such an underconstrained problem, we observe that variances are quite low, indicating the overall accuracy.

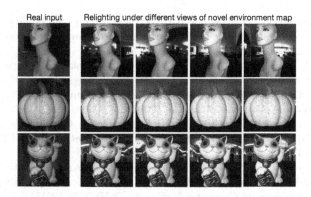

Fig. 11. Given a single real image as input, our network relights it under a new environment map. Four different views are shown in the figure. Note the recovery of fine details, such as the green, violet and red tinges on objects in the three rows, reflecting the colors in the corresponding environment maps. (Color figure online)

5   Conclusion and Future Work

We present a joint learning approach to reconstruct object shape and SVBRDF, while relighting it under a new light source given only a single image captured by a mobile phone camera. We achieve this by training a cascaded CNN with feature sharing mechanism between the two branches, following the intuition of a physically-based rendering process. Our model is able to progressively refine the estimates, leading to high-quality reconstruction and relighting results on both synthetic and real data. Our future work includes extending the light sources from point lights to a more general illumination. Another direction that can be explored in the future is to study how multiple highly-correlated tasks in forward and inverse rendering can benefit from a joint learning strategy.

Acknowledgments. This work was supported by NSF CAREER 1751365, along with generous gifts from a Google Research Award and Adobe Research. This work was done during Shen Sang's graduate studies at UC San Diego.

References

1. Aittala, M., Weyrich, T., Lehtinen, J., et al.: Two-shot SVBRDF capture for stationary materials. ACM Trans. Graph. **34**(4), 110-1 (2015)
2. Bansal, A., Russell, B., Gupta, A.: Marr revisited: 2D–3D alignment via surface normal prediction. In: Proceedings of the IEEE Conference on Computer Vision and Pattern Recognition, pp. 5965–5974 (2016)
3. Barron, J.T., Malik, J.: Shape, illumination, and reflectance from shading. IEEE Trans. Pattern Anal. Mach. Intell. **37**(8), 1670–1687 (2014)
4. Bell, S., Upchurch, P., Snavely, N., Bala, K.: Material recognition in the wild with the materials in context database. In: Proceedings of the IEEE Conference on Computer Vision and Pattern Recognition, pp. 3479–3487 (2015)

5. Cai, Z., Vasconcelos, N.: Cascade R-CNN: delving into high quality object detection. In: Proceedings of the IEEE Conference on Computer Vision and Pattern Recognition, pp. 6154–6162 (2018)
6. Debevec, P., Hawkins, T., Tchou, C., Duiker, H.P., Sarokin, W., Sagar, M.: Acquiring the reflectance field of a human face. In: Proceedings of the 27th Annual Conference on Computer Graphics and Interactive Techniques, pp. 145–156. ACM Press/Addison-Wesley Publishing Co. (2000)
7. Deschaintre, V., Aittala, M., Durand, F., Drettakis, G., Bousseau, A.: Single-image SVBRDF capture with a rendering-aware deep network. ACM Trans. Graph. (TOG) 37(4), 128 (2018)
8. Eigen, D., Fergus, R.: Predicting depth, surface normals and semantic labels with a common multi-scale convolutional architecture. In: Proceedings of the IEEE International Conference on Computer Vision, pp. 2650–2658 (2015)
9. Gardner, M.A., et al.: Learning to predict indoor illumination from a single image. arXiv preprint arXiv:1704.00090 (2017)
10. Georgoulis, S., Rematas, K., Ritschel, T., Fritz, M., Tuytelaars, T., Van Gool, L.: What is around the camera? In: Proceedings of the IEEE International Conference on Computer Vision, pp. 5170–5178 (2017)
11. Hold-Geoffroy, Y., Sunkavalli, K., Hadap, S., Gambaretto, E., Lalonde, J.F.: Deep outdoor illumination estimation. In: Proceedings of the IEEE Conference on Computer Vision and Pattern Recognition, pp. 7312–7321 (2017)
12. Hui, Z., Sankaranarayanan, A.C.: Shape and spatially-varying reflectance estimation from virtual exemplars. IEEE Trans. Pattern Anal. Mach. Intell. 39(10), 2060–2073 (2016)
13. Isola, P., Zhu, J.Y., Zhou, T., Efros, A.A.: Image-to-image translation with conditional adversarial networks. arXiv (2016)
14. Johnson, M.K., Adelson, E.H.: Shape estimation in natural illumination. In: CVPR 2011, pp. 2553–2560. IEEE (2011)
15. Karis, B., Games, E.: Real shading in unreal engine 4. In: Proceedings of the Physically Based Shading Theory Practice, vol. 4 (2013)
16. Li, H., Lin, Z., Shen, X., Brandt, J., Hua, G.: A convolutional neural network cascade for face detection. In: Proceedings of the IEEE Conference on Computer Vision and Pattern Recognition, pp. 5325–5334 (2015)
17. Li, X., Dong, Y., Peers, P., Tong, X.: Modeling surface appearance from a single photograph using self-augmented convolutional neural networks. ACM Trans. Graph. (TOG) 36(4), 45 (2017)
18. Li, Z., Sunkavalli, K., Chandraker, M.: Materials for masses: SVBRDF acquisition with a single mobile phone image. In: Ferrari, V., Hebert, M., Sminchisescu, C., Weiss, Y. (eds.) ECCV 2018. LNCS, vol. 11207, pp. 74–90. Springer, Cham (2018). https://doi.org/10.1007/978-3-030-01219-9_5
19. Li, Z., Xu, Z., Ramamoorthi, R., Sunkavalli, K., Chandraker, M.: Learning to reconstruct shape and spatially-varying reflectance from a single image. In: SIGGRAPH Asia 2018 Technical Papers, p. 269. ACM (2018)
20. Matusik, W., Loper, M., Pfister, H.: Progressively-refined reflectance functions from natural illumination. In: Rendering Techniques, pp. 299–308 (2004)
21. Meka, A., et al.: Lime: live intrinsic material estimation. In: Proceedings of the IEEE Conference on Computer Vision and Pattern Recognition, pp. 6315–6324 (2018)

22. Newell, A., Yang, K., Deng, J.: Stacked hourglass networks for human pose estimation. In: Leibe, B., Matas, J., Sebe, N., Welling, M. (eds.) ECCV 2016. LNCS, vol. 9912, pp. 483–499. Springer, Cham (2016). https://doi.org/10.1007/978-3-319-46484-8_29

23. Oxholm, G., Nishino, K.: Shape and reflectance estimation in the wild. IEEE Trans. Pattern Anal. Mach. Intell. **38**(2), 376–389 (2015)

24. Paszke, A., et al.: Automatic differentiation in PyTorch (2017)

25. Peers, P., Dutré, P.: Inferring reflectance functions from wavelet noise. In: Proceedings of the Sixteenth Eurographics conference on Rendering Techniques, pp. 173–182. Eurographics Association (2005)

26. Peers, P., et al.: Compressive light transport sensing. ACM Trans. Graph. (TOG) **28**(1), 3 (2009)

27. Rematas, K., Ritschel, T., Fritz, M., Gavves, E., Tuytelaars, T.: Deep reflectance maps. In: Proceedings of the IEEE Conference on Computer Vision and Pattern Recognition, pp. 4508–4516 (2016)

28. Ren, P., Dong, Y., Lin, S., Tong, X., Guo, B.: Image based relighting using neural networks. ACM Trans. Graph. (TOG) **34**(4), 111 (2015)

29. Riviere, J., Peers, P., Ghosh, A.: Mobile surface reflectometry. In: Computer Graphics Forum, vol. 35, pp. 191–202. Wiley Online Library (2016)

30. Ronneberger, O., Fischer, P., Brox, T.: U-Net: convolutional networks for biomedical image segmentation. In: Navab, N., Hornegger, J., Wells, W.M., Frangi, A.F. (eds.) MICCAI 2015. LNCS, vol. 9351, pp. 234–241. Springer, Cham (2015). https://doi.org/10.1007/978-3-319-24574-4_28

31. Shi, B., Wu, Z., Mo, Z., Duan, D., Yeung, S.K., Tan, P.: A benchmark dataset and evaluation for non-Lambertian and uncalibrated photometric stereo. In: Proceedings of the IEEE Conference on Computer Vision and Pattern Recognition, pp. 3707–3716 (2016)

32. Shi, J., Dong, Y., Su, H., Yu, S.X.: Learning non-Lambertian object intrinsics across ShapeNet categories. In: Proceedings of the IEEE Conference on Computer Vision and Pattern Recognition, pp. 1685–1694 (2017)

33. Sun, T., et al.: Single image portrait relighting. ACM Trans. Graph. **38**(4), 79-1 (2019)

34. Wei, S.E., Ramakrishna, V., Kanade, T., Sheikh, Y.: Convolutional pose machines. In: Proceedings of the IEEE Conference on Computer Vision and Pattern Recognition, pp. 4724–4732 (2016)

35. Xu, Z., Sunkavalli, K., Hadap, S., Ramamoorthi, R.: Deep image-based relighting from optimal sparse samples. ACM Trans. Graph. (TOG) **37**(4), 126 (2018)

36. Zhou, H., Hadap, S., Sunkavalli, K., Jacobs, D.W.: Deep single-image portrait relighting. In: Proceedings of the IEEE International Conference on Computer Vision, pp. 7194–7202 (2019)

37. Zhu, J.Y., Park, T., Isola, P., Efros, A.A.: Unpaired image-to-image translation using cycle-consistent adversarial networks. In: 2017 IEEE International Conference on Computer Vision (ICCV) (2017)

Unsupervised 3D Human Pose Representation with Viewpoint and Pose Disentanglement

Qiang Nie[1,2] ⬤, Ziwei Liu[1] ⬤, and Yunhui Liu[1,2(✉)] ⬤

[1] The Chinese University of Hong Kong, Shatin, N.T., Hong Kong
{qnie,yhliu}@mae.cuhk.edu.hk, zwliu@ie.cuhk.edu.hk
[2] T Stone Robotics Institute of CUHK, Shatin, Hong Kong

Abstract. Learning a good 3D human pose representation is important for human pose related tasks, *e.g.* human 3D pose estimation and action recognition. Within all these problems, *preserving the intrinsic pose information* and *adapting to view variations* are two critical issues. In this work, we propose a novel Siamese denoising autoencoder to learn a 3D pose representation by disentangling the pose-dependent and view-dependent feature from the human skeleton data, in a fully unsupervised manner. These two disentangled features are utilized together as the representation of the 3D pose. To consider both the kinematic and geometric dependencies, a sequential bidirectional recursive network (SeBiReNet) is further proposed to model the human skeleton data. Extensive experiments demonstrate that the learned representation 1) preserves the intrinsic information of human pose, 2) shows good transferability across datasets and tasks. Notably, our approach achieves state-of-the-art performance on two inherently different tasks: pose denoising and unsupervised action recognition. Code and models are available at: https://github.com/NIEQiang001/unsupervised-human-pose.git.

Keywords: Representation learning · 3D human pose · Pose denoising · Unsupervised action recognition

1 Introduction

Human action recognition and human behavior analysis have extensive applications on human-robot interaction (HRI) systems, such as health caring, entertainment, education, security and many other intelligent surveillance scenarios, which also makes the 3D human pose estimation a hot research topic for many decades. Learning a good human 3D pose representation has great significance both to the research of human action recognition and the human pose estimation.

Electronic supplementary material The online version of this chapter (https://doi.org/10.1007/978-3-030-58529-7_7) contains supplementary material, which is available to authorized users.

While understanding the human pose is a challenging task, which requires the computer to learn the dependencies between joints of the human skeleton robustly in different viewpoints. These dependencies include kinematic relationships between joints and geometric features of the human body. The kinematic relationship describes the motion transmission process between joints and the role of each joint in an action. The geometric feature refers to those specific appearance characteristics of the human body, such as fixed bone lengths and the symmetry between left and right limbs. Many existing works have utilized the geometric features of the human body [13,17,18,22,36], but few works are capable to model the kinematic relationships between human body joints. Kinematics is a physical process and hard to be modeled by regular CNN, RNN or MLP neural networks. Hence, we proposed a sequential bidirectional recursive network (SeBiReNet) to model the dependencies of the human skeleton.

Besides the dependencies between joints, the human 3D pose presents infinite modalities when recorded or observed from different viewpoints, which makes the processing of the human 3D pose quite intractable for the intelligent system. Increasing the size of training dataset with different views may be effective. However, it's impossible to record the data from all possible viewpoints. To tackle the view variation, some previous works applied preprocessing treatment to eliminate the view variation [3,12]. These methods are always dataset dependent because of the specifically designed preprocessing method. Many other methods [6,16,23,29,32,32] extracted hand-crafted view-invariant features as pose descriptors based on the prior knowledge of human beings. Although these hand-crafted features are view-invariant, there is information loss in extracting these features as only a few explanatory factors are considered. There are some methods [3,9,35] trying to learn discriminative pose representations using the deep learning method. However, the transferability of the representations learned by existing approaches in different datasets and different tasks is limited.

Human pose result from the rich interaction of many factors, such as the subject, the action, and the viewpoint. Learning view-invariant features means to extract features that are insensitive to the direction of view variation, which also means some features that are sensitive to the variations but informative are discarded. As Bengio et al. [2] mentioned, "a better way to overcome these challenges is to leverage the data itself, ..., to disentangle as many factors as possible and discarding as little information about the data as in practice".

Motivated by aforementioned issues, we propose an unsupervised method for learning a latent representation of the human 3D pose by disentangling the pose-dependent and view-dependent features from human skeleton data. We introduce a novel SeBiReNet to model the human skeleton data. A Siamese denoising autoencoder based on the SeBiReNet is designed to learn the latent human pose representation. Ability of denoising corrupted skeletons from an unseen dataset proves the learned representation preserves the intrinsic information of human pose, including both the kinematic and geometric dependencies. Disentangling the pose-dependent (view-invariant) and view-dependent (view-variant) feature from skeleton data other than extracting the view-invariant feature enables us to transfer the viewpoint of human pose in the latent space, which is used as a strengthened regularization in our training process.

We summarize our contributions as follows:

- We propose a novel SeBiReNet to model the kinematic dependencies between body joints in the human skeleton data.
- Based on SeBiReNet, a Siamese denosing autoencoder is proposed for learning 3D human pose representation with feature disentanglement. The unsupervisedly learned pose representation 1) preserves the intrinsic information of human pose, 2) shows good transferability across datasets and tasks.
- Extensive experiments demonstrate that state-of-the-art performance can be achieved when applying the learned representation on two inherently different tasks: pose denoising and unsupervised action recognition.

2   Related Works

2.1   Modeling Human 3D Poses

To understand the human 3D pose, the most important is to figure out the dependencies between body joints, which should include both the kinematic and the geometric dependency. Compared to kinematic dependency between joints, geometric characteristic is much easier to model. Ramakrishna et al. [17] used normalized limb lengths as anthropometric regularity to reconstruct 3D human pose from the 2D image landmarks. Sun et al. [22] proposed to use the summation of bone lengths as a supervision loss. The summation of bone length considers all bones between every paired two joints. In essence, the summation of bone lengths is a pairwise geodesic distance. Their work proved that the accuracy of human pose regression can be improved based on the summations of bone length. As ratios between bone lengths remain relatively fixed in a human skeleton, Zhou et al. [36] utilized the length ratios of bones as a weak supervision for reconstructing 3D pose from wild images without 3D annotations. Though human skeleton is similar to the tree structure, few works have applied the recursive network for the human pose modeling. Wei et al. [28] introduced a vanilla tree network for skeleton-based action recognition. However, only the output from the single tree root node is utilized, which is inherently different from the structure of our SeBiReNet proposed to model the human 3D pose.

2.2   Learning Pose Representations

Demisse et al. [3] proposed a denoising autoencoder for unsupervised skeleton-based action recognition by using MLP layers. But to evaluate the extracted features in cross-view action recognition, a preprocessing treatment is applied to estimate the view variation. Li et al. [9] proposed a method to learn pose representation from sequential RGB data by adding a view discriminator to decide which view the learned feature comes from. Using view classifier indicates that their views are depend on the training data and view labels were given. While in our method, the poses are randomly rotated and no view label is given. Zheng et al. [35] presented an adversarial training strategy to learn representations of skeleton sequences for action recognition. Compared to these methods, the proposed method is able to learn a view-invariant pose-dependent feature from single pose without any additional label or auxiliary network. Requiring no temporal information makes our representation can be applied to both time-related or time-independent tasks, as verified in our experiments. It's interesting to find that Aberman et al. [1] applied a similar feature decomposition and re-composition process in their work of retargeting video-captured motion between different human performers. Our method differs with theirs in two aspects: 1) we embed a denoising process in the learning, which helps the network capture the intrinsic feature of skeleton pose; and 2) our disentangled features have more interaction by sharing some weights in the decomposition and multiplying with each other in the re-composition process.

3   Our Approach

3.1   Problem Formulation

Given a human 3D pose x, a latent representation h can be learned by assigning a function f with parameters θ, i.e., $h = f(x; \theta)$. In order to make sure the learned representation contains useful information of original data, h is required to be able to recover the original pose through another function g with parameters ζ. The reconstructed pose can be formulated as $\hat{x} = g(h; \zeta)$, which is the basic idea of autoencoder in representation learning. Vincent et al. [24] has proven that using the denoising autoencoder to reconstruct the clean data from its corrupted version is helpful in avoiding trivial solutions and improving the performance of learned latent representations. Therefore, basically, learning the human 3D pose representation can be formulated as the following equation.

$$\underset{\theta,\zeta}{\arg\min} \, \mathbb{E}_{q(\tilde{x}|x)} L(x, g(h; \zeta)) \tag{1}$$

where $h = f_\theta(\tilde{x})$ is the learned latent representation of the human 3D pose and $\tilde{x}$ is the corrupted pose corresponding to the clean pose x. However, the representation learned in Eq. 1 contains both the pose-dependent and the view-dependent information. As analyzed in Sect. 1, we hope to learn a view-invariant representation as well as avoid discarding the view-dependent feature of human pose for the sake of information preservation. Thus different from traditional methods, we attempt to disentangle the view-invariant feature h_{vi} from view-dependent feature h_v and using the combination of $[h_{vi}, h_v]$ as a latent representation of the human 3D pose. Under this consideration, the representation learning is reformulated as Eq. 2.

$$\underset{\theta_{vi},\theta_v,\zeta}{\arg\min} \, \mathbb{E}_{q(\tilde{x}|x)} L(x, g(h_v \otimes h_{vi}; \zeta)) \tag{2}$$

where $h_{vi} = f(\tilde{x}; \theta_{vi})$ and $h_v = f(\tilde{x}; \theta_v)$. $\otimes$ is an operation to couple h_{vi} and h_v together, which can be matrix multiplication or concatenation. From a generative perspective, the learning process in Eq. 2 can also be written as

$$\underset{\theta_{vi},\theta_v,\zeta}{\arg\max} \mathbb{E}_{q(\tilde{x}|x)} \log \left[p(x|h_{vi}, h_v; \zeta)p(h_{vi}, h_v|\tilde{x}; \theta_{vi}, \theta_v)p(\theta_{vi}, \theta_v) \right] \quad (3)$$

where $q(\tilde{x}|x)$ denotes the pose corruption process. If we assume the prior distribution $p(\theta_{vi}, \theta_v)$ can be factorized as $p(\theta_{vi}, \theta_v) = p(\theta_{vi})p(\theta_v)$, i.e., they are independent. Then we have

$$\log p(h_{vi}, h_v|\tilde{x}; \theta_{vi}, \theta_v)p(\theta_{vi}, \theta_v) = \log p(h_{vi}|\tilde{x}; \theta_{vi})p(\theta_{vi}) + \log p(h_v|\tilde{x}; \theta_v)p(\theta_v) \quad (4)$$

According to Eq. 4, learning of the view-dependent feature and pose-dependent feature don't have much influence on each other. To strengthen the interaction between these two features and disentangle them smoothly, we propose to have $p(h_{vi}|\tilde{x}; \theta_{vi}) = f(\phi(\tilde{x}; \eta); \theta_{vi} \backslash \eta)$ and $p(h_v|\tilde{x}; \theta_v) = f(\phi(\tilde{x}; \eta); \theta_v \backslash \eta)$, where η is the shared parameters in the parameter space. In this manner, h_v and h_{vi} are disentangled and affect each other through the common latent feature $\phi(\tilde{x})$. Although we are trying to disentangle the view-dependent and pose-dependent feature from original pose, this is not necessarily induced so far, as the learned latent representation $[h_{vi}, h_v]$ is still not well constrained. To introduce the concept of viewpoint into the learning process, an additional transformation is added to the corrupted pose $\tilde{x}$ by randomly rotating it in the 3D space. At this circumstance, Eq. 3 becomes

$$\underset{\theta_{vi},\theta_v,\zeta}{\arg\max} \mathbb{E}_{q(\tilde{x}|x)q_r(\tilde{x}_r|\tilde{x})} \log \left[p(x|h_{vi}, h_v; \zeta)p(h_{vi}, h_v|\tilde{x}_r; \theta_{vi}, \theta_v)p(\theta_{vi}, \theta_v) \right] \quad (5)$$

where $\tilde{x}_r$ is the randomly rotated corrupted pose corresponding to $\tilde{x}$, $q_r(\tilde{x}_r|\tilde{x})$ denotes the random rotation process. A marginal distribution consistency of $p(h_{vi})$ should be satisfied from corrupted pose $\tilde{x}$ and randomly rotated pose $\tilde{x}_r$. Thus, besides the pose reconstruction loss, we regularize the pose-dependent feature by minimizing the Kullback–Leibler divergence between pose-dependent features of poses under different observation angles as shown in Eq. 6.

$$\underset{\theta_{vi},\theta_v}{\arg\min} D_{KL}(p(h_{vi}|\tilde{x}; \theta_{vi})||p(h_{vi}|\tilde{x}_r; \theta_{vi})) \quad (6)$$

Putting all together, our human 3D pose representation learning process is modelled as

$$\underset{\theta_{vi},\theta_v,\zeta}{\arg\min} \mathbb{E}_{q(\tilde{x}|x)} \left[L(x, g(h_v \otimes h_{vi}, \tilde{x}; \zeta)) + q_r(\tilde{x}_r|\tilde{x})L(x, g(h_v \otimes h_{vi}, \tilde{x}_r; \zeta)) \right] +$$

$$D_{KL}(p(h_{vi}|\tilde{x}; \theta_{vi})||p(h_{vi}|\tilde{x}_r; \theta_{vi})) \quad (7)$$

3.2   Sequential Bidirectional Recursive Network

In order to capture the kinematic dependencies of human skeleton structure, a sequential bidirectional recursive neural network (SeBiReNet) is proposed. The

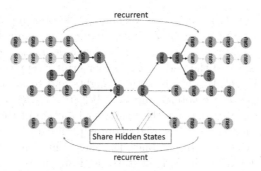

Fig. 1. The proposed sequential bidirectional recursive neural network (SeBiReNet). Each node corresponds to a real joint of the human body and different colors represent different body parts

bidirectional recursive neural network has two tree structures as shown in Fig. 1, which models the human skeleton structure intuitively. The recursive neural network is widely used for text or language analysis [7, 21] due to its ability in summarising the semantic meanings. However, the conventional recursive neural network has only one direction, which means the information can only flow from leaf nodes to the root node. On the contrary, the motion of the human body is transmitted from parent joint to child joints. Usually, to determine the position of a joint, both the position of parent joint and the positions of child joints have to be considered. In this regards, the proposed SeBiReNet models the dependency $p(J_{parent}|J_{child})$ and $p(J_{child}|J_{parent})$ between parent joint and child joint respectively through a recursive subnet (left part in Fig. 1) and a diffuse subnet (right part in Fig. 1). The two subnets have independent kernel weights but share the hidden states $h \in \mathbb{R}^{J \times m}$, where J is the joint number and m is the feature size. The shared hidden states store the intermediate inference results when information flows in the network, and the intermediate results will be continually refined when the network recurrently runs. This network is named SeBiReNet because information flows sequentially and reversely in the two subnets. The proposed architecture not only models the forward and inverse kinematic process but also imitates the repeated thinking process of human.

The node number of SeBiReNet can be adjusted according to the joint number of a human skeleton model. As most skeleton models contain 17 joints, the basic version of our proposed model is designed to have 34 nodes. In SeBiReNet, each node is a GRU cell. Other node types, such as LSTM, can also be used. The forgetting mechanism GRU cell enables the network to tackle noisy input. The inference process of SeBiReNet can be formulated as Eq. 8.

$$
\begin{aligned}
h_i^r &= \varphi(W_{xi}^r x_i^r + W_{hi}^r h_i + b_i^r) \\
O_i^r &= \mathcal{O}(W_o^r h_i^r + b_o^r) \\
h_i^d &= \varphi(W_{xi}^d x_i^d + W_{hi}^d h_i + b_i^d) \\
O_i^d &= \mathcal{O}(W_o^d h_i^d + b_o^d)
\end{aligned}
\tag{8}
$$

where $x_i^r = (p_i, h_{children})$ and $x_i^d = (p_i, h_{parent})$ are the input of the node i, which contains the 3D position p_i of corresponding joint i and the hidden states output from all its child nodes $h_{children}$ or parent node h_{parent}. $h_i \in \mathbb{R}^m$ denotes the shared hidden state of the node i. The superscript r represents the recursive subnet and $W_{xi}^r, W_{hi}^r, b_i^r, W_o^r, b_o^r$ are kernel weights and biases of it. The superscript d denotes the diffuse subnet and $W_{xi}^d, W_{hi}^d, b_i^d, W_o^d, b_o^d$ are kernel weights and biases belong to it. φ denotes the nonlinear function of the GRU cell. $\mathcal{O}$ is the activation function and $tanh$ is used in our experiments. After each inference in the recursive subnet or diffuse subnet, the shared hidden states and network output will be updated by the hidden states and output of corresponding subnet. Outputs of all nodes are concatenated together as the final output of the SeBiReNet.

Complexity of the SeBiReNet. Assuming the hidden units of each GRU node is n_h and the dimension of input feature is n_x. The number of parameters in a node with N child nodes (in recursive subnetwork) or parent node (in diffuse subnetwork) is $l_N = [3n_x + (3N + 4)n_h + 1]n_h$. In a SeBiReNet with 17 joints, there are 6 leaf nodes (l_0), 26 nodes with one child node or parent node (l_1), 2 nodes have 3 child nodes (l_3).

3.3 Learning Framework Based on SeBiReNet

According to the analysis in Sect. 3.1, we designed a denoising autoencoder (DAE) to learn the representation of the human 3D pose based on SeBiReNet. Different from general practice [25] that adds Gaussian noise to the clean input and achieves a gently polluted version, we directly destroy the skeleton to an unreasonable version where some randomly selected joints are moved to illegal positions. The network is expected to distinguish valid human pose from invalid human pose and recover the correct position of those invalid joints.

Though the kinematic dependency has intrinsically modeled by the SeBiReNet, the geometric characteristics haven't been well considered. To this end, we added a bone length loss L_B and a symmetry loss L_S to the pose reconstruction loss, as shown in Eq. 9.

$$L(p, g(h_v \otimes h_{vi}, \tilde{p}; \zeta)) = \sum_s (L_P + L_B + L_S) \tag{9}$$

where the first part $L_P = \sum_{i=1}^{J} \|p_i^s - \hat{p}_i^s)\|_2$ is the reconstruction error of joint position, p_i^s denotes the 3D position of joint i of sample s, $\hat{p}_i^s$ is the corresponding recovered position. The second term $L_B = \sum_{ij} \|b_{ij}^s - \hat{b}_{ij}^s\|_2$ calculates the bone length loss, which requires the recovered bone length $\hat{b}_{ij}^s$ between joint i and j to be equal to the ground truth length b_{ij}^s. The third term $L_S = \sum_{mn,kl} \|\hat{b}_{mn}^s - \hat{b}_{kl}^s\|_2$ constrains the recovered bone lengths of the left limb must be equal to the corresponding bone lengths of recovered right limb.

The view-dependent feature and pose-dependent feature are disentangled after the SeBiReNet in the encoder. Sharing some weights before disentanglement can strengthen the interaction between h_v and h_{vi} as explained in

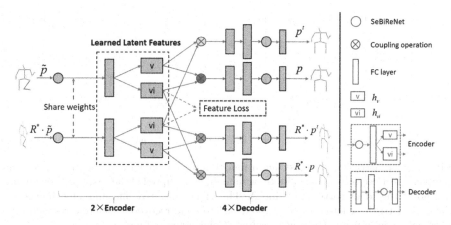

Fig. 2. The proposed architecture for the human 3D pose representation learning, which takes randomly corrupted 3D skeletons as inputs and reconstructs their correct version. Blue stream processes the non-rotated poses and green stream processes the randomly rotated poses (Color figure online)

Sect. 3.1 and make the network more compact. It's a reasonable requirement that view-dependent feature should not change the metrics of pose-dependent feature space. As the coupling operation $\otimes$ we adopt is matrix multiplication, the requirement is satisfied only when the view-dependent feature plays a role of unit unitary transformation. For our real domain problem, we regularize the view-variant feature $h_v \in \mathbb{R}^{z \times z}$ in the $SO(z)$ space as shown in Eq. 10, where $z \times z$ is the dimension of h_v. λ is a weight factor and I is an identity matrix. The orthogonal regularization is also capable of preventing the pose-related information from leaking into view-dependent feature.

$$L_O = \lambda \|I - h_v^T h_v\|_2 \tag{10}$$

To regularize the learned pose-dependent feature being view-invariant, random rotation is added to those corrupted human poses and keeping consistency between distribution $p(h_{vi}|\tilde{p})$ and $p(h_{vi}|R^* \cdot \tilde{p})$ by using a feature loss, as shown in Fig. 2. In Fig. 2, there are two pipelines to process the corrupted pose $\tilde{p}$ and the randomly rotated pose $R^* \cdot \tilde{p}$ separately. R^* is a randomly generated rotation matrix. The SeBiReNet is utilized both in the encoder and decoder. Weights are shared between all the encoders and decoders to make sure that poses under different views are encoded and decoded in the same manner. The feature loss L_f of learned pose-dependent features from different views is defined as the Frobenius norm $L_f = \|h_{vi}^1 - h_{vi}^2\|_F$. We believe that, if features are well disentangled from human pose, poses can be transferred between different views by exchanging their pose-dependent features and view-dependent features. This belief is utilized as a reinforced regularization for learning the pose representation in our method, as shown in Fig. 2 where p^t and $R^* p^t$ are view-transferred poses. Therefore, writing all together, our optimization target of learning a human 3D

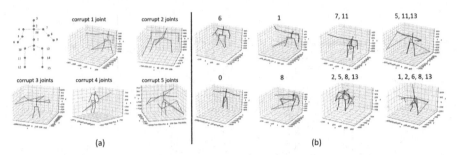

(a)   (b)

Fig. 3. (a) Illustration of the skeleton model and some generated corrupted skeleton samples, (b) Pose recovery results from randomly corrupted skeletons, the above number notes the id of corrupted joint(s). The green line, red line and blue line draw the ground truth skeleton, the corrupted skeleton and recovered skeleton, respectively. Better to view in color mode with scaling (Color figure online)

pose representation is formulated as Eq. 11, where $L(p), L(R^*p), L(p^t), L(R^*p^t)$ are the pose reconstruction loss defined in Eq. 9, $\omega_1, \omega_2, \omega_3$ are weights to adjust the influence of each loss, $R(w)$ is the L2 weight regularization term to avoid overfitting.

$$\arg\min_{\theta_{vi},\theta_v,\zeta} \left\{ L(p) + L(R^*p) + \omega_1 L(p^t) + \omega_2 L(R^*p^t) + \omega_3 L_f + L_O + R(w) \right\} \quad (11)$$

4   Experiments

4.1   Experimental Setup

Implementation Details. The hidden unit number of GRU cell in SeBiReNet is 32. Except the output layer, nonlinear activation function $tanh$ is utilized after each MLP layer. Gradient descent optimizer with an initial learning rate of $5e-5$ is used in training the DAE. Weights of different losses defined in Eq. 11 are $\omega_1 = 0.01, \omega_2 = 0.01, \omega_3 = 0.1$. λ in Eq. 10 is set to 0.1. The batch size is 64.

Training Set. The Cambridge-Imperial APE (Action-Pose-Estimation) dataset is used to train the proposed Siamese DAE. The Cambridge-Imperial APE dataset, which contains 245 sequences from 7 subjects performing 7 different categories of actions, is collected for 3D human pose estimation. Corrupted skeletons are generated by randomly selecting 1–5 joints from each skeleton and moving the them to unreasonable positions with a relatively large displacement. As shown in Fig. 3(a), these corrupted skeletons violate bio-constraints, such as bone length and allowed motion angle limits. Totally, 52500 corrupted poses are generated for training and 14000 skeletons are generated for testing. The Mean Per Joint Position Error (MPJPE) is adopted as a performance measurement of reconstructed skeletons and the trained model.

Table 1. Comparison of the performance on pose denoising among different network structures. The proposed structure achieves the best results

Network structure	MPJPE (mm)
Conventional tree (only has the recursive subnet) [28]	65.76
The diffuse subnet	64.94
Concatenated structure	75.17
SeBiReNet	**42.03**
Recurrent SeBiReNet	**41.58**

Test Sets. To verify the effectiveness of learned representations, we evaluate them on two different tasks: pose denoising and unsupervised cross-view action recognition. Two benchmark action datasets are used: Northwestern-UCLA (N-UCLA) dataset [27] and NTU RGB+D dataset [19]. Both of the two datasets contain skeletons captured from different views and performed by different subjects. NTU RGB+D dataset is one of the largest skeleton datasets and N-UCLA is one of the most commonly used datasets. Pretrained encoder is applied on them to extract pose representations without any additional training, i.e., these two datasets are not used in the training phase of DAE. A 1-layer LSTM with 128 hidden units is used as the classifier in action recognition task.

4.2 Evaluation on Pose Denoising

Our model is trained and validated on the Cambridge-Imperial APE dataset. Figure 3(b) shows several recovered skeletons. Although we destroy the skeleton randomly and extremely, our network is still able to recover the correct positions of those invalid joints. To further show the effectiveness of our network design, we compared the performance of the proposed SeBiReNet with some baseline structures: conventional tree structure (only has the recursive part), the diffuse subnet, the concatenated structure, and the recurrent SeBiReNet. Different from the SeBiReNet which shares hidden states between the recursive subnet and the diffuse subnet, the concatenated structure takes the concatenation of the outputs from the recursive subnet and the diffuse subnet as its output. The recurrent SeBiReNet means the SeBiReNet runs in a recurrent mode as shown in Fig. 1. In this experiment, we only implement it one more times.

For a fair comparison of the capability of different structures in encoding the human 3D pose, results in Table 1 is achieved by replacing the decoder in Fig. 2 with a three-layer MLP. As shown in Table 1, even with a simple decoder, using the proposed SeBiReNet as encoder achieves an MPJPE of 42.03 mm, which is a 35% improvement compared to the first three structures in recovering corrupted skeletons. Recurrently running the SeBiReNet doesn't bring too much promotion. As skeleton data is relatively simple and low dimension, implementing the SeBiReNet only once is enough to obtain a good result. Compared to structures that only has SeBiReNet in encoder, the proposed structure in Fig. 2

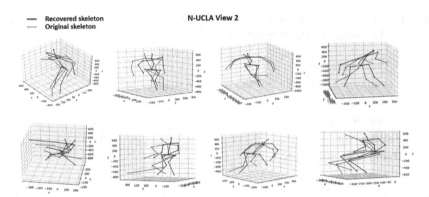

Fig. 4. Pose recovery results on N-UCLA dataset which is an unseen dataset to our pretrained DAE (Better to view in color mode with scaling) (Color figure online)

which embeds the SeBiReNet both in encoder and decoder attains the best performance 33.39 mm. The noteworthy result indicates that the SeBiReNet is superior to MLP layers in processing skeleton data.

To further demonstrate that the learned representation does encode the intrinsic feature of human 3D pose, we applied the pretrained network on unseen N-UCLA dataset for a qualitative pose denoising evaluation. As Fig. 4 shows, from perspectives of fixed bone length, symmetry, and motion limit of human joints, the recovered skeletons are much more stable and reasonable compared to the original skeletons captured by the 3D sensor. The capability of denoising unseen skeleton verifies that our network has learned the intrinsic feature of human 3D pose.

4.3   Evaluation on Unsupervised Cross-view Action Recognition

To evaluate the learned pose-dependent feature, we further exploit it for unsupervised cross-view action recognition on the N-UCLA dataset and NTU RGB+D dataset. The results are shown in Table 2. In unsupervised action recognition, it's a general way to keep the pre-trained encoder fixed and only train the classifier [3,9,14]. As our target is to evaluate the performance of learned pose-dependent representation in cross-view action recognition, a simple 1-layer LSTM is adopted as classifier to reduce the influence of classifier design. Also, to this end, we only compare with those state-of-the-art methods based on RNN. Though our classifier is much simpler than those compared methods, the accuracy we achieved is competitive and even surpass some of the supervised methods. Action recognitions that are directly based on skeleton coordinates are used as baselines. Among them, the "raw coordinates" means directly feeding the raw coordinates of skeletons into classifier. The "normalized coordinates" means the poses are further normalized according to the mean position and standard deviation of joints. Translation of human pose is neglected when training the DAE.

Table 2. Results of the cross-view action recognition on the N-UCLA dataset and the NTU RGB+D dataset (* means the result is reproduced by implementing the model reported)

Dataset		Method	Acc. (%)	# of params.
N-UCLA	Baselines	Raw coordinates	38.72	-
		Normalized coordinates	48.69	-
	Supervised	TLDS [4]	74.6	-
		HBRNN-L [5]	78.52	-
		Multi-task RNN [26]	87.3	-
		AGC-LSTM [20]	93.3	-
	Unsupervised	Li et al. [9]	62.5	-
		LongT GAN [35]	74.3*	-
		Denoised-LSTM [3]	76.81	-
		Ours (1-layer LSTM)	**80.30**	-
NTU RGB+D	Baseline	Normalized coordinates	69.08	-
	Supervised	Hand-crafted LARP [23]	52.76	-
		LieGroups [6]	66.95	-
		Part-aware LSTM [19]	70.27	-
		ST-LSTM+TG [10]	77.70	15.37M
		Two-stream GCA-LSTM [11]	85.10	24.54M
		Bayesian GC-LSTM [34]	89.0	-
		AGC-LSTM [20]	95.0	>10.75M
	Unsupervised	LongT GAN [35]	48.1*	40.18M
		EnGAN-PoseRNN [8]	77.8	>0.7M
		Ours (1-layer LSTM)	**79.71**	0.27M

But for action recognition, the translation, which should be a part of the human motion, is concatenated together with the learned pose-dependent feature.

It shows explicitly in Table 2 that the learned pose-dependent feature improves the cross-view action recognition accuracy significantly compared with baseline results, about improving by 30% on N-UCLA dataset and 10% on NTU RGB+D dataset. Among those unsupervised methods on N-UCLA dataset, our method achieves the best performance with an increment of 18% compared to the work of [9]. The method of [9] is exclusively designed for learning a temporal representation using sequential skeletons in action recognition, while our method is designed for learning a representation from single pose. The accuracy of Denoised-LSTM [3] which is based on conventional DAE is quite close to our result, but the feature they learned is not view-invariant and a preprocessing treatment is needed to alleviate the influence of view changing. A similar performance is reported on NTU RGB+D dataset. Even compared with supervised methods, the accuracy is better than some of them that have more complex

Table 3. Ablation study based on the N-UCLA and NTU datasets. All components contribute to the overall performance and a better feature disentanglement

Model	Accuracy (%)	
	N-UCLA	NTU RGB+D
Baseline (relative coordinates)	51.53	69.08
raw DAE	58.66	71.11
raw DAE + Feature Decomposition (FD)	60.61	73.99
raw DAE + FD + L_O	62.55	74.46
raw DAE + FD + L_O + L_f	73.81	75.72
raw DAE + FD + L_O + L_f + $L(R*p)$	76.84	77.07
Full architecture	**80.30**	**79.71**

classifier. Performance attained on these two benchmark datasets sufficiently demonstrates the effectiveness and robustness of the learned pose representation in our method.

Though temporal information is not considered in learning pose representation, the performance in action recognition indicates that informative temporal features still can be extracted from sequential learned representations with simple LSTM layer, which should be attributed to the intrinsic feature of human pose it has learned.

Moreover, as shown in Table 2, we also contrast the size of model with other state-of-the-art works that evaluated on the NTU dataset. Considering the SeBiReNet and all MLP layers used in our learning architecture, the learnable parameters in our method is about 0.27 million. As some details missed in several works, we can only estimate the lowest number of parameters in those methods, such as EnGAN-PoseRNN [8] and AGC-LSTM [20]. It can be seen that our method achieves a competitive result with the least parameters, which also shows the efficiency of our method from another perspective.

4.4   Ablation Study

To evaluate the contribution of each part in the learning architecture, we have an ablation study based on the N-UCLA and NTU RGB+D dataset as shown in Table 3. In Table 3, the raw DAE means the structure denoted in Eq. 1. "FD" means the learned latent feature is disentangled to view-dependent feature and pose-dependent feature as denoted in Eq. 2. L_O refers to the unit orthogonal matrix constraint on view-dependent feature, as denoted in Eq. 10. L_f and $L(R*p)$ are the feature loss and reconstruction loss of randomly rotated pose as defined in Sect. 3.3. "full architecture" means integrating all the components defined in Eq. 11 for a better disentanglement and representation learning.

As shown in Table 3, the raw DAE with skeleton corruption achieved an accuracy of 58.66%, which is 10% higher than the baseline result. By disentangling

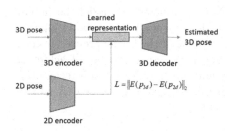

Fig. 5. Extension for 3D pose estimation

Table 4. 3D pose estimation from the generated 2D pose of H3.6M dataset

Method	MPJPE (mm)
aGCN [31]	82.9
ST-GCN [30]	57.4
Martinez et al. [15]	45.5
SemGraph [33]	43.8
Ours	53.1

the latent feature and adding orthogonal loss to view-dependent feature, another 4% improvement is obtained. However, the accuracy steeply increase to 73.81% when adding the feature loss to pose-dependent feature, which indicates that the network learns better view-invariant pose feature in this case. The reconstruction losses of randomly rotated pose and generated view-transferred poses can further help improve the performance to 80.3% in cross-view action recognition, which indicates the features are better disentangled. The improvements brought by different components are steady on the NTU RGB+D dataset, but all the components designed in our method contribute to the final performance. Feature loss and view-transferred pose losses are strong regularizations in preserving all the intrinsic pose information and learning view-invariant representations. The results, in turn, demonstrate the effectiveness of disentangling features rather than only extracting the view-invariant feature.

4.5   Extension Evaluation on 3D Pose Estimation

We further design a simple frame to explore the extension of the learned representation for 3D pose estimation from 2D pose. The extension frame contains a 3D encoder, a 2D encoder, and a decoder as shown in Fig. 5. The 3D encoder and decoder form a 3D stream and are pre-trained using 3D poses as we did in the former section. Encoder and decoder are the same with DAE in Fig. 2. In the second step, by regularizing the 2D encoder to learn a representation similar to the representation obtained in the 3D stream, 3D pose is expected to be estimated from the 2D pose. The result achieved by finetuning the 3D stream on H3.6M dataset as shown in Table 4. It can be seen that the learned representation is also applicable to the 3D pose estimation with a simple frame.

5   Conclusion

In this paper, we propose a neural network architecture to learn a human 3D pose representation by disentangling the view-dependent and pose-dependent features. Different from previous methods, the proposed method use the view-dependent and pose-dependent feature together as a pose representation for sake of preserving information. A SeBiReNet is proposed to model the human skeleton data, which considers the kinematic dependency between body joints of the human skeleton. Extensive experiments prove that the learned representation keeps the intrinsic feature of the human 3D pose and is capable of achieving excellent performance in skeleton denoising and unsupervised action recognition tasks. Utilizing the disentangled pose feature, our extension research will be focused on the view transfer between different poses.

Acknowledgements. This work is supported in part by Hong Kong RGC via project 14202918, the InnoHK programme of the HKSAR government via the Hong Kong Centre for Logistics Robotics.

References

1. Aberman, K., Wu, R., Lischinski, D., Chen, B., Cohen-Or, D.: Learning character-agnostic motion for motion retargeting in 2D. ACM Trans. Graph. (TOG) **38**(4), 1–14 (2019)
2. Bengio, Y., Courville, A., Vincent, P.: Representation learning: a review and new perspectives. IEEE Trans. Pattern Anal. Mach. Intell. **35**(8), 1798–1828 (2013)
3. Demisse, G.G., Papadopoulos, K., Aouada, D., Ottersten, B.: Pose encoding for robust skeleton-based action recognition. In: Proceedings of the IEEE Conference on Computer Vision and Pattern Recognition Workshops, pp. 188–194 (2018)
4. Ding, W., Liu, K., Belyaev, E., Cheng, F.: Tensor-based linear dynamical systems for action recognition from 3D skeletons. Pattern Recogn. **77**, 75–86 (2018)
5. Du, Y., Wang, W., Wang, L.: Hierarchical recurrent neural network for skeleton based action recognition. In: Proceedings of the IEEE Conference on Computer Vision and Pattern Recognition, pp. 1110–1118 (2015)
6. Huang, Z., Wan, C., Probst, T., Van Gool, L.: Deep learning on lie groups for skeleton-based action recognition. In: Proceedings of the 2017 IEEE Conference on Computer Vision and Pattern Recognition (CVPR), pp. 6099–6108. IEEE Computer Society (2017)
7. Irsoy, O., Cardie, C.: Deep recursive neural networks for compositionality in language. In: Advances in Neural Information Processing Systems, pp. 2096–2104 (2014)
8. Kundu, J.N., Gor, M., Uppala, P.K., Radhakrishnan, V.B.: Unsupervised feature learning of human actions as trajectories in pose embedding manifold. In: 2019 IEEE Winter Conference on Applications of Computer Vision (WACV), pp. 1459–1467. IEEE (2019)
9. Li, J., Wong, Y., Zhao, Q., Kankanhalli, M.: Unsupervised learning of view-invariant action representations. In: Advances in Neural Information Processing Systems, pp. 1262–1272 (2018)
10. Liu, J., Shahroudy, A., Xu, D., Wang, G.: Spatio-temporal LSTM with trust gates for 3D human action recognition. In: Leibe, B., Matas, J., Sebe, N., Welling, M. (eds.) ECCV 2016. LNCS, vol. 9907, pp. 816–833. Springer, Cham (2016). https://doi.org/10.1007/978-3-319-46487-9_50
11. Liu, J., Wang, G., Duan, L.Y., Abdiyeva, K., Kot, A.C.: Skeleton-based human action recognition with global context-aware attention LSTM networks. IEEE Trans. Image Process. **27**(4), 1586–1599 (2018)

12. Liu, M., Liu, H., Chen, C.: Enhanced skeleton visualization for view invariant human action recognition. Pattern Recogn. **68**, 346–362 (2017)
13. Liu, Z., Yan, S., Luo, P., Wang, X., Tang, X.: Fashion landmark detection in the wild. In: Leibe, B., Matas, J., Sebe, N., Welling, M. (eds.) ECCV 2016. LNCS, vol. 9906, pp. 229–245. Springer, Cham (2016). https://doi.org/10.1007/978-3-319-46475-6_15
14. Luo, Z., Peng, B., Huang, D.A., Alahi, A., Fei-Fei, L.: Unsupervised learning of long-term motion dynamics for videos. In: Proceedings of the IEEE Conference on Computer Vision and Pattern Recognition, pp. 2203–2212 (2017)
15. Martinez, J., Hossain, R., Romero, J., Little, J.J.: A simple yet effective baseline for 3D human pose estimation. In: Proceedings of the IEEE International Conference on Computer Vision, pp. 2640–2649 (2017)
16. Nie, Q., Wang, J., Wang, X., Liu, Y.: View-invariant human action recognition based on a 3D bio-constrained skeleton model. IEEE Trans. Image Process. **28**(8), 3959–3972 (2019)
17. Ramakrishna, V., Kanade, T., Sheikh, Y.: Reconstructing 3D human pose from 2D image landmarks. In: Fitzgibbon, A., Lazebnik, S., Perona, P., Sato, Y., Schmid, C. (eds.) ECCV 2012. LNCS, vol. 7575, pp. 573–586. Springer, Heidelberg (2012). https://doi.org/10.1007/978-3-642-33765-9_41
18. Rong, Y., Liu, Z., Li, C., Cao, K., Loy, C.C.: Delving deep into hybrid annotations for 3D human recovery in the wild. In: Proceedings of the IEEE International Conference on Computer Vision, pp. 5340–5348 (2019)
19. Shahroudy, A., Liu, J., Ng, T.T., Wang, G.: NTU RGB+D: a large scale dataset for 3D human activity analysis. In: Proceedings of the IEEE Conference on Computer Vision and Pattern Recognition, June 2016
20. Si, C., Chen, W., Wang, W., Wang, L., Tan, T.: An attention enhanced graph convolutional LSTM network for skeleton-based action recognition. In: Proceedings of the IEEE Conference on Computer Vision and Pattern Recognition, pp. 1227–1236 (2019)
21. Socher, R., Manning, C.D., Ng, A.Y.: Learning continuous phrase representations and syntactic parsing with recursive neural networks. In: Proceedings of the NIPS-2010 Deep Learning and Unsupervised Feature Learning Workshop, vol. 2010, pp. 1–9 (2010)
22. Sun, X., Shang, J., Liang, S., Wei, Y.: Compositional human pose regression. In: Proceedings of the IEEE International Conference on Computer Vision, pp. 2602–2611 (2017)
23. Vemulapalli, R., Arrate, F., Chellappa, R.: Human action recognition by representing 3D skeletons as points in a lie group. In: Proceedings of the IEEE Conference on Computer Vision and Pattern Recognition, pp. 588–595 (2014)
24. Vincent, P., Larochelle, H., Bengio, Y., Manzagol, P.A.: Extracting and composing robust features with denoising autoencoders. In: Proceedings of the 25th International Conference on Machine Learning, pp. 1096–1103. ACM (2008)
25. Vincent, P., Larochelle, H., Lajoie, I., Bengio, Y., Manzagol, P.A.: Stacked denoising autoencoders: learning useful representations in a deep network with a local denoising criterion. J. Mach. Learn. Res. **11**, 3371–3408 (2010)
26. Wang, H., Wang, L.: Learning content and style: joint action recognition and person identification from human skeletons. Pattern Recogn. **81**, 23–35 (2018)
27. Wang, J., Nie, X., Xia, Y., Wu, Y., Zhu, S.C.: Cross-view action modeling, learning and recognition. In: Proceedings of the IEEE Conference on Computer Vision and Pattern Recognition, pp. 2649–2656 (2014)

28. Wei, S., Song, Y., Zhang, Y.: Human skeleton tree recurrent neural network with joint relative motion feature for skeleton based action recognition. In: 2017 IEEE International Conference on Image Processing (ICIP), pp. 91–95. IEEE (2017)
29. Xia, L., Chen, C.C., Aggarwal, J.: View invariant human action recognition using histograms of 3D joints. In: 2012 IEEE Computer Society Conference on Computer Vision and Pattern Recognition Workshops (CVPRW), pp. 20–27. IEEE (2012)
30. Yan, S., Xiong, Y., Lin, D.: Spatial temporal graph convolutional networks for skeleton-based action recognition. In: Thirty-Second AAAI Conference on Artificial Intelligence (2018)
31. Yang, J., Lu, J., Lee, S., Batra, D., Parikh, D.: Graph R-CNN for scene graph generation. In: Ferrari, V., Hebert, M., Sminchisescu, C., Weiss, Y. (eds.) ECCV 2018. LNCS, vol. 11205, pp. 690–706. Springer, Cham (2018). https://doi.org/10.1007/978-3-030-01246-5_41
32. Yang, X., Tian, Y.L.: EigenJoints-based action recognition using Naive-Bayes-nearest-neighbor. In: 2012 IEEE Computer Society Conference on Computer Vision and Pattern Recognition Workshops (CVPRW), pp. 14–19. IEEE (2012)
33. Zhao, L., Peng, X., Tian, Y., Kapadia, M., Metaxas, D.N.: Semantic graph convolutional networks for 3D human pose regression. In: Proceedings of the IEEE Conference on Computer Vision and Pattern Recognition, pp. 3425–3435 (2019)
34. Zhao, R., Wang, K., Su, H., Ji, Q.: Bayesian graph convolution LSTM for skeleton based action recognition. In: Proceedings of the IEEE International Conference on Computer Vision, pp. 6882–6892 (2019)
35. Zheng, N., Wen, J., Liu, R., Long, L., Dai, J., Gong, Z.: Unsupervised representation learning with long-term dynamics for skeleton based action recognition. In: Thirty-Second AAAI Conference on Artificial Intelligence (2018)
36. Zhou, X., Huang, Q., Sun, X., Xue, X., Wei, Y.: Weakly-supervised transfer for 3D human pose estimation in the wild. In: IEEE International Conference on Computer Vision, ICCV, vol. 3, p. 7 (2017)

Angle-Based Search Space Shrinking for Neural Architecture Search

Yiming Hu[1,3], Yuding Liang[2], Zichao Guo[2(✉)], Ruosi Wan[2], Xiangyu Zhang[2], Yichen Wei[2], Qingyi Gu[1], and Jian Sun[2]

[1] Institute of Automation, Chinese Academy of Sciences, Beijing, China
{huyiming2016,qingyi.gu}@ia.ac.cn
[2] MEGVII Technology, Beijing, China
{liangyuding,guozichao,wanruosi,zhangxiangyu,
weiyichen,sunjian}@megvii.com
[3] School of Artificial Intelligence, University of Chinese Academy of Sciences, Beijing, China

Abstract. In this work, we present a simple and general search space shrinking method, called Angle-Based search space Shrinking (ABS), for Neural Architecture Search (NAS). Our approach progressively simplifies the original search space by dropping unpromising candidates, thus can reduce difficulties for existing NAS methods to find superior architectures. In particular, we propose an angle-based metric to guide the shrinking process. We provide comprehensive evidences showing that, in weight-sharing supernet, the proposed metric is more stable and accurate than accuracy-based and magnitude-based metrics to predict the capability of child models. We also show that the angle-based metric can converge fast while training supernet, enabling us to get promising shrunk search spaces efficiently. ABS can easily apply to most of NAS approaches (e.g. SPOS, FairNAS, ProxylessNAS, DARTS and PDARTS). Comprehensive experiments show that ABS can dramatically enhance existing NAS approaches by providing a promising shrunk search space.

Keywords: Angle · Search space shrinking · NAS

1 Introduction

Neural Architecture Search (NAS), the process of automatic model design has achieved significant progress in various computer vision tasks [8,22,34,36]. They usually search over a large search space covering billions of options to find the

---

Y. Hu and Y. Liang—Equal contribution. The work was done during the internship of Yiming Hu at MEGVII Technology.

Electronic supplementary material The online version of this chapter (https://doi.org/10.1007/978-3-030-58529-7_8) contains supplementary material, which is available to authorized users.

A. Vedaldi et al. (Eds.): ECCV 2020, LNCS 12364, pp. 119–134, 2020.
https://doi.org/10.1007/978-3-030-58529-7_8

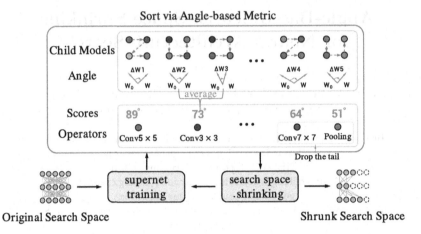

Fig. 1. Overview of the proposed angle-based search space shrinking method. We first train the supernet for some epochs with uniform sampling. After this, all operators are ranked by their scores and those of them whose rankings fall at the tail are dropped

superior ones, which is time-consuming and challenging. Though many weight-sharing NAS methods [5,15,23,24,33] have been proposed to relieve the search efficiency problem, the challenge brought by the large and complicated search space still remains.

Shrinking search space seems to be a feasible solution to relieve the optimization and efficiency problem of NAS over large and complicated search spaces. In fact, recent studies [4,7,20,26,27] have adopted different shrinking methods to simplify the large search space dynamically. These methods either speed up the search process or reduce the optimization difficulty in training stage by progressively dropping unpromising candidate operators. Though existing shrinking methods have obtained decent results, it's still challenging to detect unpromising operators among lots of candidate ones. The key is to predict the capacity of candidates by an accurate metric. Existing NAS methods usually use accuracy-based metric [4,20,23,28] or magnitude-based metric [7,26,27] to guide the shrinking process. However, neither of them is satisfactory: the former one is unstable and unable to accurately predict the performance of candidates in weight-sharing setting [35]; while the later one entails the rich-get-richer problem [1,7].

In this work, we propose a novel angle-based metric to guide the shrinking process. It's obtained via computing the angle between the model's weight vector and its initialization. Recent work [6] has used the similar metric to measure the generality of stand-alone models and demonstrates its effectiveness. For the first time, we introduce the angle-based metric to weight-sharing NAS. Compared with accuracy-based and magnitude-based metrics, the proposed angle-based metric is more effective and efficient. First, it can save heavy computation overhead by eliminating inference procedure. Second, it has higher stability and ranking correlation than accuracy-based metric in weight-sharing supernet. Third, it converges faster than its counterparts, which enables us to detect and remove unpromising candidates during early training stage.

Based on the angle-based metric, we further present a conceptually simple, flexible, and general method for search space shrinking, named as Angle-Based search space Shrinking (ABS). As shown in Fig. 1, we divide the pipeline of ABS into multiple stages and progressively discard unpromising candidates according to our angle-based metric. ABS aims to get a shrunk search space covering many promising network architectures. Contrast to existing shrinking methods, the shrunk search spaces ABS find don't rely on specific search algorithms, thus are available for different NAS approaches to get immediate accuracy improvement.

ABS applies to various NAS algorithms easily. We evaluate its effectiveness on Benchmark-201 [12] and ImageNet [19]. Our experiments show several NAS algorithms consistently discover more powerful architectures from the shrunk search spaces found by ABS. To sum up, our main contributions are as follows:

1. We clarify and verify the effectiveness of elaborately shrunk search spaces to enhance the performance of existing NAS methods.
2. We design a novel angle-based metric to guide the process of search space shrinking, and verify its advantages including efficiency, stability, and fast convergence by lots of analysis experiments.
3. We propose a dynamic search space shrinking method that can be considered as a general plug-in to improve various NAS algorithms including SPOS [15], FairNAS [9], ProxylessNAS [5], DARTS [24] and PDARTS [7].

2   Related Work

Weight-Sharing NAS. To reduce computation cost, many works [3,5,7,15,24] adopt weight-sharing mechanisms for efficient NAS. Latest approaches on efficient NAS fall into two categories: one-shot methods [3,9,15] and gradient-based methods [5,24,33]. One-shot methods train an over-parameterized supernet based on various sample strategies [3,9,15]. After this, they evaluate many child models with the well-trained supernet as alternatives, and choose those with the best performance. Gradient-based algorithms [5,24,33] jointly optimize the network weights and architecture parameters by back-propagation. Finally, they choose operators by the magnitudes of architecture parameters.

Search Space Shrinking. Several recent works [4,7,20,23,26,26-28] perform search space shrinking for efficient NAS. For example, PDARTS [7] proposes to shrink the search space for reducing computational overhead when increasing network depth. In order to improve the ranking quality of candidate networks, PCNAS [20] attempts to drop unpromising operators layer by layer based on one-shot methods. However, existing shrinking techniques are strongly associated with specific algorithms, thus unable to easily apply to other NAS methods. In contrast, our search space shrinking method is simple and general, which can be considered as a plug-in to enhance the performance of different NAS algorithms. Moreover, an effective metric is vital to discover less promising models or operators for search space shrinking. Accuracy-based metric [4,20,23,28] and magnitude-based metric [7,26,27] are two widely used metrics in NAS area. In contrast, our angle-based metric is much more stable and predictive without the poor ranking consistence and the rich-get-richer problem.

Angle-Based Metric. Recently, deep learning community comes to realize the angle of weights is very useful to measure the training behavior of neural networks: some works [2,21] theoretically prove that due to widely used normalization layers in neural network, the angle of weights is more accurate than euclidean distance to represent the update of weights; [6] uses the angle between the weights of a well-trained network and the initialized weights, to measure the generalization of the well-trained network on real data experiments. But the angle calculation method in [6] can't deal with none-parameter operators like identity and average pooling. To our best knowledge, no angle-based method was proposed before in NAS filed. Therefore we design a special strategy to apply the angle-based metric in NAS methods.

3   Search Space Shrinking

In this section, firstly we verify our claim that a elaborately shrunk search space can improve existing NAS algorithms by experiments. Then we propose an angle-based metric to guide the process of search space shrinking. Finally, we demonstrate the pipeline of the overall angle-based search space shrinking method.

3.1   Elaborately Shrunk Search Space Is Better

In this section, we investigate behaviors of NAS methods on various shrunk search spaces and point out that an elaborately shrunk search space can enhance existing NAS approaches. Our experiments are conducted on NAS-Bench-201 [12], which contains 15625 child models with ground-truths. We design 7 shrunk search spaces of various size on NAS-Bench-201, and evaluate five NAS algorithms [10,11,15,24,29] over shrunk search spaces plus the original one.

Figure 2 summaries the experiment results. It shows the elaborately shrunk search space can improve the given NAS methods with a clear margin. For example, GDAS finds the best model on CIFAR-10 from $S2$. On CIFAR-100 dataset, all algorithms discover the best networks from $S8$. For SPOS, the best networks found on ImageNet-16-120 are from $S5$. However, not all shrunk search spaces are beneficial to NAS algorithms. Most of shrunk search spaces show no superiority to the original one ($S1$), and some of them even get worse performance. Only a few shrunk search spaces can outperform the original ones, which makes it non-trivial to shrink search space wisely. To deal with such issue, we propose an angle-based shrinking method to discover the promising shrunk search space efficiently. The proposed shrinking procedure can apply to all existing NAS algorithms. We'll demonstrate its procedure and effectiveness later.

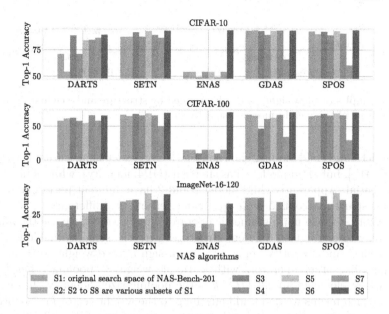

Fig. 2. Elaborately shrunk Search Space is better. We evaluate five different NAS algorithms [10,11,15,24,29] on eight search spaces

3.2   Angle-Based Metric

Angle of Weights. According to [2,21], the weights of a neural network with Batch Normalization [17,31] are "scale invariant", which means the Frobenius norm of weights can't affect the performance of the neural network and only direction of weights matters. Due to "scale invariant" property, the angle Δ_W (defined as Eq. (1)) between trained weights W and initialized weights W_0 is better than euclidean distance of weights to represent the difference between initialized neural networks and trained ones:

$$\Delta_W = arccos(\frac{< W, W_0 >}{||W||_F \cdot ||W_0||_F}), \tag{1}$$

where $< W, W_0 >$ denotes the inner product of W and W_0, $|| \cdot ||_F$ denotes the Frobenius norm. [6] shows Δ_W is an efficient metric to measure the generalization of a well-trained stand-alone model.

Angle-Based Metric for Child Model from Supernet. Since the angle shows close connection to generalization of trained networks, we consider using it to compare the performance of different child models. However, directly using angle Δ_W of a child model may meet severe problems in weight sharing settings: **the procedure of computing Δ_W can't distinguish different structures with exact same learnable weights.** Such dilemma is caused by non-parametric alternative operators ("none", "identity", "pooling"). For example,

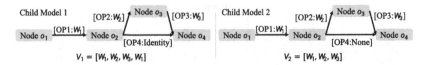

Fig. 3. Examples of the weight vector determined by structure and weights. V_1, V_2 are weight vectors of these child models respectively

child model 1 and child model 2 shown in Fig. 3 have exact same learnable weights $[\boldsymbol{W}_1, \boldsymbol{W}_2, \boldsymbol{W}_3]$, but child model 1 has shortcut (OP4: identity), while child model 2 is sequential. Apparently child model 1 and 2 have different performance due to diverse structures, but $\Delta_{[\boldsymbol{W}_1, \boldsymbol{W}_2, \boldsymbol{W}_3]}$ can't reflect such difference.

Therefore, to take non-parametric operators into account, we use the following strategy to distinguish different structures with the same learnable weights. For "pooling" and "identity" operators, we assign a fixed weight to them, and treat them like other operators with learnable weights: "pooling"[1] has $k \times k$ kernel, where elements are all $1/k^2$, k is the pooling size; "identity" has empty weights, which means we don't add anything to the weight vector for "identity". For "none" operator, it can totally change the connectivity of the child model, we can't simply treat it as the other operators. Hence we design a new angle-based metric as following to take connectivity of child model into account.

Definition of Angle-based Metric. Supernet is seen as a directed acyclic graph $\mathcal{G}(\boldsymbol{O}, \boldsymbol{E})$, where $\boldsymbol{O} = \{o_1, o_2, ..., o_M\}$ is the set of nodes, o_1 is the only root node (input of the supernet), o_M is the only leaf node (output of the supernet); $\boldsymbol{E} = \{(o_i, o_j, w_k)|$ alternative operators (including non-parametric operators except "none") from o_i to o_j with $w_k\}$. Assume a child model is sampled from the supernet, and it can be represented as a sub-graph $g(\boldsymbol{O}, \tilde{\boldsymbol{E}})$ from $\mathcal{G}$, where $\tilde{\boldsymbol{E}} \subset \boldsymbol{E}$, $o_1, o_M \in \tilde{\boldsymbol{E}}$; The angle-based metric Δ_g given g is defined as:

$$\Delta_g = arccos(\frac{< \boldsymbol{V}(g, \boldsymbol{W}_0), \boldsymbol{V}(g, \boldsymbol{W}) >}{||\boldsymbol{V}(g, \boldsymbol{W}_0)||_F \cdot ||\boldsymbol{V}(g, \boldsymbol{W})||_F}), \tag{2}$$

where $\boldsymbol{W}_0$ is the initialized weights of the supernet $\mathcal{G}$; $\boldsymbol{V}(g, \boldsymbol{W})$ denotes the weight vector of g, and it's constructed by concatenating the weights of all paths[2] from o_1 to o_M in g, its construction procedure is shown in Algorithm 1.

The construction procedure described in Algorithm 1 can make sure child models with diverse structures must have different weight vectors, even with the same learnable weights. As an example, Fig. 3 illustrates the difference between the weight vectors of child models with "none" and "identity" (comparing child model 1 and 2). Since $\boldsymbol{V}(g, \boldsymbol{W})$ is well defined on child models from any type of supernet, we compute the angel-based metric on all child models no matter whether there's "none" in supernet as an alternative.

---

[1] In this work, we do not distinguish "max pooling" and "average pooling".

[2] Path from node o_{i_1} to node o_{i_k} in a directed acyclic graph $\mathcal{G}(\boldsymbol{O}, \boldsymbol{E})$ means there exists a subset $P \subset \tilde{\boldsymbol{E}}$, where $P = \{(o_{i_1}, o_{i_2}, w_{j_1}), (o_{i_2}, o_{i_3}, w_{j_2}), ..., (o_{i_{k-1}}, o_{i_k}, w_{j_{k-1}})\}$.

Algorithm 1: Construction of weight vector $\boldsymbol{V}(g, \boldsymbol{W})$ for Model g

---

Input: A child model $g(\boldsymbol{O}, \tilde{\boldsymbol{E}})$ from the supernet, weights of supernet $\boldsymbol{W} = \{w\}$.

Output: weight vector $\boldsymbol{V}(g, \boldsymbol{W})$

1 Find all paths from the root node o_1 to the leaf node o_M in g:
$\boldsymbol{P} = \{P \subset \tilde{\boldsymbol{E}} | P \text{ is a path from } o_1 \text{ to } o_M\}$;

2 $\boldsymbol{V} = [\emptyset]([\emptyset] \text{ means empty vector})$;

3 **for** P *in* $\boldsymbol{P}$ **do**

4     $\quad V_P = concatenate(\{w_k | (o_i, o_j, w_k) \in P\})$;

5     $\quad \boldsymbol{V} = concatenate[\boldsymbol{V}, V_P]$;

6 **end**

7 $\boldsymbol{V}(g, \boldsymbol{W}) = \boldsymbol{V}$;

Constructing Weight Vector on Cell-Like/Block-Like Supernet. Algorithm 1 presents the general construction procedure of weight vector given a child model. It works well when the topology of supernet isn't too complex. However, in the worst case, the length of weight vector is of exponential complexity given the number of nodes. Hence it can make massive computational burden when number of nodes is too large in practice. Luckily, existing popular NAS search spaces all consist of several non-intersect cells, which allows us to compute the angle-based metric within each cell instead of the whole network. Specifically, we propose the following strategy as a computation-saving option:

1. Divide the whole network into several non-intersecting blocks;
2. Construct weight vector within each block respectively by Algorithm 1;
3. Obtain weight vector of the child model by concatenating each block.

3.3 Angle-Based Shrinking Method

Scores of Candidate Operators. Before demonstrating the pipeline of angle-based shrinking method, we firstly define the angle-based score to evaluate alternative operators. Assume $\boldsymbol{P} = \{p_1, p_2, \cdots, p_N\}$ represents the collection of all candidate operators from supernet, N is the number of candidate operators. We define the score of an operator by the expected angle-based metric of child models containing the operator:

$$Score(p_i) = \mathbb{E}_{g \in \{g | g \subset \mathcal{G}, g \text{ contains } p_i\}} \Delta_g, \quad i \in \{1, 2, \cdots, N\}, \tag{3}$$

where g, $\mathcal{G}$ and Δ_g have been defined in Sect. 3.2, g is uniformly sampled from $\{g | g \subset \mathcal{G}, g \text{ contains } p_i\}$. In practice, rather than computing the expectation in Eq. (3) precisely, we randomly sample finite number of child models containing the operator, and use the sample mean of angle-based metric instead.

Algorithm of Angle-Based Shrinking Method. Based on the angle-based metric, we present Algorithm 2 to describe the pipeline shown in Fig. 1. Note

---

Algorithm 2: Angle-based Search Space Shrinking Method (ABS)

Input: A supernet $\mathcal{G}$, threshold of search space size $\mathcal{T}$, number of operators dropped out per iteration k.

Output: A shrunk supernet $\tilde{\mathcal{G}}$

1 Let $\tilde{\mathcal{G}} = \mathcal{G}$;

2 **while** $|\tilde{\mathcal{G}}| > \mathcal{T}$ **do**

3 | Training the supernet $\tilde{\mathcal{G}}$ for several epochs following [15];

4 | Computing score of each operator from $\tilde{\mathcal{G}}$ by Eq. (3);

5 | Removing k operators from $\tilde{\mathcal{G}}$ with the lowest k scores;

6 **end**

Table 1. The mean Kendall's Tau of 10 repeat experiments on NAS-Bench-201 for different initialization policies

Initialization	CIFAR-10	CIFAR-100	ImageNet-16-120
Kaiming-norm [16]	0.622	0.608	0.534
Xavier-uniform [13]	0.609	0.614	0.544
Orthogonal	0.609	0.612	0.533

that during the shrinking process, at least one operator is preserved in each edge, since ABS should not change the connectivity of the supernet.

4 Experiments

In this section, we demonstrate the power of ABS in two aspects: first, we conduct adequate experiments to verify and analyze the effectiveness of our angle-based metric in stability and convergence; second, we show that various NAS algorithms can achieve better performance by combining with ABS.

4.1 Empirical Study on Angle-Based Metric

How Important Is the Specific Network Initialization? There are several different ways to initialize a network, while almost all initialization methods are gaussian type, thus the direction of initialized weights is always uniformly random. Theoretically, various initialization methods make no difference to the angle-based metric. The results in Table 1 prove our justification. Our proposed metric is reasonably robust to various initialization settings on different datasets.

Ranking Correlation in Stand-Alone Model. First of all, we conduct experiments to verify if the angle-based metric defined in Eq. (2) can really reflect the capability of stand-alone models with different structures. In detail, we uniformly select 50 child models from NAS-Bench-201 and train them from scratch

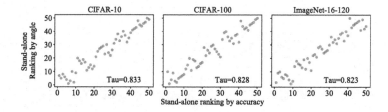

Fig. 4. The correlation between the angle-based ranking and ground-truth ranking. We uniformly choose 50 models from NAS-Bench-201 [12], and train them from scratch. After this, we leverage the angle and accuracy of these models to rank them respectively.

Table 2. The mean Kendall's Tau of 10 repeat experiments on NAS-Bench-201

Method	CIFAR-10	CIFAR-100	ImageNet-16-120
Random	0.0022	−0.0019	−0.0014
Acc. w/ Re-BN[a] [15]	0.5436	0.5329	0.5391
Angle	0.5748	0.6040	0.5445

[a] *Re-BN* means that before inferring the selected child model, we reset the batch normalization's [17] mean and variance and re-calculate them on the training dataset.

to obtain the fully optimized weights. Since the initialized weights are known, the angle of a model can be calculated as Eq. (2). To quantify the correlation between the networks' capability and their angles, we rank chosen 50 models according to their angle, and compute the Kendall rank correlation coefficient [18] (Kendall's Tau for short) with their accuracy in standalone setting.

Figure 4 shows the correlation between the network ranking by angle and the ranking of ground-truth on three datasets (CIFAR-10, CIFAR-100, ImageNet-16-120). It's obvious that the Kendall's Tau on all three different datasets are greater than 0.8, which suggests the angle of a model has significant linear correlation with its capability. Therefore, it's reasonable to use the angle-based metric to compare the performance of trained models even with different structures.

Ranking Correlation in Weight-Sharing Supernet. In this section, we verify the effectiveness of our angel-based metric in weight-sharing supernet. In detail, we firstly train a weight-sharing supernet constructed on NAS-Bench-201 following [15]. Then we calculate different metrics, such as accuracy and angle, of all child models by inheriting optimized weights from supernet. At last, we rank child models by the metric and ground-truth respectively, and compute the Kendall's Tau between these two types of ranks as the ranking correlation. Since the magnitude-based metric can only rank operators, it's not compared here.

Table 2 shows the ranking correlations based on three metrics (random, accuracy with Re-BN, angle-based metric) on three different datasets (CIFAR-10, CIFAR-100, ImageNet-16-120). Accuracy-based metric with Re-BN and

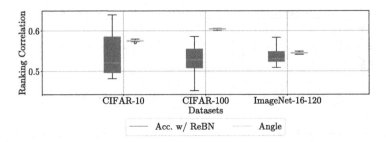

Fig. 5. The ranking stability on NAS-Bench-201. Every column is the range of ranking correlation for a metric and dataset pair. The smaller column means more stable

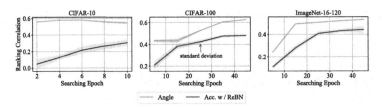

Fig. 6. Ranking correlation of metrics at early training stage on NAS-Bench-201

angle-based metric are both dramatically better than random selection. Importantly, our angle-based metric outperforms accuracy-based metric with a clear margin on all three datasets, which suggests that our angle-based metric is more effective to evaluate the capability of child models from supernet.

Ranking Stability. We have shown that our angle-based metric can achieve higher ranking correlation than the accuracy-based metric. In this section, we further discuss the ranking stability of our metric. In detail, we conduct 9 experiments on three different datasets and calculate means and variances of ranking correlation obtained by accuracy-based metric and angle-based metric. As Fig. 5 shows, our angle-based metric is extremely stable compared with accuracy-based metric. It has much smaller variance and higher mean on all three datasets. This is a crucial advantage for NAS methods, which can relieve the problem of reproducibility in weight-sharing NAS approaches. Magnitude-based metric is still not included in discussion, because it can't rank child models.

Convergence in Supernet Training. In this section, we further investigate convergence behaviors of angle-based metric and accuracy-based metric in supernet training. In search space shrinking procedure, unpromising operators are usually removed when supernet isn't well trained. Hence the performance of the metric to evaluate child models' capability at early training stage will severely influence the final results. Figure 6 shows different metrics' ranking correlation with ground-truth at early training stage. Our angle-based metric has higher

Table 3. The processing time (100 models) of different metrics on NAS-Bench-201

Method	CIFAR-10 (s)	CIFAR-100 (s)	ImageNet-16-120 (s)
Acc. w/ Re-BN [15]	$561.75_{\pm 126.58}$	$332.43_{\pm 59.18}$	$259.84_{\pm 31.90}$
Angle	$0.92_{\pm 0.06}$	$0.77_{\pm 0.02}$	$0.73_{\pm 0.04}$

ranking correlation on all three datasets during the first 10 epochs. Especially, there is a huge gap between such two metrics during the first 5 epochs. It suggests that our metric converges faster than accuracy-based metric in supernet training, which makes it more powerful to guide shrinking procedure at early training stage.

Time Cost for Metric Calculation. Magnitude-based metric needs to train extra architecture parameters as metric except network weights, which costs nearly double time for supernet training. Instead, accuracy-based metric only requires inference time by inheriting weights from supernet. But it still costs much time when evaluating a large number of child models. And our angle-based metric can further save the inference time. To compare the time cost of calculating metrics, we train a supernet and apply the specific metric to 100 randomly selected models from NAS-Bench-201. Experiments are run ten times on *NVIDIA GTX 2080Ti* GPU to calculate the mean and standard deviation. From Table 3, the time cost of our metric on three datasets are all less than 1 s while accuracy-based metric's time cost are greater than 250 s.

Select Promising Operators. The experiments above prove the superiority of angle-based metric as an indicator to evaluate child models from supernet, but we still need to verify if it's really helpful to guide the selection of promising operators. To this end, we directly compare the shrinking results based on different metrics. In our settings, the ground-truth score of each operator is obtained by averaging the ground-truth accuracy of all child models containing the given operator, the ground-truth ranking is based on the ground-truth score. We also rank alternative operators according to their metric-based scores: our angle-based score is defined as Eq. (3); the accuracy-based score is similar to the ground-truth score but the accuracy is obtained from the well-trained supernet. It shares the same algorithm pipeline (see Algorithm 2) and the hyper-parameters as our approach except the specific metric; the magnitude-based metric takes the magnitudes of corresponding architecture parameters as operator scores. It trains supernet following [32], but has the identical training and shrinking setting as our method. After getting the metric based rank, we drop 20 operators with the lowest ranking, and check the ground-truth ranking of the reserved operators.

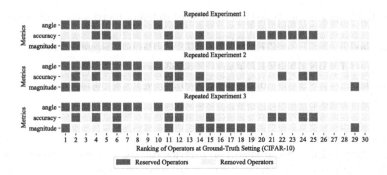

Fig. 7. The operator distribution after shrinking in three repeated CIFAR-10 experiments on NAS-Bench-201 with different random seeds

From Fig. 7, magnitude-based and accuracy-based metrics both remove most of operators in the first 8 ground-truth ranking, while the angle-based metric reserves all of them. Moreover, almost all reserved operators our approach finds have higher ground-truth scores than the removed ones', while other two methods seem to choose operators randomly. Besides, we repeat the experiments for three times with different random seeds, the result shows that angle-based shrinking method can stably select the promising operators with top ground-truth scores, while the shrunk spaces based on the other metrics are of great uncertainty.

Though there's no guarantee that the child models with best performance must be hidden in the shrunk search space, it's reasonable to believe we are more likely to discover well-behaved structures from elaborately shrunk search spaces with high ground-truth scores. Based on this motivation, the angle-based metric allows us to select those operators with high performance efficiently.

4.2   NAS Algorithms with Angle-Based Shrinking

In this part, we verify the power of ABS combined with existing NAS algorithms. We choose five NAS algorithms (SPOS [15], FairNAS [9], ProxylessNAS [5], DARTS [24], and PDARTS [7]), whose public codes are available, to apply ABS. All experiments are conducted on ImageNet. The original training set is split into two parts: 50000 images for validation and the rest for training.

MobileNet-Like Search Space. MobileNet-like Search Space consists of MobileNetV2 blocks with kernel size $\{3, 5, 7\}$, expansion ratio $\{3, 6\}$ and identity as alternative operators. We test the performance of ABS with SPOS [15], ProxylessNAS [5] and FairNAS [9] on MobileNet-like search space. SPOS and ProxylessNAS are applied on the Proxyless (GPU) search space [5], while FairNAS is applied on the same search space as [9]. We shrink the MobileNet-like search spaces by ABS at first, then apply three NAS algorithms to the shrunk spaces.

Table 4. Search results on MobileNet-like search space. * The searched models in their papers are retrained using our training setting

	Flops	Top1 Acc.	Flops(ABS)	Top1 Acc.(ABS)
FairNAS [9]	322M	74.24%*	325M	**74.42%**
SPOS [15]	465M	75.33%*	472M	**75.97%**
ProxylessNAS [5]	467M	75.56%*	470M	**76.14%**

Table 5. ImageNet results on DARTS search space. * For the form x(y), x means models searched by us using codes, y means the searched models in their papers

Method	Channels	Flops	Top1 Acc.
DARTS [24]	48(48)*	446M(530M)*	73.39%(74.88%)*
DARTS(ABS)	48	619M	**75.59**
DARTS(ABS, scale down)	45	547M	**75.19**
PDARTS [7]	48(48)*	564M(553M)*	75.02%(75.58%)*
PDARTS(ABS)	48	645M	**75.89**
PDARTS(ABS, scale down)	45	570M	**75.64**

In detail, supernet is trained for 100 and 5 epochs in the first and other shrinking stages. We follow the block-like weight vector construction procedure to compute the angle-based metric. The score of each operator is acquired by averaging the angle of 1000 child models containing the given operator. Moreover, the base weight W_0 used to compute angle is reset when over 50 operators are removed from the original search space. Because our exploratory experiments (see Fig. 4 in appendix) show that after training models for several epochs, the angle between the current weight W and the initialized weight W_0 is always close to 90° due to very high dimension of weights. It doesn't mean the training is close to be finished, but the change of angle is too tiny to distinguish the change of weights. Therefore, to represent the change of weights effectively during the mid-term of training, we need to reset the base weight to compute the angle.

When sampling child models, ABS dumps models that don't satisfy flops constraint. For SPOS and ProxylessNAS, ABS removes 7 operators whose rankings fall at the tail. For FairNAS, ABS removes one operator for each layer each time because of its fair constraint. The shrinking process finishes when the size of search space is less than 10^5. For re-training, we use the same training setting as [15] to retrain all the searched models from scratch, with an exception: dropout is added before the final fully-connected and the dropout rate is 0.2.

As Table 4 shows, all algorithms can obtain significant benefits with ABS. SPOS and ProxylessNAS find models from the shrunk search space with 0.6% higher accuracy than from the original search space respectively. FairNAS also finds better model on shrunk search space with 0.2% accuracy improvement.

DARTS Search Space. Following the experiment settings in [24], we apply the search procedure on CIFAR-10, then retrain the selected models from scratch and evaluate them on ImageNet. In detail, the block-like weight vector construction procedure is adopted while using ABS. Supernet is trained for 150 and 20 epochs in the first and other shrinking stages respectively. More epochs are adopted for training supernet due to its slow convergence on DARTS search space. ABS removes one operator for each edge each time. The shrinking process stops when the size of shrunk search space is less than a threshold. DARTS and PDARTS share the same threshold as the MobileNet-like search space. During re-training, all algorithms use the same training setting as [7] to retrain the searched models.

From Table 5, the architectures found by DARTS and PDARTS with ABS on CIFAR10 perform well on ImageNet. Equipped with ABS, DARTS and PDARTS get 2.2% and 0.87% accuracy improvement respectively without any human interference (0.71% and 0.31% improvement even compared with reported results in [7,24]). Such vast improvement is probably due to the fact that the architectures found from the shrunk search space have more flops. But it's reasonable that models with higher flops are more likely to have better capability if the flops are not constrained. Furthermore, to fairly compare the performance with constrained flops, the channels of the architecture we found from shrunk space are scaled down to fit with the constraint of flops. Table 5 shows that even the constrained models from the shrunk search space can still get better results.

Discussion. Search space shrinking is very useful for NAS [7,20], and the angle-based metric is extremely suitable for shrinking due to its high correlation with the performance of DNN and fast convergence (see Fig. 6). Our results show ABS can enhance existing NAS algorithms (see Table 4, 5). But the metric is not a perfect indicator (see Table 2), so directly searching with our metric shows no superiority to combining it and other NAS methods: on the Mobilenet-like search space, our experiments indicate SPOS gets only 0.19% improvement by replacing the accuracy-based metric with the metric, while combining with ABS, SPOS can get 0.64% improvement. Thus we leverage the metric to perform shrinking.

5   Conclusion and Future Work

In this paper, we point out that elaborately shrunk search space can improve performance of existing NAS algorithms. Based on this observation, we propose an angle-based search space shrinking method available for existing NAS algorithms, named as ABS. While applying ABS, we adopt a novel angle-based metric to evaluate capability of child models and guide the shrinking procedure. We verify the effectiveness of the angle-based metric on NAS-bench-201, and demonstrate the power of ABS by combining with various NAS algorithms on multiple search spaces and datasets. All experiments prove that the proposed method is highly efficient, and can significantly improve existing NAS algorithms.

However, there are some problems not solved yet. For example, how to discriminate average pooling and max pooling; how to process more non-parametric operators such as different activation functions [14,25,30]). In the future, we will spend more time on discriminating more non-parametric operators using the angle-based metric in NAS. Additionally, we plan to apply our proposed metric to some downstream tasks (e.g., detection, segmentation) in our future work.

Acknowledgement. This work is supported by the National Key Research and Development Program of China (No. 2017YFA0700800), Beijing Academy of Artificial Intelligence (BAAI) and the National Natural Science Foundation of China (No. 61673376).

References

1. Adam, G., Lorraine, J.: Understanding neural architecture search techniques. arXiv preprint arXiv:1904.00438 (2019)
2. Arora, S., Li, Z., Lyu, K.: Theoretical analysis of auto rate-tuning by batch normalization. arXiv preprint arXiv:1812.03981 (2018)
3. Bender, G., Kindermans, P.J., Zoph, B., Vasudevan, V., Le, Q.: Understanding and simplifying one-shot architecture search. In: International Conference on Machine Learning, pp. 549–558 (2018)
4. Cai, H., Gan, C., Han, S.: Once for all: train one network and specialize it for efficient deployment. arXiv preprint arXiv:1908.09791 (2019)
5. Cai, H., Zhu, L., Han, S.: ProxylessNAS: direct neural architecture search on target task and hardware. arXiv preprint arXiv:1812.00332 (2018)
6. Carbonnelle, S., De Vleeschouwer, C.: Layer rotation: a surprisingly simple indicator of generalization in deep networks? (2019)
7. Chen, X., Xie, L., Wu, J., Tian, Q.: Progressive differentiable architecture search: bridging the depth gap between search and evaluation. arXiv preprint arXiv:1904.12760 (2019)
8. Chen, Y., Yang, T., Zhang, X., Meng, G., Xiao, X., Sun, J.: DetNAS: backbone search for object detection. In: Advances in Neural Information Processing Systems, pp. 6638–6648 (2019)
9. Chu, X., Zhang, B., Xu, R., Li, J.: FairNAS: rethinking evaluation fairness of weight sharing neural architecture search. arXiv preprint arXiv:1907.01845 (2019)
10. Dong, X., Yang, Y.: One-shot neural architecture search via self-evaluated template network. In: Proceedings of the IEEE International Conference on Computer Vision (ICCV), pp. 3681–3690 (2019)
11. Dong, X., Yang, Y.: Searching for a robust neural architecture in four GPU hours. In: Proceedings of the IEEE Conference on Computer Vision and Pattern Recognition, pp. 1761–1770 (2019)
12. Dong, X., Yang, Y.: NAS-Bench-201: extending the scope of reproducible neural architecture search. In: International Conference on Learning Representations (ICLR) (2020). https://openreview.net/forum?id=HJxyZkBKDr
13. Glorot, X., Bengio, Y.: Understanding the difficulty of training deep feedforward neural networks. In: Proceedings of the Thirteenth International Conference on Artificial Intelligence and Statistics, pp. 249–256 (2010)
14. Glorot, X., Bordes, A., Bengio, Y.: Deep sparse rectifier neural networks. In: Proceedings of the Fourteenth International Conference on Artificial Intelligence and Statistics, pp. 315–323 (2011)
15. Guo, Z., et al.: Single path one-shot neural architecture search with uniform sampling. arXiv preprint arXiv:1904.00420 (2019)

16. He, K., Zhang, X., Ren, S., Sun, J.: Delving deep into rectifiers: surpassing human-level performance on ImageNet classification. In: 2015 IEEE International Conference on Computer Vision (ICCV), pp. 1026–1034 (2015)
17. Ioffe, S., Szegedy, C.: Batch normalization: accelerating deep network training by reducing internal covariate shift. arXiv preprint arXiv:1502.03167 (2015)
18. Kendall, M.G.: A new measure of rank correlation. Biometrika **30**(1/2), 81–93 (1938)
19. Krizhevsky, A., Sutskever, I., Hinton, G.E.: ImageNet classification with deep convolutional neural networks. Commun. ACM **60**(6), 84–90 (2017)
20. Li, X., et al.: Improving one-shot NAS by suppressing the posterior fading. arXiv preprint arXiv:1910.02543 (2019)
21. Li, Z., Arora, S.: An exponential learning rate schedule for deep learning. arXiv preprint arXiv:1910.07454 (2019)
22. Liu, C., et al.: Auto-DeepLab: hierarchical neural architecture search for semantic image segmentation. In: Proceedings of the IEEE Conference on Computer Vision and Pattern Recognition, pp. 82–92 (2019)
23. Liu, C., et al.: Progressive neural architecture search. In: Ferrari, V., Hebert, M., Sminchisescu, C., Weiss, Y. (eds.) ECCV 2018. LNCS, vol. 11205, pp. 19–35. Springer, Cham (2018). https://doi.org/10.1007/978-3-030-01246-5_2
24. Liu, H., Simonyan, K., Yang, Y.: Darts: differentiable architecture search. arXiv preprint arXiv:1806.09055 (2018)
25. Maas, A.L., Hannun, A.Y., Ng, A.Y.: Rectifier nonlinearities improve neural network acoustic models. In: Proceedings of the ICML, vol. 30, p. 3 (2013)
26. Nayman, N., Noy, A., Ridnik, T., Friedman, I., Jin, R., Zelnik, L.: XNAS: neural architecture search with expert advice. In: Advances in Neural Information Processing Systems, pp. 1975–1985 (2019)
27. Noy, A., et al.: ASAP: architecture search, anneal and prune. arXiv preprint arXiv:1904.04123 (2019)
28. Pérez-Rúa, J.M., Baccouche, M., Pateux, S.: Efficient progressive neural architecture search. arXiv preprint arXiv:1808.00391 (2018)
29. Pham, H., Guan, M.Y., Zoph, B., Le, Q.V., Dean, J.: Efficient neural architecture search via parameter sharing. arXiv preprint arXiv:1802.03268 (2018)
30. Ramachandran, P., Zoph, B., Le, Q.V.: Searching for activation functions. arXiv preprint arXiv:1710.05941 (2017)
31. Wan, R., Zhu, Z., Zhang, X., Sun, J.: Spherical motion dynamics of deep neural networks with batch normalization and weight decay. arXiv preprint arXiv:2006.08419 (2020)
32. Wang, L., Xie, L., Zhang, T., Guo, J., Tian, Q.: Scalable NAS with factorizable architectural parameters. arXiv preprint arXiv:1912.13256 (2019)
33. Wu, B., et al.: FBNeT: hardware-aware efficient convnet design via differentiable neural architecture search. In: Proceedings of the IEEE Conference on Computer Vision and Pattern Recognition, pp. 10734–10742 (2019)
34. Xu, H., Yao, L., Zhang, W., Liang, X., Li, Z.: Auto-FPN: automatic network architecture adaptation for object detection beyond classification. In: Proceedings of the IEEE International Conference on Computer Vision, pp. 6649–6658 (2019)
35. Zhang, Y., et al.: Deeper insights into weight sharing in neural architecture search. arXiv preprint arXiv:2001.01431 (2020)
36. Zoph, B., Vasudevan, V., Shlens, J., Le, Q.V.: Learning transferable architectures for scalable image recognition. In: Proceedings of the IEEE Conference on Computer Vision and Pattern Recognition, pp. 8697–8710 (2018)

RobustScanner: Dynamically Enhancing Positional Clues for Robust Text Recognition

Xiaoyu Yue[1], Zhanghui Kuang[1](✉), Chenhao Lin[2], Hongbin Sun[1], and Wayne Zhang[1]

[1] SenseTime Research, Hong Kong, China
{yuexiaoyu,kuangzhanghui,sunhongbin,wayne.zhang}@sensetime.com
[2] School of Cyber Science and Engineering, Xi'an Jiaotong University, Xi'an, China
linchenhao@xjtu.edu.cn

Abstract. The attention-based encoder-decoder framework has recently achieved impressive results for scene text recognition, and many variants have emerged with improvements in recognition quality. However, it performs poorly on contextless texts (*e.g.*, random character sequences) which is unacceptable in most of real application scenarios. In this paper, we first deeply investigate the decoding process of the decoder. We empirically find that a representative character-level sequence decoder utilizes not only context information but also positional information. Contextual information, which the existing approaches heavily rely on, causes the problem of attention drift. To suppress such side-effect, we propose a novel position enhancement branch, and dynamically fuse its outputs with those of the decoder attention module for scene text recognition. Specifically, it contains a position aware module to enable the encoder to output feature vectors encoding their own spatial positions, and an attention module to estimate glimpses using the positional clue (*i.e.*, the current decoding time step) only. The dynamic fusion is conducted for more robust feature via an element-wise gate mechanism. Theoretically, our proposed method, dubbed *RobustScanner*, decodes individual characters with dynamic ratio between context and positional clues, and utilizes more positional ones when the decoding sequences with scarce context, and thus is robust and practical. Empirically, it has achieved new state-of-the-art results on popular regular and irregular text recognition benchmarks while without much performance drop on contextless benchmarks, validating its robustness in both contextual and contextless application scenarios.

1 Introduction

Scene text recognition is crucial for visual understanding and reasoning in many application scenarios [5,44]. Despite great progress recently, it remains

---

Electronic supplementary material The online version of this chapter (https://doi.org/10.1007/978-3-030-58529-7_9) contains supplementary material, which is available to authorized users.

A. Vedaldi et al. (Eds.): ECCV 2020, LNCS 12364, pp. 135–151, 2020.
https://doi.org/10.1007/978-3-030-58529-7_9

a challenging task because the potential irregularity and diversity of text shapes and layouts in the wild, which can be curved, oriented or distorted, make the misalignment between the output character sequence and the two-dimensional input image [25,29,42,50,57]. The prevalent approaches for scene text recognition are inspired by machine translation [2,30,46] and image caption [54] following the encoder-decoder framework with varied attention mechanisms [25,39,42,50,56].

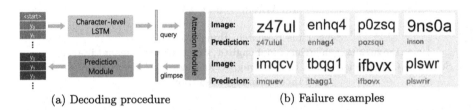

(a) Decoding procedure   (b) Failure examples

Fig. 1. Illustration of the decoding procedure of encoder-decoder with attention framework and its failure cases.

Typically, the encoder-decoder with attention framework [25,56] consists of one encoder, and one decoder. The decoder contains one character-level LSTM, one attention module, and one prediction module. During decoding, at each step, the LSTM takes the previously predicted character and the hidden state as inputs, and outputs one *query* feature vector, which is fed into the attention module to estimate attention map and compute one *glimpse* feature vector. The glimpse vector is finally classified into one character category or the <EOS> token in the prediction module as illustrated in Fig. 1(a). In spite of the appealing effectiveness of the encoder-decoder with attention framework on academic benchmarks, it performs poorly on contextless text sequence images, which hinders it from being widely used in real application scenarios. To demonstrate it, we synthesize one benchmark of random character sequence images, dubbed *RandText*, to evaluate existing encoder-decoder with attention based methods. Surprisingly, the official released model of the state-of-the-art method SAR [25] obtains a low accuracy of 59.6% on it. Figure 1(b) shows some failure samples, all of which are without background clutter, low resolutions, varied illumination or distortions, and thus considered as easy cases by human.

To explore the underlying reasons of the failure recognition, in this work, we deeply investigate the decoding process of encoder-decoder with attention based methods. By computing the averaged cosine similarity between the *query* feature vectors of the ith and j^{th} time steps on ICDAR 2013 [20] test set, we observed the high averaged similarity between those of the same time step (as shown in Fig. 2) although their corresponding characters are different. The observation suggests that the *query* vectors encode not only context information but also the positional information. We also observed that the averaged similarity between the *query* vectors of neighborhood time steps increases as the time step increases, which suggests that the positional information is drowned with the introduction of others including context information at latter time steps. It can easily lead to alignment drift and misrecognition of latter characters of contextless sequences, which coincides with most of the failure samples in Fig. 1(b).

To mitigate the above misrecognition, in this paper, we propose RobustScanner for text recognition via dynamically enhancing the positional clues of the decoder. Specifically, besides the conventional decoder, it consists of one position enhancement branch and one dynamic fusion module. The former is tailored for enhancing the conventional decoder in terms of positional encoding capability via estimating the *glimpses* with positional clues (*i.e.*, the current decoding time step) only. The latter is designed to dynamically fuse the *glimpses* of the position enhancement branch, and those of the conventional decoder via one element-wise gate mechanism. In such a way, the fusion ratio between positional and context information at each time step can be dynamically and adaptively adjusted according to the their own importance.

Our **contributions** can be summarized as follows:

- We investigate the intrinsic mechanism of the decoding procedure of the encoder-decoder with attention framework for the first time. We find out that the *query* feature vectors of the LSTM encodes not only context but also positional information, and the context information dominates the *query* at latter decoding time steps, which can lead to misrecognition on contextless text images.
- We propose RobustScanner to mitigate the issue of misrecognition in contextless scenarios via introducing a novel position enhancement branch and a dynamic fusion module.
- We extensively evaluate our proposed RobustScanner, which achieves new state-of-the-art performances on popular regular and irregular text recognition benchmarks while without much performance drop on contextless *RandText*, validating its robustness in both context and contextless application scenarios.

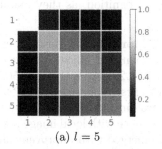 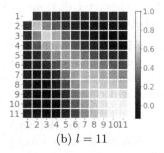

(a) $l = 5$ (b) $l = 11$

Fig. 2. Visualization of the averaged similarity matrix. The x-axis and the y-axis indicate the position index in sequences, while the color indicate the averaged similarity. The block at (i, j) indicates $S_l(i, j)$. (a) visualizes the averaged similarity matrix when $l = 5$ while (b) $l = 11$.

2 Related Work

Most of traditional methods for scene text recognition [23,33,34,48,49] adopt the bottom-up approach in which individual character is first detected by sliding window, and then integrated for taking the dependence with its neighbors into consideration. These methods might fail to detect small characters, and are easily disturbed by background clutter, illumination, and low image quality, *e.g.*, blurring, noise, *etc.* Later, top-down methods [1,3,7,8,11,12,15,16,24,25,35,40–42,45,50,55,57] were proposed, in which text sequences are end-to-end predicted without the single character detection. Recently, approaches which target at challenging arbitrary-shaped text recognition become dominant. These approaches can be roughly categorized into rectification-based, segmentation-based and encoder-decoder with attention-based.

Rectification-Based Approaches. They attempt to rectify irregular images to regular ones before recognition. STN [18] was first introduced into text recognition network by Shi *et al.* [41], which was extended by considering more flexible Transformation Thin-Plate-Spline (TPS) in [42,55] and conducting rectification iteratively in [57]. Rather than rectifying the whole text region, Liu *et al.* [27] detected individual characters first and then rectified them separately. The shortness of this strategy is that, if some important information missed during rectification process, it cannot be compensated in the latter part of the network, which may be fatal at times.

Segmentation-Based Approaches. They segment each character individually to avoid the issue of irregular layout. Liao *et al.* [26] employed fully convolutional network to detect and recognize individual characters followed by character-combination in post-processing. However, they need character-level annotations which are unavailable in most public datasets. Xing *et al.* [53] alleviated this issue by an iterative character detection, which can transform the ability of character detection learned from synthetic data to real-world images. All the segmentation-based approaches cannot trivially extend to the text recognition with huge character dictionary, such as Chinese recognition, as they maintain one probability heat map for each character.

Encoder-Decoder with Attention-Based Approaches. Most of existing state-of-the-art methods for irregular text recognition follow the encoder-decoder framework with attention mechanisms [1,7,25,27,35,41,45,50,56,56]. The encoder-decoder with attention framework was first proposed for NLP tasks such as machine translation [2,30,46]. Later, it was introduced into scene text recognition to align the character in the output sequence with local image regions in [41]. Since then, many variants [7,25,56] were emerged with improvements in recognition quality. Cheng *et al.* [7] introduced a focus network to suppress the attention drift problem. SAR [25] employed a tailored 2D attention mechanism to recognize irregular texts and achieved impressive results. Recently, [39,50] introduced Transformer to replace RNN structure to capture long distance context. Wang *et al.* [51] proposed Decoupled Attention Network (DAN) to mitigate the alignment drift problem. Our approach falls into the encoder-decoder with attention framework. Similar to DAN [51], we also target at suppressing the misrecognition caused by alignment drift. Instead of decoupling attention from historical decoding results as done in [51], we propose the position enhancement branch and dynamically fusion module to adaptively adjust the ratio of positional and context clues during decoding. Besides, we deeply investigate the intrinsic mechanism of the decoding procedure in the decoder for the first time.

Our approach is related to the positional encoding model [9,38,47]. We do not target at enumerating all possible architectures and finding the optimal one of positional encoding model. In contrast, we focus on enhancing positional clues of the attention-based decoder.

3   Methodology

In this section, we first review the encoder-decoder with attention-based scene text recognition, and then dissect the decoder and analyze what information the *query* feature vectors contain. Finally, we introduce our proposed approach RobustScanner.

3.1   Background

As [25,56], one representative encoder-decoder with attention-based scene text recognition approach consists of one encoder and one decoder. The decoder has one LSTM-based sequence module, one attention module and one prediction module. Given one input image, the encoder extracts one feature map $\mathbf{F} \in \mathbb{R}^{H \times W \times C}$. During decoding, at time step t, the LSTM-based sequence model first generates one hidden feature vector $\mathbf{h_t}$. Formally,

$$\mathbf{h_t} = \mathrm{LSTM}(\mathbf{x_t}, \mathbf{h_{t-1}}), \mathbf{x_t} = \begin{cases} \mathbf{y_{t-1}} & \text{if } t > 1 \\ <\text{start}> & \text{if } t = 1 \end{cases}, \tag{1}$$

where $<\text{start}>$ is a special start token, and $\mathbf{y_{t-1}}$ is the output of decoding process at time step $t - 1$. $\mathbf{h_t}$ is considered as the *query* feature vector of the attention module to compute one attention map as follows:

$$\alpha_{ij}^t = \mathrm{softmax}(\mathbf{h_t}^T \mathbf{f_{i,j}}), \tag{2}$$

where $\mathbf{h_t}^T$ indicates the transpose of the vector $\mathbf{h_t}$, and $\mathbf{f_{i,j}}$ represents the feature vector at the position (i, j) of $\mathbf{F}$. The *glimpse* vector $\mathbf{g_t}$ is then computed by the weighted aggregation of the convolutional feature map $\mathbf{F}$ as follows:

$$\mathbf{g_t} = \sum_{ij} \alpha_{ij}^t \mathbf{f_{i,j}}. \tag{3}$$

Finally, the glimpse vector $\mathbf{g_t}$ is classified into one character or the $<\text{EOS}>$ token. Formally,

$$\mathbf{y_t} = \mathrm{softmax}(\mathbf{W} \mathbf{g_t} + b), \tag{4}$$

where $\mathbf{W}$ and b indicate the linear transformation and the bias of the classifier respectively.

3.2   Decoder Dissection

From Eq. (1), (2), (3), and (4), we conclude that given the feature map $\mathbf{F}$ and learned network parameters, the recognized character $\mathbf{y_t}$ depends on the *query* vector $\mathbf{h_t}$ only. What information does the *query* vector $\mathbf{h_t}$ encode so that its corresponding attention weight α^t can highlight and the classifier can correctly recognize the tth character on the input image? Obviously, the *query* vector contains context information since it depends on previously-predicted characters from Eq. (1).

We observe that the *query* vector $\mathbf{h_1}$ keeps unchanged for different text sequences, and does not encode any context information. However, the first character can still be correctly recognized. This implies that the *query* vector $\mathbf{h_t}$ (including $\mathbf{h_1}$) contains the positional information. *i.e.*, the character index in one sequence.

To verify the above conjecture, we analyze the similarity of the *query* for different text sequences at the same time step. We conduct experiments on test set of ICDAR 2013 [20]. Let $\mathcal{I}$ denote the set of all text sequences, and $\widehat{\mathcal{I}_l}$ be the subset of $\mathcal{I}$ with all text sequences of length l. We compute the average cosine similarity $S_l(i,j)$ between the *query* vectors at position i and j over $\widehat{\mathcal{I}_l}$ as follows:

$$S_l(i,j) = \frac{\sum_{m \neq n}^{|\widehat{\mathcal{I}_l}|} \cos(\mathbf{h_i^{m,l}}, \mathbf{h_j^{n,l}})}{|\widehat{\mathcal{I}_l}|(|\widehat{\mathcal{I}_l}| - 1)}, \tag{5}$$

where $|\widehat{\mathcal{I}_l}|$ denotes the cardinality of $\mathcal{I}_l$, and $\mathbf{h_i^m}$ denotes the ith *query* vector for the mth sequence in $\mathcal{I}_l$.

Figure 2 visualizes the averaged similarity matrixes when $l = 5$ and $l = 11$. We have two observations:

- Averaged similarities between the *query* vectors of the same position are obviously higher than those of different positions.
- As the time step increases, the contrast between the averaged similarities between the *query* vectors of the same position, and those of neighbor positions become smaller.

Note that the ith character of sequences in $\mathcal{I}_l$ varies from one sequence to another. High value of $S_l(i,i)$ suggests queries can be well separated into groups corresponding to their steps using kernel methods. We further conduct the linear regression between queries ($\mathbf{h_t}$) and positions (t) via fitting $t = \mathbf{W_r}\mathbf{h_t} + b_r$ on the data with $l = 5$ (90% for training, 10% for test). We report the classic R-squared R^2 which indicates the proportion of the variance of the dependent variable that is predictable. We get $R^2 = 0.994$ and $R^2 = 0.956$ on training and test set. High R^2 scores prove queries can reliably predict positions. Thus, queries encode them. The second observation suggests that the positional information is drowned with the introduction of others including the context information.

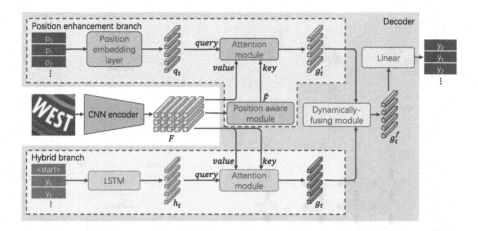

Fig. 3. Architecture of RobustScanner. Given an input image, we first extract its feature map $\mathbf{F}$ by the CNN encoder. $\mathbf{F}$ is then fed into the hybrid branch, and the position enhancement branch, obtaining the *glimpses* $\mathbf{g_t}$ and $\mathbf{g'_t}$, which are dynamically fused by the dynamically-fusing module before predicting the tth character.

3.3   RobustScanner

Overview. As discussed in Sect. 3.2, the *query* vectors in the encoder-decoder with attention based framework contain the hybrid information of context and position. The positional clues become weaker while the contextual ones become stronger as the time step increases during decoding, which may lead to alignment drift and misrecognition, especially on contextless text images. To enhance the positional information, we propose one position enhancement branch and dynamically fuse its outputs with those of the conventional decoder. As shown in Fig. 3, our RobustScanner consists of one encoder and one decoder. In the encoder, we adapt one 31-layer ResNet [14] as backbone as done in [25]. The decoder consists of one hybrid branch, one position enhancement branch, one dynamically-fusing module, and one prediction module.

Hybrid Branch. The hybrid branch consists of one two-layer LSTM with 128 hidden state size and one attention module. The LSTM takes the previously-predicted character and its hidden variable as input and generates the *query* vector $\mathbf{h_t}$. Then the *query* vector is fed into the attention module to estimate *glimpse* vector $\mathbf{g_t}$ for the character prediction during decoding (see Eq. (1) and (3)). It utilizes both contextual and positional information simultaneously.

Position Enhancement Branch. The positional information becomes weak while the contextual information becomes strong in the latter time steps during decoding. It would lead to the alignment drift and serious misrecognition on contextless text images where context cannot be used to reliably predict characters. Our position enhancement branch is designed to mitigate this problem. It consists one position embedding layer, one position aware module and one attention module.

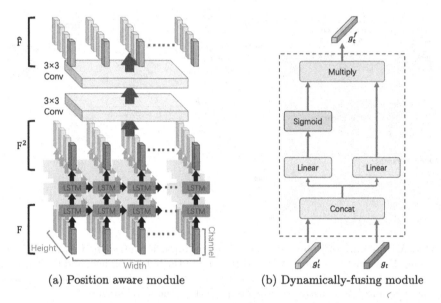

(a) Position aware module   (b) Dynamically-fusing module

Fig. 4. Architecture of the position aware module and that of the dynamically-fusing module. (a) the position aware module inputs $\mathbf{F}$, then obtains $\mathbf{F^2}$ after two LSTM layers, and finally outputs $\widehat{\mathbf{F}}$ after two 3×3 convolutional layers. (b)the dynamically-fusing module takes $\mathbf{g_t}$ and $\mathbf{g'_t}$ as inputs and output one adaptively fused glimpse $\mathbf{g^f_t}$.

The position embedding layer encodes the decoding time step. It inputs one hot vectors and outputs one specific embedding vector $\mathbf{q_t}$ for each time step t. Note that the embedding vector of each time step keeps unchanged across different decoding sequences.

Position Aware Module. Although the position embedding layer encodes the character index in sequences, precisely locating the tth character on the encoder output feature map $\mathbf{F}$, which requires the global information, is still challenging. However, the width of input image might be beyond the receptive field size of the CNN encoder. Moreover, counting the indexes of characters in images needs to understand the shapes and directions of the text sequences. To this end, we propose a position aware module to capture the global and high-level information so that the encoder output feature map is position-aware. Figure 4(a) shows the detailed architecture of the proposed position aware module. We employ two-layer LSTM with 128 hidden state size for each row of the feature map $\mathbf{F}$ to capture the global context. For all rows, the LSTMs share parameters to overcome overfitting and reduce parameter amount. We then employ two 3×3 convolutional layers with one ReLU between them to generate the *key* vectors $\widehat{\mathbf{F}}$ of its following attention module. Formally,

$$\mathbf{f}^1_{i,j} = \text{LSTM}(\mathbf{f}_{i,j}, \mathbf{f}^1_{i,j-1}), \qquad (6)$$

$$\mathbf{f}^2_{i,j} = \text{LSTM}(\mathbf{f}^1_{i,j}, \mathbf{f}^2_{i,j-1}), \qquad (7)$$

$$\widehat{\mathbf{F}} = f(\mathbf{F}^2), \qquad (8)$$

where $\mathbf{f}^1_{i,j}$ and $\mathbf{f}^2_{i,j}$ are the first and the second LSTM hidden variables respectively. $\mathbf{F}^2$ is the tensor consisting of $\mathbf{f}^2_{i,j}$, and $f(\cdot)$ is the stack of 3×3 *conv*, ReLU, and 3×3 *conv* operations.

We feed the output vectors $\mathbf{q}_t$ of the embedding layer into the attention module as *key* vectors to estimate attention maps, which are used to compute the final *glimpse* vectors $\mathbf{g}'_t$ as done in Eq. (2) and (3). Different from conventional methods, we use the position aware feature map $\widehat{\mathbf{F}}$ instead of $\mathbf{F}$ when computing the attention maps.

Note that position aware module injects the global context so that it has the capability to output position aware features. The query vectors in the position enhancement branch explicitly encode the character order indexes (positions). The end-to-end training enforces the position aware module to output feature maps correlated with positions so that the attention module in the branch can correctly output the feature glimpse at each decoding step (position) with the position aware module output feature maps and position-specific query vector as inputs (see Fig. 3). Otherwise, texts cannot be correctly decoded.

Dynamically-Fusing Module. As shown in Fig. 4(b), we propose to dynamically fuse the hybrid branch output $\mathbf{g}_t$ and the position enhancement branch output $\mathbf{g}'_t$ at each time step t. We design one gate mechanism to predict one attention weight for each dimension of their concatenation, which is used to enhance or suppress their corresponding feature. Formally,

$$\mathbf{w}_t = \text{sigmoid}(\mathbf{W}_a[\mathbf{g}_t; \mathbf{g}'_t]), \qquad (9)$$

$$\mathbf{g}^f_t = \mathbf{w}_t \odot (\mathbf{W}_p[\mathbf{g}_t; \mathbf{g}'_t]), \qquad (10)$$

where $\mathbf{W}_a$ and $\mathbf{W}_p$ are two learned linear transformations. $\odot$ indicates the element-wise multiplication operation. $\mathbf{g}^f_t$ is the final output of our dynamically-fusion module, which is used to predict the character via the prediction module.

4   Experiments

4.1   Datasets

For fair comparison with previous state-of-the-art approaches, we follow their settings to train the proposed network by using two public available synthetic datasets, *i.e.* MJSynth [17] and SynthText [13]. We conduct extensively experiments on 6 standard benchmarks including 3 regular text datasets (IIIT 5K-words [32], Street View Text [48], ICDAR 2013 [20]), 3 irregular text datasets (ICDAR 2015 [19], Street View Text Perspective [36], CUTE 80 [37]).

IIIT 5K-words (IIIT5K) [32] is a large dataset containing 5000 word patches cropped from natural scene images collected from Google image search, in which 2000 images are used for training and 3000 for test. Text instances in these patches are regular with the horizontal layout.

Street View Text (SVT) [48] consists of 647 word patches cropped from Google Street View for testing. Most images are horizontal, but severely corrupted by noise and blur, or with low-resolution.

ICDAR 2013 (IC 2013) [20] has 848 cropped word patches for training and 1095 for test. For fair comparison with other reported results, we discard images that contain non-alphanumeric characters, which results in 1015 test patches. Words in this dataset are mostly regular.

ICDAR 2015 (IC 2015) [19] contains word patches cropped from incidental scene images captured under arbitrary angles. Hence most word patches in this dataset are irregular (oriented, perspective or curved). It contains 4468 patches for training and 2077 for test.

Street View Text Perspective (SVTP) [36] consists of 639 word patches, which are cropped from side view snapshots in Google Street View and encounter severe perspective distortions. All patches are used for test.

CUTE 80 [37] contains 288 cropped high resolution images for test and many of them are curved irregular text images.

RandText contains 500 test images. We synthesize them by pasting black random character sequences on white background images. The character set contains small and capital letters, and numbers. Some examples can be found in Fig. 1(b). We will publicly release RandText to facilitate the future research.

4.2 Implementation Details

The proposed framework is implemented by using PyTorch. All experiments are conducted on servers with 4 NVIDIA Titan X GPUs with 12 GB memory.

. Our RobustScanner is trained from scratch using Adam optimizer [21] with the base learning rate 1×10^{-3}. The whole training process contains 5 epochs, while the learning rate decreases to 1×10^{-4} at the 3rd epoch and 1×10^{-5} at the 4th epoch. The batch size at training phase is set to 128. For both training and test, heights of all image patches are set to 48, while widths are proportionally scaled with heights, but no longer than 160 and no smaller than 48 pixels. Our models recognizes 91 token classes, including 10 digits, 52 case sensitive letters, 28 punctuation characters and an <EOS> token.

To reduce the computation time of two attention module, the dimension of the hybrid query vector h_t and the position embedding q_t is set to 128. Before feeding F to the hybrid attention module and the position aware module, a 1×1 *conv* layer is added to reduce the channel dimension to 128. The maximum number of position embeddings is set to 36.

In the test stage, for images with height larger than width, we will rotate the image by $90°$ clockwise and anticlockwise respectively, and recognize them together with the original image. For the recognition results of each 3-sibling image group, the top-score one will be chosen as the final recognition result.

Table 1. Comparison with state-of-the-art methods. "MJ", "ST" and "R" are the training data of MJSynth [17], SynthText [13] and training splits of real datasets, respectively.

Method	Training data	Regular text			Irregular text		
		IIIT5K	SVT	IC 2013	IC 2015	SVTP	CUTE 80
Shi et al. [42]	MJ + ST	93.4	**93.6**	91.8	76.1	78.5	79.5
Zhan and Lu [57]	MJ + ST	93.3	90.2	91.3	76.9	79.6	83.3
Gao et al. [10]	MJ + ST	94.0	88.6	93.2	**77.1**	80.6	88.5
Bai et al. [3]	MJ + ST	88.3	87.5	94.4	73.9	-	-
Luo et al. [29]	MJ + ST	91.2	88.3	92.4	68.8	76.1	77.4
Wang et al. [50]	MJ + ST	93.3	88.1	91.3	74.0	80.2	85.1
Lyu et al. [31]	MJ + ST	94.0	90.1	92.7	76.3	82.3	86.8
Xie et al. [52]	MJ + ST	82.3	82.6	89.7	68.9	70.1	82.6
DAN [51]	MJ + ST	94.3	89.2	93.9	74.5	80.0	84.4
Bartz et al. [4]	MJ + ST	94.6	89.2	93.1	74.2	**83.1**	89.6
Bleeker et al. [6]	MJ + ST	94.7	89.0	93.4	75.7	80.6	82.5
Long et al. [28]	MJ + ST	93.7	88.9	92.4	76.6	78.8	86.8
Baek et al. [1]	MJ + ST	87.9	87.5	92.3	71.8	79.2	74.0
RobustScanner	MJ + ST	**95.3**	88.1	**94.8**	**77.1**	79.5	**90.3**
SAR [25]	MJ + ST + R	95.0	**91.2**	94.0	78.8	**86.4**	89.6
RobustScanner	MJ + ST + R	**95.4**	89.3	94.1	**79.2**	82.9	**92.4**

4.3   Comparison with State-of-the-Art Approaches

We compare our approach with previous state-of-the-art methods in Table 1. It has been shown that our proposed RobustScanner achieves best results on four datasets including IIIT5K, ICDAR 2013, ICDAR 2015 and CUTE 80 when only synthetic training datasets are used. To demonstrate the potential of our proposed method, we further train it on MJSynth, SynthText, and training sets of real datasets in Sect. 4.1 following the training setting of SAR [25]. We have observed that RobustScanner outperforms its competitor SAR on four out of six benchmarks. Especially, it obtains the accuracy of 92.4%, and outperforms SAR with impressive margins on the challenging irregular text dataset CUTE 80. It can be noticed that our method performs worse than SAR [25] on two street view text datasets, we attribute the performance gap to that SVT and SVTP consist of contextual words and suffer from low resolution, blur and distortion, where context is more important than positions when recognizing texts.

This paper targets at mitigating the misrecongition issue on contextless text images of the encoder-decoder with attention based framework. Therefore, we evaluate our proposed RobustScanner on RandText dataset. Table 2 compared it with representative encoder-decoder with attention based approaches. Again, our proposed RobustScanner obviously outperforms its counterparts including

Table 2. Comparison on RandText. All methods are trained on the training data of MJSynth [17] and SynthText [13] for fair comparison.

Method	SAR [25]	DAN [51]	Wang *et al.* [50]	RobustScanner
Accuracy	59.6	76.4	78.8	**81.2**

LSTM based methods [25] and [51] and the Transformer based method [50]. Especially, DAN [51] decouples the historical decoded characters from the attention estimation to suppress the alignment drift problem. However, it still performs worse than our RobustScanner by absolute 4.8%. The effectiveness of RobustScanner on both context and contextless benchmarks validate its robustness in real application scenarios.

4.4   Ablation Study

The Effectiveness of Each Branch. To show the effectiveness of each branch, we evaluate our RobustScanner without the position enhancement branch or the hybrid branch in Table 3. In these experiments, the *glimpse* vectors are fed directly into the classifier to decode the character at each time step without dynamic fusion. We have two observations. First, RobustScanner greatly outperforms its counterpart without the hybrid branch on all academical regular and irregular benchmarks, and performs slightly worse on RandText. Due to the collection bias, all academical benchmarks have abundant context. It suggests that the context clues introduced via the hybrid branch can boost the recognition performances on context text images, and causes side effect on contextless text images. Second, the performance of RobustScanner drops drastically when without applying the position enhancement branch on both context and contextless text images. Particularly, RobustScanner without the position enhancement branch obtains a low accuracy of 46.8% on RandText, which is lower than it with both branches by absolutely 34.4%. We conclude that the capacity of encoding positional clues in the decoder with attention should be enhanced, especially when recognizing contextless text images.

Table 3. Evaluation of the effectiveness of each branch in RobustScanner. HB and PEB indicate the hybrid branch and the position enhancement branch respectively.

	IIIT5K	SVT	IC 2013	IC 2015	SVTP	CUTE 80	RandText
w/o HB	92.5	84.4	91.4	70.7	74.4	83.3	**83.4**
w/o PEB	91.0	**88.3**	91.7	72.0	75.4	84.0	46.8
RobustScanner	**95.3**	88.1	**94.8**	**77.1**	**79.5**	**90.3**	81.2

The Effectiveness of the Position Aware Module. Enhancing position encoding is nontrivial since it requires the global context of the input image and the comprehension of the shapes and directions of text sequences. Our proposed position aware module is the core component of the position enhancement branch. Table 4 evaluates its effect. If we take out the position aware module, our RobustScanner decreases from 92.5%, 84.4%, 91.4%, 70.7%, 74.4%, 83.3% and 83.4% to 88.7%, 84.1%, 89.0%, 61.8%, 62.3%, 76.7% and 68.0% on IIIT5K, SVT, ICDAR 2013, ICDAR 2015, SVTP, CUTE 80 and RandText respectively. We also compare our position aware module with sine and cosine positional encoding [47]. We compute the 128-dimensional sine and cosine positional encoding via $pe(pos, 2i) = \sin(pos/1000^{2i/128})$ and $pe(pos, 2i + 1) = \cos(pos/1000^{2i/128})$ with pos being the horizontal coordinate of the current encoder output feature vector in the spatial space, and $2i$ and $2i + 1$ being the encoding indexes. We pad the sine and cosine positional encoding with $\mathbf{F}$ and obtain $\widehat{\mathbf{F}}$, which is fed into the attention module as key vectors. As shown in Table 4, sine and cosine positional encoding leads to obvious performance drop. Arguably, it is because since and cosine positional encoding contain absolute coordinate information only while relative character indexes in sequences are required in the position enhancement branch.

Table 4. Evaluation of the effectiveness of the position aware module, and other position encoding method. PAM indicates the position aware module. sine&cosine indicates padding sine and cosine positional encoding with the encoder output feature maps.

	IIIT5K	SVT	IC 2013	IC 2015	SVTP	CUTE 80	RandText
w/o PAM	88.7	84.1	89.0	61.8	62.3	76.7	68.0
sine&cosine	86.1	83.2	87.8	57.5	56.1	74.0	49.0
RobustScanner	**92.5**	**84.4**	**91.4**	**70.7**	**74.4**	**83.3**	**83.4**

The Effectiveness of the Dynamically-Fusing Module. Table 5 compares our proposed dynamically-fusing module with other baseline fusion methods. Namely, element-wise addition and concatenation. They element-wise addition or concatenate the $glimpse$ vectors $\mathbf{g_t}$ and $\mathbf{g'_t}$ from the hybrid branch and the position enhancement branch before feeding them into the classifier at the tth time step during decoding. Different from dynamically-fusing, they are static and keep unchanged across different time steps and different decoding sequences. Our proposed dynamically-fusing module achieves best results on all 6 academical benchmarks and the second best result on RandText. Therefore, it is more robust than its static competitors, and applicable in more general application scenarios including those with or without context.

Performance on License Plate Recognition. To verify the effectiveness of our RobustScanner on contextless data, we conduct experiments on the license plate recognition task. We crop 97 license plate images from Cars dataset [22] as the test set by using the character-level training annotations introduced in [43]. Noted that all methods are trained on the training data of MJSynth [17] and

Table 5. Comparison with different fusion methods.

Method	IIIT5K	SVT	IC 2013	IC 2015	SVTP	CUTE 80	RandText
Element-wise addition	94.8	87.9	94.3	75.5	78.6	89.2	**82.4**
Concatenation	95	**88.1**	94.2	75.2	78.6	88.2	80.4
Dynamically-fusing	**95.3**	**88.1**	**94.8**	**77.1**	**79.5**	**90.3**	81.2

Table 6. Comparison on the license plate dataset.

Method	SAR [25]	DAN [51]	Wang et al. [50]	RobustScanner
Accuracy	29.9	51.1	46.4	**55.7**

Fig. 5. Samples of recognition results of our RobustScanner and SAR [25] on the license plate dataset.

SynthText [13]. Therefore, the training and test data are very different in terms of background, font, and layout. All methods get relatively low accuracy on it. However, our RobustScanner outperforms other encoder-decoder with attention based methods with impressive margins, as shown in Table 6. Figure 5 shows some results of our method and SAR [25] on the license plate test set.

5   Conclusions

In this paper, we target at mitigating the misrecognition problem of the encoder-decoder with attention framework on contextless text images. We have investigated the decoding procedure and have found that the *query* vectors of attention in the decoder contains both positional and context information, and positional clues become weak while contextual ones become strong as the decoding time step increases. Motivated by this finding, we have proposed RobustScanner for scene text recognition, which contains one hybrid branch and one position enhancement branch, and dynamically fuses the two branches at each time step during decoding. Moreover, we have proposed one novel position aware module, which can strengthen the positional encoding capacity of the position enhancement branch. We have extensively evaluated our proposed RobustScanner on both academical benchmarks and our synthesized RandText. The experimental results show that our approach has achieved new state-of-the-art results on popular regular and irregular text benchmarks while without much performance drop on contextless benchmarks. It has been validated that our proposed RobustScanner is robust in both context and contextless application scenarios.

References

1. Baek, J., et al.: What is wrong with scene text recognition model comparisons? Dataset and model analysis. In: Proceedings of the IEEE International Conference on Computer Vision, pp. 4715–4723 (2019)
2. Bahdanau, D., Cho, K., Bengio, Y.: Neural machine translation by jointly learning to align and translate. In: ICLR, pp. 1–15 (2015)
3. Bai, F., Cheng, Z., Niu, Y., Pu, S., Zhou, S.: Edit probability for scene text recognition. In: CVPR, pp. 1508–1516 (2018)
4. Bartz, C., Bethge, J., Yang, H., Meinel, C.: KISS: keeping it simple for scene text recognition. arXiv preprint arXiv:1911.08400 (2019)
5. Biten, A.F., et al.: Scene text visual question answering. In: Proceedings of the IEEE International Conference on Computer Vision, pp. 4291–4301 (2019)
6. Bleeker, M., de Rijke, M.: Bidirectional scene text recognition with a single decoder. arXiv preprint arXiv:1912.03656 (2019)
7. Cheng, Z., Bai, F., Xu, Y., Zheng, G., Pu, S., Zhou, S.: Focusing attention: towards accurate text recognition in natural images. In: ICCV, pp. 5076–5084 (2017)
8. Cheng, Z., Xu, Y., Bai, F., Niu, Y., Pu, S., Zhou, S.: AON: towards arbitrarily-oriented text recognition. In: CVPR, pp. 5571–5579 (2018)
9. Dai, Z., et al.: Transformer-XL: attentive language models beyond a fixed-length context. arXiv preprint arXiv:1901.02860 (2019)
10. Gao, Y., Chen, Y., Wang, J., Lei, Z., Zhang, X.Y., Lu, H.: Recurrent calibration network for irregular text recognition. arXiv preprint arXiv:1812.07145 (2018)
11. Gao, Y., Chen, Y., Wang, J., Lu, H.: Reading scene text with attention convolutional sequence modeling. arXiv preprint arXiv:1709.04303 (2017)
12. Graves, A., Fernández, S., Gomez, F., Schmidhuber, J.: Connectionist temporal classification: labelling unsegmented sequence data with recurrent neural networks. In: Proceedings of the 23rd International Conference on Machine Learning, pp. 369–376. ACM (2006)
13. Gupta, A., Vedaldi, A., Zisserman, A.: Synthetic data for text localisation in natural images. In: CVPR (2016)
14. He, K., Zhang, X., Ren, S., Sun, J.: Deep residual learning for image recognition. In: CVPR, pp. 770–778 (2016)
15. He, P., Huang, W., Qiao, Y., Loy, C.C., Tang, X.: Reading scene text in deep convolutional sequences. In: AAAI (2016)
16. He, W., Yin, F., Zhang, X.-Y., Liu, C.-L.: TextDragon: an end-to-end framework for arbitrary shaped text spotting. In: ICCV, pp. 9076–9085 (2019)
17. Jaderberg, M., Simonyan, K., Vedaldi, A., Zisserman, A.: Synthetic data and artificial neural networks for natural scene text recognition. arXiv preprint arXiv:1406.2227 (2014)
18. Jaderberg, M., Simonyan, K., Zisserman, A., et al.: Spatial transformer networks. In: NIPS, pp. 2017–2025 (2015)
19. Karatzas, D., et al.: ICDAR 2015 competition on robust reading. In: ICDAR, pp. 1156–1160. IEEE (2015)
20. Karatzas, D., et al.: ICDAR 2013 robust reading competition. In: ICDAR, pp. 1484–1493 (2013)
21. Kingma, D.P., Ba, J.: Adam: a method for stochastic optimization. arXiv preprint arXiv:1412.6980 (2014)
22. Krause, J., Stark, M., Deng, J., Fei-Fei, L.: 3D object representations for fine-grained categorization. In: 4th International IEEE Workshop on 3D Representation and Recognition (3dRR 2013), Sydney, Australia (2013)

23. Lee, C.Y., Bhardwaj, A., Di, W., Jagadeesh, V., Piramuthu, R.: Region-based discriminative feature pooling for scene text recognition. In: Proceedings of the IEEE Conference on Computer Vision and Pattern Recognition, pp. 4050–4057 (2014)
24. Lee, C.Y., Osindero, S.: Recursive recurrent nets with attention modeling for OCR in the wild. In: CVPR, pp. 2231–2239 (2016)
25. Li, H., Wang, P., Shen, C., Zhang, G.: Show, attend and read: a simple and strong baseline for irregular text recognition. In: AAAI (2019)
26. Liao, M., et al.: Scene text recognition from two-dimensional perspective. arXiv preprint arXiv:1809.06508 (2018)
27. Liu, W., Chen, C., Wong, K.Y.K.: Char-Net: a character-aware neural network for distorted scene text recognition. In: AAAI (2018)
28. Long, S., Guan, Y., Bian, K., Yao, C.: A new perspective for flexible feature gathering in scene text recognition via character anchor pooling. arXiv preprint arXiv:2002.03509 (2020)
29. Luo, C., Jin, L., Sun, Z.: MORAN: a multi-object rectified attention network for scene text recognition. Pattern Recogn. **90**, 109–118 (2019)
30. Luong, M.T., Pham, H., Manning, C.D.: Effective approaches to attention-based neural machine translation. In: EMNLP (2015)
31. Lyu, P., Yang, Z., Leng, X., Wu, X., Li, R., Shen, X.: 2D attentional irregular scene text recognizer. arXiv preprint arXiv:1906.05708 (2019)
32. Mishra, A., Alahari, K., Jawahar, C.V.: Scene text recognition using higher order language priors. In: BMVC-British Machine Vision Conference. BMVA (2012)
33. Mishra, A., Alahari, K., Jawahar, C.V.: Top-down and bottom-up cues for scene text recognition. In: IEEE Conference on Computer Vision and Pattern Recognition, pp. 2687–2694 (2012)
34. Mishra, A., Alahari, K., Jawahar, C.V.: Enhancing energy minimization framework for scene text recognition with top-down cues. Comput. Vis. Image Underst. **145**, 30–42 (2016)
35. Qin, S., Bissacco, A., Raptis, M., Fujii, Y., Xiao, Y.: Towards unconstrained end-to-end text spotting. In: ICCV (2019)
36. Quy Phan, T., Shivakumara, P., Tian, S., Lim Tan, C.: Recognizing text with perspective distortion in natural scenes. In: Proceedings of the IEEE International Conference on Computer Vision, pp. 569–576 (2013)
37. Risnumawan, A., Shivakumara, P., Chan, C.S., Tan, C.L.: A robust arbitrary text detection system for natural scene images. Expert Syst. Appl. **41**(18), 8027–8048 (2014)
38. Shaw, P., Uszkoreit, J., Vaswani, A.: Self-attention with relative position representations. arXiv preprint arXiv:1803.02155 (2018)
39. Sheng, F., Chen, Z., Xu, B.: NRTR: a no-recurrence sequence-to-sequence model for scene text recognition. arXiv preprint (2017)
40. Shi, B., Bai, X., Yao, C.: An end-to-end trainable neural network for image-based sequence recognition and its application to scene text recognition. PAMI **39**(11), 2298–2304 (2016)
41. Shi, B., Wang, X., Lyu, P., Yao, C., Bai, X.: Robust scene text recognition with automatic rectification. In: CVPR, pp. 4168–4176 (2016)
42. Shi, B., Yang, M., Wang, X., Lyu, P., Yao, C., Bai, X.: ASTER: an attentional scene text recognizer with flexible rectification. PAMI **41**(9), 2035–2048 (2018)

43. Silva, S.M., Jung, C.R.: License plate detection and recognition in unconstrained scenarios. In: Ferrari, V., Hebert, M., Sminchisescu, C., Weiss, Y. (eds.) ECCV 2018. LNCS, vol. 11216, pp. 593–609. Springer, Cham (2018). https://doi.org/10.1007/978-3-030-01258-8_36

44. Singh, A., et al.: Towards VQA models that can read. In: Proceedings of the IEEE Conference on Computer Vision and Pattern Recognition, pp. 8317–8326 (2019)

45. Sun, Y., Liu, J., Liu, W., Han, J., Ding, E., Liu, J.: Chinese street view text: large-scale Chinese text reading with partially supervised learning. In: ICCV, pp. 9086–9095 (2019)

46. Sutskever, I., Vinyals, O., Le, Q.V.: Sequence to sequence learning with neural networks. In: NIPS (2014)

47. Vaswani, A., et al.: Attention is all you need. In: Advances in Neural Information Processing Systems, pp. 5998–6008 (2017)

48. Wang, K., Babenko, B., Belongie, S.: End-to-end scene text recognition. In: 2011 International Conference on Computer Vision, pp. 1457–1464 (2011)

49. Wang, K., Belongie, S.: Word spotting in the wild. In: Daniilidis, K., Maragos, P., Paragios, N. (eds.) ECCV 2010. LNCS, vol. 6311, pp. 591–604. Springer, Heidelberg (2010). https://doi.org/10.1007/978-3-642-15549-9_43

50. Wang, P., Yang, L., Li, H., Deng, Y., Shen, C., Zhang, Y.: A simple and robust convolutional-attention network for irregular text recognition. aXiv preprint (2019)

51. Wang, T., et al.: Decoupled attention network for text recognition. In: AAAI Conference on Artificial Intelligence (2020)

52. Xie, Z., Huang, Y., Zhu, Y., Jin, L., Liu, Y., Xie, L.: Aggregation cross-entropy for sequence recognition. In: Proceedings of the IEEE Conference on Computer Vision and Pattern Recognition, pp. 6538–6547 (2019)

53. Xing, L., Tian, Z., Huang, W., Scott, M.R.: Convolutional character networks. In: ICCV, pp. 9126–9136 (2019)

54. Xu, K., Courville, A., Zemel, R.S., Bengio, Y.: Show, attend and tell: neural image caption generation with visual attention. In: ICML (2015)

55. Yang, M., et al.: Symmetry-constrained rectification network for scene text recognition. In: Proceedings of the IEEE International Conference on Computer Vision, pp. 9147–9156 (2019)

56. Yang, X., He, D., Zhou, Z., Kifer, D., Giles, C.L.: Learning to read irregular text with attention mechanisms. In: IJCAI (2017)

57. Zhan, F., Lu, S.: ESIR: end-to-end scene text recognition via iterative image rectification. arXiv preprint arXiv:1812.05824 (2018)

Towards Fast, Accurate and Stable 3D Dense Face Alignment

Jianzhu Guo[1,2] (ID), Xiangyu Zhu[1,2] (ID), Yang Yang[1,2] (ID), Fan Yang[3] (ID), Zhen Lei[1,2(✉)] (ID), and Stan Z. Li[4] (ID)

[1] CBSR&NLPR, Institute of Automation, Chinese Academy of Sciences, Beijing, China
{jianzhu.guo,xiangyu.zhu,yang.yang,zlei}@nlpr.ia.ac.cn
[2] School of Artificial Intelligence, University of Chinese Academy of Sciences, Beijing, China
[3] College of Software, Beihang University, Beijing, China
fanyang@buaa.edu.cn
[4] School of Engineering, Westlake University, Hangzhou, China
szli@nlpr.ia.ac.cn

Abstract. Existing methods of 3D dthus limiting the scope of their practical applications. In this paper, we propose a novel regression framework which makes a balance among speed, accuracy and stability. Firstly, on the basis of a lightweight backbone, we propose a meta-joint optimization strategy to dynamically regress a small set of 3DMM parameters, which greatly enhances speed and accuracy simultaneously. To further improve the stability on videos, we present a virtual synthesis method to transform one still image to a short-video which incorporates in-plane and out-of-plane face moving. On the premise of high accuracy and stability, our model runs at 50 fps on a single CPU core and outperforms other state-of-the-art heavy models simultaneously. Experiments on several challenging datasets validate the efficiency of our method. The code and models will be available at https://github.com/cleardusk/3DDFA_V2.

Keywords: 3D dense face alignment · 3D face reconstruction

1 Introduction

3D dense face alignment is essential for many face related tasks, e.g., recognition [6,12,23,25,41], animation [9], avatar retargeting [8], tracking [46], attribute classification [3,20,21], image restoration [10,11,47], anti-spoofing [24,37,45,49,

---

J. Guo and X. Zhu—Equal contribution.

Electronic supplementary material The online version of this chapter (https://doi.org/10.1007/978-3-030-58529-7_10) contains supplementary material, which is available to authorized users.

50]. Recent studies are mainly divided into two categories: 3D Morphable Model (3DMM) parameters regression [22,31,33,44,54,55,57] and dense vertices regression [17,26]. Dense vertices regression methods directly regress the coordinates of all the 3D points (usually more than 20,000) through a fully convolutional network [17,26], achieving the state-of-the-art performance. However, the resolution of reconstructed faces relies on the size of the feature map and these methods rely on heavy networks like hourglass [35] or its variants, which are slow and memory-consuming in inference. The natural way of speeding it up is to prune channels. We try to prune 77.5% channels on the state-of-the-art PRNet [17] to achieve real-time speed on CPU, but find the error greatly increases 44.8% (3.62% vs. 5.24%). Besides, an obvious disadvantage is the presence of checkerboard artifacts due to the deconvolution operators, which is present in the supplementary material. Another strategy is to regress a small set of 3DMM parameters (usually less than 200). Compared with dense vertices, 3DMM parameters have low dimensionality and low redundancy, which are appropriate to regress by a lightweight network. However, different 3DMM parameters influence the reconstructed 3D face [54] differently, making the regression challenging since we have to dynamically re-weight each parameter according to their importance during training. Cascaded structures [33,54,55] are always adopted to progressively update the parameters but the computation cost is increased linearly with the number of cascaded stages.

Fig. 1. A few results from our *MobileNet (M+R+S)* model, which runs at 50 fps on a single CPU core or 130 fps on multiple CPU cores.

In this paper, we aim to accelerate the speed to CPU real time and achieve the state-of-the-art performance simultaneously (Fig. 1). To this end, we choose to regress 3DMM parameters with a fast backbone, e.g. MobileNet. To handle the optimization problem of the parameters regression framework, we exploit two different loss terms WPDC and VDC [54] (see Sect. 2.2) and propose our meta-joint optimization to combine the advantages of them. The meta-joint optimization looks ahead by k-steps with WPDC and VDC on the meta-train batches, then dynamically selects the better one according to the error on the meta-test batch. By doing so, the whole optimization converges faster and achieves better performance than the vanilla-joint optimization. Besides, a landmark-regression regularization is introduced to further alleviate the optimization problem to achieve higher accuracy. In addition to single image, 3D face applications on videos are becoming more and more popular [8,9,27,28], where reconstructing stable results across consecutive frames is important, but it is often ignored by recent methods [17,26,54,55]. Video-based training [16,32,36,40] is always adopted to improve the stability in 2D face alignment. However, no video databases are publicly available for 3D dense face alignment. To address it, we propose a 3D aided short-video-synthesis method, which simulates both in-plane and out-of-plane face moving to transform one still image to a short video, so that our network can adjust results of consecutive frames. Experiments show our short-video-synthesis method significantly improves the stability on videos.

In general, our proposed methods are (i) *fast*: It takes about 7.2ms with an single image as input (almost 24× faster than PRNet) and runs at over 50fps (19.2ms) on a single CPU core or over 130fps (7.2ms) on multiple CPU cores (i5-8259U processor), (ii) *accurate*: By dynamically optimizing 3DMM parameters through a novel meta-optimization strategy combining the fast WPDC and VDC, we surpass the state-of-the-art results [17,26,54,55] under a strict computation burden in inference, and (iii) *stable*: In a mini-batch, one still image is transformed slightly and smoothly into a short synthetic video, involving both in-plane and out-of-plane rotations, which provides temporal information of adjacent frames for training. Extensive experimental results on four datasets show that the overall performance of our method is the best.

2   Methodology

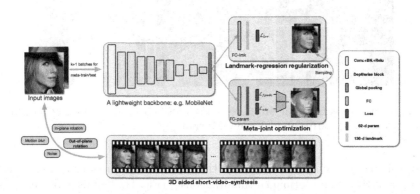

Fig. 2. Overview of our method. Our architecture consists of four parts: the lightweight backbone like MobileNet for predicting 3DMM parameters, the meta-joint optimization of fWPDC and VDC, the landmark-regression regularization and the short-video-synthesis for training. The landmark-regression branch is discarded in inference, thus not increasing any computation burden.

This section details our proposed approach. We first discuss 3D Morphable Model (3DMM) [5]. Then, we introduce the proposed methods of the meta-joint optimization, landmark-regression regularization and 3D aided short-video-synthesis. The overall pipeline is illustrated in Fig. 2 and the algorithm is described in Algorithm 1.

Algorithm 1: The overall algorithm of our proposed methods.

Input: Training data $\mathcal{X} = \{(x^l, p^l)\}_{l=1}^M$.
Init: Model parameters θ initialized randomly, the learning rate α, look-ahead step k, length of 3D aided short-video-synthesis n, and batch-size of B.

1   **for** i *in* $max\_iterations$ **do**
2   Randomly sampling k batches $\{\mathcal{X}_{mtr}^l\}_{l=1}^k$ for meta-train and one disjoint batch $\mathcal{X}_{mte}$ for meta-test, each batch contains B pairs: $\{(x^l, p^l)\}_{l=1}^B$.
    // short-video-synthesis
3   **for** *each* $x \in \mathcal{X}_{mtr}$ *or* $\mathcal{X}_{mte}$ **do**
4   Synthesize a short-video with n adjacent frames: $\{(x_0, p_0|x_0)|x_0 = x\} \cup \{(x_j', p_j'|x_j')|x_j' = (M \circ P)(x_j), x_j = (T \circ F)(x_{j-1}), 1 \le j \le n - 1\}$.
5   **end**
    // Meta-joint optimization with landmark-regression regularization
6   Let $\theta_i^f, \theta_i^v \leftarrow \theta_i$;
7   **for** $j = 1 \cdots k$ **do**
8       $\theta_{i+j}^f \leftarrow \alpha \nabla_{\theta_{i+j-1}^f} \left(\mathcal{L}_{fwpdc}(\theta_{i+j-1}^f, \mathcal{X}_{mtr}^j) + \frac{|l_{fwpdc}|}{|l_{lrr}|} \cdot \mathcal{L}_{lrr}(\theta_{i+j-1}^f, \mathcal{X}_{mtr}^j) \right)$;
      $\theta_{i+j}^v \leftarrow \alpha \nabla_{\theta_{i+j-1}^v} \left(\mathcal{L}_{vdc}(\theta_{i+j-1}^v, \mathcal{X}_{mtr}^j) + \frac{|l_{vdc}|}{|l_{lrr}|} \cdot \mathcal{L}_{lrr}(\theta_{i+j-1}^v, \mathcal{X}_{mtr}^j) \right)$;
9   **end**
10   Select $\theta_{i+1} \leftarrow \arg\min_{\theta_{i+k}} \left(\mathcal{L}_{vdc}(\theta_{i+k}^f, \mathcal{X}_{mte}), \mathcal{L}_{vdc}(\theta_{i+k}^v, \mathcal{X}_{mte}) \right)$;
11 **end**

2.1 Preliminary of 3DMM

The original 3DMM can be described as:

$$\mathbf{S} = \overline{\mathbf{S}} + \mathbf{A}_{id}\boldsymbol{\alpha}_{id} + \mathbf{A}_{exp}\boldsymbol{\alpha}_{exp}, \tag{1}$$

where $\mathbf{S}$ is the 3D face mesh, $\overline{\mathbf{S}}$ is the mean 3D shape, $\boldsymbol{\alpha}_{id}$ is the shape parameter corresponding to the 3D shape base $\mathbf{A}_{id}$, $\mathbf{A}_{exp}$ is the expression base and $\boldsymbol{\alpha}_{exp}$ is the expression parameter. After the 3D face is reconstructed, it can be projected onto the image plane with the scale orthographic projection:

$$V_{2d}(\mathbf{p}) = f * \mathbf{Pr} * \mathbf{R} * \left(\overline{\mathbf{S}} + \mathbf{A}_{id}\boldsymbol{\alpha}_{id} + \mathbf{A}_{exp}\boldsymbol{\alpha}_{exp}\right) + \mathbf{t}_{2d}, \tag{2}$$

where $V_{2d}(\mathbf{p})$ is the projection function generating the 2D positions of model vertices, f is the scale factor, $\mathbf{Pr}$ is the orthographic projection matrix, $\mathbf{R}$ is the rotation matrix constructed by Euler angles including pitch, yaw, roll and $\mathbf{t}_{2d}$ is the translation vector. The complete parameters of 3DMM are $\mathbf{p} = [f, \text{pitch}, \text{yaw}, \text{roll}, \mathbf{t}_{2d}, \boldsymbol{\alpha}_{id}, \boldsymbol{\alpha}_{exp}]$.

However, the three Euler angles will cause the gimbal lock [30] when faces are close to the profile view. This ambiguity will confuse the regressor to degrade the performance, so we choose to regress the similarity transformation matrix instead of $[f, \text{pitch}, \text{yaw}, \text{roll}, \mathbf{t}_{2d}]$ to reduce the regression difficulty: $\mathbf{T} = f[\mathbf{R}; \mathbf{t}_{3d}]$, where $\mathbf{T} \in \mathbb{R}^{3 \times 4}$ is constructed by a scale factor f, a rotation matrix $\mathbf{R}$ and a translation vector $\mathbf{t}_{3d} = \begin{bmatrix} \mathbf{t}_{2d} \\ 0 \end{bmatrix}$. Therefore, the scale orthographic projection in Eq. 2 can be simplified as:

$$V_{2d}(\mathbf{p}) = \mathbf{Pr} * \mathbf{T} * \begin{bmatrix} \mathbf{S} + \mathbf{A}\boldsymbol{\alpha} \\ 1 \end{bmatrix}, \tag{3}$$

where $\mathbf{A} = [\mathbf{A}_{id}, \mathbf{A}_{exp}]$ and $\boldsymbol{\alpha} = [\boldsymbol{\alpha}_{id}, \boldsymbol{\alpha}_{exp}]$. Our regression objective is described as $\mathbf{p} = [\mathbf{T}, \boldsymbol{\alpha}]$.

The high-dimensional parameters $\boldsymbol{\alpha}_{shp} \in \mathbb{R}^{199}$, $\boldsymbol{\alpha}_{exp} \in \mathbb{R}^{29}$ are redundant, since 3DMM models the 3D face shape with PCA and the last parts of parameters have little effect on the face shape. We choose only the first 40 dimensions of $\boldsymbol{\alpha}_{shp}$ and the first 10 dimensions of $\boldsymbol{\alpha}_{exp}$ as our regression target, since the NME increase is acceptable and the reconstruction can be greatly accelerated. The NME error heatmap caused by different size of shape and expression dimensions is present in the supplementary material. Therefore, our complete regression target is simplified as $\mathbf{p} = [\mathbf{T}^{3 \times 4}, \boldsymbol{\alpha}^{50}]$, with 62 dimensions in total, where $\boldsymbol{\alpha} = [\boldsymbol{\alpha}_{shp}^{40}, \boldsymbol{\alpha}_{exp}^{10}]$. To eliminate the negative impact of magnitude differences between $\mathbf{T}$ and $\boldsymbol{\alpha}$, Z-score normalizing is adopted: $\mathbf{p} = (\mathbf{p} - \boldsymbol{\mu}_p)/\boldsymbol{\sigma}_p$, where $\boldsymbol{\mu}_p \in \mathbb{R}^{62}$ is the mean of parameters and $\boldsymbol{\sigma}_p \in \mathbb{R}^{62}$ indicates the standard deviation of parameters.

2.2   Meta-Joint Optimization

We first review the Vertex Distance Cost (VDC) and Weighted Parameter Distance Cost (WPDC) in [54], then derivate the meta-joint optimization to facilitate the parameters regression.

The VDC term $\mathcal{L}_{vdc}$ directly optimizes $\mathbf{p}$ by minimizing the vertex distances between the fitted 3D face and the ground truth:

$$\mathcal{L}_{vdc} = \|V_{3d}(\mathbf{p}) - V_{3d}(\mathbf{p}^g)\|^2, \tag{4}$$

where $\mathbf{p}^g$ is the ground truth parameter, $\mathbf{p}$ is the predicted parameter and $V_{3d}(\cdot)$ is the 3D face reconstruction formulated as:

$$V_{3d}(\mathbf{p}) = \mathbf{T} * \begin{bmatrix} \mathbf{S} + \mathbf{A}\boldsymbol{\alpha} \\ 1 \end{bmatrix}. \tag{5}$$

Different from VDC, the WPDC term [54] $\mathcal{L}_{wpdc}$ assigns different weights to each parameter:

$$\mathcal{L}_{wpdc} = \|\mathbf{w} \cdot (\mathbf{p} - \mathbf{p}^g)\|^2, \tag{6}$$

where $\mathbf{w}$ indicates the importance weight as follows:

$$\mathbf{w} = (w_1, w_2, \ldots, w_i, \ldots, w_n),$$
$$w_i = \|V_{3d}(\mathbf{p}^{de,i}) - V_{3d}(\mathbf{p}^g)\| / Z, \tag{7}$$
$$\mathbf{p}^{de,i} = (\mathbf{p}_1^g, \mathbf{p}_2^g, \ldots, \mathbf{p}_i, \ldots, \mathbf{p}_n^g),$$

where n is the number of parameters ($n = 62$ in our regression framework), $\mathbf{p}^{de,i}$ is the i-degraded parameter whose i-th element is from the predicted $\mathbf{p}$, Z is the maximum of $\mathbf{w}$ for regularization. The term $\left\|V_{3d}(\mathbf{p}^{de,i}) - V_{3d}(\mathbf{p}^g)\right\|$ models the importance of i-th parameter.

Algorithm 2: fWPDC: Fast WPDC Algorithm.

Input : Shape and expression base: $\mathbf{A} = [\mathbf{A}_{id}, \mathbf{A}_{exp}] \in \mathbb{R}^{3N \times 50}$
Mean shape: $\overline{\mathbf{S}} \in \mathbb{R}^{3 \times N}$
Predicted parameters: $\mathbf{p} = [\mathbf{T} \in \mathbb{R}^{3 \times 4}, \alpha \in \mathbb{R}^{50}]$
Ground truth parameters: $\mathbf{p}^g = [\mathbf{T}^g \in \mathbb{R}^{3 \times 4}, \alpha^g \in \mathbb{R}^{50}]$
Scale factor scalar: f

Output: WPDC item

1 Initialize the weights of the parameter $\mathbf{T}$ and α: $\mathbf{w}_T \in \mathbb{R}^{3 \times 4}$, $\mathbf{w}_\alpha \in \mathbb{R}^{50}$;
   // Calculating the weight of transform matrix
2 Reconstruct the vertices without projection: $\mathbf{S} = \overline{\mathbf{S}} + \mathbf{A}\alpha \in \mathbb{R}^{3 \times N}$;
3 **for** $i = 1, 2, 3$ **do**
4 $\quad$ $\mathbf{w}_T(:,i) = \left(\mathbf{T}(:,i) - \mathbf{T}^g(:,i)\right) \cdot \|\mathbf{S}(i,:)\|$;
5 **end**
6 $\mathbf{w}_T(:,4) = \left(\mathbf{T}(:,4) - \mathbf{T}^g(:,4)\right) \cdot \sqrt{N/3}$ and then flatten $\mathbf{w}_T$ to the vector form in row-major order;
   // Calculating the weight of shape and expression parameters
7 **for** $i = 1 \ldots 50$ **do**
8 $\quad$ $\mathbf{w}_\alpha(i) = f \cdot \left(\alpha(i) - \alpha^g(i)\right) \cdot \|\mathbf{A}(:,i)\|$;
9 **end**
   // Calculating the fWPDC item
10 Get the maximum value Z of the weights $(\mathbf{w}_T, \mathbf{w}_\alpha)$ and normalize them: $\mathbf{w}_T = \mathbf{w}_T/Z$, $\mathbf{w}_\alpha = \mathbf{w}_\alpha/Z$;
11 Calculate the WPDC item: $\mathcal{L}_{fwpdc} = \|\mathbf{w}_T \cdot (\mathbf{T} - \mathbf{T}^g)\|^2 + \|\mathbf{w}_\alpha \cdot (\alpha - \alpha^g)\|^2$

---

fWPDC. The original calculation of $\mathbf{w}$ in WPDC is rather slow as the calculation of each w_i needs to reconstruct all the vertices once, which is a bottleneck for fast training. We find that the vertices can be only reconstructed once by decomposing the weight calculation into two parts: the similarity transformation matrix $\mathbf{T}$, and the combination of shape and expression parameters α. Therefore, we design a fast implementation of WPDC named fWPDC: (i) reconstructing the vertices without projection $\mathbf{S} = \overline{\mathbf{S}} + \mathbf{A}\alpha$ and calculating $\mathbf{w}_T$ using the norm of row vectors; (ii) calculating $\mathbf{w}_\alpha$ using the norm of column vectors of $\mathbf{A}$ and the input scale f: $\mathbf{w}_\alpha(i) = f \cdot \left(\alpha(i) - \alpha^g(i)\right) \cdot \|\mathbf{A}(:,i)\|$; (iii) Combining them to calculate the final cost. The detailed algorithm of fWPDC is described in Algorithm 2. fWPDC only reconstructs dense vertices once, not 62 times as WPDC, thus greatly reducing the computation cost. With 128 samples as a batch input, the original WPDC takes 41.7 ms while fWPDC only takes 3.6 ms. fWPDC is over 10× faster than the original WPDC while preserving the same outputs.

Exploitation of VDC and fWPDC. Through Eq. 4 and Eq. 6, we find: WPDC/fWPDC is suitable for parameters regression since each parameter is appropriately weighted, while VDC can directly reflect the goodness of the 3D face reconstructed from parameters. In Fig. 3, we investigate how these two losses converge as the training progresses. It is shown that the optimization is difficult for VDC since the vertex error is still over 15 when training converges. The work in [55] also demonstrates that optimizing VDC with gradient descent converges

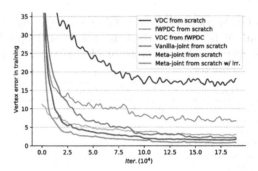

Fig. 3. The vertex error in training on 300W-LP supervised by different loss terms. VDC from scratch has the highest error, fWPDC is lower than VDC, and VDC from fWPDC is better than both. When combining VDC and fWPDC, the proposed meta-joint optimization converges faster and reaches lower error than vanilla-joint, and achieves even better convergence when incorporating the landmark-regression regularization.

very slowly due to the "zig-zagging" problem. In contrast, the convergence of fWPDC is much faster than VDC and the error is about 7 when training converges. Surprisingly, if the fWPDC-trained model is fine-tuned by VDC, we can get a much lower error than fWPDC. Based on the above observation, we conclude that: *training from scratch with VDC is hard to converge* and *the network is not fully trained by fWPDC in the late stage*.

Meta-Joint Optimization. Based on above discussions, it is natural to weight two terms to perform a vanilla-joint optimization: $\mathcal{L}_{vanilla\text{-}joint} = \beta \mathcal{L}_{fwpdc} + (1 - \beta)\frac{|l_{fwpdc}|}{|l_{vdc}|} \cdot \mathcal{L}_{vdc}$, where $\beta \in [0,1]$ controls the importance between fWPDC and VDC. However, the vanilla-joint optimization relies on the manually set hyperparameter β and does not achieves satisfactory results in Fig. 3. Inspired by Lookahead [52] and MAML [18], we propose a meta-joint optimization strategy to dynamically combine fWPDC and VDC. The overview of the meta-joint optimization is shown in Fig. 4. In the training process, the model looks ahead by k-steps with the cost fWPDC or VDC on k meta-train batches $\mathcal{X}_{mtr}$, then selects the better one between fWPDC and VDC according to the vertex error on the meta-test batch. Specifically, the whole meta-joint optimization consists of four steps: (i) sampling k batches of training samples $\mathcal{X}_{mtr}$ for meta-train and one batch $\mathcal{X}_{mte}$ for meta-test; (ii) meta-train: updating the current model parameters θ_i with fWPDC and VDC on $\mathcal{X}_{mtr}$ by k-steps, respectively, getting two parameter states θ_{i+k}^f and θ_{i+k}^v; (iii) meta-test: evaluating the vertex error θ_{i+k}^f and θ_{i+k}^v on $\mathcal{X}_{mte}$; (iv) selecting the parameters which have the lower error to update θ_i. The proposed meta-joint optimization can be directly embedded into the standard training regime. From Fig. 3, we can observe that the meta-joint optimization converges faster than vanilla-joint and has the lower error.

2.3   Landmark-Regression Regularization

In 3D face reconstruction [14,15,19,42,43], the 2D sparse landmarks after projecting are usually used as an extra regularization to facilitate the parameters regression. In our regression framework, we find that treating 2D sparse landmarks as a auxiliary regression task benefits more.

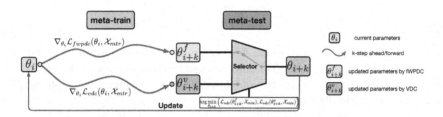

Fig. 4. Overview of the meta-joint optimization.

As shown in Fig. 2, we add an additional landmark-regression task on the global pooling layer, trained by L2 loss. The difference between the former landmark-regularization and the latter landmark-regression regularization is that the latter introduces extra parameters to regress the landmarks. In other words, the landmark-regression regularization is a task-level regularization. From the tomato curve in Fig. 3, we get a lower error by incorporating the landmark-regression regularization. The comparative results in Table 3 show our proposed landmark-regression regularization is better than landmark-regularization (3.59% vs. 3.71% on AFLW2000-3D). The landmark-regression regularization is formulated as: $\mathcal{L}_{lrr} = \frac{1}{N}\sum_{i=1}^{N}\|l_i - l_i^g\|_2^2$, where N is 136 here as we utilize 68 2D landmarks and flatten them into a 136-d vector.

2.4   3D Aided Short-video-synthesis

Video based 3D face applications have become more and more popular [8,9,27, 28] recently. In these applications, 3D dense face alignment methods are required to run on videos and provide stable reconstruction results across adjacent frames. The stability means that the changing of the reconstructed 3D faces across adjacent frames should be consistent with the true face moving in a fine-grained level. However, most of existing methods [17,26,54,55] omit this requirement and the predictions suffer from random jittering. In 2D face alignment, post-processing like temporal filtering is a common strategy to reduce the jittering, but it degrades the precision and causes the frame delay. Besides, since no public video databases for 3D dense face alignment are available, the video training strategies [16,32,36,40] cannot work here. A challenge arises: *can we improve the stability on videos with only still images available when training?*

To address this challenge, we propose a batch-level 3D aided short-video-synthesis strategy, which expands one still image to several adjacent frames, forming a short synthetic video in a mini-batch. The common patterns in a video can be modelled as: (i) Noise. We model noise as $P(x) = x + \mathcal{N}(0, \Sigma)$, where $\Sigma = \sigma^2 I$. (ii) Motion Blur. Motion blur can be formulated as $M(x) = K * x$, where K is the convolution kernel (the operator $*$ denotes a convolution). (iii) In-plane rotation. Given two adjacent frames x_t and x_{t+1}, the in-plane temporal change from x_t to x_{t+1} can be described as a similarity transform $T(\cdot)$:

$$T(\cdot) = \Delta s \begin{bmatrix} \cos(\Delta\theta) & -\sin(\Delta\theta) & \Delta t_1 \\ \sin(\Delta\theta) & \cos(\Delta\theta) & \Delta t_2 \end{bmatrix}, \tag{8}$$

where Δs is the scale perturbation, $\Delta\theta$ is the rotation perturbation, Δt_1 and Δt_2 are translation perturbations. (iv) Since human faces share similar 3D structure, we are also able to synthesize the out-of-plane face moving. Face profiling [54] $F(\cdot)$, which is originally proposed to solving large-pose face alignment, is utilized to progressively increase the yaw angle $\Delta\phi$ and pitch angle $\Delta\gamma$ of the face. Specifically, we sample several still images in a mini-batch and for each still image x_0, we transform it slightly and smoothly to generate a synthetic video with n adjacent frames: $\{x'_j | x'_j = (M \circ P)(x_j), x_j = (T \circ F)(x_{j-1}), 1 \leq j \leq n-1\} \cup \{x_0\}$. In Fig. 5, we give an illustration of how these transformations are applied on an image to generate several adjacent frames.

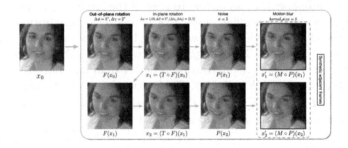

Fig. 5. An illustration of how two adjacent frames are synthesized in our 3D aided short-video-synthesis.

3   Experiments

In this section, we first introduce the datasets and protocols; then, we give comparison experiments on the accuracy and stability; thirdly, the complexity and running speed are evaluated; extensive discussions are finally made. The implementation details, generalization and scaling-up ability of our proposed method are in the supplementary material.

3.1 Datasets and Evaluation Protocols

Five datasets are used in our experiments: **300W-LP** [54] (300W Across Large Poses) is composed of the synthesized large-pose face images from 300W [38], including AFW [56], LFPW [2], HELEN [53], IBUG [38], and XM2VTS [34]. Specifically, the face profiling method [54] is adopted to generate 122,450 samples across large poses. **AFLW** [29] consists of 21,080 in-the-wild faces (following [22,55]) with large poses (yaw from -90° to 90°). Each image is annotated up to 21 visible landmarks. **AFLW2000-3D** [54] is constructed by [54] for evaluating 3D face alignment performance, which contains the ground truth 3D faces and the corresponding 68 landmarks of the first 2,000 AFLW samples. **Florence** [1] is a 3D face dataset containing 53 subjects with its ground truth 3D mesh acquired from a structured-light scanning system. For evaluation, we generate renderings with different poses for each subject following VRN [26] and PRNet [17]. **Menpo-3D** [51] provides a benchmark for evaluating 3D facial landmark localization algorithms in the wild in arbitrary poses. Specifically, Menpo-3D provides 3D facial landmarks for 55 videos from 300-VW [39] competition.

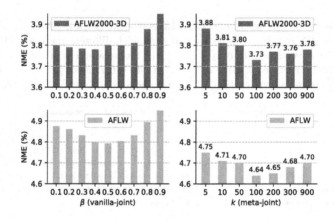

Fig. 6. Ablative results of the vanilla-joint optimization with different β and meta-joint optimization with different k. Lower NME (%) is better.

Protocols. The protocol on AFLW follows [54] and Normalized Mean Error (NME) by bounding box size is reported. Two protocols on AFLW2000-3D are applied: the first one follows AFLW, and the other one follows [17] to evaluate the NME of 3D face reconstruction normalized by the bounding box size. For Florence, we follow [17,26] to evaluate the NME of 3D face reconstruction normalized by outer interocular distance. As for Menpo-3D, we evaluate the NME on still frames and the stability across adjacent frames. We calculate the stability following [40] by measuring the NME between the predicted offsets and the ground-truth offsets of adjacent frames. Specifically, at frame $t-1$ and t,

Table 1. The NME (%) of different methods on AFLW2000-3D and AFLW. The first and the second best results are highlighted. M, R, S denote the meta-joint optimization, landmark-regression regularization and short-video-synthesis, respectively.

Method	AFLW2000-3D (68 pts)				AFLW (21 pts)			
	[0, 30]	[30, 60]	[60, 90]	Mean	[0, 30]	[30, 60]	[60, 90]	Mean
ESR [13]	4.60	6.70	12.67	7.99	5.66	7.12	11.94	8.24
SDM [46]	3.67	4.94	9.67	6.12	4.75	5.55	9.34	6.55
3DDFA [54]	3.78	4.54	7.93	5.42	5.00	5.06	6.74	5.60
3DDFA+SDM [54]	3.43	4.24	7.17	4.94	4.75	4.83	6.38	5.32
Yu et al. [48]	3.62	6.06	9.56	6.41	–	–	–	–
DeFA [33]	–	–	–	4.50	–	–	–	–
3DSTN [4]	3.15	4.33	5.98	4.49	**3.55**	**3.92**	5.21	**4.23**
3D-FAN [7]	3.15	3.53	4.60	3.76	4.40	4.52	5.17	4.69
3DDFA-TPAMI [55]	2.84	3.57	4.96	3.79	4.11	4.38	5.16	4.55
PRNet [17]	**2.75**	3.51	4.61	3.62	4.19	4.69	5.45	4.77
MobileNet (M+R)	**2.75**	**3.49**	**4.53**	**3.59**	4.06	4.41	**5.02**	4.50
MobileNet (M+R+S)	**2.63**	**3.42**	**4.48**	**3.51**	**3.98**	**4.31**	**4.99**	**4.43**

Table 2. The NME (%) on Florence, AFLW2000-3D (Dense), NME (%) / Stability (%) on Menpo-3D, running complexity and time with different methods. Our method outputs 3D dense vertices with only 2.1 ms (2 ms for parameters prediction and 0.1 ms for vertices reconstruction) in GPU or 7.2 ms in CPU (6.2 ms for parameters prediction and 1 ms for vertices reconstruction). The first and second best results are highlighted.

Methods	Florence	AFLW2000-3D (Dense)	Menpo-3D	Params	MACs	Run time (ms)
3DDFA [54]	6.38	6.56	–	–	–	75.7 = 23.2 (GPU)+52.5 (CPU)
VRN [26]	5.27	–	–	–	–	69.0 (GPU)
DeFA [33]	–	6.04	–	–	1426M	35.4=11.8 (GPU)+23.6 (CPU)
PRNet [17]	3.76	4.41	1.90 / 0.54	13.4M	6190M	9.8 (GPU) / 175.0 (CPU)
MobileNet (M+R)	**3.59**	**4.20**	**1.86 / 0.52**	3.27M	183M	**2.1 (GPU) / 7.2 (CPU)**
MobileNet (M+R+S)	**3.56**	**4.18**	**1.71 / 0.48**			

the ground-truth landmark offset is $\Delta p = p_t - p_{t-1}$, the prediction offset is $\Delta q = q_t - q_{t-1}$, the error $\Delta p - \Delta q$ normalized by the bounding box size represents the stability. Since 300W-LP only has the indices of 68 landmarks, we use 68 landmarks of Menpo-3D for consistency.

3.2   Ablation Study

To evaluate the effectiveness of the meta-joint optimization and the landmark-regression regularization, we carry out comparative experiments including our two baselines: *VDC* and *fWPDC*, three joint options: (i) *VDC from fWPDC*: fine-tune the model with VDC loss from the pre-trained model by fWPDC; (ii) *Vanilla-joint*: weight VDC and fWPDC by the best scalar $\beta = 0.5$; (iii) *Meta-joint*: the proposed meta-joint optimization with best $k = 100$ and four options

Table 3. The comparative and ablative results on AFLW2000-3D and AFLW. The mean NMEs (%) across small, medium and large poses on AFLW2000-3D and AFLW are reported. lmk. indicates landmark constraint on the parameter regression like [43] and lrr. is the proposed landmark-regression regularization.

	Method	AFLW2000-3D	AFLW
Baseline	VDC	5.23	6.37
	fWDPC	4.04	5.10
Joint-optimization options	VDC from fWPDC	3.88	4.83
	Vanilla-joint	3.80	4.80
	Meta-joint	**3.73**	**4.64**
Utilization of 2D landmarks	VDC w/ lrr	3.92	4.92
	fWPDC w/ lrr	3.89	4.84
	Meta-joint w/ lmk	3.71	4.80
	Meta-joint w/ lrr.	**3.59**	**4.50**

Table 4. Comparisons of NME (%)/Stability (%) on Menpo-3D. svs. indicates short-video-synthesis, rnd. indicates applying in-plane and out-of-plane rotations randomly in one mini-batch.

Method	Menpo-3D
fWPDC w/o svs	1.96 / 0.54
fWPDC w/ svs	**1.84 / 0.51**
Meta-joint+lrr. w/o svs	1.86 / 0.52
Meta-joint+lrr. w/ rnd	1.76 / 0.50
Meta-joint+lrr. w/ svs	**1.71/0.48**

of how the 2D landmarks are utilized. From Table 3, Table 4, Fig. 3 and Fig. 6, we can draw the following conclusions:

Meta-Joint Optimization Performs Better. Comparing with two baselines *VDC* and *fWPDC*, all three joint optimization methods perform better. Among three joint optimization methods, the proposed meta-joint performs better than *VDC from fWPDC* and *vanilla-joint*: the mean NME drops from 4.04% to 3.73% on AFLW2000-3D and 5.10% to 4.64% on AFLW when compared with the baseline *fWPDC*. Furthermore, we conduct ablative experiments with different β for *vanilla-joint* and different look-ahead step k in Fig. 6. We can observe that $\beta = 0.5$ is the best setting for *vanilla-joint*, but *meta-joint* still outperforms it and $k = 100$ performs best on both AFLW2000-3D and AFLW. Overall, the proposed meta-joint optimization is effective in alleviate the training and promoting the performance.

Landmark-Regression Regularization Benefits. Another contribution is the landmark-regression regularization, which can also be regarded as an auxiliary task to parameters regression. From Table 3, the improvements from *fWPDC* to *fWPDC w/ lrr.* on AFLW2000-3D and AFLW are 0.15% and 0.26%, and the improvements from *Meta-joint* to *Meta-joint w/ lrr.* on AFLW2000-3D and AFLW are 0.14% and 0.14%. We also compare the proposed landmark-regression regularization with prior methods [42,43] which directly impose landmark constraint on the parameter regression, the results show ours is significantly better: 3.59% vs. 3.71% on AFLW2000-3D. We further evaluate the performance of the landmark-regression branch on AFLW2000-3D and AFLW. The performances are 3.58% and 4.52% respectively, which are close to the parameter branch. It indicates that these two tasks are highly related. Overall, the landmark-regression regularization benefits the training and promotes the performance.

Short-Video-Synthesis Improves Stability. The last contribution is 3D aided short-video-synthesis, which is designed to enhance stability on videos by augmenting one still image to a short video in a mini-batch. The results in Table 4 indicate that short-video-synthesis works for both the fWPDC and meta-joint optimization. With short-video-synthesis and landmark-regression regularization, the performance on still frames improves from 1.86% to 1.71% and the stability improves from 0.52% to 0.48%. We also evaluate the performance by randomly applying in-plane and out-of-plane rotations in each mini-batch and find it is worse than short-video-synthesis: 1.76%/0.50% v.s. 1.71%/0.48%. These results validate the effectiveness of the 3D aided short-video-synthesis.

3.3   Evaluations of Accuracy and Stability

Sparse Face Alignment. We use AFLW2000-3D and AFLW to evaluate sparse face alignment performance with small, medium and large yaw angles. The results in Table 1 indicate that our method performs better than PRNet (3.51% vs. 3.62%) in AFLW2000-3D and better than 3DDFA-TPAMI [55] in AFLW (4.43% vs. 4.55%). Note that these results are achieved with only 3.27M parameters (24% of PRNet) and it takes 6.2 ms (3.5% of PRNet) in CPU. The sampling of 68/21 landmarks from 3DMM is extremely fast, only 0.01 ms (CPU), which can be ignored.

Dense Face Alignment. Dense face alignment is evaluated on Florence and AFLW2000-3D. Our evaluation settings follow [17] to keep consistency. The results in Table 2 show that the proposed method significantly outperforms others. As for 3D dense vertices reconstruction, 45K vertices only takes 1 ms in CPU (0.1 ms in GPU) with our regression framework.

Video-based 3D Face Alignment. We use Menpo-3D to evaluate both the accuracy and stability. Table 4 has already shown the superiority of short-video-synthesis. We choose to compare our method with recent PRNet [17] in Table 2.

The results indicate that our method significantly surpasses PRNet in both the accuracy and stability on videos of Menpo-3D with a much lower computation cost.

3.4 Evaluations of Speed

We compare parameter numbers, MACs (Multiply-Accumulates) measuring the number of fused Multiplication and Addition operations, and the running time of our method with others in Table 2. As for the running speed, 3DDFA [54] takes 23.2 ms (GPU) for predicting parameters and 52.5 ms (CPU) for PNCC construction, DeFA [17] needs 11.8 ms (GPU) to predict 3DMM parameters and 23.6 ms (CPU) for post-processing, VRN [26] detects 68 2D landmarks with 28.4 ms (GPU) and regresses the 3D dense vertices with 40.6 ms (GPU), PRNet [17] predicts the 3D dense vertices with 9.8 ms (GPU) or 175 ms (CPU). Compared with them, our method takes only 2 ms (GPU) or 6.2 ms (CPU) to predict 3DMM parameters and 0.1 ms (GPU) or 1 ms (CPU) to reconstruct 3D dense vertices.

Specifically, compared with the recent PRNet [17], the parameters of our model (3.27M) are less than one-quarter of PRNet (13.4M), and the MACs are less than 1/30 (183.5M vs. 6190M). We measure the overall running time on GeForce GTX 1080 GPU and i5-8259U CPU with 4 cores. Note that our method takes only 7.2 ms, which is almost 24× faster than PRNet (175 ms). Besides, we benchmark our method on a single CPU core (using only one thread) and *the running speed of our method is about 19.2 ms (over 50 fps), including the reconstruction time*. The specific CPU configuration is i5-8259U CPU @ 2.30 GHz on a 13-inch MacBook Pro.

3.5 Analysis of Meta-Joint Optimization

We visualize the auto-selection result of fWPDC and VDC in the meta-joint optimization, as shown in Fig. 7. We can observe that both $k = 100$ and $k = 200$ show the same trend: fPWDC dominates in the early stage and VDC guides in the late stage. This trend is consistent with the previous observations and gives a clear description of why our proposed meta-joint optimization works.

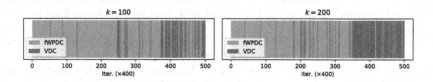

Fig. 7. Auto-selection result of the selector in the meta-joint optimization.

4 Conclusion

In this paper, we have successfully pursued the fast, accurate and stable 3D dense face alignment simultaneously. Towards this target, we make three main efforts: (i) proposing a fast WPDC named fWPDC and the meta-joint optimization to combine fWPDC and VDC to alleviate the problem of optimization; (ii) imposing an extra landmark-regression regularization to promote the performance to state-of-the-art; (iii) proposing the 3D aided short-video-synthesis method to improve the stability on videos. The experimental results demonstrate the effectiveness and efficiency of our proposed methods. Our promising results pave the way for real-time 3D dense face alignment in practical use and the proposed methods may improve the environment by reducing the amount of carbon dioxide released by the huge amounts of energy consumed by GPUs.

Acknowledgement. This work was supported in part by the National Key Research & Development Program (No. 2020YFC2003901), Chinese National Natural Science Foundation Projects #61872367, #61876178, #61806196, #61976229.

References

1. Bagdanov, A.D., Bimbo, A.D., Masi, I.: The florence 2D/3D hybrid face dataset. In: ACM workshop on Human gesture and behavior understanding (2011)
2. Belhumeur, P.N., Jacobs, D.W., Kriegman, D.J., Kumar, N.: Localizing parts of faces using a consensus of exemplars. TPAMI **35**, 2930–2940 (2013)
3. Bettadapura, V.: Face expression recognition and analysis: the state of the art. arXiv:1203.6722 (2012)
4. Bhagavatula, C., Zhu, C., Luu, K., Savvides, M.: Faster than real-time facial alignment: a 3D spatial transformer network approach in unconstrained poses. In: ICCV (2017)
5. Blanz, V., Vetter, T., et al.: A morphable model for the synthesis of 3D faces. In: SIGGRAPH (1999)
6. Booth, J., Roussos, A., Zafeiriou, S., Ponniah, A., Dunaway, D.: A 3D morphable model learnt from 10,000 faces. In: CVPR (2016)
7. Bulat, A., Tzimiropoulos, G.: How far are we from solving the 2D & 3D face alignment problem? (and a dataset of 230,000 3D facial landmarks). In: ICCV (2017)
8. Cao, C., Chai, M., Woodford, O., Luo, L.: Stabilized real-time face tracking via a learned dynamic rigidity prior. In: SIGGRAPH Asia 2018 Technical Papers. ACM (2018)
9. Cao, C., Weng, Y., Lin, S., Zhou, K.: 3D shape regression for real-time facial animation. ACM Trans. Graph. (TOG) **32**, 1–10 (2013)
10. Cao, J., Hu, Y., Zhang, H., He, R., Sun, Z.: Learning a high fidelity pose invariant model for high-resolution face frontalization. In: Advances in Neural Information Processing Systems, pp. 2867–2877 (2018)
11. Cao, J., Hu, Y., Zhang, H., He, R., Sun, Z.: Towards high fidelity face frontalization in the wild. Int. J. Comput. Vision **128**, 1–20 (2019)
12. Cao, J., Huang, H., Li, Y., He, R., Sun, Z.: Informative sample mining network for multi-domain image-to-image translation. In: Proceedings of the European Conference on Computer Vision (ECCV) (2020)

13. Cao, X., Wei, Y., Wen, F., Sun, J.: Face alignment by explicit shape regression. IJCV **107**, 177–190 (2014)
14. Chinaev, N., Chigorin, A., Laptev, I.: Mobileface: 3D face reconstruction with efficient cnn regression. In: ECCV (2018)
15. Deng, Y., Yang, J., Xu, S., Chen, D., Jia, Y., Tong, X.: Accurate 3D face reconstruction with weakly-supervised learning: from single image to image set. In: CVPR Workshop (2019)
16. Dong, X., Yu, S.I., Weng, X., Wei, S.E., Yang, Y., Sheikh, Y.: Supervision-by-registration: an unsupervised approach to improve the precision of facial landmark detectors. In: CVPR (2018)
17. Feng, Y., Wu, F., Shao, X., Wang, Y., Zhou, X.: Joint 3D face reconstruction and dense alignment with position map regression network. In: ECCV (2018)
18. Finn, C., Abbeel, P., Levine, S.: Model-agnostic meta-learning for fast adaptation of deep networks. In: ICML (2017)
19. Gecer, B., Ploumpis, S., Kotsia, I., Zafeiriou, S.: Ganfit: generative adversarial network fitting for high fidelity 3D face reconstruction. In: CVPR (2019)
20. Guo, J., et al.: Dominant and complementary emotion recognition from still images of faces. IEEE Access **6**, 26391–26403 (2018)
21. Guo, J., et al.: Multi-modality network with visual and geometrical information for micro emotion recognition. In: 2017 12th IEEE International Conference on Automatic Face & Gesture Recognition (FG 2017), pp. 814–819. IEEE (2017)
22. Guo, J., Zhu, X., Lei, Z.: 3ddfa (2018). https://github.com/cleardusk/3DDFA
23. Guo, J., Zhu, X., Lei, Z., Li, S.Z.: Face synthesis for eyeglass-robust face recognition. In: Zhou, J., et al. (eds.) CCBR 2018. LNCS, vol. 10996, pp. 275–284. Springer, Cham (2018). https://doi.org/10.1007/978-3-319-97909-0_30
24. Guo, J., Zhu, X., Xiao, J., Lei, Z., Wan, G., Li, S.Z.: Improving face anti-spoofing by 3D virtual synthesis. In: 2019 International Conference on Biometrics (ICB), pp. 1–8. IEEE (2019)
25. Guo, J., Zhu, X., Zhao, C., Cao, D., Lei, Z., Li, S.Z.: Learning meta face recognition in unseen domains. In: Proceedings of the IEEE/CVF Conference on Computer Vision and Pattern Recognition, pp. 6163–6172 (2020)
26. Jackson, A., Bulat, A., Argyriou, V., Tzimiropoulos, G.: Large pose 3D face reconstruction from a single image via direct volumetric cnn regression. In: ICCV (2017)
27. Kim, H., et al.: Neural style-preserving visual dubbing. ACM Trans. Graph. (TOG) **38**, 1–13 (2019)
28. Kim, H., et al.: Deep video portraits. ACM Trans. Graph. (TOG) **37**, 1–14 (2018)
29. Koestinger, M., Wohlhart, P., Roth, P.M., Bischof, H.: Annotated facial landmarks in the wild: a large-scale, real-world database for facial landmark localization. In: ICCV Workshop (2011)
30. Lepetit, V., Fua, P., et al.: Monocular model-based 3D tracking of rigid objects: A survey. Found. Trends® Comput. Graph. Vision (2005)
31. Liu, F., Zeng, D., Zhao, Q., Liu, X.: Joint face alignment and 3D face reconstruction. In: Leibe, B., Matas, J., Sebe, N., Welling, M. (eds.) ECCV 2016. LNCS, vol. 9909, pp. 545–560. Springer, Cham (2016). https://doi.org/10.1007/978-3-319-46454-1_33
32. Liu, H., Lu, J., Feng, J., Zhou, J.: Two-stream transformer networks for video-based face alignment. TPAMI **40**, 2546–2554 (2018)
33. Liu, Y., Jourabloo, A., Ren, W., Liu, X.: Dense face alignment. In: ICCV (2017)
34. Messer, K., Matas, J., Kittler, J., Luettin, J., Maitre, G.: Xm2vtsdb: the extended m2vts database. In: Second International Conference on Audio and Video-Based Biometric Person Authentication (1999)

35. Newell, A., Yang, K., Deng, J.: Stacked hourglass networks for human pose estimation. In: Leibe, B., Matas, J., Sebe, N., Welling, M. (eds.) ECCV 2016. LNCS, vol. 9912, pp. 483–499. Springer, Cham (2016). https://doi.org/10.1007/978-3-319-46484-8_29
36. Peng, X., Feris, R.S., Wang, X., Metaxas, D.N.: A recurrent encoder-decoder network for sequential face alignment. In: Leibe, B., Matas, J., Sebe, N., Welling, M. (eds.) ECCV 2016. LNCS, vol. 9905, pp. 38–56. Springer, Cham (2016). https://doi.org/10.1007/978-3-319-46448-0_3
37. Qin, Y., et al.: Learning meta model for zero-and few-shot face anti-spoofing. In: The Thirty-Fourth AAAI Conference on Artificial Intelligence (AAAI) (2020)
38. Sagonas, C., Tzimiropoulos, G., Zafeiriou, S., Pantic, M.: 300 faces in-the-wild challenge: the first facial landmark localization challenge. In: CVPRW (2013)
39. Shen, J., Zafeiriou, S., Chrysos, G.G., Kossaifi, J., Tzimiropoulos, G., Pantic, M.: The first facial landmark tracking in-the-wild challenge: Benchmark and results. In: ICCV Workshops (2015)
40. Tai, Y., et al.: Towards highly accurate and stable face alignment for high-resolution videos. arXiv:1811.00342 (2018)
41. Taigman, Y., Yang., M., Ranzato, M., Wolf, L.: Deepface: closing the gap to human-level performance in face verification. In: CVPR (2014)
42. Tewari, A., et al.: Fml: face model learning from videos. In: CVPR (2019)
43. Tewari, A., et al.: Mofa: model-based deep convolutional face autoencoder for unsupervised monocular reconstruction. In: ICCV (2017)
44. Tuan, T., Hassner, T., Masi, I., Medioni, G.: Regressing robust and discriminative 3d morphable models with a very deep neural network. In: CVPR (2017)
45. Wang, Z., et al.: Deep spatial gradient and temporal depth learning for face anti-spoofing. In: Proceedings of the IEEE/CVF Conference on Computer Vision and Pattern Recognition, pp. 5042–5051 (2020)
46. Xiong, X., De, T.F.: Global supervised descent method. In: CVPR (2015)
47. Yang, C.Y., Liu, S., Yang, M.H.: Structured face hallucination. In: CVPR (2013)
48. Yu, R., Saito, S., Li, H., Ceylan, D., Li, H.: Learning dense facial correspondences in unconstrained images. In: ICCV (2017)
49. Yu, Z., Li, X., Niu, X., Shi, J., Zhao, G.: Face anti-spoofing with human material perception. In: Proceedings of the European Conference on Computer Vision (ECCV) (2020)
50. Yu, Z., et al.: Searching central difference convolutional networks for face anti-spoofing. In: Proceedings of the IEEE/CVF Conference on Computer Vision and Pattern Recognition, pp. 5295–5305 (2020)
51. Zafeiriou, S., Chrysos, G.G., Roussos, A., Ververas, E., Deng, J., Trigeorgis, G.: The 3D menpo facial landmark tracking challenge. In: ICCV (2017)
52. Zhang, M., Lucas, J., Ba, J., Hinton, G.E.: Lookahead optimizer: k steps forward, 1 step back. In: NeurIPS (2019)
53. Zhou, E., Fan, H., Cao, Z., Jiang, Y., Yin, Q.: Extensive facial landmark localization with coarse-to-fine convolutional network cascade. In: CVPRW (2013)
54. Zhu, X., Lei, Z., Liu, X., Shi, H., Li, S.Z.: Face alignment across large poses: a 3D solution. In: CVPR (2016)
55. Zhu, X., Liu, X., Lei, Z., Li, S.Z.: Face alignment in full pose range: a 3D total solution. TPAMI 41, 78–92 (2019)
56. Zhu, X., Ramanan, D.: Face detection, pose estimation, and landmark localization in the wild. In: CVPR (2012)
57. Zhu, X., et al.: Beyond 3D mm space: towards fine-grained 3D face reconstruction. In: Proceedings of the European Conference on Computer Vision (ECCV) (2020)

Iterative Feature Transformation for Fast and Versatile Universal Style Transfer

Tai-Yin Chiu$^{(\boxtimes)}$ and Danna Gurari

University of Texas at Austin, Austin, USA
`chiu.taiyin@utexas.edu`

Abstract. The general framework for fast universal style transfer consists of an autoencoder and a feature transformation at the bottleneck. We propose a new transformation that iteratively stylizes features with analytical gradient descent (Implementation is open-sourced at https://github.com/chiutaiyin/Iterative-feature-transformation-for-style-transfer). Experiments show this transformation is advantageous in part because it is fast. With control knobs to balance content preservation and style effect transferal, we also show this method can switch between artistic and photo-realistic style transfers and reduce distortion and artifacts. Finally, we show it can be used for applications requiring spatial control and multiple-style transfer.

1 Introduction

Style transfer is a task that renders a content image with the style from another image. Modern methods typically rely on neural networks to extract high level features for content and style representations. While achieving remarkable results, they can suffer from a *slow stylizing process* [5] or lack the ability to support *universal style transfer* [4,9,11,14,22,23,26], i.e., the ability to deal with arbitrary style images. To address these limitations, the recent trend has been to design frameworks that consist of an autoencoder that embeds a feature transformation to support the style transfer [2,8,13,15,21], as shown in Fig. 1(A).

At present, the feature transformations used for style transfer mostly focus on transferring style. For some methods [2,8,21], this leads to a distorted content in the resulting stylized images. This limits their applicability to scenarios when a user is performing artistic style transfer. In contrast, some methods are better suited to preserve the content and so produce photo-realistic transfer results [13, 15]. However, these methods can result in unnecessary artifacts and distortions in detailed content as initially examined in prior work [12,17,19] and expanded upon in our experiments.

Electronic supplementary material The online version of this chapter (https://doi.org/10.1007/978-3-030-58529-7_11) contains supplementary material, which is available to authorized users.

A. Vedaldi et al. (Eds.): ECCV 2020, LNCS 12364, pp. 169–184, 2020.
https://doi.org/10.1007/978-3-030-58529-7_11

In this paper, we propose an iterative feature transformation. We conduct experiments to show it realizes fast universal style transfer that can preserve content. More generally, this transformation provides control knobs to change the amount of style effect transferal, enabling it to switch between artistic and photo-realistic style transfers. We also demonstrate that our method is versatile in that it can be applied for spatial control and (non-linear) multi-style transfer.

2   Related Works

A summary of how our work differs from prior work is shown in Table 1. We elaborate in this section on the details conveyed in this table, and how our approach is uniquely able to meet the many interests of the style transfer community.

Neural Style Transfer. Gatys et al. [5] proposed a method of neural style transfer (NST) which has opened a new era of using a deep neural network to extract content and style representations of images, based on which we can synthesize an image whose content and style are from two distinct images. Variants of this algorithm include adding a Markov random field as a regularizer to reduce artifacts [10] and introducing extra histogram losses to help improve quality and convergence [20]. Neural style transfer also allows fine-grained control such as spatial/semantic control [1,6]. The drawback of Gatys's framework [5] and variants is that solving for stylized images is time-consuming due to many iterations of feed-forward and back-propagation to adjust pixel values. In the experiments, we will demonstrate our approach leads to considerable speed ups and so addresses the limitation that NST is very slow.

Table 1. Shown is a summary of the differences between our proposed approach and existing style transfer methods. The first four items are general characteristics of a method, while the last four exemplify versatility. Our method realizes every listed item. (**Ava:** Avatar-net. **SS:** Style swap. **Ada:** AdaIN. **Learn-free:** Style-learning-free. **Balance:** Content-style balance. **Art:** For artistic style transfer only but no photorealistic transfer. **NL/L:** Non-linear/Linear fashion.) * [13] does not mention if LST realizes multi-style transfer, but we believe it can as indicated in the table.

	NST [5]	WCT [15]	Ava [21]	SS [2]	Ada [8]	LST [13]	Ours
Universal	✓	✓	Art	Art	Art	✓	✓
Learn-free	✓	✓	✓				✓
Fast		✓	✓	✓	✓	✓	✓
Balance	✓						✓
Artistic	✓	✓	✓	✓	✓	✓	✓
Photo-realistic	✓	✓				✓	✓
Spatial control	✓	✓	✓		✓	✓	✓
Multi transfer	NL	L	L		L	L*	NL/L

Feed-Forward Style Networks. Numerous methods address the issue that NST is slow by training feed-forward networks [9,11,22,23] on a pre-defined set of style images to reduce the content and style losses used in [5]. In testing time, content images can then be stylized with learned styles fast or even in real time for images that are not high resolution in one forward pass. However, these algorithms did so at the cost of limiting how many styles they can transfer to a few styles up to 1,000 styles [4,14,26]. In other words, this adaptation leads to a limitation that such methods do not support universal style transfer. Our work, in contrast, supports universal style transfer.

Universal Style Transfer. Chen and Schmidt [2] introduce a framework of an autoencoder with a "Style swap" feature transformation at the bottleneck, with the transformation the key behind it being able to learn to generalize to unseen styles and virtually realize universal style transfer after trained on a large corpus of 80k paintings. Other works [7], with the most recent being AdaIN [8] and Linear Style Transfer (LST) [13], follow the same idea of training on a large dataset of style images but use different transformation mechanisms to achieve universality. In contrast, style-learning-free methods, including whitening and coloring transform (WCT) [15] and Avatar-net [21], realize universal artistic style transfer without the need to learn from style images. In our experiments, we compare our method to five modern universal style transfer methods to reveal its advantage in being able to support a larger range of tasks, also often more effectively than existing more constrained methods. It does so without pre-training.

Photo-Realistic Transfer. Compared to artistic transfer, photo-realistic transfer is more constrained in that the results need to look convincingly realistic to an end user. NST and its variant [18] pioneered the use of neural networks for photo-realistic transfer. Among the aforementioned autoencoder-based methods for universal style transfer, the transformations in WCT and LST are applicable [13, 16], while other transformations [2,8,21] are only suitable for artistic transfer. Our experiments demonstrate an advantage of our transformation for photo-realistic transfer in balancing content preservation and style transfer, with it considerably reducing artifacts and distortion compared to WCT and LST.

3 Method

In this section, we show how we derive our new transformation for style transfer. Throughout the derivation, we will explain why this transformation is GPU-friendly, how it balances content information and style effect, and how it can be employed for the applications of spatial control and multi-style transfer.

3.1 General Framework - Background

The general framework for fast style transfer consists of an autoencoder (i.e., an encoder-decoder pair) and a feature transformation at the bottleneck, as shown

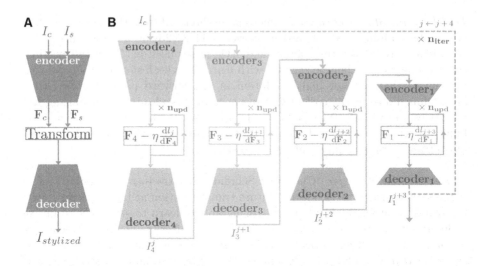

Fig. 1. (A) General framework for universal style transfer: an encoder extracts features $\mathbf{F}_c$ and $\mathbf{F}_s$ from content and style images I_c and I_s respectively. $\mathbf{F}_c$ is transformed with reference to $\mathbf{F}_s$ and then decoded to a stylized image $I_{stylized}$. (B) Schematic diagram of our style transfer algorithm by analytical gradient descent. Style image I_s is suppressed for clarity and style information resides in the gradients $\frac{dl}{d\mathbf{F}}$'s. Content image I_c is first encoded as a feature $\mathbf{F}_4$. $\mathbf{F}_4$ is gradually stylized by our new iterative transformation with gradient descent and then decoded to a coarsely stylized image I_4^j, which is treated as a new content image to the next autoencoder for finer stylization. The same procedure applies iteratively until the last autoencoder to derive the final result I_1^{j+3}. If more style effect is wanted, a user can repeat from the first autoencoder by setting I_1^{j+3} as the content.

in Fig. 1(A). An encoder first extracts features from content and style images, features are transformed by the transformation method, and a transformed feature is mapped to an image by the decoder.

Transferring style features from multiple layers can be done by a cascade of autoencoders as in WCT [15]. A standard approach pioneered by Gatys et al. with NST [5] is to use as the *content information* of the image a feature map of the image that comes from a higher layer of VGG network and use as the *style information* of an image the Gram matrices of feature maps from different layers in VGG network. Formally, the set-up consists of *relu4_1* layer for content feature extraction and *relu1_1*, *relu2_1*, *relu3_1*, and *relu4_1* layers for style feature extraction.

We denote the reshaped feature map of the image I from the layer *reluN_1* as $\mathbf{F}_N(I) \in \mathbb{R}^{C_N \times H_N(I)W_N(I)}$, where $H_N(I)$, $W_N(I)$, and C_N are height, width, and channel length of the layer output. Suppose I_c and I_s are the content and style images, respectively, and $\mathbf{F}_N(I_c) \triangleq \mathbf{F}_{N,c}$ and $\mathbf{F}_N(I_s) \triangleq \mathbf{F}_{N,s}$. Then the stylized image I of the same size of I_c can be derived by solving the following optimization problem:

$$\min_{I} \underbrace{||\mathbf{F}_4(I) - \mathbf{F}_{4,c}||_F^2}_{\text{content loss}} + \underbrace{\sum_{N=1}^{4} \lambda_N || \frac{1}{n_N} \mathbf{F}_N(I) \mathbf{F}_N(I)^{\mathrm{T}} - \frac{1}{m_N} \mathbf{F}_{N,s} \mathbf{F}_{N,s}^{\mathrm{T}} ||_F^2}_{\text{style loss}}, \quad (1)$$

where λ_N's are weights between content and style losses, n_N and m_N equal to $H_N(I)W_N(I)$ and $H_N(I_s)W_N(I_s)$, respectively.

3.2 New Iterative Transformation with Analytical Gradient Descent

Our novelty lies in approximating the solution to the NST [5] objective by embedding a new transformation that iteratively updates features in the cascade of four autoencoders using analytical gradient descent. An overview of our method is illustrated in Fig. 1(B).

We introduce our approach to address the limitation that Eq. 1 cannot be analytically solved and optimization requires gradient descent with backpropagation, which is time consuming. We borrow the idea of alternating minimization used in convex optimization to speed up and approximately solve this equation. In alternating minimization of a function $f(x,y)$, we first fix y to an initial value y_0 and optimize over x to x_1, then we optimize over y to y_1 with x fixed to x_1, and repeat, alternating until convergence. By analogy, we first optimize for $\mathbf{F}_4$ in Eq. 1:

$$\min_{\mathbf{F}_4} ||\mathbf{F}_4 - \mathbf{F}_{4,c}||_F^2 + \lambda_4 || \frac{1}{n_4} \mathbf{F}_4 \mathbf{F}_4^{\mathrm{T}} - \frac{1}{m_4} \mathbf{F}_{4,s} \mathbf{F}_{4,s}^{\mathrm{T}} ||_F^2. \quad (2)$$

Suppose the value of $\mathbf{F}_4$ found by solving Eq. 2 is $\mathbf{F}_4^{(1)}$, which is the feature map of image $I_4^{(1)}$ from layer *relu4_1*. Note that this image can be derived by exploiting an autoencoder as in [15]. Since feature maps from different layers are coupled through the image $I_4^{(1)}$, we also have feature maps $\mathbf{F}_N^{(1)} = \mathbf{F}_N(I_4^{(1)})$, $N = 3, 2, 1$. Due to the coupling, fixing $\mathbf{F}_4$, $\mathbf{F}_2$, and $\mathbf{F}_1$ to $\mathbf{F}_4^{(1)}$, $\mathbf{F}_2^{(1)}$, and $\mathbf{F}_1^{(1)}$, respectively, can be done by fixing $\mathbf{F}_3$ to $\mathbf{F}_3^{(1)}$. Therefore, in the next step where we optimize for $\mathbf{F}_3$ with other feature maps fixed, we solve the following problem:

$$\min_{\mathbf{F}_3} ||\mathbf{F}_3 - \mathbf{F}_3^{(1)}||_F^2 + \lambda_3 || \frac{1}{n_3} \mathbf{F}_3 \mathbf{F}_3^{\mathrm{T}} - \frac{1}{m_3} \mathbf{F}_{3,s} \mathbf{F}_{3,s}^{\mathrm{T}} ||_F^2, \quad (3)$$

where the first term captures the concept of the hard fixation $\mathbf{F}_3 = \mathbf{F}_3^{(1)}$ that is relaxed to a soft proximity. Let $\mathbf{F}_3^{(2)} \triangleq \mathbf{F}_3(I_3^{(2)})$ be the result of optimization and $\mathbf{F}_2^{(2)} = \mathbf{F}_2(I_3^{(2)})$. Similarly, we can solve for $\mathbf{F}_2$ in Eq. 1 with extra soft proximity $||\mathbf{F}_2 - \mathbf{F}_2^{(2)}||_F^2$. In general, with $\mathbf{F}_4^{(0)} \triangleq \mathbf{F}_{4,c}$ the objective of each step is as follows:

$$\min_{\mathbf{F}_N} l_j(\mathbf{F}_N) = \min_{\mathbf{F}_N} \underbrace{||\mathbf{F}_N - \mathbf{F}_N^{(j)}||_F^2}_{\text{soft proximity loss}} + \underbrace{\lambda_N || \frac{1}{n_N} \mathbf{F}_N \mathbf{F}_N^{\mathrm{T}} - \frac{1}{m_N} \mathbf{F}_{N,s} \mathbf{F}_{N,s}^{\mathrm{T}} ||_F^2}_{\text{style loss}}. \quad (4)$$

We alternate between the minimization of $\mathbf{F}_N$'s until convergence.

To incorporate soft proximity, we use gradient descent to solve the optimization problem in Eq. 4.[1] Unlike solving Eq. 1 that uses back-propagation to compute the gradients, the gradient $\frac{dl_j(\mathbf{F}_N)}{d\mathbf{F}_N}$ has an analytical form, and the optimization process can be done fast using GPU acceleration. Specifically, the gradient can be written in the following form (detailed derivation is given in Supplementary Material):

$$\frac{dl_j}{d\mathbf{F}_N} = 2(\mathbf{F}_N - \mathbf{F}_N^{(j)}) + \frac{4\lambda_N}{n_N}(\frac{1}{n_N}\mathbf{F}_N\mathbf{F}_N^{\mathrm{T}} - \frac{1}{m_N}\mathbf{F}_{N,s}\mathbf{F}_{N,s}^{\mathrm{T}})\mathbf{F}_N, \qquad (5)$$

and the gradient descent updates $\mathbf{F}_N$ by repeating the following update rule n_{upd} times:

$$\mathbf{F}_N \leftarrow \mathbf{F}_N - \eta\frac{dl_j}{d\mathbf{F}_N}, \qquad (6)$$

where η is the learning rate. **Equations 5 and 6 together form the iterative feature transformation method.** We can observe that the computation of it is a mix of matrix multiplication and matrix addition, and thus is GPU-friendly.

The whole style transfer algorithm by analytical gradient descent is summarized in Fig. 1. The cascade of four autoencoders is the same structure as used in WCT style transfer algorithm [15]. Here $encoder_N$ denotes the part of the VGG network from the input layer to $reluN\_1$ layer. The structure of $decoder_N$ is symmetrical to $encoder_N$ and implements an inverse function of $encoder_N$. At the bottleneck of each autoencoder, the feature map updates n_{upd} times, where the value can be decided by trial and error. If more style effect is wanted, we can iterate over the autoencoder cascade for multiple rounds, say n_{iter} times[2]. These two parameters n_{upd} and n_{iter} together with the learning rate η and the weights λ_N's are the four knobs that control how much style effect to be transferred.

3.3   Applications that Demonstrate the Versatility of Our Method

Spatial Control. In spatial control of style transfer [6], a content image I_c and a style image I_s are segmented into regions. The r-th region of the content image is stylized with the corresponding r-th region in the style image (exemplified in Fig. 4). Suppose the set $\mathcal{S}_{N,c}^r$ of indices $\{r_{N,c}^1, r_{N,c}^2, \dots\}$ indicates the columns of feature $\mathbf{F}_{N,c}$ that correspond to the pixels of the r-th region of I_c, and similarly we have $\mathcal{S}_{N,s}^r$ for $\mathbf{F}_{N,s}$ and I_s. Let $\mathbf{F}_N^r \in \mathbb{R}^{C_N \times |\mathcal{S}_{N,c}^r|}$ be $\mathbf{F}_N[:, \mathcal{S}_{N,c}^r]$ and $\mathbf{F}_{N,s}^r \in \mathbb{R}^{C_N \times |\mathcal{S}_{N,s}^r|}$ be $\mathbf{F}_{N,s}[:, \mathcal{S}_{N,s}^r]$, where $|\mathcal{S}|$ is the size of $\mathcal{S}$. To realize spatial control with our style transfer method, we modify Eq. 5 as follows:

---

[1] Previous analysis [3] shows that the feature $\mathbf{F}_{wct}$ derived by applying WCT to $\mathbf{F}_{N,c}$ and $\mathbf{F}_{N,s}$ makes the value of the style loss in Eq. 4 go to zero, and hence could serve as an approximate solution. However, WCT does not consider the balance between soft proximity loss and style loss.

[2] We found $n_{iter} = 3$ is sufficient for convergence with little difference from $n_{iter} = 2$.

$$\frac{\mathrm{d}l_j}{\mathrm{d}\mathbf{F}_N^r} = 2(\mathbf{F}_N^r - (\mathbf{F}_N^{(j)})^r) + \frac{4\lambda_N}{n_N}(\frac{1}{|\mathcal{S}_{N,c}^r|}\mathbf{F}_N^r(\mathbf{F}_N^r)^{\mathrm{T}} - \frac{1}{|\mathcal{S}_{N,s}^r|}\mathbf{F}_{N,s}^r(\mathbf{F}_{N,s}^r)^{\mathrm{T}})\mathbf{F}_N^r, \forall r,$$

$$(7)$$

and $\frac{\mathrm{d}l_j}{\mathrm{d}\mathbf{F}_N}$ is the collection of $\frac{\mathrm{d}l_j}{\mathrm{d}\mathbf{F}_N^r}$'s.

Multiple-Style Transfer. Our algorithm can be easily extended from single-style transfer to multiple-style transfer (exemplified in Fig. 5). In particular, if now we have q style images $I_{s,1}$, $I_{s,2}$, ..., $I_{s,q}$ with feature maps $\mathbf{F}_{N,s}^1$, $\mathbf{F}_{N,s}^2$, ..., $\mathbf{F}_{N,s}^q$, the optimization problem in Eq. 4 should be modified as

$$\min_{\mathbf{F}_N} ||\mathbf{F}_N - \mathbf{F}_N^{(j)}||_F^2 + \sum_{k=1}^q \lambda_N^k ||\frac{1}{n_N}\mathbf{F}_N\mathbf{F}_N^{\mathrm{T}} - \frac{1}{m_N^k}\mathbf{F}_{N,s}^k(\mathbf{F}_{N,s}^k)^{\mathrm{T}}||_F^2. \qquad (8)$$

Unlike Eq. 4 where λ_N controls only the balance between content and style losses, λ_N^k's in Eq. 8 are also the weights between different style effects. We provide the derivation of the gradient equation to solve this objective in the Supplementary Materials

4   Experiments

In the experiments, we first validate that our transformation is GPU-friendly. To do so, we show our approach is the fastest among modern universal transfer methods that do not require pre-training. Our next experiments demonstrate that the knobs controlling the balance between content preservation and style effect transfer benefit photo-realistic style transfer by reducing artifacts and distortion. Finally, we demonstrate the versatility of our method by showing it can be used for two additional applications.

4.1   Single-Style Transfer

We first demonstrate how our method compares to existing style transfer methods in terms of speed. We also show qualitative results.

Baselines. We evaluate two groups of methods that support universal transfer style transfer. Their properties are summarized in Table 1.

One subset of existing methods requires pre-training on style images: Style swap [2], AdaIN [8], and LST [13]. Style swap is the first to introduce the framework of an autoencoder with an embedded feature transform to realize universal style transfer. To achieve faster speed, AdaIN replaces the computationally expensive style swap layer with a lightweight transformation that matches variances between style images and stylized images. Furthermore, LST introduces a transformation that aims to match covariances.

Our method is more similar to the second group which are methods that can perform style transfer *without pre-training*. These methods include: NST [5], WCT [15], and Avatar-net [21]. NST is the first deep learning method that realized style transfer. WCT is the first style-learning-free method for fast style transfer. For WCT, we use the version of a cascade of four autoencoders due to its better performance [16]. Avatar-net introduces a style decorator that combines the transforms of WCT and Style swap.

Implementation Details for Our Method. We use the following hyperparameter setting for our algorithm for artistic style transfer: learning rate $\eta = 0.01$, weights $\{\lambda_1, \lambda_2, \lambda_3, \lambda_4\} = \{10^4, 10^4, 10^3, 10^2\}$, number of update $n_{upd} = 20$, and number of iteration $n_{iter} = 2$.

Experimental Design. We benchmarked speed performance for each method on an Nvidia GTX 1080 Ti with 11 GB memory. To enrich our analysis, we analyzed speed across four different resolutions for the content image: 256×256, 512×512, 768×768, and 1024×1024. In doing so, we captured common image resolutions for the two use cases we study: photo-realistic and artistic style transfer. While photo-realistic transfer typically is conducted with higher resolution images, artistic transfer supports the range of resolutions from low to high. This analysis also enables us to identify limitations of some methods in handling the full range of image resolutions. The size of style images are fixed to 512×512. We conducted experiments with 20 style images each applied to 5 content images. Elapsed time in seconds is estimated by averaging the time from 100 experimental results.

Speed Performance Results. Results are shown in Table 2.[3]
As shown, our method is consistently faster than all baselines which similarly do not require pre-training. For example, our method is approximately 100 times faster than NST and approximately 3–10 times faster than WCT and Avatar-net. We attribute the slowest speed observed from NST to it using gradient descent with back-propagation to solve the Eq. 1. While our method consistently outperforms all these methods, we observe that the performance gains can fall with higher resolution images. Specifically, at the largest resolution of 1024×1024, we observe our method is roughly 1.5 times faster than WCT and Avatar-net. We attribute this to the repeated computation of $\mathbf{F}_N \mathbf{F}_N^{\mathrm{T}}$ in Eq. 5 with a large size of $\mathbf{F}_N$. While our advantage is still shown over existing methods, further speed-ups could be achieved by increasing the learning rate η and accordingly decreasing the number of updates n_{upd}. We also observe that Avatar-net works slightly faster than WCT, despite the fact that both avoid any pre-training. This is because Avatar-net only exploits one autoencoder composed of *encoder*$_4$ and *decoder*$_4$. The drawback of Avatar-net though is that the style transfer primarily results from the *relu4_1* style feature, while the features from *relu1_1*, *relu2_1*, and *relu3_1* layers are marginally transferred.

---

[3] Our reported times include the computation time for style image encoding and its relevant terms, as done for some papers [2,8,13,15] but not others [21].

Table 2. Speed performance of universal style transfer methods. Four different sizes of content images are considered. For WCT and our algorithms, we report two values for $n_{iter} = 1$ and $n_{iter} = 2$ (in parentheses). The former value transfers less of the style, which is better-suited for photo-realistic transfer. The latter value transfers more style, which is better-suited for artistic transfer. Results show our method is consistently faster than all baselines which similarly do not require pre-training. **OOM**: Out of memory. **Unit**: Second. (* means average over three results, due to out-of-memory error midway)

Content image size	No pre-training				Pre-training		
	NST [5]	WCT [15]	Ava [21]	Ours	SS [2]	Ada [8]	LST [13]
256 × 256	15.28	1.15 (2.31)	0.96	**0.15 (0.28)**	0.55	**0.036**	0.04
512 × 512	33.29	1.24 (2.47)	1.08	**0.33 (0.65)**	1.89	**0.046**	0.05
768 × 768	64.50	1.38 (2.69)	1.28	**0.64 (1.29)**	4.29*	**0.068**	0.10
1024 × 1024	108.94	1.63 (3.28)	1.54	**1.07 (2.15)**	OOM	**0.105**	0.15

Compared to the methods which require pre-training, our method is both slightly better and slightly worse. For example, we observe that Style swap is both slower and cannot handle large content images; e.g.., at least roughly three times slower. In contrast, we observe speed gains for AdaIN and LST. We attribute this advantage to their training on a large dataset of style images and so embedding knowledge of styles in the values of the learned model parameters. However, this pre-training brings a downside in that users have less flexible control on the transfer effect which can lead to distorted content. We quantify such disadvantages below in Sect. 4.2.

Qualitative Style-Transfer Results. Examples of style transfer results are shown in Figs. 2 and 3 for artistic style transfer and photo-realistic style transfer respectively. Of note, only a subset of the methods support photo-realistic style transfer: NST, WCT, LST, and ours. As shown, like prior methods, our approach can produce visually-pleasing style transfer results.

Qualitatively, the strength of our approach is more evident for the photo-realistic results, which is the setting where the content must be convincing that it is plausibly real. We observe that our method can preserve content well while NST, WCT, and LST suffer from some artifacts and distorted content. In the first example of the canal, NST introduces extra light strokes, WCT produces unpleasant artifacts in the clouds and their reflection on the water, and LST does not hold content well (as shown in the zoomed-in picture). In the second example of the monastery, we can clearly see in the result of our method the boundaries on the brick wall and the pattern and the reflection on the ground. These are ruined to some extent in the results from other methods. Furthermore, LST shows no reflection of light on the river in the third example. In the next section, we quantify this disadvantage.

4.2   Photo-Realistic Style Transfer - Quantitative Analysis

We aim to show that our method can preserve content better/produce fewer artifacts than existing methods while still transferring style effects.

Baselines. We compare our method with NST, WCT and LST, which have been considered for photo-realistic style transfer. For the other related methods, Avatar-net, Style swap and AdaIN are prone to distort content much and hence only suitable for artistic style transfer. NST was the first to show the possibility of applying deep neural networks for photo-realistic style transfer. LST shows that a network pre-trained on paintings is also applicable to real photos as style images. WCT is more widely studied: PhotoWCT [16] makes stylized images from WCT more realistic by post-processing to reduce artifacts. WCT2 [25] embeds WCT in an autoencoder that better preserves content using wavelet transform. Here we focus on the effect from feature transformations rather than post-processing and fancy autoencoders. Therefore, only vanilla autoencoders are used for WCT, LST, and our method and we do not apply post-processing in the experiment.[4]

Implementation Details for Our Method. In photo-realistic style transfer, we need to avoid transferring too much style effect to prevent artifacts and distorted content. Therefore, we use the same values of η and λ_N's as in artistic style transfer but reduce the values n_{upd} and n_{iter} to 15 and 1.

Experimental Design. We generated 30 stylized images from 30 pairs of a real content image and real style image (shown in the Supplementary Materials). To quantify the amount of distortion, we calculate SSIM (structural similarity) [24] and FSIM (feature similarity) [27] values between content images and stylized images in grayscale.[5] SSIM is the product of three comparison measurements: luminance, contrast, and structure, where the structure measurement directly captures the level of distortion.[6] We report both SSIM and structure index values. FSIM is based on two feature maps: phase congruency and gradient magnitude, both of which evaluate local structure similarity from different angles.[7]

---

[4] While a fancy autoencoder such as WCT2 [25] using wavelet pooling can further prevent distortion, that is beyond the scope of this paper.

[5] Our aim was to capture the distortion level caused by different transformations. While a user study can reflect aesthetics, it is hard for users to notice all distortions in an image and the score scale can be only coarse-grained (eg, 0 = no distortion, 5 = worst distortion). That motivated our choice to use quantitative metrics.

[6] We use the MATLAB implementation, setting the luminance, contrast, and structural exponents to 1 and regularization constants to 0.01^2, 0.03^2, and $0.03^2/2$.

[7] We adopt the official implementation with default hyper-parameters, which computes phase congruency with Kovesi's method and log-Gabor filters and the gradient magnitude based on the Scharr operator.

Fig. 2. Comparison of artistic style transfer for universal style transfer algorithms. **Green panel:** methods that do not require pre-training: NST [5], WCT [15], Avatarnet [21], and ours. **Orange panel:** methods that require pre-training: Style swap [2], AdaIN [8], and LST [13]. Like prior methods, our approach can produce visually-pleasing style transfer results. (Color figure online)

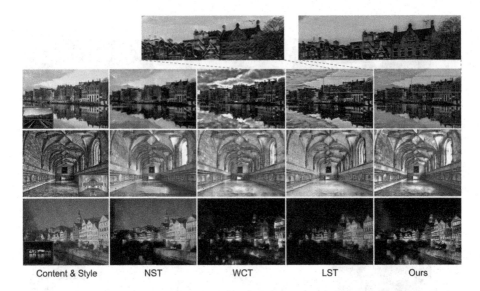

Content & Style   NST   WCT   LST   Ours

Fig. 3. Photo-realistic style transfer results for our algorithm and NST [5], WCT [15], and LST [13]. Note that no post-processing and no spatial control is applied. Results show that our method can preserve content better and cause fewer artifacts (discussed in the text).

Results. As mentioned previously, our transformation balances between content preservation and style effect transferal. This is unlike WCT and LST, which invest mostly in the latter and thus distort content more. This is justified in the results shown in Table 3, where NST sets a reference line for the other three fast methods. As shown, NST gets the highest score in SSIM. Our method outperforms the other autoencoder-based methods and has a score close to that of NST. With respect to the FSIM metric, our method gets the highest score. Altogether, these results suggest that our feature transformation preserves content better than WCT and LST.

Table 3. Evaluation of distortion level in photo-realistic style transfer. For SSIM, both SSIM values and structure indices (in parentheses) are reported. Among three autoencoder-based algorithms, our feature transformation results in highest scores in both SSIM and FSIM metrics, preserving content best.

	NST [5]	Autoencoder-based		
		WCT [15]	LST [13]	Ours
SSIM	**0.5644 (0.7567)**	0.4476 (0.7265)	0.4429 (0.6919)	0.5301 (0.7513)
FSIM	0.7870	0.7643	0.7658	**0.8197**

We show resulting stylized images in the Supplementary Materials to demonstrate that our method transfers style. instead of conducting a user study that only allows coarse-grained scores (eg, 0 = no distortion, 5 = worst distortion),

4.3   Other Applications

To highlight the versatility of our method, we also demonstrate that our method can be applied for style transfer with spatial control and multi-style transfer.

Fig. 4. Style transfer with spatial control with our algorithm. Style from a segment in a style image is transferred to the segment denoted the same color in a content image. Results show that with slight re-formulation our method can support spatial control.

Style Transfer Results Using Spatial Control. Results for style transfer with spatial control are shown in Fig. 4. Content images and style images are segmented into regions denoted by different colors. A segment in a content image is stylized with the style from the segment denoted the same color in a style image. The results demonstrate that our work is suitable for the spatial control task.

Multi-style Transfer. Among the universal style transfer methods considered, only NST and our algorithm can mix multiple styles in a non-linear fashion, while AdaIN, Avatar-net, and WCT blend different styles by linear interpolation of transformed features. It is not explicitly mentioned in the original paper of NST [5], but extending NST to multiple-style transfer is straightforward. We

NST	WCT	Ours

Fig. 5. Results of double-style transfer using NST [5], WCT [15], and our methods **Upper**: Three sets of a content image and two style images. **Lower**: Smaller stylized images are single-style transfer results from each style image. Larger images are the results of double-style transfer. Our method preserves the integrity of each style better than WCT and has more pleasant results than NST.

describe these details as well as how to use WCT or multi-style transfer in the Supplementary Materials.

We show three examples of double-style transfer using NST, WCT, and our methods in Fig. 5.[8] In each example, the weights for two styles are equal. By observing the change of color, we can tell that each double-style transfer result from WCT is somewhat an average of two single-style transfer results: the dark grey sky in the first example is the mean of light grey and black skies, the light green tint in the second example is the mean of dark green and light grey, and the orange leaves in the third example is the mean of red and green leaves. Moreover, in the second example the effect of sketch is covered by that of the painting of shipwreck and is barely present.

In contrast, our method preserves each style in the double-style transfer results. In the first example, the glowing and dark effect is in the sky and the ink stroke effect is on the buildings. The style of the painting of shipwreck in the second example is on the buildings and their reflection on the sea, and the sketch style can be found in the sky and the sea. In the third example, the leaves overhead are the mixture of red and green leaves, and more green leaves can be

---

[8] Due to limited space and a similar trend of linear transition from one style to the other, we show results from AdaIN and Avatar-net in the Supplementary Materials.

noted on the wall. NST, on the other hand, also produces non-linear effects, but might result in an unsatisfactory outcome, for instance, the third example.

5   Conclusion

We introduce an iterative feature transformation for universal style transfer that arises from approximating the solution to the objective of NST. Our method provides control knobs that balance content preservation and style effect transferal and helps switch between artistic and photo-realistic style transfers. For versatility, we show that our method supports semantic control and multiple-style transfer. We show the effectiveness of our method by comparing it with NST and the representative transformations for fast universal style transfer.

References

1. Champandard, A.J.: Semantic style transfer and turning two-bit doodles into fine artworks. arXiv preprint arXiv:1603.01768 (2016)
2. Chen, T.Q., Schmidt, M.: Fast patch-based style transfer of arbitrary style. arXiv preprint arXiv:1612.04337 (2016)
3. Chiu, T.Y.: Understanding generalized whitening and coloring transform for universal style transfer. In: Proceedings of the IEEE International Conference on Computer Vision, pp. 4452–4460 (2019)
4. Dumoulin, V., Shlens, J., Kudlur, M.: A learned representation for artistic style. In: 5th International Conference on Learning Representations, ICLR 2017, Toulon, France, 24–26 April 2017, Conference Track Proceedings. OpenReview.net (2017). https://openreview.net/forum?id=BJO-BuT1g
5. Gatys, L.A., Ecker, A.S., Bethge, M.: Image style transfer using convolutional neural networks. In: Proceedings of the IEEE Conference on Computer Vision and Pattern Recognition, pp. 2414–2423 (2016)
6. Gatys, L.A., Ecker, A.S., Bethge, M., Hertzmann, A., Shechtman, E.: Controlling perceptual factors in neural style transfer. In: Proceedings of the IEEE Conference on Computer Vision and Pattern Recognition, pp. 3985–3993 (2017)
7. Ghiasi, G., Lee, H., Kudlur, M., Dumoulin, V., Shlens, J.: Exploring the structure of a real-time, arbitrary neural artistic stylization network. In: Kim, T.K., Zafeiriou, S., Brostow, G., Mikolajczyk, K. (eds.) Proceedings of the British Machine Vision Conference (BMVC), pp. 114.1–114.12. BMVA Press, September 2017. http://doi.org/10.5244/C.31.114
8. Huang, X., Belongie, S.: Arbitrary style transfer in real-time with adaptive instance normalization. In: Proceedings of the IEEE International Conference on Computer Vision, pp. 1501–1510 (2017)
9. Johnson, J., Alahi, A., Fei-Fei, L.: Perceptual losses for real-time style transfer and super-resolution. In: Leibe, B., Matas, J., Sebe, N., Welling, M. (eds.) ECCV 2016. LNCS, vol. 9906, pp. 694–711. Springer, Cham (2016). https://doi.org/10.1007/978-3-319-46475-6_43
10. Li, C., Wand, M.: Combining Markov random fields and convolutional neural networks for image synthesis. In: Proceedings of the IEEE Conference on Computer Vision and Pattern Recognition, pp. 2479–2486 (2016)

11. Li, C., Wand, M.: Precomputed real-time texture synthesis with Markovian generative adversarial networks. In: Leibe, B., Matas, J., Sebe, N., Welling, M. (eds.) ECCV 2016. LNCS, vol. 9907, pp. 702–716. Springer, Cham (2016). https://doi.org/10.1007/978-3-319-46487-9_43

12. Li, P., Zhao, L., Xu, D., Lu, D.: Optimal transport of deep feature for image style transfer. In: Proceedings of the 2019 4th International Conference on Multimedia Systems and Signal Processing, pp. 167–171 (2019)

13. Li, X., Liu, S., Kautz, J., Yang, M.H.: Learning linear transformations for fast image and video style transfer. In: Proceedings of the IEEE Conference on Computer Vision and Pattern Recognition, pp. 3809–3817 (2019)

14. Li, Y., Fang, C., Yang, J., Wang, Z., Lu, X., Yang, M.H.: Diversified texture synthesis with feed-forward networks. In: Proceedings of the IEEE Conference on Computer Vision and Pattern Recognition, pp. 3920–3928 (2017)

15. Li, Y., Fang, C., Yang, J., Wang, Z., Lu, X., Yang, M.H.: Universal style transfer via feature transforms. In: Guyon, I., et al. (eds.) Advances in Neural Information Processing Systems, pp. 386–396 (2017)

16. Li, Y., Liu, M.-Y., Li, X., Yang, M.-H., Kautz, J.: A closed-form solution to photorealistic image stylization. In: Ferrari, V., Hebert, M., Sminchisescu, C., Weiss, Y. (eds.) ECCV 2018. LNCS, vol. 11207, pp. 468–483. Springer, Cham (2018). https://doi.org/10.1007/978-3-030-01219-9_28

17. Lu, M., Zhao, H., Yao, A., Chen, Y., Xu, F., Zhang, L.: A closed-form solution to universal style transfer. In: Proceedings of the IEEE International Conference on Computer Vision, pp. 5952–5961 (2019)

18. Luan, F., Paris, S., Shechtman, E., Bala, K.: Deep photo style transfer. In: Proceedings of the IEEE Conference on Computer Vision and Pattern Recognition, pp. 4990–4998 (2017)

19. Mroueh, Y.: Wasserstein style transfer. arXiv preprint arXiv:1905.12828 (2019)

20. Risser, E., Wilmot, P., Barnes, C.: Stable and controllable neural texture synthesis and style transfer using histogram losses. arXiv preprint arXiv:1701.08893 (2017)

21. Sheng, L., Lin, Z., Shao, J., Wang, X.: Avatar-Net: multi-scale zero-shot style transfer by feature decoration. In: Proceedings of the IEEE Conference on Computer Vision and Pattern Recognition, pp. 8242–8250 (2018)

22. Ulyanov, D., Lebedev, V., Vedaldi, A., Lempitsky, V.S.: Texture networks: feed-forward synthesis of textures and stylized images. In: Balcan, M.F., Weinberger, K.Q. (eds.) ICML, vol. 1, p. 4 (2016)

23. Ulyanov, D., Vedaldi, A., Lempitsky, V.: Improved texture networks: maximizing quality and diversity in feed-forward stylization and texture synthesis. In: Proceedings of the IEEE Conference on Computer Vision and Pattern Recognition, pp. 6924–6932 (2017)

24. Wang, Z., Bovik, A.C., Sheikh, H.R., Simoncelli, E.P.: Image quality assessment: from error visibility to structural similarity. IEEE Trans. Image Process. **13**(4), 600–612 (2004)

25. Yoo, J., Uh, Y., Chun, S., Kang, B., Ha, J.W.: Photorealistic style transfer via wavelet transforms. In: Proceedings of the IEEE International Conference on Computer Vision, pp. 9036–9045 (2019)

26. Zhang, H., Dana, K.: Multi-style generative network for real-time transfer. In: Leal-Taixé, L., Roth, S. (eds.) ECCV 2018. LNCS, vol. 11132, pp. 349–365. Springer, Cham (2019). https://doi.org/10.1007/978-3-030-11018-5_32

27. Zhang, L., Zhang, L., Mou, X., Zhang, D.: FSIM: a feature similarity index for image quality assessment. IEEE Trans. Image Process. **20**(8), 2378–2386 (2011)

CATCH: Context-Based Meta Reinforcement Learning for Transferrable Architecture Search

Xin Chen[1], Yawen Duan[1], Zewei Chen[2], Hang Xu[2], Zihao Chen[2],
Xiaodan Liang[3], Tong Zhang[4(✉)], and Zhenguo Li[2]

[1] The University of Hong Kong, Hong Kong, China
[2] Huawei Noah's Ark Lab, Hong Kong, China
[3] Sun Yat-sen University, Guangzhou, China
[4] The Hong Kong University of Science and Technology, Hong Kong, China
tongzhang@tongzhang-ml.org

Abstract. Neural Architecture Search (NAS) achieved many break-throughs in recent years. In spite of its remarkable progress, many algorithms are restricted to particular search spaces. They also lack efficient mechanisms to reuse knowledge when confronting multiple tasks. These challenges preclude their applicability, and motivate our proposal of CATCH, a novel Context-bAsed meTa reinforcement learning (RL) algorithm for transferrable arChitecture searcH. The combination of meta-learning and RL allows CATCH to efficiently adapt to new tasks while being agnostic to search spaces. CATCH utilizes a probabilistic encoder to encode task properties into latent context variables, which then guide CATCH's controller to quickly "catch" top-performing networks. The contexts also assist a network evaluator in filtering inferior candidates and speed up learning. Extensive experiments demonstrate CATCH's universality and search efficiency over many other widely-recognized algorithms. It is also capable of handling cross-domain architecture search as competitive networks on ImageNet, COCO, and Cityscapes are identified. This is the first work to our knowledge that proposes an efficient transferrable NAS solution while maintaining robustness across various settings.

Keywords: Neural architecture search · Meta reinforcement learning

1 Introduction

The emergence of many high-performance neural networks has been one of the pivotal forces pushing forward the progress of deep learning research and production. Recently, many neural networks discovered by Neural Architecture Search

---

X. Chen and Y. Duan—Equal contribution.

Electronic supplementary material The online version of this chapter (https://doi.org/10.1007/978-3-030-58529-7_12) contains supplementary material, which is available to authorized users.

A. Vedaldi et al. (Eds.): ECCV 2020, LNCS 12364, pp. 185–202, 2020.
https://doi.org/10.1007/978-3-030-58529-7_12

(NAS) methods have surpassed manually designed ones on a variety of domains including image classification [47,61], object detection [61], semantic segmentation [5], and recommendation systems [31]. Many potential applications of practical interests are calling for solutions that can (1) efficiently handle a myriad of tasks, (2) be widely applicable to different search spaces, and (3) maintain their levels of competency across various settings. We believe these are important yet somewhat neglected aspects in the past research, and a transformative NAS algorithm should be able to respond to these needs to make a real influence.

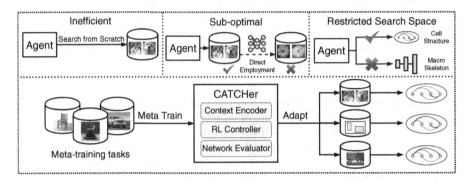

Fig. 1. Upper: drawbacks of current NAS schemes. Lower: the overall framework of CATCH. Our search agent, CATCHer, consists of three core components: context encoder, RL controller and network evaluator. CATCHer first goes through the meta-training phase to learn an initial search policy, then it adapts to target tasks efficiently.

Many algorithms [33,37] have been proposed to improve the efficiency of NAS. However, they lack mechanisms to seek and preserve information that can be meaningfully reused. Hence, these algorithms can only repeatedly and inefficiently search from scratch when encountering new tasks. To tackle this problem, a rising direction of NAS attempts to create efficient transferrable algorithms. Several works [23,36] try to search for architectures that perform well across tasks, but the solutions may not be optimal on the target tasks, especially when the target task distributions are distant from the training task distributions. Some recent works [15,28] use meta-learning [16,27] for one-shot NAS instead. With recent critiques [26,56] pointing out some one-shot solutions' dependence on particular search spaces and sensitivity to hyperparameters, many concerns arise on the practicality of these meta NAS works based on one-shot methods. To avoid ambiguity, throughout this paper, *tasks* are defined as problems that share the same action space, but differ in reward functions. In NAS, the change of either the dataset or domain (e.g. from classification to detection) alters the underlying reward function, and thus can be treated as different tasks.

Striking a balance between universality and efficiency is hard. Solving the universality problem needs a policy to disentangle from specifics of search spaces, which uproots an important foundation of many efficient algorithms. The aim to improve efficiency on multiple tasks naturally links us to a transfer/meta learning paradigm. Meta Reinforcement Learning (RL) [25,38] offers a solution to achieving both efficiency and universality, which largely inspired our proposal of CATCH, a novel context-guided meta reinforcement learning framework that is both search space-agnostic and swiftly adaptive to new tasks.

The search agent in our framework, namely CATCHer, acts as the decision-maker to quickly "catch" top-performing networks on a task. As is shown in Fig. 1, it is first trained on a set of meta-training tasks then deployed to target tasks for fast adaptation. CATCHer leverages three core components: context encoder, RL controller, and network evaluator. The context encoder adopts an amortized variational inference approach [1,24,38] to encode task properties into latent context variables that guide the controller and evaluator. The RL controller makes sequential decisions to generate candidate networks in a stochastic manner. The network evaluator predicts the performance of the candidate networks and decides which nets are valuable for training. All three components are optimized in an end-to-end manner.

We test the method's universality and adaptation efficiency on two fundamentally different search spaces: cell-based search space [13] and Residual block-based [19,57] search space. The former focuses on cell structure design, while the latter targets macro skeleton search. With NAS-Bench-201 [13], we can compare CATCH fairly with other algorithms by eliminating performance fluctuations rising from different search spaces and training settings. Our experiments demonstrate CATCH's superiority over various other works, including R-EA [40] and DARTS [33]. On Residual block-based search space, we use image classification tasks on sub-datasets of ImageNet [10] as meta-training tasks, and then adapt the CATCHer to target tasks, such as image classification on full ImageNet, object detection on COCO [30], and semantic segmentation on Cityscapes [9]. CATCH discovered networks on these tasks with competitive performance and inference latency. Our results demonstrated CATCH's robustness across various settings, easing previously raised concerns of NAS algorithms' sensitivity to search space, random seeds, and tendencies to overfit to only one or two reported tasks.

Our key contribution is the first attempt to design an efficient and universal transferrable NAS framework. It swiftly handles various tasks through fast adaptation, and robustly maintains competitive performance across different settings. Our work brings along new perspectives on solving NAS problems, including using amortized variational inference to generate task characteristics that inform network designs. It also demonstrates the possibility of creating efficient sample-based NAS solutions that are comparable with widely-recognized one-shot methods. With competitive networks identified across classification, detection, and segmentation domains, it further opens the investigation on the feasibility of cross-domain architecture search.

2   Related Work

NAS is an algorithmic approach to design neural networks through searching over candidate architectures. Many harness the power of Reinforcement Learning (RL) [60], Bayesian Optimization [3,4], Evolutionary Algorithm [14,39], and Monte Carlo Tree Search [35,52]. The field gradually gains its tractions with the emergence of highly-efficient algorithms [33,37,39] and architectures [40,47] with remarkable performance.

Our method is inspired by PEARL [38], a recent work in context-based meta reinforcement learning, which captures knowledge about a task with probabilistic latent contexts. The knowledge is then leveraged for informed policy training. There are a few key challenges in efficiently applying it to NAS: (1) PEARL models the latent context embeddings of RL tasks as distributions over Markov Decision Processes (MDP), but it is less clear how a task in NAS can be meaningfully encoded. (2) RL is notoriously famous for its sample inefficiency, but it is extremely expensive to obtain reward signals on NAS. We address these challenges by (1) proposing the use of network-reward pairs to represent a task, (2) introducing meta-training tasks that can be cheaply evaluated to obtain more data for learning, and including a network evaluator that acts like Q-learning agents to speed up learning.

Previous works also explored the possibility of using meta-learning for NAS. Some [23,36] aimed to identify a single architecture that simultaneously works well on all considered tasks. These solutions may not be scalable when confronting a large pool of target tasks. An early work [53] aimed to learn a general policy across tasks. However, it generates task embeddings from images, which may fail at datasets with the same images, and is unable to differentiate among classification, detection, and segmentation tasks on the same dataset. A few recent papers [15,28] combined gradient-based meta-learning with DARTS, but the algorithms are only applicable to search spaces compatible with DARTS. Additionally, none of the above proposals reported their performance on large-scale tasks like ImageNet full dataset. This leaves questions on these proposals' generalizability and adaptation efficiency on more challenging datasets, where scientists expect meta-NAS algorithms should have an edge over typical NAS methods. CATCH is the first NAS algorithm to our knowledge that deploys meta-learning while maintaining universality, robustness across different search spaces, and capability to handle large-scale tasks.

3   CATCH Framework

In NAS, the change of dataset (e.g. CIFAR-10 vs. ImageNet) or domain (e.g. image classification vs. object detection) essentially indicates the shift of underlying reward distribution. The goal of a cross-task transfer algorithm is hence to quickly identify the best actions under the changed reward dynamics. To handle this challenge, the CATCH framework consists of two phases: a meta-training phase and an adaptation phase, as is presented in Algorithm 1. In the meta-training phase, we train the CATCHer on a pool of meta-training tasks that can be cheaply evaluated. A key goal of this phase is to present the context encoder with sufficiently diversified tasks, and encourage it to consistently encode meaningful information for different tasks. Meanwhile, both the controller and the evaluator may gain a good initialization for adaptation. In the adaptation phase, the meta-trained CATCHer then learns to find networks on the target task efficiently through the guidance of the latent context encoding.

We show the search procedure on any single task in Fig. 2, which corresponds to line 3–13 of Algorithm 1.

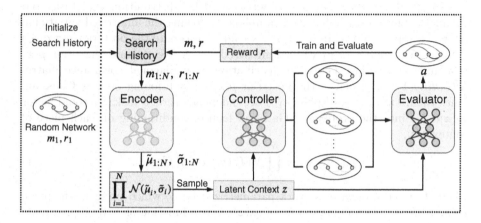

Fig. 2. The search procedure of CATCH on a given task. The procedure starts from initializing the search history by storing a randomly selected network m and its reward r. The encoder applies amortized variational inference approach to generate latent context encoding z by encoding network-reward pairs from the search history. The controller then generates candidate networks for the evaluator to choose the most promising ones to train and evaluate. Newly selected networks and their rewards will be stored in the search history. The loop continues after the three components are optimized.

3.1 Context Encoding

The use of latent context encoding is a crucial part of CATCH. The question is what information about the task is reliable to construct such latent contexts. Directly extracting feature maps of images of the dataset is an intuitive solution. However, for the same dataset, the best network configurations to perform different tasks like object detection and semantic segmentation may differ a lot. Hence, simply extracting information directly from images may not be a viable approach.

We instead believe that the task-specific contextual knowledge can be mined from the search history (i.e. sets of network-reward pairs). If the same group of networks have similar relative strengths on two tasks, it might mean these tasks are "close" to each other. It is also helpful to break the barriers for cross-task architecture search, since the network-reward pair of information is universal across tasks.

Before searching on a task, we randomly form a few networks m and evaluate their performance r to initialize the search history. The retrieved network-reward pairs are stored in the search history for its initialization. To start the search, we sample a number of network-reward pairs $\{(m, r)_i\}_1^N$ (denoted by $c_{1:N}$ for simplicity) from the search history, which will be fed into the encoder to generate a latent context vector z representing the salient knowledge about the task.

We model the latent context encoding process in a probabilistic manner, because it allows the context encoder to model a distribution over tasks and conduct exploration via posterior sampling. Following the amortized variational inference approach used in [1,24,38], we aim to estimate the posterior $p(z|c_{1:N})$ with the encoder $q_\phi(z|c_{1:N})$, parametrized by ϕ. We assume the prior $p(z)$ is a unit multivariate Gaussian distribution with diagonal covariance matrix $\mathcal{N}(0, diag(1))$, and hence, the posterior $p(z|c)$ conditioning on c is Gaussian. Since the network-reward pairs $c_{1:N}$ are independent on a task, we could factor $q_\phi(z|c_{1:N})$ into the product of Gaussian factors conditioning on each piece of contexts c_i,

$$q_\phi(z|c_{1:N}) \propto \prod_{i=1}^N \mathcal{N}(f_\phi^{\tilde{\mu}}(c_i), diag(f_\phi^{\tilde{\sigma}}(c_i))), \tag{1}$$

where f_ϕ is an inference network parametrized by ϕ, which predicts the mean $\tilde{\mu}_i$ and the standard deviation $\tilde{\sigma}_i$ of $q_\phi(z|c_i)$ as a function of c_i to approximate Gaussian $p(z|c_i)$.

During the forward pass, the encoder network f_ϕ outputs $\tilde{\mu}_i, \tilde{\sigma}_i$ of the Gaussian posterior $q_\phi(z|c_i)$ conditioning on each context, then we take their product $q_\phi(z|c_{1:N})$. Each context c_i is $(m, r)_i$, where r is normalized among $\{r\}_{1:N}$ to reflect the relative advantage of each network. All the network-reward pairs in the search history are utilized. We then sample z from $q_\phi(z|c_{1:N})$. Further implementation details can be found in the Appendix.

3.2   Network Sampling

The generation of a network can be treated as a decision-making problem, where each of the RL controller's actions determines one attribute of the resulting architecture. The attribute can be an operation type to form a certain edge in a cell-based search (e.g. skip-connect, convolution operations, etc.), or the shape of a network in a macro-skeleton search (e.g. width, depth, etc.). Both ways are explored in our work.

A network, denoted by m, is represented as a list of actions $[a_1, a_2, ..., a_L]$ taken by the controller in a sequential manner. At each time step l, the controller makes a decision a_l according to its policy π_{θ_c}, parametrized by θ_c. The controller policy takes z and the previous actions $[a_1...a_{l-1}, 0, ..., 0]$ as inputs, and outputs the probability distribution of choosing a certain action $\pi_{\theta_c}(a^l|[a_1...a_{l-1}, 0, ..., 0], z)$, where the actions will be sampled accordingly. z is

---

Algorithm 1. Context-based Meta Architecture Search (CATCH)

Inputs: $\{\mathcal{T}_{meta}\}$ (meta-training task pool), $\{\mathcal{T}_{target}\}$ (target task pool), N_{meta} (# of meta epochs), N_{search} (# of search epochs), C (# of contexts to sample), M (# of models to sample)

Meta-training Phase:
1: **for** N_{meta} meta epochs **do**
2:     Select meta-training task $\mathcal{T}$ from $\{\mathcal{T}_{meta}\}$
3:     Initialize SearchHistory
4:     **for** $n = 1$ to N_{search} **do**
5:         $\{(m,r)_i\}_1^C$ = SearchHistory.sample_contexts(C)
6:         z = Encoder.encode($\{(m,r)_i\}_1^C$)
7:         $\{m\}_1^M \leftarrow$ Controller.sample_networks(z, M)
8:         $m' \leftarrow$ Evaluator.choose_best($\{m_j\}_1^M$, z)
9:         $r \leftarrow$ train_and_evaluate(m', $\mathcal{T}$)
10:        SearchHistory.add((m', z, r))
11:        Encoder, Controller, Evaluator optimization
12:     **end for**
13: **end for**
    Adaptation Phase:
14: Select target task $\mathcal{T}$ from $\{\mathcal{T}_{target}\}$
15: **Repeat** Line 3-13
16: BestModel $\leftarrow$ SearchHistory.best_model()
17: **return** BestModel

---

the latent context vector generated by the encoder, and $[a_1...a_{l-1}, \mathbf{0}, ..., \mathbf{0}]$ is a collection of one-hot vectors indicating all the actions taken so far at l-th timestep, leaving untaken actions $[a_l, ..., a_L]$ as zero vectors. The reward for each action is the normalized performance score of the network. The controller samples M networks stochastically as candidates for the network evaluator.

3.3 Network Scoring and Evaluation

Since the candidate networks are sampled stochastically by the controller, it is almost inevitable that some inferior models will be generated. We set up a filtering mechanism, namely network evaluator, which acts like a Q-learning agent that predicts the actual performance of each network, and selects the top one for training. The predicted value is not necessarily an accurate prediction of the training performance, but should be able to provide a ranking among candidate models roughly similar to their true performance.

The evaluator $f_{\theta_e}(m, z)$ is parameterized by θ_e. It takes M tuples of network-context pairs (m, z) as inputs, and outputs the predicted performance of input architectures. The network with the highest predicted performance score will be trained to obtain the true reward r. The network-context-reward tuple (m, z, r) is then stored in the evaluator's local memory for future gradient updates.

3.4   Optimization of CATCHer

To optimize the controller policy, we maximize the expected reward for the task it is performed on. The controller is trained using Proximal Policy Optimization (PPO) [43] with a clipped surrogate objective $\mathcal{L}_c$.

To optimize the evaluator, we deploy Prioritized Experience Replay (PER) [42], a Deep Q-learning [34] optimization technique. During the update, it prompts the evaluator to prioritize sampling entries that it makes the most mistakes on, and thus improves sample efficiency. The loss of the evaluator $\mathcal{L}_e$ is the Huber loss [22] between the evaluator's prediction $\tilde{r}$ and the normalized true performance score. Further details of $\mathcal{L}_c$ and $\mathcal{L}_e$ can be found in the Appendix.

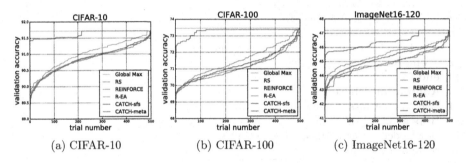

(a) CIFAR-10   (b) CIFAR-100   (c) ImageNet16-120

Fig. 3. (a)–(c) show the results of 500 trials for CATCH-meta, CATCH-sfs(search from scratch) and other sample-based algorithms. Each individual trial is sorted by the final validation accuracy of the searched network.

To optimize the encoder, we take $\mathcal{L}_c$ and $\mathcal{L}_e$ as part of the objective. The resulting variational lower bound for each task $\mathcal{T}$ is

$$\mathcal{L} = \mathbb{E}_{z \sim q_\phi(z|c^{\mathcal{T}})}[\mathcal{L}_c + \mathcal{L}_e + \beta D_{KL}(q_\phi(z|c^{\mathcal{T}})||p(z))], \qquad (2)$$

where D_{KL} serves as an approximation to a variational information bottleneck that constrains the mutual information between z and c, as is shown in [1,38]. This information bottleneck acts as a regularizer to avoid overfitting to training tasks. β is the weight of D_{KL} in the objective, and $p(z)$ is a unit Gaussian prior. Since (1) the latent context z serves as input to both controller and evaluator, and (2) $q_\phi(z|c)$ and $p(z)$ are Gaussian, with D_{KL} computed using their mean and variance, gradient of Eq. 2 can be back-propagated end-to-end to the encoder with the reparameterization trick.

4   Experiments

4.1   Implementation Details

We use Multi-layer Perceptrons (MLP) as the controller policy network to generate the probability of choosing a certain action. The parameters θ_c of the controller is trained on-policy via the PPO algorithm. We mask invalid actions by zeroing out their probabilities in the controller's outputs, then softmax the remaining probabilities and sample actions accordingly.

The evaluator is an MLP to generate the predicted score of a network. In the meta-training phase, we reset ϵ in the ϵ-greedy exploration strategy each time when the agent initializes a new task. We sample 80% of the entries as a batch from the replay buffer using PER.

The encoder MLP outputs a 10-dim latent context vector z, and the weight of the KL-Divergence β in the combined loss is set to be 0.1. More details of the components' hyperparameters can be found in the Appendix.

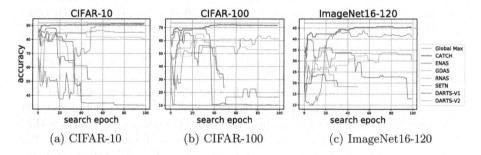

(a) CIFAR-10   (b) CIFAR-100   (c) ImageNet16-120

Fig. 4. Learning curves of one-shot algorithms and CATCH. Each curve is an average of three runs. We plot the first 100 search epochs for algorithms except for DARTS, which is trained only for 50 search epochs.

4.2   Benchmark on NAS-Bench-201

As recent work [56] indicated, NAS algorithms are usually compared unfairly under different settings. To mitigate such problems, we first tested CATCH on NAS-Bench-201. It is a benchmark dataset that enables fair comparisons among NAS methods under the same configurations. It supports searching over cell-based architectures, where a directed acyclic graph represents each cell with 4 nodes and 5 possible connection operations on each edge. It provides the validation and test accuracies of 15,625 architectures on CIFAR-10, CIFAR-100, and ImageNet16-120 datasets. ImageNet16-120 is a subdataset for ImageNet, which downsampled all its images to 16×16, and contains only the first 120 classes of ImageNet.

Experiment Settings. In the meta-training phase, each task is formed as a classification task on an X-class sub-dataset of ImageNet16 (ImageNet downsampled to 16×16) to maintain consistency with the configurations in NAS-Bench-201. The number of classes $X \in [10, 20, 30]$. In each meta-epoch, the agent searches 20 networks whose validation accuracies after 12 training epochs are used as the reward signals. The hyperparameters used for training the networks in both phases are identical to those in NAS-Bench-201. In the following experiments, CATCH-meta is meta-trained with 25 meta epochs for 10.5 GPU hours on Tesla V100. We apply the same configurations as those in NAS-Bench-201.

Comparison with Sample-Based Algorithms. We display the search results of the meta-trained version (CATCH-meta) and the search-from-scratch version (CATCH-sfs where the meta-training phase is skipped) of our method, and compare them with other sample-based algorithms: Random Search (RS) [2], Regularized Evolution Algorithm (R-EA) [40], and REINFORCE [51]. The results of other methods are reproduced by running the code and configurations originally provided by NAS-bench-201. Each experiment is repeated for 500 trials with different seeds. The algorithms are trained for 50 search epochs in each trial. Figure 3 presents the search results on CIFAR-10, CIFAR-100, ImageNet16-120, with the highest validation accuracy on each task.

The reproduced results are consistent with the experiments performed in NAS-Bench-201. The performance of CATCH-sfs is similar to the other four methods, but CATCH-meta dominates all other algorithms in the searched network accuracies. On CIFAR-10, CATCH-meta finds the best model in 280/500 trials. On CIFAR-100, over half of them find top-3 performance networks within 50 samples, while other algorithms barely touch the roof. On ImageNet16-120, CATCH reaches the best network for more than 22% trials. We can see tremendous benefits for using the meta-trained CATCH to reduce time and cost.

Table 1. Comparison of CATCH with one-shot algorithms. The top accuracies of identified models, standard deviations, search time (hour), total search time (hour), and the highest validation accuracies among all the networks in NAS-Bench-201 are reported. The same three random seeds are used to run through each algorithm. The time budget for search on CIFAR-10, CIFAR-100, and ImageNet16-120 are 3, 4, and 5 hours respectively.

Algorithm	CIFAR-10		CIFAR-100		ImageNet16-120		Total time
	Acc±std	Time	Acc±std	Time	Acc±std	Time	
DARTS-V1 [33]	88.08±1.89	2.46	68.99±1.93	2.44	23.66±0	4.55	9.45
DARTS-V2 [33]	87.16±0.39	9	65.06±2.95	7.91	26.29±0	22.14	39.05
GDAS [12]	90.32±0.08	6	70.33±0.85	6.23	44.81±0.97	17	29.23
R-NAS [26]	90.45±0.43	2.19	70.39±1.36	2.26	44.12±1.04	5.94	10.39
ENAS [37]	90.2±0.63	4.22	69.99±1.03	4.26	44.92±0.51	5.18	13.66
SETN [11]	90.26±0.75	7.62	68.01±0.21	7.74	41.04±1.64	20.33	35.69
CATCH-meta	**91.33±0.07**	3	**72.57±0.81**	4	**46.07±0.6**	5	22.5
Max Acc	91.719		73.45		47.19		—

Comparison with One-Shot Algorithms. One of the central controversies around meta-NAS algorithms is: given the high searching efficiency of one-shot methods, can sample-based algorithms outperform them? We therefore compare the performance of CATCH with many state-of-the-art one-shot NAS solutions. For fair comparisons, instead of querying the NAS-Bench-201 network database, we train each child network for 12 epochs and obtain their early-stop validation accuracies as training feedbacks. The early-stop training setup is the same as the one in the meta-training phase. The one-shot algorithms involved are first-order DARTS (DARTS-V1) [33], second-order DARTS (DARTS-V2), GDAS [12], Random NAS (R-NAS) [26], ENAS [37], and SETN [11]. We run the algorithms with the original code and configurations released from NAS-Bench-201. DARTS-V1 and DARTS-V2 are run for 50 search epochs, and other algorithms are trained for 250 search epochs.

Table 2. Results on ImageNet compared to manually designed and NAS searched architectures. Latency is measured on one Tesla V100 with one image with shape (3, 720, 1080).

Network	Top-1 Acc (%)	Top-5 Acc (%)	Latency (ms)
ResNet50 [19]	77.15	93.29	16.4
DenseNet201 [20]	77.42	93.66	31.6
ResNext101 [54]	79.31	94.5	76.7
Inception-V3 [45]	78.8	94.4	16.4
EfficientNet-B1 [47]	77.3	93.5	29.5
EfficientNet-B2	79.2	94.5	47.6
NASNet-A [61]	78.6	94.2	–
BASE [44]	74.3	91.9	–
CATCH-Net-A	79.04	94.43	**16.9**
CATCH-Net-B	**79.46**	**94.7**	33.7

Figure 4 presents the learning curves of each algorithm in the first 100 search epochs. For CATCH, at each search epoch, we identify networks with the best partially trained accuracy found so far, and report their fully trained accuracies. Both DARTS and ENAS have a relatively strong performance at the beginning, but the curves drop significantly afterward. SETN resembles Random NAS a lot. GDAS is among the best one-shot algorithms, but it seems to plateau at local maximums after a few search epochs. CATCH has the best performance among all, as it quickly adapts and identifies promising architectures that are beyond other algorithms' search capacity.

In Table 1, we report the best fully trained accuracy of networks that each algorithm identifies over their complete training process. We set the time budget for CATCH to search on CIFAR-10, CIFAR-100, and ImageNet16-120 as 3, 4, and 5 hours. It is roughly equivalent to cutting the search on these tasks at 70, 50, and 40 search epochs, respectively. Although DARTS-V1, R-NAS, and ENAS spend less time in total, they are highly unstable and the performance of DARTS and ENAS tends to deteriorate over time. CATCH spends 22.5 (10.5 meta + 12 adaptation) hours on all three tasks, and its searched networks surpass all other algorithms. The presented results have proved that CATCH is swiftly adaptive, and it is able to identify networks beyond many one-shot algorithms' reach within a reasonable time.

4.3 Experiments on Residual Block-Based Search Space

Having proved that CATCH can adapt to new tasks efficiently with meta-training, we further inquire whether CATCH has the ability to transfer across different domains including image classification, objection detection, and semantic segmentation. In this section, we consider a more challenging setting where the meta-training phase contain only image classification tasks while tasks in all the three domains are targeted in the adaptation phase. The architectures are very different among these domains, so we search for their common component - the feature extractor (backbone). ResNet is one popular backbone for these tasks, thus we design the search space following [49,57].

Table 3. Results on COCO compared to manually designed and NAS searched backbones. Latency results of networks except CATCH are referred from [57].

Method	Backbone	Input size	Latency (ms)	mAP
RetinaNet [29]	ResNet101-FPN	1333×800	91.7 (V100)	39.1
FSAF [59]	ResNet101-FPN	1333×800	92.5 (V100)	40.9
GA-Faster RCNN [48]	ResNet50-FPN	1333x800	104.2 (V100)	39.8
Faster-RCNN [41]	ResNet101-FPN	1333×800	84.0 (V100)	39.4
Mask-RCNN [18]	ResNet101-FPN	1333×800	105.0 (V100)	40.2
DetNAS [8]	Searched backbone	1333×800	–	42.0
SM-NAS: E3	Searched backbone	800×600	50.7(V100)	42.8
SM-NAS: E5	Searched backbone	1333×800	108.1(V100)	45.9
Auto-FPN [55]	Searched backbone	1333×800	–	40.5
CATCH	CATCH-Net-C	1333×800	123.5 (V100)	**43.2**

Constructing a model in the Residual block-based search space requires the controller to make several decisions: (1) select the network's base channel from $[48, 56, 64, 72]$, (2) decide the network's depth within $[15, 20, 25, 30]$, (3) choose the number of stages s, which is either 4 or 5, (4) schedule the number of blocks contained in each stage, and (5) arrange the distribution of blocks holding different channels. Details of the Residual block-based search space can be found in the Appendix.

Experiment Settings. We use the same meta-training settings as the ones we used in NAS-Bench-201. For each meta epoch, an ImageNet sub-dataset is created. To form such sub-datasets, we sample X classes from all classes of ImageNet, where $X \in [10, 20, 30]$. Then the images are resize to 16×16, 32×32, or 224×224. Thus there are $3 \times \left[\binom{1000}{10} + \binom{1000}{20} + \binom{1000}{30} \right]$ possible sub-datasets.

To achieve the balance between inference latency and network performance, we adopt the multi-objectve reward function $R = P(m) \times [\frac{LAT(m)}{T_{target}}]^w$ in [46], where $P(m)$ denotes the model's performance (e.g. validation accuracy for classification, mAP for object detection or mIoU for semantic segmentation), $LAT(m)$ measures the model's inference latency, and T_{target} is the target latency. w serves as a hyperparameter adjusting the performance-latency tradeoff. In our experiments, we set $w = -0.05$. With this reward, we hope to find models that excel not only in performance but also in inference speed. We meta train CATCHer for 5 GPU days, and adapt on each target task to search for 10 architectures. We target ImageNet dataset for image classification, COCO dataset for object detection and Cityscapes dataset for semantic segmentation. The detailed settings can be found in the Appendix.

Table 4. Results on Cityscapes compared to manually designed and NAS searched backbones. Latency is measured on Tesla V100 with one image with shape (3, 1024, 1024). SS and MS denote for single scale and multiple scale testing respectively.

Method	Backbone	Latency (ms)	mIoU (SS)	mIoU (MS)
BiSeNet [58]	ResNet101	41	–	80.3
DeepLabv3+ [7]	Xception-65	85	77.82	79.3
CCNet [21]	ResNet50	175	–	78.5
DUC [50]	ResNet152	–	76.7	–
DANet [17]	ResNet50	–	76.34	–
Auto-DeepLab [32]	Searched Backbone	–	79.94	–
DPC [6]	Xception-71	–	80.1	–
CATCH	CATCH-Net-D	**27**	79.52	**81.12**

Search Results. Table 2 compares the searched architectures with other widely-recognized networks on ImageNet. CATCH-Net-A outperforms many listed networks. Its accuracy is comparable with EfficientNet-B1 and ResNext-101, yet it is 2.82X and 4.54X faster. CATCH-Net-B outperforms ResNext-101 while shortens the latency by 2.28X. The network comparison on COCO and Cityscapes is presented in Table 3 and Table 4. Our network again shows faster inference time and competitive performance. We also transfer CATCH-Net-B found during the search on ImageNet to COCO and Cityscapes, which yield 42% mAP with 136 ms inference time and 80.87% mIoU (MS) with 52 ms latency, respectively. Our results again show that directly transferring top architectures from one task to another cannot guarantee optimality. It also reveals CATCH's potentials to transfer across tasks even when they are distant from the meta-training ones.

5   Ablation Study

The context encoder is the spotlight component of our algorithm. We are especially curious about: (1) Is the encoder actually helpful for adaptation (compared with simply plugging in the meta-learned controller and evaluator priors)? (2) If so, does the improvement come from good estimates of the posterior, or is it from the stochastic generation of z that encourages exploration and benefits generalization?

To answer these questions, we designed two extra sets of experiments: (1) CATCH-zero: We set $z = 0$, and thereby completely eliminate the encoder's effect on both the controller and the evaluator; (2) CATCH-random: We sample each z from a unit Gaussian prior $\mathcal{N}(0, diag(1))$ during the search as random inputs. The results are presented in Fig. 5 (a)–(c). In both settings, the agents are still meta-trained for 10.5 h before they are plugged in for adaptation.

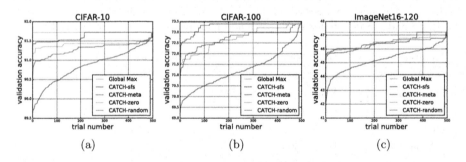

Fig. 5. (a)–(c) compare results of 500 trials for CATCH-meta, CATCH-sfs(search from scratch), CATCH-zero, CATCH-random.

The gaps among the lines in Fig. 5 answered our questions. The encoder not only helps with adaptation (through comparing CATCH-meta and CATCH-zero), but also provides assistance in a much more meaningful way than using random inputs for exploration, as CATCH-meta outperforms CATCH-random on both CIFAR-10 and CIFAR-100. Interestingly, we observe less significant improvement on ImageNet16-120. One hypothesis is since we perform the meta-training phase on sub-datasets of ImageNet16, the meta-trained controller and evaluator are already tuned towards policies that fit the search on ImageNet16. Hence, the transferred policies require less adaptation assistance from the encoder. More ablation studies can be found in the Appendix.

6   Conclusion and Discussion

In this work, we propose CATCH, a transferrable NAS approach, by designing an efficient learning framework that leverages the benefits of context-based meta reinforcement learning. The key contribution of CATCH is to boost NAS efficiency by extracting and utilizing task-specific latent contexts, while maintaining universality and robustness in various settings. Experiments and ablation studies show its dominant position in search efficiency and performance over non-transferrable schemes on NAS-Bench-201. Extensive experiments on residual block-based search space also demonstrate its capability in handling cross-task architecture search. As a task-agnostic transferrable NAS framework, CATCH possesses great potentials in scaling NAS to large datasets and various domains efficiently.

During our research into transferrable NAS frameworks, we identified many potentially valuable questions to be explored. Efficient adaptation among domains is challenging, and we demonstrated a first attempt to simplify it by searching for backbones with a shared search space. A possible future investigation would be to generalize cross-task architecture search to flexibly include more decisions, such as searching for detection and segmentation heads. Meanwhile, our meta-training tasks involve only classification tasks, but it is also possible to diversify the pool and explore whether it leads to further performance boosts.

References

1. Alemi, A.A., Fischer, I., Dillon, J.V., Murphy, K.: Deep variational information bottleneck. arXiv preprint arXiv:1612.00410 (2016)
2. Bergstra, J., Bengio, Y.: Random search for hyper-parameter optimization. J. Mach. Learn. Res. **13**(Feb), 281–305 (2012)
3. Bergstra, J., Yamins, D., Cox, D.: Making a science of model search: hyperparameter optimization in hundreds of dimensions for vision architectures. In: International Conference on Machine Learning, pp. 115–123 (2013)
4. Bergstra, J.S., Bardenet, R., Bengio, Y., Kégl, B.: Algorithms for hyper-parameter optimization. In: Advances in Neural Information Processing Systems, pp. 2546–2554 (2011)
5. Chen, L.C., et al.: Searching for efficient multi-scale architectures for dense image prediction. In: Advances in Neural Information Processing Systems, pp. 8699–8710 (2018)
6. Chen, L.C., et al.: Searching for efficient multi-scale architectures for dense image prediction. In: Bengio, S., Wallach, H., Larochelle, H., Grauman, K., Cesa-Bianchi, N., Garnett, R. (eds.) Advances in Neural Information Processing Systems, vol. 31, pp. 8699–8710. Curran Associates Inc., Red Hook (2018)
7. Chen, L.C., Zhu, Y., Papandreou, G., Schroff, F., Adam, H.: Encoder-decoder with atrous separable convolution for semantic image segmentation. In: The European Conference on Computer Vision (ECCV) (2018)
8. Chen, Y., Yang, T., Zhang, X., Meng, G., Pan, C., Sun, J.: Detnas: Neural architecture search on object detection. arXiv preprint arXiv:1903.10979 (2019)

9. Cordts, M., et al.: The cityscapes dataset for semantic urban scene understanding. In: Proceedings of the IEEE Conference on Computer Vision and Pattern Recognition (CVPR) (2016)
10. Deng,J., Dong, W., Socher, R., Li, L.J., Li, K., Fei-Fei, L.: Imagenet: a large-scale hierarchical image database. In: 2009 IEEE Conference on Computer Vision and Pattern Recognition, pp. 248–255. IEEE (2009)
11. Dong, X., Yang, Y.: One-shot neural architecture search via self-evaluated template network. In: Proceedings of the IEEE International Conference on Computer Vision, pp. 3681–3690 (2019)
12. Dong, X., Yang, Y.: Searching for a robust neural architecture in four gpu hours. In: Proceedings of the IEEE Conference on Computer Vision and Pattern Recognition, pp. 1761–1770 (2019)
13. Dong, X., Yang, Y.: Nas-bench-201: extending the scope of reproducible neural architecture search. arXiv preprint arXiv:2001.00326 (2020)
14. Elsken, T., Metzen, J.H., Hutter, F.: Efficient multi-objective neural architecture search via lamarckian evolution. arXiv preprint arXiv:1804.09081 (2018)
15. Elsken, T., Staffler, B., Metzen, J., Hutter, F.: Meta-learning of neural architectures for few-shot learning. arXiv preprint arXiv:1911.11090 (2019)
16. Finn, C., Abbeel, P., Levine, S.: Model-agnostic meta-learning for fast adaptation of deep networks. arXiv preprint arXiv:1703.03400 (2017)
17. Fu, J., et al.: Dual attention network for scene segmentation. In: The IEEE Conference on Computer Vision and Pattern Recognition (CVPR) (2019)
18. He, K., Gkioxari, G., Dollár, P., Girshick, R.: Mask r-cnn. In: Proceedings of the IEEE International Conference on Computer Vision, pp. 2961–2969 (2017)
19. He, K., Zhang, X., Ren, S., Sun, J.: Deep residual learning for image recognition. In: Proceedings of the IEEE Conference on Computer Vision and Pattern Recognition, pp. 770–778 (2016)
20. Huang, G., Liu, Z., Van Der Maaten, L., Weinberger, K.Q.: Densely connected convolutional networks. In Proceedings of the IEEE Conference on Computer Vision and Pattern Recognition, pp. 4700–4708 (2017)
21. Huang, Z., Wang, X., Huang, L., Huang, C., Wei, Y., Liu, W.: Ccnet: criss-cross attention for semantic segmentation. In: The IEEE International Conference on Computer Vision (ICCV) (2019)
22. Huber, P.J.: Robust estimation of a location parameter. In: Kotz, S., Johnson, N.L. (eds.) Breakthroughs in Statistics. Springer Series in Statistics (Perspectives in Statistics), pp. 492–518. Springer, New York (1992). https://doi.org/10.1007/978-1-4612-4380-9_35
23. Kim, J., et al.: Auto-meta: Automated gradient based meta learner search. arXiv preprint arXiv:1806.06927 (2018)
24. Kingma, D.P., Welling, M.: Auto-encoding variational bayes. arXiv preprint arXiv:1312.6114 (2013)
25. Lan, L., Li, Z., Guan, X., Wang, P.: Meta reinforcement learning with task embedding and shared policy. arXiv preprint arXiv:1905.06527 (2019)
26. Li, L., Talwalkar, A.: Random search and reproducibility for neural architecture search. arXiv preprint arXiv:1902.07638 (2019)
27. Li, Z., Zhou, F., Chen, F., Li, H.: Meta-sgd: learning to learn quickly for few-shot learning. arXiv preprint arXiv:1707.09835 (2017)
28. Lian, D., et al.: Towards fast adaptation of neural architectures with meta learning. In: International Conference on Learning Representations (2020)

29. Lin, T.Y., Goyal, P., Girshick, R., He, K., Dollár, P.: Focal loss for dense object detection. In: Proceedings of the IEEE International Conference on Computer Vision, pp. 2980–2988 (2017)
30. Lin, T.Y., et al.: Microsoft COCO: common objects in context. In: Fleet, D., Pajdla, T., Schiele, B., Tuytelaars, T. (eds.) ECCV 2014. LNCS, vol. 8693, pp. 740–755. Springer, Cham (2014). https://doi.org/10.1007/978-3-319-10602-1_48
31. Liu, B., et al.: Autofis: Automatic feature interaction selection in factorization models for click-through rate prediction. arXiv preprint arXiv:2003.11235 (2020)
32. Liu, C., et al.: Auto-deeplab: hierarchical neural architecture search for semantic image segmentation. In: Proceedings of the IEEE Conference on Computer Vision and Pattern Recognition, pp. 82–92 (2019)
33. Liu, H., Simonyan, K., Yang, Y.: Darts: Differentiable architecture search. arXiv preprint arXiv:1806.09055 (2018)
34. Mnih, V., et al.: Playing atari with deep reinforcement learning. arXiv preprint arXiv:1312.5602 (2013)
35. Negrinho, R., Gordon, G.: Deeparchitect: Automatically designing and training deep architectures. arXiv preprint arXiv:1704.08792 (2017)
36. Pasunuru, R., Bansal, M.: Continual and multi-task architecture search. arXiv preprint arXiv:1906.05226 (2019)
37. Pham, H., Guan, M.Y., Zoph, B., Le, Q.V., Dean, J.: Efficient neural architecture search via parameter sharing. arXiv preprint arXiv:1802.03268 (2018)
38. Rakelly, K., Zhou, A., Quillen, D., Finn, C., Levine, S.: Efficient off-policy meta-reinforcement learning via probabilistic context variables. arXiv preprint arXiv:1903.08254 (2019)
39. Real, E., Aggarwal, A., Huang, Y., Le, Q.V.: Aging evolution for image classifier architecture search. In: AAAI Conference on Artificial Intelligence (2019)
40. Real, E., Aggarwal, A., Huang, Y., Le, Q.V.: Regularized evolution for image classifier architecture search. In: Proceedings of the AAAI Conference on Artificial Intelligence, vol. 33, pp. 4780–4789 (2019)
41. Ren, S., He, K., Girshick, R., Sun, J.: Faster r-cnn: towards real-time object detection with region proposal networks. In: Advances in Neural Information Processing Systems, pp. 91–99 (2015)
42. Schaul, T., Quan, J., Antonoglou, I., Silver, D.: Prioritized experience replay. arXiv preprint arXiv:1511.05952 (2015)
43. Schulman, J., Wolski, F., Dhariwal, P., Radford, A., Klimov, O.: Proximal policy optimization algorithms. arXiv preprint arXiv:1707.06347 (2017)
44. Shaw, A., Wei, W., Liu, W., Song, L., Dai, B.: Meta architecture search. In: Advances in Neural Information Processing Systems, pp. 11225–11235 (2019)
45. Szegedy, C., Vanhoucke, V., Ioffe, S., Shlens, J., Wojna, Z.: Rethinking the inception architecture for computer vision. In: Proceedings of the IEEE Conference on Computer Vision and Pattern Recognition, pp. 2818–2826 (2016)
46. Tan, M., et al.: Mnasnet: platform-aware neural architecture search for mobile. In The IEEE Conference on Computer Vision and Pattern Recognition (CVPR) (2019)
47. Tan, M., Le, Q.V.: Efficientnet: Rethinking model scaling for convolutional neural networks. arXiv preprint arXiv:1905.11946 (2019)
48. Wang, J., Chen, K., Yang, S., Loy, C.C., Lin, D.: Region proposal by guided anchoring. In: Proceedings of the IEEE Conference on Computer Vision and Pattern Recognition, pp. 2965–2974 (2019)
49. Wang, N., Gao, Y., Chen, H., Wang, P., Tian, Z., Shen, C.: NAS-FCOS: fast neural architecture search for object detection. CoRR, abs/1906.04423 (2019)

50. Wang, P., et al.: Understanding convolution for semantic segmentation. In: 2018 IEEE Winter Conference on Applications of Computer Vision (WACV), pp. 1451–1460 (2018)

51. Williams, R.J.: Simple statistical gradient-following algorithms for connectionist reinforcement learning. Mach. Learn. **8**(3–4), 229–256 (1992)

52. Wistuba, M.: Finding competitive network architectures within a day using uct. arXiv preprint arXiv:1712.07420 (2017)

53. Wong, C., Houlsby, N., Lu, Y., Gesmundo, A.: Transfer learning with neural automl. In: Advances in Neural Information Processing Systems, pp. 8356–8365 (2018)

54. Xie, S., Girshick, R., Dollár, P., Tu, Z., He, K.: Aggregated residual transformations for deep neural networks. In: Proceedings of the IEEE Conference on Computer Vision and Pattern Recognition, pp. 1492–1500 (2017)

55. Xu, H., Yao, L., Zhang, W., Liang, X., Li, Z.: Auto-FPN: automatic network architecture adaptation for object detection beyond classification. In: Proceedings of the IEEE International Conference on Computer Vision, pp. 6649–6658 (2019)

56. Yang, A., Esperança, P.M., Carlucci, F.F.: NAS evaluation is frustratingly hard. In: International Conference on Learning Representations (2020)

57. Yao, L., Xu, H., Zhang, W., Liang, X., Li, Z.: SM-NAS: structural-to-modular neural architecture search for object detection. arXiv preprint arXiv:1911.09929 (2019)

58. Yu, C., Wang, J., Peng, C., Gao, C., Yu, G., Sang, N.: Bisenet: bilateral segmentation network for real-time semantic segmentation. In: The European Conference on Computer Vision (ECCV) (2018)

59. Zhu, C., He, Y., Savvides, M.: Feature selective anchor-free module for single-shot object detection. In: Proceedings of the IEEE Conference on Computer Vision and Pattern Recognition, pp. 840–849 (2019)

60. Zoph, B., Le, Q.V.: Neural architecture search with reinforcement learning. arXiv preprint arXiv:1611.01578 (2016)

61. Zoph, B., Vasudevan, V., Shlens, J., Le, Q.V.: Learning transferable architectures for scalable image recognition. In: Proceedings of the IEEE Conference on Computer Vision and Pattern Recognition, pp. 8697–8710 (2018)

Toward Faster and Simpler Matrix Normalization via Rank-1 Update

Tan Yu[1,2(✉)], Yunfeng Cai[1,2], and Ping Li[1,2]

[1] Cognitive Computing Lab, Baidu Research, 10900 NE 8th Street,
Bellevue, WA 98004, USA
{tanyu01,caiyunfeng,liping11}@baidu.com
[2] Cognitive Computing Lab, Baidu Research, No. 10 Xibeiwang East Road,
Beijing 100085, China

Abstract. Bilinear pooling has been used in many computer vision tasks and recent studies discover that matrix normalization is a vital step for achieving impressive performance of bilinear pooling. The standard matrix normalization, however, needs singular value decomposition (SVD), which is not well suited in the GPU platform, limiting its efficiency in training and inference. To resolve this issue, the Newton-Schulz (NS) iteration method has been proposed to approximate the matrix square-root. Although it is GPU-friendly, the NS iteration still takes several (expensive) iterations of matrix-matrix multiplications. Furthermore, the NS iteration is incompatible with the compact bilinear features obtained from Tensor Sketch (TS) or Random Maclaurin (RM). To overcome those known limitations, in this paper we propose a "rank-1 update normalization" (RUN), which only needs matrix-vector multiplications and is hence substantially more efficient than the NS iteration using matrix-matrix multiplications. Moreover, RUN readily supports the normalization on compact bilinear features from TS or RM. Besides, RUN is simpler than the NS iteration and easier for implementation in practice. As RUN is a differentiable procedure, we can plug it in a CNN-based an end-to-end training setting. Extensive experiments on four public benchmarks demonstrates that, for the full bilinear pooling, RUN achieves comparable accuracy with a substantial speedup over the NS iteration. For the compact bilinear pooling, RUN achieves comparable accuracy with a significant speedup over SVD-based normalization.

1 Introduction

Bilinear pooling has achieved excellent performance in many computer vision tasks, such as fine-grained recognition [19,20,22,29,30], generic image recognition [18], visual question answering [7,36] and action classification [3,14,28,31]. Recent studies [11,15,18–20] show that, the normalization on singular values of

Electronic supplementary material The online version of this chapter (https://doi.org/10.1007/978-3-030-58529-7_13) contains supplementary material, which is available to authorized users.

© Springer Nature Switzerland AG 2020
A. Vedaldi et al. (Eds.): ECCV 2020, LNCS 12364, pp. 203–219, 2020.
https://doi.org/10.1007/978-3-030-58529-7_13

the bilinear matrix is vital for achieving high recognition performance. To be specific, DeepO^{2}P [11] adopts the logarithm normalization on the singular values to approximate the Log-Euclidean metric [1] for exploiting geometry of covariance spaces. MPN-COV [19] explains the advantage of the power normalization on singular values from the perspective of robust covariance estimation. In parallel, HoK [15], Improved BCNN [20], MHBN [35], Second-order Democratic Aggregation [21] and Power Normalization [16] demonstrate the importance of the normalization on singular values in remedying the burstiness phenomenon and equalizing contributions of singular values into the final image descriptor.

To conduct normalization on the singular values of the bilinear matrix, traditional methods such as matrix square-root normalization [19] and matrix logarithm normalization [11] rely on the singular value decomposition (SVD) to explicitly obtain the singular values. But SVD is not easily parallelizable and hence not well suited in the GPU platform, limiting its efficiency. To boost the efficiency in the GPU platform, improved B-CNN [20] attempts to approximate the matrix square root via the Newton-Schulz (NS) iteration [10] in the forward propagation. Since NS iteration only needs matrix-matrix product, it is easily parallelizable and well suited in the GPU platform in the inference time. But in the backward propagation of, the improved B-CNN uses Lyapunov equation, which is still expensive in computation. iSQRT [18] further makes the NS iteration differentiable and thus makes it feasible in the backward propagation. In each iteration, the NS method calculates several times of matrix-matrix multiplications. We denote the iteration number by K and denote the bilinear matrix by $\mathbf{B} \in \mathbb{R}^{D \times D}$, and NS method has a computation complexity of $\mathcal{O}(KD^3)$, which is expensive. In parallel, power-normalization methods are proposed in [16], which also rely on a series of matrix-matrix multiplications, taking a $\mathcal{O}(\log(\eta)D^3)$ computation complexity where η is the level of power normalization. In addition, NS iteration and power normalization only support normalization on the full bilinear matrix, and cannot support the normalization on the compact bilinear features [8] from Tensor Sketch [25] or Random Maclaurin [12]. This limits their usefulness in cases when low-dimension features are required.

To further improve the efficiency and overcome the limitation of the NS iteration, we propose a rank-1 update normalization (RUN). The proposed RUN is an iterative algorithm inspired by a classical numerical algorithm, power method [2]. In each iteration, it only needs twice matrix-vector multiplications, taking low computation cost. Meanwhile, it is easily parallelizable and well suited in the GPU platform. In each iteration, the computation complexity of the proposed RUN is $\mathcal{O}(DN)$. Here, N is the number of local features per image, which is in a comparable scale with D. In this case, the per-iteration cost of RUN, $\mathcal{O}(DN)$, is much lower than NS's per-iteration cost $\mathcal{O}(D^3)$. Moreover, in practice, our RUN needs less iterations to achieve the optimal recognition accuracy than NS method, making its efficiency advantage over the NS iteration more significant. Besides, the proposed RUN is much simpler than NS iteration and thus much easier for implementation in practice. In addition, the proposed RUN readily supports the normalization on a compact bilinear features generated from Tensor

Table 1. Differences between the proposed RUN and other bilinear pooling methods, O^2P [11], G^2DeNet [29], MPN-COV [19], Improved B-CNN [20], iSQRT [18], Power-Norm [16] and MoNet [9]. Here, K_1 is the number of iterations used in Newton-Schulz (NS) method, and K_2 is that in the proposed RUN, η is the level of power normalization, D is the local feature dimension and N is the number of local features. In practice, N is in a comparable scale with D, $K_2 < K_1$. Thus, the complexity $\mathcal{O}(K_2DN)$ of ours is significantly lower than the complexity $\mathcal{O}(K_1D^3)$ of the NS method. Meanwhile, our RUN is well suited in the GPU and readily supports compact bilinear pooling (CBP) based on Tensor Sketch or Random Maclaurin.

Method	Algorithm	Complexity	GPU support	CBP support
O^2P	SVD	$\mathcal{O}(D^3)$	Limited	No
G^2DeNet	SVD	$\mathcal{O}(D^3)$	Limited	No
MPN-COV	Eigen Decomp	$\mathcal{O}(D^3)$	Limited	No
Improved B-CNN	Newton-Schulz in FP	$\mathcal{O}(D^3)$	Good in FP	No
iSQRT	Newton-Schulz	$\mathcal{O}(K_1D^3)$	Good	No
Power Normalization	MaxExp	$\mathcal{O}(\log(\eta)D^3)$	Good	No
MoNet	SVD	$\mathcal{O}(D^3)$	Limited	Yes
RUN (Ours)	Power Method	$\mathcal{O}(K_2DN)$	Good	Yes

Sketch or Random Maclaurin. Thus, our RUN is especially useful for the cases when compact features are necessary. Power method is also used in obtaining the largest singular value for spectral normalization [24]. The spectral normalization is conducted on the weight matrix whereas ours is conducted on the feature. Table 1 compares our RUN with several bilinear pooling methods. In summary, our contributions in this paper are three-fold:

- We propose "rank-1 update normalization" (RUN), which only needs several matrix-vector multiplications and is considerably more efficient than existing GPU-friendly normalization methods based on the NS iteration.
- The proposed RUN readily supports normalization on compact bilinear features from Tensor Sketch or Random Maclaurin, which cannot be achieved by existing matrix normalization methods based on the NS iteration.
- The proposed RUN is a differentiable procedure. We plug it into a neural network and achieve an end-to-end training. The systematic experiments conducted on four public benchmarks demonstrate its excellence.

2   Background

We denote the feature map from a convolutional layer by $\mathcal{F} \in \mathbb{R}^{W \times H \times D}$, where W is the width, H is the height and D is the depth. We reshape $\mathcal{F}$ into a matrix

$\mathbf{F} \in \mathbb{R}^{WH \times D}$. Bilinear pooling obtains the bilinear matrix by $\mathbf{B} = \mathbf{F}^\top \mathbf{F} \in \mathbb{R}^{D \times D}$. A pioneering work, B-CNN [22], implements the bilinear pooling as a layer of a convolutional neural network to support an end-to-end training. It achieves a better performance on fine-grained classification than standard AlexNet. The following research on bilinear pooling in deep neural network proceeds along two main directions: 1) improve the effectiveness of bilinear features [17,19,20,29,38]; 2) reduce the dimension of bilinear features [5,8,13]. Our work is related with both directions since we propose a fast matrix normalization method to boost its effectiveness, and make it compatible with compact bilinear pooling to obtain a compact and normalized bilinear feature. Below we review existing matrix normalization methods and compact bilinear pooling methods, respectively.

2.1   Matrix Normalization

We first review two traditional methods, matrix square-root normalization in improved B-CNN [20] and matrix logarithm normalization in O^2P [11]. They first conduct singular value decomposition (SVD) on the bilinear matrix $\mathbf{B}$ by

$$\mathbf{B} \to \mathbf{U}\mathbf{\Sigma}\mathbf{U}^\top.$$

Normalization is conducted on singular values and the normalized feature is

$$\hat{\mathbf{B}} \leftarrow \mathbf{U}g(\mathbf{\Sigma})\mathbf{U}^\top,$$

where $g(\mathbf{\Sigma})$ is conducted on singular values in an element-wise manner. Matrix square-root normalization adopts $g(\mathbf{\Sigma}) = \mathbf{\Sigma}^{1/2}$ and matrix logarithm normalization adopts $g(\mathbf{\Sigma}) = \log(\mathbf{\Sigma})$. However, as mentioned before, SVD is not easily parallelizable and not well supported in the GPU platform, limiting its efficiency in training and inference. Improved B-CNN [20] utilizes Newton-Schulz (NS) iteration to approximate the matrix square root in the forward propagation. iSQRT [18] makes the NS iteration differentiable and makes it support backward propagation as well. Given a bilinear matrix $\mathbf{B}$, the NS method initializes $\mathbf{Y}_0 = \mathbf{B}$ and $\mathbf{Z}_0 = \mathbf{I}$. In each iteration, the NS method updates $\mathbf{Z}_k$ and $\mathbf{Y}_k$ by

$$\mathbf{Y}_k = \frac{1}{2}\mathbf{Y}_{k-1}(3\mathbf{I} - \mathbf{Z}_{k-1}\mathbf{Y}_{k-1}), \quad \mathbf{Z}_k = \frac{1}{2}(3\mathbf{I} - \mathbf{Z}_{k-1}\mathbf{Y}_{k-1})\mathbf{Z}_{k-1},$$

where $\mathbf{Y}_k$ converges to $\mathbf{B}^{1/2}$. Since it involves only matrix-matrix product, it is easily parallelizable and well supported in the GPU platform. The computation complexity of each iteration is $\mathcal{O}(D^3)$, where D is the local feature dimension. Since D is large, computing Newton-Schulz (NS) iteration is still expensive. In contrast, our method is based on iterations of matrix-vector multiplications, which are computationally cheaper than the matrix-matrix multiplications used in the NS iteration. What's more, we will show in Sect. 2.2 that, the NS iteration is not compatible with compact bilinear pooling methods based on Random Maclaurin and Tensor Sketch, whereas ours readily supports normalization on compact bilinear pooling features.

2.2 Compact Bilinear Pooling

The dimension of a bilinear feature is $D \times D$, which is extremely high. On one hand, it is prone to over-fitting due to huge number of model parameters in the classifier, and thus requires a large number of training sample. On the other hand, it is extremely expensive in memory and computation when training the classifier. To overcome these drawbacks, CBP [8] is proposed. It treats the outer product used in bilinear pooling as a polynomial kernel embedding, and seeks to approximate the explicit kernel feature map. To be specific, by rearranging the feature map $\mathcal{F}$ to $\mathbf{F} = [\mathbf{f}_1, \cdots, \mathbf{f}_{WH}]^\top$, the bilinear matrix $\mathbf{B}$ is obtained by

$$\mathbf{B} = \mathbf{F}^\top \mathbf{F} = \sum_{i=1}^{WH} \mathbf{f}_i \mathbf{f}_i^\top = \sum_{i=1}^{WH} \mathrm{h}(\mathbf{f}_i),$$

where $\mathrm{h}(\mathbf{f}_i) = \mathbf{f}_i \mathbf{f}_i^\top \in \mathbb{R}^{D \times D}$ is the explicit feature map of the second-order polynomial kernel. CBP seeks for a low-dimensional projection function $\phi(\mathbf{f}_i) \in \mathbb{R}^d$ with $d \ll D^2$ such that

$$\langle \phi(\mathbf{x}), \phi(\mathbf{y}) \rangle \approx \langle \mathrm{vec}(\mathrm{h}(\mathbf{x})), \mathrm{vec}(\mathrm{h}(\mathbf{y})) \rangle,$$

where $\mathrm{vec}(\cdot)$ is the operation to unfold a 2D matrix to a 1D vector. In this case, the approximated low-dimensional bilinear feature is obtained by $\tilde{\mathbf{B}} = \sum_{i=1}^{WH} \phi(\mathbf{f}_i)$. The advantages of low-dimensional features are two-fold: 1) less prone to over-fitting, 2) faster in training the classifier.

CBP investigates two types of approximation methods: Random Maclaurin [12] and Tensor Sketch [25]. Since the compact bilinear feature $\tilde{\mathbf{B}}$ has broken the matrix structure, the matrix normalization methods conducted on the bilinear feature $\mathbf{B}$, such as Newton-Schulz iteration, is no longer feasible for normalizing $\tilde{\mathbf{B}}$. To tackle this challenge, MoNet [9] conducts SVD directly on the original local feature $\mathbf{F}$ instead of the bilinear matrix $\mathbf{B}$ and then conducts compact bilinear pooling. Nevertheless, as we mentioned, the SVD is not well supported on GPU platform, limiting the training and inference efficiency. In contrast, we will see in the next section that our method only relies on matrix-vector multiplications, and hence is easily parallelizable and well supported in the GPU platform. Meanwhile, the proposed RUN supports the normalization on a compact bilinear feature generated from Tensor Sketch or Random Maclaurin.

3 Rank-1 Update Normalization (RUN)

To overcome the limitations of previous methods, we propose a rank-1 update normalization (RUN). Below we give the details of the proposed RUN method and then summarize the method in Algorithm 1.

We first define some notations. Assuming that, through SVD, the bilinear feature $\mathbf{B}$ can be decomposed into $\mathbf{B} = \mathbf{U}\mathbf{\Sigma}\mathbf{U}^\top$. $\mathbf{U} = [\mathbf{u}_1, \cdots, \mathbf{u}_D]$ consists of singular vectors, which are orthogonal to each other. $\mathbf{\Sigma} = \mathrm{diag}([\sigma_1, \cdots, \sigma_D])$ is a diagonal matrix where $\{\sigma_d\}_{d=1}^D$ are singular values and $\sigma_1 \geq \sigma_2 \geq \cdots \geq \sigma_D$. Next we introduce the process of the proposed RUN.

In the first step, we initialize a random vector $\mathbf{v}_0 = [v_1, ..., v_D] \sim \mathcal{N}(\mathbf{0}, \mathbf{I})$. That is, $\{v_i\}_{i=1}^D$ are $i.i.d.$ random variables with standard normal distribution. Then, we perform K iterations of power method as follows:

$$\mathbf{v}_k = \mathbf{B}\mathbf{v}_{k-1}, \text{ for } k = 1, \ldots, K. \tag{1}$$

After that, the rank-1 matrix is constructed by

$$\mathbf{R}_K = \mathbf{B}\mathbf{v}_K\mathbf{v}_K^\top / \|\mathbf{v}_K\|_2^2.$$

At last, we update the matrix $\mathbf{B}$ by subtracting $\mathbf{R}_K$:

$$\mathbf{B}_K = \mathbf{B} - \epsilon\mathbf{R}_K, \tag{2}$$

where $\epsilon \in (0, 1]$ is a small positive constant. The classic convergence property of power method tells that if $\sigma_1 > \sigma_2$, $\mathbf{v}_K/\|\mathbf{v}_K\|_2$ will converge to $\mathbf{u}_1$. Therefore, $\mathbf{B}_K$ converges to $\mathbf{B} - \epsilon\sigma_1\mathbf{u}_1\mathbf{u}_1^\top$. That is

$$\lim_{K\to\infty} \mathbf{B}_K = \mathbf{U}\operatorname{diag}([\sigma_1(1 - \epsilon), \sigma_2, \ldots, \sigma_D])\mathbf{U}^\top, \tag{3}$$

$i.e.$, the eigenvalues of $\mathbf{B}_\infty$ remain unchanged except the largest one, which is decreased by $\epsilon\sigma_1$. More generally, $\mathbf{B}_K$ is an estimation of a normalized bilinear matrix. To be specific, it satisfies the following theorem:

Theorem 1. *Let* $\mathbf{B}_K$ *be obtained via Eq. (1)-(2), where* $\mathbf{v}_0 \sim \mathcal{N}(\mathbf{0}, \mathbf{I})$. *Then the expectation of* $\mathbf{B}_K$ *is given by*

$$\mathbb{E}(\mathbf{B}_K) = \mathbf{U}\operatorname{diag}([\sigma_1(1 - \epsilon\alpha_1), \cdots, \sigma_D(1 - \epsilon\alpha_D))\mathbf{U}^\top, \tag{4}$$

where $1 \geq \alpha_1 \geq \alpha_2 \geq \cdots \geq \alpha_D$.

Due to limitation of the space, the proof of the Theorem 1 is given in the supplementary material. The operation in the right-hand side of Eq. (4) scales each singular value σ_i by $(1 - \epsilon\alpha_i)$. As $1 \geq \alpha_1 \geq \alpha_2 \geq \cdots \geq \alpha_D$ and $\epsilon \in [0, 1]$, thus

$$0 \leq 1 - \epsilon\alpha_1 \leq 1 - \epsilon\alpha_2 \leq \cdots \leq 1 - \epsilon\alpha_D \leq 1.$$

That is, it gives a smaller scale factor to a larger singular value, making the contributions of singular values to the final image feature more balanced and achieving the same goal as the spectral power normalization used in [15, 20].

Since computing $\mathbf{B}_K$ only requires $2K$ times matrix-vector multiplications, it only takes $\mathcal{O}(KD^2)$ complexity and is well supported in GPU platform. In experiments section, we will show when K is small, $e.g.$, $K = 2$, it has achieved an excellent performance. Nevertheless, obtaining the above approximated normalized bilinear feature $\mathbf{B}_K$ requires the original bilinear matrix $\mathbf{B}$ obtained from bilinear pooling. Thus, it is not applicable to the compact bilinear feature which has broken the structure of square matrix. To make the proposed fast matrix normalization method compatible with compact bilinear pooling, we seek to directly conduct normalization on the original feature map $\mathbf{F} \in \mathbb{R}^{N \times D}$, where $N = WH$ is the number of local features and D is the local feature dimension. It is based on following iterations:

$$\mathbf{v}_k = \mathbf{F}^\top \mathbf{F} \mathbf{v}_{k-1}, \text{for } k = 1, \ldots, K, \qquad (5)$$

where the entries of $\mathbf{v}_0$ are *i.i.d.* random variables with standard normal distribution. Then we construct the updated feature map $\mathbf{F}_K$ by

$$\mathbf{F}_K = \mathbf{F} - \eta \mathbf{F} \mathbf{v}_K \mathbf{v}_K^\top / \|\mathbf{v}_K\|_2^2, \qquad (6)$$

where $\mathbf{v}_K$ is obtained via (5) and $\eta \in (0, 1]$ is a constant. The above procedure is summarized in Algorithm 1. Since in each iteration, it only needs twice matrix-vector multiplications, in total, the computational complexity of obtaining $\mathbf{F}_K$ is $\mathcal{O}(KDN)$. Let $\mathbf{u}_{F,i}$ and $\mathbf{v}_{F,i}$ be the left and right singular vectors of $\mathbf{F}$ corresponding with its ith largest singular value $\sigma_{F,i}$. If $\sigma_{F,1} \neq \sigma_{F,2}$, $\mathbf{F} \mathbf{v}_k / \|\mathbf{v}_k\|_2$ and $\mathbf{v}_k / \|\mathbf{v}_k\|_2$ will converge to $\mathbf{u}_{F,1}$ and $\mathbf{v}_{F,1}$, respectively. In limit, we have

$$\lim_{K \to \infty} \mathbf{F}_K = \mathbf{F} - \eta \sigma_{F,1} \mathbf{u}_{F,1} \mathbf{v}_{F,1}^\top,$$

whose singular values are the same as that of $\mathbf{F}$, except the largest one, which is decreased by $\eta \sigma_{F,1}$. In fact, similar to Theorem 1, we have

Theorem 2. *Let $\mathbf{F}_K$ be obtained through Algorithm 1. Then the expectation of $\mathbf{F}_K$ can be given by*

$$\mathbb{E}(\mathbf{F}_K) = \mathbf{U}_F \widehat{\Sigma}_F \mathbf{V}_F^\top, \qquad (7)$$

where $\mathbf{U}_F$, $\mathbf{V}_F$ are the left and right singular vector matrices of $\mathbf{F}$, respectively, $\widehat{\Sigma}_F$ is the diagonal matrix $\mathrm{diag}[(\sigma_{F,1}(1 - \eta\beta_1), \cdots, \sigma_{F,D}(1 - \eta\beta_D))]$ with $0 \leq 1 - \eta\beta_1 \leq 1 - \eta\beta_2 \leq \cdots \leq 1 - \eta\beta_D \leq 1$.

Its proof is similar to Theorem 1, and thus we omit it. Using the standard bilinear pooling, the normalized bilinear matrix feature can be obtained by $\bar{\mathbf{B}}_K = \mathbf{F}_K^\top \mathbf{F}_K$. When $\sigma_{F,1} \neq \sigma_{F,2}$, $\bar{\mathbf{B}}_K$ satisfies

$$\lim_{K \to \infty} \bar{\mathbf{B}}_K = \mathbf{V}_F \, \mathrm{diag}([\sigma_{F,1}^2 (1 - \eta)^2, \cdots, \sigma_{F,D}^2]) \mathbf{V}_F^\top. \qquad (8)$$

Since $\mathbf{V}_F$ in Eq. (8) is equal to $\mathbf{U}$ in Eq. (3), if we set $(1 - \epsilon)$ in Eq. (8) equal to $(1 - \eta)^2$ in Eq. (3), $\mathbf{B}_K$ and $\bar{\mathbf{B}}_K$ will converge to the same matrix. But the advantage of updating $\mathbf{F}$ as Eq. (6) over updating $\mathbf{B}$ as Eq. (2) is that, the former is compatible with compact bilinear pooling, which cannot be achieved by the latter. The compact normalized bilinear feature is obtained by

$$\bar{\mathbf{b}}_K = \sum_{i=1}^{N} \phi(\mathbf{F}_K[i, :]),$$

Algorithm 1. Rank-1 Update Normalization (RUN).

Input: Local features $\mathbf{F} \in \mathbb{R}^{N \times D}, \eta, K$.
Output: Normalized local features $\mathbf{F}_K$.
1: Generate $\mathbf{v}_0 = [v_1, ..., v_D] \in \mathbb{R}^D$, where $\{v_i\}_{i=1}^D$ are *i.i.d.* random variables with normal distribution.
2: **for** $k \in [1, K]$ **do**
3:     $\mathbf{v}_k = \mathbf{F}^\top \mathbf{F} \mathbf{v}_{k-1}$.
4: $\mathbf{F}_K = \mathbf{F} - \eta \frac{\mathbf{F} \mathbf{v}_K \mathbf{v}_K^\top}{\|\mathbf{v}_K\|_2^2}$.
5: **return** $\mathbf{F}_K$.

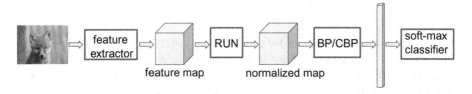

Fig. 1. The architecture of the proposed convolutional neural network. RUN denotes the proposed rank-1 update normalization, which takes input the feature map of the last convolutional layer. BP denotes the bilinear pooling and CBP represents compact bilinear pooling. The obtained BP/CBP feature is fed into the soft-max classifier.

where $\mathbf{F}_K[i, :]$ is the i-th row of $\mathbf{F}_K$, ϕ is implemented by TS or RM, and $\bar{\mathbf{b}}_K \in \mathbb{R}^D$ is the compact and normalized bilinear feature where $D \ll d^2$.

The proposed RUN is summarized in Algorithm 1. We implement the proposed RUN as a layer of a CNN. The layer takes the feature map $\mathbf{F}$ as input and outputs the normalized feature map $\mathbf{F}_K$. In the forward propagation, $\mathbf{F}_K$ is computed by Eq. (6). After obtaining $\mathbf{F}_K$, it is feasible to conduct bilinear pooling (BP) or compact bilinear pooling (CBP). Figure 1 illustrates the architecture of the proposed network. Note that, despite that one can rely on auto-grad tool in existing deep learning frameworks to automatically obtain the backward propagation based on the forward propagation, we still derive it in the supplementary material for readers to better understand the proposed algorithm.

4 Experiments

We first introduce the testing datasets and implementation details. Then we conduct ablation studies on two scenarios: 1) RUN with the standard bilinear pooling and 2) RUN with the compact bilinear pooling. After that, the comparisons with existing state-of-the-art bilinear pooling methods are conducted.

4.1 Datasets and Evaluation Metrics

As summarized in Table 2, we conduct experiments on three tasks: 1) fine-grained recognition, 2) scene recognition and 3) texture recognition. On the

Table 2. The number of training/testing samples of four datasets.

	Fine-grained		Scene	Texture
	CUB	Aircraft	MIT	DTD
Classes	200	100	67	47
Training	5,994	6,667	4,014	1,880
Testing	5,794	3,333	1,339	3,760

fine-grained recognition task, experiments are conducted on CUB [33] and Aircraft [23] datasets. On the scene recognition task, experiments are conducted on MIT [26] dataset. On the texture recognition task, we test our method on DTD [4] dataset. Since we tackle the recognition task, we evaluate the performance of the proposed method through the average classification accuracy.

4.2 Implementation Details

Following [19,20], we use VGG16 [27] as the backbone network to make a fair comparison with existing methods. After scaling and cropping, the input size of an input image is $448 \times 448 \times 3$ and the size of the last convolutional feature map is $28 \times 28 \times 512$. After we obtain the normalized bilinear feature from our RUN, we further conduct element-wise signed square-root normalization followed by ℓ_2-normalization as BCNN [22]. Following [9], we adopt a two-phase training strategy. In the first phase, we update the weights of the last fully-connected linear layer and keep other layers unchanged. The initial learning rate is set as 0.2 on aircraft dataset and 1 on other datasets, and it decreases to 0.1 of current learning rate. We set weight decay as 10^{-8} in the first phase. The first phase finishes in 50 epochs. In the second phase, we update the weights of all layers and the initial learning rate is set as 0.02 on CUB dataset and 0.01 on other datasets, and it decreases to 0.1 of the current learning rate if the validation error does not drop in continuous 5 epochs. We set weight decay as 10^{-5} in the second phase. The second phase finishes in 40 epochs. We use paddlepaddle. Note that, iSQRT [18] pre-trains the network on ImageNet dataset.

4.3 Ablation Study on RUN with Original Bilinear Pooling

In this section, we test the proposed RUN using original high-dimensional bilinear pooling features. The feature dimension is $512 * 512 = 262K$.

Influence of η. η in Eq. (8) controls the strength of suppressing the large singular values. Recall from Eq. (8) that, $\bar{\mathbf{B}}_K$ converges to:

$$\mathbf{V}^F \mathrm{diag}[(1 - \eta)^2 \sigma_{F,1}^2, \cdots, \sigma_{F,d}^2] \mathbf{V}_F^\top.$$

From the above equation, we observe that, when $\eta \in (2, +\infty) \cup (-\infty, 0)$, the largest value of the normalized bilinear matrix $\bar{\mathbf{B}}_K$ is even larger than that of

Table 3. The influence of η on the proposed RUN.

η	CUB	Aircraft	MIT	DTD
0.0	84.1	88.9	79.8	65.6
0.1	84.8	89.3	80.6	66.6
0.2	85.3	89.5	**81.0**	67.8
0.4	86.0	89.6	80.5	68.3
0.6	86.3	**89.8**	80.8	**68.4**
0.8	86.2	89.7	80.7	**68.4**
1.0	**86.4**	**89.8**	80.9	68.3
1.2	86.0	**89.8**	80.9	68.2
1.5	86.2	89.7	80.5	68.3
2.0	83.9	89.0	79.7	65.7

Table 4. The average $\sigma_{F,1}/\sigma_{F,2}$ on four datasets.

	CUB	Aircraft	MIT	DTD
First epoch	2.23	1.53	2.38	5.09
Last epoch	3.68	1.69	4.53	7.40

the original bilinear matrix **B**. Hence a good value of η should be in the range $[0, 2]$. Ideally, we can select the value of η according to the gap between $\sigma_{F,1}$ and $\sigma_{F,2}$. Since singular values change for different samples or different epochs, we can compute $\sigma_{F,1}$ and $\sigma_{F,2}$ online for each sample in each epoch. But computing $\sigma_{F,1}$ and $\sigma_{F,2}$ will double the time cost compared with using a manually set η which only needs compute $\sigma_{F,1}$. Thus, we simply use a manually set η.

As shown in Table 3, when $\eta = 0$, i.e., without RUN, the accuracies are not as good as that when $\eta \in [0.4, 1.5]$. Note that, on Aircraft dataset, the accuracy gap between the case when $\eta \in [0.4, 1.5]$ and the case when $\eta = 0$ is not significant. This is due to that the value of $\sigma_{F,1}/\sigma_{F,2}$ on Aircraft dataset (shown in Table 4) is small. It means that, the singular values are already balanced and thus the matrix normalization does not play an important role. In contrast, on DTD dataset, the accuracy gap is considerable, it is also in accordance with the large value of $\sigma_{F,1}/\sigma_{F,2}$ on DTD dataset as shown in Table 4.

As Table 4 shows that the average value of $\sigma_{F,1}/\sigma_{F,2}$ varies significantly on four datasets, thus we might expect that the optimal η are different on four dataset. Surprisingly, as shown in Table 3, when $\eta \in [0.4, 1.5]$ the performance is stable and not sensitive to the change of η. That is, in practice, the choice of η is quite easy for the user. By default, we set $\eta = 0.6$ on all datasets. Another observation is that, when $\eta = 2.0$, its performance is as bad as that when $\eta = 0.0$. The bad performance when $\eta = 2.0$ is expected since it leads to the condition that $(1 - \eta)^2 = 1$. It is equivalent to removing the matrix normalization.

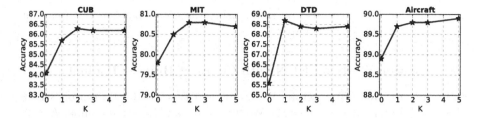

Fig. 2. The influence of K on the proposed RUN.

Influence of K. K in Eq. (6) represents the number of iterations in our RUN. The time cost of the proposed RUN is linear with K. Recall from Eq. (8) that, when K is large, the normalization focuses only on the largest singular value and keeps the others unchanged. In contrast, if K is not large, it also normalizes other large singular values besides the largest one. As shown in Fig. 2, on CUB, MIT and DTD datasets, our RUN achieves the optimal accuracy within 2 iterations. In contrast, on Aircraft dataset, it achieves the best accuracy with 5 iterations. But using 2 iterations, the accuracy on Aircraft dataset is comparable with that using 5 iterations. By default, we set $K = 2$ on all datasets.

Table 5. Comparisons with Lyapunov equation [20] and Newton-Schulz (NS) iteration.

Algorithm	FLOPs	GPU Time	Accuracy			
			CUB	Aircraft	MIT	DTD
Lyapunov equation	8.83G	1841 ms	85.8	88.5	80.6	68.4
NS iteration	4.03G	833 ms	85.7	89.6	80.5	68.3
RUN (ours)	3.2M	2.5 ms	86.3	89.8	80.8	68.4

Time Cost Evaluation. We compare the time cost in matrix normalization in the GPU platform of the proposed method with existing methods based on Lyapunov equation [20] and Newton-Schulz (NS) iteration. We conduct experiments based on 4 NVIDIA K40 GPU cards and set the batch size as 32. As shown in Table 5, the FLOPs of ours is less than 0.1% of the NS iteration. Meanwhile, considering the GPU time, the factual speed-up ratio of ours over the NS iteration is beyond 330. The significant reduction in FLOPs and GPU time is contributed by two factors. Firstly, in each iteration, we only need two matrix-vector multiplications whereas NS iteration takes three times of matrix-matrix multiplications. Secondly, ours takes only 2 iterations for a good performance whereas NS iteration takes 5 iterations to achieve a good performance suggested by [18]. Note that, iSQRT [18] reduces the dimension of local convolutional features from 512 to 256 through a convolution layer, reducing the computation cost of the NS iteration. Our RUN can also be faster using the 256-dimension features, but that is not the focus of this paper.

4.4   Ablation Study on RUN with Compact Bilinear Pooling

Influence of the Dimension. We adopt two types of CBP, Tensor Sketch (TS) and Random Maclaurin (RM). We set $\eta = 0.6$ and iteration number $K = 2$, and change the dimension after CBP among $\{1K, 2K, 4K, 8K, 10K\}$. As shown in Fig. 3, the accuracies generally increase as the dimension increases. It is expected since a larger dimension leads to a better approximation for the polynomial kernel. Meanwhile, the accuracies achieved by TS are comparable with that achieved by RM. By default, we use TS for compact bilinear pooling.

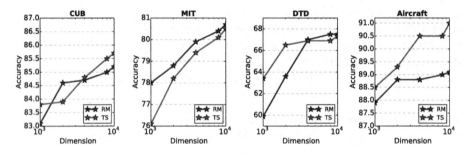

Fig. 3. The influence of the feature dimension of compact features from RM and TS.

Time Cost Evaluation. We evaluate the time cost used in matrix normalization for compact bilinear pooling (CBP). Since the Lyapunov equation and Newton-Schulz iteration cannot be conducted on the original feature $\mathbf{F}$, it is incompatible with CBP. Thus, we only compare with Monet-2 [9] which conducts SVD on $\mathbf{F}$. $\mathbf{F} \in \mathbb{R}^{784 \times 512}$ is in a larger size than $\mathbf{B} \in \mathbb{R}^{512 \times 512}$. Meanwhile, $\mathbf{B}$ is symmetric and only needs compute its left singular vectors $\mathbf{U}$ as well as the singular values $\mathbf{\Sigma}$. But $\mathbf{F}$ is asymmetric and thus needs compute its right singular vectors $\mathbf{V}_F$, left singular vectors $\mathbf{U}_F$ and singular values $\mathbf{\Sigma}_F$. Therefore, the FLOPs of computing SVD on $\mathbf{F}$ shown in Table 6 is larger than the FLOPs of computing SVD on $\mathbf{B}$ shown in Table 5. In contrast, the FLOPs of our RUN used for CBP is as the same as that used for original BP. As shown in Table 6, achieving comparable or even better accuracies, we reduce the FLOPs from 4.21G to 3.2M. Moreover, we reduce the time cost in the GPU from 13850 ms to 2.5 ms, *i.e.*, we achieve a 5540× speedup. Note that, the GPU time cost speedup is larger than the FLOPs reduction ratio since the proposed RUN better supported than SVD in the GPU platform. We also test the time cost of SVD using CPU with 16 threads, it takes 7.6 s, which is still much slower than our RUN using only 2.5 ms.

Table 6. Comparisons between ours and MoNet-2 [9].

Method	Algorithm	Dimension	FLOPs	GPU time	Accuracy	
					CUB	Aircraft
MoNet-2 [9]	SVD	10,000	4.21G	13850 ms	85.7	86.7
Ours	Power method	10,000	3.2M	2.5 ms	85.7	91.0

Table 7. Comparisons with other pooling methods. We compare the feature dimension, the algorithm as well as the time cost for matrix normalization per batch (Normalization Algorithm/Time) and the accuricies on four public benchmarks.

Method	Dimension	Normalization Method/Time	CUB	Aircraft	MIT	DTD
Max-pooling	512	–	69.6	78.9	50.4	55.1
Sum-pooling	512	–	71.7	82.1	58.7	58.2
BCNN [22]	262K	–	84.0	84.1	–	–
Improved BCNN [20]	262K	SVD/6.3 s	85.8	88.5	–	–
BCNN + NS	262K	NS/833 ms	85.7	89.6	80.5	68.3
iSQRT [18]	32K	NS/107 ms	87.2	90.0	–	–
CBP [8]	8.2K	–	84.0	–	76.2	64.5
LRBP [13]	8.2K	–	84.2	87.3	–	65.8
MoNet-2 [9]	10K	SVD/13.9 s	85.7	86.7	–	–
MoNet [9]	10K	SVD/13.9 s	86.4	89.3	–	–
KP [5]	12.8K	–	86.2	86.9	–	–
HBP [34]	24K	–	87.1	90.3	–	–
GP [32]	4K	SVD/15.6 s	85.8	89.8	–	–
DeepKSPD [6]	262K	SVD/6.3 s	86.5	91.0	**81.0**	–
DBTNet-50 [37]	2K	–	**87.5**	**91.2**	–	–
BP + RUN (Ours)	262K	RUN/2.5 ms	86.3	89.8	80.8	**68.4**
CBP + RUN (Ours)	10K	RUN/2.5 ms	85.7	91.0	80.5	67.3

4.5 Comparison with Other Pooling Methods

Firstly, we compare with two baselines, which replace bilinear pooling by max-pooling and sum-pooling, respectively. As shown in Table 7, features from max-pooling and sum-pooling are compact. But accuracies achieved by them are lower than methods based on bilinear pooling. We further compare with B-CNN [22]. Benefited from bilinear pooling, B-CNN has achieved a good performance but the obtained bilinear features are high-dimensional. Nevertheless, since there is no matrix normalization, the performance of B-CNN is not as good as its counterparts with matrix normalization. We further compare with CBP [8] and LRBP [13]. CBP uses Tensor Sketch and Random Maclaurin to reduce the feature dimension, whereas LRBP adopts the low-rank strategy for a compact feature. Nevertheless, neither CBP nor LRBP adopts matrix normalization. Thus their classification accuracies are not as high as compact bilinear methods with matrix normalization such as MoNet [9], GP [32] and our RUN.

We then compare with Improved BCNN [20] and BCNN + Newton-Schulz (NS). To make a fair comparison with BCNN + NS, we directly use the NS layer released by the authors of iSQRT [18], and keep all other settings identical. As shown in Table 7, they achieve high accuracies but generate high-dimension features and take high cost in matrix normalization. We further compare with iSQRT [18]. In iSQRT [18], the authors conduct an additional feature dimension reduction operation on the local feature, and reduces the feature dimension from 512 to 256. The dimension reduction on local features decreases the normalization time 833 ms from 107 ms. Using the 256-dimension local features, the normalization cost of our RUN can also be reduced, but that is not the focus of this paper. Meanwhile, as shown in Table 7, on CUB dataset, iSQRT achieves a higher accuracy than ours and other compared methods. The better performance might be contributed to that iSQRT is pre-trained on ImageNet dataset. In contrast, ours and other methods adopt a vanilla VGG16 pretrained model and adds the bilinear pooling operation only in the fine-tuning stage. More promising results might be achieved if we pre-train VGG16 with our RUN layer on ImageNet dataset, but that is not the focus of this paper, either.

After that, we compare with MoNet-2 and MoNet [9]. MoNet-2 achieves high accuracies and generate compact feature, but the time cost in matrix normalization is extremely high. MoNet improves MoNet-2 by fusing the first-order information, achieving higher accuracies, but is also slow in matrix normalization. By fusing higher-order features, KP [5] achieves an excellent performance on CUB dataset even without normalization. A better performance of the proposed RUN might be achieved by fusing the first-order and higher-order features likewise MoNet and KP, but it is not the focus of this paper. We also compare with HBP [34] and GP [32]. HBP ensembles three types of features and achieves a better performance than ours on CUB dataset. We can also achieve a better performance by ensembling several features, but that is not the focus on this paper, either. GP conducts SVD along the feature map and selects the first a few singular vectors as the image representation. It achieves a comparable performance with the proposed RUN on CUB and Aircraft datasets, using only 4K-dimension features. But it takes twice SVD, which is inefficient on the GPU.

We further compare with two recent work DeepKSPD [6] and DBTNet-50 [37]. By exploiting the Gaussian RBF kernel, DeepKSPD achieves an excellent performance. Our RUN is orthogonal to the kernel used in DeepKSPD and the RUN can also be used for normalization the bilinear matrix from DeepKSPD. DBTNet-50 [37] exploits the bilinear transformation in early layers, which relies on pretraining on a large-scale dataset. In contrast, we only exploit bilinear pooling in the late stage of the network, and does not reply on the pre-training.

5 Conclusion

We propose a simple and fast rank-1 update normalization (RUN) to improve the effectiveness of the bilinear matrix. Since it only takes several iterations of matrix-vector multiplications, the proposed RUN not only takes cheap computation and memory complexity in theory but also is well supported in the GPU platform in practice. More importantly, the proposed RUN supports normalization on compact bilinear features, which cannot be achieved by existing fast normalization methods based on the NS iteration. In addition, our RUN is much simpler than NS iteration and considerably easier for implementation. Meanwhile, RUN is differentiable and hence we plug it into a convolutional neural network, achieving an end-to-end training. Our systematic experiments on four datasets show that, combined with original bilinear pooling, we achieve comparable or even better accuracies with a substantial speedup over NS iteration on the GPU. When using compact bilinear pooling, we achieve comparable accuracies with a significant speedup over the SVD-based method on the GPU.

References

1. Arsigny, V., Fillard, P., Pennec, X., Ayache, N.: Geometric means in a novel vector space structure on symmetric positive-definite matrices. Siam J. Matrix Anal. Appl. **29**(1), 328–347 (2006)
2. Burden, R.L., Faires, J.D.: Numerical Analysis, 4th edn. (1988)
3. Cherian, A., Koniusz, P., Gould, S.: Higher-order pooling of CNN features via kernel linearization for action recognition. In: Applications of Computer Vision (2017)
4. Cimpoi, M., Maji, S., Kokkinos, I., Mohamed, S., Vedaldi, A.: Describing textures in the wild. In: CVPR (2014)
5. Cui, Y., Zhou, F., Wang, J., Liu, X., Lin, Y., Belongie, S.: Kernel pooling for convolutional neural networks. In: CVPR. IEEE (2017)
6. Engin, M., Wang, L., Zhou, L., Liu, X.: DeepKSPD: learning kernel-matrix-based SPD representation for fine-grained image recognition. In: Ferrari, V., Hebert, M., Sminchisescu, C., Weiss, Y. (eds.) ECCV 2018. LNCS, vol. 11206, pp. 629–645. Springer, Cham (2018). https://doi.org/10.1007/978-3-030-01216-8_38
7. Fukui, A., Park, D.H., Yang, D., Rohrbach, A., Darrell, T., Rohrbach, M.: Multimodal compact bilinear pooling for visual question answering and visual grounding. In: EMNLP (2016)
8. Gao, Y., Beijbom, O., Zhang, N., Darrell, T.: Compact bilinear pooling. In: CVPR. IEEE (2016)
9. Gou, M., Xiong, F., Camps, O., Sznaier, M.: MoNet: moments embedding network. In: CVPR. IEEE (2018)
10. Higham, N.J.: Functions of Matrices: Theory and Computation, vol. 104. Siam (2008)

11. Ionescu, C., Vantzos, O., Sminchisescu, C.: Matrix backpropagation for deep networks with structured layers. In: ICCV. IEEE (2015)
12. Kar, P., Karnick, H.: Random feature maps for dot product kernels. In: AISTATS (2012)
13. Kong, S., Fowlkes, C.: Low-rank bilinear pooling for fine-grained classification. In: CVPR, pp. 365–374. IEEE (2017)
14. Koniusz, P., Cherian, A., Porikli, F.: Tensor representations via kernel linearization for action recognition from 3D skeletons. In: Leibe, B., Matas, J., Sebe, N., Welling, M. (eds.) ECCV 2016. LNCS, vol. 9908, pp. 37–53. Springer, Cham (2016). https://doi.org/10.1007/978-3-319-46493-0_3
15. Koniusz, P., Yan, F., Gosselin, P.H., Mikolajczyk, K.: Higher-order occurrence pooling for bags-of-words: visual concept detection. T-PAMI **39**(2), 313–326 (2017)
16. Koniusz, P., Zhang, H., Porikli, F.: A deeper look at power normalizations. In: CVPR. IEEE (2018)
17. Lei, W., Zhang, J., Zhou, L., Chang, T., Li, W.: Beyond covariance: feature representation with nonlinear kernel matrices. In: ICCV. IEEE (2015)
18. Li, P., Xie, J., Wang, Q., Gao, Z.: Towards faster training of global covariance pooling networks by iterative matrix square root normalization. In: CVPR. IEEE (2018)
19. Li, P., Xie, J., Wang, Q., Zuo, W.: Is second-order information helpful for large-scale visual recognition? In: ICCV. IEEE (2017)
20. Lin, T.Y., Maji, S.: Improved bilinear pooling with CNNs. In: BMVC (2017)
21. Lin, T.-Y., Maji, S., Koniusz, P.: Second-order democratic aggregation. In: Ferrari, V., Hebert, M., Sminchisescu, C., Weiss, Y. (eds.) ECCV 2018. LNCS, vol. 11207, pp. 639–656. Springer, Cham (2018). https://doi.org/10.1007/978-3-030-01219-9_38
22. Lin, T.Y., Roychowdhury, A., Maji, S.: Bilinear CNN models for fine-grained visual recognition. In: ICCV. IEEE (2015)
23. Maji, S., Kannala, J., Rahtu, E., Blaschko, M., Vedaldi, A.: Fine-grained visual classification of aircraft. Technical report (2013)
24. Miyato, T., Kataoka, T., Koyama, M., Yoshida, Y.: Spectral normalization for generative adversarial networks. In: ICLR (2018)
25. Pham, N., Pagh, R.: Fast and scalable polynomial kernels via explicit feature maps. In: SIGKDD, pp. 239–247. ACM (2013)
26. Quattoni, A., Torralba, A.: Recognizing indoor scenes. In: CVPR. IEEE (2009)
27. Simonyan, K., Zisserman, A.: Very deep convolutional networks for large-scale image recognition. arXiv preprint arXiv:1409.1556 (2014)
28. Tu, Z., et al.: Multi-stream CNN: learning representations based on human-related regions for action recognition. PR **79**, 32–43 (2018)
29. Wang, Q., Li, P., Zhang, L.: G2DeNet: global gaussian distribution embedding network and its application to visual recognition. In: CVPR. IEEE (2017)
30. Wang, Q., Li, P., Zuo, W., Lei, Z.: Raid-g: Robust estimation of approximate infinite dimensional gaussian with application to material recognition. In: CVPR. IEEE (2016)
31. Wang, Y., Long, M., Wang, J., Yu, P.S.: Spatiotemporal pyramid network for video action recognition. In: CVPR. IEEE (2017)
32. Wei, X., Zhang, Y., Gong, Y., Zhang, J., Zheng, N.: Grassmann pooling as compact homogeneous bilinear pooling for fine-grained visual classification. In: Ferrari, V., Hebert, M., Sminchisescu, C., Weiss, Y. (eds.) ECCV 2018. LNCS, vol. 11207, pp. 365–380. Springer, Cham (2018). https://doi.org/10.1007/978-3-030-01219-9_22

33. Welinder, P., et al.: Caltech-UCSD birds **200** (2010)

34. Yu, C., Zhao, X., Zheng, Q., Zhang, P., You, X.: Hierarchical bilinear pooling for fine-grained visual recognition. In: Ferrari, V., Hebert, M., Sminchisescu, C., Weiss, Y. (eds.) ECCV 2018. LNCS, vol. 11220, pp. 595–610. Springer, Cham (2018). https://doi.org/10.1007/978-3-030-01270-0_35

35. Yu, T., Meng, J., Yuan, J.: Multi-view harmonized bilinear network for 3D object recognition. In: CVPR. IEEE (2018)

36. Yu, Z., Yu, J., Fan, J., Tao, D.: Multi-modal factorized bilinear pooling with co-attention learning for visual question answering. In: ICCV. IEEE (2017)

37. Zheng, H., Fu, J., Zha, Z.J., Luo, J.: Learning deep bilinear transformation for fine-grained image representation. In: Advances in Neural Information Processing Systems, pp. 4277–4286. Curran Associates, Inc. (2019)

38. Zhou, L., Lei, W., Zhang, J., Shi, Y., Yang, G.: Revisiting metric learning for SPD matrix based visual representation. In: CVPR. IEEE (2017)

Accurate Polarimetric BRDF for Real Polarization Scene Rendering

Yuhi Kondo[(✉)], Taishi Ono, Legong Sun, Yasutaka Hirasawa,
and Jun Murayama

Sony Corporation, Tokyo, Japan
{Yuhi.Kondo,Taishi.Ono,Legong.Sun,Yasutaka.Hirasawa,
Jun.Murayama}@sony.com

Abstract. Polarization has been used to solve a lot of computer vision tasks such as Shape from Polarization (SfP). But existing methods suffer from ambiguity problems of polarization. To overcome such problems, some research works have suggested to use Convolutional Neural Network (CNN). But acquiring large scale dataset with polarization information is a very difficult task. If there is an accurate model which can describe a complicated phenomenon of polarization, we can easily produce synthetic polarized images with various situations to train CNN.

In this paper, we propose a new polarimetric BRDF (pBRDF) model. We prove its accuracy by fitting our model to measured data with variety of light and camera conditions. We render polarized images using this model and use them to estimate surface normal. Experiments show that the CNN trained by our polarized images has more accuracy than one trained by RGB only.

Keywords: Polarization · Shape from polarization · Polarimetric BRDF · Convolutional Neural Network

1 Introduction

Polarization is the property of light that is invisible to human unlike brightness or color. In the field of computer vision, various works utilizing polarization effect have been studied. In the early years, polarization had been used to remove or separate reflection components of an image [21]. From the beginning of 2000, several studies related to Shape from Polarization (SfP) [1,3,5,19,20] and Bidirectional Reflectance Distribution Function (BRDF) including polarization property [23,31] were proposed. In 2016, an image sensor which implement a polarizer on each pixel with different angles was developed [37], and it enabled a single shot capture of polarized images of $0°, 45°, 90°, 135°$. Since then, the

Electronic supplementary material The online version of this chapter (https://doi.org/10.1007/978-3-030-58529-7_14) contains supplementary material, which is available to authorized users.

A. Vedaldi et al. (Eds.): ECCV 2020, LNCS 12364, pp. 220–236, 2020.
https://doi.org/10.1007/978-3-030-58529-7_14

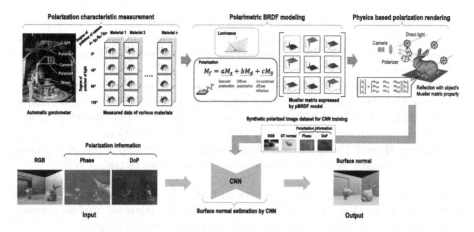

Fig. 1. Our framework: In order to create realistic polarized images, we build polarization-specific goniometer, and measure the polarization characteristic of materials with variety of light and camera conditions equipped with rotatable polarizers in front of them. Then, we estimate parameters of our polarimetric BRDF model by fitting our model to the measured data. After that, our polarization renderer simulates a large amount of synthetic polarized images reproducing polarization property by that model. Finally, synthetic polarized images are used to train CNN that estimates surface normal.

number of studies related to SfP increased [7,8], however these studies still suffer from the following two critical problems.

First, there is an ambiguity between polarization angle x and $x + 180°$ which results in the ambiguity of azimuth angle in SfP.

Second problem is that there are two kinds of reflection which are specular reflection and diffuse reflection. Many studies ignore diffuse reflection assuming that only specular reflection is polarized, but as described in [12,36], diffuse reflection is also polarized in a different way from specular reflection. Since these two reflections are always mixed in real scenes, SfP is a very challenging task.

Kadambi et al. [16] used coarse depth map obtained from Microsoft Kinect to resolve ambiguity and fused coarse depth map and fine normal map to get fine depth map.

CNN is also used to solve these problems. Ba et al. [7] proposed that it is helpful to use polarized images to train Convolutional Neural Network (CNN) for surface normal estimation without ambiguity. Ba et al. [7] acquired polarized images and surface normal using a 3D scanner, and to increase the amount of training data, they synthesized polarized images from surface normal information. Although, as they simulate polarized images with diffuse reflection only, synthesized polarized images are quite different from real scene. To solve these problems, we also use CNN but with more accurately rendered data to train CNN. As shown in Fig. 1, the process consists of the following three steps,

1. **Polarization Characteristic Measurement:** In order to obtain the polarization characteristic of real materials, we develop a measurement system which captures images with variety of light and camera positions and polarization angles.
2. **Polarimetric BRDF Model:** In order to represent the polarization property for all incident/exitant light directions, we establish the generalized polarimetric BRDF (pBRDF) model which can accurately describe actual polarization behavior for both specular and diffuse reflection.
3. **Physics Based Polarization Rendering:** We develop a renderer which produces realistic polarized images using above model to train CNN.

We apply rendered polarized images to train CNN for surface normal estimation and show that with our synthesized dataset, estimated surface normal error is reduced by 70% compared to the one trained by RGB only.

2   Related Work

Polarization has long been studied in the computer vision field to understand the behavior of the reflectance of light. Wolff and Boult [35,36] showed the differences between specular polarization and diffuse polarization, and based on these differences, Nayar et al. [21] proposed a separation of specular reflection component and diffuse reflection component. As an application, Schechner et al. [28] demonstrated a haze removal using polarization. From the beginning of 2000, several studies related to the estimation of surface normal from polarization [1,3,5,19,20] and the polarization BRDF model [23,25,27,31] were proposed.

2.1   Shape from Polarization

In this section we describe SfP which estimates surface normal from the polarization information. Rahmann and Canterakis [24] estimated surface normal from the phase angle and the degree of polarization (DoP) of specular reflection. However, surface normal estimation from the polarization of specular reflection has azimuth and zenith ambiguity. To solve these ambiguity problems, Miyazaki et al. [20] and, Atkinson and Hancock [3] proposed surface estimation of dielectric objects by analyzing the polarization of diffuse reflection. In their work, the zenith angle obtained from DoP of diffuse reflection does not have an ambiguity , but the ambiguity of azimuth angle still remains. There are several works to solve the ambiguity problem: the fusion of polarization and depth map [13,16,41], multi-view camera with polarization [1,2,5,11,14,38], optimization using light distributions [20], shape from shading constraint [18,29], and photometric stereo with polarization [4,6,17,22].

As described in the previous section, the behaviors of specular and diffuse polarization are different, and both of them must be considered. Taamazyan et al. [30] proposed surface normal estimation with mixed polarization of specular and diffuse reflection. Baek et al. [8] explicitly defined the polarization of diffuse reflection in pBRDF model and estimate surface normal. Ba et al. [7] used CNN to obtain surface normal without ambiguity using polarized images and surface normal with ambiguity.

2.2 Polarimetric BRDF

Many pBRDF models have been proposed [15,23,26,31,34,40], but they ignore diffuse reflection component. There is a model which considers both specular and diffuse reflection [8], however, it assumes light source and camera are placed at the same optical axis. In this paper, we expand their pBRDF to correctly model arbitrary light and camera position.

3   Basics of Polarization

3.1   Surface Normal from Polarized Images

Intensity of the light $I(\phi_{pol})$ captured through a linear polarizer at an angle of ϕ_{pol} is expressed by the following equation.

$$I(\phi_{pol}) = \frac{I_{max} + I_{min}}{2} + \frac{I_{max} - I_{min}}{2} \cos\left(2(\phi_{pol} - \phi)\right) \qquad (1)$$

We can infer three unknown variables (I_{max}, I_{min}, and ϕ) with more than three measurements at different polarization angles. DoP that represents how much the light is polarized, can be written as follows.

$$\rho = \frac{I_{max} - I_{min}}{I_{max} + I_{min}} \qquad (2)$$

When the light is reflected by the surface, polarization state of the light changes depending on the surface angle. Therefore, by measuring polarization status of the light, one can estimate surface normal of the object.

Obtaining Surface Normal from Specular Reflection Component: When the observed light consists of specular reflection only, we can obtain surface normal (i.e. azimuth and zenith angle) with ambiguity from specular reflection component. The azimuth angle can be calculated from (1) and is $\phi + 90°$. The zenith angle can be estimated from DoP with the following equation.

$$\rho^s = \frac{2\sin^2\theta\cos\theta\sqrt{\eta^2 - \sin^2\theta}}{\eta^2 - \sin^2\theta - \eta^2\sin^2\theta + 2\sin^4\theta} \qquad (3)$$

where η denotes the refractive index and θ denotes the zenith angle.

Obtaining Surface Normal from Diffuse Reflection Component: Likewise, when the observed light consists of diffuse reflection only, we can obtain surface normal with ambiguity from the diffuse reflection component.

The zenith angle can be calculated from DoP using the following equation.

$$\rho^d = \frac{(\eta - 1/\eta)^2 \sin^2 \theta}{2 + 2\eta^2 - (\eta + 1/\eta)^2 \sin^2 \theta + 4 \cos \theta \sqrt{\eta^2 - \sin^2 \theta}} \tag{4}$$

Obtaining Surface Normal in the Real Scene: In real scenes, surface normal estimation becomes a very challenging task. We have two ambiguities in estimating azimuth angle. One is so called 180° ambiguity due to the fact that a polarizer can not distinguish between 0° and 180°. And the other is so called 90° ambiguity which is caused by mixed polarization of specular reflection and diffuse reflection. It is also difficult to obtain correct zenith angle, since the observed DoP is a mixture of two types of reflection.

3.2   Stokes Vector and Mueller Matrix

A Stokes vector is a four dimensional vector that represents the polarization state described as $\mathbf{s} = [s0, s1, s2, s3]^{\mathbf{T}}$. $s0$ is intensity of light, $s1$ is the difference of 0° and 90° polarized intensity, $s2$ is the difference of 45° and 135° polarized intensity and $s3$ is the difference of right circular and left circular polarized intensity.

A Mueller matrix $\mathbf{M}$ represents the change of the polarization state by reflection and refraction phenomena. When we define Stokes vectors before and after reflection/refraction as s and s', their relationship is expressed as $s' = \mathbf{M}s$. When we omit circular polarization component, Mueller matrix is expressed as 3x3 matrix.

4   Our Polarimetric BRDF Based on Measurement

In this section, we propose new pBRDF model which is applicable for arbitrary light and camera position.

4.1   Polarization Measurement System

We show our polarization characteristic measurement system in Fig. 1. To acquire polarization characteristics of various materials, we build an automated capturing system which can set the light and the camera with rotatable polarizers to arbitrary positions.

The Stokes vector observed in our system is expressed by the following equation.

$$s = \begin{bmatrix} s0 \\ s1 \\ s2 \end{bmatrix} = \begin{bmatrix} (I_0 + I_{45} + I_{90} + I_{135})/4 \\ (I_0 - I_{90})/2 \\ (I_{45} - I_{135})/2 \end{bmatrix} \tag{5}$$

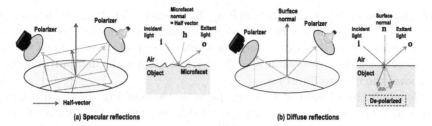

Fig. 2. Polarization of specular reflection and diffuse reflection : (a) Polarization of specular reflection is defined as the mirror-like reflection at the microfacet of the object. Incident light is reflected at the same angle to the half vector of light direction and camera direction. (b) Polarization of diffuse reflection is defined as the reflection that the light penetrate the material at first, depolarized inside the material, and then refracted back into the air.

$I_0, I_{45}, I_{90}, I_{135}$ are polarized intensities obtained by the camera with different polarizer angles.

The Stokes vectors obtained with different polarization angle of light, $0°$, $45°$, $90°$, $135°$ are the followings.

$$\begin{bmatrix} s0^0 \\ s1^0 \\ s2^0 \end{bmatrix} = \mathbf{M} \begin{bmatrix} 1 \\ 1 \\ 0 \end{bmatrix} = \begin{bmatrix} m00 + m01 \\ m10 + m11 \\ m20 + m21 \end{bmatrix}, \begin{bmatrix} s0^{90} \\ s1^{90} \\ s2^{90} \end{bmatrix} = \mathbf{M} \begin{bmatrix} 1 \\ -1 \\ 0 \end{bmatrix} = \begin{bmatrix} m00 - m01 \\ m10 - m11 \\ m20 - m21 \end{bmatrix}$$

$$\begin{bmatrix} s0^{45} \\ s1^{45} \\ s2^{45} \end{bmatrix} = \mathbf{M} \begin{bmatrix} 1 \\ 0 \\ 1 \end{bmatrix} = \begin{bmatrix} m00 + m02 \\ m10 + m12 \\ m20 + m22 \end{bmatrix}, \begin{bmatrix} s0^{135} \\ s1^{135} \\ s2^{135} \end{bmatrix} = \mathbf{M} \begin{bmatrix} 1 \\ 0 \\ -1 \end{bmatrix} = \begin{bmatrix} m00 - m02 \\ m10 - m12 \\ m20 - m22 \end{bmatrix} \quad (6)$$

We calculate Mueller matrices $\mathbf{M}$ for each light and camera position. Using (6), Mueller matrices can be obtained in the following form.

$$\mathbf{M} = \begin{bmatrix} m00 & m01 & m02 \\ m10 & m11 & m12 \\ m20 & m21 & m22 \end{bmatrix} = \begin{bmatrix} \frac{s0^0 + s0^{90}}{2} & \frac{s0^0 - s0^{90}}{2} & \frac{s0^{45} - s0^{135}}{2} \\ \frac{s1^0 + s1^{90}}{2} & \frac{s1^0 - s1^{90}}{2} & \frac{s1^{45} - s1^{135}}{2} \\ \frac{s2^0 + s2^{90}}{2} & \frac{s2^0 - s2^{90}}{2} & \frac{s2^{45} - s2^{135}}{2} \end{bmatrix} \quad (7)$$

4.2 Polarimetric BRDF Model

In the previous work [8], pBRDF has been obtained for the camera and light which are fixed to coaxial position. Here, we describe our new pBRDF model which allows us to accurately model Mueller matrix for arbitrary camera and lighting position without any approximation.

Polarization of Specular Reflection. As shown in Fig. 2, in specular reflection, the incident light is reflected directly by the plane and its reflection angle can be described by the angle of incident light, camera direction and half vector. A half vector is described as: $\mathbf{h} = \frac{\mathbf{i}+\mathbf{o}}{||\mathbf{i}+\mathbf{o}||}$ where $\mathbf{i}$ denotes the light direction and $\mathbf{o}$ denotes the camera direction.

Generally, it is assumed that the plane is composed of many microfacets which have specular reflection property at different angle. The Mueller matrix of specular reflection is described as follows.

$$\mathbf{M_{i,o}^s} = \mathbf{C_c}(\phi_c)\mathbf{L}(\delta)\mathbf{R}(\theta_s;\eta)\mathbf{C_1}(\phi_1) \tag{8}$$

where $\mathbf{C_1}(\phi_1)$ denotes a rotation matrix of the angle ϕ_l from the polarizer axis of light into the incident plane, $\mathbf{R}(\theta_s;\eta)$ is the Fresnel term of specular reflection that has the angle θ_s between a half vector $\mathbf{h}$ and light $\mathbf{i}$, and η is the refractive index, and $\mathbf{L}(\delta)$ is a delay matrix. $\mathbf{C_c}(\phi_c)$ is a rotation matrix of the angle ϕ_c from the incident plane into the polarizer axis of a camera. $\mathbf{M_{i,o}^s}$ can be denoted by the following matrix,

$$\mathbf{M_{i,o}^s} = \begin{bmatrix} R^+ & R^-\gamma_l & R^-\chi_l & 0 \\ R^-\gamma_c & R^+\gamma_l\gamma_c - R^\times\chi_l\chi_c\cos\delta & R^+\chi_l\gamma_c + R^\times\gamma_l\chi_c\cos\delta & R^\times\chi_c\sin\delta \\ -R^-\chi_c & -R^+\gamma_l\chi_c - R^\times\chi_l\gamma_c\cos\delta & -R^+\chi_l\chi_c + R^\times\gamma_l\gamma_c\cos\delta & R^\times\gamma_c\sin\delta \\ 0 & R^\times\chi_l\sin\delta & -R^\times\gamma_l\sin\delta & R^\times\cos\delta \end{bmatrix} \tag{9}$$

With reference to [8], $\chi_{l,c} = \sin 2\phi_{l,c}$ and $\gamma_{l,c} = \cos 2\phi_{l,c}$. $R^+ = (R^p + R^s)/2$, $R^- = (R^s - R^p)/2$, and $R^\times = \sqrt{R^p R^s}$ are the Fresnel reflection coefficients. For dielectric objects, $\cos\delta = -1$ when the incident angle is less than Brewster angle. Otherwise $\cos\delta = 1$ and $\sin\delta = 0$. R^p, R^s are described as follows.

$$R^p = \left(\frac{\eta^2\cos\theta_s - \sqrt{\eta^2 - \sin^2\theta_s}}{\eta^2\cos\theta_s + \sqrt{\eta^2 - \sin^2\theta_s}}\right)^2 , R^s = \left(\frac{\cos\theta_s - \sqrt{\eta^2 - \sin^2\theta_s}}{\cos\theta_s + \sqrt{\eta^2 - \sin^2\theta_s}}\right)^2 \tag{10}$$

Polarization of Diffuse Reflection. As illustrated in Fig. 2, diffuse reflection is observed when the light penetrates into the material, depolarized inside the material, and then refract back out to the air.

The Mueller matrix of diffuse reflection is described as follows.

$$\mathbf{M_{i,o}^d} = \mathbf{C_{nc}}(\phi_{nc})\mathbf{T_o}(\theta_o;\eta)\mathbf{P_0}\mathbf{T_i}(\theta_i;\eta)\mathbf{C_{ln}}(\phi_{ln}) \tag{11}$$

$\mathbf{C_{ln}}(\phi_{ln})$ denotes the rotation matrix of the angle ϕ_{ln} from the polarizer axis of light into the incident plane, $\mathbf{T_i}(\theta_i;\eta)$ is the Fresnel term of refraction from the air into the material surface, $\mathbf{P_0}$ is a depolarization matrix, $\mathbf{T_o}(\theta_o;\eta)$ is the Fresnel term of refraction back out into the air, and $\mathbf{C_{nc}}(\phi_{nc})$ is a rotation matrix of the angle ϕ_{nc} from the exitant plane into the polarizer axis of camera. In a depolarization matrix $\mathbf{P_0}$, only $m00$ is 1 and the other elements are 0.

$$\mathbf{M_{i,o}^d} = \begin{bmatrix} T_o^+ T_i^+ & T_o^+ T_i^- \beta_{ln} & T_o^+ T_i^- \alpha_{ln} & 0 \\ T_o^- T_i^+ \beta_{nc} & T_o^- T_i^- \beta_{ln}\beta_{nc} & T_o^- T_i^- \alpha_{ln}\beta_{nc} & 0 \\ -T_o^- T_i^+ \alpha_{nc} & -T_o^- T_i^- \beta_{ln}\alpha_{nc} & -T_o^- T_i^- \alpha_{ln}\alpha_{nc} & 0 \\ 0 & 0 & 0 & 0 \end{bmatrix} \tag{12}$$

$\alpha_{ln,nc} = \sin 2\phi_{ln,nc}$ and $\beta_{ln,nc} = \cos 2\phi_{ln,nc}$. $T_{i,o}^+ = (T_{i,o}^p + T_{i,o}^s)/2$, $T_{i,o}^- = (T_{i,o}^p - T_{i,o}^s)/2$ and $T_{i,o}^\times = \sqrt{T_{i,o}^p T_{i,o}^s}$ denoting the Fresnel transmission coefficients. We assume that the polarizer axis of the light and the camera are on the same incident and exitant plane, therefore $\mathbf{C_{ln}}(\phi_{ln})$ and $\mathbf{C_{nc}}(\phi_{nc})$ are identity matrices and $\alpha_{ln,nc} = 0$, $\beta_{ln,nc} = 1$. $T_{i,o}^p, T_{i,o}^s$ are described as follows.

$$T_{i,o}^p = \frac{4\eta^2 \cos\theta_{i,o}\sqrt{\eta^2 - \sin^2\theta_{i,o}}}{(\eta^2 \cos\theta_{i,o} + \sqrt{\eta^2 - \sin^2\theta_{i,o}})^2}, T_{i,o}^s = \frac{4\cos\theta_s\sqrt{\eta^2 - \sin^2\theta_{i,o}}}{(\cos\theta_{i,o} + \sqrt{\eta^2 - \sin^2\theta_{i,o}})^2} \tag{13}$$

Polarization Property Representation. As described above, our polarization characteristic measurement system captures only linear polarization since there is not much use of circular polarization in practice. Therefore, we only consider the top-left 3×3 Mueller matrix components that represent linear polarization. We estimate luminance parameters and polarization parameters separately. We normalize $\mathbf{M^s}, \mathbf{M^d}$ by their m_{00} components that represent the luminance:

$$\hat{\mathbf{M}}_{i,o}^s = \begin{bmatrix} 1 & -\rho^s \gamma_l & -\rho^s \chi_l \\ -\rho^s \gamma_c & \gamma_l\gamma_c - \frac{2R^\times}{R^+}\chi_l\chi_c \cos\delta & \chi_l\gamma_c + \frac{2R^\times}{R^+}\gamma_l\chi_c \cos\delta \\ \rho^s \chi_c & -\gamma_l\chi_c - \frac{2R^\times}{R^+}\chi_l\gamma_c \cos\delta & -\chi_l\chi_c + \frac{2R^\times}{R^+}\gamma_l\gamma_c \cos\delta \end{bmatrix} \tag{14}$$

$$\hat{\mathbf{M}}_{i,o}^d = \begin{bmatrix} 1 & \rho_i^d & 0 \\ \rho_o^d & \rho_o^d\rho_i^d & 0 \\ 0 & 0 & 0 \end{bmatrix} \tag{15}$$

where ρ^s and $\rho_{i,o}^d$ denote $(R^p - R^s)/(R^p + R^s)$ and $(T_{i,o}^p - T_{i,o}^s)/(T_{i,o}^p + T_{i,o}^s)$ that represent DoP in specular reflection and diffuse reflection.

We measure Mueller matrices of the material and express them as a linear combination of specular Mueller matrix and diffuse Mueller matrix. For each material and for each light and camera position, the normalized Mueller matrix $\mathbf{M^f}_{i,o}$ is described as follows.

$$\mathbf{M_{i,o}^f} = \mathbf{a_{i,o}}\hat{\mathbf{M}}_{i,o}^s + \mathbf{b_{i,o}}\hat{\mathbf{M}}_{i,o}^d + \mathbf{c_{i,o}}\mathbf{M_0} \tag{16}$$

$$(a_{i,o} + b_{i,o} + c_{i,o} = 1)$$

$a_{i,o}, b_{i,o}, c_{i,o}$ are the coefficients for the single light and camera position. $\mathbf{M_0}$ is a depolarization matrix which represents diffraction and scattering of light inside materials. Finally, $\mathbf{M^f_{i,o}}$ is expressed as the following matrix.

$$
\mathbf{M^f_{i,o}} = \begin{bmatrix} a+b+c & -a\rho^s\gamma_l + b\rho^d_i & -a\rho^s\chi_l \\ -a\rho^s\gamma_c + b\rho^d_o & a\gamma_l\gamma_c - a\frac{2R^\times}{R^+}\chi_l\chi_c\cos\delta + b\rho^d_o\rho^d_i & a\chi_l\gamma_c + a\frac{2R^\times}{R^+}\gamma_l\chi_c\cos\delta \\ a\rho^s\chi_c & -a\gamma_l\chi_c - a\frac{2R^\times}{R^+}\chi_l\gamma_c\cos\delta & -a\chi_l\chi_c + a\frac{2R^\times}{R^+}\gamma_l\gamma_c\cos\delta \end{bmatrix}
$$

$$\text{(17)}$$

For each light and camera position, unknown variables are $a_{i,o}, b_{i,o}, c_{i,o}$, the specular DoP ρ^s, the diffuse DoP $\rho^d_{i,o}$ and $2R^\times/R^+$. These unknown variables for each light and camera position can be estimated from the observed Mueller matrices.

From the observed Mueller matrices, we can calculate the specular DoPρ^s and the diffuse DoP$\rho^d_{i,o}$ for each light and camera position from (17). Then, we estimate refractive index from DoPs using (3) and (4). $2R^\times/R^+$ can be obtained from estimated refractive index.

Finally, we estimate the linear combination coefficients $a_{i,o}, b_{i,o}, c_{i,o}$.

BRDF Model with Polarization Property. We use the GGX BRDF model [33], to parameterize the luminance and polarization property $a_{i,o}, b_{i,o}, c_{i,o}$. GGX model consists of the specular term and the diffuse term. The specular term takes into account Fresnel function, but the diffuse term does not. Therefore, we extend the diffuse term of the GGX model:

$$
k^s\frac{D(\theta_h;\sigma)G(\theta_i,\theta_o;\sigma)F^s}{4(\mathbf{n}\cdot\mathbf{o})(\mathbf{n}\cdot\mathbf{i})}(\mathbf{n}\cdot\mathbf{i}) + (k^{pd}F^d + k^d)(\mathbf{n}\cdot\mathbf{i}) \tag{18}
$$

where k^s, k^{pd} and k^d denote the coefficients for specular, polarized diffuse and un-polarized diffuse components. θ_h is the zenith angle between normal vector of the surface $\mathbf{n}$ and half vector $\mathbf{h}$. θ_i and θ_o are the zenith angle between the normal vector $\mathbf{n}$ and the light direction $\mathbf{i}$, and the camera direction $\mathbf{o}$ respectively. σ is the surface roughness parameter of GGX distribution D. And G is the shadow/masking function. Fresnel coefficients are described as $F^s = R^+, F^d = T^+_o T^+_i$ from $m00$ component of each Mueller matrix.

Here, parameterized coefficients of specular reflection and polarimetric diffuse reflection $\hat{a}^s_{i,o}, \hat{b}^{pd}_{i,o}$ are described as follows.

$$
\hat{a}^s_{i,o} = \frac{k^s\frac{DGF^s}{4(\mathbf{n}\cdot\mathbf{o})(\mathbf{n}\cdot\mathbf{i})}(\mathbf{n}\cdot\mathbf{i})}{k^s\frac{DGF^s}{4(\mathbf{n}\cdot\mathbf{o})(\mathbf{n}\cdot\mathbf{i})}(\mathbf{n}\cdot\mathbf{i}) + (k^{pd}F^d + k^d)(\mathbf{n}\cdot\mathbf{i})} \tag{19}
$$

$$
\hat{b}^{pd}_{i,o} = \frac{k^{pd}F^d(\mathbf{n}\cdot\mathbf{i})}{k^s\frac{DGF^s}{4(\mathbf{n}\cdot\mathbf{o})(\mathbf{n}\cdot\mathbf{i})}(\mathbf{n}\cdot\mathbf{i}) + (k^{pd}F^d + k^d)(\mathbf{n}\cdot\mathbf{i})} \tag{20}
$$

Now, we estimate GGX model parameters by solving an optimization problem that consists of three energy terms as follows.

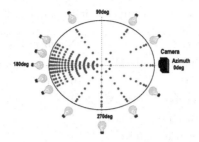

Fig. 3. Light positions: This is a top view of light positions at the camera azimuth $0°$ and zenith $30°$. We measure the data in confronting positions densely. We lack some measurement points when the light source blocks the camera.

$$E = E_a + \lambda_b E_b + \lambda_{lum} E_{lum} \tag{21}$$

$$E_a = \sum_{i,o} ||a_{i,o} - \hat{a}^s_{i,o}||_2^2, \quad E_b = \sum_{i,o} ||b_{i,o} - \hat{b}^{pd}_{i,o}||_2^2 \tag{22}$$

$$E_{lum} = \sum_{i,o} ||m00_{i,o} - (k^s \frac{DGF^s}{4(n \cdot o)(n \cdot i)}(n \cdot i) + (k^{pd} F^d + k^d)(n \cdot i))||_2^2 \tag{23}$$

where E_a, E_b are for the polarization property, E_{lum} is the luminance property, and λ_b, λ_l are the weights. The weight of luminance depends on the captured intensity. We normalize luminance values by the maximum value in every material, but most values are very low when the material has sharp specular components. Therefore, we use $\lambda_b = 1, \lambda_l = 10^3$ as weights.

Finally, we obtain all parameters by optimization. In the optimization process, with reference to [9], first we estimate the diffuse parameters from the measured data without the data where the light and camera are in confronting position, after that, we estimate only specular parameters with the data where the light and camera are in confronting position.

4.3 Evaluation of Our Polarimetric BRDF

We compare our pBRDF model with Baek et al. [8] to evaluate the accuracy of refractive index estimation and Mueller matrix modeling. Note that the model [8] uses the data where the camera and light are at the coaxial position, while we use all measured data.

Measurement Setup. In this measurement, we assume the measured samples have isotropic BRDF, so the azimuth angle of the camera is fixed. Other parameters, the zenith angle of the camera, the azimuth and zenith angle of the light, and the rotation angle of polarizers in front of the light and camera are changed as described in Table 1. It shows the measurement positions and the polarizer angles of the light and the camera. Positions are not uniform as shown in Fig. 3.

Table 1. Light and camera parameters in our system. (* Refer to Fig. 3.)

Parameters	Range	Number of positions
Light azimuth	0:330	21 *
Light zenith	0:85	9 or 18 *
Light polarizer	0,45,90,135	4
Camera azimuth	0 (fixed)	1
Camera zenith	0:85	18
Camera polarizer	0,45,90,135	4

This is because the BRDF characteristics tend to change drastically when the light and the camera positions are at the confronting position, so dense measurements are necessary in that case. With this setup, we capture about 100,000 images for each material. For each captured image, 10×10 pixels in the center of image are averaged and used.

Evaluation of Refractive Index. We first evaluate the accuracy of the refractive index estimation for the materials with known refractive index value. The refractive index changes depending on the wavelength of the light, so we only use green channel data. Table 2 shows that our results are closer to the ground truth refractive index.

Table 2. Results of the refractive index estimation

Material	GT	Proposed	[8]
Silicon nitride	2.0–2.1	2.09	2.00
Alumina	1.75–1.80	1.76	1.58
Aluminum nitride	2.1–2.2	1.99	1.58
Zirconia	2.3–2.3	1.95	1.56
PVC	1.52–1.55	1.66	1.71
PTFE	1.35	1.55	1.51

Evaluation of Mueller Matrix. To evaluate accuracy of Mueller matrices represented by our pBRDF model, we first calculate output Stokes vectors by multiplying various Stokes vectors using modeled Mueller matrix. We use 24 different Stokes vectors that correspond to polarized images of $[0°, 30°, 60°, 90°, 120°, 150°]$ with the DoP of $[0, 0.25, 0.5, 1]$. And then, we convert output Stokes vectors back into luminance images. Obtained luminance values are compared with measured values to evaluate accuracy of our model.

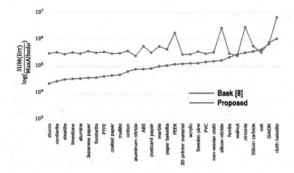

Fig. 4. Error of Mueller matrices for 30 materials: Proposed method and Baek [8] are compared. X-axis is measured materials and Y-axis is a sum of fitting errors with reference to [9]. Results are sorted by the error of proposed method.

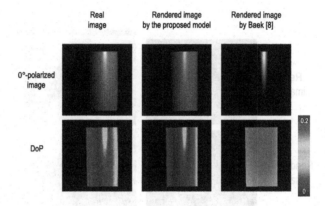

Fig. 5. Rendered results: We capture the cylinder object made of the 3D printer material in Fig. 4 and compare the 0°-polarized image and Degree of Polarization (DoP) by our model and Baek [8] to the real data.

As illustrated in Fig. 4, we measure thirty different materials and evaluate the error between modeled values and observed values. Results show that our model represents variety of materials with less error. It follows that our pBRDF model can model luminance and polarization property of various materials even without the coaxial assumption.

In addition to the quantitative error evaluation of Mueller matrices, we evaluate the rendered image qualitatively. As shown in Fig. 5, the rendered image using our model is closer to the real image. This is because the model in [8] assumes the coaxial setup of the camera and the light, and can not represent the specular components correctly when the light position is separated from the camera position.

5   Polarization Renderer

We build physics based renderer which can simulate the polarization behavior of rays based on the pBRDF of each material. In order to verify the accuracy of our polarization renderer, we set up real scene with objects whose polarization property and geometry information are known. In this evaluation, we first prepared a well-defined evaluation box and corresponding 3D model. The material characteristics of the evaluation box have been measured by our system, and to get fine geometry, we manually aligned the 3D mesh of the 3D printed Stanford bunny with the evaluation box on Blender. We rendered the same scene by our polarization renderer for comparison. Figure 6 shows the result, the average PSNR between real image and rendered image is 29 dB for nine polarization angles. Our renderer can reproduce the polarization property correctly including interreflection effect in the real scenes.

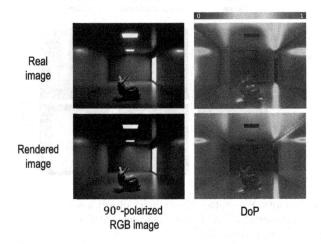

Fig. 6. Comparison between real image and rendered image: 90°-polarized image and the Degree of Polarization (DoP) is shown here.

6   Shape from Polarization by CNN Trained with Synthesized Polarization Images

Using a large number of rendered polarized images, we train CNN to estimate surface normal. In addition to RGB images, we use DoP and polarization phase derived from synthetic polarized images to train CNN.

To demonstrate the effectiveness of polarization information, we compare our surface normal results with Zhang et al. [39] which uses only the RGB images as input. Figure 7 shows the comparison of the estimated surface normal for the

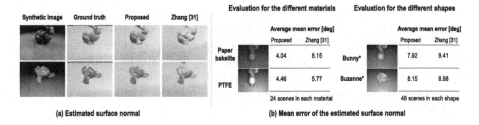

(a) Estimated surface normal   (b) Mean error of the estimated surface normal

Fig. 7. Comparison of the estimated surface normal between our method and Zhang [39]. (a) Estimated surface normal images: The surface normal results by the proposed method using polarization information have less error. (b) Mean errors of the estimated surface normals: The proposed method estimates better surface normal for various materials and shapes. (*"Stanford Bunny"[32] and "Suzanne"[10])

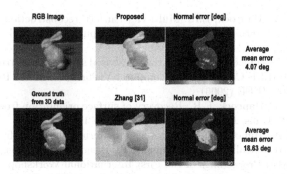

Fig. 8. Estimated surface normal for real scene by the proposed method and Zhang [39]. The ground truth of surface normal is manually adjusted 3D object data of Stanford Bunny [32].

synthetic data. Our proposed method estimate better surface normal for various materials and shapes.

Figure 8 shows the comparison of estimated surface normal for the real data. Error of the estimated surface normal reduced by 70% with the proposed method.

Refer to the *supplementary material* for more details about our CNN architecture and training dataset.

7 Conclusion

In summary, we proposed the framework for utilizing polarization information of light. We first measured the polarization property of various materials, and modeled their polarization property using new pBRDF model that can describe polarization for omnidirectional setups of the cameras and lights. We made a renderer to generate a large number of realistic polarized images and used those images to train CNN for SfP task.

However, there are still some works that have to be done in our framework. Proposed pBRDF model can be extended to treat non-dielectric material and other materials which have anisotropic polarization reflectance property or more complex reflectance property. And, although the effectiveness of polarization information was shown for SfP task, other applications which can utilize polarization information more effectively should be studied. Since our framework can generate synthetic polarized images to train CNN, we believe that our framework can encourage people to seek for the new promising applications thanks to the power of CNN.

Acknowledgment. We express our sincere thanks to our colleagues from Sony Corporation for their helpful discussion and support.

References

1. Atkinson, G.A., Hancock, E.R.: Multi-view surface reconstruction using polarization. In: IEEE International Conference on Computer Vision, vol. 1, pp. 309–316. IEEE (2005)
2. Atkinson, G.A., Hancock, E.R.: Polarization-based surface reconstruction via patch matching. In: IEEE Conference on Computer Vision and Pattern Recognition, vol. 1, pp. 495–502. IEEE (2006)
3. Atkinson, G.A., Hancock, E.R.: Recovery of surface orientation from diffuse polarization. IEEE Trans. Image Process. **15**(6), 1653–1664 (2006)
4. Atkinson, G.A., Hancock, E.R.: Recovering material reflectance from polarization and simulated annealing. In: Belhumeur, P., Ikeuchi, K., Prados, E., Soatto, S., Sturm, P. (eds.) Proceedings of the First International Workshop on Photometric Analysis For Computer Vision - PACV 2007, p. 8. INRIA, Rio de Janeiro (2007). https://hal.inria.fr/inria-00265255, iSBN 2-7261-1297 8
5. Atkinson, G.A., Hancock, E.R.: Shape estimation using polarization and shading from two views. IEEE Trans. Pattern Anal. Mach. Intell. **29**(11), 2001–2017 (2007)
6. Atkinson, G.A., Hancock, E.R.: Surface reconstruction using polarization and photometric stereo. In: Kropatsch, W.G., Kampel, M., Hanbury, A. (eds.) CAIP 2007. LNCS, vol. 4673, pp. 466–473. Springer, Heidelberg (2007). https://doi.org/10.1007/978-3-540-74272-2_58
7. Ba, Y., Chen, R., Wang, Y., Yan, L., Shi, B., Kadambi, A.: Physics-based neural networks for shape from polarization. arXiv preprint arXiv:1903.10210 (2019)
8. Baek, S.H., Jeon, D.S., Tong, X., Kim, M.H.: Simultaneous acquisition of polarimetric svbrdf and normals. ACM Trans. Graph. **37**(6), 1–4 (2018)
9. Bagher, M.M., Soler, C., Holzschuch, N.: Accurate fitting of measured reflectances using a shifted gamma micro-facet distribution. In: Computer Graphics Forum, vol. 31, pp. 1509–1518. Wiley Online Library (2012)
10. Blender: Suzanne. https://www.blender.org/. Accessed 15 Nov 2019
11. Chen, L., Zheng, Y., Subpa-Asa, A., Sato, I.: Polarimetric three-view geometry. In: Proceedings of the European Conference on Computer Vision (ECCV), pp. 20–36 (2018)
12. Collett, E.: Field Guide to Polarization. Field Guide Series, SPIE Press (2005), https://books.google.co.jp/books?id=5lJwcCsLbLsC
13. Cui, Z., Gu, J., Shi, B., Tan, P., Kautz, J.: Polarimetric multi-view stereo. In: IEEE Conference on Computer Vision and Pattern Recognition, pp. 1558–1567 (2017)

14. Cui, Z., Larsson, V., Pollefeys, M.: Polarimetric relative pose estimation. In: Proceedings of the IEEE International Conference on Computer Vision, pp. 2671–2680 (2019)
15. Hyde Iv, M., Schmidt, J., Havrilla, M.: A geometrical optics polarimetric bidirectional reflectance distribution function for dielectric and metallic surfaces. Opt. Exp. **17**(24), 22138–22153 (2009)
16. Kadambi, A., Taamazyan, V., Shi, B., Raskar, R.: Polarized 3D: high-quality depth sensing with polarization cues. In: IEEE International Conference on Computer Vision, pp. 3370–3378 (2015)
17. Logothetis, F., Mecca, R., Sgallari, F., Cipolla, R.: A differential approach to shape from polarisation: a level-set characterisation. Int. J. Comput. Vis. **127**(11–12), 1680–1693 (2019)
18. Mahmoud, A.H., El-Melegy, M.T., Farag, A.A.: Direct method for shape recovery from polarization and shading. In: IEEE International Conference on Image Processing, pp. 1769–1772. IEEE (2012)
19. Miyazaki, D., Kagesawa, M., Ikeuchi, K.: Transparent surface modeling from a pair of polarization images. IEEE Trans. Pattern Anal. Mach. Intell. **1**, 73–82 (2004)
20. Miyazaki, D., Tan, R.T., Hara, K., Ikeuchi, K.: Polarization-based inverse rendering from a single view. In: IEEE International Conference on Computer Vision, p. 982. IEEE (2003)
21. Nayar, S.K., Fang, X.S., Boult, T.: Separation of reflection components using color and polarization. Int. J. Comput. Vis. **21**(3), 163–186 (1997)
22. Ngo Thanh, T., Nagahara, H., Taniguchi, R.I.: Shape and light directions from shading and polarization. In: IEEE Conference on Computer Vision and Pattern Recognition, pp. 2310–2318 (2015)
23. Priest, R.G., Meier, S.R.: Polarimetric microfacet scattering theory with applications to absorptive and reflective surfaces. Opt. Eng. **41**, 988–993 (2002)
24. Rahmann, S., Canterakis, N.: Reconstruction of specular surfaces using polarization imaging. In: IEEE Conference on Computer Vision and Pattern Recognition, vol. 1, pp. I-I. IEEE (2001)
25. Renhorn, I.G., Boreman, G.D.: Developing a generalized BRDF model from experimental data. Opt. Exp. **26**(13), 17099–17114 (2018)
26. Renhorn, I.G., Hallberg, T., Bergström, D., Boreman, G.D.: Four-parameter model for polarization-resolved rough-surface BRDF. Opt. Exp. **19**(2), 1027–1036 (2011)
27. Renhorn, I.G., Hallberg, T., Boreman, G.D.: Efficient polarimetric BRDF model. Opt. Exp. **23**(24), 31253–31273 (2015)
28. Schechner, Y.Y., Narasimhan, S.G., Nayar, S.K.: Instant dehazing of images using polarization. In: IEEE Conference on Computer Vision and Pattern Recognition, pp. 325–332 (2001)
29. Smith, W.A., Ramamoorthi, R., Tozza, S.: Height-from-polarisation with unknown lighting or albedo. IEEE Trans. Pattern Anal. Mach. Intell. **41**(12), 2875–2888 (2018)
30. Taamazyan, V., Kadambi, A., Raskar, R.: Shape from mixed polarization. arXiv preprint arXiv:1605.02066 (2016)
31. Thilak, V., Voelz, D.G., Creusere, C.D.: Polarization-based index of refraction and reflection angle estimation for remote sensing applications. Appl. Opt. **46**(30), 7527–7536 (2007)
32. Turk, G., Levoy, M.: The stanford bunny. http://graphics.stanford.edu/data/3Dscanrep/. Accessed 15 Nov 2019

33. Walter, B., Marschner, S.R., Li, H., Torrance, K.E.: Microfacet models for refraction through rough surfaces. In: Eurographics conference on Rendering Techniques, pp. 195–206. Eurographics Association (2007)
34. Wang, K., Zhu, J.P., Liu, H.: Degree of polarization based on the three-component PBRDF model for metallic materials. Chin. Phys. B **26**(2), 024210 (2017)
35. Wolff, L.B.: Polarization-based material classification from specular reflection. IEEE Trans. Pattern Anal. Mach. Intell. **12**(11), 1059–1071 (1990)
36. Wolff, L.B., Boult, T.E.: Constraining object features using a polarization reflectance model. IEEE Trans. Pattern Anal. Mach. Intell. **7**, 635–657 (1991)
37. Yamazaki, T., et al.: Four-directional pixel-wise polarization CMOS image sensor using air-gap wire grid on 2.5-μm back-illuminated pixels. In: IEEE International Electron Devices Meeting, pp. 8–17. IEEE (2016)
38. Yang, L., Tan, F., Li, A., Cui, Z., Furukawa, Y., Tan, P.: Polarimetric dense monocular slam. In: Proceedings of the IEEE Conference on Computer Vision and Pattern Recognition, pp. 3857–3866 (2018)
39. Zhang, Y., et al.: Physically-based rendering for indoor scene understanding using convolutional neural networks. In: IEEE Conference on Computer Vision and Pattern Recognition, pp. 5287–5295 (2017)
40. Zhang, Y., Zhang, Y., Zhao, H., Wang, Z.: Improved atmospheric effects elimination method for PBRDF models of painted surfaces. Opt. Exp. **25**(14), 16458–16475 (2017)
41. Zhu, D., Smith, W.A.: Depth from a polarisation + rgb stereo pair. In: IEEE Conference on Computer Vision and Pattern Recognition (2019)

Lensless Imaging with Focusing Sparse URA Masks in Long-Wave Infrared and Its Application for Human Detection

Ilya Reshetouski[✉], Hideki Oyaizu, Kenichiro Nakamura, Ryuta Satoh,
Suguru Ushiki, Ryuichi Tadano, Atsushi Ito, and Jun Murayama

Sony Corporation, Tokyo, Japan
{Ilya.Reshetouski,Hideki.Oyaizu,Kenichiro.Nakamura,Ryuta.Satoh,
Suguru.Ushiki,Ryuichi.Tadano,Atsushi.C.Ito,Jun.Murayama}@sony.com

Abstract. We introduce a lensless imaging framework for contemporary computer vision applications in long-wavelength infrared (LWIR). The framework consists of two parts: a novel lensless imaging method that utilizes the idea of local directional focusing for optimal binary sparse coding, and lensless imaging simulator based on Fresnel-Kirchhoff diffraction approximation. Our lensless imaging approach, besides being computationally efficient, is calibration-free and allows for wide FOV imaging. We employ our lensless imaging simulation software for optimizing reconstruction parameters and for synthetic image generation for CNN training. We demonstrate the advantages of our framework on a dual-camera system (RGB-LWIR lensless), where we perform CNN-based human detection using the fused RGB-LWIR data.

Keywords: Lensless imaging · Long-wave infrared (LWIR) imaging · Diffractive optics · Image reconstruction · Diffraction simulation · Pedestrian detection · Human detection · Visible-infrared image fusion · Faster R-CNNs

1 Introduction

Lensless cameras have been extensively used in X-ray and γ-ray imaging where focusing is not feasible [11,22]. These cameras are based on the principle that the signal from the scene is encoded by specially designed aperture such that it can be successfully decoded from the sensor image. The reconstruction quality of the coded aperture imaging system is crucially dependent on the underlying aperture mask design, and the apertures based on Uniformly Redundant Arrays (URA) have theoretically the best imaging properties [14].

Electronic supplementary material The online version of this chapter (https://doi.org/10.1007/978-3-030-58529-7_15) contains supplementary material, which is available to authorized users.

A. Vedaldi et al. (Eds.): ECCV 2020, LNCS 12364, pp. 237–253, 2020.
https://doi.org/10.1007/978-3-030-58529-7_15

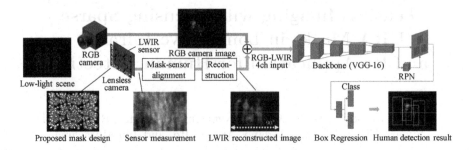

Fig. 1. The architecture of our RGB-LWIR lensless camera system for human detection: The lensless camera is equipped with our focusing sparse URA mask and has horizontal FOV ≈ 90°. Four channels (RGB and LWIR) are fed into the CNN, and a robust human detection is performed even in low-light conditions.

The growing demand for smaller and cheaper visible light or infrared cameras brings attention to lensless imaging in this area. Unfortunately, in these wavebands the sizes of sensor pixels are comparable with wavelengths which significantly increases the diffraction contribution. Therefore, it is not feasible to directly use URA or similar types of blocking masks in longer wavelengths [12].

In this paper, we present a lensless imaging framework which adopts the efficient URA coding aperture technology for LWIR. Our framework consists of novel focusing sparse URA mask design, diffraction-based lensless imaging simulation software, and fast reconstruction algorithm. Our masks features high SNR, wide Field of View (FOV) and low-cost manufacturing. We show that our lensless system produces good quality reconstructions results without hardware-based calibration, but only with lensless imaging simulation. Finally, we demonstrate an application of our lensless framework for CNN-based human detection using fused RGB and LWIR lensless input data, see Fig. 1.

2   Related Work

LWIR Imaging: LWIR cameras provide the ability to 'see' the temperature in a scene as an image [17]. Some early works showed that LWIR images can give us better performance on pedestrian detection task, which has been intensively studied in the context of autonomous driving [5,13]. In [31], LWIR images were superior to visible light images (RGB images) in terms of detection performance. In combination with RGB images, [28] achieved even more improvement than the LWIR images only case. Both owe to the informative expression of human body in LWIR images even in cluttered backgrounds or bad low intensity environments at night in which ordinal RGB cameras will suffer. In response to this trend, several benchmark datasets, which are composed of RGB images synchronized with images of invisible light such as LWIR, were released [3,21,23]. They are inviting sophisticated approaches with Convolutional Neural Network (CNN) right now [27,29,39,42].

Despite the benefit described above, there are some constrains when utilising LWIR cameras in practical products. Optical elements for LWIR are generally made with expensive materials like germanium and its compound such as chalcogenide, because of their high transmittance percentages. The challenge for exploring new designs using components made of cheap materials such as silicon or polyethylene has started now. Though these components can be massively replicated by photolithography or molding process, transmissions in the LWIR spectral band are apparently lower than germanium. Therefore, the allowable thickness of a silicon lens is thinner than a germanium lens for keeping the camera sensitivity. It means that the entire LWIR camera system size is limited by the diameter of silicon lens. It also means that detectors having small pixel number are available. In recent work [20], nearly flat Fresnel lenses on a thin substrate are proposed for improving transmittance percentages. In this paper, to overcome these limitations in LWIR optics, we will take advantage of lensless imaging modality in which compact and cost efficient manufacturing is feasible.

Lensless Imaging: Recently, multiple lensless architectures for visible and infrared light diapason have been proposed. These lensless cameras have demonstrated passive incoherent imaging using amplitude masks [2, 24], diffractive masks [18], diffuser masks [1], random reflective surfaces [16, 35], and modified microlens arrays [37].

Many of these solutions have multiple drawbacks including a) narrow FOV and/or large sensor-to-mask distance, usually due to the requirement to have constant PSF [1, 12]; b) reconstruction complexity is too high [25]; c) calibration is difficult and time consumptive [2, 24, 25]; d) calibration required for each unit [1, 25]. These drawbacks limit the application areas of existing lensless systems and make them less attractive for mass-production.

Additionally, the methods above target mostly visible light or short infrared. However, in the case of LWIR, the diffraction blur is stronger (especially for large incident light angles). In [18], even though it was aimed for thermal sensing, such side effect was not treated. We take care of this by incorporating Fresnel Zone Plates (FZP) into our mask design, which will be detailed in Sect. 3.1. FZP, which consists of concentric transparent and opaque rings (or zones), can be used to focus light and form an image using diffraction [4, 19]. Light, hitting a zone plate, diffracts around the opaque regions and interferes constructively at the focal point. Zone plates can be used in place of pinholes or lenses to form an image. One advantage of zone plates over pinholes is their large transparent area, which provides better light efficiency. In contrast with lenses, zone plates can be used for imaging wavelengths where lenses are either expensive or difficult to manufacture [10, 26].

3 Proposed Method

3.1 Mask Design

Ultimately, we want to bring exceptional reconstruction properties of URA coded apertures to lensless imaging in LWIR. Additionally, since focusing in LWIR is much simpler than in X-ray diapason, instead of simple blocking light at the opaque mask features, we can manipulate it more wisely.

Focusing Sparse URA Mask: Our basic idea is: a) To substitute binary blocking URA mask with an optical element that acts as a lens with multiple sub-lenses with optical centers distributed in the same pattern as the original binary mask and with coincident focal and sensor planes; b) To use sparse URA masks in order to reduce the diffraction crosstalk between transparent features of the mask and to increase average focusing area for each feature. In other words, sparsity allows each sub-lens to have a much larger numerical aperture than the transparent feature of the original binary mask.

The advantages of a) and b) are illustrated on the Fig. 2. Here, three different mask patterns are shown in the top row. The middle row depicts a side view of each mask together with the image sensor and two different directions of the incident light (green and yellow arrows). One dimensional charts in the bottom row indicate the intensity of projected light for the two incident light directions respectively. Note that for simplicity, projection from only three selected mask locations is described in (b) and (c). (a) Modified Uniformly Redundant Array (MURA) mask or similar kind of pseudo-random mask, which is commonly used

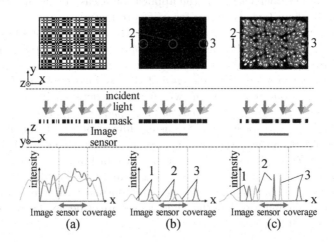

Fig. 2. Projection patterns for different mask designs: (a) MURA, (b) Sparse URA as pinhole array and (c) Sparse URA as FZP array (proposed). The mask pattern (c) resolves the drawbacks in (a) and (b) by increasing image sharpness while maintaining a large amount of light. (Color figure online)

for lensless imaging. In this case, the shadow of the mask is significantly blurred due to the diffraction. For the same reason, for incident light with large-angle (yellow line), the shadow of the mask is blurred even stronger. (b) Pinholes arrayed in a sparse URA pattern make a sharper projection on the sensor surface due to the smaller diffraction crosstalk between holes. Nevertheless, the pinhole array has two major drawbacks: less amount of light and still relatively large blur caused by diffraction. (c) is our proposed method: Focused with FZP sparse URA pattern. This mask pattern resolves the drawbacks in (a) and (b) by increasing image sharpness while maintaining a large amount of light.

Optical Axes Tuning: We aim to create a system with wide FOV. Substituting the standard binary mask with lenses with multiple optical centers helps to increase Signal-to-Noise-Ratio (SNR), but, to maintain the quality over entire FOV, each sub-lens should have a sharp focus for all meaningful light directions. Note that for a typical cyclic aperture system, the variation of scene directions passing through a transparent element depends on its position. In particular, the closer the element to the edges of the mask, the smaller is the variation, see Fig. 3. The figure shows the difference between meaningful incident light directions variation angles depending on the optical element position on the mask. These light directions are restricted by the directions (the red dotted lines) corresponding to the maximum meaningful angle defined by the relationship between the edge of the mask and that of the Focal Plane Array (FPA). The meaningful incident light variation angle from FZP B to the FPA is θ_B, and that from FZP C is θ_C. We use this observation to optimize the average sharpness of each sub-lens by aligning its optical axis with its average incoming light direction. Schematic result of the axes adjustment is illustrated in Fig. 2: for non-optimized mask (b), in the sensor area, the yellow signal is more blurred and less strong than the green signal, while for optimized mask (c) the yellow and green signals are equally sharp. Note that the shapes of FZPs in the center and near the edge of our prototype mask, as shown Fig. 4, are different for this purpose.

3.2   Scene Reconstruction

Our lensless imaging method is designed to project an $M \times N$ scene on the $M \times N$ sensor. We assume, that the imaging is linear and can be described as:

$$y = Fx + n \tag{1}$$

where F - an $(MN) \times (MN)$ real-valued matrix, $x \in R^{MN}$ - 1D column vector representing the scene intensities, $y \in R^{MN}$ - 1D column vector of the sensor measurements, $n \in R^{MN}$ - 1D column vector of the noise.

Ideally, if each scene direction can be precisely focused onto a set of uniformly bright sharp spots arranged as sparse URA pattern, we can use very efficient reconstruction algorithms [15] with computational complexity $O((MN)\log(MN))$. In this case $F = U$ - imaging matrix for ideal URA coded aperture system. However, since our implementation is based on blocking-type masks, sharp uniform focusing of light from a relatively broad spectrum over a large range of incoming light directions is problematic. Therefore, the direct application of reconstruction methods designed for URA masks is prone to artifacts.

One way to improve the reconstruction quality is to use more general reconstruction techniques, but they often require significantly larger computational and/or memory expenses. For example, scene reconstruction can be done with regularized matrix inversion approach

$$\hat{x} = F^* y \tag{2}$$

where F^* - an $(MN) \times (MN)$ real-valued matrix, calculated with, for example, Tikhonov regularization method [38]. But this method requires $O((MN)^3)$ operations to multiply F^* with y and sufficient memory to store F^*.

To balance the quality, speed and memory requirements we propose to approximate F^* with U^*:

$$U^* = \alpha U^{-1} \beta + u^T v \tag{3}$$

$$\|U^* - F^*\| \xrightarrow[\alpha, \beta, u, v]{} \min \tag{4}$$

where α, and β - $(MN) \times (MN)$ diagonal matrices and u^T, $v \in R^{MN}$ - 1D row and column vectors correspondingly, norm here is Frobenius matrix norm. Note, that the computational complexity of the calculation of the product $U^* y$ using (3) is the same as $U^{-1} y$ (i.e. URA reconstruction), can be performed with fast Fourier transform (FFT) and doesn't require explicit calculation or storage of U^* or U^{-1}. For more details regarding are computation of $U^* y$ please refer to the Supplementary Materials.

3.3 Diffraction Simulation for Imaging Matrix Estimation

As was mentioned in Sect. 3.2, due to drawbacks of binary FZP-type focusing, the imaging matrix F is not exactly URA, and therefore it has to be evaluated.

One way to estimate F is to perform calibration step, for example by capturing point light source or set of patterns. However, this method is not practical. Instead, we perform an estimation of F using diffraction simulation based on known mask design and mask to sensor distance.

Since our mask consists of multitude of FZP's with diameters not much smaller than the gap between the mask and the sensor, we decided to employ the Fresnel-Kirchhoff diffraction model [6]:

$$U(P) = -\frac{ia}{2\lambda} \int_M \frac{e^{ik(r+s)}}{rs} \left[cos(\alpha_{n,r}) - cos(\alpha_{n,s}) \right] dM \tag{5}$$

where $U(P)$ - complex amplitude at the point P on the sensor, a - magnitude of the scene point, λ - wavelength, M - transparent area of the mask, k - wavenumber, r - distance from the scene point to the mask element, s - distance from the mask element to the sensor point, $(\alpha_{n,r})$ and $(\alpha_{n,s})$ - angle between the normal to the mask and the direction from the scene (sensor) point to the mask element.

To estimate imaging matrix F, we performed simulation of the sensor image from each scene point, see details in the implementation Sect. 4.4.

4   Implementation and Results

4.1   System Overview

Our RGB-LWIR lensless camera is equipped with a LWIR sensor (PICO384 Gen2^{TM}, spectral range: 8–14 μm, resolution: 384 × 288, pixel pitch: 17 μm), and with RGB camera (resolution: 1920 × 1080, horizontal FOV: 84°), see Fig. 5 (a)–(b). These two cameras were aligned to have similar scene view.

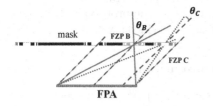

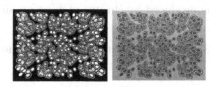

Fig. 3. θ_B is a meaningful incident light variation angle from FZP B, and θ_C is that from FZP C.

Fig. 4. Our mask design (*left*) and a photo of a real mask on Si wafer (*right*)

Fig. 5. Our prototype system: An RGB camera and an LWIR lensless camera are placed in parallel (*left*). The bare LWIR sensor is placed behind a mask (*right*).

4.2   Mask Prototyping

Because irradiance received by the FPA falls off with an incoming angle, to record a reasonable range of sensor values from the entire FOV, we chose 90° as FOV. Since the final URA mask is twice bigger than the sensor, to have FOV 90°, the distance between the mask and the sensor should be 3.2 mm. Correspondingly, given the wide FOV and relatively large spectral range of the bolometer, to maintain uniform focusing, we choose to use FZPs with maximum 3 zones. This limits the output resolution to approximately 60 μm.

Therefore, we choose sparse Singer URA mask with parameters $q = 107$ and $w = 3$, see [7]. The selected mask has basic resolution 127×91, only 0.9% of transparent features and matches the resolution of the bolometer after 3×3 pixel averaging (effective pixel size $17 \times 3 = 51$ μm). Final sparse URA mask was generated as 2×2 mosaic of the basic URA pattern and had resolution 253×181.

For each transparent feature of the final URA mask we calculated average incoming light direction, see Sect. 3.1, and generated corresponding FZP using interference model. In case if one or more FZPs partially overlap, we resolved situation with greedy approach maximizing total focused light. Finally, to reduce variation of intensities of the focused mask, we performed iterative reduction (0.1 of the zone thickness) of the FZP diameter for the most bright spots.

Figure 4 shows our mask design and the photo of the prototype. The mask was produced by chrome etching on an optical grade silicon wafer.

4.3   Implementation of the Scene Reconstruction

Our reconstruction software consists of a capturing part and a scene reconstruction part. The capturing part acquires RAW LWIR images and applies a two-points Non-Uniformity Correction (NUC) to the LWIR data in a similar manner as described in [32]. To measure NUC parameters we used an extended area blackbody radiation source. Before reconstructing lensless images, we estimated the parameters of the model, described in Eq. (3)–(4). In order to do so, we performed the following steps:

1. Calculated the imaging matrix F [$(127 * 91) \times (127 * 91)$], see Sect. 3.2, for our mask design with our diffraction simulation software, see Sect. 4.4.
2. Calculated the regularized inverse matrix F^* using Tikhonov regularization.
3. Calculated the theoretical inverse matrix U^{-1} for our URA mask.
4. Optimized the Eq. (4) with BFGS minimization algorithm and received approximation of the parameters of the model $\hat{\alpha}$, $\hat{\beta}$, $\hat{u}$, $\hat{v}$.

Finally, to recover a scene x from lensless LWIR image y, we calculated U^*y using FFT after expanding the Eq. (3) with the parameters $\hat{\alpha}$, $\hat{\beta}$, $\hat{u}$, $\hat{v}$.

Figure 6 illustrates various examples of reconstructions. Images (a) - (d) show performance of our method for scenes with people. Note, that the results are sharp enough to distinguish poses and other details. (e) shows behaviour of our solution on the edge of the FOV. (f) shows the result with hot objects (half-empty cup with hot coffee and bottles with hot water).

We analyzed the performance of our lensless prototype by measuring its modulation transfer function (MTF) for different angles of incidence. For comparison, we performed MTF evaluation for a simple LWIR camera with a molded-in plastic Fresnel lens (FL = 0.0094 m) and for the standard lensless camera with a 37×37 MURA mask (mask distance $= 0.002$ m), see Fig. 7. By comparing the results in Fig. 7, we can conclude that our system has relatively uniform quality for wide FOV ($2 \times 42°$), it outperforms MURA lensless camera and better than Fresnel lens camera when incident angle is sufficiently large (more than $12°$).

4.4 Implementation of the Imaging Matrix Simulation

We evaluated imaging F by simulating sensor image from each scene point for multiple wavelengths in the range of 8–14 μm. The final result was calculated as the weighted average of simulations for different wavelengths with weights corresponding to the sensor spectral response multiplied with expected scene spectral profile. In our implementation, we used sensor spectral response provided by the sensor manufacturer and the scene spectral profile was chosen to be the blackbody spectral profile at the average human body temperature $\approx 309K$.

The evaluation of the imaging matrix F using Fresnel-Kirchhoff integration is computationally expensive; however, we need to perform it only once. Additionally, images from each scene point and for each wavelength can be calculated independently. We implemented our simulation software with C++/CUDA. It took approximately one week to estimate the F-matrix for our prototype on a machine with a single GPU (NVIDIA GeForce RTX 2080 Ti). Figure 8 shows the comparison between real and simulated images of a point light source.

4.5 Robustness to the Alignment Error

As we explained in the previous section, position alignment between a sensor and a mask is important, especially for manufacturing real products. So we should know how large misalignment is acceptable for reconstructed image quality. We evaluated quantitative relationships between sensor-mask misalignment

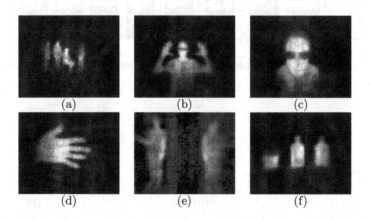

Fig. 6. Examples of reconstructed image

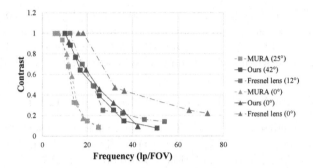

Fig. 7. Measured MTF's for different angles of incidence for Fresnel lens (*blue lines*), MURA mask (*orange lines*) and our prototype (*red lines*) (Color figure online)

	real	simulated
0°		
45°		

Fig. 8. Comparison between the real and the simulated sensor images of a point light source at 0° and 45° incidence angles: We could acquire assumed sensor image even in the corner of the image.

	ΔX		ΔZ			$\Delta\theta$		
	0.0mm	0.15mm	-0.6mm	0.0mm	0.8mm	0.0°	1.7°	3.9°
center								
side								

Fig. 9. Reconstructed samples in the robustness evaluation for misalignment

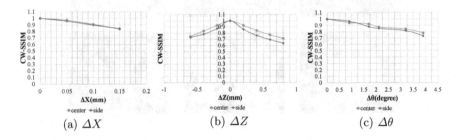

(a) ΔX (b) ΔZ (c) $\Delta\theta$

Fig. 10. Evaluation of misalignment error of our mask in CW-SSIM index: (a) parallel position misalignment, (b) gap misalignment and (c) roll misalignment

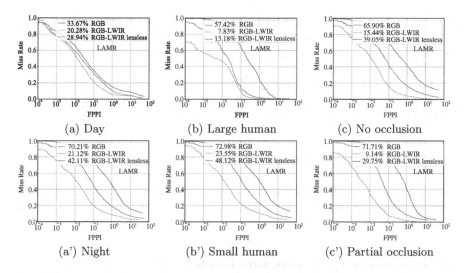

(a) Day   (b) Large human   (c) No occlusion

(a') Night   (b') Small human   (c') Partial occlusion

Fig. 11. Comparison of human detection miss rate by LAMR: (a)(a') day and night scenes, (b)(b') human size in the scenes and (c)(c') different scenes about human occluded rates

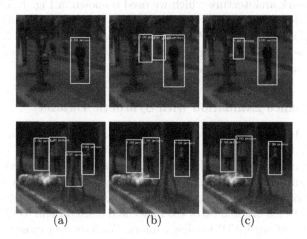

(a)   (b)   (c)

Fig. 12. Examples of false-negatives and false-positives in synthetic evaluation: (a) detected result from RGB image, (b) RGB-LWIR and (c) RGB-LWIR lensless

and reconstructed image quality. We measured a lace curtain before a black-body as a thermally textured object from two different positions. Then we evaluated them by Complex Wavelet Structural Similarity (CW-SSIM) [40] index. Its insensibility to spatial translation and size difference is suitable for our evaluation. We measured parallel shift (ΔX), gap distance shift (ΔZ), and roll ($\Delta\theta$). Figure 9 is a sample of reconstructed images. We can see that the larger misalignment, the more degradation of a lace pattern. Figure 10 is graphs of misalignment values and CW-SSIM values. In general, it is said that if the CW-SSIM value is larger than 0.9, the compared image quality can be treated as good. By these criteria, the allowable value of ΔX, ΔZ, and $\Delta \theta$ are $100\,\mu\text{m}$, $150\,\mu\text{m}$, and $1.5°$ respectively.

These values are much larger than the manufacturing accuracy, and therefore we can conclude that per-unit mask calibration will not be required in the production of our lensless camera.

5   Experiments in Inference Task

Human detection is still a current challenge in computer vision research as it is an essential task for the safety of the transportation system, including pedestrian detection in automobile applications.

5.1   Human Detection Algorithm Pipeline

For human body detection experiments, we chose a Faster R-CNN model [33] as a baseline because it is most commonly used in the image-based object detection field. The network architecture which we used is shown in Fig. 1. The Faster R-CNN has a two-stage structure with a backbone network (VGG16) followed by a Region Proposal Network (RPN) and a classifier. For the RGB-LWIR fusion, we modified the first convolution layer of the backbone CNN to accept 4ch input and fed additional LWIR plane along with RGB planes.

5.2   Performance Evaluation with Synthetic Dataset

Experimental Setup: To show the effectiveness of our LWIR lensless imaging system in an inference task, we used an open dataset i.e. KAIST Multispectral Pedestrian Detection Benchmark dataset [21] as a base for synthetic evaluation. It contains aligned RGB and LWIR images of day and night traffic taken from a vehicle. To retrieve people's images efficiently, we cropped two regions out from the lower half of each original 640×480 image and resized them to 127×91, which is the image size of our LWIR lensless camera. We took over most of the original annotations with minor modifications: We ignored "cyclist" labels and altered "person" labels to "occluded person" if the person is occluded more than 60% by other objects. Consequently, we prepared 26658 labels from 24719 frames for training, and 32981 labels from 27888 frames for testing. To acquire RGB-LWIR lensless pairs, we simulated a full lensless encoding-decoding cycle and applied it to the selected above 127×91 LWIR images. Our lensless encoding-decoding cycle was organized as follows: first, we produced synthetic lensless sensor images using simulated matrix F, see Sect. 3.3; second, we added Gaussian sensor noise with $\mu = 0$, $\sigma = 0.14\%$; finally, we reconstructed noisy synthetic sensor images.

Analysis: We created LWIR lensless training data from KAIST dataset by lensless simulation (Sect. 3.3) and utilized it as 'LWIR lensless' channel for our human detector. We trained the detector with following three configurations: 1) 3ch RGB input, 2) 4ch RGB-LWIR input, and 3) 4ch RGB-LWIR lensless input.

Evaluation results of False Positive Per Image (FPPI) to miss rate and Log Average Miss Rate (LAMR) are shown in Fig. 11. (a) and (a') show the comparison between daylight and night scenes. One can see the LWIR channel improves LAMR in night scenes (a') compared to that of daylight scenes (a). We also evaluated the miss rate between different human scales in (b) and (b'). LAMR naturally improves when detecting larger scale humans, and both LWIR and 'LWIR lensless' channels exhibit higher contribution for the near scale. (c) and (c') are the comparison of detection between no-occluded and partially-occluded person. Both LWIR and 'LWIR lensless' channels consistently maintain good LAMR improvements.

From the above, it is obvious that adding LWIR channel to RGB improves LAMR. Though the contribution of 'LWIR lensless' which was generated by lensless simulation is inferior to that of original LWIR, it is still effective to increase the ability of human detection.

Examples of false-negatives and false-positives are shown in Fig. 12. In the first row, RGB (a) missed some people in rather darker scenes while LWIR (b) and 'LWIR lensless' (c) didn't. On the other hand in the second row, (a) incorrectly detected an object as a person that (b) and (c) didn't.

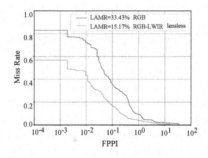

Fig. 13. Evaluation of human detection rate by our RGB-LWIR lensless camera: The result of the RGB-LWIR lensless camera is significantly better than that of the RGB camera only.

5.3   Experiment with Real-World Dataset

Experimental Setup: For the data acquisition, we used the RGB-LWIR lensless camera system described in Sect. 4.1, which simultaneously captures RGB and LWIR lensless images. The next step was to apply a geometrical calibration between an LWIR lensless camera and an RGB camera. Since the resolution of reconstructed LWIR images is relatively low, the classical camera calibration approach [43] is not reliable. Therefore, we calibrated the intrinsic parameters of

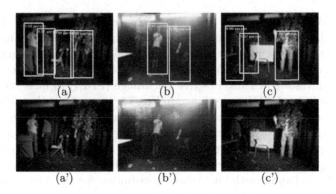

Fig. 14. Comparison of human recognition results between RGB-LWIR lensless images (*upper row*) and only RGB images (*lower row*)

the RGB camera by applying [43]'s method and of the LWIR camera by using design parameters. Then we calibrated the extrinsic parameters by showing a high-temperature halogen light at two different known positions.

Analysis: We captured real image samples of humans by RGB-LWIR lensless cameras. These images were resized to fit the KAIST dictionary and were evaluated by the human detection algorithm described in Sect. 5.1. We show the evaluation result of human detection from 531 frame images in Fig. 13. As we wrote before, we can see that the result of the RGB-LWIR lensless camera is better than that of the RGB camera only. We show human detection samples in Fig. 14, which upper side is the results of an RGB-LWIR lensless camera, and the lower side is of the RGB camera. (a) and (a') show the same scene that four persons are standing in a low-light environment. While nobody is detected in (a'), all persons are recognized in (a). (b) and (b') show a backlight situation what is a difficult scene to detect humans for RGB camera. (c) and (c') show an occluded scene. While two persons are heavily occluded by a plate or leaves, and one person is standing in a dark area, all persons are detected in (c). RGB-LWIR lensless camera can detect such an occluded person in the dark by strengthening information about the human body with two different types of images.

6   Conclusion

We have presented a novel lensless imaging framework in the long-wave infrared. We proposed a wide FOV lensless camera system with novel modulation principle and an efficient reconstruction algorithm. With our experimental prototype, we evaluated the reconstruction performance qualitatively and quantitatively. We also have shown the robustness of the misalignment between a mask and a sensor, and the required accuracy is lower than manufacturing accuracy. As a background core technology, we constructed a precise diffraction simulator that can easily create imaging matrix F without calibration. We demonstrated, that our simulator can contribute to generating a massive number of training data for CNN-based inference algorithm and evaluated its performance in human detection tasks. Throughout evaluations with fusion data of LWIR lensless and RGB images, we show that performance with our dataset was superior to with just RGB dataset, and was comparable to RGB-LWIR with a lens.

Limitations and Future Work: One limitation is the quality degradation due to difficulty to achieve sharp uniform focusing of all open features of the URA mask with diffractive mask. The solution to this problem could be to substitute FZP-type mask with free-form lens. Another limitation is the mask distance. Reducing the mask distance to the sensor increases the FOV, however, the FOV can't be extended much more than 90° due to the angular intensity fall-off.

Although our mask design provides a good starting point for LWIR lensless imaging, we believe that data-driven approach which proved to be efficient for optics optimization (see [8,9,30,34,36,41]) can be coupled with our lensless imaging simulation system for further mask design optimization.

A spectral extension is the most interesting future work. Recently, there are several proposals for improved detectors for not only long-wave infrared but middle-wave infrared or terahertz imaging. We consider that our diffraction simulation framework and focusing modulation can be applied in this direction.

References

1. Antipa, N., et al.: DiffuserCam: lensless single-exposure 3D imaging. Optica **5**(1), 1 (2018)
2. Asif, M.S., Ayremlou, A., Sankaranarayanan, A., Veeraraghavan, A., Baraniuk, R.G.: FlatCam: thin, lensless cameras using coded aperture and computation. IEEE Trans. Comput. Imaging **3**(3), 384–397 (2016)
3. Barrera Campo, F., Lumbreras Ruiz, F., Sappa, A.D.: Multimodal stereo vision system: 3D data extraction and algorithm evaluation. IEEE J. Sel. Top. Signal Process. **6**(5), 437–446 (2012)
4. Barrett, H.H.: Fresnel zone plate imaging in nuclear medicine. J. Nucl. Med. **13**(6), 382–385 (1972)
5. Benenson, R., Omran, M., Hosang, J., Schiele, B.: Ten years of pedestrian detection, what have we learned? In: Agapito, L., Bronstein, M.M., Rother, C. (eds.) ECCV 2014. LNCS, vol. 8926, pp. 613–627. Springer, Cham (2015). https://doi.org/10.1007/978-3-319-16181-5_47
6. Born, M., Wolf, E.: Principles of Optics: Electromagnetic Theory of Propagation, Interference and Diffraction of Light, 7th edn. Cambridge University Press, Cambridge (1999)
7. Busboom, A., Elders-Boll, H., Schotten, H.: Uniformly redundant arrays. Exp. Astron. **8**, 97–123 (1998). https://doi.org/10.1023/A:1007966830741
8. Chakrabarti, A.: Learning sensor multiplexing design through back-propagation. In: Advances in Neural Information Processing Systems, pp. 3089–3097 (2016)
9. Chang, J., Wetzstein, G.: Deep optics for monocular depth estimation and 3D object detection. In: Proceedings of Computer Vision and Pattern Recognition (CVPR), pp. 10192–10201 (2019)

10. Chu, Y.S., et al.: Hard-X-ray microscopy with Fresnel zone plates reaches 40 nm Rayleigh resolution. Appl. Phys. Lett. **92**(10), 103119 (2008)
11. Cieślak, M.J., Gamage, K.A., Glover, R.: Coded-aperture imaging systems: past, present and future development - a review. Radiat. Meas. **92**, 59–71 (2016)
12. DeWeert, M.J., Farm, B.P.: Lensless coded-aperture imaging with separable Doubly-Toeplitz masks. Opt. Eng. **54**(2), 023102 (2015)
13. Dollár, P., Wojek, C., Schiele, B., Perona, P.: Pedestrian detection: an evaluation of the state of the art. IEEE Trans. Pattern Anal. Mach. Intell. **34**(4), 743–761 (2012)
14. Fenimore, E.E., Cannon, T.M.: Coded aperture imaging with uniformly redundant arrays. Appl. Opt. **17**(3), 337 (1978)
15. Fenimore, E.E., Cannon, T.M.: Uniformly redundant arrays: digital reconstruction methods. Appl. Opt. **20**(10), 1858 (1981)
16. Fergus, R., Torralba, A., Freeman, W.T.: Random Lens Imaging. MIT-CSAIL-TR-2006-058, September 2006
17. Gade, R., Moeslund, T.B.: Thermal cameras and applications: a survey. Mach. Vision Appl. **25**(1), 245–262 (2014). https://doi.org/10.1007/s00138-013-0570-5
18. Gill, P.R., et al.: Thermal Escher sensors: pixel-efficient lensless imagers based on tiled optics. In: Optics InfoBase Conference Papers, vol. Part F46-COSI 2017, p. CTu3B.3. OSA - The Optical Society, June 2017
19. Goodman, J.W.: Introduction to Fourier Optics, 3rd edn. Roberts, Greenwood Village (2005)
20. Grulois, T., Druart, G., Guérineau, N., Crastes, A., Sauer, H., Chavel, P.: Extra-thin infrared camera for low-cost surveillance applications. Opt. Lett. **39**(11), 3169 (2014)
21. Hwang, S., Park, J., Kim, N., Choi, Y., Kweon, I.S.: Multispectral pedestrian detection: benchmark dataset and baseline. In: Proceedings of Computer Vision and Pattern Recognition (CVPR), 07–12 June 2015, pp. 1037–1045. IEEE Computer Society, October 2015
22. in't Zand, J.: A coded-mask imager as monitor of Galactic X-ray sources. Ph.D. thesis, Space Research Organization Netherlands, Sorbonnelaan 2, 3584 CA Utrecht, The Netherlands (1992)
23. Karasawa, T., Watanabe, K., Ha, Q., Tejero-De-Pablos, A., Ushiku, Y., Harada, T.: Multispectral object detection for autonomous vehicles. In: Proceedings of Thematic Workshops of ACM Multimedia, pp. 35–43. Association for Computing Machinery Inc, New York, October 2017
24. Khan, S.S., Adarsh, V.R., Boominathan, V., Tan, J., Veeraraghavan, A., Mitra, K.: Towards photorealistic reconstruction of highly multiplexed lensless images. In: Proceddings of International Conference on Computer Vision (ICCV), pp. 7859–7868. IEEE, October 2019
25. Kim, G., Isaacson, K., Palmer, R., Menon, R.: Lensless photography with only an image sensor. Appl. Opt. **56**(23), 6450–6456 (2017)
26. Kirz, J.: Phase zone plates for X rays and the extreme UV. J. Opt. Soc. Am. **64**(3), 301–309 (1974)
27. Konig, D., Adam, M., Jarvers, C., Layher, G., Neumann, H., Teutsch, M.: Fully convolutional region proposal networks for multispectral person detection. In: IEEE Conference on Computer Vision and Pattern Recognition Workshops (CVPRW), July 2017, pp. 243–250. IEEE Computer Society, August 2017
28. Leykin, A., Ran, Y., Hammoud, R.: Thermal-visible video fusion for moving target tracking and pedestrian classification. In: Proceedings of Computer Vision and Pattern Recognition (CVPR) (2007)

29. Liu, J., Zhang, S., Wang, S., Metaxas, D.N.: Multispectral deep neural networks for pedestrian detection. In: British Machine Vision Conference (BMVC), September 2016, pp. 73.1–73.13 (2016)
30. Metzler, C.A., Ikoma, H., Peng, Y., Wetzstein, G.: Deep optics for single-shot high-dynamic-range imaging. In: Proceedings of Computer Vision and Pattern Recognition (CVPR), August 2020
31. Miezianko, R., Pokrajac, D.: People detection in low resolution infrared videos. In: IEEE Conference on Computer Vision and Pattern Recognition Workshops (CVPRW) (2008)
32. Mudau, A.E., Willers, C.J., Griffith, D., Le Roux, F.P.: Non-uniformity correction and bad pixel replacement on LWIR and MWIR images. In: Saudi International Electronics, Communications and Photonics Conference (SIECPC) (2011)
33. Ren, S., He, K., Girshick, R., Sun, J.: Faster R-CNN: towards real-time object detection with region proposal networks. IEEE Trans. Pattern Anal. Mach. Intell. **39**(6), 1137–1149 (2017)
34. Sitzmann, V., et al.: End-to-end optimization of optics and image processing for achromatic extended depth of field and super-resolution imaging. ACM Trans. Graph. **37**(4), 1–13 (2018)
35. Stylianou, A., Pless, R.: SparkleGeometry: glitter imaging for 3D point tracking. In: IEEE Conference on Computer Vision and Pattern Recognition Workshops (CVPRW), pp. 919–926. IEEE Computer Society, December 2016
36. Sun, Q., Zhang, J., Dun, X., Ghanem, B., Peng, Y., Heidrich, W.: End-to-end learned, optically coded super-resolution SPAD camera. ACM Trans. Graph. **39**(2), 1–14 (2020)
37. Tanida, J., et al.: Thin observation module by bound optics (TOMBO): concept and experimental verification. Appl. Opt. **40**(11), 1806 (2001)
38. Tikhonov, A.N., Arsenin, V.Y.: Solutions of Ill-Posed Problems. W.H. Winston, Washington (1977)
39. Wagner, J., Fischer, V., Herman, M., Behnke, S.: Multispectral pedestrian detection using deep fusion convolutional neural networks. In: Proceedings of European Symposium on Artificial Neural Networks (ESANN) (2016)
40. Wang, Z., Simoncelli, E.P.: Translation insensitive image similarity in complex wavelet domain. In: Proceedings of International Conference on Acoustics, Speech and Signal Processing (ICASSP), vol. II (2005)
41. Wu, Y., Boominathan, V., Chen, H., Sankaranarayanan, A., Veeraraghavan, A.: PhaseCam3D - learning phase masks for passive single view depth estimation (2019)
42. Xu, D., Ouyang, W., Ricci, E., Wang, X., Sebe, N.: Learning cross-modal deep representations for robust pedestrian detection. In: Proceedings of Computer Vision and Pattern Recognition (CVPR), January 2017, pp. 4236–4244. Institute of Electrical and Electronics Engineers Inc., November 2017
43. Zhang, Z.: A flexible new technique for camera calibration. IEEE Trans. Pattern Anal. Mach. Intell. **22**(11), 1330–1334 (2000)

Topology-Preserving Class-Incremental Learning

Xiaoyu Tao[1], Xinyuan Chang[2], Xiaopeng Hong[1,3], Xing Wei[2],
and Yihong Gong[2(✉)]

[1] Faculty of Electronic and Information Engineering, Xi'an Jiaotong University,
Xi'an, China
txy666793@stu.xjtu.edu.cn, hongxiaopeng@mail.xjtu.edu.cn
[2] School of Software Engineering, Xi'an Jiaotong University, Xi'an, China
cxy19960919@stu.xjtu.edu.cn, xingxjtu@gmail.com, ygong@mail.xjtu.edu.cn
[3] Research Center for Artificial Intelligence, Peng Cheng Laboratory,
Shenzhen, China

Abstract. A well-known issue for class-incremental learning is the *catastrophic forgetting* phenomenon, where the network's recognition performance on old classes degrades severely when incrementally learning new classes. To alleviate forgetting, we put forward to preserve the old class knowledge by maintaining the topology of the network's feature space. On this basis, we propose a novel *topology-preserving class-incremental learning* (TPCIL) framework. TPCIL uses an *elastic Hebbian graph* (EHG) to model the feature space topology, which is constructed with the *competitive Hebbian learning* rule. To maintain the topology, we develop the *topology-preserving loss* (TPL) that penalizes the changes of EHG's neighboring relationships during incremental learning phases. Comprehensive experiments on CIFAR100, ImageNet, and subImageNet datasets demonstrate the power of the TPCIL for continuously learning new classes with less forgetting. The code will be released.

Keywords: Topology-Preserving Class-Incremental Learning
(TPCIL) · Class-Incremental Learning (CIL) · Elastic Hebbian Graph
(EHG) · Topology-Preserving Loss (TPL)

1 Introduction

To date, deep neural networks have been successfully applied to a large number of computer vision and pattern recognition tasks [5,8,11,16,20,22,24,33,34,40,41], etc. When applying a network to a classification problem, we generally first assume that the data classes are pre-defined and fixed, and then construct a network with the number of neural units in the output layer equal to the number of classes. In real applications, however, there often emerge new classes of data that have not been encountered before, and can not be recognized by the learnt

---

X. Tao and X. Chang—Co-first authors.

© Springer Nature Switzerland AG 2020
A. Vedaldi et al. (Eds.): ECCV 2020, LNCS 12364, pp. 254–270, 2020.
https://doi.org/10.1007/978-3-030-58529-7_16

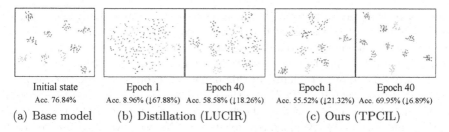

Initial state	Epoch 1	Epoch 40	Epoch 1	Epoch 40
Acc. 76.84%	Acc. 8.96% (↓67.88%)	Acc. 58.58% (↓18.26%)	Acc. 55.52% (↓21.32%)	Acc. 69.95% (↓6.89%)
(a) Base model	(b) Distillation (LUCIR)		(c) Ours (TPCIL)	

Fig. 1. t-SNE visualization of the comparison between TPCIL and the distillation approach in classifying the base class exemplars. We report the test accuracy on the base class test set during incremental learning. (a) Initially, the base class exemplars are well separated in feature space. (b) The distillation approach fails to maintain the feature space topology of the base class exemplars at the beginning of incremental learning, where *catastrophic forgetting* is clearly identified at *epoch 1* with severe degradation of the base class test accuracy. As a result, it has to take a much longer time (*e.g.*, *40* epochs here) to re-learn discriminative features for the exemplars. (c) TPCIL uses the *topology-preserving loss* (TPL) that maintains the topology of these old class exemplars, which can avoid forgetting during the entire incremental learning phase

model. Therefore, it is crucial to allow the model to incrementally expand, and to learn from data of new classes. This ability is referred to as *class-incremental learning* (CIL) in the literature [3,32].

CIL aims to incrementally learn a unified classifier to recognize *new* classes without forgetting the *old* ones at the same time. This problem is usually studied under a practical condition that the training set of old classes is unavailable when learning new classes [32]. As a consequence, it is prohibitive to retrain the model on the joint training set of both old and new classes. A straight-forward approach is to directly finetune the model on new class data. However, it is prone to *catastrophic forgetting* (CF) [10], where classification accuracies on old classes deteriorate drastically during finetuning.

To tackle catastrophic forgetting, a number of CIL methods [3,13,32,42] adopt the *knowledge distillation* [12] technique to preserve the old class knowledge contained in the network's output logits. Knowledge distillation was originally proposed for transferring 'dark knowledge' from the teacher model to a student model [12,43]. LwF [19] introduces this idea to incremental learning to alleviate the forgetting of the old tasks' knowledge when learning a new task. When applying to CIL, one typically stores a smaller set of exemplar images representative of old classes, and incorporates the distillation loss with the classification loss (i.e., cross-entropy) for learning from new class training samples.

Although the distillation approaches can mitigate forgetting to some extent, they face the bias problem [13,42] caused by imbalanced number of old/new class training samples, which hurts the recognition performance [9]. Moreover, it is observed in our experiments that the distillation-based methods seem to *forget* the old knowledge at first and then re-learn the knowledge from the old class exemplars during incremental learning, which is termed the *start-all-over* phenomenon, as shown in Fig. 1(b). As a result, it takes more additional epochs to re-acquire the old class knowledge. Besides, excessive re-learning also increases the risk of overfitting to the old class exemplars. These issues restrict the ability of incremental learning from a (potentially) infinite sequence of new classes.

To solve the above problems, in this paper, we propose a cognitive-inspired Topology-Preseving CIL (TPCIL) method. Recent advances in cognitive science reveal that forgetting is caused by the disruption of the topology of human visual working memory [6,39]. Analogously, for deep CNNs, we have also observed that catastrophic forgetting occurred together with the disruption of the feature space topology once learning new classes. Based on these discoveries, we endeavor to preserve the old class knowledge and mitigate forgetting by maintaining the topology of CNN's feature space. We model the topology using an *elastic Hebbian graph* (EHG) constructed with *competitive Hebbian learning* (CHL) [28]. During CIL, we impose new constraints, namely the *topology-preserving loss* (TPL) on EHG, to penalize the changes of its topological connections.

We conduct comprehensive experiments on popular image classification benchmarks CIFAR100, ImageNet, and subImageNet, and compare TPCIL with the state-of-the-art CIL methods. Experimental results demonstrate the effectiveness of TPCIL for improving recognition performance in a long sequence of incremental learning. To summarize, our main contributions include:

- We propose a neuroscience inspired, topology-preserving framework for effective class-incremental learning with less forgetting.
- We construct an *elastic Hebbian graph* (EHG) by *competitive Hebbian learning* to model the topology of CNN's feature space.
- We design the *topology-preserving loss* (TPL) to maintain the feature space topology and mitigate forgetting.

2   Related Work

There are two branches in recent incremental learning studies. The *multi-task* incremental learning [19,30] aims at learning a sequence of independent tasks, each of which is assigned a specific classifier, while the *single-task* incremental learning [27,38] employs a unified classifier to treat the entire incremental learning process as one task. The CIL focused by this paper belongs to the single-task incremental learning, where only one classification head is incrementally learnt to recognize all encountered data batches of different classes.

2.1   Multi-task Incremental Learning

The multi-task incremental learning [30] assumes the task identity is always known during training and testing. The model is required to learn new tasks without degrading the old tasks' performance. Research works usually adopt the following strategies to mitigate forgetting: (1) regularization strategy [14,17,19,45], (2) architectural strategy [1,25,26,35,44], and (3) rehearsal strategy [4,23,36,46]. Regularization strategy imposes regularization on the network weights or outputs when learning the new tasks. For example, EWC [14] and SI [45] impose constraints on the network weights, penalizing changing of the weights important to old tasks. Architectural strategy dynamically modifies the network's structures by expanding, pruning [21,47] or masking the neural connections. For example, PackNet [26] creates free parameters for new tasks by network pruning. HAT [35] learns the attention masks to constrain the weights for old tasks when learning new tasks. Rehearsal strategy periodically replay the memory for the past experiences of the old tasks to the network when learning new tasks. For example, GEM [23] uses an external memory to store a small set of old tasks' exemplar images and use them to constrain the old tasks' losses during incremental learning. DGR [36] and LifelongGAN [46] use a generative model to memorize the old tasks' data distribution, with a generative adversarial network learnt to produce pseudo training samples of old tasks.

In short, the *multi-task* methods perform incremental learning in task-level with task-specific classifiers. As a consequence, these methods can not be directly used by CIL, which only has a single, incrementally expanded classifier.

2.2 Class-Incremental Learning

Most *class-incremental learning* (CIL) works [3,13,32,42] alleviates forgetting using the knowledge distillation [12,18,31,43] technique, which is initially introduced by LWF [19] for multi-task incremental learning. An earlier work iCaRL [32] decouples the learning of the classifier and the feature representation, where the classifier is implemented by the nearest matching of the pre-stored exemplars in an *episodic memory*. When learning the representation for the new classes, the a distillation loss term is added to the cross-entropy loss function to maintain the representations of the old class exemplars. A later work EEIL [3] learns the network in an end-to-end fashion with the *cross-distillated loss*. It overcomes the limitation of iCaRL by learning the representation and the classifier jointly. More recent CIL studies [9,13,37,42] reveal the critical *bias* issue caused by the imbalanced number of training samples of old and new classes, where the classification layer's weights and logits are biased towards new classes after incremental learning. To eliminate the bias, LUCIR [13] normalizes the feature vectors and the weights of the classification layer, adopts the cosine similarity metric, and applies distillation to the feature space rather than the output logits. BIC [42] develops a bias correction technique that learns a linear model to unify the distribution of the output logits. IL2M [9] proposes a dual-memory approach that finetunes the model without the distillation loss. It stores the exemplars and the statistics of historical classes to rectify the prediction scores.

In short, the distillation-based CIL methods maintain the distribution of the output/feature logits [3,13,32,42] for the old class exemplars. However, it is observed that such kind of objective is not well achieved during incremental learning, where the old class knowledge is likely forgotten at the beginning of incremental learning (see Fig. 1). Besides, as the exemplar set is typically randomly sampled from the old class training set, it is only a rough approximation of the data distribution. Recent studies in *few-shot class-incremental learning* [37] show that the knowledge can be well preserved by learning the topology of the feature space manifold, even when the manifold is non-uniform and heterogeneous. Different from the above approaches, TPCIL maintains the feature space topology by constraining the relations of the representative points, while allowing the shift of the representatives to adapt to new classes.

3 Topology-Preserving Class-Incremental Learning

3.1 Problem Definition

The *class-incremental learning* (CIL) problem is defined as follows. Let X, Y, and Z denote the training set, the label set, and the test set, respectively. A CNN model θ is required to incrementally learn a unified classifier from a sequence of training sessions $X^1, X^2, \cdots, X^t, X^{t+1}, \cdots$, where $X^t = \{(x_i^t, y_i^t)\}_{i=1}^{N_t}$ is the labeled training set of the t-th session with N_t samples, and x_i^t and $y_i^t \in Y^t$ are the i-th image and its label, respectively. Y^t is the disjoint label set at session t, s.t. $\forall p \neq q$, $Y^p \cap Y^q = \varnothing$. At session $(t+1)$, a model θ^{t+1} is learnt from X^{t+1}, without the presence of the old class training sets $X^1, X^2, \cdots, X^t$. Then θ^{t+1} is evaluated on the union of all the encountered test sets $\bigcup_{j=1}^{t+1} Z^j$.

3.2 Overall Framework

A CNN can be regarded as the composition of a feature extractor $f(\cdot; \theta)$ with parameters θ and a classification layer with a weight matrix W. Given an input x, CNN outputs $o(x; \theta) = W^\top f(x; \theta)$, which is followed by a softmax layer to produce multi-class probabilities. Let $\mathcal{F} \subseteq \mathbb{R}^n$ denotes the feature space defined by $f(\cdot; \theta)$. Initially, we train θ^1 on the base class training set X^1 with the cross-entropy loss. Then, we incrementally finetune the model on $X^2, \cdots, X^t, X^{t+1}, \cdots$, to get $\theta^2, \cdots, \theta^t, \theta^{t+1}, \cdots$. At session $(t+1)$, the output layer is expanded for new classes by adding $|Y^{t+1}|$ new neurons. Directly finetuning θ^{t+1} on X^{t+1} will overwrite old weights in θ^t important for recognizing old classes, which disrupts the feature space topology and causes catastrophic forgetting, with a degradation of the recognition performance on $\bigcup_{j=1}^t Y^j$.

In this paper, we alleviate forgetting by maintaining the feature space topology for the old classes. To achieve this purpose, we first model the feature space topology using the *elastic Hebbian graph* (EHG), and then propose the *topology-preserving loss* (TPL) term to penalize changing of the feature space topology represented by EHG. Let G^t denote the EHG constructed at session t. The overall loss function at the next session $(t+1)$ is defined as:

$$\ell(X^{t+1}, G^t; \theta^{t+1}) = \ell_{CE}(X^{t+1}, G^t; \theta^{t+1}) + \lambda \ell_{TPL}(G^t; \theta^{t+1}). \tag{1}$$

In the above equation, ℓ_{CE} is the standard cross-entropy loss:

$$\ell_{CE}(X^{t+1}, G^t; \theta^{t+1}) = \sum_{(x,y)} -\log \hat{p}_y(x), \tag{2}$$

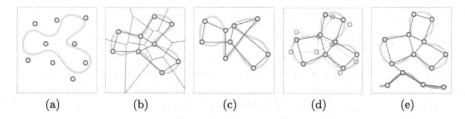

Fig. 2. Conceptual visualization of the topology-preserving mechanism. The golden curve stands for the feature space manifold; The circles and solid lines indicate the vertices and edges of EHG, respectively. (a) N points are randomly picked to initialize EHG's vertices. (b) By *competitive Hebbian learning* (CHL), the feature space is partitioned into N disjoint *Voronoi cells*, each of which is encoded by a vertex. The neighborhood relations is described by the connections between the vertices. (c) Finetuning CNN for new classes may greatly change the neighborhood relationship of vertices and disrupt the feature space topology. (d) The TPL term compels EHG to maintain the relations of the vertices. (e) After learning new class, EHG grows by inserting new vertices. Then all vertices are updated by CHL and the similarities are re-computed

where (x, y) denotes a training image and its label, and $\hat{p}_y(x)$ is the CNN's predicted probability of label y given input x. We use X^{t+1} as well as the old class images assigned to EHG's vertices (see Sect. 3.3 for details) for training. ℓ_{TPL} is the proposed TPL loss term applied to G^t. The hyper-parameter λ is used for controlling the strength of TPL. We elaborate our approach in the following subsections.

3.3 Topology Modelling via Elastic Hebbian Graph

An effective way to model the topology of a feature space is to perform *Competitive Hebbian learning* (CHL) [28] on the feature space manifold. CHL can learn a set of points representative of any manifold (e.g., non-uniform), and is proved to well preserve the topological structure [29]. To enable topology modelling for CIL and cooperate with CNN, we design the *elastic Hebbian graph* (EHG) which is constructed using CHL. The detailed algorithm is described as follows.

For computational stability, we normalize the feature space and adopt the *cosine similarity* metric. Let $\bar{\cdot}$ denotes the normalization operation, where $\bar{\mathbf{f}} = \mathbf{f}/\|\mathbf{f}\|$. Given the normalized feature space $\bar{\mathcal{F}}$, the EHG is defined as $G = \langle V, E \rangle$, where $V = \{\bar{\mathbf{v}}_1, \cdots, \bar{\mathbf{v}}_N | \bar{\mathbf{v}}_i \in \bar{\mathcal{F}}\}$ is the set of N vertices representative of $\bar{\mathcal{F}}$, and E is the edge set describing the neighborhood relations of the vertices in V. Each vertex $\bar{\mathbf{v}}_i$ is the centroid vector representing the feature vectors within a neighborhood region $\mathcal{V}_i$, which is refered to as the *Voronoi cell* [29]:

$$\mathcal{V}_i = \{\bar{\mathbf{f}} \in \bar{\mathcal{F}} | \bar{\mathbf{f}}^\top \bar{\mathbf{v}}_i \geq \bar{\mathbf{f}}^\top \bar{\mathbf{v}}_j, \ \forall j \neq i\}, \ \forall i. \tag{3}$$

To get $\bar{\mathbf{v}}_i$, we first randomly initialize its value by picking a random position in feature space, as shown in Fig. 2(a). Then we update $\bar{\mathbf{v}}_i$ iteratively using the following normalized *Hebbian* rule:

$$\mathbf{v}_i^* = \bar{\mathbf{v}}_i + \epsilon \cdot e^{-k_i/\alpha}(\bar{\mathbf{f}} - \bar{\mathbf{v}}_i), \ \bar{\mathbf{v}}_i^* = \mathbf{v}_i^*/\|\mathbf{v}_i^*\|, \ i = 1, \cdots, N, \qquad (4)$$

where $\bar{\mathbf{v}}_i^*$ denotes the updated vertex, and $e^{-k_i/\alpha}$ is the decay function to scale the updating step. The decay factor is measured by the proximity rank k_i, where $\bar{\mathbf{v}}_i$ is the k_i-th nearest neighbor of $\bar{\mathbf{f}}$ among all vertices in V. The hyper-parameter ϵ is the learning rate, and α controls the strength of the decay. Equation (4) ensures the vertex nearest to $\bar{\mathbf{f}}$ has the largest adapting step towards $\bar{\mathbf{f}}$, while other vertices are less affected. We execute Eq. (4) until $\bar{\mathbf{v}}_i^*$ is converged.

With the updated vertex set V, we may construct the corresponding *Delaunay graph* as in [29] to model the neighborhood relations of the vertices, as shown in Fig. 2(b). However, it is difficult to directly constrain the Delaunay graph under the gradient descent framework, as the adjacency of vertices are changed by the Hebbian rule, which is hard to cooperate with CNN's back-propagation. Alternatively, we convert G as a similarity graph for ease of optimization. Each edge e_{ij} is assigned with a weight s_{ij}, which is the similarity between $\bar{\mathbf{v}}_i$ and $\bar{\mathbf{v}}_j$:

$$s_{ij} = \bar{\mathbf{v}}_i^\top \bar{\mathbf{v}}_j. \qquad (5)$$

In this way, the changing of G can be back-propagated to CNN and optimized with the gradient decent algorithm. For computing the observed values of each vertex at the next incremental learning session, we assign $\bar{\mathbf{v}}_i$ with an image u_i drawn from the old training samples whose feature vector is the closet to $\bar{\mathbf{v}}_i$.

When applying EHG to incremental learning, we first construct the graph using the base class training data. When the training of θ^1 is completed, we extract the set of normalized feature vectors on X^1, by which we have $\bar{F}^1 = \{\bar{f}(x; \theta^1)|\forall(x, y) \in X^1\}$. $\bar{F}^1$ forms the feature space manifold of the base classes. We compute EHG G^1 on $\bar{F}^1$ using Eq. (4) and Eq. (5). G^1 is stored to alleviate forgetting at the next session. Iteratively, at session $(t+1)$, after learning θ^{t+1}, we grow and update the pre-stored EHG G^t to make it consistent with the adapted feature space. We insert K new vertices $\{\bar{\mathbf{v}}_{N+1}, \cdots, \bar{\mathbf{v}}_{N+K}\}$ to get V^{t+1}, and then update all vertices on $\bar{F}^{t+1}$ using Eq. (4). After that, the similarities are recomputed to get E^{t+1}. Figure 2(e) illustrates the growth of EHG. The topology of the newly formed manifold for new classes is modelled by new vertices and integrated into the EHG.

3.4   Topology-Preserving Constraint

At session $(t+1)$, given EHG $G^t = \langle V^t, E^t \rangle$, when catastrophic forgetting occurs, G^t is distorted with the disruption of the old edges, as shown in Fig. 2(c). To alleviate forgetting, the original connections in G^t should be maintained when finetuning CNN on X^{t+1}. This is achieved by constraining the neighboring relations of vertices described by the edges' weights (i.e., similarities) in E^t. For this purpose, one approach is to maintain the rank of the edges' weights during learning. However, it is difficult and inefficient to optimize the nonsmooth global ranking [2], while the local ranking can not well preserve the global relations. Alternatively, we can measure the changing of the neighboring relations by computing the correlation between the initial and observation values of the edges' weights. A lower correlation indicates a higher probability that the rank of the edges has changed during learning, which should be penalized. On this basis, we define the *topology-preserving loss* (TPL) term as:

$$\ell_{TPL}(G^t; \theta^{t+1}) = -\frac{\sum\limits_{i,j}^{N}(s_{ij} - \frac{1}{N^2}\sum\limits_{i,j}^{N} s_{ij})(\tilde{s}_{ij} - \frac{1}{N^2}\sum\limits_{i,j}^{N} \tilde{s}_{ij})}{\sqrt{\sum\limits_{i,j}^{N}(s_{ij} - \frac{1}{N^2}\sum\limits_{i,j}^{N} s_{ij})^2}\sqrt{\sum\limits_{i,j}^{N}(\tilde{s}_{ij} - \frac{1}{N^2}\sum\limits_{i,j}^{N} \tilde{s}_{ij})^2}}, \tag{6}$$

where $S = \{s_{ij}|1 \leq i,j \leq N\}$ and $\tilde{S} = \{\tilde{s_{ij}}|1 \leq i,j \leq N\}$ are the sets of the initial and observation values of edges' weights in E^t, respectively. The active value $\tilde{s}_{ij}$ is estimated by:

$$\tilde{s}_{ij} = \tilde{\mathbf{f}}_i^\top \tilde{\mathbf{f}}_j = \bar{f}(u_i; \theta^{t+1})^\top \bar{f}(u_j; \theta^{t+1}), \tag{7}$$

where u_i and u_j are the pre-stored images assigned to $\bar{\mathbf{v}}_i$ and $\bar{\mathbf{v}}_j$, respectively. As $\bar{\mathbf{v}}_i$ encodes the i-th region in feature space, the TPL term implicitly maintains the adjacency of these regions. Another choice for the loss term is to penalize the l_1 or l_2 norms of the similarities. In our experiments, we found such restrictions are not as flexible as the correlation form and behave worse, since they do not allow a linear changing of the similarities' scale.

Rather than penalizing the shift of EHG's vertices in feature space, TPL penalizes the changing of the topological relations between the vertices, while allowing the reasonable shift of vertices. Such constraint is 'soft', easier to optimize, which makes the EHG structure 'elastic' and does not interfere the learning of new classes. Figure 2(d) illustrates the effect of TPL.

3.5 Optimization

TPCIL integrates a CNN model and an EHG G^t, where G^t is used to preserve the topology of CNN's feature space manifold. It is noteworthy that the CNN model is trained with the *minibatch stochastic gradient descent* (minibatch SGD) algorithm, while G^t is constructed and updated with the *competitive Hebbian learning* (CHL). It is less efficient to update the vertices of G^t using Eq. (4) at each minibatch iteration, as the features obtained at intermediate training sessions have not been fully optimized. Therefore, we learn G^t after the training of CNN is completed. G^t is then used for the next incremental session $(t + 1)$.

3.6 Comparison with the Distillation-Based Approaches

In contrast to our approach that maintains the feature space topology, other CIL works [3,13,42] are mostly based on knowledge distillation, where a distillation loss term is appended to the cross-entropy loss:

$$\ell(\tilde{X}^{t+1}; \theta^{t+1}, \theta^t) = \ell_{CE}(\tilde{X}^{t+1}; \theta^{t+1}) + \gamma\ell_{DL}(\tilde{X}^{t+1}; \theta^{t+1}, \theta^t), \tag{8}$$

where $\tilde{X}^{t+1} = X^{t+1} \cup M^t$ denotes the joint set of new class training samples X^{t+1} and the old class exemplars M^t, and θ^t and θ^{t+1} are the parameter sets achieved at session t and $(t+1)$, correspondingly. The distillation loss term ℓ_{DL} is applied to the network's output logits corresponding to the old classes [3,32]:

$$\ell_{DL}(\tilde{X}^{t+1}; \theta^{t+1}, \theta^t) = -\sum_{(x,y)\in\tilde{X}^{t+1}} \sum_{c=1}^{C^t} \frac{e^{-o_c(x;\theta^t)/T}}{\sum_{j=1}^{C^t} e^{-o_j(x;\theta^t)/T}} \log \frac{e^{-o_c(x;\theta^{t+1})/T}}{\sum_{j=1}^{C^t} e^{-o_j(x;\theta^{t+1})/T}}, \tag{9}$$

where $C^t = |Y^t|$ is the number of the old classes and T (e.g., $T = 2$) is the temperature for distillation. Another distillation approach is to apply the distillation loss to the feature space, which is called *feature distillation loss* [13]:

$$\ell_{FDL}(\tilde{X}^{t+1}; \theta^{t+1}, \theta^t) = \sum_{(x,y)\in\tilde{X}^{t+1}} (1 - \bar{f}(x; \theta^t)^\top \bar{f}(x; \theta^{t+1})), \tag{10}$$

where $\bar{f}(x; \theta^t)$ denotes the normalized feature vector.

The distillation losses ℓ_{DL} and ℓ_{FDL} penalize the changing of the output logits or feature vectors computed by the old model. Such a restriction is too strict and difficult to satisfy, as the cross-entropy loss ℓ_{CE} dominantly brings adaptation to new classes in the feature or output space. We have observed the *start-all-over* phenomenon, where the features of the base class exemplars in M^t are 'forgotten' at the beginning of incremental learning, as illustrated in Fig. 1(b). In comparison, the TPL term in Eq. (6) constrains the neighboring relations between the EHG vertices, allowing the feature space to adapt to new classes more freely without losing discriminative power. In this way, the plummeting of the old classes' recognition performance at the initial training iterations can be avoid. Detailed experimental comparisons are described in Sect. 4.3.

4   Experiments

We conduct comprehensive experiments under the CIL setting in [13] on three popular image classification datasets CIFAR100 [15], ImageNet [7] and subImageNet [13,32]. Following [13], for each dataset, we choose half of the classes as the base classes for the base session and divide the rest of the classes into 5 or 10 incremental sessions. Detailed setups are described as follows.

4.1   Datasets and Experimental Setups

CIFAR100. It contains 60,000 natural RGB images of the size 32×32 over 100 classes, including 50,000 training and 10,000 test images. We follow the protocols in [13] to process the dataset, where 50 classes are selected as the base classes, and the rest 50 classes are equally divided for incremental learning phases. We randomly flip each image for data augmentation during training.

ImageNet. The large-scale ImageNet (1k) dataset has 1.28 million training and 50,000 validation images over 1000 classes. We select 500 classes as the base classes and split the rest 500 classes for incremental learning. We randomly flip the image and crop a 224 × 224 patch for data augmentation during training, and use the single-crop center image patch for testing.

SubImageNet. This dataset is the 100-class subset of ImageNet, which contains about 130,000 images for training and 5,000 images for testing. We select 50 classes as the base classes and equally divide the rest 50 classes for incremental learning. For data augmentation, we use the same technique as ImageNet.

Experimental Setups. All the experiments are performed using PyTorch. As in [13], we choose the popular 32-layer ResNet as the baseline CNN for CIFAR100 and the 18-layer ResNet for ImageNet and subImageNet, respectively.

Initially, we train the base model for 120 epochs using minibatch SGD with the minibatch size of 128. The learning rate is initialized to 0.1 and decreased to 0.01 and 0.001 at epoch 60 and 100, respectively. At each incremental learning session, we finetune the model for 90 epochs, where the learning rate is initially set to 0.01 for CIFAR100 and 5e−4 for ImageNet and subImageNet, respectively, and decreased by 10 times at epoch 30 and 60. We set the hyper-parameter $\lambda = 15$ in Eq. (1) for CIFAR100 and $\lambda = 10$ for subImageNet and ImageNet, respectively. For EHG, we insert 20 vertices for each new class, which leads to 2,000 vertices for CIFAR100 and subImageNet, and 20,000 vertices for ImageNet. We set $\epsilon = 0.1$ and $\alpha = 10$ in Eq. (4). At the end of each session, we evaluate the model on the union of all the encountered test sets.

We compare TPCIL with the representative CIL methods, including the classical iCARL [32], EEIL [3] and recent state of the arts LUCIR [13] and BiC [42]. To show the effectiveness of alleviate forgetting, we also directly finetune the CNN model using both the new class training samples and the old class exemplars without forgetting-reduction techniques. We denote this baseline method as "Ft-CNN". For the upper-bound, we follow [13] and retrain the model at each session on a joint set of all training images of encountered classes, which is denoted as "Joint-CNN". The distillation temperature in Eq. (9) is set to $T = 2$. For fair comparisons, we use the equal number of old class exemplars for all comparative methods. All results are averaged over 5 runs. We report the top-1 test accuracy of each session, as well as the accuracy averaged over all sessions.

4.2   Comparison Results

Figure 3 shows the comparison results between TPCIL and other CIL methods. Each curve reports the changing of the test accuracy at each session. The green curve stands for the baseline "Ft-CNN", while the yellow curve indicates the *upper-bound* "Joint-CNN". The orange curve reports the accuracy achieved by TPCIL, while the cyan, blue and purple curves report the accuracies of LUCIR, iCARL and EEIL, respectively. We summarize the results as follows:

- For training with both the 5 and 10-session settings on all datasets, TPCIL greatly outperforms all other CIL methods on each incremental session by a

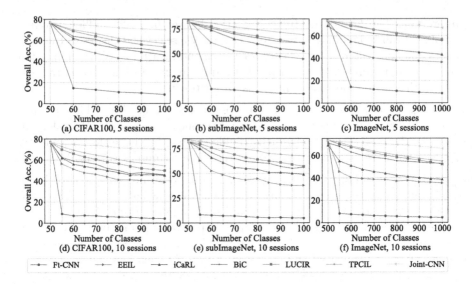

Fig. 3. Comparison results on CIFAR100, subImageNet, and ImageNet under the 5-session (a)–(c) and 10-session (d)–(f) settings. Noting that the original EEIL in [3] uses more data augmentation techniques to boost the performance, which has higher accuracy than iCaRL. In our experiments, we apply the same data augmentation operation to all methods for fair comparisons, which causes the accuracy of EEIL lower (Color figure online)

large margin, and is the closest to the upper-bound joint training method. By comparing each pair of the orange and cyan curves in Fig. 3, we observe that TPCIL achieves higher accuracy than the state-of-the-art LUCIR. Moreover, the superiority of TPCIL is more obvious after learning all the sessions. It shows the effectiveness of TPCIL for long-term incremental learning.

- On CIFAR100, TPCIL achieves the average accuracy of **65.34%** and **63.58%** with the 5 and 10-session settings, respectively. In comparison, the second-best LUCIR achieves the average accuracy of 63.42% and 60.18%, correspondingly. TPCIL outperforms LUCIR by up to **3.40%**. After learning all the sessions, TPCIL greatly outperforms LUCIR by up to **4.28%**.
- On subImageNet, TPCIL has the average accuracy of **76.27%** and **74.81%** with the 5 and 10-session settings, respectively, while the second-best LUCIR has the average accuracy of 70.47% and 68.09%, correspondingly. TPCIL greatly outperforms LUCIR by up to **6.72%**. Furthermore, at the last session, TPCIL significantly outperforms LUCIR by up to **10.60%**.
- On ImageNet, with the 5-session CIL setting, the average accuracy of TPCIL is **64.89%**, exceeding the second-best LUCIR (64.34%) by up to **0.55%**. With the 10-session setting, TPCIL achieves the average accuracy of **62.88%**, surpassing LUCIR (61.28%) by up to **1.60%**. After learning all the sessions, TPCIL outperforms LUCIR by up to **1.43%** and **2.53%**, correspondingly.

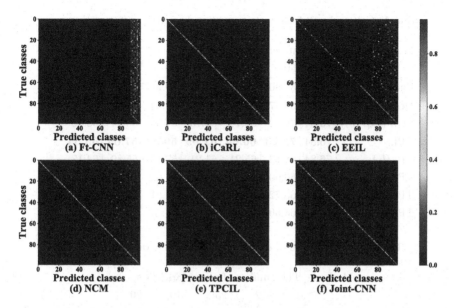

Fig. 4. Confusion matrices of different methods on CIFAR100 under the 5-session setting. The horizontal/vertical axes indicate the predicted/true classes, respectively. The color bar at the right side indicates the activation intensity (Color figure online)

In addition to the 5 and 10-session setting, we have also evaluated 1 and 2-session incremental learning and permuted the order of the sessions. We find the rank of the methods' accuracies remains the same, by which we can draw the same conclusion for the comparison results.

Figure 4 shows the confusion matrices of classification results produced by different CIL methods. In Fig. 4(a), simply finetuning for new class will cause severe misclassifications, where the old class samples are prone to be classified as new classes. The iCARL (b), EEIL (c), and LUCIR (d) methods can correct some misclassified cases, but there are still many unsatisfactory activations outside the diagonal. In comparison, our TPCIL (e) produces a much better confusion matrix, where the activations are mostly distributed at the diagonal, which is the closest to the upper-bound Joint-CNN (f) method. It demonstrates the effectiveness of TPCIL for alleviating forgetting and improving the accuracy.

4.3 Analysis of the TPCIL Components

We perform ablation studies on CIFAR100 under the 5-session incremental learning setting to analyse the effect of TPCIL components, as described in follows.

The Effect of Different Loss Terms. We explore how different loss terms affect the recognition performance, including the *distillation loss* (DL) and *feature distillation loss* (FDL) in Sect. 3.6, and different choices (i.e., Eq. (6), l_1 or l_2) of the TPL form. The experiments are performed on CIFAR100 under

Table 1. Comparison of the test accuracy achieved by different loss terms

Method	Encountered classes						Avg. acc.
	50	60	70	80	90	100	
Finetuning	76.84	51.90	49.66	43.23	40.21	39.40	50.21
DL (Eq. (9))	76.84	61.57	55.27	48.76	46.04	45.20	55.61
FDL (Eq. (6))	76.84	66.32	62.11	55.73	51.56	50.74	60.55
TPL	76.84	**70.23**	**66.64**	**61.99**	**59.32**	**57.04**	**65.34**
TPL(l_1)	76.84	68.33	65.21	61.21	57.63	55.80	64.17
TPL(l_2)	76.84	66.60	63.23	59.11	56.64	54.08	62.75
TPL+DL	76.84	63.72	57.44	48.75	45.31	45.07	56.19
TPL+FDL	76.84	68.60	61.04	52.33	47.41	45.76	58.66

Table 2. Comparison of different exemplar generation techniques

Method	The number of exemplars/class				
	1	2	5	10	20
Random	33.86	45.83	48.89	58.26	64.70
k-means	39.45	48.75	52.24	60.67	65.03
EHG	**42.26**	**51.27**	**52.89**	**61.47**	**65.34**

the 5-session setting. For fair comparisons, all loss terms use the same set of representative images given by EHG. Additionally, we also combine TPL with DL and FDL and evaluate their performances.

Table 1 reports the comparison results. The TPL term achieves the best accuracy after learning all sessions, exceeding FDL significantly by up to **6.3%** and DL by up to **11.84%**. While the combinations of TPL and distillation losses degrade the performance of using TPL alone. It demonstrates that maintaining the feature space topology is more effective to alleviate forgetting than maintaining the stability of the output logits or feature vectors using distillation.

Comparison of Different Exemplar Generation Techniques. In TPCIL, the EHG vertices learned by Hebbian rules can be seen as the exemplars of the feature space. Alternatively, we can randomly sample points in feature space, or run a clustering method (e.g., k-means) and treat the cluster centroids as the exemplars. Table 2 compares the average test accuracy achieved by the three exemplar generations approaches under different number of the exemplars. Apparently, using a large number of exemplars can achieve higher accuracy even for random sampling, while EHG behaves better especially when the number of exemplars is small, thanks to the topology-preservation mechanism [29].

The Effect of the Number of the Exemplars. In the experiments, the CIL methods use an external memory to store the old class exemplars. Though storing more representatives is helpful for the recognition performance, it also

Table 3. Average accuracy of different methods with different number of exemplars

Method	The number of exemplars				
	10	20	30	40	50
iCaRL [32]	52.5	56.5	60.0	61.0	62.0
EEIL [3]	41.8	50.3	55.2	57.1	59.7
LUCIR [13]	61.0	64.0	64.5	65.5	66.0
TPCIL (ours)	**61.5**	**65.3**	**66.2**	**66.5**	**67.0**

Table 4. Average accuracy with different λ on CIFAR100 with the 5-session setting

λ	0	0.1	1	5	10	15	50	100
Average acc.	22.34	58.39	63.07	64.99	65.33	65.34	64.48	61.99

brings more memory overhead. Table 3 reports the average accuracy achieved by using different numbers of vertices/exemplars *per class*. It is observed that the test accuracy is prone to be saturated when the number of exemplars per class is greater than 30. For a better trade-off, we use 20 exemplars per class. Besides, we can also observe that TPCIL achieves better performance than other methods when fixing the memory size, which demonstrates the efficiency of TPCIL.

4.4 Sensitivity Study of the Hyper-parameter λ

The hyper-parameter λ in Eq. (1) controls the strength of TPL term. We perform the sensitivity study to see how the recognition performance is influenced by changing λ. For other hyper-parameters ϵ and α in Eq. (4), we follow their settings in [29] and ensure the vertices of EHG well converged after *competitive Hebbian learning*. We run TPCIL on CIFAR100 with the 5-session setting and change λ in the range of $\{0.1, 1, 5, 10, 15, 50, 100\}$. Table 4 shows the average test accuracy achieved by different values of λ. We observe that with the increasing of λ within a reasonably wide range, the average test accuracy is improved, indicating the effectiveness of TPL. While too large λ (e.g., $\lambda = 100$) could weaken the contribution of the classification loss and hurt the accuracy.

5 Conclusion

This work focuses on the CIL task and addresses the catastrophic forgetting problem from a new, cognitive-inspired perspective. To alleviate forgetting, we put forward to preserve the old class knowledge by maintaining the topology of feature space. We propose a novel TPCIL framework, which uses an EHG graph to model the topology of the feature space manifold, and a TPL term to constrain EHG, penalizing the changing of the topology. Extensive experiments demonstrate that the proposed TPCIL greatly outperforms state-of-the-art CIL methods. In future works, we will generalize TPCIL to more applications.

Acknowledgements. This work is sponsored by National Key R&D Program of China under Grand No.2019YFB1312000, National Major Project under Grant No.2017YFC0803905 and SHAANXI Province Joint Key Laboratory of Machine Learning.

References

1. Aljundi, R., Babiloni, F., Elhoseiny, M., Rohrbach, M., Tuytelaars, T.: Memory aware synapses: learning what (not) to forget. In: Ferrari, V., Hebert, M., Sminchisescu, C., Weiss, Y. (eds.) ECCV 2018. LNCS, vol. 11207, pp. 144–161. Springer, Cham (2018). https://doi.org/10.1007/978-3-030-01219-9_9
2. Burges, C.J., Ragno, R., Le, Q.V.: Learning to rank with nonsmooth cost functions. In: NeurIPS (2007)
3. Castro, F.M., Marín-Jiménez, M.J., Guil, N., Schmid, C., Alahari, K.: End-to-end incremental learning. In: Ferrari, V., Hebert, M., Sminchisescu, C., Weiss, Y. (eds.) ECCV 2018. LNCS, vol. 11216, pp. 241–257. Springer, Cham (2018). https://doi.org/10.1007/978-3-030-01258-8_15
4. Chaudhry, A., Ranzato, M., Rohrbach, M., Elhoseiny, M.: Efficient lifelong learning with A-GEM. arXiv preprint arXiv:1812.00420 (2018)
5. Chen, L.C., Papandreou, G., Schroff, F., Adam, H.: Rethinking atrous convolution for semantic image segmentation. arXiv preprint arXiv:1706.05587 (2017)
6. Chen, L.: The topological approach to perceptual organization. Vis. Cogn. **12**(4), 553–637 (2005)
7. Deng, J., Dong, W., Socher, R., Li, L.J., Li, K., Li, F.F.: ImageNet: a large-scale hierarchical image database. In: CVPR (2009)
8. Deng, J., Guo, J., Xue, N., Zafeiriou, S.: ArcFace: additive angular margin loss for deep face recognition. arXiv preprint arXiv:1801.07698 (2018)
9. Eden, B., Adrian, P.: IL2M: class incremental learning with dual memory. In: ICCV (2019)
10. French, R.M.: Catastrophic forgetting in connectionist networks. Trends Cogn. Sci. **3**(4), 128–135 (1999)
11. He, K., Zhang, X., Ren, S., Sun, J.: Deep residual learning for image recognition. arXiv preprint arXiv:1512.03385 (2015)
12. Hinton, G., Vinyals, O., Dean, J.: Distilling the knowledge in a neural network. Comput. Sci. **14**(7), 38–39 (2015)
13. Hou, S., Pan, X., Loy, C.C., Wang, Z., Lin, D.: Learning a unified classifier incrementally via rebalancing. In: CVPR (2019)
14. Kirkpatrick, J., et al.: Overcoming catastrophic forgetting in neural networks. Proc. Nat. Acad. Sci. **114**(13), 3521–3526 (2017)
15. Krizhevsky, A., Hinton, G.: Learning multiple layers of features from tiny images. Tech. rep. Citeseer (2009)
16. Krizhevsky, A., Sutskever, I., Hinton, G.E.: ImageNet classification with deep convolutional neural networks. In: NeurIPS (2012)
17. Lee, S.W., Kim, J.H., Jun, J., Ha, J.W., Zhang, B.T.: Overcoming catastrophic forgetting by incremental moment matching. In: NeurIPS (2017)
18. Lee, S., Song, B.C.: Graph-based knowledge distillation by multi-head attention network. In: BMVC (2019)
19. Li, Z., Hoiem, D.: Learning without forgetting. T-PAMI **40**(12), 2935–2947 (2018)
20. Liu, W., Wen, Y., Yu, Z., Li, M., Raj, B., Song, L.: SphereFace: deep hypersphere embedding for face recognition. In: CVPR (2017)

21. Liu, Z., Sun, M., Zhou, T., Huang, G., Darrell, T.: Rethinking the value of network pruning. In: ICLR (2019)
22. Long, J., Shelhamer, E., Darrell, T.: Fully convolutional networks for semantic segmentation. In: CVPR (2015)
23. Lopez-Paz, D., et al.: Gradient episodic memory for continual learning. In: NeurIPS (2017)
24. Ma, Z., Wei, X., Hong, X., Gong, Y.: Bayesian loss for crowd count estimation with point supervision. In: ICCV (2019)
25. Mallya, A., Davis, D., Lazebnik, S.: Piggyback: adapting a single network to multiple tasks by learning to mask weights. In: Ferrari, V., Hebert, M., Sminchisescu, C., Weiss, Y. (eds.) ECCV 2018. LNCS, vol. 11208, pp. 72–88. Springer, Cham (2018). https://doi.org/10.1007/978-3-030-01225-0_5
26. Mallya, A., Lazebnik, S.: PackNet: adding multiple tasks to a single network by iterative pruning. In: CVPR (2018)
27. Maltoni, D., Lomonaco, V.: Continuous learning in single-incremental-task scenarios. arXiv preprint arXiv:1806.08568 (2018)
28. Martinetz, T.M.: Competitive Hebbian learning rule forms perfectly topology preserving maps. In: International Conference on Artificial Neural Networks, pp. 427–434 (1993)
29. Martinetz, T., Schulten, K.: Topology representing networks. Neural Netw. **7**(3), 507–522 (1994)
30. Parisi, G.I., Kemker, R., Part, J.L., Kanan, C., Wermter, S.: Continual lifelong learning with neural networks: a review. Neural Netw. **113**, 54–71 (2019)
31. Park, W., Kim, D., Lu, Y., Cho, M.: Relational knowledge distillation. In: CVPR (2019)
32. Rebuffi, S.A., Kolesnikov, A., Sperl, G., Lampert, C.H.: iCaRL: incremental classifier and representation learning. In: CVPR (2017)
33. Redmon, J., Divvala, S., Girshick, R., Farhadi, A.: You only look once: unified, real-time object detection. arXiv preprint arXiv:1506.02640 (2015)
34. Ren, S., He, K., Girshick, R., Sun, J.: Faster R-CNN: towards real-time object detection with region proposal networks. In: NeurIPS (2015)
35. Serrà, J., Suris, D., Miron, M., Karatzoglou, A.: Overcoming catastrophic forgetting with hard attention to the task. arXiv preprint arXiv:1801.01423 (2018)
36. Shin, H., Lee, J.K., Kim, J., Kim, J.: Continual learning with deep generative replay. In: NeurIPS (2017)
37. Tao, X., Hong, X., Chang, X., Dong, S., Xing, W., Yihong, G.: Few-shot class-incremental learning. In: CVPR (2020)
38. Tao, X., Hong, X., Chang, X., Gong, Y.: Bi-objective continual learning: learning 'new' while consolidating 'known'. In: AAAI, February 2020
39. Wei, N., Zhou, T., Zhang, Z., Zhuo, Y., Chen, L.: Visual working memory representation as a topological defined perceptual object. J. Vis. **19**(7), 1–12 (2019)
40. Wei, X., Zhang, Y., Gong, Y., Zhang, J., Zheng, N.: Grassmann pooling as compact homogeneous bilinear pooling for fine-grained visual classification. In: Ferrari, V., Hebert, M., Sminchisescu, C., Weiss, Y. (eds.) ECCV 2018. LNCS, vol. 11207, pp. 365–380. Springer, Cham (2018). https://doi.org/10.1007/978-3-030-01219-9_22
41. Wei, X., Zhang, Y., Gong, Y., Zheng, N.: Kernelized subspace pooling for deep local descriptors. In: CVPR (2018)
42. Wu, Y., et al.: Large scale incremental learning. In: CVPR (2019)
43. Yim, J., Joo, D., Bae, J., Kim, J.: A gift from knowledge distillation: fast optimization, network minimization and transfer learning. In: CVPR (2017)

44. Yoon, J., Yang, E., Lee, J., Hwang, S.J.: Lifelong learning with dynamically expandable networks. arXiv preprint arXiv:1708.01547 (2017)
45. Zenke, F., Poole, B., Ganguli, S.: Continual learning through synaptic intelligence. In: ICML (2017)
46. Zhai, M., Chen, L., Tung, F., He, J., Nawhal, M., Mori, G.: Lifelong GAN: continual learning for conditional image generation. In: ICCV (2019)
47. Zhuo, L., et al.: Cogradient descent for bilinear optimization. In: CVPR (2020)

Inter-Image Communication for Weakly Supervised Localization

Xiaolin Zhang$^{(\boxtimes)}$, Yunchao Wei, and Yi Yang

ReLER, AAII, University of Technology Sydney, Ultimo, Australia
Xiaolin.Zhang-3@student.uts.edu.au, {Yunchao.Wei,Yi.Yang}@uts.edu.au

Abstract. Weakly supervised localization aims at finding target object regions using only image-level supervision. However, localization maps extracted from classification networks are often not accurate due to the lack of fine pixel-level supervision. In this paper, we propose to leverage pixel-level similarities across different objects for learning more accurate object locations in a complementary way. Particularly, two kinds of constraints are proposed to prompt the consistency of object features within the same categories. The first constraint is to learn the stochastic feature consistency among discriminative pixels that are randomly sampled from different images within a batch. The discriminative information embedded in one image can be leveraged to benefit its counterpart with inter-image communication. The second constraint is to learn the global consistency of object features throughout the entire dataset. We learn a feature center for each category and realize the global feature consistency by forcing the object features to approach class-specific centers. The global centers are actively updated with the training process. The two constraints can benefit each other to learn consistent pixel-level features within the same categories, and finally improve the quality of localization maps. We conduct extensive experiments on two popular benchmarks, *i.e.*, ILSVRC and CUB-200-2011. Our method achieves the Top-1 localization error rate of 45.17% on the ILSVRC validation set, surpassing the current state-of-the-art method by a large margin. The code is available at https://github.com/xiaomengyc/I2C.

1 Introduction

Deep learning has achieved great success on various tasks, *e.g.*, classification [30,33], detection [13,26], segmentation [3,5,6,18,45] *et al.*In this paper, we focus on the Weakly Supervised Object Localization (WSOL) problem. Briefly, WSOL tries to locate object regions within given images using only image-level labels as supervision. Currently, the standard practice for this task is to train a convolutional classification network supervised by the given image-level labels. The convolutional operations can preserve relative positions of the input pixels so that activations from high-level layers can roughly indicate the position of target objects. Some previous works [42,43,46] have already explored how to produce object localization maps effectively. These methods obtain localization

© Springer Nature Switzerland AG 2020
A. Vedaldi et al. (Eds.): ECCV 2020, LNCS 12364, pp. 271–287, 2020.
https://doi.org/10.1007/978-3-030-58529-7_17

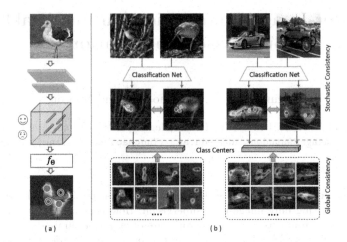

Fig. 1. (a) Convolutional operations preserve the relative pixel positions. Inconsistent response scores of different pixels on the class activation map are essentially caused by the inconsistent learned features. (b) The proposed Stochastic Consistency (SC) and Global Consistency (GC) are to align the object-related feature vectors. *Upper:* Pixel features of images sampled from the same category can reach consistency between the highly confident points within the same mini-batch. *Bottom:* We actively learn class-specific centers and push object features of the same category across different mini-batch towards the centers. (Color figure online)

maps by aggregating feature maps with a fully connected layer. Figure 1a shows the general pipeline for generating localization maps. Given an image of a bird, it is firstly fed into some convolution layers to yield the feature maps. These feature maps are then processed by a function f_Θ to get the localization maps of the right class using the methods in CAM [46], ACoL [42], ADL [8], *etc.*. Ideally, the localization maps are expected to highlight all the object regions and depress the background. Unfortunately, only some sparse parts are highlighted and cannot cover the entire target objects, which is a major problem in practice. We try to alleviate this issue based on the following intuition. Theoretically, for a specific output score of a pixel, the input features of the function f_Θ may be various. However, there are two observations in practice, *i.e.*, 1) convolution operations preserve the relative positions between the input and output feature maps [42,46]; 2) features of the same category objects tend to lie in the same clusters and similar input features produce similar output values [47]. Therefore, the root cause for this problem is that the network fails to learn consistent feature representations for pixels belonging to the object of interest. In Fig. 1a, the low response scores in the localization maps (pink circles) of the bird are caused by the low-quality or non-discriminative features in the intermediate feature maps, while the high response scores (orange dots) are produced by the decent and discriminative features. Several efforts have been taken to alleviate this issue. MDC [39] attempt to learn consistent features of different parts by enlarging receptive fields with dilated convolutions [4], but it is prone to draw into background noises. SPG [43] employs an auxiliary loss to enforce the consistency of object features using self-produced pseudo-masks as supervision. Nevertheless, the both methods only consider inter-pixel correlations within an image, and involve sophisticated network modules and many extra computational resources.

In this paper, we alleviate this issue by employing two constraints on the object pixels across images with the cost of negligible extra resources. Different from MDC and SPG, we argue that not only pixels within a object should keep close, but more importantly, object pixels of different images in the same category should also semantically keep consistent in the high-level feature space. In Fig. 1b, different parts of the same category objects $e.g.$, heads and bodies of the birds, the wheels and bodies of the vehicles, are highlighted in different images. The corresponding features of these highlighted pixels do not necessarily very close, but we force them to communicate with each other to learn more consistent and robust features, and thereby, produce better localization maps. We propose to realize the pixel-level communications by employing two constraints $i.e.$, Stochastic Consistency (SC) and Global Consistency (GC). The two constraints act as auxiliary loss functions to train classification networks. With the training process, convolution networks are not only looking for discriminative patterns to support the classification purpose, but communicating between different object patterns for learning more consistent and robust features. Consequently, more accurate object regions will be discovered as we desired. Specifically, the proposed SC is to constrain the object features of the same category within a batch. We firstly feed training images through a classification network for obtaining localization maps. Then, we select several confident seed points among the pixels with high scores in the maps. Finally, features of these seed pixels can communicate with each other across images within the same category. We attain the inter-image communication by optimizing the Euclidean distance between high-level features of the seed pixels. In Fig. 1b, given two images of the same class, different parts of the target objects are highlighted. Object features can reach consistencies by narrowing the distances between the seed points of different images. Notably, due to the lack of pixel annotations in our task, we firstly ascertain a portion of object pixels for each image. Pixels with high scores in localization maps usually lie in object regions with high confidence [42,43]. Meanwhile, it is also significant to avoid the influence from the background by only considering the confident object regions. Then, inter-image pixel-level communication can be explicitly accomplished.

Due to the limitation of the Stochastic Gradient Descent (SGD) optimization methodology, SC can only keep the semantic consistency within a batch. It cannot guarantee the class-specific consistency of the entire dataset. To tackle this issue, we further introduce the Global Consistency (GC) to augment SC by constraining images across the entire training set. As in Fig. 1b, image features are forced towards their class-specific global centers. In detail, the class-specific centers are actively maintained. We adopt a momentum strategy to update the class centers. During each training step, class-specific centers are updated using the seed features and memory centers. The ultimate goal of GC is to push object features approaching their global centers throughout the training set. GC constrains the object features across images. It is noticeable that the proposed SC constraint does not bring any extra parameters. GC brings a few parameters which is negligible compared to the backbone parameters.

We name the proposed method as Inter-Image Communication (I^2C) model. We conduct extensive experiments on the ILSVRC [9,27] and CUB-200-2011 [34] datasets. Our main contributions are three-fold:

- We propose to employ inter-image communication of objects in the same category for learning more robust and reliable localization maps under the supervision of image-level annotations.
- We propose two constraints. Stochastic consistency can keep the features of the same semantic within a batch close in the high-level feature space. Global consistency can learn a class-specific center for each category and keep the features of the same category close throughout the training set.
- This work achieves a new state-of-the-art with the localization error rate of Top-1 45.17% on the ILSVRC [9,27] validation set and 44.01% on the CUB-200-2011 [34] test set.

2   Related Work

Weakly supervised segmentation has a strong connection with our WSOL task [1,2,16,19,21,25,36–39]. It normally and firstly applies similar techniques to obtain pseudo masks, and then trains segmentation networks for predicting accurate masks. DD-Net [28] studies the method of generating pseudo masks from localization maps, and proposes to improve the accuracy by removing noises via self-supervised learning. OAA [19] accumulates localization maps with respect to different training epochs with the optimization process. ICD [12] utilizes an intra-class discriminator to learn better boundaries between classes. SEAM [35] proposes to use consistency regularization on predicted activation maps of various transforms as self-supervision for network learning.

Weakly supervised detection and localization aims to apply an alternative cheaper way by only using image-level supervision [11,23,24,31,48]. Recently, ADL [8] borrows the adversarial erasing idea from ACoL [42] to provide a more neat and powerful approach without bringing much more parameters and computational resources. CutMix [41] also explores the techniques of erasing patches of images. In addition to the erasing operation, CutMix mixes ground truth labels along with image patches. SEM [44] and [7] reformulate the evaluation of WSOL problem. SEM also proposes an enhancement alternative approach to produce high-quality localization maps.

3   Methodology

Figure 2 depicts the framework of the proposed approach. Given a pair of images (I_i^y, I_j^y) sharing the same category y, we firstly forward them to obtain high-level

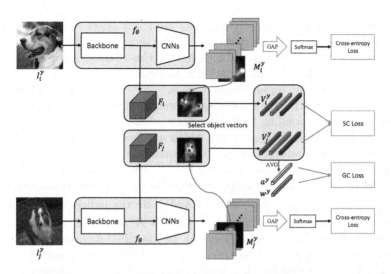

Fig. 2. The structure of the proposed approach. Given a pair of images (I_i^y, I_j^y) of the same category y, the localization maps (M_i^y, M_j^y) can be obtained by forwarding them through the classification network f_θ. Object seed vectors (V_i^y, V_j^y) are extracted from the high-level feature maps (F_i, F_j) according to the confident regions in the maps. Finally, the SC loss is employed on the object seed vectors. Also, the GC loss is employed on the averaged object feature a^y from a batch and the global class-specific center w^y. GAP refers to Global Average Pooling. AVG refers to the average operation.

feature maps (F_i, F_j) and localization maps (M_i^y, M_j^y). Then, we identify the reliable object regions according to the response scores in the produced localization maps. We randomly sample K representative seeds from the object regions. K object vectors of the seeds, denoted as (V_i^y, V_j^y), are extracted from the high-level feature maps (F_i, F_j) for each image according to the spatial localization. Next, we optimize the similarity between different object seed vectors using the Stochastic Consistency (SC) loss across images. Additionally, the Global Consistency (GC) loss is also employed to encourage the object representative vector of each minibatch to approach the global class-specific vector w^y throughout the training set. We will describe the details of constructing the object seed vectors, the SC and GC losses in the following sections.

3.1 Object Seed Vectors

Object seeds serve as the bridge for inter-image communication to narrow the distance between object pixels of the same category. Our target is to consistently high-light object pixels in localization maps, which is equivalent to get consistent high-level object features as the analysis in Sect. 1. The first obstacle we are facing is the lack of object pixel cues. Some previous works [36,42,43] employ a trade-off strategy of mining the confident object regions according to the scores in localization maps. We further randomly select some seed pixels as the object representation, and optimize the distance of the seeds across images. Such that intact object regions are high-lighted consistently, and robustness can be improved by exchanging information with different objects.

In detail, given an input image $I \in \mathbb{R}^{3 \times W_0 \times H_0}$ and its class label $y \in \{0, 1, ..., Y-1\}$, we pick out the localization map from the output of the last convolution layer corresponding to the category y following the simplified method in [42], where W_0 and H_0 denote the width and height of the image, Y is the number of total categories. Suppose the normalized map is $M^y \in [0, 1]^{W \times H}$ and the map before normalization is $M^{*y} \in \mathbb{R}^{W \times H}$, where W and H are the width and height of the localization map, we calculate the normalized map by following $M_{i,j}^y = \frac{M_{i,j}^{*y} - \min(M^{*y})}{\max(M^{*y}) - \min(M^{*y})}$, where i and j are the indices of the map. For each image in a batch, we extract $K \in [1, W \times H]$ object-related seeds within the object regions. The object regions can be identified according to the scores in the localization maps. To be specific, pixels whose corresponding values in localization maps are higher than a threshold $\delta \in (0, 1)$ are considered as reliable object regions. We randomly select K pixels from the object regions as the object representation seeds of the image I. We denote the object seed vectors as $V \in \mathbb{R}^{K \times D}$ which is extracted from high-level feature maps, where D is the dimension of the vectors, $i.e.$, the number of the channels in the feature maps. In this way, we finally obtain K vectors of the most discriminative object regions. Next, these vectors are employed to communicate with the other images in the same category.

3.2   Stochastic Consistency

Features of pixels belonging to the same category should be close. Although classification loss can drive networks to find the most discriminative patterns to produce correct classification scores, the learned features of the same objects are not necessarily similar due to the lack of pixel-level supervision. In other words, features between different pixels of objects are not consistent, which deviates from the requirement of highlighting integral object regions. We argue that more accurate localization maps can be obtained by keeping the consistency between features of objects in the same class. Object features of different images can communicate in a complementary approach, and thus the entire object regions can be consistently highlighted. We propose a Stochastic Constraint (SC) to drive the consistency of pixels from different objects of the same category in a minibatch. Given a batch $B = \{(I_i, y_i) | i = 0, 1, ..., N^B\}$ of randomly sampled images, we can find any two images I_i and I_j whose class labels are the same, namely, $y_i = y_j$, where N^B is the batch size. After forwarding them through the network, we obtain the object seed vectors according to Sect. 3.1. We denote the object seed features as $V_i \in \mathbb{R}^{K \times D}$ and $V_j \in \mathbb{R}^{K \times D}$, respectively. We expect the two images can communicate by explicitly constraining the pixels belonging to the same category. Particularly, we propose a constraint to optimize the L2-norm between the object features of I_i and I_j according to Eq. (1).

$$L_{sc} = \frac{1}{K} \sum_{k=0}^{K-1} ||v_i^k - v_j^k||_2^2, \tag{1}$$

where K is the number of randomly selected seeds, and $v^k \in \mathbb{R}^D$ is the k_{th} row of V. Thus, object features can communicate with each other across images in a batch, and influences from the background is not involved.

3.3 Global Consistency

Deep networks are trained with the SGD based optimization algorithms, *e.g.*, Adam [20], Adagrad [10] and RMSprop [14]. These methods construct mini-batches by randomly sampling images to perform training steps, which means SC can only constrain images within the same minibatch. To overcome this limitation, we propose to learn a global feature center for each category, so that features extracted from a batch can be optimized to approach the class-specific global centers. The object features of each class are hence gradually consistent with the global vectors.

We maintain a memory bank $W \in \mathbb{R}^{Y \times D}$. The y_{th} row of W denoted as w_y is the global center of category y. For each batch, we obtain one representation vector for each category by averaging the object seed vectors sharing the same class labels. Formally, we denote $B^y = \{(I_i, y_i)|y_i = y\}$ and $\{V_k^y|k = 0, 1, ..., K|B^y|\}$ as the class-specific subset and the object seed vectors corresponding to the category y in a batch , where $|B^y|$ is the image number in the subset B^y. We extract one representation vector a^y for category y from every minibatch. Formally, the representation vector a^y of class y in a batch is obtained according to Eq. (2).

$$a^y = \frac{1}{K|B^y|} \sum_{k=0}^{K|B^y|-1} V_k^y. \tag{2}$$

Global vector w_y *w.r.t.* class y in a minibatch is updated during each training step. We do *not* update the memory bank during the backward process. We propose a simple yet effective updating procedure for learning the memory matrix. For the class y, its global representation w_y is as in Eq. (3).

$$w^y = (1 - \eta_{t^y}^y)w^y + \eta_{t^y}^y a^y, 0 < \eta_{t^y}^y < 1, \tag{3}$$

where $\eta_{t^c}^c$ is the updating rate of the class y at step t^y. We adopt a class-specific updating rate as given in Eq. (4) for learning the global centers.

$$\eta_{t^y}^y = e^{-\alpha t^y}, 0 < \alpha < 1, \tag{4}$$

where t^y counts the updating steps of class y, and $\eta_{t^y}^y$ is the update rate of the class y at learning step t^y. Note the updating step t^y is also class-specific and maintained throughout the training process, because the updated counters of different categories are not the same due to the random sampling procedure of each batch. α is a hyper-parameter for decaying the learning rate of the global representation w^y. Thereby, w^y will be gradually stable with the training process.

The features of each batch can be optimized to approach the global representation as in Eq (5).

$$L_{gc} = \frac{1}{|Y^B|} \sum_{y \in Y^B} ||a^y - w^y||_2^2, \qquad (5)$$

where Y^B is the label set of the mini-batch.

We further apply a typical cross-entropy loss for classification and denote it as L_{cls}. In total, the optimization of our approach is a joint training process with three items following Eq. (6)

$$L = L_{cls} + \lambda_1 L_{sc} + \lambda_2 L_{gc}, \qquad (6)$$

where λ_1 and λ_2 are for trading-off the three loss items.

In *testing*, we simply feed testing images into the network, and obtain the localization maps *w.r.t.*the predicted class labels. The extracted localization map is then normalized and resized to the original size of the input image by the bilinear interpolation. Following the baseline methods [42,43,46], we leverage the same strategy in CAM [46] for generating the bounding boxes of the target objects. Specifically, we firstly binarize the localization maps by a threshold for separating the object regions from the background. Afterward, we draw tight bounding boxes that can cover the largest connected area of the foreground pixels. The thresholds for splitting the object regions are adjusted to the optimal values. For more details, please refer to [46].

4   Experiments

4.1   Experiment Setup

Datasets. We evaluate the proposed method following the previous methods, *e.g.*, CAM [46], ACoL [42], SPG [43] and ADL [8]. Two datasets, *i.e.*, ILSVRC [9, 27] and CUB-200-2011 [34] are applied to train classification networks for a fair comparison with the baselines. ILSVRC is a widely recognized large-scale classification dataset including 1.2 million images of 1,000 categories for training and 50,000 images for validation. Images in both the training and validation sets are well annotated with image categories and tight bounding boxes of objects. CUB-200-2011 [34] includes 11,788 images from 200 different species of birds. It is splitted into the training set of 5,994 images and the testing set of 5,794 images. Similarly, all images are annotated with class labels and tight bounding boxes. In our experiments, the proposed method is learned with the training sets using only image-level labels as supervision. The annotated bounding boxes on the validation set of ILSVRC and the testing set of CUB-200-2011 are employed for the evaluation.

Evaluation Metrics. We apply the recommended metric in [27] to evaluate the localization maps following the baseline algorithms [8,42,43,46]. To be specific, it calculates the percentage of the images that satisfy the following two conditions. First, the predicted classification labels match the ground-truth categories. Second, the predicted bounding boxes have over 50% IoU with at least one of the ground-truth boxes. In order to have a more explicit and pure comparison in localization ability, we calculate and compare the localization accuracy given ground-truth labels. We denote these results as the Gt-known localization accuracy. This Gt-known localization accuracy removes the influence of classification results and is much fairer in comparing the localization ability.

Implementation Details. We implement the proposed algorithm based on three popular backbone networks, *e.g.*VGG16 [30], ResNet50 [15] and InceptionV3 [33]. We make the same modifications on the networks to obtain localization maps following ACoL [42] and SPG [43]. We use the simplified method in ACoL [42] to produce localization maps, while the erasing branch is not applied. We enable the proposed constraints after finetuning the parameters for a few epoches to obtain a good initialization of the newly added parameters. In the ablation experiments, we compare a plain version network without SC and GC for comparison, named InceptionV3-plain. In order to assure that each batch contains images of the same category, we randomly draw 40 categories and then randomly sample two images from the selected categories, constructing the image batch size of 80. We apply multiple hyper-parameters *i.e.*, λ_1, λ_2, δ, α and K, and conduct extensive experiments for studying the impact of these variables. The global memory centers are randomly initialized. We set $\delta = 0.7$ following SPG [43].

4.2 Comparison with the State-of-the-Arts

ILSVRC. Table 1 compares the proposed method with various baselines on the ILSVRC validation set. I^2C surpasses all the baseline methods in Top-1 and Gt-known localization error. I^2C based on ResNet50 achieves the lowest error rate of 45.17%, significantly surpassing ADL by a large margin of 6.30%. It is notable ADL uses a stronger backbone network, *i.e.*, ResNet50-SE. I^2C based on InceptionV3 significantly surpasses the current state-of-the-art method, ADL, by 4.40%. The results based on VGG16 are also notably better than the currently reported results by 1.58% in Top-1. Additionally, the classification errors of our I^2C method are competitive with all the counterparts based on the same backbones. As demonstrated in Sect. 4.1, the Gt-known localization metric can reflect the pure localization ability regardless the affect from classification results. The proposed method achieves the best localization ability among the existing methods. The lowest Gt-known localization error of I^2C is 31.50%, outperforming the SPG approach by 3.81%. The I^2C model based on VGG16 achieves 36.10% in Gt-known localization error, which is also better than the counterparts.

Table 1. Comparison of the localization error rate on ILSVRC validation set. Classification error rates is also presented for reference.

Methods	Backbone	Loc Err.			Cls Err.	
		Top-1	Top-5	Gt-known	Top-1	Top-5
CAM [46]	AlexNet [22]	67.19	52.16	45.01	42.6	19.5
CAM [46]	GoogLeNet [32]	56.40	43.00	41.34	31.9	11.3
HaS-32 [31]	GoogLeNet [32]	54.53	–	39.43	32.5	–
ACoL [42]	GoogLeNet [32]	53.28	42.58	–	29.0	11.8
DANet [40]	GoogLeNet [30]	52.47	41.72	–	27.5	8.6
Backprop [29]	VGG16 [30]	61.12	51.46	–	–	
CAM [46]	VGG16 [30]	57.20	45.14	–	31.2	11.4
CutMix [41]	VGG16 [30]	56.55	–	–	–	–
ADL [8]	VGG16 [30]	55.08	–	–	32.2	–
ACoL [42]	VGG16 [30]	54.17	**40.57**	37.04	32.5	12.0
I^2C-Ours	VGG16 [30]	**52.59**	41.49	**36.10**	30.6	10.7
CAM [46]	ResNet50-SE [15,17]	53.81	–	–	23.44	–
CutMix [41]	ResNet50 [15]	52.75	–	–	21.4	5.92
ADL [8]	ResNet50-SE [15,17]	51.47	–	–	24.15	–
I^2C-Ours	ResNet50 [15]	**45.17**	**35.40**	**31.50**	23.3	6.9
CAM [46]	InceptionV3 [33]	53.71	41.81	37.32	26.7	8.2
SPG [43]	InceptionV3 [33]	51.40	40.00	35.31	30.3	9.9
ADL [8]	InceptionV3 [33]	51.29	–	–	27.2	–
I^2C-Ours	InceptionV3 [33]	**46.89**	**35.87**	**31.50**	26.7	8.4

CUB. We implement the proposed method on the CUB-200-2011 dataset following the baseline methods, e.g., ACoL [42], SPG [43] and CAM [46]. InceptionV3 is chosen as the backbone network following [8,43]. Table 2 compares our method with the baselines. I^2C surpasses all the baseline methods on both Top-1 and Top-5 metrics, yielding the accuracies of Top-1 44.01% and Top-5 31.66% and significantly outperforming the current reported state-of-the-art errors by 2.95% in Top-1 and 6.38% in Top-5.

Visualization. In Fig. 3, we compare localization maps and the corresponding bounding boxes between the proposed method and ACoL [42]. We can observe that localization maps produced by I^2C can accurately highlight the object regions of interest. The proposed method can not only reduce the noises from the irrelevant objects or stuff in the background regions, but find more object-related regions accurately.

Table 2. Localization error on the CUB-200-2011 test set. I^2C significantly surpasses all the baselines.

Methods	Top-1	Top-5
CAM [46]	56.33	46.47
ACoL [42]	54.08	43.49
SPG [43]	53.36	42.28
DANet [40]	47.48	38.04
ADL [8]	46.96	–
I^2C-Ours	**44.01**	**31.66**

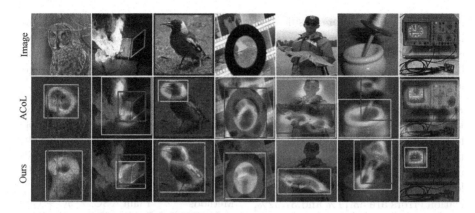

Fig. 3. Comparison of the predicted bounding boxes with ACoL [42]. Our method obtains better localization maps and better bounding boxes. *The predicted boxes are in green and the ground-truth boxes are in red.* (Color figure online)

As a result, it is easy to draw bounding boxes which can better match the target object regions as shown in Fig. 3.

In summary, our method can successfully obtain better localization maps and accurate bounding boxes. I^2C surpasses all the baseline methods on both ILSVRC and CUB-200-2011. We believe that there are two aspects accounting for the success of I^2C. First, the proposed two constraints can retain pixel-level consistent between object features of different images, so that images can benefit from each other to obtain better localization maps. Second, I^2 can not only increase the localization accuracy, but can get competitive classification results.

4.3 Ablation Study

In this section, we analyse the insights and effectiveness of the different modules in the proposed method. We conduct the ablation experiments based on InceptionV3. The experiments are on the most convincing large-scale dataset *i.e.*, ILSVRC, with the input resolution of 320 by 320, unless specifically specified. When testing the classification and localization results, we do *NOT* apply the ten-crop operation to enhance classification accuracies for convenience.

Table 3. Gt-known localization error with different input resolutions. Enlarging input resolution slightly improve the localization on ILSVRC, while dramatically boost the localization performance on CUB.

DataSet	Resolution	Gt-known
ILSVRC	224×224	31.50
	320×320	31.04
CUB	224×224	27.40
	320×320	22.99

Does Input Resolution Affect the Localization Ability? Table 3 depicts the Gt-known localization errors *w.r.t.* different resolutions of input images. We exclude the influences of classification results by comparing the Gt-known localization errors. We see that enlarging the resolutions can decrease the localization errors with other configuration unchanged. For ILSVRC, the gain is slight of only 0.46%, Dislike ILSVRC, CUB is more sensitive to the resolution of input images and the Gt-known error drops significantly by 4.41%.

Are SC and GC Really Effective? Table 4 compares the localization errors of the proposed constraints to the plain version network. When using only the cross-entropy loss, the localization and the Gt-known localization errors are 53.71% and 37.32%, respectively. After adding the SC constraint, the localization accuracy is significantly improved and the error rate drops to 49.07%. The Gt-known

Table 4. Localization error on ILSVRC validation set using different configurations of the proposed constraints. (∗ indicates the numbers obtained with the classification results using the ten-crop operation.)

Methods	Plain	SC	SC + GC
Loc	53.71*	49.07	**48.08**
Gt-known Loc	37.32	31.63	**31.04**

localization error also decreases to 31.63% by a large margin of 5.69%. Furthermore, the localization performance can be boosted with the GC constraint. By adding the proposed two constraints simultaneously, the localization and Gt-known errors can finally be reduced to 48.45% and 31.30%, respectively. Moreover, to verify the superiority of the proposed updating strategy in GC, we conduct an experiment of updating the global memory matrix with the back-propagation process. The localization accuracies of such an updating method obtains 49.03% and 32.09% in localization and Gt-known error rates, respectively. The back-propagation updating strategy is worse than the proposed updating strategy. Moreover, although the global constraint introduces a vector for each class, these vectors only involve negligible computational resources. In particular, the number of parameters for the backbone network is 27M (InceptionV3). GC only increase 0.8M parameters by 2.9%. During the forward stage of training, the Flops is 21.42G. GC only gain 3K Flops which can be totally ignored. SC does not involve extra Flops nor parameters. During the testing phase, neither SC nor GC involve any extra Flops.

Is I^2C Sensitive to λ_1, λ_2 and K? λ_1 controls the relative importance of SC in training. In order to maximize the performance of the proposed method and study the robustness to λ_1, we test the localization accuracy $w.r.t.$ various values of λ_1. We remove the GC constraint and only add the SC constraint. Figure 5a illustrates the classification error, localization error and Gt-known localization errors when λ_1 changes in 40 times of scale from 0.002 to 0.08. We obtain the best results of 29.24%, 49.07% and 31.63% and the worst results of 32.13%, 50.82% and 34.44% in terms of the classification, localization and Gt-known localization error, respectively. In general, with the increase of λ_1, the classification ability is getting better while Gt. localization is getting worse. The localization errors with respect to the predicted labels achieve the best value of 49.07% at 0.008, because only the generated bounding boxes are counted as correct hits when the predicted labels of classification meet the ground-truth labels in this criterion.

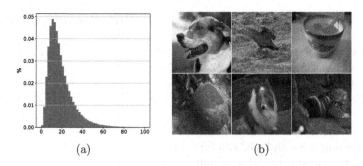

(a)   (b)

Fig. 4. *(a)*: histogram of the number of object pixels with the threshold of 0.7 on the ILSVRC training set. *(b)*: identified object regions (in magenta) according to the localization maps (Color figure online)

It is notable that the gap between the best and worst values of the localization error is *only* 1.75% *over the changes of* 40 *times in* λ_1, which means the proposed method is quite robust to the values of λ_1.

λ_2 controls the relative importance of GC in training. According to Fig. 5a, we leverage the best value of $\lambda_1 = 0.008$ to study the performance with λ_2 changing from 0.0001 to 0.1. Figure 5b shows the accuracies of the proposed model adding both SC and GC. The classification errors remain stable at around 30% after applying GC. The localization accuracy achieve lower error rates of 48.07% compared to only using SC, which reflects the effectiveness of the proposed global consistency strategy. As for the Gt-known localization metric, the error rates decrease to 31.04% by adding GC. It is also notable that the model is robust to the change of the hyper-parameter λ_2 in *a large range of 1,000 times from* 0.0001 *to* 0.1. The localization error *only fluctuates within a range of 0.96%*.

K is the number of the chosen object seeds. For an input image with the resolution of 320 by 320, the networks downsample the resolution by a factor of 8 and obtain the corresponding localization maps of 40 by 40 with 1600 pixels. Following the recommended threshold in SPG [43], we set the threshold δ to 0.7 for discovering the object regions in each image. Figure 4 illustrates the histogram of the number of the identified object pixels on the ILSVRC training set. We observe that most of the images contain object pixels in the range from 1 to 60. Particularly, we choose $K = \{3, 20, 40, 60, 80, 100\}$ to study the performance changes with the variant number of sampled representative pixels in each image. Figure 5c shows the classification and localization accuracies with different K values. The classification error is lower when the number of sampled pixels is relatively larger. The classification error rate reaches the lowest point of 28.40% at $K = 60$. On the contrary, the localization error increases when we adopt a larger value of K, and the localization error is lowest at $K = 3$.

We believe the reason for this phenomenon is that the larger number may include more noises in the sampled object pixels, and more sampled pixels implicitly make the constraints stronger. The proposed I^2C is robust to the change of seed numbers, and *the localization accuracy only fluctuates within a small range of 0.46% with K changing of 33 times from 3 to 100.*

In total, we can summarize that the improvement of the proposed method mainly attribute to three aspects. First, SC can semantically drive the consistency between the object features in a batch, which improves the localization maps. Second, GC can further drive the consistency throughout the entire dataset by forcing the object features towards their class-specific centers. Third, the proposed updating strategy can effectively learn the class-specific centers with the training process. Also, we have studied the robustness of the hyper-parameters. λ_1 and λ_2 are for balancing the costs of SC and GC. The experiment results show that the network performs superiorly in a very large range. In addition, according to the changes of the

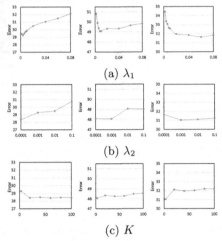

(a) λ_1

(b) λ_2

(c) K

Fig. 5. Classification (*left*), localization (*middle*) and Gt-known Loc (*right*) error rates with the changes of hyper-parameters, *i.e.*, λ_1, λ_2 and K.

localization performance *w.r.t.* the change of K. We can obtain satisfied accuracies just selecting a small value of K, *e.g.*, $K = 3$.

5 Conclusion

We propose an Inter-Image Communication approach (I^2C) to improve the accuracy of localization maps through training classification networks. First, we randomly select several object seeds according to the activated area of localization maps. These seed points are further employed to extract representation vectors of class-specific objects. Second, the extracted vectors are leveraged to communicate between different objects of the same classes. Concretely, stochastic consistency (SC) is proposed to optimize the objects within a mini-batch. Global consistency (GC) is designed to keep consistency across minibatchs. Also, a strategy is applied to update the global memory matrix. Finally, the proposed I^2C approach achieves the Top-1 localization error rate of 45.17% on the ILSVRC validation set, surpassing the current state-of-the-art method.

Acknowledgement. This work is partially supported by ARC DECRA DE190101315 and ARC DP200100938. Xiaolin Zhang (No. 201606180026) is partially supported by the Chinese Scholarship Council.

References

1. Ahn, J., Cho, S., Kwak, S.: Weakly supervised learning of instance segmentation with inter-pixel relations. In: IEEE CVPR, pp. 2209–2218 (2019)

2. Ahn, J., Kwak, S.: Learning pixel-level semantic affinity with image-level supervision for weakly supervised semantic segmentation. In: IEEE CVPR, pp. 4981–4990 (2018)
3. Chen, L.C., Papandreou, G., Kokkinos, I., Murphy, K., Yuille, A.L.: Semantic image segmentation with deep convolutional nets and fully connected CRFs. preprint arXiv:1412.7062 (2014)
4. Chen, L.C., Papandreou, G., Kokkinos, I., Murphy, K., Yuille, A.L.: DeepLab: semantic image segmentation with deep convolutional nets, atrous convolution, and fully connected CRFs. IEEE TPAMI **40**(4), 834–848 (2017)
5. Chen, L.C., Zhu, Y., Papandreou, G., Schroff, F., Adam, H.: Encoder-decoder with atrous separable convolution for semantic image segmentation. arXiv preprint arXiv:1802.02611 (2018)
6. Cheng, B., et al.: SPGNet: semantic prediction guidance for scene parsing. In: IEEE ICCV, pp. 5218–5228 (2019)
7. Choe, J., Oh, S.J., Lee, S., Chun, S., Akata, Z., Shim, H.: Evaluating weakly supervised object localization methods right. In: Proceedings of the IEEE/CVF Conference on Computer Vision and Pattern Recognition, pp. 3133–3142 (2020)
8. Choe, J., Shim, H.: Attention-based dropout layer for weakly supervised object localization. In: IEEE CVPR, June 2019
9. Deng, J., Dong, W., Socher, R., Li, L.J., Li, K., Fei-Fei, L.: ImageNet: a large-scale hierarchical image database. In: IEEE CVPR, pp. 248–255 (2009)
10. Duchi, J., Hazan, E., Singer, Y.: Adaptive subgradient methods for online learning and stochastic optimization. JMLR **12**, 2121–2159 (2011)
11. Durand, T., Mordan, T., Thome, N., Cord, M.: WILDCAT: weakly supervised learning of deep convnets for image classification, pointwise localization and segmentation. In: IEEE CVPR, pp. 642–651 (2017)
12. Fan, J., Zhang, Z., Song, C., Tan, T.: Learning integral objects with intra-class discriminator for weakly-supervised semantic segmentation. In: IEEE CVPR, June 2020
13. Girshick, R.: Fast R-CNN. arXiv preprint arXiv:1504.08083 (2015)
14. Graves, A.: Generating sequences with recurrent neural networks. arXiv preprint arXiv:1308.0850 (2013)
15. He, K., Zhang, X., Ren, S., Sun, J.: Deep residual learning for image recognition. In: IEEE CVPR, pp. 770–778 (2016)
16. Hou, Q., Jiang, P., Wei, Y., Cheng, M.M.: Self-erasing network for integral object attention. In: NIPS, pp. 549–559 (2018)
17. Hu, J., Shen, L., Sun, G.: Squeeze-and-excitation networks. In: IEEE CVPR, pp. 7132–7141 (2018)
18. Huang, Z., et al.: CCNet: criss-cross attention for semantic segmentation. IEEE TPAMI (2020)
19. Jiang, P.T., Hou, Q., Cao, Y., Cheng, M.M., Wei, Y., Xiong, H.K.: Integral object mining via online attention accumulation. In: IEEE ICCV, pp. 2070–2079 (2019)
20. Kingma, D.P., Ba, J.: Adam: a method for stochastic optimization. arXiv preprint arXiv:1412.6980 (2014)
21. Kolesnikov, A., Lampert, C.H.: Seed, expand and constrain: three principles for weakly-supervised image segmentation. In: Leibe, B., Matas, J., Sebe, N., Welling, M. (eds.) ECCV 2016. LNCS, vol. 9908, pp. 695–711. Springer, Cham (2016). https://doi.org/10.1007/978-3-319-46493-0_42
22. Krizhevsky, A., Sutskever, I., Hinton, G.E.: ImageNet classification with deep convolutional neural networks. In: NIPS, pp. 1097–1105 (2012)

23. Liang, X., Liu, S., Wei, Y., Liu, L., Lin, L., Yan, S.: Towards computational baby learning: a weakly-supervised approach for object detection. In: IEEE ICCV, pp. 999–1007 (2015)
24. Oquab, M., Bottou, L., Laptev, I., Sivic, J.: Is object localization for free?-Weakly-supervised learning with convolutional neural networks. In: IEEE CVPR, pp. 685–694 (2015)
25. Papandreou, G., Chen, L.C., Murphy, K., Yuille, A.L.: Weakly-and semi-supervised learning of a DCNN for semantic image segmentation. In: IEEE ICCV (2015)
26. Ren, S., He, K., Girshick, R., Sun, J.: Faster R-CNN: towards real-time object detection with region proposal networks. In: NIPS, pp. 91–99 (2015)
27. Russakovsky, O., et al.: ImageNet large scale visual recognition challenge. Int. J. Comput. Vis. **115**(3), 211–252 (2015). https://doi.org/10.1007/s11263-015-0816-y
28. Shimoda, W., Yanai, K.: Distinct class-specific saliency maps for weakly supervised semantic segmentation. In: Leibe, B., Matas, J., Sebe, N., Welling, M. (eds.) ECCV 2016. LNCS, vol. 9908, pp. 218–234. Springer, Cham (2016). https://doi.org/10.1007/978-3-319-46493-0_14
29. Simonyan, K., Vedaldi, A., Zisserman, A.: Deep inside convolutional networks: visualising image classification models and saliency maps. arXiv preprint arXiv:1312.6034 (2013)
30. Simonyan, K., Zisserman, A.: Very deep convolutional networks for large-scale image recognition. In: ICLR (2015)
31. Singh, K.K., Lee, Y.J.: Hide-and-seek: forcing a network to be meticulous for weakly-supervised object and action localization. arXiv preprint arXiv:1704.04232 (2017)
32. Szegedy, C., et al.: Going deeper with convolutions. In: IEEE CVPR, pp. 1–9 (2015)
33. Szegedy, C., Vanhoucke, V., Ioffe, S., Shlens, J., Wojna, Z.: Rethinking the inception architecture for computer vision. In: IEEE CVPR, pp. 2818–2826 (2016)
34. Wah, C., Branson, S., Welinder, P., Perona, P., Belongie, S.: The Caltech-UCSD Birds-200-2011 Dataset. Tech. Rep. CNS-TR-2011-001, California Institute of Technology (2011)
35. Wang, Y., Zhang, J., Kan, M., Shan, S., Chen, X.: Self-supervised equivariant attention mechanism for weakly supervised semantic segmentation. In: IEEE/CVF Conference on Computer Vision and Pattern Recognition (CVPR), June 2020
36. Wei, Y., Feng, J., Liang, X., Cheng, M.M., Zhao, Y., Yan, S.: Object region mining with adversarial erasing: a simple classification to semantic segmentation approach. In: IEEE CVPR (2017)
37. Wei, Y., et al.: Learning to segment with image-level annotations. PR **59**, 234–244 (2016)
38. Wei, Y., et al.: STC: a simple to complex framework for weakly-supervised semantic segmentation. IEEE TPAMI **39**(11), 2314–2320 (2016)
39. Wei, Y., Xiao, H., Shi, H., Jie, Z., Feng, J., Huang, T.S.: Revisiting dilated convolution: a simple approach for weakly-and semi-supervised semantic segmentation. In: IEEE CVPR, pp. 7268–7277 (2018)
40. Xue, H., Liu, C., Wan, F., Jiao, J., Ji, X., Ye, Q.: DANet: divergent activation for weakly supervised object localization. In: IEEE ICCV, pp. 6589–6598 (2019)
41. Yun, S., Han, D., Oh, S.J., Chun, S., Choe, J., Yoo, Y.: CutMix: regularization strategy to train strong classifiers with localizable features. In: IEEE ICCV, pp. 6023–6032 (2019)
42. Zhang, X., Wei, Y., Feng, J., Yang, Y., Huang, T.: Adversarial complementary learning for weakly supervised object localization. In: IEEE CVPR (2018)

43. Zhang, X., Wei, Y., Kang, G., Yang, Y., Huang, T.: Self-produced guidance for weakly-supervised object localization. In: Ferrari, V., Hebert, M., Sminchisescu, C., Weiss, Y. (eds.) ECCV 2018. LNCS, vol. 11216, pp. 610–625. Springer, Cham (2018). https://doi.org/10.1007/978-3-030-01258-8_37
44. Zhang, X., Wei, Y., Yang, Y., Wu, F.: Rethinking localization map: towards accurate object perception with self-enhancement maps. arXiv preprint arXiv:2006.05220 (2020)
45. Zhao, H., Shi, J., Qi, X., Wang, X., Jia, J.: Pyramid scene parsing network. In: IEEE CVPR, pp. 2881–2890 (2017)
46. Zhou, B., Khosla, A., A., L., Oliva, A., Torralba, A.: Learning Deep Features for Discriminative Localization. In: IEEE CVPR (2016)
47. Zhou, B., Bau, D., Oliva, A., Torralba, A.: Interpreting deep visual representations via network dissection. IEEE TPAMI **41**(9), 2131–2145 (2018)
48. Zhu, Y., Zhou, Y., Ye, Q., Qiu, Q., Jiao, J.: Soft proposal networks for weakly supervised object localization. arXiv preprint arXiv:1709.01829 (2017)

UFO²: A Unified Framework Towards Omni-supervised Object Detection

Zhongzheng Ren[1,2(✉)], Zhiding Yu[2], Xiaodong Yang[2], Ming-Yu Liu[2], Alexander G. Schwing[1], and Jan Kautz[2]

[1] University of Illinois at Urbana-Champaign, Champaign, USA
zr5@illinois.edu
[2] NVIDIA, Santa Clara, USA

Abstract. Existing work on object detection often relies on a single form of annotation: the model is trained using either accurate yet costly bounding boxes or cheaper but less expressive image-level tags. However, real-world annotations are often diverse in form, which challenges these existing works. In this paper, we present UFO², a unified object detection framework that can handle different forms of supervision simultaneously. Specifically, UFO² incorporates strong supervision (*e.g.*, boxes), various forms of partial supervision (*e.g.*, class tags, points, and scribbles), and unlabeled data. Through rigorous evaluations, we demonstrate that each form of label can be utilized to either train a model from scratch or to further improve a pre-trained model. We also use UFO² to investigate budget-aware omni-supervised learning, *i.e.*, various annotation policies are studied under a fixed annotation budget: we show that competitive performance needs no strong labels for all data. Finally, we demonstrate the generalization of UFO², detecting more than 1,000 different objects without bounding box annotations.

Keywords: Omni-supervised · Weakly-supervised · Object detection

1 Introduction

State-of-the-art object detection methods benefit greatly from supervised data, which comes in the form of bounding boxes on many datasets. However, annotating images with bounding boxes is time-consuming and hence expensive. To ease this dependence on expensive annotations, '*omni-supervised learning*' [40] has been proposed: models should be trained via all types of available labeled data plus internet-scale sources of unlabeled data.

Z. Ren and X. Yang—Work partially done at NVIDIA.

Electronic supplementary material The online version of this chapter (https://doi.org/10.1007/978-3-030-58529-7_18) contains supplementary material, which is available to authorized users.

A. Vedaldi et al. (Eds.): ECCV 2020, LNCS 12364, pp. 288–313, 2020.
https://doi.org/10.1007/978-3-030-58529-7_18

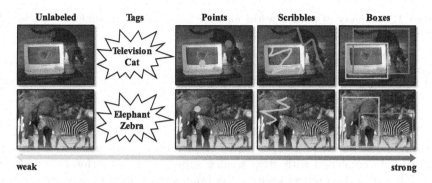

Fig. 1. Illustrative example of the supervision hierarchy.

Omni-supervised learning is particularly beneficial in practice. Compared to the enormous amounts of visual data uploaded to the internet (*e.g.*, over 100 million photos uploaded to Instagram every day [1]; 300 hours of new video on YouTube each minute [2]), fully-annotated training data remains a negligible fraction. Most data is either unlabeled, or comes with a diverse set of weak labels. Hence, directly leveraging web data often requires handling labels that are incomplete, inexact, or even incorrect (noisy).

Towards the goal of handling real-world messy data, we aim to study omni-supervised *object detection* where a plethora of unlabeled, partially labeled (with image-level class tags, points, or scribbles), and strongly labeled (with bounding boxes) images are utilized to train detection models. Examples of the considered supervisions are shown in Fig. 1. Designing a framework for omni-supervised detection is non-trivial. A big challenge is the conflict of the different architectures that have been proposed for each annotation. To address this issue, prior work either ensembles different networks trained from different annotations [25,55] or uses iterative knowledge distillation [37,50]. However, the conflict between different modules remains as it is largely addressed in a post-processing step.

In contrast, we propose UFO^2, a unified omni-supervised object detection framework that addresses the above challenges with a principled and computationally efficient solution. To the best of our knowledge, the proposed framework is the first to simultaneously handle direct supervision, various forms of partial supervision, and unlabeled data for object detection. UFO^2 (1) integrates a **unified task head** which handles various forms of supervision (Sect. 3.1), and (2) incorporates a **proposal refinement** module that utilizes the localization information contained in the labels to restrict the assignment of object candidates to class labels (Sect. 3.2). Importantly, the model is **end-to-end trainable**.

We note that assessing the efficacy of the proposed approach is non-trivial. Partial labels are hardly available in popular object detection data [30]. We thus create a simulated set of partial annotations, whose labels are synthesized to closely mimic human annotator behavior (Sect. 4). We then conduct rigorous evaluations to show that: (1) each type of label can be effectively uti-

Table 1. Summary of related works for object detection using different labels. (B: boxes, T: tags, P: points, S: scribbles, U: unlabeled.)

B	T	P	S	B+U	B+T	B+T+P+S+U
[13,17,27,31,41,43]	[6,45,53,62]	[34,35]	None	[9,40,47]	[14,22,42,55,59]	UFO^2 (ours)

lized to either train a model from scratch or to boost the performance of an existing model (Sect. 5.1); (2) a model trained on a small portion of strongly labeled data combined with other weaker supervision can perform comparably to a fully-supervised model under a fixed annotation budget, suggesting a better annotation strategy in practice (Sect. 5.4); (3) the proposed model can be seamlessly generalized to utilize large-scale classification (only tags are used) data. This permits to scale the detection model to more than 1,000 categories (Appendix A).

2   Related Work

In the following we first discuss related works for each single supervision type. Afterwards we introduce prior works to jointly leverage multiple labels for visual tasks. Training data usage of prior object detection works are given in Table 1.

Object Detection. Object detection has been one of the most fundamental problems in computer vision research. Early works [13] focus on designing hand-crafted features and multi-stage pipelines to solve the problem. Recently, Deep Neural Nets (DNNs) have greatly improved the performance and simplified the frameworks. Girshick *et al.* [16,17] leverage DNNs to classify and refine pre-computed object proposals. However, those methods are slow during inference because the proposals need to be computed online using time-consuming classical methods [56,65]. To alleviate this issue, researchers have designed DNNs that learn to generate proposals [20,43] or one-shot object detectors [31,41]. Recently, top-down solutions have emerged, re-formulating detection as key-point estimation [27]. These methods achieve impressive results. However, to train these methods, supervision in the form of accurate localization information (bounding boxes) for each object is required. Collecting this supervision is not only costly in terms of time and money, but also prevents detectors from generalizing to new environments with scarce labeled data.

Weakly-supervised Learning. Weak labels in the form of image-level category tags are studied in various tasks [26,36,49,63]. For object detection, existing works [6,45,53,60] formulate a multiple instance learning task: the input image acts as a bag of pre-computed proposals [3,56,65] and several most representative proposals are picked as detections. Bilen and Vedaldi [6] are among the first to implement the above idea in an end-to-end trainable DNN. Follow-up works boost the performance by including extra information, such as spatial relations [39,45,62] or context information [24,45]. In addition, better optimization strategies like curriculum learning [61], self-taught learning [23], and iterative refinement [15,39,48] have shown success. However, due to the limited representation ability of weak labels, these methods often suffer from two issues: (1) they cannot differentiate multiple instances of the same class when instances are spatially close; (2) they tend to focus on the most discriminative parts of an object instead of its full extent. This suggests that training object detectors solely from weak labels is not satisfactory and motivates to study a hybrid approach.

Partially-supervised Learning. Points and scribbles are two user-friendly ways of interacting with machines. Thus they are widely used in various visual tasks such as semantic segmentation [4,29,58], instance segmentation [64], and image synthesis [38]. From a data annotation perspective, these partial labels are easier to acquire than labeling bounding boxes or masks [29]. However, partial labels are in general understudied in object detection. A few examples on this topic include Papadopoulos *et al.* [34,35] which collect click annotation for the VOC [12] dataset and train an object detector through iterative multiple instance learning. Different from their approach, however, we propose an end-to-end trainable framework and evaluate on more challenging data [18,30].

Semi-supervised Learning. Semi-supervised learning [8,33,46] aims to augment the limited annotated training set with large-scale unlabeled data to boost the performance. Recent approaches [5,32,46,54,57,66,67] on classification often utilize unlabeled data through self-training combined with various regularization techniques including consistency regularization through data augmentation [5,54,57], entropy minimization [28,32], and weight decay [5]. In this paper, we adopt the entropy regularization [32] and pseudo-labeling [28] methods to efficiently utilize unlabeled data.

For object detection, Rosenberg *et al.* [47] demonstrate that self-training is still effective. Ensemble methods [5,40] and representation learning [9,11,19,44] are shown to be useful. Nevertheless, these methods are heavily pipelined and usually assume existence of a portion of strong labels to initialize the teacher model. In contrast, our UFO^2 learns from an arbitrary combination of either strong or partial labels and unlabeled data, it is unified and end-to-end trainable.

Omni-supervised Learning. Omni-supervised learning is a more general case of semi-supervised learning in the sense that several types of available labels are mixed to train visual models jointly. Xu *et al.* [58] develop a non-deep learning method to jointly utilize image tags, partial supervision, and unlabeled data for semantic segmentation and perform competitively. Chéron *et al.* [10] extend this idea to video data by training an action localization network using various labels. However, their method cannot deal with unlabeled data.

For object detection, prior works [14,22,42,55,59] have studied to combine bounding boxes and image tags. However, these methods are either pipelined and iterative [14,22,55] or require extra activity labels and human bounding boxes

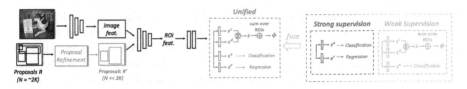

Fig. 2. The UFO^2 framework: green modules are newly proposed in this paper. (Color figure online)

to guide the detection [59]. Compared to those works, the proposed framework can handle more types of labels and, importantly, our proposed approach is end-to-end trainable.

3 UFO^2

We aim to solve omni-supervised object detection: a single object detector is learned jointly from various forms of labeled and unlabeled data. Formally, the training dataset contains two parts: an unlabeled set $\mathcal{U} = (u_i; i \in \{1, \ldots, |\mathcal{U}|\})$ and a labeled set $\mathcal{X} = (x_i; i \in \{1, \ldots, |\mathcal{X}|\})$. Each x_i is associated with one annotated label coming in one of the following four forms: (1) accurate bounding boxes, (2) a single point on the object, (3) a scribble overlaying the object in some form, or (4) image-level class tags. Note, for the first three forms of annotations we also know the semantic class. In this paper, we make **no assumptions on labels**: every form of label can make up any fraction of the training data. This is in contrast to most prior work on mixed supervision [14,42,55,59] which assumes a certain amount of strongly labeled data (bounding boxes) is always available.

Since each form of annotation has been separately studied in prior work, different frameworks have been specifically tailored for each annotation. In contrast, we present a novel unified framework UFO^2 which inherits merits of prior single supervision methods and permits to exploit arbitrary combinations of labeled and unlabeled data as shown in Fig. 2. We introduce the specific solution to handle each supervision in Sect. 3.1. We further devise an improved proposal refinement module [16,43] so as to incorporate localization information in partial labels (see Sect. 3.2).

3.1 Unified Model

As shown in Fig. 2, for a labeled input image $x \in \mathcal{X}$ or an unlabeled $u \in \mathcal{U}$, convolutional layers from an ImageNet pre-trained neural network are used to extract image features. A set of pre-computed object proposals R is refined to the set R' and then used to generate ROI features through ROI-Pooling [20]. Note that not all the proposals are used since they are usually redundant. We discuss our refinement technique in Sect. 3.2. In our proposed model, the ROI features are processed via several intermediate layers followed by a new task head as shown in Fig. 2 (center, green), which differs from classical methods.

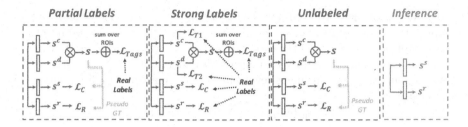

Fig. 3. Task head behavior for training (w/ partial, strong, or no labels), and inference.

Classical Methods. In strongly supervised frameworks [16,43], the task head consists of two fully-connected layers to produce the classification logits $s^s(r, c) \in \mathbb{R}$ for every region $r \in R'$ and class $c \in C$, and the region coordinates $s^r(r) \in \mathbb{R}^4$ for every region $r \in R'$ for bounding box regression. This is highlighted via a blue box in Fig. 2.

In weakly-supervised frameworks [6,45,53] which handle image-level tags, the task head contains three fully-connected layers to produce a class confidence score $s^c(r, c) \in \mathbb{R}$, an objectness score $s^d(r, c) \in \mathbb{R}$, and similarly, classification logits $s^s(r, c) \in \mathbb{R}$ for every region $r \in R'$ and class $c \in C$ (Fig. 2 yellow box). The class confidence score $s^c(r, c)$ and objectness score $s^d(r, c)$ are first normalized via:

$$s^c(r, c) = \frac{\exp s^c(r, c)}{\sum_{c \in C} \exp s^c(r, c)}, \text{ and } s^d(r, c) = \frac{\exp s^d(r, c)}{\sum_{r \in R} \exp s^d(r, c)}. \quad (1)$$

They are then used for image-level classification. Also, $s^s(r, c)$ is used similarly for region classification using online-computed pseudo-labels.

UFO^2 Loss. We propose to fuse both heads into a unified task head to produce the four aforementioned scores simultaneously as shown in Fig. 2 (center green box). A joint objective is optimized via

$$\mathcal{L}_{\text{joint}} = \mathcal{L}_I + \frac{1}{|R'|} \sum_{r \in R', c \in C} \mathcal{L}_R(s^r(r), t(r)) + \mathcal{L}_C(s^s(r, c), y(r, c)), \quad (2)$$

where $\mathcal{L}_I$ subsumes different losses for different labels and $\mathcal{L}_C, \mathcal{L}_R$ are standard cross-entropy loss and smooth-L1 loss for region classification and regression respectively. Moreover, $y(r, c) \in \{0, 1\}$ and $t(r) \in \mathbb{R}^4$ are either ground-truth region labels and regression targets from strong labels, or pseudo labels and pseudo targets generated online for partial labels and unlabeled data. We provide detailed explanations for $\mathcal{L}_I$ and how to generate pseudo labels $y(r, c)$ and pseudo targets $t(r)$ in the following. We discuss each form of annotation separately.

Tags. As illustrated in Fig. 3 left, when input images x come with image-level class tags $q(c) \in \{0, 1\}$ for class $c \in C$, we neither know the exact assignment of class labels to each proposal nor the exact target location. Therefore, we first compute the image scores via $s(r,c) = s^c(r,c) \cdot s^d(r,c)$, i.e., as a product of the class confidence score s^c and the objectness score s^d. Then image level evidence ϕ is obtained by summing up $s(r,c)$ across all regions: $\phi(c) = \sum_{r \in R'} s(r,c)$. We then compute $\mathcal{L}_{\text{Tags}}$ as an image-level binary cross-entropy loss for multi-label classification:

$$\mathcal{L}_{\text{Tags}}(\phi, q) = -\sum_{c \in C} q(c) \log \phi(c).$$

For samples with image-level tags we set $\mathcal{L}_I = \mathcal{L}_{\text{Tags}}$ in Eq. (2) during training. This yields semantically meaningful ROI scores $s(c,r)$, which can then be used to generate pseudo ROI-level ground-truth to augment the training via the two region-level losses $\mathcal{L}_C$ and $\mathcal{L}_R$ as detailed in Eq. (2). We follow Ren et al. [45] to generate pseudo ground-truth, taking one or few diverse confident predictions.

Points and Scribbles. Similar to image-level tags, points and scribbles also don't contain the exact region-level ground-truth. However, they provide some level of localization information (e.g., scribbles can be very rough or accurate depending on the annotator). Therefore, we employ the same loss developed for 'Tags', (illustrated in Fig. 3 left) but introduce extra constraints to restrict the assignment of ROIs to class labels based on the labels. Specifically, pseudo label $y(r,c) = 1$ if and only if region r contains the given point or scribble, and class c is the same as the category label of this point or scribble. These constraints filter out a lot of false-positives during training and help the framework select high quality candidate regions.

Boxes. When the input image is annotated with bounding boxes, the most naïve solution is to directly train the network using $\mathcal{L}_C$ and $\mathcal{L}_R$ losses: the real label and target are given and the scores s^s and s^r will be used for inference. Most supervised work [16,43] follows the above procedure and impressive results are achieved. Importantly, only applying these two losses in our framework will not optimize the scores s^c and s^d when learning from strong labels. However, these two scores are used as a 'teacher' to compute pseudo ground-truth for optimizing s^s and s^r when partial labels are given, as described in the previous two sections. Hence, when training with mixed annotations, we found the 'student' to be stronger than the 'teacher', rendering weakly labeled data useless.

To address this concern, i.e., to enable training with mixed annotations, we found a *balanced teacher-student model* to be crucial. Specifically, for any fully labeled sample we introduce three extra losses on the latent modules, i.e., on s^c, s^d, ϕ, as shown in Fig. 3 second column:

$$\mathcal{L}_I = \mathcal{L}_{\text{Tags}}(\phi, q) + \frac{1}{|R|} \sum_{r \in R} (\mathcal{L}_{T1}(s^c, y, r) + \mathcal{L}_{T2}(s^d, \psi, r)). \tag{3}$$

These three losses provide a signal to the 'teacher' when using strong labels. Specifically, since s^c is normalized across all classes via a softmax, as mentioned in Eq. (1), we can naturally apply as the first strong-teacher loss a standard cross-entropy on s^c for region classification:

$$\mathcal{L}_{T1}(s^c, y, r) = -\sum_{c \in C} y'(c, r) \log s^c(c, r).$$

Hereby $y'(c, r) = 1$ for all regions r which overlap with any ground-truth boxes in class c by more than a threshold. In practice, we set this threshold to 0.5 and we use the class of the biggest overlapping ground-truth as the label if assignment conflicts occur. The second strong-teacher loss encourages the latent distribution s^d to approach the real objectness distribution. Hence we use a KL-divergence applied on s^d:

$$\mathcal{L}_{T2}(s^d, \psi, r) = \sum_{c \in C} \psi(c, r) \log \frac{\psi(c, r)}{s^d(c, r)}.$$

Here, $\psi(c, r)$ is constructed to represent the objectness of each ROI. ψ is zero initialized and $\psi(c, r) = \text{IoU}(r, r')$ for ground-truth region r' with class c. We then normalize ψ across all $r \in R'$, following $s^d(c, r)$ normalization in Eq. (1).

In addition, we also construct an image-level class label q from the ground-truth annotations and compute the image-level classification loss $\mathcal{L}_{\text{Tags}}$ following the 'Tags' setting. This loss term improves network consistency when switching between partial labels and strong labels.

Unlabeled. For unlabeled data, we employ a simple yet effective strategy as shown in Fig. 3 third column. We use a single threshold τ on $\phi(c)$ to first pick out a set of confident classes $\hat{q}(c)$. This set of classes is used as tags to train the framework as descried in the 'Tags' section. In addition, we apply entropy regularization on s^s to encourage the model to output confident predictions on unlabeled data. The overall loss is:

$$\mathcal{L}_I = \mathcal{L}_{\text{Tags}}(\phi, \hat{q}) + H(s^s) = -\sum_{c \in C} \hat{q}(c) \log \phi(c) - \sum_{r \in R', c \in C} s^s(r, c) \log s^s(r, c),$$

where $\hat{q}(c) = \delta(\phi(c) > \tau)$ and $\delta(\cdot)$ is the delta function. As pointed out in [40,53,60], self-ensembling is helpful when utilizing unlabeled data. We thus stack multiple ROI-classification and regression layers. Pseudo ground-truth will be computed from the ROI-classification logits of one layer to supervise another one. For inference, the average prediction is adopted.

3.2 Proposal Refinement

Given strong labels, it's a standard technique [16,43] to reject most false positive proposals and re-balance the training batch using the ground-truth boxes. However, proposal refinement using partial labels has not been studied before. Specifically, we keep a specific positive and negative proposal ratio in each mini-batch. Positive proposals satisfy two requirements: (1) one of the ground-truth

Fig. 4. Top row: labels for single instance (suitcase and person). Bottom row: labels for all the objects (see appendix for more).

points or scribbles should be contained in each positive ROI; (2) all the selected positive ROIs together need to cover all the annotations. Negative proposals from the ROIs contain no labels. When generating a training batch we sample according to a pre-defined ratio. This practice dramatically decreases the number of proposals and thus simplifies subsequent optimization. We refer to the proposal set after sampling and re-balancing using R', as shown in Fig. 2 left.

4   Partial Labels Simulation

Partial labels (*e.g.*, points and scribbles) are much easier and natural to annotate than bounding boxes. They also provide much stronger localization information compared to tags. However, these types of annotations are either incomplete (*e.g.*, part of the VOC images are labeled with points [34,35]) or missing (*e.g.*, no partial labels have been annotated for COCO or LVIS) for object detection.

As a proof-of-concept for the proposed framework, we therefore develop an approach to synthesize partial labels when ground-truth instance masks are available. It is our goal to mimic practical human labeling behavior. We are aware that the quality of the generated labels is sub-optimal. Yet these labels provide a surrogate to test and demonstrate the effectiveness of UFO². In this work, we generate the semantic partial labels for every object in the scene, and leave manual collection of labels to future work.

Points. When annotating points, humans tend to click close to the center of the objects [34]. However, different objects differ in shapes and poses. Hence, their center usually does not coincide with the bounding box center. To mimic human behavior, we first apply a distance transform on each instance mask. The obtained intensity maps represent the distance between the points inside the body region and the closest boundary. This distance transform usually generates a 'ridge' inside the object. We thus further normalize it and multiply with a Gaussian probability restricted to the bounding box. The final probabilistic maps are used to randomly sample one point as the annotation.

Scribbles. Scribbles are harder to simulate since human annotators generate very diverse labels. Here we provide a way to generate relatively simple scribbles. The obtained labels likely don't perfectly mimic human annotations, yet

Table 2. Training on COCO-80 from scratch using a single form of annotation and testing on COCO-val. All results are obtained with a VGG-16 backbone.

Methods	Test-scale	Label	AP	AP-50
PCL [52]	Multi	Tags	8.5	19.4
C-MIDN [14]	Multi	Tags	9.6	21.4
WSOD2 [60]	Multi	Tags	10.8	22.7
Ours	Multi	Tags	**11.4**	**24.3**
Ours	Single	Tags	**10.8**	**23.1**
Ours	Single	Points	**12.4**	**27.0**
Ours	Single	Scribbles	**13.7**	**29.8**
Fast-RCNN [16]	Single	Boxes	18.9	38.6
Faster-RCNN [43]	Single	Boxes	21.2	41.5
Ours	Single	Boxes	**25.7**	**46.3**

they serve as a proof-of-concept to show the effectiveness of the proposed framework. Given the instance mask, we first compute the topological skeleton, *i.e.*, a connected graph, using OpenCV's [7] skeleton function. Using this graph, we start from a random point and seek a long path by extending in both directions. At intersections we randomly choose. We post-process the paths to avoid that their ends are close to the boundary. This latter constraint is inspired by the observation that humans usually don't draw scribbles close to the boundary.

Representative generated labels are visualized in Fig. 4, where the top row shows examples for a single object (*i.e.*, suitcase and rider) and the bottom row shows the labels for all objects in the scene. We observe the partial labels to be correctly located within each object. They also exhibit great diversity in terms of location and length across different instances.

5 Experiments

We assess the proposed framework subsequently after detailing dataset, evaluation metrics and implementation.

Dataset and Evaluation Metrics. We conduct experiments on COCO [30] – the most popular dataset for object detection. Standard metrics are reported including AP (averaged over IoU thresholds) and AP-50 (IoU threshold at 50%). We use several COCO splits in this paper: (1) COCO-80: COCO 2014 train set of 80K images. (2) COCO-35 (a.k.a. valminusminival): a 35K subset of COCO 2017 train set. (3) COCO-115: COCO 2017 train set, equals union of COCO-80 and COCO-35. (4) COCO-val: COCO 2014 val set of 40K images. (5) minival: COCO 2017 val set of 5K images. (6) Un-120: COCO unlabeled set of 120k images.

Table 3. Fine-tuning to improve an existing model using each single supervision. Results are reported by testing on `minival`.

Train	Methods	Backbone	Labels	AP	Extra	Labels	AP	Δ
COCO-35	ours	VGG-16	Tags	4.9	COCO-80	–	5.3	**8.2%**
COCO-115	ours	VGG-16	Tags	12.9	Un-120	–	13.6	**5.4%**
COCO-35	ours	ResNet-50	Tags	9.8	COCO-80	–	10.5	**7.1%**
COCO-35	ours	ResNet-50	Boxes	29.1	COCO-80	tags	29.4	**1.0%**
COCO-35	ours	ResNet-50	Boxes	29.1	COCO-80	points	30.1	**5.5%**
COCO-35	ours	ResNet-50	Boxes	29.1	COCO-80	scribbles	30.9	**6.2%**
COCO-115	ours	ResNet-50	Boxes	32.7	Un-120	–	33.9	**3.7%**

Implementation Details. For a fair comparison to prior work with different forms of a single supervision, we use the most common VGG-16 and ResNet-50 backbones. SGD is used for optimization. After proposal refinement, we keep 1024 ROIs for points and scribbles and 512 for boxes as those have the most localization information and thus a reduced need for abundant ROIs.

5.1   Evaluation of Single Labels

Train from Scratch. We fist study the scenario where each single supervision is used to train a model from scratch. A VGG-16 model is trained on COCO-80 and evaluated on COCO-val for a fair comparison to both weakly-supervised (tags) and strongly-supervised (boxes) work. The results are reported in Table 2. Following prior work, we report both single-scale and multi-scale testing results ('Test-scale' column in Table 2).

When using tags, our model performs comparable to prior work. We slightly increase AP and AP-50 by 0.6% and 1.6% (Table 2 top block). When using strong labels, our method also outperforms Fast- and Faster-RCNN baselines (Table 2 bottom block). We found improvements to be due to the strong teacher losses introduced in Sect. 3.1. In addition, we also report the results of partial labels (tags, points, and scribbles) in the center block of Table 2, where we observe a natural correlation of performance with complexity of the labels. Note that the performance boost from tag to point (+1.6% AP/3.9% AP-50) is bigger than the boost from point to scribble (+1.3% AP/2.8% AP-50). Also, strong labels still result in the biggest performance boost: it is significantly larger than that of partial labels. Hence, bounding boxes are necessary for accurate performance.

Improve Existing Models. We now study the use of each label to boost a pre-trained object detector. Results are shown in Table 3. This experimental setup follows semi-supervised learning studies and mimics a common practical scenario: we want to apply a pre-trained object detector to new environments

Fig. 5. Qualitative comparison of models trained by using different labels.

while keeping annotation cost low or while having weak labels readily available. Motivated by this scenario, pre-trained models are only fine-tuned by integrating extra weaker labels (*e.g.*, first train with boxes, and then fine-tune with points, scribbles, or unlabeled data). We study two cases in Table 3: (1) small scale: from COCO-35 to COCO-80 where the model sees more unlabeled data; (2) large scale: from COCO-115 to Un-120 where labeled and unlabeled data are of similar size.

In Table 3 (top block), we show that unlabeled data can be utilized to improve the performance of a weakly-supervised model where the VGG-16 and ResNet-50 based model are improved by 8.2% (relative) and 7.1% (relative), respectively. In Table 3 (center), we further demonstrate that partial labels are effective for improving a strongly-supervised model. Similarly, the relative performance improvement from tag to point (+4.5% Δ) is bigger than the improvement from point to scribble (+0.7% Δ). In Table 3 (bottom), we use unlabeled data for a strongly supervised ResNet-50 based model, where unlabeled data improves its performance by 1.2% AP (3.7% relative improvement).

5.2 Qualitative Results

Qualitative comparisons of the same model trained using different forms of supervision are shown in Fig. 5. From top to bottom we show predicted boxes and their confidence score when using tags, points, scribbles, and boxes. We observe stronger labels to help the model reject false positive predictions (*e.g.*, the noisy small boxes on the sea and around the human head, the cars and books in the background), and also localize better true positive predictions (*e.g.*, the giraffe, surfing man, and each person in a crowd). More results and some failure modes are provided in the Appendix.

5.3 Ablation Study

Next we study the effectiveness of each proposed module in the UFO^2 framework.

Table 4. Ablation study for the three strong teacher losses.

Loss	$\mathcal{L}_C + \mathcal{L}_R$	$+\mathcal{L}_{T1}$	$+\mathcal{L}_{T2}$	$+\mathcal{L}_{T1} + \mathcal{L}_{T2}$	$+\mathcal{L}_{T1} + \mathcal{L}_{T2} + \mathcal{L}_{\text{Tags}}$
AP	22.6	24.8	25.1	25.5	25.7
AP-50	42.4	44.1	45.0	46.0	46.3

Table 5. Ablation study for localization constraints (Con_P and Con_S for points and scribbles) and proposal refinement (Ref_P, Ref_S).

Methods	Tags	Ref_P	Ref_S	$\text{Ref}_P + \text{Con}_P$	$\text{Ref}_S + \text{Con}_S$
AP	10.8	11.1	11.6	12.4	13.7
AP-50	23.1	24.2	25.1	27.0	29.8

Do Strong Teacher Losses Help? In Sect. 3.1, we introduce three extra losses for a balanced teacher student model when using boxes. Theses losses provide two advantages: (1) the model trained with strong labels improves as reported in Table 4. These results are obtained using the same setting as those given in Table 2. In the table, $\mathcal{L}_C + \mathcal{L}_R$ represents the vanilla version, *i.e.*, only ROI classification and regression heads are trained following supervised methods [16,43]. We then add each teacher loss and illustrate that each one of them is beneficial. The best number is achieved when all three are combined. (2) strong losses help omni-supervised learning. Without those losses, using tags, points, and scribbles will hurt the performance of a strongly pre-trained model by -5.6%, -5.2%, and -6.3% compared to the performance improvement gained in Table 3 (middle).

Does Proposal Refinement Help? We evaluate the localization constraints proposed in Sect. 3.1 'Points & Scribbles' and the proposal refinement module (Sect. 3.2) following the settings of Table 2. The results are reported in Table 5. Both proposed modules improve the final performance. The localization constraints play a more important role than proposal refinement. This is reasonable as the localization constraints also consider the semantic information of partial labels.

5.4   Omni-supervised Learning

Given a fixed annotation budget, we can either choose to annotate more data with cheaper labels or less data with strong labels. With the proposed unified model, we empirically study and compare several annotation policies, and we provide a new insight regarding a suitable strategy.

Annotation Time Estimation. We use the labeling time as the annotation cost and ignore other factors in this work. We approximate the annotation time of each supervision relying on the annotation and dataset statistics reported in the literature [4,30].

Table 6. Budget-aware omni-supervised detection (T: tags, P: points, S: scribbles, B: boxes, U: unlabeled). Mean and standard deviation of Average Precision (AP) are reported over three runs.

Policy	Image amount	Labels	AP
MOST	10000	T	3.0 ± 0.57
STRONG	$2312 + 7688$	B+U	13.97 ± 0.98
EQUAL	$2500 + 2255 + 1250 + 578 + 5417$	T+P+S+B+U	5.87 ± 0.70
EQUAL-NUM	$1185 \times 4 + 5260$	T+P+S+B+U	9.43 ± 0.68
80%B	$1804 + 1850 + 6346$	P+B+U	**14.11 ± 1.01**
50%B	$4510 + 1156 + 4334$	P+B+U	11.13 ± 1.12
20%B	$7215 + 462 + 2323$	P+B+U	4.47 ± 0.75

- **Tags:** Collecting image-level class labels takes 1 s per category according to [4]. Thus, the expected annotation time on COCO is 80 s/img.
- **Points:** COCO [30] contains 3.5 categories and 7.7 instances per image on average. Similarly to above, it takes 1 s to annotate every non-exist classes, for $80 - 3.5 = 76.5$ s in total. [4] reports that annotators take a median of 2.4 s to click on the first instance of a class, and 0.9 s for every additional instances. Thus the total labeling time is $76.5 + 3.5 \times 2.4 + (7.7 - 3.5) \times 0.9 = 88.7$ s/img. Note that point supervision is only 1.1 times more expensive than tags which is very efficient.
- **Scribbles:** For each existing class, drawing a free-form scribble takes 10.9 s on average [4,29]. Hence, the total time is $76.5 + 7.7 \times 10.9 = 160.4$ s/img. This number is roughly twice the time of labeling tags or points.
- **Boxes:** It took 35s for one high quality box according to [51]. Hence, the total annotation time is $76.5 + 7.7 \times 35 = 346$ s/img.

Given above approximations, we roughly know that annotating 1 image with bounding boxes takes as much time as annotating 4.33/3.9/2.16 images with tags/points/scribbles.

Budget-aware Omni-supervised Detection. We wonder: *what annotation policy maximizes performance given a budget?* Let's assume the total budget is fixed, *e.g.*., 800,000 s. We empirically study several policies as listed below: (1) MOST: we aim to maximize the number of images thus the entire budget is used to acquire tag annotation; (2) STRONG: all the budget is used to annotate bounding boxes, which is widely-adopted in practice; (3) EQUAL: use one quarter of the budget for each label; (4) EQUAL-NUM: same amount labeled for each.

Via above labeling time analysis and single-label experiments, we find that annotating points is a good choice among partial labels: roughly as efficient as tags but leads to better results; only half the price of scribbles but performs comparably well. We thus also study scenarios with different combinations of boxes and points: (1) 80%B: 80% budget on boxes; 20% on points; (2) 50%B: 50% budget on boxes; 50% on points; (3) 20%B: 20% budget on boxes; 80% on points.

As reported in Table 6, for the fixed budget of 800,000s, we first 'annotate' (sample from COCO-35) 10,000 images with tags for the MOST policy. The other settings will only annotate less images. Annotations are then sampled from those 10,000 images. For example, STRONG will annotate 2,312 images with boxes and the rest remains unlabeled, which will also be utilized in our method given in Sect. 3.1. Therefore, training will use the same 10,000 images, albeit different policies make use of different labels. A VGG-16 based model is trained as described above and evaluated on minival. We observe: (1) strong labels are still very important and the policy STRONG outperforms other popular polices by a great margin (Table 6 top half). (2) It's not necessary to annotate every image with boxes to achieve competitive results. 80%B is slightly better than STRONG and 50%B also performs better than EQUAL-NUM. This result suggests that spending a certain amount of cost annotating more images with points is a better annotation strategy than the commonly adopted bounding box annotation (STRONG).

6 Conclusions

We present UFO^2, a novel unified framework for omni-supervised object detection. It handles strong labels, several forms of partial annotations (tags, points, and scribbles), and unlabeled data simultaneously. UFO^2 is able to utilize each label effectively, permitting to study budget-aware omni-supervised object detection. We also assess a promising annotation policy.

Acknowledgement. ZR is supported by Yunni & Maxine Pao Memorial Fellowship. This work is supported in part by NSF under Grant No. 1718221 and MRI #1725729, UIUC, Samsung, 3M, Cisco Systems Inc. (Gift Award CG 1377144) and Adobe.

Appendix

In this document, we provide:

- An extensive study on the LVIS [18] dataset where UFO^2 learns to detect more than 1k different objects without bounding box annotation (Sect. A), which demonstrates the generalizability and applicability of UFO^2
- Details regarding the annotation policies mentioned in Sect. 5.4 'Budget-aware Omni-supervised Detection' of the main paper
- Additional visualizations of the simulated partial labels
- Additional qualitative results on COCO (complementary to main paper Sect. 5.2)

A   Extensions: Learning to Detect Everything

In this section we show that without any architecture changes UFO^2 can be generalized to detect any objects given image-level tags. Hence we follow [21] and refer to this setting as 'learning to detect everything.'

Specifically, we aim to detect objects from the LVIS [18] dataset: it contains 1239 categories and we only use tags as annotation. We use COCO*[1] with boxes and train UFO^2 on it first. Our model achieves 32.7% AP and 52.3% AP-50 on minival. We then jointly fine-tune this model using tags from LVIS and boxes from COCO*. The final model performs comparably on minival (31.6% AP, 50.1% AP-50) and also decent on LVIS validation of over 1k classes (3.5% AP, 6.3% AP-50 where a supervised model achieves 8.6% AP, 14.8% AP-50). To the best of our knowledge, no numbers have been reported on this dataset using weak labels. Our results are also not directly comparable to strongly supervised results [18] as we don't use the bounding box annotation on LVIS.

Qualitative results are shown in Fig. 6. We observe that UFO^2 is able to detect objects accurately even though no bounding box supervision is used for the new classes (e.g., short pants, street light, parking meter, frisbee, etc.). Specifically, UFO^2 can (1) detect spatially adjacent or even clustered instances with great recall (e.g., goose, cow, zebra, giraffe); (2) recognize some obscure or hard objects (e.g., wet suite, short pants, knee pad); (3) localize different objects with tight and accurate bounding boxes. Importantly, note that we don't need to change the architecture of UFO^2 at all to integrate both boxes and tags as supervision.

B   Annotation Policies

To study budget-aware omni-supervised object detection, we defined the following policies: 80%B, 50%B, 20%B motivated by the following findings: (1) among the three partial labels (tags, points, and scribbles), labeling of points (88.7 s/img; see Sect. 5.4 in the main paper) is roughly as efficient as annotating tags (80 s/img), both of which require half the time/cost of scribbles (160.4 s/img); (2) using points achieves a consistent performance boost compared to using tags (12.4 over 10.8 AP in Table 2; 30.1 over 29.4 AP in Table 3); (3) using scribbles is just slightly better than using points (13.7 over 12.4 AP in Table 2; 30.9 over 30.1 AP in Table 3) but twice as expensive to annotate; and (4) strong supervision (boxes) is still necessary to achieve good results (strongly supervised models are significantly better than others in Table 2 and Table 3).

Therefore, we choose to combine points and boxes as a new annotation policy which we found to work well under the fixed-budget setting as shown in Table 6: 80%B is slightly better than STRONG and 50%B also performs better than EQUAL-NUM. These results suggest that spending some amount of cost to annotate more images with points is a better annotation strategy than the commonly-adopted bounding box only annotation (STRONG). Meanwhile, the optimal annotation policy remains an open question and better policies may exist if more accurate scribbles are collected or advanced algorithms are developed to utilize partial labels.

---

[1] COCO*: because LVIS is a subset of COCO-115, we construct COCO* by taking COCO-115 images excluded from LVIS.

Fig. 6. Visualization of results on LVIS data.

C   Additional Visualization of Partial Labels

We show additional results together with the ground-truth bounding boxes in
Figs. 7–10. Figure 7 and Fig. 8 show labels for single objects (*e.g.*, car, motor,
sheep, chair, person, and bus) and Fig. 9 and Fig. 10 visualize labels for all the
instances in the images.

We observe: (1) both points and scribbles are correctly located within the objects; (2) points are mainly located around the center area of the objects and with a certain amount of randomness, which aligns with our goal to mimic human labeling behavior as discussed in Sect. 4 of the main paper; (3) the generated scribbles are relatively simple yet effective in capturing the rough shape of the

Fig. 7. Additional visualization of the ground-truth boxes and the simulated partial labels.

Fig. 8. Additional visualization of the ground-truth boxes and the simulated partial labels.

objects. Also, they exhibit a reasonable diversity. These partial labels serve as a proof-of-concept to show the effectiveness of the proposed UFO^2 framework.

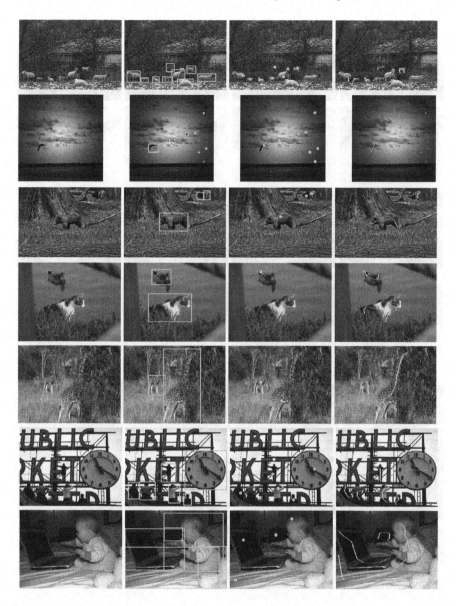

Fig. 9. Additional visualization of the ground-truth boxes and the simulated partial labels.

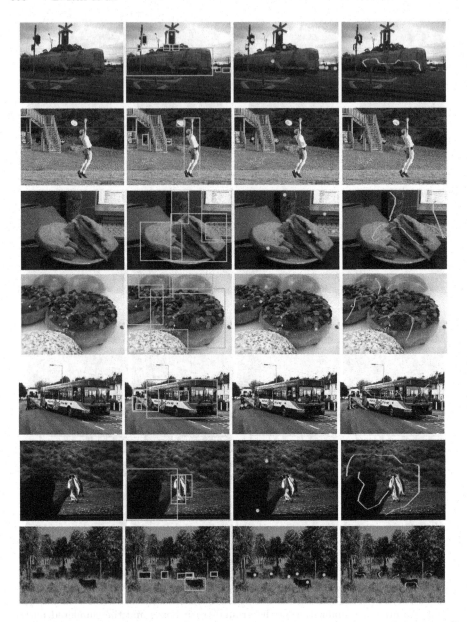

Fig. 10. Additional visualization of the ground-truth boxes and the simulated partial labels.

D   Additional Qualitative Results

In Fig. 11 and Fig. 12 we show additional qualitative results. We compare the same VGG-16 based model trained on COCO-80 with different forms of supervision. From left to right we show predicted boxes and their confidence scores when

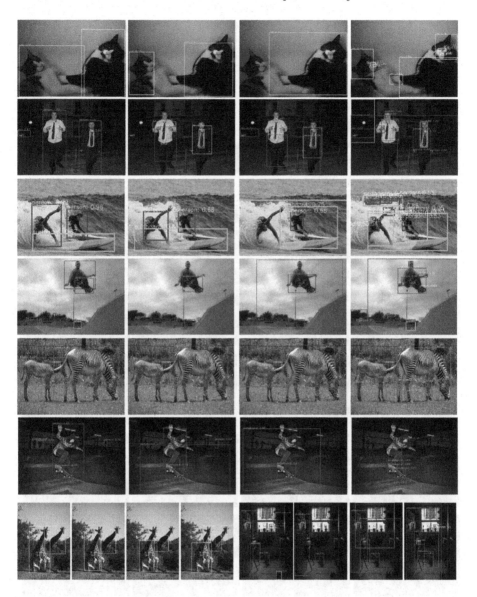

Fig. 11. Additional qualitative comparison of models trained with different labels on COCO (left to right: boxes, scribbles, points, tags).

using boxes, scribbles, points, and tags. Similar to the results in Sect. 5.2 of the main paper, we find that stronger labels better reduce false positive predictions and better localize true positive predictions.

Fig. 12. Additional qualitative comparison of models trained with different labels on COCO (left to right: boxes, scribbles, points, tags).

References

1. Instagram statistics 2019. www.omnicoreagency.com/instagram-statistics/
2. Youtube statistics 2019. https://merchdope.com/youtube-stats/

3. Arbeláez, P., Pont-Tuset, J., Barron, J., Marques, F., Malik, J.: Multiscale combinatorial grouping. In: CVPR (2014)
4. Bearman, A., Russakovsky, O., Ferrari, V., Fei-Fei, L.: What's the point: semantic segmentation with point supervision. In: Leibe, B., Matas, J., Sebe, N., Welling, M. (eds.) ECCV 2016. LNCS, vol. 9911, pp. 549–565. Springer, Cham (2016). https://doi.org/10.1007/978-3-319-46478-7_34
5. Berthelot, D., Carlini, N., Goodfellow, I.J., Papernot, N., Oliver, A., Raffel, C.: MixMatch: a holistic approach to semi-supervised learning. In: NeurIPS (2019)
6. Bilen, H., Vedaldi, A.: Weakly supervised deep detection networks. In: CVPR (2016)
7. Bradski, G.: The OpenCV Library. Dobb's J. Softw. Tools **25**, 120–125 (2000)
8. Chapelle, O., Schölkopf, B., Zien, A. (eds.): Semi-Supervised Learning. The MIT Press, Cambridge (2006)
9. Chen, Y., Li, W., Sakaridis, C., Dai, D., Gool, L.V.: Domain adaptive faster R-CNN for object detection in the wild. In: CVPR (2018)
10. Chéron, G., Alayrac, J.B., Laptev, I., Schmid, C.: A flexible model for training action localization with varying levels of supervision. In: NIPS (2018)
11. Doersch, C., Gupta, A., Efros, A.A.: Unsupervised visual representation learning by context prediction. In: ICCV (2015)
12. Everingham, M., Van Gool, L., Williams, C.K.I., Winn, J., Zisserman, A.: The PASCAL visual object classes (VOC) challenge. IJCV **88**, 303–338 (2010). https://doi.org/10.1007/s11263-009-0275-4
13. Felzenszwalb, P.F., Girshick, R.B., McAllester, D.A., Ramanan, D.: Object detection with discriminatively trained part-based models. T-PAMI **32**(9), 1627–1645 (2010)
14. Gao, Y., et al.: C-MIDN: coupled multiple instance detection network with segmentation guidance for weakly supervised object detection. In: ICCV (2019)
15. Ge, W., Yang, S., Yu, Y.: Multi-evidence filtering and fusion for multi-label classification, object detection and semantic segmentation based on weakly supervised learning. In: CVPR (2018)
16. Girshick, R.B.: Fast R-CNN. In: ICCV (2015)
17. Girshick, R.B., Donahue, J., Darrell, T., Malik, J.: Rich feature hierarchies for accurate object detection and semantic segmentation. In: CVPR (2014)
18. Gupta, A., Dollar, P., Girshick, R.: LVIS: a dataset for large vocabulary instance segmentation. In: CVPR (2019)
19. He, K., Fan, H., Wu, Y., Xie, S., Girshick, R.: Momentum contrast for unsupervised visual representation learning. In: CVPR (2019)
20. He, K., Gkioxari, G., Dollár, P., Girshick, R.: Mask R-CNN. In: ICCV (2017)
21. Hu, R., Dollár, P., He, K., Darrell, T., Girshick, R.: Learning to segment every thing. In: CVPR (2018)
22. Inoue, N., Furuta, R., Yamasaki, T., Aizawa, K.: Cross-domain weakly-supervised object detection through progressive domain adaptation. In: CVPR (2018)
23. Jie, Z., Wei, Y., Jin, X., Feng, J., Liu, W.: Deep self-taught learning for weakly supervised object localization. In: CVPR (2017)
24. Kantorov, V., Oquab, M., Cho, M., Laptev, I.: ContextLocNet: context-aware deep network models for weakly supervised localization. In: Leibe, B., Matas, J., Sebe, N., Welling, M. (eds.) ECCV 2016. LNCS, vol. 9909, pp. 350–365. Springer, Cham (2016). https://doi.org/10.1007/978-3-319-46454-1_22
25. Khodabandeh, M., Vahdat, A., Ranjbar, M., Macready, W.G.: A robust learning approach to domain adaptive object detection. In: ICCV (2019)

26. Khoreva, A., Benenson, R., Hosang, J., Hein, M., Schiele, B.: Simple does it: weakly supervised instance and semantic segmentation. In: CVPR (2017)
27. Law, H., Deng, J.: CornerNet: detecting objects as paired keypoints. In: Ferrari, V., Hebert, M., Sminchisescu, C., Weiss, Y. (eds.) Computer Vision – ECCV 2018. LNCS, vol. 11218, pp. 765–781. Springer, Cham (2018). https://doi.org/10.1007/978-3-030-01264-9_45
28. Lee, D.H.: Pseudo-label: the simple and efficient semi-supervised learning method for deep neural networks. In: ICML 2013 Workshop (2013)
29. Lin, D., Dai, J., Jia, J., He, K., Sun, J.: ScribbleSup: scribble-supervised convolutional networks for semantic segmentation. In: CVPR (2016)
30. Lin, T., et al.: Microsoft COCO: common objects in context. CoRR (2014)
31. Liu, W., et al.: SSD: single shot multibox detector. In: Leibe, B., Matas, J., Sebe, N., Welling, M. (eds.) ECCV 2016. LNCS, vol. 9905, pp. 21–37. Springer, Cham (2016). https://doi.org/10.1007/978-3-319-46448-0_2
32. Miyato, T., Maeda, S., Koyama, M., Ishii, S.: Virtual adversarial training: a regularization method for supervised and semi-supervised learning. T-PAMI 41(8), 1979–1993 (2019)
33. Oliver, A., Odena, A., Raffel, C.A., Cubuk, E.D., Goodfellow, I.: Realistic evaluation of deep semi-supervised learning algorithms. In: NeurIPS (2018)
34. Papadopoulos, D.P., Uijlings, J.R.R., Keller, F., Ferrari, V.: Extreme clicking for efficient object annotation. In: ICCV (2017)
35. Papadopoulos, D.P., Uijlings, J.R.R., Keller, F., Ferrari, V.: Training object class detectors with click supervision. In: CVPR (2017)
36. Papandreou, G., Chen, L., Murphy, K.P., Yuille, A.L.: Weakly-and semi-supervised learning of a deep convolutional network for semantic image segmentation. In: ICCV (2015)
37. Pardo, A., Xu, M., Thabet, A.K., Arbelaez, P., Ghanem, B.: BAOD: budget-aware object detection. CoRR abs/1904.05443 (2019)
38. Park, T., Liu, M.Y., Wang, T.C., Zhu, J.Y.: Semantic image synthesis with spatially-adaptive normalization. In: CVPR (2019)
39. Peng, X., Sun, B., Ali, K., Saenko, K.: Learning deep object detectors from 3D models. In: ICCV (2015)
40. Radosavovic, I., Dollár, P., Girshick, R.B., Gkioxari, G., He, K.: Data distillation: towards omni-supervised learning. In: CVPR (2018)
41. Redmon, J., Divvala, S.K., Girshick, R.B., Farhadi, A.: You only look once: unified, real-time object detection. In: CVPR (2016)
42. Redmon, J., Farhadi, A.: YOLO9000: better, faster, stronger. In: CVPR (2017)
43. Ren, S., He, K., Girshick, R., Sun, J.: Faster R-CNN: towards real-time object detection with region proposal networks. TPAMI 39(6), 1137–1149 (2016)
44. Ren, Z., Lee, Y.J.: Cross-domain self-supervised multi-task feature learning using synthetic imagery. In: CVPR (2018)
45. Ren, Z., et al.: Instance-aware, context-focused, and memory-efficient weakly supervised object detection. In: CVPR (2020)
46. Ren, Z., Yeh, R.A., Schwing, A.G.: Not all unlabeled data are equal: learning to weight data in semi-supervised learning. arXiv preprint arXiv:2007.01293 (2020)
47. Rosenberg, C., Hebert, M., Schneiderman, H.: Semi-supervised self-training of object detection models. In: WACV/MOTION (2005)
48. Shen, Y., Ji, R., Zhang, S., Zuo, W., Wang, Y.: Generative adversarial learning towards fast weakly supervised detection. In: CVPR (2018)

49. Singh, G., Saha, S., Sapienza, M., Torr, P., Cuzzolin, F.: Online real time multiple spatiotemporal action localisation and prediction on a single platform. In: ICCV (2017)
50. Singh, K.K., Xiao, F., Lee, Y.J.: Track and transfer: watching videos to simulate strong human supervision for weakly-supervised object detection. In: CVPR (2016)
51. Su, H., Deng, J., Fei-Fei, L.: Crowdsourcing annotations for visual object detection. In: AAAI Technical Report, 4th Human Computation Workshop (2012)
52. Tang, P., et al.: PCL: proposal cluster learning for weakly supervised object detection. T-PAMI **42**(1), 176–191 (2018)
53. Tang, P., Wang, X., Bai, X., Liu, W.: Multiple instance detection network with online instance classifier refinement. In: CVPR (2017)
54. Tarvainen, A., Valpola, H.: Weight-averaged consistency targets improve semi-supervised deep learning results. In: NeurIPS (2017)
55. Uijlings, J.R.R., Popov, S., Ferrari, V.: Revisiting knowledge transfer for training object class detectors. In: CVPR (2018)
56. Uijlings, J., van de Sande, K., Gevers, T., Smeulders, A.: Selective search for object recognition. IJCV **104**, 154–171 (2013)
57. Xie, Q., Dai, Z., Hovy, E., Luong, M.T., Le, Q.V.: Unsupervised data augmentation for consistency training. arXiv preprint arXiv:1904.12848 (2019)
58. Xu, J., Schwing, A.G., Urtasun, R.: Learning to segment under various forms of weak supervision. In: CVPR (2015)
59. Yang, Z., Mahajan, D., Ghadiyaram, D., Nevatia, R., Ramanathan, V.: Activity driven weakly supervised object detection. In: CVPR (2019)
60. Zeng, Z., Liu, B., Fu, J., Chao, H., Zhang, L.: WSOD2: learning bottom-up and top-down objectness distillation for weakly-supervised object detection. In: ICCV (2019)
61. Zhang, X., Feng, J., Xiong, H., Tian, Q.: Zigzag learning for weakly supervised object detection. In: CVPR (2018)
62. Zhang, Y., Bai, Y., Ding, M., Li, Y., Ghanem, B.: W2F: a weakly-supervised to fully-supervised framework for object detection. In: CVPR (2018)
63. Zhou, B., Khosla, A., A., L., Oliva, A., Torralba, A.: Learning deep features for discriminative localization. In: CVPR (2016)
64. Zhou, X., Zhuo, J., Krähenbühl, P.: Bottom-up object detection by grouping extreme and center points. In: CVPR (2019)
65. Zitnick, C.L., Dollár, P.: Edge boxes: locating object proposals from edges. In: Fleet, D., Pajdla, T., Schiele, B., Tuytelaars, T. (eds.) ECCV 2014. LNCS, vol. 8693, pp. 391–405. Springer, Cham (2014). https://doi.org/10.1007/978-3-319-10602-1_26
66. Zou, Y., Yu, Z., Liu, X., Kumar, B., Wang, J.: Confidence regularized self-training. In: ICCV (2019)
67. Zou, Y., Yu, Z., Vijaya Kumar, B.V.K., Wang, J.: Unsupervised domain adaptation for semantic segmentation via class-balanced self-training. In: Ferrari, V., Hebert, M., Sminchisescu, C., Weiss, Y. (eds.) ECCV 2018. LNCS, vol. 11207, pp. 297–313. Springer, Cham (2018). https://doi.org/10.1007/978-3-030-01219-9_18

iCaps: An Interpretable Classifier via Disentangled Capsule Networks

Dahuin Jung, Jonghyun Lee, Jihun Yi, and Sungroh Yoon[✉]

Electrical and Computer Engineering, ASRI, INMC, and Institute of Engineering Research, Seoul National University, Seoul 08826, South Korea
{annajung0625,leejh9611,t080205,sryoon}@snu.ac.kr

Abstract. We propose an interpretable Capsule Network, *iCaps*, for image classification. A capsule is a group of neurons nested inside each layer, and the one in the last layer is called a class capsule, which is a vector whose norm indicates a predicted probability for the class. Using the class capsule, existing Capsule Networks already provide some level of interpretability. However, there are two limitations which degrade its interpretability: 1) the class capsule also includes classification-irrelevant information, and 2) entities represented by the class capsule overlap. In this work, we address these two limitations using a novel class-supervised disentanglement algorithm and an additional regularizer, respectively. Through quantitative and qualitative evaluations on three datasets, we demonstrate that the resulting classifier, *iCaps*, provides a prediction along with clear rationales behind it with no performance degradation.

Keywords: Capsule Networks · Interpretable neural networks · Class-supervised disentanglement · Generative Adversarial Networks (GANs)

1 Introduction

Despite the success of deep learning in a broad range of tasks, including image classification and segmentation, speech synthesis, and medical decision-making, the reliability of decisions made by artificial intelligence is still questionable. Hence, many promising studies have been conducted regarding explainable artificial intelligence (XAI). The main task of XAI is to provide explanations that can aid the comprehension of provided decisions to users. Using these explanations, users can check whether a model performs as expected or identify potential bias/problems inherent to the model.

Several different approaches have been proposed to explain deep learning models. In some studies, models that can provide human-understandable explanations of their predictions without retraining or modification have been proposed. These studies aim for built-in interpretability. We herein propose a new

Electronic supplementary material The online version of this chapter (https://doi.org/10.1007/978-3-030-58529-7_19) contains supplementary material, which is available to authorized users.

A. Vedaldi et al. (Eds.): ECCV 2020, LNCS 12364, pp. 314–330, 2020.
https://doi.org/10.1007/978-3-030-58529-7_19

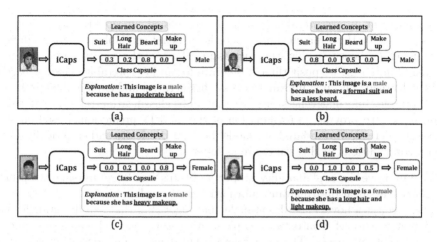

Fig. 1. Overview of our study. We propose a new interpretable classifier, iCaps, which classifies an observation by only considering class-relevant variables; these class-relevant variables are human-understandable concepts. By analyzing the values of the class-relevant variables (concepts), we can understand the decisions made by iCaps.

built-in interpretable model that offers a concept-based explanation using Capsule Networks (CapsNets) [38].

As the main building block, CapsNets use capsules - a group of neurons – that encapsulates the instantiation parameters of an entity, such as an object or its fragments. The magnitude of the output vector of a capsule indicates the probability that the encoded instantiation parameter is present in the input. The capsules in the final layer are called class capsules, and the norm of each class capsule indicates the predicted probability of each class. The instantiation parameters of the class capsule can represent the position, color, texture, and scaling of an object or its fragments, and these can be interpreted as concepts to humans.

Therefore, the instantiation parameters represented by the class capsule and its magnitudes can be used, to an extent, to explain a model's prediction. However, two factors degrade interpretability. First, some instantiation parameters of the class capsule represent classification-irrelevant concepts. Next, a single concept can be encoded in multiple elements of the class capsule. Therefore, a single concept can be represented by different magnitudes in two different elements.

By addressing these two problems, we propose an interpretable CapsNet architecture, *iCaps*, that only contains classification-relevant distinct concepts in the class capsule. The overview of iCaps is described in Fig. 1. To address the first problem, we propose a novel class-supervised disentanglement method that disentangles class-relevant and -irrelevant features within an observation, without any leakage. For the second problem, we use an additional regularizer based on latent traversal to prevent the same concept from being encapsulated several times in the class capsule.

Some built-in interpretable models use predefined concepts to provide explanations [21,22]. However, such prior knowledge is not available or costly to define in most cases; hence, in this study, we assumed where the concepts were learned instead. Moreover, we posit three desiderata for an interpretable classifier based on the learned concepts: informativeness, distinctness, and explainability where, for example, informativeness ensures that only classification-relevant information is used to provide an explanation of the model's prediction. Based on the three desiderata, we validated our model both theoretically and empirically. Our main contributions in this study are as follows:

1. We improve the explainability property of CapsNets by addressing two problems: classification-irrelevant information and overlapping.
2. We suggest a novel class-disentanglement algorithm that can disentangle the latent feature of x into two complementary subspaces: class-relevant and -irrelevant subspaces. The class-relevant subspace of our algorithm contains intra-class variation, unlike prior studies, which contain only inter-class variation.
3. We posit three desiderata for an interpretable classifier based on learned concepts and demonstrate the effectiveness of iCaps based on the three desiderata.

2   Related Work

2.1   Capsule Networks

CapsNet [38] is a neural network based on a group of neurons – a vector. The original CapsNet has a simple network structure comprising three layers. First, an observation x undergoes a convolution layer to transfer pixel-level information into a latent space, followed by the Primary-Capsule (PC) layer and Class-Capsule (CC) layer. Information contained in the PC layer is transferred to the CC layer above using a dynamic routing method, and this method is called "routing by agreement". The coupling coefficients between the capsules in the PC and CC layers are updated in a direction that can increase the classification performance (a top-down mechanism). The output of the CC layer is a class capsule of classes, and the norm of each class capsule indicates the predicted probability for each class. The elements of the class capsules represent the instantiation parameters of a type of entity. To encode these instantiation parameters for the class capsules, margin loss and reconstruction loss are used. The margin loss, $\mathcal{L}_M$, is:

$$\mathcal{L}_M = \lambda_M \left(y^i \max(0,\, m^+ - \|c\|)^2 + 0.5 \left((1 - y^i) \max(0,\, \|c^{\neq i}\| - m^-)^2\right)\right), \quad (1)$$

where $y^i = 1$ iff the ground-truth class label is i, c is the class capsule for the ground-truth class i, $c^{\neq i}$ are the class capsules except for c, $m^+ = 0.9$, and $m^- = 0.1$. The reconstruction loss, $\mathcal{L}_{\text{recon}}$, is used, which is expressed as

$$\mathcal{L}_{\text{recon}} = \lambda_{\text{recon}} \, \mathbb{E} \, \|\hat{x} - x\|_F^2, \quad (2)$$

where $\hat{x}$ is reconstructed x using an additional decoder, which uses c as the input. The original CapsNet presents some computational and structural limitations. Hence, some advanced studies based on CapsNet have been performed [2,15,19, 36]. Among these, our study uses DeepCaps [36] as a base because it yields better classification performance than the original CapsNet on more complex images by utilizing a skip connection and a three-dimensional convolution-inspired routing method and is easy to apply to our work. More detailed information regarding CapsNets is available in [36,38].

2.2 Disentanglement

Our work utilizes class-supervised disentanglement to create an interpretable classifier that provides an explanation using only classification-relevant information. Class-supervised disentanglement learning aims to disentangle the latent feature of x into two complementary subspaces - class-relevant and -irrelevant subspaces - in a setting where the class label for images in the training set is provided. Two approaches can be used in class-supervised disentanglement: adversarial and non-adversarial. DrNet [9] and Szabo et al. [46] are adversarial methods, whereas Cycle-VAE [20], ML-VAE [4], and LORD [12] are non-adversarial methods. Implicitly or explicitly, all class-supervised disentanglement methods assume that inter-class variation is much larger than intra-class variation; therefore, intra-class variation can be ignored. On the contrary, our work assumes that intra-class variation should not be ignored even though it is relatively small. From the perspective of an interpretable classifier, intra-class variation is an important feature to explain a model's prediction. Also, our method has some level of similarity with InfoGAN [7] (unsupervised disentanglement method) in a structural way. The comparison is given in Sect. S10 of the supplementary.

2.3 Interpretable Methods

Two topics of research in XAI provide two different notions of interpretability of deep models: (1) post-hoc interpretability and (2) built-in interpretability. (1) Post-hoc interpretability methods aim to interpret models or decisions of already trained neural networks. By contrast, networks that are inherently interpretable provide (2) built-in interpretability.

Post-Hoc Interpretability. Starting from the Saliency map [42], a number of post-hoc interpretation methods have been suggested to visually explain the decision of a classifier. These methods generate a heatmap of the same size as the input image and highlight the decisive regions within the input image. Post-hoc methods are based on backpropagation [1,3,40–45], local perturbation [47,48], or mask optimization [5,8,10,11,34]. The resulting heatmap of post-hoc methods are easily interpretable. However, evaluating the quality of their results is non-trivial, and both the method and the evaluation metrics are active research areas. Recently, several interpretable methods that offer explanations based on

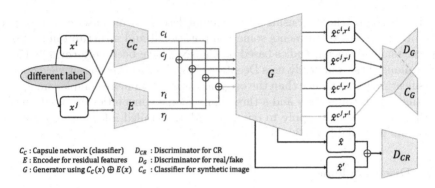

Fig. 2. Network architecture. x^i and x^j are two images of different labels. C_C encodes only class-relevant features of x^i and x^j to c^i and c^j, respectively. E encodes only class-irrelevant (residual) features of x^i and x^j to r^i and r^j, respectively. G constructs the images $\hat{x}^{c^i,r^i}$ and $\hat{x}^{c^j,r^j}$ using $c^i \oplus r^i$ and $c^j \oplus r^j$, respectively. Also, G generates the images $\hat{x}^{c^i,r^j}$ and $\hat{x}^{c^j,r^i}$ using swapped $c^i \oplus r^j$ and $c^i \oplus r^j$, respectively. These images are distinguished as real or fake and classified by D_G and C_G. D_{CR} takes two images $\hat{x}$ and $\hat{x}'$ that share the same c and r except for a single index l of c, and it is trained to identify l.

concepts and prototypes have been proposed [6,22,27,31]. TCAV [22] is a post-hoc method based on predefined concepts. TCAV offers an explanation by finding the closest predefined concepts to the corresponding class in the feature space. Unlike most post-hoc methods, TCAV only offers an explanation for a class, not for a single data point.

Built-In Interpretability. SENN [31] suggests an interpretable classifier structure that predicts a class by combining concepts and relevances. SENN encodes input features into two representations: concepts and relevances. The importance of a given concept for classification can be explained through the relevance score of the corresponding concept. However, the learned concepts of SENN are not clearly human-understandable, as analyzed in Sect. S3 of the supplementary. ProtoPNet [6] proposes an interpretable classifier based on prototypes. ProtoPNet learns prototypical patches of each class from the training dataset. After finding the prototypes, the model makes a decision by measuring the distance between local patches of the test observation and the found prototypes of each class.

3   iCaps: An Interpretable Classifier via Disentangled Capsule Networks

iCaps comprises six components, as illustrated in Fig. 2.

- C_C: a capsule network (classifier) that represents the class-relevant latent space.

- E: an encoder that represents the class-irrelevant (residual) latent space.
- G: a generator that creates synthetic images using $C_C(x) \oplus E(x)$, where $\oplus$ represents concatenation.
- D_G: a discriminator for image generation, that distinguishes whether an observation is from the dataset or from G.
- C_G: a classifier for image generation, that estimates class labels.
- D_{CR}: a discriminator for contrastive regularization (CR), that maximizes the distance between the concepts represented by C_C

Assume that a collection of n images $x_1, x_2, ..., x_n \in \mathcal{X}$ and their corresponding labels $y_i \in [k]$ is provided. k and $[k]$ ($= [1, ..., k]$) are the number and the set of classes, respectively. $\mathcal{X}^i$ represents all images corresponding to a class index i. As described in Fig. 2, iCaps uses two images of different class labels as input in the training phase. In the case of binary classification, the input pairs are images of the opposite class labels. In multiclass classification, two class labels are randomly selected in each batch.

We assume that the representation of images can be disentangled into two complementary latent spaces, $\mathcal{C}$ and $\mathcal{R}$. Our objective is to find a class-relevant representation $c_i \in \mathcal{C}$ and a class-irrelevant (we call as residual) representation $r_i \in \mathcal{R}$ for each image x_i. The size of output vector of the class-relevant representation is L.

3.1 Disentanglement Between Class-Relevant and Class-Irrelevant Information

The class-relevant subspace, $\mathcal{C}$, is represented by C_C, and the residual subspace, $\mathcal{R}$, is represented by E. The class-relevant representation, c_i, contains all the information relevant for classification, whereas the residual representation, r_i, contains residual information irrelevant for classification. The previous class-supervised disentanglement methods [4,9,12,20] contain only information shared by each class (inter-class variation) in c_i, assuming that $\|c_i - c_j\|_F^2 = 0$ if $y_i = y_j$. However, under this assumption, c_i cannot include classification-relevant intra-class variation. For example, if a model is trained using a dataset labeled as female and male, and most of the males are wearing suits, then wearing a suit should be a classification-relevant variable. In other words, this variable should be included in c. However, to satisfy the assumption: $\|c_i - c_j\|_F^2 = 0$ if $y_i = y_j$ above, every man should be defined as wearing a suit. This is not true. If this variable is not included in c, it should be included in r. Consequently, information leakage is implied because wearing a suit is classification-relevant information in this model.

We wish to include classification-relevant intra-class variation in c_i. By analyzing only c_i, we can understand the rationale behind the model's prediction. More information-theoretically, when the mutual information between c and y is:

$$I(c; y) = \int_y \int_c p(y) \, q(c|y) \log \frac{q(c|y)}{q(c)} \, dc \, dy, \tag{3}$$

where $q(c) = \int_y p(y) \, q(c|y) \, dy$, $I(c; \, y)$ should be non-zero, and $I(r; \, y)$ should be zero. To obtain $I(c; \, y) > 0$ and $I(r; \, y) = 0$, we utilize three objective functions.

The first objective is a cross-entropy loss that includes two images generated by swapping r of two inputof latent traversal. However,s. The loss term is:

$$\mathcal{L}_{C_G} = \lambda_{C_G} \, (\mathbb{E}[(1 - y_t) \cdot C_G(x)] + \mathbb{E}[(1 - y_t^i) \cdot C_G(\hat{x}^{c^i, r^i})]$$
$$+ \, \mathbb{E}[(1 - y_t^i) \cdot C_G(\hat{x}^{c^i, r^j})] - \mathbb{E}[y_t \cdot C_G(x)]] \qquad (4)$$
$$- \, \mathbb{E}[y_t^i \cdot C_G(\hat{x}^{c^i, r^i})]] - \mathbb{E}[y_t^i \cdot C_G(\hat{x}^{c^i, r^j})]]),$$

where i and j are two different class indices, $x \sim p_{\text{data}}(x)$, $x^i \sim p_{\text{data}}(x^i)$, $x^j \sim p_{\text{data}}(x^j)$, y_t is an one-hot encoding of $y \in [k]$, $\hat{x}^{c^i, r^i} \sim G(C_C(x^i), E(x^i))$, and $\hat{x}^{c^i, r^j} \sim G(C_C(x^i), E(x^j))$. The class labels of the two synthetic images, $\hat{x}^{c^i, r^i}$ and $\hat{x}^{c^i, r^j}$, are the same as y_t^i. For all images in Eq. 4, the higher the probability of class i, the smaller the loss.

Furthermore, we use the prediction confidence of the model as a loss. We propose a class-similarity (CS) loss:

$$\mathcal{L}_{\text{CS}} = \lambda_{\text{CS}} \, \mathbb{E} \left\| C_G^{\text{logit}}(\hat{x}^{c^i, r^i}) - C_G^{\text{logit}}(\hat{x}^{c^i, r^j}) \right\|_F^2, \qquad (5)$$

where C_G^{logit} represents the logit of C_G. In Eq. 5, we can compare the likelihood distributions of two images generated based on the same c yet different r. That is, the images generated with the same c should have exactly the same likelihood distributions in our framework. $\mathcal{L}_{C_G}$ and $\mathcal{L}_{\text{CS}}$ cause information relevant to the classification to be included in c.

The third loss is for the residual features independent of classification. Other similar studies use either an adversarial loss [9], KL-divergence term [4], or asymmetric noise regularization [12] to encode class-irrelevant features in r. Unlike these methods, we allow r to include the remaining information by causing c to include all the relevant information for classification. The residual similarity (RS) loss is defined as follows:

$$\mathcal{L}_{\text{RS}} = \lambda_{\text{RS}} \, \mathbb{E} \left\| E(x^i) - E(\hat{x}^{c^j, r^i}) \right\|_F^2. \qquad (6)$$

To minimize $\mathcal{L}_{\text{RS}}$, the class-irrelevant (residual) feature, r, of the real image x^i corresponding to class index i and the class-irrelevant (residual) feature, r, of $\hat{x}^{c^j, r^i}$ should be the same. This is only possible when c contains all the classification-relevant information.

In addition, in our study, we assume that all dimensions of c are used to represent class-relevant concepts. More formally,

$$\min_{l \in L} \mathbb{E}[I(C_C(x); y)_l] > 0 \qquad (7)$$

where L is the size of c. However, $\mathcal{L}_M$, $\mathcal{L}_{C_G}$ and $\mathcal{L}_{\text{CS}}$ do not guarantee the above assumption. Therefore, we propose the loss as follows:

$$\mathcal{L}_{\text{concept}} = - \lambda_{\text{concept}} \, (\min_{l \in L} \left| \mathbb{E}[C_C(x^i)] - \mathbb{E}[C_C(x^j)] \right|_l). \qquad (8)$$

$\mathcal{L}_{concept}$ is additionally suggested to maximize the mutual information between all elements of c and y. By using $\mathcal{L}_M$ and $\mathcal{L}_{concept}$ together, we enforce all dimensions of c to represent discriminative concepts by maximizing the smallest distance between different classes i, j among all the dimensions. We elaborate the benefits of the proposed losses and components in Sects. 4 and S2.

3.2 Latent Traversal

We add a discriminator, D_{CR}, to prevent overlapping concepts, which is the second problem we wish to solve. The idea of D_{CR} comes from latent traversal. Latent traversal refers to generating images by traversing a single element of a latent space; it is widely used to measure disentanglement in evaluation [18,23]. Lin et al. [28] first used the idea of latent traversal in the training phase, and named as contrastive regularization. By following it, we also call our loss as $\mathcal{L}_{CR}$. $\mathcal{L}_{CR}$ can be expressed as follows:

$$\mathcal{L}_{CR} = -\lambda_{CR}\, \mathbb{E}_{l\sim U[L],\,(\hat{x},\hat{x}')\sim G(C_C(x),E(x))}\left[\langle I,\, \log D_{CR}(\hat{x},\hat{x}')\rangle\right], \qquad (9)$$

where l is a random index over L, $\hat{x}$ and $\hat{x}'$ are two images generated with different value of $C_C(x)_l$ while fixing the remaining elements. $< \cdot >$ represents a dot product, and I denotes the one-hot encoding of the random index l. $\mathcal{L}_{CR}$ forces changes in the elements of c to be visually noticeable and easy to distinguish between each other. The difference between our L_{CR} and that reported in [28] is that we directly used the definition of latent traversal. However, Lin et al. [28] fixed a single element and changes all the remaining elements, and tries to identify the fixed element.

3.3 Interpretable Classifier Based on Learned Concepts

In addition, we replace the decoder part of DeepCaps with Generative Adversarial Networks (GANs) [13] to encourage $\hat{x}^{c^i,r^j}$ to be realistic. To enable $\mathcal{L}_{C_G}$ and $\mathcal{L}_{CS}$ to function as intended, the quality of generated image $\hat{x}^{c^i,r^j}$ is important. Unlike $\hat{x}^{c^i,r^i}$, $\hat{x}^{c^i,r^j}$ does not have a ground-truth image. Therefore, we used an adversarial game of GANs and the ACGAN [33] structure; as such, C_G and D_G share the weight except for the last fully connected layer. The losses for G and D_G are as follows:

$$\mathcal{L}_G = -\lambda_G\, \mathbb{E}[D_G(\hat{x})], \quad \mathcal{L}_{D_G} = \lambda_{D_G}\,(\mathbb{E}[D_G(\hat{x})] - \mathbb{E}[D_G(x)]). \qquad (10)$$

L_G is a loss to create a realistic image, and L_{D_G} is a WGAN [14] based loss to distinguish generated images by G from real images. For the gradient penalty, we used a Lipschitz gradient penalty term [35]:

$$\mathcal{L}_{LGP} = \lambda_{LGP}\, \mathbb{E}(\|\nabla_{\hat{x}} D_G(\hat{x})\|_2 - 1)_+^2. \qquad (11)$$

The built-in interpretable model domain is still new. By analyzing similar studies, we posit a reasonable set of desiderata for an interpretable classifier based on learned concepts as follows:

Table 1. Classification accuracy (C_C) of $p(y|c)$ (higher is better).

Architecture	MNIST	SVHN	CelebA
ResNet-18 [16]	0.992	0.945	0.977
DeepCaps [36]	0.997	0.971	0.974
Ours	0.992	0.920	0.984

1. **Informativeness**: the concept representation of x for explanations should preserve only classification-relevant information,
2. **Distinctness**: the learned concepts should be non-overlapping,
3. **Explainability**: a decision should be explained with human-understandable concepts.

We obtained these conditions by (i) encoding only the class-relevant information in c, (ii) enforcing distinctness by an additional discriminator and (iii) exploiting the fact that the instantiation parameters represented by the class capsule are human-understandable concepts.

To train iCaps, we alternatively trained C_C, E, D_G & C_G, G, and D_{CR} using the following gradients:

$$\theta_{C_C} \overset{+}{\leftarrow} -\Delta_{\theta_{C_C}}(\mathcal{L}_M + \mathcal{L}_{\text{recon}} + \mathcal{L}_{\text{concept}} + \mathcal{L}_{C_G} + \mathcal{L}_{\text{CS}} + \mathcal{L}_{\text{RS}} + \mathcal{L}_{\text{CR}}) \quad (12)$$

$$\theta_E \overset{+}{\leftarrow} -\Delta_{\theta_E}(\mathcal{L}_{\text{recon}} + \mathcal{L}_{\text{KL}} + \mathcal{L}_{\text{CS}} + \mathcal{L}_{\text{RS}} + \mathcal{L}_{C_G}) \quad (13)$$

$$\theta_{(D_G, C_G)} \overset{+}{\leftarrow} -\Delta_{\theta_{(D_G, C_G)}}(\mathcal{L}_{D_G} + \mathcal{L}_{C_G} + \mathcal{L}_{\text{CS}} + \mathcal{L}_{\text{LGP}}) \quad (14)$$

$$\theta_G \overset{+}{\leftarrow} -\Delta_{\theta_G}(\mathcal{L}_G + \mathcal{L}_{C_G} + \mathcal{L}_{\text{recon}} + \mathcal{L}_{\text{CS}} + \mathcal{L}_{\text{RS}} + \mathcal{L}_{\text{CR}}) \quad (15)$$

$$\theta_{D_{CR}} \overset{+}{\leftarrow} -\Delta_{\theta_{D_{CR}}}\mathcal{L}_{\text{CR}} \quad (16)$$

$\mathcal{L}_{\text{KL}}$ represents the KL term of a variational autoencoder [24]; $\mathcal{L}_{\text{KL}}$ is scaled down by a small hyperparameter such that it does not reduce the reconstruction ability [23]. $\mathcal{L}_M$ and $\mathcal{L}_{\text{recon}}$ are provided in Sect. 2.1. In case of $\mathcal{L}_{\text{recon}}$, $\hat{x}$ is from $G(C_C(x), E(x))$.

4   Experiments

We evaluated the performance of our method and the comparison methods on three datasets: MNIST [25] (digit number as a class label), SVHN [32] (digit number as a class label), and CelebA [29] (gender as a class label). In CelebA, we used gender as a class label. Unlike person identity or other CelebA attributes, such as smiling and beard, several factors should be considered when selecting whether an observation is a female or a male. To demonstrate the effectiveness of our study, a classification task is required, in which several consistent factors are considered to classify an observation.

Table 2. Classification accuracy of $p(y|r)$. We trained a classifier using r of ours and the comparison methods. The classifier would have a random chance for test datasets if there is no class-relevant information in r (lower is better).

Architecture	MNIST	SVHN	CelebA
Cycle-VAE [20]	0.176	0.436	0.793
ML-VAE [4]	0.717	0.445	0.786
LORD [12]	0.099	0.163	0.517
Ours	0.099	0.099	0.501
Random chance	0.100	0.100	0.500

We predetermined the sizes of c and r for the three datasets. In MNIST and SVHN, $c \in \mathbb{R}^4$ and $r \in \mathbb{R}^8$. In CelebA, $c \in \mathbb{R}^8$ and $r \in \mathbb{R}^{16}$. Sect. S6 of the supplementary discusses the sizes of c and r in detail. In addition, Sect. S1 of the supplementary provides details of experiment information of our work.

4.1 Informativeness

We measured the classification performance of our model and compared it with those of ResNet-18 [16] and DeepCaps [36]. Our method shows similar accuracies on all three datasets, as shown in Table 1. Our model can provide an explanation of the model's prediction without degradation in classification performance. We verified the informativeness of c using quantitative and qualitative methods.

Quantitative Experiments. By following the protocol from Cycle-VAE [20], we trained a simple classifier to classify class labels from the residual representation r. This experiment was conducted to evaluate whether the class-relevant information is present in r. For comparison, we used recent class-supervised disentanglement methods [4,12,20]. The details of hyperparameters used for the comparison methods are provided in Sect. S9 of the supplementary.

As shown in Table 2, only our method preserved a random chance in all the three datasets. This is because unlike the comparison methods, we did not agree with and implement the assumption that intra-class variation can be ignored. For datasets created for disentanglement learning, such as Cars3D [37], Small-Norb [26], KTH [39], etc., class-relevant intra-class variation is certainly small. However, for complex real datasets, class-relevant intra-class variation is typical (even large). Empirically, the classification accuracies of SVHN and CelebA in Table 2 show that the completely class-irrelevant r cannot be created when assumed that intra-class variation can be ignored. For further analysis, we measured the mutual information between y and c, r of our model: $I(c; y)$ and $I(r; y)$. The $c0$ to $c7$ in Fig. 3 represent each element of the output vector of the class capsule. As shown in Fig. 3(a, b, c), all the elements of c of our method are strongly correlated to y, and all the elements of r are uncorrelated to y for the datasets.

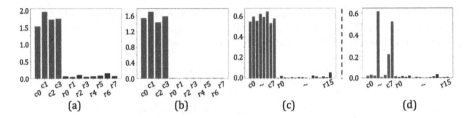

Fig. 3. Mutual information between y and c, r of (a) MNIST, (b) SVHN, (c) CelebA, and (d) CelebA w/o $\mathcal{L}_{\text{concept}}$ (higher is better for c; lower is better for r)

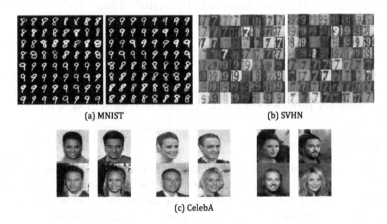

Fig. 4. Swapping. The images on the left of (a, b, c) are reconstructed using (c^i, r^i) and (c^j, r^j). The images on the right of (a, b, c) are generated by swapping c: (c^j, r^i) and (c^i, r^j).

As an ablation study, we tested the importance of $\mathcal{L}_{\text{concept}}$. As shown in Fig. 3(d), some elements of c obtained without $\mathcal{L}_{\text{concept}}$ show low correlations to y. r still does not contain any class-relevant information, however, $\mathcal{L}_{\text{concept}}$ is required to encode class-relevant information to each element of c. Also, We tested the importance of $\mathcal{L}_M$ by replacing C_C with ResNet-18. The result is discussed in Sect. S4 of the supplementary.

Qualitative Experiments. By swapping, we visually evaluated which factors of variation were encoded into c and r and whether they were semantically correct. From two test images of different class labels, we obtained (c_i, r_i) and (c_j, r_j), individually. Subsequently, we swapped c_i and c_j to generate new observations. The images on the left of Fig. 4(a, b, c) are generated using the original set: (c_i, r_i) and (c_j, r_j). The images on the right of Fig. 4(a, b, c) are generated by swapping: (c_j, r_i) and (c_i, r_j). It is clear that for MNIST, r contains factors of variation such as thickness and skew. For SVHN, r contains background color, font color, thickness, location, and skew. For CelebA, r contains background color and a person's face feature. We believe that the results show semantically

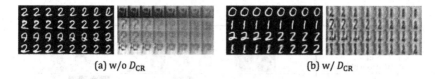

(a) w/o D_{CR} **(b)** w/ D_{CR}

Fig. 5. Ablation study of D_{CR}. For (a), changes in rows overlap, whereas changes in rows are distinct in (b).

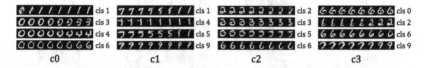

c0   c1   c2   c3

Fig. 6. Concepts learned for MNIST. c0: being a big circle, c1: being a straight line, c2: creating a small circle in the bottom part and c3: changing the upper part of the digit to a line.

correct disentanglement. A detailed analysis of c will be presented in Sect. 4.3. In addition, the T-SNE [30] results of r and c of our method are shown in Sect. S7. The measured FID [17] scores of the images by reconstruction, swapping, and random generation are provided in Sect. S8 of the supplementary.

4.2 Distinctness

Distinctness means that each concept should be represented by a single variable. The variable type varies in each method, which can be a prototype or a latent feature [6,31]. In our method, the single concept is represented by a single element of the class capsule. To enforce it, we used an additional discriminator, D_{CR}. Figure 5(a) shows the images generated by G trained without D_{CR}. Each row of image (a) indicates each element of the class capsule, and the eight images of the row are the results of linear interpolation between -1 and 1. In Fig. 5(b), the change in each element is distinct from each other, whereas in Fig. 5(a), the elements overlap. For example, the change in the left-half of the first row and the change in the right-half of the fourth row in MNIST of Fig. 5(a) are the almost same. In such a case, the values for a single concept would be contradicting. This shows that D_{CR} is required to enforce distinctness between the elements. The same trend was observed in CelebA. The qualitative and quantitative results of CelebA are given in Fig. S2 and Table S3 of the supplementary. In addition, the importance of all the six components is discussed in Sect. S2 of the supplementary.

4.3 Explainability

If explanations are provided based on concepts, these concepts should be human-understandable. In our setting, we demonstrate the learned concepts by linearly

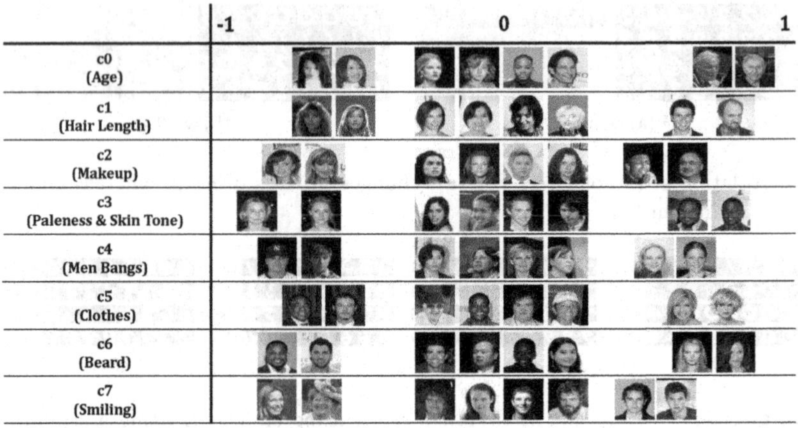

Fig. 7. Concepts learned for CelebA. For more details, $c2$ represents makeup. As the value approaches -1, people with heavy makeup appear. $c6$ represents a beard. As the value approaches -1, people who have a beard appear. Other concepts can be understood by verifying which image has a negative or positive value for each element.

interpolating or analyzing data points of similar values. In Fig. 6, the concept of each element is shown by linear interpolation. In MNIST, r contains concepts such as thickness and skew, as described in Sect. 4.1. For c, the first element represents being a large circle. As the value approaches to -1, a majority of the digits are changed to zero. The second element represents being a straight line, and the third and fourth elements represent creating a small circle in the bottom part and changing the upper part of the digit to a line, respectively. By analyzing these results, we recognized that the factors relevant to MNIST classification are the size, number, and location of the circles and lines, and this finding also fits to SVHN in a very similar way (Sect. S5).

For CelebA, we show the concept of each element by analyzing a set of test images of certain values. We discovered the concepts such as age, hair length, makeup, paleness, skin tone, men hairstyle, clothes, beard, and smile, as shown in Fig. 7. Case $c1$ represents hair length. As the value approaches 1, a person with extremely short hair appears. Case $c4$ represents men's hairstyle. A person who has men bangs and perm typically exhibits a value less than 0. In case $c5$, the majority of men exhibit values less than 0. $c5$ is close to -1 when the person wears a suit and close to 1 when the person wears open-shoulder clothes.

We discovered an interesting phenomenon: In case $c0$, the element represents age. For persons appearing young, they typically have a value less than 0. Statistically, the number of females with values less than 0 was high, and the number of females with values greater than 0 was low. For males, the situation was vice versa. The model learned data bias from the CelebA dataset. When we analyzed the attribute named "young" of the CelebA dataset, we discovered an imbalance in the number of data, i.e., a ratio 2:1 (female:male). Similar to this case, we discovered an imbalance in CelebA attributes "pale skin" (3:1) and "smiling"

		Age	Hair Length	Make up	Skin Tone	Men Bangs	Clothes	Beard	Smiling	Confidence
(a)	 F	-0.073	-0.271	-0.364	-0.469	0.306	0.175	0.408	-0.523	0.999
(b)	 M	0.439	0.411	0.325	0.300	-0.344	-0.370	-0.410	0.124	0.999
(c)	 F	-0.101	-0.261	-0.101	0.006	-0.027	0.073	-0.116	-0.063	0.335
(d)	 M	0.043	-0.016	-0.001	0.017	-0.054	0.040	0.001	0.024	0.087

Fig. 8. Explanations generated by iCaps for four samples. In the cases of (a, b), iCaps is accurate in the predictions. On the contrary, in the cases of (c, d), iCaps misclassified with a low confidence score. By analyzing the values of each concept of the samples, we can understand the high and low confidence of iCaps in making the predictions.

(2:1), and these biases were encoded as class-relevant concepts ($c0$, $c3$, and $c7$). We discovered that our model can be used as a detector of hidden data bias; this will be investigated in future studies.

Herein, we demonstrate the explainability of our method using samples. In Fig. 8, we present classification success cases of a female and a male, as well as misclassification cases of a female and a male. By analyzing the values of the concepts, we understood why the model classified Fig. 8(a) as a female with such high confidence. Figure 8(a) was predicted as a female owing to observations of long hair, pale skin, no men bangs, no beard, and a smiling face. In the misclassification case (d), the model showed very low confidence in the classification because the model could not find a strong relevance to any concepts.

5   Conclusion and Future Work

We propose a novel disentanglement method that the class-relevant subspace contains both class-relevant inter- and intra-class variation. Using the proposed method, we build a new interpretable model that provides explanations of the model's prediction based on class-relevant distinct concepts.

In addition, the generator of our model can generate an image of the desired combination of the concepts. Hence, it can be used for data augmentation or additional explanations. Also, we will keep analyzing the possibility of our model as a detector of data bias. In future studies, we try to improve reconstruction ability and further, add a sentence generation phase at the end so that the model can generate an explanation as a sentence automatically.

Acknowledgments. This work was supported by the National Research Foundation of Korea (NRF) grant funded by the Korea government (Ministry of Science and ICT) [2018R1A2B3001628], the Brain Korea 21 Plus Project in 2020, Samsung Advanced Institute of Technology and Institute for Information & Communications Technology Planning & Evaluation (IITP) grant funded by the Korea government (MSIT)

(No.2019-0-01367, BabyMind), and AIR Lab in Hyundai Motor Company through HMC-SNU AI Consortium Fund.

References

1. Adebayo, J., Gilmer, J., Goodfellow, I., Kim, B.: Local explanation methods for deep neural networks lack sensitivity to parameter values. arXiv preprint arXiv:1810.03307 (2018)
2. Ahmed, K., Torresani, L.: STAR-Caps: capsule networks with straight-through attentive routing. In: Advances in Neural Information Processing Systems, pp. 9098–9107 (2019)
3. Bach, S., Binder, A., Montavon, G., Klauschen, F., Müller, K.R., Samek, W.: On pixel-wise explanations for non-linear classifier decisions by layer-wise relevance propagation. PloS ONE **10**(7), e0130140 (2015)
4. Bouchacourt, D., Tomioka, R., Nowozin, S.: Multi-level variational autoencoder: learning disentangled representations from grouped observations. In: Thirty-Second AAAI Conference on Artificial Intelligence (2018)
5. Chang, C.H., Creager, E., Goldenberg, A., Duvenaud, D.: Explaining image classifiers by counterfactual generation (2018)
6. Chen, C., Li, O., Tao, D., Barnett, A., Rudin, C., Su, J.K.: This looks like that: deep learning for interpretable image recognition. In: Advances in Neural Information Processing Systems, pp. 8928–8939 (2019)
7. Chen, X., Duan, Y., Houthooft, R., Schulman, J., Sutskever, I., Abbeel, P.: Info-GAN: interpretable representation learning by information maximizing generative adversarial nets. In: Advances in Neural Information Processing Systems, pp. 2172–2180 (2016)
8. Dabkowski, P., Gal, Y.: Real time image saliency for black box classifiers. In: Advances in Neural Information Processing Systems, pp. 6967–6976 (2017)
9. Denton, E.L., et al.: Unsupervised learning of disentangled representations from video. In: Advances in Neural Information Processing Systems, pp. 4414–4423 (2017)
10. Fong, R., Patrick, M., Vedaldi, A.: Understanding deep networks via extremal perturbations and smooth masks. arXiv preprint arXiv:1910.08485 (2019)
11. Fong, R.C., Vedaldi, A.: Interpretable explanations of black boxes by meaningful perturbation. In: Proceedings of the IEEE International Conference on Computer Vision, pp. 3429–3437 (2017)
12. Gabbay, A., Hoshen, Y.: Demystifying inter-class disentanglement. In: International Conference on Learning Representations (2020). https://openreview.net/forum?id=Hyl9xxHYPr
13. Goodfellow, I., et al.: Generative adversarial nets. In: Advances in Neural Information Processing Systems, pp. 2672–2680 (2014)
14. Gulrajani, I., Ahmed, F., Arjovsky, M., Dumoulin, V., Courville, A.C.: Improved training of wasserstein GANs. In: Advances in Neural Information Processing Systems, pp. 5767–5777 (2017)
15. Hahn, T., Pyeon, M., Kim, G.: Self-routing capsule networks. In: Advances in Neural Information Processing Systems, pp. 7656–7665 (2019)
16. He, K., Zhang, X., Ren, S., Sun, J.: Deep residual learning for image recognition. In: Proceedings of the IEEE Conference on Computer Vision and Pattern Recognition, pp. 770–778 (2016)

17. Heusel, M., Ramsauer, H., Unterthiner, T., Nessler, B., Hochreiter, S.: GANs trained by a two time-scale update rule converge to a local nash equilibrium. In: Advances in Neural Information Processing Systems, pp. 6626–6637 (2017)
18. Higgins, I., et al.: Beta-VAE: learning basic visual concepts with a constrained variational framework. In: ICLR, vol. 2, no. 5, p. 6 (2017)
19. Jeong, T., Lee, Y., Kim, H.: Ladder capsule network. In: International Conference on Machine Learning. pp, 3071–3079 (2019)
20. Jha, A.H., Anand, S., Singh, M., Veeravasarapu, V.S.R.: Disentangling factors of variation with cycle-consistent variational auto-encoders. In: Ferrari, V., Hebert, M., Sminchisescu, C., Weiss, Y. (eds.) ECCV 2018. LNCS, vol. 11207, pp. 829–845. Springer, Cham (2018). https://doi.org/10.1007/978-3-030-01219-9_49
21. Kim, B., Gilmer, J., Wattenberg, M., Viégas, F.: TCAV: relative concept importance testing with linear concept activation vectors (2018)
22. Kim, B., Wattenberg, M., Gilmer, J., Cai, C., Wexler, J., Viegas, F., et al.: Interpretability beyond feature attribution: quantitative testing with concept activation vectors (TCAV). In: International Conference on Machine Learning, pp. 2668–2677 (2018)
23. Kim, H., Mnih, A.: Disentangling by factorising. In: Dy, J., Krause, A. (eds.) Proceedings of the 35th International Conference on Machine Learning. Proceedings of Machine Learning Research. PMLR, Stockholmsmässan, Stockholm, Sweden, 10–15 July 2018, vol. 80, pp. 2649–2658 (2018)
24. Kingma, D.P., Welling, M.: Auto-encoding variational bayes. arXiv preprint arXiv:1312.6114 (2013)
25. LeCun, Y., Bottou, L., Bengio, Y., Haffner, P.: Gradient-based learning applied to document recognition. Proc. IEEE **86**(11), 2278–2324 (1998)
26. LeCun, Y., Huang, F.J., Bottou, L.: Learning methods for generic object recognition with invariance to pose and lighting. In: Proceedings of the 2004 IEEE Computer Society Conference on Computer Vision and Pattern Recognition, 2004. CVPR 2004, vol. 2, pp. II-104. IEEE (2004)
27. Li, O., Liu, H., Chen, C., Rudin, C.: Deep learning for case-based reasoning through prototypes: a neural network that explains its predictions. In: Thirty-Second AAAI Conference on Artificial Intelligence (2018)
28. Lin, Z., Thekumparampil, K.K., Fanti, G., Oh, S.: InfoGAN-CR: disentangling generative adversarial networks with contrastive regularizers. arXiv preprint arXiv:1906.06034 (2019)
29. Liu, Z., Luo, P., Wang, X., Tang, X.: Deep learning face attributes in the wild. In: Proceedings of International Conference on Computer Vision (ICCV), December 2015
30. Maaten, L.V.D., Hinton, G.: Visualizing data using t-SNE. J. Mach. Learn. Res. **9**, 2579–2605 (2008)
31. Melis, D.A., Jaakkola, T.: Towards robust interpretability with self-explaining neural networks. In: Advances in Neural Information Processing Systems, pp. 7775–7784 (2018)
32. Netzer, Y., Wang, T., Coates, A., Bissacco, A., Wu, B., Ng, A.Y.: Reading digits in natural images with unsupervised feature learning (2011)
33. Odena, A., Olah, C., Shlens, J.: Conditional image synthesis with auxiliary classifier GANs. In: Proceedings of the 34th International Conference on Machine Learning, vol. 70, pp. 2642–2651. JMLR. org (2017)
34. Petsiuk, V., Das, A., Saenko, K.: RISE: randomized input sampling for explanation of black-box models. arXiv preprint arXiv:1806.07421 (2018)

35. Petzka, H., Fischer, A., Lukovnikov, D.: On the regularization of wasserstein GANs. In: International Conference on Learning Representations (2018). https://openreview.net/forum?id=B1hYRMbCW
36. Rajasegaran, J., Jayasundara, V., Jayasekara, S., Jayasekara, H., Seneviratne, S., Rodrigo, R.: DeepCaps: going deeper with capsule networks. In: Proceedings of the IEEE Conference on Computer Vision and Pattern Recognition, pp. 10725–10733 (2019)
37. Reed, S.E., Zhang, Y., Zhang, Y., Lee, H.: Deep visual analogy-making. In: Advances in Neural Information Processing Systems, pp. 1252–1260 (2015)
38. Sabour, S., Frosst, N., Hinton, G.E.: Dynamic routing between capsules. In: Advances in Neural Information Processing Systems, pp. 3856–3866 (2017)
39. Schuldt, C., Laptev, I., Caputo, B.: Recognizing human actions: a local SVM approach. In: Proceedings of the 17th International Conference on Pattern Recognition, 2004. ICPR 2004, vol. 3, pp. 32–36. IEEE (2004)
40. Selvaraju, R.R., Cogswell, M., Das, A., Vedantam, R., Parikh, D., Batra, D.: Grad-CAM: visual explanations from deep networks via gradient-based localization. In: Proceedings of the IEEE International Conference on Computer Vision, pp. 618–626 (2017)
41. Shrikumar, A., Greenside, P., Kundaje, A.: Learning important features through propagating activation differences. In: Proceedings of the 34th International Conference on Machine Learning, vol. 70, pp. 3145–3153. JMLR. org (2017)
42. Simonyan, K., Vedaldi, A., Zisserman, A.: Deep inside convolutional networks: visualising image classification models and saliency maps. arXiv preprint arXiv:1312.6034 (2013)
43. Smilkov, D., Thorat, N., Kim, B., Viégas, F., Wattenberg, M.: Smoothgrad: removing noise by adding noise. arXiv preprint arXiv:1706.03825 (2017)
44. Springenberg, J.T., Dosovitskiy, A., Brox, T., Riedmiller, M.: Striving for simplicity: the all convolutional net. arXiv preprint arXiv:1412.6806 (2014)
45. Sundararajan, M., Taly, A., Yan, Q.: Axiomatic attribution for deep networks. In: Proceedings of the 34th International Conference on Machine Learning, vol. 70, pp. 3319–3328. JMLR. org (2017)
46. Szabó, A., Hu, Q., Portenier, T., Zwicker, M., Favaro, P.: Challenges in disentangling independent factors of variation. arXiv preprint arXiv:1711.02245 (2017)
47. Zeiler, M.D., Fergus, R.: Visualizing and understanding convolutional networks. In: Fleet, D., Pajdla, T., Schiele, B., Tuytelaars, T. (eds.) ECCV 2014. LNCS, vol. 8689, pp. 818–833. Springer, Cham (2014). https://doi.org/10.1007/978-3-319-10590-1_53
48. Zintgraf, L.M., Cohen, T.S., Adel, T., Welling, M.: Visualizing deep neural network decisions: prediction difference analysis. arXiv preprint arXiv:1702.04595 (2017)

Detecting Natural Disasters, Damage, and Incidents in the Wild

Ethan Weber[1(✉)], Nuria Marzo[1], Dim P. Papadopoulos[1], Aritro Biswas[1],
Agata Lapedriza[1,3], Ferda Ofli[2], Muhammad Imran[2], and Antonio Torralba[1]

[1] Massachusetts Institute of Technology, Cambridge, USA
{ejweber,nmarzo,dimpapa,abiswas,agata,torralba}@mit.edu
[2] Qatar Computing Research Institute, HBKU, Ar-Rayyan, Qatar
{fofli,mimran}@hbku.edu.qa
[3] Universitat Oberta de Catalunya, Barcelona, Spain

Abstract. Responding to natural disasters, such as earthquakes, floods, and wildfires, is a laborious task performed by on-the-ground emergency responders and analysts. Social media has emerged as a low-latency data source to quickly understand disaster situations. While most studies on social media are limited to text, images offer more information for understanding disaster and incident scenes. However, no large-scale image datasets for incident detection exists. In this work, we present the Incidents Dataset, which contains 446,684 images annotated by humans that cover 43 incidents across a variety of scenes. We employ a baseline classification model that mitigates false-positive errors and we perform image filtering experiments on millions of social media images from Flickr and Twitter. Through these experiments, we show how the Incidents Dataset can be used to detect images with incidents in the wild. Code, data, and models are available online at http://incidentsdataset.csail.mit.edu.

Keywords: Image classification · Visual recognition · Scene understanding · Image dataset · Social media · Disaster analysis · Incident detection

1 Introduction

Rapid detection of sudden onset disasters such as earthquakes, flash floods, and other emergencies such as road accidents is extremely important for response organizations. However, acquiring information in the occurrence of emergencies is labor-intensive and costly as it often requires manual data processing and expert assessment. To alleviate these manual efforts, there have been attempts to apply computer vision techniques on satellite imagery, synthetic aperture radar, and other remote sensing data [14,25,60,74]. Unfortunately, these approaches are still costly to deploy and they are not robust enough to obtain relevant data under time-critical situations. Moreover, satellite imagery is susceptible to noise such as clouds and smoke (i.e., common scenes during hurricanes and wildfires), and only provides an overhead view of the disaster-hit area.

© Springer Nature Switzerland AG 2020
A. Vedaldi et al. (Eds.): ECCV 2020, LNCS 12364, pp. 331–350, 2020.
https://doi.org/10.1007/978-3-030-58529-7_20

On the other hand, studies show that social media posts in the form of text messages, images, and videos are available moments after a disaster strikes and contain information pertinent to disaster response such as reports of damages to infrastructure, urgent needs of affected people, among others [13,35]. However, unlike other data sources (e.g., satellite), social media imagery remains unexplored, mainly because of two important challenges. First, image streams on social media are very noisy, and disasters are not an exception. Even after performing a text-based filter, a large percentage of images in social media are not relevant to specific disaster categories. Second, deep learning models, that are the standard techniques used for image classification, are data-hungry, and yet no large-scale ground-level image dataset exists today to build robust computational models.

In this work we address these challenges and investigate how to detect natural disasters, damage, and incidents in images. Concretely, our paper has the following three main contributions. First, we present the large-scale Incidents Dataset, which consists of 446,684 scene-centric images annotated by humans as positive for natural disasters (class-positives), types of damage or specific events that can require human attention or assistance, like traffic jams or car accidents. We use the term *incidents* to refer to the 43 categories covered by our dataset (Sect. 3). The dataset also contains an additional set of 697,464 images annotated by humans as negatives for specific incident categories (class-negatives). As discussed in Sect. 2, the Incidents Dataset is significantly larger, more complete, and much more diverse than any other dataset related to incident detection in scene-centric images. Second, using the full set of 1.1M images in our dataset, we train different deep learning models for incident classification and incident detection. In particular, we use a slightly modified binary cross-entropy loss function, which we refer to as class-negative loss, that exploits our class-negative images. Our experiments in Sect. 5 show the importance of using class-negatives in order to train a model that is robust enough to be deployed for incident detection in real scenarios, where the number of negatives is large. Third, we perform extended incident detection experiments on large-scale social media image collections, using millions of images from Flickr and Twitter. These experiments, presented in Sect. 6, show how our model, trained with the Incidents Dataset and the class-negative loss, can be effectively deployed in real situations to identify incidents in social media images. We hope that the release of the Incidents Dataset will spur more work in computer vision for humanitarian purposes, specifically natural disaster and incident analysis.

2   Related Work

Computer Vision for Social Good. Existing vision-based technologies are short of reaching out to diverse geographies and communities due to biases in the commonly used datasets. For instance, state-of-the-art object recognition models perform poorly on images of household items found in low-income countries [79]. To remedy this shortcoming, the community has made recent progress in areas

Fig. 1. Example images from the Incidents Dataset. Incidents (left) happen in many places (top), which we capture by having 43 incident and 49 place categories. Notice that a car accident can occur on a beach, farm, highway, etc. The place categories help by adding diversity to the dataset.

including agriculture [23,40,62,68], sustainable development [34,36,81], poverty mapping [59,77,80], human displacement [38,39], social welfare [10,26,27,51], health [2,50,82], urban analysis [4,11,41,52,53,85], and environment [42,70]. These studies, among many others, have shown the potential of computer vision to create impact for social good at a global scale.

Incident Detection on Satellite Imagery. There are numerous studies that combine traditional machine learning with a limited amount of airborne or satellite imagery collected over disaster zones [14,24,25,63,74,78]. For a detailed survey, see [17,19,37,60]. Oftentimes, these studies are constrained to particular disaster events. Recently, deep learning-based techniques have been applied on larger collections of remote-sensed data to assess structural damage [5,20,30,31,46,83] incurred by floods [7,56,67], hurricanes [47,75], and fires [21,64], among others. Some studies have also applied transfer learning [71] and few-shot learning [57] to deal with unseen situations in emergent disasters.

Incident Detection on Social Media. More recently, social media has emerged as an alternative data source for rapid disaster response. Most studies have focused heavily on text messages for extracting crisis-related information [35,66]. On the contrary, there are only a few studies using social media images for disaster response [1,3,15,16,45,54,55,58,61]. For example, [54] classifies images into three damage categories whereas [55] regresses continuous values indicating the level of destruction. Recently, [3] presented a system with duplicate removal, relevancy filtering, and damage assessment for analyzing social media images. [45,61] investigated adversarial networks to cope with data scarcity during an emergent disaster event.

Incident Detection Datasets. Most of the aforementioned studies use small datasets covering just a few disaster categories, which limits the possibility of creating methods for automatic incident detection. In addition, the reported results are usually not comparable due to lack of public benchmark datasets, whether it be from social media or satellites [69]. One exception is the xBD dataset [32], which contains 23,000 images annotated for building damage but covers only six disasters types (earthquake, tsunami, flood, volcanic eruption, wildfire, and wind). On the other hand, [30] has many more images but their dataset is constructed for detecting damage as anomaly using pre- and post-disaster images. There are also datasets combining social media and satellite imagery for understanding flood scenes [8,9] but they have up to 11,000 images only. In summary, existing incident datasets are small, both in number of images and categories. In particular, incident datasets are far, in size, from the current large datasets on image classification, like ImageNet [18] or Places [84], which contain millions of labeled images. Unfortunately, neither ImageNet nor Places covers incident categories. Our dataset is significantly larger, more complete, and much more diverse than any other available dataset related to incident detection, enabling the training of robust models able to detect incidents in the wild.

3   Incidents Dataset

In this section, we present the Incidents Dataset collected to train models for automatic detection of disasters, damage, and incidents in scene-centric images.

Incidents Taxonomy. We create a fine-grained vocabulary of 233 categories, covering high-level categories such as general types of damage (e.g., destroyed, blocked, collapsed), natural disasters including weather-related (e.g., heat wave, snow storm, blizzard, hurricane), water-related (e.g., coastal flood, flash flood, storm surge), fire-related (e.g., fire, wildfire, fire whirl), as well as geological (e.g., earthquake, landslide, mudslide, mudflow, volcanic eruption) events, and transportation and industrial accidents (e.g., train accident, car accident, oil spill, nuclear explosion). We then manually prune this extensive vocabulary by discarding categories that are hard to recognize from images (e.g., heat wave, infestation, famine) or by combining categories that are visually similar (e.g., snow storm and blizzard, or mudslide and mudflow). As a result of this pruning step, we obtain a final set of 43 incident categories.

Image Downloading and Duplicate Removal. Images are download from Google Images using a set of queries. To generate the queries and promote diversity on the data, we combine the 43 incident categories with place categories. For the place categories, we select the 118 outdoor categories of Places dataset [84] and merge categories belonging to the same super-category (e.g., topiary garden, Japanese garden, vegetable garden are merged into garden). After this process we obtain 49 different place categories. By combining incident and place categories, we obtain a total of 43 incidents × 49 places = 2107 pairs. Each pair is extended with incidents and places synonyms to create queries such as "car accident in highway" and "car wreck in flyover", or "blizzard in street" and "snow storm in alley." We obtain 10,188 queries in total and we download all images returned from Google Images for each query, resulting in a large collection of

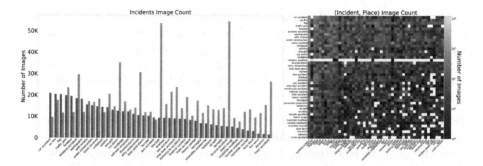

Fig. 2. Dataset composition. The number of positive and negative labeled incident images is shown on the left and the distribution of images for (incident, place) combinations is shown on the right. The dataset contains incidents in many different scenes. White cells indicate the *unlikely* (incident, place) combinations for which the Incidents Dataset does not contain any images (e.g., "car accident in volcano").

6,178,192 images. After that, we perform duplicate image removal as follows: we extract feature vectors from each image with a ResNet-18 [33] model trained on Places [84] and we cluster duplicate images with a radius-based Nearest Neighbor algorithm. This results in 3,487,339 unique images.

Image Labeling. Images obtained through Google Images are noisy, and they may not necessarily be relevant to the query they are downloaded for. Rather, the results may contain non-incident images with similar appearances (e.g., airplanes but not airplane accidents, fireplaces but not dangerous fires, bicycles and not bicycle accidents, etc.), images with other incidents, or completely random images. To clean the data we ask annotators to manually verify the images using the Amazon Mechanical Turk (MTurk) platform. Workers are shown a batch of images, and they have to answer whether each image belongs to a specific category or not. In particular, the interface used for image annotation is similar to [84]. Each image is annotated by one annotator. Each annotation batch contains 100 images, including 15 control images (10 positives and 5 negatives). Annotation batches are accepted when the accuracy in the control images is above 85%. Otherwise the annotations of the batch are discarded.

The images are annotated in several stages. First, we label 798,316 images from the initial 3,487,339 image collection, using the queries the images are downloaded from. For example, the images downloaded with the query "car accident in village" are labeled as positives or negatives for the class "car accident." This results in 193,648 class-positive incident images and 604,668 class-negatives. Class-negative images are those that we know do not show a specific incident class but they may contain another incident category. After the first annotation stage, we train a temporary incident recognition model, as described in Sect. 4, to determine which images to label next. We send images whose incident category confidence scores were greater than 0.5 to MTurk to get more class-positive and class-negative labels. This process is repeated until obtaining 446,684 positive incident images. Finally, these 446,684 images are sent to MTurk for annotation on place categories using the same interface. In this case, each image is assessed for the place category of its original query (e.g., an image downloaded with the query "wildfire in forest" is labeled as positive or negative for the "forest" category). Eventually, we obtain 167,999 images with positive place labels. The remaining images have negative place labels.

Dataset Statistics. The Incidents Dataset contains 1,144,148 labeled images in total. Of these, 446,684 are class-positive incident images, 167,999 of which have also positive place labels. Figure 1 shows some sample images from our dataset. Figure 2 shows the number of images per incident, place, and combined (incident, place). Although the common practice when collecting datasets is just to keep images with positive labels, we will show in Sect. 4 and Sect. 5 that class-negative images are particularly valuable for incident detection in the wild because they can be used as hard negatives for training.

4 Incident Model

In this section, we present our model for recognizing and detecting different incident types in scene-centric images.

Multi-task Architecture. The images in our Incidents Dataset are accompanied with an incident and a place label (see Sect. 3). We choose to build a single model that jointly recognizes incident and place categories following a standard multi-task learning paradigm [12,65,73]. This architecture offers efficiency as it can jointly recognize incidents and places, and we also did not observe any difference in the performance when training a model for a single task. In our experiments, we employ a Convolutional Neural Network (CNN) architecture with two task-specific output layers. Specifically, our network is composed of a sequence of shared convolutional layers followed by two parallel branches of fully-connected layers, corresponding to incident and place recognition tasks.

Training with a Cross-Entropy Loss. The standard and most successful strategy for training an image classification model (either for incidents or places) is to employ a cross-entropy loss on top of a softmax activation function for both outputs of the network. Note that this is the standard procedure for single-label classification of objects [18], scenes [84] or actions [73].

In our real-world scenario of detecting incidents in social media images, many of the test scene-centric images do not belong to any of the incidents categories and they should be classified as images with "no incident." This can be handled by adding an extra neuron in the output layer that should fire on "no incident" images. Notice that this requires training the model with additional absolute negative images, i.e., images that do not show any incident.

Training with a Class-Negative Loss. Even during an incident, the number of images depicting the incident is only a small proportion of all the images shared in social media. For this reason, our task of finding incidents in social media imagery is more closely related to that of detection [28,49,72] than classification. In particular, our model must find positive examples out of a pool of many challenging negatives (e.g. a chimney with smoke or a fireplace are not disaster situations, yet they share visual features similar to our "with smoke" and "on fire" incident categories). To handle this problem and mitigate false positive detections, either the training process can be improved [22,43] or the predictions can be adjusted at test time [44,48]. For our task, we choose to modify our training process to incorporate class-negatives.

In particular, similar to [22], we modify a binary cross entropy (BCE) loss to use partial labels for single-label predictions. Our partial labels consist of both the class-positive and class-negative labels obtained during the image annotation process (Sect. 3). Notice that class-negative images are, in fact, hard negatives for the corresponding classes because of the way they were selected during labeling: they are either false-positive results returned from the image search engine or false-positive predictions with high confidence scores using our model. More formally, we modify BCE by introducing a weight vector to mask the loss where we've obtained partial labels. This is given by the equation:

$$\text{Loss} = \sum_{x_i, y_i, w_i \in X, Y, W} [w_i[y_i \log(A(x_i)) + (1 - y_i) \log(1 - A(x_i))]] \quad (1)$$

where A is the activation function (typically a sigmoid), X the prediction, Y the target, and W the weight vector. $X, Y, W \in \mathbb{R}^N$, and N is the number of classes.

For a training image with a class-positive label, we set $y_i = 1$ and $W = 1^N$ because we can conclude all information is known (i.e., due to our single-label assumption, the image is considered as negative for all the other classes). For a class-negative training image of the class i, we set $y_i = 0$ and $w_i = 1$. We do not set $W = 1^N$ in this case because we do not have ground truth positive or negative labels for the rest of the classes (different incidents may or may not appear in the image). Hence, for any unknown class j, i.e., $j \neq i$, we set $w_j = 0$.

The final loss $\mathcal{L}$ is given by the sum of the incidents loss $\mathcal{L}_d$ and the place loss $\mathcal{L}_p$, where both $\mathcal{L}_d$ and $\mathcal{L}_p$ are given by Eq. (1).

5   Experiments on the Incidents Dataset

Data. We split the images of the Incidents Dataset into training (90%), validation (5%), and a test (5%). As a reference, the training set contains 1,029,726 images, with 401,875 class-positive and 683,572 class-negative incident labels, and 151,665 class-positive and 265,415 class-negative place labels. Note that an image may have more than one class-negative label. Since the number of class-positive place labels is much lower than the number of class-positive incident labels, we augment the training set with 42,318 images from the Places dataset [84]. However, while training, we do not back-propagate the incidents loss on the additional Places images (which have no incident) since we already

Table 1. Ablation study. Performance comparison of the proposed model under different settings on both test sets. The best mAP is achieved by the model that uses CN loss with additional Places images as well as class negatives.

Architecture	Training with			Test set		Augmented test set	
	Loss	Class negatives	Additional places Images	Incident mAP	Place mAP	Incident mAP	Place mAP
ResNet-18	CE		✓	62.04	**47.85**	60.60	53.60
ResNet-18	CN		✓	61.15	46.61	59.88	53.41
ResNet-18	CN	✓		66.59	46.59	65.39	52.82
ResNet-18	CN	✓	✓	66.35	46.71	65.76	62.04
ResNet-50	CN	✓	✓	**67.65**	**47.56**	**67.19**	**63.20**

have class-negatives for the incidents that are better negative examples than these images from Places with no incidents.

The *test set* contains 57,215 images, and we also construct an *augmented test set* that is enriched with 2,365 extra images from Places that we assume contain no incidents. Unlike other image classification datasets, our *test set* contains class-negative images, which are important to evaluate the ability of a model to detect incidents in test images.

Incident Classification. We first evaluate the ability of our model to classify an image to the correct incident category, using just the images from the test set that belong to an incident category. Note that this experiment is similar to a within-the-dataset classification task where every test image belongs to a target category. We use a ResNet-18 [33] as backbone and train the model using the class-negative loss. We evaluate the incidents classification accuracy only on the part of test set that has positive incident labels. The top-1 accuracy is 77.3%, while the top-5 accuracy is 95.9%. As a reference, the performance of the same architecture trained on the same images but with a cross-entropy loss, which is a more standard choice for this classification task, is only slightly better, with 78.9% top-1 and 96.3% top-5 accuracy.

Incident Detection. We consider here a more realistic scenario of detecting incidents in images, evaluating the performance of the model on the whole test set that also includes images with negative labels. We measure this performance using the average precision (AP) metric, and we report the mean over all categories (mAP) for both the incidents and the places.

The obtained results are shown in Table 1, that presents, in fact, an ablation study exploring the use of different model architectures (ResNet-18 and ResNet-50), losses (cross-entropy and class-negative), and training data. Each model is pre-trained on the Places365 dataset [84] for the task of scene classification and then fine-tuned with the corresponding Incidents training data until convergence (at least 10 epochs). We used the Adam optimizer with an initial learning rate of 1e−4 and a batch size of 256 images, with shuffling. For each model, we report the incident and the place mAP on both the *test set* and the *augmented test set*.

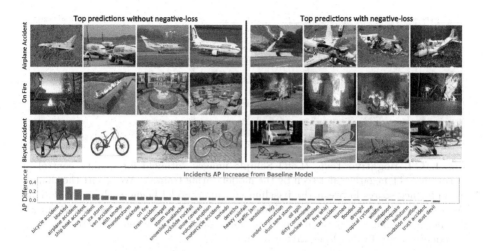

Fig. 3. Using the class-negative loss. Top confidence images for "airplane accident", "on fire", and "bicycle accident" categories when training without (left) and with (right) the class-negative loss. (Bottom) We report incident AP increments achieved by our model over the baseline model.

We observe that the incident mAP significantly improves by 4.3% (on the test set) to 5.2% (on the augmented test set) when we move from the cross-entropy (CE) loss to the class-negative loss (CN) using the class negatives (first and fourth row of Table 1). Figure 3 shows some top-ranked images for three incident categories by these two models. We can observe that, without using the class negatives during training, the model is not able to distinguish the difference between a fireplace and a house on fire or detect when a bicycle is broken because of an accident. The bottom of Fig. 3 shows the change in AP per incident category achieved by the CN model over the CE model. Notice that for nearly all incident categories the AP is much higher with CN model.

As a reference, the performance of the CN loss without using any class negatives, which corresponds to the standard BCE loss, is only less than 1% worse than the CE (first and second row of Table 1). Using additional Places images during training does not affect the incident detection but it vastly improves the place detection, especially in the case of the augmented test set, where mAP increases by 9.2% (third and fourth row of Table 1). Switching from a ResNet-18 to a deeper ResNet-50 architecture gives an extra final boost of incident mAP performance by 1.3% (fifth row of Table 1).

To further demonstrate the improved performance of our model trained with the CN loss (final), we compare it against the model trained with a CE loss (baseline) on 208 hand-selected hard-negative images used for MTurk quality control and not seen during training. Our final model recognizes 176 images correctly as true negatives with confidence score below 0.5 (85% accuracy) while the baseline model predicts the majority of them as false positives (30% accuracy).

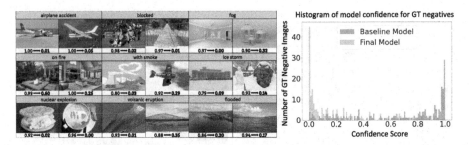

Fig. 4. GT negative test. (Left) Sample images withheld for quality control on MTurk are GT negatives not seen by the model during training. We report the changes in confidence scores between the baseline and final model below each image. (Right) We visualize the distribution of confidence scores obtained by both models for all 208 GT negative images. Our final model is more conservative when predicting incident confidence scores for hard-negative examples.

In Fig. 4, we investigate the changes in the confidence scores between the baseline and final models. Figure 4 (left) displays some qualitative examples of false positives for different incident categories. We observe that the confidence scores significantly decrease when using the final model. More concretely, the final model does not associate airplane features blindly to airplane accident, does not confuse rivers with flood scenes, or does not mistake clouds as smoke. Figure 4 (right) shows the distribution of confidence scores obtained by the baseline and final models. Notice that a perfect detector should assign 0 score to all of these images. Overall, this analysis shows, consistently with the other experiments explained in this section, how our final model is more robust against difficult cases, which is very important for filtering disaster images in the wild.

6   Detecting Incidents in Social Media Images

In this section, we examine how our incident detection model, trained with class-negative loss, performs in three different real-world scenarios using millions of images collected from two popular social media platforms: Flickr and Twitter.

6.1   Incident Detection from Flickr Images

The goal of this experiment is to illustrate how our model can be used to detect specific incident categories in the wild. For this purpose, we use 40 million geo-tagged Flickr images obtained from the YFCC100M dataset [76]. Since the images have precise geo-coordinates from EXIF data, we can use our incident detection model to filter for specific incidents and compare distance to ground-truth locations. We evaluate only earthquake and volcanic eruption incidents in this experiment as we could find reasonable ground-truth data to compare the results. Specifically, we downloaded the GPS coordinates, i.e., latitude and

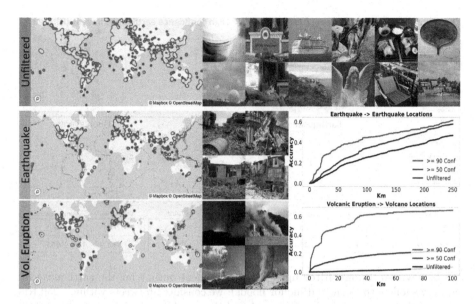

Fig. 5. Filtering Flickr images. (Top) Left: map visualization of Flickr image locations (complete unfiltered set). Right: random Flickr images. (Middle) Earthquake filtering. Left: map visualization of the location of images filtered by the earthquake category (earthquake epicenters are displayed as red dots). Middle: examples of images filtered with the earthquake category. Right: Accuracy@XKm, defined as the percent of images within X kilometers from an epicenter. When filtering with a confidence threshold above 0.9 (green), images are much closer to epicenters than in the unfiltered case (black). (Bottom) Volcanic eruptions and volcanoes, with the same structure as the earthquake experiment. (Color figure online)

longitude, of volcanoes from the National Oceanic and Atmospheric Administration (NOAA) website[1] and a public compilation of earthquake epicenters[2]. We employ an Accuracy@XKm metric [29] to determine whether the predicted incident is correct or not. More concretely, we compute the percentage of images within X Km from the closest earthquake epicenter or volcano, respectively. We randomly sample images and report metrics for (i) unfiltered images, (ii) images with model confidence above 0.5, and (iii) images with model confidence above 0.9. Figure 5 shows that detected earthquake and volcanic eruption incidents appear much closer to expected locations when compared to random images.

6.2   Incident Detection from Twitter Images

In this experiment we aim to detect earthquakes and floods in noisy Twitter data posted during actual disaster events. We collected data from five earthquake and two flood events using event-specific hashtags and keywords. In total, 901,127

---

[1] https://www.noaa.gov/.

[2] https://raw.githubusercontent.com/plotly/datasets/master/earthquakes-23k.csv.

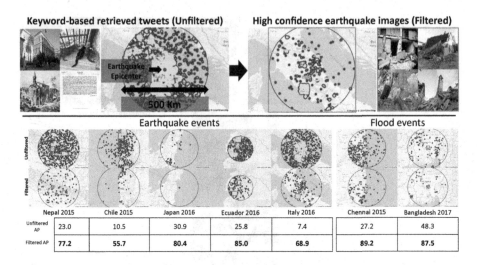

Fig. 6. Twitter image filtering. (Top) Experiment outline for the earthquake filtering (we follow the same outline for floods): we consider all tweets within a 250 Km radius of the epicenter of a specific event and then we filter the images for the earthquake category. Left part shows image examples and location of the unfiltered images, while right part shows locations and examples of filtered images. (Middle) Locations of unfiltered (top) and filtered images (bottom) are shown for each one of the seven events (five earthquakes and two floods), respectively. (Bottom) Ground-truth labels obtained from MTurk for each event are used to compute the AP for unfiltered (top row) and filtered (bottom row) images. Notice that our model significantly outperforms the unfiltered baseline.

images were downloaded. Twitter GPS coordinates are not nearly as precise as the Flickr ones, so we consider only the 39,494 geo-located images within 250 Km from either (i) the earthquake epicenter or (ii) the flooded city center.

For all seven events shown in Fig. 6, we use MTurk to obtain ground-truth human labels (i.e., earthquake or not, and flood or not) for images within the considered radius. Then, we compare the quality of the initial set of the keyword-based retrieved Twitter images (unfiltered) to the quality of images retained by our model (filtered). We report the average precision (AP) per event for both earthquakes and floods. When considering all earthquake events and flood events, we obtain a average AP of 73.9% and 89.1% compared to the baseline AP of 11.9% and 28.2%, respectively. The baseline AP is the AP averaged over multiple trials of randomly shuffling the images, and it is given as a reference.

6.3   Temporal Monitoring of Incidents on Twitter

In this section we demonstrate how our model can be used on Twitter data stream to detect specific incidents in time. To test this, we downloaded 1,946,850 images from tweets containing natural disaster keywords (e.g., blizzard, tornado, hurricane, earthquake, active volcano, coastal flood, wildfire, landslide)

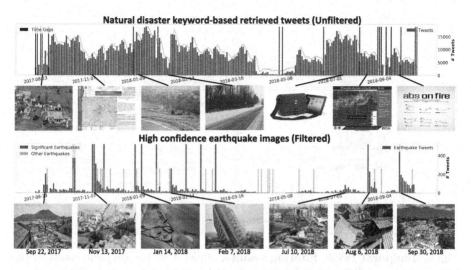

Fig. 7. Finding peaks in earthquake tweets. (Top) Histogram of tweets obtained from Twitter using natural disaster keywords from 2017–2018. Black lines indicate periods of time when our data collection server was inactive. (Bottom) Number of tweets with earthquake images per day after filtering with at least 0.5 confidence. For significant earthquakes (above 6.5 magnitude), we notice an increase in earthquake images immediately after the event. Furthermore, we notice a spike on July 20, 2018 not reported in the NOAA database. We manually checked the tweets and found images referring to a severe flood in Japan, indicating that the flood damage may resemble earthquake damage.

from Aug. 23, 2017 to Oct. 15, 2018. To quantify detection results, we obtained ground-truth event records from the "Significant Earthquake Database", the "Significant Volcanic Eruption Database", and the "Storm Events Database" of NOAA. The earthquake and volcanic eruptions ground-truth events are rare *global* events, while the storms (floods, tornadoes, snowstorms and wildfires) are much more frequent but reported only for the *United States*. We filter images with at least 0.5 confidence and compare against the databases (Fig. 7).

For earthquakes and volcanic eruptions, we report average Relative Tweet Increase (RTI) inspired by [6]. $RTI_e = \sum_{d=e}^{e+w} N_d / \sum_{d=e}^{e-w} N_d$, where N_d is the number of relevant images posted on day d, e is the event day (e.g., day of earthquake), and w is an interval of days. We use $w = 7$ for our analysis to represent a week before and after an event. An *RTI* of 2 means that the average number of tweets in the week following an event is twice as high as the average number the week before. After filtering, the mean RTI (mRTI $= \sum_{e \in E} RTI_e / |E|$) shows an average of 2.42 folds increase in tweets the week after an earthquake and 1.31 folds after a volcanic eruption (Fig. 8).

We notice that the mRTI would be even better if the ground truth databases were exhaustive. On Nov. 27, 2017 we detect the highest number of volcanic eruption images, but observe no significant eruption in the database. Looking

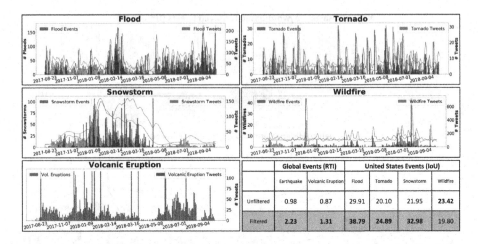

Fig. 8. Temporal tweet filtering results. (Rows 1–2) For frequent events in the United States, we filter tweets for floods, tornadoes, snowstorms, and wildfires images and compare with ground truth frequency events obtained from NOAA. (Bottom Left) Filtered volcanic eruption images with ground truth events. (Bottom Right) Reported mRTI for global events and IoU for common US events.

into this, we found that Mount Agung erupted the same day, which caused the airport in Bali, Indonesia to close and left many tourists stranded[3].

For the more common events (e.g., tornadoes and snowstorms), we measure the correlation between tweet frequency and event frequency. We normalize both histograms, smooth with a low-pass filter, and report intersection over union (IoU) for United States incidents in Fig. 8. We notice an increase in IoU after filtering for flood, tornado, and snowstorm images. For wildfires, we notice a decrease in IoU and attribute this to the large spike in tweets in December 2017. Frequency correlation does not represent damage extent. In fact, a destructive wildfire occurred in California on Dec. 4, 2017 burning 281,893 acres[4].

7 Conclusion

In this paper, we explored how to automatically and systematically detect disasters, damage, and incidents in social media images in the wild. We presented the large-scale Incidents Dataset, which consists of 446,684 human-labeled scene-centric images that cover a diverse set of 43 incident categories (e.g., earthquake, wildfire, landslide, tornado, ice storm, car accident, nuclear explosion, etc.) in various scene contexts. Different from common practice, the Incidents Dataset includes an additional 697,464 class-negative images which can be used as hard negatives to train a robust model for detecting incidents in the wild. To that end,

---

[3] https://en.wikipedia.org/wiki/Mount_Agung.
[4] https://en.wikipedia.org/wiki/Thomas_Fire.

we also used a class-negative loss that capitalizes on this phenomenon. We then showed how the resulting model can be used in different settings for identifying incidents in large collections of social media images. We hope that these contributions will motivate further research on detecting incidents in images, and also promote the development of automatic tools that can be used by humanitarian organizations and emergency response agencies.

Acknowledgments. This work is supported by the CSAIL-QCRI collaboration project and RTI2018-095232-B-C22 grant from the Spanish Ministry of Science, Innovation and Universities.

References

1. Abavisani, M., Wu, L., Hu, S., Tetreault, J., Jaimes, A.: Multimodal categorization of crisis events in social media. In: Proceedings of the IEEE/CVF Conference on Computer Vision and Pattern Recognition (CVPR) (2020)
2. Abdur Rehman, N., Saif, U., Chunara, R.: Deep landscape features for improving vector-borne disease prediction. In: The IEEE Conference on Computer Vision and Pattern Recognition (CVPR) Workshops (2019)
3. Alam, F., Ofli, F., Imran, M.: Processing social media images by combining human and machine computing during crises. Int. J. Hum. Comput. Interact. **34**(4), 311–327 (2018)
4. Arietta, S.M., Efros, A.A., Ramamoorthi, R., Agrawala, M.: City forensics: using visual elements to predict non-visual city attributes. IEEE Trans. Visual Comput. Graphics **20**(12), 2624–2633 (2014)
5. Attari, N., Ofli, F., Awad, M., Lucas, J., Chawla, S.: Nazr-CNN: object detection and fine-grained classification in crowdsourced UAV images. In: IEEE International Conference on Data Science and Advanced Analytics (DSAA) (2016)
6. Avvenuti, M., Cresci, S., Marchetti, A., Meletti, C., Tesconi, M.: Ears (earthquake alert and report system) a real time decision support system for earthquake crisis management. In: SIGKDD International Conference on Knowledge Discovery and Data Mining (KDD), pp. 1749–1758. ACM (2014)
7. Ben-Haim, Z., et al.: Inundation modeling in data scarce regions. In: NeurIPS Workshop on Artificial Intelligence for Humanitarian Assistance and Disaster Response (2019)
8. Bischke, B., Helber, P., Schulze, C., Venkat, S., Dengel, A., Borth, D.: The multimedia satellite task at mediaeval 2017: emergency response for flooding events. In: Proceedings of the MediaEval 2017 Workshop, pp. 1–3 (2017)
9. Bischke, B., Helber, P., Zhao, Z., De Bruijn, J., Borth, D.: The multimedia satellite task at mediaeval 2018: emergency response for flooding events. In: Proceedings of the MediaEval 2018 Workshop, pp. 1–3 (2018)
10. Bonafilia, D., Gill, J., Basu, S., Yang, D.: Building high resolution maps for humanitarian aid and development with weakly- and semi-supervised learning. In: The IEEE Conference on Computer Vision and Pattern Recognition (CVPR) Workshops (2019)
11. Can, G., Benkhedda, Y., Gatica-Perez, D.: Ambiance in social media venues: visual cue interpretation by machines and crowds. In: The IEEE Conference on Computer Vision and Pattern Recognition (CVPR) Workshops (2018)

12. Caruana, R.: Multitask learning. Mach. Learn. **28**(1), 41–75 (1997). https://doi.org/10.1023/A:1007379606734
13. Castillo, C.: Big Crisis Data. Cambridge University Press, New York (2016)
14. Chehata, N., Orny, C., Boukir, S., Guyon, D., Wigneron, J.: Object-based change detection in wind storm-damaged forest using high-resolution multispectral images. Int. J. Remote Sens. **35**(13), 4758–4777 (2014)
15. Chen, T., Lu, D., Kan, M.Y., Cui, P.: Understanding and classifying image tweets. In: ACM International Conference on Multimedia, pp. 781–784 (2013)
16. Daly, S., Thom, J.: Mining and classifying image posts on social media to analyse fires. In: 13th International Conference on Information Systems for Crisis Response and Management (ISCRAM), pp. 1–14 (2016)
17. Dell'Acqua, F., Gamba, P.: Remote sensing and earthquake damage assessment: experiences, limits, and perspectives. Proc. IEEE **100**(10), 2876–2890 (2012)
18. Deng, J., Dong, W., Socher, R., Li, L., Kai, L., Li, F.-F.: ImageNet: a large-scale hierarchical image database. In: The IEEE Conference on Computer Vision and Pattern Recognition (CVPR), pp. 248–255 (2009)
19. Dong, L., Shan, J.: A comprehensive review of earthquake-induced building damage detection with remote sensing techniques. ISPRS J. Photogrammetry Remote Sens. **84**, 85–99 (2013)
20. Doshi, J., Basu, S., Pang, G.: From satellite imagery to disaster insights. In: NeurIPS Workshop on Artificial Intelligence for Social Good (2018)
21. Doshi, J., et al.: FireNet: real-time segmentation of fire perimeter from aerial video. In: NeurIPS Workshop on Artificial Intelligence for Humanitarian Assistance and Disaster Response (2019)
22. Durand, T., Mehrasa, N., Mori, G.: Learning a deep convnet for multi-label classification with partial labels. In: Proceedings of the IEEE/CVF Conference on Computer Vision and Pattern Recognition (CVPR) (2019)
23. Efremova, N., West, D., Zausaev, D.: AI-based evaluation of the SDGs: the case of crop detection with earth observation data. In: ICLR Workshop on Artificial Intelligence for Social Good (2019)
24. Fernandez Galarreta, J., Kerle, N., Gerke, M.: UAV-based urban structural damage assessment using object-based image analysis and semantic reasoning. Nat. Hazards Earth Syst. Sci. **15**(6), 1087–1101 (2015)
25. Gamba, P., Dell'Acqua, F., Trianni, G.: Rapid damage detection in the bam area using multitemporal SAR and exploiting ancillary data. IEEE Trans. Geosci. Remote Sens. **45**(6), 1582–1589 (2007)
26. Gebru, T., et al.: Using deep learning and google street view to estimate the demographic makeup of neighborhoods across the United States. Proc. Nat. Acad. Sci. **114**(50), 13108–13113 (2017)
27. Gebru, T., Krause, J., Wang, Y., Chen, D., Deng, J., Fei-Fei, L.: Fine-grained car detection for visual census estimation. In: The AAAI Conference on Artificial Intelligence (2017)
28. Girshick, R., Donahue, J., Darrell, T., Malik, J.: Rich feature hierarchies for accurate object detection and semantic segmentation. In: Proceedings of the IEEE Conference on Computer Vision and Pattern Recognition (CVPR) (2014)
29. Gritta, M., Pilevar, M.T., Collier, N.: A pragmatic guide to geoparsing evaluation: toponyms, named entity recognition and pragmatics. Lang. Resour. Eval. (2019). https://doi.org/10.1007/s10579-019-09475-3
30. Gueguen, L., Hamid, R.: Large-scale damage detection using satellite imagery. In: The IEEE Conference on Computer Vision and Pattern Recognition (CVPR), pp. 1321–1328 (2015)

31. Gupta, R., et al.: Creating xBD: a dataset for assessing building damage from satellite imagery. In: The IEEE Conference on Computer Vision and Pattern Recognition (CVPR) Workshops (2019)
32. Gupta, R., et al.: xBD: a dataset for assessing building damage from satellite imagery. arXiv preprint arXiv:1911.09296 (2019)
33. He, K., Zhang, X., Ren, S., Sun, J.: Deep residual learning for image recognition. In: The IEEE Conference on Computer Vision and Pattern Recognition (CVPR), pp. 770–778 (2016)
34. Helber, P., et al.: Mapping informal settlements in developing countries with multi-resolution, multi-spectral data. In: ICLR Workshop on Artificial Intelligence for Social Good (2019)
35. Imran, M., Castillo, C., Diaz, F., Vieweg, S.: Processing social media messages in mass emergency: a survey. ACM Comput. Surv. **47**(4), 67 (2015)
36. Jean, N., Burke, M., Xie, M., Davis, W.M., Lobell, D.B., Ermon, S.: Combining satellite imagery and machine learning to predict poverty. Science **353**(6301), 790–794 (2016)
37. Joyce, K.E., Belliss, S.E., Samsonov, S.V., McNeill, S.J., Glassey, P.J.: A review of the status of satellite remote sensing and image processing techniques for mapping natural hazards and disasters. Prog. Phys. Geogr. **33**(2), 183–207 (2009)
38. Kalliatakis, G., Ehsan, S., Fasli, M., D McDonald-Maier, K.: DisplaceNet: recognising displaced people from images by exploiting dominance level. In: The IEEE Conference on Computer Vision and Pattern Recognition (CVPR) Workshops (2019)
39. Kalliatakis, G., Ehsan, S., Leonardis, A., Fasli, M., McDonald-Maier, K.D.: Exploring object-centric and scene-centric CNN features and their complementarity for human rights violations recognition in images. IEEE Access **7**, 10045–10056 (2019)
40. Kaneko, A., et al.: Deep learning for crop yield prediction in Africa. In: ICML Workshop on Artificial Intelligence for Social Good (2019)
41. Kataoka, H., Satoh, Y., Abe, K., Minoguchi, M., Nakamura, A.: Ten-million-order human database for world-wide fashion culture analysis. In: The IEEE Conference on Computer Vision and Pattern Recognition (CVPR) Workshops (2019)
42. Kellenberger, B., Marcos, D., Tuia, D.: When a few clicks make all the difference: improving weakly-supervised wildlife detection in UAV images. In: The IEEE Conference on Computer Vision and Pattern Recognition (CVPR) Workshops (2019)
43. Lee, K., Lee, H., Lee, K., Shin, J.: Training confidence-calibrated classifiers for detecting out-of-distribution samples. In: International Conference on Learning Representations (2018)
44. Lee, K., Lee, K., Lee, H., Shin, J.: A simple unified framework for detecting out-of-distribution samples and adversarial attacks. In: Bengio, S., Wallach, H., Larochelle, H., Grauman, K., Cesa-Bianchi, N., Garnett, R. (eds.) Advances in Neural Information Processing Systems 31, pp. 7167–7177. Curran Associates, Inc. (2018)
45. Li, X., Caragea, D., Caragea, C., Imran, M., Ofli, F.: Identifying disaster damage images using a domain adaptation approach. In: 16th International Conference on Information Systems for Crisis Response and Management (ISCRAM) (2019)
46. Li, Y., Hu, W., Dong, H., Zhang, X.: Building damage detection from post-event aerial imagery using single shot multibox detector. Appl. Sci. **9**(6), 1128 (2019)
47. Li, Y., Ye, S., Bartoli, I.: Semisupervised classification of hurricane damage from postevent aerial imagery using deep learning. J. Appl. Remote Sens. **12**(4), 045008 (2018)
48. Liang, S., Li, Y., Srikant, R.: Enhancing the reliability of out-of-distribution image detection in neural networks. arXiv preprint arXiv:1706.02690 (2017)

49. Lin, T.Y., Goyal, P., Girshick, R., He, K., Dollar, P.: Focal loss for dense object detection. In: Proceedings of the IEEE International Conference on Computer Vision (ICCV) (2017)
50. McKinney, S.M., et al.: International evaluation of an AI system for breast cancer screening. Nature **577**(7788), 89–94 (2020)
51. Nachmany, Y., Alemohammad, H.: Detecting roads from satellite imagery in the developing world. In: The IEEE Conference on Computer Vision and Pattern Recognition (CVPR) Workshops (2019)
52. Naik, N., Philipoom, J., Raskar, R., Hidalgo, C.: Streetscore - predicting the perceived safety of one million streetscapes. In: The IEEE Conference on Computer Vision and Pattern Recognition (CVPR) Workshops, pp. 793–799 (2014)
53. Naik, N., Kominers, S.D., Raskar, R., Glaeser, E.L., Hidalgo, C.A.: Computer vision uncovers predictors of physical urban change. Proc. Nat. Acad. Sci. (2017). https://doi.org/10.1073/pnas.1619003114
54. Nguyen, D.T., Ofli, F., Imran, M., Mitra, P.: Damage assessment from social media imagery data during disasters. In: International Conference on Advances in Social Networks Analysis and Mining (ASONAM), pp. 1–8 (2017)
55. Nia, K.R., Mori, G.: Building damage assessment using deep learning and ground-level image data. In: 14th Conference on Computer and Robot Vision (CRV), pp. 95–102. IEEE (2017)
56. Nogueira, K., et al.: Exploiting convnet diversity for flooding identification. IEEE Geosci. Remote Sens. Lett. **15**(9), 1446–1450 (2018)
57. Oh, J., Hebert, M., Jeon, H.G., Perez, X., Dai, C., Song, Y.: Explainable semantic mapping for first responders. In: NeurIPS Workshop on Artificial Intelligence for Humanitarian Assistance and Disaster Response (2019)
58. Peters, R., de Albuquerque, J.P.: Investigating images as indicators for relevant social media messages in disaster management. In: 12th International Conference on Information Systems for Crisis Response and Management (ISCRAM) (2015)
59. Piaggesi, S., et al.: Predicting city poverty using satellite imagery. In: The IEEE Conference on Computer Vision and Pattern Recognition (CVPR) Workshops (2019)
60. Plank, S.: Rapid damage assessment by means of multi-temporal SAR–a comprehensive review and outlook to sentinel-1. Remote Sens. **6**(6), 4870–4906 (2014)
61. Pouyanfar, S., et al.: Unconstrained flood event detection using adversarial data augmentation. In: IEEE International Conference on Image Processing (ICIP), pp. 155–159 (2019)
62. Pryzant, R., Ermon, S., Lobell, D.: Monitoring ethiopian wheat fungus with satellite imagery and deep feature learning. In: The IEEE Conference on Computer Vision and Pattern Recognition (CVPR) Workshops (2017)
63. Radhika, S., Tamura, Y., Matsui, M.: Cyclone damage detection on building structures from pre-and post-satellite images using wavelet based pattern recognition. J. Wind Eng. Ind. Aerodyn. **136**, 23–33 (2015)
64. Radke, D., Hessler, A., Ellsworth, D.: FireCast: leveraging deep learning to predict wildfire spread. In: International Joint Conference on Artificial Intelligence (IJCAI), pp. 4575–4581 (2019)
65. Rebuffi, S.A., Bilen, H., Vedaldi, A.: Learning multiple visual domains with residual adapters. In: Advances in Neural Information Processing Systems (NeurIPS), pp. 506–516 (2017)
66. Reuter, C., Kaufhold, M.A.: Fifteen years of social media in emergencies: a retrospective review and future directions for crisis informatics. J. Contingencies Crisis Manage. **26**(1), 41–57 (2018)

67. Rudner, T.G.J., et al.: Multi^{3}Net: segmenting flooded buildings via fusion of multiresolution, multisensor, and multitemporal satellite imagery. In: The AAAI Conference on Artificial Intelligence, pp. 702–709 (2019)
68. Rustowicz, R., Cheong, R., Wang, L., Ermon, S., Burke, M., Lobell, D.: Semantic segmentation of crop type in Africa: a novel dataset and analysis of deep learning methods. In: The IEEE Conference on Computer Vision and Pattern Recognition (CVPR) Workshops (2019)
69. Said, N., et al.: Natural disasters detection in social media and satellite imagery: a survey. Multimedia Tools Appl. **78**, 31267–31302 (2019)
70. Schmidt, V., et al.: Visualizing the consequences of climate change using cycle-consistent adversarial networks. In: ICLR Workshop on Artificial Intelligence for Social Good (2019)
71. Seo, J., Lee, S., Kim, B., Jeon, T.: Revisiting classical bagging with modern transfer learning for on-the-fly disaster damage detector. In: NeurIPS Workshop on Artificial Intelligence for Humanitarian Assistance and Disaster Response (2019)
72. Shrivastava, A., Gupta, A., Girshick, R.: Training region-based object detectors with online hard example mining. In: Proceedings of the IEEE Conference on Computer Vision and Pattern Recognition (CVPR) (2016)
73. Simonyan, K., Zisserman, A.: Two-stream convolutional networks for action recognition in videos. In: Advances in Neural Information Processing Systems, pp. 568–576 (2014)
74. Skakun, S., Kussul, N., Shelestov, A., Kussul, O.: Flood hazard and flood risk assessment using a time series of satellite images: a case study in Namibia. Risk Anal. **34**(8), 1521–1537 (2014)
75. Sublime, J., Kalinicheva, E.: Automatic post-disaster damage mapping using deep-learning techniques for change detection: Case study of the Tohoku Tsunami. Remote Sens. **11**(9), 1123 (2019)
76. Thomee, B., et al.: YFCC100M: the new data in multimedia research. Commun. ACM **59**(2), 64–73 (2016)
77. Tingzon, I., et al.: Mapping poverty in the Philippines using machine learning, satellite imagery, and crowd-sourced geospatial information. In: ICML Workshop on Artificial Intelligence for Social Good (2019)
78. Turker, M., San, B.T.: Detection of collapsed buildings caused by the 1999 Izmit, Turkey earthquake through digital analysis of post-event aerial photographs. Int. J. Remote Sens. **25**(21), 4701–4714 (2004)
79. de Vries, T., Misra, I., Wang, C., van der Maaten, L.: Does object recognition work for everyone? In: The IEEE Conference on Computer Vision and Pattern Recognition (CVPR) Workshops (2019)
80. Watmough, G.R., et al.: Socioecologically informed use of remote sensing data to predict rural household poverty. Proc. Nat. Acad. Sci. **116**(4), 1213–1218 (2019)
81. Workman, S., Zhai, M., Crandall, D.J., Jacobs, N.: A unified model for near and remote sensing. In: The IEEE International Conference on Computer Vision (ICCV) (2017)
82. Wu, N., et al.: Deep neural networks improve radiologists' performance in breast cancer screening. IEEE Trans. Med. Imaging **39**(1), 1184–1194 (2019)

83. Xu, J.Z., Lu, W., Li, Z., Khaitan, P., Zaytseva, V.: Building damage detection in satellite imagery using convolutional neural networks. In: NeurIPS Workshop on Artificial Intelligence for Humanitarian Assistance and Disaster Response (2019)
84. Zhou, B., Lapedriza, A., Khosla, A., Oliva, A., Torralba, A.: Places: a 10 million image database for scene recognition. IEEE Trans. Pattern Anal. Mach. Intell. **40**, 1452–1464 (2018)
85. Zhou, B., Liu, L., Oliva, A., Torralba, A.: Recognizing city identity via attribute analysis of geo-tagged images. In: Fleet, D., Pajdla, T., Schiele, B., Tuytelaars, T. (eds.) ECCV 2014. LNCS, vol. 8691, pp. 519–534. Springer, Cham (2014). https://doi.org/10.1007/978-3-319-10578-9_34

Dynamic ReLU

Yinpeng Chen$^{(\boxtimes)}$ (ID), Xiyang Dai (ID), Mengchen Liu (ID), Dongdong Chen (ID),
Lu Yuan (ID), and Zicheng Liu (ID)

Microsoft Corporation, Redmond, WA 98052, USA
{yiche,xidai,mengcliu,dochen,luyuan,zliu}@microsoft.com

Abstract. Rectified linear units (ReLU) are commonly used in deep
neural networks. So far ReLU and its generalizations (non-parametric or
parametric) are **static**, performing identically for all input samples. In
this paper, we propose **Dynamic ReLU** (DY-ReLU), a dynamic rectifier of which parameters are generated by a hyper function over all
input elements. The key insight is that DY-ReLU *encodes the global context into the hyper function, and adapts the piecewise linear activation
function accordingly.* Compared to its static counterpart, DY-ReLU has
negligible extra computational cost, but significantly more representation
capability, especially for light-weight neural networks. By simply using
DY-ReLU for MobileNetV2, the top-1 accuracy on ImageNet classification is boosted from 72.0% to 76.2% with only 5% additional FLOPs.

Keywords: ReLU · Convolutional Neural Networks · Dynamic

1 Introduction

Rectified linear unit (ReLU) [17,27] is one of the few milestones in the deep learning revolution. It is simple and powerful, greatly improving the performance of
feed-forward networks. Thus, it has been widely used in many successful architectures (e.g. ResNet [11], MobileNet[12,13,30] and ShuffleNet [24,44]) for different
vision tasks (e.g. recognition, detection, segmentation). ReLU and its generalizations, either non-parametric (leaky ReLU [25]) or parametric(PReLU [10]) are
static. They perform in the exactly same way for different inputs (e.g. images).
This naturally raises an issue: *should rectifiers be fixed or adaptive to input (e.g.
images)?* In this paper, we investigate *dynamic* rectifiers to answer this question.

We propose dynamic ReLU (DY-ReLU), a piecewise function $f_{\theta(x)}(x)$ whose
parameters are computed from a hyper function $\theta(x)$ over input x. Figure 1
shows an example that the slopes of two linear functions are determined by the
hyper function. The key idea is that the *global context of all input elements* $x =
\{x_c\}$ is encoded in the hyper function $\theta(x)$ for adapting the activation function

Electronic supplementary material The online version of this chapter (https://
doi.org/10.1007/978-3-030-58529-7_21) contains supplementary material, which is
available to authorized users.

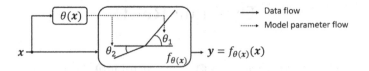

Fig. 1. Dynamic ReLU. The piecewise linear function is determined by the input x.

$f_{\theta(x)}(x)$. This enables significantly more representation capability, especially for light-weight neural networks (e.g. MobileNet). Meanwhile, it is computationally efficient as the hyper function $\theta(x)$ is simple with negligible computational cost.

Furthermore, we explore three variations of dynamic ReLU, which share activation functions across spatial locations and channels differently: (a) spatial and channel-shared DY-ReLU-A, (b) spatial-shared and channel-wise DY-ReLU-B, and (c) spatial and channel-wise DY-ReLU-C. They perform differently at different tasks. Channel-wise variations (DY-ReLU-B and DY-ReLU-C) are more suitable for image classification. When dealing with keypoint detection, DY-ReLU-B and DY-ReLU-C are more suitable for the backbone network while the spatial-wise DY-ReLU-C is more suitable for the head network.

We demonstrate the effectiveness of DY-ReLU on both ImageNet classification and COCO keypoint detection. Without bells and whistles, simply replacing static ReLU with dynamic ReLU in multiple networks (ResNet, MobileNet V2 and V3) achieves solid improvement with only a slight increase (5%) of computational cost. For instance, when using MobileNetV2, our method gains 4.2% top-1 accuracy on image classification and 3.5 AP on keypoint detection, respectively.

2   Related Work

Activation Functions: activation function introduces non-linearity in deep neural networks. Among various activation functions, ReLU [9,17,27] is widely used. Three generalizations of ReLU are based on using a nonzero slopes α for negative input. Absolute value rectification [17] fixes $\alpha = -1$. LeakyReLU [25] fixes α to a small value, while PReLU [10] treats α as a learnable parameter. RReLU took a further step by making the trainable parameter a random number sampled from a uniform distribution [40]. Maxout [7] generalizes ReLU further, by dividing input into groups and outputs the maximum. One problem of ReLU is that it is not smooth. A number of smooth activation functions have been developed to address this, such as softplus [6], ELU [4], SELU [19], Mish [26]. PELU [33] introduced three trainable parameters into ELU. Recently, empowered by neural architecture search (NAS) techniques [2,22,29,32,35,39,45,46], Ramachandran et al. [28] found several novel activation functions, such as Swish function. Different with these static activation functions that are input independent, our dynamic ReLU adapts the activation function to the input.

Dynamic Neural Networks: Our method is related to recent work of dynamic neural networks [3,14,15,20,23,34,37,41,42]. D²NN [23], SkipNet [34] and BlockDrop [37] learn a controller for skipping part of an existing model by using reinforcement learning. MSDNet [15] allows early-exit based on the prediction confidence. Slimmable Net [42] learns a single network executable at different widths. Once-for-all [1] proposes a progressive shrinking algorithm to train one network that supports multiple sub-networks. Hypernetworks [8] generates network parameters using anther network. SENet [14] squeezes global context to reweight channels. Dynamic convolution [3,41] adapts convolution kernels based on their attentions that are input dependent. Compared with these works, our method shifts the focus from kernel weights to activation functions.

Efficient CNNs: Recently, designing efficient CNN architectures [12,13,16,24, 30,44] has been an active research area. MobileNetV1 [13] decomposes a 3×3 convolution to a depthwise convolution and a pointwise convolution. MobileNetV2 [30] introduces inverted residual and linear bottlenecks. MobileNetV3 [12] applies squeeze-and-excitation [14], and employs a platform-aware neural architecture search approach [32] to find the optimal network structure. ShuffleNet further reduces MAdds for 1 × 1 convolution by group convolution. ShiftNet [36] replaces expensive spatial convolution by the shift operation and pointwise convolution. Our method provides an effective activation function, which can be easily used in these networks (by replacing ReLU) to improve representation capability with low computational cost.

3   Dynamic ReLU

Dynamic ReLU (DY-ReLU) is a **dynamic** piecewise function, of which parameters are input dependent. It does NOT increase either the depth or the width of the network, but increases the model capability efficiently with negligible extra computational cost. This section is organized as follows. We firstly introduce the generic dynamic activation. Then, we present the mathematical definition of DY-ReLU, and how to implement it. Finally, we compare it with prior work.

3.1   Dynamic Activation

For a given input vector (or tensor) x, the dynamic activation is defined as a function $f_{\theta(x)}(x)$ with learnable parameters $\theta(x)$, which *adapt to the input* x. As shown in Fig. 1, it includes two functions:

1. *hyper function* $\theta(x)$: that computes parameters for the activation function.
2. *activation function* $f_{\theta(x)}(x)$: that uses the parameters $\theta(x)$ to generate activation for all channels.

Note that the hyper function encodes the global context of all input elements ($x_c \in x$) to determine the appropriate activation function. This enables significantly more representation power than its static counterpart, especially for light-weight models (e.g. MobileNet). Next, we will discuss dynamic ReLU.

3.2 Definition and Implementation of Dynamic ReLU

Definition: Let us denote the traditional or static ReLU as $y = \max\{x, 0\}$, where x is the input vector. For the input x_c at the cth channel, the activation is computed as $y_c = \max\{x_c, 0\}$. ReLU can be generalized to a parametric piecewise linear function $y_c = \max_k\{a^k x_c + b^k_c\}$. We propose dynamic ReLU to further extend this piecewise linear function from static to dynamic by adapting a^k_c, b^k_c based upon all input elements $x = \{x_c\}$ as follows:

$$y_c = f_{\theta(x)}(x_c) = \max_{1 \le k \le K}\{a^k_c(x)x_c + b^k_c(x)\}, \qquad (1)$$

where the coefficients (a^k_c, b^k_c) are the output of a hyper function $\theta(x)$ as:

$$[a^1_1, \ldots, a^1_C, \ldots, a^K_1, \ldots, a^K_C, b^1_1, \ldots, b^1_C, \ldots, b^K_1, \ldots, b^K_C]^T = \theta(x), \qquad (2)$$

where K is the number of functions, and C is the number of channels. Note that the activation parameters (a^k_c, b^k_c) are not only related to its corresponding input x_c, but also related to other input elements $x_{j \ne c}$.

Implementation of Hyper Function $\theta(x)$: We use a light-weight network to model the hyper function that is similar to Squeeze-and-Excitation (SE) [14]. For an input tensor x with dimension $C \times H \times W$, the spatial information is firstly squeezed by global average pooling. It is then followed by two fully connected layers (with a ReLU between them) and a normalization layer. The output has $2KC$ elements, corresponding to the **residual** of $a^{1:K}_{1:C}$ and $b^{1:K}_{1:C}$, which are denoted as $\Delta a^{1:K}_{1:C}$ and $\Delta b^{1:K}_{1:C}$. We simply use $2\sigma(x) - 1$ to normalize the residual between -1 to 1, where $\sigma(x)$ denotes sigmoid function. The final output is computed as the sum of initialization and residual as follows:

$$a^k_c(x) = \alpha^k + \lambda_a \Delta a^k_c(x), \ b^k_c(x) = \beta^k + \lambda_b \Delta b^k_c(x), \qquad (3)$$

where α^k and β^k are initialization values of a^k_c and b^k_c, respectively. λ_a and λ_b are scalars that control the range of residual. α^k, β^k, λ_a and λ_b are hyper parameters. For the case of $K = 2$, the default values are $\alpha^1 = 1$, $\alpha^2 = \beta^1 = \beta^2 = 0$, corresponding to static ReLU. The default λ_a and λ_b are 1.0 and 0.5, respectively.

3.3 Relation to Prior Work

Table 1 shows the relationship between DY-ReLU and prior work. The three special cases of DY-ReLU are equivalent to ReLU [17,27], LeakyReLU [25] and PReLU [10], where the hyper function becomes static. SE [14] is another special case of DY-ReLU, with a *single* linear function $K = 1$ and zero intercept $b^1_c = 0$.

DY-ReLU is a *dynamic* and *efficient* Maxout [7], with significantly less computations but even better performance. Different with Maxout that requires multiple (K) convolutional kernels, DY-ReLU applies K *dynamic* linear transforms on the results of a *single* convolutional kernel, and outputs the maximum of them. This results in much less computations and even better performance.

Table 1. Relation to prior work. ReLU, LeakyReLU, PReLU and SE are special cases of DY-ReLU. DY-ReLU is a *dynamic* and *efficient* version of Maxout. α in LeakyReLU is a small number (e.g. 0.01). a_c in PReLU is a parameter to learn.

		Type	K	relation to DY-ReLU
ReLU [27, 17]		static	2	special case $a_c^1(x) = 1,\ b_c^1(x) = 0$ $a_c^2(x) = 0,\ b_c^2(x) = 0$
LeakyReLU [25]		static	2	special case $a_c^1(x) = 1,\ b_c^1(x) = 0$ $a_c^2(x) = \alpha,\ b_c^2(x) = 0$
PReLU [10]		static	2	special case $a_c^1(x) = 1,\ b_c^1(x) = 0$ $a_c^2(x) = a_c,\ b_c^2(x) = 0$
SE [14]		dynamic	1	special case $a_c^1(x) = a_c(x),\ b_c^1(x) = 0$ $0 \le a_c(x) \le 1$
Maxout [7]		static	1,2,3,...	DY-ReLU is a dynamic and efficient Maxout.
DY-ReLU		dynamic	1,2,3,...	identical

4   Variations of Dynamic ReLU

In this section, we introduce another two variations of dynamic ReLU in addition to the option discussed in Sect. 3.2. These three options have different ways of sharing activation functions as follows:

DY-ReLU-A: the activation function is *spatial and channel-shared*.
DY-ReLU-B: the activation function is *spatial-shared and channel-wise*.
DY-ReLU-C: the activation function is *spatial and channel-wise*.

DY-ReLU-B has been discussed in Sect. 3.2.

4.1   Network Structure and Complexity

The network structures of three variations are shown in Fig. 2. The detailed explanation is discussed as follows:

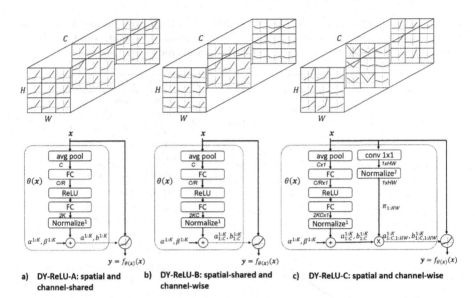

Fig. 2. Three DY-ReLU variations. They have different ways of sharing activation functions. The top row illustrates the piecewise linear function across spatial locations and channels, and the bottom row shows the network structure for the hyper function. Note that the first FC layer reduces the dimension by R, which is a hyper parameter.

DY-ReLU-A (Spatial and Channel-Shared): the same piecewise linear activation function is shared across all spatial positions and channels. Its hyper function has similar network structure (shown in Fig. 2-(a)) to DY-ReLU-B, except the number of outputs is reduced to $2K$. Compared to DY-ReLU-B, DY-ReLU-A has less computational cost, but less representation capability.

DY-ReLU-B (Spatial-shared and Channel-wise): the implementation details are introduced in Sect. 3.2 and the network structure is shown in Fig. 2-(b). The hyper function outputs $2KC$ parameters ($2K$ per channel).

DY-ReLU-C (Spatial and Channel-wise): as shown in Fig. 2-(c), each input element $x_{c,h,w}$ has a unique activation function $\max_k\{a_{c,h,w}^k x_{c,h,w} + b_{c,h,w}^k\}$, where the subscript c,h,w indicates the cth channel at the hth row and wth column of the feature map that has dimension $C \times H \times W$. This introduces an issue that the output dimension is too large ($2KCHW$), resulting in significantly more parameters in the fully connected layer. We address it by decoupling spatial locations from channels. Specifically, another branch for computing spatial attention $\pi_{h,w}$ is introduced. The final output is computed as the product of channel-wise parameters ($[a_{1:C}^{1:K}, b_{1:C}^{1:K}]^T$) and spatial attentions ($[\pi_{1:HW}]$). The spatial attention branch is simple, including a 1×1 convolution with a single output channel and a normalization that is a softmax function with upper cutoff as follows:

Table 2. Comparing three DY-ReLU variations on Imagenet [5] classification. MobileNetV2 with width multiplier ×0.35 is used. The mean and standard deviations of three runs are shown. The numbers in brackets denote the performance improvement over the baseline. Channel-wise variations (DY-ReLU-B and DY-ReLU-C) are more effective than the channel-shared (DY-ReLU-A). Spatial-wise (DY-ReLU-C) does NOT introduce additional improvement.

	Top-1
ReLU	60.32 ± 0.13
DY-ReLU-A	$63.28 \pm 0.12_{(2.96)}$
DY-ReLU-B	$\mathbf{66.36 \pm 0.12}_{(6.04)}$
DY-ReLU-C	$66.31 \pm 0.14_{(5.99)}$

Table 3. Comparing three DY-ReLU variations on COCO [21] keypoint detection. We use MobileNetV2 ×0.5 as backbone and use up-sampling and inverted residual bottleneck blocks [3] in the head. The mean and standard deviations of three runs are shown. The numbers in brackets denote the performance improvement over the baseline. Channel-wise variations (DY-ReLU-B and DY-ReLU-C) are more effective in the backbone and the spatial-wise variation (DY-ReLU-C) is more effective in the head.

Backbone	Head	AP
ReLU	ReLU	59.26 ± 0.21
DY-ReLU-A	ReLU	$58.97 \pm 0.15_{(-0.29)}$
DY-ReLU-B	ReLU	$61.76 \pm 0.27_{(+2.50)}$
DY-ReLU-C	ReLU	$62.23 \pm 0.32_{(+2.97)}$
ReLU	DY-ReLU-A	$57.12 \pm 0.25_{(-2.14)}$
ReLU	DY-ReLU-B	$58.72 \pm 0.35_{(-0.54)}$
ReLU	DY-ReLU-C	$61.03 \pm 0.11_{(+1.77)}$
DY-ReLU-C	DY-ReLU-C	$\mathbf{63.27 \pm 0.15}_{(+4.01)}$

$$\pi_{h,w} = \min\left\{\frac{\gamma \exp(z_{h,w}/\tau)}{\sum_{h,w} \exp(z_{h,w}/\tau)}, 1\right\}, \tag{4}$$

where $z_{h,w}$ is the output of 1×1 convolution, τ is the temperature, and γ is a scalar. The softmax is scaled up by γ is to prevent gradient vanishing. We empirically set $\gamma = \frac{HW}{3}$, making the average attention $\pi_{h,w}$ to $\frac{1}{3}$. A large temperature ($\tau = 10$) is used to prevent sparsity during the early training stage. The upper bound 1 constrains the attention between zero and one.

Computational Complexity: DY-ReLU is computationally efficient. It includes four components: (a) average pooling, (b) the first FC layer (with ReLU), (c) the second FC layer (with normalization), and (d) piecewise function $f_{\theta(x)}(x)$. For a feature map with dimension $C \times H \times W$, all three DY-ReLU variations share complexity for average pooling $O(CHW)$, the first FC layer $O(C^2/R)$ and piecewise function $O(CHW)$. The second FC layer has complexity $O(2KC/R)$ for DY-ReLU-A and $O(2KC^2/R)$ for DY-ReLU-B and DY-ReLU-C. Note that DY-ReLU-C spends additional $O(CHW)$ on computing spatial attentions. In most of the layers of MobileNet and ResNet, DY-ReLU has much less computation than a 1×1 convolution, which has complexity $O(C^2HW)$.

4.2 Ablations

Next, we study the three DY-ReLU variations on image classification and keypoint detection. Our goal is to understand their differences when performing different tasks. The details of datasets, implementation and training setup will be shown later in the next section.

The comparison among three DY-ReLU variations on ImageNet [21] classification is shown in Table 2. MobileNetV2 ×0.35 is used. Although all three variations achieve improvement from the baseline, *channel-wise DY-ReLUs (variation B and C) are clearly better than the channel-shared DY-ReLU (variation A)*. Variation B and C have similar accuracy, showing that spatial-wise is not critical for image classification.

Table 3 shows the comparison on COCO keypoint detection. Similar to image classification, *channel-wise variations (B and C) are better than channel-shared variation A in the backbone*. In contrast, *the spatial-wise variation C is critical in the head*. Using DY-ReLU-C in both backbone and head achieves 4 AP improvement. We also observe that the performance is even worse than the baseline if we use DY-ReLU-A in the backbone or use DY-ReLU-A and DY-ReLU-B in the head. We believe the spatially-shared hyper function in DY-ReLU-A or DY-ReLU-B is difficult to learn when dealing with spatially sensitive task (e.g. distinguishes body joints in pixel level), especially in the head that has higher resolutions. This difficulty can be effectively alleviated by making hyper function spatial-wise, which encourages learning different activation functions at different positions. We observe that the training converges much faster when using spatial attention in the head network.

Base upon these ablations, we use DY-ReLU-B for ImageNet classification and use DY-ReLU-C for COCO keypoint detection in the next section.

5   Experimental Results

In this section, we present experimental results on image classification and single person pose estimation to demonstrate the effectiveness of DY-ReLU. We also report ablation studies to analyze different components of our approach.

5.1   ImageNet Classification

We use ImageNet [5] for all classification experiments. ImageNet has 1000 classes, including 1,281,167 images for training and 50,000 images for validation. We evaluate DY-ReLU on three CNN architectures (MobileNetV2 [30], MobileNetV3 [12] and ResNet [11]). We replace their default activation functions (ReLU in ResNet and MobileNetV2, ReLU/hswish/SE in MobileNetV3) with DY-ReLU. The main results are obtained by using spatial-shared and channel-wise DY-ReLU-B with two piecewise linear functions ($K = 2$). Note that MobileNetV2 and V3 have no activation after the last convolution layer in each block, where we add DY-ReLU with $K = 1$. The batch size is 256. We use different training setups for the three architectures as follows:

Training Setup for MobileNetV2: The initial learning rate is 0.05, and is scheduled to arrive at zero within a single cosine cycle. All models are trained using SGD optimizer with 0.9 momentum for 300 epochs. The label smoothing

Table 4. Comparing DY-ReLU with baseline activation functions (ReLU, SE or h-swish, denoted as HS) on ImageNet [5] classification in three network architectures. DY-ReLU-B with $K = 2$ linear functions is used. Note that SE blocks are removed when using DY-ReLU in MobileNetV3. The numbers in brackets denote the performance improvement over the baseline. DY-ReLU outperforms its counterpart for all networks.

Network	Activation	#Param	MAdds	Top-1	Top-5
MobileNetV2 ×1.0	ReLU	3.5M	300.0M	72.0	91.0
	DY-ReLU	7.5M	315.5M	$76.2_{(4.2)}$	$93.1_{(2.1)}$
MobileNetV2 ×0.75	ReLU	2.6M	209.0M	69.8	89.6
	DY-ReLU	5.0M	221.7M	$74.3_{(4.5)}$	$91.7_{(2.1)}$
MobileNetV2 ×0.5	ReLU	2.0M	97.0M	65.4	86.4
	DY-ReLU	3.1M	104.5M	$70.3_{(4.9)}$	$89.3_{(2.9)}$
MobileNetV2 ×0.35	ReLU	1.7M	59.2M	60.3	82.9
	DY-ReLU	2.7M	65.0M	$66.4_{(6.1)}$	$86.5_{(3.6)}$
MobileNetV3-Large	ReLU/SE/HS	5.4M	219.0M	75.2	92.2
	DY-ReLU	9.8M	230.5M	$75.9_{(0.7)}$	$92.7_{(0.5)}$
MobileNetV3-Small	ReLU/SE/HS	2.9M	66.0M	67.4	86.4
	DY-ReLU	4.0M	68.7M	$69.7_{(2.3)}$	$88.3_{(1.9)}$
ResNet-50	ReLU	23.5M	3.86G	76.2	92.9
	DY-ReLU	27.6M	3.88G	$77.2_{(1.0)}$	$93.4_{(0.5)}$
ResNet-34	ReLU	21.3M	3.64G	73.3	91.4
	DY-ReLU	24.5M	3.65G	$74.4_{(1.1)}$	$92.0_{(0.6)}$
ResNet-18	ReLU	11.1M	1.81G	69.8	89.1
	DY-ReLU	12.8M	1.82G	$71.8_{(2.0)}$	$90.6_{(1.5)}$
ResNet-10	ReLU	5.2M	0.89G	63.0	84.7
	DY-ReLU	6.3M	0.90G	$66.3_{(3.3)}$	$86.7_{(2.0)}$

0.1 is used. We use weight decay 2e-5 and dropout 0.1 for width ×0.35, and increase weight decay 3e-5 and dropout 0.2 for width ×0.5, ×0.75, ×1.0. Random cropping/flipping and color jittering are used for all width multipliers. Mixup [43] is used for width ×1.0 to prevent overfitting.

Training Setup for MobileNetV3: The initial learning rate is 0.1 and is scheduled to arrive at zero within a single cosine cycle. The weight decay is $3e-5$ and label smoothing is 0.1. We use SGD optimizer with 0.9 momentum for 300 epochs. We use dropout rate of 0.1 and 0.2 before the last layer for MobileNetV3-Small and MobileNetV3-Large respectively. We use more data augmentation (color jittering and Mixup [43]) for MobileNetV3-Large.

Training Setup for ResNet: The initial learning rate is 0.1 and drops by 10 at epoch 30, 60. The weight decay is $1e-4$. All models are trained using SGD

Table 5. Comparing DY-ReLU with related activation functions on ImageNet [5] classification. MobileNetV2 with width multiplier ×0.35 and ×1.0 are used. We use spatial-shared and channel-wise DY-ReLU-B with $K = 2, 3$ linear functions. The numbers in brackets denote the performance improvement over the baseline. DY-ReLU outperforms all prior work including Maxout, which has significantly more computations.

Activation	K	MobileNetV2 ×0.35			MobileNetV2 ×1.0		
		#Param	MAdds	Top-1	#Param	MAdds	Top-1
ReLU	2	1.7M	59.2M	60.3	3.5M	300.0M	72.0
RReLU [40]	2	1.7M	59.2M	$60.0_{(-0.3)}$	3.5M	300.0M	$72.5_{(+0.5)}$
LeakyReLU [25]	2	1.7M	59.2M	$60.9_{(+0.6)}$	3.5M	300.0M	$72.7_{(+0.7)}$
PReLU [10]	2	1.7M	59.2M	$63.1_{(+2.8)}$	3.5M	300.0M	$73.3_{(+1.3)}$
SE[14]+ReLU	2	2.1M	62.0M	$62.8_{(+2.5)}$	5.1M	307.5M	$74.2_{(+2.2)}$
Maxout [7]	2	2.1M	106.6M	$64.9_{(+4.6)}$	5.7M	575.8M	$75.1_{(+3.1)}$
Maxout [7]	3	2.4M	157.6M	$65.4_{(+5.1)}$	7.8M	860.2M	$75.8_{(+3.8)}$
DY-ReLU-B	2	2.7M	65.0M	$66.4_{(+6.1)}$	7.5M	315.5M	$\mathbf{76.2}_{(+4.2)}$
DY-ReLU-B	3	3.1M	67.8M	$\mathbf{66.6}_{(+6.3)}$	9.2M	322.8M	$\mathbf{76.2}_{(+4.2)}$

optimizer with 0.9 momentum for 90 epochs. We use dropout rate 0.1 before the last layer and label smoothing for ResNet-18, ResNet-34 and ResNet-50.

Main Results: We compare DY-ReLU with its static counterpart in three CNN architectures (MobileNetV2, MobileNetV3 and ResNet) in Table 4. Without bells and whistles, DY-ReLU outperforms its static counterpart by a clear margin for all three architectures, with small extra computational cost (∼5%). DY-ReLU gains more than 1.0% top-1 accuracy in ResNet and gains more than 4.2% top-1 accuracy in MobileNetV2. For the state-of-the-art MobileNetV3, our DY-ReLU outperforms the combination of SE and h-swish (key contributions of MobileNetV3). The top-1 accuracy is improved by 2.3% and 0.7% for MobileNetV3-Small and MobileNetV3-Large, respectively. Note that DY-ReLU achieves more improvement for smaller models (e.g. MobileNetV2 ×0.35, MobileNetV3-Small, ResNet-10). This is because the smaller models are underfitted due to their model size, and dynamic ReLU significantly boosts their representation capability.

The comparison between DY-ReLU and prior work is shown in Table 5. Here we use MobileNetV2 (×0.35 and ×1.0), and replace ReLU with different activation functions in prior work. Our method outperforms all prior work with a clear margin, including Maxout that has significantly more computational cost. This demonstrates that DY-ReLU not only has more representation capability, but also is computationally efficient.

5.2   Inspecting DY-ReLU: Is It Dynamic?

We check if DY-ReLU is dynamic by examining its input and output over multiple images. Different activation values (y) across different images for a given

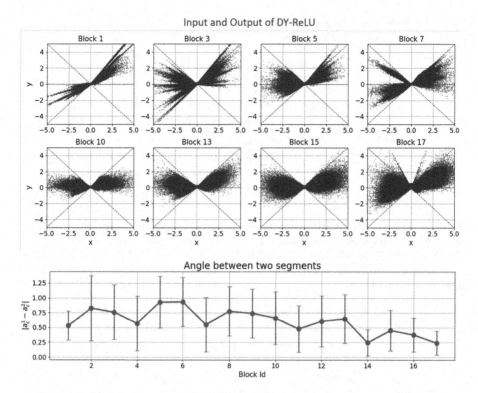

Fig. 3. Top: plots of input and output values of DY-ReLU in a well trained model (using MobileNetV2 ×0.35) over 50,000 validation images in ImageNet [5]. We choose the dynamic ReLU after the depthwise convolution in every other mobile block. Block 1 corresponds to the lowest block, and Block 17 corresponds to the highest block. The two red lines correspond to $y = x$ and $y = -x$, respectively. **Bottom:** Angle (or slope difference $|a_c^1 - a_c^2|$) between two segments in DY-ReLU across blocks. The bending of the activation functions decreases from low levels to high levels. Best viewed in color. (Color figure online)

input value (e.g. $x = 0.5$) is expected to differentiate from static ReLU, which has a fixed output (e.g. $y = 0.5$ when $x = 0.5$).

Figure 3-(Top) plots the input and output values of DY-ReLU at different blocks (from low level to high level) for 50,000 validation images in ImageNet [5]. Clearly, the learnt DY-ReLU is dynamic over features as activation values (y) vary in a range (that blue dots cover) for a given input x. The dynamic range varies across different blocks, indicating different dynamic functions learnt across levels. We also observe many positive activations for negative inputs. Statistically, 51% of DY-ReLU have segments with either negative slope or slope above 1, and 37% of DY-ReLU have at least one segment with intercept more than 0.05. These cases cannot be handled by ReLU, SE or MaxOut of two SEs.

We also analyzed the angle between two segments in DY-ReLU (i.e. slope difference $|a_c^1 - a_c^2|$). The slope difference decreases from lower to higher levels

Table 6. Different dynamic piecewise functions evaluated on ImageNet classification. MobileNetV2 ×0.35 is used.

	K	Intercept b_c^k	Activation Function	Top-1	Top-5
ReLU	2		$\max\{x_c, 0\}$	60.3	82.9
	2		$\max\{a_c(\boldsymbol{x})x_c, 0\}$	63.8	85.1
	2	✓	$\max\{a_c(\boldsymbol{x})x_c + b_c(\boldsymbol{x}), 0\}$	64.0	85.2
DY-ReLU	2		$\max_{k=1}^2\{a_c^k(\boldsymbol{x})x_c\}$	65.7	86.2
	2	✓	$\max_{k=1}^2(a_c^k(\boldsymbol{x})x_c + b_c^k(\boldsymbol{x}))$	66.4	86.5
	3		$\max_{k=1}^3\{a_c^k(\boldsymbol{x})x_c\}$	65.9	86.3
	3	✓	$\max_{k=1}^3\{a_c^k(\boldsymbol{x})x_c + b_c^k(\boldsymbol{x})\}$	66.6	86.8

Table 7. DY-ReLU at different layers evaluated on ImageNet. MobileNetV2 ×0.35 is used. A_1, A_2, A_3 indicate activations after three convolution layers in an inverted residual block.

	A_1	A_2	A_3	Top-1	Top-5
ReLU	–	–	–	60.3	82.9
	✓	–	–	64.2	84.9
	–	✓	–	65.3	85.9
	–	–	✓	62.7	83.8
DY-ReLU	✓	✓	–	66.2	86.4
	✓	–	✓	64.5	85.3
	–	✓	✓	65.9	86.2
	✓	✓	✓	66.4	86.5

Table 8. Different reduction ratios R for the first fully connected layer in the hyper function (see Fig. 2). Evaluation is on ImageNet classification. MobileNetV2 ×0.35 is used. Setting $R = 8$ achieves a good trade-off.

	R	#param	MAdds	Top-1	Top-5
ReLU	–	1.7M	59.2M	60.3	82.9
	64	2.0M	64.3M	65.0	85.7
	32	2.1M	64.4M	65.5	86.0
DY-ReLU	16	2.3M	64.6M	65.9	86.3
	8	2.7M	65.0M	66.4	86.5
	4	3.6M	65.9M	66.5	86.7

(shown in Fig. 3-(Bottom)). This indicates that the activation functions tend to have lower bending in higher levels.

5.3   Ablation Studies on ImageNet

We run a number of ablations to analyze DY-ReLU. We focus on spatial-shared and channel-wise DY-ReLU-B, and use MobileNetV2 ×0.35 for all ablations. By default, the number of linear functions in DY-ReLU is set as $K = 2$. The initialization values of slope and intercept are set as $\alpha^1 = 1$, $\alpha^2 = \beta^1 = \beta^2 = 0$. The range of slope and intercept are set as $\lambda_a = 1$ and $\lambda_b = 0.5$, respectively. The reduction ratio of the first FC layer in the hyper function is set as $R = 8$.

Dynamic Piecewise Functions: Table 6 shows the classification accuracy using different piecewise functions. The major gain is due to making ReLU dynamic. Specifically, making the first segment dynamic boosts top-1 accuracy from 60.3% to 63.8%. Making the second segment gains additional

Table 9. Ablations of three hyper parameters in DY-ReLU on Imagenet classification.

α^1	α^2	Top-1	Top-5
1.0	0.0	66.4	86.5
1.5	0.0	65.7	86.2
0.5	0.0	66.1	86.3
0.0	0.0	not converge	
1.0	-0.5	65.2	85.5
1.0	0.5	66.4	86.2
1.0	1.0	66.0	86.1

β^1	β^2	Top-1	Top-5
0.0	0.0	66.4	86.5
-0.1	0.0	66.4	86.5
0.1	0.0	66.2	86.4
0.0	-0.1	65.8	86.2
0.0	0.1	65.3	85.8

λ_a	Top-1	Top-5
0.5	65.3	86.0
1.0	66.4	86.5
2.0	66.3	86.5
3.0	65.5	86.1

(a) **Initialization of α^k.**   (b) **Initialization of β^k.**   (c) **Range of slope λ_a.**

1.9%. The intercept b_c^k is helpful consistently. The gap between $K = 2$ and 3 is small. In most of DY-ReLU with $K = 3$ segments, 2 of the 3 segments have similar slopes.

Dynamic ReLU at Different Layers: Table 7 shows the classification accuracy for using DY-ReLU at three different layers (after 1×1 conv, 3×3 depthwise conv, 1×1 conv) in an inverted residual block in MobileNetV2 $\times 0.35$. The accuracy is improved if DY-ReLU is used for more layers. Using DY-ReLU for all three layers yields the best accuracy. If only one layer is allowed to use DY-ReLU, using it after 3×3 depth-wise convolution yields the best performance.

Reduction Ratio R: The reduction ratio of the first FC layer in the hyper function $\theta(x)$ controls the representation capacity and computational cost of DY-ReLU. The comparison across different reduction ratios is shown in Table 8. Setting $R = 8$ achieves a good trade-off.

Initialization of Slope (α^k in Eq. (3)): As shown in Table 9-(a), the classification accuracy is not sensitive to the initialization values of slopes if the first slope is not close to zero and the second slope is non-negative.

Initialization of Intercept (β^k in Eq. (3)): the performance is stable (shown in Table 9-(b)) when both intercepts are close to zero. The second intercept is more sensitive than the first one, as it moves the interception of two lines further away from the origin diagonally.

Range of slope (λ_a in Eq. (3)): Making slope range either too wide or too narrow is not optimal, as shown in Table 9-(c). A good choice is to keep λ_a between 1 and 2.

5.4   COCO Single-Person Keypoint Detection

We use COCO 2017 dataset [21] to evaluate dynamic ReLU on single-person keypoint detection. All models are trained on train2017, including $57K$ images

Table 10. Comparing DY-ReLU with baseline activation functions (ReLU, SE or h-swish, denoted as HS) on COCO Keypoint detection. The evaluation is on validation set. The head structure in [3] is used. DY-ReLU-C with $K = 2$ is used in both backbone and head. Note that SE blocks are removed when using DY-ReLU in MobileNetV3. The numbers in brackets denote the performance improvement over the baseline. DY-ReLU outperforms its static counterpart by a clear margin.

Backbone	Activation	Param	MAdds	AP	$AP^{0.5}$	$AP^{0.75}$	AP^M	AP^L
MBNetV2 ×1.0	ReLU	3.4M	993.7M	64.6	87.0	72.4	61.3	71.0
	DY-ReLU	9.0M	1026.9M	$68.1_{(3.5)}$	88.5	76.2	64.8	74.3
MBNetV2 ×0.5	ReLU	1.9M	794.8M	59.3	84.3	66.4	56.2	65.0
	DY-ReLU	4.6M	820.3M	$63.3_{(4.0)}$	86.3	71.4	60.3	69.2
MBNetV3 Large	ReLU/SE/HS	4.1M	896.4M	65.7	87.4	74.1	62.3	72.2
	DY-ReLU	10.1M	926.6M	$67.2_{(1.5)}$	88.2	75.4	64.1	73.2
MBNetV3 Small	ReLU/SE/HS	2.1M	726.9M	57.1	83.8	63.7	55.0	62.2
	DY-ReLU	4.8M	747.9M	$60.7_{(3.6)}$	85.7	68.1	58.1	66.3

and $150K$ person instances labeled with 17 keypoints. These models are evaluated on `val2017` containing 5000 images by using the mean average precision (AP) over 10 object key point similarity (OKS) thresholds as the metric.

Implementation Details: We evaluate DY-ReLU on two backbone networks (MobileNetV2 and MobileNetV3) and one head network used in [3]. The head simply uses upsampling and four MobileNetV2's inverted residual bottleneck blocks. We compare DY-ReLU with its static counterpart in both *backbone* and *head*. The spatial and channel-wise DY-ReLU-C is used here, as we show that the spatial attention is important for keypoint detection, especially in the head network (see Sect. 4.2). Note that when using MobileNetV3 as backbone, we remove Squeeze-and-Excitation and replace either ReLU or h-swish by DY-ReLU. The number of linear functions in DY-ReLU is set as $K = 2$. The initialization values of slope and intercept are set as $\alpha^1 = 1$, $\alpha^2 = \beta^1 = \beta^2 = 0$. The range of slope and intercept are set as $\lambda_a = 1$ and $\lambda_b = 0.5$, respectively.

Training Setup: We follow the training setup in [31]. All models are trained from scratch for 210 epochs, using Adam optimizer [18]. The initial learning rate is set as 1e-3 and is dropped to 1e-4 and 1e-5 at the 170th and 200th epoch, respectively. All human detection boxes are cropped from the image and resized to 256×192. The data augmentation includes random rotation ($[-45°, 45°]$), random scale ($[0.65, 1.35]$), flipping, and half body data augmentation.

Testing: We use the person detectors provided by [38] and follow the evaluation procedure in [31,38]. The keypoints are predicted on the average heatmap of the original and flipped images. The highest heat value location is then adjusted by a quarter offset from the highest response to the second highest response.

Main Results: Table 10 shows the comparison between DY-ReLU and its static counterpart in four different backbone networks (MobileNetV2 ×0.5 and ×1.0,

MobileNetV3 Small and Large). The head network [3] is shared for these four experiments. DY-ReLU outperforms baselines by a clear margin. It gains 3.5 and 4.0 AP when using MobileNetV2 with width multipler ×1.0 and ×0.5, respectively. It also gains 1.5 and 3.6 AP when using MobileNetV3-Large and MobileNetV3-Small, respectively. These results demonstrate that our method is also effective on keypoint detection.

6   Conclusion

In this paper, we introduce dynamic ReLU (DY-ReLU), which adapts a piece-wise linear activation function dynamically for each input. Compared to its static counterpart (ReLU and its generalizations), DY-ReLU significantly improves the representation capability with negligible extra computation cost, thus is more friendly to efficient CNNs. Our dynamic ReLU can be easily integrated into existing CNN architectures. By simply replacing ReLU (or h-swish) in ResNet and MobileNet (V2 and V3) with DY-ReLU, we achieve solid improvement for both image classification and human pose estimation. We hope DY-ReLU becomes a useful component for efficient network architecture.

References   ·

1. Cai, H., Gan, C., Han, S.: Once for all: train one network and specialize it for efficient deployment. arXiv:abs/1908.09791 (2019)
2. Cai, H., Zhu, L., Han, S.: ProxylessNAS: direct neural architecture search on target task and hardware. In: International Conference on Learning Representations (2019). https://openreview.net/forum?id=HylVB3AqYm
3. Chen, Y., Dai, X., Liu, M., Chen, D., Yuan, L., Liu, Z.: Dynamic convolution: attention over convolution kernels. arXiv:abs/1912.03458 (2019)
4. Clevert, D.A., Unterthiner, T., Hochreiter, S.: Fast and accurate deep network learning by exponential linear units (ELUS). arXiv preprint arXiv:1511.07289 (2015)
5. Deng, J., Dong, W., Socher, R., Li, L.J., Li, K., Fei-Fei, L.: ImageNet: a large-scale hierarchical image database. In: 2009 IEEE Conference on Computer Vision and Pattern Recognition, pp. 248–255. IEEE (2009)
6. Dugas, C., Bengio, Y., Bélisle, F., Nadeau, C., Garcia, R.: Incorporating second-order functional knowledge for better option pricing. In: Advances in Neural Information Processing Systems, pp. 472–478 (2001)
7. Goodfellow, I.J., Warde-Farley, D., Mirza, M., Courville, A., Bengio, Y.: Maxout networks. arXiv preprint arXiv:1302.4389 (2013)
8. Ha, D., Dai, A.M., Le, Q.V.: Hypernetworks. In: ICLR (2017)
9. Hahnloser, R.H., Sarpeshkar, R., Mahowald, M.A., Douglas, R.J., Seung, H.S.: Digital selection and analogue amplification coexist in a cortex-inspired silicon circuit. Nature **405**(6789), 947–951 (2000)
10. He, K., Zhang, X., Ren, S., Sun, J.: Delving deep into rectifiers: surpassing human-level performance on ImageNet classification. In: ICCV (2015)
11. He, K., Zhang, X., Ren, S., Sun, J.: Deep residual learning for image recognition. In: Proceedings of the IEEE Conference on Computer Vision and Pattern Recognition, pp. 770–778 (2016)

12. Howard, A., et al.: Searching for MobileNetv3. CoRR abs/1905.02244 (2019). http://arxiv.org/abs/1905.02244

13. Howard, A.G., et al.: MobileNets: efficient convolutional neural networks for mobile vision applications. arXiv preprint arXiv:1704.04861 (2017)

14. Hu, J., Shen, L., Sun, G.: Squeeze-and-excitation networks. In: The IEEE Conference on Computer Vision and Pattern Recognition (CVPR), June 2018

15. Huang, G., Chen, D., Li, T., Wu, F., van der Maaten, L., Weinberger, K.: Multi-scale dense networks for resource efficient image classification. In: International Conference on Learning Representations (2018). https://openreview.net/forum?id=Hk2aImxAb

16. Iandola, F.N., Moskewicz, M.W., Ashraf, K., Han, S., Dally, W.J., Keutzer, K.: SqueezeNet: alexnet-level accuracy with $50\times$ fewer parameters and <1 mb model size. CoRR abs/1602.07360 (2016). http://arxiv.org/abs/1602.07360

17. Jarrett, K., Kavukcuoglu, K., Ranzato, M., LeCun, Y.: What is the best multi-stage architecture for object recognition? In: The IEEE International Conference on Computer Vision (ICCV) (2009)

18. Kingma, D.P., Ba, J.: Adam: a method for stochastic optimization. In: International Conference on Learning Representations (ICLR) (2015)

19. Klambauer, G., Unterthiner, T., Mayr, A., Hochreiter, S.: Self-normalizing neural networks. In: Advances in Neural Information Processing Systems, pp. 971–980 (2017)

20. Lin, J., Rao, Y., Lu, J., Zhou, J.: Runtime neural pruning. In: Advances in Neural Information Processing Systems, pp. 2181–2191 (2017). http://papers.nips.cc/paper/6813-runtime-neural-pruning.pdf

21. Lin, T.-Y., et al.: Microsoft COCO: common objects in context. In: Fleet, D., Pajdla, T., Schiele, B., Tuytelaars, T. (eds.) ECCV 2014. LNCS, vol. 8693, pp. 740–755. Springer, Cham (2014). https://doi.org/10.1007/978-3-319-10602-1_48

22. Liu, H., Simonyan, K., Yang, Y.: DARTS: differentiable architecture search. In: International Conference on Learning Representations (2019). https://openreview.net/forum?id=S1eYHoC5FX

23. Liu, L., Deng, J.: Dynamic deep neural networks: optimizing accuracy-efficiency trade-offs by selective execution. In: AAAI Conference on Artificial Intelligence (AAAI) (2018)

24. Ma, N., Zhang, X., Zheng, H.-T., Sun, J.: ShuffleNet V2: practical guidelines for efficient CNN architecture design. In: Ferrari, V., Hebert, M., Sminchisescu, C., Weiss, Y. (eds.) Computer Vision – ECCV 2018. LNCS, vol. 11218, pp. 122–138. Springer, Cham (2018). https://doi.org/10.1007/978-3-030-01264-9_8

25. Maas, A.L., Hannun, A.Y., Ng, A.Y.: Rectifier nonlinearities improve neural network acoustic models. In: in ICML Workshop on Deep Learning for Audio, Speech and Language Processing (2013)

26. Misra, D.: Mish: a self regularized non-monotonic neural activation function. arXiv preprint arXiv:1908.08681 (2019)

27. Nair, V., Hinton, G.E.: Rectified linear units improve restricted Boltzmann machines. In: ICML (2010)

28. Ramachandran, P., Zoph, B., Le, Q.V.: Searching for activation functions. arXiv preprint arXiv:1710.05941 (2017)

29. Real, E., Aggarwal, A., Huang, Y., Le, Q.V.: Regularized evolution for image classifier architecture search. In: AAAI Conference on Artificial Intelligence (AAAI) (2018)

30. Sandler, M., Howard, A., Zhu, M., Zhmoginov, A., Chen, L.C.: MobileNetV2: inverted residuals and linear bottlenecks. In: Proceedings of the IEEE Conference on Computer Vision and Pattern Recognition, pp. 4510–4520 (2018)
31. Sun, K., Xiao, B., Liu, D., Wang, J.: Deep high-resolution representation learning for human pose estimation. In: CVPR (2019)
32. Tan, M., et al.: MnasNet: platform-aware neural architecture search for mobile. In: The IEEE Conference on Computer Vision and Pattern Recognition (CVPR), June 2019
33. Trottier, L., Gigu, P., Chaib-draa, B., et al.: Parametric exponential linear unit for deep convolutional neural networks. In: 2017 16th IEEE International Conference on Machine Learning and Applications (ICMLA), pp. 207–214. IEEE (2017)
34. Wang, X., Yu, F., Dou, Z.-Y., Darrell, T., Gonzalez, J.E.: SkipNet: learning dynamic routing in convolutional networks. In: Ferrari, V., Hebert, M., Sminchisescu, C., Weiss, Y. (eds.) ECCV 2018. LNCS, vol. 11217, pp. 420–436. Springer, Cham (2018). https://doi.org/10.1007/978-3-030-01261-8_25
35. Wu, B., et al.: FBNet: hardware-aware efficient convnet design via differentiable neural architecture search. In: The IEEE Conference on Computer Vision and Pattern Recognition (CVPR), June 2019
36. Wu, B., et al.: Shift: a zero flop, zero parameter alternative to spatial convolutions (2017)
37. Wu, Z., et al.: BlockDrop: dynamic inference paths in residual networks. In: The IEEE Conference on Computer Vision and Pattern Recognition (CVPR), June 2018
38. Xiao, B., Wu, H., Wei, Y.: Simple baselines for human pose estimation and tracking. In: Ferrari, V., Hebert, M., Sminchisescu, C., Weiss, Y. (eds.) ECCV 2018. LNCS, vol. 11210, pp. 472–487. Springer, Cham (2018). https://doi.org/10.1007/978-3-030-01231-1_29
39. Xie, S., Zheng, H., Liu, C., Lin, L.: SNAS: stochastic neural architecture search. In: International Conference on Learning Representations (2019). https://openreview.net/forum?id=rylqooRqK7
40. Xu, B., Wang, N., Chen, T., Li, M.: Empirical evaluation of rectified activations in convolutional network. CoRR (2015)
41. Yang, B., Bender, G., Le, Q.V., Ngiam, J.: CondConv: conditionally parameterized convolutions for efficient inference. In: NeurIPS (2019)
42. Yu, J., Yang, L., Xu, N., Yang, J., Huang, T.: Slimmable neural networks. In: International Conference on Learning Representations (2019). https://openreview.net/forum?id=H1gMCsAqY7
43. Zhang, H., Cisse, M., Dauphin, Y.N., Lopez-Paz, D.: mixup: beyond empirical risk minimization. In: International Conference on Learning Representations (2018). https://openreview.net/forum?id=r1Ddp1-Rb
44. Zhang, X., Zhou, X., Lin, M., Sun, J.: ShuffleNet: an extremely efficient convolutional neural network for mobile devices. In: The IEEE Conference on Computer Vision and Pattern Recognition (CVPR), June 2018
45. Zoph, B., Le, Q.V.: Neural architecture search with reinforcement learning. CoRR abs/1611.01578 (2017)
46. Zoph, B., Vasudevan, V., Shlens, J., Le, Q.V.: Learning transferable architectures for scalable image recognition. In: The IEEE Conference on Computer Vision and Pattern Recognition (CVPR), June 2018

Acquiring Dynamic Light Fields Through Coded Aperture Camera

Kohei Sakai[1(✉)] [ID], Keita Takahashi[1] [ID], Toshiaki Fujii[1] [ID],
and Hajime Nagahara[2] [ID]

[1] Graduate School of Engineering, Nagoya University, Nagoya, Japan
{sakai.kohei,takahasi,fujii}@fujii.nuee.nagoya-u.ac.jp
[2] Institute for Datability Science, Osaka University, Suita, Japan
nagahara@ids.osaka-u.ac.jp

Abstract. We investigate the problem of compressive acquisition of a dynamic light field. A promising solution for compressive light field acquisition is to use a coded aperture camera, with which an entire light field can be computationally reconstructed from several images captured through differently-coded aperture patterns. With this method, it was assumed that the scene should not move throughout the complete acquisition process, which restricted real applications. In this study, however, we assume that the target scene may change over time, and propose a method for acquiring a dynamic light field (a moving scene) using a coded aperture camera and a convolutional neural network (CNN). To successfully handle scene motions, we develop a new configuration of image observation, called V-shape observation, and train the CNN using a dynamic-light-field dataset with pseudo motions. Our method is validated through experiments using both a computer-generated scene and a real camera.

Keywords: Light field · CNN · Coded aperture camera

1 Introduction

The concept of a light field, which is a 4-D signal representation that describes all light rays traveling in 3-D space [1,12,23], has been used in various applications, such as view synthesis [19,27,34,54], depth estimation [35,44,48,51], synthetic refocusing [18,32], super resolution [5,48], 3-D display [16,22,39,49], and object recognition [25,45]. A light field is usually represented as a set of dense multi-view images, where many (tens to hundreds) views are aligned in parallel with tiny viewpoint intervals.

Electronic supplementary material The online version of this chapter (https://doi.org/10.1007/978-3-030-58529-7_22) contains supplementary material, which is available to authorized users.

© Springer Nature Switzerland AG 2020
A. Vedaldi et al. (Eds.): ECCV 2020, LNCS 12364, pp. 368–385, 2020.
https://doi.org/10.1007/978-3-030-58529-7_22

Acquiring a light field is challenging due to the large amount of data, for which several approaches have been investigated. The most straightforward approach is to use a moving camera gantry [23] or multiple cameras [11,38,50] to capture a target scene from different viewpoints. This approach is costly in terms of the hardware or time required to acquire the entire light field. Another approach is to use lens-array based cameras that can capture both the spatial and directional information of the light rays [2,3,31,32]. These cameras can acquire an entire light field in a single image, but the spatial resolution of each viewpoint image is in a trade-off relationship with the number of viewpoints.[1] The final approach we mention is compressed acquisition using, e.g., a coded aperture/mask camera [4,17,24,26,30,40,43,53]. We are interested in the final approach due to its potential advantage in efficiency and the ability to acquire a light field in the full spatial resolution of the image sensor.

With this final approach, the target light field is computationally reconstructed from several observed images of the same target scene with different encoding (aperture/mask) patterns.[2] The number of images required for reconstruction can be successfully reduced by optimizing the encoding process (e.g., finding optimal aperture/mask patterns) and corresponding reconstruction algorithm. In earlier studies, this problem was tackled in the context of compressed sensing [6,7,10], and reconstruction methods were developed on the basis of sparse representation on a learned dictionary [26,40] and approximation using the most significant basis vectors [53]. In more recent studies, deep neural networks were successfully applied for better reconstruction from fewer observed images [13,17,29,42]. For example, Inagaki et al. [17] reported that only a few observed images were sufficient for reconstructing a light field with 5×5 or 8×8 views. This successful result came with the learning-based optimization of the entire acquisition process modeled using a deep convolutional neural network (CNN). However, most of the methods mentioned here have been applied only to static light fields (stationary scenes).

In this study, we focused on the problem of compressive acquisition of dynamic light fields (moving scenes). Specifically, we extended Inagaki et al.'s method [17], which was designed exclusively for static light fields, to dynamic light fields. In short, we propose a method for acquiring a dynamic light field using a coded aperture camera and a CNN. To our knowledge, this is the first work that achieves compressive acquisition of a dynamic light field based on the concept of "deep optics", where the optical elements (aperture patterns) and reconstruction algorithm are jointly optimized through deep learning.

---

[1] The combination of a lens-array based camera and ordinary camera has also been explored to increase the temporal resolution [46], but the trade-off between the spatial and directional resolutions still remains unsolved.

[2] A related topic is angular super resolution [19,27,47,52,54], where the target light field is synthesized from sparser (e.g., located at the four corners) views. This is regarded as a special case of compressive acquisition where the encoding process is limited to view subsampling.

Given successful results [17] for static light fields, one might easily conceive of the following two naive strategies for dynamic light fields, both of which are unsuccessful, as shown from our experiments. The first strategy is to reconstruct a light field at each time from only a single observed image [26], which helps avoid the effect of scene motions. Thanks to the recent deep-learning-based optimization, the quality of light field reconstruction from a single image has improved [8,29,37]. However, it is essentially difficult for this strategy to achieve geometrically-correct reconstruction, because in principle, the disparity information cannot be extracted from a single observed image alone. In particular, when an ordinary image (without aperture/mask coding) is used as the input [8,37], the resulting light field is only "hallucinated" based on the implicit knowledge learned from the training dataset rather than the apparent geometric cues. Another naive strategy is to assume that the scene is stationary for a short time and directly apply a method designed for static light fields. In this case, a light field at a certain time can be reconstructed from several images observed over different times [40]. Using several images helps in obtaining 3-D information embedded as disparities related to different aperture patterns. This strategy was expected to work well for scenes with few motions. However, it fails in practice because scene motions are non-negligible even between two consecutive times.

To summarize, we need several (at least two) images to obtain sufficient geometric cues for reconstructing a 3-D structure of the target scene, which are embedded as disparity information among the images captured through different aperture patterns. At the same time, the observed images are also affected by the scene motions over time. In other words, the difference among the observed images is not only due to the disparities but also by scene motions, which greatly complicates the reconstruction problem. To address this issue in our method, we first introduced a new configuration of image observation, called V-shape observation, to help the CNN successfully separate the disparity information from scene motions. We then constructed a dynamic-light-field dataset from static light fields with pseudo motions, and used it for training the CNN to make the CNN more adaptable to dynamic scenes. Our method was quantitatively evaluated through simulation experiments using a computer-generated dynamic scene. We also applied our method for a coded aperture camera and succeeded in capturing a real dynamic scene with fine quality.

2   Proposed Method

We present a method for acquiring a dynamic light field (a moving scene) with a coded aperture camera and a CNN. Our method can be regarded as an extension of the method by Inagaki et al. [17] that was designed exclusively for static light fields. However, to our knowledge, our work is the first to achieve compressive acquisition of a dynamic light field based on the concept of deep optics, where the optical elements (aperture patterns) and reconstruction algorithm are jointly optimized for dynamic light fields through deep learning.

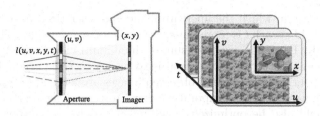

Fig. 1. Coded aperture camera (left) and example of dynamic light field (right)

In this section, we first introduce notations and the problem formulation in Sect. 2.1. Next, we explore several possible configurations for dynamic light-field reconstruction and discuss the proposed method in Sect. 2.2. We explain the architecture of the CNN in Sect. 2.3 then describe the datasets, training procedure, and the optimized aperture patterns in Sect. 2.4.

2.1 Notations and Problem Formulation

A schematic diagram of a coded aperture camera is shown in Fig. 1 (left). All incoming light rays to the camera are parameterized with four variables (u, v, x, y), where (u, v) and (x, y) denote the intersections with the aperture and imaging planes, respectively. The light field is defined over 4-D space (u, v, x, y), with which the light intensity is described as $l(u, v, x, y)$. When we consider scene motions over time t, the light intensity is described as $l(u, v, x, y, t)$ on 5-D space.

We consider a coded aperture design with which the transmittance of the aperture can be controlled at any position and time. The transmittance at position (u, v) and t is defined as $a(u, v, t)$. The image-formation process through a coded aperture camera is described as

$$i_t(x, y) = \frac{1}{|\mathcal{E}_t|} \iiint_{\mathcal{E}_t \times \mathcal{U} \times \mathcal{V}} a(u, v, \tau) l(u, v, x, y, \tau) du dv d\tau, \tag{1}$$

where $i_t(x, y)$ is the observed image at t, $\mathcal{E}_t$ is the exposure time around t, and $\mathcal{U} \times \mathcal{V}$ denotes the effective aperture area.

We next transform Eq. 1 into a discretized representation on the time and aperture domains. We assume that the light field and aperture pattern are constant during each exposure time, i.e., $l(u, v, x, y, \tau) = l_t(u, v, x, y)$ and $a(u, v, \tau) = a_t(u, v)$ for $\tau \in \mathcal{E}_t$. In this case, t can be considered as an index instead of a real value. We also assume that the aperture plane is discretized into several square blocks indexed by a pair of integers (u, v). We can simplify Eq. 1 as

$$i_t(x, y) = \sum_{u,v} a_t(u, v) l_{u,v,t}(x, y). \tag{2}$$

We rewrite $l_t(u, v, x, y)$ as $l_{u,v,t}(x, y)$, which can be regarded as one of the rectified sub-aperture images observed from viewpoint (u, v) at t. Figure 1 (right) illustrates a case in which the aperture plane was discretized in 5×5 regions; thus, a light field at each t is represented as 5×5 multi-view images. The observed image given by Eq. 2 is a weighted sum of those multi-view images.

Given the model of Eq. 2, our goal is to reconstruct the original light field at each t, $l_{u,v,t}(x, y)$, from several observed images around t: $i_{t'}(x, y)$ for $t' \in \mathcal{T}_t$, where $\mathcal{T}_t$ denotes the local temporal window around t. The aperture patterns, $a_t(u, v)$, should also be optimized simultaneously. This is a problem of compressed sensing with an extreme compression ratio, where a set of multi-view images (e.g., 5×5 views) is compressed into a single observed image at each t. However, in the reconstruction stage, we can use the information not only from the corresponding time ($i_t(x, y)$) but also from other adjacent times $t' \in \mathcal{T}_t$ (e.g., $i_{t-1}(x, y)$ and $i_{t+1}(x, y)$), which will help improve reconstruction quality.

The observation and reconstruction processes of a dynamic light field can be translated into a neural network model. The observation process at t, which is given by Eq. 2, can be written in a form of a mapping as $f: L_t \rightarrow I_t$ where L_t represents a tensor that contains all the pixels of $l_{u,v,t}(x, y)$ for all viewpoints (u, v) for a specific t, and I_t represents a tensor that contains all the pixels of $i_t(x, y)$ at t. The reconstruction process is written as $g: \{I_{t'} | t' \in \mathcal{T}_t\} \rightarrow \hat{L}_t$ where $\hat{L}_t$ corresponds to an estimate of L_t. The composite mapping $h = g \circ f$ can be regarded as an auto-encoder, where f and g correspond to the encoder and decoder, respectively, and a set of observed images, $i_{t'}(x, y)$ for $t' \in \mathcal{T}_t$, is regarded as a latent representation. The goal of optimization is formulated, e.g., with the squared error loss, as

$$\hat{f}, \hat{g} = \arg \min_{f,g} ||L_t - \hat{L}_t||^2. \tag{3}$$

As detailed later, we implemented the composite mapping as a deep CNN, using 2-D convolutional neural layers exclusively. The entire network can be trained end-to-end by using a training dataset. The learned parameters in $\hat{f}$ and $\hat{g}$ correspond to the aperture patterns $a_t(u, v)$ and reconstruction algorithm, respectively, both of which are jointly optimized. When applied to a real coded aperture camera, $\hat{f}$ is conducted by the physical imaging process on the camera and the aperture patterns of which are configured in accordance with the learned parameters in $\hat{f}$. The images acquired from the camera are fed to the network corresponding to $\hat{g}$, then, the target light field is reconstructed on the computer.

Our problem described above is similar but more challenging than that of Inagaki et al. [17]. In [17], the target light field is assumed to be static and the observation process is described as

$$i_t(x, y) = \sum_{u,v} a_t(u, v) l_{u,v}(x, y). \tag{4}$$

Time t still appears in $a_t(u, v)$ and $i_t(x, y)$ but disappears from $l_{u,v}(x, y)$. In this case, the same light field can be observed several times as several images $i_t(u, v)$ observed through different aperture patterns $a_t(u, v)$ over t. The target light field was reconstructed with reasonable fidelity because the difference in the observed images was caused solely by the difference in the aperture patterns. More intuitively, due to the difference in the masking patterns on the aperture plane, the observed images have disparities in accordance with the depth of each pixel (x, y), from which the reconstruction algorithm can deduce 3-D information of the target scene. In our case, however, the target light field $l_{u,v,t}(x, y)$ changes over t; thus, each light-field instance $l_{u,v,t}(x, y)$ can be observed only once. Similarly to Inagaki et al. [17], we change the aperture patterns over t, but the differences in the observed images are due to not solely by the difference in the aperture patterns, which is known and even controllable, but also by the scene motions, which are unknown and should be estimated from the observed images.

2.2 Reconstruction of Dynamic Light Field

As mentioned earlier, we can use several observed images $I_{t'}$ ($t' \in \mathcal{T}_t$) to reconstruct a light field $\hat{L}_t$ at t. We now discuss how to do this more specifically considering several design factors. We then present our method, V-shape observation trained with our dynamic-light-field dataset.

The first factor is the number of aperture patterns used for observation. According to Inagaki et al. [17], only two images observed through two different aperture patterns are sufficient to reconstruct a static light field consisting of 5×5 or 8×8 views. Therefore, we determined to use at most two aperture patterns; using more patterns would be helpful to improve the reconstruction quality, but we did not do this to avoid increasing complexity. As shown at the bottom of Fig. 2, two aperture patterns, A and B, are alternately repeated over t. Therefore, at each t, we have only one observed image with one of the aperture patterns. An image observed through aperture pattern A at t is denoted as I_t^A. Note that the target light field changes over t.

The second and third factors are the number of observed images used for reconstruction and the type of training data: static or dynamic light fields. The possible reconstruction methods we considered along with the proposed method are summarized in the top-left table of Fig. 2 and discussed in detail below.

(i) **Single:** reconstruction from only a single observed image (top-right in Fig. 2). At each t, L_t is reconstructed from a single observed image I_t^A, using a pre-trained decoder $\hat{g}$, denoted as "CNN" in the figure. In this case, $\mathcal{T}_t = \{t\}$; thus, the model is free from scene motions; the training can be conducted with a static dataset, and the reconstruction is not affected by scene motions. However, it is difficult to expect good reconstruction quality because the disparity information cannot be obtained from a single image alone in principle.

(ii) **2-S:** reconstruction from two consecutive images using a model trained on a static dataset (bottom-left in Fig. 2). This is a naive application of Inagaki et al.'s method [17] for reconstructing a dynamic light field. We assume that the scene is static over t in which two images are captured and simply apply the model trained on a static dataset. We adopt $\mathcal{T}_t = \{t - 1, t\}$ and try to reconstruct L_t from I_{t-1}^A and I_t^B. One might expect that this would work well with little motion because Inagaki et al.'s method [17] worked perfectly for static

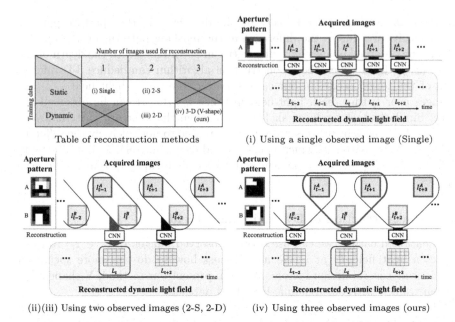

Fig. 2. Reconstruction of dynamic light field with several possible configurations

scenes. However, from our experiments, the scene motion cannot be negligible even between two consecutive images, which leads to poor reconstruction quality.

(iii) **2-D:** reconstruction from two consecutive images using a model trained on a dynamic dataset. This is the same as (ii) except for the training dataset; the model is trained on a dynamic dataset, which will make the model more adaptable to dynamic scenes. However, even in this case, the reconstruction quality is insufficient. One possible reason is that the scene motion and disparity information are inseparable on the two observed images. As mentioned earlier, the difference between the two images is caused by the difference in the aperture patterns (which induces disparities) and scene motions.

(iv) **3-D (V-shape):** reconstruction from three consecutive images using a model trained on a dynamic dataset (bottom right in Fig. 2). This is our proposed method. We adopt $\mathcal{T}_t = \{t - 1, t, t + 1\}$ and try to reconstruct L_t from the three observed images, I_{t-1}^A, I_t^B, and I_{t+1}^A. Images I_{t-1}^A and I_{t+1}^A are captured with the same aperture pattern, i.e., A, so that the difference between these images is exclusively attributed to scene motions. Image I_t^B contains both disparity and motion information with respect to the other two images. We expect that feeding these three images can help the CNN successfully separate disparity information from scene motions, which leads to better reconstruction quality of L_t. We call this "V-shape" observation because the locus tracing the three images constitutes a "V" shape.

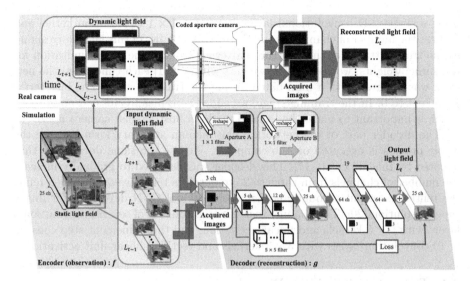

Fig. 3. Network structure for dynamic light field acquisition, where encoder and decoder parts are shown in blue and orange background, respectively.

2.3 Network Architecture

Figure 3 illustrates an example of the networks we constructed where the light field is composed of 25 (5 × 5) viewpoints and the temporal window is set to $T_t = \{t - 1, t, t + 1\}$. The basic architecture is similar to that of Inagaki et al.'s [17], which was dedicated to static light fields, but our network can handle dynamic light fields thanks to the extensions described in Sect. 2.2. We now briefly summarize the architecture.

The network is composed solely of 2-D convolutional layers; thus, it is agnostic of the spatial resolution. An instance of a light field at t (L_t) is treated as a 2-D image having multiple channels. More specifically, a light field with 25 viewpoints is translated into a 2-D image with 25 channels[3]. Therefore, the input and output of the network have 25 channels. For each convolution layer, we use one-pixel stride and appropriate zero padding to maintain the image size before and after the convolution. The number of channels can be changed at each convolution layer. Therefore, the image size (height and width) is kept constant throughout the network but only the number of channels is changed as the data proceed in the network.

The encoder part of the network f is designed with some constraints because it corresponds to the physical-image-capturing process of a coded aperture camera. Specifically, the transmittance of the aperture pattern ($a_t(u, v)$) should be limited within $[0, 1]$, and each pixel (x, y) on the imaging plane cannot be mixed with its neighbors. Similarly to Inagaki et al. [17], we implemented this process

---

[3] We assume that the light field has only one color channel for simplicity. For a color light field, RGB color channels are treated individually.

using a single 2-D convolutional layer that has a 1×1 convolution kernel and reduces the number of channels from 25 to 1 (the weights of this layer correspond to the transmittance of the aperture pattern). To keep the range limitation for the kernel weights, we clipped the weights within $[0, 1]$ each time when the network was updated with a mini-batch during the training stage. The bias terms were kept to 0. In the training stage, we added zero-mean Gaussian noise to I_t, which is important to make the learned model robust against camera noise.

The decoder part of the network g can take an arbitrary form because the whole process is executed on the computer. We use the same decoder as that adopted by Inagaki et al. [17]. This decoder was designed to gradually increase the number of channels from three to 25 to obtain a tentative output then refine the tentative output through another deep residual CNN developed for image super-resolution [20]. The channel-increase step consists of several convolutional layers with 5×5 kernels and linear activation, and the refinement step consists of 19 convolution layers with 3×3 kernels and rectified-linear-unit activation.

2.4   Dataset and Training Procedure

We first explain how we prepared static and dynamic light field datasets used to train the networks. We then mentioned the details of the training procedure and the obtained aperture patterns. The number of views for a light field was set to 5×5 and 8×8.

We followed the procedure of Inagaki et al. [17] in preparing the static-light-field dataset. The training samples were collected from many light-field datasets [9,14,15,28], which are summarized in Table 1. From each light field, we extracted image patches with 64×64 pixels at the same position from all 25 or 64 views and combined them to compose a light-field sample. The position of the image patches was changed to obtain many samples from each light field; we took patches every 32 pixels both in the horizontal and vertical directions but discarded those with almost uniform intensities. Three (RGB) color channels of each light field were used as three individual light fields. We augmented the data by changing the intensity levels of each sample uniformly. We multiplied 1.0, 0.9, 0.8, 0.7, 0.6 and 0.5 with the original samples. Finally, we collected 295,200 and 166,680 samples for 5×5 and 8×8 views, respectively, which were used to train the networks for Single and 2-S.

We next prepared a dynamic light field dataset, which was necessary to train the networks for 2-D and 3-D (V-shape). We need a dataset in which each sample consists of 5×5 or 8×8 views over three consecutive times. To the best of our knowledge, there are no public datasets suitable for our purpose. Therefore, we created such a dataset from the static-light-field dataset by giving it pseudo motions. As illustrated in Fig. 4, we clipped out three slightly different regions from a single image patch and regarded them as a temporal sequence. More specifically, we extracted three image patches with 60×60 pixels from each of the patches (64×64 pixels) of the static-light-field dataset. The extracted patches, gathered from all the views, constituted a sample of dynamic light field corresponding to a set of L_{t-1}, L_t and L_{t+1}. We assume that the pseudo motions

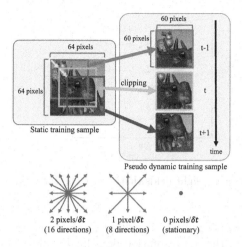

Fig. 4. Creating dynamic training samples with pseudo motions

Table 1. Datasets used for training

5 × 5 views (51 light fields)

Chess, Lego Bulldozer, Lego Truck, Eucalyptus Flowers, Amethyst, Bracelet, The Stanford Bunny, Jelly Beans, Lego Knights, Tarot Cards and Crystal Ball (small angular extent), Treasure Chest (Stanford [9]), Red Dragon, Happy Buddha, Messerschmitt, Dice, Green Dragon, Mini Cooper, Butterfly, Lucy (MIT [28]), Bedroom, Bicycle, Herbs, Origami, Boxes, Cotton, Sideboard, Antinous, Boardgames, Dishes, Greek, Museum, Pens, Pillows, Platonic, Rosemary, Table, Tomb, Town, Vinyl (New HCI [15]), Buddha, Buddha 2, StillLife, Papillon, MonaRoom, Medieval, Horse, Couple, Cube, Maria, Pyramide, Statue (Old HCI [14])

8 × 8 views (30 light fields)

Chess, Lego Bulldozer, Lego Truck, Eucalyptus Flowers, Amethyst, Bracelet, The Stanford Bunny, Jelly Beans, Lego Knights, Tarot Cards and Crystal Ball (small angular extent), Treasure Chest Bedroom (Stanford [9]), Bicycle, Herbs, Origami, Boxes, Cotton, Sideboard, Antinous, Boardgames, Dishes, Greek, Museum, Pens, Pillows, Platonic, Rosemary, Table, Tomb, Town, Vinyl (New HCI [15])

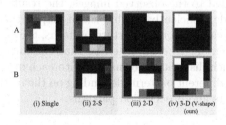

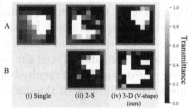

Fig. 5. Aperture patterns optimized through deep learning (left: 5 × 5, right: 8 × 8)

over t are linear and of a constant velocity limited within 2 pixels between the time intervals (δt). Specifically, we applied 25 motion patterns to each static light-field sample, resulting in 7,380,000 and 4,167,000 samples for 5 × 5 and 8 × 8 views, respectively. The motion patterns included linear motions in 16 directions with 2 pixels/δt, 8 directions with 1 pixel/δt, and a stationary one, as illustrated at the bottom of Fig. 4.

For each of the cases with 5 × 5 and 8 × 8 views, we used almost the same network for Single, 2-S, 2-D, and 3-D (V-shape) to make the comparison as fair as possible. The only difference was the joint between the encoder and decoder parts because the number of observed images used for reconstruction differs depending on the method (one to three). We used and extended the source code provided by Inagaki et al. [17]. The software was implemented using Python version 3.6.6 and Chainer [41] version 5.4.0. The batch size for training was set to 15. We used a built-in Adam optimizer [21]. The standard deviation of noise added to the observed image I_t was set to $\sigma = 0.005$ with respect to the image-intensity range $[0, 1]$ of I_t. The number of epochs was fixed to 20 throughout the experiments. The training with V-shape observation (our proposal) took approximately 5 days

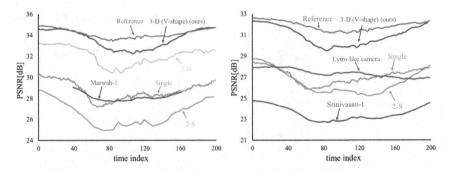

Fig. 6. Quantitative comparison of reconstructed light fields (left: 5 × 5, right: 8 × 8)

on a PC equipped with NVIDIA Geforce GTX 1080 Ti. Although the training was conducted with small image patches, the full-resolution light field could be processed at once in the testing stage because our network is fully convolutional.

The aperture patterns obtained with Single, 2-S, 2-D, and 3-D (V-shape) are shown in Fig. 5. Due to the noise added to the observed images, the resulting aperture patterns were seemingly made sufficiently bright, which helped them to be robust against the noise. For the case with two aperture patterns, they are optimized to be partial and complementary to each other, so that the images acquired with them should contain much disparity information with each other. Moreover, the optimization resulted in different patterns depending on the methods due to the difference of the datasets and observation patterns.

3   Experiments

We first present quantitative evaluations using a computer-generated dynamic scene. We then mention an experiment using a physical coded-aperture camera to capture a real dynamic scene.

3.1   Quantitative Evaluation

We compared the four methods denoted as Single, 2-S, 2-D, and 3-D (V-shape). Note that Single and 2-S correspond to the methods proposed by Inagaki et al. [17], which were designed exclusively for static light fields. In addition, we tested several methods that can obtain a light field from a single image at each time t: Marwah-1, Srinivasan-1, and Lytro-like camera. Marwah-1 [26] is a compressed-sensing-based method constructed on the learned dictionary and sparsity prior, where a light field with 5 × 5 views is reconstructed from a single coded image. Srinivasan-1 [37] is a deep-learning-based method that reconstructs 8 × 8 views from an ordinary image. Lytro-like camera is a simulation of a lens-array based camera [31,32] that obtains 8 × 8 views simultaneously but with a less (1/8 × 1/8) spatial resolution (the resulting images were upsampled to the original resolution using bicubic interpolation). We also tested a method (Reference) with

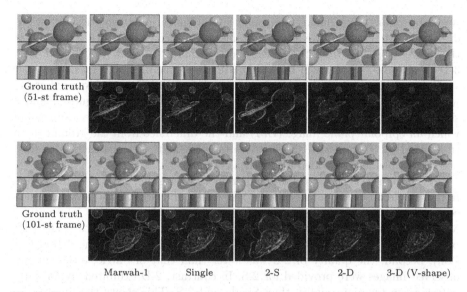

Fig. 7. Reconstructed light fields of computer-generated dynamic scene (5 × 5 views)

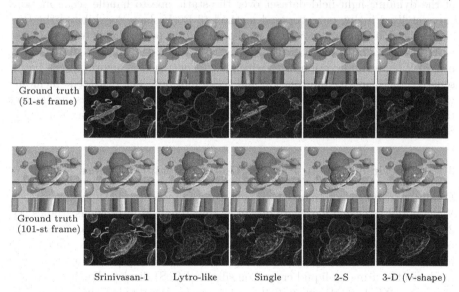

Fig. 8. Reconstructed light fields of computer-generated dynamic scene (8 × 8 views)

which L_t is reconstructed using the same network as the one for 2-S but from two images (I_t^A and I_t^B) observed at the same t, which is practically impossible but serves as the reference that shows the upper-bound reconstruction quality.

For quantitative evaluation, we generated a light-field sequence of a dynamic scene using POV-Ray [33], which is composed of 840 × 593 pixels and 5 × 5 or 8 × 8 views over 200 temporal frames. This test scene contains several slowly revolving planets, producing scene motions with various velocities in various directions. At test time, we added zero-mean Gaussian noise with $\sigma = 0.005$ to the images observed from the coded aperture/mask cameras (Single, 2-S, 2-D, 3-D (V-shape), and Marwah-1) to simulate noisy imaging conditions.

Figure 6 shows the peak signal-to-noise ratios (PSNRs) (the squared errors were averaged over 25 or 64 views) over t for each method[4]. Figures 7 and 8 show the reconstructed top-left views at the 51-st and 101-st frames, for each of which an epipolar plane image (EPI) and the difference from the ground truth (magnified by 3) were also shown to better present the reconstruction quality. See the supplementary video for further details.

Several observations can be found from those results. First, reconstruction from a single observed image (Single, Marwah-1, and Srinivasan-1) was not successful because a single image alone cannot carry the disparity information. Meanwhile, Lytro-like camera can obtain correct disparities with a single shot but with the limited ($1/8 \times 1/8$) spatial resolution (zoom in on the digital version). Second, the quality of 2-S was lower than that of Single, although two observed images were provided for 2-S. In contrast, 2-D exhibited significantly better reconstruction quality than Single and 2-S. This shows the importance of the dynamic-light-field dataset over the static one to handle scene motions successfully. Finally, our proposed method (3-D (V-shape)) exhibited the best reconstruction quality among the methods, and its performance was even close to Reference. The superiority of our method over 2-D indicates the effectiveness of V-shape observation, with which the reconstruction algorithm can better separate the disparity information and scene motions. The test scene including various motions was successfully reconstructed with our method despite the fact that the dataset used for training contained only rather simple linear motions. See Appendix for more results with larger scene motions.

3.2   Experiment Using Physical Coded Aperture Camera

Finally, we acquired a dynamic light field using a physical coded aperture camera. We adopted the same hardware design as that reported in previous studies [17, 26, 30, 36]. The resolution of the camera (FLIR GRAS-14S5C-C) was 1384×1036 pixels, which is equivalent to the spatial resolution of light field acquired with it. We used a Nikon Rayfact lens (25 mm F1.4 SF2514MC). The aperture was implemented using an liquid crystal on silicon (LCoS) display (Forth Dimension Displays, SXGA-3DM) with 1280×1024 pixels. We divided the central area (750×750 pixels) of the LCoS display into 5×5 regions (each with 150×150 pixels), which corresponded to the angular resolution (the number of views) of 5×5. The exposure time was set to 40 ms. Due to the hardware constraint, the frame rate for the observed images was approximately 12 frames per second, and the light field video was reconstructed with 6 frames per second.

---

[4] For Marwah-1, only some of the frames were reconstructed due to heavy computation. It took approximately 20 h to reconstruct a single light field.

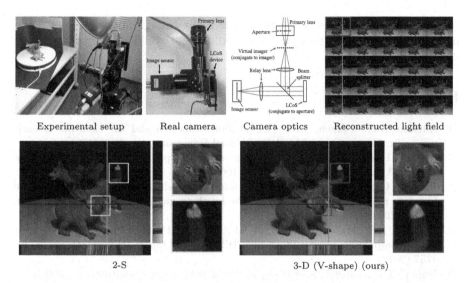

Fig. 9. Experiment using physical coded-aperture camera (see supplementary video)

The experimental setup and camera we used are illustrated in Fig. 9 (top-left and top-center). The target scene consisted of three objects located on a motorized turntable, which produced various scene motions. We used two sets of aperture patterns corresponding to 2-S and 3-D (V-shape). The reconstruction was carried out with the respective reconstruction networks. Some examples of the reconstructed top-left views and EPIs are shown in Fig. 9 (bottom). The result from 2-S seems quite poor; unnatural object edges and incorrect disparities are noticeable. Our method exhibited fine reconstruction quality over all the viewpoints over t. See the supplementary video for more details.

4   Conclusions

We developed a method of acquiring a dynamic light field through a coded aperture camera, where the entire process of light field acquisition (including the aperture patterns for the camera) is modeled as a deep CNN and optimized through training on a large amount of light-field data. Our contribution is twofold, both of which are indispensable to successfully handle a dynamic light field. We first introduced a new configuration of image observation called V-shape observation to help the CNN successfully separate the disparity information from scene motions. We then constructed a dynamic light field dataset (constructed from the static dataset with pseudo motions) to train the CNN, which makes it more adaptable to dynamic scenes. To our knowledge, this is the first work that achieves compressive acquisition of a dynamic light field based on the concept of deep optics, which will inspire further development of computational cameras. Our future work will include extending the training dataset to cover a larger amount of motions and exploring better network structures and color-processing methods. Exploring other input configurations (with different numbers of aperture patterns and observed images) would also be an interesting direction.

References

1. Adelson, E.H., Bergen, J.R.: The plenoptic function and the elements of early vision. In: Computational Models of Visual Processing, pp. 3–20 (1991)
2. Adelson, E.H., Wang, J.Y.: Single lens stereo with a plenoptic camera. IEEE Trans. Pattern Anal. Mach. Intell. **14**(2), 99–106 (1992)
3. Arai, J., Okano, F., Hoshino, H., Yuyama, I.: Gradient-index lens-array method based on real-time integral photography for three-dimensional images. Appl. Opt. **37**(11), 2034–2045 (1998)
4. Babacan, S.D., Ansorge, R., Luessi, M., Mataran, P.R., Molina, R., Katsaggelos, A.K.: Compressive light field sensing. IEEE Trans. Image Process. **21**(12), 4746–4757 (2012)
5. Bishop, T.E., Zanetti, S., Favaro, P.: Light field super resolution. In: 2009 IEEE International Conference on Computational Photography (ICCP), pp. 1–9. IEEE (2009)
6. Candes, E.J., Eldar, Y.C., Needell, D., Randall, P.: Compressed sensing with coherent and redundant dictionaries. Appl. Comput. Harmonic Anal. **31**(1), 59–73 (2011)
7. Candès, E.J., Wakin, M.B.: An introduction to compressive sampling. IEEE Signal Process. Mag. **25**(2), 21–30 (2008)
8. Chen, B., Ruan, L., Lam, M.L.: LFGAN: 4D light field synthesis from a single RGB image. ACM Trans. Multimedia Comput. Commun. Appl. **16**(1) (2020)
9. Computer Graphics Laboratory, Stanford University: The (new) stanford light field archive (2018). http://lightfield.stanford.edu
10. Donoho, D.L.: Compressed sensing. IEEE Trans. Inf. Theory **52**(4), 1289–1306 (2006)
11. Fujii, T., Mori, K., Takeda, K., Mase, K., Tanimoto, M., Suenaga, Y.: Multipoint measuring system for video and sound-100-camera and microphone system. In: 2006 IEEE International Conference on Multimedia and Expo, pp. 437–440. IEEE (2006)
12. Gortler, S.J., Grzeszczuk, R., Szeliski, R., Cohen, M.F.: The lumigraph. In: Proceedings of the 23rd Annual Conference on Computer Graphics and Interactive Techniques, pp. 43–54 (1996)
13. Gupta, M., Jauhari, A., Kulkarni, K., Jayasuriya, S., Molnar, A., Turaga, P.: Compressive light field reconstructions using deep learning. In: 2017 IEEE Conference on Computer Vision and Pattern Recognition Workshops (CVPRW), pp. 1277–1286 (2017)
14. Heidelberg Collaboratory for Image Processing: Datasets and benchmarks for densely sampled 4D light fields (2016). http://lightfieldgroup.iwr.uni-heidelberg.de/?page_id=713
15. Heidelberg Collaboratory for Image Processing: 4D light field dataset (2018). http://hci-lightfield.iwr.uni-heidelberg.de/
16. Huang, F.C., Chen, K., Wetzstein, G.: The light field stereoscope: immersive computer graphics via factored near-eye light field displays with focus cues. ACM Trans. Graph. (TOG) **34**(4), 60 (2015)

17. Inagaki, Y., Kobayashi, Y., Takahashi, K., Fujii, T., Nagahara, H.: Learning to capture light fields through a coded aperture camera. In: Ferrari, V., Hebert, M., Sminchisescu, C., Weiss, Y. (eds.) ECCV 2018. LNCS, vol. 11211, pp. 431–448. Springer, Cham (2018). https://doi.org/10.1007/978-3-030-01234-2_26
18. Isaksen, A., McMillan, L., Gortler, S.J.: Dynamically reparameterized light fields. In: Proceedings of the 27th Annual Conference on Computer Graphics and Interactive Techniques, pp. 297–306 (2000)
19. Kalantari, N.K., Wang, T.C., Ramamoorthi, R.: Learning-based view synthesis for light field cameras. ACM Trans. Graph. (Proc. SIGGRAPH Asia 2016) $35(6)$ (2016)
20. Kim, J., Kwon Lee, J., Mu Lee, K.: Accurate image super-resolution using very deep convolutional networks. In: IEEE Computer Society Conference on Computer Vision and Pattern Recognition, pp. 1646–1654 (2016)
21. Kingma, D., Ba, J.: Adam: a method for stochastic optimization. In: The International Conference on Learning Representations (ICLR) (2015)
22. Lee, S., Jang, C., Moon, S., Cho, J., Lee, B.: Additive light field displays: realization of augmented reality with holographic optical elements. ACM Trans. Graph. (TOG) $35(4)$, 60 (2016)
23. Levoy, M., Hanrahan, P.: Light field rendering. In: Proceedings of the 23rd Annual Conference on Computer Graphics and Interactive Techniques, pp. 31–42. ACM (1996)
24. Liang, C.K., Lin, T.H., Wong, B.Y., Liu, C., Chen, H.H.: Programmable aperture photography: multiplexed light field acquisition. ACM Trans. Graph. (TOG) $27(3)$, 55 (2008)
25. Maeno, K., Nagahara, H., Shimada, A., Taniguchi, R.I.: Light field distortion feature for transparent object recognition. In: IEEE Conference on Computer Vision and Pattern Recognition, pp. 2786–2793 (2013)
26. Marwah, K., Wetzstein, G., Bando, Y., Raskar, R.: Compressive light field photography using overcomplete dictionaries and optimized projections. ACM Trans. Graph. (TOG) $32(4)$, 46 (2013)
27. Mildenhall, B., et al.: Local light field fusion: Practical view synthesis with prescriptive sampling guidelines. ACM Trans. Graph. (TOG) (2019)
28. MIT Media Lab's Camera Culture Group: Compressive light field camera. http://cameraculture.media.mit.edu/projects/compressive-light-field-camera/
29. Nabati, O., Mendlovic, D., Giryes, R.: Fast and accurate reconstruction of compressed color light field. In: 2018 IEEE International Conference on Computational Photography (ICCP), pp. 1–11, May 2018
30. Nagahara, H., Zhou, C., Watanabe, T., Ishiguro, H., Nayar, S.K.: Programmable aperture camera using LCoS. In: Daniilidis, K., Maragos, P., Paragios, N. (eds.) ECCV 2010. LNCS, vol. 6316, pp. 337–350. Springer, Heidelberg (2010). https://doi.org/10.1007/978-3-642-15567-3_25
31. Ng, R.: Digital light field photography. Ph.D. thesis, Stanford University (2006)
32. Ng, R., Levoy, M., Brédif, M., Duval, G., Horowitz, M., Hanrahan, P.: Light field photography with a hand-held plenoptic camera. Comput. Sci. Tech. Rep. CSTR $2(11)$, 1–11 (2005)
33. Persistence of Vision Pty. Ltd.: Persistence of vision raytracer (version 3.6) (2004). http://www.povray.org/
34. Shi, L., Hassanieh, H., Davis, A., Katabi, D., Durand, F.: Light field reconstruction using sparsity in the continuous Fourier domain. ACM Trans. Graph. (TOG) $34(1)$, 12 (2014)

35. Shin, C., Jeon, H.G., Yoon, Y., Kweon, I.S., Kim, S.J.: EPINET: a fully-convolutional neural network using Epipolar geometry for depth from light field images. In: IEEE CVPR, pp. 4748–4757 (2018)
36. Sonoda, T., Nagahara, H., Taniguchi, R.: Motion-invariant coding using a programmable aperture camera. IPSJ Trans. Comput. Vis. Appl. **6**, 25–33 (2014)
37. Srinivasan, P.P., Wang, T., Sreelal, A., Ramamoorthi, R., Ng, R.: Learning to synthesize a 4D RGBD light field from a single image. In: IEEE International Conference on Computer Vision, pp. 2262–2270 (2017)
38. Taguchi, Y., Koike, T., Takahashi, K., Naemura, T.: TransCAIP: a live 3D TV system using a camera array and an integral photography display with interactive control of viewing parameters. IEEE Trans. Visual Comput. Graphics **15**(5), 841–852 (2009)
39. Takahashi, K., Kobayashi, Y., Fujii, T.: From focal stack to tensor light-field display. IEEE Trans. Image Process. **27**(9), 4571–4584 (2018)
40. Tambe, S., Veeraraghavan, A., Agrawal, A.: Towards motion aware light field video for dynamic scenes. In: Proceedings of the IEEE International Conference on Computer Vision, pp. 1009–1016 (2013)
41. Tokui, S., Oono, K., Hido, S., Clayton, J.: Chainer: a next-ngeneration open source framework for deep learning. In: Workshop on Machine Learning Systems (LearningSys) in the Twenty-ninth Annual Conference on Neural Information Processing Systems (NIPS) (2015)
42. Vadathya, A.K., Girish, S., Mitra, K.: A unified learning based framework for light field reconstruction from coded projections. IEEE Trans. Comput. Imaging, 1 (2019)
43. Veeraraghavan, A., Raskar, R., Agrawal, A., Mohan, A., Tumblin, J.: Dappled photography: mask enhanced cameras for heterodyned light fields and coded aperture refocusing. ACM Trans. Graph. (TOG) **26**(3), 69 (2007)
44. Wang, T.C., Efros, A.A., Ramamoorthi, R.: Depth estimation with occlusion modeling using light-field cameras. IEEE Trans. Pattern Anal. Mach. Intell. **38**(11), 2170–2181 (2016)
45. Wang, T.C., Zhu, J.Y., Hiroaki, E., Chandraker, M., Efros, A., Ramamoorthi, R.: A 4d light-field dataset and CNN architectures for material recognition. In: European Conference on Computer Vision (ECCV), pp. 121–138 (2016)
46. Wang, T.C., Zhu, J.Y., Kalantari, N.K., Efros, A.A., Ramamoorthi, R.: Light field video capture using a learning-based hybrid imaging system. ACM Trans. Graph. **36**(4), 133:1–133:13 (2017)
47. Wang, Y., Liu, F., Wang, Z., Hou, G., Sun, Z., Tan, T.: End-to-End view synthesis for light field imaging with pseudo 4DCNN. In: Ferrari, V., Hebert, M., Sminchisescu, C., Weiss, Y. (eds.) ECCV 2018. LNCS, vol. 11206, pp. 340–355. Springer, Cham (2018). https://doi.org/10.1007/978-3-030-01216-8_21
48. Wanner, S., Goldluecke, B.: Variational light field analysis for disparity estimation and super-resolution. IEEE Trans. Pattern Anal. Mach. Intell. **36**(3), 606–619 (2014)
49. Wetzstein, G., Lanman, D., Hirsch, M., Raskar, R.: Tensor displays: compressive light field synthesis using multilayer displays with directional backlighting. ACM Trans. Graph. (Proc. SIGGRAPH) **31**(4), 1–11 (2012)
50. Wilburn, B., et al.: High performance imaging using large camera arrays. ACM Trans. Graph. (TOG) **24**(3), 765–776 (2005)
51. Williem, W., Park, I.K., Lee, K.M.: Robust light field depth estimation using occlusion-noise aware data costs. IEEE Trans. Pattern Anal. Mach. Intell. **PP**(99), 1 (2017)

52. Wu, G., Zhao, M., Wang, L., Dai, Q., Chai, T., Liu, Y.: Light field reconstruction using deep convolutional network on EPI. In: 2017 IEEE Conference on Computer Vision and Pattern Recognition (CVPR), pp. 1638–1646, July 2017
53. Yagi, Y., Takahashi, K., Fujii, T., Sonoda, T., Nagahara, H.: PCA-coded aperture for light field photography. In: IEEE International Conference on Image Processing (ICIP) (2017)
54. Zhou, T., Tucker, R., Flynn, J., Fyffe, G., Snavely, N.: Stereo magnification: Learning view synthesis using multiplane images. In: SIGGRAPH (2018)

Gait Recognition from a Single Image Using a Phase-Aware Gait Cycle Reconstruction Network

Chi Xu[1,2(✉)], Yasushi Makihara[2], Xiang Li[1,2], Yasushi Yagi[2], and Jianfeng Lu[1]

[1] Nanjing University of Science and Technology, Nanjing 210094, China
lujf@njust.edu.cn
[2] ISIR, Osaka University, Osaka 567-0047, Japan
{xu,makihara,li,yagi}@am.sanken.osaka-u.ac.jp

Abstract. We propose a method of gait recognition just from a single image for the first time, which enables latency-free gait recognition. To mitigate large intra-subject variations caused by a phase (gait pose) difference between a matching pair of input single images, we first reconstruct full gait cycles of image sequences from the single images using an auto-encoder framework, and then feed them into a state-of-the-art gait recognition network for matching. Specifically, a phase estimation network is introduced for the input single image, and the gait cycle reconstruction network exploits the estimated phase to mitigate the dependence of an encoded feature on the phase of that single image. This is called phase-aware gait cycle reconstructor (PA-GCR). In the training phase, the PA-GCR and recognition network are simultaneously optimized to achieve a good trade-off between reconstruction and recognition accuracies. Experiments on three gait datasets demonstrate the significant performance improvement of this method.

Keywords: Gait cycle reconstruction · Gait recognition · Single image

1 Introduction

Gait is a common biometric modality used to identify a person. Gait has unique advantages compared with other biometrics such as DNA, fingerprints, the iris, and the face. For example, it can be authenticated at a long distance even without subject cooperation. Gait recognition has therefore received great attention for applications such as surveillance, forensics, and criminal investigation with CCTV footage [6,19,25].

Extensive studies on gait recognition have mainly used a silhouette sequence itself [7,40,41] or gait features extracted from a gait cycle of silhouette

Electronic supplementary material The online version of this chapter (https://doi.org/10.1007/978-3-030-58529-7_23) contains supplementary material, which is available to authorized users.

A. Vedaldi et al. (Eds.): ECCV 2020, LNCS 12364, pp. 386–403, 2020.
https://doi.org/10.1007/978-3-030-58529-7_23

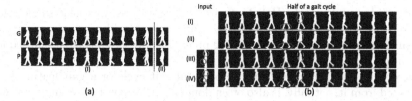

Fig. 1. Examples of different scenarios of gait recognition. (a) A matching pair (G and P) from the same subject for different problem settings. Left (I): gait recognition using a full gait cycle; right (II): gait recognition from a single image. There are significant differences between the pair of single images owing to the phase difference (i.e., double vs. single support). (b) A matching pair from different subject. (I) and (II) are the real silhouette images of a half gait cycles (i.e., ground truth). (III) and (IV) are the corresponding reconstructed half cycles from the single input image using our method. Clear motion differences (e.g., stoop by green circles and stride by red circles) are observed between real cycles (I) and (II), and also the reconstructions (III) and (IV), which means our method can successfully reconstruct the individual gait motion patterns to some extent.

sequences [14,37,38,42,45,47,48]. However, capturing a video containing a certain time length or a full gait cycle usually requires waiting for some time (e.g., about one second for a full gait cycle), which is undesirable for real-time online applications. An extreme way to reduce latency in capturing is to try identifying a subject using just a single image, which has not been especially targeted in prior work to our knowledge. Besides latency, gait recognition from a single image is also applicable to a case of temporal partial occlusion, which is another challenging factor in the real world. For example, in crowded scenes, a subject may be heavily occluded for most of the frames and those frames are useless, whereas the single-image gait recognition can still work once a single frame without occlusion is obtained.

Gait recognition from a single image, however, is quite challenging because gait phase differences (e.g., single vs. double support) introduce great intra-subject variations, as shown in Fig. 1(a). This largely degrades the performances of existing gait recognition methods such as the state-of-the-art network Gait-Set [7] and conventional techniques using gait features such as a gait energy image (GEI) [13] (i.e., averaged silhouette over a full gait cycle).

On the other hand, a snapshot in an action video has proven to imply dynamic information that can predict past/future motions (i.e., implied motion) [21], which has been applied to video synthesis and action recognition [9,33]. Similarly, a single gait image captured from a gait sequence, also intimates pose sequences before or after the frame while keeping the individuality of his/her gait thanks to temporally continuous variables (e.g., knee joint and back bending angles) [16], and hence provides the possibility of gait recognition from a single image. For example, a subject bending his/her back in the single-support is likely to bend his/her back in the double-support too (see Fig. 1(b)(I)), and a single-support phase with a greater knee flexion probably results in a double-support with a larger stride (see Fig. 1(b)(II)). Motivated by these facts, we tackle single-image gait recognition by first reconstructing a gait cycle of a silhouette sequence from the single image, which contains all the phases, before exploiting the subsequent matcher.

Recovering a silhouette sequence of a full gait cycle or a gait feature to be extracted from it, actually, is also often done in gait recognition from videos with low frame-rates [1,2,4]. However, most of these methods does not work well for a very limited number of input frames (i.e., a single frame), and moreover, these approaches optimize only gait cycle reconstruction quality, and hence cannot guarantee the optimal recognition accuracy essentially.

We therefore propose a unified framework of a phase-aware gait cycle reconstruction network (PA-GCRNet) for gait recognition from a single image. This consists of a phase-aware gait cycle reconstructor (PA-GCR) module and a subsequent recognition network. Instead of simply minimizing the gait cycle reconstruction error, the proposed PA-GCRNet learns an appropriate gait cycle reconstruction, where the reconstruction quality is well maintained while ensuring optimal recognition performance simultaneously. The contributions of this work are threefold:

1. The first work aiming at gait recognition from a single image

To our knowledge, this is the first work specially aimed at gait recognition from a single image. Compared with most existing gait recognition studies, which require acquisition of a gait video containing a certain time length (e.g., a gait cycle), single-image gait recognition is more suitable for real-time online applications because the result can be obtained once a single image is captured (i.e., without latency).

2. Gait cycle reconstruction from an arbitrary input phase

While most existing works focus on generating future action frames from an initial frame [9,33], the proposed PA-GCR can reconstruct a gait cycle including future and past frames from an arbitrary input phase. To reduce the intra-subject variations in the reconstructed gait cycles caused by input phase difference, an phase estimation network is incorporated to mitigate the dependence of an encoded feature on the input phase. The proposed PA-GCR is further combined with the state-of-the-art sequence-based gait recognition network Gait-Set [7], in an end-to-end training manner to achieve a good trade-off between gait cycle reconstruction performance and recognition accuracy, unlike traditional low frame-rate gait recognition methods that just focus on reconstruction quality instead of recognition performance.

3. State-of-the-art performance on three publicly available datasets

The proposed method was evaluated on three publicly available gait datasets: the OU-ISIR Gait Database, Multi-View Large Population Dataset (OU-MVLP) [39], CASIA Gait Database, Dataset B (CASIA-B) [46], and OU-ISIR Treadmill Dataset D (OUTD-D) [26]. The proposed method yields significantly improved recognition performance on all three datasets compared with pure sequence-based GaitSet [7] and other state-of-the-art approaches to low frame-rate gait recognition.

2   Related Work

2.1   Gait Recognition from Low Frame-Rate Videos

Temporal Interpolation and Super-Resolution-Based Approaches. Temporal interpolation and super-resolution-based approaches were developed to increase the number of frames to cope with the low frame-rate. Al-Huseiny et al. [3] proposed level-set morphing for temporal interpolation, and Prismall et al. [34] used linear interpolation for moment descriptors. These are, however, not applicable for very low frame-rates.

Makihara et al. [27] proposed reconstructing a gait period with a high frame-rate using phase registration data among multiple periods from a sequence with a low frame-rate and a manifold expressing a periodic temporal super-resolution (TSR) image sequence via energy minimization. Akae et al. [1] later used an exemplar of a gait image sequence with a high frame-rate to overcome the wagon wheel effect in [27]. A unified example-based and reconstruction-based periodic TSR was proposed in [2] to further solve the stroboscopic problem with good reconstruction even when the sequence has such a low frame-rate as to appear nearly still.

However, these methods only ensure optimal reconstruction quality rather than recognition accuracy, which is the main goal of gait recognition.

Metric Learning-Based Approach. Unlike temporal interpolation and super-resolution-based approaches, metric learning-based approach directly applies a metric learning technique to videos with low frame-rates. Guan et al. [12] first extracted a gait feature just by averaging a sequence with a low frame-rate and applied a random subspace method (RSM) to reduce the generalization errors caused by the low frame-rate. However, this does not work well for extremely low frame-rates (e.g., 1 fps) because it is difficult to find robust subspaces with good generalizations for very few input frames.

Direct Gait Feature Reconstruction-Based Approach. Recently, a direct gait feature reconstruction-based approach [4] was proposed that takes the average of a low frame-rate sequence as an input feature (e.g., an incomplete GEI) and reconstructs a GEI to be progressively extracted from a full gait cycle using a fully convolutional neural network. Similarly to traditional temporal interpolation and super-resolution-based approaches, this network only optimizes the reconstruction performance of the GEI, and still works poorly for very low frame-rates.

2.2   Gait Representation

Most studies on gait recognition cope with normal frame-rates under various covariates, such as view [28,42], walking speed [11,43], clothing [10,17], and carried objects [23,29]. Rather than directly using silhouette image sequences, most traditional methods exploit feature templates (e.g., GEI and frequency-domain

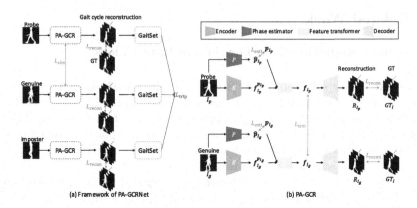

Fig. 2. Overview of the proposed method. GT denotes the ground truth. (a) shows the whole framework of the PA-GCRNet, which contains a PA-GCR for full gait cycle reconstruction and GaitSet [7] as the subsequent recognition network for discrimination learning. A triplet of samples (probe, genuine, and imposter) is fed into the PA-GCRNet in the training stage, where the network parameters are shared among each stream. (b) illustrates the details of the PA-GCR module, which consists of four components: an encoder, a phase estimator, a feature transformer, and a decoder. The imposter is omitted here because the similarity loss L_{sim} is only defined for the genuine pair.

features [28]) extracted from the full gait cycle of a silhouette sequence for further processing such as feature transformation [22,28] and spatial metric learning [5,11,29]. Recently, gait recognition performance has been greatly improved by introducing the convolutional neural network (CNN) framework, where the GEI is mainly used as the network input [37,38,42,45,47,48]. Additionally, a few CNN-based approaches directly handle silhouette sequences [7,40,41] to use more temporal information than a single GEI template. Among them, GaitSet [7] achieves remarkable state-of-the-art recognition performance; hence, we combine the proposed PA-GCR with GaitSet for further feature discrimination learning from the reconstructed full gait cycles.

3   Gait Recognition Using PA-GCRNet

3.1   Overview

An overview of the proposed PA-GCRNet is shown in Fig. 2(a). Given a captured gait image, a silhouette can be first extracted using graph-cut segmentation based on background subtraction [30], or recent state-of-the-art semantic segmentation methods such as RefineNet [24] based on deep learning. A normalized silhouette is then obtained via height normalization and registration using the center of gravity [28], after which it is used as an input for the proposed method.

The proposed PA-GCRNet consists of two parts: PA-GCR and the recognition network (GaitSet in our implementation). Similarly to GaitSet [7], the proposed PA-GCRNet takes a triplet of inputs in the training stage, where the network parameters are shared among the three inputs. The PA-GCR tries fully reconstructing a gait cycle of a silhouette sequence that contains a fixed number of frames with corresponding phases (e.g., left-leg-forward double-support in the first frame) by considering the phase of a single input silhouette. The reconstructed full gait cycle of silhouettes is then fed into the subsequent recognition network to learn more discriminative features for gait recognition. In the testing stage, the dissimilarity between a matching pair is computed as the L2 distance between the discriminative features learnt by the recognition network.

3.2 PA-GCR

The proposed PA-GCR has four components: an encoder, a phase estimator, a feature transformer, and a decoder, as shown in Fig. 2(b). One potential issue is that the phase difference among input silhouettes may affect gait cycle reconstruction results. For example, a double-support silhouette reconstructed from a single-support input silhouette may be different from that reconstructed from a double-support silhouette, because the poses in dynamic parts such as legs and arms in the double-support phase are not observed in the single-support phase. There may be large intra-subject variations in the reconstructed gait cycle of silhouettes if we directly use encoded features from input silhouettes with various phases (kinds of phase-dependent encoded features). We therefore introduce the feature transformer to transform the phase-dependent encoded features into more phase-independent features by taking the estimated phase information into account for the following decoder. This is more advantageous because it reduces intra-subject variations in the reconstructed gait cycle of silhouettes.

Phase Representation. Considering the periodicity of human gait, it is necessary to represent the phase (gait stance) using a periodically continuous label. The phase can be defined by a cyclic angle representation with the domain $[0, 2\pi)$ similarly to a general periodic variable. The cyclic angle representation, however, is discontinuous from 2π to 0; hence we use a redundant two-dimensional vector representation without discontinuity consisting of sine and cosine functions. Assuming that a gait cycle has T frames and that the phase evolves linearly over the frames. The phase vector $\boldsymbol{p}_t \in \mathbb{R}^2$ at the t-th frame is expressed as

$$\boldsymbol{p}_t = [\cos \theta_t, \sin \theta_t]^T, \tag{1}$$

where $\theta_t = \theta_0 + 2\pi \frac{t}{T}$, and θ_0 is a phase shift.

Gait Cycle of a Silhouette Sequence for Training. We need full gait cycles of silhouette sequences from multiple training subjects (i.e., ground truth) to train the proposed network, and the cycles should be phase-synchronized among the training subjects to mitigate the impact of phase inconsistency on reconstruction performance in the training data. However, the real gait cycle needs to be first interpolated into the common gait cycle (e.g., 100 frames per cycle) because the number of frames of a real cycle might be different among the training subjects (e.g., 25 frames per cycle for subject A, 32 frames per cycle for subject B). We therefore apply a geometric transformation based on free-form deformation (FFD) [36] to interpolate intermediate frames between original frames and to generate the silhouette sequence with the common gait cycle because the FFD is suitable for expressing the transformation of a non-rigid human body and helps preserve gait individuality in the transformed image [8,44].

After obtaining the silhouette sequences with the common gait cycle, we synchronize them among the training subjects using a baseline algorithm [35]. More specifically, we first choose a subject as the standard, and then compute the sum of silhouette differences over the common gait cycle between another subject and this standard. We compute the sum for each shift amount of the starting frame, and we adopt the silhouette sequence with the shift amount that minimizes the summed difference as the training data for the reconstructor.

Networks *1) Encoder.* The encoder E first extracts a low-dimensional feature from the input silhouette, which somewhat depends on the phase of the input silhouette. Given the input silhouette I, the obtained low-dimensional feature from the encoder is denoted as

$$f_I^{p_I} = E(I), \tag{2}$$

where p_I is the phase of input I.

The encoder is designed as a CNN with an input size of $1 \times 64 \times 64$. Four convolutional layers are used with a filter size of 4×4 and stride of two, and the number of filters is increased from 64 to 512 in successive doubling steps. We apply a batch-normalization layer [18] and the rectified linear unit (ReLU) activation function [31] after each convolutional layer. Finally, a 100-dimensional feature is obtained through a fully connected layer.

2) Phase Estimator. A phase estimator P is used to estimate the phase label of the input silhouette to make the phase-dependent encoded feature more phase-independent in the next step. The phase estimator is represented as

$$\hat{p}_I = P(I) \in \mathbb{R}^2. \tag{3}$$

The phase estimator has a structure similar to that of the encoder, but with one more fully connected layer to regress the 2D phase label. A normalization layer is used to ensure that $\|\hat{p}_I\|_2 = 1$, which is a characteristic of the sine and cosine functions. The output phase label is compared with the ground truth label p_I to compute an estimation loss as

$$L_{\text{esti}} = \|\hat{p}_I - p_I\|_2^2. \tag{4}$$

3) Feature Transformer. A feature transformer T is inserted between the encoder and the decoder to reduce the reconstruction difference caused by the input phase difference for the same subject. The feature transformer transforms the phase-dependent encoded feature $\boldsymbol{f}_I^{\boldsymbol{p}_I}$ into the phase-independent feature $\boldsymbol{f}_I$, which is formulated as

$$\boldsymbol{f}_I = T(\text{cat}(\boldsymbol{f}_I^{\boldsymbol{p}_I}, \hat{\boldsymbol{p}}_I)), \tag{5}$$

where cat indicates a concatenation.

We implement the feature transformation using a fully connected layer to obtain the transformed 100D feature $\boldsymbol{f}_I \in \mathbb{R}^{100}$ from the 102D concatenated vector of the encoded feature $\boldsymbol{f}_I^{\boldsymbol{p}_I} \in \mathbb{R}^{100}$ and the estimated phase $\hat{\boldsymbol{p}}_I \in \mathbb{R}^2$. We expect the transformed feature $\boldsymbol{f}_I$ to be more independent of the input phase than the encoded feature $\boldsymbol{f}_I^{\boldsymbol{p}_I}$, i.e., those for the same subjects are more similar to each other among different phases of the input silhouettes. Therefore, we minimize the similarity loss for the phase-independent feature $\boldsymbol{f}_I$ via

$$L_{\text{sim}} = \|\boldsymbol{f}_{I_p} - \boldsymbol{f}_{I_g}\|_2^2, \tag{6}$$

where I_p and I_g denote the probe and genuine in a training triplet sample, respectively.

4) Decoder. The output feature of the feature transformer is then fed into the decoder D to fully reconstruct a gait cycle with a predefined number of frames M, and the decoding process is formulated as

$$R_I = D(\boldsymbol{f}_I), \tag{7}$$

where R_I denotes the gait cycle of M silhouettes reconstructed from the input silhouette I.

The structure of the decoder is symmetrical to that of the encoder. A fully connected layer along with reshaping is first used to convert the input 100D feature into the same size as the feature output from the last convolutional layer in the encoder, and then four deconvolutional layers are used for up-sampling. A sigmoid activation function is applied after the last deconvolutional layer that outputs the reconstructions with a size of $M \times 64 \times 64$, where each channel indicates a reconstructed image at a specific phase common to all subjects. A reconstruction loss is computed to ensure the reconstructed gait cycle is similar to the corresponding ground truth (training data) GT_I, which is defined as

$$L_{\text{recon}} = \|R_I - GT_I\|_2^2. \tag{8}$$

3.3 Combining PA-GCR with GaitSet

Next, the reconstructed gait cycle from the PA-GCR is fed into GaitSet to obtain a more discriminative feature.

GaitSet [7] is a set-based gait recognition network that takes a set of silhouettes as an input. After obtaining features from each input silhouette independently using a CNN, set pooling is applied to aggregate features over frames into a set-level feature. The set-level feature is then used for discrimination learning via horizontal pyramid mapping, which extracts features of different spatial locations on different scales. The feature output from GaitSet G for the reconstructed gait cycle of silhouettes R_I is formulated as

$$h_I = G(R_I). \tag{9}$$

For a batch size of $S \times K$ in the training stage, where S is the number of subjects and K is the number of samples per subject, the batch all triplet loss is [15]

$$L_{\text{trip}} = \frac{1}{N} \sum_{i=1}^{S} \sum_{a=1}^{K} \sum_{\substack{s=1 \\ s \neq a}}^{K} \sum_{\substack{j=1 \\ j \neq i}}^{S} \sum_{n=1}^{K} \max(\text{margin} + d_{i,s}^{i,a} - d_{j,n}^{i,a}, 0), \tag{10}$$

where $N = SK(SK - K)(K - 1)$ is the number of all triplets in a batch, $d_{i,s}^{i,a} = \|h_{I_{i,s}} - h_{I_{i,a}}\|_2^2$ is the dissimilarity score of the genuine pair, and $d_{j,n}^{i,a} = \|h_{I_{j,n}} - h_{I_{i,a}}\|_2^2$ is the dissimilarity score of the imposter pair.

3.4 Unified Loss Function

Because the phase estimator directly works on the input image, we train it separately from the main pipeline (i.e., the encoder, the feature transformer, the decoder, and GaitSet). We therefore define a unified loss function to optimize the whole main pipeline jointly to achieve a trade-off between reconstruction and recognition accuracy. The unified loss function is calculated as the weighted sum of the three aforementioned loss functions:

$$L_{\text{uni}} = w_{\text{sim}} L_{\text{sim}} + w_{\text{recon}} L_{\text{recon}} + w_{\text{trip}} L_{\text{trip}}, \tag{11}$$

where w_{sim}, w_{recon}, and w_{trip} are the respective weights for the three losses.

4 Experiments

4.1 Datasets

We evaluated the proposed method on three publicly available datasets: OU-MVLP [39], CASIA-B [46], and OUTD-D [26].

OU-MVLP contains image sequences of 10,307 subjects captured from 14 views at a frame rate of 25 fps, and is the largest gait dataset with a wide view variation in the world. We only focused on the side view (90°) to investigate the recognition performance using a single frame without other covariates. According to the original protocol [39], 5,153 subjects were used for training and the other disjoint 5,154 subjects were used for testing, with one probe sequence and one gallery sequence for each subject. We used this as the main dataset for the following experiments because of its high statistical reliability.

CASIA-B is one of the most widely used gait datasets and consists of gait sequences of 124 subjects captured at 25 fps. Each subject has six normal walking sequences for each of the 11 views. Similarly to the OU-MVLP experiment, only sequences at 90° were used for our evaluation (Sect. 4.4). We adopted the same challenging protocol as in [4], where the first 24 subjects were used for training and the last 100 were used for testing, with one gallery sequence (NM #01) and five probe sequences (NM #02–06).

OUTD-D is a dataset that focuses on gait fluctuations (i.e., silhouette differences of the same phase) over several periods. Hence, it includes a larger number of frames, 360 in each sequence. 185 subjects with two sequences (probe and gallery) for each subject were captured at 60 fps from the side view in this dataset. Using the same protocol as in [1,2], we used 85 subjects for training and the other 100 for testing (Sect. 4.4).

We randomly selected a single frame from a sequence as the input for evaluation for all the datasets.

4.2 Implementation Details

We trained the proposed network using the Adam optimizer [20] with a batch size of $S \times K = 8 \times 16$. We used the same number of channels in GaitSet for OU-MVLP and CASIA-B as in [7], and used the same number for OUTD-D as that for CASIA-B. The margin in Eq. 10 was set to 0.2 for all three datasets. We first prepared the ground truth of a full gait cycle containing 100 frames for the phase synchronization introduced in Sect. 3.2. Considering the computational complexity and memory size needed to train the network, we set the number of frames in the reconstructions as $M = 25$, and evenly down-sampled 25 frames from the original 100 frames to correspond to the training ground truth.

The weights in Eq. 11 were set as $w_{\mathrm{sim}} = 0.0005$ and $w_{\mathrm{recon}} = w_{\mathrm{trip}} = 1$. To first achieve stable reconstruction results, L_{trip} was excluded (i.e., only PA-GCR was included) for the first 30K training iterations with an initial learning rate of 10^{-4} for OU-MVLP, and for the first 20K iterations with an initial learning rate of 10^{-5} for CASIA-B and OUTD-D. We then involved L_{trip} with a learning rate of 10^{-4} for GaitSet while reducing the learning rate for PA-GCR by 0.1. The whole network was trained with 50K more iterations for CASIA-B and OUTD-D and 250K more iterations for OU-MVLP, where the learning rates for both PA-GCR and GaitSet were again reduced by 0.1 for the last 100K iterations.

The recognition performance was evaluated using rank-1 identification rate and equal error rate (EER) [32].

4.3 Visualizing Gait Cycle Reconstruction

We first visualize gait cycles reconstructed by PA-GCRNet using a **test** example of a genuine pair. We choose the challenging case of a large phase difference between the matching pair, where the input probe and gallery image are in the single-support and double-support phase, respectively. Figure 3 shows that the reconstruction results are similar to the corresponding ground truths. We also

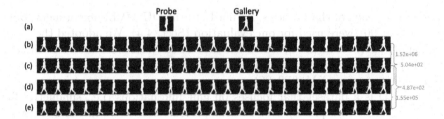

Fig. 3. Examples of gait cycle reconstruction. (a) Input silhouette; left: probe; right: gallery. (b) Ground truth of probe gait cycle. (c) Ground truth of gallery gait cycle. (d) Reconstructed probe gait cycle. (e) Reconstructed gallery gait cycle. Blue digits indicate the errors between the reconstruction and corresponding ground truth, and orange digits indicate the mean squared L2 distances between the corresponding probe and gallery pairs.

give the mean squared error (MSE) as a measure of the difference between the reconstruction result and ground truth [2]:

$$\text{MSE} = \frac{1}{MWH} \sum_{m=1}^{M} \sum_{i=1}^{W} \sum_{j=1}^{H} \|R_I(i,j,m) - GT_I(i,j,m)\|_2^2, \qquad (12)$$

where W and H are the image width and height, respectively, and M is the number of images in the gait cycle (25 in this case). The figure also shows the mean squared L2 distance between the ground truth pair and reconstruction pair to illustrate the difference between the matching pair.

Using the single input silhouette, the proposed method successfully reconstructs a natural gait cycle with a continuous phase change. Although there is still a reconstruction error, the body shapes and poses in the reconstruction are similar to those in the ground truth. The reconstructed gallery and probe pair are also quite similar (see Figs. 3(d) and (e)), which demonstrates that the PA-GCRNet reconstructions are independent of the phase of the input silhouettes to some extent.

On the other hand, the ground truth pair in Fig. 3(b) and (c) has a larger difference because there may be pose variations even for the same phase. This implies that the proposed network not only forces the reconstruction results to be similar to the ground truth, but also reduces the intra-subject variation between the reconstructed same subject pair, which is more beneficial for matching. This is because the end-to-end training includes both reconstruction and recognition, which makes the PA-GCRNet achieve a good trade-off between reconstruction quality and recognition performance. More reconstruction examples are shown in the supplementary material.

In addition, taking a look at the case that a pair of inputs are in the same phase but from different **test** subjects (see Figs. 1(b)(III) and (IV)), the pose differences (e.g., different back bending and stride) are continuously observed between the reconstructed gait cycle pair, which demonstrates the proposed

Table 1. Rank-1 identification rate [%] (denoted as Rank-1) and EER [%] of the proposed method and other benchmarks for OU-MVLP. Bold and bold italic indicate the best and second-best results, respectively. This font convention is used to indicate performance throughout this paper.

Method	Rank-1	EER
DM	4.4	41.3
Gaitset [7]	*14.0*	*19.6*
PA-GCRNet (proposed)	**80.3**	**1.3**

network can keep the gait pose individuality to some extent. That is, an individual gait pose sequence is able to be reconstructed from a single gait image by the network, which provides more gait characteristics of a specific subject, and hence possibly helps improve the recognition accuracy.

4.4   Comparison with State-of-the-Art Methods

OU-MVLP. In this section, the proposed method is compared with state-of-the-art methods for OU-MVLP. There is no existing work on this topic, and only GaitSet [7] has been used to test performance based on a single input image. Therefore, we compare our method with GaitSet[1] and the baseline, i.e., direct matching (DM) between the selected single probe and gallery image pair, as shown in Table 1.

The proposed method significantly outperforms the benchmarks. For example, the rank-1 identification rate is over five times higher than that of the benchmarks, which makes it possible to achieve gait recognition from a single image. The proposed method completes a matching task and obtains the dissimilarity score between a matching image pair in 5 milliseconds using a Quadro RTX 6000 GPU, demonstrating its real-time executability.

CASIA-B. Considering the very limited number of training subjects in CASIA-B, we adopted two strategies for the proposed method: training the network from scratch only using 24 training subjects in CASIA-B, and fine-tuning the network from the model pre-trained for OU-MVLP. For the latter, we only fine-tuned the PA-GCR from the OU-MVLP while still training the GaitSet part from scratch because of the different settings of GaitSet for these two datasets [7]. Additionally, to validate the generalization capability of the proposed network, we also investigated the performance of cross-dataset testing, i.e., directly tested with CASIA-B using the pre-trained PA-GCRNet on OU-MVLP.

Table 2 (left) shows the results for GaitSet, DM and our method along with that of ITCNet, which was reported [4] using a single input image for this dataset.

---

[1] The results were obtained by using their model on our test set (selected single image from a sequence).

Table 2. Rank-1 identification rate [%] (denoted as Rank-1) and EER [%] of the proposed method and other benchmarks for CASIA-B and OUTD-D. Note that ITC-Net [4], NoTSR [2], Morph [3], TSR [1], and Unified TSR [2] used different protocols from ours.

Dataset	CASIA-B		OUTD-D	
Method	Rank-1	EER	Rank-1	EER
DM	14.1	39.7	17	39.0
Gaitset [7]	33.3	17.7	42	13.0
PA-GCRNet (scratch)	39.4	14.7	73	6.4
PA-GCRNet (cross-dataset)	**74.7**	*9.9*	*75*	*4.1*
PA-GCRNet (fine-tune)	**74.7**	**8.1**	**91**	**3.5**
ITCNet [4]	50.0	22.8	–	–
NoTSR [2]	–	–	51	15.0
Morph [3]	–	–	52	14.0
TSR [1]	–	–	44	16.5
Unified TSR [2]	–	–	87	3.5

Note that the ITCNet protocol differed from ours by choosing 14 different frames for each probe and gallery sequence and then obtaining the result via fusion. The other benchmarks and our method used only a single image.

Because of the severe overfitting caused by the very limited training samples, the proposed method cannot perform well by training from scratch on this dataset but still gains a little improvement compared with GaitSet. The overfitting problem can be solved and the performance of the proposed method largely improved by fine-tuning the PA-GCR pre-trained via OU-MVLP with a better generalization capability. Although the result is not as good as for OU-MVLP, this is understandable because some low-quality silhouettes with segmentation errors are included in this dataset. These may affect the recognition performance if the selected matching image pair has different segmented silhouettes.

It is worth mentioning to that the cross-dataset testing achieves a quite good performance, which is only slightly worse than the fine-tuned model in terms of EER. That means, the proposed network trained on a large-scale dataset (i.e., OU-MVLP) has a good generalization to be directly used for another dataset, and hence has a chance to be directly applied in real application scenarios.

OUTD-D. We finally compare the methods for OUTD-D. Table 2 (right) shows the results of our method using both training from scratch and fine-tuning, as well as cross-dataset testing, as was done for CASIA-B. The results for NoTSR [2] (direct matching between the averaged silhouettes over selected frames), Morph [3], TSR [1], and Unified TSR [2] were obtained for 1 fps, which means six frames from one sequence were simultaneously used in those methods.

Table 3. Ablation experiments evaluated using rank-1 identification rate [%] (denoted as Rank-1) on OU-MVLP. Ground truth is denoted as GT. "×" indicates phase information is not used.

Model	Removed component	Phase info	#Training input frame	Test input	Rank-1
GaitSet [7]	–	×	30	1 real frame	14.0
GaitSet	PA-GCR	×	1	1 real frame	34.4
PA-GCR + GaitSet	Unified training	Estimated	1	1 real frame	50.5
GCRNet	Use of phase info	×	1	1 real frame	**77.4**
PA-GCRNet (proposed)	-	Estimated	1	1 real frame	**80.3**
PA-GCRNet (upper bound of phase-aware framework)	–	GT	1	1 real frame	80.6
GaitSet (upper bound of reconstruction)	–	×	30	GT gait cycle (25 frames)	97.7

Compared with the benchmarks using the same protocol, the proposed method achieves much better results even for training from scratch. The performance of the proposed method can be further improved by fine-tuning the PA-GCR from the pre-trained model for OU-MVLP. This even outperforms the state-of-the-art method for low frame-rate gait recognition (Unified TSR [2]), which uses more than one frame for each sequence simultaneously. Again, the cross-dataset testing works well and gains a better result than the model trained from scratch, which further demonstrates the good generalization capability of the proposed method[2].

4.5 Ablation Study

We analyzed the effects of each component of the proposed method on OU-MVLP, as shown in Table 3. The first row shows the result of the baseline GaitSet, which used the same settings as in the original paper [7]. One component of our method was removed for each row from the second to the fourth row. Specifically, we did the following: in the second row, the GaitSet was retrained using the same strategy (a single image) as the proposed method to fairly confirm the effectiveness of PA-GCR reconstruction; in the third row, PA-GCR and GaitSet were separately trained to verify the effectiveness of the proposed unified framework; in the fourth row, the phase estimator and feature transformer with the similarity loss (Eq. 6) were removed from the proposed network to validate the effects of using the phase information of the input image. The fifth row shows the result of our method. For reference, the sixth row reports the upper bound of the proposed phase-aware framework (i.e., using the ground truth phase label

---

[2] Reconstruction results for cross-dataset testing are shown in the supplementary material.

rather than the estimate by the phase estimator). The last row shows the upper bound of reconstruction (i.e., test results for the ground truth of the gait cycle using the pre-trained GaitSet model in the first row).

Comparing the results in the second and fifth rows, it is obvious that removing the proposed PA-GCR significantly reduces the recognition performance. This demonstrates the need to involve gait cycle reconstruction in this task. The proposed unified framework performs much better than the separated training strategy in the third row because it achieves a trade-off between reconstruction and recognition accuracy through its unified optimization. The effectiveness of using input phase information is also confirmed by comparing the fourth and fifth rows. Additionally, the phase estimator yields an error of only 0.02, which is the mean squared L2 distance between the estimated and ground truth phases[3]. Therefore, the difference in performance between the real test (i.e., using the estimated phase) and the upper bound of using the ground truth phase is quite small for the proposed method.

5   Conclusion

This paper presented PA-GCRNet for gait recognition from a single image. Given a single input image, the PA-GCR fully reconstructs the gait cycle of a silhouette in conjunction with the phase estimator and then feeds the reconstruction into a subsequent recognition network like GaitSet for matching. This method achieved significantly higher recognition performance on three publicly available gait datasets.

One future research goal is to extend the proposed PA-GCR to accept multiple input images for low frame-rate gait recognition. Additionally, the proposed method can also potentially be extended to general actions to generate both future and past frames from an arbitrary frame, which is beneficial for video synthesis and action recognition, and this remains future work.

Acknowledgment. This work was supported by JSPS KAKENHI Grant No. JP18H04115, JP19H05692, and JP20H00607, Jiangsu Provincial Science and Technology Support Program (No. BE2014714), the 111 Project (No. B13022), and the Priority Academic Program Development of Jiangsu Higher Education Institutions.

References

1. Akae, N., Makihara, Y., Yagi, Y.: Gait recognition using periodic temporal super resolution for low frame-rate videos. In: Proceedings of the International Joint Conference on Biometrics (IJCB2011), Washington D.C., USA, pp. 1–7, October 2011

---

[3] A mean squared L2 distance of 0.02 is equivalent to approximately 9° of the circumference, i.e., less than one phase for a gait cycle containing 25 phases.

2. Akae, N., Mansur, A., Makihara, Y., Yagi, Y.: Video from nearly still: an application to low frame-rate gait recognition. In: Proceedings of the 25th IEEE Conference on Computer Vision and Pattern Recognition (CVPR2012), Providence, RI, USA, pp. 1537–1543, June 2012
3. Al-Huseiny, M.S., Mahmoodi, S., Nixon, M.S.: Gait learning-based regenerative model: a level set approach. In: The 20th International Conference on Pattern Recognition, Istanbul, Turkey, pp. 2644–2647, August 2010
4. Babaee, M., Li, L., Rigoll, G.: Person identification from partial gait cycle using fully convolutional neural networks. Neurocomputing **338**, 116–125 (2019)
5. Bashir, K., Xiang, T., Gong, S.: Cross view gait recognition using correlation strength. In: BMVC (2010)
6. Bouchrika, I., Goffredo, M., Carter, J., Nixon, M.: On using gait in forensic biometrics. J. Forensic Sci. **56**(4), 882–889 (2011)
7. Chao, H., He, Y., Zhang, J., Feng, J.: GaitSet: regarding gait as a set for cross-view gait recognition. In: Proceedings of the 33th AAAI Conference on Artificial Intelligence (AAAI 2019) (2019)
8. El-Alfy, H., Xu, C., Makihara, Y., Muramatsu, D., Yagi, Y.: A geometric view transformation model using free-form deformation for cross-view gait recognition. In: Proceedings of the 4th Asian Conference on Pattern Recognition (ACPR 2017). IEEE, November 2017
9. Gao, R., Xiong, B., Grauman, K.: Im2Flow: motion hallucination from static images for action recognition. In: CVPR (2018)
10. Guan, Y., Li, C., Roli, F.: On reducing the effect of covariate factors in gait recognition: a classifier ensemble method. IEEE Trans. Pattern Anal. Mach. Intell. **37**(7), 1521–1528 (2015)
11. Guan, Y., Li, C.T.: A robust speed-invariant gait recognition system for walker and runner identification. In: Proceedings of the 6th IAPR International Conference on Biometrics, pp. 1–8 (2013)
12. Guan, Y., Li, C.T., Choudhury, S.: Robust gait recognition from extremely low frame-rate videos. In: 2013 International Workshop on Biometrics and Forensics (IWBF), pp. 1–4, April 2013. https://doi.org/10.1109/IWBF.2013.6547319
13. Han, J., Bhanu, B.: Individual recognition using gait energy image. IEEE Trans. Pattern Anal. Mach. Intell. **28**(2), 316–322 (2006)
14. He, Y., Zhang, J., Shan, H., Wang, L.: Multi-task GANs for view-specific feature learning in gait recognition. IEEE Trans. Inf. Forensics Secur. **14**(1), 102–113 (2019). https://doi.org/10.1109/TIFS.2018.2844819
15. Hermans, A., Beyer, L., Leibe, B.: In defense of the triplet loss for person re-identification. CoRR abs/1703.07737 (2017). http://arxiv.org/abs/1703.07737
16. Horst, F., Lapuschkin, S., Samek, W., Müller, K., Schöllhorn, W.: Explaining the unique nature of individual gait patterns with deep learning. Sci. Rep. **9**, 2391 (2019). https://doi.org/10.1038/s41598-019-38748-8
17. Hossain, M.A., Makihara, Y., Wang, J., Yagi, Y.: Clothing-invariant gait identification using part-based clothing categorization and adaptive weight control. Pattern Recogn. **43**(6), 2281–2291 (2010)
18. Ioffe, S., Szegedy, C.: Batch normalization: accelerating deep network training by reducing internal covariate shift. CoRR abs/1502.03167 (2015). http://arxiv.org/abs/1502.03167
19. Iwama, H., Muramatsu, D., Makihara, Y., Yagi, Y.: Gait verification system for criminal investigation. IPSJ Trans. Comput. Vis. Appl. **5**, 163–175 (2013)
20. Kingma, D.P., Ba, J.: Adam: a method for stochastic optimization. arXiv preprint arXiv: 1412.6980 (2014)

21. Kourtzi, Z., Kanwisher, N.: Activation in human MT/MST by static images with implied motion. J. Cogn. Neurosci. **12**, 48–55 (2000). https://doi.org/10.1162/08989290051137594

22. Kusakunniran, W., Wu, Q., Zhang, J., Li, H.: Support vector regression for multiview gait recognition based on local motion feature selection. In: Proceedings of IEEE Computer Society Conference on Computer Vision and Pattern Recognition 2010, San Francisco, CA, USA, pp. 1–8, June 2010

23. Li, X., Makihara, Y., Xu, C., Yagi, Y., Ren, M.: Joint intensity transformer network for gait recognition robust against clothing and carrying status. IEEE Trans. Inf. Forensics Secur. **14**(12), 3102–3115 (2019)

24. Lin, G., Milan, A., Shen, C., Reid, I.: RefineNet: multi-path refinement networks for high-resolution semantic segmentation. In: CVPR, July 2017

25. Lynnerup, N., Larsen, P.: Gait as evidence. IET Biometrics **3**(2), 47–54 (2014). https://doi.org/10.1049/iet-bmt.2013.0090

26. Makihara, Y., et al.: The OU-ISIR gait database comprising the treadmill dataset. IPSJ Trans. Comput. Vis. Appl. **4**, 53–62 (2012)

27. Makihara, Y., Mori, A., Yagi, Y.: Temporal super resolution from a single quasiperiodic image sequence based on phase registration. In: Proceedings of the 10th Asian Conference on Computer Vision, Queenstown, New Zealand, pp. 107–120, November 2010

28. Makihara, Y., Sagawa, R., Mukaigawa, Y., Echigo, T., Yagi, Y.: Gait recognition using a view transformation model in the frequency domain. In: Leonardis, A., Bischof, H., Pinz, A. (eds.) ECCV 2006. LNCS, vol. 3953, pp. 151–163. Springer, Heidelberg (2006). https://doi.org/10.1007/11744078_12

29. Makihara, Y., Suzuki, A., Muramatsu, D., Li, X., Yagi, Y.: Joint intensity and spatial metric learning for robust gait recognition. In: 2017 IEEE Conference on Computer Vision and Pattern Recognition (CVPR), pp. 6786–6796, July 2017. https://doi.org/10.1109/CVPR.2017.718

30. Makihara, Y., Yagi, Y.: Silhouette extraction based on iterative spatio-temporal local color transformation and graph-cut segmentation. In: Proceedings of the 19th International Conference on Pattern Recognition, Tampa, Florida, USA, December 2008

31. Nair, V., Hinton, G.E.: Rectified linear units improve restricted Boltzmann machines. In: Proceedings of the 27th International Conference on International Conference on Machine Learning, ICML 2010, Omnipress, USA, pp. 807–814 (2010). http://dl.acm.org/citation.cfm?id=3104322.3104425

32. Phillips, P., Moon, H., Rizvi, S., Rauss, P.: The FERET evaluation methodology for face-recognition algorithms. IEEE Trans. Pattern Anal. Mach. Intell. **22**(10), 1090–1104 (2000)

33. Pintea, S.L., Gemert, J.C., Smeulders, A.W.M.: Déjàvu: motion prediction in static images. In: ECCV (2014)

34. Prismall, S.P., Nixon, M.S., Carter, J.N.: Novel temporal views of moving objects for gait biometrics. In: Kittler, J., Nixon, M.S. (eds.) AVBPA 2003. LNCS, vol. 2688, pp. 725–733. Springer, Heidelberg (2003). https://doi.org/10.1007/3-540-44887-X_84

35. Sarkar, S., Phillips, P.J., Liu, Z., Vega, I.R., Grother, P., Bowyer, K.W.: The humanID gait challenge problem: data sets, performance, and analysis. IEEE Trans. Pattern Anal. Mach. Intell. **27**(2), 162–177 (2005). https://doi.org/10.1109/TPAMI.2005.39

36. Sederberg, T.W., Parry, S.R.: Free-form deformation of solid geometric models. SIGGRAPH Comput. Graph. **20**(4), 151–160 (1986). https://doi.org/10.1145/15886.15903
37. Shiraga, K., Makihara, Y., Muramatsu, D., Echigo, T., Yagi, Y.: GeiNet: view-invariant gait recognition using a convolutional neural network. In: 2016 International Conference on Biometrics (ICB), pp. 1–8 (2016)
38. Takemura, N., Makihara, Y., Muramatsu, D., Echigo, T., Yagi, Y.: On input/output architectures for convolutional neural network-based cross-view gait recognition. IEEE Trans. Circ. Syst. Video Technol., 1 (2018). https://doi.org/10.1109/TCSVT.2017.2760835
39. Takemura, N., Makihara, Y., Muramatsu, D., Echigo, T., Yagi, Y.: Multi-view large population gait dataset and its performance evaluation for cross-view gait recognition. IPSJ Trans. Comput. Vis. Appl. **10**(1), 1–14 (2018). https://doi.org/10.1186/s41074-018-0039-6
40. Wolf, T., Babaee, M., Rigoll, G.: Multi-view gait recognition using 3D convolutional neural networks. In: 2016 IEEE International Conference on Image Processing (ICIP), pp. 4165–4169 (2016)
41. Wu, Z., Huang, Y., Wang, L.: Learning representative deep features for image set analysis. IEEE Trans. Multimedia **17**(11), 1960–1968 (2015). https://doi.org/10.1109/TMM.2015.2477681
42. Wu, Z., Huang, Y., Wang, L., Wang, X., Tan, T.: A comprehensive study on cross-view gait based human identification with deep CNNs. IEEE Trans. Pattern Anal. Mach. Intell. **39**(2), 209–226 (2017)
43. Xu, C., Makihara, Y., Li, X., Yagi, Y., Lu, J.: Speed Invariance vs. stability: cross-speed gait recognition using single-support gait energy image. In: Lai, S.-H., Lepetit, V., Nishino, K., Sato, Y. (eds.) ACCV 2016. LNCS, vol. 10112, pp. 52–67. Springer, Cham (2017). https://doi.org/10.1007/978-3-319-54184-6_4
44. Xu, C., Makihara, Y., Yagi, Y., Lu, J.: Gait-based age progression/regression: a baseline and performance evaluation by age group classification and cross-age gait identification. Mach. Vis. Appl. **30**(4), 629–644 (2019). https://doi.org/10.1007/s00138-019-01015-x
45. Yu, S., Chen, H., Reyes, E.B.G., Poh, N.: GaitGAN: invariant gait feature extraction using generative adversarial networks. In: 2017 IEEE Conference on Computer Vision and Pattern Recognition Workshops (CVPRW), pp. 532–539, July 2017. https://doi.org/10.1109/CVPRW.2017.80
46. Yu, S., Tan, D., Tan, T.: A framework for evaluating the effect of view angle, clothing and carrying condition on gait recognition. In: Proceedings of the 18th International Conference on Pattern Recognition, Hong Kong, China, vol. 4, pp. 441–444, August 2006
47. Zhang, C., Liu, W., Ma, H., Fu, H.: Siamese neural network based gait recognition for human identification. In: 2016 IEEE International Conference on Acoustics, Speech and Signal Processing (ICASSP), pp. 2832–2836 (2016)
48. Zhang, K., Luo, W., Ma, L., Liu, W., Li, H.: Learning joint gait representation via quintuplet loss minimization. In: 2019 Conference on Computer Vision and Pattern Recognition (CVPR 2019) (2019)

Informative Sample Mining Network for Multi-domain Image-to-Image Translation

Jie Cao[1,3], Huaibo Huang[1,3], Yi Li[1,3], Ran He[1,2,3(✉)],
and Zhenan Sun[1,2,3]

[1] Center for Research on Intelligent Perception and Computing, NLPR, CASIA,
Beijing, China
{jie.cao,huaibo.huang,yi.li}@cripac.ia.ac.cn, {rhe,znsun}@nlpr.ia.ac.cn
[2] Center for Excellence in Brain Science and Intelligence Technology, CAS,
Beijing, China
[3] School of Artificial Intelligence, University of Chinese Academy of Sciences,
Beijing, China

Abstract. The performance of multi-domain image-to-image translation has been significantly improved by recent progress in deep generative
models. Existing approaches can use a unified model to achieve translations between all the visual domains. However, their outcomes are far
from satisfying when there are large domain variations. In this paper,
we reveal that improving the sample selection strategy is an effective
solution. To select informative samples, we dynamically estimate sample importance during the training of Generative Adversarial Networks,
presenting Informative Sample Mining Network. We theoretically analyze the relationship between the sample importance and the prediction
of the global optimal discriminator. Then a practical importance estimation function for general conditions is derived. Furthermore, we propose
a novel multi-stage sample training scheme to reduce sample hardness
while preserving sample informativeness. Extensive experiments on a
wide range of specific image-to-image translation tasks are conducted,
and the results demonstrate our superiority over current state-of-the-art
methods.

Keywords: Image-to-image translation · Multi-domain image
generation · Generative adversarial networks

1 Introduction

Multi-domain image-to-image translation (I2I) aims at learning the mappings
between visual domains. These domains can be instantiated by a set of attributes,
each of which represents a meaningful visual property. Since each possible combination of the attributes specifies a unique domain [28], the total domain number

Electronic supplementary material The online version of this chapter (https://
doi.org/10.1007/978-3-030-58529-7_24) contains supplementary material, which is
available to authorized users.

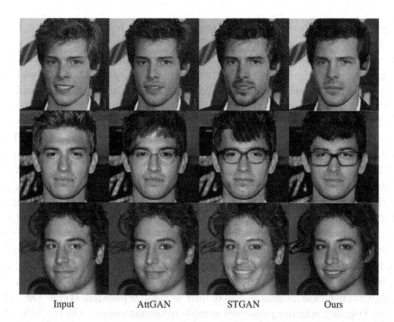

Fig. 1. Facial attribute transfer results of different methods. From top to bottom, the target attributes of each row are *"beard, no_smiling, black_hair"*, *"bangs, eyeglasses, black_hair"*, and *"female, smiling, brown_hair"*, respectively. While AttGAN [11] and STGAN [21] show degraded results in these challenging cases, our approach achieves effective attribute transfer and maintains the realism of texture details.

can be huge in practical applications. For instance, if there are 10 independent binary attributes, we need to handle the translations among 1024 visual domains, which is far more challenging than the two-domain translation. Fortunately, thanks to the recent advances in deep generative models [7,18], current methods [2,11,21,36] can achieve multi-domain I2I by a single model. However, these methods only produce promising results when translating images within similar visual domains, e.g., changing human hair color. The translations between domains with large semantic discrepancies are still not well addressed yet.

To further illustrate the limitation of existing approaches, we take the task of facial attribute transfer as a prime example. Figure 1 shows the results of some challenging translations. Due to the large gap between the source and the target domain, it is difficult to transfer target attributes without impairing visual realism. Even the current state-of-the-art methods [11,21] produce degraded results, although they can address most of the easy translations (we will show these cases in the following experiments). This phenomenon indicates that existing methods mainly focus on easy cases during training but neglect hard ones.

We argue that effective sample selection strategies greatly help to address this problem. Sample selection is within the scope of deep metric learning, which contributes to many computer vision tasks. The studies in deep metric learning [14,29,38,40] point out that a large fraction of training samples may satisfy the loss constraints, providing no progress for model learning. That is, the vast majority of samples are too easy, so their contributions to our training are only marginal. Unfortunately, current multi-domain I2I methods merely adopt the naive random sample selection that treats all training samples equally and thus selects the easy ones mostly. It intuitively hinders training efficiency and consequently leads to the degradation discussed above.

In this paper, we propose **Informative** sample mining network (INIT) to enhance training efficiency and improve performance in multi-domain I2I tasks. Concretely, we integrate Importance Sampling into the generation framework under Generative Adversarial Networks (GAN). Adversarial Importance Weighting is proposed to select informative samples and assign them greater weight. We derive the weighting function based on the assumption that the global optimal discriminator is known. Then we consider more general conditions and introduce the guidance from the prior model to rescale the importance weight. Furthermore, we propose Multi-hop Sample Training to avoid the potential problems [29,35,40] in model training caused by sample mining. Based on the principle of divide-and-conquer, we produce target images by multiple hops, which means the image translation is decomposed into several separated steps. On the one hand, our training scheme preserves sample informativeness. On the other hand, step-by-step training ensures that the generator can learn complex translations. Combining with Adversarial Importance Weighting and Multi-hop Sample Training, our approach can probe and then fully utilize informative training samples.

To verify the effectiveness of our approach, we conduct experiments on facial attribute transfer, season transfer, and edge&photo transfer. We make extensive comparisons with current state-of-the-art multi-domain I2I methods. The experimental results demonstrate our improvements in both attribute transfer and content preservation.

Our contributions can be summarized as follows:

- We analyze the importance of sample selection in image-to-image translation and propose Informative Sample Mining Network.
- We propose Adversarial Importance Weighting, which integrates Importance Sampling into GAN, to achieve effective training sample mining.
- We propose Multi-hop Sample Training to reduce the hardness of the probed informative samples, making them easy to train.
- We provide extensive experimental results on facial attribute transfer, season transfer, and edge&photo transfer, showing our superiority over existing approaches.

2 Related Work

Image-to-Image Translation. Recent advances in deep generative models [7,18,26] have brought much progress in the field of image-to-image translation [2,3,11,15,19,21,22,36,41]. At the early stage, the studies are focused on translations between two visual domains. Zhu et al. have done pioneering works on learning the translations with paired data [15] and unpaired data [41]. FaderNet [19] disentangles the salient information in the latent space to control attribute intensity. UNIT [22] combines Variational AutoEncoder [18] with GAN, and present high-quality results on unsupervised translation tasks. Later on, a lot of efforts are made to deal with the multi-domain condition. StarGAN [2] is the first unified model that produces visually plausible multi-domain translation results. AttGAN [11] introduces an attribute-aware constraint as well as a reconstruction-based regularization to achieve "only change what you want". Following AttGAN, Liu et al. [21] propose a novel selective transfer unit to enhance image quality. RelGAN [36] introduces the notion of relative attribute and employs multiple discriminators to improve both attribute translation and interpolation. Different from previous approaches, we make improvements from a new perspective: we probe informative samples during training, making our network aware of the most challenging cases.

Deep Metric Learning. Deep metric learning aims at learning good representations. The core idea is to narrow the distances of similar images in the embedding space and enlarge the distances of dissimilar ones. Existing works mainly focus on how to choose proper loss functions and sample selection strategies. In the studies of loss function, contrastive loss [13] and triplet loss [34] are the most representative works. The two losses are widely adopted and extended by successive methods. Huang et al. [14] explore the structure of quadruplets. Wang et al. [33] improve triplet loss by introducing a third-order geometry relationship. Sample selection strategies have also been widely studied. For example, hard negative sample mining [30] is proposed to replace the random sample selection in the contrastive loss. FaceNet [29] first adopts semi-hard negative mining within a batch for face recognition. Harwood et al. [9] utilize approximate nearest neighbor search to select harder samples adaptively. Recently proposed methods [4,39] introduce adversarial learning to generate potentially informative samples to train the model. At present, sample selection strategies have been adopted in many computer vision tasks, including image classification [20], face recognition [1,8,13,29], and person re-identification [37]. In this work, we show that sample strategy is also important to image generation but rarely studied. To this end, we propose a novel sampling strategy specifically for multi-domain I2I.

Importance Sampling. Importance Sampling (IS) [6] is a method for estimating properties of a target distribution $p_{data}(\boldsymbol{x})$ which is difficult to sample from directly. Samples are instead drawn from a proposal distribution $p_g(\boldsymbol{x})$ that over-weights the important region. IS is essential for many statistical theories, including Bayesian inference [6] and sequential Monte Carlo methods [25,32]. Applying IS, we can draw samples from $p_g(\boldsymbol{x})$ to estimate $\mathbb{E}_{p_{data}}[\mathcal{L}(\boldsymbol{X})]$ for any known function $\mathcal{L}$. Specifically, we have

$$\mathbb{E}_{p_{data}}[\mathcal{L}(\boldsymbol{X})] = \int \frac{p_{data}(\boldsymbol{x})}{p_g(\boldsymbol{x})} \mathcal{L}(\boldsymbol{x}) p_g(\boldsymbol{x}) \mathrm{d}\boldsymbol{x} = \mathbb{E}_{p_g}\left[\frac{p_{data}(\boldsymbol{X})}{p_g(\boldsymbol{X})} \mathcal{L}(\boldsymbol{X})\right], \quad (1)$$

where for any $\boldsymbol{x}$ in the sample space, we have $p_g(\boldsymbol{x}) > 0$ whenever $p_g(\boldsymbol{x}) \cdot p_{data}(\boldsymbol{x}) \neq 0$. The likelihood ratio $\frac{p_{data}(\boldsymbol{x})}{p_g(\boldsymbol{x})}$ is also referred to as the importance

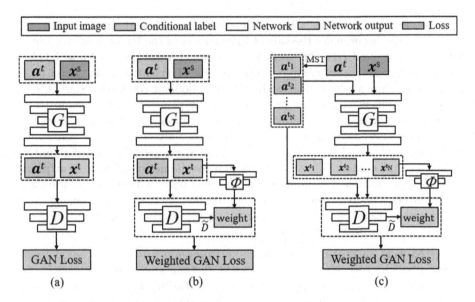

Fig. 2. A illustration about our framework. (a) is our backbone model, which is a Conditional GAN. (b) is the improved version with the proposed AIW (see Sect. 3.1). Our full model, which combines AIW and MST (see Sect. 3.2), is represented as (c).

weight. In the following section, we will integrate IS into the GAN-based multi-domain I2I methods.

3   Proposed Method

We consider visual domains characterized by an n-dimensional binary attribute vector $\boldsymbol{a} = [a_1, a_2, \cdots, a_n]^T$, where each bit a_i represents a meaningful visual attribute. We build Informative Sample Mining Network to learn all the mappings between these domains from unpaired training data. Our network takes a source image $\boldsymbol{x}^s$ with a target attribute $\boldsymbol{a}^t$ to produce the corresponding fake target image $\boldsymbol{x}^t$.

We adopt a Conditional GAN [24] as our backbone model, which is illustrated in Fig. 2 (a). That is, we train the generator and make the generator distribution p_g to capture the true data distribution p_{data}. Meanwhile, a discriminator tries to distinguish the real data from the synthesized fake data. The generator and the discriminator are trained jointly by optimizing the adversarial loss, which can be written as:

$$\min_{G} \max_{D} \mathcal{L} = \overbrace{\mathbb{E}_{\boldsymbol{x}^s, \boldsymbol{a}^s \sim p_{data}} [\log D(\boldsymbol{x}^s, \boldsymbol{a}^s)]}^{\mathcal{L}_{data}} + \overbrace{\mathbb{E}_{\boldsymbol{x}^t, \boldsymbol{a}^t \sim p_g} [\log(1 - D(\boldsymbol{x}^t, \boldsymbol{a}^t))]}^{\mathcal{L}_g}, \quad (2)$$

where $\boldsymbol{x}^t = G(\boldsymbol{x}^s, \boldsymbol{a}^t)$. For brevity, We use G and D to denote the generator and the discriminator, respectively. The inputs of G and D are the concatenation of an image and an attribute vector. We apply spatial replication on the attribute vector, making the sizes of the image and the attribute vector matched.

3.1 Adversarial Importance Weighting

In this section, we describe how to improve the sampling strategy of our backbone model, proposing Adversarial Importance Weighting. We will first consider the situation where we have the global optimal discriminator and then discuss the generalized situation.

To emphasize the contributions of informative samples, we improve the estimation of $\mathcal{L}_g$ by introducing an importance weight for each fake sample x^t. Specifically, we aim to calculate the weight $\frac{p_{data}(x^t)}{p_g(x^t)}$, which is introduced in Eq. 1. To this end, we need to find a solution to make the weight computable. Recall the proposition made by Goodfellow et al. [7]: for any fixed G and any sample point x^t, we have

$$D^*(x^t) = \frac{p_{data}(x^t)}{p_{data}(x^t) + p_g(x^t)}, \tag{3}$$

where D^* is the global optimal discriminator. To reveal the relation between the discriminator and the importance weight, let $D^*(x^t) = S(\widetilde{D}^*(x^t))$, where S denotes the sigmoid function. That is, we have

$$D^*(x^t) = \frac{1}{1 + e^{-\widetilde{D}^*(x^t)}}. \tag{4}$$

Combining Eq. 3 and Eq. 4, we can derive that $\frac{p_{data}(x^t)}{p_g(x^t)} = e^{\widetilde{D}^*(x^t)}$. Hence, the weighted $\mathcal{L}_g$ can be formulated as:

$$\mathcal{L}_g = \mathbb{E}_{x^t, a^t \sim p_g}[e^{\widetilde{D}^*(x^t)} \cdot \log(1 - D(x^t, a^t))]. \tag{5}$$

Equation 5 indicates that a greater $\widetilde{D}^*(x^t)$ brings x^t a bigger sample weight, which means x^t is more informative. In the meantime, a greater $\widetilde{D}^*(x^t)$ also indicates x^t is harder to distinguish for the discriminator. Hence, similar to existing sample selection strategies [29,35,40], **mining the informative samples in GAN means finding the hard fake samples.**

Now we consider the practical situation, where we cannot get the optimal discriminator. A straightforward way to sidestep the need of D^* is replacing it with D. However, D may not provide accurate estimation if it is too far away from the optimality. Hence, we aim at measuring how close D is to D^*. Inspired by the fact [7] that D is close to D^* when p_g is similar to p_{data}, we propose a heuristic metric. Concretely, we first project each training batch $\{x_1^s, x_2^s, \cdots, x_n^s\}$ and the corresponding generated results $\{x_1^t, x_2^t, \cdots, x_n^t\}$ onto a hypersphere whose radius is r by a pre-trained embedding model ϕ. Then, we can calculate the

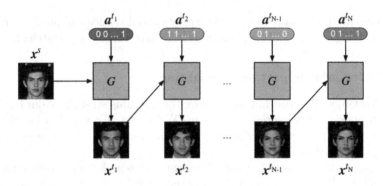

Fig. 3. An illustration about N-hop target image generation. After N times of translations, the generator produces the N-hop target image $\boldsymbol{x}^{t_N}$.

distance matrix $\boldsymbol{E}$, where $e_{ij} = ||\phi(\boldsymbol{x}_i^s) - \phi(\boldsymbol{x}_j^t)||$, i.e., the Euclidean distance between $\boldsymbol{x}_i^s$ and $\boldsymbol{x}_j^t$ in the embedding space. We define that

$$\Delta l = (\overbrace{\sum_{i,j} e_{ij} - \sum_i e_i}^{\Delta l_n}) - \overbrace{\sum_i e_i}^{\Delta l_p} = \sum_{i,j} e_{ij} - 2 \cdot \text{trace}(\boldsymbol{E}), \tag{6}$$

where Δl_p denotes the sum of the distances between the relative image pairs (e.g., e_{11}, e_{33}), and Δl_n denotes the sum of the distances between the permuted image pairs (e.g., e_{12}, e_{31}). Since only the source and the generated images that form a relative pair have the same content information, Δl_p should be as small as possible, and Δl_n should be as large as possible. In the optimal situation, we have $\Delta l_n^* = 2r$ and $\Delta l_p^* = 0$. Hence, Δl^* is a determined constant namely $2r$. In practical conditions, we can calculate $(\Delta l^* - \Delta l)$ to measure how close our network is to the global optimality. Formally, introducing the resale factor $(\Delta l^* - \Delta l)$ into the importance weight, we propose Adversarial Importance Weighting, which can be formulated as:

$$\text{AIW}(\boldsymbol{x}^t) = ||1 + (\Delta l^* - \Delta l)||^2 \cdot e^{\widetilde{D}(\boldsymbol{x}^t)}. \tag{7}$$

We have introduced AIW into our backbone model, as depicted in Fig. 2 (b). Accordingly, the formula of $\mathcal{L}_g$ is updated to:

$$\mathcal{L}_g = \mathbb{E}_{\boldsymbol{x}^t, a^t \sim p_g}[\text{AIW}(\boldsymbol{x}^t) \cdot \log(1 - D(\boldsymbol{x}^t, \boldsymbol{a}^t))]. \tag{8}$$

3.2   Multi-hop Sample Training

The proposed AIW makes the discriminator aware of hard samples and thus strengthens its power. However, since D and G are rivals during training, the training of G may become problematic due to the superior D. To address this

Algorithm 1: Training algorithm of INIT

---
1 Pretrain the embedding model ϕ
2 Initialize the generator G and the discriminator D
3 **for** *the number of training epochs* **do**
4 | Darw a training sample batch
5 | G forward propagates, producing 1-hop target images
6 | D forward propagates
7 | Calculate sample importance weights by Eq. 7
8 | Draw intermediate attributes
9 | G forward propagates, producing multi-hop target images
10 | D forward propagates
11 | Calculate $\mathcal{L}_{data} = \mathbb{E}_{x^s,a^s \sim p_{data}}[\log D(x^s, a^s)]$
12 | Calculate $\mathcal{L}_g$ by Eq. 10
13 | Calculate $\mathcal{L} = \mathcal{L}_{data} + \mathcal{L}_g$
14 | Optimize G by minimizing $\mathcal{L}$
15 | Optimize D by maximizing $\mathcal{L}$
16 **end**

---

issue, we introduce Multi-hop Sample Training which reduces sample hardness for the generator in a divide-and-conquer manner.

Let "hop" denote translation time a model takes to produce the target result. Figure 3 provides a visual illustration, and here we give a formal definition:

$$x^{t_N} = \overbrace{G(\cdots G(G(x^s, a^{t_1}), a^{t_2}), \cdots), a^{t_N})}^{N}, \qquad (9)$$

where generator transforms x^s into x^{t_N} via N separate steps, and x^{t_N} is denoted as N-hop target image. We define $\{a^{t_1}, a^{t_2}, \cdots, a^{t_{N-1}}\}$ as intermediate attributes, and $\{x^{t_1}, x^{t_2}, \cdots, x^{t_{N-1}}\}$ are inferred to as intermediate images.

Previous approaches only consider the situation where $N = 1$. Consequently, some complex transformations may be too hard to learn for the generator. However, any complex transformation can be shrunk step-by-step (e.g., transfer multiple target attributes one-by-one), and it suffices to construct a feasible solution step-by-step. Therefore, we propose to reduce sample hardness by generating the target image in a multi-hop manner. Concretely, we introduce Multi-hop Sample Training, which considers $\{$1-hop, 2-hop, $\cdots$, N-hop$\}$ target images. During training, we calculate losses on both the target images and the intermediate images, providing supervision information for each single step in the multi-hop image generation. Equipping the backbone model with MST, we update the formula of $\mathcal{L}_g$ to:

$$\mathcal{L}_g = \sum_{n=1}^{N} \mathbb{E}_{p_g}[\text{AIW}(x^t) \cdot \mathbb{E}_{p_{n\text{-hop}}}[\sum_{i=1}^{n} \log(1 - D(x^{t_i}, a^{t_i}))]], \qquad (10)$$

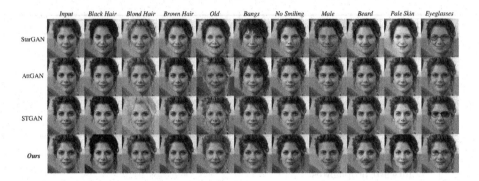

Fig. 4. Visual examples of single facial attribute editing results. From top to bottom, the rows are results of StarGAN [2], AttGAN [11], STGAN [21], and our INIT.

where $\{a^{t_1}, a^{t_2}, \cdots, a^{t_{n-1}}\} \sim p_{\text{n-hop}}$ $(n = 1, 2, \cdots, N)$, and we draw these intermediate attributes randomly in our experiments. Note that we also add AIW, which is proposed in Eq. 7, to this equation.

3.3 Implementation Details

Combining AIW and MST, our full model is able to select informative samples and then train them effectively. The complete diagram is depicted in Fig. 2 (c). During training, we follow the methodology of classical GAN [7] and optimize G and D iteratively. We first produce 1-hop target images, just like the previous approaches. Then, we estimate the importance weight by Eq. 7. Next, we draw intermediate attributes and produce multi-hop target images. Finally, we update model parameters by optimizing the weighted adversarial loss on multi-hop images. The training process is summarized in Algorithm 1.

In our experiments, we adopt 2-hop MST. We build a fully convolutional network as our generator and use a patch discriminator similar to [41]. The pre-trained VGG [31] is employed as the embedding model. Specifically, we use VGGFace [27] for facial attribute transfer. We optimize model parameters by Adam optimizer [17] with $\beta_1 = 0.5$, $\beta_2 = 0.999$, and a learning rate of 1e-4. During testing, our generator directly produces the 1-hop target images as the output, which is the same as existing I2I methods.

4 Experiments

To validate the effectiveness of our approach, we perform extensive experiments on facial attribute transfer, season transfer, and edge&photo transfer. We produce 256×256 results and train our model as well as other competing models for 100 epochs. Our batch size is set to 16. In the following part, we first describe the datasets in our experiments (Sect. 4.1). Then we make comparisons with existing methods and report experimental results (Sect. 4.2, 4.3, and 4.4). Finally, we present an ablation study (Sect. 4.5).

Table 1. The comparisons of the classification accuracy (%) [36] of each attribute (higher is better) and Fréchet Inception Distance [12] (FID, lower is better) on facial attribute transfer.

	StarGAN [2]	AttGAN [11]	STGAN [21]	Ours	Real data
Hair Color	91.02	93.10	92.45	**94.47**	96.12
Aging	92.38	95.41	95.22	**97.90**	98.42
Bangs	87.97	91.03	91.84	**93.26**	93.67
Smile	85.53	90.47	87.41	**90.94**	91.00
Gender	90.72	**96.77**	94.76	96.57	98.25
Beard	87.90	93.53	93.09	**95.58**	95.34
Skin Color	89.35	92.65	94.03	**94.69**	94.22
Eyeglasses	93.38	96.44	96.09	**98.46**	99.31
FID	19.28	13.62	15.94	**11.16**	–

4.1 Dataset

CelebA [23] is the largest publicly available dataset for multi-domain I2I tasks at present. There are annotations of 40 binary attributes for each image. In our experiment, we use the high-quality version, CelebA-HQ [16], for facial attribute transfer. We choose the following 10 attributes to construct the attribute vector: *Black_Hair*, *Blond_Hair*, *Brown_Hair*, *Bangs*, *Smiling*, *Male*, *No_Beard*, *Pale_Skin*, and *Eyeglasses*. We randomly select 300 images as the testing set and use all the remaining images for training.

Yosemite Flickr Dataset [41] consists of 1,200 winter photos and 1,540 summer photos of Yosemite National Park. It is widely used for season transfer, which is an unpaired I2I problem. In our experiment, we follow the training and testing data divisions of CycleGAN [41].

Edge2Photo Dataset [5] contains photos of 250 categories of objects and the corresponding edges. Pix2pix [15] first uses the shoes category for edge-to-photo transfer. We follow the training and testing data divisions in Pix2pix to train our model.

4.2 Facial Attribute Transfer

We compare with StarGAN [2], AttGAN [11], and STGAN [21] on facial attribute transfer. We reproduce their results by the released source codes. The training and testing data for all the methods are the same.

Figure 4 shows single attribute transfer results. Given an input image, each method produces 10 transformed images. For each output result, one specific attribute is toggled. For the relatively easy tasks like changing hair color, all the methods produce plausible results. By contrast, when dealing with the challenging ones like aging, our method produces more realistic results. In general, our INIT can achieve effective attribute transfer and outperform other methods.

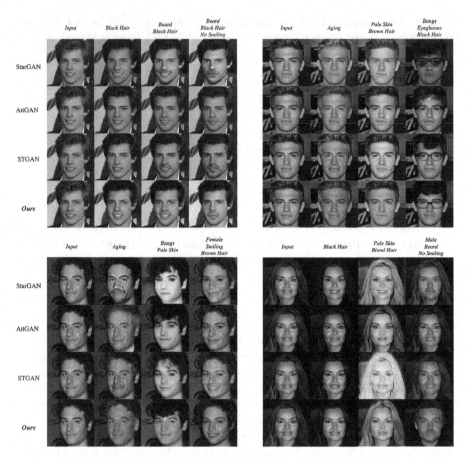

Fig. 5. Visual examples of multiple facial attribute editing, which is a very challenging case in multi-domain I2I. Please zoom in for better visualization. We make comparisons with StarGAN [2], AttGAN [11], STGAN [21].

We argue that **multiple attribute transfer** should also be emphasized. Transferring multiple attributes is at least no easier than transferring a single attribute, and the number of possible combinations is significantly larger. Hence, the hard cases are mainly from the multiple attribute conditions. We report comparison results of multiple facial attribute transfer in Fig. 1 and Fig. 5. In these cases, keeping visual quality and achieving effective attribute transfer become far more challenging. However, our INIT can still produce the desired results. Thanks to the weighting strategies, our method pays more attention to the hard cases and therefore yields better performance. Our superiority provides strong evidence on the effectiveness of sample selection.

We also calculate Fréchet Inception Distance (FID) [12] and the classification accuracy [36] to make objective comparisons. Lower FID is better since it means that the Wasserstein distance between the real distribution and the generated

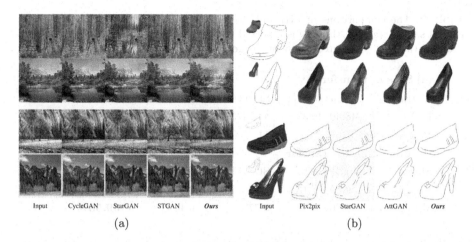

Input   CycleGAN   StarGAN   STGAN   *Ours*   Input   Pix2pix   StarGAN   AttGAN   *Ours*

(a)   (b)

Fig. 6. Visual examples of (a) season transfer and (b) edge&photo transfer. (a) The two rows on the top are *summer → winter*, and the two rows on the bottom are *winter → summer*. We make comparisons with CycleGAN [41], StarGAN [2], and STGAN [21]. (b) The top two rows are *edge → shoes*, and the bottom two rows are *shoes → edge*. We compare with Pix2pix [15], StarGAN [2], and AttGAN [11]. The ground truths are on the upper left corner of the inputs.

distribution is smaller. The classification accuracy reflects the effectiveness of attribute transfer, and thus higher is better. Following [21], we train a Resnet-18 [10] as the classifier and calculate the accuracy on the transformed results. To train this classifier, we use the same data division of CelebA-HQ [16] as the division for our generation tasks. In Table 1, we summarize FID and the classification accuracy of each class. It can be observed that our method has the best performance, indicating our improvements in visual realism and attribute transfer.

4.3   Season Transfer

For season transfer, we make comparisons with CycleGAN [41], StarGAN [2], and STGAN [21]. Note that only CycleGAN trains a pair of networks to achieve *summer → winter* and *winter → summer*, respectively. The other approaches can achieve season transfer by a single model.

We summarize the visual examples of translation results in Fig. 6a. We also calculate FID as an objective metric. Since real summer and winter photos have an apparent perceptual discrepancy, we calculate FID on the two seasons separately. Furthermore, we conduct a user study. We invite volunteers to select the best result among the transformed images from the four methods. All the testing images are compared, and we report the percent of votes for each method. The quantitative comparison results are summarized in the upper part of Table 2. The comparison on FID indicates that our approach favorably outperforms the competing methods, and we obtain the majority of the user votes.

Table 2. The comparisons of FID and the percent of user votes (higher is better). For (a) season transfer, the FID is reported as "summer/winter". For (b) edge&photo transfer, the FID is reported as "photo/edge".

(a) **Season transfer**

Metric	CycleGAN [41]	StarGAN [2]	STGAN [21]	Ours
FID	48.40/49.39	44.84/52.16	45.61/50.37	**40.09/44.91**
Vote Percent	3.73%	11.07%	21.52%	**63.68%**

(b) **Edge&photo transfer**

Metric	Pix2pix [15]	StarGAN [2]	AttGAN [11]	Ours
FID	39.59/17.13	33.23/13.92	29.01/13.86	**28.44/12.30**
Vote percent	30.26%	3.77%	6.44%	**59.53%**

Table 3. Comparison results of different variations of our method. $w/$ and w/o are the abbreviations of "with" and "without", respectively. Our full model is equivalent to the variation (c).

Model	AIW	MST	Hop Number	FID	Mean Acc
(a)	w/o	$w/$	2	18.91	92.86
(b)	$w/$	$w/$	3	11.23	94.98
(c)	$w/$	$w/$	2	**11.16**	**95.08**
(d)	$w/$	w/o	1	14.52	93.78
(e)	w/o	w/o	1	21.38	91.44

4.4   Edge&Photo Transfer

In this subsection, our method is compared with Pix2pix [15], StarGAN [2], and AttGAN [11] on edge&photo transfer. Pix2pix needs to learn edge-to-photo and photo-to-edge separately, and the other methods can deal with the two translations simultaneously. Since we have paired data in this dataset, we add the L1 distance loss [15] in the pixel space, which is useful for paired I2I tasks. Note that we also add the L1 loss for the other competing methods to make fair comparisons.

We report the examples of translation results and the ground truth in Fig. 6b. Similar to season transfer, we calculate FID and conduct user study, the results of which are reported in the lower part of Table 2. Learning edge-to-photo and photo-to-edge as two separate tasks brings Pix2pix obvious advantages, but our method still has the best performance. Compared with StarGAN and AttGAN, our method produces more plausible results, showing stronger generalization ability for paired I2I tasks.

4.5 Ablation Study

In this subsection, we conduct an ablation study to verify the effectiveness of AIW and MST. To this end, we implement several variations of our approach and evaluate them on facial attribute transfer. Concretely, we consider the following variations: (a) INIT without any importance sampling schemes, (b–d) INIT with n-hop sample training, where $n = 3, 2, 1$, respectively. (e) INIT that removes both AIW and MST, i.e., simply a conditional GAN [24]. Note that our full model is equivalent to variation (c).

We use the same experiment setting and train these variations for the same number of iterations. Note that variations with a smaller hop number will have more iterations for training new samples since they have fewer intermediate results to optimize. Tabel 3 shows comparison results on quantitative metrics, and please refer to our Supplementary for visual examples. Through the ablation study, we can verify the following two points:

Mining Informative Samples Plays an Important Role. Without the important sampling scheme, the performances of variations (a) and (e) drop sharply. Even when we double the training iterations of variation (e), its performance is still obviously inferior. Hence, merely taking more training time is not an effective option.

The Optimal Choice is 2-hop Sample Training. As the hop number increases, more intermediate samples are drawn during training. It means that we pay more attention to reduce the sample hardness for the generator. However, as indicated by Eq. 10, it also means 1-hop samples contribute less to the loss function. Note that during testing, the evaluations are based on 1-hop target images. Hence, a larger hop number does not guarantee better performance in practice.

5 Conclusion

In this paper, we propose to integrate Importance Sampling into a GAN-based model, resulting in Adversarial Importance Weighting for high-quality multi-domain image-to-image translation. Furthermore, Multi-hop Sample Training subtly reduces sample hardness while preserving sample informativeness. Thanks to the improvements in training efficiency, our approach achieves effective translation even when dealing with a large number of challenging visual domains. We conduct extensive experiments on practical tasks, including facial attribute transfer, season transfer, and edge&photo transfer. The results consistently demonstrate our superiority over existing methods.

Acknowledgement. This work is funded by the National Natural Science Foundation of China (Grant No. U1836217), Beijing Natural Science Foundation (Grant No. JQ18017) and Youth Innovation Promotion Association CAS (Grant No. Y201929).

References

1. Cao, D., Zhu, X., Huang, X., Guo, J., Lei, Z.: Domain balancing: Face recognition on long-tailed domains. In: CVPR (2020)
2. Choi, Y., Choi, M., Kim, M., Ha, J.W., Kim, S., Choo, J.: StarGAN: unified generative adversarial networks for multi-domain image-to-image translation. In: CVPR (2018)
3. Deng, Q., Cao, J., Liu, Y., Chai, Z., Li, Q., Sun, Z.: Reference guided face component editing (2020)
4. Duan, Y., Zheng, W., Lin, X., Lu, J., Zhou, J.: Deep adversarial metric learning. In: CVPR (2018)
5. Eitz, M., Hays, J., Alexa, M.: How do humans sketch objects? In: SIGGRAPH (2012)
6. Evans, M., Swartz, T., et al.: Methods for approximating integrals in statistics with special emphasis on Bayesian integration problems. Stat. Sci. (1995)
7. Goodfellow, I., et al.: Generative adversarial nets. In: NeurIPS (2014)
8. Guo, J., Zhu, X., Zhao, C., Cao, D., Lei, Z., Li, S.Z.: Learning meta face recognition in unseen domains. In: CVPR (2020)
9. Harwood, B., Kumar, B., Carneiro, G., Reid, I., Drummond, T., et al.: Smart mining for deep metric learning. In: ICCV (2017)
10. He, K., Zhang, X., Ren, S., Sun, J.: Deep residual learning for image recognition. In: CVPR (2016)
11. He, Z., Zuo, W., Kan, M., Shan, S., Chen, X.: AttGAN: facial attribute editing by only changing what you want. TIP (2019)
12. Heusel, M., Ramsauer, H., Unterthiner, T., Nessler, B., Klambauer, G., Hochreiter, S.: GANs trained by a two time-scale update rule converge to a Nash equilibrium. In: NeurIPS (2017)
13. Hu, J., Lu, J., Tan, Y.P.: Discriminative deep metric learning for face verification in the wild. In: CVPR (2014)
14. Huang, C., Loy, C.C., Tang, X.: Local similarity-aware deep feature embedding. In: NeurIPS (2016)
15. Isola, P., Zhu, J.Y., Zhou, T., Efros, A.A.: Image-to-image translation with conditional adversarial networks. In: CVPR (2017)
16. Karras, T., Aila, T., Laine, S., Lehtinen, J.: Progressive growing of GANs for improved quality, stability, and variation. In: ICLR (2018)
17. Kingma, D.P., Ba, J.: Adam: a method for stochastic optimization. In: ICLR (2015)
18. Kingma, D.P., Welling, M.: Auto-encoding variational Bayes. In: ICLR (2014)
19. Lample, G., Zeghidour, N., Usunier, N., Bordes, A., Denoyer, L., Ranzato, M.: Fader networks: manipulating images by sliding attributes. In: NeurIPS (2017)
20. Law, M.T., Thome, N., Cord, M.: Quadruplet-wise image similarity learning. In: ICCV (2013)
21. Liu, M., et al.: STGAN: a unified selective transfer network for arbitrary image attribute editing. In: CVPR (2019)
22. Liu, M.Y., Breuel, T., Kautz, J.: Unsupervised image-to-image translation networks. In: NeurIPS (2017)
23. Liu, Z., Luo, P., Wang, X., Tang, X.: Deep learning face attributes in the wild. In: ICCV (2015)
24. Mirza, M., Osindero, S.: Conditional generative adversarial nets. arXiv preprint arXiv:1411.1784 (2014)

25. Oh, M.S., Berger, J.O.: Integration of multimodal functions by Monte Carlo importance sampling. J. Am. Stat. Assoc. (1993)
26. Oord, A.V.D., Kalchbrenner, N., Kavukcuoglu, K.: Pixel recurrent neural networks. In: ICML (2016)
27. Parkhi, O.M., Vedaldi, A., Zisserman, A., et al.: Deep face recognition. In: BMVC (2015)
28. Patel, V.M., Gopalan, R., Li, R., Chellappa, R.: Visual domain adaptation: a survey of recent advances. Signal Process. Mag. (2015)
29. Schroff, F., Kalenichenko, D., Philbin, J.: FaceNet: a unified embedding for face recognition and clustering. In: CVPR (2015)
30. Simo-Serra, E., Trulls, E., Ferraz, L., Kokkinos, I., Fua, P., Moreno-Noguer, F.: Discriminative learning of deep convolutional feature point descriptors. In: ICCV (2015)
31. Simonyan, K., Zisserman, A.: Very deep convolutional networks for large-scale image recognition. arXiv preprint arXiv:1409.1556 (2014)
32. Veach, E., Guibas, L.J.: Optimally combining sampling techniques for Monte Carlo rendering. In: SIGGRAPH (1995)
33. Wang, J., Zhou, F., Wen, S., Liu, X., Lin, Y.: Deep metric learning with angular loss. In: ICCV (2017)
34. Wang, J., et al.: Learning fine-grained image similarity with deep ranking. In: CVPR (2014)
35. Wu, C.Y., Manmatha, R., Smola, A.J., Krahenbuhl, P.: Sampling matters in deep embedding learning. In: ICCV (2017)
36. Wu, P.W., Lin, Y.J., Chang, C.H., Chang, E.Y., Liao, S.W.: RelGAN: multi-domain image-to-image translation via relative attributes. In: ICCV (2019)
37. Yu, R., Dou, Z., Bai, S., Zhang, Z., Xu, Y., Bai, X.: Hard-aware point-to-set deep metric for person re-identification. In: Ferrari, V., Hebert, M., Sminchisescu, C., Weiss, Y. (eds.) ECCV 2018. LNCS, vol. 11220, pp. 196–212. Springer, Cham (2018). https://doi.org/10.1007/978-3-030-01270-0_12
38. Yuan, Y., Yang, K., Zhang, C.: Hard-aware deeply cascaded embedding. In: ICCV (2017)
39. Zhao, Y., Jin, Z., Qi, G., Lu, H., Hua, X.: An adversarial approach to hard triplet generation. In: Ferrari, V., Hebert, M., Sminchisescu, C., Weiss, Y. (eds.) ECCV 2018. LNCS, vol. 11213, pp. 508–524. Springer, Cham (2018). https://doi.org/10.1007/978-3-030-01240-3_31
40. Zheng, W., Chen, Z., Lu, J., Zhou, J.: Hardness-aware deep metric learning. In: CVPR (2019)
41. Zhu, J.Y., Park, T., Isola, P., Efros, A.A.: Unpaired image-to-image translation using cycle-consistent adversarial networks. In: ICCV (2017)

Spherical Feature Transform
for Deep Metric Learning

Yuke Zhu[1], Yan Bai[2], and Yichen Wei[1(✉)]

[1] MEGVII Inc., Beijing, China
{zhuyuke,weiyichen}@megvii.com
[2] Tongji Unversity, Shanghai, China
yan.bai@tongji.edu.cn

Abstract. Data augmentation in feature space is effective to increase data diversity. Previous methods assume that different classes have the same covariance in their feature distributions. Thus, feature transform between different classes is performed via translation. However, this approach is no longer valid for recent deep metric learning scenarios, where feature normalization is widely adopted and all features lie on a hypersphere.

This work proposes a novel spherical feature transform approach. It relaxes the assumption of identical covariance between classes to an assumption of similar covariances of different classes on a hypersphere. Consequently, the feature transform is performed by a rotation that respects the spherical data distributions. We provide a simple and effective training method, and in depth analysis on the relation between the two different transforms. Comprehensive experiments on various deep metric learning benchmarks and different baselines verify that our method achieves consistent performance improvement and state-of-the-art results.

1 Introduction

It is crucial to have sufficient data diversity in deep metric learning. A common practice is to augment data in the image space. This is effective but has limited effect. Specifically, it is hard to generate variances in one class using the information in the other classes.

Directly augmenting data in the feature space has become a new trend [6, 12,13,17,31,33,34]. Specifically, Yin et al. [31] propose a simple method that requires no extra labeling and is easy to implement. It assumes that the example

Y. Zhu and Y. Bai—Equal contribution.

Electronic supplementary material The online version of this chapter (https://doi.org/10.1007/978-3-030-58529-7_25) contains supplementary material, which is available to authorized users.

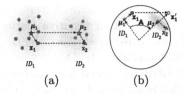

Fig. 1. Illustration of two feature transforms. (a) *translation transform* [31]. The feature of ID_1 and ID_2 are sampled from Gaussian distributions with mean value μ_1, μ_2 and identical covariance. To increase the intra-class variances of ID_2, feature x_2 is generated by translating x_1 by $\mu_2 - \mu_1$. (b) Illustration of *translation transform* and SFT on a sphere. Directly translating x_1 from ID_1 to ID_2 will result in x'_1, which is out of the surface of the sphere. Our spherical feature transform performs a rotation, such that feature x_1 of ID_1 is transferred to x_2 of ID_2.

features in each class follow a Gaussian distribution, and the covariance between all classes is the same, thus shared. Each feature is the summation of the class-dependent mean and a class-independent variance. Thus, given existing features in one class, their variance parts can be transferred to generate *new* features in other classes, via a translation. This is illustrated in Fig. 1(a). It is shown effective in [31].

Recently, feature normalization is widely adopted in deep metric learning [4, 18, 26–29]. In this case, all features lie on the surface of a hypersphere. The feature transfer approach [31] becomes inappropriate. First, a Gaussian distribution is no longer correct. A proper spherical distribution should be used instead. Second, although each class can be approximated as a local Gaussian on the sphere, the assumption of identical covariance between classes is less valid. Last, feature translation would produce an invalid feature that is out of the surface of the hypersphere, as shown in Fig. 1(b). Therefore, both the prior and the feature transform should be adapted for the spherical case.

This work proposes *spherical feature transform* to resolve above problems. It assumes that distributions of features of different classes are spherical-homoscedastic [9]. This relaxes the previous assumption that identical covariance between classes. Instead, it assumes all classes have *similar* covariances, where the similarity is measured by equivalence of eigenvalues of the covariance matrices. Consequently, the transformation between two classes is a rotation that is characterized by the classes' means. This is illustrated in Fig. 1(b). Theoretical analysis reveals that our approach is a generalization of [31].

Our method is simple and general. It is validated on several deep metric learning tasks. Comprehensive experiments and ablation studies demonstrate its effectiveness.

2   Related Work

Feature augmentation is a relatively new topic. Some researchers [6,21,33,34] adopt an adversarial approach to generate hard features from the observed negative samples utilizing the Generative Adversarial Networks (GAN) [7]. Their main focus is to generate hard negative features. While the structure of feature distributions is not considered. Also, the training process with GAN is usually complicated and unstable [1]. Dixit et al. [5] propose a data augmentation method using attribute-guided feature descriptor for generation. Liu et al. [13] propose to learn a pose manifold in the feature space and use it to synthesize pose-augmented features. However, these works need extra labeling for supervision.

Recently, Lin et al. [12] utilize the variational inference to disentangle intraclass variance and leverages the distribution to generate discriminative samples to improve robustness. This work and ours share similar insight that the variances of different class can be regarded as similar. But their method is based on the assumption that the variances can be fully disentangled and can be modeled using a Gaussian. While our method makes no assumptions about this. In fact, we will show that when features are on a hypersphere, the intra-class variances can not be modeled using one distribution. The most similar work to ours is in [31]. This work also models the variances using a Gaussian. It proposes to transfer the variance part from one class to the other for feature augmentation. It will be detailedly introduced in Sect. 3.1. However, both two works do not considering the widely adopted feature normalization techniques and its influence on feature distributions.

3   Proposed Approach

3.1   Review of Feature Transform

Feature transform is an approach for feature generation by transferring the intraclass variance from one class to the others. It is based on the assumption that features from each class follow a Gaussian distribution and the distributions of different classes have different mean values but shared covariances. Using this assumption, a feature $\mathbf{x}$ is represented by two parts:

$$\mathbf{x} = \boldsymbol{\mu} + \boldsymbol{\sigma}, \tag{1}$$

where $\boldsymbol{\mu}$ is the mean value of the class that $\mathbf{x}$ belongs to. $\boldsymbol{\sigma}$ is the variance part sampled from a zero-mean Gaussian. $\boldsymbol{\mu}$ contains the information of identity of the class. $\boldsymbol{\sigma}$ contains the information of intra-class variance that is shared among classes.

Following this prior, Feature Transfer Learning (FTL) [31] is proposed to transfer the variance part from one class to the others for feature generation. Specifically, given a feature $\mathbf{x}_1$ with $\mathbf{x}_1 = \boldsymbol{\mu}_1 + \boldsymbol{\sigma}_1$ and the center of a target class $\boldsymbol{\mu}_2$. The feature generation is proceeded by $\tilde{\mathbf{x}}_2 = \boldsymbol{\mu}_2 + \boldsymbol{\sigma}_1$, where $\tilde{\mathbf{x}}_2$ is regarded as belonging to the target class but shares identical variance with $\mathbf{x}_1$. We illustrate this process in Fig. 1(a). The feature transform can also be written as

$$\tilde{\mathbf{x}}_2 = \mathbf{x}_1 + \boldsymbol{\mu}_2 - \boldsymbol{\mu}_1. \tag{2}$$

It can be interpreted as translating the feature $\mathbf{x}_1$ by $\boldsymbol{\mu}_2 - \boldsymbol{\mu}_1$. Thus, this method is referred to as *translation transform*.

3.2   Review of Spherical-Homoscedasticity

Spherical-homoscedasticity is a property describing the relationship between a set of data distributions on the sphere, which we refer to as spherical distributions. It is proposed by Onur C et al. [9].

The definition of spherical-homoscedasticity resorts to the Gaussian approximation. We first give the definition of Gaussian approximation and then give the definition of spherical-homoscedasticity.

Definition 1. *Suppose $\mathbf{x}_i$ is a sample from the spherical distribution. Then the Gaussian approximation is given as $N(E(\mathbf{x}_i), Var(\mathbf{x}_i))$, where $E(.)$ and $Var(.)$ are the functions for expectation and variances.*

Definition 2. *Suppose distribution $N_1(\boldsymbol{\mu}, \Sigma)$ is the Gaussian approximation of spherical distribution F_1 and $\mathbf{A}$ is an orthogonal matrix. Suppose $\mathbf{A}$ is spanned by $\boldsymbol{\mu}$ and one of the eigenvectors of Σ. Suppose $N_2 \left(\mathbf{A}\boldsymbol{\mu}, \mathbf{A}^T \Sigma \mathbf{A} \right)$ is the Gaussian approximation of spherical distribution F_2. Then N_1 and N_2 (F_1 and F_2) are spherical-homoscedastic.*

Spherical-homoscedasticity requires the covariances of distributions to have identical eigenvalues. Geometrically, this property indicates that distributions share identical shape. In other words, distributions can be transformed to be totally overlapped.

3.3   Spherical Feature Transform

Recently, *feature normalization* has been widely discussed [18,26,27] and adopted in DML frameworks [4,27–29]. This technique scales all the features to the same norm. Thus, the features are restricted to lie on the surface of a hypersphere. In this case, the feature transform in Eq. 2 is no longer valid. There are two reasons. First, the identical-variance prior is too restrictive for spherical distributions. In general (e.g. the two distributions in Fig. 1(b)), spherical distributions are unlikely to have the same covariance. Second, *translation transform* produces features lying out of the surface of the hypersphere. This breaks the manifold structure of the feature space as shown in Fig. 1(b). Therefore, both the identical-variance prior and the *translation transform* should be modified for the spherical case.

We propose a new approach. It relaxes the identical-variance prior to the prior of identical eigen values of variances, which is the spherical-homoscedasticity as defined in Sect. 3.2. This relaxation is validated Fig. 2. The experiment is performed on CUB dataset (see experiments for details). We choose four classes with sufficient number of samples so that their feature distributions can be faithfully estimated. We compare their covariance matrices and the eigenvalues. As shown

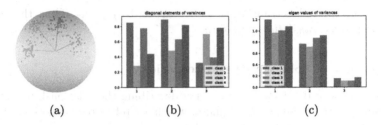

Fig. 2. (a) Visualization of features on CUB dataset. Features are projected to 3D using PCA. (b) Diagonal elements of four classes' variances from CUB. The values from the same position on the diagonal are plotted together. They differ a lot. (c) Eigen values of four classes' variances from CUB. The eigen values from the same position on the eigen matrices are plotted together. They are much closer.

in Fig. 2(b), their covariance matrices are significantly different, but the difference of the eigen values of these covariance matrices are much smaller (about 8% on average) as shown in Fig. 2(c). This shows that the identical-variance prior does not hold. And our assumption of identical eigenvalues of covariances is more valid. The similar observation is also found on other datasets in face recognition, vehicle recognition and etc.

Geometrically, our assumption implies that a distribution can be transformed to overlap with another via an orthogonal rotation matrix as in the Definition 2. Thus, a feature vector in one class can be transformed to another class to generate augmented features. We denote the Gaussian approximation of two classes distributions as $N_1(\boldsymbol{\mu_1}, \Sigma_1)$ and $N_2(\boldsymbol{\mu_2}, \Sigma_2)$. Given a feature $\mathbf{x}_1$ sampled from N_1, we have:

$$\tilde{\mathbf{x}}_2 = \mathbf{A}\mathbf{x}_1, \tag{3}$$

where $\tilde{\mathbf{x}}_2$ is considered as belonging to the class of N_2. This method is called *Spherical Feature Transform (SFT)*.

However, we note that solving the orthogonal matrix $\mathbf{A}$ according to Definition 2. is non-trivial. A brute force approach would be complex. We propose a simpler and more elegant approach to calculate $\mathbf{A}$ without solving matrix equations. It is presented in the Proposition 1.

Proposition 1. *Suppose $N_1(\boldsymbol{\mu_1}, \Sigma_1)$ and $N_2(\boldsymbol{\mu_2}, \Sigma_2)$ are two Gaussian approximations of spherical distributions. If they are spherical-homoscedastic, then the rotation matrix between them is spanned by $\boldsymbol{\mu}_1$ and $\boldsymbol{\mu}_2$.*

The proof of Proposition 1 is left in the supplement. The rotation matrix $\mathbf{A}$ is calculated as following. First, we apply Schmidt orthogonalization to obtain $\boldsymbol{\mu}_1$ and $\boldsymbol{\mu}_2$: $\mathbf{n}_1 = \boldsymbol{\mu}_1$, $\mathbf{n}_2 = \frac{\boldsymbol{\mu}_2 - (\boldsymbol{\mu}_2^T \mathbf{n}_1)\mathbf{n}_1}{\left\| \boldsymbol{\mu}_2 - (\boldsymbol{\mu}_2^T \mathbf{n}_1)\mathbf{n}_1 \right\|_2}$. Then, we use Rodrigues rotation formula to calculate the rotation matrix:

$$\mathbf{A} = \mathbf{I} + (\mathbf{n}_2 \mathbf{n}_1^T - \mathbf{n}_1 \mathbf{n}_2^T)\sin(\alpha) + (\mathbf{n}_1 \mathbf{n}_1^T + \mathbf{n}_2 \mathbf{n}_2^T)(\cos(\alpha) - 1), \tag{4}$$

where $\mathbf{I}$ is the identity matrix and α is the rotation angle between $\boldsymbol{\mu}_1$ and $\boldsymbol{\mu}_2$.

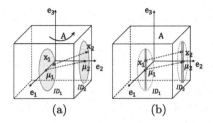

(a)   (b)

Fig. 3. Illustration of the degeneration from SFT to *translation transform* by taking a three-dimensional example. The e_1, e_2, e_3 are three axis of the coordinate. The red and blue ellipses represents the distribution of ID_1 and ID_2. Suppose they are spherical-homoscedastic and the rotation matrix between them is $\mathbf{A}$ and $\mathbf{x}_2 = \mathbf{A}\mathbf{x}_1$ (a) In general $\mu_2 - \mu_1$ is not equivalent to $\mathbf{x}_2 - \mathbf{x}_1$. (b) Special case: The intra-class variances are now encoded by the one-dimensional space spanned by e_3 and the $\mu_2 - \mu_1$ is equivalent to $\mathbf{x}_2 - \mathbf{x}_1$.

3.4 Theoretical Analysis

We discuss the relation between proposed SFT in Eq. (3) and the *translation transform* in Eq. (2). In general, the two transforms are different. However, we show that a simple variant of the *translation transform* (for normalized features) under some special cases is a degenerated form of SFT. Actually, we use this variant as a baseline method in our experiment.

In *translation transform*, the variance part σ defined in Eq. (1) is assumed to have the same distribution among all the classes. Differently, we propose SFT by showing that this term should be orthogonal transformed when features are normed. We observed that, when well trained, the features sampled from σ are likely to lie in the invariant subspace of the orthogonal matrix $\mathbf{A}$, as defined in Definition 2. This observation is experimentally validated in Sect. 4.2. We show that in this case SFT degenerates to *translation transform* defined in Eq. 2. With this condition $\mathbf{A}\sigma_1 = \sigma_1$, Eq. (3) is simplified as

$$\tilde{\mathbf{x}}_2 = \mathbf{A}\mathbf{x}_1 = \mathbf{A}(\mu_1 + \sigma_1) = \mu_2 + \sigma_1. \tag{5}$$

The right side is the *translation transform* in Eq. (2).

This degeneration case is a bit hard to understand, especially in high dimensional space. For an intuitive illustration, we show an example in three-dimensional space. As shown in Fig. 3(a), in general, the result of SFT $\mathbf{x}_2 = \mathbf{A}\mathbf{x}_1$ is not equal to $\mathbf{x}_1 + \mu_2 - \mu_1$. While, some special features stay equal after rotation and translation, as shown in Fig. 3(b). In such a case, the direction of σ_1 is parallel to the rotation axis of $\mathbf{A}$. That is, σ_1 lie in the invariant subspace of $\mathbf{A}$.

Proposition 2. *The degeneration happens only before feature normalization.*

Proof. Suppose feature $\mathbf{x} = \mu + \sigma$ and its variance part σ lie in the invariant subspace of $\mathbf{A}$. As $\mathbf{A}$ is spanned by μ and one of the other vector, μ is orthogonal to the invariant subspace of $\mathbf{A}$. So $\boldsymbol{\mu}$ is orthogonal to σ. Then the norm of $\mathbf{x}$ is evaluated as:

$$\|\mathbf{x}\| = \|\boldsymbol{\mu} + \boldsymbol{\sigma}\| = \sqrt{(\boldsymbol{\mu} + \boldsymbol{\sigma})^T (\boldsymbol{\mu} + \boldsymbol{\sigma})} = \sqrt{\boldsymbol{\mu}^T \boldsymbol{\mu} + \boldsymbol{\sigma}^T \boldsymbol{\sigma}} \tag{6}$$

As $\boldsymbol{\mu}$ is a constant for one class and the $\boldsymbol{\sigma}$ varies, the norm of $\mathbf{x}$ can not be a constant for each features of a class. In other words, the feature norms are not constant. □

Based on Proposition 2, we can make a simple modification to the *translation transform* to make it able to produce valid features in spherical case. Specifically, we use Eq. 2 before feature normalization and then reproject them back to the hypersphere. This variant is referred to as the degenerated form of SFT.

However, the degenerated form will produce identical augmented features as SFT only when degeneration takes place. There are still features that won't obey the condition of degeneration. Directly applying the degenerated form on them may curse the augmentation process. We further investigate into whether there is an ideal case where the degeneration will always take place thus the degenerated form can be treated as an alternative of SFT. Considering the condition of degeneration, this special case should satisfy $\mathbf{A}\boldsymbol{\sigma} = \boldsymbol{\sigma}$ for any rotation matrix $\mathbf{A}$ and any $\boldsymbol{\sigma}$. The three-dimensional example in Fig. 3(b) gives a clear clue that this special case exist mathematically. Specifically, if the feature distributions are shrunk in the plane defined by $\{\mathbf{e_1}, \mathbf{e_2}\}$, then all $\boldsymbol{\sigma}$ will lie in the invariant subspace of $\mathbf{A}$. The exact mathematical description for such case is presented in Proposition 3

Proposition 3. *SFT degenerates to the* translation transform *iff for* ∀ *feature* $\mathbf{x}$ *with* $\mathbf{x} = \boldsymbol{\mu} + \boldsymbol{\sigma}$, $\boldsymbol{\mu} \perp \boldsymbol{\sigma}$.

The proof is presented in the supplement. Proposition 3 has revealed a extremely restrictive condition that the mean vectors $\boldsymbol{\mu}$ and $\boldsymbol{\sigma}$ lie in two orthogonal subspaces. Intuitively, this condition is hard to be satisfied. While surprisingly, it is found, although not clear why, but in general, that deep neural networks tend to learn an orthogonal subspaces for $\boldsymbol{\mu}$ and $\boldsymbol{\sigma}$. For revealing this phenomenon, we define a measure of how much the subspaces of $\boldsymbol{\mu}$ and $\boldsymbol{\sigma}$ are orthogonal. We first define two covariance matrices:

$$\mathbf{S}_c = \frac{1}{C} \sum_{i=1}^{C} \boldsymbol{\mu}_i^T \boldsymbol{\mu}_i, \mathbf{S}_w = \frac{1}{C} \sum_{i=1}^{C} \frac{1}{N_k} \sum_{k=0}^{N_k} (\mathbf{x}_k - \boldsymbol{\mu}_i)^T (\mathbf{x}_k - \boldsymbol{\mu}_i), \tag{7}$$

where y_k is the label of embedding $\mathbf{x_k}$. C is the number of classes. N_k is the number of samples for k-th class. Then, we estimate the eigenvalue space for $\mathbf{S}_c$ and denote them as $\mathbf{U}$, where $\mathbf{U} = \{\mathbf{u_1}, \mathbf{u_2}, ..., \mathbf{u_k}\}$ corresponds to the k largest eigenvalues. The subspace spanned by $\mathbf{U}$ will cover most energy of the mean vectors while the energy of σ will distribute over these components. We calculate the remaining energy percent of σ in this subspace by evaluating:

$$r_w = trace\left(\mathbf{U}^T \mathbf{S}_w \mathbf{U}\right) / trace(\mathbf{S}_w), \tag{8}$$

where $trace(.)$ is the sum of the diagonal elements. r_w measures that how much energy percent of σ is distributed over the subspace spanned by $\mathbf{U}$. r_w is between 0 and 1. If $r_w = 0$, then the subspaces for μ and σ are orthogonal. So the smaller r_w, the nearer of the state being orthogonal.

3.5 Training Scheme

Both the *translation transform* defined in Eq. 2 and SFT defined in Eq. 3 rely on the accurate estimation of the feature center of each class. We denote the feature centers as $\{\mu_1, \mu_2, ..., \mu_C\}$ where C is the number of classes. In every mini-batch, we update them by:

$$\Delta\mu_j = \frac{\sum_{i=1}^{m} \delta\left(y_i = j\right) \cdot \left(\mu_j - \mathbf{x}_i\right)}{1 + \sum_{i=1}^{m} \delta\left(y_i = j\right)}, \tag{9}$$

where y_i is the label of feature $\mathbf{x}_i$ and m is the mini-batch size. $\delta(.)$ is the indicator function. For training, we propose two train schemes depending on the whether the training set is balanced.

Balanced Train. When the dataset is balanced in the number of samples for each class, we will generate new features for every class. In specific, for a feature, we randomly choose a different class as target and transform the feature to that class. We do this for every feature in the mini-batch. After that, we get a new batch of features with different labels.

Unbalanced Train. When the dataset is unbalanced in the number of samples for each class, we only generate new features for classes that are short of samples. In specific, we set a threshold for the number of samples and use it to separate the whole training data into head classes and tail classes. For any head features in a mini-batch, we randomly choose a tail class as target and transform it into the tail distributions.

For both training schemes, we get two batch of training data. Let $\mathbf{X} = [\mathbf{x}_1, \cdots, \mathbf{x}_n]$ be the original features and $\mathbf{Y} = [y_1, \cdots, y_n]$ be the corresponding labels, where $y_i \in \{1, \cdots, C\}$. Let $\mathbf{X}_{gen} = [\mathbf{x}_{gen,1}, \cdots, \mathbf{x}_{gen,m}]$ be the generated batch and $\mathbf{Y}_{gen} = [y_{gen,1}, \cdots, y_{gen,m}]$ be the corresponding labels. As our augmentation method is applicable to any DML frameworks, we denote $J(\theta; \mathbf{X}, \mathbf{Y})$ as a general target function with θ denoting the parameters to be optimized and $\mathbf{X}, \mathbf{Y}$ denoting the batch data and labels. Similar to DVML [12] and HDML [34], we also apply the metric learning losses on the original features besides the augmented features. It is because that the augmentation process relies on a well trained feature space. Omitting the original features or applying too much weight on the augmented features will curse the training process. It is shown in Sect. 4.2. We formulate our losses as:

$$\min_{\theta} J = J(\theta; \mathbf{X}, \mathbf{Y}) + \lambda J(\theta; \mathbf{X}_{gen}, \mathbf{Y}_{gen}), \tag{10}$$

where λ is a weighting factor controlling the balance between the original batch data and the generated batch data. The total training scheme for feature transform is illustrated in Algorithm 1.

Algorithm 1. Training with Feature Transform

Input: Training image set, network f, target function J, parameters λ and number of iteration numbers T.
Output: Parameters of network θ
1: Initialize θ
2: **for** $iter = 1, ..., T$ **do**
3:    Sample mini-batch of m training images.
4:    Extract embeddings using f to get $\mathbf{X}$ with labels $\mathbf{Y}$.
5:    Produce data $\{\mathbf{X_{gen}}, \mathbf{Y_{gen}}\}$ using (3) or (2).
6:    Update geometric centers using (9).
7:    Optimize θ using (10).
8: **end for**

---

4   Experiments

Datasets and Metrics. We conduct experiments on two types of benchmark datasets: Metric Learning and Face Recognition. For metric learning, we experiment on three widely-used benchmarks to evaluate the our approach: (1) **Cars196** [11], (2) **CUB-200-2011** [25], (3) Stanford Online Products (**SOP**) [16]. To evaluate the performance of each method, we follow [6] to perform the K-means algorithm in the test set and report normalized mutual information (NMI) and F_1 metrics as well as Recall@K for retrieval task. For face recognition, we use a cleaned version of MS-Celeb-1M [8] as our training set that contains 3M facial images and 80920 classes. We present evaluation results on three face verification benchmarks: **LFW** [10], **YTF** [30] and **IJB-C** [15]. For LFW and YTF, we follow the unrestricted with labeled outside data protocol and report the performance of 6,000 face pairs on LFW and 5,000 video pairs on YTF. For IJB-C, we follow the 1:1 verification protocol to evaluate 19,557 positive matches and 15,638,932 negative matches and report the results of TARs at various FARs.

Implementation Details. For the metric learning task, we use GoogleNet [23] (or GoogleNet-V2) pre-trained with ImageNet [3] as a backbone network and add a fully connected layer at the end to output the feature embedding. We use the same data preprocessing and augmentation as in Multi-Similarity Loss [29]. We set the embedding size to 512 and perform ℓ_2-normalization on the feature. We use the SGD optimizer with a weight decay of 1e−4 and train for 30,000 iterations. For learning rate, we set 1e−2 for Cars196 and SOP and 1e−3 for CUB-200-2011 as base learning rate for backbone and newly added layers 10× the base learning rate, and decay the learning rate by multiply 0.1 every 10,000 iterations. We set the batch size to be 60 made up of 20 classes and 3 images per class. The balanced train scheme is adopted when SFT is used. For face recognition, the CNN architecture used in our work is similar to [14]. We change the number of residual units to $[3, 4, 6, 3]$ to construct a 34-layer residual network. We preprocess all face images by MTCNN [32]. Then the 5 facial points are adopted to perform alignment to the face image. After that, we resize the cropped

Table 1. Comparison on Cars196 and CUB-200-2011.

	Cars196					CUB-200-2011				
	R@1	R@2	R@4	MNI	F1	R@1	R@2	R@4	NMI	F1
GoogleNet										
Triplet	58.4	70.3	80.2	57.0	27.2	42.8	55.2	55.6	52.4	19.1
Triplet+HDML [34]	62.0	73.3	82.9	57.7	27.8	44.3	56.0	68.0	55.5	26.7
Triplet+DVML [12]	64.4	73.5	78.6	**60.5**	28.4	43.3	55.8	68.0	55.0	25.2
Triplet+FTL	60.1	71.5	80.5	57.9	25.0	46.8	59.2	70.2	57.3	24.3
Triplet+SFT-d	60.3	71.7	81.4	57.9	28.1	46.5	59.3	70.0	57.9	28.1
Triplet+SFT	**65.1**	**75.7**	**84.0**	58.1	**28.6**	**48.3**	**60.0**	**71.2**	**58.1**	**28.6**
NPair	72.8	82.3	88.5	61.3	29.4	53.5	64.9	72.3	60.4	27.8
NPair+HDML [34]	78.9	87.0	91.0	67.1	37.3	53.9	65.8	76.7	62.0	30.0
NPair+DVML [12]	**80.2**	85.6	91.9	66.1	34.8	54.2	66.2	77.3	62.0	31.5
NPair+FTL	73.1	82.2	88.6	60.0	27.4	54.0	66.0	77.0	61.9	29.7
NPair+SFT-d	76.2	85.0	90.9	64.2	33.1	54.5	67.0	**77.7**	62.0	30.1
NPair+SFT	79.4	**87.1**	**92.4**	**67.2**	**37.3**	**54.7**	**67.0**	77.5	**62.2**	**30.5**
GoogleNet-V2										
RLL [28]	74.2	83.2	89.0	62.2	32.9	59.6	71.0	80.5	64.3	32.9
RLL+DVML [12]	79.0	86.6	91.3	65.5	34.9	60.2	71.7	81.0	64.7	33.0
RLL + SFT-d	78.8	86.7	92.1	65.4	34.4	59.4	71.2	80.9	64.2	32.8
RLL + SFT	**80.2**	**88.1**	**92.8**	66.1	35.3	**60.3**	**71.8**	**81.1**	**64.9**	**33.6**
MS [29]	84.0	90.2	94.1	72.8	45.3	65.7	76.6	84.6	69.0	39.6
MS+DVML [12]	84.4	**90.8**	92.4	72.0	45.3	66.2	76.7	85.1	69.6	40.0
MS + SFT-d	83.8	90.4	94.6	73.1	45.3	66.1	76.8	85.2	70.0	**41.6**
MS + SFT	**84.5**	90.6	**94.6**	**73.2**	**45.8**	**66.8**	**77.5**	**85.8**	**70.3**	40.4

image to 112×112. Each pixel(in [0, 255]) in RGB images is normalized by subtracting 127.5 then being divided by 128. We use SGD optimizer with a weight decay of 5e−4 and train for 120K iterations. The learning rate is set to 0.1 initially and is divided by 10 at the 70K, 90K and 110K iterations. The unbalanced train scheme is adopted when SFT is used, where we set the classes that have less than 15 samples as tail classes.

Compared Methods. We compare our method to other feature generation methods, including HDML [34], DVML [12] and FTL [31]. These methods are introduced in Sect. 2. They require no extra labeling and can be compared fairly on metric learning tasks. Also the degenerated SFT will be included for comparison. It is denoted as SFT-d in the results. The comparison is made on two traditional representative baseline losses, aka, triplet loss [19] and NPair loss [20] and two most recent baseline losses that achieved high results, aka, Ranked List Loss (RLL) [28] and Multi-Similarity Loss (MS) [29]. Most of the comparison is made on GoogleNet [23] because almost all of the chosen competitors report their results on this backbone. For comparison with the SOTA, we also make some comparison on GoogleNet-V2. For fair comparison, we implement all of these methods and report the results from our experiments.

For FTL [31], the features are normed in our implementation as we found that feature normalization will outperform the original method greatly. The FTL differs from the degenerated form of SFT in that it requires a pre-training of the network and is applied in the fine-tuning stage while this is not needed in both SFT and the degenerated form. Also, FTL requires a decoder network and only transfers a part of the energy of σ using PCA. In our implementation, we follows them to use 95%.

4.1   Quantitative Results

Table 1, Table 3, Table 2 and Table 4 present the experimental results of SFT on three popular deep metric learning benchmarks and three face recognition benchmarks respectively.

By comparing with baseline methods, it is noticed that SFT can significantly improve the performance of them, especially on Cars196 and CUB-200-2011. For example, when coupled with NPair loss, SFT improves the baseline by 7 point on Cars196. SFT can also boost performance on higher baselines that reported by two most recent losses, Multi-Similarity loss and Ranked-List loss. While SFT is relatively less effective on SOP (Table 3). The reason is that the number of samples for each class in SOP is too small (about 5).

To sum up, SFT performs better than HDML [34], FTL [31] and DVML [12]. For example, when coupled with NPair loss, SFT outperforms the HDML by 1.0 on Cars196.

On higher baselines, such as Multi-Similarity Loss, our SFT outperforms DVML by 0.7 on CUB. The degenerated form of SFT can be effective on most baseline methods. While averagely, it surpass the performance of SFT. Besides the metric learning losses, SFT can also be used together with softmax-based losses. This is mainly used in face recognition tasks. On LFW dataset and YTF dataset(Shown in Table 2), the performance of deep neural networks are nearly saturated, but we still report the performance for comparison with

Table 2. Face verification (%) on the LFW and YTF datasets.

Method	Training Data	LFW	YTF
DeepFace+ [24]	4M	97.35	91.4
FaceNet [19]	200M	99.63	95.1
DeepID2+ [22]	300K	99.47	93.2
SphereFace [14]	0.5M	99.42	95.0
CosFace [27]	5M	99.73	97.6
ArcFace [4]	5.8M	99.83	98.02
L2-Face [18]	3.7M	99.78	96.08
L2-Face [18] (ours)	3M	99.45	96.0
L2-Face(ours) + SFT-d	3M	99.41	95.9
L2-Face(ours) + SFT	3M	99.50	96.5
CosFace [27] (ours)	3M	99.68	96.2
CosFace (ours) + SFT-d	3M	99.70	96.5
CosFace (ours) + SFT	3M	99.73	97.2

the other works. On IJB-C(Shown in Table 4), we provide a competitive baseline for both L2-Face [18] and CosFace [27], while it is observed that SFT can still boost the performance when compared with the baselines.

Table 3. Experimental results on Stanford Online Products (SOP). SFT is less effective on SOP as the number of samples for each class is only 5.

	SOP				
	R@1	R@10	R@100	NMI	F1
Triplet (ours)	70.8	85.5	93.8	88.2	28.0
Triplet + SFT-d	71.9	86.4	94.4	88.5	29.3
Triplet + SFT	72.3	86.5	94.5	88.6	29.9
RLL [28] (ours)	77.5	89.9	95.8	89.7	35.3
RLL + SFT-d	77.9	90.3	96.1	89.8	35.9
RLL + SFT	77.8	90.2	96.0	89.9	36.4
MS [29] (ours)	73.1	87.2	94.7	88.5	29.6
MS + SFT-d	73.5	87.5	94.9	88.6	29.8
MS + SFT	73.4	87.1	94.7	88.8	30.9

Table 4. Comparison with the state-of-art methods on IJB-C. The '-' denotes the corresponding results are not reported in the original paper.

Method	Training Data	IJB-C(TAR@FAR)		
		0.001%	0.01%	0.1%
Vggface2 [2]	3.3M	74.7	84.0	91.0
L2-Face [18]	3.3M	78.54	87.01	92.10
Arcface [4]	5.8M	-	92.10	-
L2-Face [18](ours)	3M	79.3	87.3	93.3
L2-Face(ours) + SFT-d	3M	79.4	87.9	93.3
L2-Face(ours) + SFT	3M	**80.6**	**88.2**	**93.6**
CosFace [27] (ours)	3M	85.67	92.11	95.4
CosFace (ours) + SFT-d	3M	86.85	**92.78**	**95.72**
CosFace (ours) + SFT	3M	**87.19**	92.63	95.6

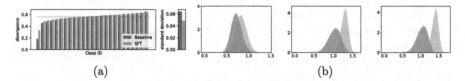

(a)   (b)

Fig. 4. Effect of SFT on feature distributions. (a) **Left**: Divergences of each class in baseline and SFT. The blue dashed line represents the average divergence of baseline. **Right**: The standard deviation of divergences in baseline and SFT. (b) Histograms of positive(blue) and negative(orange) distance distributions on the Cars196 test set for(from left to right), initial state with pre-trained model, training with ranked list loss, training with ranked list loss together with SFT.

4.2   Ablation Study

In this part, we conduct the ablation study on Cars-196 with the ranked list loss. The conclusions from these experiments are also applicable to other datasets and loss functions.

Effect on Feature Distributions. We find that SFT can make feature distributions more similar than the baseline method. This is consistent with our prior that feature distributions should be similar to each other. In other words, the SFT can make the eigenvalues of variances from different classes to be closer. In specific, we compare the similarity by comparing the trace of the scattering matrix of each class. We refer to the trace of the matrix as the divergence. The scattering matrix of each class is defined as:

$$\mathbf{S}_{w,k} = \frac{1}{N_k} \sum_{k=0}^{N_k} (\mathbf{x}_k - \boldsymbol{\mu}_i)^T (\mathbf{x}_k - \boldsymbol{\mu}_i). \tag{11}$$

Figure 4(a) shows the divergences of each class, and the standard deviation of the divergences. The class IDs are sorted according to the divergences of the baseline. For clarity, one for every four values is chosen to shown in the histogram. It is observed that the divergences among classes are more balanced when SFT is applied. In general, the divergences below the average(blue dashed line) are increased and those above the average are decreased. The right part of Fig. 4 displays the standard deviations of the divergence values. It is consistent with the conclusion.

Furthermore, the distributions of pair distance are compared. It is shown in Figure 4(b). It is observed that the overlap between the positive parts and negative parts is reduced when SFT is applied. This indicates that SFT helps the network to learn a more discriminative feature space.

Effect on Unbalanced Datasets. The face recognition datasets differ from DML datasets in that they are usually long-tailed. Among then, plenty of classes are in short of samples. These classes are usually called the tail classes. Experimentally, we find SFT can improve the performance of tail classes. In specific, we select all classes in MS-Celeb-1M that contains more than 100 samples to construct a mini-dataset. In total, we get 2,445

Table 5. Effect of SFT on an unbalanced dataset. Head represents classes with rich samples. Tail represents classes in short of training samples. The results are the classification accuracy (%).

	Baseline	Balanced train	Unbalanced train
Head	95.61	**95.77**	95.49
Tail	73.91	78.35	**82.32**

classes. Then, we random choose 1,500 classes to be the head classes and choose 50 samples each for training. For the remaining 945 classes, we treat them as the tail classes and choose 5 samples each for training. All the other samples are left for testing. As the training set is much smaller than that of MS-Celeb-1M, we adopt a smaller network for training. In specific, we use a similar CNN architecture for training except that we change the number of residual units to $[1, 1, 1, 1]$. The results are shown in Table 5. We can see that the baseline method performs worst in the tail classes. But when SFT is applied, the performance of the tail classes is increased by a large margin. The best performance in tail classes is achieved by the unbalanced train scheme, which outperforms the baseline by 8.4%, while the performance drop in the head classes is negligible. In summary, the SFT can effectively improve the accuracy of the tail classes.

Impact of Center Estimation. As the rotation matrix of SFT is estimated based on feature centers, the center estimation is essential. To evaluate the importance, we compare the image retrieval performance under three circumstances: (1) "Random", skip the center

Table 6. Impact of center estimation.

	Baseline	SFT	Random	Pick
R@1	74.2	**80.2**	74.4	74.6

estimation step in line 6 of Algorithm 1. (2) "Pick", randomly pick one sample from the same class as center. (3) SFT, the standard SFT procedure. The results are shown in Table 6. The performances of SFT are almost the same as the baseline when Random or Pick is adopted. While only when SFT is adopted will the performance be improved by a noticeable number. This illustrate that the accurate estimation of class centers is crucial for feature transform. Moreover, it is noticed that even when the center estimation is not accurate, the feature transform will not harm the training too much. This suggests that training with feature transform is stable.

Batch Size. The batch size is usually important in deep metric learning as it determines the number of positive pairs and negative pairs used for constructing target loss. While when implemented with our method, the number of positive pairs and negative pairs are enlarged. We then conduct experiments on

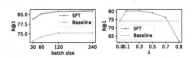

Fig. 5. Performance with different **Left**: batch size; **Right** λ.

different batch sizes to "fairly" compare the performance under an equal number of positive and negative pairs. The comparison results are shown in the left part of Fig. 5. It is observed that SFT can beat the baseline with the largest batch size 240 even evaluated under a small batch size 30. This suggests that the improvement when SFT is applied is not due to the increase of batch size.

Effect of λ. We conduct experiments to explore the influence of the weight factor. As shown in the Fig. 5, when increasing the λ, the performance of the method first increases and then decreases. When the λ is too large, the performance drops significantly. We blame the performance drop to that the gradients from the generated features will dominate the optimization process and infect the optimization of the regular ones. In practice, the optimal λ is data-dependent. We do not investigate into what is the optimal value of λ. In most of our experiments, the value is set to 0.2.

Discussion of Degeneration. In Sect. 3.4, it is hypothesized that σ defined in Eq. 1 is likely to lie in the invariant subspace of $\mathbf{A}$. To investigate into whether the hypothesis holds, we evaluate the value of $d = \|\mathbf{A}\sigma - \sigma\|_2$ on five versions of ResNet. The distribution of d on ResNet50 is shown in Fig. 6(a). It is noticed that a large number of d values are near zero. For these features, the augmented features by SFT and the degenerated form are close. For each backbone, d is evaluated 10000 times and the mean value is reported. The result is shown in Fig. 6(b). As observed, the hypothesis is more likely to hold in deeper networks. This implies that the degeneration of SFT will be more likely to happen when the network gets deeper.

Our experiment also reveals that the learned subspaces for μ and σ tend to be orthogonal. This is presented in Fig. 6(c). For example, on the backbone of ResNet50, σ only distribute 10% energy on the subspace that covers 99% energy of μ. It means that, although the ideal condition in Proposition 3 can not be reached, the learned feature space tend to approach it. These experimental results support our analysis that the degeneration of SFT happens for most features. Considering the comparison shows that the SFT will outperform the degenerated form in most scenarios, the side effect of the degenerated form on features that won't degenerate should not be neglected.

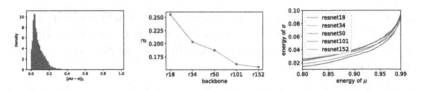

Fig. 6. Experiment on the condition of the degeneration. (a) The distribution of $\|\mathbf{A}\sigma - \sigma\|_2$ sampled from features of backbone ResNet50. (b) The mean values of the distributions of $\|\mathbf{A}\sigma - \sigma\|_2$ from different backbones. (c) s_r defined in Eq. 8 with respect to the energy of μ.

5   Conclusion

In this paper, we propose Spherical Feature Transform (SFT) to generate new features from existing ones. The proposed SFT can effectively enrich the intra-class variances of both regular classes and under-represented ones. We have demonstrated the effectiveness of SFT by applying it to several most recent DML frameworks in three popular deep metric learning benchmark datasets and three face recognition benchmark datasets.

Acknowledgment. This work was supported in part by the National Key Research and Development Program of China under Grant 2017YFA0700800.

References

1. Brock, A., Donahue, J., Simonyan, K.: Large scale GAN training for high fidelity natural image synthesis. arXiv preprint arXiv:1809.11096 (2018)
2. Cao, Q., Shen, L., Xie, W., Parkhi, O.M., Zisserman, A.: VGGFace2: a dataset for recognising faces across pose and age. In: 2018 13th IEEE International Conference on Automatic Face & Gesture Recognition (FG 2018), pp. 67–74. IEEE (2018)
3. Deng, J., Dong, W., Socher, R., Li, L.J., Li, K., Fei-Fei, L.: ImageNet: a large-scale hierarchical image database. In: CVPR 2009 (2009)
4. Deng, J., Guo, J., Xue, N., Zafeiriou, S.: ArcFace: additive angular margin loss for deep face recognition. In: Proceedings of the IEEE Conference on Computer Vision and Pattern Recognition, pp. 4690–4699 (2019)
5. Dixit, M., Kwitt, R., Niethammer, M., Vasconcelos, N.: AGA: attribute-guided augmentation. In: Proceedings of the IEEE Conference on Computer Vision and Pattern Recognition, pp. 7455–7463 (2017)
6. Duan, Y., Zheng, W., Lin, X., Lu, J., Zhou, J.: Deep adversarial metric learning. In: Proceedings of the IEEE Conference on Computer Vision and Pattern Recognition, pp. 2780–2789 (2018)
7. Goodfellow, I., et al.: Generative adversarial nets. In: Advances in Neural Information Processing Systems, pp. 2672–2680 (2014)
8. Guo, Y., Zhang, L., Hu, Y., He, X., Gao, J.: MS-Celeb-1M: a dataset and benchmark for large-scale face recognition. In: Leibe, B., Matas, J., Sebe, N., Welling, M. (eds.) ECCV 2016. LNCS, vol. 9907, pp. 87–102. Springer, Cham (2016). https://doi.org/10.1007/978-3-319-46487-9_6

9. Hamsici, O.C., Martinez, A.M.: Spherical-homoscedastic distributions: the equivalency of spherical and normal distributions in classification. J. Mach. Learn. Res. **8**, 1583–1623 (2007)
10. Huang, G.B., Mattar, M., Berg, T., Learned-Miller, E.: Labeled faces in the wild: a database for studying face recognition in unconstrained environments (2008)
11. Krause, J., Stark, M., Deng, J., Fei-Fei, L.: 3D object representations for fine-grained categorization. In: Proceedings of the IEEE International Conference on Computer Vision Workshops, pp. 554–561 (2013)
12. Lin, X., Duan, Y., Dong, Q., Lu, J., Zhou, J.: Deep variational metric learning. In: Ferrari, V., Hebert, M., Sminchisescu, C., Weiss, Y. (eds.) ECCV 2018. LNCS, vol. 11219, pp. 714–729. Springer, Cham (2018). https://doi.org/10.1007/978-3-030-01267-0_42
13. Liu, B., Wang, X., Dixit, M., Kwitt, R., Vasconcelos, N.: Feature space transfer for data augmentation. In: Proceedings of the IEEE Conference on Computer Vision and Pattern Recognition, pp. 9090–9098 (2018)
14. Liu, W., Wen, Y., Yu, Z., Li, M., Raj, B., Song, L.: SphereFace: deep hypersphere embedding for face recognition. In: Proceedings of the IEEE Conference on Computer Vision and Pattern Recognition, pp. 212–220 (2017)
15. Maze, B., et al.: IARPA Janus benchmark-C: face dataset and protocol. In: 2018 International Conference on Biometrics (ICB), pp. 158–165. IEEE (2018)
16. Oh Song, H., Xiang, Y., Jegelka, S., Savarese, S.: Deep metric learning via lifted structured feature embedding. In: Proceedings of the IEEE Conference on Computer Vision and Pattern Recognition, pp. 4004–4012 (2016)
17. Radford, A., Metz, L., Chintala, S.: Unsupervised representation learning with deep convolutional generative adversarial networks. arXiv preprint arXiv:1511.06434 (2015)
18. Ranjan, R., Castillo, C.D., Chellappa, R.: L2-constrained softmax loss for discriminative face verification. arXiv preprint arXiv:1703.09507 (2017)
19. Schroff, F., Kalenichenko, D., Philbin, J.: FaceNet: a unified embedding for face recognition and clustering. In: Proceedings of the IEEE Conference on Computer Vision and Pattern Recognition, pp. 815–823 (2015)
20. Sohn, K.: Improved deep metric learning with multi-class n-pair loss objective. In: Advances in Neural Information Processing Systems, pp. 1857–1865 (2016)
21. Sohn, K., Liu, S., Zhong, G., Yu, X., Yang, M.H., Chandraker, M.: Unsupervised domain adaptation for face recognition in unlabeled videos. In: Proceedings of the IEEE International Conference on Computer Vision, pp. 3210–3218 (2017)
22. Sun, Y., Wang, X., Tang, X.: Deeply learned face representations are sparse, selective, and robust. In: Proceedings of the IEEE Conference on Computer Vision and Pattern Recognition, pp. 2892–2900 (2015)
23. Szegedy, C., et al.: Going deeper with convolutions. In: Computer Vision and Pattern Recognition (CVPR) (2015). http://arxiv.org/abs/1409.4842
24. Taigman, Y., Yang, M., Ranzato, M., Wolf, L.: DeepFace: closing the gap to human-level performance in face verification. In: Proceedings of the IEEE Conference on Computer Vision and Pattern Recognition, pp. 1701–1708 (2014)
25. Wah, C., Branson, S., Welinder, P., Perona, P., Belongie, S.: The Caltech-UCSD birds-200-2011 dataset (2011)
26. Wang, F., Xiang, X., Cheng, J., Yuille, A.L.: NormFace: L2 hypersphere embedding for face verification. In: Proceedings of the 25th ACM International Conference on Multimedia, pp. 1041–1049. ACM (2017)

27. Wang, H., et al.: CosFace: large margin cosine loss for deep face recognition. In: Proceedings of the IEEE Conference on Computer Vision and Pattern Recognition, pp. 5265–5274 (2018)
28. Wang, X., Hua, Y., Kodirov, E., Hu, G., Garnier, R., Robertson, N.M.: Ranked list loss for deep metric learning. arXiv preprint arXiv:1903.03238 (2019)
29. Wang, X., Han, X., Huang, W., Dong, D., Scott, M.R.: Multi-similarity loss with general pair weighting for deep metric learning. In: Proceedings of the IEEE Conference on Computer Vision and Pattern Recognition, pp. 5022–5030 (2019)
30. Wolf, L., Hassner, T., Maoz, I.: Face recognition in unconstrained videos with matched background similarity. IEEE (2011)
31. Yin, X., Yu, X., Sohn, K., Liu, X., Chandraker, M.: Feature transfer learning for face recognition with under-represented data. In: In Proceeding of IEEE Computer Vision and Pattern Recognition, Long Beach, CA, June 2019
32. Zhang, K., Zhang, Z., Li, Z., Qiao, Y.: Joint face detection and alignment using multitask cascaded convolutional networks. IEEE Sig. Process. Lett. **23**(10), 1499–1503 (2016)
33. Zhao, Y., Jin, Z., Qi, G., Lu, H., Hua, X.: An adversarial approach to hard triplet generation. In: Ferrari, V., Hebert, M., Sminchisescu, C., Weiss, Y. (eds.) ECCV 2018. LNCS, vol. 11213, pp. 508–524. Springer, Cham (2018). https://doi.org/10.1007/978-3-030-01240-3_31
34. Zheng, W., Chen, Z., Lu, J., Zhou, J.: Hardness-aware deep metric learning. In: Proceedings of the IEEE Conference on Computer Vision and Pattern Recognition, pp. 72–81 (2019)

Semantic Equivalent Adversarial Data Augmentation for Visual Question Answering

Ruixue Tang[1], Chao Ma[1(✉)], Wei Emma Zhang[2], Qi Wu[2], and Xiaokang Yang[1]

[1] MoE Key Lab of Artificial Intelligence, AI Institute, Shanghai Jiao Tong University, Shanghai, China
{alicetang,chaoma,xkyang}@sjtu.edu.cn
[2] University of Adelaide, Adelaide, Australia
{wei.e.zhang,qi.wu01}@adelaide.edu.au

Abstract. Visual Question Answering (VQA) has achieved great success thanks to the fast development of deep neural networks (DNN). On the other hand, the data augmentation, as one of the major tricks for DNN, has been widely used in many computer vision tasks. However, there are few works studying the data augmentation problem for VQA and none of the existing image based augmentation schemes (such as rotation and flipping) can be directly applied to VQA due to its semantic structure – an ⟨image, question, answer⟩ triplet needs to be maintained correctly. For example, a direction related Question-Answer (QA) pair may not be true if the associated image is rotated or flipped. In this paper, instead of directly manipulating images and questions, we use generated adversarial examples for both images and questions as the augmented data. The augmented examples do not change the visual properties presented in the image as well as the **semantic** meaning of the question, the correctness of the ⟨image, question, answer⟩ is thus still maintained. We then use adversarial learning to train a classic VQA model (BUTD) with our augmented data. We find that we not only improve the overall performance on VQAv2, but also can withstand adversarial attack effectively, compared to the baseline model. The source code is available at https://github.com/zaynmi/seada-vqa.

Keywords: VQA · Data augmentation · Adversarial learning

1 Introduction

Both computer vision and natural language processing (NLP) have made enormous progress on many problems using deep learning in recent years. Visual question answering (VQA) is a field of study that fuses computer vision and

Electronic supplementary material The online version of this chapter (https://doi.org/10.1007/978-3-030-58529-7_26) contains supplementary material, which is available to authorized users.

A. Vedaldi et al. (Eds.): ECCV 2020, LNCS 12364, pp. 437–453, 2020.
https://doi.org/10.1007/978-3-030-58529-7_26

NLP to achieve these successes. The VQA algorithm aims to predict a correct answer to the given question referring to an image. The recent benchmark study [17] demonstrates that the performance of VQA algorithms hinges on the amount of training data. Existing algorithms can always benefit greatly from more training data. This suggests that data augmentation without manual annotations is an intuitive attempt to improve the VQA performance, just like its success on the other deep learning applications.

Existing Data augmentation approaches enlarge the training dataset size by either data warping or oversampling [37]. Data warping transforms data and keeps their labels. Typical examples include geometric and color transformations, random erasing, adversarial training, and neural style transfer. Oversampling generates synthetic instances and adds them to the training set. Data augmentation has shown to be effective in alleviating the overfitting problem of DNNs [37]. However, data augmentation in VQA is barely studied due to the challenge of maintaining an ⟨image, question, answer⟩ triplet semantically correct. Neither geometric transform nor randomly erasing the image could preserve the answer. For example, when asking about *What is the position of the computer?*, *Is the car to the left or right of the trash can?*, flipping or rotating images results in the opposite answers. Randomly erasing the image associated with the question *How many ...?* would miss the number of objects. Such transforms need tailored answers which are unavailable. On the textual side, it is challenging to come up with generalized rules for language transformation. Universal data augmentation techniques in NLP have not been thoroughly explored. Therefore, it is non-trivial to explore the data augmentation technique to facilitate VQA.

Previous works have generated reasonable questions based on the image content [16] and the given answer [25], namely Visual Question Generation (VQG). However, a significant portion of the generated questions either have grammatical errors or are oddly phrased. In addition, they learn from the questions and images in the same target dataset, thus the generated data are drawn from the same distribution of the original data. Since the training and test data usually do not share the same distribution, the generated data could not help to relieve the overfitting.

In this paper, we propose to generate semantic equivalent adversarial examples of both visual and textual data as augmented data. Adversarial examples are strategically modified samples that could successfully fool the deep models to make incorrect predictions. However, the modification is imperceptible that keeps the semantics of data while driving the underlying distribution of adversarial examples away from that of the original data [41]. In our method, visual adversarial examples are generated by an un-targeted gradient-based attacker [24], and textual adversarial examples are paraphrases that could fool the VQA model (predicting a wrong answer) while keeping the questions semantically equivalent. The existence of adversarial examples not only reveals the limited generalization ability of ConvNets, but also poses security threats on the real-world deployment of these models.

We adversarially train the strong baseline method Bottom-Up-Attention and Top-Down (BUTD) [2] on VQAv2 dataset [13] with clean examples and adversarial examples generated on-the-fly. We regard the adversarial training as a regularizer acting in a period of training time. Experimental results demonstrate that our proposed adversarial training framework not only better boosts the model performance on clean examples than other data augmentation techniques, but also improves the model robustness against adversarial attacks. Although there are few works studying the data augmentation problem for VQA [1,18,33,35], they merely generate either new questions or images. To our best knowledge, our work is the first to augment both visual and textual data in VQA.

To summarize, our major contributions are threefold:

- We propose to generate visual and textual adversarial examples to augment the VQA dataset. Our generated data preserve the semantics and explore the learned decision boundary to help improve the model generalization.
- We propose an adversarial training scheme that enables VQA models to take advantage of the regularization power of adversarial examples.
- We show that the model trained with our method achieves 65.16% accuracy on the clean validation set, beating its vanilla training counterpart by 1.84%. Moreover, the adversarially trained model significantly increases accuracy on adversarial examples by 21.55%.

2   Related Work

VQA. A large number of VQA algorithms have been proposed, including spatial attention [2,6,26,44], compositional approaches [3,4,14], and bilinear pooling schemes [10,20]. Spatial attention [2] is one of the most widely used methods for both natural and synthetic image VQA. A large portion of prior arts [19,29, 31,46] are built upon the bottom-up top-down (BUTD) attention method [2]. We also choose the BUTD as our baseline VQA model. Instead of developing a more sophisticated answering machine, we propose a VQA data augmentation technique that can potentially benefit existing VQA methods since data is the fuel.

Data Augmentation. Compared to vision, a few efforts have been done on augmenting text for classification problems. Wei *et al.* [40] make a comprehensive extension for text editing techniques on NLP data augmentation and achieve gains on text classification. However, our study shows that it could degrade the model performance on the VQA task (see Sect. 4). Other works generate paraphrases [28,45] and add noise to smooth text data [42]. There are fewer works [1,18,30,33,35] that learn data augmentation for VQA. Kafle *et al.*[18] do a pioneer work where they generate new questions by using semantic annotations on images. Work of [33] automatically generates entailed questions for a source QA pair , but it uses additional data in Visual Genome [22] to add diversity to the generated questions. Work of [35] proposes a cyclic-consistent training scheme where it generates different rephrasings of question and train the model such that the predicted answers across the generated and original questions remain consistent. The method [1] employ a GAN-based re-synthesis technique to automatically remove objects to strengthen the model robustness against semantic visual variations. Note that all of these methods augment data in a single modality (text-only or image-only) and heavily rely on complex modules to achieve slight performance gains.

Adversarial Attack and Defense. In recent years, research works [12,38] add imperceptible perturbations to input images, named adversarial examples, to evaluate the robustness of deep neural networks against such perturbation attacks. In the NLP community, state-of-the-art textual DNN attackers [5,7,9] use a different approach from those in the visual community to generate textual adversarial examples. Our work is inspired by SCPNs [15] and SEA [34] which generate paraphrases of the sentence as textual adversarial examples. Meanwhile, previous works [12] show that training with adversarial examples can improve the model generalization on small dataset (e.g., MNIST), but degrade the performance on large datasets (e.g., ImageNet), in the fully-supervised setting. Recent notable work [41] suggests that adversarial training could boost model performance even on ImageNet with a well-designed training scheme. A number of methods [36,43] have investigated adversarial attack on the VQA task. However, they merely attack the image and do not discuss how the adversarial examples can benefit the VQA model. To summarize, how adversarial examples can facilitate VQA remains an open problem. This work sheds light on utilizing adversarial examples as augmented data for VQA.

3   Method

We now introduce our data augmentation method to train a robust VQA model. As illustrated in Fig. 1, given an ⟨*image, question, answer*⟩ triplet, we first generate the paraphrases of questions and store them, then, generate visual adversarial examples on-the-fly to obtain semantically equivalent additional training triplets, which are used in the proposed adversarial training scheme. We describe them in detail as follows.

3.1   VQA Model

Answering questions about images can be formulated as the problem of predicting an answer a given an image v and a question q according to a parametric probability measure:

$$\hat{a} = \arg\max_{a \in \mathcal{A}} p(a|v, q; \theta) \qquad (1)$$

where θ represents a vector of all parameters to learn and $\mathcal{A}$ is a set of all answers. VQA requires solving several tasks at once involving both visual and

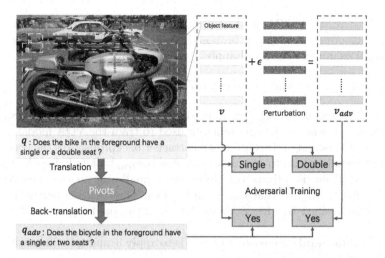

Fig. 1. Framework of the proposed data augmentation method. We generate adversarial examples of both visual and textual data as augmented data, which are passed through the VQA model to obtain incorrect answers. The augmented and original data are jointly trained using the proposed adversarial training scheme, which can boost model performance on clean data while improving model robustness against attack.

textual inputs. Here we use Bottom-Up-Attention and Top-Down (BUTD) [2] as our backbone model because it has become a golden baseline in VQA. In BUTD, region-specific image features extracted by fine-tuned Faster R-CNN [11] are utilized as visual inputs. In this paper, let $v = \{\overrightarrow{v_1}, \overrightarrow{v_2}, ..., \overrightarrow{v_K}\}$ be a collection of visual features extracted from K image regions and the question is a sequence of words $q = \{q_1, q_2, ..., q_n\}$. The $\langle image, question, answer \rangle$ triplet has a strong semantic relation that neither image nor question can be easily transformed to augment the training data while preserving original content.

3.2 Data Augmentation

Due to the risk of affecting answers, we avoid manipulating the raw inputs (i.e., images and questions) directly, such as cropping the image or changing the word order. Inspired by the adversarial attack and defense, we propose to generate adversarial examples as additional training data. In this section, we present how to generate adversarial examples of images and questions while preserving the original labels and how to use them to augment the training data.

Visual Adversarial Examples Generation. Adversarial attacks are originated from the computer vision community. In general, the overarching goal is to add the least amount of perturbation to the input data to cause the desired misclassification. We employ an efficient gradient-based attacker Iterative Fast Gradient Sign Method (IFGSM) [23] to generate visual adversarial examples.

Before illustrating IFGSM, we firstly introduce FGSM, as IFGSM is an extension of it. Goodfellow *et al.* [12] proposed the FGSM as a simple way to generate adversarial examples. We could apply it on visual input as:

$$v_{adv} = v + \epsilon \text{sign}(\nabla_v L(\theta, v, q, a_{true})) \tag{2}$$

where v^{adv} is the adversarial example of v, θ is the set of model parameters, $L(\theta, v, q, a_{true})$ denotes the cost function used to train the VQA model, ϵ is the size of the adversarial perturbation. The attacker backpropagates the gradient to the input visual feature to calculate $\nabla_v L(\theta, v, q, a_{true})$ while fixing the network parameters. Then, it adjusts the input by a small step in the direction (i.e. $\text{sign}(\nabla_v L(\theta, v, q, a_{true}))$) that maximize the loss. The resulting perturbed, v_{adv}, is then misclassified by the VQA model (e.g., the model predicts *Double* in Fig. 1).

A straightforward extension of FGSM is to apply it multiple times with small step size, referred to IFGSM as:

$$v_{adv}^0 = v, \quad v_{adv}^{N+1} = Clip_{v,\epsilon}\left\{v_{adv}^N + \alpha\text{sign}(\nabla_v L(\theta, v_{adv}^N, q, a_{true}))\right\} \tag{3}$$

where $Clip_{v,\epsilon}(A)$ denotes element-wise clipping A, with $A_{i,j}$ clipped to the range $[v_{i,j} - \epsilon, v_{i,j} + \epsilon]$, α is step size in each iteration. In this paper, we summarize gradient-based method as VAdvGen(v, q).

One-step methods of adversarial example generation generate a candidate adversarial image after computing only one gradient. Iterative methods apply many gradient updates. They typically do not rely on any approximation of the model and typically produce more harmful adversarial examples when running for more iterations. Our experimental results show that the accuracy of the BUTD vanilla trained model on visual adversarial examples generated by IFGSM is about 17%–30% for $\epsilon \in [0.3, 1.3]$. It implies that adversarial examples have different distribution to normal examples.

Semantic Equivalent Questions Generation. To generate adversarial example q_{adv} of a question, we cannot directly apply approaches from image DNN attackers since textual data is discrete. In addition, the perturbation size that measured by L_p norm in image is also inapplicable for textual data. Moreover, the small changes in texts, e.g., character or word change, would easily destroy the grammar and semantics, rendering the possibility of attack failure. Adhere to the principle of not changing the semantics of input data, inspired by [15,28], we generate semantically equivalent adversarial questions by using a sequence-to-sequence paraphrasing model.

Here we use a paraphrasing model [28] based purely on neural networks and it is an extension of the basic encoder-decoder Neural Machine Translation (NMT) framework. In the neural encoder-decoder framework, the encoder (RNN) is used to compress the meaning of the source sentence into a sequence of vectors. The decoder, a conditional RNN language model, generates a target sentence word-by-word. The encoder takes a sequence of original question words

$X = \{x_1, ..., x_{T_x}\}$ as inputs, and produces a sequence of context. The decoder produces, given the source sentence, a probability distribution over the target sentence $Y = \{y_1, ..., y_{T_y}\}$ with a softmax function:

$$P(Y|X) = \prod_{t=1}^{T_y} P(y_t|y_{<t}, X) \tag{4}$$

However, in the case of paraphrasing, there is not a path from English to English, but a path from English to a pivot language to English can be used. For example, the source English sentence E_1, is translated into a single French sentence F. Next, F is translated back into English, giving a probability distribution over English sentences, E_2, which acts as paraphrase distribution:

$$P(E_2|E_1, F) = P(E_2|F) \tag{5}$$

Our paraphrasing model pivots through the set of K-best translations $\mathcal{F} = \{F_1, ..., F_K\}$ of E_1. This ensures that multiple aspects (semantic and syntactic) of the source sentence are captured. Translating multiple pivot sentences into one sentence producing a probability distribution over the target vocabulary could be formed as:

$$P(y_t = w|y_{<t}, \mathcal{F}) = \sum_{i=1}^{K} P(\mathcal{F}_i|E_1) \cdot P(y_t = w|y_{<t}, \mathcal{F}_i) \tag{6}$$

We further expand on the multi-pivot approach by pivoting over multiple sentences in multiple languages (e.g.., French and Portuguese). Deriving from Eq. 6, we obtain $P(y_t = w|y_{<t}, \mathcal{F}^{Fr})$ and $P(y_t = w|y_{<t}, \mathcal{F}^{Po})$. Then averaging these two distributions, producing a multi-sentence, multi-lingual paraphrase probability:

$$P(y_t = w|y_{<t}, \mathcal{F}^{Fr}, \mathcal{F}^{Po}) = \frac{1}{2}(P(y_t = w|y_{<t}, \mathcal{F}^{Fr}) + P(y_t = w|y_{<t}, \mathcal{F}^{Po})) \tag{7}$$

which is used to obtain the probability distributions over sentences:

$$P(E_2|E_1) = \prod_{t=1}^{T_{E_2}} P(y_t|y_{<t}, \mathcal{F}^{Fr}, \mathcal{F}^{Po}) \tag{8}$$

We employ the pre-trained NMT model[1] which is trained for English↔Portuguese and English↔French to generate paraphrase candidates. A score [34] that measures the semantic similarity between paraphrase and its original text is defined as:

$$S(q, q') = \min\left(1, \frac{P(q'|q)}{P(q|q)}\right) \tag{9}$$

---

[1] https://github.com/OpenNMT/OpenNMT-py.

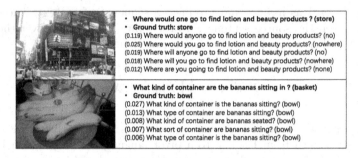

Fig. 2. Examples of our generated q_{adv}. The first question in bold in each block is the original question. The words in brackets are model predictions of the corresponding question; the numbers in brackets are the semantic score of q_{adv}.

where $P(q'|q)$ is the probability of a paraphrase q' given original question q defined in Eq. 8, $P(q|q)$, which approximates how difficult it is to recover q, is used to normalize different distributions. We penalize those candidates with edit distance more than e or unknown words by adding a large negative number λ to the similarity score. We select the paraphrase candidates with the top-k semantic scores as our q_{adv}. The generation algorithm of q_{adv} is denoted $q_{adv} =$ QAdvGen(q).

Our paraphrases edit at least words to maintain syntax and semantics rather than exploring the linguistic variations regardless of the possibility of being perceived. We illustrate two examples of our q_{adv} in Fig. 2. They show that generated paraphrases could easily "break" the BUTD model. A predicted label is considered "flipped" if it differs from the prediction on the corresponding original question (assume that we do not attack visual data in this part). We observe that q_{adv} not only flip from positive predictions to negative ones but also correct the negative predictions to positive ones in some cases. Surprisingly, the flip rate of the vanilla trained model is 36.72% causing an absolute accuracy drop of 10%. It suggests that there is brittleness in the model decision and indicates that the model exploits spurious correlations while making its predictions.

3.3   Adversarial Training with Augmented Examples

Considering the adversarial training framework [24,41], we treat adversarial examples as additional training samples and train networks with a mixture of adversarial and clean examples. The augmented questions are model-agnostic and generated before training, while visual adversarial examples are continually generated at every step of training. There are two kinds of visual adversarial examples depending on the question inputs:

$$v_{qc} = \text{VAdvGen}(v, q), \quad v_{qadv} = \text{VAdvGen}(v, q_{adv}) \qquad (10)$$

For each (v, q) pair, we have 4 additional training pairs, (v_{qc}, q), (v_{qadv}, q), (v_{qc}, q_{adv}) and (v_{qadv}, q_{adv}). All these four pairs are semantically equivalent,

---

Algorithm 1: Pseudo code of our adversarial training

Input: A set of clean visual and textual examples v, q with answers a
Output: Network parameter θ

1 $q_{adv} = \text{QAdvGen}(q)$;
2 **for** *each training step* i **do**
3   Sample a mini-batch of clean visual examples v^b, clean textual examples q^b, textual adversarial examples q^b_{adv} and answer a^b;
4   **if** i *is in adversarial training period time* **then**
5   Generating the corresponding mini-batch of additional training pairs (v^b_{qc}, q^b), (v^b_{qadv}, q^b), (v^b_{qc}, q^b_{adv}) and (v^b_{qadv}, q^b_{adv});
6   Minimize the loss in Eq. 11 w.r.t. network parameter θ
7   **else**
8   Minimize the loss $L(\theta, v^b, q^b, a^b)$ w.r.t. network parameter θ
9   **end**
10 **end**
11 **return** θ

---

which means they hold the same ground truth answer. We maintain the original $\langle image, question, answer \rangle$ triplet but augment the original example at least four times, in the case of only one q_{adv} generated. We formulate a loss function that allows control of the relative weight of additional pairs in each batch:

$$Loss = L(\theta, v, q, a_{true}) + w\Big(L(\theta, v_{qc}, q, a_{true}) + L(\theta, v_{qadv}, q, a_{true})$$

$$+ L(\theta, v_{qc}, q_{adv}, a_{true}) + L(\theta, v_{qadv}, q_{adv}, a_{true})\Big) \qquad (11)$$

where $L(\theta, v, q, a_{true})$ is a loss on a batch of v and q examples with true answer a_{true}, w is a parameter which controls the relative weight of adversarial examples in the loss. Our main goal is to improve network performance on clean images by leveraging the regularization power of adversarial examples. We empirically find that training with a mixture of adversarial and clean examples from beginning to end would not converge well on clean samples. Therefore, we mix them in a period of training time and fine-tune with clean examples in the rest epochs. Not only does this boost the performance on clean examples, but also improves the robustness of the model to adversarial examples. We present our adversarial training scheme in Algorithm 1.

4 Experiments

4.1 Experiments Setup

Dataset. We conduct experiments on the VQAv2 [13], which is improved from the previous version to emphasize visual understanding by reducing the answer bias in the dataset. VQAv2 contains 443K train, 214K validation and 453K test examples. The annotations for the test set are unavailable except for the remote evaluation servers. We provide our results on both validation and test set, and perform ablation study on the validation set.

VQA Architectures. We use a strong baseline Bottom-Up-Attention and Top-Down (BUTD) [2] which combines a bottom-up and a top-down attention mechanism to perform VQA, with the bottom-up mechanism generating object proposals from Faster R-CNN [11], and the top-down mechanism predicting an attention distribution over those proposals. Following setting in [2,39], we use a maximum of 100 object proposals per image, which are 2048 dimensional features, as visual input. We represent question words as 300 dimensional embeddings initialized with pre-trained GloVe vectors [32], and process them with a one-layer GRU to obtain a 1024 dimensional question embedding.

Training Details. For fair comparison, we train the BUTD baseline and our framework using Adamax [21] with a batch size of 256 on the training split for a total of 25 epochs. Baseline achieves 63.32% accuracy on the validation set and we save this checkpoint to evaluate the attackers in the following. We set an initial learning rate of 0.001, and then decay it after five epochs at the rate of 0.25 for every two epochs. We inject the additional data merely in a period of epochs $(start, end)$, where $start$ is the epoch when we start adversarial training and end is the epoch when we start standard training. We set the number of iterations n of IFGSM to 2 and the number of generated paraphrases per question to 1 for saving training time. In paraphrase generating, we set the edit distance threshold $e = 4$ and penalization score $\lambda = -10$. To avoid *label leaking* effect [24], we replace the true label in Eq. 2 and 3 with the most likely label predicted by the model when adversarial training. Our best result is achieved by using values $\epsilon = 0.3, \alpha = 0.0625, w = 50$. These hyperparameters are chosen based on grid search, and other settings are tested in the ablation studies.

4.2   Results

Overall Performance. Table 1 shows the results on VQAv2 validation, test-dev and test-std sets. We compare our method with the BUTD vanilla training setting. Our method outperforms vanilla trained baseline, making gains of 1.82%, 2.55%, 2.6% on validation, test-dev and test-std set, respectively. Furthermore, our training scheme only consumes a small amount of additional time (4 min for an epoch) while allows for a considerable increase in standard accuracy.

Comparison with Other Data Augmentation Methods. We compare our method with related VQA data augmentation method CC [35], and NLP data augmentation method EDA [40] and report the results on VQAv2 in Table 1. The model of CC is trained to predict the same answer for a question and its rephrasing, which are generated by a VQG module in their training scheme. Their outperforming validation accuracy is in contrast to the less competitive

Table 1. Performance and ablation studies on VQAv2.0. All models listed here are single model, which trained on the training set to report *Val* scores and trained on training and validation sets to report *Test-dev* and *Test-std* scores. The first row represents the vanilla trained baseline model. The rows begin with + represents the data augmentation method added to the first row. EDA-3 represents that we generate three augmented questions per original questions using EDA [40]. † This method is implemented based on a stronger BUTD (see [35]) and obtains a relatively small improvement (0.48%) on validation score, even so, its test-dev score is surpassed by our method.

Method	Val	Test-dev				Test-std
		Overall	Yes/no	Number	Others	
BUTD [2]	63.32	65.23	81.82	44.21	56.05	65.67
+Noise	63.28	64.80	81.03	43.96	55.70	–
+EDA-3 [40]	62.73	–	–	–	–	–
+CC [35]†	65.53	67.55	–	–	–	–
+Ours	**65.16**	**67.78**	**84.08**	**47.55**	**58.48**	**68.27**
+Ours *w/o* Aug-Q	65.05	67.58	83.85	47.34	58.31	–
+Ours *w/o* Aug-V	64.69	67.45	83.55	46.96	58.37	–

accuracy on the test-dev set. It reveals CC is less capable of generalizing on unseen data. EDA is a text editing technique boosting model performance on the text classification task. We implement it to generate three augmented questions per original question and set the percent of words in a question that are changed $\alpha = 0.1$. However, results (see Table 1) show that EDA could degrade the performance on clean data and make a 0.59% accuracy drop. It demonstrates that text editing techniques for generating question are not applicable as large numbers of questions are too short that could not be allowed to insert, delete or swap words. Moreover, sometimes the text editing may change the original semantic meaning of the question, which leads to noisy and even incorrect data.

Since our augmented data might be regarded as injecting noise to original data, we also set comparison by injecting random noise with a standard deviation of 0.3 (same as our ϵ in reported results) to visual data. Random noise, as well, could be regarded as a naive attacker that causes a 0.9% absolute accuracy drop on the vanilla model. However, jointly training with clean and noising data could not boost the performance on clean data, as reported in Table 1. It proves that our generated data are drawn from the proper distribution that let the model take full advantage of the regularization power of adversarial examples.

4.3 Analysis

Training Set Size Impact. Furthermore, we conduct experiments using a fraction of the available data in the training set. As overfitting tends to be more severe when training on smaller datasets, we show that our method has more significant improvements for smaller training sets. We run both vanilla training

Table 2. Validation accuracy (%) across BUTD with and without our framework on different training set sizes.

Training set size	BUTD	+Ours
80%	62.77	64.27 (+1.50)
60%	61.55	63.11 (+1.56)
40%	59.47	61.35 (+1.88)
20%	55.45	57.39 (+1.94)

Table 3. Validation accuracy (%) of our method using different adversarial training periods.

$(start, end)$	Accuracy
(5,25)	63.93
(10,25)	64.08
(10,15)	**65.16**
(15,20)	64.18

and our method for the following training set fractions (%): $\{20, 40, 60, 80\}$. Performances are shown in Table 2. The best accuracy without augmentation, 63.32%, was achieved using 100% of the training data. Our method surpasses it with 80% of the training data, achieving 64.27%.

Effect of Augmenting Time. We empirically find that the time when the adversarial examples are injected into training has an effect on accuracy. We demonstrate this via ablation studies in Table 3. We try several adversarial training period $(5, 25)$, $(10, 25)$, $(10, 15)$ $(15, 20)$. They respectively evaluate the effect of delaying injecting additional training data after different epochs and prove the advantage gained from fine-tuning with clean data in the last few epochs. Results show that $(10, 15)$ is the optimal adversarial training period, and it surpasses the baseline model and achieves 65.16% accuracy. One explanation is that adversarial examples have different underlying distributions to normal examples, and if boosting model performance on clean examples is our main goal, it is inappropriate to inject the perturbed examples at an early stage where the model has not warm up, and the fitting ability of model on clean examples need to be retrieved at the end of the training process.

4.4 Ablation Studies

Augmentation Decomposed. Results from ablation studies to test the contributions of our method's components are given in Table 1. The augmentation on visual and textual (question) data both make their individual contribution to improve the accuracy. We observe that visual adversarial examples are critical to our performance, and removing it causes a 0.47% accuracy drop (see Ours *w/o* Aug-V) on the validation set. The question augmentation also leads to comparable improvements, see the model of Ours *w/o* Aug-V.

Ablation on Adversarial Attackers. We now ablate the effects of attacker strength and type used in our method on network performance. To evaluate the regularization power of adversarial examples, we first compute the accuracy of the vanilla model after being attacked by the gradient-based attacker with a

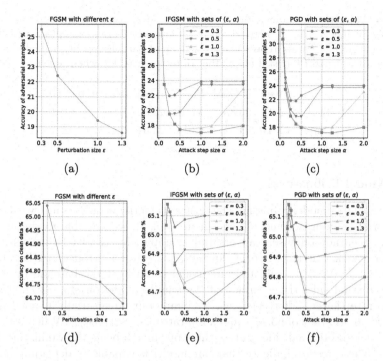

Fig. 3. Ablation on visual attacker strength and type. The top row is the accuracy of the vanilla model on adversarial examples generated by FGSM, IFGSM, and PGD, respectively. The bottom row is the standard accuracy of our model that adversarially trained with the corresponding attacker. The number of iterations is fixed to 2.

variety of sets of parameters. Since the visual input ranges from 0 to 83, we try perturbation size ϵ among $\{0.3, 0.5, 1, 1.3\}$, approximately following the ratio of ϵ to pixel value in [41], and step size α among $\left\{ \frac{1}{16}, \frac{1}{8}, \frac{1}{4}, \frac{3}{8}, \frac{1}{2}, 1, 2 \right\}$.

Figure 3(b) reflects the attacker strength changes with different parameter settings (accuracy declines implies strength increases) while Fig. 3(e) reflects how the model performance changes with attacker strength. We observe that the accuracy on clean data is inversely proportional to attacker strength. As weaker attackers push the distribution of adversarial examples less away from the distribution of clean data, the model is better at bridging domain differences. However, the extremely weak attacker (e.g., random noise, $\alpha < \frac{1}{64}$) yields negligible improvement on standard accuracy, since the generated data are drawn similar distribution with original data.

We then study the effects of applying different gradient-based attackers in our method on model performance. Specifically, we try two other attackers, FGSM and PGD [27]. Their performances are reported in Fig. 3(a), 3(d), 3(c), 3(f). We observe that all attackers substantially improve model performance over the vanilla training baseline. This result suggests that our VQA data augmentation method is not designed for a specific attacker.

Table 4. Validation accuracy (%) of vanilla and adversarially trained (using IFGSM $\epsilon = 0.3, \alpha = 0.0625, n = 2$) network on clean and adversarial examples with various test-time attackers. Parap. represents the generated paraphrases in our method. Note that the IFGSM and PGD still act as the white-box attacker when testing.

	Clean	IFGSM	Parap	IFGSM & Parap	PGD
BUTD [2]	63.32	30.83	54.03	22.09	18.05
+Ours	**65.16**	44.57	63.18	43.64	22.64

4.5 Model Robustness

Improvement of model robustness against adversarial attacks is a reward of our adversarial training scheme. As shown in Table 4, we are able to significantly increase accuracy on visual adversarial examples by 13.74%, when using the training attacker at test-time. Following [8], we test a stronger PGD attacker ($\epsilon = 0.5, \alpha = 0.125, n = 6$) and our model could beat the baseline by 4.59%. On the textual side, the accuracy of the vanilla model on q_{adv} is 54.03% and the flip rate (lower is better) is 36.72% while our adversarially trained model obtained an accuracy of 63.18% and a flip rate of 18.8% on q_{adv}. When attacking both visual and textual sides in test-time, our model beats the vanilla model by 21.55%. These results indicate that our model is capable of defending against both visual and textual common attackers.

4.6 Human Evaluation of Semantic Consistency

In order to show the semantic consistency of our generated paraphrases with original questions, we conduct a human study. We sampled 100 questions and their paraphrases with top1 semantic similarity score defined in Eq. 9, and asked 4 human evaluators to assign labels (e.g., positive for similar or negative for not similar). We averaged the opinions of different evaluations for each query to get a positive score of 84%. It demonstrates that the majority of paraphrases are similar to the originals.

5 Conclusion

In this paper, we propose to generate visual and textual adversarial examples as augmented data to train a robust VQA model with our adversarial training scheme. The visual adversaries are generated by gradient-based adversarial attacker and textual adversaries are paraphrases. Both of them keep modification imperceptible and maintain the semantics. Experimental results show that our method not only outperforms prior arts of VQA data augmentation, and also improves model robustness against adversarial attacks. To the best of our knowledge, this is the first work that uses both semantic equivalent visual and textual adversaries as data augmentation for the visual question answering problem.

Acknowledgements. This work was supported by National Key Research and Development Program of China (2016YFB1001003), NSFC (U19B2035, 61527804, 60906119), STCSM (18DZ1112300). C. Ma was sponsored by Shanghai Pujiang Program

References

1. Agarwal, V., Shetty, R., Fritz, M.: Towards causal VQA: revealing and reducing spurious correlations by invariant and covariant semantic editing. arXiv preprint arXiv:1912.07538 (2019)
2. Anderson, P., et al.: Bottom-up and top-down attention for image captioning and visual question answering. In: Proceedings of the IEEE Conference on Computer Vision and Pattern Recognition, pp. 6077–6086 (2018)
3. Andreas, J., Rohrbach, M., Darrell, T., Klein, D.: Learning to compose neural networks for question answering. arXiv preprint arXiv:1601.01705 (2016)
4. Andreas, J., Rohrbach, M., Darrell, T., Klein, D.: Neural module networks. In: Proceedings of the IEEE Conference on Computer Vision and Pattern Recognition, pp. 39–48 (2016)
5. Belinkov, Y., Bisk, Y.: Synthetic and natural noise both break neural machine translation. arXiv preprint arXiv:1711.02173 (2017)
6. Ben-Younes, H., Cadene, R., Cord, M., Thome, N.: MUTAN: multimodal tucker fusion for visual question answering. In: Proceedings of the IEEE International Conference on Computer Vision, pp. 2612–2620 (2017)
7. Blohm, M., Jagfeld, G., Sood, E., Yu, X., Vu, N.T.: Comparing attention-based convolutional and recurrent neural networks: Success and limitations in machine reading comprehension. arXiv preprint arXiv:1808.08744 (2018)
8. Carlini, N.,et al.: On evaluating adversarial robustness. arXiv preprint arXiv:1902.06705 (2019)
9. Ebrahimi, J., Lowd, D., Dou, D.: On adversarial examples for character-level neural machine translation. arXiv preprint arXiv:1806.09030 (2018)
10. Fukui, A., Park, D.H., Yang, D., Rohrbach, A., Darrell, T., Rohrbach, M.: Multimodal compact bilinear pooling for visual question answering and visual grounding. arXiv preprint arXiv:1606.01847 (2016)
11. Girshick, R.: Fast R-CNN. In: Proceedings of the IEEE International Conference on Computer Vision, pp. 1440–1448 (2015)
12. Goodfellow, I.J., Shlens, J., Szegedy, C.: Explaining and harnessing adversarial examples. arXiv preprint arXiv:1412.6572 (2014)
13. Goyal, Y., Khot, T., Summers-Stay, D., Batra, D., Parikh, D.: Making the V in VQA matter: elevating the role of image understanding in visual question answering. In: Proceedings of the IEEE Conference on Computer Vision and Pattern Recognition, pp. 6904–6913 (2017)
14. Hu, R., Andreas, J., Rohrbach, M., Darrell, T., Saenko, K.: Learning to reason: End-to-end module networks for visual question answering. In: Proceedings of the IEEE International Conference on Computer Vision, pp. 804–813 (2017)
15. Iyyer, M., Wieting, J., Gimpel, K., Zettlemoyer, L.: Adversarial example generation with syntactically controlled paraphrase networks. arXiv preprint arXiv:1804.06059 (2018)
16. Jain, U., Zhang, Z., Schwing, A.G.: Creativity: generating diverse questions using variational autoencoders. In: Proceedings of the IEEE Conference on Computer Vision and Pattern Recognition, pp. 6485–6494 (2017)

17. Kafle, K., Kanan, C.: Visual question answering: datasets, algorithms, and future challenges. Comput. Vis. Image Underst. **163**, 3–20 (2017)
18. Kafle, K., Yousefhussien, M., Kanan, C.: Data augmentation for visual question answering. In: Proceedings of the 10th International Conference on Natural Language Generation, pp. 198–202 (2017)
19. Kim, J.H., Jun, J., Zhang, B.T.: Bilinear attention networks. In: Advances in Neural Information Processing Systems, pp. 1564–1574 (2018)
20. Kim, J.H., On, K.W., Lim, W., Kim, J., Ha, J.W., Zhang, B.T.: Hadamard product for low-rank bilinear pooling. arXiv preprint arXiv:1610.04325 (2016)
21. Kingma, D.P., Ba, J.: Adam: a method for stochastic optimization. arXiv preprint arXiv:1412.6980 (2014)
22. Krishna, R., et al.: Visual genome: Connecting language and vision using crowdsourced dense image annotations. Int. J. Comput. Vis. **123**(1), 32–73 (2017). https://doi.org/10.1007/s11263-016-0981-7
23. Kurakin, A., Goodfellow, I., Bengio, S.: Adversarial examples in the physical world. arXiv preprint arXiv:1607.02533 (2016)
24. Kurakin, A., Goodfellow, I., Bengio, S.: Adversarial machine learning at scale. arXiv preprint arXiv:1611.01236 (2016)
25. Li, Y., et al.: Visual question generation as dual task of visual question answering. In: Proceedings of the IEEE Conference on Computer Vision and Pattern Recognition, pp. 6116–6124 (2018)
26. Lu, J., Yang, J., Batra, D., Parikh, D.: Hierarchical question-image co-attention for visual question answering. In: Advances in Neural Information Processing Systems, pp. 289–297 (2016)
27. Madry, A., Makelov, A., Schmidt, L., Tsipras, D., Vladu, A.: Towards deep learning models resistant to adversarial attacks. arXiv preprint arXiv:1706.06083 (2017)
28. Mallinson, J., Sennrich, R., Lapata, M.: Paraphrasing revisited with neural machine translation. In: Proceedings of the 15th Conference of the European Chapter of the Association for Computational Linguistics: Volume 1, Long Papers, pp. 881–893 (2017)
29. Norcliffe-Brown, W., Vafeias, S., Parisot, S.: Learning conditioned graph structures for interpretable visual question answering. In: Advances in Neural Information Processing Systems, pp. 8334–8343 (2018)
30. Patro, B., Namboodiri, V.P.: Differential attention for visual question answering. In: Proceedings of the IEEE Conference on Computer Vision and Pattern Recognition, pp. 7680–7688 (2018)
31. Peng, G., et al.: Dynamic fusion with intra-and inter-modality attention flow for visual question answering. arXiv preprint arXiv:1812.05252 (2018)
32. Pennington, J., Socher, R., Manning, C.D.: GloVe: global vectors for word representation. In: Proceedings of the 2014 Conference on Empirical Methods in Natural Language Processing (EMNLP), pp. 1532–1543 (2014)
33. Ray, A., Sikka, K., Divakaran, A., Lee, S., Burachas, G.: Sunny and dark outside?! Improving answer consistency in VQA through entailed question generation. arXiv preprint arXiv:1909.04696 (2019)
34. Ribeiro, M.T., Singh, S., Guestrin, C.: Semantically equivalent adversarial rules for debugging NLP models. In: Proceedings of the 56th Annual Meeting of the Association for Computational Linguistics (Volume 1: Long Papers), pp. 856–865 (2018)
35. Shah, M., Chen, X., Rohrbach, M., Parikh, D.: Cycle-consistency for robust visual question answering. In: Proceedings of the IEEE Conference on Computer Vision and Pattern Recognition, pp. 6649–6658 (2019)

36. Sharma, V., Vaibhav, A., Chaudhary, S., Patel, L., Morency, L.: Attend and attack: attention guided adversarial attacks on visual question answering models (2018)
37. Shorten, C., Khoshgoftaar, T.M.: A survey on image data augmentation for deep learning. J. Big Data **6**(1), 60 (2019). https://doi.org/10.1186/s40537-019-0197-0
38. Szegedy, C., et al.: Intriguing properties of neural networks. arXiv preprint arXiv:1312.6199 (2013)
39. Teney, D., Anderson, P., He, X., Van Den Hengel, A.: Tips and tricks for visual question answering: learnings from the 2017 challenge. In: Proceedings of the IEEE Conference on Computer Vision and Pattern Recognition, pp. 4223–4232 (2018)
40. Wei, J.W., Zou, K.: EDA: easy data augmentation techniques for boosting performance on text classification tasks. arXiv preprint arXiv:1901.11196 (2019)
41. Xie, C., Tan, M., Gong, B., Wang, J., Yuille, A., Le, Q.V.: Adversarial examples improve image recognition. arXiv preprint arXiv:1911.09665 (2019)
42. Xie, Z., et al.: Data noising as smoothing in neural network language models. arXiv preprint arXiv:1703.02573 (2017)
43. Xu, X., Chen, X., Liu, C., Rohrbach, A., Darrell, T., Song, D.: Fooling vision and language models despite localization and attention mechanism. In: Proceedings of the IEEE Conference on Computer Vision and Pattern Recognition, pp. 4951–4961 (2018)
44. Yang, Z., He, X., Gao, J., Deng, L., Smola, A.: Stacked attention networks for image question answering. In: Proceedings of the IEEE Conference on Computer Vision and Pattern Recognition, pp. 21–29 (2016)
45. Yu, A.W., et al.: QANet: combining local convolution with global self-attention for reading comprehension. arXiv preprint arXiv:1804.09541 (2018)
46. Zhang, Y., Hare, J., Prügel-Bennett, A.: Learning to count objects in natural images for visual question answering. arXiv preprint arXiv:1802.05766 (2018)

Unsupervised Multi-view CNN for Salient View Selection of 3D Objects and Scenes

Ran Song[1], Wei Zhang[1(✉)], Yitian Zhao[2], and Yonghuai Liu[3]

[1] School of Control Science and Engineering, Shandong University, Jinan, China
{ransong,davidzhang}@sdu.edu.cn
[2] Cixi Institute of Biomedical Engineering,
Ningbo Institute of Materials Technology and Engineering,
Chinese Academy of Sciences, Ningbo, China
yitian.zhao@nimte.ac.cn
[3] Department of Computer Science, Edge Hill University, Ormskirk, UK
liuyo@edgehill.ac.uk

Abstract. We present an unsupervised 3D deep learning framework based on a ubiquitously true proposition named view-object consistency as it states that a 3D object and its projected 2D views always belong to the same object class. To validate its effectiveness, we design a multi-view CNN for the salient view selection of 3D objects, which quintessentially cannot be handled by supervised learning due to the difficulty of data collection. Our unsupervised multi-view CNN branches off two channels which encode the knowledge within each 2D view and the 3D object respectively and also exploits both intra-view and inter-view knowledge of the object. It ends with a new loss layer which formulates the view-object consistency by impelling the two channels to generate consistent classification outcomes. We experimentally demonstrate the superiority of our method over state-of-the-art methods and showcase that it can be used to select salient views of 3D scenes containing multiple objects.

Keywords: Unsupervised 3D deep learning · Multi-view CNN · View-object consistency · View selection

1 Introduction

The success of Generative Adversarial Network (GAN) [8] demonstrates the great value and impact of a widely applicable unsupervised deep learning framework. One important reason is that data collection for training a deep network is laborious in many tasks. This is particularly the case for 3D tasks where data collection is generally more challenging than that in 2D tasks. Therefore, a widely applicable 3D deep learning framework is potentially of broad interest.

Electronic supplementary material The online version of this chapter (https://doi.org/10.1007/978-3-030-58529-7_27) contains supplementary material, which is available to authorized users.

© Springer Nature Switzerland AG 2020
A. Vedaldi et al. (Eds.): ECCV 2020, LNCS 12364, pp. 454–470, 2020.
https://doi.org/10.1007/978-3-030-58529-7_27

A simple but ubiquitously true proposition is that a 3D object and its projected 2D views always belong to the same object class no matter what taxonomy is applied to the classification. We name the proposition *view-object consistency* and propose an unsupervised 3D deep learning framework based on it. Since it is not feasible for us to thoroughly explore the utility of the framework via various 3D tasks in one paper, we pick salient view selection of 3D objects to demonstrate its effectiveness for three reasons. First, salient view selection is challenging as it does not only rely on low-level geometric features but also involves high-level semantics of objects. Thus a data-driven method is naturally sound. Second, however, it is the particular task where collecting a large amount of accurately and consistently annotated data is notoriously difficult. We found that all existing datasets are very small (e.g. 68 objects in [7] and 16 objects in [23]) no matter whether the annotations were collected directly (e.g.. by marking a viewpoint on a view sphere surrounding the object [7]) or indirectly (e.g. by selecting the preferred view from two views for multiple times [23]). Third, we shall further show the advantage of an unsupervised method by extending salient view selection to 3D scenes. Salient view selection of 3D scenes can hardly be addressed by a weakly supervised method relying on such annotation as a single class label as a scene often contains objects belonging to different classes.

The problem of salient view selection of 3D objects is arguably well defined. Besides related literatures in computer vision and graphics to be discussed in Section 2, researchers in psychology [2,6] have revealed that for many classes of familiar objects, the preferred views are reasonably consistent among the human subjects. To make it clear, the most salient view of a 3D object herein is defined as the view that a human subject likes most for whatever reason. And we shall evaluate our method using the publicly available benchmark [7] where subjects were asked to rotate a 3D object to directly select the view that they preferred.

To instantiate the view-object consistency in the context of salient view selection, we develop a multi-view convolutional neural network (CNN). It formulates the view-object consistency through a two-channel architecture and a new loss function. It also integrates with an important heuristic of human's view preference via a specifically designed layer. The proposed multi-view CNN is trained end-to-end in an unsupervised manner using only a collection of 3D objects without any manual annotations and is thus named as Unsupervised Multi-View CNN (UMVCNN). Overall, it exploits both intra-view and inter-view knowledge via a multi-view representation of 3D objects for salient view selection.

The contribution of our work is hence threefold:

(1) We propose an unsupervised framework of 3D deep learning where the core idea is valid ubiquitously and thus potentially has a range of applications.
(2) We propose a multi-view CNN in accordance with this unsupervised framework to address the classical problem of salient view selection of 3D objects.
(3) By the unsupervised 3D deep learning framework, we extend salient view selection from individual 3D objects to scenes containing multiple objects.

2   Related Work

We categorise the literatures into three groups. The first group is based only on handcrafted attributes of 3D objects; the second group is essentially shallow learning of a certain model to combine multiple attributes while all attributes are not learned but still handcrafted; the third group is based on deep learning where some, if not all of the attributes, are learned via deep neural networks.

Handcrafted Attributes. Polonsky et al. [21] explored general frameworks for view selection by analysing several handcrafted attributes associated to geometrical or statistical properties of a 3D object or its projected 2D views. Lee et al. [16] selected salient views using the attribute of mesh saliency computed via Gaussian-weighted mean curvatures. Yamauchi et al. [33] employed mesh saliency as the intra-view cue for finding salient views while taking into account such inter-view cue as the similarity of projected views. [17] computed a saliency measure based on both local geometrical and global topological attributes for salient view selection. However, most methods based on handcrafted attributes do not generalise well due mainly to the limited expressive capabilities of the attributes extracted by some fixed schemes for objects of different classes.

Handcrafted Attributes with Shallow Learning. Vieira et al. [29] learned good views via an SVM classifier where the candidate views were represented by a collection of handcrafted attributes. To investigate human view preference, Secord et al. [23] collected a small dataset to learn a regression model combining a list of handcrafted attributes. Mezuman and Weiss [18] leveraged Internet images to learn the view from which we most often see the object, where the handcrafted GIST descriptor was employed to measure view similarity. He et al. [10] proposed a multi-view learning framework exploiting both 2D and 3D handcrafted attributes to recommend viewpoints for photographing architectures.

Deep Learning. Apart from the psychological work [6,9,27], in computer vision, there is also evidence [19,26,32] of the relation between view selection and object recognition where view-dependent attributes were extracted via deep networks for 3D object recognition. Kim et al. [14] and Song et al. [25] leveraged CNNs for view selection instead of improving recognition accuracy. Our work is inspired by them but fundamentally different for two reasons: 1) both [14] and [25] require annotated data for training while our work is unsupervised; 2) both of them cannot be trained end-to-end where the former trains two CNNs and a Random Forest classifier separately and the latter trains a CNN and a Markov Random Field individually while our UMVCNN is trained fully end-to-end.

3   Salient View Selection via UMVCNN

In this section, we first describe each component of our method in a piecewise manner. We then elaborate the implementation as a whole where each component is situated in the context of the complete pipeline.

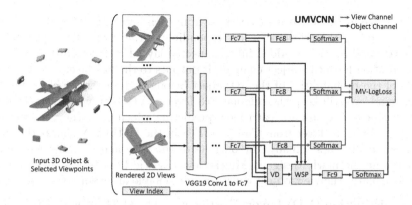

Fig. 1. Overview of the proposed UMVCNN containing two channels. The green and the red arrows denote the view channel and the object channel respectively. "VD" and "WSP" denote the view distinction and the weighted sum pooling layers respectively. (Color figure online)

3.1 Multi-view Representation of a 3D Object

Multi-view CNNs have been used to adapt image-based deep networks to 3D objects where an object is represented as a set of its projected views. Compared with other methods which generalise deep learning to non-Euclidean domains, multi-view CNNs showed state-of-the-art performance in various 3D shape understanding tasks [12,13,22,26]. One consensus is that we should avoid using the very 'bad' views usually defined as the ones that cause misunderstanding of objects. We propose a scheme considering two low-level attributes to ensure that the selected 2D views for representing a 3D object are at least 'not very bad'.

We start with an icosahedron to uniformly sample a view sphere surrounding the input object. Then we iteratively subdivide the icosahedron to produce more viewpoints on the view sphere. We end with a polyhedron with 162 vertices. Next, we rank the views taken from these viewpoints based on the attributes of view area and silhouette length. View area is calculated as the area of the projection of the object as seen from a particular viewpoint. Silhouette length is the length of the outer contour of the silhouette of the object as seen from a particular viewpoint. We collect the top $N = 20$ views with the highest ranks on average based on the two attributes as the multi-view representation of the 3D object.

3.2 UMVCNN Architecture

Overview. Figure 1 illustrates the architecture of the UMVCNN. It starts with VGG-19 [3] as the backbone and then branches off the view and the object channels after the Fc7 layers. Through the view distinction (VD) layer, it generates an inter-view heuristic using the deep features extracted from the 2D views. A weighted sum pooling (WSP) layer is then employed to incorporate this heuristic and multiple intra-view features derived from each individual view into a single tensor encoding the information corresponding to the entire 3D object. These two layers and the newly added fully connected layer Fc9 followed by a Softmax normalisation form the object channel. It outputs to the loss layer a vector composed of the probabilities of the 3D object belonging to a certain class. On the other hand, we still keep the original Fc8 layer of VGG-19 in the view channel that generates a vector for each view predicting which class the view belongs to. Every VGG-19 layer from Conv1 to Fc8 in the UMVCNN shares the same weights for all views. Finally, the outputs of the view and the object channels converge at the newly designed Multi-View Logistic Loss (MV-LogLoss) layer that formulates the view-object consistency to enable an unsupervised learning.

View Distinction (VD) Layer. Existing work [23,33,34] showed that humans subjects find a good view by not only scrutinising its own intra-view content, but also comparing it with other views of the same object. Note that a limitation of most previous work is the lack of the consideration of such inter-view knowledge in their algorithms. In this work, we propose a heuristic mechanism to formulate the inter-view knowledge via paired comparisons of views. Previous work [15,31] in psychology pointed out that a basic principle in human visual system is to suppress the response to frequently occurring features, while at the same time it remains sensitive to features that deviate from the norm. We thus propose the VD layer as a heuristic method to formulate this principle where the view most different from all other views are regarded as the most distinct one. The VD layer takes as input the outputs of all Fc7 layers. Since one 3D object is represented as N views, the input of the VD layer is a matrix of size $4096 \times N$ for a given object. Each of its columns can be regarded as a feature descriptor of one view. The VD layer outputs an N-dimensional vector to the WSP layer. Each element of the vector corresponds to the distinction of a particular view.

Given two views V_i and V_j, their difference can be measured as the Euclidean distance between their feature descriptors F_i and F_j output by the Fc7 layer (with ReLU activation). However, this measure is insufficient as a view tends to have similar content with its neighbouring views. If a view is even very different from its neighbouring views, it is likely to contain some unique content and thus be considered confidently distinct from the other views. Hence, the dissimilarity of two views should be proportional to the difference computed as the Euclidean distance between their feature descriptors and inversely proportional to the geodesic distance between their corresponding viewpoints. Such a heuristic also computationally holds for symmetric objects. For symmetric views, the dissimilarity is always 0 as $F_i = F_j$ and thus has nothing to do with the geodesic distance between them. Besides the N projected views, the UMVCNN also requires as input the view index $\text{VInd}_i \in \{1, 2, ..., 162\}$ generated as a byproduct when creating the multi-view presentation of the object (see Sect. 3.1).

Let $\text{Geod}(\text{VInd}_i, \text{VInd}_j)$ be the geodesic distance between the viewpoints corresponding to V_i and V_j, the dissimilarity between them is defined as:

$$D_{ij} = \frac{\|F_i - F_j\|}{1 + \alpha \cdot \text{Geod}(\text{VInd}_i, \text{VInd}_j)}, \quad \text{s.t. } i, j \in \{1, 2 \ldots, N\} \text{ and } i \neq j \quad (1)$$

where $\alpha = 2$ in our implementation. The distinction of V_i is then computed as the sum of its pairwise dissimilarity to all the other views.

$$S_i = \sum_{j \neq i} D_{ij}. \quad (2)$$

Equations (1) and (2) are both differentiable. Thus for back-propagation, given that the gradient passed to the VD layer is an N-dimensional vector $\mathcal{S}$, according to the chain rule, the gradient $\mathcal{F}$ with regard to its input can be computed as

$$\mathcal{F}_i = \mathcal{S}_i \frac{\partial S_i}{\partial F_i} \quad (3)$$

Considering Eqs. (1) and (2) and the partial derivative of the Euclidean distance function $\frac{\partial \|x\|}{\partial x_i} = \frac{x_i}{\|x\|}$, it can be computed as

$$\frac{\partial S_i}{\partial F_i} = \sum_{j \neq i} \frac{F_i - F_j}{(1 + \alpha \cdot \text{Geod}(\text{VInd}_i, \text{VInd}_j)) \cdot \|F_i - F_j\|}. \quad (4)$$

Weighted Sum Pooling (Wsp) Layer. To implement the view-object consistency through the loss layer requiring the outputs of the view and the object channels to have the same dimensions, we need to pool to aggregate the learned knowledge across all 2D views to create a single descriptor for the 3D object. Also, we need to consider how to cast the influence of view distinction into this aggregation process where distinct views should have larger weights. Thus instead of the popular element-wise max pooling [13, 26] in multi-view CNNs, we carry out a WSP to incorporate view distinction as the weights into the pooling

$$P = \sum_{i=1}^{N} F_i S_i \quad (5)$$

where F_i is the column vector of the output of the Fc7 layer F which denotes the feature descriptor of V_i. S_i is its distinction output by the VD layer. The output of the WSP layer P regarded as the feature descriptor of the 3D object is thus estimated as the weighted sum of the feature descriptors of all views where the weights are their distinctions. Equation (5) can be expressed in a bilinear form as $P = FS$. Thus with the gradient $\mathcal{P}$ passed to the WSP layer, the gradients $\mathcal{F}$ and $\mathcal{S}$ with regard to the inputs F and S respectively can be computed as

$$\mathcal{F} = \mathcal{P}S^T, \quad \mathcal{S} = F^T\mathcal{P}. \quad (6)$$

MV-LogLoss Layer. We propose the MV-LogLoss layer to formulate the view-object consistency enabling an unsupervised learning. No matter what the taxonomy is, the outcome of the classification based on each 2D view should be consistent with that based on the entire 3D object. As illustrated in Fig. 1, either of the view and the object channels alone is specifically designed to have the architecture of a classification network, which facilitates the formulation of the view-object consistency. Moreover, such a design benefits salient view selection as the features vital for object classification are usually important for the selection of a salient view. Psychological studies [6,9,27] validated that a good view of an object can significantly help people to correctly recognise it.

The MV-LogLoss simply adapts the log loss in a multi-view scenario. This loss layer first computes the individual log loss of the softmax-normalised output of each Fc8 layer, $\mathcal{V}(i)$ with regard to that of the Fc9 layer, $\mathcal{O}$, which represent the final outputs of the view channel and the object channel respectively. The multi-view loss is then computed as the sum of all individual log losses:

$$\mathcal{L} = -\sum_{i=1}^{N}\sum_{c=1}^{C} \mathcal{O}_c \cdot \log\left(\mathcal{V}_c(i)\right) \tag{7}$$

where for simplicity, we write the output of the view channel $\mathcal{V}_c(V_i)$ as $\mathcal{V}_c(i)$. Through training, Eq. (7) is minimised by impelling $\mathcal{O}$ to be consistent with $\mathcal{V}(i)$ and the view-object consistency is thus realised.

It can be clearly seen that the MV-LogLoss defined as Eq. (7) does not rely on any annotations as $\mathcal{O}_c$ and $\mathcal{V}_c(i)$ are internally generated by the object channel and the view channel of the UMVCNN respectively. C in Eq. (7) is a picked integer defining the output dimension of the Fc8/Fc9 layer when building the UMVCNN. And the influence of varying C will be studied in Sect. 4.4.

3.3   Salient View Selection

In the deployment, given an object represented as a set of N views, we first feed the views into the UMVCNN and hijack the output of the Softmax layer connected with the Fc9 layer during the forward-propagation to predict its object class $\mathcal{C}$. Then, we back-propagate a C-dimensional one-hot vector where only the entry of index $\mathcal{C}$ is 1 from this Softmax layer to the input views with all network weights fixed. It leads to a per-pixel saliency map I_i for all pixels in each view V_i based on their influence on the predicted class $\mathcal{C}$. I_i can be interpreted as a measure of pixel importance with regard to the recognition of the object. Like previous methods [16,17,23] and also to facilitate evaluations, we are keen to obtain the goodness of any viewpoint, which requires to generate a per-vertex saliency map. We thus employed the 2D-to-3D saliency transfer scheme proposed in [25] to derive a 3D saliency map H_i from I_i. Finally, we hijack the output of the VD layer S_i as the weighting parameters which represent the learned view distinction to aggregate multi-view saliency maps H_is into a single one:

$$H = \sum_{i=1}^{N} S_i H_i. \tag{8}$$

We then select the viewpoint that maximises the sum of the saliency map H for the visible regions of the 3D object as the salient viewpoint:

$$v_s = \arg\max_v \left(\sum_{m \in B(v)} H(m) \right) \tag{9}$$

where $B(v)$ is the set of the vertices visible from the viewpoint v and $H(m)$ denotes the saliency of the vertex m. $M(v) = \sum_{m \in B(v)} H(m)$ can be regarded as the saliency map of the viewpoints. Figure 2 shows the 2D representation of the unwarped viewpoint saliency map on a view sphere normalised to the interval of $[0, 1]$. It is generated via the Mercator projection where the x and the y axes correspond to the latitude and the longitude respectively. Note that initially the model is not up oriented in the view sphere.

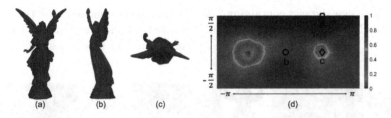

Fig. 2. Viewpoint saliency map. (a)–(c) are the projected views of the Lucy model. (d) is the viewpoint saliency map where the black square, circle and diamond mark the locations of the viewpoints corresponding to the views shown in (a)–(c) respectively.

3.4   Implementation

The proposed method is fully unsupervised. All we need to do is to pick an integer C for defining the output dimension of the Fc8/Fc9 layer.

We first render each 3D object as 20 views as described in Sect. 3.1 using a standard OpenGL renderer with perspective projection mode. The strengths of the ambient light, the diffuse light and the specular reflection are set to 0.2, 0.6 and 0.1 respectively. We apply flat shading to the meshed object. Using different illumination models or shading coefficients does not affect our method due to the invariance of the learned convolutional filters to illumination changes, as observed in image-based CNNs. All of the 20 views are then printed at 200 dpi, also in the OpenGL mode, and further resized to the resolution of 224×224. Then for training we feed these views into the UMVCNN wherein the convolutional layers and the first fully connected layer Fc6 are initialised with the weights pretrained on ImageNet while other fully connected layers Fc7, Fc8 and Fc9 are all initialised with random weights using the popular method proposed in [11]. The UMVCNN is trained end-to-end by stochastic gradient descent with the learning rate of 10^{-5}. As we observed, the training always converged within 50 epochs for all of the variants of the UMVCNN that we shall discuss in Sects. 4.4.

When deploying the UMVCNN to select the salient view of a given 3D object, we again render the object as 20 views with the same rendering settings and then use the scheme described in Sects. 3.3 to output the salient viewpoint.

4 Experimental Results

In this section, we first introduce the datasets used in the experiments and evaluate our method qualitatively. Then, we show that our method can be directly used to select the salient view of a 3D scene to attract further interest. Finally, we evaluate both the proposed UMVCNN and its variants via quantitative comparisons for demonstrating its superiority and better understanding it.

4.1 Datasets

We create a new dataset containing 2747 3D models downloaded from the Princeton ModelNet dataset [32], the Schelling dataset [4] and the Trimble 3D Warehouse [30]. These models are originally from 30 object categories while in this

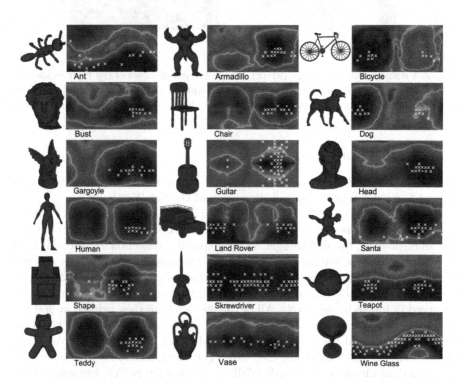

Fig. 3. Qualitative results of the salient views and the viewpoint saliency maps generated by our method. The black square corresponds to the salient viewpoints selected by our method. The white "X"s correspond to the ground truth best viewpoints picked by 26 human subjects (including their symmetric viewpoints) provided by [7].

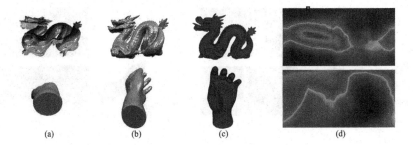

(a)   (b)   (c)   (d)

Fig. 4. Qualitative comparisons with [16] and [33]. (a) The best views selected by [16] (as implemented and shown in [33]). (b) The best views selected by [33]. (c) The best views selected by our method. (d) The viewpoint saliency maps generated by our method where the black squares mark the most salient viewpoints.

work, all categorical annotations are removed in training and validation for an unsupervised learning. We use the same data split as in [32] where 80% of the objects in each category are used for training and 20% are used for validation.

We test our method on the Best View Selection benchmark [7] which might be the only publicly available benchmark suitable for quantitatively evaluating view selection methods. It contains 68 3D objects of various classes including some that do not belong to any of the 30 categories from the perspective of human recognition. It provides a quantitative benchmarking measure, the ground truth best viewpoints picked by 26 people and the results of 7 competing methods. We also used objects from the Stanford 3D Scanning Repository [5], the Princeton Shape Benchmark [24] and the Watertight Track of SHREC'07 for evaluations. Data and codes are available at https://github.com/rsong/UMVCNN.

4.2   Qualitative Results

Figure 3 shows our results for a variety of 3D objects with the ground truth best viewpoints supplied by [7]. The ground truth best viewpoints could be more or less than 26 as 1) several participants could select the same viewpoint and 2) the symmetry of each object is taken into account and thus the symmetric viewpoints of those picked by the participants are also included. It can be seen that the consistency of human preferred viewpoints varies over different objects. Even though, most ground truth best viewpoints fall into the red or orange areas in the viewpoint saliency maps, which demonstrates that our method is good at predicting human's viewpoint preference over various objects. Also, for most objects, the salient viewpoint found by our method is, or at least very close to, a ground truth viewpoint picked by a participant. Due to the default distortion of the Mercator projection, for the Ant, the viewpoints on the bottom boundary of the viewpoint saliency map that look distant from each other are actually very close on the view sphere since they are both close to its bottom pole.

We next compare our method with some state-of-the-art methods. Since some of them require tuning of parameters and some are not open-sourced, we used

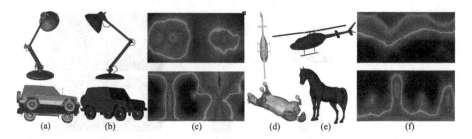

Fig. 5. Qualitative comparisons with [17, 25]. (a) and (d) The best views selected by [17] and [25] respectively. (b) and (e) The best views selected by our method. (c) and (f) The viewpoint saliency maps with black squares marking the most salient viewpoints.

our method to select salient views for the same objects used in the papers where the methods were reported. Figure 4 compared our method with [16] and [33]. It can be seen that the our method is less influenced by some local geometric features such as the sharp edges at the bottom of the hand model if semantically they do not help the recognition of the object. Similarly, Fig. 5 shows that [17] chose a back view of the lamp containing many local details such as wires and screws. In comparison, for both the lamp and the jeep, our method tends to select views natural and good for recognising the objects. Figure 5 also shows that our method outperforms [25] over a helicopter and a horse while more convincing quantitative comparisons using a variety of 3D objects are provided in Sect. 4.3. Note that [25] is essentially based on a weakly supervised deep learning framework where the class labels of the objects are available during training.

Since the UMVCNN does not rely on the knowledge about object classes, our method can be directly used to select the salient view of a 3D scene which usually contains objects of different classes and thus is unlikely to be reliably categorised in most datasets. According to the results shown in Fig. 6, our method successfully selects good views for various 3D scenes. The viewpoint saliency maps of 3D scenes generated by our method are also informative. For instance, by observing the corresponding locations of the best and the worst views in the viewpoint saliency maps of most scenes, we find that the views with positive elevation angles are generally much more salient than those with negative ones, which is consistent with human's viewpoint preference. We also observed that the best view of a scene is not necessarily the best view of each individual object in it. For example, in the living room scene, the best view of the entire scene is not that of one of the three sofas. Similarly, in the work site scene, the best view of the scene is not that of the person in the middle and some chairs.

Please refer to the supplemental material for more qualitative results.

4.3   Quantitative Results

We tested our method on the benchmark supplied by [7] which contains 68 objects using a computer with an Intel i7-4790 3.6 GHz CPU and 32GB RAM

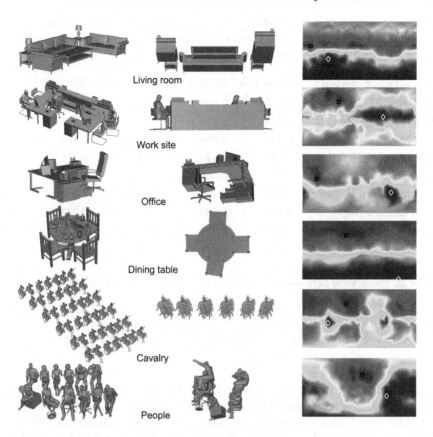

Fig. 6. Salient and non-salient views of 3D scenes (courtesy of Trimble 3D Warehouse [30]) selected by our method. Left column: the most salient views; Middle column: the least salient views; Right column: the viewpoint saliency maps where the black square marks the most salient view and the white diamond marks the least salient view.

without any GPU acceleration. The salient views of most objects can be computed within 1 min where the vertex visibility to each viewpoint is precomputed.

Table 1 gives the statistics of the View Selection Error (VSE) of 9 automatic view selection methods over all of 68 objects. The VSE proposed by [7] measures the geodesic distance between the viewpoint found by a method and the ground truth supplied by a human subject on a unit view sphere and is averaged over the choices of all subjects, with the consideration of object-specific symmetry.

According to Table 1, our method yields the best performance in terms of the mean VSE, the median VSE and the number of objects for which a method gave the lowest VSE among all competing methods. Here UMVCNN-30 refers to the UMVCNN with C set to 30. As mentioned at the end of Sect. 3.2, this means that the output dimension of the Fc8 and Fc9 layers is set to 30 when we build the UMVCNN, which indicates that either of the view and the object channels categorises the objects into 30 classes. As shown in Fig. 3, due to

Table 1. Statistics of the VSE of 9 methods over 68 objects. SD and IQR represent the standard deviation and the interquartile range respectively. n gives the number of objects for which a method gave the lowest VSE among all competing methods.

View selection method	Mean VSE	Median VSE	SD of VSE	IQR of VSE	n
View area [7]	0.517	0.539	0.186	0.306	6
Ratio of visible area [21]	0.473	0.473	0.196	0.338	1
Surface area entropy [28]	0.396	0.386	0.144	0.195	8
Silhouette length [21]	0.446	0.445	0.172	0.275	7
Silhouette entropy [20]	0.484	0.469	0.153	0.241	5
Curvature entropy [20]	0.474	0.466	0.139	0.239	8
Mesh saliency [16]	0.430	0.395	0.165	0.233	2
Deep mesh distinction [25]	0.380	0.346	0.173	0.314	11
UMVCNN-30	0.367	0.336	0.165	0.236	20

Table 2. Mean View Selection Error of the variants of the UMVCNN over 68 objects

UMVCNN Variants	$C = 10$	$C = 15$	$C = 20$	$C = 25$	$C = 30$	$C = 30$, max-pooling	$C = 30$, 30 views	$C = 35$	$C = 40$
Mean VSE	0.379	0.373	0.382	0.381	0.367	0.384	0.366	0.377	0.380

the inconsistency of the ground truth choices of human subjects over the same object, reaching a zero mean VSE is impossible and improving the VSE is very challenging if it is already low. In most cases, a viewpoint with a mean VSE lower than 0.3 corresponds to a good view. Even though, our method outperforms [25] by 3.4%, 2.9%, 4.6% and 24.8% in terms of the mean, the median, the standard deviation and the interquartile range of the VSE respectively. Note that their method is also based on deep learning but trained, in a weakly supervised manner, on a large dataset with the annotations of object class membership.

No method is consistently the best over all 68 objects although our method accomplishes the best results for 20 objects, the most over all competing methods. This is in agreement with the conclusions in [1,23] which argued that human's view preference is driven by a variety of attributes. In general, the methods based on low-level attributes perform significantly worse than the two based on deep neural networks which learn high-level attributes of 3D objects.

In particular, Table 1 shows that our method significantly outperforms [7] based on view area and [21] based on silhouette length in terms of the VSE. This demonstrates that the improvement of the VSE does come from the UMVCNN rather than the handcrafted features, i.e. view area and silhouette length that we use for the multi-view representation of a 3D object (see Sect. 3.1).

Fig. 7. Limitation. Our method tends to select views good for recognition but not necessarily "natural". Left: the view selected by a subject; Middle: the view selected by our method; Right: the viewpoint saliency map where the diamond and the square mark the views selected by the subject and our method respectively.

4.4 Evaluations over the Variants of UMVCNN

Effect of Varying C. Table 2 gives the mean VSE of the UMVCNN variants. It can be seen that redesigning the UMVCNN by varying C from 30 leads to an insignificant degradation of performance. As mentioned in Sect. 4.1, the 3D objects used for training are originally from 30 categories while we removed all categorical annotations for an unsupervised learning. Presumably, that $C = 30$ is indeed a good choice for the UMVCNN can be interpreted by the fact that salient view selection is highly related to classification as we observe that the objects of the same class tend to have analogous salient viewpoints while it is not the case the other way round. However, we cannot observe any obvious rule that suggests a way for deciding C. In a supervised learning, the network is forced to adopt the taxonomy of object classification consistent with human annotations while there is no guarantee that this taxonomy is optimal to the particular task such as salient view selection. Thus in different tasks, C might need to be tuned, but not necessarily fine-tuned as the UMVCNN is not very sensitive to it.

Ablation Study for Validating VD and WSP. We are interested in the heuristic component of the UMVCNN, i.e. the VD and the WSP layers. To validate its effectiveness, we replace the VD and the WSP layers with the popular element-wise max pooling which have demonstrated state-of-the-art performances in various 3D shape understanding tasks such as classification [26], retrieval [26] and segmentation [14]. The variant corresponds to '$C = 30$, max pooling' in Table 2. To aggregate the multi-view 3D saliency maps H_i in Eq. (8), we set S_i to 1 as it is not available via this variant. Table 2 shows that the performance of the UMVCNN is significantly worse without the VD and the WSP layers. This demonstrates the effectiveness of the view distinction heuristic. It also suggests that the unsupervised learning based on the view-object consistency is likely to benefit from some heuristics introduced for the specific task.

Effect of the Number of Views. We tested the variant corresponding to '$C = 30$, 30 views' in Table 2 where a 3D object is projected into 30 instead of 20 views. All the other variants in Table 2 used the 20-view setup. It can be seen that using 30 views merely reduces the mean VSE slightly from 0.367 to 0.366. Using more or different views is trivial, however, we found that a 20-view setup is already enough to achieve high performance.

5   Conclusions

This work reveals that the view-object consistency is promising for the establishment of an unsupervised framework of 3D deep learning. We validate its effectiveness on the challenging task of salient view selection of 3D objects through the relatively naive design of a multi-view deep architecture. While the performance of our method is impressive, it has some limitations as shown in Fig. 7. Our method tends to select a view good for recognising the object, such as the view that better shows some features important for recognising the airplane (e.g. the wings and the engines). However, most subjects prefer a "natural" side view.

Future work will focus on implementing the unsupervised learning framework in more applications to demonstrate that it is amenable to a wide range of 3D shape understanding tasks. Particularly interesting applications might be some 3D scene understanding tasks hindered by the difficulty of collecting large amounts of accurately and consistently annotated data for training.

Acknowledgements. We acknowledge the support of the Young Taishan Scholars Program of Shandong Province tsqn20190929 and the Qilu Young Scholars Program of Shandong University 31400082063101, the National Natural Science Foundation of China under Grant 61991411 and U1913204, the National Key Research and Development Plan of China under Grant 2017YFB1300205, and the Shandong Major Scientific and Technological Innovation Project 2018CXGC1503.

References

1. Biederman, I.: Recognition-by-components: a theory of human image understanding. Psychol. Rev. **94**(2), 115 (1987)
2. Blanz, V., Tarr, M.J., Bülthoff, H.H.: What object attributes determine canonical views? Perception **28**(5), 575–599 (1999)
3. Chatfield, K., Simonyan, K., Vedaldi, A., Zisserman, A.: Return of the devil in the details: delving deep into convolutional nets. In: Proceedings of the BMVC (2014)
4. Chen, X., Saparov, A., Pang, B., Funkhouser, T.: Schelling points on 3D surface meshes. ACM Trans. Graph. (Proc. SIGGRAPH) **31**(4), 29 (2012)
5. Curless, B., Levoy, M.: A volumetric method for building complex models from range images. In: 1996 Proceedings of the SIGGRAPH, pp. 303–312 (1996)
6. Cutzu, F., Edelman, S.: Canonical views in object representation and recognition. Vis. Res. **34**(22), 3037–3056 (1994)
7. Dutagaci, H., Cheung, C.P., Godil, A.: A benchmark for best view selection of 3D objects. In: Proceedings of the ACM Workshop on 3DOR, pp. 45–50 (2010)
8. Goodfellow, I., et al.: Generative adversarial nets. In: Advances in Neural Information Processing Systems, pp. 2672–2680 (2014)
9. Hayward, W.G.: Effects of outline shape in object recognition. J. Exp. Psychol. Hum. Percept. Perform. **24**(2), 427 (1998)
10. He, J., Wang, L., Zhou, W., Zhang, H., Cui, X., Guo, Y.: Viewpoint assessment and recommendation for photographing architectures. IEEE Trans. Vis. Comput. Graph **25**, 2636–2649 (2018)
11. He, K., Zhang, X., Ren, S., Sun, J.: Delving deep into rectifiers: surpassing human-level performance on imagenet classification. In: Proceedings of the ICCV, pp. 1026–1034 (2015)

12. Huang, H., Kalogerakis, E., Chaudhuri, S., Ceylan, D., Kim, V.G., Yumer, E.: Learning local shape descriptors from part correspondences with multi-view convolutional networks. ACM Trans. Graph. **37**(1), 6 (2018)
13. Kalogerakis, E., Averkiou, M., Maji, S., Chaudhuri, S.: 3D shape segmentation with projective convolutional networks. In: Proceedings of the CVPR, vol. 1, p. 8 (2017)
14. Kim, S.h., Tai, Y.W., Lee, J.Y., Park, J., Kweon, I.S.: Category-specific salient view selection via deep convolutional neural networks. In: Computer Graphics Forum, vol. 36, pp. 313–328. Wiley Online Library (2017)
15. Koch, C., Poggio, T.: Predicting the visual world: silence is golden. Nat. Neurosci. **2**, 9–10 (1999)
16. Lee, C.H., Varshney, A., Jacobs, D.W.: Mesh saliency. ACM Trans. Graph. (Proc. SIGGRAPH) **24**(3), 659–666 (2005)
17. Leifman, G., Shtrom, E., Tal, A.: Surface regions of interest for viewpoint selection. IEEE Trans. Pattern Anal. Mach. Intell. **38**(12), 2544–2556 (2016)
18. Mezuman, E., Weiss, Y.: Learning about canonical views from internet image collections. In: Proceedings of the NIPS, pp. 719–727 (2012)
19. Novotny, D., Larlus, D., Vedaldi, A.: Learning 3D object categories by looking around them. In: Proceedings of the ICCV, October 2017
20. Page, D.L., Koschan, A.F., Sukumar, S.R., Roui-Abidi, B., Abidi, M.A.: Shape analysis algorithm based on information theory. In: Proceedings of the ICIP, vol. 1, p. I-229 (2003)
21. Polonsky, O., Patané, G., Biasotti, S., Gotsman, C., Spagnuolo, M.: What's in an image? Vis. Comput. **21**(8–10), 840–847 (2005)
22. Qi, C.R., Su, H., Nießner, M., Dai, A., Yan, M., Guibas, L.: Volumetric and multi-view CNNs for object classification on 3D data. In: Proceedings of the CVPR, pp. 5648–5656 (2016)
23. Secord, A., Lu, J., Finkelstein, A., Singh, M., Nealen, A.: Perceptual models of viewpoint preference. ACM Trans. Graph. **30**(5), 109 (2011)
24. Shilane, P., Min, P., Kazhdan, M., Funkhouser, T.: The Princeton shape benchmark. In: Proceedings of Shape Modeling Applications (2004)
25. Song, R., Liu, Y., Rosin, P.L.: Distinction of 3D objects and scenes via classification network and Markov random field. IEEE Trans. Vis. Comput. Graph **26**(6), 2204–2218 (2020)
26. Su, H., Maji, S., Kalogerakis, E., Learned-Miller, E.G.: Multi-view convolutional neural networks for 3D shape recognition. In: Proceedings of the ICCV, pp. 945–953 (2015)
27. Tarr, M.J., Pinker, S.: Mental rotation and orientation-dependence in shape recognition. Cogn. Psychol. **21**(2), 233–282 (1989)
28. Vázquez, P.P., Feixas, M., Sbert, M., Heidrich, W.: Viewpoint selection using viewpoint entropy. In: VMV, vol. 1, pp. 273–280 (2001)
29. Vieira, T., et al.: Learning good views through intelligent galleries. In: Computer Graphics Forum, vol. 28, pp. 717–726. Wiley Online Library (2009)
30. 3D Warehouse: https://3dwarehouse.sketchup.com
31. Wolfe, J.M.: Guided search 2.0 A revised model of visual search. Psychon. Bull. Rev. **1**(2), 202–238 (1994). https://doi.org/10.3758/BF03200774

32. Wu, Z., et al.: 3D shapeNets: a deep representation for volumetric shapes. In: Proceedings of the CVPR, pp. 1912–1920 (2015)
33. Yamauchi, H., Saleem, W., Yoshizawa, S., Karni, Z., Belyaev, A., Seidel, H.P.: Towards stable and salient multi-view representation of 3D shapes. In: IEEE International Conference on Shape Modeling and Applications (2006)
34. Zhao, S., Ooi, W.T.: Modeling 3D synthetic view dissimilarity. Vis. Comput. **32**(4), 429–443 (2016). https://doi.org/10.1007/s00371-015-1069-z

Representation Sharing for Fast Object Detector Search and Beyond

Yujie Zhong, Zelu Deng, Sheng Guo, Matthew R. Scott, and Weilin Huang[✉]

Malong LLC, Wilmington, USA
{jaszhong,zeldeng,sheng,mscott,whuang}@malong.com

Abstract. Region Proposal Network (RPN) provides strong support for handling the scale variation of objects in two-stage object detection. For one-stage detectors which do not have RPN, it is more demanding to have powerful sub-networks capable of directly capturing objects of unknown sizes. To enhance such capability, we propose an extremely efficient neural architecture search method, named Fast And Diverse (FAD), to better explore the optimal configuration of receptive fields and convolution types in the sub-networks for one-stage detectors. FAD consists of a designed search space and an efficient architecture search algorithm. The search space contains a rich set of diverse transformations designed specifically for object detection. To cope with the designed search space, a novel search algorithm termed Representation Sharing (RepShare) is proposed to effectively identify the best combinations of the defined transformations. In our experiments, FAD obtains prominent improvements on two types of one-stage detectors with various backbones. In particular, our FAD detector achieves 46.4 AP on MS-COCO (under single-scale testing), outperforming the state-of-the-art detectors, including the most recent NAS-based detectors, Auto-FPN [42] (searched for 16 GPU-days) and NAS-FCOS [39] (28 GPU-days), while significantly reduces the search cost to 0.6 GPU-days. Beyond object detection, we further demonstrate the generality of FAD on the more challenging instance segmentation, and expect it to benefit more tasks.

1 Introduction

Object detection is a fundamental task in computer vision [15,17,18,23,24,30, 31,38,45], but it remains challenging due to the large variation in object scales. To handle the scale variation, a straightforward method is to utilize multi-scale image inputs [34,35], which usually lacks efficiency. A line of more efficient methods is to tackle the scale variation on the intermediate features [17,24]. For example, Feature Pyramid Networks (FPN) [17] is a representative work that implements the detection of objects with different scales in multiple levels of feature pyramids. On the other hand, recent works also attempt to improve the

Electronic supplementary material The online version of this chapter (https://doi.org/10.1007/978-3-030-58529-7_28) contains supplementary material, which is available to authorized users.

A. Vedaldi et al. (Eds.): ECCV 2020, LNCS 12364, pp. 471–487, 2020.
https://doi.org/10.1007/978-3-030-58529-7_28

Table 1. Comparison against other NAS methods for object detection on MS-COCO [19]. *Trans.* indicates the number of transformation types in the search space ('skip-connect' is excluded). *Counterpart* denotes the baseline detectors (and backbone) for direct comparison. * means only the dilation rates are varied.

Method	Search method	Trans.	GPU-days	Counterpart	Relative AP Imp
NAS-FPN [7]	RL	2	> 100	RetinaNet (Res-50)	↑ 2.9
DetNAS [1]	EA	4	44	FPN (ShuffleNetv2)	↑ 2.0
NATS-det [26]	EA	9*	20	RetinaNet (Res-50)	↑ 1.3
Auto-FPN [42]	Gradient	6	16	FPN (Res-50)	↑ 1.9
NAS-FCOS [39]	RL	6	28	FCOS (Res-50)	↑ 1.7
SM-NAS [43]	EA	–	> 100	–	–
FAD (ours)	Gradient	12	**0.6**	FCOS (Res-50)	↑ 1.7

detectors from the perspective of receptive fields (RFs) [15,23]. They enhance the scale-awareness of the detectors by having multi-branch transformations with different combinations of kernel sizes and/or dilation rates. Then the features of different RFs are aggregated to enrich the information of different scales at each spatial location.

An object detector often has a backbone network followed by the detection-specific sub-networks (i.e. heads), which play an important role in object detection. The sub-networks compute the deep features which are used to directly predict the object category, localization and size. Unlike two-stage detectors in which the sub-networks operate on the fixed-size feature maps computed from each object proposal, generated by a region proposal network with ROI-pooling [31], the sub-networks in one-stage detectors should be capable of 'looking for' objects of arbitrary sizes directly. It becomes more challenging for an anchor-free detector. Because the multi-scale anchor boxes can be considered as a way to explicitly handle various sizes and shapes of objects, whereas an anchor-free detector only predicts a single object at each spatial location, without any prior information about the object size. Therefore, for one-stage detectors, especially the anchor-free ones, the capability of the sub-networks for capturing the objects with large scale variation becomes the key. In this work, we aim to enhance the power of the sub-networks in one-stage detectors, by searching for the optimal combination of the RFs and convolutions in a learning-based manner.

Neural Architecture Search (NAS) has gained increasing attention. It transfers the task of neural networks design from a heuristics-guided process to an optimization problem. Recently, it has been shown that NAS can achieve prominent results on object detection [1,7,26,39,42,43]. In most of the work, the operations in the search space are directly extended from those used for image classification [22,48] with limited variation on dilation rates. Therefore, their search spaces with respect to *transformations* are relatively limited, as listed in Table 1. Apart from the combination of RFs, we also investigate the importance of the diversity of the transformations in NAS search space for object detection.

However, searching through such a large number of candidate transformations can be computationally expensive, especially for the RL-based [27,48] and EA-based [29] approaches. Additionally, this problem can be more significant for object detection than image classification, due to the more complicated pipelines with larger input images.

To this end, we propose a computation-friendly method, named Fast And Diverse (FAD), to search for the task-specific sub-networks in one-stage object detectors. FAD consists of a designed search space and an efficient search algorithm. We first design a rich set of diverse transformations tailored for object detection, covering multiple RFs and various convolution types. To learn the optimal combinations more efficiently, a search method via *representation sharing* (RepShare) is proposed accordingly. By sharing intermediate representations, the proposed RepShare significantly reduces the searching time and memory cost for the architecture search. Furthermore, we propose an efficient method to reduce the interference between the transformations sharing the same representations, and at the same time, alleviate the degradation of search quality caused by RepShare.

To demonstrate the effectiveness of the proposed method, we redesign the sub-networks for modern one-stage object detectors, and propose a searchable module for replacement. *The architecture search for the module is extremely efficient using our FAD, which is more than 25× faster than the fastest NAS approach for object detectors so far, while achieving a comparable AP improvement* (see Table 1). With ResNeXt-101 [41] as the backbone, our FAD detector achieves 46.4 AP on the MS-COCO [19] *test-dev* set using a single model under single-scale testing, without using any additional regularization or modules (e.g. deformable conv [3]). Moreover, we show that FAD can also benefit more challenging tasks, such as instance segmentation. The contributions of this work are summarized as:

- We present a novel method, named Fast And Diverse (FAD), to search meaningful transformations in the task-specific sub-networks for one-stage object detection. The search space is designed specifically for object detection, and we empirically investigate the importance of the RFs coverage and convolution types for object detection.
- We propose an efficient search method with a novel representation sharing (RepShare) algorithm, which can significantly reduce the search cost in both time and memory usage, e.g. being more than 25× faster than all previous methods. To ensure the search quality, a new method is introduced to decouple the transformation selection from the shared representations.
- To evaluate our methods, we design a searchable module for one-stage object detection and instance segmentation. Extensive experiments show that our FAD detector obtains consistent performance improvements on different detection frameworks with various backbones, and even has fewer parameters.

2   Related Work

2.1   Object Detection and Instance Segmentation

In general, object detectors can be categorized into two groups: two-stage detectors and one-stage detectors. Modern two-stage detectors [2,31] first adopt a regional proposal network (RPN) to generate a set of object proposals, which are then fed to the R-CNN heads for object classification and bounding box regression. On the other hand, one-stage object detectors [18,24,30] directly perform object classification and box regression simultaneously at each spatial location on the feature maps produced from a backbone network. Taking RetinaNet as an example, it consists of a backbone network with a feature pyramid network (FPN) [17] and two sub-networks for classification and bounding box regression. Recent works attempt to get rid of hand-designed anchor boxes while achieving comparable performance [4,14,38,47]. For instance, FCOS [38] additionally predicts a centerness score which indicates the distance of current location to the center of the corresponding object, and can even outperform RetinaNet.

Receptive Fields (RF). RF is proved to be very important for object detectors [15,23]. For instance, Liu et al. [23] designed a combination of kernel sizes and dilation rates, to simulate the impact of the eccentricities of population receptive fields in human visual cortex. TridentNet [15] tackles the scale variation using multi-branch modules with different dilation rates. In this work, we aim to search for an optimal combination of different conv layers and dilation rates jointly.

Instance Segmentation. Instance segmentation is closely related to object detection, and the dominant instance segmentation methods often have two stages [10,13]: they first detect the objects in an image, and then predict an object mask on each detected region. Mask R-CNN [10] is a representative work in this paradigm, which has an additional mask head on top of Faster R-CNN [31] to perform mask prediction on each object proposal. In this work, we apply the proposed FAD search method to instance segmentation, which has not been explored previously.

2.2   Neural Architecture Search

Recent attention has been moved from network design by hand to neural architecture search (NAS) [21,22,25,27,48]. A stream of efficient NAS methods is the differentiable NAS [22,25]. In particular, DARTS [22] significantly increases the search efficiency by relaxing the categorical choice of operation to be continuous, so that the architecture can be optimized by gradient descent. In this work, we develop an efficient NAS algorithm for object detectors, by fast searching the optimized transformations.

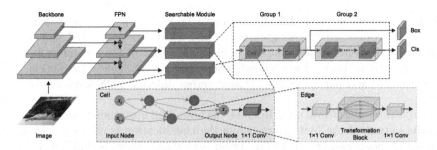

Fig. 1. Search space of FAD for one-stage object detectors. The backbone and FPN [17] in detectors remain the same, while each FPN level is connected to a searchable module. It consists of two groups of cells, with same cell architectures within each group. In a cell, the edges connecting nodes consist of two standard 1×1 conv layers and a transformation block in between. The cell structures and the transformations are to be searched. Each edge might have different RFs, resulting in combinations of RFs at each node which enrich the features for capturing information of various scales.

NAS for Object Detection. NAS has been applied to many vision tasks apart from image classification, such as object detection [1,7,26,42]. For example, NAS-FPN [7] uses a RL-based NAS to search for an optimal FPN [17] on the RetinaNet. DetNAS [1] aims at finding the optimal shuffle-block-based backbone network in object detectors using an evolution algorithm [8,28]. A channel-level NAS is proposed in NATS [26] to search for the backbone in object detectors. Alternatively, some recent works search for the detection-specific parts rather than the backbone for object detection. For instance, Auto-FPN [42] searches for a FPN structure and head structures. SM-NAS [43] also searches for two-stage detectors by first conducting a structural-level search and then a modular-level search. Instead of exploring novel structures, CR-NAS [16] aims to re-allocate the computation resources in the backbone. NAS-FCOS [39] is a FCOS-based detector in which the structure of its FPN and the following sub-networks are computed using RL-based NAS. In this work, we design the search space specifically, and propose the FAD method to search for the sub-networks in one-stage detectors.

3   Fast Diverse-Transformation Search

3.1   Search Space of FAD

One-stage detectors like RetinaNet [18] and FCOS [38] consist of a backbone network with FPN [17] and two parallel sub-networks for object classification and bounding box regression, respectively. In this section, we design a searchable module to replace the commonly-used sub-networks. This module is searched by the proposed FAD, and can be adapted to one-stage object detectors that follow a similar structure as RetinaNet [18] in a plug-and-play fashion. We then describe the novel search space of FAD which is tailored for object detection, including a variety of diverse transformations with different RFs.

Object Detector with FAD. As shown in Fig. 1, the proposed searchable module is comprised of two groups of cells, which are connected sequentially with a shortcut from the input of the module to that of the second group. The module outputs both object classification and bounding box prediction. The architectures and parameters are shared across different FPN levels.

Classification and Regression. In FAD, the bounding box prediction is performed on the output of the first group, while the classification is computed from the output of the second group. The intuition behind this design is that the two tasks should not be implemented on the exactly same feature maps due to different objectives: bounding box regression needs to focus on the local detailed information, while object classification is implemented on the features with more semantic information (i.e. the feature maps on deeper layers). Therefore, we perform bounding box regression on the output of the first group.

Design of Search Space. In the following, we describe the design of the search space for FAD, which is inspired by the insights from modern neural architectures [11,37] and object detectors [15,23]. Three important considerations in our design are the coverage of RFs, the diversity in convolution types and the computational efficiency.

Groups and Cells. A group contains M repeated cells, and each cell is defined as a module that contains multiple nodes and edges. Similar to [20,22], each cell is formulated as a directed acyclic graph of nodes. Each node is a stack of feature maps and each edge is an atomic block for search. In this work, we empirically set the number of nodes in each cell to be 3, excluding the input and output nodes. In our design, an edge consists of two 1×1 conv layers f and a transformation block T between the two (Fig. 1 bottom-right). The transformation block contains a set of candidate transformations which will be described in Sect. 3.2. Each conv layer in the transformation is followed by a group-normalization layer [40] and a ReLU. Given a node x_j, all the predecessors x_i connected to it, and an edge pointing from x_i to x_j, we can have the following expression:

$$x_j = \sum_{i<N}^{N} f_{i,j}^{c',c}(T_{i,j}^{c',c'}(f_{i,j}^{c,c'}(x_i))),$$ (1)

where $f_{i,j}^{c,c'}$ and $f_{i,j}^{c',c}$ are the two 1×1 conv layers, with one transforming the input channel c to the channel used in the transformation block $T_{i,j}^{c',c'}$ and the other vice versa. x_j is computed based on N total number of predecessors. The two 1×1 convolution enable a flexibility in the channel size in T, similar to the inception module [37], while maintaining the same channel size for all the nodes. We empirically found that maintaining a relatively large channel size for nodes is beneficial to the performance. The representations of the intermediate nodes in a cell are concatenated and passed to a 1×1 conv layer to reduce the number of channels back to c. This additional conv layer ensures the consistent channel size between the input and output of each cell. Furthermore, the idea of having two groups of cells enables a larger flexibility for the architecture search, i.e. a larger search space. Within each group, the cells share the same structure. Therefore, once the search is completed, the cells in each group can be repeated for multiple times, offering a great scalability in architecture depth.

Diverse Transformations. Our initial design of the candidate transformations covers 4 different sizes of RFs (Fig. 2 bottom left). In particular, for the transformations that are responsible for a RF larger than 5, we use more efficient operations by having a base filter followed by a dilated convolution which spreads out the base filter to reach larger RFs. Moreover, the dilated conv layers are depthwise separable [12,32], in order to keep the computation efficient. The memory-efficient design introduced in Sect. 3.2, allows us to include more types of convolutions. Hence we have two streams of transformations: the standard conv and the depthwise separable conv. Namely, for the 6 transformations shown in the bottom-left corner of Fig. 2, the 'conv' layers can be all standard convolution or depthwise separable convolution.

There are no pooling layers involved in the search space as we empirically found that they are not helpful in our scenario. This is probably because the spatial resolution of the feature maps remains the same in the sub-networks. Moreover, skip-connection is not included in the transformation. Lastly, a 'none' path, indicating the importance of input edges with respect to each node, is added to the transformation block. In summary, the proposed transformation block contains 13 distinct transformations in total, including 2 types of conv layers and 3 dilation rates, and covering 4 sizes of RFs, as illustrated in Fig. 2. Therefore, we build a meaningful search space with strongly diverse transformations. The resultant search space has roughly 2.3×10^{13} unique paths in total, with one cell per group in search time.

FAD for Instance Segmentation. We expect that the mask prediction task can also benefit from the combination of RFs and diverse transformations. With minimal modification, FAD readily applicable to general instance segmentation frameworks, e.g. Mask R-CNN [10] and Mask Scoring R-CNN [13]. Specifically, we replace the conv layers before the deconvolutional layer in the mask head by the proposed searchable module, and search for its architecture in an end-to-end fashion. The search space is designed by following that of object detectors.

3.2   Fast Search with Representation Sharing

In this section, we propose a novel algorithm to significantly reduce the search cost in both time and memory, followed by the description of search procedure.

Representation Sharing. The proposed acceleration method for architecture search, named RepShare, is performed in two steps: filter decomposing and intermediate representation sharing. We elaborate these two steps in the following.

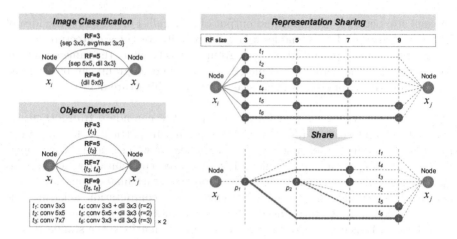

Fig. 2. Transformations and representation sharing. Left: comparison between the transformations used for image classification and those proposed for object detection in the search space. The proposed transformations are listed at the bottom. *conv* can be the standard or the depthwise separable convolution. **Right**: RepShare. Each sphere and solid line denotes a representation and a conv layer, respectively. First, large filters are decomposed into stacks of 3×3 filters. Second, p_1 and p_2 are shared across transformations. Note that the 1×1 conv layers are not shown for simplicity.

Decomposing Large Filters. As proposed in [33], filters with large kernel sizes can be replaced by multiple 3×3 filters. For example, a stack of three 3×3 filters in fact has an equivalent size of receptive filed as a 7×7 filter. The stacked filters have the advantages of fewer parameters and more non-linearities in between for learning more discriminative representations. Following this intuition, we decompose the filters with large kernel size and construct a transformation block only containing filters of size 3×3 (t_1 to t_6 shown in Fig. 2 top-right). However, the replacement of large filters with stacks of small ones significantly increases the memory overhead during the search. Taking the proposed transformations as an example, more than twice intermediate representations are generated after the decomposition.

Representation Sharing. To reduce this memory overhead, we further propose a novel approach. Namely, for each receptive field (RF) level, all the intermediate representations that are not directly connected to node x_j are shared (Fig. 2 bottom-right). To be specific, we denote t_3 in top-right of Fig. 2 as the stem. In the stem, there are 3 intermediate representations having different sizes of RFs with respect to the node x_i. We merge the transformations by sharing the intermediate representations in the stem. For example in Figure 2 (top-right), to merge the t_1 into the stem, we directly connect the first intermediate representation in the stem to node x_j, and therefore the original t_1 (conv 3×3) transformation is replaced by this new transformation. Specifically, the RepSharereduces the number of representations computed in each transformation block from 26 to 12. Therefore, it can significantly speed up the search process. Moreover, the search speed is further boosted by the memory-efficiency of RepSharesince the search can be done using a single GPU, which avoids the computational overhead introduced by training with multiple GPUs (e.g. parameter update).

Relation to Other Efficient Search Methods. The proposed RepSharehas similar spirits to some recent approaches. For instance, parameter sharing introduced in [27] takes the advantage of sharing the same sets of parameters among child models to greatly speed up the search in RL-based NAS methods. It is inspired by parameter inheritance [29] which also reuses the same parameters for child models across mutation to avoid training from scratch. RepShareis more than using the same parameters, but also the same computation. Furthermore, apart from accelerating the search, RepSharefurther reduces the memory consumption. Single-path NAS [36] also share computations, but is different from ours. It considers a small kernel (e.g. 3×3) as the core of a large one (e.g. 5×5), and uses a learnable threshold to compare the importance of the two kernels, and selects the optimal one.

Decoupling Shared Representations. Similar to parameter sharing described in [27] in which child models are coupled to some extent due to reusing the same weights, RepSharealso exhibits such behaviour. In RepShare, transformations sharing the same representations might interfere with each other, and thus the parameters directly corresponding to the shared representations are not well optimized in the search. It causes that those transformations are difficult to outstand in the architecture derivation. For example, in Fig. 2 (bottom-right), two intermediate representations are shared. Namely, p_1 is shared across all six transformations and p_2 is shared across t_2, t_3 and t_5. Due to the coupling effect (i.e. interference between transformations), t_1 and t_2 are not able to learn the optimal parameters on their own, which may degrade the search quality. Notably, this effect mainly happens on t_1 and t_2, since their outputs are exactly the shared representations; while other transformations (t_3 to t_6) have the flexibility to compensate this effect due to additional operations on the share representations.

Decoupling with Extra Functions. To address this issue in RepShare, we propose a simple yet effective method to decouple the transformations (that directly depend on the shared representations, i.e. t_1 and t_2) from the shared representations. Namely, an additional function H is applied between each shared representation and its corresponding transformation output. With this additional function, for example, the output of t_1 is no longer p_1, but $H(p_1)$. In this case, t_1 and t_2 are decoupled from p_1 and p_2, respectively. For the choice of H, we use a standard 1×1 conv layer followed by a ReLU. This light-weight extra function produces minimal computational overhead and is applied to both conv streams (i.e. the standard and depthwise separable convolution streams).

Optimization and Deriving Architectures. In a cell, each edge contains a transformation block in which the final transformation is determined from a set of candidates illustrated in Fig. 2. In order to search using back-propagation, we follow the continuous relaxation for the search space as [22], and adapt it to the proposed RepShareparadigm. For each of the two streams (Fig. 2 bottom-right) in the transformation block, the output of a transformation $(T_{i,j})$ is essentially the sum of all the intermediate representations multiplied with corresponding α. Therefore, we can have:

$$T_{i,j}(x_i') = \sum_{p \in P} \frac{\exp\left(\alpha_{i,j}^p\right)}{\sum_{p' \in P} \exp\left(\alpha_{i,j}^{p'}\right)} \, p, \tag{2}$$

where x_i' is the output of the first 1×1 conv layer in the transformation block. p and p' are the intermediate representations out of all representations P. α^p is the α corresponding to p.

Optimization and Derivation of Discrete Architectures. During the architecture search, α and the network weights w are jointly optimized in a bilevel optimization scheme, as in [20,22]. In particular, the first-order approximation is adopted. At the end of the search, a discrete architecture is decoded by retaining one transformation per edge and two input edges for each node based on the largest α in each transformation block. Since the intermediate representations are selected instead of operations, they should then be mapped to the corresponding actual transformations in the derived architecture, i.e. the transformations in Fig. 2 (top-right).

4 Experiments

In this section, the proposed FAD is evaluated in two tasks: object detection and instance segmentation. In the Supplementary Material (SM), we further conduct experiments for image classification to analyze the effect of decoupling in RepShare.

4.1 Object Detection

Implementation Details. Although the proposed module can be adopted to different one-stage object detectors, we perform the architecture search using FAD on FCOS [38], due to its efficiency. The search is conducted on the PAS-CAL VOC [5]. We also perform the search directly on MS-COCO [19] and make comparisons in Table 2. More implementation details, including the search and the detector training, can be found in the SM.

Ablation Study. We conduct ablation study on the search cost, search spaces, as well as different backbones and detectors. More studies on the marco-structure of the module, and network width and depth are presented in SM.

Table 2. Comparison for the architecture search. *Memory* and *bs* denotes the memory usage and images per GPU. Both *Subset* and *Full* refer to the proposed search space. *Sep.* and *Std.* mean that only depthwise and standard conv are used, respectively. ResNet-50 is used as the backbone. Results are obtained on the MS-COCO *minival* split. All the searches are performed on VOC, expect for [†] which is on MS-COCO.

Method	RepShare	Search Space	Trans.	RFs	Memory (G)	GPU-days	AP
FCOS [38]	–	–	–	–	–	–	38.6
Random	–	Full	12	3,5,7,9	–	–	39.0
FAD	✗	DARTS [22]	7	5,7,9	~ 10 (bs = 4)	0.4	39.0
FAD	✓	Subset 1	4	3,5	~ 7 (bs = 4)	0.25	39.2
FAD	✓	Subset 2	8	3,5,7	~ 11 (bs = 4)	0.5	39.7
FAD	✓	Sep. only	6	3,5,7,9	~ 10 (bs = 4)	0.36	39.5
FAD	✓	Std. only	6	3,5,7,9	~ 9.5 (bs = 4)	0.4	39.9
FAD	✓	w/o decouple	12	3,5,7,9	~ 12 (bs = 4)	0.6	40.0
FAD	✓	Full	12	3,5,7,9	~ 12 (bs = 4)	0.6	**40.3**
FAD	✗	Full	12	3,5,7,9	~ 9 (bs = 1)	2.3	**40.3**
FAD[†]	✓	Full	12	3,5,7,9	~ 9 (bs = 4)	5.5	**40.3**

Search Cost. The time required for a complete architecture search using our FAD is 0.6 GPU-days. A single TITAN XP is used for the search. Table 1 compares the search cost of FAD against other NAS-based methods for object detection. As we can see, the search speed for FAD is at least 25× faster than other recent approaches, while achieving a similar relative AP improvement on MS-COCO. Meanwhile, the architecture explored by FAD is scalable in depth by simply adding the repetitive cells in the groups, which provides greater flexibility to the module.

Search Space. To demonstrate the superiority of the proposed search space, we reuse the same search procedure but replace the proposed search operations with that in DARTS [22], which are listed in Fig. 2 (top-left). Note that the depthwise separable convolution is doubled in DARTS, and hence the RFs change accordingly. As we can see from Table 2, the operations used in DARTS only bring a marginal improvement of 0.4 AP, compared to the original FCOS, while *the proposed transformations improve the performance significantly, from 38.6 to 40.3.* To further study the importance of the full transformation set, we search by using two transformation subsets. Namely, the two subsets contain transformations with the RFs smaller than 7 and 9, respectively. Our results show that with less transformations in the search space, the performance degrades accordingly. Moreover, we search by using only one type of convolution (either the standard or the depthwise separable) for the conv layers with dilation rate of 1. Not surprisingly, both of them fail to achieve a similar performance as the full search space. This illustrates the power of the proposed transformations which fully benefit from the better combinations of RFs and convolution types. Besides, the performance slightly degrades without decoupling. More results on

Table 3. FAD on different detectors and backbones. The → indicates the change from original detector to FAD. *Dim.* is the channel size in the subnets, or c' in the transformation block in FAD. Results are obtained on MS-COCO *minival*.

Method	Backbone	Dim.	Params (M)	FLOPs (G)	AP
FCOS	MobileNetV2	256 → 96	9.8 → 9.0	124 → 108	31.3 → 32.7
	Res-50	256 → 96	32.2 → 31.5	201 → 185	38.6 → 40.3
	Res-101	256 → 96	51.2 → 50.4	277 → 261	43.0 → 44.2
	Res-X-101	256 → 96	90.0 → 89.2	439 → 423	44.7 → 45.8
	Res-X-101	256 → 128	90.0 → 91.2	439 → 465	44.7 → **46.0**
RetinaNet	Res-50	256 → 96	33.8 → 33.0	234 → 218	36.1 → 37.7
	Res-101	256 → 96	52.7 → 52.0	310 → 294	37.7 → 39.4
	Res-X-101	256 → 128	91.5 → 92.7	472 → 498	39.8 → **41.6**
Subnet only	-	256 → 96	4.9 → 4.1	105 → 89	-

decoupling can be found in the SM. Another observation is that the proxyless search on MS-COCO can achieve similar performance on detection, but it takes much longer search time. Hence, we use the architecture searched on VOC for object detection for the rest of this work.

In addition, our FAD is also compared with the 'random' baseline. Namely, a transformation is randomly sampled in each block and two edges are randomly sampled for each node. It can be found that the proposed FAD indeed finds much better architectures. The last conclusion to draw in Table 2 is that, comparing to the search without RepShare, *RepShare enables an almost* 4× *faster search with only one third of the GPU memory usage*, without harming the performance.

Adaptation to Different Backbone Networks. We replace the ResNet-50 in the detector by using three different networks: MobileNetV2 [12], ResNet-101 [11] and ResNeXt-101 [41]. As shown in Table 3, our FAD obtains a consistent improvement (about 1.4 AP on average) for all the backbones compared, with even fewer parameters and FLOPs. This indicates that the architecture of FAD generalizes well to the backbone networks with different capacity. A direct comparison on the sub-networks (without the backbone and FPN) shows a 16.3% and 15.2% decrease on the number of parameters and the FLOPs. Hence, we can conclude that the performance gain is obtained from the better architecture searched rather than the network capacity itself.

Transferability. Our FAD is expected to be readily applicable to different types of one-stage object detectors (with the two-subnet structure). To examine this property, we further plug the proposed searchable module into RetinaNet [18]. Table 3 reveals that FAD can also improve the performance of RetinaNet by a large margin even with fewer parameters. Therefore, we see that the searched sub-networks can boost the performance of different types of detectors (and potentially more powerful detectors in the future) in a plug-and-play fashion.

Table 4. Comparison with the state-of-the-art object detectors on the MS-COCO *test-dev* split (including concurrent work [9,39,44,46]). FCOS [38] is used as the base detector for FAD. All the results are tested under the single-scale and single-model setting. Note that models using additional regularization method [6] and deformable convolution [3] are excluded in the table (except for NAS-FCOS [39]).

Two-stage detectors	Backbone	**AP**	AP_{50}	AP_{75}	AP_S	AP_M	AP_L
TridentNet[15]	ResNet-101	42.7	63.6	46.5	23.9	46.6	56.6
Auto-FPN [42]	ResNeXt-64x4d-101	44.3	–	–	–	–	–
SM-NAS: E5 [43]	Searched	45.9	64.6	49.6	27.1	49.0	58.0
Hit-Detector [9]	Searched	44.5	–	–	–	–	–
One-stage detectors							
RetinaNet [18]	ResNeXt-101	40.8	61.1	44.1	24.1	44.2	51.2
CenterNet511 [4]	Hourglass-104	44.9	62.4	48.1	25.6	47.4	57.4
FSAF [47]	ResNeXt-64x4d-101	42.9	63.8	46.3	26.6	46.2	52.7
FCOS [38]	ResNeXt-64x4d-101	44.7	64.1	48.4	27.6	47.5	55.6
FreeAnchor [45]	ResNeXt-101	44.9	64.3	48.5	26.8	48.3	55.9
SAPD [46]	ResNeXt-64x4d-101	45.4	65.6	48.9	27.3	48.7	56.8
ATSS [44]	ResNeXt-64x4d-101	45.6	64.6	49.7	28.5	48.9	55.6
NAS-FPN [7] (7 @ 384)	ResNet-50	45.4	–	–	–	–	–
NAS-FCOS [39]	ResNeXt-64x4d-101	46.1	–	–	–	–	–
FAD @ 96	ResNet-101	44.1	62.7	47.9	26.8	47.1	54.6
FAD @ 128	ResNet-101	44.5	63.0	48.3	27.1	47.4	55.0
FAD @ 128	ResNeXt-64x4d-101	46.0	64.9	50.0	29.1	48.8	56.6
FAD @ 128-256	ResNeXt-64x4d-101	**46.4**	65.4	50.4	29.4	49.3	57.4

Comparison with the State-of-the-Art. We compare FAD with the state-of-the-art object detectors on the MS-COCO *test–dev* split, including some recent NAS-based object detectors. All the methods are evaluated under the single-model and single-scale setting. Table 4 shows that, by having 128 channels in the first group and 256 in the second (with 98.3M parameters), FAD @128-256 achieves 46.4 AP which surpasses all the recent object detectors, including two concurrent work, NAS-FCOS [39] and Hit-Detector [9]. Note that NAS-FCOS includes the deformable convolution [3] in the search space, which is not considered in other NAS-based detectors (including our FAD), and it is well-known for giving large AP improvements. On the other hand, the search of FAD is almost 50× faster than that of NAS-FCOS on the same dataset (i.e. VOC).

Searched Architectures. The derived architectures by FAD are presented in Fig. 3. We have two interesting observations. First, the edges correspond to a mixture of RFs (especially for the cell group for classification) and convolution

Fig. 3. Architectures searched for object detection. The left and right cells are for the first and second group, respectively. *std*, *sep* and *dil* denote the standard, depthwise separable and dilated conv.

Table 5. Comparison on instance segmentation *mask* AP on the MS-COCO *minival* split. *P.* is for parameters (M) and *F.* is for FLOPs (G).

Method	Backbone	P.	F.	AP	AP$_{50}$	AP$_{75}$	AP$_S$	AP$_M$	AP$_L$
Mask R-CNN [10]	Res-50	44.3	285	34.2	55.7	36.3	15.4	36.8	50.9
	Res-101	63.3	362	36.1	58.1	38.3	16.4	38.9	53.4
Mask FAD	Res-50	44.4	287	35.5	56.8	37.9	16.0	38.4	52.7
	Res-101	63.4	364	37.0	58.6	39.5	17.0	39.8	54.9
MS R-CNN [13]	Res-50	60.7	326	35.6	56.2	38.2	16.6	37.8	52.0
	Res-101	79.6	402	37.4	58.3	40.2	17.5	40.2	54.4
MS FAD	Res-50	60.8	328	36.3	56.3	39.2	16.1	38.8	53.4
	Res-101	79.7	404	**38.0**	58.7	41.0	17.6	41.0	55.1

types, which again validates our motivation. Another important insight is that the transformations with large RFs (i.e. 7 and 9) appear near the input node, while those with small RFs (i.e. 3 and 5) are closer to the output node. This is consistent with the DetNAS architecture explored in [1].

4.2   Instance Segmentation

To showcase the generality of the proposed FAD, we apply it to another useful task – instance segmentation. Different from object detection, only one group of cell is searched in the mask head. The search is conducted on MS-COCO, which takes 2.6 GPU-days. For a fair comparison, we exactly follow [10,13] for training the searched networks. The search and training details are described in the SM.

Results. Table 5 shows that, with similar number of parameters and FLOPs, all FAD outperform their counterparts with same backbones on both Mask R-CNN and MS R-CNN. Notably, Mask FAD has relatively larger improvements in terms of AP$_M$ and AP$_L$ (e.g. 1.6 and 1.8 AP on ResNet-50) than AP$_S$ (0.6 AP), possibly due to the transformations with larger RFs. Another surprising result is that Mask FAD (ResNet-50) achieves similar AP as MS R-CNN (ResNet-50), i.e. 35.5 vs. 35.6, despite a simpler pipeline and 26.9% fewer parameters. The improvements are prominent since we only modify the mask head architecture which only accounts for 2.25M parameters, i.e. 2.8% to 5% of the whole networks.

5   Conclusion

In this work, we propose FAD to efficiently search for better sub-networks with diverse transformations and optimal combinations of RFs for one-stage object detection and instance segmentation. To demonstrate the effectiveness of the proposed search space and search method, we design a searchable module for the two tasks at hand (and potentially applicable to other tasks). Extensive experiments show that the architectures searched by our FAD can consistently outperform their counterparts on different detectors and segmentation networks.

References

1. Chen, Y., Yang, T., Zhang, X., Meng, G., Pan, C., Sun, J.: DetNAS: backbone search for object detection. arXiv preprint arXiv:1903.10979 (2019)
2. Dai, J., Li, Y., He, K., Sun, J.: R-FCN: object detection via region-based fully convolutional networks. In: Advances in Neural Information Processing Systems, pp. 379–387 (2016)
3. Dai, J., et al.: Deformable convolutional networks. In: Proceedings of the IEEE International Conference on Computer Vision, pp. 764–773 (2017)
4. Duan, K., Bai, S., Xie, L., Qi, H., Huang, Q., Tian, Q.: CenterNet: keypoint triplets for object detection. In: Proceedings of the IEEE International Conference on Computer Vision, pp. 6569–6578 (2019)
5. Everingham, M., Van Gool, L., Williams, C.K., Winn, J., Zisserman, A.: The pascal visual object classes (VOC) challenge. Int. J. Comput. Vis. 88(2), 303–338 (2010). https://doi.org/10.1007/s11263-009-0275-4
6. Ghiasi, G., Lin, T.Y., Le, Q.V.: DropBlock: a regularization method for convolutional networks. In: Advances in Neural Information Processing Systems, pp. 10727–10737 (2018)
7. Ghiasi, G., Lin, T.Y., Le, Q.V.: NAS-FPN: learning scalable feature pyramid architecture for object detection. In: Proceedings of the IEEE Conference on Computer Vision and Pattern Recognition, pp. 7036–7045 (2019)
8. Goldberg, D.E., Deb, K.: A comparative analysis of selection schemes used in genetic algorithms. In: Foundations of Genetic Algorithms, vol. 1, pp. 69–93. Elsevier (1991)
9. Guo, J., et al.: Hit-detector: hierarchical trinity architecture search for object detection. In: Proceedings of the IEEE/CVF Conference on Computer Vision and Pattern Recognition, pp. 11405–11414 (2020)
10. He, K., Gkioxari, G., Dollár, P., Girshick, R.: Mask R-CNN. In: Proceedings of the IEEE International Conference on Computer Vision, pp. 2961–2969 (2017)
11. He, K., Zhang, X., Ren, S., Sun, J.: Deep residual learning for image recognition. In: Proceedings of the IEEE Conference on Computer Vision and Pattern Recognition, pp. 770–778 (2016)
12. Howard, A.G., et al.: MobileNets: efficient convolutional neural networks for mobile vision applications. arXiv preprint arXiv:1704.04861 (2017)
13. Huang, Z., Huang, L., Gong, Y., Huang, C., Wang, X.: Mask scoring R-CNN. In: Proceedings of the IEEE Conference on Computer Vision and Pattern Recognition, pp. 6409–6418 (2019)

14. Law, H., Deng, J.: CornerNet: detecting objects as paired keypoints. In: Ferrari, V., Hebert, M., Sminchisescu, C., Weiss, Y. (eds.) Computer Vision – ECCV 2018. LNCS, vol. 11218, pp. 765–781. Springer, Cham (2018). https://doi.org/10.1007/978-3-030-01264-9_45

15. Li, Y., Chen, Y., Wang, N., Zhang, Z.: Scale-aware trident networks for object detection. arXiv preprint arXiv:1901.01892 (2019)

16. Liang, F., et al.: Computation reallocation for object detection. arXiv preprint arXiv:1912.11234 (2019)

17. Lin, T.Y., Dollár, P., Girshick, R., He, K., Hariharan, B., Belongie, S.: Feature pyramid networks for object detection. In: Proceedings of the IEEE Conference on Computer Vision and Pattern Recognition, pp. 2117–2125 (2017)

18. Lin, T.Y., Goyal, P., Girshick, R., He, K., Dollár, P.: Focal loss for dense object detection. In: Proceedings of the IEEE International Conference on Computer Vision, pp. 2980–2988 (2017)

19. Lin, T.-Y., et al.: Microsoft COCO: common objects in context. In: Fleet, D., Pajdla, T., Schiele, B., Tuytelaars, T. (eds.) ECCV 2014. LNCS, vol. 8693, pp. 740–755. Springer, Cham (2014). https://doi.org/10.1007/978-3-319-10602-1_48

20. Liu, C., et al.: Auto-DeepLab: hierarchical neural architecture search for semantic image segmentation. In: Proceedings of the IEEE Conference on Computer Vision and Pattern Recognition, pp. 82–92 (2019)

21. Liu, C., et al.: Progressive neural architecture search. In: Ferrari, V., Hebert, M., Sminchisescu, C., Weiss, Y. (eds.) ECCV 2018. LNCS, vol. 11205, pp. 19–35. Springer, Cham (2018). https://doi.org/10.1007/978-3-030-01246-5_2

22. Liu, H., Simonyan, K., Yang, Y.: DARTS: differentiable architecture search. arXiv preprint arXiv:1806.09055 (2018)

23. Liu, S., Huang, D., Wang, Y.: Receptive field block net for accurate and fast object detection. In: Ferrari, V., Hebert, M., Sminchisescu, C., Weiss, Y. (eds.) ECCV 2018. LNCS, vol. 11215, pp. 404–419. Springer, Cham (2018). https://doi.org/10.1007/978-3-030-01252-6_24

24. Liu, W., et al.: SSD: single shot MultiBox detector. In: Leibe, B., Matas, J., Sebe, N., Welling, M. (eds.) ECCV 2016. LNCS, vol. 9905, pp. 21–37. Springer, Cham (2016). https://doi.org/10.1007/978-3-319-46448-0_2

25. Luo, R., Tian, F., Qin, T., Chen, E., Liu, T.Y.: Neural architecture optimization. In: Advances in Neural Information Processing Systems, pp. 7816–7827 (2018)

26. Peng, J., Sun, M., Zhang, Z., Tan, T., Yan, J.: Efficient neural architecture transformation searchin channel-level for object detection. arXiv preprint arXiv:1909.02293 (2019)

27. Pham, H., Guan, M.Y., Zoph, B., Le, Q.V., Dean, J.: Efficient neural architecture search via parameter sharing. arXiv preprint arXiv:1802.03268 (2018)

28. Real, E., Aggarwal, A., Huang, Y., Le, Q.V.: Regularized evolution for image classifier architecture search. In: Proceedings of the AAAI Conference on Artificial Intelligence, vol. 33, pp. 4780–4789 (2019)

29. Real, E., et al.: Large-scale evolution of image classifiers. In: Proceedings of the 34th International Conference on Machine Learning-Volume 70, pp. 2902–2911. JMLR. org (2017)

30. Redmon, J., Farhadi, A.: YOLOv3: an incremental improvement. arXiv preprint arXiv:1804.02767 (2018)

31. Ren, S., He, K., Girshick, R., Sun, J.: Faster R-CNN: towards real-time object detection with region proposal networks. In: Advances in Neural Information Processing Systems, pp. 91–99 (2015)

32. Sifre, L., Mallat, S.: Rigid-motion scattering for image classification. Ph.D. dissertation (2014)
33. Simonyan, K., Zisserman, A.: Very deep convolutional networks for large-scale image recognition. arXiv preprint arXiv:1409.1556 (2014)
34. Singh, B., Davis, L.S.: An analysis of scale invariance in object detection SNIP. In: Proceedings of the IEEE Conference on Computer Vision and Pattern Recognition, pp. 3578–3587 (2018)
35. Singh, B., Najibi, M., Davis, L.S.: SNIPER: efficient multi-scale training. In: Advances in Neural Information Processing Systems, pp. 9310–9320 (2018)
36. Stamoulis, D., et al.: Single-Path NAS: designing hardware-efficient convnets in less than 4 hours. arXiv preprint arXiv:1904.02877 (2019)
37. Szegedy, C., et al.: Going deeper with convolutions. In: Proceedings of the IEEE Conference on Computer Vision and Pattern Recognition, pp. 1–9 (2015)
38. Tian, Z., Shen, C., Chen, H., He, T.: FCOS: fully convolutional one-stage object detection. arXiv preprint arXiv:1904.01355 (2019)
39. Wang, N., Gao, Y., Chen, H., Wang, P., Tian, Z., Shen, C.: NAS-FCOS: fast neural architecture search for object detection. arXiv preprint arXiv:1906.04423 (2019)
40. Wu, Y., He, K.: Group normalization. In: Ferrari, V., Hebert, M., Sminchisescu, C., Weiss, Y. (eds.) ECCV 2018. LNCS, vol. 11217, pp. 3–19. Springer, Cham (2018). https://doi.org/10.1007/978-3-030-01261-8_1
41. Xie, S., Girshick, R., Dollár, P., Tu, Z., He, K.: Aggregated residual transformations for deep neural networks (2017)
42. Xu, H., Yao, L., Zhang, W., Liang, X., Li, Z.: Auto-FPN: automatic network architecture adaptation for object detection beyond classification. In: Proceedings of the IEEE International Conference on Computer Vision, pp. 6649–6658 (2019)
43. Yao, L., Xu, H., Zhang, W., Liang, X., Li, Z.: SM-NAS: structural-to-modular neural architecture search for object detection. arXiv preprint arXiv:1911.09929 (2019)
44. Zhang, S., Chi, C., Yao, Y., Lei, Z., Li, S.Z.: Bridging the gap between anchor-based and anchor-free detection via adaptive training sample selection. In: Proceedings of the IEEE/CVF Conference on Computer Vision and Pattern Recognition, pp. 9759–9768 (2020)
45. Zhang, X., Wan, F., Liu, C., Ji, R., Ye, Q.: FreeAnchor: learning to match anchors for visual object detection. In: Advances in Neural Information Processing Systems, pp. 147–155 (2019)
46. Zhu, C., Chen, F., Shen, Z., Savvides, M.: Soft anchor-point object detection. arXiv preprint arXiv:1911.12448 (2019)
47. Zhu, C., He, Y., Savvides, M.: Feature selective anchor-free module for single-shot object detection. arXiv preprint arXiv:1903.00621 (2019)
48. Zoph, B., Le, Q.V.: Neural architecture search with reinforcement learning. arXiv preprint arXiv:1611.01578 (2016)

Peeking into Occluded Joints: A Novel Framework for Crowd Pose Estimation

Lingteng Qiu[1,2,3], Xuanye Zhang[1,2], Yanran Li[4], Guanbin Li[5], Xiaojun Wu[3], Zixiang Xiong[6], Xiaoguang Han[1,2(✉)], and Shuguang Cui[1,2]

[1] The Chinese University of Hong Kong, Shenzhen, China
hanxiaoguang@cuhk.edu.cn
[2] Shenzhen Research Institute of Big Data, Shenzhen, China
[3] Harbin Institute of Technology, Shenzhen, China
[4] Bournemouth University, Poole, UK
[5] Sun Yat-sen University, Guangzhou, China
[6] Texas A and M University, College Station, USA

Abstract. Although occlusion widely exists in nature and remains a fundamental challenge for pose estimation, existing heatmap-based approaches suffer serious degradation on occlusions. Their intrinsic problem is that they directly localize the joints based on visual information; however, the invisible joints are lack of that. In contrast to localization, our framework estimates the invisible joints from an inference perspective by proposing an Image-Guided Progressive GCN module which provides a comprehensive understanding of both image context and pose structure. Moreover, existing benchmarks contain limited occlusions for evaluation. Therefore, we thoroughly pursue this problem and propose a novel OPEC-Net framework together with a new Occluded Pose (OCPose) dataset with 9k annotated images. Extensive quantitative and qualitative evaluations on benchmarks demonstrate that OPEC-Net achieves significant improvements over recent leading works. Notably, our OCPose is the most complex occlusion dataset with respect to average IoU between adjacent instances. Source code and OCPose will be publicly available.

Keywords: Pose estimation · Occlusion · Progressive GCN

1 Introduction

Human pose estimation is a long-standing problem in Computer Vision. It has still attracted increasing attentions in recent years due to rising demands for wide range of applications which require human pose as input [2,4,7,11,16,18,22].

L. Qiu and X. Zhang—Equal contributions.

Electronic supplementary material The online version of this chapter (https://doi.org/10.1007/978-3-030-58529-7_29) contains supplementary material, which is available to authorized users.

© Springer Nature Switzerland AG 2020
A. Vedaldi et al. (Eds.): ECCV 2020, LNCS 12364, pp. 488–504, 2020.
https://doi.org/10.1007/978-3-030-58529-7_29

Despite the significant progress achieved in this area by advanced deep learning techniques [3,6,8,13,24], pose estimation in crowd scenarios still remains extremely challenging due to the intractable occlusion problem.

Trending models for crowd pose estimation strongly rely on heatmap representation for joints estimation: albeit being effective for visible joints, these methods still suffer performance degradation on occlusions and this is due to the fact that, since invisible joints are hidden, it is infeasible to directly localize them. To date, researchers have made painstaking efforts and complicated remedies in developing heatmap models and improving their accuracy of localization. However, the occlusion problem has only received little attention and only few attempts have been made into solving it. As illustrated in Fig. 1, the current state-of-the-art work still produces very awkward poses and fails to estimate the occluded joints.

Fig. 1. The current SOTA method [13] (left) vs. our method (right). Our method demonstrates a more natural and accurate estimation for occluded joints

Occlusion is an intractable challenge in pose estimation due to the complicated background context, complex intertwined human poses and arbitrary occluded shape. To reveal the hidden joints, it becomes necessary to have a comprehensive inference method rather than simple localization. *Our key insight is that the invisible joints are strongly related to contextual understanding of the image and structural understanding of the human pose.* For example, humans can easily infer the location of invisible joints using clues derived from the action type and the image context. Therefore, we delve deeper into the clues needed for invisible joints inference and propose a novel framework OPEC-Net to incorporate these clues for multi-person pose estimation. To achieve this goal, two stages are proposed in our framework: Initial Pose Estimation and GCN-based Pose Correction. The first stage generates heatmaps to produce an initial pose and the subsequent correction stage adjusts the initial pose obtained from the heatmaps by an Image-Guided Progressive GCN (IGP-GCN) module.

The correction module deals with the image context and pose structure clues in the following aspects: (1) The human body structure provides the essential constraint information between joints. For this reason, the correction module is designed as a GCN-based network, which offers an explicit way of modeling the body structural information that is advantageous for correcting the joints.

(2) Another important clue to infer the invisible joints is their related image context. Considering that, our GCN network is specially designed in an Image-Guided way: The IGP-GCN feeds both the coordinate of joints and also the image features extracted at the location of joints as input to each graph node. Therefore, the multi-scale image features from the heatmap modules are fed into the IGP-GCN in a progressive way, so that large displacements can be learned steadily. This enables the IGP-GCN to not only capture pose structural information but also the contextual image information at the same time. (3) In a crowd scenario, human interaction information becomes vital to infer poses. Therefore, we further formulate a CoupleGraph by connecting the corresponding joints of two instances, making the interaction between the pair of people contribute to our estimation results as well. However, the multi-scale image features learnt for heatmap estimation are not compatible for the coordinate correction module. Thus, a Cascaded Feature Adaption (CFA) strategy is introduced to process the features first: since the finer image feature has lost more global contextual information, we fuse the low-level features with high-level features following a cascaded design in order to strengthen their contextual information.

Finally, our framework is trained in an end-to-end fashion and addresses occlusion problem in an elegant way. Interestingly, the heatmap module and coordinate GCN module are complementary in our framework: the quantisation error introduced from the heatmap modules can be addressed by the IGP-GCN and, at the same time, the heatmap modules offer a more accurate initial value for IGP-GCN that benefits the correction.

We conduct comprehensive experiments and introduce a new dataset to evaluate our framework. While occlusion cases are ubiquitous in crowded scenarios, only few existing benchmarks include enough complex examples tailored to the evaluation of this problem. Thus, it becomes necessary to have datasets that that not only contain light occlusions but also include heavily occluded scenes, such as waltz and wrestling, in which individuals are intertwined in complex ways. However, this field is still lacking such datasets because annotating human poses in heavily occluded scenes is very difficult and requires massive manual work. Therefore, we introduce a new dataset called **Occluded Pose (OCPose)** that includes more complex occlusions. We manually label all the 18k groundtruth human poses of the 9k images in OCPose. We also compare the average intersection over union (IoU) with typical datasets. MSCOCO [15] and MPII [1] have less than 5% data with IoU higher than 30%, in contrast, our dataset OCPose contains 90% data with IoU higher than 30%.

In summary, the contributions of this work are:

- To the best of our knowledge, this is the first attempt at tackling the challenging problem of occluded joints from digging the image context and pose structure clues in an inference perspective. A novel framework, named OPEC-Net, is proposed, which significantly outperforms existing methods.
- Our approach designs a novel Image-Guided Progressive GCN to accommodate the structural pose information and contextual image information for correction in a single pass.

– We contribute a carefully-annotated 9 K human pose dataset **OCPose** that includes highly challenging occluded scenes. To the best of our knowledge, OCPose is one of the datasets that contains the most complex occlusions to date. The OCPose dataset will be released to the public to facilitate research in the pose estimation field.

2   Related Works

Heatmap-Based Models for Pose Estimation

Models for multi-person pose estimation (MPPE) can be divided into two categories, namely bottom-up and top-down approaches. The bottom-up methods first detect the joints and then assign them to the matching person. Pioneer works of bottom-up methods [3,10,17,21,26] attempted to design different joint grouping strategies. Newell *et al.* [17] introduced a stacked hourglass network to utilize the tagging heatmap. DeepCut [21] presented an Integer Linear Program (ILP) and Zanfir *et al.* [26] grouped joints by learned scoring functions. Cao *et al.* [3] proposed a novel 2d vector field Part Affinity Fields (PAFs) for association as well. However, these prior works all have a serious deficiency that the invisible joints will decrease the performance drastically.

In the second category, the top-down methods first detect all people in the scene and then perform pose estimation for each person. Most of the existing top-down approaches [6,8,19] focused on proposing a more effective human detector to obtain better results. Fang *et al.* [6] proposed a framework which is more robust for the redundant human bounding box. Li *et al.* [13] designed a global maximum joints association algorithm to address the association problem in crowd scenarios. Nevertheless, all of these strategies are unable to adequately reduce errors, especially in the severe occlusion cases, where one bounding box captures joints of multiple people. Most of the mainstream approaches are heatmap-based and thus are limited to estimating invisible joints which are lack of visual information. Therefore, we propose an OPEC-Net which completely differ from these works and is able to estimate invisible joints by inference rather than by localization.

GCN for Pose Modelling. The human body shows a natural graph structure, so that some advanced work constructed graph networks to address human pose related problems, such as action recognition [25], motion prediction [14], 3D pose regression [5,28]. These work intuitively form the natural human pose as a graph and apply convolutional layers on it. Compared to other approaches, Graph Convolutional Networks demonstrate one compelling advantage when deal with human pose modeling problem: they are more effective in capturing dependency relationships between joints.

Previous work [14,25] achieved a significant gap of improvements in human motion understanding by forming the spatial and temporal relationships as edges in graph. Moreover, pose regression from 2D to 3D is a natural graph prediction problem so that a new SemGCN [28] is proposed in this field. However, GCN frameworks are never introduced for keypoints detection problem such as MPPE.

In comparison, our graph network is specially designed for keypoints detection and contains a progressive learning strategy and guided by image features.

3   OPEC-Net: Occluded Pose Estimation and Correction

Existing pose estimation approaches achieve striking results on visible joints but produce wildly inaccurate outcomes on invisible ones. This is mainly due to the fact that localizing invisible joints from the heatmap is very challenging since they are occluded and there is a lack of visual information. To rectify this shortcoming, we introduce a novel framework that infers invisible joints from the image contextual and pose structural clues.

Considering that, we generate an initial pose from a heatmap-based module and process it into an GCN-based joints correction module to learn their precise position. An Image-Guided GCN network (IGP-GCN) and a Cascaded Feature Adaption module is proposed in the correction stage. The IGP-GCN network exploits the human body structure and image context together to optimize the estimation results. By learning the displacements in a progressive way, it also offers a stable way to achieve more accurate results.

The heatmap and coordinate modules in our framework are actually inter-dependent. Due to our heatmap inference network, the IGP-GCN module has a more accurate pose initialization, which also contributes to a more precise local contextual understanding, before conducting corrections. On the other hand, coordinate based IGP-GCN also addresses the limitation of heatmap modules: due to a size limit, heatmap representation usually causes quantisation error for joints estimations. Our IGP-GCN design tackles this issue by converting the heatmap into coordinate representation. The overall framework and the proposed OPEC-Net module is illustrated in Fig. 2.

3.1   Initial Pose Estimation from Heatmap-Based Modules

In this stage, AlphaPose+ [13] is employed as the base module to generate a heatmap for visible joints. This is a top-down approach, which first detects a bounding box for each person and then performs instance-level human pose estimation. We describe the process for an instance-level human pose in the following.

Firstly, the three layers of the decoder of the base module generate three corresponding feature maps with different levels of fine details: a coarse feature map $\mathcal{F}_1$, a middle feature map $\mathcal{F}_2$ and a fine feature map $\mathcal{F}_3$. The base module outputs a heatmap which has high confidence for visible joints. The estimated pose from the heatmap H can be denoted as P, which contains estimation results for each joint:

$$\{< x^1, y^1, c^1 >, \ < x^2, y^2, c^2 >, \ \ldots, < x^k, y^k, c^k >\} \tag{1}$$

where x^j and y^j are the position of the jth joint, c^j the confidence score, and k is the number of joints in the skeleton.

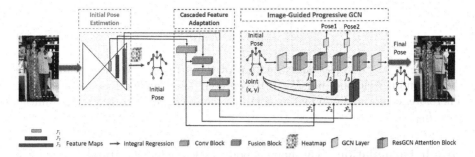

Fig. 2. The schematic diagram of our pipeline. This figure depicts the two stages of estimation for one single pose. The GCN-based pose correction stage contains two modules: the Cascaded Feature Adaptation and the Image-Guided Progressive GCN. Firstly a base module is employed to generate heatmaps. After that, an integral regression method [23] is employed to transform the heatmap representation into a coordinate representation, which can be the initial pose for GCN network. The initial pose and the three feature maps from the base module are processed in Image-Guided Progressive GCN. The multi-scale feature maps are updated through the Cascaded Feature Adaptation module and put into each ResGCN Attention blocks. $\hat{J}_1$, $\hat{J}_2$ and $\hat{J}_3$ are the node features excavated on related location (x, y) from image features. The error of Initial Pose, Pose1, Pose2, and Final Pose are all considered in the objective function. Then the OPEC-Net is trained entirely to estimate the human pose. The details of the whole framework are described in Sect. 3

3.2 GCN-Based Joints Correction

The occluded poses can be inferred easily by humans mostly because of their abundant prior knowledge of implicit body structure and pose properties. More specifically, a natural human pose is highly constrained by the environments and human body property, such as the biomechanical structure of the human body and implications in the environments. In light of that, we propose an Image-Guided graph network for correction which takes the initial pose generated from the above modules and adjusts the estimation results according to the implicit relationship of joints.

Heatmap Representation to Coordinate Representation. First of all, we generate the initial pose for the GCN network from the heatmaps of the first two stages. An important factor to consider in obtaining the initial pose is that the translation from heatmap to coordinate representation needs to be differential for the end to end training purpose, so the initial pose cannot be grasped directly from the heatmap by searching max values as P. Finally, we find out that a coordinate initial pose $\hat{J}_i$ can be generated from $Heatmap$ and estimated by an *integral regression* method [23].

Specifically, the heatmap is propagated into a Softmax layer which normalizes the values into likelihood values [0, 1]. After that, an integral operation is applied on the likelihood map to sum up the values and estimate joints positions.

$$\hat{J}_i^k = \int_{p \in A} p \cdot H_k(p), \tag{2}$$

where $\hat{J}_i^k$ is the position estimation of the kth joint. We use A to denote the region of likelihood and $H_k(p)$ to represent the likelihood value on point p. Therefore, every heatmap matrix contains the information to produce an initial pose P_{init}.

Graph Formulation. The human body skeleton has a natural hierarchical graph structure. Previous researches on MPPE merely utilize this information by a primitive graph matching strategy. We claim that the implicit relationships between different joints are helpful to guide position estimation. We thus construct an intuitive graph $G = (V, E)$ to formulate the human pose with N joints. V is the node set in G which can be denoted as $V = \{v_i \,| i = 1, 2, ..., N\}$. $E = \{v_i v_j \,|$ if i and j are connected in the human body$\}$ is the edge set which refers to limbs of the human body. The adjacent matrix of G refers to matrix $A = \{a_{ij}\}$, with $a_{ij} = 1$ when v_i and v_j are neighbors in G or $i = j$, otherwise $a_{ij} = 0$.

For every node, the input feature G_i^j is the joint estimation result $< x_i^j, y_i^j, c_i^j >$, where i is ith pose and j is the jth joint of the skeleton. We denote $G_i \in \mathbb{R}^{L \times N}$ as the input feature of the ith pose in the training set, where L is the feature dimension.

Image-Guided Progressive GCN Network. The core methodology proposed in our work is the Image-Guided Progressive GCN for Correction. In this network, the image context and pose structure clues for invisible joints inference are merged together in an innovative way. The details of each layers and ResGCN Attention Blocks are describe in supplementary materials.

(1) The estimated position of invisible joints from the base module is sometimes far from their correct locations and this makes it challenging to directly regress their displacements. Therefore, we design an intuitive coarse-to-fine learning mechanism in the coordinate-based module, which builds a ***progressive GCN architecture*** and leverages the performance steadily by enforcing multi-scale image features in a progressive manner.

(2) The coordinate-based module lacks ***local context information***. Consequently, we excavate the related image features for each joints position and fuse them into the module. In another word, we improve the pose estimation results by incorporating image feature maps $\hat{\mathcal{F}}_1, \hat{\mathcal{F}}_2$, and $\hat{\mathcal{F}}_3$. Specifically, we design cascaded ResGCN attention blocks to grasp the useful information that is stored in the feature maps but lost in initial pose $\hat{P}_i$. The three feature maps are ordered from coarse to fine according to their size of receptive fields. After that, we employ a grid sample method that obtains the jth joint feature by excavating the feature located in $< x_i^j, y_i^j >$ on the related coordinate weight feature map. Every pose leads to three node feature vectors $\hat{J}_1$,

$\hat{J}_2$, and $\hat{J}_3$ extracted following this process. Finally, these node features are fed into the ResGCN attention blocks accordingly.

Cascaded Feature Adaption (CFA). Feature maps $\mathcal{F}_1, \mathcal{F}_2$, and $\mathcal{F}_3$ should be adaptive to provide more effective information to the IGP-GCN. Moreover, the low-level feature and high-level feature are fused in the cascaded design in order to enlarge their respective fields resulting the updated feature are more informative. The details of Conv Blocks and Fusion Blocks used in this module is in supplementary materials.

CoupleGraph. We extend the single human graph into a CoupleGraph that captures more human interactions and this is achieved by connecting the corresponding joints to capture human interaction information. The couple graph can be denoted as $G' = (V', E')$. The joints number of a single person is N so that there is $2N$ joints in total in the couple graph. It can be formulated as $V' = \{v_i \,|i = 1,\ 2,\ ...,\ 2N\}$. There are two types of edges in E', the edges representing the human skeleton E_s and the edges connecting the two humans E_c. The human skeleton edges are noted as $E_s = \{v_i v_j \mid$ if i and j are connected in the human body$\}$. The human interaction edges can be written as $E_c = \{v_i v_{i+N}\}$, where the v_i and v_{i+N} are correspond to the same components of the two human skeletons. The CoupleGraph module is appended after OPEC-Graph module to enhance the performance of estimation. Each pair of people is processed by CoupleGraph.

3.3   Loss Functions

The objective function of our OPEC-Net module can now be formulated. We denote the training set as Ω, the ground truth pose in Ω as P_i, and the output pose of jth ResGCN Attention block as $\hat{P}_{ij}$. From heatmap representation to coordinate representation, the integral regression method produces an initial pose $\hat{P}_{init}$. Hence, the total loss is defined as the sum of the rectified loss of poses from IGP-GCN and initial loss of initial pose:

$$Loss = \min_{\theta} \sum_{i \in \Omega} (\sum_{j=1}^{n} \lambda_j |(\hat{P}_{ij} - P_i) \odot M| + |(\hat{P}_{init} - P_i) \odot M|) \qquad (3)$$

The term $|\hat{P}_{ij} - P_i|$ indicates the calculation of the L_1 loss between our estimated pose and the ground truth, n is the number of ResGCN attention blocks in the model. In this work, we set $n = 3$. We sum up all the errors of the produced pose from each block and assign a parameter λ_j to control the weight. All the trainable parameters in our network are denoted as θ. $M \in \mathbb{Z}_2^N$ is a binary mask where the element in M corresponds to 1 when the related joint has a ground truth label, otherwise it is 0. The $\odot$ denotes the element-wise product operation so that we only take into account the errors on the joints with ground truth.

The lasted generated pose will correspond to the best estimation result, so we treat the final one as our estimated result.

4 Our Occluded Pose Dataset

We build a new dataset, called **Occluded Pose** (OCPose), that includes more heavy occlusions to evaluate the MPPE. It contains challenging invisible joints and complex intertwined human poses. We mostly consider the couple pose scenes, such as dancing, skating, and wrestling, because they have more reliable annotations and practical utility. This section gives details of data collection, data annotation, and data statistics.

Data Collection. The ground truth of human pose can be hard to recognize when the occlusions are extremely heavy. Thus, we majorly collect videos of two-person interactions since they are much easier to annotate because the volunteer can infer the pose from contextual information. We first search for videos from the Internet by using keywords such as boxing, dancing, and wrestling. We then capture the distinctive images which contain diverse poses and humans from these videos by restricting the interval to be at least 3 s. Finally, we manually sift through the clips to select high-quality images. All the images are collected under the permission of privacy issues.

Data Annotation. We develop an annotation tool for the user to bound the area of the couple and then locate two template skeletons to their right positions. Six volunteers are recruited for manual labelling. Each skeleton has 12 joints and the left and right components are distinct. In addition to annotating the bounding box and the human body poses, the volunteers also need to indicate whether the joint is visible or not. To ensure accuracy, we use cross annotation for every image. At least two volunteers are required to provide their annotations on the same image. If an intolerant deviation exists between their results, the image is annotated again. The final joint positions are the mean value of the two annotations.

Table 1. The comparison of occlusion level. We count the number of images of each dataset with different level of occlusion. As shown above, MSCOCO and MPII almost have no heavily occlusions. OCHuman is the state-of-the-art dataset for occlusions but our dataset is larger and contains more severe occlusion

Dataset	Total	IoU>0.3	IoU>0.5	IoU>0.75	Average
CrowdPose	20000	8706 (44%)	2909 (15%)	309 (2%)	0.27
MSCOCO	118287	6504 (5%)	1209 (1%)	106 (<1%)	0.06
MPII	24987	0	0	0	0.11
OCHuman	4773	3264(68 %)	3244(68%)	1082(23%)	0.46
Ours	9000	8105 (**90%**)	6843 (**76%**)	2442 (**27%**)	**0.47**

Data Statistics. In total, our dataset contains 9000 images and 18000 fully annotated persons. For the training process, the training dataset consists of 5000 images, whereas validation and test dataset each contains 2000 images.

To compare the occlusion level, we evaluate the average intersection over union (IoU) of bounding box on the other public benchmarks, such as CrowdPose [13], OCHuman [27], MSCOCO [15] and MPII [1]. We report the comparison result of these benchmarks in Table 1, which illustrates that our dataset beats down all the other benchmarks on the occlusion level.

Other Dataset. In our approach, we carried out extensive experiments on public benchmarks. Following the typical training procedure, we evaluate the OPEC-Net on our OCPose, CrowdPose [13], MSCOCO [15] and particular occluded dataset OCHuman [27]. CrowdPose dataset is split in a ratio of 5 : 4 : 1 for training, testing and validation respectively. We regard the validation set of OCHuman with 2500 images as our training dataset, and the rest 2273 images for testing. Then we follow the typical training strategy on MSCOCO.

5   Experiments

In this section, extensive quantitative and qualitative experiments are demonstrated to evaluate the effectiveness of our OPEC-Net. Comprehensive ablation studies are carried out to validate the effectiveness of each components.

5.1   Experiments Settings

Implementation Details. For training, we set the parameters $\lambda_1 = 0.3$, $\lambda_2 = 0.5$, $\lambda_3 = 1$ and *epochs* $= 30$. We feed 10 images in a batch to train the whole framework. The initial learning rate is set to $1e^{-3}$ and decays in a cosine way. The input image size are 384×288 for MSCOCO and 320×256 for the other datasets. An AdamOptimizer is employed to optimize the parameters by backpropagation. For a fair comparison, we filter the proposal of the instances in the background and only focus on the Object Keypoint Similarity (OKS) of targets when we evaluate baselines on our dataset. We implement our model in PyTorch [20] and conduct experiments on one Nvidia GeForce GTX 1080 Ti with 11GB memory. More details are described in the supplementary materials.

Evaluation Metric. We follow the standard evaluation metric of MSCOCO, which is widely used by existing work as well [3,6,9,13]. Specifically, we report the mean Average Precision (mAP) value at 0.5:0.95, 0.5, 0.75, 0.80 and 0.90. In order to grasp the qualified poses for OPEC-Net training procedure, two rules are formulated to select the proposal. The proposal poses must contain more than 5 visible points and OKS value more than 0.3 to ensure the quality. To enrich the dataset, we also flip the images as a data augmentation strategy. Furthermore, we provide the visualization results of pose estimation.

Baselines. For comparison, we assess the performance with our OPEC-Net module using the three state-of-the-art approaches for MPPE: Mask RCNN [8],

AlphaPose+[1] [13] and SimplePose [24]. For a fair comparison, we quote the results of Mask RCNN and SimplePose directly from paper [13] and re-train AlphaPose+ from their public code. For the evaluation on OCPose, CrowdPose and OCHuman, we take AlphaPose+ for the initial pose estimation stage with ResNet-101 as backbone and Yolo V3 as detector. For MSCOCO dataset, we take the public code of SimplePose[2] for the first stage for it has higher performance than AlphaPose+ on MSCOCO. Mask RCNN is used as the detector and ResNet-152 is used as the backbone on MSCOCO. OPEC-Net here denotes the framework with a single person as graph, and CoupleGraph denotes the baseline that performs a CoupleGraph based framework after OPEC-Net.

Fig. 3. The qualitative evaluation of CoupleGraph and OPEC-Net. The left images are generated from OPEC-Net and the right ones come from CoupleGraph

Table 2. The comparison on our OCPose dataset

Method	mAP@0.5:0.95	AP^{50}	AP^{75}	AP^{80}	AP^{90}
Mask RCNN [8]	21.5	49.8	15.9	7.7	0.1
Simple Pose [24]	27.1	54.3	24.2	16.8	4.7
AlphaPose+ [13]	30.8	58.4	28.5	22.4	8.2
OPEC-Net	32.8(+2.0)	60.5	31.1	24.0	9.2
CoupleGraph	**33.6(+2.8)**	**60.8**	**32.5**	**25.0**	**9.8**

5.2 Performance Comparison on Our OCPose Dataset

Quantitative Comparison. The quantitative results are presented in Table 2. Our approach attains the best mAP comparing to all the baselines with a considerable margin. OPEC-Net achieves a significant gain which is surprisingly 2.0 mAP@0.5:0.95 improvement compared to AlphaPose+. Despite of that, a significant 1.0 AP^{90} improvement has been achieved which proves that our OPEC-Net has great ability of inference especially for high level of occlusions compared to localization methods. In conclusion, these results validate the prominent effectiveness of our OPEC-Net module on MPPE tasks.

---

[1] https://github.com/MVIG-SJTU/AlphaPose/tree/pytorch.
[2] https://github.com/leoxiaobin/pose.pytorch.

Fig. 4. The results on OCPose, OCHuman and CrowdPose. These are the qualitative comparison results of AlphaPose+ method and OPEC-Net on our datasets. The left pose is estimated by AlphaPose+ method and the right one is ours. The first row is OCPose and the second row represents OCHuman, the rest represents CrowdPose

Qualitative Comparison. As illustrated in the first row of Fig. 4, our OPEC-Net is capable of correcting the wrong link between joints and estimating the occluded joints while maintaining high performance on visible joints. We make these observations from the results: (1) For the first sample, a superior pose estimation result is provided by our method. Even an error with large displacement can be corrected by OPEC-Net. (2) Moreover, although the second case has difficult sunlight interference, our approach can also adjust the joints to their correct locations. (3) The third group also shows an evidence that our OPEC-Net module produces more natural poses that conform to human body constraints. (4) The fourth figure shows that our method can find the correct link between joints.

CoupleGraph. The evaluations of CoupleGraph are given in Table 2 and Fig. 3. Comparing to OPEC-Net, CoupleGraph baseline also shows an advanced lifting 0.8 mAP@0.5:0.95, which validates the human interaction clues are quite prominent. As illustrated in Fig. 3, CoupleGraph outperforms OPEC-Net significantly in quality. In these human interactive scenarios, the poses estimated by Couple-Graph are more concordant and superior.

5.3   Comparison Against State-of-the-Arts on Other Benchmarks

Extensive evaluations on heavily benchmarked dataset demonstrate the effectiveness of our model for occlusion problem. The experimental results on existing benchmarks are presented in Table 3, 4 and Fig. 4. Our model surpasses all the baselines by a considerable margin.

Table 3. The qualitative result on occlusion dataset

Method	Dataset									
	OCHuman [27]					CrowdPose [13]				
	mAP@0.5:0.95	AP^{50}	AP^{75}	AP^{80}	AP^{90}	mAP@0.5:0.95	AP^{50}	AP^{75}	AP^{80}	AP^{90}
Mask RCNN [8]	20.2	33.2	24.5	18.3	2.1	57.2	83.5	60.3	–	–
SimplePose [24]	24.1	37.4	26.8	22.6	4.5	60.8	81.4	65.7	–	–
AlphaPose+ [13]	27.5	40.8	29.9	24.8	9.5	68.5	86.7	73.2	66.9	45.9
OPEC-Net	**29.1(+1.6)**	**41.3**	**31.4**	**27.0**	**12.8(+3.3)**	**70.6(+2.1)**	**86.8**	**75.6**	**70.1**	**48.8(+2.9)**

Table 4. MSCOCO 2017 test-dev set [15]

Method	mAP@0.5:0.95	mAP@0.5	mAP@0.75
AlphaPose+ [13]	72.2	90.1	79.3
Simple Pose [24]	73.7	91.9	81.8
OPEC-Net	**73.9(+0.2)**	**91.9**	**82.2**

OCHuman. As OCHuman is a new benchmark proposed mainly for pose segmentation, we are the first to report all the baseline results on this challenging occlusion dataset. Comparing to AlphaPose+, we achieve maximal 3.3 improvements on AP^{90}. This further validates that our OPEC-Net model is robust even for highly challenging occlusion scenarios.

CrowdPose. As shown in Table 3, OPEC-Net drastically lifts 2.1 mAP@0.5:0.95 of the estimation result over AlphaPose+. It is also worth noting that the improvements remain high when the comparison AP terms are high. For example, our model achieves 0.1, 2.4, 3.2 and 2.9 on AP 50, 75, 80 and 90 respectively.

MSCOCO. We also present our results on the largest benchmark MSCOCO. Our model only contributes slightly accuracy improvements. The reason is the key difference between MSCOCO and other datasets – it contains too few occlusion scenarios, especially the severe ones. Moreover, a lot of invisible joints lack annotations on MSCOCO.

Invisible vs. Visible. To investigate of the effectiveness on invisible (Inv) and visible (V) joints separately, we report the statistics of each type of joints according to the similar rule of OKS. From Table 5, our OPEC-Net improves mostly on the invisible joints rather than visible joints. In terms of Inv@75, our framwork achieves a considerable marginal 3.3% and 4.9% gains on CrowdPose and

OCPose respectively. On the contrary, the OPEC-Net only improves a maximal 1% on visible joints because our main focus is the invisible joints. This comparison also explains why the gains are smaller on MSCOCO datasets than the other datasets that contains more occlusions.

Table 5. Results for Visible and Invisible Joints on CrowdPose and OCPose !

Datasets	CrowdPose				OCPose			
Method	Inv@75	Inv@90	V@75	V@90	Inv@75	Inv@90	V@75	V@90
AlphaPose+	76.2%	57.2%	89.5%	67.8%	50.7%	17.7%	85.2%	**55.3%**
OPEC-Net	**79.5%**	**58.4%**	**90.0%**	**67.8%**	**55.6%**	**20.5%**	**86.2%**	55.1%

Table 6. Ablation study of our OPEC-Net framework (mAP@0.5:0.95)

The evaluation of removal each component	OCHuman	CrowdPose	OCPose
The AlphaPose+ baseline	30.8	27.5	68.5
(a)Without the Image-Guided strategy in GCN	30.8	27.7	68.6
(b)Without the Progressive design in the GCN	32.2	28.3	69.3
(c)Use one feature F_3 instead of multi-scale features	32.5	28.5	69.7
(d)Remove the Cascaded Feature Adaption module	32.1	28.4	69.9
(e)Remove the Fusion Block in CFA module	32.4	28.7	69.6
The full OPEC-Net	32.8	29.1	70.6

5.4 Alabtion Studies

To analyze our model in details, we conduct comprehensive ablative experiments to evaluate the capability of each component and clues we claimed. As illustrated in Table 6, we present the baselines to investigate the impact of each component.

Firstly, we investigate the impact of image guided strategy that blends the image context with GCN. From (a), a clear decrease around 2.0 mAP@0.5:0.95 is observed, which points out the importance of the Image-Guide strategy. Without the Image-Guided part, a single GCN network improves the performance poorly. This evidence validates that the GCN module must learn under the guidance of image features.

We further investigate each design of the IGP-GCN. From (b) and (c), we can conclude that the strategy of progressive and coarse to fine feature learning is effective. Moreover, the proposed Cascaded Feature Adaption module is analysed as well. In Table 6, the mAP value of three datasets falls down significantly, demonstrating that the CFA module plays an indispensable role in the whole framework. We remove the Fusion Blocks and report the results in (c), which further proves the effectiveness of the fusion part in the CFA module. We can conclude that the image guidance is the most imperative in the framework. The CFA module brings an average 0.7 mAP@0.5:0.95 gain on three datasets, which manifests the necessity to make image features adaptive for coordinate module. Overall, these ablation studies overwhelmingly validate that every component is effective and the clues are informative for invisible joints inference.

6 Conclusion

In this paper, we proposed a novel OPEC-Net module and a challenging Occluded Pose (OCPose) dataset to address the occlusion problem in Crowd Pose Estimation. Two elaborate components, Image-Guided Progressive GCN and Cascaded Feature Adaptation, are designed to exploit the natural human body constraints and image context. We conduct thorough experiments on four benchmarks and ablation studies to demonstrate the effectiveness and provide a variety of insights. The heatmap and coordinate module are proved to work cooperatively and achieve remarkable improvements in all aspects. By making this dataset available, we hope to arouse the attention and increase the interest in the investigation of the occlusion problem in pose estimation.

Acknowledgment. The work was supported in part by grants No. 2018YFB1800800, No. 2018B030338001, No. 2017ZT0 7X152, No. ZDSYS201707251409055 and in part by National Natural Science Foundation of China (Grant No.: 61902334 and 61629101). The authors also would like to thank Running Gu and Yuheng Qiu for their early efforts on data labeling.

References

1. Andriluka, M., Pishchulin, L., Gehler, P., Schiele, B.: 2D human pose estimation: new benchmark and state of the art analysis. In: Proceedings of the IEEE Conference on computer Vision and Pattern Recognition, pp. 3686–3693 (2014)
2. Bansal, A., Ma, S., Ramanan, D., Sheikh, Y.: Recycle-GAN: unsupervised video retargeting. In: Proceedings of the European Conference on Computer Vision (ECCV), pp. 119–135 (2018)
3. Cao, Z., Simon, T., Wei, S.E., Sheikh, Y.: Realtime multi-person 2D pose estimation using part affinity fields. In: Proceedings of the IEEE Conference on Computer Vision and Pattern Recognition, pp. 7291–7299 (2017)
4. Chan, C., Ginosar, S., Zhou, T., Efros, A.A.: Everybody dance now. arXiv preprint arXiv:1808.07371 (2018)
5. Ci, H., Wang, C., Ma, X., Wang, Y.: Optimizing network structures for 3D human pose estimation. In: ICCV (2019)
6. Fang, H., Xie, S., Tai, Y.W., Lu, C.: RMPE: regional multi-person pose estimation. In: The IEEE International Conference on Computer Vision (ICCV), vol. 2 (2017)
7. Gui, L.Y., Zhang, K., Wang, Y.X., Liang, X., Moura, J.M., Veloso, M.: Teaching robots to predict human motion. In: 2018 IEEE/RSJ International Conference on Intelligent Robots and Systems (IROS), pp. 562–567. IEEE (2018)

8. He, K., Gkioxari, G., Dollár, P., Girshick, R.: Mask R-CNN. In: 2017 IEEE International Conference on Computer Vision (ICCV), pp. 2980–2988. IEEE (2017)
9. Huang, Z., Huang, L., Gong, Y., Huang, C., Wang, X.: Mask scoring R-CNN. In: Proceedings of the IEEE Conference on Computer Vision and Pattern Recognition, pp. 6409–6418 (2019)
10. Insafutdinov, E., Pishchulin, L., Andres, B., Andriluka, M., Schiele, B.: DeeperCut: a deeper, stronger, and faster multi-person pose estimation model. In: Leibe, B., Matas, J., Sebe, N., Welling, M. (eds.) ECCV 2016. LNCS, vol. 9910, pp. 34–50. Springer, Cham (2016). https://doi.org/10.1007/978-3-319-46466-4_3
11. Joo, H., Simon, T., Sheikh, Y.: Total capture: a 3D deformation model for tracking faces, hands, and bodies. In: Proceedings of the IEEE Conference on Computer Vision and Pattern Recognition, pp. 8320–8329 (2018)
12. Li, G., Muller, M., Thabet, A., Ghanem, B.: DeepGCNs: Can GCNs go as deep as CNNs? In: Proceedings of the IEEE International Conference on Computer Vision, pp. 9267–9276 (2019)
13. Li, J., Wang, C., Zhu, H., Mao, Y., Fang, H.S., Lu, C.: CrowdPose: efficient crowded scenes pose estimation and a new benchmark. In: Proceedings of the IEEE Conference on Computer Vision and Pattern Recognition, pp. 10863–10872 (2019)
14. Li, M., Chen, S., Chen, X., Zhang, Y., Wang, Y., Tian, Q.: Actional-structural graph convolutional networks for skeleton-based action recognition. In: Proceedings of the IEEE Conference on Computer Vision and Pattern Recognition, pp. 3595–3603 (2019)
15. Lin, T.-Y., et al.: Microsoft COCO: common objects in context. In: Fleet, D., Pajdla, T., Schiele, B., Tuytelaars, T. (eds.) ECCV 2014. LNCS, vol. 8693, pp. 740–755. Springer, Cham (2014). https://doi.org/10.1007/978-3-319-10602-1_48
16. Mehta, D., Sridhar, S., Sotnychenko, O., Rhodin, H., Shafiei, M., Seidel, H.P., Xu, W., Casas, D., Theobalt, C.: VNect: real-time 3D human pose estimation with a single RGB camera. ACM Trans. Graph. (TOG) 36(4), 44 (2017)
17. Newell, A., Huang, Z., Deng, J.: Associative embedding: end-to-end learning for joint detection and grouping. In: Advances in Neural Information Processing Systems, pp. 2277–2287 (2017)
18. Panteleris, P., Oikonomidis, I., Argyros, A.: Using a single RGB frame for real time 3D hand pose estimation in the wild. In: 2018 IEEE Winter Conference on Applications of Computer Vision (WACV), pp. 436–445. IEEE (2018)
19. Papandreou, G., et al.: Towards accurate multi-person pose estimation in the wild. In: CVPR, vol. 3, p. 6 (2017)
20. Paszke, A., et al.: Automatic differentiation in PyTorch (2017)
21. Pishchulin, L., et al.: DeepCut: joint subset partition and labeling for multi person pose estimation. In: Proceedings of the IEEE Conference on Computer Vision and Pattern Recognition, pp. 4929–4937 (2016)
22. Qian, X., et al.: Pose-normalized image generation for person re-identification. In: Proceedings of the European Conference on Computer Vision (ECCV), pp. 650–667 (2018)
23. Sun, X., Xiao, B., Wei, F., Liang, S., Wei, Y.: Integral human pose regression. In: Proceedings of the European Conference on Computer Vision (ECCV), pp. 529–545 (2018)
24. Xiao, B., Wu, H., Wei, Y.: Simple baselines for human pose estimation and tracking. In: Proceedings of the European Conference on Computer Vision (ECCV), pp. 466–481 (2018)

25. Yan, S., Xiong, Y., Lin, D.: Spatial temporal graph convolutional networks for skeleton-based action recognition. In: Thirty-Second AAAI Conference on Artificial Intelligence (2018)
26. Zanfir, A., Marinoiu, E., Zanfir, M., Popa, A.I., Sminchisescu, C.: Deep network for the integrated 3D sensing of multiple people in natural images. In: Advances in Neural Information Processing Systems, pp. 8410–8419 (2018)
27. Zhang, S.H., et al.: Pose2Seg: detection free human instance segmentation. In: Proceedings of the IEEE Conference on Computer Vision and Pattern Recognition, pp. 889–898 (2019)
28. Zhao, L., Peng, X., Tian, Y., Kapadia, M., Metaxas, D.N.: Semantic graph convolutional networks for 3D human pose regression. In: Proceedings of the IEEE Conference on Computer Vision and Pattern Recognition, pp. 3425–3435 (2019)

RubiksNet: Learnable 3D-Shift for Efficient Video Action Recognition

Linxi Fan[1]([✉]), Shyamal Buch[1], Guanzhi Wang[1], Ryan Cao[1], Yuke Zhu[2,3], Juan Carlos Niebles[1], and Li Fei-Fei[1]

[1] Stanford Vision and Learning Lab, Stanford, USA
{jimfan,shyamal}@cs.stanford.edu
[2] UT Austin, Austin, USA
[3] NVIDIA, Santa Clara, USA

Abstract. Video action recognition is a complex task dependent on modeling spatial and temporal context. Standard approaches rely on 2D or 3D convolutions to process such context, resulting in expensive operations with millions of parameters. Recent efficient architectures leverage a channel-wise shift-based primitive as a replacement for temporal convolutions, but remain bottlenecked by spatial convolution operations to maintain strong accuracy and a fixed-shift scheme. Naively extending such developments to a 3D setting is a difficult, intractable goal. To this end, we introduce RubiksNet, a new efficient architecture for video action recognition which is based on a proposed *learnable* 3D spatiotemporal shift operation instead. We analyze the suitability of our new primitive for video action recognition and explore several novel variations of our approach to enable stronger representational flexibility while maintaining an efficient design. We benchmark our approach on several standard video recognition datasets, and observe that our method achieves comparable or better accuracy than prior work on efficient video action recognition at a fraction of the performance cost, with 2.9–5.9× fewer parameters and 2.1–3.7× fewer FLOPs. We also perform a series of controlled ablation studies to verify our significant boost in the efficiency-accuracy tradeoff curve is rooted in the core contributions of our RubiksNet architecture.

Keywords: Efficient action recognition · Spatiotemporal · Learnable shift · Budget-constrained · Video understanding

1 Introduction

Analyzing videos to recognize human actions is a critical task for general-purpose video understanding algorithms. However, action recognition can be

---

L. Fan and S. Buch—Equal contribution lead author.

Electronic supplementary material The online version of this chapter (https://doi.org/10.1007/978-3-030-58529-7_30) contains supplementary material, which is available to authorized users.

A. Vedaldi et al. (Eds.): ECCV 2020, LNCS 12364, pp. 505–521, 2020.
https://doi.org/10.1007/978-3-030-58529-7_30

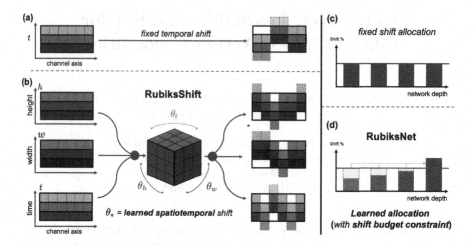

Fig. 1. *Top:* Prior work for efficient shift-based video recognition [16] has explored **(a)** fixed temporal shift operation on expensive 2D convolution features, with **(c)** a fixed shift allocation network design. *Bottom:* We introduce **RubiksNet**, a new architecture based on a **(b)** learnable 3D-shift layer (RubiksShift) that learns to perform spatial (h, w) and temporal (t) shift operations jointly end-to-end, while also **(d)** learning an effective layer-wise network allocation of a constrained shift budget. Our model significantly improves the accuracy-efficiency boundary.

computationally costly, requiring processing of several frames spatiotemporally to ascertain the correct action. As embodied applications of video recognition for autonomous agents and mobile devices continue to scale, the need for efficient recognition architectures with fewer parameters and compute operations remains ever-growing.

Prior efforts for video action recognition [1,23] rely on deep neural network architectures with expensive convolution operations across spatial and temporal context, which are often prohibitive for resource-constrained application domains. Recent work has proposed to improve the efficiency of the spatial and temporal operations separately [16,18,25,31]. However, they are still largely bounded by the efficiency of the base spatial aggregation method through spatial convolutions.

In images, spatial shift operations [11,29] have been proposed as a GPU-efficient alternative to traditional convolution operations, and architectures built using these operations have shown promise for efficient image recognition, though accuracy is limited. Recently, a temporal shift module (TSM) [16] based on hand-designed fixed temporal shift (Fig. 1, *top*) has been proposed to be used with existing 2D convolutional image recognition methods [26] for action recognition. However, the efficiency of their architecture family remains limited by the parameter and computation cost for spatial operations, as in other prior work.

A crucial observation is that much of the input spatiotemporal context contained in consecutive frames of a video sequence is often redundant to the action recognition task. Furthermore, the impact of modeling capacity on the action recognition task likely varies significantly at different depths in the architecture. In other words, action recognition in videos poses a unique opportunity for pushing the boundaries of the efficiency-accuracy tradeoff curve by considering efficient shift operations in both space and time dimensions with flexible allocations.

However, a **key limitation** towards a naive generalization from fixed temporal shift [16] to a spatiotemporal shift scheme is that the design space becomes intractable. In particular, we would need to exhaustively explore the number of channels that are shifted for each dimension, the magnitude of these shifts, and the underlying layer design combining each of these operations, among other design choices. Thus, there is a clear motivation for enabling the architecture to learn the shift operations during training itself. Recent work [11] has explored the possibility of learning shifts for 2D image processing. However, the challenge of generalizing this formulation to enable stable and effective spatiotemporal optimization of shift-based operations on high-dimensional video input has remained unexplored.

To this end, we propose **RubiksNet**: a new video action recognition architecture based on a novel **spatiotemporal** shift layer (*RubiksShift*) that **learns** to perform shift operations jointly on spatial and temporal context. We explore several variations of our design, and find that our architecture **learns effective allocations** of shift operations within a **constrained shift budget**. We benchmark our overall approach on several standard action recognition benchmarks, including large-scale temporal-focused datasets like Something-Something-v1 [6] and Something-Something-v2 [17], as well as others like UCF-101 [22] and HMDB [15]. We observe that our architecture can maintain competitive accuracy with the prior state-of-the-art on efficient shift-based action recognition [16] while simultaneously improving the efficiency and number of parameters by a large margin, up to 5.9x fewer parameters and 3.7x fewer FLOPs. Our controlled ablation analyses also demonstrate that these efficiency-accuracy gains come from the joint ability of our architecture to synergize spatial and temporal shift learning, as well as effective learned allocation of shift across the network.

2   Related Work

Action Recognition. The action recognition task in videos focuses on the classification of activities in video clips amongst a set of action classes. The initial set of deep network-based approaches processed frames individually using 2D convolutional neural networks [13,21,26]. For example, Temporal Segment Network (TSN) extracts features from sampled frames before averaging them for the final prediction [26]. While such methods are relatively efficient and parallelizable, they also do not model the temporal dynamics well. As such, the dominant paradigm in video action recognition is centered around the usage of spatial and temporal convolutions over the 3D space [1,5,12,23]. There are also other action recognition works that exploit temporal information [32]. While these deep networks are more accurate, the increase in computational cost has proven to be substantial and prohibitive for efficiency-conscious applications.

Recent progress in action recognition has largely focused on two directions: (1) improving efficiency by considering a mixture of 3D convolutions and separate spatial + temporal convolution operations [18,25,31,36], and (2) incorporating longer term temporal reasoning [27,34,36] to further improve the accuracy of the methods. We differentiate this work from prior efforts along both axes. Along the first, we note that the above methods make progress towards bringing cubic scaling of 3D convolutions towards the quadratic scaling of 2D convolutions, but the spatial kernel remains an inherent strong bound on performance. Our approach offers an alternative that is much more efficient and has much fewer parameters by eliminating the need for 2D or 3D convolutions in the architecture. Along the second, our method introduces a learnable spatiotemporal shift operation that efficiently increases the effective receptive field capacity of the network, and allows it to flexibly allocate its capacity across the network, in contrast with prior efforts that leveraged fixed shift operations throughout the network [16].

Efficient Neural Networks for Images and Video. Convolutions have been the main computational primitive in deep neural network approaches for computer vision tasks [3,8,9,29,33]. Recently, the shift operation has been proposed as a more hardware efficient alternative to spatial convolution for image classification [11,29,35]. While shift has been examined as a replacement for 1D temporal convolutions recently [16], the possibility of a learnable 3D shift operation has remained unexplored due to the challenges afforded by joint learning of the shift primitive across spatial and temporal context, and the traditional advantage spatial convolutions hold in action recognition architectures in terms of accuracy. We aim to propose a technique that need not depend on any spatial convolution operations during inference – only shift and pointwise convolution.

Additionally, our work remains complementary to literature on neural network compression [30], so while our proposed method saves substantially on model size and computation cost, it is possible that application of such techniques can lead to further gains. We also highlight work that ShuffleNet [33], MobileNet [9,20], and SqueezeNet [10] for efficient 2D image classification. Tran et al. [24] factorizes 3D group convolutions while preserving channel interactions. The aim of our work is to develop video models that can similarly be applied in embodied vision applications, where efficiency is essential.

3   Technical Approach

In this section, we describe our proposed method for efficient action recognition, where the task is to take an input video clip and classify which of a set of human action categories is present. We first describe our proposed RubiksShift layers for replacing spatiotemporal convolutions with learnable spatiotemporal shifts. Then, we detail how we compose these operations into the RubiksNet architecture.

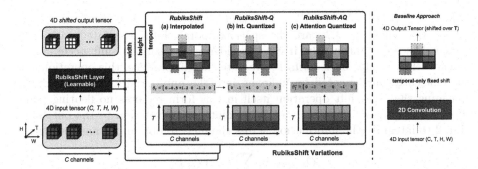

Fig. 2. Our proposed RubiksShift layer (Sect. 3.1) is the primary driver of our overall RubiksNet architecture (Sect. 3.2). RubiksShift aims to perform a spatiotemporal shift operation on input 4D tensor along each of the input channels, for spatial and temporal axes. **(a)** Our primary RubiksShift layer is based on a continuous interpolated shift primitive, which enables a true gradient with low additional overhead, and **(b)** our RubiksShift-Q alternative is a quantized variant. **(c)** Finally, our RubiksShift-AQ variant enables learning integer shift using a temporal attention layer (also see Fig. 3).

3.1 RubiksShift: Learnable 3D Shift

Spatiotemporal Convolution. In a traditional convolutional network with 3D spatiotemporal convolutions, the input to each layer of the network is a 4D tensor $F \in \mathbb{R}^{C \times T \times H \times W}$, C is the number of input channels, T the temporal length, and H, W are the height and width respectively. The 3D spatiotemporal convolution operation [23] is then defined as:

$$O_{c',t,h,w} = \sum_{c,i,j,k} K_{c',c,k,i,j} F_{c,t+\hat{k},h+\hat{i},w+\hat{j}} \tag{1}$$

where $O \in \mathcal{R}^{C' \times T \times H \times W}$ is the output tensor, $K \in \mathbb{R}^{C' \times C \times T_K \times H_K \times W_K}$ is the 3D convolution kernel, i, j, k index along the temporal, height, and width dimensions of the kernel, and c, c' index along the channel dimensions. The indices $\hat{i}, \hat{j}, \hat{k}$ are the re-centered spatial and temporal indices, with $\hat{k} = k - \lfloor T_K/2 \rfloor, \hat{i} = i - \lfloor H_K/2 \rfloor, \hat{j} = j - \lfloor W_K/2 \rfloor$. Assuming $H = W$ for simplicity, the total number of parameters in this operation is thus $C \times C' \times T_K \times H_K{}^2$ and the computational cost is $C \times C' \times (T \times H^2) \times (T_K \times H_K{}^2)$. Indeed, this operation scales quadratically with the spatial input and cubically when considering temporal dimensions as well, both in parameters and number of operations (Fig. 2).

Fixed Spatiotemporal Shift. In this context, we propose a spatiotemporal shift operation as an alternative to traditional 3D convolutions. Since the shift primitive proposed in prior work can be considered an efficient special case of depthwise-separable convolutions with fewer memory access calls [3,29,35], we can formalize the spatiotemporal shift operation as follows:

$$O'_{c,t,h,w} = \sum_{i,j,k} S_{c,k,i,j} F_{c,t+\hat{k},h+\hat{i},w+\hat{j}} \tag{2}$$

where $S \in \{0,1\}^{C \times T_K \times H_K \times W_K}$, such that $S_{c,k,i,j} = 1$ if and only if $(i,j,k) = (i_c, j_c, k_c)$, where i_c, j_c, k_c are the spatiotemporal shifts associated with each channel index c. Intuitively, if S is the identity tensor, no shift occurs since every element maps back to itself. We note that in practice, this operation can be efficiently implemented by indexing into the appropriate memory address, meaning that the shift operation itself in this form requires no floating point operations (FLOPs). We then apply a pointwise convolution to the output of Eq. 2 to integrate the information across channels to obtain our final output:

$$O_{c',t,h,w} = \sum_c P_{c',c} O'_{c,t,h,w} \tag{3}$$

where P is the pointwise convolution kernel with only $C \times C'$ parameters. Assuming $H = W$, the computational cost is $C \times C' \times (T \times H^2)$, much lower than the spatiotemporal convolution. Notably, when deploying such an architecture, we can fuse the shift and pointwise convolution operations into a single efficient kernel call, meaning the final parameters and operation complexity from the spatiotemporal shift operation itself is subsumed entirely.

Learnable Spatiotemporal Shift. Finally, a key design aspect of our proposed spatiotemporal shift operation which differentiates itself from prior work in temporal modeling [16] is the ability of our model to *learn* the temporal shift primitive. In particular, our method learns to shift over the joint spatiotemporal context jointly, which affords the network the ability to efficiently consider a significant span of spatiotemporal context with fewer overall parameters.

Following prior work in spatial shift [11], we consider a continuous form of the traditionally discrete shift operation, allowing us to optimize the shift parameters directly by backpropagation. We define the 3D shift learnable parameters as:

$$\theta = \{(\gamma_c, \alpha_c, \beta_c) \mid c \in C\} \tag{4}$$

where $\gamma_c, \alpha_c, \beta_c$ are the temporal, vertical, and horizontal shift *parameters* for each channel c. With this, we consider an alternative formulation of Eq. 2:

$$O'_{c,t,h,w} = \sum_{i,j,k} S^\theta_{c,k,i,j} F_{c,t+\hat{k},h+\hat{i},w+\hat{j}} \tag{5}$$

$$S^\theta_{c,k,i,j} = \prod_{(z,g) \in \{(\gamma_c,k),(\alpha_c,i),(\beta_c,j)\}} \begin{cases} \Delta z & \text{if } g = \lceil z \rceil, \\ 1 - \Delta z & \text{if } g = \lfloor z \rfloor, \\ 0 & \text{otherwise} \end{cases} \tag{6}$$

with $\Delta z = z - \lfloor z \rfloor$ and g is the corresponding index to the z parameter dimension (e.g., γ_c corresponds to the time index k). Here, each sparse entry $S^\theta_{c,k,i,j}$ is a coefficient representing the *product* of interpolated shift contributions from all 3 dimensions. Intuitively, we are constructing a shift operation over an implicit continuous trilinearly-interpolated input activation tensor, where the interpolation is evaluated *sparsely* around the local neighborhood (2^3-point cube) around

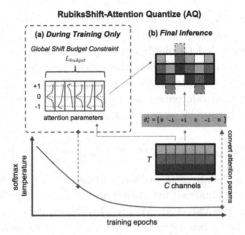

Fig. 3. (a) During training, our RubiksShift-AQ variant parameterizes shift with an attention distribution corresponding to integer shift values. We can then train quantized temporal shift with a true gradient (under a budget constraint), in contrast with interpolated quantized methods [2]. Attention softmax temperature is annealed during training. **(b)** After training, the resulting one-hot attention parameters are converted to final integer shift values for efficient inference at test time.

each shift operation at the location of each shift parameter. We note that this equation is once again a formalism; in practice, the operation can still be written efficiently on the GPU with minimal additional overhead with respect to discrete shift. We provide additional technical discussion in the supplement.

Taken together, we term this combined learnable spatiotemporal shift operation *RubiksShift* as shown in Fig. 1. We observe that it enables our overall architecture to learn a joint spatiotemporal shift kernel that aggregates discriminative features over the full activation in an efficient manner.

Interpolated Quantized Shift. While the interpolated formulation above remains efficient, we can push efficiency a little higher by considering a quantized version of the above spatiotemporal shift scheme. Our second RubiksShift variant is a *naive* spatiotemporal extension based on an interpolated shift quantization mechanism on images [2]. Briefly, during training, the model maintains a copy of the interpolated shift parameters as floats. In the forward pass, all shifts are rounded to the nearest integer. In the backward pass, gradient is computed with respect to the continuous shifts and these parameters are updated by regular gradient descent. Our ablative analysis shows that while this technique does work, the lack of a *true* gradient ends up hindering performance by a large margin.

Attention Quantized Shift. To address the shortcomings of the interpolated quantized variant, we propose RubiksShift-AQ (Fig. 3) as an alternative way to quantize temporal shifts with *exact* gradient. Related to concurrent attention pruning work [7] for 2D object recognition, we formulate *temporal attention* *shift* as an operator for video action recognition that parameterizes shift with an attention distribution corresponding to integer shift values. The attention weights are then annealed to one-hot, integer-valued shifts over the course of the training process. In this manner, the model is able to flexibly and stably learn a high-capacity spatiotemporal representation suitable for video action recognition, but at final inference time is as efficient as quantized shift. Given an attention weight tensor $\mathbf{W_{attn}}$, we compute:

$$\mathbf{W_{attnshift}} = softmax \left(\tau_a \frac{\mathbf{W_{attn}}}{std(\mathbf{W_{attn}})} \right) \quad (7)$$

where τ_a denotes the temperature of the softmax. After the softmax operation, every value in $\mathbf{W}$ is normalized between 0 and 1, which represents the attention weight. At high τ_a, the values in $\mathbf{W}$ are close to uniform, while at extremely low τ_a, $\mathbf{W}$ approaches a binary tensor with only one non-zero entry along each channel slice. During training, we anneal τ_a exponentially to a low value, typically 10^{-3}, at which stage we take the hard max operation to convert attention shift $\mathbf{W_{attnshift}}$ to the equivalent discrete integer shift operation S for efficient inference.

Shift Operations Budget Constraint. Prior work [11,16] has noted that while shift operations save parameters and FLOPs, they can still incur latency cost through memory management. We incorporate this important aspect into our RubikShift design. A key feature of our proposed temporal attention shift is that we can apply a novel flexible constraint that corresponds to an overall "global shift budget", which penalizes the model for aggressively shifting. Importantly, the constraint is flexible in that it only penalizes a global metric for the shift – the specific allocation across layers at various depths in the network can then be learned by the network. Specifically, our budget constraint loss takes the form:

$$L_{budget} = \left\| \frac{1}{N_L} \sum_{l=1}^{N_L} \left(\frac{1}{C'} \sum_{c,*} \mathbf{W}^{(l)}_{nonzero} \right) - B \right\| \quad (8)$$

where N_L is the number of layers, B is the shift budget between 0 and 1, and $\mathbf{W}^{(l)}_{nonzero}$ denotes the attention weights in $\mathbf{W_{attnshift}}$ at layer l corresponding to the non-zero shift positions. We find that our proposed RubiksShift-AQ under budget constraint enables RubiksNet to discover interesting, non-uniform allocations of the shift budget across the network layers while preserving the global fraction of shift operations. To our knowledge, this is the first such method with learnable discrete shift under a shift resource constraint. Further, we find such learned allocation is critical to our overall design in careful ablation analysis.

3.2   RubiksNet: Model Architecture Design

Our overall architecture mirrors the residual block design in the ResNet architecture [8]. Each RubiksShift layer includes shift operations as described in Sect. 3.1

Table 1. Benchmark results on the Something-Something-v2 dataset [17]. RubiksNet offers strong performance across a range of base architectures as compared with TSM [16] architecture family. 2-clip accuracy metric per [16]; FLOPs reported for 1 clip, center crop for all architectures. (-) indicates value not reported. (#x) denotes efficiency savings factor relative to analogous size TSM model.

Method	Size	Input	1-Clip Val		2-Clip Val		#Param.	FLOPs/Video
			Top-1	Top-5	Top-1	Top-5		
TSN [26]	Large	8	30.0	60.5	30.4	61.0	24.3M	33G
TRN [36]	Large	8	48.8	77.6	-	-	18.3M	16G
bLVNet-TAM [4]	Large	8 × 2	59.1	86	-	-	25M	23.8G
TSM [16]	Large	8	58.8	85.6	61.3	87.3	24.3M	33G
	Medium	8	56.9	84.0	59.3	85.9	21.4M	29.4G
	Small	8	49.3	77.6	51.3	79.5	11.3M	14.6G
RubiksNet (Ours)	Large	8	59.0	85.2	61.7	87.3	8.5M (2.9×)	15.8G (2.1×)
	Medium	8	58.3	85.0	60.8	86.9	6.2M (3.5×)	11.2G (2.6×)
	Small	8	57.5	84.3	59.8	86.2	3.6M (3.1×)	6.8G (2.1×)
	Tiny	8	54.6	82.0	56.7	84.1	1.9M (5.9×)	3.9G (3.7×)

and pointwise Conv1 × 1 operations (Eq. 3) to facilitate information exchange across channels. We place RubiksShift layers at the "residual shift" position [16], which fuses temporal information inside a residual branch. While we choose ResNet-like structure as our backbone design, the RubiksShift operator is flexible to be plugged into any architecture to replace the heavy convolutional layers.

Stable Shift Training. To improve the stability of spatiotemporal shift training, we normalize the shift gradients to use only the direction of change [11], rather than the magnitude. In practice, equal normalization over all 3 axes is sub-optimal, because the spatial dimensions of video inputs (e.g., 224 × 224) are substantially larger than the temporal dimension (e.g., 8 frames). We propose *scaled* gradient normalization, which scales the gradient vector for the spatial shifts $\Delta\theta_h$, $\Delta\theta_w$ and temporal shift $\Delta\theta_t$ onto an ellipsoid rather than a unit sphere:

$$\overline{\Delta\theta_h} = \frac{\Delta\theta_h}{Z}; \quad \overline{\Delta\theta_w} = \frac{\Delta\theta_w}{Z}; \quad \overline{\Delta\theta_t} = \frac{\lambda\Delta\theta_t}{Z}, \tag{9}$$

where λ is the temporal gradient scaling factor and Z is the normalization factor:

$$Z = \sqrt{||\Delta\theta_h||^2 + ||\Delta\theta_w||^2 + \lambda||\Delta\theta_t||^2}. \tag{10}$$

Architecture Size Versions. We design several variants of RubiksNet models with different sizes to accommodate different computational budgets, analogous to prior work on shift for image classification [11]. Please refer to our supplementary material for full architecture breakdown tables. In our experiments (e.g., Table 1), we consider different size *classes* of our architecture, RubiksNet-Large, Medium, Small which all have the same channel width but different layer depths.

Table 2. Benchmark results on the Something-Something-v1 dataset [6]. Results are reported as 1-clip accuracy; FLOPs are reported for 1 clip, center crop for all architectures. (-) indicates value not reported.

Method	Input	Val Top-1	Val Top-5	#Param.	FLOPs/Video
I3D [1]	64	45.8	76.5	12.7M	111G
NL I3D + GCN [28]	32+32	46.1	76.8	303M	62.2G
S3D [31]	64	47.3	78.1	8.8M	66G
bLVNet-TAM [4]	8 × 2	46.4	76.6	25M	23.8G
TSN [26]	8	19.5	-	10.7M	16G
TRN [36]	8	34.4	-	18.3M	16G
ECO [37]	8	39.6	-	47.5M	32G
TSM [16]	8	45.6	74.2	24.3M	33G
RubiksNet (Ours)	8	46.4	74.5	8.5M	15.8G

These size classes are chosen to correspond with TSM [16] operating on standard ResNet-50, ResNet-34, and ResNet-18 backbones respectively. Our RubiksNet-Tiny model has the same depth as RubiksNet-Small, but a thinner width. We leverage this spectrum of models to generate our Pareto curves in Sect. 4.

4   Experiments and Analysis

In this section, we describe the experimental details (Sect. 4.1) and results of our method. In Sect. 4.2, we detail our comparisons and analysis against the prior art methods on several standard benchmarks, and we show our architecture significantly pushes the state-of-the-art on the accuracy-efficiency frontier across large and smaller scale benchmarks. Finally, in Sect. 4.3, we conduct a series of controlled ablation studies and analysis to verify that the core scientific aspects of our architecture are responsible for this significant gain.

4.1   Experimental Setup

Overview. We leverage the Something-Something-v1 [6], Something-Something-v2 [17], UCF-101 [22], and HMDB [15] datasets to benchmark our approach. As a general rule, we follow training and evaluation protocols established in recent work [4,16] for fair comparison, including input and metrics. We implement our RubiksNet architecture and training pipeline in PyTorch, and write the RubiksShift operators in CUDA and Pytorch C++ for efficiency.[1]

Spatial Shift Pretraining. Per prior works [4,16], we pretrain the spatial portion of our RubiksNet models on ImageNet-1k [19] to reach comparable accuracy with spatial-shift image classification literature [11,29]. Analogous to

---

[1] See rubiksnet.stanford.edu project page for supplementary material.

Table 3. Quantitative results on UCF-101 [22] and HMDB-51 [15]. 2-clip metric, 1-clip FLOPs per [16]. Pareto curve results in Fig. 4 and supplement.

Method	Size	UCF-101		HMDB-51		#Param.	FLOPs
		Val Top-1	Val Top-5	Val Top-1	Val Top-5		
TSN [26]	Large	91.7	99.2	64.7	89.9	23.7M	33G
TSM [16]	Large	95.2	99.5	73.5	94.3	23.7M	33G
RubiksNet	Large	95.5	99.6	74.6	94.4	8.5M	15.8G

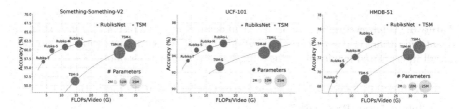

Fig. 4. We report the Pareto curves for our method compared with prior work [16], with size of the circle corresponding to the number of model parameters, as per Tables 1, 2 and 3. Our RubiksNet architecture family consistently offers better performance-efficiency tradeoff across datasets. (Additional vis. in supplement)

inflated convolution kernels [1], we initialize the spatial components of the 3D RubiksShift layers with the learned 2D shift patterns before benchmark training.

Something-Something-V2 and -V1. Something-Something-(v2,v1) are both large-scale datasets; SS-v2 in particular has 220k video clips and 174 action classes. The action labels, such as "pushing something from left to right" and "putting something next to something", cannot be predicted by looking at only a single frame. This challenging aspect separates this benchmark from similar large-scale benchmarks like Kinetics [14], as also noted in [4,16]. Our spatial-pretrained RubiksNet is jointly trained end-to-end on the full benchmark, with the gradient normalization described in Eq. 9 for stability. For temporal attention shift, we initialize all the attention weights by sampling from $Uniform[1, 1.05]$, so that the initial attention distribution is roughly uniform over all possible shift locations. The softmax temperature is exponentially annealed from $T = 2.0$ to 10^{-3} over 40 epochs, before conversion to discrete integer shifts for evaluation.

UCF-101 and HMDB-51. These standard benchmarks have 101 and 51 action classes, respectively, and are smaller scale than the SS-v1/2 datasets. We follow the standard practice from prior work [16,26] and pretrain our model on Kinetics [1] before fine-tuning on each benchmark. For fine-tuning, we follow the same general learning schedule protocol as Something-Something-v2, normalizing gradients again per Eq. 9 and following a similar attention shift annealing schedule.

Table 4. Ablation analysis: effect of learnable spatial and temporal shifts (Sect. 4.3). RubiksNet's ability to learn spatial and temporal shift jointly significantly improves over fixed, heuristic methods over spatial [29] and time [16] dimensions.

Spatial Shift Type	Temporal Shift Type	Val Top-1 (Large)	Val Top-1 (Small)
Learned	**Learned**	**71.4**	**69.5**
Learned	Fixed [16]	69.5	67.8
Fixed [29]	Learned	70.0	67.5
Fixed [29]	Fixed [16]	68.3	65.7

Table 5. Ablation analysis: impact of RubiksShift design (Sect. 4.3). Our attention-quantized variant is able to learn discrete shift operations with comparable performance to full interpolated, while observing shift/latency budget constraints.

RubiksShift Type	Val Top-1	Exact Gradient	Integer Shift	Budget
Interpolated (RS)	61.7	✓		
Interpolated Quantized (RS-IQ)	58.2		✓	
Attention Quantized (RS-AQ)	61.6	✓	✓	✓ (0.125)

4.2   Benchmark Comparisons and Analysis

Baselines. Our key point of comparison is the recent state-of-the-art shift-based action recognition architecture TSM [16] from ICCV 2019. In contrast with our technique, TSM operates with a hand-designed, fixed shift approach on the time dimension only, with heuristics found by extensive architecture tuning. TSM also has a fixed allocation scheme across its network. In our benchmark comparisons, we also include comparisons against much heavier but well-known architectures, like I3D, S3D, and others [1,4,28,31] for reference. Other networks, like TSN [26] and ECO [37] are also included as comparison points.

Evaluation. We follow the evaluation convention in prior work [16,27,28] and report results from two evaluation protocols. For "1-Clip Val" (Table 1), we sample only a single clip per video and the center 224×224 crop for evaluation. For "2-Clip Val", we sample 2 clips per video and take 3 equally spaced 224×224 crops from the full resolution image scaled to 256 pixels on the shorter side. 2-Clip evaluation yields higher accuracy, but requires more computation than 1-Clip evaluation. We employ the same protocol for all methods in all the tables.

Quantitative Analysis. In Tables 1, 2 and 3, we demonstrate that our proposed architectures consistently achieve competitive or better accuracies than their baseline counterparts at a range of model capacities, while achieving

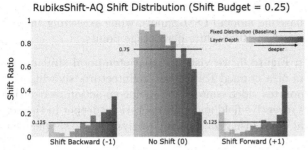

Shift-T Budget (Latency) (Ratio of Non-Zero Shift)		
Layers	Rubiks-AQ	Fixed
all	**0.25**	**0.25**
1-4	0.23	0.25
5-12	0.15	0.25
13-48	0.23	0.25
49-51	0.74	0.25

Fig. 5. We visualize our learned shifts distribution using our proposed attention quantized shift RubiksNet. The bottom labels are the different shifts $(-1, 0, +1)$ for a kernel size 3 RubiksShift-AQ temporal kernel, and the y-axis shows the proportion of channels with that temporal shift operation. Each colored bar represents a different layer, and we increase the depth of the network moving left to right. We observe that RubiksNet is able to learn to save its shift operations budget from early layers (few nonzero shift operations) to increase temporal modeling ability at deeper ones. Table 4 shows how this learned allocation consistently improves over heuristic techniques like TSM [16] that have a fixed shift budget allocation regardless of depth (shown by black horizontal bars above).

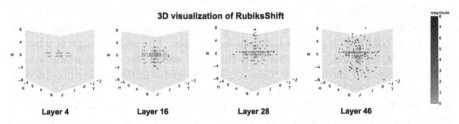

Fig. 6. We visualize the overall learned interpolated shift distribution across spatial (H, W) and temporal (T) dimensions at different layers in the RubiksNet architecture. RubiksNet is conservative with shift operations in early layers, while increasing the 3D receptive field in deeper layers for better spatiotemporal modeling. Please refer to supplement for additional video visualizations.

significantly higher efficiency in both parameter counts and FLOPs. Additionally, we provide a detailed efficiency analysis breakdown in our supplement.

We also benchmark several sizes of our model to draw a Pareto curve of performance and efficiency. In Fig. 4, we visualize Pareto curves for our approach against TSM on multiple benchmarks. We observe a consistent trend that our method significantly improves the accuracy-efficiency tradeoff for efficient action recognition architectures. On Something-Something-v2 datasets (Table 1), our most efficient model, RubiksNet-Tiny, outperforms TSM-Small by 5.3 absolute percentage points, while reducing parameters by 5.9x and FLOPs by 3.7x. This indicates that RubiksNet performs especially well in the low-resource regime when compared against prior work. Towards the other extreme, our highest-end model (RubiksNet-Large) consumes 24.1% *fewer* parameters and comparable FLOPs to the *lowest-end* baseline model (TSM-Small), while exceeding the latter's top 1 accuracy by more than 10 absolute percentage points.

Qualitative Analysis. In Figure 6, we visualize spatiotemporal shift operations across different layers of a trained RubiksNet architecture, showing how the model efficiently incorporates video context to provide an action recognition prediction by increasing its receptive field and shift operations deeper in the network. We include additional video visualizations and analysis in the supplement.

4.3   Ablations and Analysis

Finally, we provide controlled ablations and analysis over our core RubiksNet design principles. In particular, we verify that *jointly learning* our 3D-shift operations is key to our accuracy-efficiency improvements by synergizing both spatial and temporal shift learning. Further, we verify our RubiksShift-AQ variant provides strong performance under a strict global shift (latency) budget.

Ablation: Learned vs. Fixed. Our first ablation experiment provides a controlled analysis on the effect of learning the spatial and temporal shift aspects respectively. We describe our results in Table 4. We report top-1 accuracy results on the HMDB dataset for both Large and Small model size class. Critically, the architecture in all cases remains *constant* within a given model class size so there is no confounder due to different backbones. The only change is whether an aspect is "learned" or "fixed". In the fixed cases, we initialize the spatial and temporal shift parameters based on the heuristic initialization provided by ShiftNet [29] and TSM [16], respectively. Spatial and temporal learned cases are based on the RubiksNet (RubiksShift-AQ) method. For learned temporal, we set our budget constraint to 0.25 to exactly match that of the TSM [16] fixed setting for fair comparison and to ensure the same number of shift operations are performed. We find that our RubiksNet approach for learning spatial and temporal dimensions jointly consistently outperforms the ablations.

Ablation: RubiksShift-AQ. Our second ablation verifies the efficacy of the proposed RubiksShift layers and its variations. We report our results in Table 5. Here, we highlight that our RubiksShift-AQ is able to achieve comparable accuracy with a budget constraint of only 0.125 shift ratio, in comparison to the full RubikShift variant. In contrast with the naive RubiksShift-IQ variant, RubiksShift-AQ enables discrete shift learned with true gradient and substantially outperforms. We observe that given a shift budget constraint, our attention shift mechanism is able to learn nontrivial temporal patterns (Fig. 5) without hand-engineered prior knowledge. The network chooses to allocate more nonzero shifts for deeper layers, likely because heavier information exchange in the more abstract feature space is beneficial to the network's temporal modeling capability. Such findings are in alignment with traditional hand-designed "top-heavy" spatiotemporal convolutional networks [31]. Importantly, RubiksNet's learned temporal shift pattern can be thought of as an allocation of the limited "temporal modeling power budget". Prior works like [31] enumerate many configurations of temporal modeling allocation (i.e. permutations of Conv2D and Conv3D layers), and test them individually to find the best candidate. In contrast, our proposed method discovers a good temporal allocation pattern from random temporal initialization.

5 Conclusion

We introduced RubiksNet, a new efficient architecture for video action recognition. We examined the potential for a model based on our proposed 3D-spatiotemporal RubiksShift operations, and explored several novel variations of our design that enable stable joint training with flexible shift budget allocation. We benchmarked our method on several standard action recognition benchmarks, and find that RubiksNet can match or exceed the accuracies given by the previous state-of-the-art shift-based action recognition architecture at a fraction of the parameter and FLOP cost. Through careful and controlled ablations, we verified these gains are rooted in our core architecture contributions, from the joint learning of the spatial and temporal shifts to RubiksNet's ability to learn a flexible allocation of shift budget to maximize accuracy at minimal shift cost.

Acknowledgements. L. Fan and S. Buch are supported by SGF and NDSEG fellowships, respectively. This research was sponsored in part by grants from Toyota Research Institute (TRI). Some computational support for experiments was provided by Google Cloud and NVIDIA. This article reflects the authors' opinions and conclusions, and not any other entity. We thank Ji Lin, Song Han, De-An Huang, Danfei Xu, the general Stanford Vision Lab (SVL) community, and our anonymous reviewers for helpful comments and discussion.

References

1. Carreira, J., Zisserman, A.: Quo vadis, action recognition? A new model and the kinetics dataset. In: Proceedings of the IEEE Conference on Computer Vision and Pattern Recognition, pp. 6299–6308 (2017)
2. Chen, W., Xie, D., Zhang, Y., Pu, S.: All you need is a few shifts: designing efficient convolutional neural networks for image classification. In: Proceedings of the IEEE Conference on Computer Vision and Pattern Recognition, pp. 7241–7250 (2019)
3. Chollet, F.: Xception: deep learning with depthwise separable convolutions. In: Proceedings of the IEEE Conference on Computer Vision and Pattern Recognition, pp. 1251–1258 (2017)
4. Fan, Q., Chen, C.F.R., Kuehne, H., Pistoia, M., Cox, D.: More is less: learning efficient video representations by big-little network and depthwise temporal aggregation. In: Advances in Neural Information Processing Systems, pp. 2261–2270 (2019)
5. Feichtenhofer, C., Pinz, A., Wildes, R.: Spatiotemporal residual networks for video action recognition. In: Advances in Neural Information Processing Systems, pp. 3468–3476 (2016)

6. Goyal, R., et al.: The "something something" video database for learning and evaluating visual common sense. In: The IEEE International Conference on Computer Vision (ICCV), October 2017
7. Hacene, G.B., Lassance, C., Gripon, V., Courbariaux, M., Bengio, Y.: Attention based pruning for shift networks. arXiv:1905.12300 [cs] (May 2019)
8. He, K., Zhang, X., Ren, S., Sun, J.: Deep residual learning for image recognition. In: Proceedings of the IEEE Conference on Computer Vision and Pattern Recognition, pp. 770–778 (2016)
9. Howard, A.G., et al.: MobileNets: efficient convolutional neural networks for mobile vision applications. arXiv preprint arXiv:1704.04861 (2017)
10. Iandola, F.N., Han, S., Moskewicz, M.W., Ashraf, K., Dally, W.J., Keutzer, K.:SqueezeNet: AlexNet-level accuracy with 50x fewer parameters and<0.5 mb model size. arXiv preprint arXiv:1602.07360 (2016)
11. Jeon, Y., Kim, J.: Constructing fast network through deconstruction of convolution. In: Advances in Neural Information Processing Systems, pp. 5951–5961 (2018)
12. Ji, S., Xu, W., Yang, M., Yu, K.: 3D convolutional neural networks for human action recognition. IEEE Trans. Pattern Anal. Mach. Intell. **35**(1), 221–231 (2012)
13. Karpathy, A., Toderici, G., Shetty, S., Leung, T., Sukthankar, R., Fei-Fei, L.: Large-scale video classification with convolutional neural networks. In: Proceedings of the IEEE Conference on Computer Vision and Pattern Recognition, pp. 1725–1732 (2014)
14. Kay, W., et al.: The kinetics human action video dataset. arXiv preprint arXiv:1705.06950 (2017)
15. Kuehne, H., Jhuang, H., Garrote, E., Poggio, T., Serre, T.: HMDB: a large video database for human motion recognition. In: 2011 IEEE International Conference on Computer Vision (ICCV), pp. 2556–2563. IEEE (2011)
16. Lin, J., Gan, C., Han, S.: TSM: temporal shift module for efficient video understanding (2018)
17. Mahdisoltani, F., Berger, G., Gharbieh, W., Fleet, D., Memisevic, R.: On the effectiveness of task granularity for transfer learning. arXiv preprint arXiv:1804.09235 (2018)
18. Qiu, Z., Yao, T., Mei, T.: Learning spatio-temporal representation with pseudo-3D residual networks. In: proceedings of the IEEE International Conference on Computer Vision, pp. 5533–5541 (2017)
19. Russakovsky, O., et al.: ImageNet large scale visual recognition challenge. Int. J. Comput. Vis. **115**(3), 211–252 (2015). https://doi.org/10.1007/s11263-015-0816-y
20. Sandler, M., Howard, A., Zhu, M., Zhmoginov, A., Chen, L.C.: MobileNetV2: inverted residuals and linear bottlenecks. In: Proceedings of the IEEE Conference on Computer Vision and Pattern Recognition, pp. 4510–4520 (2018)
21. Simonyan, K., Zisserman, A.: Two-stream convolutional networks for action recognition in videos. In: Advances in Neural Information Processing Systems, pp. 568–576 (2014)
22. Soomro, K., Zamir, A.R., Shah, M.: UCF101: a dataset of 101 human actions classes from videos in the wild. arXiv preprint arXiv:1212.0402 (2012)
23. Tran, D., Bourdev, L., Fergus, R., Torresani, L., Paluri, M.: Learning spatiotemporal features with 3D convolutional networks. In: Proceedings of the IEEE International Conference on Computer Vision, pp. 4489–4497 (2015)
24. Tran, D., Wang, H., Torresani, L., Feiszli, M.: Video classification with channel-separated convolutional networks. In: Proceedings of the IEEE International Conference on Computer Vision, pp. 5552–5561 (2019)

25. Tran, D., Wang, H., Torresani, L., Ray, J., LeCun, Y., Paluri, M.: A closer look at spatiotemporal convolutions for action recognition. In: Proceedings of the IEEE Conference on Computer Vision and Pattern Recognition, pp. 6450–6459 (2018)
26. Wang, L., et al.: Temporal segment networks: towards good practices for deep action recognition. In: Leibe, B., Matas, J., Sebe, N., Welling, M. (eds.) ECCV 2016. LNCS, vol. 9912, pp. 20–36. Springer, Cham (2016). https://doi.org/10.1007/978-3-319-46484-8_2
27. Wang, X., Girshick, R., Gupta, A., He, K.: Non-local neural networks. In: Proceedings of the IEEE Conference on Computer Vision and Pattern Recognition, pp. 7794–7803 (2018)
28. Wang, X., Gupta, A.: Videos as space-time region graphs. In: Ferrari, V., Hebert, M., Sminchisescu, C., Weiss, Y. (eds.) ECCV 2018. LNCS, vol. 11209, pp. 413–431. Springer, Cham (2018). https://doi.org/10.1007/978-3-030-01228-1_25
29. Wu, B., et al.: Shift: A zero flop, zero parameter alternative to spatial convolutions. In: Proceedings of the IEEE Conference on Computer Vision and Pattern Recognition, pp. 9127–9135 (2018)
30. Wu, C.Y., Zaheer, M., Hu, H., Manmatha, R., Smola, A.J., Krähenbühl, P.: Compressed video action recognition. In: Proceedings of the IEEE Conference on Computer Vision and Pattern Recognition, pp. 6026–6035 (2018)
31. Xie, S., Sun, C., Huang, J., Tu, Z., Murphy, K.: Rethinking spatiotemporal feature learning: speed-accuracy trade-offs in video classification. In: Ferrari, V., Hebert, M., Sminchisescu, C., Weiss, Y. (eds.) ECCV 2018. LNCS, vol. 11219, pp. 318–335. Springer, Cham (2018). https://doi.org/10.1007/978-3-030-01267-0_19
32. Yao, G., Lei, T., Zhong, J.: A review of convolutional-neural-network-based action recognition. Pattern Recogn. Lett. 118, 14–22 (2019)
33. Zhang, X., Zhou, X., Lin, M., Sun, J.: ShuffleNet: an extremely efficient convolutional neural network for mobile devices. In: Proceedings of the IEEE Conference on Computer Vision and Pattern Recognition, pp. 6848–6856 (2018)
34. Zhao, Y., Xiong, Y., Lin, D.: Trajectory convolution for action recognition. In: Advances in Neural Information Processing Systems, pp. 2204–2215 (2018)
35. Zhong, H., Liu, X., He, Y., Ma, Y., Kitani, K.: Shift-based primitives for efficient convolutional neural networks. arXiv preprint arXiv:1809.08458 (2018)
36. Zhou, B., Andonian, A., Oliva, A., Torralba, A.: Temporal relational reasoning in videos. In: Ferrari, V., Hebert, M., Sminchisescu, C., Weiss, Y. (eds.) ECCV 2018. LNCS, vol. 11205, pp. 831–846. Springer, Cham (2018). https://doi.org/10.1007/978-3-030-01246-5_49
37. Zolfaghari, M., Singh, K., Brox, T.: ECO: efficient convolutional network for online video understanding. In: Ferrari, V., Hebert, M., Sminchisescu, C., Weiss, Y. (eds.) ECCV 2018. LNCS, vol. 11206, pp. 713–730. Springer, Cham (2018). https://doi.org/10.1007/978-3-030-01216-8_43

Deep Hashing with Active Pairwise Supervision

Ziwei Wang[1,2,3], Quan Zheng[1,2,3], Jiwen Lu[1,2,3(✉)], and Jie Zhou[1,2,3,4]

[1] Department of Automation, Tsinghua University, Beijing, China
{wang-zw18,zhengq16}@mails.tsinghua.edu.cn,
{lujiwen,jzhou}@tsinghua.edu.cn
[2] State Key Lab of Intelligent Technologies and Systems, Beijing, China
[3] Beijing National Research Center for Information Science and Technology, Beijing, China
[4] Tsinghua Shenzhen International Graduate School, Tsinghua University, Shenzhen, China

Abstract. In this paper, we propose a Deep Hashing method with Active Pairwise Supervision (DH-APS). Conventional methods with passive pairwise supervision obtain labeled data for training and require large amount of annotations to reach their full potential, which are not feasible in realistic retrieval tasks. On the contrary, we actively select a small quantity of informative samples for annotation to provide effective pairwise supervision so that discriminative hash codes can be obtained with limited annotation budget. Specifically, we generalize the structural risk minimization principle and obtain three criteria for the pairwise supervision acquisition: uncertainty, representativeness and diversity. Accordingly, samples involved in the following training pairs should be labeled: pairs with most uncertain similarity, pairs that minimize the discrepancy between labeled and unlabeled data, and pairs which are most different from the annotated data, so that the discriminality and generalization ability of the learned hash codes are significantly strengthened. Moreover, our DH-APS can also be employed as a plug-and-play module for semi-supervised hashing methods to further enhance the performance. Experiments demonstrate that the presented DH-APS achieves the accuracy of supervised hashing methods with only 30% labeled training samples and improves the semi-supervised binary codes by a sizable margin.

Keywords: Active learning · Deep hashing · Structural risk minimization

Electronic supplementary material The online version of this chapter (https://doi.org/10.1007/978-3-030-58529-7_31) contains supplementary material, which is available to authorized users.

© Springer Nature Switzerland AG 2020
A. Vedaldi et al. (Eds.): ECCV 2020, LNCS 12364, pp. 522–538, 2020.
https://doi.org/10.1007/978-3-030-58529-7_31

1   Introduction

Large scale image search, which aims to retrieve images with similar content from the database given a query image, has aroused extensive interest in computer vision due to its wide application [1,17,21]. Although conventional methods based on trees [49], nearest neighbor search [36] and quantization [20] have been broadly employed in low-dimensional data retrieval, they are not feasible for high-dimensional visual data due to the unbearable computational complexity and storage cost. Hence, it is desirable to extract compact features for the high-dimensional data in image search.   Recently, hashing-based approximating

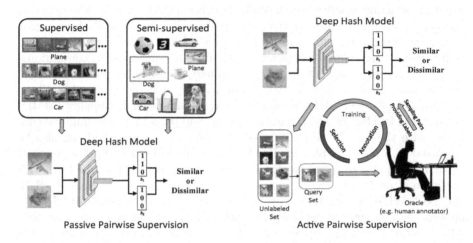

Fig. 1. Deep hashing methods with the passive and active pairwise supervision. For the former, supervised methods require exhaustive annotation with unbearable annotation cost to reach the full potential, and semi-supervised methods randomly select a few samples to label so that effective supervision is not provided. Our DH-APS selects samples providing effective pairwise supervision to label so that discriminative and generalizable binary codes are learned with limited annotation budget.

nearest neighbor search method have been presented to learn binary codes [10–12,29,41,53]. The storage and the computational cost of retrieval is decreased significantly, as Hamming distance instead of Euclidean distance between different hash codes is calculated when comparing the similarity of various instances. The objective of hashing-based methods is to learn a set of hash functions that maps each visual sample into a compact binary feature vector, where conceptually similar samples are hashed into similar binary codes. As limited bitwidth degrades the representational capacity of the representations, deep neural networks are applied to learn informative hash codes. Because unsupervised deep hashing methods suffer from low discriminative power due to the lack of supervision, supervised deep hash models boost the performance of the learned binary codes. However, exhaustive labeling for learning supervised hash codes require large amount of cost, which is prohibited in realistic applications with limited annotation budget. Moreover, semi-supervised deep hashing methods randomly select partial instances for annotation and fail to provide effective pairwise supervision for hash code learning.

In this paper, we propose a Deep Hashing method with Active Pairwise Supervision (DH-APS) to learn effective binary codes for image search with limited annotation budget. Unlike methods applying passive pairwise supervision which require to label all training samples to reach the full potential, our method only annotates a few samples which provide effective pairwise supervision, so that discriminative and generalizable binary codes are learned with limited annotation cost. More specifically, we extend the structural risk minimization principle to active deep hashing and obtain three annotation acquisition criteria: uncertainty, representativeness and diversity. As the goal of hashing is similarity preservation, our acquisition function is based on the pairwise relationship instead of individual samples that are usually considered in conventional active learning methods [28,48,54]. Accordingly, we label samples involved in the following pairs: pairs with highest uncertainty which is measured by Shannon Entropy [37], pairs which minimize the maximum mean discrepancy (MMD) between the labeled set and the unlabeled set, and pairs that have minimal similarity with the samples in the labeled set. Moreover, our method can also be employed as a plug-and-play module for semi-supervised deep hashing method to further enhance the performance. Figure 1 shows deep hashing methods with passive and active pairwise supervision. Extensive experiments on CIFAR-10 [23], NUS-WIDE [8] and ImageNet [9] demonstrate that the proposed DH-APS obtains the competitive performance with supervised binary codes with only 30% annotated training samples and enhances the semi-supervised hash models by a large margin.

2   Related Work

Deep Hashing: Deep hashing has been widely studied in recent years due to strong discriminative power and the high efficiency in large scale visual search. Deep hashing obtains much better performance compared with hand-crafted and shallow binary codes due to the data-dependent hash functions and the employment of deep architectures. Existing deep hashing methods can be divided into three categories according to the type of supervision: unsupervised [12,15,42], supervised [24,29,50] and semi-supervised [46,51] methods. For the first category, Liong et al. [12] utilized the deep neural networks with energy constraint objectives to enhance the discriminative ability of hash codes. Ghasedi et al. [15] applied the Generative Adversarial Networks (GANs) [16] to learn hash codes through which the reconstructed images were enforced to have minimum discrepancy with the real ones, so that the obtained binary representations acquired informativeness and independency. For supervised methods, relation among different samples or explicit class labels are usually employed as supervision for hash code learning. Liu et al. [29] enforced the similar samples to obtain closer binary codes and punished semantically dissimilar samples whose hash codes have short Hamming distance so that the learned binary representations could precisely preserve the topology of the semantic space. Yang *et al.* [50] used the category information to supervise the hash model, and the learned hash codes extracted the class-dependent information for image retrieval. For semi-supervised methods, Zhang *et al.* [51] mined the semantic topology between labeled and unlabeled samples and generated pseudo labels for unlabeled samples to leverage the limited supervision. Zhang *et al.* [52] utilized the knowledge distillation to train the student model for hash code generation, and the teacher network was assembled by multiple students. Nevertheless, exhaustive labeling is not feasible in realistic application due to the large scale database and limited annotation budget, and randomly annotating part of samples in hash code learning fails to provide effective supervision.

Active Learning: Active learning aims to acquire better performance when learning with fewer labeled training samples by actively annotating part of the training data from a pool of unlabeled set. The criteria for active sample selection can be divided into two types: informativeness and representativeness. For the former category, the unlabeled data which the learner is most uncertain about is selected to annotate as effective supervision can enhance discriminality of the learner. The uncertainty can be defined as the entropy of the posterior probabilities [22,30,39], distance to the classification boundaries [27,45], margin between the largest and the second largest posterior probabilities [2] and disagreement among independent classifiers [32,44]. Gal *et al.* [14] utilized the neural networks to estimate the task-specific uncertainty through multiple forward passes in a data-driven manner. Beluch *et al.* [4] constructed a classifier committee comprising five deep neural networks to obtain accurate estimation of uncertainty disagreement. For the latter category, the samples that can represent the unlabeled pool are chosen to label as the learning over a representative subset is competitive over the whole pool. The representativeness can be measured by clustering [33], knowledge propagation [19,31], expected model change [13,40] and optimal experimental design which tries to query the representative samples directly [7]. Sener *et al.* [38] selected the core-set for annotation by minimizing the gap between an average loss over any given subset and the remaining data points. Meanwhile, as combining informativeness and representativeness can enhance the learner, a variety of hybrid strategies have been proposed for specific tasks [28,34]. Active hashing has also been proposed in Zhen *et al.* [54] and Wang *et al.* [48], which only measured the uncertainty of individuals to select samples for annotation and failed to consider the representativeness and diversity. Meanwhile, pairwise relationship should be considered in the acquisition function because the goal of hashing is similarity preservation. However, existing methods just calculate the acquisition function according to individual samples, which leads to uninformative annotation. In this paper, we extend active learning to deep hashing by considering pairwise relationship so that samples providing effective pairwise supervision are labeled to learn discriminative and generalizable binary codes with limited annotation budget.

3 Approach

In this section, we first introduce the problem setting of deep hashing with active pairwise supervision and then build the link between the acquisition function for active annotation and the structural risk minimization principle. Finally, we design the acquisition function by considering pairwise relationship for active deep hashing.

3.1 Deep Hashing with Active Pairwise Supervision

The training data set $\mathcal{X}$ consists of an active seed set $\mathcal{L}$ including a few labeled samples $\{\boldsymbol{x}_L\}$, a large pool set $\mathcal{U}$ containing unlabeled data $\{\boldsymbol{x}_U\}$ and a query set $\mathcal{Q}$ comprising samples $\{\boldsymbol{x}_Q\}$ that are selected from $\mathcal{U}$ for the Oracle to label. For the initialization of active deep hashing, we randomly move only a few samples from $\mathcal{U}$ to $\mathcal{L}$, and $\mathcal{Q}$ is an empty set. Active deep hashing algorithms undergo three iterative steps listed as follows: (1) training the hash model $\mathcal{H}$ with the pairs sampled from $\mathcal{L}$; (2) selecting samples that can provide the most effective supervision from $\mathcal{U}$ based on the acquisition function $s(\mathcal{H}, \mathcal{U}, \mathcal{L})$ and adding them to $\mathcal{Q}$; (3) asking the Oracle to label the samples in $\mathcal{Q}$ and updating $\mathcal{L}$, $\mathcal{U}$ and $\mathcal{Q}$.

Let $\boldsymbol{f}^k$ be the k_{th} byte of the float feature for the input image, which is obtained after the projection of the hash model $\mathcal{H}$. The k_{th} bit of the hash code $\boldsymbol{b}^k$ is obtained as follows:

$$\boldsymbol{b}^k = sgn(\boldsymbol{f}^k) \tag{1}$$

where $sgn(x)$ means the sign function which equals to zero if x is negative and equals to one otherwise. Following the typical hinge loss in supervised hash model training [29], we optimize the following objective to learn the optimal binary codes:

$$J = y||\boldsymbol{b}_a - \boldsymbol{b}_b||_2^2 + (1 - y)\max(m - ||\boldsymbol{b}_a - \boldsymbol{b}_b||_2^2, 0)$$
$$s.t. \quad \boldsymbol{b}_a, \boldsymbol{b}_b \in \{+1, -1\}^d \tag{2}$$

where $\boldsymbol{b}_a$ and $\boldsymbol{b}_b$ are the learned binary codes of $\boldsymbol{x}_a$ and $\boldsymbol{x}_b$ in the labeled set, and sampling the labeled set constructs pairs for training. y is the label providing pairwise supervision, which equals to one if $\boldsymbol{x}_a$ and $\boldsymbol{x}_b$ are similar and zero otherwise. m is a margin threshold parameter assigned to be positive. The objective enforces the similar samples to be mapped into binary codes with short distance and punishes dissimilar sample pairs whose hash codes are close when their Hamming distance falls below m. As the sign function is non-differentiable and searching for the optimal solution of binary codes is NP-hard, we relax the optimization in (2) as the following problem:

$$J = y||\boldsymbol{f}_a - \boldsymbol{f}_b||_2^2 + (1 - y)\max(m - ||\boldsymbol{f}_a - \boldsymbol{f}_b||_2^2, 0)$$
$$+ \gamma(|||\boldsymbol{f}_a| - \mathbf{1}^d||_1 + |||\boldsymbol{f}_b| - \mathbf{1}^d||_1) \tag{3}$$

where $\mathbf{1}^d$ is a all-one vector in d dimensions and $|\cdot|$ is the element-wise absolute value operation. f_a and f_b are the float feature for b_a and b_b, and γ is an hyperparameter to balance the term for similarity preservation and quantization error minimization. In active deep hashing, pairs sampled from the labeled set are utilized to train the hash model via (3). Moreover, active deep hashing can also be integrated with semi-supervised methods [52] so that the performance of the semi-supervised binary codes can be further enhanced due to the effective supervision.

3.2   Structural Risk Minimization for Active Hashing

The target for supervised hashing is to learn a hash model that preserves similarity among all samples and generalizes well on unseen data. The structural risk minimization (SRM) principle illustrates the objective via minimizing the upper bound of the true risk under unknown data distribution, which holds for dataset containing n samples with the probability at least $1 - \delta$ [3]:

$$\mathbb{E}(J(z)) \leqslant \hat{\mathbb{E}}(J(z)) + 2R_n(\Omega) + \sqrt{\frac{\ln 1/\delta}{n}} \tag{4}$$

where $J(z)$ means the loss over the data z. $\mathbb{E}(J(z))$ and $\hat{\mathbb{E}}(J(z))$ are the loss expectation over true distribution of z and the distribution sampled from the dataset, which are named true risk and empirical risk respectively. $R_n(\Omega)$ represents the Rademacher complexity of the loss function class Ω. The SRM principle requires the data to be i.i.d. sampled from the original data distribution. However, the pairs sampled from available labeled instances in active hashing follow different distribution compared with the whole training set as the chosen data is usually more informative and representative. In order to extend the SRM principle in active deep hashing, we reformulate the risk bound inequality with z omitted and the detailed formulation is in the supplementary material:

$$\mathbb{E}(J) \leqslant (\mathbb{E}(J) - \mathbb{E}_M(J)) + \hat{\mathbb{E}}_M(J) + \Phi \tag{5}$$

where $\mathbb{E}_M(J)$ and $\hat{\mathbb{E}}_M(J)$ are the true risk and empirical risk of available labeled data which includes the labeled set and query set. $\Phi = 2R_c(\Omega) + \sqrt{\frac{\ln 1/\delta}{c}}$ means the model complexity, and c is the size of the available labeled training pairs. In active hashing, the data z consists of sample pairs $\mathbf{x} = (\mathbf{x}_a, \mathbf{x}_b)$ and their labels y, we can rewrite the first term of (5) as follows:

$$\mathbb{E}(J) - \mathbb{E}_M(J) = \int p(\mathbf{x}|\mathbf{x} \in \mathcal{X}) \int J \cdot p(y|\mathbf{x}) d\mathbf{x} dy$$

$$- \int p(\mathbf{x}|\mathbf{x} \in \mathcal{M}) \int J \cdot p(y|\mathbf{x}) d\mathbf{x} dy$$

$$= \int g(\mathbf{x})p(\mathbf{x}|\mathbf{x} \in \mathcal{X}) d\mathbf{x} - \int g(\mathbf{x})p(\mathbf{x}|\mathbf{x} \in \mathcal{M}) d\mathbf{x} \tag{6}$$

where $\mathcal{M}$ means the labeled set $\mathcal{L}$ and the query set $\mathcal{Q}$. $p(\mathbf{x}|\mathbf{x} \in \mathcal{X})$ and $p(\mathbf{x}|\mathbf{x} \in \mathcal{M})$ are the distribution of all training pairs and available labeled pairs respectively, and $p(y|\boldsymbol{x})$ is the probability of the pair $\boldsymbol{x}$ to be similar. As $g(\boldsymbol{x}) = \int J \cdot p(y|\boldsymbol{x})dy$ is bounded and measurable, a bounded and continuous function $\hat{g}(\boldsymbol{x})$ can guarantee the boundness of (6):

$$\mathbb{E}(J) - \mathbb{E}_M(J) \leqslant \sup_{\hat{g} \in S}[\int g(\boldsymbol{x})p(\mathcal{X})d\boldsymbol{x} - \int g(\boldsymbol{x})p(\mathcal{M})d\boldsymbol{x}]$$
$$= MMD_S(p(\mathcal{X}), p(\mathcal{M})) \tag{7}$$

where we rewrite $p(\boldsymbol{x}|\boldsymbol{x} \in \mathcal{X})$ as $p(\mathcal{X})$ and $p(\boldsymbol{x}|\boldsymbol{x} \in \mathcal{M})$ as $p(\mathcal{M})$ for simplicity. $MMD_S(p_1, p_2)$ represents the maximum mean discrepancy between distribution p_1 and p_2, which is measured by functions from class S. Finally, the SRM principle can be directly employed in deep hashing with active pairwise supervision and rewritten as follows:

$$\mathbb{E}(J) \leqslant \hat{\mathbb{E}}_M(J) + \varPhi + MMD_S(p(\mathcal{X}), p(\mathcal{M})) \tag{8}$$

Minimizing the upper bound in (8) can actively distinguish the sample pairs that provide effective supervision.

3.3   Designing the Acquisition Function via Structural Risk Minimization

We propose a batch mode active deep hashing algorithm by minimizing the structural risk bound illustrated in (8) with pairwise relationship. The query set is selected via the following optimization objectives:

$$\min_{\mathcal{Q},\mathcal{H}} \frac{1}{l+q} \sum_{x \in \mathcal{L} \cup \mathcal{Q}} J + \lambda ||\mathcal{H}||_F^2 + MMD_S[p(\mathcal{X}), p(\mathcal{L} \cup \mathcal{Q})]$$

where l and q are the size of the labeled set and the query set. $||\mathcal{H}||_F$ is the Frobenius norm of the weight matrix in deep hash model, which demonstrates the model complexity $\varPhi$ [3] equally. In the above objective function, we denote the first two terms as L_1 which corresponds to the regularized empirical risk for all labeled sample pairs. Minimizing L_1 enforces the learned hash codes to be discriminative to learn the topology of semantic space of images in visual retrieval according to the supervision. The last term is notated as L_2, which relates to the generalization ability of the active deep hash model. Optimizing L_2 requires the distribution difference between labeled pairs and all pairs in the training set to be small, which encourages the labeled set to capture the representative information of the whole training set for enhanced generalization ability.

According to the definition of J presented in (3), we should minimize the worst-case regularized empirical risk as labels for sample pairs in the query set is unknown. We can write the worst-case regularized empirical risk explicitly as follows:

$$\min_{\mathcal{Q},\mathcal{H}} L_1 = \frac{1}{l+q} \sum_{x \in \mathcal{L}} J + \lambda ||\mathcal{H}||_F^2 + \frac{1}{l+q} \sup_y \sum_{x \in \mathcal{Q}} J \tag{9}$$

The label of pairs sampled from the query set with the worst-case risk is $y = -sign(\frac{m}{2} - ||f_a - f_b||_2^2)$. The first two terms in (9) train the hash model with pairwise supervision. The last term measures the similarity uncertainty of pairs sampled from the query set and contributes to the acquisition function, as hard pairs leading to high training loss should acquire label information to provide effective supervision.

The distribution difference between pairs sampled from the labeled and training sets is measured by their mean maximum discrepancy (MMD). The MMD objective ensures the labeled sample pairs are similar to the overall sample pairs so that representative information of the training data is captured. The hash model $\mathcal{H}$ yields two binary vectors to represent the sample pair, and the distance between binary code pairs is defined as follows:

$$d(\mathcal{H}(\boldsymbol{x}), \mathcal{H}(\boldsymbol{t})) = \inf_k ||\mathcal{H}(\boldsymbol{x}) - \mathcal{T}_k(\mathcal{H}(\boldsymbol{t}))||_F$$

$$= \min(||\mathcal{H}(\boldsymbol{x}_a) - \mathcal{H}(\boldsymbol{t}_a)||_F + ||\mathcal{H}(\boldsymbol{x}_b) - \mathcal{H}(\boldsymbol{t}_b)||_F,$$

$$||\mathcal{H}(\boldsymbol{x}_b) - \mathcal{H}(\boldsymbol{t}_a)||_F + ||\mathcal{H}(\boldsymbol{x}_a) - \mathcal{H}(\boldsymbol{t}_b)||_F) \tag{10}$$

where $\mathcal{T}_k$ and $k \in \{0, 1\}$ is the permutation operator and indicator respectively. $\mathcal{T}_1(\mathcal{H}(\boldsymbol{t}))$ means to permute the pair $(\mathcal{H}(\boldsymbol{t}_a), \mathcal{H}(\boldsymbol{t}_b))$ to $(\mathcal{H}(\boldsymbol{t}_b), \mathcal{H}(\boldsymbol{t}_a))$ when calculating the Hamming distance with other pairs, and $\mathcal{T}_0(\mathcal{H}(\boldsymbol{t}))$ remains $\mathcal{H}(\boldsymbol{t})$ unchanged. When large distance is caused by the sampling order for semantically similar pairs, we permute the instances in pairs to obtain the real semantic distance. As proved in the supplementary materials, the defined distance is nonnegative, symmetric and follows the triangle inequality. According to the distance definition in (10), we write the MMD objectives for active deep hashing in the following [5,18]:

$$\inf_{k_1, k_2} \left\| \frac{1}{l+q} \sum_{i=1}^{l+q} \mathcal{T}_{k_{1,i}}(\mathcal{H}(\boldsymbol{x}_{1,i})) - \frac{1}{u-q} \sum_{i=1}^{u-q} \mathcal{T}_{k_{2,i}}(\mathcal{H}(\boldsymbol{x}_{2,i})) \right\|_F^2$$

where $\boldsymbol{x}_{1,i} \in \mathcal{L} \bigcup \mathcal{Q}$ is the i_{th} pair sampled from the labeled and query sets, and $\boldsymbol{x}_{2,i} \in \mathcal{U} \setminus \mathcal{Q}$ is the i_{th} pair sampled from the unlabeled set excluding query instances. $k_{1,i}$ and $k_{2,i}$ is the i_{th} element of the permutation indicator $\boldsymbol{k}_1 \in \{0, 1\}^{l+q}$ and $\boldsymbol{k}_2 \in \{0, 1\}^{u-q}$. Similar to [7], we transfer the MMD objective for active deep hashing as follows during the optimization process:

$$\min_{\boldsymbol{\alpha}} L_2 = \frac{1}{2}\boldsymbol{\alpha}^T \boldsymbol{K}_{UU} \boldsymbol{\alpha} + \frac{u-q}{n} \mathbf{1}^l \boldsymbol{K}_{LU} \boldsymbol{\alpha} - \frac{l+q}{n} \mathbf{1}^u \boldsymbol{K}_{UU} \boldsymbol{\alpha}$$

$$s.t. \quad \boldsymbol{\alpha} \in \{0, 1\}^u, ||\boldsymbol{\alpha}||_1 = q \tag{11}$$

where the k_{th} element of $\boldsymbol{\alpha}$ is one if the k_{th} pair sampled from the unlabeled set is require to obtain annotation and otherwise equals to zero. $\mathbf{1}^d$ is an all one vector in d dimensions. $\boldsymbol{K}_{UU}$ illustrates the self-correlation matrix of pairs sampled from the unlabeled set, and $\boldsymbol{K}_{LU}$ demonstrates the correlation between pairs sampled from the labeled set and the unlabeled pool. We denote the element in the i_{th} row and j_{th} column of $\boldsymbol{K}_{UU}$ and $\boldsymbol{K}_{LU}$ as $K_{UU,ij}$ and $K_{LU,ij}$ and represent them as $K_{UU,ij} = \inf_{k} \mathcal{H}(\boldsymbol{x}_{U,i})^T \mathcal{T}_k(\mathcal{H}(\boldsymbol{x}_{U,j}))$ and $K_{LU,ij} = \inf_{k} \mathcal{H}(\boldsymbol{x}_{L,i})^T \mathcal{T}_k(\mathcal{H}(\boldsymbol{x}_{U,j}))$ respectively, where $\boldsymbol{x}_{U,i}$ and $\boldsymbol{x}_{L,i}$ are the i_{th} pair sampled from the unlabeled and labeled sets. The MMD objective contributes to the acquisition function. In (11), the first term aims to minimize the self-correlation of pairs sampled from the query set in a batch so that the Oracle provides more information, and the second term purposes to encourage pairs sampled from the query set to be different from those sampled from the labeled set so that the provided supervision is not redundant. The above two terms increase the diversity of information with redundancy elimination in batch mode deep active hashing. The goal of the last term is to ensure the pairs sampled from the query set are comprehensively similar to all unlabeled ones as they are representative for the whole dataset.

Finally, we obtain different terms of the acquisition function in the proposed DH-APS method with respect to uncertainty, representativeness and diversity:

$$Uncertainty: \quad s_1 = \frac{1}{l+q} \sup_{y} \sum J\alpha$$

$$Representativeness: \quad s_2 = -\frac{l+q}{n} \mathbf{1}^u K_{UU}\alpha$$

$$Diversity: \quad s_3 = \frac{1}{2}\alpha^T K_{UU}\alpha + \frac{u-q}{n} \mathbf{1}^l K_{LU}\alpha$$

where the i_{th} element of $J \in \mathcal{R}^{1 \times u}$ represents the training loss of the i_{th} pair sampled from the unlabeled set. As searching for the optimal α is an NP-hard problem, we employ the alternating direction method of multipliers (ADMM) algorithm [6] to solve the following problem in active deep hashing:

$$\min_{\alpha} s = s_1 + s_2 + s_3 \tag{12}$$

Because α indicates the selection of pairs instead of instances, we rank all unlabeled samples based on the number of selected pairs containing them in a descent order. Then we add the top q instances to the query set before the annotation process. Labeling the selected samples provides effective supervision and enforces the hash model to learn discriminative and generalizable binary codes.

4   Experiments

In this section, we evaluated our method on three datasets for image retrieval: CIFAR-10, NUS-WIDE and ImageNet. We first introduce the implementation details, and then investigate the influence of the acquisition function by ablation study. Meanwhile, we compare the proposed DH-APS with the state-of-the-art hash codes to show the benefits of effective supervision from actively selected samples. Finally, we visualize the query set to demonstrate our intuition.

Table 1. Effect of different components in the acquisition function and the ratio of labeled samples on mean average precision (%), where Unc., Rep. and Div. represent uncertainty, representativeness and diversity respectively. The proposed DH-APS was evaluated with the 32-bit hash codes on CIFAR-10.

Unc.	Rep.	Div.	Ratio of labeled samples									
			0%	1%	5%	10%	15%	20%	30%	50%	80%	100%
√	√	√	18.1	32.6	41.0	49.5	54.2	57.3	63.5	64.7	65.4	66.1
		×	18.1	31.8	39.5	47.6	51.9	55.9	62.9	64.1	65.1	66.1
	×	√	18.1	31.5	38.9	48.0	52.1	55.2	61.8	64.3	65.0	66.1
		×	18.1	28.7	36.6	46.0	49.3	53.1	59.5	63.8	64.8	66.1
×	√	√	18.1	29.0	36.4	44.3	49.2	52.5	58.8	63.6	64.7	66.1
		×	18.1	26.8	34.9	41.0	45.5	49.6	56.0	62.4	64.2	66.1
	×	√	18.1	26.4	35.4	41.2	45.3	48.9	54.7	62.3	64.4	66.1
		×	18.1	25.5	33.7	38.1	44.6	48.1	54.3	62.0	63.9	66.1

4.1 Datasets and Implementation Details

We first introduce the datasets our DH-APS carried out experiments on and corresponding data preprocessing techniques:

CIFAR-10: The CIFAR-10 dataset consists of $60,000$ images of size 32×32 and is categorized into 10 classes. We randomly selected 1,000 images (100 images per class) as the query set, the rest 59,000 images as the training set and the retrieval database. We padded 4 pixels on each side of the image and cropped it into the size of 32×32 randomly with normalization.

NUS-WIDE: The NUS-WIDE dataset contains $269,648$ images collected from Flicker with 81 manually annotated concepts. Two images are regarded as positive if they share at least one positive label and are negative otherwise. Only the 21 most frequent concepts were used, resulting in a total of $166,047$ images. We randomly chose 2,100 images (100 images per class) as the query set and regarded the rest as the training set and the retrieval database. The images were warped to 64×64 before feeding forward to the networks and normalized.

ImageNet-100: ImageNet (ILSVRC12) contains approximately 1.2 million training and 50K validation images from 1,000 categories. ImageNet is much more challenging because of its large scale and high diversity. Images of 100 randomly sampled categories were selected to construct the training set, and we applied all images in the selected classes from the validation set as queries. Followed by data augmentation of bias subtraction applied in CIFAR-10, a 224×224 region was randomly cropped for training from the resized image whose shorter side was 256. For inference, we employed the 224×224 center crop.

We trained our DH-APS with VGG16-like [43] architectures, where the softmax layer in the original VGG16 was replaced with a fully-connected layer to obtain the binary codes. In each iteration, we trained the hash model for 60 epochs, selected the samples for annotation and labeled the query samples by an Oracle until reaching the annotation cost limit. For hash model training, the SGD optimizer with the momentum of 0.9 and weight decay of 0 was leveraged. The learning rate started from 0.01 and changed to $1e^{-3}$ and $1e^{-4}$ at the 20_{th} and 40_{th} epoch. For sample selection, we randomly sampled $\frac{\eta n^2}{100}$ pairs from the unlabeled instances to construct the unlabeled pairs and then actively selected $\frac{\eta n^2}{1000}$ pairs by solving (12) via ADMM, where η is the assigned ratio of labeled data representing the annotation budget and n is the size of the dataset. We ranked all unlabeled samples based on the number of selected pairs containing them and added the top $\frac{\eta n}{1000}$ samples to the query set.

4.2   Ablation Study

As DH-APS selects samples that provide effective pairwise supervision for annotation, the learned binary codes are enhanced significantly with discriminative information and strong generalization ability. To verify the importance of the proposed acquisition function and supervision, we implemented our DH-APS with different annotation budget and utilization of various terms in the acquisition function. Because the uncertainty, representativeness and diversity terms in the acquisition function contribute differently to sample selection, we conducted orthogonal ablation study w.r.t. them. We adopted VGG16-like architecture as the deep hash model, which was evaluated on the CIFAR-10 dataset. Mean Average Precision (MAP) in 32-bit binary codes was reported in Table 1. Based on the results, we observe the influence of different component in the proposed acquisition function and the ratio of labeled samples.

- Comparing the accuracy obtained with different ratio of labeled samples, we know that annotating a small quantity of informative samples improves the MAP of retrieval very significantly. The effective pairwise supervision benefits the hash code learning obviously especially when extremely little annotation budget is accessible for training. Although the ratio of labeled samples is positively related to the performance, the margin of the MAP enhancement caused by the extra annotation declines for the large labeled set, which means most samples fail to provide effective supervision and do not contribute to deep hash code learning. Our DH-APS achieves competitive accuracy compared with the fully supervised deep hashing methods by utilizing only 30% labeled data for training, which significantly saves the labeling cost.
- All components in the acquisition function including uncertainty, representativeness and diversity improve the MAP at various degrees, which implies the DH-APS method are universally suitable for various deep hash model. The uncertainty enhances the binary codes most significantly, because hard pairs with the most uncertain similarity provide large gradients in the back-propagation so that the deep hash model is supervised effectively. Because the representative samples capture the global topology of the semantic space and the diverse samples eliminate information redundancy in supervision, combining all components in the acquisition function further increases the MAP.

Table 2. Comparison of mean average precision (%) with state-of-the-art unsupervised, semi-supervised and supervised deep binary descriptors under varying code lengths. 12b, 24b, 32b and 48b means the hash codes in 12, 24, 36 and 48 bits. SSH[†] means that we integrate the method with deep hash models. DH-APS (1%, 10%, 30%) stands for our method with different ratio of labeled samples, and DH-APS (∗) means that we adopt the same annotation setting as semi-supervised hashing methods. DH-APS+PTS³H represents the presented DH-APS combined with PTS³H.

Methods	CIFAR-10				NUS-WIDE				ImageNet-100			
	12b	24b	32b	48b	12b	24b	32b	48b	12b	24b	32b	48b
Unsupervised Hashing												
DH	22.3	23.0	23.6	23.7	22.5	23.1	23.4	23.3	12.5	13.8	14.0	14.2
GraphBit	26.9	27.2	27.0	27.3	26.7	27.0	27.2	27.4	12.9	14.5	14.7	15.1
Semi-supervised Hashing												
SSH[†]	35.3	37.0	38.1	38.2	30.0	31.6	35.8	32.6	19.9	21.0	21.6	23.1
SSDH	80.1	81.3	81.2	81.4	77.3	77.9	77.8	77.8	–	–	–	–
PTS³H	79.8	82.8	83.5	84.3	75.2	77.4	78.3	78.9	66.1	67.5	68.0	69.7
Supervised Hashing												
DSH	61.6	65.6	66.1	67.3	54.5	55.3	55.9	56.0	47.9	50.3	50.7	51.4
DPSH	71.3	72.7	74.4	75.7	79.4	82.2	83.8	85.1	–	–	–	–
SDSH	93.9	93.9	93.9	93.4	–	81.7	82.1	82.1	–	–	–	–
Active Hashing												
DH-APS (1%)	30.5	31.9	32.6	32.8	30.1	30.6	31.2	31.8	17.9	18.1	19.5	19.6
DH-APS (∗)	44.9	46.4	47.8	47.7	36.0	36.8	38.5	38.8	24.9	25.1	26.3	26.8
DH-APS (10%)	47.2	48.6	49.5	49.7	38.1	39.6	40.2	40.7	26.1	27.3	27.8	28.0
DH-APS (30%)	61.8	62.4	63.5	64.3	51.8	53.0	53.5	54.3	43.5	43.6	45.2	46.9
DH-APS+PTS³H	82.1	85.3	86.7	86.9	79.1	81.1	82.2	82.3	68.9	70.0	70.3	71.8

4.3 Comparison with the State-of-the-art Methods

In this section, we compare the performance of our DH-APS with existing unsupervised methods DH [12] and GraphBit [11], semi-supervised methods SSH [47], SSDH [51] and PTS³H [52] and supervised methods DSH [29], DPSH [26] and SDSH [35] in image retrieval tasks on the CIFAR-10, NUS-WIDE and ImageNet datasets, and the applied backbone of the above methods were all VGG16 in our comparison. Table 2 illustrates the MAP of different methods in various code lengths, where SSH[†] means that we reimplemented the method with deep hash models. DH-APS (1%, 10%, 30%) represents the proposed active deep hashing method with corresponding ratio of labeled samples. We also implemented our DH-APS with the same annotation setting as semi-supervised methods [47,51,52] which is denoted as DH-APS (*). For DH-APS (*), we randomly selected 500, 500 and 100 images of each class on CIFAR-10, NUS-WIDE and ImageNet-100 for labeling respectively. DH-APS+PTS³H represent DH-APS

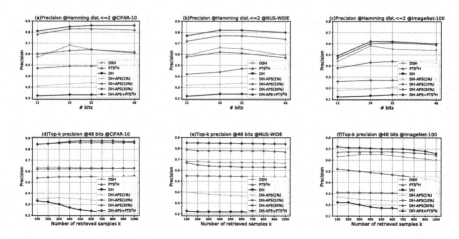

Fig. 2. The performance on image retrieval of different binary codes.

deployed as a plug-and-play module in PTS³H for labeled instance sampling. Table 2 illustrates the MAP of different hash methods. Figure 2 depicts the precision within Hamming 2 for 12, 24, 32 and 48-bit hash codes and w.r.t. top-k in 48-bit binary representations on the three datasets. The performance of DH, GraphBit, SSH†, PTS³H and DSH was obtained by rerunning the codes and the results of other baselines were copied from the referenced paper.

The results indicate DH-APS achieves the competitive accuracy with the supervised method DSH with only 30% labeled samples on both the CIFAR-10 and NUS-WIDE datasets, and the underperformance on ImageNet-100 is caused by the rich information of the dataset where the global structure of the semantic space is difficult to represent by few samples. Meanwhile, DH-APS enhances the semi-supervised method PTS³H significantly due to the effective supervision from actively selected samples. Compared with unsupervised methods, DH-APS outperforms GraphBit across all datasets with only 1% data labeled. With better discriminality and generalization ability, DH-APS mines the global structure of the semantic space with few labeled samples.

4.4   Visualization

In order to demonstrate the intuition of the proposed method, we provide the visualization of DH-APS. We trained an active deep hash model with the LeNet5 architecture on the MNIST dataset [25] through our method. The MNIST dataset consists of $60,000$ digit images with the size 28×28, which are divided into 10 categories. We scaled and biased all images into the range $[-0.5, 0.5]$. We randomly sampled $2,000$ images with 200 samples for each class to construct the training set and selected 10 images to annotate according to the acquisition function only consisting of uncertainty, representativeness and diversity terms respectively. Figure 3(a) shows the 2-d projection of the samples via the t-SNE method, where dots in different colors represent various digits and dots with

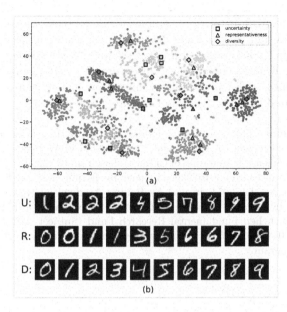

Fig. 3. Visualization of DH-APS. (a) The 2-d projection of the samples via the t-SNE method, where dots in different colors represent various digits. Dots with square, triangle and rhombus borders mean the selected instances based on acquisition function only containing uncertainty, representativeness and diversity terms respectively. (b) Selected images according to acquisition function only composed of uncertainty (U), representativeness (R) and diversity (D) respectively (best viewed in color).

different borders stand for the selected instances based on various acquisition function. Figure 3(b) demonstrate the selected images according to acquisition function composed by uncertainty, representativeness and diversity terms respectively.

When only applying the uncertainty term, the ambiguous samples which remain far from the original distribution are selected. As these hard instances provide large gradient for the hash model learning, the discriminality of the learned hash codes is enhanced. Selecting samples for annotation based on the representativeness term encourages samples near the center of different classes to be labeled. The representative instances capture the semantic information of the whole dataset instead of local structure, so that the learned hash model can be generalized to image retrieval in large scale. When the diversity term is employed as the acquisition function, samples in different classes are chosen evenly for annotation. The diverse instances offer effective supervision without redundancy to fully utilize the representation capacity of the binary codes.

5   Conclusion

In this paper, we have proposed an deep hashing method with active pairwise supervision called DH-APS for large scale image search. The proposed DH-APS actively selects a small quantity of samples for annotation via considering pairwise relationship and generalizing the structural risk minimization principle, so that uncertain, representative and diverse samples are labeled. The effective supervision significantly enhances the discriminality and generalization ability of the learned hash codes with limited annotation cost. Extensive experiments have demonstrated the effectiveness of the proposed approach.

Acknowledgement. This work was supported in part by the National Key Research and Development Program of China under Grant 2017YFA0700802, in part by the National Natural Science Foundation of China under Grant 61822603, Grant U1813218, Grant U1713214, and Grant 61672306, in part by Beijing Natural Science Foundation under Grant No. L172051, in part by Beijing Academy of Artificial Intelligence (BAAI), in part by a grant from the Institute for Guo Qiang, Tsinghua University, in part by the Shenzhen Fundamental Research Fund (Subject Arrangement) under Grant JCYJ20170412170602564, and in part by Tsinghua University Initiative Scientific Research Program.

References

1. Babenko, A., Lempitsky, V.: Aggregating local deep features for image retrieval. In: ICCV, pp. 1269–1277 (2015)
2. Balcan, M.-F., Broder, A., Zhang, T.: Margin based active learning. In: Bshouty, N.H., Gentile, C. (eds.) COLT 2007. LNCS (LNAI), vol. 4539, pp. 35–50. Springer, Heidelberg (2007). https://doi.org/10.1007/978-3-540-72927-3_5
3. Bartlett, P.L., Mendelson, S.: Rademacher and Gaussian complexities: risk bounds and structural results. JMLR **3**(Nov), 463–482 (2002)
4. Beluch, W.H., Genewein, T., Nürnberger, A., Köhler, J.M.: The power of ensembles for active learning in image classification. In: CVPR, pp. 9368–9377 (2018)
5. Borgwardt, K.M., Gretton, A., Rasch, M.J., Kriegel, H.P., Schölkopf, B., Smola, A.J.: Integrating structured biological data by kernel maximum mean discrepancy. Bioinformatics **22**(14), 49–57 (2006)
6. Boyd, S., Parikh, N., Chu, E., Peleato, B., Eckstein, J., et al.: Distributed optimization and statistical learning via the alternating direction method of multipliers. Found. Trends® Mach. Learn. **3**(1), 1–122 (2011)
7. Chattopadhyay, R., Wang, Z., Fan, W., Davidson, I., Panchanathan, S., Ye, J.: Batch mode active sampling based on marginal probability distribution matching. TKDD **7**(3), 13 (2013)
8. Chua, T.S., Tang, J., Hong, R., Li, H., Luo, Z., Zheng, Y.: NUS-WIDE: a real-world web image database from national university of Singapore. In: Proceedings of the ACM International Conference on Image and Video Retrieval, p. 48 (2009)
9. Deng, J., Dong, W., Socher, R., Li, L.J., Li, K., Fei-Fei, L.: ImageNet: a large-scale hierarchical image database. In: CVPR, pp. 248–255 (2009)
10. Duan, Y., Lu, J., Wang, Z., Feng, J., Zhou, J.: Learning deep binary descriptor with multi-quantization. In: CVPR, pp. 1183–1192 (2017)
11. Duan, Y., Wang, Z., Lu, J., Lin, X., Zhou, J.: GraphBit: bitwise interaction mining via deep reinforcement learning. In: CVPR, pp. 8270–8279 (2018)
12. Erin Liong, V., Lu, J., Wang, G., Moulin, P., Zhou, J.: Deep hashing for compact binary codes learning. In: CVPR, pp. 2475–2483 (2015)

13. Freytag, A., Rodner, E., Denzler, J.: Selecting influential examples: active learning with expected model output changes. In: Fleet, D., Pajdla, T., Schiele, B., Tuytelaars, T. (eds.) ECCV 2014. LNCS, vol. 8692, pp. 562–577. Springer, Cham (2014). https://doi.org/10.1007/978-3-319-10593-2_37

14. Gal, Y., Islam, R., Ghahramani, Z.: Deep Bayesian active learning with image data. In: ICML, pp. 1183–1192 (2017)

15. Ghasedi Dizaji, K., Zheng, F., Sadoughi, N., Yang, Y., Deng, C., Huang, H.: Unsupervised deep generative adversarial hashing network. In: CVPR, pp. 3664–3673 (2018)

16. Goodfellow, I., et al.: Generative adversarial nets. In: NIPS, pp. 2672–2680 (2014)

17. Gordo, A., Almazán, J., Revaud, J., Larlus, D.: Deep image retrieval: learning global representations for image search. In: Leibe, B., Matas, J., Sebe, N., Welling, M. (eds.) ECCV 2016. LNCS, vol. 9910, pp. 241–257. Springer, Cham (2016). https://doi.org/10.1007/978-3-319-46466-4_15

18. Gretton, A., Borgwardt, K.M., Rasch, M.J., Schölkopf, B., Smola, A.: A kernel two-sample test. JMLR 13(Mar), 723–773 (2012)

19. Hasan, M., Roy-Chowdhury, A.K.: Context aware active learning of activity recognition models. In: ICCV, pp. 4543–4551 (2015)

20. Jegou, H., Douze, M., Schmid, C.: Product quantization for nearest neighbor search. TPAMI 33(1), 117–128 (2010)

21. Johnson, J., et al.: Image retrieval using scene graphs. In: CVPR, pp. 3668–3678 (2015)

22. Joshi, A.J., Porikli, F., Papanikolopoulos, N.: Multi-class active learning for image classification. In: CVPR, pp. 2372–2379 (2009)

23. Krizhevsky, A., Hinton, G., et al.: Learning multiple layers of features from tiny images. Technical report (2009)

24. Lai, H., Pan, Y., Liu, Y., Yan, S.: Simultaneous feature learning and hash coding with deep neural networks. In: CVPR, pp. 3270–3278 (2015)

25. LeCun, Y., Bottou, L., Bengio, Y., Haffner, P., et al.: Gradient-based learning applied to document recognition. Proc. IEEE 86(11), 2278–2324 (1998)

26. Li, W.J., Wang, S., Kang, W.C.: Feature learning based deep supervised hashing with pairwise labels. In: IJCAI, pp. 1711–1717 (2016)

27. Li, X., Guo, Y.: Multi-level adaptive active learning for scene classification. In: Fleet, D., Pajdla, T., Schiele, B., Tuytelaars, T. (eds.) ECCV 2014. LNCS, vol. 8695, pp. 234–249. Springer, Cham (2014). https://doi.org/10.1007/978-3-319-10584-0_16

28. Liu, B., Ferrari, V.: Active learning for human pose estimation. In: ICCV, pp. 4363–4372 (2017)

29. Liu, H., Wang, R., Shan, S., Chen, X.: Deep supervised hashing for fast image retrieval. In: CVPR, pp. 2064–2072 (2016)

30. Luo, W., Schwing, A., Urtasun, R.: Latent structured active learning. In: NIPS, pp. 728–736 (2013)

31. Mac Aodha, O., Campbell, N.D., Kautz, J., Brostow, G.J.: Hierarchical subquery evaluation for active learning on a graph. In: CVPR, pp. 564–571 (2014)

32. Melville, P., Mooney, R.J.: Diverse ensembles for active learning. In: ICML, p. 74 (2004)

33. Nguyen, H.T., Smeulders, A.: Active learning using pre-clustering. In: ICML, p. 79 (2004)

34. Paul, S., Bappy, J.H., Roy-Chowdhury, A.K.: Non-uniform subset selection for active learning in structured data. In: CVPR, pp. 6846–6855 (2017)

35. Pidhorskyi, S., Jones, Q., Motiian, S., Adjeroh, D., Doretto, G.: Deep supervised hashing with spherical embedding. In: Jawahar, C.V., Li, H., Mori, G., Schindler, K. (eds.) ACCV 2018. LNCS, vol. 11364, pp. 417–434. Springer, Cham (2019). https://doi.org/10.1007/978-3-030-20870-7_26

36. Qin, D., Gammeter, S., Bossard, L., Quack, T., Van Gool, L.: Hello neighbor: accurate object retrieval with k-reciprocal nearest neighbors. In: CVPR, pp. 777–784 (2011)

37. Rényi, A., et al.: On measures of entropy and information. In: Proceedings of the Fourth Berkeley Symposium on Mathematical Statistics and Probability, Volume 1: Contributions to the Theory of Statistics (1961)

38. Sener, O., Savarese, S.: Active learning for convolutional neural networks: a core-set approach. arXiv preprint arXiv:1708.00489 (2017)

39. Settles, B., Craven, M.: An analysis of active learning strategies for sequence labeling tasks. In: EMNLP, pp. 1070–1079 (2008)

40. Settles, B., Craven, M., Ray, S.: Multiple-instance active learning. In: NIPS, pp. 1289–1296 (2008)

41. Shen, F., Shen, C., Liu, W., Tao Shen, H.: Supervised discrete hashing. In: CVPR, pp. 37–45 (2015)

42. Shen, F., Xu, Y., Liu, L., Yang, Y., Huang, Z., Shen, H.T.: Unsupervised deep hashing with similarity-adaptive and discrete optimization. TPAMI **40**(12), 3034–3044 (2018)

43. Simonyan, K., Zisserman, A.: Very deep convolutional networks for large-scale image recognition. arXiv preprint arXiv:1409.1556 (2014)

44. Vasisht, D., Damianou, A., Varma, M., Kapoor, A.: Active learning for sparse Bayesian multilabel classification. In: KDD, pp. 472–481 (2014)

45. Vijayanarasimhan, S., Grauman, K.: Large-scale live active learning: training object detectors with crawled data and crowds. IJCV **108**(1–2), 97–114 (2014). https://doi.org/10.1007/s11263-014-0721-9

46. Wang, G., Hu, Q., Cheng, J., Hou, Z.: Semi-supervised generative adversarial hashing for image retrieval. In: Ferrari, V., Hebert, M., Sminchisescu, C., Weiss, Y. (eds.) ECCV 2018. LNCS, vol. 11219, pp. 491–507. Springer, Cham (2018). https://doi.org/10.1007/978-3-030-01267-0_29

47. Wang, J., Kumar, S., Chang, S.F.: Semi-supervised hashing for large-scale search. TPAMI **34**(12), 2393–2406 (2012)

48. Wang, Q., Si, L., Zhang, Z., Zhang, N.: Active hashing with joint data example and tag selection. In: SIGIR, pp. 405–414 (2014)

49. Wang, X., Yang, M., Cour, T., Zhu, S., Yu, K., Han, T.X.: Contextual weighting for vocabulary tree based image retrieval. In: ICCV, pp. 209–216 (2011)

50. Yang, H.F., Lin, K., Chen, C.S.: Supervised learning of semantics-preserving hash via deep convolutional neural networks. TPAMI **40**(2), 437–451 (2017)

51. Zhang, J., Peng, Y.: SSDH: semi-supervised deep hashing for large scale image retrieval. TCSVT **29**(1), 212–225 (2017)

52. Zhang, S., Li, J., Zhang, B.: Pairwise teacher-student network for semi-supervised hashing. In: CVPR, pp. 0–0 (2019)

53. Zhao, F., Huang, Y., Wang, L., Tan, T.: Deep semantic ranking based hashing for multi-label image retrieval. In: CVPR, pp. 1556–1564 (2015)

54. Zhen, Y., Yeung, D.Y.: Active hashing and its application to image and text retrieval. Data Min. Knowl. Disc. **26**(2), 255–274 (2013). https://doi.org/10.1007/s10618-012-0249-y

Graph Edit Distance Reward:
Learning to Edit Scene Graph

Lichang Chen[1,2], Guosheng Lin[1(✉)], Shijie Wang[1,3], and Qingyao Wu[4,5]

[1] Nanyang Technological University, Singapore, Singapore
gslin@ntu.edu.sg
[2] Zhejiang University, Hangzhou, China
bobchen@zju.edu.cn
[3] Huazhong University of Science and Technology, Wuhan, China
[4] School of Software Engineering, South China University of Technology,
Guangzhou, China
[5] Key Laboratory of Big Data and Intelligent Robot, Ministry of Education,
Beijing, China

Abstract. Scene Graph, as a vital tool to bridge the gap between language domain and image domain, has been widely adopted in the cross-modality task like VQA. In this paper, we propose a new method to edit the scene graph according to the user instructions, which has never been explored. To be specific, in order to learn editing scene graphs as the semantics given by texts, we propose a Graph Edit Distance Reward, which is based on the Policy Gradient and Graph Matching algorithm, to optimize neural symbolic model. In the context of text-editing image retrieval, we validate the effectiveness of our method in CSS and CRIR dataset. Besides, CRIR is a new synthetic dataset generated by us, which we will publish soon for future use.

Keywords: Scene graph editing · Policy gradient · Graph matching

1 Introduction

Nowadays, in our daily life, more and more people have grown accustomed to typing in texts to obtain images from search engine. However, if they are not satisfied with searching results or they would like to modify the previous results, the only thing they can do is altering the language, then searching again. If users can provide their instructions about how to edit the searching results, it will be more than convenient for them to retrieve satisfied images. Figure 1 shows the simulation of such a scenario in the synthetic dataset. Vo *et al.* [26] firstly propose this text-editing image retrieval task, where the input query is composed by an input image I_{input} and an input text T_{input}, describing the desired modifications

This work was done when L. Chen was an intern student in NTU.

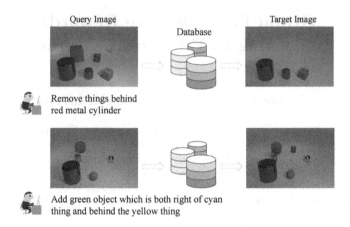

Fig. 1. Examples about cross-modal image retrieval. Given a query image and a query text describing the modification to the query image, we expect to edit the scene graph of the query image then retrieve a target image from database.

of I_{input}. Here, T_{input} can be viewed as user instructions and I_{input} can be viewed as the unsatisfactory image. We believe it is a superb platform for simulating the cross-modal task in real life.

Teaching machines to comprehend interaction between language and vision is an essential step for solving the Text+Image problem. There are some visual question answering (VQA [2,10]) systems [11,30] succeeding in crossing modalities by reasoning over Scene Graphs [12] following the semantics given by the texts, which proves Scene Graphs can bridge the gap between vision and language. Some image captioning models [18,29] also adopted Scene Graphs and achieves good results, demonstrating that Scene Graphs are a fantastic representation of image scenes. We represent our scene by Scene Graph owing to the advantages of Scene Graphs. In this way, we transform the image editing problem into Scene Graph editing problem.

Due to the booming of computation resources, "old school" symbolic models lose its position from the competition with numeric model [19], which need less human intervening. However, it is undeniable that symbolism has one secret weapon, neat representation, which the high dimensional numeric does not possess. Recently, utilizing the advantage of symbolism, Yi *et al.* [30] propose applying neural symbolic model on CLEVR [10] with fully transparent reasoning. In details, firstly they use a scene parser to derender the scenes from images. Then they train a seq2seq program generator to predict the latent program from a question. Finally, their program executor will execute these predicted programs over symbolic scene representations to produce answer. Motivated by their model's neat representations and fully explainable characteristics, we employ it to parse the user instructions. We design a Scene Graph Generation Engine to parse each image into a symbolic scene graph, whose nodes represent the objects while edges represent the relation between nodes. We also design a module to edit

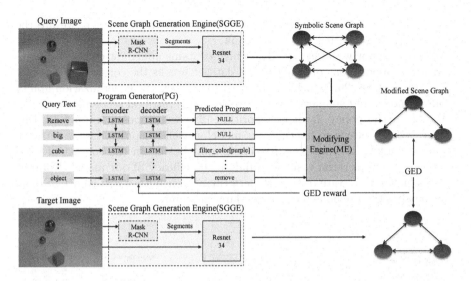

Fig. 2. Model Overview. The intact query text is "remove big cube to the right of purple object". The intact Predicted Program is "remove", "filter_size[large]", "filter_shape[cube]", "relate[right]", "filter_color[purple]". Because the query text is longer than the predicted program, our Program Generator will pad "NULL" program to fix the length inconsistency.

the scene graph. After that, the retrieval problem can be converted to a graph matching problem [5], which has low combinatorial space due to the symbolic representation.

We notice that REINFORCE [28] algorithm applied to finetune the Neural Symbolic Model [30] is the most vital part in achieving marvelous results. Following Johnson *et al.* [11], Yi *et al.* apply 0, 1 reward to finetune their program generator. This reward, however, is quite coarse if applying to our task. To be specific, only when exact matching [5] happens, which means all the nodes and all the edges in two generated symbolic scene graphs (one is generated from query image, another is generated from target image) matching, it is set to 1. To refine it, we propose applying Graph Edit Distance [22] based reward, which can optimize our model better.

In our experiment, we discover the CSS dataset [26] is simple because it has plenty of exact location information. To validate our model's efficacy further, we follow CLEVR's [10] generation process and generate our own Complex Reasoning Image Retrieval, called CRIR, which contains multi-hop queries thus the scene graphs are hard to be accurately edited. Moreover, our dataset breaks the constraints of exact location so it is more close to the real world scenes.

To summarize, our contributions are:

- We propose a GED reward to explore editing the scene graph with user instruction in the context of text-editing image retrieval. We refine the previous neural symbolic model aiming at VQA and make it suitable for our cross-modal image retrieval task. To the best of our knowledge, we are the first to propose editing the scene graph.

- We propose a new dataset, CRIR, which contains abundant complex queries with full annotations of images. The dataset breaks the constraints of exact location in CSS [26], which can be used to validate the generalization ability of our model and simulate the real-world image retrieval scene better.
- Based on the policy gradient algorithm [28], we propose Graph Edit Distance(GED) reward to finetune our model as well as apply GED as retrieval metric, making it learn to edit scene graphs better. In the context of text-editing image retrieval task, we validate the efficacy of our model. Notably, we achieves new state-of-the-art performance on both CRIR and CSS [26], surpassing the previous methods by large margins.

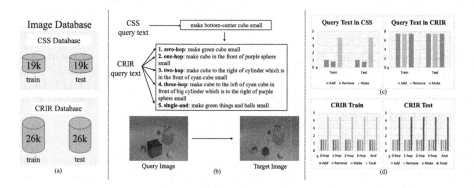

Fig. 3. (a) Image database scale – CRIR vs. CSS. (b) CSS only has zero-hop query. CRIR has 5 different types of queries. (c) Query Text Scale – CRIR vs. CSS. In CSS dataset, both training set and testing set contain 6k queries, while in CRIR dataset, both training set and testing set have 4.5k queries in each type of templates, totally 22.5k queries. (d) Query text type details. CRIR eliminates the dataset bias, each template generating the same number of queries.

2   Related Work

Image Retrieval. Conventional image retrieval [14] is a task to retrieve the most similar image to the query image from database, which is also viewed as image to image matching problem. In recent year, with much stronger image feature extractor [7,25], conventional image retrieval has also made a huge progress [3,6,15] and has been extended to different real-world scenes like face retrieval. [17,24].

Johnson *et al.* [12] first proposed cross-modality image retrieval. The task can be defined as given a text T_{input}, the model should retrieve an image I_{target} which is the most relevant to the T_{input}. They also give the definition of scene graph and use it to represent the content of the scene, which builds a bridge between image domain and text domain. What's more, cross-modality image retrieval is also extended to real-world scenes such as recipe to food image retrieval where the input query is recipe, food image to recipe retrieval, using deep metric learning method [27].

Visual Question Answering. Visual Question Answering [2] requires model to answer question given by text based on the input image. Solving this problem is a vital step to cross the modalities between language and vision.

Recently, Johnson et al. [10] utilize Blender to render images and they obtain a synthetic, virtual, and diagnostic dataset named CLEVR with full annotations of objects, such as 3D coordinates, size, shape, color, material, etc. The low cost of rendering virtual datasets allows for the appearance of CLEVR based datasets. For instance, Liu et al. [16] refine the CLEVR program generation engine and propose CLEVR-REF+ for referring expression task. They also modify the rendering engine which generates images with segments and bounding box information. There are also some real-world VQA datasets like VQA v1.0, v2.0 [2] and GQA [9], etc. Though the annotations cost is high, they provide a more realistic platform for validating the methods.

Neural Module Network. NMN is firstly proposed by Andreas et al. [1]. They parsed the natural language sentences into programs and applied it to instantiate different neural modules, then executing them to obtain the answer. Following their work, Johnson et al. [11] and Hu et al. [8] extend the Neural Module Network to the CLEVR dataset. But their neural modules are numeric one with executing programs and reasoning on high dimensional features. Yi et al. [30] propose symbolic module network to execute programs over symbolic scenes generated by scene parser achieving new state-of-the-art result in CLEVR, 99.9%. Due to the efficacy of their model, we adapt them to text-editing image retrieval task.

3   Method

In Sect. 3.1, we introduce our model. In Sect. 3.2, we give the definition of Graph Edit Distance. In Sect. 3.3, we introduce policy gradient with new method we proposed to estimate the gradient in this task.

3.1   Our Model

Figure 2 shows the overview of our model. Our model is adapted from neural symbolic reasoning model in [30]. The first step to train our model is supervised training separately on both Scene Graph Generation Engine (SGGE) and Program Generator (PG) with Images and small number of ground truth latent programs(We provide the training details in Sects. 5.1 and 5.2). In finetuning, the input of our model contains T_{input} and I_{input}. From SGGE, We obtain the symbolic scene graph of the I_{input} while the latent program can be parsed by

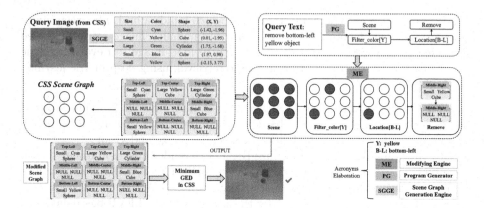

Fig. 4. A scene graph editing case in CSS dataset. CSS Scene Graph does not have any edges. So Modifying Engine just reason over nodes. In final `remove` program, we keep structure of the scene graph by just substituting the attribute values in operation. Red nodes in ME means attended nodes. Minimum GED means the minimum Graph Edit Distance between Modified Scene Graph and other Scene Graphs in CSS.

PG. The output of PG will be put into Modifying Engine (ME) with the generated scene graph. Then ME will execute programs sequentially and output the modified scene graph. Finally, the modified scene graph is compared with the target scene graph, which is generated from target image by the same SGGE, in Graph Edit Distance metric. After the computation of GED, the GED based reward can be backpropagated to finetune the PG.

The details about three main components, Scene Graph Generation Engine, Program Generator, Modifying Engine show as follows:

Scene Graph Generation Engine. We use SGGE to obtain the 3D coordinates with attribute values, including shape, size, color, material, for each objects in the image. In detail, Mask R-CNN is applied to generate segment proposals of each object in the image. Then we input the segment of each object with original image, resized to 224 by 224, into a Resnet-34 [7] to predict 3D coordinates.

Program Generator. The program generator follows the language model proposed by [30] which is improved version of [11] with attention. It is a seq2seq model. We set the dimension of input word vector to 300, 2 hidden layers in both encoder and decoder to 256 dimension. As the Fig. 2 shows, we return a reward from the final part to finetune our program generator. Because the Modifying Engine (ME) execution part is symbolic, the gradient stream will be cut down there, which means the model is undifferentiable when entering ME. Therefore, we exploit small number of ground truth programs to pretrain our PG, then using GED reward to finetune it. Because training and finetuning details are different in different datasets, we will elaborate them in Experiment (Sect. 5).

Modifying Engine. The modifying engine will execute programs predicted by program generator over symbolic scene graphs. Thanks to the neat representation of symbolic representation, the reasoning and modifying operations over symbolic scene graphs are fully transparent and make our image retrieval process explainable. We adopt different modifying engines in two experiments. The details about 2 modifying engines show in Sects. 5.1 and 5.2. We implement our Modifying Engine as a set of modules in Python. Each program has one counterpart module in ME. The programs will first be converted to the corresponding modules and then be executed in Modifying Engine sequentially.

3.2   Graph Edit Distance

Graph Edit Distance (GED) is a graph matching [5] approach first proposed by Sanfeliu et al. [22]. The concept of GED is finding the optimal set of edit operation which can transform Graph G_1 into Graph G_2.

Definition1. (Graph G)
A graph G can be represented by a 3-tuple (V, α, β), such that: V is a set of nodes. $\alpha : V \rightarrow L$ is the node labeling function. $\beta : V \times V \rightarrow L$ is the edge labeling function.

Definition2. (Graph Isomorphism)
A graph isomorphism between $G_1 = (V_1, \alpha_1, \beta_1)$ and $G_2 = (V_2, \alpha_2, \beta_2)$ is a bijective mapping $f : V_1 \rightarrow V_2$ such that $\alpha_1(x) = \alpha_2(f(x))$ for all $x \in V_1$ and $\beta_1((x,y)) = \beta_2((f(x), f(y)))$ for all $(x,y) \in V_1 \times V_1$.

Definition3. (Common Subgraph)
Let $G'_1 \subseteq G_1$ and $G'_2 \subseteq G_2$, if there exists a graph isomorphism between G'_1 and G'_2, both G'_1 and G'_2 will be called a common subgraph of G_1 and G_2. Moreover, a graph G is called a maximum common subgraph of G_1 and G_2 if G is a common subgraph of G_1 and G_2 and there exists no other common subgraph of G_1 and G_2 that has more nodes than G.

Definition4. (error-correcting graph matching)
An error-correcting graph matching from G_1 to G_2 is a bijective function $f : \hat{V}_1 \rightarrow \hat{V}_2$ where $\hat{V}_1 \subseteq V_1$ and $\hat{V}_2 \subseteq V_2$.

Definition5. (Graph Edit Distance)
Let $G_1 = (V_1, \alpha_1, \beta_1)$, $G_2 = (V_2, \alpha_2, \beta_2)$ be two graphs, the GED between these 2 graphs is defined as

$$GED(G_1, G_2) = \min_{e_1, \cdots, e_k \in \gamma(f)} \sum_{i=1}^{k} c(e_i), \tag{1}$$

where f is an error-correcting graph matching $f : \hat{V}_1 \rightarrow \hat{V}_2$ from Graph G_1 to Graph G_2 and c denotes the cost function measuring the strength $c(e_i)$ of an edit operation e_i and $\gamma(f)$ denotes the set of edit paths transforming G_1 into G_2. Insertions, deletions, and substitutions of both edges and nodes are 4 types of edit operations allowed. Thus, the right part of Eq. 1 can be denoted as [4]

$$
\min_{e_1,\cdots,e_k \in \gamma(G_1,G_2)} \sum_{i=1}^{k} c(e_i) = \min \Bigg(\sum_{x \in V_1 - \hat{V}_1} c_{nd}(x)
$$
$$
+ \sum_{x \in V_2 - \hat{V}_2} c_{ni}(x) + \sum_{x \in \hat{V}_1} c_{ns}(x) + \sum_{e \in \hat{E}_1} c_{es}(e) \Bigg), \tag{2}
$$

where $c_{nd}(x)$ is the cost of deleting a node $x \in V_1 - \hat{V}_1$ from G_1. $c_{ni}(x)$ is the cost of inserting a node $x \in V_2 - \hat{V}_2$ in G_2, $c_{ns}(x)$ is the cost of inserting a node $x \in \hat{V}_1$ by $f(x) \in \hat{V}_2$, and $c_{es}(e)$ is the cost substituting a node $x \in \hat{V}_1$ by $f(x) \in \hat{V}_2$ and $c_{es}(e)$ is the cost of substituting an egde $e = (x,y) \in \hat{V}_1 \times V_1$ by $e' = (f(x), f(y)) \in V_2 \times \hat{V}_2$. The cost of 4 operations are hyperparameter in our model. In experiment part Sect. 5, we will show the best hyperparameters in different datasets.

We follow the widely used quick GED computation algorithm proposed by Riesen et al. [21] which is referred to as A*GED to compute GED in our paper.

3.3 Policy Gradient + GED reward

In Reinforcement Learning, unlike the image classification and segmentation, the problems are usually undifferentiable with high-dimensional discrete states and learning (state, action) pair is very hard. However, the policy, such as make a robot move left or kick a ball, is easier to learn. Thus, we can formally define a class of parametrized policies as $\Pi = \{\pi_\theta, \theta \in \mathbb{R}^m\}$. And for each policy, the value is defined as Eq. 3, where r_t is the reward in the time step t, γ^t is the attenuation coefficient in the time step t.

$$
J(\theta) = \mathbb{E}\left[\sum_{t \geq 0} \gamma^t r_t | \pi_\theta \right] \tag{3}
$$

Our goal is to find the optimal policy $\theta^* = \arg\max_\theta J(\theta)$. And one of simple algorithms to solve this problem is REINFORCE [28] which applies gradient ascent to optimize the parameter θ. The expected future reward can be written as

$$
J(\theta) = \mathbb{E}_{\tau \sim p(\tau;\theta)}[r(\tau)]
$$
$$
= \int_\tau r(\tau)p(\tau;\theta)\mathrm{d}\tau, \tag{4}
$$

where the $p(\tau;\theta)$ is the probability of trajectory τ in sampling. And by differentiating the Eq. 4, we can obtain:

$$
\nabla_\theta J(\theta) = \int_\tau r(\tau)\nabla_\theta p(\tau;\theta)\mathrm{d}\tau. \tag{5}
$$

$\nabla_\theta p(\tau;\theta)$ in Eq. 5 can be rewritten as

$$
\nabla_\theta p(\tau;\theta) = p(\tau;\theta)\frac{\nabla_\theta p(\tau;\theta)}{p(\tau;\theta)} = p(\tau;\theta)\nabla_\theta \log p(\tau;\theta). \tag{6}
$$

Finally, we can estimate $J(\theta)$ as Eq. 6:

$$\nabla_\theta J(\theta) \approx \sum_{t \geq 0} r(\tau) \nabla_\theta \log \pi_\theta \left(a_t | s_t \right), \tag{7}$$

where s_t is the state in time step t.

As previously state in Sect. 1, the simple 0, 1 reward is coarse in our task. Thanks to the graph matching algorithm, we have a better measurement about the similarity of 2 graphs. To measure the reward after a number of programs executing in Modifying Engine better, we propose a new reward (See Eq. 8) combining Graph Edit Distance with policy gradient algorithm named GED reward. In experiment, we will validate the efficacy of this reward when it is applied to finetune our program generator.

$$reward = 1 - GED. \tag{8}$$

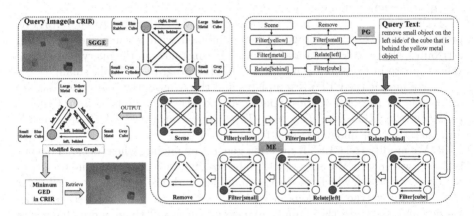

Fig. 5. A scene graph editing case in CRIR dataset. ME is Modifying Engine. PG is Program Generator. SGGE is Scene Graph Generation Engine. Symbolic Reasoning over CRIR scene graphs need utilizing edge information, as shows in "Relate" program reasoning part. Here, we display the reasoning details of ME. The reasoning process in CRIR is more complex than in CSS.

4   CRIR Dataset

After exploring the Color, Shape, Size(CSS) [26] dataset carefully, we find it just adopt one simplest kind of template, zero-hop, in CLEVR's [10] template universe, which means it does not need any reasoning process before editing the scene graphs. Thus, inheriting the CLEVR template universe, we generate more complex reasoning dataset called CRIR to validate the reasoning and generalization ability of our model.

Our dataset generation can be split into 2 parts, image generation and query text generation, which will be discussed in Sect. 4.1 and Sect. 4.2 respectively.

4.1   Image Generation

Firstly, we select 3k images from CSS [26] Dataset, which should have at least 4 objects in the scenes. Then we add material information to these objects, which means randomly choosing the metal or rubber for the object. According to the query answer (generation process is explained in Sect. 4.2), we modify the scene files in CSS. Then following the image generation engine provided by Liu [16] *et al.*, we create our own image database, which contains 26k images in the training set and 26k images in the testing set. The image database is larger than the previous CSS image database, we show details in Fig. 3a. Our objects contain 4-dimension information, color, shape, size, material, comparing to 3-dimension in CSS.

4.2   Query Generation

The queries' generation can be summarized as follows:

1. We add 3 types of programs, add, remove and make, to the CLEVR-programs universe. Make programs are combined with a value chosen from 4 attributes, shape, color, material and size. For instance, in the query text "make yellow sphere in front of green cube small", the program is "make[small]".

2. We inherit the CLEVR templates and throw away the templates that are unsuitable for retrieval queries. Specifically, we select 5 templates from CLEVR [10]: *Zere Hop, One Hop, Two Hop, Three Hop, Single And*, which are suitable for generating our image retrieval text queries.

3. We modify the CLEVR question generation engine, whose original output is the answer in CLEVR answer set. To be specific, we force our engine to output the objects' indices which need to be modified with the text query suitable for this task, unlike the questions in CLEVR. Firstly, we generate remove, make queries and maintain the number of remove queries 2 times more than make queries. Then we use these queries to change the image scenes according to the remove or make type and objects' indices. After that, we apply these scenes to render new images. For add query generation, we compare the original scene with the generated scene one by one, if it reduces one object, we put it to an addition candidate list. After that, we randomly choose pairs from the list then change query type from add to remove and convert the I_{target} to I_{input} until the number of add query text is equal to the remove query text. Finally, we obtain 22.5k queries in training set and 22.5k queries in testing set.

Results. We compare CRIR dataset with CSS dataset which shows in Fig. 3. To conclude, CRIR's image database is larger than CSS, Fig. 3a. CRIR's query text is more versatile than CSS's, Fig. 3b. Additionally, CRIR's scale in query texts is larger than CSS's, Fig. 3c. In Fig. 3d, we show the details about the types of query text in CRIR. All these perspectives above demonstrate we generate a more complex reasoning and hard-to-edit dataset for text-editing image retrieval task.

5 Experiment

To display the effectiveness of our model on editing the scene graphs, we carry out experiments on CSS and CRIR. Our measurement is set to recall at rank 1 in order to better compare with other methods.

5.1 Experiment on CSS Dataset

Because nearly 85% query texts in CSS dataset has exact location word, we create exact location program for this dataset, such as "Location[B-L]" program in Fig. 4, which can attend the object at Bottom-Left grid. The location boundaries used to split the 3 by 3 grids are $(-0.99, 0.86)$ horizontally and $(-0.47, 2.35)$ vertically. In CSS training, we randomly select 30 text queries (add, remove, make, each 10) and annotate them for pretraining our program generator, with learning rate 6×10^{-4}, 12000 iterations, and batch size 64. Especially, in CSS, we keep the structure of Scene Graph when ME executing programs to modify it. We show an example of ME's reasoning details in Fig. 4.

Table 1. Quantitative results in CSS. The retrieval metric is Recall at rank 1. ImageO and TextO means Image Only and Text Only, respectively. Concate is a method just concatenating language feature and image feature without other processing. As show above, our model with GED reward surpasses all other models by large margins in all three types of queries.

Method	ImageO	TextO	Concate	MRN [13]	Relat [23]	FiLM [20]	TIRG [26]	Ours
Add	0.1	0.1	73.6	72.9	74.7	75.9	83.6	**99.7**
Remove	0.2	0.1	45.3	42.8	49.8	52.3	64.3	**99.8**
Make	9.1	0.1	63.2	64.6	61.8	68.6	73.3	**99.9**
Overall	6.3	0.1	60.6	60.1	62.1	65.6	73.7	**99.8**

In Modifying Engine, we inherit programs which have prefix `filter` from CLEVR and create corresponding modules for them. Here we list some special programs outside CLEVR-programs universe and its corresponding modules' operation details, which shows as follows:

Location Modules. Location modules are instantiated from location programs and they will select the exact location like "Top-Left" for operating modification later on. There are totally 9 different location modules corresponding to 3 by 3 grids.

Remove, Add, Make Modules. According to the start word of the query text we can obtain `Remove`, `Add`, or `Make` programs to instantiate modules and execute operations over structural scene graph. All these three types of modules will be executed last. We also create 2 reasoning modes, "normal" and "add". Mode "normal" is created for `Remove` and `Make` modules while mode "add" for

Add module. Remove module is applied to change every attribute value of the attended nodes into NULL while Make modules change the specific attribute that attended by the previous modules. But in Add type queries, some attributes will not be assigned value, for example, in query text "Add small cube to the top-left", the color information is not assigned. Thus we create value 1 for these unassigned attributes when modifying the node in Add. In Graph Edit Distance [22] computation, value 1 can match any value except NULL.

Graph Edit Distance in CSS. In the CSS settings, scene graphs are structural and each graph has 9 nodes with rigid location. Thus in Eq. 2, only substituting cost exists. The Graph Edit Distance [22] computation can be simplified as:

$$GED = \min \big(\sum_{x \in \hat{V}_1} c_{ns}(x) \big). \tag{9}$$

For every node having 3 attributes, we set the cost of substituting every attribute to $1/3$ and force the reward to be 0 if GED between 2 graphs is larger than 1. In the testing, we apply graph edit distance as our retrieval metric. If GED of two pairs' graphs happen to be the same, we will randomly choose one as our target image. We return this reward to finetune the program generator with 50,000 iterations and early-stopping strategy. Batch size is fixed to 64 in finetuning.

Results and Analysis. As Table 1 shows, our model achieves state-of-the-art result and surpass the previous baseline model TIRG [26] drastically no matter in which query text type. Additionally, We give an example in CSS and display our symbolic model's transparent and powerful reasoning ability in Fig. 4. The results and the visualization prove our method's effectiveness on editing symbolic scene graph according to the instructions.

One biggest problem in CSS is that if our model predicts the correct location program, it will attend to the correct object because of the exact location information text provided. Besides, all queries in CSS are *Zero Hop*, which does not need any edge information for reasoning. Only through attribute filter or location programs can the model attend to correct nodes. Therefore, we propose a more complex dataset to validate our model's reasoning ability: 1. To simulate the real-world scene, the dataset should just provide the relational location information, not exact locations. 2. The dataset should also contain more complex queries, not just *Zero Hop*. Aiming at this, we generate CRIR. Details can be referred to Sect. 4.2.

5.2 Experiment on CRIR Dataset

In CRIR dataset, we remove the location programs to simulate a more realistic situation. Though we can still generate the structural scene graph shown as Fig. 4, we consider that 3 by 3 grid structural scene graph is a special case in the real world. Therefore, we cancel this rigid location and generate relational scene graphs for the images in the CRIR dataset then editing relational scene graphs. In training procedure, we randomly select 300 programs (add, remove, make type

Table 2. Quantitative results in CRIR. The retrieval metric is Recall at rank 1. We adapt Vo's [26] code to train TIRG and Concat models in CRIR. 0, 1 means applying 0, 1 reward to finetune our model. GED means applying GED reward to optimize our model. In particular, our model with GED reward optimizing surpass all the other models in every type of query.

Model	Zero_Hop	One_Hop	Two_Hop	Three_Hop	Single_And	Overall
Concatenate	45.1	25.2	16.7	3.7	15.8	21.3
MRN [13]	44.8	28.3	19.4	3.5	19.6	23.1
Relat [23]	51.9	28.2	21.3	4.0	18.1	24.7
FiLM [20]	50.2	28.1	21.1	3.6	16.3	23.9
TIRG [26]	53.8	29.6	22.9	4.8	19.4	26.1
0,1 Reward	95.9	95.4	95.8	95.3	94.5	95.4
GED Reward	**99.0**	**98.4**	**98.2**	**97.9**	**98.4**	**98.4**

each 100 programs) to pretrain our program generator with 16,000 iterations and 7×10^{-4} learning rate. Add, Remove modules in CRIR settings are different from CSS. To illustrate, Add module in CRIR Modifying Engine will add a pseudo node to the scene graph, unlike Add module in CSS just changing the attended node. We give an instance here. Assuming the query text is "Add red large sphere to the left of large yellow cylinder", our Modifying Engine will execute Add module to create one pseudo node. The pseudo node will create edges linking to all other nodes in scene graphs. Then if PG outputs "Relate[left]" program, it will assign edge linking to the "large yellow cylinder" Left value. For Remove module, unlike the example shows in Fig. 4 just changing the attributes to NULL, in CRIR, Remove module will remove the attended objects and all the edges of the nodes as example shows in Fig. 5.

Graph Edit Distance in CRIR. We apply graph edit distance to finetune our program generator. Unlike the graph edit distance in CSS dataset without edge information, in this part, our graph edit distance has all costs (four parts) in Eq. 2. And we set the cost of inserting a node to 1, the cost of deleting to 1, substituting an attribute value to 1/4, and substituting an edge to 1/16. We only return the positive reward and force negative reward to 0. We return this reward to finetune PG with 60, 000 iterations, early-stopping training strategy and batch size is fixed to 64.

Results and Analysis. We provide the quantitative results in Table 2. As it shows, our model can still maintain high-level performance in all five types of queries while TIRG [26] and Concat models drop its performance on CRIR drastically. *Zero Hop* is the easiest type query text so all the model achieve its best performance on this type of query text. From Table 2, we also discover that *Three Hop* is so complicated that TIRG and Concat model can not learn this type of query text well, but our models are able to comprehend this type of queries. Notably, Our GED reward is more efficient than simple 0, 1 reward according to the last 2 columns of Table 2. The performance of our model with

GED reward surpasses all other models in all types of queries, which proves the GED reward is a precise measurement of the final modified graph to the target graph. We also show one case of our model's (optimized by GED reward) symbolic reasoning insight in Fig. 5.

We compare the performance of feature combination model and ours qualitatively and show a case in Fig. 6. As case shows, the TIRG [26] just retrieve the image with similar objects while our scene-graph-editing based model can understand the true meaning of this text and retrieve the correct image in CRIR dataset. In conclusion, our model has more powerful generalization ability than TIRG [26].

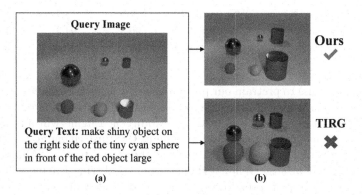

Fig. 6. The qualitative results in CRIR. (a) represents the input query while (b) is the retrieval results by applying our model (with GED reward optimizing) and TIRG [26]

6   Conclusion

In this paper, we have proposed a GED reward for learning to edit scene graph in the context of text-editing image retrieval. By exploiting CLEVR toolkit, we generate a Complex Reasoning Image Retrieval dataset, simulating a harder case of editing. To the best of our knowledge, we are the first to apply Graph Edit Distance as retrieval metric. Furthermore, we validate our model on both CSS and CRIR dataset and achieve nearly perfect results, surpassing other models by large margins, proving the effectiveness of editing scene graphs in the context of text-editing image retrieval. However, our model still need prior information like the annotations of some latent programs to pretrain the PG. We expect our machine can own the reasoning ability without using any prior information in the future.

Acknowledgments. This research was supported by the National Research Foundation Singapore under its AI Singapore Programme (Award Number: AISG-RP-2018-003) and the MOE Tier-1 research grants: RG28/18 (S) and RG22/19 (S). Q. Wu's participation was supported by NSFC 61876208, Key-Area Research and Development Program of Guangdong 2018B010108002.

References

1. Andreas, J., Rohrbach, M., Darrell, T., Klein, D.: Neural module networks. In: CVPR (2016)
2. Antol, S., et al.: VQA: visual question answering. In: CVPR (2015)
3. Babenko, A., Lempitsky, V.: Aggregating local deep features for image retrieval. In: CVPR (2015)
4. Bunke, H.: Error correcting graph matching: on the influence of the underlying cost function. TPAMI **21**(9), 917–922 (1999)
5. Conte, D., Foggia, P., Sansone, C., Vento, M.: Thirty years of graph matching in pattern recognition. Int. J. Pattern Recognit. Artif. Intell. **18**(03), 265–298 (2004)
6. Gordo, A., Almazán, J., Revaud, J., Larlus, D.: Deep image retrieval: learning global representations for image search. In: Leibe, B., Matas, J., Sebe, N., Welling, M. (eds.) ECCV 2016. LNCS, vol. 9910, pp. 241–257. Springer, Cham (2016). https://doi.org/10.1007/978-3-319-46466-4_15
7. He, K., Zhang, X., Ren, S., Sun, J.: Deep residual learning for image recognition. In: CVPR (2016)
8. Hu, R., Andreas, J., Rohrbach, M., Darrell, T., Saenko, K.: Learning to reason: end-to-end module networks for visual question answering. In: ICCV (2017)
9. Hudson, D.A., Manning, C.D.: GQA: a new dataset for real-world visual reasoning and compositional question answering. In: CVPR (2019)
10. Johnson, J., Hariharan, B., van der Maaten, L., Fei-Fei, L., Lawrence Zitnick, C., Girshick, R.: CLEVR: a diagnostic dataset for compositional language and elementary visual reasoning. In: CVPR (2017)
11. Johnson, J., et al.: Inferring and executing programs for visual reasoning. In: CVPR (2017)
12. Johnson, J., et al.: Image retrieval using scene graphs. In: CVPR (2015)
13. Kim, J.H., et al.: Multimodal residual learning for visual QA. In: Advances in Neural Information Processing Systems, pp. 361–369 (2016)
14. Lin, K., Yang, H.F., Hsiao, J.H., Chen, C.S.: Deep learning of binary hash codes for fast image retrieval. In: CVPR Workshops (2015)
15. Liu, H., Wang, R., Shan, S., Chen, X.: Deep supervised hashing for fast image retrieval. In: CVPR (2016)
16. Liu, R., Liu, C., Bai, Y., Yuille, A.L.: CLEVR-REF+: diagnosing visual reasoning with referring expressions. In: CVPR (2019)
17. Liu, Z., Luo, P., Qiu, S., Wang, X., Tang, X.: DeepFashion: powering robust clothes recognition and retrieval with rich annotations. In: CVPR (2016)
18. Luo, R., Price, B., Cohen, S., Shakhnarovich, G.: Discriminability objective for training descriptive captions. In: Proceedings of the IEEE Conference on Computer Vision and Pattern Recognition, pp. 6964–6974 (2018)
19. Minsky, M.L.: Logical versus analogical or symbolic versus connectionist or neat versus scruffy. AI Mag. **12**(2), 34–34 (1991)
20. Perez, E., Strub, F., De Vries, H., Dumoulin, V., Courville, A.: FILM: visual reasoning with a general conditioning layer. In: Thirty-Second AAAI Conference on Artificial Intelligence (2018)
21. Riesen, K., Fankhauser, S., Bunke, H.: Speeding up graph edit distance computation with a bipartite heuristic. In: MLG (2007)
22. Sanfeliu, A., Fu, K.S.: A distance measure between attributed relational graphs for pattern recognition. IEEE Trans. Syst. Man Cybern. **SMC-13**(3), 353–362 (1983)

23. Santoro, A., et al.: A simple neural network module for relational reasoning. In: Advances in Neural Information Processing Systems, pp. 4967–4976 (2017)
24. Schroff, F., Kalenichenko, D., Philbin, J.: FaceNet: a unified embedding for face recognition and clustering. In: CVPR (2015)
25. Simonyan, K., Zisserman, A.: Very deep convolutional networks for large-scale image recognition. arXiv preprint arXiv:1409.1556 (2014)
26. Vo, N., et al.: Composing text and image for image retrieval-an empirical odyssey. In: CVPR (2019)
27. Wang, H., Sahoo, D., Liu, C., Lim, E.P., Hoi, S.C.H.: Learning cross-modal embeddings with adversarial networks for cooking recipes and food images. In: CVPR (2019)
28. Williams, R.J.: Simple statistical gradient-following algorithms for connectionist reinforcement learning. Mach. Learn. 8(3–4), 229–256 (1992)
29. Yang, X., Tang, K., Zhang, H., Cai, J.: Auto-encoding scene graphs for image captioning. In: Proceedings of the IEEE Conference on Computer Vision and Pattern Recognition, pp. 10685–10694 (2019)
30. Yi, K., Wu, J., Gan, C., Torralba, A., Kohli, P., Tenenbaum, J.B.: Neural-symbolic VQA: disentangling reasoning from vision and language understanding. In: NIPS (2018)

Malleable 2.5D Convolution: Learning Receptive Fields Along the Depth-Axis for RGB-D Scene Parsing

Yajie Xing[1]([✉]) [ID], Jingbo Wang[2] [ID], and Gang Zeng[1] [ID]

[1] Key Laboratory of Machine Perception, Peking University, Beijing, China
{yajie_xing,zeng}@hust.edu.cn
[2] The Chinese University of Hong Kong, Shatin, Hong Kong
jbwang@ie.cuhk.edu.hk

Abstract. Depth data provide geometric information that can bring progress in RGB-D scene parsing tasks. Several recent works propose RGB-D convolution operators that construct receptive fields along the depth-axis to handle 3D neighborhood relations between pixels. However, these methods pre-define depth receptive fields by hyperparameters, making them rely on parameter selection. In this paper, we propose a novel operator called malleable 2.5D convolution to learn the receptive field along the depth-axis. A malleable 2.5D convolution has one or more 2D convolution kernels. Our method assigns each pixel to one of the kernels or none of them according to their relative depth differences, and the assigning process is formulated as a differentiable form so that it can be learnt by gradient descent. The proposed operator runs on standard 2D feature maps and can be seamlessly incorporated into pre-trained CNNs. We conduct extensive experiments on two challenging RGB-D semantic segmentation dataset NYUDv2 and Cityscapes to validate the effectiveness and the generalization ability of our method.

Keywords: RGB-D scene parsing · Geometry in CNN · Malleable 2.5D convolution

1 Introduction

Recent progresses [2,3,25] in CNN have achieved great success in scene parsing tasks such as semantic segmentation. Depth data provide geometric information that is not captured by the color channels and therefore can assist feature extraction and improve segmentation performance. With the availability of commercial RGB-D sensors such as Kinect, there comes an increasing interest in exploiting the additional depth data and incorporating geometric information into CNNs.

Electronic supplementary material The online version of this chapter (https://doi.org/10.1007/978-3-030-58529-7_33) contains supplementary material, which is available to authorized users.

A. Vedaldi et al. (Eds.): ECCV 2020, LNCS 12364, pp. 555–571, 2020.
https://doi.org/10.1007/978-3-030-58529-7_33

Many works [6,10,16,17,25] take RGB images and depth maps or HHA [9] encodings as two separate inputs and adopt two-stream style networks to process them. These methods only take depth information as features and keep the fixed geometric structures of 2D CNN, which neglects the available 3D geometric relations between pixels. The most direct method to leverage the 3D relations between pixels is to project RGB-D data into 3D pointclouds [23] or volumes [29,39], and exploit 3D networks to handle geometry. However, 3D networks are computationally more expensive than 2D CNN and cannot benefit from prevalent ImageNet-pretrained models.

Recently, some works turn to introduce geometric information into the 2D convolution operators. Depth-aware CNN [31] augments the standard convolution with a depth similarity term. It applies masks to suppress the contribution of pixels whose depths are different from the center of the kernel. Consequently, it constructs a soft receptive field along the depth-axis where more distant pixels are partially occluded by the mask. 2.5D convolution [34] moves a step forward to utilizing more kernels to capture richer geometric relations. It builds a grid receptive field in 3D space, assigns each pixel to one of the kernels according to the relative depth differences with the center of the kernel, and thus mimics a real 3D convolution kernel. These methods successfully leverage geometric information by introducing a receptive field along the depth-axis. And they can be easily incorporated into pre-trained CNNs while not bring much computational cost. However, in these methods, the depth receptive fields are determined by pre-defined hyperparameters.

In different environments, the scene structures and depth quality can be very different. For example, NYUDv2 [27] consists of indoor scenes and captures depth data by Kinect, which has good accuracy. Cityscapes [7] uses a stereo camera to capture outdoor street scenes, resulting in a much longer depth range and noisier depth data. Naturally, the receptive field along the depth-axis should not be the same across different environment settings. If we artificially pre-define depth receptive fields for different environments, it would bring many parameter-adjusting works, and the selected parameters are possibly still not suitable for the specific environment. Therefore, we need a method that can not only build a receptive field along the depth-axis to handle 3D geometry, but also flexibly learn the receptive field for different environments.

To address the aforementioned problems, in this paper, we propose a novel convolution operator called malleable 2.5D convolution (illustrated in Fig. 1). Similar to 2.5D convolution, the malleable 2.5D convolution can have either one or more 2D convolution kernels sequentially arranged along the depth-axis. To determine the depth receptive field of each kernel, we adopt a softmax classification to assign each pixel to kernels according to pixels' relative depth differences. The assigning process is differentiable and can be learnt by gradient descent. We also introduce learnable "kernel rebalancing weights" parameters to rebalance the output scale of each kernel, since pixels are not distributed evenly in each class. The malleable 2.5D convolution can flexibly learn the depth receptive field for different environments (as shown in Fig. 4 while only introducing a small

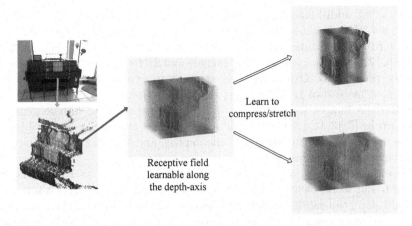

Fig. 1. Illustration of the malleable 2.5D convolution with 3 kernels. Best view in color. The blue, green, and red colors respectively represent the receptive field of each kernel. The malleable 2.5D convolution arranges its kernels sequentially along the depth-axis and adopts differentiable functions to construct soft depth receptive fields for its kernels. It samples pixels on the 2D plane, the same as standard 2D convolution. And it assigns pixels to its kernels according to depth data and its depth receptive fields. During the training process, the depth receptive fields can be learnt to compress or stretch automatically according to the dataset, making the convolution "malleable" (Color figure online)

number of additional parameters ($2k + 3$ parameters if it has k kernels). Meanwhile, because malleable 2.5D convolutions are based on 2D convolution kernels, they can be easily incorporated into pre-trained 2D CNNs by simply replacing standard 2D convolutions.

Our contributions can be summarized as follows:

- We propose a novel convolution operator called malleable 2.5D convolution that has learnable receptive fields along the depth-axis.
- Two techniques are proposed in the malleable 2.5D convolution: 1) We propose a differentiable pixel assigning method to achieve learnable depth receptive field; 2) We introduce "kernel rebalancing weights" parameters to rebalance the uneven pixel distribution in the kernels.
- We conduct extensive experiments on both indoor RGB-D semantic segmentation dataset NYUDv2 [27] and outdoor dataset Cityscapes [7], and validate the effectiveness and generalization ability of our method.

2   Related Works

RGB-D Scene Parsing. Benefiting from the great success of deep convolutional networks [11,15,28], Fully Convolutional Networks (FCNs) [21] and its successors [2,4,19,26,36,38] have achieved promising results for RGB semantic segmentation. RGB-D segmentation extends RGB semantic segmentation by providing additional depth data. A widely applied method is to encode depth into HHA features [9]: horizontal disparity, height above the ground and angle with gravity direction. It is usually used in two-stream style networks [9,10,16,17,25,35] to process RGB images and HHA images and fuse the features or predictions. Other methods attempt to exploit geometric clues from depth data instead of treating them as features. Some works [23,29,39] transform RGB-D images into 3D data and use 3D networks to handle geometry. Other works [5,13,14,18] take advantage of the fact that the scales of objects in images are inversely proportional to the depths, and change the receptive fields of convolutions according to the depth information.

Depth-aware CNN [31] and 2.5D Convolution [34] are two methods most related to our work. Depth-aware CNN applies a mask to construct a soft receptive field along the depth-axis where more distant pixels are weakened and nearer pixels have more contribution to the output. 2.5D convolution seeks to mimic a 3D convolution kernel with several 2D convolution kernels on 2D plane. It builds a grid receptive field in 3D space, and accordingly assigns each pixel to one of the kernels in a similar way a 3D convolution does. Both methods pre-define the receptive field along the depth-axis by hyperparameters, making them rely on parameter adjusting and therefore more difficult to be applied in different environments. Our method solves this problem by building a learnable depth receptive field, and yields better effectiveness and generalization ability.

Convolutions with Learnable Receptive Fields. In 2D CNNs, there are several works attempting to break the fixed grid kernel structure of convolution and construct learnable receptive fields. Spatial Transformer Networks [12] warps feature maps with a learned global spatial transformation. SAC [37] learns the scale of receptive fields according to the contents of local features. Deformable convolution [8,40] learns 2D offsets and adds them to the regular grid sampling locations in the standard convolution. These works change their receptive field on the 2D plane, which can be implemented by linear transformation and interpolation. However, along the depth-axis, we are facing a very different problem. We cannot determine a sample point and then calculate the corresponding feature because pixels in 3D space are very sparse. We have to do it inversely, assigning pixels to sample points. And that makes the process more difficult to be differentiable. Despite the difficulty, our method manages to construct a learnable receptive field along the depth-axis in a novel way. Another difference is that in this work, we aim to learn the depth receptive field suitable for the given dataset instead of each pixel.

Neural Architecture Search. Some neural architecture search works [1,20, 30,33] try to determine the best convolution kernel shapes (or their combination) for the specific dataset. They use different methods including searching techniques or differentiable optimization. Our method can also be considered as searching the kernel shapes of malleable 2.5D convolutions, but we only search the receptive fields along the depth-axis and we achieve it through learning by gradient descent.

3   Malleable 2.5D Convolution

In this section, we describe and analyze the proposed malleable 2.5D convolution. We firstly introduce the method to construct learnable receptive fields along the depth-axis. Then we introduce the kernel rebalancing mechanism in the operator. Finally, we give some analysis of malleable 2.5D convolution and present how we integrate it into pre-trained CNN.

3.1   Learning Receptive Fields Along the Depth-Axis

Relative Depth Differences. First of all, we define the relative depth differences that are used when we construct receptive fields along the depth-axis. For a convolution kernel, if input map has a downsampling rate r_{down} to the original input image, and the dilation rate is r_{dilate}, then the distance between two neighborhood points sampled by the convolution is $\Delta d_p = r_{down} * r_{dilate}$. Note that Δd_p is a distance on the original input image plane.

For a pixel p_i whose coordinate at the input image is c_i, and the depth at p_i is $d(c_i)$, the coordinate of p_i in 3D space is $\hat{c}_i = (c_i - (c_x, c_y)) * d(c_i)/f$, where c_x, c_y are the coordinates of the principal point and f is the focal length. c_x, c_y, f are all given by camera parameters (usually two focal lengths f_x, f_y are given, but in most cases they are very close and we can approximately treat them as the same value).

If we project the local sampling grid of the convolution kernel around p_i to 3D space, then the distance between two neighborhood points would be $\Delta d_s(c_i) = \Delta d_p * d(c_i)/f$. The grid size along the depth-axis should be the same with the other two directions. Therefore, we define $\Delta d_s(c_i)$ as the unit of relative depth difference at image coordinate c_i. And the relative depth difference between pixel at c_j and c_i within the local grid centered at c_i is given by

$$d(c_i, c_j) = (d(c_i) - d(c_j))/\Delta d_s(c_i) \tag{1}$$

Depth Receptive Field Functions. For each pixel p_i whose coordinate at the input image is c_i, a standard 2D convolution performs a weighted sum within the receptive field around p_i:

$$y(c_i) = \sum_{c_p \in \mathcal{R}_p} w(c_p) \cdot x(c_i + c_p), \tag{2}$$

where $\mathcal{R}_p$ is the local grid that describes the 2D receptive field around p_i in the input x, and w is the convolution kernel. Typically, $\mathcal{R}_p$ is a regular grid defined by kernel size and dilation rate.

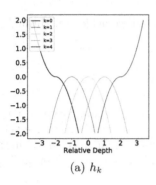
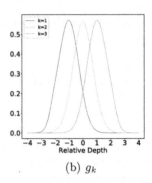

(a) h_k (b) g_k

Fig. 2. Image of h_k and g_k when $K = 3$, $[a_0, a_1, a_2, a_3, a_4] = [-2, -1, 0, 1, 2]$ and $t = 1$. Best view in color

A malleable 2.5D convolution has K convolution kernels whose receptive fields are sequentially arranged along the depth-axis. And the pixels are assigned to the kernels according to depth map $\mathbf{d}$:

$$\mathbf{y}(\mathbf{c}_i) = \sum_{k=1}^{K} \sum_{\mathbf{c}_p \in \mathcal{R}_p} g_k(\mathbf{d}(\mathbf{c}_i), \mathbf{d}(\mathbf{c}_i + \mathbf{c}_p)) \cdot \mathbf{w}_k(\mathbf{c}_p) \cdot \mathbf{x}(\mathbf{c}_i + \mathbf{c}_p), \qquad (3)$$

where g_k is the assigning function for kernel k. g_k defines the depth receptive field of kernel k, and satisfies

$$\sum_{k=1}^{K} g_k(\mathbf{d}(\mathbf{c}_i), \mathbf{d}(\mathbf{c}_i + \mathbf{c}_p)) \leq 1, \forall \mathbf{c}_p \in \mathcal{R}_p. \qquad (4)$$

To make the assigning functions differentiable, we implement them as a softmax classification:

$$g_k(\mathbf{d}(\mathbf{c}_i), \mathbf{d}(\mathbf{c}_i + \mathbf{c}_p)) = \frac{exp(h_k(\mathbf{d}(\mathbf{c}_i), \mathbf{d}(\mathbf{c}_i + \mathbf{c}_p)))}{\sum_{m=0}^{K+1} exp(h_m(\mathbf{d}(\mathbf{c}_i), \mathbf{d}(\mathbf{c}_i + \mathbf{c}_p)))}. \qquad (5)$$

Here h_0 and h_{K+1} are the functions for the two classes outside of all receptive fields (in front of and behind). For $k = 1, 2, \cdots, K$, h_k are defined by the relative depth difference as

$$h_k(\mathbf{d}(\mathbf{c}_i), \mathbf{d}(\mathbf{c}_i + \mathbf{c}_p)) = -(d(\mathbf{c}_i, \mathbf{c}_i + \mathbf{c}_p) - a_k)^2 / t, \qquad (6)$$

where a_k is a learnable parameter that determines the center of the kernel's depth receptive field, and t is a learnable temperature parameter that can sharpen/soften the activation of softmax. h_0 and h_{K+1} are defined as

$$h_0 = -sgn(d(\mathbf{c}_i, \mathbf{c}_i + \mathbf{c}_p) - a_0) \cdot (d(\mathbf{c}_i, \mathbf{c}_i + \mathbf{c}_p) - a_0)^2 / t,$$
$$h_{K+1} = sgn(d(\mathbf{c}_i, \mathbf{c}_i + \mathbf{c}_p) - a_{K+1}) \cdot (d(\mathbf{c}_i, \mathbf{c}_i + \mathbf{c}_p) - a_{K+1})^2 / t. \qquad (7)$$

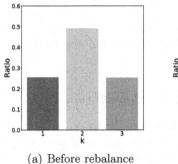
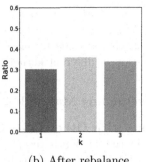

(a) Before rebalance   (b) After rebalance

Fig. 3. The ratio of pixels assigned to each kernel, before and after rebalance. The figure shows the malleable 2.5D convolution at res5 stage of a trained model. We count the sum of g_k and $s_k \cdot g_k$ for each kernel across the whole NYUDv2 dataset and calculate the ratio. More cases will be presented in the supplementary material.

Here *sgn* denotes the signum function, which is used to make h_0 and h_{K+1} monotonic so that they construct borders of the receptive field.

The constructed depth receptive fields are controlled by parameters t and $a_k, k = 0, 1, \cdots, K + 1$. And both sets of parameters are learnable by gradient descent. Figure 2 gives an example of the image of h_k and g_k.

3.2 Kernel Rebalancing

Through the receptive field functions g_k, we can assign pixels to convolution kernels. However, pixels are not evenly distributed along the depth-axis. In other words, the expectation $\mathbb{E}[g_k(\mathbf{d}(\mathbf{c}_i), \mathbf{d}(\mathbf{c}_i + \mathbf{c}_p))]$ are not equal for different parameters of g_k. This implies that the outputs of different kernels might have different value scales, and the scales change with parameters of g_k. Theoretically, the scale change can be adjusted by $\mathbf{w}_k$, but implicitly learning a scale factor in convolution kernel weights could increase learning difficulty. Therefore, we introduce a scale factor s_k to rebalance the output scales of different kernel. Then Eq. 3 is modified as

$$\mathbf{y}(\mathbf{c}_i) = \sum_{k=1}^{K} \sum_{\mathbf{c}_p \in \mathcal{R}_p} s_k \cdot g_k(\mathbf{d}(\mathbf{c}_i), \mathbf{d}(\mathbf{c}_i + \mathbf{c}_p)) \cdot \mathbf{w}_k(\mathbf{c}_p) \cdot \mathbf{x}(\mathbf{c}_i + \mathbf{c}_p), \qquad (8)$$

And s_k-s must satisfy $s_k \geq 0, \forall k = 1, 2, \cdots, K$ and $\sum_{k=1}^{K} s_k = 1$. Note that $\sum_{k=1}^{K} s_k$ can actually equal to any constant considering that in modern CNNs, a convolution layer is almost always followed by a normalization layer. To ensure that s_k-s satisfy the conditions, we implement them as

$$s_k = \frac{exp(b_k)}{\sum_{k=1}^{K} exp(b_k)} \qquad (9)$$

And the malleable 2.5D convolution learns b_k by gradient descent.

Figure 3 shows the effect of kernel rebalancing. We can see that the kernel rebalancing mechanism meets our expectation and successfully rebalance the pixel distribution in different kernels.

3.3   Understanding Malleable 2.5D Convolution

Comparisons with Other RGB-D Convolutions. To get a better understanding of learnable depth receptive fields, we compare our malleable 2.5D convolution with the two previous RGB-D convolutions, Depth-aware Convolution and the 2.5D Convolution. These two convolutions can both be written as the form of Eq. 3. In Depth-aware Convolution, K is 1, and g_1 is defined as

$$g_1(\mathbf{d}(\mathbf{c}_i), \mathbf{d}(\mathbf{c}_i + \mathbf{c}_p)) = exp(-\alpha|\mathbf{d}(\mathbf{c}_i) - \mathbf{d}(\mathbf{c}_i + \mathbf{c}_p)|), \tag{10}$$

where α is a pre-defined constant. And in 2.5D convolution, K can be any positive integer, and g_k is defined as

$$g_k(\mathbf{d}(\mathbf{c}_i), \mathbf{d}(\mathbf{c}_i + \mathbf{c}_p)) = \begin{cases} 1, & k - 1 - \dfrac{K}{2} \leq d(\mathbf{c}_i, \mathbf{c}_i + \mathbf{c}_p) < k - \dfrac{K}{2} \\ 0, & otherwise \end{cases} \tag{11}$$

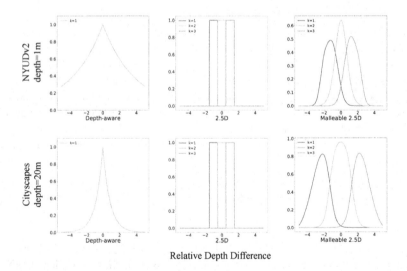

Fig. 4. Comparison of depth receptive field functions g_k. Best view in color. We compare the depth receptive fields at res5 stage after training. The first row shows a case in NYUDv2 where the depth $\mathbf{d}(\mathbf{c}_i) = 1$ m. The second row shows a case in Cityscapes where the depth $\mathbf{d}(\mathbf{c}_i) = 20$ m. Note that we scale the y-axis to see better. The overall scale does not affect output results because of batch normalizations

In Fig. 4, we compare depth receptive fields of these two convolutions and our method. We visualize depth receptive fields in two typical cases in NYUDv2 and Cityscapes respectively. In the two datasets, both focal lengths and the depth ranges are different. The Depth-aware Convolution uses absolute depth difference to control the receptive field. When the depths and focal length changes, the 3D distance between two adjacent pixels on the image could be very different. And we can see that Depth-aware Convolution cannot fit both cases with the same parameter setting. 2.5D convolution adopts relative depth differences, which makes it more robust to varying depth and focal length. However, 2.5D convolution's receptive field along the depth-axis is also pre-determined and cannot adapt to different datasets without handcraft adjusting. In contrast, malleable 2.5D convolution not only can avoid the influence of varying depth and focal length, but also automatically learn the depth receptive field for different environments. As an outdoor dataset, Cityscapes has a larger range of depth. And the depth maps in Cityscapes are relatively noisy, not as sharp as those in NYUDv2. Intuitively, the depth receptive field for Cityscapes should be larger and less sharp. We can see from the figure that malleable 2.5D convolution learns a wider depth receptive field for Cityscapes than that for NYUDv2, and the edges drop slower.

Table 1. Comparison of the computational cost of different convolutions. The input size is 768 × 768. "kernels" means the kernel number of used RGB-D convolutions

Method	Kernels	FLOPs (G)	Params (M)
Baseline	1	215.673	59.468
Depth-aware [31]	1	215.675	59.468
Malleable 2.5D	1	215.679	59.468
2.5D [34]	3	234.701	65.734
Malleable 2.5D	3	234.711	65.734

In Table 1, we compare the FLOPs and parameter number of different convolutions. We present ResNet-based DeepLabv3+[4] as the baseline, and replace the 3 × 3 convolution with a RGB-D convolution in the first residual unit in each stage of the ResNet. It shows that when using the same number of kernels, the malleable 2.5D convolution only brings very minor additional computational cost to achieve learnable depth receptive fields.

Usage of Malleable 2.5D Convolution. Malleable 2.5D convolutions can be easily incorporated into CNNs by replacing standard 2D convolutions. The inputs of malleable 2.5D convolutions are standard feature maps, depth maps, and camera parameters. And the outputs of malleable 2.5D convolutions are the same with standard 2D convolutions.

In RGB-D semantic segmentation, utilizing pre-trained models is essential to attain good performance. When replacing standard convolutions with malleable 2.5D convolutions, we do not abandon the pre-trained weights of the original convolutions but adopt a simple parameter loading strategy to make use of them. We duplicate the pre-trained weights and load them into each kernel of the malleable 2.5D convolution. in finetuning time, the k kernels start from the same initialization and gradually learn to model geometric relations.

4 Experiments

4.1 Datasets

We evaluate our method on two popular RGB-D scene parsing datasets: NYUDv2 [27] and Cityscapes [7]. These two datasets respectively contains indoor and outdoor scenes and the depth sources are different. Therefore, the depth ranges, object sizes and the quality of depth data are very different in them. Evaluating on these two datasets is challenging and can validate the robustness and generalization ability of RGB-D scene parsing methods. We will introduce these two datasets in detail in the supplementary material.

4.2 Implementation Details

Model Implementation. DeepLabv3+[4] is a widely recognized state-of-the-art method for semantic segmentation. We adopt ResNet-based DeepLabv3+ pre-trained on ImageNet [24] as our baseline network. And for NYUDv2, we moreover adopt a multi-stage merging block inspired by previous works [16, 19]. Details of the network structures will be illustrated in the supplementary material. To evaluate the our method, we replace the 3×3 convolution with a malleable 2.5D convolution in the first residual unit in each stage of the ResNet.

Our implementation is based on PyTorch [22]. Synchronized batch normalization are adopted for better batch statistics. By default, we use malleable 2.5D convolution with 3 kernels, and the parameter $[a_0, a_1, a_2, a_3, a_4]$ are initialized as $[-2, -1, 0, 1, 2]$, t is initialized as 1, and b_k-s are all initialized as 0.

Training Settings. We use SGD optimizer with momentum to train our model. The momentum is fixed as 0.9 and the weight decay is set to 0.0001. We employ a "poly" learning rate policy where the initial learning rate is multiplied by $(1 - \frac{iter}{max\_iter})^{power}$. The initial learning rate is set to 0.01 and the power is set to 0.9. We use batch size of 16 and train our model for 40k iterations for NYUDv2 and 60k iterations for Cityscapes. For data augmentation, we use random cropping, random horizontal flipping and random scaling with scale $\in \{0.75, 1, 1.25, 1.5, 1.75, 2\}$. Besides, we adopt the bootstrapped cross-entropy loss as in [32] for Cityscapes experiments.

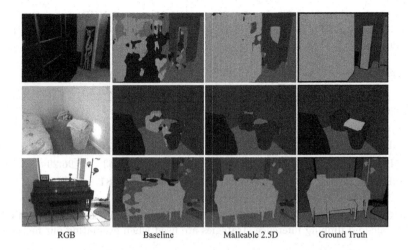

RGB   Baseline   Malleable 2.5D   Ground Truth

Fig. 5. Segmentation results on NYUDv2 test dataset. Black regions in "Ground Truth" is are the ignoring category. Models are based on ResNet-50

4.3   Main Results

First of all, we compare our method with previous RGB-D convolutions to validate the benefits of learnable receptive fields along the depth-axis. The results are
shown in Table 2. We compare Depth-aware, 2.5D and malleable 2.5D convolution on both NYUDv2 and Cityscapes datasets. When implementing the other
two methods, we use the default parameters provided in their papers [31,34]
which are tuned on NYUDv2. All evaluations are conducted without multi-scale
and flip testing tricks. For fairness, we compare malleable 2.5D convolution with
other convolutions in the case that they have the same kernel number. And the
single-kernel version of malleable 2.5D convolution's parameter $[a_0, a_1, a_2]$ are
initialized as $[-1, 0, 1]$. The results show that the malleable 2.5D convolution
consistently outperforms other methods and baselines. It is worth noting that
Depth-aware and 2.5D convolutions fail on Cityscapes. They decrease the performance even depth information is incorporated. However, our malleable 2.5D
convolution still works well on Cityscapes with the same parameter initialization
on NYUDv2. It adaptively learns the depth receptive field that fits the outdoor
environment and improves segmentation performance. Figure 5 visualizes qualitative comparison results between the baseline and our method on NYUv2 test
set.

NYUDv2 provides high-quality depth data, and most RGB-D scene parsing
methods take it as the main benchmark. Therefore, we then compare with more
state-of-the-art RGB-D scene parsing methods on NYUDv2, shown in Table 3.
As other works do [16,34,35], we adopt test-time multi-scale and flip inference
to obtain best performance. We evaluate models based on both ResNet-50 and
ResNet-101 backbones. And we use malleable 2.5D convolutions with 3 kernels.
Different from many works that adopt two-stream network design to process

Table 2. Comparison with other RGB-D convolutions on NYUDv2 and Cityscapes. The backbone model is ResNet-50. "kernels" means the kernel number of used RGB-D convolutions

Method	kernels	NYUDv2		Cityscapes	
		mIoU(%)	Pixel Acc (%)	mIoU(%)	Pixel Acc (%)
Baseline	1	44.56	73.01	79.94	96.34
Depth-aware [31]	1	46.69	74.27	79.01	96.32
Malleable 2.5D	1	**47.08**	**75.13**	**80.26**	**96.40**
2.5D [34]	3	48.23	75.73	78.63	96.29
Malleable 2.5D	3	**48.80**	**76.03**	**80.81**	**96.51**

Table 3. Comparison with state-of-the-art RGB-D scene parsing methods on NYUDv2. Multi-scale and flipping inference strategies are used when evaluating our method.

Method	Backbone	mIoU (%)	Pixel Acc (%)
FCN+HHA [25]	VGG-16 ×2	34.0	65.4
Depth-aware+HHA [31]	VGG-16 ×2	43.9	-
CFN (RefineNet-152) [18]	ResNet-152 ×2	47.7	-
2.5D [34]	ResNet-101 ×1	48.4	75.3
2.5D+HHA [34]	ResNet-101 ×2	49.1	75.9
RDF-101 [16]	ResNet-101 ×2	49.1	75.6
RDF-152 [16]	ResNet-152 ×2	50.1	76.0
Idempotent [35]	ResNet-101 ×2	50.6	76.3
Malleable 2.5D	ResNet-50 ×1	49.7	76.3
Malleable 2.5D	ResNet-101 ×1	**50.9**	**76.9**

RGB+HHA inputs, we do not use HHA input and thus do not double the computational cost brought by backbones. The results show that even without doubling the backbone, our model achieves promising performance and outperforms other methods.

4.4   Ablation Studies

In this subsection, we conduct ablation studies on NYUDv2 dataset to validate the efficacy of our method.

Number of Kernels. In Table 4, we conduct experiments that compare different numbers of convolutional kernels in malleable 2.5D convolutions. While the performance improves when the number increases from 1 to 3, the performance of the 5-kernel case drops slightly compared to the 3-kernel case. We suppose the reason is that 3 kernels are enough to model 3D relations between pixels, and in the 5-kernel case there are too few pixels assigned to the two outer kernels and they cannot be sufficiently trained.

Table 4. Ablation study for number of convolution kernels. The backbone is ResNet-50

Kernel numbers	mIoU (%)	Pixel Acc (%)
1	47.08	75.13
3	**48.80**	**76.03**
5	48.17	75.59

Learnable Parameters. In Table 5, we evaluate the effects of introduced learnable parameters. We fix part of the introduced parameters $\{a_k, t, b_k\}$ at the initialized values, and set rest of them learnable. The results demonstrate that when we fix all the parameters and thus fix the depth receptive fields, the performance is the worst. And the fixed malleable 2.5D convolution gets a very similar result to 2.5D convolution. When only the kernel center a_k is learnable, the performance stays almost the same. And when both a_k and t are learnable, the mIoU improves from 48.33% to 48.62% and pixel accuracy improves from 75.74% to 75.91%. We argue that this is because the temperature term T controls the sharpness of depth receptive fields, and therefore it is crucial to set both a_k and t learnable for assigning pixels to different kernels more accurately. When the kernel rebalancing parameter b_k is introduced, the performance moreover improves to the result of complete malleable 2.5D convolution. These results validate that the improvement is indeed brought by the introduced learnable parameters.

Table 5. Ablation study for introduced learnable parameters in malleable 2.5D convolution. The backbone model is ResNet-50Ablation study for introduced learnable parameters in malleable 2.5D convolution. The backbone model is ResNet-50

Method	Learnable params	mIoU(%)	Pixel Acc(%)
Baseline	-	44.56	73.01
2.5D [34]	-	48.23	75.73
Malleable 2.5D	None	48.28	75.68
	a_k	48.33	75.74
	a_k, t	48.62	75.91
	a_k, t, b_k	**48.80**	**76.03**

Initialization of Introduced Parameters. The parameter a_k serves as the center of kernel k's receptive field along the depth-axis. It is the most direct factor that controls the learnt depth receptive field. In Table 6, we evaluate the effects of different initialization of a_k for 3-kernel malleable 2.5D convolution. When we use large values to initialize a_k, the performance drops slightly. However, both results outperform the baseline and 2.5D convolution. This validates the effectiveness and the robustness of the learnable depth receptive field in our method. More experiments of different parameter initializations will be included in the supplementary material.

Table 6. Results of different initialization of a_k. The backbone model is ResNet-50

Method	Initialization	mIoU(%)	Pixel Acc(%)
Baseline	-	44.56	73.01
2.5D [34]	-	48.23	75.73
Malleable 2.5D	$[-4, -2, 0, 2, 4]$	48.66	75.94
	$[-2, -1, 0, 1, 2]$	**48.80**	**76.03**

Malleable 2.5D Convolution in Different Layers. To reveal the effects of using malleable 2.5D convolution in different locations in the backbone network, we conduct a series of experiments. The results are shown in Table 7. When using more malleable 2.5D convolution, the network gains more capability to handle 3D geometric information and achieves better segmentation performance.

Table 7. Results of using malleable 2.5D convolutions in different layers. "Replaced Location" means in which stage in the ResNet the first 3×3 convolution is replaced by malleable 2.5D convolution. The backbone model is ResNet-50

Method	Replaced location	mIoU(%)	Pixel Acc(%)
Baseline	-	44.56	73.01
Malleable 2.5D	res2, res3	48.27	75.83
	res4, res5	48.34	75.77
	res3, res4, res5	48.58	75.93
	res2, res3, res4, res5	**48.80**	**76.03**

5 Conclusion

We propose a novel RGB-D convolution operator called malleable 2.5D convolution, which has learnable receptive fields along the depth-axis. By learning the receptive field along the depth-axis, malleable 2.5D convolution can learn to adapt to different environments without handcraft parameter adjusting and improve RGB-D scene parsing performance. And malleable 2.5D convolution can be easily incorporated into pre-trained standard CNNs. Our extensive experiments on NYUDv2 and Cityscapes validate the effectiveness and the generalization ability of our method.

Acknowledgments. This work is supported by the National Key Research and Development Program of China (2017YFB1002601, 2016QY02D0304), National Natural Science Foundation of China (61375022, 61403005, 61632003), Beijing Advanced Innovation Center for Intelligent Robots and Systems (2018IRS11), and PEK-SenseTime Joint Laboratory of Machine Vision.

References

1. Chen, L., et al.: Searching for efficient multi-scale architectures for dense image prediction. In: NeurIPS, pp. 8713–8724 (2018)
2. Chen, L., Papandreou, G., Kokkinos, I., Murphy, K., Yuille, A.L.: Deeplab: semantic image segmentation with deep convolutional nets, atrous convolution, and fully connected CRFs. IEEE Trans. Pattern Anal. Mach. Intell. **40**(4), 834–848 (2018)
3. Chen, L., Papandreou, G., Schroff, F., Adam, H.: Rethinking atrous convolution for semantic image segmentation. CoRR abs/1706.05587 (2017)
4. Chen, L.-C., Zhu, Y., Papandreou, G., Schroff, F., Adam, H.: Encoder-decoder with atrous separable convolution for semantic image segmentation. In: Ferrari, V., Hebert, M., Sminchisescu, C., Weiss, Y. (eds.) ECCV 2018. LNCS, vol. 11211, pp. 833–851. Springer, Cham (2018). https://doi.org/10.1007/978-3-030-01234-2_49
5. Chen, Y., Mensink, T., Gavves, E.: 3D neighborhood convolution: learning depth-aware features for RGB-D and RGB semantic segmentation. In: 3DV, pp. 173–182. IEEE (2019)
6. Cheng, Y., Cai, R., Li, Z., Zhao, X., Huang, K.: Locality-sensitive deconvolution networks with gated fusion for RGB-D indoor semantic segmentation. In: CVPR, pp. 1475–1483. IEEE Computer Society (2017)
7. Cordts, M., et al.: The cityscapes dataset for semantic urban scene understanding. In: 2016 IEEE Conference on Computer Vision and Pattern Recognition, CVPR 2016, Las Vegas, NV, USA, 27–30 June, 2016, pp. 3213–3223. IEEE Computer Society (2016). https://doi.org/10.1109/CVPR.2016.350,https://doi.org/10.1109/CVPR.2016.350
8. Dai, J., Qi, H., Xiong, Y., Li, Y., Zhang, G., Hu, H., Wei, Y.: Deformable convolutional networks. In: ICCV, pp. 764–773. IEEE Computer Society (2017)
9. Gupta, S., Girshick, R., Arbeláez, P., Malik, J.: Learning Rich Features from RGB-D Images for Object Detection and Segmentation. In: Fleet, D., Pajdla, T., Schiele, B., Tuytelaars, T. (eds.) ECCV 2014. LNCS, vol. 8695, pp. 345–360. Springer, Cham (2014). https://doi.org/10.1007/978-3-319-10584-0_23
10. Hazirbas, C., Ma, L., Domokos, C., Cremers, D.: FuseNet: incorporating depth into semantic segmentation via fusion-based CNN architecture. In: Lai, S.-H., Lepetit, V., Nishino, K., Sato, Y. (eds.) ACCV 2016. LNCS, vol. 10111, pp. 213–228. Springer, Cham (2017). https://doi.org/10.1007/978-3-319-54181-5_14
11. He, K., Zhang, X., Ren, S., Sun, J.: Deep residual learning for image recognition. In: CVPR, pp. 770–778. IEEE Computer Society (2016)
12. Jaderberg, M., Simonyan, K., Zisserman, A., Kavukcuoglu, K.: Spatial transformer networks. In: NIPS, pp. 2017–2025 (2015)
13. Kang, B., Lee, Y., Nguyen, T.Q.: Depth-adaptive deep neural network for semantic segmentation. IEEE Trans. Multimed. **20**(9), 2478–2490 (2018)
14. Kong, S., Fowlkes, C.C.: Recurrent scene parsing with perspective understanding in the loop. In: CVPR, pp. 956–965. IEEE Computer Society (2018)
15. Krizhevsky, A., Sutskever, I., Hinton, G.E.: ImageNet classification with deep convolutional neural networks. In: NIPS, pp. 1106–1114 (2012)

16. Lee, S., Park, S., Hong, K.: RDFNet: RGB-D multi-level residual feature fusion for indoor semantic segmentation. In: ICCV, pp. 4990–4999. IEEE Computer Society (2017)

17. Li, Z., Gan, Y., Liang, X., Yu, Y., Cheng, H., Lin, L.: LSTM-CF: unifying context modeling and fusion with LSTMs for RGB-D scene labeling. In: Leibe, B., Matas, J., Sebe, N., Welling, M. (eds.) ECCV 2016. LNCS, vol. 9906, pp. 541–557. Springer, Cham (2016). https://doi.org/10.1007/978-3-319-46475-6_34

18. Lin, D., Chen, G., Cohen-Or, D., Heng, P., Huang, H.: Cascaded feature network for semantic segmentation of RGB-D images. In: ICCV, pp. 1320–1328. IEEE Computer Society (2017)

19. Lin, G., Milan, A., Shen, C., Reid, I.D.: RefineNet: multi-path refinement networks for high-resolution semantic segmentation. In: CVPR, pp. 5168–5177. IEEE Computer Society (2017)

20. Liu, H., Simonyan, K., Yang, Y.: DARTS: differentiable architecture search. In: ICLR (Poster). OpenReview.net (2019)

21. Long, J., Shelhamer, E., Darrell, T.: Fully convolutional networks for semantic segmentation. In: CVPR, pp. 3431–3440. IEEE Computer Society (2015)

22. Paszke, A., et al.: Automatic differentiation in PyTorch. In: NIPS Autodiff Workshop (2017)

23. Qi, X., Liao, R., Jia, J., Fidler, S., Urtasun, R.: 3D graph neural networks for RGBD semantic segmentation. In: ICCV, pp. 5209–5218. IEEE Computer Society (2017)

24. Russakovsky, O., Deng, J., Su, H., Krause, J., Satheesh, S., Ma, S., Huang, Z., Karpathy, A., Khosla, A., Bernstein, M.S., Berg, A.C., Li, F.: Imagenet large scale visual recognition challenge. Int. J. Comput. Vision 115(3), 211–252 (2015)

25. Shelhamer, E., Long, J., Darrell, T.: Fully convolutional networks for semantic segmentation. IEEE Trans. Pattern Anal. Mach. Intell. 39(4), 640–651 (2017)

26. Shen, F., Gan, R., Yan, S., Zeng, G.: Semantic segmentation via structured patch prediction, context CRF and guidance CRF. In: CVPR, pp. 5178–5186. IEEE Computer Society (2017)

27. Silberman, N., Hoiem, D., Kohli, P., Fergus, R.: Indoor segmentation and support inference from RGBD images. In: Fitzgibbon, A., Lazebnik, S., Perona, P., Sato, Y., Schmid, C. (eds.) ECCV 2012. LNCS, vol. 7576, pp. 746–760. Springer, Heidelberg (2012). https://doi.org/10.1007/978-3-642-33715-4_54

28. Simonyan, K., Zisserman, A.: Very deep convolutional networks for large-scale image recognition. CoRR abs/1409.1556 (2014)

29. Song, S., Yu, F., Zeng, A., Chang, A.X., Savva, M., Funkhouser, T.A.: Semantic scene completion from a single depth image. In: CVPR, pp. 190–198. IEEE Computer Society (2017)

30. Tan, M., Le, Q.V.: MixConv: mixed depthwise convolutional kernels. CoRR abs/1907.09595 (2019)

31. Wang, W., Neumann, U.: Depth-aware CNN for RGB-D segmentation. In: Ferrari, V., Hebert, M., Sminchisescu, C., Weiss, Y. (eds.) ECCV 2018. LNCS, vol. 11215, pp. 144–161. Springer, Cham (2018). https://doi.org/10.1007/978-3-030-01252-6_9

32. Wu, Z., Shen, C., van den Hengel, A.: High-performance semantic segmentation using very deep fully convolutional networks. CoRR abs/1604.04339 (2016)

33. Xie, S., Zheng, H., Liu, C., Lin, L.: SNAS: stochastic neural architecture search. In: ICLR (Poster). OpenReview.net (2019)

34. Xing, Y., Wang, J., Chen, X., Zeng, G.: 2.5D convolution for RGB-D semantic segmentation. In: 2019 IEEE International Conference on Image Processing (ICIP), pp. 1410–1414. IEEE (2019)

35. Xing, Y., Wang, J., Chen, X., Zeng, G.: Coupling two-stream RGB-D semantic segmentation network by idempotent mappings. In: 2019 IEEE International Conference on Image Processing (ICIP), pp. 1850–1854. IEEE (2019)
36. Yu, F., Koltun, V.: Multi-scale context aggregation by dilated convolutions. CoRR abs/1511.07122 (2015)
37. Zhang, R., Tang, S., Zhang, Y., Li, J., Yan, S.: Scale-adaptive convolutions for scene parsing. In: IEEE International Conference on Computer Vision, ICCV 2017, Venice, Italy, 22–29 October, 2017, pp. 2050–2058. IEEE Computer Society (2017). https://doi.org/10.1109/ICCV.2017.224
38. Zhao, H., Shi, J., Qi, X., Wang, X., Jia, J.: Pyramid scene parsing network. In: CVPR, pp. 6230–6239. IEEE Computer Society (2017)
39. Zhong, Y., Dai, Y., Li, H.: 3D geometry-aware semantic labeling of outdoor street scenes. In: ICPR, pp. 2343–2349. IEEE Computer Society (2018)
40. Zhu, X., Hu, H., Lin, S., Dai, J.: Deformable convNets V2: more deformable, better results. In: CVPR, pp. 9308–9316. Computer Vision Foundation/IEEE (2019)

Feature-Metric Loss for Self-supervised Learning of Depth and Egomotion

Chang Shu[1], Kun Yu[2], Zhixiang Duan[2], and Kuiyuan Yang[2(✉)]

[1] Meituan Dianping Group, Beijing, China
shuchang02@meituan.com
[2] DeepMotion, Beijing, China
{kunyu,zhixiangduan,kuiyuanyang}@deepmotion.ai

Abstract. Photometric loss is widely used for self-supervised depth and egomotion estimation. However, the loss landscapes induced by photometric differences are often problematic for optimization, caused by plateau landscapes for pixels in textureless regions or multiple local minima for less discriminative pixels. In this work, feature-metric loss is proposed and defined on feature representation, where the feature representation is also learned in a self-supervised manner and regularized by both first-order and second-order derivatives to constrain the loss landscapes to form proper convergence basins. Comprehensive experiments and detailed analysis via visualization demonstrate the effectiveness of the proposed feature-metric loss. In particular, our method improves state-of-the-art methods on KITTI from 0.885 to 0.925 measured by δ_1 for depth estimation, and significantly outperforms previous method for visual odometry.

1 Introduction

Estimating depth and egomotion from monocular camera is a fundamental and valuable task in computer vision, which has wide applications in augmented reality [35], robotics navigation [8] and autonomous driving [31]. Though monocular camera is cheap and lightweight, the task is hard for conventional SfM/SLAM algorithms [12,34,42] and continues challenging deep learning based approaches [1,2,4,24,56].

Deep learning for depth and egomotion estimation can be broadly categorized into supervised and self-supervised learning. For depth estimation, supervised learning takes images paired with depth maps as input [11,13,23], where depth maps are sparsely collected from expensive LiDAR sensors [14] or densely rendered from simulation engines [29], while supervision from LiDAR limits the generalization to new cameras and supervision from rendering limits the generalization to real scenes. For egomotion estimation, supervised signals come from trajectories computed by classical methods with high precision sensors

---

This work is done when Chang Shu is an intern at DeepMotion.

© Springer Nature Switzerland AG 2020
A. Vedaldi et al. (Eds.): ECCV 2020, LNCS 12364, pp. 572–588, 2020.
https://doi.org/10.1007/978-3-030-58529-7_34

like IMU and GPS, which are also costly and can not guarantee absolute accuracy. Self-supervised learning unifies these two tasks into one framework, and only uses monocular videos as inputs, and supervision is from view synthesis [15,16,27,52,56]. The setup is simpler, and easy to generalize among cameras.

However, self-supervised approaches are still inferior to supervised ones by large margins when compared on standard benchmarks. The main problem lies in the weak supervision added as photometric loss, which is defined as the photometric difference between a pixel warped from source view by estimated depth and pose and the pixel captured in the target view. Nevertheless, small photometric loss does not necessarily guarantee accurate depth and pose, especially for pixels in textureless regions. The problem can be partially solved by adding smoothness loss on depth map, which encourages first-order smoothness [4,15,16] or second-order smoothness [26,49–51], and forces depth propagation from discriminative regions to textureless regions. However, such propagation is with limited range and tends to cause over-smooth results around boundaries.

Considering the basic limitation is from representation, feature-metric loss is proposed to use learned feature representation for each pixel, which is explicitly constrained to be discriminative even in textureless regions. For learning feature representation, a single view reconstruction pathway is added as an auto-encoder network. To ensure loss landscapes defined on the learned feature representation having desired shapes, two additional regularizing losses are added to the auto-encoder loss, $i.e.$, discriminative loss and convergent loss. The discriminative loss encourages feature differences across pixels modeled by first-order gradients, while the convergent loss ensures a wide convergence basin by penalizing feature gradients' variances across pixels.

In total, our network architecture contains three sub-networks, $i.e.$, DepthNet and PoseNet for cross-view reconstruction, and FeatureNet for single-view reconstruction, where features generated by FeatureNet are used to define feature-metric loss for DepthNet and PoseNet.

In experiment, feature-metric loss outperforms widely used first-order and second-order smoothness losses, and improves state-of-the-art depth estimation from 0.885 to 0.925 measured by δ_1 on KITTI dataset. In addition, our method generates better egomotion estimation and results in more accurate visual odometry.

In general, our contributions are summarized as three-fold:

- Feature-metric loss is proposed for self-supervised depth and egomotion estimation.
- FeatureNet is proposed for feature representation learning for depth and egomotion estimation.
- State-of-the-art performances on depth and egomotion estimation are achieved on KITTI dataset.

2   Related Work

In this section, we review related works of self-supervised learning for two tasks, *i.e.*, monocular depth and egomotion estimation, as well as visual representation learning.

Monocular Depth and Egomotion Estimation: SfMLearner is a pioneering work [56] for this task, where geometry estimation from DepthNet and PoseNet is supervised by photometric loss. To tackle moving objects that break the assumption of static scenes, optical flow is estimated to compensate these moving pixels [26,49,52,57], segmentation masks provided by pre-trained segmentation models are also to handle potential moving objects separately [4,17,30].

More geometric priors are also used to strengthen the self-supervised learning. Depth-normal consistency loss is proposed as extra constraint [50,51]. 3D consistency between point clouds backprojected from adjacent views is considered in [2,5,27]. In addition, binocular videos are used for training to solve both scale ambiguity and scene dynamics [15,24,26,49], where only inference can be carried on monocular video.

In contrast to all above methods where focuses are on the geometry parts of the task, deep feature reconstruction [53] proposed to use deep features from pre-trained models to define reconstruction loss. Our method shares the same spirit, but takes a step further to explicitly learn deep features from the geometry problem under the same self-supervised learning framework.

Visual Representation Learning: It is of great interest of self-supervised visual representation learning for downstream tasks. Without explicitly provided labels, the losses are defined by manipulating the data itself in different ways, which could be reconstructing input data [10,28,32,45], predicting spatial transformations [9,36–38], coloring grayscale input images [7,21,22,54] etc. Our work belongs to reconstruct the input through an auto-encoder network. Different from previous works mainly aiming for learning better features for recognition tasks, our method is designed to learn better features for the geometry task.

3   Method

In this section, we firstly introduce geometry models with required notations, then define two reconstruction losses, one for depth and ego-motion learning, the other for feature representation learning. Finally, we present our overall pipeline and implementation details about loss settings and network architectures.

3.1   Geometry Models

Camera Model and Depth. The camera operator $\pi : \mathbb{R}^3 \to \mathbb{R}^2$ projects a 3D point $P = (X, Y, Z)$ to a 2D pixel $p = (u, v)$ by:

$$\pi(P) = (f_x \frac{X}{Z} + c_x, f_y \frac{Y}{Z} + c_y) \tag{1}$$

where (f_x, f_y, c_x, c_y) are the camera intrinsic parameters. Similarly, a pixel p is projected to a 3D point P given its depth $D(p)$, i.e., backprojection π^{-1} : $\mathbb{R}^2 \times \mathbb{R} \to \mathbb{R}^3$:

$$\pi^{-1}(p, D(p)) = D(p)\left(\frac{x - c_x}{f_x}, \frac{y - c_y}{f_y}, 1\right)^\top \tag{2}$$

Ego-Motion. Ego-motion is modeled by transformation $G \in \mathbb{SE}(3)$, together with π and π^{-1}, we can define a projective warping function $\omega : \mathbb{R}^2 \times \mathbb{R} \times \mathbb{SE}(3) \to \mathbb{R}^2$, which maps a pixel p in one frame to the other frame transformed by G:

$$\widehat{p} = \omega(p, D(p), G) = \pi\left(G \cdot \pi^{-1}(p, D(p))\right) \tag{3}$$

3.2 Cross-View Reconstruction

With the above geometry models, target frame I_t can be reconstructed from source frame I_s via,

$$\widehat{I}_{s \to t}(p) = I_s(\widehat{p}) \tag{4}$$

where $\widehat{p}$ is defined in Eq. 3 and depends on both depth and ego-motion. $I_t(p)$ and $I_s(\widehat{p})$ should be similar given a set of assumptions, including both depth and ego-motion are correct; the corresponding 3D point is static with Lambertian reflectance and not occluded in both views. Then, a multi-view reconstruction loss can be defined for learning depth and motion, i.e.,

$$\mathcal{L}_{s \to t} = \sum_p \ell(I_s(\widehat{p}), I_t(p)), \tag{5}$$

where $\ell(,)$ is the per-pixel loss which measures the photometric difference, i.e, photometric loss.

Though the loss works, it is fundamentally problematic since correct depth and pose is sufficient but not necessary for small photometric error, e.g., pixels in a textureless with the same photometric values can have small photometric losses even the depth and pose are wrongly estimated. The problem can be formally analysed from the optimization perspective by deriving the gradients with respect to both depth $D(p)$ and egomotion G,

$$\frac{\partial \mathcal{L}_{s \to t}}{\partial D(p)} = \frac{\partial \ell(I_s(\widehat{p}), I_t(p))}{\partial I_s(\widehat{p})} \cdot \frac{\partial I_s(\widehat{p})}{\partial \widehat{p}} \cdot \frac{\partial \widehat{p}}{\partial D(p)}, \tag{6}$$

$$\frac{\partial \mathcal{L}_{s \to t}}{\partial G} = \sum_p \frac{\partial \ell(I_s(\widehat{p}), I_t(p))}{\partial I_s(\widehat{p})} \cdot \frac{\partial I_s(\widehat{p})}{\partial \widehat{p}} \cdot \frac{\partial \widehat{p}}{\partial G}, \tag{7}$$

where both gradients depend on the image gradient $\frac{\partial I_s(\widehat{p})}{\partial \widehat{p}}$. For textureless region, the image gradients are close to zero which further causes zero gradients for Eq. 6 and contributes zero to Eq. 7 for egomotion estimation. In addition, locally non-smooth gradient directions are also challenging convergence due to inconsistent update directions towards minima.

Therefore, we propose to learn feature representation $\phi_s(p)$ with better gradient $\frac{\partial \phi_s(\hat{p})}{\partial \hat{p}}$ to overcome the above problems, and generalizes photometric loss to feature-metric loss accordingly,

$$\mathcal{L}_{s \to t} = \sum_p \ell\big(\phi_s(\hat{p}), \phi_t(p)\big). \tag{8}$$

3.3   Single-View Reconstruction

The feature representation $\phi(p)$ is also learned in self-supervised manner with single-view reconstruction through an auto-encoder network. The auto-encoder network contains an encoder for deep feature extractions from an image and an decoder to reconstruct the input image based on the deep features. The deep features are learned to encode large patterns in an image where redundancies and noises are removed. To ensure the learned representation with good properties for optimizing Eq. 8, we add two extra regularizers $\mathcal{L}_{dis}$ and $\mathcal{L}_{cvt}$ to the image reconstruction loss $\mathcal{L}_{rec}$, i.e.,

$$\mathcal{L}_s = \mathcal{L}_{rec} + \alpha \mathcal{L}_{dis} + \beta \mathcal{L}_{cvt} \tag{9}$$

where α and β are set to $1e^{-3}$ via cross validation. These three loss terms are described in detail below.

For simplicity, we denote first-order derivative and second-order derivative with respect to image coordinates by ∇^1 and ∇^2, which equals $\partial_x + \partial_y$ and $\partial_{xx} + 2\partial_{xy} + \partial_{yy}$ respectively.

Image Reconstruction Loss. Image reconstruction loss $\mathcal{L}_{rec}$ is the standard loss function for an auto-encoder network, which requires the encoded features can be used to reconstruct its input, i.e.,

$$\mathcal{L}_{rec} = \sum_p |I(p) - I_{rec}(p)|_1 \tag{10}$$

where $I(p)$ is the input image, and $I_{rec}(p)$ is the image reconstructed from the auto-encoder network.

Discriminative Loss. $\mathcal{L}_{dis}$ is defined to ensure the learned features have gradients $\frac{\partial \phi(\hat{p})}{\partial \hat{p}}$ by explicitly encouraging large gradient, i.e.,

$$\mathcal{L}_{dis} = -\sum_p |\nabla^1 \phi(p)|_1 \tag{11}$$

Furthermore, image gradients are used to emphasize low-texture regions,

$$\mathcal{L}_{dis} = -\sum_p e^{-|\nabla^1 I(p)|_1} |\nabla^1 \phi(p)|_1 \tag{12}$$

where low-texture regions receive large weights.

Convergent Loss. $\mathcal{L}_{cvt}$ is defined to encourage smoothness of feature gradients, which ensures consistent gradients during optimization and large convergence radii accordingly. The loss is defined to penalize the second-order gradients, i.e.,

$$\mathcal{L}_{cvt} = \sum_p |\nabla^2 \phi(p)|_1 \tag{13}$$

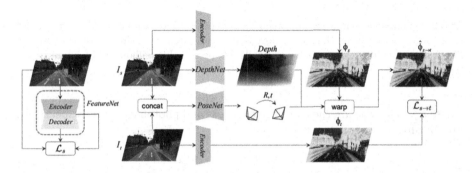

Fig. 1. An illustration of the overall framework, which contains DepthNet, PoseNet and FeatureNet for depth map prediction, egomotion prediction and feature learning respectively. FeatureNet uses $\mathcal{L}_s$ to learn require visual representation, the encoder from FeatureNet is used to extract features for cross-view reconstruction loss $\mathcal{L}_{s \to t}$.

3.4 Overall Pipeline

Single-view reconstruction and cross-view reconstruction are unified to form the final framework as illustrated in Fig. 1. DepthNet is a monodepth estimator which takes the target frame as input and outputs a depth map. PoseNet is an egomotion estimator, which takes two frames from both source and target view and outputs the relative pose between them. DepthNet and PoseNet provide the geometry information to establish point-to-point correspondences for cross-view reconstruction. FeatureNet is for feature representation learning, which follows the auto-encoder architecture and supervised by single-view reconstruction loss. Features from FeatureNet are used to define the cross-view reconstruction loss.

Therefore, the total loss for the whole architecture contains two parts, where $\mathcal{L}_s$ constrains the quality of learned features through single-view reconstruction, whilst $\mathcal{L}_{s \to t}$ penalizes the discrepancy from cross-view reconstruction, i.e.,

$$\mathcal{L}_{total} = \mathcal{L}_s + \mathcal{L}_{s \to t} \tag{14}$$

Toward better performance, the proposed feature-metric loss is combined with used photometric loss, i.e.,

$$\mathcal{L}_{s \to t} = \sum_p \mathcal{L}_{fm}\big(\phi_s(\hat{p}), \phi_t(p)\big) \\ + \sum_p \mathcal{L}_{ph}(I_s(\hat{p}), I_t(p)) \tag{15}$$

Fig. 2. Qualitative comparison between Monodepth2 [15] (second row) and our method (last row). It can be seen that we achieve better performance on the low-texture regions like walls and billboards, and finer details are present like silhouette of humans and poles.

where $\mathcal{L}_{fm}$ and $\mathcal{L}_{ph}$ are the feature-metric loss and photometric loss respectively. Specifically, feature-metric loss is defined by

$$\mathcal{L}_{fm} = |\phi_s(\widehat{p}) - \phi_t(p)|_1, \tag{16}$$

and photometric loss is defined following [16] using a combination of L_1 and SSIM losses, i.e.,

$$\mathcal{L}_{ph} = 0.15 \sum_p |I_s(\widehat{p}) - I_t(p)|_1 \\ + 0.85 \frac{1 - \text{SSIM}(I_s(\widehat{p}), I_t(p))}{2} \tag{17}$$

Furthermore, we resolve the occlusion problem following the practices in [6,15,46,53], where two source views are used to define the cross-view reconstruction loss,

$$\mathcal{L}'_{s\rightarrow t} = \sum_p \min_{s \in V} \mathcal{L}_{s\rightarrow t}\big(\phi_s(\widehat{p}), \phi_t(p)\big) \tag{18}$$

Where V is a set composed of source frames. When trained on the monocular videos, V contains the previous and posterior source frames of current target frame; when trained on the calibrated binocular videos, an extra frame of opposite stereo pair is added.

3.5   Implementation Details

For FeatureNet, ResNet-50 [18] with fully-connected layer removed is used as the encoder, where deepest feature map goes through 5 downsampling stages and reduces to 1/32 resolution of input image, the decoder contains five 3×3 convolutional layers and each followed by a bilinear upsampling layer. Multi-scale feature maps from convolutional layers of the decoder are used to generate multi-scale reconstructed images, where feature map of each scale further goes through a 3×3 convolution with sigmoid function for image reconstruction. The largest feature map with 64 channels from encoder is regularized by $\mathcal{L}_{dis}$ and $\mathcal{L}_{cvt}$ and will be used for feature-metric loss.

DepthNet also adopts an encoder-decoder structure, where ResNet-50 without fully-connected layer is used as encoder and multi-scale feature maps are outputted. The decoder for depth is implemented in a cascaded refinement manner, which decodes depth maps in a top-down pathway. Specifically, multiple-scale features from encoder are used to predict maps of corresponding sizes via a 3×3 convolution followed by sigmoid, and these maps are refined in a coarse-to-fine manner towards the final depth map. Both FeatureNet and DepthNet take image size of 320×1024 as inputs.

The PoseNet is a pose estimator with a structure of ResNet-18 [18], which is modified to receive a concatenated image pair and predicts a relative pose therein. Here axis angle is chosen to represent the 3D rotation. The input resolution is 192×640. Comparing with both FeatureNet and DepthNet, PoseNet uses lower image resolution and more light-weight backbone, which observes this has no obvious influence to pose accuracy, but significantly save both memory and computation.

We adopt the setting in [15] for data preprocessing. Our models are implemented on PyTorch [39] with distributed computing, and trained for 40 epochs using Adam [20] optimizer, with a batch size of 2, on the 8 GTX 1080Ti GPUs. The learning rate is gradually warmed up to $1e^{-4}$ in 3 steps, where each step increases learning rate by $1e^{-4}/3$ in 500 iterations. After warmping, learning rate $1e^{-4}$ is used for the first 20 epochs and halved twices at 20th and 30th epoch. As for online refinement technique we used during testing, we follow the practice proposed by [4,5]. We keep the model training while performing inference. The batch size is set to 1. Each batch consists of the test image and its two adjacent frames. Online refinement is performed for 20 iterations on one test sample with the same setting introduced before. No data augmentation is used in the inference phase.

4   Experiments

In this section we show extensive experiments for evaluating the performance of our approach. We make a fair comparison on KITTI 2015 dataset [14] with prior art on both single view depth and visual odometry estimation tasks. And detailed ablation studies of our approach are done to show the effectiveness of the **feature-metric loss**.

KITTI 2015 dataset contains videos in 200 street scenes captured by RGB cameras, with sparse depth ground truths captured by Velodyne laser scanner. We follow [56] to remove static frames as pre-processing step. We use the Eigen split of [11] to divide KITTI raw data, and resulting in 39,810 monocular triplets for training, 4,424 for validation and 697 for testing.

For depth evaluation, we test our depth model on divided 697 KITTI testing data. For odometry evaluation, we test our system to the official KITTI odometry split which containing 11 driving sequences with ground truth odometry obtained through the IMU and GPS readings. Following previous works [2,53,56], we train our model on the sequence 00–08 and use the sequence 09–10 for testing.

Table 1. Performance metrics for depth evaluation. d and d^* respectively denotes predicted and ground truth depth, D presents a set of all the predicted depth values of an image, $|.|$ returns the number of the elements in the input set.

Abs Rel : $\frac{1}{|D|} \sum_{d \in D} |d^* - d|/d^*$	**RMSE** : $\sqrt{\frac{1}{|D|} \sum_{d \in D} ||d^* - d||^2}$
Sq Rel : $\frac{1}{|D|} \sum_{d \in D} ||d^* - d||^2/d^*$	**RMSE log** : $\sqrt{\frac{1}{|D|} \sum_{d \in D} ||logd^* - logd||^2}$
$\delta_t : \frac{1}{|D|} |\{d \in D|\ max(\frac{d^*}{d}, \frac{d}{d^*}) < 1.25^t\}| \times 100\%$	

4.1 Depth Evaluation

Performance Metrics. Standard metrics are used for depth evaluation, as shown in Table 1. During evaluation, depth is capped to 80 m. For the methods trained on monocular videos, the depth is defined up to scale factor [56], which is computed by

$$scale = median(D_{gt})/median(D_{pred}) \qquad (19)$$

For evaluation, those predicted depth maps are multiplied by computed *scale* to match the median with the ground truth, this step is called **median scaling**.

Comparison with State-of-the-Art. Table 2 shows performances of current state-of-the-art approaches for monocular depth estimation. They are trained on different kinds of data—monocular videos (M), stereo pairs (S), binocular videos (MS) and labelled single images (Sup), while all of them are tested with single image as input.

We achieve the best performance compared to all self-supervised methods, no matter which training data is used. Our method achieves more significant improvement in the performance metric Sq Rel. According to Table 1, this metric penalizes more on large errors in short range, where more textureless regions exist due near objects are large in images and our method handles well. The closest results in self-supervised methods are from DepthHint [47], which uses the same input size but adds an extra post processing step. It utilizes a traditional stereo matching method—SGM [19] to provide extra supervisory signals for training, since SGM is less likely to be trapped by local minimums. However, in its settings, the object function of SGM is still photometric loss, the drawbacks of photometric loss are still inevitable. In contrast, proposed feature-metric loss will largely avoid the interference of local minimums.

Moreover, compared with state-of-the-art **supervised** methods [13,23], which achieve top performances on the KITTI depth prediction competition, our model with online refinement technique even exceeds in many metrics. Our advantage over supervised methods is that the gap between the distributions of training and testing data does exist, we can make full use of online refinement technique. What is more, as shown in Sect. 4.3, the introduction of feature-metric loss can obtain more performance gain from online refinement technique.

Table 2. Comparison of performances are reported on the KITTI dataset. Best results are in bold, second best are underlined. M: trained on monocular videos. S: trained on stereo pairs. MS: trained on calibrated binocular videos. Sup: trained on labelled single images. *: using the online refinement technique [4], which advocated keeping the model training while performing inference. †: using post processing steps.

Method	Train	The lower the better				The higher the better		
		Abs Rel	Sq Rel	RMSE	RMSE log	δ_1	δ_2	δ_3
SfMLearner [56]	M	0.208	1.768	6.958	0.283	0.678	0.885	0.957
DNC [51]	M	0.182	1.481	6.501	0.267	0.725	0.906	0.963
Vid2Depth [27]	M	0.163	1.240	6.220	0.250	0.762	0.916	0.968
LEGO [50]	M	0.162	1.352	6.276	0.252	0.783	0.921	0.969
GeoNet [52]	M	0.155	1.296	5.857	0.233	0.793	0.931	0.973
DF-Net [57]	M	0.150	1.124	5.507	0.223	0.806	0.933	0.973
DDVO [46]	M	0.151	1.257	5.583	0.228	0.810	0.936	0.974
EPC++ [26]	M	0.141	1.029	5.350	0.216	0.816	0.941	0.976
Struct2Depth [4]	M	0.141	1.036	5.291	0.215	0.816	0.945	0.979
SIGNet [30]	M	0.133	0.905	5.181	0.208	0.825	0.947	0.981
CC [43]	M	0.140	1.070	5.326	0.217	0.826	0.941	0.975
LearnK [17]	M	0.128	0.959	5.230	0.212	0.845	0.947	0.976
DualNet [55]	M	0.121	<u>0.837</u>	4.945	0.197	0.853	0.955	<u>0.982</u>
SuperDepth [40]	M	0.116	1.055	-	0.209	0.853	0.948	0.977
Monodepth2 [15]	M	<u>0.115</u>	0.882	<u>4.701</u>	<u>0.190</u>	<u>0.879</u>	<u>0.961</u>	<u>0.982</u>
Ours	M	**0.104**	**0.729**	**4.481**	**0.179**	**0.893**	**0.965**	**0.984**
Struct2Depth [4]	M*	0.109	0.825	4.750	0.187	0.874	<u>0.958</u>	**0.983**
GLNet [5]	M*	<u>0.099</u>	<u>0.796</u>	<u>4.743</u>	<u>0.186</u>	<u>0.884</u>	0.955	0.979
Ours	M*	**0.088**	**0.712**	**4.137**	**0.169**	**0.915**	**0.965**	<u>0.982</u>
Dorn [13]	Sup	0.099	0.593	3.714	0.161	0.897	0.966	0.986
BTS [23]	Sup	0.091	0.555	4.033	0.174	0.904	0.967	0.984
MonoDepth [16]	S	0.133	1.142	5.533	0.230	0.830	0.936	0.970
MonoDispNet [48]	S	0.126	0.832	**4.172**	0.217	0.840	0.941	0.973
MonoResMatch [44]	S	0.111	0.867	4.714	0.199	0.864	0.954	<u>0.979</u>
MonoDepth2 [15]	S	0.107	0.849	4.764	0.201	0.874	0.953	0.977
RefineDistill [41]	S	**0.098**	0.831	4.656	0.202	0.882	0.948	0.973
UnDeepVO [24]	MS	0.183	1.730	6.570	0.268	-	-	-
DFR [53]	MS	0.135	1.132	5.585	0.229	0.820	0.933	0.971
EPC++ [26]	MS	0.128	0.935	5.011	0.209	0.831	0.945	<u>0.979</u>
MonoDepth2 [15]	MS	0.106	0.818	4.750	0.196	0.874	0.957	<u>0.979</u>
DepthHint [47]	MS†	0.100	<u>0.728</u>	4.469	<u>0.185</u>	<u>0.885</u>	<u>0.962</u>	**0.982**
Ours	MS	<u>0.099</u>	**0.697**	<u>4.427</u>	**0.184**	**0.889**	**0.963**	**0.982**
Ours	MS*	0.079	0.666	3.922	0.163	0.925	0.970	0.984

Figure 2 shows the qualitative results. Compared with state-of-the-art method MonoDepth2 [15], we achieve better performance on low-texture regions and finer details, e.g., walls, billboards, silhouette of humans and poles.

Table 3. Comparison of performances are reported on the KITTI odometry dataset [14]. Best results are in bold.

Method	Seq. 09		Seq. 10	
	t_{err}	r_{err}	t_{err}	r_{err}
ORB-SLAM [33]	15.30	0.26	3.68	0.48
SfMLearner [56]	17.84	6.78	37.91	17.78
DFR [53]	11.93	3.91	12.45	3.46
MonoDepth2 [15]	10.85	2.86	11.60	5.72
NeuralBundler [25]	**8.10**	2.81	12.90	**3.17**
SC-SfMlearner [2]	8.24	2.19	10.70	4.58
Ours	8.75	**2.11**	**10.67**	4.91

However, MonoDepth2 is built on the photometric loss, which is easily trapped by local minimums especially on low-texture regions like walls and billboards. In contrast, the introduction of feature-metric loss leads the network into jumping out of local minimums, since our features are designed to form a desirable loss for easier optimization.

4.2   Odometry Evaluation

Performance Metric. Average translational root mean square error drift (t_{err}) and average rotational root mean square error drift (r_{err}) on length of 100 m–800 m are adopted for evaluation. For the methods who suffer from scale ambiguity, one global scale that best align the whole sequence is used.

Comparison with State-of-the-Art. As shown in Table 3, we report the performance of ORB-SLAM[33] as a reference and compare with recent deep methods. Our method gets top performances in two metrics and comparable performance in the rest metrics compared to other deep learning methods. When compared to traditional SLAM method [33], our translation performance is comparable, while in the rotation estimation we still fall short like other deep learning methods. We believe that it is because the bundle adjustment of the traditional SLAM method can optimize subtler rotation errors along a long sequence which can't be observed in a small sequence used by current deep learning based methods. Moreover current reconstruction process may be not sensible to variation of rotation [3].

4.3   Ablation Study

To get a better understanding of the contribution of proposed losses—feature-metric loss, discriminative loss and convergent loss—to the overall performance, we perform an ablation study in Table 4.

Table 4. The ablation study of different loss settings of our work.

Method	OR	The lower the better				The higher the better		
		Abs Rel	Sq Rel	RMSE	RMSE log	δ_1	δ_2	δ_3
$\mathcal{L}_{ph} + \mathcal{L}_{ds}^1$	×	0.105	0.748	4.835	0.191	0.878	0.956	0.979
$\mathcal{L}_{ph} + \mathcal{L}_{ds}^2$	×	0.103	0.740	4.754	0.187	0.881	0.959	0.981
$\mathcal{L}_{ph} + \mathcal{L}_{ds}^1 + \mathcal{L}_{ds}^2$	×	0.103	0.735	4.554	0.187	0.883	0.961	0.981
$\mathcal{L}_{ph} + \mathcal{L}_{ds}^1 + \mathcal{L}_{ds}^2$	✓	0.088	0.712	4.237	0.175	0.905	0.965	0.982
$\mathcal{L}_{ph} + \mathcal{L}_{fm}$	×	0.099	0.697	4.427	0.184	0.889	0.963	0.982
$\mathcal{L}_{ph} + \mathcal{L}_{fm}$	✓	**0.079**	**0.666**	**3.922**	**0.163**	**0.925**	**0.970**	**0.984**

(a) **Different loss combinations in $\mathcal{L}_{s \to t}$** (Eq. 8), the term 'OR' denotes whether the online refinement [4] is used.

Loss	The lower the better				The higher the better			Seq. 09		Seq. 10	
	Abs Rel	Sq Rel	RMSE	RMSE log	δ_1	δ_2	δ_3	t_{err}	r_{err}	t_{err}	r_{err}
$\mathcal{L}_{rec}$	0.105	0.739	4.585	0.191	0.883	0.961	**0.982**	4.30	1.18	8.50	4.06
$\mathcal{L}_{rec} + \mathcal{L}_{dis}$	0.103	0.723	4.535	0.187	0.884	0.961	**0.982**	4.10	1.07	8.03	3.94
$\mathcal{L}_{rec} + \mathcal{L}_{cvt}$	0.100	0.721	4.474	0.187	0.885	0.962	**0.982**	3.29	1.16	5.91	3.48
$\mathcal{L}_{rec} + \mathcal{L}_{dis} + \mathcal{L}_{cvt}$	**0.099**	**0.697**	**4.427**	**0.184**	**0.889**	**0.963**	0.982	**3.07**	**0.89**	**3.83**	**1.78**

(b) **Different loss combinations in $\mathcal{L}_s$** (Eq. 9).

The Losses for Cross-View Reconstruction. In Table 4a, different components of $\mathcal{L}_{s \to t}$ have been tried. The smoothness losses which are widely used are used as baselines:

$$\mathcal{L}_{ds}^i = \sum_p e^{-|\nabla^i I(p)|_1} |\nabla^i \widehat{D}(p)|_1 \tag{20}$$

where $\widehat{D}(p) = D(p)/\bar{D}$, this operation is the mean normalization technique advocated by [46]. i denotes the order of the derivatives. These smoothness losses are used as baselines to verify the effectiveness of the feature-metric loss.

Compared with smoothness losses, feature-metric loss leads to much better effect. We can see that a biggest performance boost is gained by introducing the feature-metric loss. As we discussed before, the propagation range of smoothness losses is limited, in contrast, the feature-metric loss enable a long-range propagation, since it has a large convergence radius. We also observe that when feature-metric loss can benefit more from the performance gain provided by online refinement than other loss combination. Higher performance gain is attributed to better supervised signal provided by feature-metric loss during online refinement phase, where incorrect depth values can be appropriately penalized with larger losses based on more discriminative features.

The Losses for Single-View Reconstruction. Table 4b shows that the model without any of our contributions performs the worst. When combined together, all our components lead to a significant improvement.

And as shown in right part of Table 4b, although small deviations are less obvious in some metrics of the depth evaluation, small errors will be magnified via accumulation and propagation during trajectory prediction, big differences

Fig. 3. A visualization of a learned visual representation, which is achieved by selecting one principle channel through PCA decomposition, then showing the feature map as a heat map, hotter color indicates a higher feature value. First row shows a typical image which is full of textureless regions like walls and shadows. The visualization of corresponding feature maps is shown in second to fourth rows. The feature maps are respectively learned with different loss combinations, which sequentially correspond with the settings in the first three rows in Table 4b. In order to get a better understanding, we crop three typical textureless regions as shown in (a–c), cropped feature maps are visualized according to the dynamic range after cropping.

are shown in the odometry evaluation. Note that different from previous odometry evaluation, we directly applied the model trained on the kitti raw data to sequence 09–10 to get t_{err} and r_{err}.

Merely using $\mathcal{L}_{rec}$ gets similar performance as merely using photometric loss (the third row in Table 4a), since it plays a similar role as the photometric loss at textureless regions. Results get better when equipped with $\mathcal{L}_{dis}$, since discrimination at low-texture regions is improved. Best performance is achieved when added $\mathcal{L}_{cvt}$, which means discrimination is not enough, a correct optimization direction is also important.

Visualization Analysis. In order to see whether learned visual representations have promised properties, we visualize it in Fig. 3. The feature maps learned with different loss combinations: $\mathcal{L}_{rec}$, $\mathcal{L}_{rec} + \mathcal{L}_{dis}$ and $\mathcal{L}_{rec} + \mathcal{L}_{dis} + \mathcal{L}_{cvt}$ are sequentially shown from the second to the fourth row. Although we require our feature to be discriminative, this effect is not sufficient to be shown in a large view, since the gap between the features of different sorts are much larger than that of spatially adjacent features. Therefore, we cropped three typical textureless regions, and visualize them again according to the dynamic range after cropping.

We can see that merely using $\mathcal{L}_{rec}$ get small variations at textureless regions. The close-ups of original images are similar to feature maps only trained with $\mathcal{L}_{rec}$, which verifies the proposed losses in improving feature representations. The feature map learned with $\mathcal{L}_{rec} + \mathcal{L}_{dis}$ is not smooth and disordered, since $\mathcal{L}_{dis}$ overemphasizes the discrepancy between adjacent features, the network degenerates to form a landscape of a zigzag shape. This phenomenon can be approved by the results in the second row of Table 4b, which is only slightly higher than merely using $\mathcal{L}_{rec}$.

A desired landscape for feature maps is a smooth slope, in this way, feature-metric loss will be able to form a basin-like landscape. The feature map learned with all the proposed losses approximates this ideal landscape, from zoom-in views we can see a clear and smooth transition along a certain direction. On this landscape, gradient descent approaches can move smoothly toward optimal solutions.

5   Conclusion

In this work, feature-metric loss is proposed for self-supervised learning of depth and egomotion, where feature representation is additionally learned with two extra regularizers to ensure convergence towards correct depth and pose. The whole framework is end-to-end trainable in self-supervised setting, and achieves state-of-the-art depth estimation which is even comparable to supervised learning methods. Furthermore, visual odometry based on estimated egomotion also significantly outperforms previous state-of-the-art methods.

Acknowledgements. This research is supported by Beijing Science and Technology Project (No. Z181100008918018).

References

1. Andraghetti, L., et al.: Enhancing self-supervised monocular depth estimation with traditional visual odometry. arXiv:1908.03127 (2019)

2. Bian, J.W., et al.: Unsupervised scale-consistent depth and ego-motion learning from monocular video. In: NeurIPS (2019)
3. Bian, J.W., Zhan, H., Wang, N., Chin, T.J., Shen, C., Reid, I.: Unsupervised depth learning in challenging indoor video: Weak rectification to rescue. arXiv:2006.02708 (2020)
4. Casser, V., Pirk, S., Mahjourian, R., Angelova, A.: Depth prediction without the sensors: leveraging structure for unsupervised learning from monocular videos. In: AAAI (2019)
5. Chen, Y., Schmid, C., Sminchisescu, C.: Self-supervised learning with geometric constraints in monocular video: connecting flow, depth, and camera. In: ICCV (2019)
6. Cheng, X., Zhong, Y., Dai, Y., Ji, P., Li, H.: Noise-aware unsupervised deep lidar-stereo fusion. In: CVPR (2019)
7. Deshpande, A., Rock, J., Forsyth, D.: Learning large-scale automatic image colorization. In: ICCV (2015)
8. DeSouza, G.N., Kak, A.C.: Vision for mobile robot navigation: a survey. TPAMI (2002)
9. Doersch, C., Gupta, A., Efros, A.A.: Unsupervised visual representation learning by context prediction. In: ICCV (2015)
10. Donahue, J., Krähenbühl, P., Darrell, T.: Adversarial feature learning. arXiv preprint arXiv:1605.09782 (2016)
11. Eigen, D., Puhrsch, C., Fergus, R.: Depth map prediction from a single image using a multi-scale deep network. In: NeurIPS (2014)
12. Engel, J., Koltun, V., Cremers, D.: Direct sparse odometry. TPAMI (2017)
13. Fu, H., Gong, M., Wang, C., Batmanghelich, K., Tao, D.: Deep ordinal regression network for monocular depth estimation. In: CVPR (2018)
14. Geiger, A., Lenz, P., Urtasun, R.: Are we ready for autonomous driving? The KITTI vision benchmark suite. In: CVPR (2012)
15. Godard, C., Mac Aodha, O., Brostow, G.: Digging into self-supervised monocular depth estimation. In: ICCV (2019)
16. Godard, C., Mac Aodha, O., Brostow, G.J.: Unsupervised monocular depth estimation with left-right consistency. In: CVPR (2017)
17. Gordon, A., Li, H., Jonschkowski, R., Angelova, A.: Depth from videos in the wild: unsupervised monocular depth learning from unknown cameras. In: ICCV (2019)
18. He, K., Zhang, X., Ren, S., Sun, J.: Deep residual learning for image recognition. In: CVPR (2016)
19. Hirschmuller, H.: Stereo processing by semiglobal matching and mutual information. TPAMI (2007)
20. Kingma, D.P., Ba, J.: Adam: a method for stochastic optimization. arXiv:1412.6980 (2014)
21. Larsson, G., Maire, M., Shakhnarovich, G.: Learning representations for automatic colorization. In: Leibe, B., Matas, J., Sebe, N., Welling, M. (eds.) ECCV 2016. LNCS, vol. 9908, pp. 577–593. Springer, Cham (2016). https://doi.org/10.1007/978-3-319-46493-0_35
22. Larsson, G., Maire, M., Shakhnarovich, G.: Colorization as a proxy task for visual understanding. In: CVPR (2017)
23. Lee, J.H., Han, M.K., Ko, D.W., Suh, I.H.: From big to small: multi-scale local planar guidance for monocular depth estimation. arXiv:1907.10326 (2019)
24. Li, R., Wang, S., Long, Z., Gu, D.: Undeepvo: Monocular visual odometry through unsupervised deep learning. In: ICRA (2018)

25. Li, Y., Ushiku, Y., Harada, T.: Pose graph optimization for unsupervised monocular visual odometry. arXiv:1903.06315 (2019)
26. Luo, C., et al.: Every pixel counts++: joint learning of geometry and motion with 3d holistic understanding. arXiv:1810.06125 (2018)
27. Mahjourian, R., Wicke, M., Angelova, A.: Unsupervised learning of depth and egomotion from monocular video using 3D geometric constraints. In: CVPR (2018)
28. Masci, J., Meier, U., Cireşan, D., Schmidhuber, J.: Stacked convolutional autoencoders for hierarchical feature extraction. In: ICANN (2011)
29. Mayer, N., et al.: A large dataset to train convolutional networks for disparity, optical flow, and scene flow estimation. In: Proceedings of the IEEE Conference on Computer Vision and Pattern Recognition, pp. 4040–4048 (2016)
30. Meng, Y., et al.: Signet: semantic instance aided unsupervised 3D geometry perception. In: CVPR (2019)
31. Menze, M., Geiger, A.: Object scene flow for autonomous vehicles. In: CVPR (2015)
32. Mescheder, L., Nowozin, S., Geiger, A.: Adversarial variational Bayes: unifying variational autoencoders and generative adversarial networks. In: ICML (2017)
33. Mur-Artal, R., Montiel, J.M.M., Tardos, J.D.: ORB-SLAM: a versatile and accurate monocular slam system. TR (2017)
34. Mur-Artal, R., Montiel, J.M.M., Tardos, J.D.: ORB-SLAM: a versatile and accurate monocular slam system. IEEE Trans. Rob. **31**(5), 1147–1163 (2015)
35. Newcombe, R.A., Lovegrove, S.J., Davison, A.J.: DTAM: dense tracking and mapping in real-time. In: ICCV (2011)
36. Noroozi, M., Favaro, P.: Unsupervised learning of visual representations by solving jigsaw puzzles. In: Leibe, B., Matas, J., Sebe, N., Welling, M. (eds.) ECCV 2016. LNCS, vol. 9910, pp. 69–84. Springer, Cham (2016). https://doi.org/10.1007/978-3-319-46466-4_5
37. Noroozi, M., Pirsiavash, H., Favaro, P.: Representation learning by learning to count. In: ICCV (2017)
38. Noroozi, M., Vinjimoor, A., Favaro, P., Pirsiavash, H.: Boosting self-supervised learning via knowledge transfer. In: CVPR (2018)
39. Paszke, A., et al.: Automatic differentiation in Pytorch. In: NeurIPS-W (2017)
40. Pillai, S., Ambrus, R., Gaidon, A.: SuperDepth: self-supervised, super-resolved monocular depth estimation. In: ICRA (2019)
41. Pilzer, A., Lathuilière, S., Sebe, N., Ricci, E.: Refine and distill: exploiting cycle-inconsistency and knowledge distillation for unsupervised monocular depth estimation. In: CVPR (2019)
42. Pire, T., Fischer, T., Castro, G., De Cristóforis, P., Civera, J., Berlles, J.J.: S-PTAM: stereo parallel tracking and mapping. Rob. Auton. Syst. **93**, 27–42 (2017)
43. Ranjan, A., Jampani, V., Kim, K., Sun, D., Wulff, J., Black, M.J.: Competitive collaboration: joint unsupervised learning of depth, camera motion, optical flow and motion segmentation. In: CVPR (2019)
44. Tosi, F., Aleotti, F., Poggi, M., Mattoccia, S.: Learning monocular depth estimation infusing traditional stereo knowledge. In: CVPR (2019)
45. Vincent, P., Larochelle, H., Bengio, Y., Manzagol, P.A.: Extracting and composing robust features with denoising autoencoders. In: ICML (2008)
46. Wang, C., Buenaposada, J.M., Zhu, R., Lucey, S.: Learning depth from monocular videos using direct methods. In: CVPR (2018)
47. Watson, J., Firman, M., Brostow, G.J., Turmukhambetov, D.: Self-supervised monocular depth hints. In: ICCV (2019)
48. Wong, A., Hong, B.W., Soatto, S.: Bilateral cyclic constraint and adaptive regularization for unsupervised monocular depth prediction. In: CVPR (2019)

49. Yang, Z., Wang, P., Wang, Y., Xu, W., Nevatia, R.: Every pixel counts: unsupervised geometry learning with holistic 3D motion understanding. In: Leal-Taixé, L., Roth, S. (eds.) ECCV 2018. LNCS, vol. 11133, pp. 691–709. Springer, Cham (2019). https://doi.org/10.1007/978-3-030-11021-5_43
50. Yang, Z., Wang, P., Wang, Y., Xu, W., Nevatia, R.: Lego: Learning edge with geometry all at once by watching videos. In: CVPR (2018)
51. Yang, Z., Wang, P., Xu, W., Zhao, L., Nevatia, R.: Unsupervised learning of geometry with edge-aware depth-normal consistency. In: AAAI (2018)
52. Yin, Z., Shi, J.: GeoNet: unsupervised learning of dense depth, optical flow and camera pose. In: CVPR (2018)
53. Zhan, H., Garg, R., Weerasekera, C.S., Li, K., Agarwal, H., Reid, I.: Unsupervised learning of monocular depth estimation and visual odometry with deep feature reconstruction. In: CVPR (2018)
54. Zhang, R., Isola, P., Efros, A.A.: Colorful image colorization. In: Leibe, B., Matas, J., Sebe, N., Welling, M. (eds.) ECCV 2016. LNCS, vol. 9907, pp. 649–666. Springer, Cham (2016). https://doi.org/10.1007/978-3-319-46487-9_40
55. Zhou, J., Wang, Y., Qin, K., Zeng, W.: Unsupervised high-resolution depth learning from videos with dual networks. In: ICCV (2019)
56. Zhou, T., Brown, M., Snavely, N., Lowe, D.G.: Unsupervised learning of depth and ego-motion from video. In: CVPR (2017)
57. Zou, Y., Luo, Z., Huang, J.-B.: DF-net: unsupervised joint learning of depth and flow using cross-task consistency. In: Ferrari, V., Hebert, M., Sminchisescu, C., Weiss, Y. (eds.) ECCV 2018. LNCS, vol. 11209, pp. 38–55. Springer, Cham (2018). https://doi.org/10.1007/978-3-030-01228-1_3

Propagating Over Phrase Relations for One-Stage Visual Grounding

Sibei Yang[1], Guanbin Li[2], and Yizhou Yu[1]($\boxtimes$)

[1] The University of Hong Kong, Pokfulam, Hong Kong
sbyang9@hku.hk, yizhouy@acm.org
[2] Sun Yat-sen University, Guangzhou, China
liguanbin@mail.sysu.edu.cn

Abstract. Phrase level visual grounding aims to locate in an image the corresponding visual regions referred to by multiple noun phrases in a given sentence. Its challenge comes not only from large variations in visual contents and unrestricted phrase descriptions but also from unambiguous referrals derived from phrase relational reasoning. In this paper, we propose a linguistic structure guided propagation network for one-stage phrase grounding. It explicitly explores the linguistic structure of the sentence and performs relational propagation among noun phrases under the guidance of the linguistic relations between them. Specifically, we first construct a linguistic graph parsed from the sentence and then capture multimodal feature maps for all the phrasal nodes independently. The node features are then propagated over the edges with a tailor-designed relational propagation module and ultimately integrated for final prediction. Experiments on Flickr30K Entities dataset show that our model outperforms state-of-the-art methods and demonstrate the effectiveness of propagating among phrases with linguistic relations (Source code will be available at https://github.com/sibeiyang/lspn.).

Keywords: One-stage phrase grounding · Linguistic graph · Relational propagation · Visual grounding

1 Introduction

A fundamental yet challenging problem of AI for achieving communication between humans and machines in the real world is to perform jointly understanding of natural language and visual scene. To bridge language and vision, it is necessary to align visual contents in a given visual scene with the corresponding linguistic elements in the natural language which describes the visual scene. Phrase grounding [14], a basic task on language grounding to vision, has attracted increasing attention [3,12,19,29].

The phrase grounding is typically defined as locating corresponding visual regions in an image referred to by multiple noun phrases in a natural language

---

The first author is supported by the Hong Kong PhD Fellowship.

© Springer Nature Switzerland AG 2020
A. Vedaldi et al. (Eds.): ECCV 2020, LNCS 12364, pp. 589–605, 2020.
https://doi.org/10.1007/978-3-030-58529-7_35

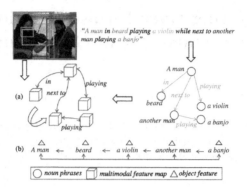

Fig. 1. Comparison of the proposed LSPN (a) with existing methods (b) on relational propagation among noun phrases for phrase grounding. LSPN (a) encodes language-vision information at nodes as multimodal feature maps. Then it propagates multi-modal information over the parsed linguistic graph which encodes the linguistic structure. As a comparison, the existing methods (b) consider the object-level features and propagate the object information without considering explicit linguistic relations among phrases. They pass messages over all the pairs of phrases or sequential phrases following the reverse lexical order of the sentence.

description. Beyond object detection [15,17], a traditional vision task, phrase grounding introduces the natural language description and presents two extra challenges. First, phrase grounding generalizes the restricted object categories into unrestricted noun phrases description, which increases the difficulty for matching a separate noun phrase with a visual region due to the large variations in the pairs of object appearance and its related phrase description. Second, a noun phrase may only be able to unambiguously locate its corresponding visual region by cooperating with other specific phrases in the sentence. The noun phrases existing in a natural language description have phrase contexts, *i.e.*, the relations among phrases. For the sentence given in Fig. 1, its phrase contexts include relational triplets of *"A man-in-beard"*, *"A man-playing-a violin"*, *"A man-next to-another man"* and *"another man-playing-beard"*. Note that there are two men and a unique violin in the image, the grounding result of the unique *"violin"* can be leveraged to distinguish the target man from the other man for the noun phrase *"A man"* by considering the relation of *"A man-playing-a violin"*. Similarly, other phrase relations (*i.e.*, *"A man-in-beard"*, *"A man-next to-another man"* and *"another man-playing-a banjo"*) in the sentence can also help to ground noun phrases and refine the grounding results. Significantly, the indirect relations among phrases, *i.e.*, multi-order relations, may also be useful. For example, the relations of *"A man-in-beard"* and *"A man-playing to-a violin"* jointly help to identify the target beard for the noun phrase *"beard"*.

However, most of existing works on phrase grounding ground noun phrases of a language description in an image individually without modeling the relations among phrases. They focus on learning the feature fusion in language and vision modalities [4,19,29], reconstructing the phrases from phrase-region features [7,

18] or matching the phrase embedding with the encoded phrase-related/phrase-unrelated region features [12,23] to address the first challenge mentioned above. There are few works taking phrase contexts into consideration, but they capture the partial or coarse phrase contexts without explicit linguistic relations among phrases (shown in Fig. 1(b)), including coreference relations [24], phrase-pair cues [1,13], contextual rewards [2] and sequential phrases following the reverse lexical order of the sentence [3].

To address the limitations mentioned above, we propose a Linguistic Structure guided Propagation Network (LSPN) for phrase grounding. The core ideas behind the proposed LSPN come from three aspects which include linguistic graph parsing from the input description, relational propagation for each pair of phrases with their relation, and one-stage grounding framework cooperated with iteratively relational propagation over the parsed linguistic graph. First, we parse the natural language description into a linguistic graph [27] and refine the graph based on the given noun phrases, where the nodes and edges of the graph are corresponding to the noun phrases and their relations respectively. The linguistic graph involves globally structured linguistic information, which also provides the possibility for indirectly relational propagation. Second, we propose a relational propagation module to perform message passing between a pair of subject and object phrases with their relation (*i.e.*, the relational triplet of *subject-relation-object*). Note that the relation between two phrases should be bidirectional, and the message from one phrase helps to unambiguously identify the corresponding visual region or refine the grounding result for the other phrase. Last but not least, we iteratively propagate language-vision multimodal information over the parsed linguistic graph to locate corresponding visual regions for the noun phrases in a single stage.

In summary, this paper has the following contributions:

- A relational propagation module (RPM) is proposed to perform bidirectional message passing for each pair of phrases with their linguistic relation.
- A linguistic structure guided propagation network is proposed for one-stage phrase grounding, which iteratively propagates the language-vision multimodal information for noun phrases using RPM under the guidance of parsed linguistic graph of the description.
- The experimental results on the common benchmark Flickr30K Entities dataset demonstrate that the proposed model outperforms state-of-the-art methods and shows the effectiveness of propagating over phrase relations.

2   Related Work

Phrase Grounding. Building a direct connection between textual phrases and visual contents is necessary for phrase grounding. Some works first fuse the representations in vision and language modalities, and then predict the visual regions [19,29] or learn the multimodal similarities for pairs of phrases and visual regions [4,22]. Another works [7,18] address phrase grounding from the view of phrase construction. Plummer et al. [12] group phrases into different sets and learn the group-conditional embeddings for phrases.

However, the above works treat phrases in isolation and neglect relations among them. Wang et al. [24] focus on one specific type of relations between phrases, *i.e.*, coreference relations (*e.g.*, "man" and "his hand"), and learn the structured matching with relation constraints. Plummer et al. [13] perform joint inference over phrases during test stage by combining extracted image and language cues, and they only consider the phrase-pair spatial cues. The works [2] and [3] implicitly consider phrase contexts, the former refines grounding results by using contextual information from all other phrases as rewards, and the latter sequentially predicts the grounding results for the phrases following their reverse lexical order in the sentence.

Different from existing methods, we explicitly extract the relations between phrases by parsing the linguistic structure of the sentence and propagate over phrase relations to build the interactions among phrases.

Referring expression comprehension aims to locate in an image a visual object described by a natural language expression. Recent works on it also try to explore the relational contexts for objects to help distinguish the referent from other objects. Yang et al. [25,28] encode the expression-guided multi-order relations by performing a gated graph convolutional networks over a multimodal relation graph based on objects in the image. Some works [6,26,31] capture the context-related language information by using self-attention mechanism over words in the expressions. In particular, Yu et al. [31] compute the matching scores between the attended relation embedding and the referent's relative location differences with its surrounding objects to capture the relational context. Yang et al. [26] highlight language information about objects and relations in a step-wise manner, and locate its corresponding visual evidence in the image.

However, most of the existing works on referring expression comprehension also neglect the syntax of the referring expression and only consider very limited contextual relations. Yang et al. [27] and Liu et al. [10] use the parsed linguistic structure of the expression to guide the process of locating the referent, but the relation models they build are not very suitable for phrase grounding. Specifically, noun phrases, except referent phrase, and their relations are used to modify the referent, and the process of locating the referent is from bottom to up. Instead of finding the referent, the aim of phrase grounding is to ground all the noun phrases in the sentence, and every noun phrase deserves attention. Thus, the relations between noun phrases on phrase grounding should be bidirectional.

Single-stage networks for object detection are widely used due to their fast inference speed and high accuracy. Recently, single-stage grounding networks have been proposed for phrase grounding. Yeh et al. [30] minimizes the energy based on a set of visual concepts over a large number of bounding boxes. However, the visual concepts used by it are based on multiple extra pre-trained models, and it is not clear how to optimize the visual concepts and the grounding

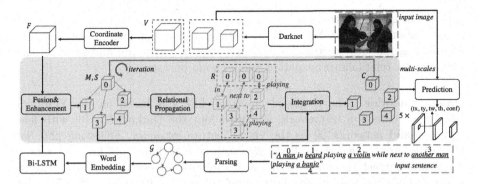

Fig. 2. The overall architecture of the proposed LSPN for one-stage phrase grounding. First, LSPN encodes the input image as spatial-aware feature map F by fusing the visual feature map V with spatial coordinates P. Second, the linguistic graph $\mathcal{G}$ is parsed from the input sentence. Third, for each node, LSPN obtains the multimodal feature map M and phrase-conditional enhance map S from the language representation of node and spatial-aware feature map. Next, LSPN captures relational enhance map R and combined enhance map C by passing messages over edges using relational propagation module and integrating messages for nodes. The propagation can be performed multiple times. Finally, LSPN predicts the grounding results from the final combined feature map.

model from end to end. Yang et al. [29] and Sadhu et al. [19] directly fuse the language feature of the input phrase and the spatial features of the image feature maps into single-stage object detection frameworks, *i.e.*, YOLOv3 [16] and SSD [11], respectively. However, existing one-stage grounding approaches ignore the fact that the referential meaning of noun phrases may depend on other word components of the sentence. Thus, we propose a one-stage grounding network which allows relational propagation between phrases under the guidance of the linguistic structure of the sentence.

3 Approach

The proposed linguistic structure guided propagation network (LSPN) iteratively propagates the language-vision multimodal information among noun phrases under the guidance of a linguistic graph parsed from a natural language description and grounds noun phrases corresponding visual regions in an image. The framework of LSPN is illustrated in Fig. 2, and it consists of three main modules, *i.e.*, image and language representation, relational propagation and prediction.

3.1 Image and Language Representation

We represent an input image and a natural language description as spatial-aware feature maps and a linguistic graph respectively. The spatial-aware feature maps capture the global image contexts. They are obtained by fusing the visual feature maps extracted from a CNN backbone with spatial coordinates embedding. The linguistic graph encodes the description's linguistic structure and provides the guidance for relational propagation among noun phrases.

Image Encoder. The proposed one-stage LSPN is based on the YOLOv3 [16] object detection framework, and we adopt the Darknet-53 [16] with feature pyramid networks [8] as the visual feature extractor. Following [29], we resize the input image I to 256×256 with zero padding and keep its aspect ratio, and extract the outputs of feature pyramid networks as visual feature maps with spatial resolutions and channels of $8 \times 8 \times 1024$, $16 \times 16 \times 512$ and $32 \times 32 \times 256$, respectively. To simplify writing, we denote a feature map with the size of $W \times H \times D_v$ as V to introduce the computations of LSPN.

A noun phrase may describe not only the appearance of a visual region itself but also its location in the image, such as *"right man"* and *"the bottle in the middle"*. Thus, similar to previous methods [19,29], we embed the spatial coordinates of a feature map into the visual features to form a spatial-aware version. In particular, the spatial map P is of the same spatial resolution as its corresponding visual feature map V, *i.e.*, $W \times H$, and the spatial feature at each position $(x, y) \in \{(0,0), (0,1), ..., (W-1, H-1)\}$ is defined as,

$$P_{x,y} = [\frac{x}{W}, \frac{y}{H}, \frac{x+0.5}{W}, \frac{y+0.5}{H}, \frac{x+1}{W}, \frac{y+1}{H}, \frac{1}{W}, \frac{1}{H}], \tag{1}$$

where the vector $P_{x,y} \in \mathbb{R}^8$ encodes the normalized coordinates of top-left, center, bottom-right, width and height of the grid at position (x, y). Next, we fuse the visual feature map V with the spatial map P to obtain the spatial-aware feature map $F \in \mathbb{R}^{W \times H \times D_f}$,

$$F = [\text{L2Norm}(\text{Conv}_0(V)); P]. \tag{2}$$

where the $\text{Conv}_0(\cdot)$ is a convolutional layer with kernel size 1×1, $\text{L2Norm}(\cdot)$ is the L2 normalization over the feature channel, and $[;]$ refers to the concatenation operation.

Linguistic Graph Parsing. The linguistic graph encodes the description as a graph where the nodes and edges respectively correspond to the noun phrases and the linguistic relations (*i.e.*, preposition or verb phrases) between noun phrases mentioned in the description. We construct the linguistic graph by parsing the description as an initial scene graph and then refining the initial scene graph based on given noun phrases. Given a natural language description L and a set of noun phrases $\mathcal{P}_g$ in L, the construction process for the linguistic graph $\mathcal{G}$ is summarized as follows,

- We first parse the natural language description L into an initial scene graph [27] using an off-the-shelf scene graph parser [20]. The nodes and edges of the initial scene graph correspond to nouns with modifiers (*e.g.*, determinants and adjectives) and linguistic relations between nouns in L.

- Then, for each node, we reorganize it as a noun phrase by sorting the noun and its modifiers following their original order in the description. The set of reorganized noun phrases is denoted as $\mathcal{P}_r$.
- However, the given noun phrases $\mathcal{P}_g$ in the description L sometimes may not exactly match with the noun phrases $\mathcal{P}_r$ in the parsed scene graph. Therefore, we associate each given noun phrase with one parsed noun phrase which has maximum overlap words with the given noun phrase. Then, we replace the parsed noun phrase by the given noun phrase.
- Next, for each parsed edge, we further insert or delete the words in it based on the replaced noun phrases connected by it. Finally, we obtain the resulted linguistic graph $\mathcal{G}$ from the refined edges and noun phrases in the scene graph.

The linguistic graph $\mathcal{G}$ parsed from the language description L is defined as $\mathcal{G} = (\mathcal{V}, \mathcal{E})$, where $\mathcal{V} = \{v_n\}_{n=1}^{N}$ is a set of nodes and $\mathcal{E} = \{e_k\}_{k=1}^{K}$ is a set of directed edges. Specifically, each node v_n corresponds to a noun phrase L_n with a sequence of words in L, and each edge e_k is a triplet $e_k = (e_k^{(s)}, e_k^{(r)}, e_k^{(o)})$. In the triplet, $e_k^{(s)} \in \mathcal{V}$ and $e_k^{(o)} \in \mathcal{V}$ are the subject node and the object node respectively, and $e_k^{(r)}$ associating with a preposition or verb phrase E_k in L is the linguistic relation from $e_k^{(s)}$ to $e_k^{(o)}$. In addition, we adopt $\mathcal{E}_n^{\mathrm{in}} \subset \mathcal{E}$ to denote the set of edges whose object node is v_n, use $\mathcal{E}_n^{\mathrm{out}} \subset \mathcal{E}$ to denote the set of edges whose subject node is v_n and denote de_n as the degree of node v_n.

3.2   Relational Propagation

The proposed relational propagation is implemented by passing messages at individual nodes over the parsed linguistic graph $\mathcal{G}$. We first obtain the relation-unrelated multimodal features for all the nodes $\mathcal{V}$ independently, and then propagate them over all the edges $\mathcal{E}$ by considering each edge separately and integrate the passed information for nodes. In particular, the bidirectional propagation over a single edge is achieved by the relational propagation module.

Propagation over Linguistic Graph. We first obtain the multimodal features for all the nodes $\mathcal{V}$ in graph $\mathcal{G}$ by fusing the spatial-aware feature map F mentioned in Sect. 3.1 with the language representations of noun phrases at nodes. In particular, we encode each word as a word embedding vector, and the initial phrasal embedding at a node is set to the mean pooling of the embedding vectors of all the words in the phrase. For a node v_n with noun phrase L_n and its phrasal embedding vector $w_n \in \mathbb{R}^{D_w}$, we learn its phrase feature $w_n' \in \mathbb{R}^{D_{w'}}$ from initial phrasal embedding via a nonlinear transformation,

$$w_n' = \mathrm{L2Norm}(\mathrm{MLP}_0(w_n)), \tag{3}$$

where the $\mathrm{MLP}_0(\cdot)$ consists of multiple linear layers with ReLU activation functions, and the $\mathrm{L2Norm}(\cdot)$ is the L2 normalization. Next, we obtain a multimodal feature map $M_n \in \mathbb{R}^{W \times H \times D_m}$ by fusing the phrase feature w_n' with the feature map F and meanwhile learn a phrase-conditional enhance map $S_n \in \mathbb{R}^{W \times H \times D_s}$, which is formulated as,

$$M_n = \text{L2Norm}(\text{Conv}_1([F; \text{Tile}(w_n')])),$$
$$S_n = \sigma(\text{Conv}_3(\text{Conv}_2(F) + \text{Tile}(\text{Fc}_0(w_n')))),$$
(4)

where $\text{Tile}(\cdot)$ is to tile a vector to each spatial position of a feature map with resolution $W \times H$, $\text{Conv}_1(\cdot)$ is a series of convolutional layers along with Batch-Norm and ReLU, $\text{Fc}_0(\cdot)$ is a fully connected layer, $\sigma(\cdot)$ is the sigmoid activation, and $\text{Conv}_2(\cdot)$ and $\text{Conv}_3(\cdot)$ are two convolutional layers with kernel size 1×1.

After obtaining the multimodal information for all the nodes $\mathcal{V}$, we pass it over the edges $\mathcal{E}$ in linguistic graph $\mathcal{G}$. For an edge $e_k = (e_k^{(s)}, e_k^{(r)}, e_k^{(o)})$, we first encode its linguistic feature. Specifically, we integrate the phrases associated with $e_k^{(s)}$, $e_k^{(r)}$ and $e_k^{(o)}$ as a sequence and pass the word embedding vectors in the sequence into a bidirectional LSTM [5], and the linguistic feature is the concatenation of the last hidden states of both the forward and backward LSTMs. The linguistic feature is denoted as h_k. Then, we feed its linguistic feature and multimodal information (*i.e.*, the multimodal feature maps and the phrase-conditional enhance maps) at subject node $e_k^{(s)}$ and object node $e_k^{(o)}$ into the **relational propagation module** to obtain the relational enhance maps, which are denoted as $R_k^{(s)} \in \mathbb{R}^{W \times H \times D_s}$ and $R_k^{(o)} \in \mathbb{R}^{W \times H \times D_s}$.

Next, for each node v_n, we integrate the relational enhance maps obtained from edges in the sets $\mathcal{E}_n^{\text{out}}$ and $\mathcal{E}_n^{\text{in}}$ to get the final relational enhance map, and further combine it with the initial phrase-conditional enhance map S_n. The combined enhance map $C_n \in \mathbb{R}^{W \times H \times D_s}$ at node v_n is computed as follows,

$$R_n = \frac{\sum_{e_{k'} \in \mathcal{E}_n^{\text{out}}} R_{k'}^{(s)} + \sum_{e_{k''} \in \mathcal{E}_n^{\text{in}}} R_{k''}^{(o)}}{de_n}$$
$$C_n = \begin{cases} S_n, & \text{if } de_n = 0, \\ (S_n + R_n)/2, & \text{otherwise,} \end{cases}$$
(5)

where de_n is the degree of node v_n (defined in Sect. 3.1).

Note that we can iteratively perform the propagation over the linguistic graph multiple times. At each time step, we can use the combined enhance maps at the last time step to replace the phrase-conditional enhance maps as the inputs of the relational propagation module to update the combined enhance maps. Iterative propagation can help to capture indirect relations among nodes. For each node v_n, M_n is the fundamental multimodal feature map and is not changed during each iterative relational propagation. S_n, which is used to enhance M_n, is updated after each iterative relational propagation. At each time step, M_n is replaced as the combined enhance map C_n of the last time step.

Relational Propagation Module. The relational propagation module passes the message of a single edge over its pair of nodes under the guidance of its linguistic feature and outputs the relational enhance maps for the nodes. Note that although the edge from the subject node to the object node is directed, the relational propagation between the subject node and object node should be bidirectional as the message from one node helps to unambiguously ground and refine the result for the other phrase.

Given the multimodal feature map M_{sub} and the phrase-conditional enhance map S_{sub} at subject node v_{sub}, M_{obj} and S_{obj} at object node v_{obj} and the edge's linguistic feature h, the relational enhance map $R_{sub} \in \mathbb{R}^{W \times H \times D_s}$ for the subject node is computed as follows,

$$g_{obj} = \text{MLP}_{obj}([\text{AvgPool}(M_{obj} \circ S_{obj}); h]),$$
$$M'_{sub} = \text{Conv}_{sub0}(M_{sub} \circ S_{sub}), \qquad (6)$$
$$R_{sub} = \sigma(\text{Conv}_{sub1}(\gamma(M'_{sub} + \text{Tile}(g_{obj})))),$$

where $\text{MLP}_{obj}(\cdot)$ is a multi-layer perceptron, $\text{AvgPool}(\cdot)$ means the global average pooling, $\circ$ represents element-wise multiplication, $\text{Conv}_{sub0}(\cdot)$ and $\text{Conv}_{sub1}(\cdot)$ are two convolutional layers and γ refers to the ReLU activation function. S_{obj} and S_{sub} are used to enhance M_{obj} and M_{sub}, respectively. g_{obj} provides the relational guidance for subject node, and it encodes the linguistic feature of edge and the global multimodal feature from object node.

Moreover, the relational enhance map $R_{obj} \in \mathbb{R}^{W \times H \times D_s}$ for the object node can be obtained following the similar computation.

3.3   Prediction and Loss

The prediction of phrase grounding is similar to the bounding boxes detection in YOLOv3 [16]. Following [29], we match three anchor boxes to every spatial position of a feature map, choose the candidate box with highest confidence score over all the anchor boxes of three feature maps at various spatial resolutions, and obtain the final grounding result by regressing the candidate box using the predicted regression offsets.

For each node v_n in graph $\mathcal{G}$, the regression offsets and confidence scores $pred_n \in \mathbb{R}^{W \times H \times 15}$ for the three anchor boxes at a single spatial resolution $W \times H$ are computed as follows,

$$pred_n = \text{Conv}_{pred}(M_n \circ C_n), \qquad (7)$$

where the multimodal feature map M_n and the final combined enhance map C_n are mentioned in Sect. 3.1 and $\text{Conv}_{pred}(\cdot)$ is a series of convolutional layers.

During training, we compute two types of losses (*i.e.*, a classification cross-entropy loss $Loss_{conf}$ and a L1 regression loss $Loss_{reg}$) and combine them as the final loss,

$$Loss = Loss_{conf} + \lambda Loss_{reg}, \qquad (8)$$

where λ is used to balance the $Loss_{conf}$ and $Loss_{reg}$. In particular, the classification loss $Loss_{conf}$ is the cross entropy loss between the output of a softmax function over all anchor boxes of three feature maps at various spatial resolutions and an one-hot vector labeling the anchor box with highest Intersection over Union (IoU) with the ground truth region set as 1. And the regression loss $Loss_{reg}$ is the L1 loss between the predicted regression offsets and the target regression offsets. Specifically, the target regression offsets $\mathbf{t} = [t_x, t_y, t_w, t_h] \in \mathbb{R}^4$ are defined as,

$$t_x = (g_x - r_x)/r_w, \qquad t_y = (g_y - r_y)/r_h, \tag{9}$$
$$t_w = \log(g_w/r_w), \qquad t_h = \log(g_h/r_h), \tag{10}$$

where $\mathbf{g} = [g_x, g_y, g_w, g_h] \in \mathbb{R}^4$ and $\mathbf{r} = [r_x, r_y, r_w, r_h] \in \mathbb{R}^4$ are the coordinates of the ground truth box and the candidate box, respectively.

During inference, we obtain the predicted box $\hat{\mathbf{g}} = [\hat{g}_x, \hat{g}_y, \hat{g}_w, \hat{g}_h]$ based on the chosen box $\mathbf{r}$ and the predicted regression offsets $\mathbf{t}'$,

$$\hat{g}_x = r_w * t'_x + r_x, \qquad \hat{g}_y = r_h t'_y + r_y, \tag{11}$$
$$\hat{g}_w = r_w \exp(t'_w), \qquad \hat{g}_h = r_h \exp(t'_h). \tag{12}$$

4   Experiments

4.1   Dataset and Evaluation

Dataset. We have conducted experiments on the commonly used Flickr30K Entities dataset [14] for phrase grounding. The phrase contexts in a natural language description are considered for bounding box annotations on Flickr30K Entities dataset. In Flickrr30K, a single noun phrase may be associated with multiple ground truth bounding boxes, while a single bounding box can also be matched with multiple noun phrases. Following previous works [3,29], if a noun phrase has multiple ground truth bounding boxes, it will be associated with the union of its all correlated boxes. We adopt the same training, validation and test split used in previous methods [3,29].

Evaluation Metric. The grounding *accuracy* is adopted as the evaluation metric, which is defined as the fraction of correct predictions for noun phrases grounding, and one prediction is considered correct if the IoU between the predicted bounding box and the ground truth region is larger than 0.5. Besides, the *inference speed* is important for models in real-time applications. The inference time is also reported, and all the tests are conducted on a desktop with the Intel Xeon Gold 5118@2.30GHz and NVIDIA RTX 2080TI.

4.2   Implementation

We extract visual feature maps from the Darknet-53 [16] with feature pyramid networks [8] pre-trained on MSCOCO object detection [9] following previous one-stage model [29]. The channel dimension of a spatial-aware feature map is set to

1024 (*i.e.*, $D_f = 1024$). The dimension of the hidden state of the bidirectional LSTM is set to 512. Thus, the linguistic features of edges are 1024-dimensional vectors, *i.e.*, $D_h = 1024$. The remaining hyper-parameters about the feature dimensions are set to 512. The RMSProp optimizer [21] is adopted to update network parameters, and the learning rate is initially set to 1e-4 and decreases following a polynomial schedule with power of 1. The learning rate for learnable parameters in Darknet-53 is set to one-tenth of the main learning rate. The loss balancing factor λ is set to 5. We train the model for 140k iterations with the batch size set to 16.

4.3   Comparison with the State of the Art

We evaluate the proposed LSPN on the Flickr30K Entities dataset and compare it with state-of-the-art methods. The results are shown in Table 1, LSPN achieves the best performance at 69.53% in accuracy and outperforms all the state-of-the-art models. It improves the accuracy achieved by the existing best performing method by 1.91%, which demonstrates the effectiveness of propagation over phrase relations in LSPN.

Table 1. Comparison with the state-of-the-art methods on Flickr30K Entities w.r.t accuracy metric and inference time for one image-query pair. We use * to indicate one-stage models. None-superscript indicates that model is from a two-stage method. The best performing method is marked in bold.

Method	Accuracy (%)	Time (ms)
GroundeR [18]	47.81	-
RtP [14]	50.89	-
IGOP [30]	53.97	-
SPC+PPC [13]	55.49	-
SS+QRN [2]	55.99	-
SimNet-ResNet [22]	60.89	140
CITE-ResNet [12]	61.33	149
SeqGROUND [3]	61.60	-
ZSGNet* [19]	63.39	-
G³RAPH++ [1]	66.93	-
FAOS* [29]	67.62	**16**
Ours LSPN*	**69.53**	20

As shown in the rightmost column of Table 1, the inference speed of one-stage methods (*i.e.*, FAOS and ours LSPN) is much faster than that of the two-stage methods (*i.e.*, SimNet-ResNet and CITE-ResNet). It takes the two-stage methods generally more than 140ms to ground a language query in an image. Most of the time is spent on generating region proposals in the image and extracting features for them. In contrast, the one-stage methods take less than 20ms to process one image-query pair without generating region proposals. Compared to FAOS, the proposed LSPN propagating contexts over noun phrases with linguistic relations achieves a higher grounding accuracy, though at the expense of a little bit of time cost.

Table 2. Comparison over coarse categories on Flickr30K Entities using accuracy metric (in percentage). The best performing method is marked in bold.

Method	People	Clothing	Body parts	Animals	Vehicles	Instruments	Scene	Other
SMPL	57.89	34.61	15.87	55.98	52.25	23.46	34.22	26.23
GroundeR	61.00	38.12	10.33	62.55	68.75	36.42	58.18	29.08
RtP	64.73	46.88	17.21	65.83	68.72	37.65	51.39	31.77
IGOP	68.71	56.83	19.50	70.07	73.72	39.50	60.38	32.45
SPC+PPC	71.69	50.95	25.24	76.23	66.50	35.80	51.51	35.98
CITE	73.20	52.34	30.59	76.25	75.75	48.15	55.64	42.83
SeqGROUND	76.02	56.94	26.18	75.56	66.00	39.36	68.69	40.60
G^{3}RAPH++	78.86	**68.34**	39.80	**81.38**	76.58	42.35	68.82	45.08
Ours LSPN	**80.69**	67.17	**44.17**	79.92	**83.23**	**62.96**	**70.91**	**52.82**

Moreover, we provide the phrase grounding performance over coarse categories. As shown in Table 2, LSPN consistently surpasses all the state-of-the-art methods on six categories, and achieves consistent improvement in overall accuracy over all the categories compared to all other methods. It significantly improves the accuracy on categories of instruments, vehicles, body parts and other by 14.81%, 7.07%, 4.37% and 7.74% respectively.

4.4 Ablation Study

We conduct an ablation study on the proposed LSPN to demonstrate the effectiveness and necessity of each component and have trained six additional variants of our model for comparison. The results are shown in Table 3.

- The *multimodal* model is the baseline, which predicts the confidence scores and regression offsets of each anchor box from the multimodal feature maps that are incorporated with the visual feature, spatial information and phrase feature.
- The *enhance* model extends the multimodal model by using the phrase-conditional enhance maps to enhance the multimodal feature maps, which improves the performance by 0.31% in accuracy.
- The *linguistic graph propagation(1)* model performs the relational propagation over the linguistic graph once. It achieves the best accuracy of 69.53% among the seven models and improves the accuracy by 1.38% over that achieved by the multimodal model, which demonstrates the effectiveness of

Table 3. Ablation study on variances of the proposed LSPN on Flickr30K Entities using accuracy metric. The number in parentheses refers to the number of propagation steps in our model.

Method	Accuracy (%)
Multimodal	68.15
Enhance	68.46
Linguistic graph propagation(1)	69.53
Linguistic graph propagation(2)	69.52
Subject graph propagation(1)	68.81
Object graph propagation(1)	68.97
Contextual propagation(1)	67.14

considering the relational propagation between noun phrases. The *linguistic graph propagation(2)* model is similar to linguistic graph propagation(1) model but propagates over the phrase relations twice. It does not further improve the performance and achieves similar accuracy as lingtuistic graph propagation(1). The reason may be that the number of phrases that need to rely on indirect phrase relations to be unambiguously grounded accounts for a relatively small proportion, and multiple propagations may instead introduce context noise.

- The *subject graph propagation(1)* model and the *object graph propagation(1)* model perform one-way subject-to-object and object-to-subject propagation over noun phrases. Compared to linguistic graph propagation(1) model performing bidirectional propagation, the performance of subject graph propagation(1) model and the object graph propagation(1) model is worse than that of it in accuracy by 0.72% and 0.56% respectively. The results demonstrate that the importance of bidirectional message passing for pairs of noun phrases.
- The *contextual propagation* model explores the message passing over another constructed graph without the explicit guidance of the linguistic structure. For each noun phrase in a sentence, we separately connect its three nearest noun phrases as three edges and learns relational weights for these edges by using the global context of the sentence. We then perform relational propagation over the constructed graph which is built on noun phrase and edges with learned weights and evaluate on this algorithmic variant. The worse experimental performance has demonstrated that the propagation over incompletely correct relations may adversely affect the model, and adopting the parsed linguistic graph as guidance is crucial for relational propagation.

Fig. 3. Qualitative results showing noun phrases in sentences and their grounding results predicted by LSPN.

4.5 Qualitative Evaluation

The qualitative evaluation results for phrase grounding are shown in Fig. 3. The proposed LSPN is able to successfully locate the visual regions referred to by noun phrases in different kinds of challenging scenarios.

In (a) and (e), LSPN grounds multiple noun phrases in long sentences, and it correctly identifies the corresponding object for each phrase. In (b), (c), (f) and (h), LSPN unambiguously distinguishes the referred objects from other objects belonging to the same categories by considering their relations to other objects in the sentence. For the example in (b), "*one older man*" can be identified by considering its relation ("*holding*") to "a beer". Samples (c) and (g) show that a single object in the image can be referred by multiple noun phrases. In (d) and (h), a noun phrase may be associated with multiple visual objects, LSPN is able to successfully locate them from the single noun phrase. For the example in (h), LSPN finds the two "*green chairs*" while excludes the chair on the right.

5 Conclusions

In this paper, we have proposed a linguistic structure guided propagation network (LSPN) for one-stage phrase grounding. LSPN works by iteratively propagating the language-vision multimodal information between noun phrases under the guidance of the linguistic graph and locating the image region corresponding to each noun phrase in the referring sentence. The context relation between each pair of noun phrases is captured by a relational propagation module. Experimental results on the common benchmark Flickr30K Entities dataset demonstrate that the proposed model outperforms state-of-the-art methods and shows the effectiveness of propagating over phrase relations.

Acknowledgment. This work is partially supported by the Guangdong Basic and Applied Basic Research Foundation under Grant No. 2020B1515020048 and the National Natural Science Foundation of China under Grant No. U1811463.

References

1. Bajaj, M., Wang, L., Sigal, L.: G3raphground: graph-based language grounding. In: Proceedings of the IEEE International Conference on Computer Vision (ICCV), October 2019
2. Chen, K., Kovvuri, R., Nevatia, R.: Query-guided regression network with context policy for phrase grounding. In: Proceedings of the IEEE International Conference on Computer Vision, pp. 824–832 (2017)
3. Dogan, P., Sigal, L., Gross, M.: Neural sequential phrase grounding (seqground). In: Proceedings of the IEEE Conference on Computer Vision and Pattern Recognition, pp. 4175–4184 (2019)
4. Fukui, A., Park, D.H., Yang, D., Rohrbach, A., Darrell, T., Rohrbach, M.: Multimodal compact bilinear pooling for visual question answering and visual grounding. In: Proceedings of the Conference on Empirical Methods in Natural Language Processing (2016)
5. Hochreiter, S., Schmidhuber, J.: Long short-term memory. Neural Comput. **9**(8), 1735–1780 (1997)
6. Hu, R., Rohrbach, M., Andreas, J., Darrell, T., Saenko, K.: Modeling relationships in referential expressions with compositional modular networks. In: Proceedings of the IEEE Conference on Computer Vision and Pattern Recognition, pp. 1115–1124 (2017)
7. Hu, R., Xu, H., Rohrbach, M., Feng, J., Saenko, K., Darrell, T.: Natural language object retrieval. In: Proceedings of the IEEE Conference on Computer Vision and Pattern Recognition, pp. 4555–4564 (2016)
8. Lin, T.Y., Dollár, P., Girshick, R., He, K., Hariharan, B., Belongie, S.: Feature pyramid networks for object detection. In: Proceedings of the IEEE Conference on Computer Vision and Pattern Recognition, pp. 2117–2125 (2017)
9. Lin, T.-Y., et al.: Microsoft COCO: common objects in context. In: Fleet, D., Pajdla, T., Schiele, B., Tuytelaars, T. (eds.) ECCV 2014. LNCS, vol. 8693, pp. 740–755. Springer, Cham (2014). https://doi.org/10.1007/978-3-319-10602-1_48
10. Liu, D., Zhang, H., Zha, Z.J., Feng, W.: Learning to assemble neural module tree networks for visual grounding. In: The IEEE International Conference on Computer Vision (ICCV) (2019)
11. Liu, W., et al.: SSD: single shot MultiBox detector. In: Leibe, B., Matas, J., Sebe, N., Welling, M. (eds.) ECCV 2016. LNCS, vol. 9905, pp. 21–37. Springer, Cham (2016). https://doi.org/10.1007/978-3-319-46448-0_2
12. Plummer, B.A., Kordas, P., Kiapour, M.H., Zheng, S., Piramuthu, R., Lazebnik, S.: Conditional image-text embedding networks. In: Ferrari, V., Hebert, M., Sminchisescu, C., Weiss, Y. (eds.) ECCV 2018. LNCS, vol. 11216, pp. 258–274. Springer, Cham (2018). https://doi.org/10.1007/978-3-030-01258-8_16
13. Plummer, B.A., Mallya, A., Cervantes, C.M., Hockenmaier, J., Lazebnik, S.: Phrase localization and visual relationship detection with comprehensive image-language cues. In: Proceedings of the IEEE International Conference on Computer Vision, pp. 1928–1937 (2017)

14. Plummer, B.A., Wang, L., Cervantes, C.M., Caicedo, J.C., Hockenmaier, J., Lazebnik, S.: Flickr30k entities: Collecting region-to-phrase correspondences for richer image-to-sentence models. In: Proceedings of the IEEE International Conference on Computer VIsion, pp. 2641–2649 (2015)
15. Redmon, J., Divvala, S., Girshick, R., Farhadi, A.: You only look once: unified, real-time object detection. In: Proceedings of the IEEE Conference on Computer Vision and Pattern Recognition, pp. 779–788 (2016)
16. Redmon, J., Farhadi, A.: Yolov3: an incremental improvement. arXiv preprint arXiv:1804.02767 (2018)
17. Ren, S., He, K., Girshick, R., Sun, J.: Faster r-cnn: Towards real-time object detection with region proposal networks. In: Advances in Neural Information Processing Systems, pp. 91–99 (2015)
18. Rohrbach, A., Rohrbach, M., Hu, R., Darrell, T., Schiele, B.: Grounding of textual phrases in images by reconstruction. In: Leibe, B., Matas, J., Sebe, N., Welling, M. (eds.) ECCV 2016. LNCS, vol. 9905, pp. 817–834. Springer, Cham (2016). https://doi.org/10.1007/978-3-319-46448-0_49
19. Sadhu, A., Chen, K., Nevatia, R.: Zero-shot grounding of objects from natural language queries. In: Proceedings of the IEEE International Conference on Computer Vision, pp. 4694–4703 (2019)
20. Schuster, S., Krishna, R., Chang, A., Fei-Fei, L., Manning, C.D.: Generating semantically precise scene graphs from textual descriptions for improved image retrieval. In: Workshop on Vision and Language (VL15). Association for Computational Linguistics, Lisbon, Portugal, September 2015
21. Tieleman, T., Hinton, G.: Lecture 6.5–RmsProp: divide the gradient by a running average of its recent magnitude. COURSERA: Neural Networks for Machine Learning (2012)
22. Wang, L., Li, Y., Huang, J., Lazebnik, S.: Learning two-branch neural networks for image-text matching tasks. IEEE Trans. Pattern Anal. Mach. Intell. **41**(2), 394–407 (2018)
23. Wang, L., Li, Y., Lazebnik, S.: Learning deep structure-preserving image-text embeddings. In: Proceedings of the IEEE Conference on Computer Vision and Pattern Recognition, pp. 5005–5013 (2016)
24. Wang, M., Azab, M., Kojima, N., Mihalcea, R., Deng, J.: Structured matching for phrase localization. In: Leibe, B., Matas, J., Sebe, N., Welling, M. (eds.) ECCV 2016. LNCS, vol. 9912, pp. 696–711. Springer, Cham (2016). https://doi.org/10.1007/978-3-319-46484-8_42
25. Yang, S., Li, G., Yu, Y.: Cross-modal relationship inference for grounding referring expressions. In: Proceedings of the IEEE Conference on Computer Vision and Pattern Recognition, pp. 4145–4154 (2019)
26. Yang, S., Li, G., Yu, Y.: Dynamic graph attention for referring expression comprehension. In: Proceedings of the IEEE International Conference on Computer Vision, pp. 4644–4653 (2019)
27. Yang, S., Li, G., Yu, Y.: Graph-structured referring expression reasoning in the wild. In: Proceedings of the IEEE Conference on Computer Vision and Pattern Recognition (CVPR) (2020)
28. Yang, S., Li, G., Yu, Y.: Relationship-embedded representation learning for grounding referring expressions. In: IEEE Transactions on Pattern Analysis and Machine Intelligence (TPAMI) (2020)
29. Yang, Z., Gong, B., Wang, L., Huang, W., Yu, D., Luo, J.: A fast and accurate one-stage approach to visual grounding. In: Proceedings of the IEEE International Conference on Computer Vision, pp. 4683–4693 (2019)

30. Yeh, R., Xiong, J., Hwu, W.M., Do, M., Schwing, A.: Interpretable and globally optimal prediction for textual grounding using image concepts. In: Advances in Neural Information Processing Systems, pp. 1912–1922 (2017)
31. Yu, L., et al.: MattNet: modular attention network for referring expression comprehension. In: Proceedings of the IEEE Conference on Computer Vision and Pattern Recognition, pp. 1307–1315 (2018)

Adversarial Semantic Data Augmentation for Human Pose Estimation

Yanrui Bin[1], Xuan Cao[2], Xinya Chen[1], Yanhao Ge[2], Ying Tai[2],
Chengjie Wang[2], Jilin Li[2], Feiyue Huang[2], Changxin Gao[1],
and Nong Sang[1]

[1] Key Laboratory of Image Processing and Intelligent Control, School of Artificial
Intelligence and Automation, Huazhong University of Science and Technology,
Wuhan, China
{yrbin,hust_cxy,cgao,nsang}@hust.edu.cn
[2] Tencent Youtu Lab, Shanghai, China
{marscao,halege,yingtai,jasoncjwang,jerolinli,garyhuang}@tencent.com

Abstract. Human pose estimation is the task of localizing body keypoints from still images. The state-of-the-art methods suffer from insufficient examples of challenging cases such as symmetric appearance,
heavy occlusion and nearby person. To enlarge the amounts of challenging cases, previous methods augmented images by cropping and pasting
image patches with weak semantics, which leads to unrealistic appearance and limited diversity. We instead propose Semantic Data Augmentation (SDA), a method that augments images by pasting segmented body
parts with various semantic granularity. Furthermore, we propose Adversarial Semantic Data Augmentation (ASDA), which exploits a generative
network to dynamically predict tailored pasting configuration. Given off-
the-shelf pose estimation network as discriminator, the generator seeks
the most confusing transformation to increase the loss of the discriminator while the discriminator takes the generated sample as input and
learns from it. The whole pipeline is optimized in an adversarial manner. State-of-the-art results are achieved on challenging benchmarks. The
code has been publicly available at https://github.com/Binyr/ASDA.

Keywords: Pose estimation · Semantic data augmentation

1 Introduction

Human Pose Estimation (HPE) is the task of localizing body keypoint from
still images. It serves as a fundamental technique for numerous computer vision
applications. Recently, deep convolutional neural networks (DCNN) [13,23,33]
have achieved drastic improvements on standard benchmark datasets. However,
as shown in Fig. 1, they are still prone to fail in some challenging cases such as
symmetric appearance, heavy occlusion, and nearby persons.

© Springer Nature Switzerland AG 2020
A. Vedaldi et al. (Eds.): ECCV 2020, LNCS 12364, pp. 606–622, 2020.
https://doi.org/10.1007/978-3-030-58529-7_36

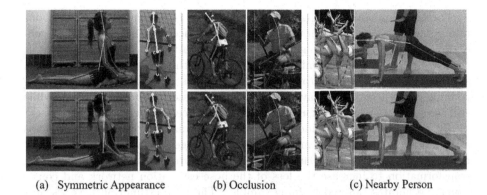

(a) Symmetric Appearance   (b) Occlusion   (c) Nearby Person

Fig. 1. Pairs of pose predictions obtained by HRNet [23] (top) and our approach (bottom) in the challenging cases. Incorrect predictions are highlighted by the red dotted circles. Note that image in Fig. 1 (c) {*cols. 1*} is an extremely challenging case so that few of the keypoints are correctly predicted by the original HRNet. After equipped with our ASDA (bottom), HRNet improve the robustness to the challenging cases. (Color figure online)

The reason for the inferior performance of the DCNN-based methods in the challenging cases is that there exists an insufficient amount of examples that contain these challenging cases to train a deep network for accurate keypoint localization. However, obtaining the annotations of keypoint localization is costly.

One promising way to tackle this problem is data augmentation. Conventional data augmentation performs global image transformations (e.g., scaling, rotating, flipping or color jittering). Although it enhances the global translational invariance of the network and largely improves the generalizability, it contributes little to solving the challenging cases. Recently, Ke et al. [13] proposes keypoints masking training to force the network better recognize poses from difficult training samples. They simulate the keypoint occlusion by copying a background patch and putting it onto a keypoint or simulate the multiple existing keypoints by copying a body keypoint patch and putting it onto a nearby background. However, this data augmentation method only brings marginal improvement. On the one hand, the used patch is cropped from the input image, resulting in a limited variance of the generated images. On the other hand, the cropped keypoint patch is surrounded by some background, which makes the generated image unrealistic.

In this paper, we propose a novel Adversarial Semantic Data Augmentation (ASDA) scheme. Human parsing is applied to the training images to get a large amount of pure body part patches. These body parts are organized, according to their semantic types, to build a semantic part pool. As the human body could be represented as a hierarchy of parts and subparts, we combine several subparts, according to the structure of the human body, to get body parts with various semantic granularity. For each input image, several parts will be randomly selected from the semantic part pool and properly pasted to the image.

Further, randomly pasting parts to the image is still suboptimal. Without taking the difference between training image instances into account, it may generate ineffective examples that are too easy to boost the network. Moreover, it can hardly match the dynamic training status of the pose estimation network, since it is usually sampled from static distributions [21]. For instance, with the training of the network, it may gradually learn to associate occluded wrists while still have difficulty in distinguish similar appearance with legs.

Based on the above consideration, we parameterize the parts pasting process as an affine transformation matrix and exploit a generative network to online predict the transformation parameters. The generator seeks the most confusing transformation to increase the loss of the pose estimation network and consequently generates tailored training samples. The pose estimation network acts as a discriminator, which takes the tailored samples as input and tries to learn from it. By leveraging the spatial transformer network, the whole process is differentiable and trained in an adversarial manner.

Additionally, our Adversarial Semantic Data Augmentation is a universal solution that can be easily applied to different datasets and networks for human pose estimation.

In summary, the main contributions are three-fold:

- We design a novel Semantic Data Augmentation (SDA) which augments images by pasting segmented body parts of various semantic granularity to simulate examples that contain challenging cases.
- We propose to utilize a generative network to dynamically adjust the augmentation parameters of the SDA and produce tailored training samples against the pose estimation network, which largely elevates the performance of the SDA.
- We comprehensively evaluate our methods on various benchmark datasets and consistently outperforms the state-of-the-art methods.

2   Related Work

The advances of DCNN-based human pose estimation benefit from multiple factors. We compare our methods with literature from three most related aspects.

2.1   Human Pose Estimation

Recently, pose estimation using DCNNs has shown superior performance. Deep-Pose [27] first applied deep neural networks to human pose estimation by directly regressing the 2D coordinates of keypoints from the input image. [26] proposed a heatmap representation for each keypoint and largely improved the spatial generalization. Following the heatmap-based framework, various methods [18,22,23,23,24,29,30] focused on designing the structure of the network and indeed achieved significant improvement. However they still suffered from insufficient amounts of samples that contains challenging cases. In this work, standing on the shoulder of the well-designed network structure, we propose a universal data augmentation solution to further improve the performance of human pose estimation.

2.2   Data Augmentation

Typical data augmentation [4,18,23,30] mainly performed global spatial transformation like scaling, rotating and flipping *etc.* These common data augmentation schemes helped the network to resist the global image deformation but
fail to improve the immunity to the challenging cases. Recently, some novel
data augmentations were proposed. PoseRefiner [8] transformed the keypoint
annotations to mimic the most common failure cases of human pose estima-
tors, so that the proposed refiner network could be trained well. MSR-net [13]
introduced keypoint-masking which cropped and pasted patches from the input
image to simulate challenging cases. Different from the existing data augmentation strategies, we propose a novel semantic data augmentation scheme which
takes advantage of the human semantic segmentation to obtain the pure segmented body parts rather than noisy image patches. Furthermore, we compose
the related parts to form a set of new parts with higher semantic granularity.

2.3   Adversarial Learning

Inspired by the minimax mechanism of Generative Adversarial Networks (GANs)
[10], some literature [5] generated hard training samples in an adversarial way.
Semantic Jitter [32] proposed to overcome the sparsity of supervision problem via
synthetically generated images. A-Fast-RCNN [28] used GANs to generate deformations for object detection. Recently, GANs were introduced into human pose
estimation. Such as Adversarial PoseNet [4] designed discriminators to distinguish
the real poses from the fake ones. Jointly Optimize [21] designed an augmentation network that competed against a target network by generating "hard" augmentation operations. In this paper, we designed a generative network to adjust
the semantic data augmentation then to produce challenging training data. The
generative network takes the difference between training instances into consideration, and produce tailored training samples for the pose estimation network. Hard
mining, as an alternative strategy to feed challenging training data to network, is
totally different from ours. Hard mining can only "select" rather than "produce"
challenging samples, which essentially limits its improvement of accuracy on challenging cases.

3   Methodology

3.1   Semantic Data Augmentation

Building Semantic Part Pool. For common human pose estimation schemes
[18,23,25,30], data augmentations such as global scaling, rotation, flipping are
usually applied, which bring the global translational invariances to the network
and largely improves the generalizability.

However, the remained problem of pose estimation task is the challenging
cases, e.g., symmetric appearance, heavy occlusion, and nearby person, where
the global spatial transformation helps little. In contrast to the global spatial

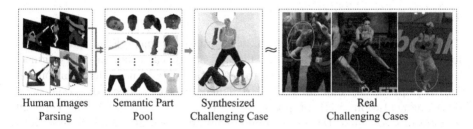

| Human Images | Semantic Part | Synthesized | Real |
| Parsing | Pool | Challenging Case | Challenging Cases |

Fig. 2. Illustration of Semantic Data Augmentation (SDA). We first apply human parsing on training images and get a large amount of segmented body parts. The segmented body parts are organized, according to their semantics, to build semantic part pool. For each training image, several part patches will be randomly sampled and properly placed on the image to synthesize the real challenging cases such as symmetric appearance (green circle), occlusion (perple circle) and nearby person (yellow circle). (Color figure online)

transformations, local pixel patch manipulation provide more degrees of freedom to augment image and is able to synthesize the challenging case realistically.

A human image is assembled by semantic part patches, such as arm, leg, shoe, trousers and so on. Inspired by these semantic cues, we can synthesize plentiful human image instances by elaborately combining these local part patches. Here, we propose a novel augmentation scheme, as shown in Fig. 2. By firstly segmenting all human images through the human parsing method [17], then we can build a data pool $\mathbb{D}_{part}$ filled with various semantic body part patches. We follow the definition of LIP dataset [9] and segment the human image into $\hat{N} = 26$ part patches. Finally, the body part patches from the data pool can be properly mounted on the current person's body to synthesize challenging cases.

As human parsing aims to analyze every detail region of a person as well as different categories of clothes, LIP defines 6 body parts and 13 clothes categories in fine semantic granularity. However, body parts of various semantic granularity will appear in images of real-world scenarios with complex multi-person activities. For the above considerations, we combine some of the parts (e.g., left shoe and left leg) to form a set of new parts with higher semantic granularity and then add them to our part pool. After the cutting step, we filter out scattered segments, segments with the area below 35^2 and segments with low semantics.

Augmentation Parameter Formulation. Given a semantic part patch I_p and a training image I_o, the placement of this semantic part can be defined by the affine transformation matrix

$$\boldsymbol{H} = \begin{bmatrix} s\cos r & s\sin r & t_x \\ -s\sin r & s\cos r & t_y \\ 0 & 0 & 1 \end{bmatrix}, \qquad (1)$$

where s denotes the scale of the part patch, r denotes the rotation, and t_x, t_y is the translation in horizontal and vertical direction respectively. Thus the placement of the part patch I_p can be uniquely determined by a 4D tuple $\theta(s, r, t_x, t_y)$.

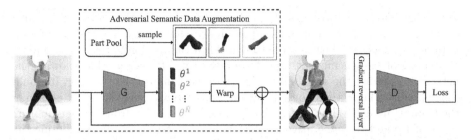

Fig. 3. Overview of our approach. The input image is fed to the generator $\mathcal{G}$ to obtain $\hat{N}$ groups of tailored augmentation parameters which are used to warp the randomly selected semantic part patches. Each group parameters is used to warp the patch of the specific part type. $\mathcal{G}$ seeks the most confusing transformation to increase the loss of the pose estimation network and consequently generates tailored training samples. The pose estimation network acts as a discriminator $\mathcal{D}$, which takes the tailored sample as input and tries to learn from it. The whole pipeline is optimized in an adversarial manner.

The scale of the part patch will be aligned with the target person in advance according to the human bounding box. Initially, the part patch could be pasted in the center of the training image without rotation. In other words, the tuple $(1, 0, 0, 0)$ is served as our original paste configuration.

Random Semantic Augmentation. With 4D augmentation parameters defined in Eq. 1, a straight augmentation method can be realized by sampling a 4D tuple augmentation parameter from a uniform distribution in the neighborhood space of $(1, 0, 0, 0)$. N different body parts will be pasted to the target person. The value of N is set manually as a hyper-parameter. Sensitivity Analysis of N is detailed in Sect. 4.5.

3.2   Adversarial Learning

Our goal is to generate the confusing transformation to improve the performance of pose estimation networks. However, the augmentation parameters of SDA are sampled from the neighborhood of $(1, 0, 0, 0)$. On the one hand, the confusing transformation naturally varies with different training instances and different part types. On the other hand, random sampling augmentation parameters from the static distribution can hardly perceive the dynamic training status. Thus it is prone to generate ineffective training samples which are so easy that it may not bring positive or even put negative effect on network training.

To overcome such issues, we propose to leverage Spatial Transformer Network (STN) to manipulate semantic parts within the network and optimize it in an adversarial manner. The main idea is to utilize an STN as the generator, which seeks the most confusing transformation to increase the pose estimation network loss. On the other hand, the pose estimation network acts as a discriminator, which tries to learn from the tailored semantic augmentation.

Generate Tailored Samples. The core module of our method is an STN, which takes the target person image as input and predicts $\hat{N}$ groups transformation parameters, each of which is used to transform the randomly selected semantic body parts of the specific part type. In our experiments, we find that allowing the network to predict the scale s of the part would collapse the training. It would easily predict a large scale, so that the part completely covers the target person in the training images. Thus, we randomly sample the scale s from the neighboring space of 1.0 and the generative network is mainly responsible for predicting the (r, t_x, t_y). The affine transformation matrix is generated as defined in Eq. 1.

Each pixel in the transformed image is computed by applying a sampling kernel centered at a particular location in the original image. Mathematically, the pointwise transformation is shown in Eq. (2).

$$\begin{pmatrix} x_i^s \\ y_i^s \\ 1 \end{pmatrix} = \boldsymbol{H} \begin{pmatrix} x_i^t \\ y_i^t \\ 1 \end{pmatrix}, \tag{2}$$

where (x_i^s, y_i^s) and (x_i^t, y_i^t) denote the coordinates of the i-th pixel in the original and transformed image respectively. The transformed parts thus can be pasted to the target person image in the order they were sampled.

It is the not the first time to determine the augmentation parameters through a network. Xi Peng et al. [21] jointly optimizes the conventional data augmentation (i.e., global scaling, rotating and feature erasing.) and network training to enhance the global transformation invariance of the network. Our contributions are quite different with [21]. We design a novel SDA which augments images by pasting segmented body parts of various semantic granularity to simulate examples that contain challenging cases. Then we further propose ASDA that utilize a generative network to dynamically adjust the augmentation parameters of the SDA and produce tailored training samples for the pose estimation network.

Joint Training. As shown in the Fig. 3, the networks training follow the pipeline of training standard GANs [10]. Generative network acting as generator $\mathcal{G}$ try to produce challenging cases. Meanwhile, the pose estimation network acting as a discriminator $\mathcal{D}$ try to learn from the generated training samples.

The discriminator is supervised by ground-truth heatmaps and try to decrease the loss $\mathcal{L}_\mathcal{D}$ which is formulated as Eq. (4). On the contrary, the generator try to increase the loss $\mathcal{L}_\mathcal{D}$. So the loss for generator is simply set as negative discriminator loss as formulated in Eq. (5).

$$I_{aug} = \mathcal{F}_{aff}(\mathcal{G}(I_o), \{I_p\}), \tag{3}$$

$$\mathcal{L}_\mathcal{D} = \|\mathcal{D}(I_{aug}) - H_{gt}\|_{\ell_2}, \tag{4}$$

$$\mathcal{L}_\mathcal{G} = -\mathcal{L}_\mathcal{D}, \tag{5}$$

where I_o is the original training image, $\{I_p\}$ is a set of randomly sampled part patches, $\mathcal{F}_{aff}(\cdot, \cdot)$ denotes the affine transformation function and H_{gt} denote ground-truth heatmap. The network weights of $\mathcal{G}$ and $\mathcal{D}$ are updated alternately.

4   Experiments

4.1   Datasets and Evaluation Protocols

We conduct experiments on three representative benchmark datasets, *i.e.* extended Leeds Sports Poses (LSP) dataset [12], MPII human pose dataset [1] and MS COCO dataset [16].

LSP Dataset. The extended LSP dataset consists of 11k training images and 1k testing images of mostly sports people. Standard Percentage of Correct Keypoints (PCK) metric is used for evaluation. It reports the percentage of keypoint that fall into a normalized distance of the ground-truth, where the torso size is used as the normalized distance.

MPII Dataset. The MPII dataset includes around 25k images containing over 40k people with annotated body keypoint (28k training and 11k testing). Following [18], 3k samples are taken as a validation set to tune the hyper-parameters. PCK is also utilized to evaluate MPII, but distance is normalized by head size. MPII evaluation metric is referred to PCKh.

COCO Dataset. The COCO dataset involves multi-person pose estimation task which requires simultaneously detecting people and localizing their key points. The COCO training dataset (train2017) includes 57k images and validation dataset (val2017) includes 5000 images. The COCO evaluation defines the object keypoint similarity (OKS) which plays the same role as the IoU.

4.2   Implementation Details

Both generator $\mathcal{G}$ and discriminator $\mathcal{D}$ are the off-the-shelf networks. For generator, the ResNet-18 is utilized to regress $(3 \times \hat{N})$ parameters, where $\hat{N}$ is the class number of the human parsing. For discriminator, we adopt HRNet [23].

During building the semantic part pool, in order to avoid the inference of different human parsing algorithms, we obtain body parts from LIP dataset [9]. Beside our semantic data augmentation, we keep original data augmentation as adopted in HRNet, including global random flip, rotation and scale.

Network training is implemented on the open-platform PyTorch. For training details, we employ Adam [14] with a learning rate 0.001 as the optimizer of both generator and discriminator network. We drop the learning rate by a factor of 10 at the 170-th and 200-th epochs. Training ends at 210 epochs. The HRNet is initialized with weight of pre-trained model on public-released ImageNet [7].

MPII. For both MPII training and testing set, body scale and center are provided. We first utilize these value to crop the image around the target person and resized to 256×256 or 384×384. Data augmentation includes random flip, random rotation $(-30°, 30°)$ and random scale $(0.75, 1.25)$.

LSP. For LSP training set, we crop image by estimating the body scale and position according to keypoint positions. The data augmentation strategy are the same to MPII. For the LSP testing set, we perform similar cropping and resizing, but simply use the image center as the body position, and estimate the body scale by the image size following [31]. We follow previous methods [29, 31] to train our model by adding the MPII training set to the extended LSP training set with person-centric annotations. For both MPII and LSP, testing is conducted on six-scale image pyramids (0.8, 0.9, 1.0, 1.1, 1.2 1.3).

COCO. For COCO training set, each ground-truth human box is extended to fixed aspect ratio, e.g., height: width = 4 : 3 and enlarged to contain more context by a rescale factor 1.25. Then the resulting box is cropped from image without distorting image aspect ratio and resized to a fixed resolution. The default resolution is 256: 192. We apply random flip, random rotation $(-40°, 40°)$ and random scale $(0.7, 1.3)$. For COCO testing set, we utilized the predicted bounding box released by Li et al. [15]. We also predict the pose of the corresponding flipped image and average the heat maps to get the final prediction.

4.3 Quantitative Results

We report the performance of our methods on the three benchmark datasets following the public evaluation protocols. We adopt the HRNet as the backbone network. "W32" and "W48" represent the channel dimentions of the high-resolution subnetworks in last three stages of HRNet, respectively. "s7" indicates the we expand the HRNet to 7 stages by repeating the last stage of the original HRNet.

Results on LSP. Table 1 presents the PCK@0.2 scores on LSP test set. Our method outperforms the state-of-the-art methods especially on some challenging keypoints, e.g., wrist, knee and ankle, we have 0.8%, 1.0% and 1.0% improvements respectively.

Table 1. Comparisons on the LSP test set (PCK@0.2).

Method	Hea.	Sho.	Elb.	Wri.	Hip.	Kne.	Ank.	Total
Insafutdinov et al., 2016 [11]	97.4	92.7	87.5	84.4	91.5	89.9	87.2	90.1
Wei et al., 2016 [29]	97.8	92.5	87.0	83.9	91.5	90.8	89.9	90.5
Bulat et al., 2016 [2]	97.2	92.1	88.1	85.2	92.2	91.4	88.7	90.7
Chu et al., 2017 [6]	98.1	93.7	89.3	86.9	93.4	94.0	92.5	92.6
Chen et al., 2017 [4]	98.5	94.0	89.8	87.5	93.9	94.1	93.0	93.1
Yang et al., 2017 [31]	98.3	94.5	92.2	88.9	94.4	95.0	93.7	93.9
Zhang et al., 2019 [33]	98.4	94.8	92.0	89.4	94.4	94.8	93.8	94.0
Ours-W32	**98.8**	**95.2**	**92.5**	**90.2**	**94.7**	**95.8**	**94.8**	**94.6**

Results on MPII. The performance of our methods on MPII test set is shown in Table 2. We can observe that Ours-W48-s7 achieves 94.1% PCKh@0.5, which is the new state-of-the-art result. In particular, Ours-W48-s7 achieves 0.5%, 0.5%

Table 2. Comparisons on the MPII test set (PCKh@0.5).

Method	Hea.	Sho.	Elb.	Wri.	Hip.	Kne.	Ank.	Total
Wei et al., 2016 [29]	97.8	95.0	88.7	84.0	88.4	82.8	79.4	88.5
Bulat et al., 2016 [2]	97.9	95.1	89.9	85.3	89.4	85.7	81.7	89.7
Newell et al., 2016 [18]	98.2	96.3	91.2	87.1	90.1	87.4	83.6	90.9
Ning et al., 2018 [20]	98.1	96.3	92.2	87.8	90.6	87.6	82.7	91.2
Chu et al., 2017 [6]	98.5	96.3	91.9	88.1	90.6	88.0	85.0	91.5
Chen et al., 2017 [4]	98.1	96.5	92.5	88.5	90.2	89.6	86.0	91.9
Yang et al., 2017 [31]	98.5	96.7	92.5	88.7	91.1	88.6	86.0	92.0
Xiao et al., 2018 [30]	98.5	96.6	91.9	87.6	91.1	88.1	84.1	91.5
Ke et al., 2018 [13]	98.5	96.8	92.7	88.4	90.6	89.4	86.3	92.1
Nie et al., 2018 [19]	98.6	96.9	93.0	89.1	91.7	89.0	86.2	92.4
Tang et al., 2018 [25]	98.4	96.9	92.6	88.7	91.8	89.4	86.2	92.3
Sun et al., 2019 [23]	98.6	96.9	92.8	89.0	91.5	89.0	85.7	92.3
Zhang et al., 2019 [33]	98.6	97.0	92.8	88.8	91.7	89.8	86.6	92.5
Su et al., 2019 [22]*	98.7	97.5	94.3	90.7	**93.4**	92.2	88.4	93.9
Ours-W48-s7*	**98.9**	**97.6**	**94.6**	**91.2**	93.1	**92.7**	**89.1**	**94.1**

"*" indicates the network take image size 384 × 384 as input.

and 0.7% improvements on wrist, knee and ankle which are considered as the most challenging keypoints.

Results on COCO. Table 3 compares our methods with classic and SOTA methods on COCO val2017 dataset. All the methods use standard top-down paradigm which sequentially performs human detection and single-person pose estimation. Our model outperforms SIM [30] and HRNet [23] by 4.8% and 0.8% for input size 256 × 192 respectively. When input size is 384 × 288, our model achieve better AP than SIM [30] and HRNet [23] by 4.5% and 0.9%.

Table 3. Comparison with SOTA methods on COCO val2017 dataset. Their results are cited from Chen et al. [3] and Sun et al. [23].

Method	Backbone	Input Size	Params	GFLOPs	AP	AP^{50}	AP^{75}	AP^M	AP^L	AR
Hourglass [18]	HG-8stage	256 × 192	25.1M	14.3	66.9	-	-	-	-	-
CPN [3]	ResNet-50	256 × 192	27.0M	6.20	69.4	-	-	-	-	-
CPN [3]	ResNet-50	384 × 288	27.0M	13.9	71.6	-	-	-	-	-
SIM [30]	ResNet-50	256 × 192	34.0M	8.9	70.4	88.6	78.3	67.1	77.2	76.3
SIM [30]	ResNet-50	384 × 288	34.0M	20.0	72.2	89.3	78.9	68.1	79.7	77.6
HRNet [23]	HRNet-W32	256 × 192	28.5M	7.10	74.4	90.5	81.9	70.8	81.0	79.8
HRNet [23]	HRNet-W32	384 × 288	28.5M	16.0	75.8	90.6	82.7	71.9	82.8	81.0
Ours	HRNet-W32	256 × 192	28.5M	7.10	**75.2**	**91.0**	**82.4**	**72.2**	**81.3**	**80.4**
Ours	HRNet-W32	384 × 288	28.5M	16.0	**76.7**	**91.2**	**83.5**	**73.2**	**83.4**	**81.5**

Fig. 4. Comparisons of the HRNet [23] trained without (left side) and with (right side) our Adversarial Semantic Data Augmentation.

4.4 Qualitative Results

Figure 4 displays some pose estimation results obtained by HRNet without (left size) and with (right side) our ASDA. We can observe that original HRNet is confused by symmetric appearance (e.g. the left and right legs in {*rows.1, cols. 3*}), heavy occlusion (e.g., the right ankle in {*rows.1 cols. 2*}) and nearby person (e.g., multiple similar legs and arms in {*rows.1, cols. 1*}). Note that image in {*rows.1, cols. 1*} is an extremely challenging case so that few of the keyponts are correctly predicted by the original HRNet. By generating tailored semantic augmentation for each input image, our ASDA largely improves the performance of the original HRNet in the extremely challenging cases. Figure 5 shows some pose estimation results obtained by our approach on the COCO test dataset.

4.5 Ablation Studies

In this section, we conduct ablative analysis on the validation set of MPII dataset. The baseline is HRNet-W32 [23] which achieved PCKh@0.5 at 90.3% by performing flipping and single scale in inference. During baseline training, the data augmentation adopts global spatial transformation including random rotation $(-30°, 30°)$, random scale $(0.75, 1.25)$ and flipping. The results are shown in Table 4(a).

The MPII dataset provide visibility annotations for each keypoint, which enables us to conduct ablative analysis on the subset of invisible keypoints and study the effect of our method on improving the occlusion cases. The results are shown in Table 4(b).

Table 4. Ablation studies on the MPII validation set (PCKh@0.5)

(a) Results evaluated on all keypoints							
Method	Hea	Sho	Elb	Wri	Hip	Kne	Ank	Total
Baseline	97.1	95.9	90.3	86.4	89.1	87.1	83.3	90.3
+ROR	97.0	96.2	90.9	86.9	89.3	86.9	82.9	90.5
+SDA (Ours)	97.2	96.3	91.2	86.9	90.0	87.2	83.7	90.8
+ASDA (Ours)	**97.6**	**96.6**	**91.5**	**87.3**	**90.5**	**87.5**	**84.5**	**91.2**
(b) Results evaluated only on invisible keypoints							
Baseline	-	90.9	73.6	61.9	81.8	71.7	61.8	74.2
+ROR	-	92.0	74.9	63.2	82.7	71.6	61.6	74.9
+SDA (Ours)	-	91.8	75.1	63.0	84.1	71.7	63.3	75.4
+ASDA (Ours)	-	**92.7**	**75.1**	**65.1**	**84.8**	**71.8**	**63.4**	**76.1**

Baseline: The original HRNet-W32 [23]. The following experiments is all based on this baseline.

+ROR: Adopt data augmentation of Randomly Occluding and Repeating (ROR) the keypoints patch [13] on training HRNet-W32.

+SDA: Adopt our Semantic Data Augmentation (SDA) scheme on training HRNet-W32, the augmentation parameters are adjusted randomly from a uniform distribution in the neighborhood space of $(1, 0, 0, 0)$.

+ASDA: Adop our Adversarial Semantic Data Augmentation (ASDA) scheme on training HRNet-W32, the augmentation parameters are online adjusted by the generative network in an adversarial way.

With vs. Without Semantic Data Augmentation. We first evaluate the effect of the Semantic Data Augmentation scheme. As shown in Table 4(a), **+SDA** outperforms the **Baseline** with a large margin by 0.5%. Note that our SDA scheme consistently achieved improvements on all keypoints. Especially, our SDA achieves 0.9%, 0.5% and 0.4% improvements on elbow, wrist and ankle respectly, which are considered as the most challenging keypoints to be localized. In Table 4(b), we can observe a more significant improvement brought by SDA. The result demonstrate that the semantic local pixel manipulation of our SDA effectively augment training data and elevate the performance of pose estimation.

Both SDA and Randomly Occluding and Repeating (ROR) the keypoints patch [13] augment training data by manipulate the local pixel. However, ROR achieves 0.3% lower average PCKh@0.5 than our SDA. Moreover, ROR even brings negative effects to baseline model when localizing keypoints like knee and ankle. These results demonstrate that various segmented body parts with high semantics used in our SDA play an key role for improving pose estimation performance.

Random vs. Adversarial Augmentation. Based on the SDA scheme, we found that Adversarial SDA can further improve the accuracy by online adjusting augmentation parameters. As shown in the Table 4(a), **+ASDA** consistently

Table 5. Ablation studies of different number of body parts N.

Part Num.	Hea.	Sho.	Elb.	Wri.	Hip.	Kne.	Ank.	Total
1	**97.6**	96.6	**91.5**	**87.3**	90.5	**87.5**	**84.5**	**91.2**
2	97.5	96.6	**91.5**	86.9	90.1	87.4	83.8	91.0
3	97.3	**96.8**	91.3	86.9	**90.6**	87.4	83.6	91.0
4	97.4	96.3	91.1	86.2	90.3	87.0	83.6	90.7
6	97.2	96.2	90.4	85.2	90.0	86.0	82.1	90.1
8	97.0	95.7	89.3	83.8	89.3	85.6	81.4	89.4

outperforms **+SDA** on all keypoints and achieve 0.4% higher average PCKh@0.5. For invisible keypoints, ASDA outperforms baseline and SDA by 1.9% and 0.7% PCKh@0.5 score. As discussed in Sect. 3.2, our ASDA can further improve performance due to the adversarial learning strategy which generates tailored samples for training pose estimation network.

Sensitivity Analysis. The part number N as a hyper-parameter is configured manually. We test different N values during training and the PCKh@0.5 score on the MPII validation set is shown in Table 5. Less than 3 parts, the performance maintain roughly the same. Begin with 4 parts, the performance sharply drop along the increasing of part number. We infer that too many parts will generate too hard training samples for pose estimation network which misleads network to learn unrealistic cases.

Table 6. Result of applying on different network.

Method	Hea.	Sho.	Elb.	Wri.	Hip.	Kne.	Ank.	Total
2-Stacked HG	96.6	95.4	89.7	84.7	88.7	84.1	80.7	89.1
2-Stacked HG+ASDA	**96.8**	**95.8**	**90.5**	**85.5**	**89.3**	**85.5**	**81.9**	**89.8**
8-Stacked HG	96.9	95.9	90.8	86.0	89.5	86.5	82.9	90.2
8-Stacked HG+ASDA	**97.5**	**96.5**	**91.6**	**87.3**	**90.5**	**87.7**	**83.5**	**91.1**
SIM-ResNet50	96.4	95.3	89.0	83.2	88.4	84.0	79.6	88.5
SIM-ResNet50+ASDA	**96.8**	**95.8**	**89.7**	**83.9**	**89.5**	**85.1**	**80.5**	**89.3**
SIM-ResNet101	96.9	**95.9**	89.5	84.4	88.4	84.5	80.7	89.1
SIM-ResNet101+ASDA	**97.2**	**95.9**	**90.0**	**85.2**	**89.7**	**86.0**	**82.3**	**90.0**
HRNet-W32	97.1	95.9	90.3	86.4	89.1	87.1	83.3	90.3
HRNet-W32+ASDA	**97.6**	**96.6**	**91.5**	**87.3**	**90.5**	**87.5**	**84.5**	**91.2**
HRNet-W48	97.2	96.1	90.8	86.3	89.3	86.6	83.1	90.4
HRNet-W48+ASDA	**97.3**	**96.5**	**91.7**	**87.9**	**90.8**	**88.2**	**84.2**	**91.4**

Fig. 5. Examples of estimated poses on the COCO test set.

Apply on Different Networks. As shown in Table 6, we report the performance of different networks trained with our ASDA. By applying our ASDA, the SOTA networks consistently achieved improvements. Especially on the challenging keypoints such as elbow, wrist, knee and ankle, our ADSA enhances the network significantly. This result exhibits the universality of our ADSA scheme.

Compare with Methods that also use Parsing Information. Nie et al. [19] also use parsing information and improves the 8-stacked hourglass from 90.2% to 91.0% on MPII validation set. The improvement is slightly lower than ASDA that improves the 8-stacked hourglass from 90.2% to 91.1%. In addition, [19] uses 2-stacked hourglass as Parsing Encoder to predict the parameters of an adaptive convolution, which introduces extra parameters and computation burden. Moreover, the parsing annotation and keypoints annotation of LIP are both used in the training of Parsing Encoder while our ASDA only uses the parsing annotation.

5   Conclusions

In this work, we proposed Semantic Data Augmentation (SDA) which locally pasted segmented body parts with various semantic granularity to synthesize challenging cases. Based on the SDA, we further proposed Adversarial Semantic Data Augmentation which exploit a generative network to online adjust the augmentation parameters for each individual training image in an adversarial way. Improved results on public benchmark and comprehensive experiments have demonstrated the effectiveness of our methods. Our ASDA is general and independent on network. We hope our work can provide inspiration on how to generate tailored training samples for other tasks.

Acknowledgement. This work was supported by the National Natural Science Foundation of China under grant 61871435 and the Fundamental Research Funds for the Central Universities no. 2019kfyXKJC024.

References

1. Andriluka, M., Pishchulin, L., Gehler, P., Schiele, B.: 2D human pose estimation: new benchmark and state of the art analysis. In: CVPR, pp. 3686–3693 (2014)
2. Bulat, A., Tzimiropoulos, G.: Human pose estimation via convolutional part heatmap regression. In: Leibe, B., Matas, J., Sebe, N., Welling, M. (eds.) ECCV 2016. LNCS, vol. 9911, pp. 717–732. Springer, Cham (2016). https://doi.org/10.1007/978-3-319-46478-7_44
3. Chen, Y., Wang, Z., Peng, Y., Zhang, Z., Yu, G., Sun, J.: Cascaded pyramid network for multi-person pose estimation. In: CVPR, pp. 7103–7112 (2018)
4. Chen, Y., Shen, C., Wei, X.S., Liu, L., Yang, J.: Adversarial posenet: a structure-aware convolutional network for human pose estimation. In: ICCV, pp. 1212–1221 (2017)
5. Chu, W., Hung, W.C., Tsai, Y.H., Cai, D., Yang, M.H.: Weakly-supervised caricature face parsing through domain adaptation. ICIP (2019)
6. Chu, X., Yang, W., Ouyang, W., Ma, C., Yuille, A.L., Wang, X.: Multi-context attention for human pose estimation. In: CVPR, pp. 1831–1840 (2017)
7. Deng, J., Dong, W., Socher, R., Li, L.J., Li, K., Fei-Fei, L.: ImageNet: a large-scale hierarchical image database. In: CVPR, pp. 248–255 (2009)
8. Fieraru, M., Khoreva, A., Pishchulin, L., Schiele, B.: Learning to refine human pose estimation. In: CVPR Workshops, pp. 205–214 (2018)
9. Gong, K., Liang, X., Zhang, D., Shen, X., Lin, L.: Look into person: self-supervised structure-sensitive learning and a new benchmark for human parsing. In: CVPR, pp. 932–940 (2017)
10. Goodfellow, I., et al.: Generative adversarial nets. In: NIPS, pp. 2672–2680 (2014)
11. Insafutdinov, E., Pishchulin, L., Andres, B., Andriluka, M., Schiele, B.: DeeperCut: a deeper, stronger, and faster multi-person pose estimation model. In: Leibe, B., Matas, J., Sebe, N., Welling, M. (eds.) ECCV 2016. LNCS, vol. 9910, pp. 34–50. Springer, Cham (2016). https://doi.org/10.1007/978-3-319-46466-4_3

12. Johnson, S., Everingham, M.: Clustered pose and nonlinear appearance models for human pose estimation. In: BMVC, vol. 2, p. 5 (2010)
13. Ke, L., Chang, M.-C., Qi, H., Lyu, S.: Multi-scale structure-aware network for human pose estimation. In: Ferrari, V., Hebert, M., Sminchisescu, C., Weiss, Y. (eds.) ECCV 2018. LNCS, vol. 11206, pp. 731–746. Springer, Cham (2018). https://doi.org/10.1007/978-3-030-01216-8_44
14. Kingma, D.P., Ba, J.: Adam: a method for stochastic optimization. ICLR
15. Li, W., et al.: Rethinking on multi-stage networks for human pose estimation. arXiv preprint arXiv:1901.00148 (2019)
16. Lin, T.-Y., et al.: Microsoft COCO: common objects in context. In: Fleet, D., Pajdla, T., Schiele, B., Tuytelaars, T. (eds.) ECCV 2014. LNCS, vol. 8693, pp. 740–755. Springer, Cham (2014). https://doi.org/10.1007/978-3-319-10602-1_48
17. Liu, T., et al.: Devil in the details: towards accurate single and multiple human parsing. arXiv preprint arXiv:1809.05996 (2018)
18. Newell, A., Yang, K., Deng, J.: Stacked hourglass networks for human pose estimation. In: Leibe, B., Matas, J., Sebe, N., Welling, M. (eds.) ECCV 2016. LNCS, vol. 9912, pp. 483–499. Springer, Cham (2016). https://doi.org/10.1007/978-3-319-46484-8_29
19. Nie, X., Feng, J., Zuo, Y., Yan, S.: Human pose estimation with parsing induced learner. In: CVPR (2018)
20. Ning, G., Zhang, Z., He, Z.: Knowledge-guided deep fractal neural networks for human pose estimation. IEEE Trans. Multimed. 20(5), 1246–1259 (2018)
21. Peng, X., Tang, Z., Yang, F., Feris, R.S., Metaxas, D.: Jointly optimize data augmentation and network training: Adversarial data augmentation in human pose estimation. In: CVPR (2018)
22. Su, Z., Ye, M., Zhang, G., Dai, L., Sheng, J.: Cascade feature aggregation for human pose estimation. arXiv preprint arXiv:1902.07837 (2019)
23. Sun, K., Xiao, B., Liu, D., Wang, J.: Deep high-resolution representation learning for human pose estimation. arXiv preprint arXiv:1902.09212 (2019)
24. Tang, W., Wu, Y.: Does learning specific features for related parts help human pose estimation? In: CVPR, pp. 1107–1116 (2019)
25. Tang, W., Yu, P., Wu, Y.: Deeply learned compositional models for human pose estimation. In: Ferrari, V., Hebert, M., Sminchisescu, C., Weiss, Y. (eds.) ECCV 2018. LNCS, vol. 11207, pp. 197–214. Springer, Cham (2018). https://doi.org/10.1007/978-3-030-01219-9_12
26. Tompson, J.J., Jain, A., LeCun, Y., Bregler, C.: Joint training of a convolutional network and a graphical model for human pose estimation. In: NIPS, pp. 1799–1807 (2014)
27. Toshev, A., Szegedy, C.: DeepPose: human pose estimation via deep neural networks. In: CVPR, pp. 1653–1660 (2014)
28. Wang, X., Shrivastava, A., Gupta, A.: A-fast-RCNN: hard positive generation via adversary for object detection. In: CVPR, pp. 2606–2615 (2017)
29. Wei, S.E., Ramakrishna, V., Kanade, T., Sheikh, Y.: Convolutional pose machines. In: CVPR. pp. 4724–4732 (2016)
30. Xiao, B., Wu, H., Wei, Y.: Simple baselines for human pose estimation and tracking. In: Ferrari, V., Hebert, M., Sminchisescu, C., Weiss, Y. (eds.) ECCV 2018. LNCS, vol. 11210, pp. 472–487. Springer, Cham (2018). https://doi.org/10.1007/978-3-030-01231-1_29
31. Yang, W., Li, S., Ouyang, W., Li, H., Wang, X.: Learning feature pyramids for human pose estimation. In: ICCV, pp. 1281–1290 (2017)

32. Yu, A., Grauman, K.: Semantic jitter: dense supervision for visual comparisons via synthetic images. In: ICCV, pp. 5570–5579 (2017)
33. Zhang, H., et al.: Human pose estimation with spatial contextual information. arXiv preprint arXiv:1901.01760 (2019)

Free View Synthesis

Gernot Riegler[(✉)] and Vladlen Koltun

Intel Labs, Neubiberg, Germany
`gernot.riegler@intel.com`

Abstract. We present a method for novel view synthesis from input images that are freely distributed around a scene. Our method does not rely on a regular arrangement of input views, can synthesize images for free camera movement through the scene, and works for general scenes with unconstrained geometric layouts. We calibrate the input images via SfM and erect a coarse geometric scaffold via MVS. This scaffold is used to create a proxy depth map for a novel view of the scene. Based on this depth map, a recurrent encoder-decoder network processes reprojected features from nearby views and synthesizes the new view. Our network does not need to be optimized for a given scene. After training on a dataset, it works in previously unseen environments with no fine-tuning or per-scene optimization. We evaluate the presented approach on challenging real-world datasets, including Tanks and Temples, where we demonstrate successful view synthesis for the first time and substantially outperform prior and concurrent work.

Keywords: View synthesis · Image-based rendering

1 Introduction

Suppose you want to visit the Sagrada Família in Barcelona but cannot travel there in person due to a coronavirus pandemic that shut down travel across the globe. Virtual reality could offer a surrogate for physically being there. For the experience to be maximally compelling, two requirements must be met. First, you should be free to move through the scene: you should be able to go anywhere in the environment, freely moving your head and body. Second, the synthesized images should be photorealistic: perceptually indistinguishable from reality.

In this paper, we present a method for free view synthesis from unstructured input images in general scenes. Given a set of images or a video of a scene, our approach enables the rendering of a completely new camera path. See Fig. 1 and the supplementary video for examples. We use 3D proxy geometry to map information from the source images to the novel target view. Rather than mapping

Electronic supplementary material The online version of this chapter (https://doi.org/10.1007/978-3-030-58529-7_37) contains supplementary material, which is available to authorized users.

A. Vedaldi et al. (Eds.): ECCV 2020, LNCS 12364, pp. 623–640, 2020.
https://doi.org/10.1007/978-3-030-58529-7_37

Fig. 1. Novel view synthesis from unstructured input images. The first three images show our synthesized results on the *Truck* scene from Tanks and Temples [21]. The unstructured image sequence was recorded using a handheld camera in natural motion. We repurpose the Tanks and Temples dataset to evaluate view synthesis by using a subset of the images as input (green cameras in the bottom right image). The other views, which significantly deviate from the input, act as target poses for view synthesis (red cameras). (Color figure online)

the color values of the source images, we first encode them using a deep convolutional network. Utilizing the proxy geometry, we map the encoded features from the source images into the target view and blend them via a second network. Since the target views can deviate significantly from the source views, we develop a recurrent blending network that is invariant to the number of input images.

Experimental results indicate that our approach works much better than state-of-the-art methods across challenging real-world datasets. On the Tanks and Temples dataset [21], we reduce the LPIPS error [48] by more than a factor of 2 on all scenes with respect to state-of-the-art methods such as EVS [8] and LLFF [26]. On the DTU dataset [1], we also significantly reduce LPIPS relative to EVS and LLFF.

Furthermore, we convincingly outperform methods that are published *concurrently* with our work: Neural Radiance Fields (NeRF) [27] and Neural Point-Based Graphics (NPBG) [2]. We reduce LPIPS relative to these concurrent methods on Tanks and Temples and perform on par on DTU. We also observe that NPBG performs well on Tanks and Temples and poorly on DTU, NeRF performs well on DTU and poorly on Tanks and Temples, while our approach performs well across datasets.

2   Related Work

Image-based Rendering without Deep Learning. Image-based rendering aims to enable the synthesis of new views of a scene directly from a set of input images [6,11,14,17,24,36,37,50]. Different methods map information from the input images to the target view in different ways. Early light-field methods [14,24,36] do not require any information about the scene geometry, but either require a fairly dense and regularly-spaced camera grid, or restrict the target view to be a linear combination of the source views. Heigl et al. [17] compute depth maps per view via stereo matching and use them for view synthesis. Bilinear blending of viewpoints is possible if the cameras are located approximately on the surface of a sphere and the object is centered [10]. These approaches impose restrictions on the layout of the input views, while we target unstructured settings in which the input views are distributed freely around the scene, for example with a single handheld video sequence.

Approaches for unstructured view synthesis are commonly based on constructing 3D proxy geometry that guides the synthesis. Buehler et al. [3] describe the Unstructured Lumigraph, which utilizes dense and accurate 3D geometry to map and blend the input images in a novel target view. Chaurasia et al. [4] estimate a per-view depth map and use these to map color values and blending weights into the target view. The method leverages superpixels to make up for missing depth values. Hyperlapse [22] also uses 3D proxy geometry obtained via structure-from-motion (SfM) and multi-view stereo (MVS). To composite a clean image in the target view, the method optimizes a Markov random field.

Rather than estimate depth from input color images, some systems assume that the input views were acquired by an RGB-D sensor that provided dense depth maps of the scene. Hedman et al. [16] utilize such an RGB-D sensor to aid their fast rendering pipeline. Penner and Zhang [32] use a volumetric approach that associates each voxel with a confidence value which indicates whether the voxel encloses free space or a physical surface.

Image-based Rendering with Deep Learning. Deep learning has come to play an important role in image-based rendering. Deep networks have been used to blend input images in the target view [15,43], to construct neural scene representations [2,29,39,40,42], and to unify geometry estimation and blending in a single model [12,19].

Flynn et al. [13] used a plane-sweep volume [9] within a network architecture for image-based rendering. A color branch predicts the color values for each depth plane in the target view and a second branch predicts the probability for a given depth plane. Kalantari et al. [19] propose a similar system for a light-field setting: four cameras placed on a plane with the same viewing direction. Their method also constructs a plane-sweep volume with the four given images and computes mean and standard deviation per plane as features. Based on these features, one network estimates a disparity map and another reprojects the images and processes them. Hedman et al. [15] use a deep convolutional network to blend source images that have been warped into the target view. Given a dense and accurate proxy geometry obtained by two independent MVS methods, four image mosaics are generated and are then fed to a network to estimate blending weights. Our work is related as we also emphasize the role of the mapping and blending network, but we do not require the construction of input mosaics based on hand-crafted heuristics. Instead, our method can handle an arbitrary number of input images and we output full color images together with blending weights, which enables a certain degree of inpainting. Thies et al. [43] extend the ideas of Hedman et al. [15] to better handle view-dependent effects. They train an additional network per scene that estimates view-dependent effects given a depth map of the target view. Xu et al. [45] also focus on view-dependent effects, but use a structured setup and directional lighting.

Zhou et al. [49] introduce a multi-plane image representation that is estimated by a convolutional network for stereo magnification. The image is represented over multiple RGB-α planes, where each plane is related to a certain depth. Given this representation, new views can be rendered using back-to-front composition. Choi et al. [8] build upon MVSNet [46] for view extrapolation. The method estimates a depth probability volume for each input view that is then warped and fused into the target view. From the fused volume an initial novel view is synthesized. This is then further refined by comparing and integrating candidate patches from the source images. Similarly, the method of Srinivasan et al. [41] synthesizes views from a narrow-baseline pair of images. The work extends the idea of multi-plane images [49] and shows the relation between the range of views that can be rendered from a multi-plane image and the depth plane sampling frequency. Mildenhall et al. [26] further improve this method with practical user guidance and refined network architectures together with local layered scene representations. Flynn et al. [12] considerably improve the view synthesis quality of light-field setups. They use plane sweep volume inputs [9] and multi-plane image outputs [49] together with a network based on regularized gradient descent to gradually refine the generated images.

Instead of mapping features from source images to novel target views, some very recent methods train neural scene representations. In a work that is published concurrently with ours, Aliev et al. [2] describe Neural Point-Based Graphics, where each 3D point is associated with a learned feature vector. These features are splatted into the target view and translated via a rendering network to synthesize the output image. The feature vectors are optimized per scene: application to a new scene requires training the feature extractor for that scene. Thies et al. [42] use a mesh instead of 3D points to embed the feature vectors. Sitzmann et al. [39] avoid explicit proxy geometry and project source images into a neural voxel grid, where each voxel is associated with a trainable feature vector. This representation is likewise trained for each object it is applied to. Lombardi et al. [25] avoid memory-intensive high-resolution neural voxel grids by computing warp fields. In another concurrent work, Mildenhall et al. [27] represent the 5D radiance field by an MLP that can be queried in a volume rendering framework to synthesize new views. In all these methods, dedicated per-scene training is required to apply the representation to a new scene. We train our image encoding and blending networks only once on a training set and apply them to new scenes without any per-scene adaptation or fine-tuning.

In a related line of work, new views are synthesized from a single input image [30,44]. These approaches only allow small deviations from the initial viewpoint, rather than the unrestricted travel through the scene that motivates our work.

3 Method

Our method begins with a preprocessing stage that involves estimating the poses of the input images and computing 3D proxy geometry via multi-view stereo and meshing. Given a target view, we select nearby source images, map them into the target view, and blend them using a recurrent convolutional network. We now describe each step in detail.

3.1 Preprocessing

Pose Estimation. Our input is a set of N images $\{I_n\}_{n=1}^{N}$, for example from a handheld video of a scene. We begin by estimating the poses of these images. For this purpose, we rely on well-established structure-from-motion (SfM) techniques. Specifically, we utilize COLMAP [35] to compute camera poses and a sparse 3D point cloud of the scene. The poses are represented by rotation matrices $\{\mathbf{R}_n\}_{n=1}^{N}$ and translation vectors $\{\mathbf{t}_n\}_{n=1}^{N}$. The SfM pipeline also estimates the intrinsic parameters of the cameras $\{\mathbf{K}_n\}_{n=1}^{N}$ and distortion coefficients.[1] We use these to undistort all images. In the remainder of the paper, the set of images $\{I_n\}_{n=1}^{N}$ refers to the set of undistorted images.

Proxy Geometry. For the mapping of the source images to the target view and also for the selection of the source images that are used to synthesize a novel view $\hat{I}_t$, we need 3D proxy geometry $\mathcal{M}$. We run a standard multi-view stereo (MVS) method [34] to estimate a depth map for each source image. The depth maps are further fused into a coherent 3D point cloud using the fusion algorithm implemented in COLMAP [34,35]. We also experimented with more recent MVS methods [46,47], but did not observe significant improvements in the mapping and blending performance on large scale scenes.

For the mapping of the source image features, we rely on a depth map in the novel target view D_t that is derived from the proxy geometry. However, rendering depth maps from 3D point clouds is problematic for two reasons. First, 3D points that are in the background and should be occluded by a surface can be projected into the foreground, leading to invalid depth values. Second, in larger untextured regions it is likely that no 3D points are reconstructed. Both problems can be alleviated by fitting a surface mesh to the 3D point cloud. We utilize a Delaunay-based reconstruction [18,23] as it can tolerate a certain amount of outliers.

---

[1] In the case of video input data we assume that the intrinsics are shared for all views. $\forall i \neq j : \mathbf{K}_i = \mathbf{K}_j$.

(a) Point cloud   (b) Mesh

Fig. 2. Proxy geometry for view synthesis. We use a surface mesh extracted from a Delaunay tetrahedralization (right). While it is more complete than the point cloud from MVS (left), it also introduces spurious triangles.

The roughness of the resulting surface can be handled by our subsequent blending network. The resulting surface mesh $\mathcal{M}$ is used to derive depth maps of the source views $\{D_n\}_{n=1}^{N}$ and of any target view D_t. Figure 2 shows our computed proxy geometry for a Tanks and Temples scene [21].

3.2 Selection of Source Images

A core advantage of the mapping and blending network described in the next section is that it supports an arbitrary number of source input images. However, in practical situations, many source images will have no overlap with the target view, because they are facing into the opposite direction, or are taken from a very different location. Also during network training, we are limited by GPU memory and can only use a fixed number of input images. For these reasons, we have a simple but effective source selection strategy. Based on the proxy geometry $\mathcal{M}$ we select the K out of N source images that maximize the overlap with the target view.

Specifically, we derive for each target view a depth map D_t. Each pixel of the depth map D_t with a valid depth value is projected into the domains of all source images based on the user defined intrinsic and extrinsic parameters of the target view $\mathbf{K}_t$, $\mathbf{R}_t$, and $\mathbf{t}_t$ and the estimated intrinsic and extrinsic parameters of the source images $\{\mathbf{K}_n\}_{n=1}^{N}$, $\{\mathbf{R}_n\}_{n=1}^{N}$, and $\{\mathbf{t}_n\}_{n=1}^{N}$. For each source image, we count the number of pixels from the target view that are mapped to the valid source image domain and select the top K images that maximize that score. To further handle occlusions and other outliers in this process, we only count pixels where the projected target depth is within 1% of the source depth.

3.3 Mapping and Blending

Once we have selected the source images $\{I_k\}_{k=1}^{K}$, we need to map them into the novel target view and blend the information to an output image $\hat{I}_t$. For this purpose, we have developed a recurrent mapping and blending network. We first encode each source image via a U-Net based convolutional network [33]. The features are then mapped into the novel target view and sequentially processed by a blending network that is based on convolutional gated recurrent units (GRU) [7]. For each source image I_k, the blending network outputs per-pixel confidence values and a color image in the target view. The final image $\hat{I}_t$ is then generated by a soft-argmax over these confidence values and color images. Figure 3 provides an overview of the recurrent mapping and blending network.

Encoding Source Images. In the first part of the mapping and blending network, we encode each source image I_k with a U-Net based convolutional network. The encoder of the U-Net consists of the first three stages of an ImageNet pretrained VGG network [38] where we replaced the max-pooling with average pooling layers. In the decoder of the U-Net, we upsample the output features of the previous stage using nearest-neighbor interpolation, concatenate them with the encoder output of the same resolution, and process this by two additional convolutional layers. All convolutional layers are followed by a ReLU [28].

Mapping into the Target View. The encoded source images must then be mapped into the target view. For this, we rely on the depth map in the target view D_t that is derived from the proxy geometry $\mathcal{M}$. We can gather the feature vectors from the source views via a warping operation $W_k(D_t)$. For a pixel in homogeneous coordinates $\mathbf{u}_t$ in the target view, we select the feature vector in the source image k at the location $\mathbf{u}_k = \mathbf{K}_k(\mathbf{R}_r D_t(\mathbf{u}_t)\mathbf{K}_t^{-1}\mathbf{u}_t + \mathbf{t}_r)$, with relative rotation $\mathbf{R}_r = \mathbf{R}_k \mathbf{R}_t^T$ and relative translation $\mathbf{t}_r = \mathbf{t}_s - \mathbf{R}_r \mathbf{t}_t$. As the locations $\mathbf{u}_k$ will not be located at the center of the pixel in general, we bilinearly interpolate the features in the warping. Further, in several cases $\mathbf{u}_k$ will not be inside the source image domain. In those instances, we set the warped feature to zero and additionally indicate those locations in a mask that is concatenated to the warped features. A major problem with the proxy geometry is that several areas do not have associated depth values, especially structures that are far away, or the sky. To alleviate this problem, we warp features that do not have a valid depth value associated using $+\infty$ as depth value and also concatenate a mask that indicates those features. This greatly reduces artifacts in the background.

Blending. At this point, we have the feature maps of K source images warped into the target view and now we need to aggregate the information to obtain a single blended output image I_t. A suitable network structure for this kind of problem is a recurrent architecture. More specifically, we utilize a U-Net based convolutional architecture with gated recurrent units (GRU) [7] that regularizes and blends the source feature maps along the spatial dimensions and across the source views. In principle, all convolutional layers of the blending network can be replaced by a convolutional GRU. However, we observed that just replacing the last convolutional layer per stage in the encoder, and the first convolutional layer per stage in the decoder works as well and decreases the time needed for training and evaluation of the overall network. For each source image I_k, the blending decoder outputs confidence values C_k and color information $\hat{I}_{t_k}$ per pixel in the target view. The final output $\hat{I}_t$ is then generated by a soft-

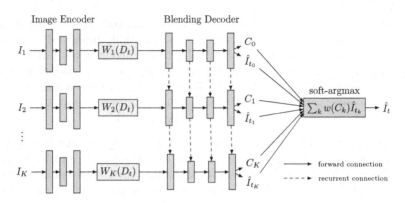

Fig. 3. Overview of the recurrent mapping and blending network. The input is a set of source images $\{I_k\}_{k=1}^{K}$ that are first encoded by a shared convolutional network, the *image encoder*. We map the resulting features into the target view using the depth map D_t, derived from the proxy geometry $\mathcal{M}$. The features are then aggregated by a recurrent network, the *blending decoder*. For each input image I_k, we output a confidence image C_k and a color image $\hat{I}_{t_k}$, which are then aggregated to a final output $\hat{I}_t$ via a soft-argmax using $w(C_k) = \exp(C_k)/\sum_j \exp(C_j)$.

argmax $\hat{I}_t = \sum_k w(C_k)\hat{I}_{t_k}$, where w are weights computed by a softmax over the confidence values.

Training. To train the mapping and blending network we require a supervision signal. We use a natural setup [12,15,43]: sample one of the source images, withhold it, and use it as ground-truth I_t.

As training loss we utilize the perceptual loss of Chen and Koltun [5]. Given our estimated image $\hat{I}_t$ and the ground-truth target I_t, the loss is

$$\mathcal{L}(\hat{I}_t, I_t) = ||\hat{I}_t - I_t||_1 + \sum_l \lambda_l ||\phi_l(\hat{I}) - \phi_l(I_t)||_1, \qquad (1)$$

where ϕ_l are the outputs of the layers 'conv1_2', 'conv2_2', 'conv3_2', 'conv4_2', and 'conv5_2' of a pretrained VGG-19 network [38]. The weighting coefficients $\{\lambda_l\}_{l=1}^{5}$ are set as in [5].

We use ADAM [20] with a learning rate of 10^{-4} and set $\beta_1 = 0.9$, $\beta_2 = 0.9999$, and $\epsilon = 10^{-8}$ to train the recurrent mapping and blending network. We train the model for 450,000 iterations with a batch size of 1.

Acceleration. The recurrent nature of our mapping and blending network allows the integration of an arbitrary number of source images with a low memory footprint. To further speed up processing, we precompute the feature embeddings of the source images. This avoids the repeated encoding of the source images for different synthesized views.

Table 1. Evaluation of architectural choices on the Tanks and Temples dataset. (Leave-one-out protocol.) See the text for a detailed description of the conditions.

	Truck			Train			M60			Playground		
	↓LPIPS	↑SSIM	↑PSNR	↓LPIPS	↑SSIM	↑PSNR	↓LPIPS	↑SSIM	↑PSNR	↓LPIPS	↑SSIM	↑PSNR
Fixed Identity	0.116	0.819	21.22	0.201	0.751	18.53	0.110	0.871	22.67	0.119	0.824	22.38
Fixed Encoding	0.096	0.828	21.19	0.168	0.769	19.01	0.096	0.876	22.80	0.107	0.831	22.40
Cat Global Avg.	0.089	0.842	21.49	0.175	0.773	18.73	0.093	0.887	23.41	0.098	0.845	22.92
Ours w/o Encoding	0.093	0.849	**22.13**	0.174	0.778	19.33	0.094	0.887	23.79	0.099	0.851	23.45
Ours w/o GRU	0.094	0.845	21.74	0.159	0.782	19.26	0.087	0.893	23.49	0.095	0.849	23.30
Ours w/o Masks	0.087	0.847	21.58	0.152	0.784	19.42	0.082	**0.897**	24.07	0.087	0.850	23.16
Ours w/o inf. depth	0.093	0.847	21.94	0.169	0.782	18.96	0.087	0.896	**24.08**	0.094	0.853	23.47
Ours w/o soft-argmax	0.091	0.845	21.74	0.159	0.786	19.43	0.086	0.891	23.79	0.090	0.857	23.50
Ours full	**0.082**	**0.852**	22.03	**0.147**	**0.794**	**19.54**	**0.081**	0.894	23.98	**0.084**	**0.859**	**23.51**

4 Experimental Evaluation

We first evaluate our design choices in controlled experiments and then compare to the state of the art. For each scene, we first run the COLMAP SfM pipeline [35] to get camera poses and a sparse reconstruction as described in Sect. 3.1. We also create a dense reconstruction of all models using MVS [34] and Delaunay-based surface reconstruction [18,23] as outlined in Sect. 3.1. To train the network we use the Tanks and Temples dataset [21]. We select 17 of the 21 scenes in the dataset for training and supervise the model by designating one image as the ground-truth target and using the remaining ones as source images. For testing we use scenes that are not included in our training set: *Truck, Train, M60,* and *Playground.* We chose these scenes for evaluation because the camera paths in these scenes were amenable to extraction of longer subsequences that can be withheld to evaluate significant deviations from the source images. Note that none of the images from the evaluation scenes have been seen during the training of our method. See Fig. 1 for a visualization of the target and source cameras for the *Truck* scene. For training, we downsample the images by scaling the image height and width by a factor of four each. We implemented our recurrent mapping and blending network in PyTorch [31].

In all of our evaluations, we report three different image metrics. We include PSNR and SSIM to evaluate low-level image differences. However, those metrics have only weak correlation with human perception [48]. Therefore, we also include the LPIPS metric, which is based on perceptual features in trained convolutional networks and was shown to better correlate with human perception [48].

Architectural Choices. In the first set of experiments we evaluate our architectural design choices. See Table 1 for an overview of the results on the Tanks and Temples test scenes. For these experiments, we also use the quarter resolution images for evaluation. This evaluation is conducted in the leave-one-out setting, i.e., we select each image per scene once as the unseen ground-truth target and utilize the other images as source images.

Our first baseline, *Fixed Identity*, is a network that is related to the one presented in [15]. It is a U-Net architecture with the same capacity as our blending network, but it receives as input a fixed number ($K = 4$) of mapped source images concatenated along the channel dimension and directly outputs the image

Table 2. Results on Tanks and Temples. (Whole sequences withheld.)

	Truck			Train			M60			Playground		
	↓LPIPS	↑SSIM	↑PSNR	↓LPIPS	↑SSIM	↑PSNR	↓LPIPS	↑SSIM	↑PSNR	↓LPIPS	↑SSIM	↑PSNR
EVS [8]	0.41	0.563	14.99	0.64	0.454	11.81	0.62	0.473	9.66	0.39	0.610	16.34
LLFF [26]	0.61	0.432	10.66	0.70	0.356	8.88	0.69	0.427	8.98	0.56	0.517	13.27
NeRF [27]	0.61	0.690	19.47	0.74	0.532	13.16	0.62	0.691	15.99	0.54	0.734	21.16
NPBG [2]	0.22	0.822	20.32	0.25	**0.801**	**18.08**	0.36	0.716	12.35	0.17	**0.876**	**23.03**
Our	**0.11**	**0.867**	**22.62**	**0.22**	0.758	17.90	**0.29**	**0.785**	**17.14**	**0.16**	0.837	22.03

in the target view. We use the same source image selection strategy as in our method. *Fixed Encoding* differs in that we use the same VGG-19 based encoding network prior to mapping as in our approach. *Cat Global Avg.* is the same architecture as our proposed one without recurrent units, but a global average concatenated to each blending head. We also ablate our recurrent mapping and blending architecture. *Ours w/o GRU* uses no GRU in the blending decoder. In *Ours w/o Encoding* we directly map the input images to the recurrent blending network, and in *Ours w/o Masks* we do not append the mapping masks to the blending network input. *Ours w/o inf. depth* does not set the invalid depth values in D_t to $+\infty$, and *Ours w/o soft-argmax* uses a single output head after the evaluation of the last blending decoder instead of the soft-argmax.

The results presented in Table 1 validate the design choices of our method. A clear advantage is the encoding of the source images before mapping and blending. We see an overall improvement for the fixed input architecture and our recurrent mapping and blending network. The difference between our results and the results of *Ours w/o GRU* and *Cat Global Avg.* also highlights the benefit of the recurrent network, i.e., propagating blending information between source images via a recurrent unit.

In Fig. 4 we evaluate the performance of our method with an increasing number of source images. We see that image fidelity improves with the number of source images up to 7 images and then saturates. Note that a higher number of source images is especially important if the novel view is farther away from the scene or object than any of the source images. In this setting, more source images are needed to cover the view frustum.

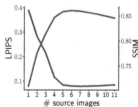

Fig. 4. The effect of increasing the number of source views.

Tanks and Temples. In this evaluation, we compare our approach to state-of-the-art methods on novel view sequences extracted from Tanks and Temples [21]. As we want to evaluate novel view synthesis from unstructured source images, we manually select a subset of camera poses from the test scenes as targets that we want to reconstruct. These target images are taken out of the dataset and only serve as ground truth for evaluation of our synthesized results. The scenes we use for evaluation have never been seen during the training of our method. An example of the setup for the *Truck* scene is depicted in Fig. 1.

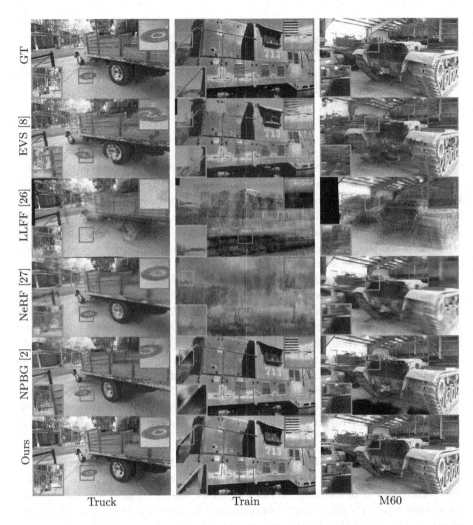

Fig. 5. Qualitative results on Tanks and Temples. (Whole sequences withheld.)

We compare our method to two recent state-of-the-art and two concurrent methods. Extreme View Synthesis (*EVS*) [8] mainly focuses on extreme stereo baseline magnification and utilizes the multi-view stereo network MVSNet [46]. Specifically, it warps the 3D feature volumes of the source images into the target view and fuses them. We utilize the code provided by the authors and as no training code is available, we also apply the pretrained model that is provided. Local Light Field Fusion (*LLFF*) [26] is based on the multi-plane image idea and assumes that the poses of the source images lie on a plane. For this method as well, we use the code provided by the authors and the provided pretrained model weights as no training code is available.

Fig. 6. Qualitative results on new recordings.

We also compare to Neural Radiance Fields (*NeRF*), which is concurrent work that is published alongside ours [27]. Finally, we benchmark Neural Point-Based Graphics (*NPBG*), which is likewise a concurrent publication [2]. We train the descriptors per 3D point and fine-tune the provided rendering network per scene, utilizing the available code. Note that *NeRF* and *NPBG* have to be trained on the test scenes, whereas our approach does not need any adaptation or fine-tuning on new scenes.

Quantitative results are summarized in Table 2 and qualitative results are shown in Fig. 5 and the supplementary video. *LLFF* clearly fails in this challenging unstructured setting: The assumptions of *LLFF* are not met, which leads to strong ghosting artifacts. *EVS* works better, but often fails on fine details and sometimes misses whole parts of the image, although we used the very same set of source images as input as we selected for our method. The latter artifacts are the main reason for the low quantitative performance of *EVS*. *NeRF* struggles on the Tanks and Temples scenes. The results are either blurry or fail completely, for example on the *Train* scene. *NPBG* produces good images that are competitive with ours. Our method produces sharp details and is superior to all other methods is terms of the LPIPS metric.

New Recordings. We also evaluate the presented method on new recordings that stress the unstructured setting. We use a handheld camera in natural motion and record videos of different scenes to extract source images. We then record each scene again to gather ground-truth data for new target views. Results are shown in Fig. 6 and the supplementary video.

DTU. We now compare our method to state-of-the-art alternatives in a more constrained view interpolation and extrapolation setting. For this we use the DTU dataset [1], which includes over 100 tabletop scenes. The image poses are identical for all scenes, as the camera has been mounted on a robotic arm and the views roughly cover an octant of a sphere. Figure 7 visualizes the poses.

Fig. 7. DTU evaluation setup. Gray cameras denote the source views. Green and blue cameras denote interpolation and extrapolation poses, respectively.

Of the 49 camera poses we selected 10 as targets for novel view synthesis and used the rest as source images. We test the view extrapolation capabilities of all methods by having four target views on the corners of the camera grid. Interpolation is tested on 6 center views. We use the object masks for scenes 65, 106, and 118, which are provided by [29] for all source images.

Table 3. Quantitative results on the DTU dataset. Numbers on the left are for view interpolation, numbers on the right are for extrapolation.

	Scan 65			Scan 106			Scan 118		
	↓LPIPS	↑SSIM	↑PSNR	↓LPIPS	↑SSIM	↑PSNR	↓LPIPS	↑SSIM	↑PSNR
EVS [8]	0.61/0.53	0.938/0.917	23.07/21.23	0.75/0.53	0.903/0.880	19.95/18.62	0.47/0.42	0.931/0.911	23.00/20.47
LLFF [26]	0.51/0.44	0.939/0.926	22.44/22.04	0.61/0.39	0.907/0.893	24.08/24.61	0.47/0.30	0.932/0.929	28.95/27.40
NeRF [27]	**0.17**/0.32	**0.987/0.963**	**34.41/27.81**	0.36/0.40	**0.973**/0.931	**34.52**/24.36	0.24/0.27	**0.985/0.952**	**37.16/28.39**
NPBG [2]	0.82/0.96	0.896/0.839	17.77/15.59	0.94/0.53	0.856/0.879	20.70/22.54	0.74/0.41	0.876/0.905	24.10/24.97
Our	0.25/**0.30**	0.972/0.950	26.96/24.08	**0.25/0.26**	0.963/**0.938**	27.24/**24.63**	**0.16/0.20**	0.975/0.951	29.21/25.75

We summarize the quantitative results in Table 3. Qualitative results are shown in Fig. 8 and the supplementary video. We notice blending artifacts in the images produced by *EVS* [8], which are reflected in the lower quantitative performance. On the other hand, the results of *LLFF* [26] and especially of *NeRF* [27] are clearly better compared to their performance on Tanks and Temples. This comes as no surprise because the DTU setup is much closer to the basic assumptions of these methods: the scene is a clearly bounded object and the camera poses are densely and regularly sampled by the source views. *NPBG* [2] struggles in this setting and often intermixes background and foreground. In contrast, our method yields sharp results, including in the extrapolation setting, and performs reasonable inpainting when geometry is missing. Note that the illumination varies with the viewing direction in DTU scenes. While we are still able to synthesize realistic results, low-level metrics such as PSNR are not very reliable.

Limitations. While our method is a clear step forward compared to prior work, it has limitations. The first limitation is apparent when we examine videos rendered from a sequence of new views. We only synthesize images frame-by-frame and do not enforce any temporal consistency. Thus synthesized videos exhibit

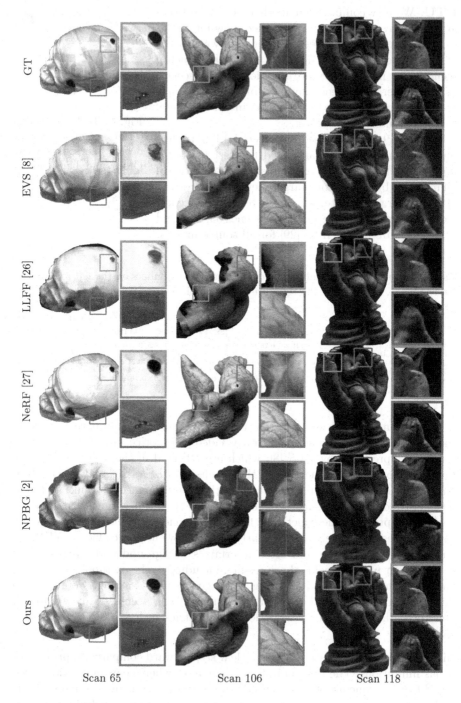

Fig. 8. View extrapolation results on the DTU dataset.

temporal instability. The second limitation stems from the use of proxy 3D geometry. If the 3D model used for mapping misses large parts of the scene or has gross outliers, our pipeline will produce visible artifacts. The flip side is that our approach can directly benefit from future improvements in SfM and MVS pipelines [21].

5   Conclusion

We presented a method for novel view synthesis in the challenging setting of unstructured input images acquired by natural motion through the scene. After preprocessing the input using standard SfM and MVS to get camera parameters and 3D proxy geometry, we showed that a recurrent mapping and blending architecture can produce sharp images for new views of the scene that depart significantly from the input. The recurrent architecture enables using an arbitrary number of source images per target view, which mostly eliminates the need for hand-crafted heuristics for source image selection and demonstrably helps in the unstructured setting. In future work, we plan to improve temporal consistency. We also expect that the results of our method will continue to improve as new techniques for SfM, MVS, and surface reconstruction are introduced.

Acknowledgements. We thank Kai Zhang for the evaluation of NeRF.

References

1. Aanæs, H., Jensen, R.R., Vogiatzis, G., Tola, E., Dahl, A.B.: Large-scale data for multiple-view stereopsis. Int. J. Comput. Vis. (IJCV) **120**(2), 153–168 (2016). https://doi.org/10.1007/s11263-016-0902-9
2. Aliev, K.A., Sevastopolsky, A., Kolos, M., Ulyanov, D., Lempitsky, V.: Neural point-based graphics. In: European Conference on Computer Vision (ECCV) (2020)
3. Buehler, C., Bosse, M., McMillan, L., Gortler, S., Cohen, M.: Unstructured lumigraph rendering. In: ACM Transactions on Graphics (SIGGRAPH). ACM (2001)
4. Chaurasia, G., Duchene, S., Sorkine-Hornung, O., Drettakis, G.: Depth synthesis and local warps for plausible image-based navigation. ACM Trans. Graph. (SIGGRAPH) **32**(3), 1–12 (2013)
5. Chen, Q., Koltun, V.: Photographic image synthesis with cascaded refinement networks. In: International Conference on Computer Vision (ICCV) (2017)
6. Chen, S.E., Williams, L.: View interpolation for image synthesis. In: ACM Transactions on Graphics (SIGGRAPH) (1993)
7. Cho, K., et al.: Learning phrase representations using RNN encoder-decoder for statistical machine translation. In: Empirical Methods in Natural Language Processing (EMNLP) (2014)
8. Choi, I., Gallo, O., Troccoli, A., Kim, M.H., Kautz, J.: Extreme view synthesis. In: International Conference on Computer Vision (ICCV) (2019)
9. Collins, R.T.: A space-sweep approach to true multi-image matching. In: Computer Vision and Pattern Recognition (CVPR) (1996)

10. Davis, A., Levoy, M., Durand, F.: Unstructured light fields. In: Computer Graphics Forum, vol. 31 (2012)
11. Debevec, P.E., Taylor, C.J., Malik, J.: Modeling and rendering architecture from photographs: a hybrid geometry-and image-based approach. In: ACM Transactions on Graphics (SIGGRAPH) (1996)
12. Flynn, J., et al.: DeepView: view synthesis with learned gradient descent. In: Computer Vision and Pattern Recognition (CVPR) (2019)
13. Flynn, J., Neulander, I., Philbin, J., Snavely, N.: DeepStereo: learning to predict new views from the world's imagery. In: Computer Vision and Pattern Recognition (CVPR) (2016)
14. Gortler, S.J., Grzeszczuk, R., Szeliski, R., Cohen, M.F.: The lumigraph. ACM Trans. Graph. (SIGGRAPH) **96**, 30 (1996)
15. Hedman, P., Philip, J., Price, T., Frahm, J.M., Drettakis, G., Brostow, G.: Deep blending for free-viewpoint image-based rendering. ACM Trans. Graph. (SIGGRAPH Asia) **37**(6), 1–15 (2018)
16. Hedman, P., Ritschel, T., Drettakis, G., Brostow, G.: Scalable inside-out image-based rendering. ACM Trans. Graph. (SIGGRAPH Asia) **35**(6), 1–11 (2016)
17. Heigl, B., Koch, R., Pollefeys, M., Denzler, J., Van Gool, L.: Plenoptic modeling and rendering from image sequences taken by a hand held camera. In: German Conference on Pattern Recognition (GCPR) (1999)
18. Jancosek, M., Pajdla, T.: Multi-view reconstruction preserving weakly-supported surfaces. In: Computer Vision and Pattern Recognition (CVPR) (2011)
19. Kalantari, N.K., Wang, T.C., Ramamoorthi, R.: Learning-based view synthesis for light field cameras. ACM Trans. Graph. (SIGGRAPH) **35**(6), 1–10 (2016)
20. Kingma, D.P., Ba, J.: Adam: a method for stochastic optimization. In: International Conference on Learning Representations (ICLR) (2015)
21. Knapitsch, A., Park, J., Zhou, Q.Y., Koltun, V.: Tanks and Temples: benchmarking large-scale scene reconstruction. ACM Trans. Graph. (SIGGRAPH) **36**(4), 1–13 (2017)
22. Kopf, J., Cohen, M.F., Szeliski, R.: First-person hyper-lapse videos. ACM Trans. Graph. (SIGGRAPH) **33**(4), 1–10 (2014)
23. Labatut, P., Pons, J.P., Keriven, R.: Efficient multi-view reconstruction of large-scale scenes using interest points, delaunay triangulation and graph cuts. In: International Conference on Computer Vision (ICCV) (2007)
24. Levoy, M., Hanrahan, P.: Light field rendering. In: ACM Transactions on Graphics (SIGGRAPH) (1996)
25. Lombardi, S., Simon, T., Saragih, J., Schwartz, G., Lehrmann, A., Sheikh, Y.: Neural volumes: learning dynamic renderable volumes from images. ACM Trans. Graph. (SIGGRAPH) **38**(4) (2019)
26. Mildenhall, B., et al.: Local light field fusion: practical view synthesis with prescriptive sampling guidelines. ACM Trans. Graph. (SIGGRAPH) **38**(4), 1–14 (2019)
27. Mildenhall, B., Srinivasan, P.P., Tancik, M., Barron, J.T., Ramamoorthi, R., Ng, R.: NeRF: representing scenes as neural radiance fields for view synthesis. In: European Conference on Computer Vision (ECCV) (2020)
28. Nair, V., Hinton, G.E.: Rectified linear units improve restricted boltzmann machines. In: International Conference on Machine Learning (ICML) (2010)
29. Niemeyer, M., Mescheder, L., Oechsle, M., Geiger, A.: Differentiable volumetric rendering: learning implicit 3D representations without 3D supervision. In: Computer Vision and Pattern Recognition (CVPR) (2020)
30. Niklaus, S., Mai, L., Yang, J., Liu, F.: 3D ken burns effect from a single image. ACM Trans. Graph. (SIGGRAPH Asia) **38**(6), 1–15 (2019)

31. Paszke, A., et al.: PyTorch: an imperative style. In: Neural Information Processing Systems, High-Performance Deep Learning Library (2019)
32. Penner, E., Zhang, L.: Soft 3D reconstruction for view synthesis. ACM Trans. Graph. (SIGGRAPH) **36**(6), 1–11 (2017)
33. Ronneberger, O., Fischer, P., Brox, T.: U-Net: convolutional networks for biomedical image segmentation. In: Navab, N., Hornegger, J., Wells, W.M., Frangi, A.F. (eds.) MICCAI 2015. LNCS, vol. 9351, pp. 234–241. Springer, Cham (2015). https://doi.org/10.1007/978-3-319-24574-4_28
34. Schönberger, J.L., Zheng, E., Frahm, J.M., Pollefeys, M.: Pixelwise view selection for unstructured multi-view stereo. In: Leibe, B., Matas, J., Sebe, N., Welling, M. (eds.) ECCV 2016. LNCS, vol. 9907, pp. 501–518. Springer, Cham (2016). https://doi.org/10.1007/978-3-319-46487-9_31
35. Schönberger, J.L., Frahm, J.M.: Structure-from-motion revisited. In: Computer Vision and Pattern Recognition (CVPR) (2016)
36. Seitz, S.M., Dyer, C.R.: View morphing. In: ACM Transactions on Graphics (SIGGRAPH) (1996)
37. Shum, H., Kang, S.B.: Review of image-based rendering techniques. In: Visual Communications and Image Processing (2000)
38. Simonyan, K., Zisserman, A.: Very deep convolutional networks for large-scale image recognition. In: International Conference on Learning Representations (ICLR) (2015)
39. Sitzmann, V., Thies, J., Heide, F., Nießner, M., Wetzstein, G., Zollhöfer, M.: Deepvoxels: learning persistent 3d feature embeddings. In: Computer Vision and Pattern Recognition (CVPR) (2019)
40. Sitzmann, V., Zollhöfer, M., Wetzstein, G.: Scene representation networks: continuous 3D-structure-aware neural scene representations. In: Neural Information Processing Systems (2019)
41. Srinivasan, P.P., Tucker, R., Barron, J.T., Ramamoorthi, R., Ng, R., Snavely, N.: Pushing the boundaries of view extrapolation with multiplane images. In: Computer Vision and Pattern Recognition (CVPR) (2019)
42. Thies, J., Zollhöfer, M., Nießner, M.: Deferred neural rendering: image synthesis using neural textures. ACM Trans. Graph. (SIGGRAPH) **38**(4), 1–12 (2019)
43. Thies, J., Zollhöfer, M., Theobalt, C., Stamminger, M., Nießner, M.: Image-guided neural object rendering. In: International Conference on Learning Representations (ICLR) (2020)
44. Wiles, O., Gkioxari, G., Szeliski, R., Johnson, J.: SynSin: end-to-end view synthesis from a single image. In: Computer Vision and Pattern Recognition (CVPR) (2020)
45. Xu, Z., Bi, S., Sunkavalli, K., Hadap, S., Su, H., Ramamoorthi, R.: Deep view synthesis from sparse photometric images. ACM Trans. Graph. (SIGGRAPH) **38**(4), 1–13 (2019)
46. Yao, Y., Luo, Z., Li, S., Fang, T., Quan, L.: MVSNet: depth inference for unstructured multi-view stereo. In: European Conference on Computer Vision (ECCV) (2018)
47. Yao, Y., Luo, Z., Li, S., Shen, T., Fang, T., Quan, L.: Recurrent MVSNet for high-resolution multi-view stereo depth inference. In: Computer Vision and Pattern Recognition (CVPR) (2019)
48. Zhang, R., Isola, P., Efros, A.A., Shechtman, E., Wang, O.: The unreasonable effectiveness of deep features as a perceptual metric. In: Computer Vision and Pattern Recognition (CVPR) (2018)

49. Zhou, T., Tucker, R., Flynn, J., Fyffe, G., Snavely, N.: Stereo magnification: learning view synthesis using multiplane images. ACM Trans. Graph. (SIGGRAPH) **37**(4) (2018)
50. Zitnick, C.L., Kang, S.B., Uyttendaele, M., Winder, S., Szeliski, R.: High-quality video view interpolation using a layered representation. ACM Trans. Graph. (SIGGRAPH) **23**(3), 600–608 (2004)

Face Anti-Spoofing via Disentangled Representation Learning

Ke-Yue Zhang[1,2], Taiping Yao[2], Jian Zhang[2], Ying Tai[2(✉)], Shouhong Ding[2], Jilin Li[2], Feiyue Huang[2], Haichuan Song[1], and Lizhuang Ma[1]

[1] East China Normal University, Shanghai, China
51184501178@stu.ecnu.edu.cn, hcsong@cs.ecnu.edu.cn, lzma@sei.ecnu.edu.cn
[2] Youtu Lab, Tencent, Shanghai, China
{taipingyao,timmmyzhang,yingtai,ericshding,jerolinli,
garyhuang}@tencent.com

Abstract. Face anti-spoofing is crucial to security of face recognition systems. Previous approaches focus on developing discriminative models based on the features extracted from images, which may be still entangled between spoof patterns and real persons. In this paper, motivated by the disentangled representation learning, we propose a novel perspective of face anti-spoofing that disentangles the liveness features and content features from images, and the liveness features is further used for classification. We also put forward a Convolutional Neural Network (CNN) architecture with the process of disentanglement and combination of low-level and high-level supervision to improve the generalization capabilities. We evaluate our method on public benchmark datasets and extensive experimental results demonstrate the effectiveness of our method against the state-of-the-art competitors. Finally, we further visualize some results to help understand the effect and advantage of disentanglement.

Keywords: Face anti-spoofing · Generative model · Disentangled representation

1 Introduction

With superior performance than human, face recognition techniques are widely used in smart devices, access control and security scenarios. However, the associated safety issues raise concern of public since the accessment of human face is low-cost and a well-designed makeup can easily fool this biometric mechanism. These face spoofs, also called Presentation Attacks (PA), vary from simpler printed facial images, video replays to more complicated 3D mask and facial

---

K. Zhang and T. Yao—Equal Contribution.

Electronic supplementary material The online version of this chapter (https://doi.org/10.1007/978-3-030-58529-7_38) contains supplementary material, which is available to authorized users.

A. Vedaldi et al. (Eds.): ECCV 2020, LNCS 12364, pp. 641–657, 2020.
https://doi.org/10.1007/978-3-030-58529-7_38

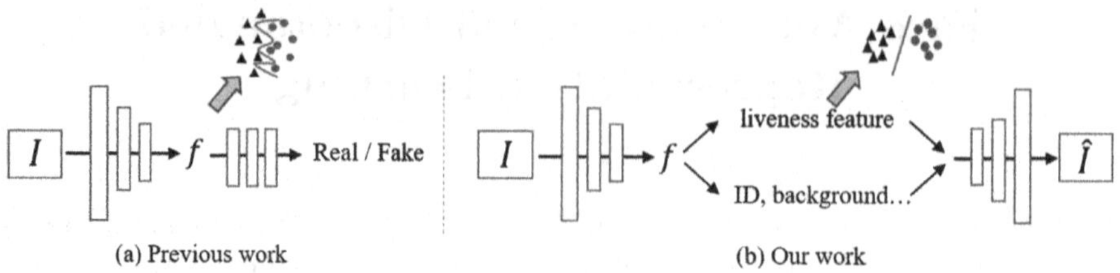

(a) Previous work   (b) Our work

Fig. 1. Comparison between previous entangled framework and our disentangled framework. Previous works learn entangled features which are easily overfitting to the training dataset. In contrast, our disentangled framework distills the liveness features with proper constraints and supervision.

cosmetic makeup. Theoretically, face recognition systems are vulnerable to all spoofs without specific defense, which incurs malicious attacks of hackers, but also encourages the boosting of robust face anti-spoofing algorithm.

Since the primary facial spoof images or videos contain artifacts, researchers put forward several methods based on texture analysis. Some handcrafted features are combined with anti-spoofing algorithms, such as Local Binary Pattern(LBP) [6,14,15,27], Histogram of Oriented Gridients(HOG) [21,41], Scale Invariant Feature Transform(SIFT) [30], *etc.* These cue-based methods use handcrafted features to detect the motion cues such as lip movement or eye blinking for authentication. However, these methods couldn't deal with the replay attacks with high-fidelity. Recently, Convolutional Neural Network(CNN)-based methods have achieved great progress in face anti-spoofing [23,29,40]. Basically, these methods treat the security issue as a binary classification problem with softmax loss. However, they are lack of generalization capability for overfitting on the training dataset. Despite many methods use auxiliary information (*i.e.*, facial depth map, rppg signals, *etc.*) to further guide the network in telling the difference between real and spoof [18,19,24], these pre-defined characteristics are still insufficient for depicting the authentic abstract spoof patterns since exhausting all possible constraints is impossible.

Thus the crucial step of face anti-spoofing does not lie in how to precisely pre-define the spoof patterns, but how to achieve the spoof patterns from high-dimensional extracted representations. One possible solution is disentangling representations into separate parts. In disentangle learning [17,38], it's a consensus that high-dimensional data can be explained by substantially lower dimensional and semantically meaningful latent representation variables. While in face anti-spoofing, the spoof patterns can be viewed as one kind of attributes of face, not just a certain irrelevant noise type or the combination. Hence, the problem is transformed into how we can directly target to the liveness information from all the variations of facial images.

As shown in Fig. 1, we propose a novel disentangled face anti-spoofing technique via separating the latent representation. Motivated by [17], we assume the latent space of facial images can be decomposed into two sub-spaces: liveness space and content space. Liveness features corresponds to the liveness-related information, while content features integrate remaining liveness-irrelated information in the input images, such as ID and lighting. However, in disentangled learning procedure, there exist two challenges on missing 1) corresponding genuine images for spoof images in translation process and vice versa, 2) clear research about properties of liveness features in face anti-spoofing literature.

To tackle above challenges, we introduce low-level texture and high-level depth characteristics to further facilitate disentanglement. For the first challenge, we adopt a Generative Adversarial Network(GAN)-like discriminator to guarantee the plausibility of the translated images. An auxiliary depth estimator is then introduced to ensure that the liveness information has also been exchanged between genuine and spoof images. For the second challenge, checking the properties of liveness features is equivalent to making liveness and content features independent in disentangled framework. In order to spilt liveness and content space, we encode the translated images to get reconstructed liveness features again. With bidirectional reconstruction loss on images and latent codes, liveness features of diverse spoof patterns are thoroughly extracted in a self-supervised way. To further regularize liveness space, we introduce a novel LBP map supervision. Finally, the spoof classification could be solved in a smaller and more discriminative liveness feature space. Hence, our architecture is more likely to achieve good generalization capability.

To sum up, the contributions of this work are three-fold:

- We address face anti-spoofing via disentangled representation learning, which separates latent representation into liveness features and content features.
- We combine low-level texture and high-level depth characteristics to regularize liveness space, which facilitates disentangled representation learning.
- Abundant experiments and visualizations are presented to reveal the properties of liveness features, which demonstrates the effectiveness of our method against the state-of-the-art competitors.

2   Related Work

Our method introduces disentangled representation learning to solve face anti-spoofing. Previous related work lies in two perspectives: face anti-spoofing and attributes disentanglement.

Face Anti-spoofing. Early researches focused on hand-crafted feature descriptors, such as LBP [6,14,15,27], HOG [21,41], SIFT [30] and SURF [7], to project the faces into a low-dimension feature space, where traditional classifiers such as SVM are utilized for judgement. There are also some methods using information from different domains, such as HSV and YCrCb color space [6,8], temporal domain [2,12,34,39], and Fourier spectrum [22]. However, these hand-crafted feature-based methods cannot achieve high accuracy due to limited representation capacity.

With the rise of deep learning, researchers attempted to tackle the face anti-spoofing with CNN-based features. Initially, [23,29,40] treated the task as a binary classification problem with softmax loss. Compared to hand-crafted features, such models gained higher accuracy in intra-testing settings. However, due to the overfitting on training data, their generalization ability are relatively poor. In order to improve the generalization ability, many methods attempted to utilize auxiliary supervision to guide networks. [24] attempted to guide networks with auxiliary supervision of facial depth information and remote-photoplethysmo-graphy (r-ppg) signal. [18] utilized the spoof images to estimate the spoofing-relevant noise pattern. [33] adopted the strategy of domain generalization to achieve improvements in cross-testing. These auxiliary supervision indeed improve generalization. However these methods all handle this problem in the whole feature space, which is disturbed by irrelevant factors.

Disentangled Representation. The key intuition about disentangling is that disentangled representation could factorize the data into distinct informative factors of variations [25]. [10,16] aimed to learn disentangled representations without supervision. [38] divided latent features of an facial image into different parts, where each part encodes a single attribute. [17] assumed that latent space of images can be decomposed into a content space and a style space.

These works inspire us decompose the features of an facial image into content features and liveness features. In face anti-spoofing, content features correspond to the liveness-irrelated information in the images, such as ID, background, Scene lighting, *etc.* On the contrary, liveness features are the key to distinguishing between real persons and attacks. Obviously, we could tackle the face anti-spoofing in the liveness feature space. However, there are many challenges in disentangled learning procedure, such as without the ground truth of the recombined images, diverse styles of spoof, *etc.* In this paper, we combine low-level texture and high-level depth characteristics to facilitate disentangled representation learning.

3   Disentanglement Framework

Our framework mainly consists of two parts: the disentanglement process and the auxiliary supervision. As the core component of our framework explained in Sect. 3.1, the disentanglement process separates the representation into two independent factors, which are liveness features and content features, respectively. As illustrated in Sect. 3.2, depth, texture, and discriminative constraints are utilized as auxiliary supervision. By introducing these three auxiliary nets, we consolidate liveness features and further facilitate the disentanglement process. Figure 2 illustrates the overview of our method and the entire learning process.

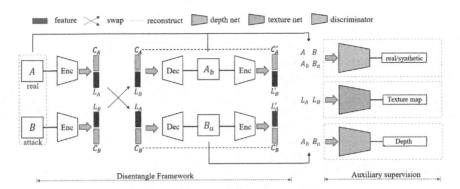

Fig. 2. Overview of our disentanglement framework. The features of an image are divided into two parts, content features and liveness features. By exchanging the liveness features of the real person and the attack, we can get different reconstructed images with the same content but their liveness attributes are changed. Texture net, depth net and discriminator are proposed to facilitate disentangled representation learning.

3.1 Disentanglement Process

Disentanglement process is designed to separate liveness features and content features by exchanging and recombining these two features. Inputs of the disentanglement part are two unpaired images A and B, where A is randomly chosen from live face images and B is chosen from spoof images. In the encoder part, we first use a convolution block to extract latent code Z from inputs. And then two independent convolutional sub-networks encode latent code Z into liveness features L and content features C respectively. This specific structure separates two features from convolving with each other. According to the above process, we can get L_A, C_A and L_B, C_B respectively by encoding images A, B. Then, we exchange the liveness part L_A and L_B to obtain images A_b and B_a.

$$A_b = Dec(C_A, L_B), B_a = Dec(C_B, L_A). \tag{1}$$

Because the liveness features determine the liveness attributes of the image, we suppose that A_b is a spoof version of image A, and B_a is a genuine version of image B. To better decode the latent code back into images, the architecture we used for the decoder is symmetrical with the encoder. Besides, following the U-Net [32] structure, the shortcuts are added from the middle layers in encoder to the corresponding layers in decoder to bring the original information as an auxiliary context for improving visual quality. To further guarantee that liveness information and content information can be split completely, we encode images A_b, B_a again to get C'_A, L'_B and C'_B, L'_A, and introduce a bidirectional reconstruction loss [17] to encourage reconstruction in two sequential processes (*i.e.*, from images to images and from latent features to latent features).

Table 1. The details of Auxiliary nets of our method.

LBP Net			Depth Net			Discriminator		
Layer	Chan./Stri	Out.Size	Layer	Chan./Stri	Out.Size	Layer	Chan./Stri	Out.Size
Input:liveness features			**Input:image**			**Input:image**		
			Conv2-0	64/1	256			
Conv1-0	384/1	32	Conv2-1	128/1	256	Conv3-1	64/1	256
			Conv2-2	196/1	256	Pool3-1	-/2	128
			Conv2-3	128/1	256			
			Pool2-1	-/2	128			
Conv1-1	128/1	32	Conv2-4	128/1	128	Conv3-2	128/1	128
			Conv2-5	196/1	128	Pool3-2	-/2	64
			Conv2-6	128/1	128			
			Pool2-2	-/2	64			
Conv1-2	64/1	32	Conv2-7	128/1	64	Conv3-3	256/1	64
			Conv2-8	196/1	64	Pool3-3	-/2	32
			Conv2-9	128/1	64			
			Pool2-3	-/2	32			
conv1-2			pool2-1+pool2-2+pool2-3			vectorize		
			Conv2-10	128/1	32			
			Conv2-11	64/1	32			
Conv1-3	1/1	32	Conv2-12	1/1	32	Fc3-1	1/1	2

Image Reconstruction. The combination of the encoder and decoder should be capable of reconstructing any image x_i from the datasets:

$$\mathcal{L}_{x_i}^{rec} = \mathbb{E}_{x_i \sim p(x_i)} \left\| D(E(x_i)) - x_i \right\|_1, \tag{2}$$

where $p(x_i)$ is the distribution of original images in the datasets, E is the encoder and D is the decoder.

Latent Reconstruction. Given a pair of liveness features and content features at translation time, we should be able to reconstruct it after decoding and encoding.

$$\mathcal{L}_{z_i}^{rec} = \mathbb{E}_{z_i \sim q(z_i)} \left\| E(D(z_i)) - z_i \right\|_1 \tag{3}$$

where z_i is the combination of liveness features L_i and content features C_i, and $q(z_i)$ is the distribution of latent code.

3.2   Auxiliary Supervision

In this section, we introduce three auxiliary supervision: LBP map, depth map and discrimination supervision, which promote the disentanglement process collaboratively. Discrimination supervision ensures the visual quality of generated image. Depth and LBP supervision are plugged into different parts to guarantee the generated image being in correct category when their liveness features are exchanged. The LBP map and depth map together regularize the liveness feature space, making it the key factor to distinguish between real persons and spoof patterns. The detailed structure of three auxiliary nets are illustrated in Table 1. Each convolutional layer is followed by a batch normalization layer and a Rectified Linear Unit (ReLU) activation function with 3×3 kernel size.

Texture Auxiliary Supervision. Liveness features are the essential characteristic of a face image, which determine the liveness categories of the image. Thus when swapping liveness features between a real person and an attack, categories of images and estimated depth maps should be changed simultaneously. And the estimated depth map is usually considered to be related to factors such as facial lighting and shadows, which are contained in the texture information of the face. What's more, previous works have proven that texture is an important clue in face anti-spoofing. Therefore, LBP map is adopted to regularize the liveness features in disentanglement framework. Although LBP features contain some additional information, proposed disentanglement framework utilize Latent Reconstruction Loss to constrain liveness features to learn only essential information. To make the features distinctive, for the genuine faces, we use the LBP map extracted by the algorithm in [1] as texture supervision. While for the spoof face, a zero map serves as the ground truth.

$$\mathcal{L}_{lbp} = \mathbb{E}_{l_i \sim P(l_i), x_i \sim P(x_i)} \left\| LBP(l_i) - lbp_{x_i} \right\|_1 \\ + \mathbb{E}_{l_i \sim N(l_i), x_i \sim N(x_i)} \left\| LBP(l_i) - \mathbf{0} \right\|_1 \tag{4}$$

where LBP is the LBP Estimator Net, $P(x_i)$ is the distribution of live face images in the datasets, $P(l_i)$ is the distribution of liveness space of live face images, $N(x_i)$ is the distribution of spoof images in the datasets, $N(l_i)$ is the distribution of liveness space of spoof images, lbp_{x_i} means the lbp map of live face images x_i and $\mathbf{0}$ means the zero maps for spoof images.

Depth Supervision. Depth map is commonly used as an auxiliary supervision in face anti-spoofing tasks. In our disentanglement framework, we combine LBP map and depth map supervision to regularize the liveness feature space. Similarly as LBP branch, we use pseudo-depth as ground truth for live face images and zero map for spoof images. The pseudo-depth is estimated by the 3D face alignment algorithm in [13]. During training stage, depth net only provides the supervision and does not update parameters. Since the reconstructed images A' and generated B_a are live images, and the reconstructed images B' and generated A_b are spoof images, the corresponding depth map of above images should be the depth of the face in images A, B and two zero maps. Then the loss of depth is formulated as:

$$\mathcal{L}_{dep} = \mathbb{E}_{x_i \sim N(x_i)} \left\| Dep(x_i) - \mathbf{0} \right\|_1 + \mathbb{E}_{x_i \sim P(x_i)} \left\| Dep(x_i) - dep_{x_i} \right\|_1 \tag{5}$$

where Dep is the parameters fixed depth net, $P(x_i)$ is the distribution of live face images, $N(x_i)$ is the distribution of spoof images, dep_{x_i} is the depth map of live face images x_i and $\mathbf{0}$ means the zero maps for spoof images correspondingly.

Discriminative Supervision. For ensuring the visual plausibility of generated images, we apply discriminative supervision on the generated images. Discriminative supervision is used for distinguishing between the generated images (A', B', A_b, B_a) and the original images (A, B). At the same time, disentanglement framework aims to produce plausible images which would be classified as non-synthetic images under discriminative supervision. Nevertheless, the receptive field of a single discriminator is limited for large images. We use multi-scale discriminators [36] to address this problem. Specifically, we deploy two identical discriminators with varied input resolution. The discriminator with a larger input scale is denoted as D_1, which guides the disentanglement net to generate finer details. And the other discriminator with a smaller input scale is denoted as D_2, which guides the disentanglement net to preserve more global information. In the training process, there are two consecutive steps in each iteration. In the first step, we fix disentanglement net and update the discriminator,

$$
\begin{aligned}
\mathcal{L}_D^{Dis} = &- \mathbb{E}_{I \in R} log(D_1(I)) - \mathbb{E}_{I \in G} log(1 - D_1(I)) \\
&- \mathbb{E}_{I \in R} log(D_2(I)) - \mathbb{E}_{I \in G} log(1 - D_2(I))
\end{aligned}
\tag{6}
$$

where R and G are the sets of real and generated images respectively. In the second step, we fix the discriminator and update the disentanglement net,

$$
\mathcal{L}_D^{Gen} = -\mathbb{E}_{I \in G} log(D_1(I)) - \mathbb{E}_{I \in G} log(D_2(I))
\tag{7}
$$

Loss Function. The final loss function of training process is the weighted summation of the loss functions above,

$$
\mathcal{L} = \mathcal{L}_D^{Gen} + \lambda_1 \mathcal{L}_{x_i}^{rec} + \lambda_2 \mathcal{L}_{z_i}^{rec} + \lambda_3 \mathcal{L}_{dep} + \lambda_4 \mathcal{L}_{lbp}
\tag{8}
$$

where $\lambda_1, \lambda_2, \lambda_3, \lambda_4$ are the weights. Following common adversarial training pipeline, we alternately optimize discriminator and disentanglement net. The weights are empirically selected to balance each loss term.

4   Experimental Results

4.1   Experimental Setting

Databases. We test our method on four face anti-spoofing databases: Oulu-NPU [9], SiW [24], CASIA-MFSD [43] and Replay-Attack [11]. We evaluate our intra-testing performance on Oulu-NPU and SiW datasets, and conduct cross-testing by training on Replay-Attack or CASIA-MFSD and testing on the other.

Metrics. To compare with previous works, we report the performance via the following metrics: Attack Presentation Classification Error Rate (APCER) [4], Bona Fide Presentation Classification Error Rate (BPCER) [4], Average Classification Error Rate (ACER) = (APCER+BPCER)/2 [4] and Half Total Error Rate (HTER) = (False Acceptance Rate + False Rejection Rate)/2 [4].

Implementation Details. All datasets above are stored in video format. We use a face detector or face location files in datasets to crop the face and resize it to 256×256. For each frame, we combine scores of estimated LBP map and Depth map to detect attack for fully utilizing the low-level texture information and high-level global information, as the methods in [18], *i.e.*, $score = (\|map_{lbp}\| + \|map_{depth}\|)/2$. We implement method in Pytorch [28]. Models are trained with batch size of 4. In each epoch, we select negative images and positive images with the ratio 1 : 1. To train network, we use learning rate of 1e-5 with Adam optimizer [20] and set λ_1 to λ_4 in Eq. 8 as 10, 1, 1 and 2. Depth net is pre-trained and remains fixed during the training of other three nets, and all networks are trained with the same data in each protocol. In inference stage, reconstruction and translation procedure are both detached, thus the speed of our method is acceptable, which achieves 77.97±0.18 FPS on GeForce GTX 1080.

4.2 Experimental Comparison

In this section, we show the superiority of disentanglement and further illustrate translation results. To verify the performance of our method, we conduct experiments on Oulu-NPU and SiW for intra-testing results, CASIA and Replay-Attack for cross-testing results. Then we demonstrate some examples to show details of translation, which verifies the validity of the liveness features.

Table 2. The intra-testing results of four protocols of Oulu-NPU dataset.

Protocol	Method	APCER(%)	BPCER(%)	ACER(%)
1	STASN [42]	1.2	2.5	1.9
	Auxiliary [24]	1.6	1.6	1.6
	FaceDe-S [18]	**1.2**	1.7	1.5
	FAS-TD [37]	2.5	**0.0**	**1.3**
	Ours	1.7	0.8	**1.3**
2	Auxiliary [24]	2.7	2.7	2.7
	GRADIANT [5]	3.1	1.9	2.5
	STASN [42]	4.2	**0.3**	2.2
	FAS-TD [37]	1.7	2.0	**1.9**
	Ours	**1.1**	3.6	2.4
3	FaceDe-S [18]	4.0±1.8	3.8±1.2	3.6±1.6
	Auxiliary [24]	2.7±1.3	3.1±1.7	2.9±1.5
	STASN [42]	4.7±3.9	**0.9±1.2**	2.8±1.6
	BASN [19]	**1.8±1.1**	3.6±3.5	2.7±1.6
	Ours	2.8±2.2	1.7±2.6	**2.2±2.2**
4	FAS-TD [37]	14.2±8.7	4.2±3.8	9.2±6.0
	STASN [42]	6.7±10.6	8.3±8.4	7.5±4.7
	FaceDe-S [18]	**5.1±6.3**	6.1±5.1	5.6±5.7
	BASN [19]	6.4±8.6	**3.2±5.3**	4.8±6.4
	Ours	5.4±2.9	3.3±6.0	**4.4±3.0**

Table 3. The intra-testing results of three protocols of SiW dataset.

Protocol	Method	APCER(%)	BPCER(%)	ACER(%)
1	Auxiliary [24]	3.58	3.58	3.58
	STASN [42]	-	-	1.00
	FAS-TD [37]	0.96	0.50	0.73
	BASN [19]	-	-	0.37
	Ours	0.07	0.50	**0.28**
2	Auxiliary [24]	0.57±0.69	0.57±0.69	0.57±0.69
	STASN [42]	-	-	0.28±0.05
	FAS-TD [37]	0.08±0.17	0.21±0.16	0.15±0.14
	BASN [19]	-	-	0.12±0.03
	Ours	0.08±0.17	0.13±0.09	**0.10±0.04**
3	STASN [42]	-	-	12.10±1.50
	Auxiliary [24]	8.31±3.81	8.31±3.80	8.31±3.81
	BASN [19]	-	-	6.45±1.80
	FAS-TD [37]	3.10±0.79	3.09±0.83	**3.10±0.81**
	Ours	9.35±6.14	1.84±2.60	5.59±4.37

Table 4. The cross-testing results on CASIA-MFSD and Replay-Attack.

Method	Train	Test	Train	Test
	CASIA MFSD	Replay Attack	Replay Attack	CASIA MFSD
Motion-Mag [3]	50.1%		47.0%	
Spectral cubes [31]	34.4%		50.0%	
LowPower [35]	30.1%		35.6%	
CNN [40]	48.5%		45.5%	
STASN [42]	31.5%		30.9%	
FaceDe-S [18]	28.5%		41.1%	
Auxiliary [24]	27.6%		**28.4%**	
BASN [19]	23.6%		29.9%	
Ours	**22.4%**		30.3%	

Intra-testing. Intra-testing is evaluated on Oulu-NPU and SiW datasets. We utilize the protocols defined in each dataset. Table 2 shows the comparison of our method with the best four methods on Oulu dataset. Our method achieves better results in protocols 1, 3 and 4, while gets slightly worse ACER in protocol 2. For protocol 4 evaluating all variations in Oulu, our method gets the best results, which verifies that our method has better generalization performance. Following [19], we report the ACER on three protocols of SiW. Table 3 shows that our method achieves better results among the frame based methods.

Cross-Testing. We evaluate the generalization capability by conducting cross-dataset evaluations. Following the related work, CASIA-MFSD and Replay-Attack are used for the experiments and the results are measured in HTER. The results are shown in Table 4. For fair comparison, we compare with methods using only single frame information. Our method achieves 1.2 pp lower HTER than the state-of-the-art from CASIA-MFSD to Replay-Attack and gets comparable HTER from Replay-Attack to CASIA-MFSD. This results also prove that our method with disentanglement has better generalization capability.

Translation Result. We demonstrate some examples of translation from Oulu protocol 1 in three groups: live-spoof, live-live, spoof-spoof, as shown in Fig. 3. In the live-spoof group, depth map changes with the exchange of the liveness features. While in live-live group and spoof-spoof group, the liveness features changing doesn't result in the change of depth map, which implies that liveness features indeed determine whether the image is live. The difference between each two columns of live face and spoof images is **light, ID, background** respectively. As the translation shows, there are no changes about these factors with the category changing, which means that liveness features do not contain these factors. Figure 4 shows two sets of live and attack images and their local area details. As shown in the figure, there is a big difference between the local details of the real person and the attack, and the attack images often have some repetitive streaks. And after combining the liveness features from the attack images, the local details of

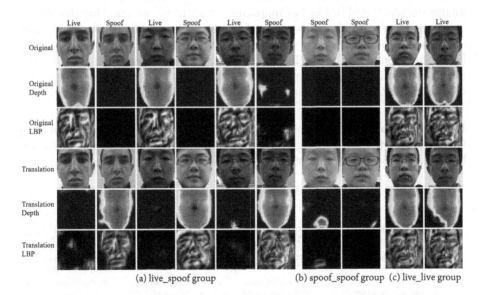

(a) live_spoof group   (b) spoof_spoof group (c) live_live group

Fig. 3. Illustrations of translation results with corresponding depth map and LBP map. We swap liveness features between every two columns. The exchanging of depth and LBP map verifies that liveness features are the key part of live face images.

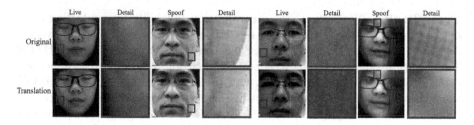

Fig. 4. Illustrations of exchanging live and spoof details. The first row is the original image, and the second row is the translation results. Red rectangular is referred as the details of live images while blue refer to the details of the spoof images.

the translation results are similar to the corresponding attacks, which shows that the liveness features have not only learned the difference between real people and attacks, but also learned different attack details.

4.3   Ablation Study

To study the effect of disentanglement, different supervision and score fusion methods, we conduct ablation experiments on Oulu-NPU protocol 1 respectively.

Liveness Feature Distribution. We use t-SNE [26] to visualize the features from different methods, which includes 500 live face images and 2, 000 spoof images, as illustrated in Fig. 5. Comparing (a) with (b), we conclude that disentanglement indeed finds a sub-space where the features of live and spoof can be distinguished more easily. For comparison between (b) and our method (c), low level LBP supervision on the liveness features improves discrimination between live and attack. The difference between (c) and (d) proves that liveness features indeed can distinguish between real and attack while content features can't.

Different Supervision. In our method, we propose the supervision combining low-level LBP texture and high-level depth information. We compare this combination of supervision with other five ablation methods, which are all based on

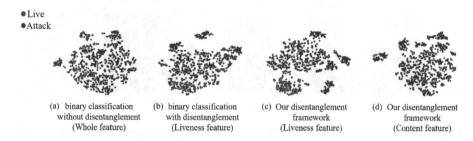

Fig. 5. Visualization of feature distributions from different methods. We use different constraint on livness feature or whole feature and draw the corresponding feature in brackets by t-SNE [26].

Table 5. The comparison of different supervision and combination.

ACER	Method					
	BC-Depth	0/1 Map-Depth	LBP-LBP	Depth-Depth	Depth-LBP	Ours
Liveness features	3.64	3.02	1.87	1.69	1.65	**1.56**
Fusion	2.78	2.50	2.40	1.80	1.50	**1.25**

●liveness ●print1 ●print2 ●display1 ●display2   ●Samsung●HTC ●MEIZU ●ASUS ●Sony ○OPPO

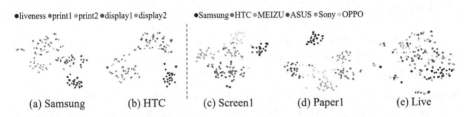

(a) Samsung   (b) HTC   (c) Screen1   (d) Paper1   (e) Live

Fig. 6. Distribution of liveness features under two different settings: (a) and (b) display liveness features of different attack and live with the same devices; (c) (d) and (e) are about features of different devices with the same attack or live.

Table 6. The results of score fusion.

Method	LBP Map	Depth Map	Fusion	
			Maximum	Average
APCER	1.25	2.50	2.92	1.67
BPCER	1.67	0.83	0.83	0.83
ACER	1.56	1.67	1.88	1.25

the proposed disentanglement framework: (1) Binary classification (BC-Depth) method which uses binary classification on the liveness space. (2) 0/1 Map-Depth method means restricting liveness space by regressing the features to 0/1 Map, where 0 map is for attack and 1 map is for live. (3) LBP-LBP method supervises feature space and translated images with LBP map. (4) Depth-Depth method refers to two depth supervision on feature space and image space. (5) Depth-LBP method uses depth supervision on feature space and LBP supervision on translated images, which is a reverse version of our method.

Table 5 shows the performance of each method on liveness features and the fusion results with depth network. Compared with different supervison on liveness features, LBP as a low-level texture supervision regularizes the feature space efficiently and performs better. The results of four combinations about LBP and Depth supervision show that the same supervision on feature space and images performs worse than different supervision. And the order of the two supervisions has little effect on the results, but the result of our method is slightly better.

Score Fusion. Using Oulu-NPU protocol 1, we perform studies on the effect of score fusion. Table 6 shows the results of each output and the fusion with maximum and average. It shows using LBP map or depth map, the performance is similiar. And the fusion of LBP map and depth map achieves the best performance. Hence, for all experiments, we evaluate the performance by utilizing the fusion score of the LBP map and the depth map, $score = (\|map_{lbp}\| + \|map_{depth}\|)/2$.

5   Further Exploration

We have ruled out the effects of some factors on liveness features in Sect. 4.2. For better understanding the essence of the liveness features, we do some qualitative experiments to explore what factors are related to it.

Spoof Type. We randomly pick up 200 images, which are collected by one certain device. Then we extract the liveness features of images and visualize them by t-SNE [26]. We demonstrate results under Samsumng and HTC mobiles in Fig. 6(a) and (b). Although no additional constraints on attacks are used, there are at least three distinct clusters: live images, paper attack and screen attack in all equipment, which implies liveness features may be related to the spoof type.

Collection Equipment. We randomly pick up 200 images for each type of attack and live with six different devices. Then we visualize the liveness features in Fig. 6(c) (d) and (e). The liveness features from different devices are clustered for attacks, but scattered for live person. It shows that the liveness features of real person may not related to collection equipment. However, the liveness features of attack may include information on collection equipment.

We further display the pixel-wise delta map between generated images and original images of each type, as shown in Fig. 7. The original images, which are shown in the first row, exchange the liveness features with the same one live image to generate the results in the third row. Then we subtract translation images from original images to get delta maps, which are mapped into color space for a better visualization in the second row. From Fig. 7, we may get the following conclusions: (1) When exchanging liveness features between real faces, the delta maps are almost zero. However the delta maps become bigger when

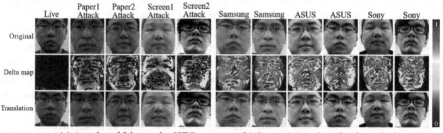

(a) Attack and Live under HTC   (b) Screen1 Attack under three devices

Fig. 7. The delta maps for different attacks with same device and different devices with same attack.

between live faces and spoof images. (2) Delta maps of the same type of attack (paper or screen) are similar but are distinguishing between two kinds of attacks. (3) For the same type of attack, delta maps are different under different collection equipment.

6   Conclusions

This paper introduces a new perspective for face anti-spoofing that disentangles the liveness and content features from images. A novel architecture combining the process of disentanglement is proposed with multiple appropriate supervisions. We combine low-level texture and high-level depth characteristics to regularize the liveness space. We visualize the translation process and analyze the content of the liveness features which provides a deeper understanding of face anti-spoofing task. Our method is evaluated on widely-used face anti-spoofing databases and achieves outstanding results.

References

1. Ahonen, T., Hadid, A., Pietikainen, M.: Face description with local binary patterns: application to face recognition. IEEE Trans. Pattern Anal. Mach. Intell. **28**(12), 2037–2041 (2006)
2. Bao, W., Li, H., Li, N., Jiang, W.: A liveness detection method for face recognition based on optical flow field. In: 2009 International Conference on Image Analysis and Signal Processing, pp. 233–236. IEEE (2009)
3. Bharadwaj, S., Dhamecha, T.I., Vatsa, M., Singh, R.: Computationally efficient face spoofing detection with motion magnification. In: Proceedings of the IEEE Conference on Computer Vision and Pattern Recognition Workshops (2013)
4. Biometcs, I.J.S.: Information technology biometric presentation attack detection part 1: framework (2016)
5. Boulkenafet, Z., et al.: A competition on generalized software-based face presentation attack detection in mobile scenarios. In: 2017 IEEE International Joint Conference on Biometrics (IJCB), pp. 688–696. IEEE (2017)
6. Boulkenafet, Z., Komulainen, J., Hadid, A.: Face anti-spoofing based on color texture analysis. In: 2015 IEEE International Conference on Image Processing (ICIP), pp. 2636–2640. IEEE (2015)
7. Boulkenafet, Z., Komulainen, J., Hadid, A.: Face antispoofing using speeded-up robust features and fisher vector encoding. IEEE Sig. Process. Lett. **24**(2), 141–145 (2016)
8. Boulkenafet, Z., Komulainen, J., Hadid, A.: Face spoofing detection using colour texture analysis. IEEE Trans. Inform. Forensics Secur. **11**(8), 1818–1830 (2016)
9. Boulkenafet, Z., Komulainen, J., Li, L., Feng, X., Hadid, A.: Oulu-npu: a mobile face presentation attack database with real-world variations. In: 2017 12th IEEE International Conference on Automatic Face & Gesture Recognition (FG 2017), pp. 612–618. IEEE (2017)
10. Chen, X., Duan, Y., Houthooft, R., Schulman, J., Sutskever, I., Abbeel, P.: Infogan: interpretable representation learning by information maximizing generative adversarial nets. In: Advances in Neural Information Processing Systems (2016)

11. Chingovska, I., Anjos, A., Marcel, S.: On the effectiveness of local binary patterns in face anti-spoofing. In: 2012 BIOSIG-Proceedings of the International Conference of Biometrics Special Interest Group (BIOSIG), pp. 1–7. IEEE (2012)

12. Feng, L., et al.: Integration of image quality and motion cues for face anti-spoofing: a neural network approach. J. Vis. Commun. Image Representation **38**, 451–460 (2016)

13. Feng, Y., Wu, F., Shao, X., Wang, Y., Zhou, X.: Joint 3d face reconstruction and dense alignment with position map regression network. In: Proceedings of the European Conference on Computer Vision (ECCV), pp. 534–551 (2018)

14. de Freitas Pereira, T., Anjos, A., De Martino, J.M., Marcel, S.: LBP - TOP based countermeasure against face spoofing attacks. In: Park, J., Kim, J. (eds.) ACCV 2012. LNCS, vol. 7728, pp. 121–132. Springer, Heidelberg (2013). https://doi.org/10.1007/978-3-642-37410-4_11

15. de Freitas Pereira, T., Anjos, A., De Martino, J.M., Marcel, S.: Can face anti-spoofing countermeasures work in a real world scenario. In: 2013 International Conference on Biometrics (ICB), pp. 1–8. IEEE (2013)

16. Higgins, I., et al.: Beta-VAE: learning basic visual concepts with a constrained variational framework. ICLR **2**(5), 6 (2017)

17. Huang, X., Liu, M.Y., Belongie, S., Kautz, J.: Multimodal unsupervised image-to-image translation. In: Proceedings of the European Conference on Computer Vision (ECCV), pp. 172–189 (2018)

18. Jourabloo, A., Liu, Y., Liu, X.: Face de-spoofing: anti-spoofing via noise modeling. In: Proceedings of the European Conference on Computer Vision (ECCV) (2018)

19. Kim, T., Kim, Y., Kim, I., Kim, D.: BASN: enriching feature representation using bipartite auxiliary supervisions for face anti-spoofing. In: Proceedings of the IEEE International Conference on Computer Vision Workshops (2019)

20. Kingma, D.P., Ba, J.: Adam: a method for stochastic optimization. arXiv preprint arXiv:1412.6980 (2014)

21. Komulainen, J., Hadid, A., Pietikäinen, M.: Context based face anti-spoofing. In: 2013 IEEE Sixth International Conference on Biometrics: Theory, Applications and Systems (BTAS), pp. 1–8. IEEE (2013)

22. Li, J., Wang, Y., Tan, T., Jain, A.K.: Live face detection based on the analysis of fourier spectra. In: Biometric Technology for Human Identification, vol. 5404, pp. 296–303. International Society for Optics and Photonics (2004)

23. Li, L., Feng, X., Boulkenafet, Z., Xia, Z., Li, M., Hadid, A.: An original face anti-spoofing approach using partial convolutional neural network. In: 2016 Sixth International Conference on Image Processing Theory, Tools and Applications (IPTA), pp. 1–6. IEEE (2016)

24. Liu, Y., Jourabloo, A., Liu, X.: Learning deep models for face anti-spoofing: binary or auxiliary supervision. In: Proceedings of the IEEE Conference on Computer Vision and Pattern Recognition, pp. 389–398 (2018)

25. Locatello, F., et al.: Challenging common assumptions in the unsupervised learning of disentangled representations. arXiv preprint arXiv:1811.12359 (2018)

26. Maaten, L., Hinton, G.: Visualizing data using t-SNE. J. Mach. Learn. Res. **9**, 2579–2605 (2008)

27. Määttä, J., Hadid, A., Pietikäinen, M.: Face spoofing detection from single images using micro-texture analysis. In: 2011 International Joint Conference on Biometrics (IJCB), pp. 1–7. IEEE (2011)

28. Paszke, A., et al.: Automatic differentiation in pytorch (2017)

29. Patel, K., Han, H., Jain, A.K.: Cross-database face antispoofing with robust feature representation. In: You, Z., et al. (eds.) CCBR 2016. LNCS, vol. 9967, pp. 611–619. Springer, Cham (2016). https://doi.org/10.1007/978-3-319-46654-5_67
30. Patel, K., Han, H., Jain, A.K.: Secure face unlock: spoof detection on smartphones. IEEE Trans. Inf. Forensics Secur. **11**(10), 2268–2283 (2016)
31. Pinto, A., Pedrini, H., Schwartz, W.R., Rocha, A.: Face spoofing detection through visual codebooks of spectral temporal cubes. IEEE Trans. Image Process. **24**(12), 4726–4740 (2015)
32. Ronneberger, O., Fischer, P., Brox, T.: U-Net: convolutional networks for biomedical image segmentation. In: Navab, N., Hornegger, J., Wells, W.M., Frangi, A.F. (eds.) MICCAI 2015. LNCS, vol. 9351, pp. 234–241. Springer, Cham (2015). https://doi.org/10.1007/978-3-319-24574-4_28
33. Shao, R., Lan, X., Li, J., Yuen, P.C.: Multi-adversarial discriminative deep domain generalization for face presentation attack detection. In: Proceedings of the IEEE Conference on Computer Vision and Pattern Recognition, pp. 10023–10031 (2019)
34. Siddiqui, T.A., et al.: Face anti-spoofing with multifeature videolet aggregation. In: 2016 23rd International Conference on Pattern Recognition (ICPR). IEEE (2016)
35. Vareto, R.H., Diniz, M.A., Schwartz, W.R.: Face spoofing detection on low-power devices using embeddings with spatial and frequency-based descriptors. In: Nyström, I., Hernández Heredia, Y., Milián Núñez, V. (eds.) CIARP 2019. LNCS, vol. 11896, pp. 187–197. Springer, Cham (2019). https://doi.org/10.1007/978-3-030-33904-3_17
36. Wang, T.C., Liu, M.Y., Zhu, J.Y., Tao, A., Kautz, J., Catanzaro, B.: High-resolution image synthesis and semantic manipulation with conditional gans. In: Proceedings of the IEEE Conference on Computer Vision and Pattern Recognition, pp. 8798–8807 (2018)
37. Wang, Z., et al.: Exploiting temporal and depth information for multi-frame face anti-spoofing. arXiv preprint arXiv:1811.05118 (2018)
38. Xiao, T., Hong, J., Ma, J.: Elegant: exchanging latent encodings with gan for transferring multiple face attributes. In: Proceedings of the European Conference on Computer Vision (ECCV), pp. 168–184 (2018)
39. Xu, Z., Li, S., Deng, W.: Learning temporal features using LSTM-CNN architecture for face anti-spoofing. In: 2015 3rd IAPR Asian Conference on Pattern Recognition (ACPR), pp. 141–145. IEEE (2015)
40. Yang, J., Lei, Z., Li, S.Z.: Learn convolutional neural network for face anti-spoofing. arXiv preprint arXiv:1408.5601 (2014)
41. Yang, J., Lei, Z., Liao, S., Li, S.Z.: Face liveness detection with component dependent descriptor. In: 2013 International Conference on Biometrics (ICB), pp. 1–6. IEEE (2013)
42. Yang, X., et al.: Face anti-spoofing: model matters, so does data. In: Proceedings of the IEEE Conference on Computer Vision and Pattern Recognition, pp. 3507–3516 (2019)
43. Zhang, Z., Yan, J., Liu, S., Lei, Z., Yi, D., Li, S.Z.: A face antispoofing database with diverse attacks. In: 2012 5th IAPR International Conference on Biometrics (ICB), pp. 26–31. IEEE (2012)

Prime-Aware Adaptive Distillation

Youcai Zhang[1], Zhonghao Lan[2], Yuchen Dai[1], Fangao Zeng[1], Yan Bai[3],
Jie Chang[1], and Yichen Wei[1(✉)]

[1] Megvii Inc., Beijing, China
{daiyuchen,zengfangao,changjie,weiyichen}@megvii.com
[2] University of Science and Technology of China, Hefei, China
lans@mail.ustc.edu.cn
[3] Tongji University, Shanghai, China
yan.bai@tongji.edu.cn, yczhang12@fudan.edu.cn

Abstract. Knowledge distillation (KD) aims to improve the performance of a student network by mimicking the knowledge from a powerful teacher network. Existing methods focus on studying what knowledge should be transferred and treat all samples equally during training. This paper introduces the adaptive sample weighting to KD. We discover that previous effective hard mining methods are not appropriate for distillation. Furthermore, we propose Prime-Aware Adaptive Distillation (PAD) by the incorporation of uncertainty learning. PAD perceives the prime samples in distillation and then emphasizes their effect adaptively. PAD is fundamentally different from and would refine existing methods with the innovative view of unequal training. For this reason, PAD is versatile and has been applied in various tasks including classification, metric learning, and object detection. With ten teacher-student combinations on six datasets, PAD promotes the performance of existing distillation methods and outperforms recent state-of-the-art methods.

Keywords: Knowledge distillation · Adaptive weighting · Uncertainty learning

1 Introduction

Obtaining highly accurate and lightweight (small model size and low computation) deep neural networks is crucial for practical applications. Knowledge Distillation (KD) methods [6,13,24,28,32,40] are effective for this purpose and have been extensively explored in the past few years. KD aims to transfer the knowledge from a high-capacity *teacher* network with a huge amount of parameters and heavy computation to a relatively lightweight *student* network. By mimicking the "behavior" of teacher, the student model achieves better performance than as is trained from scratch.

Most knowledge distillation methods focus on studying *what knowledge* should be transferred, *e.g.*, soft predictions [13], feature maps [28], activation-based attention maps [40] or relation between samples [24], etc. However, we

This work was done when Y. Zhang worked at Megvii Inc. Research Shanghai.

A. Vedaldi et al. (Eds.): ECCV 2020, LNCS 12364, pp. 658–674, 2020.
https://doi.org/10.1007/978-3-030-58529-7_39

notice that in the current literature it is rarely studied that *which samples* contribute more to learning the student model and should be focused.

This work, for the first time, studies the problem of adaptive sample weighting in knowledge distillation. First, we note that sample weighting has been widely used in other tasks, such as object detection [20,22] and metric learning [12, 37]. In these tasks, hard samples are assigned larger weights during training as they are more important to learn the model. These samples are termed "prime samples" in a recent work [3]. However, such "hard mining" approaches are not appropriate in knowledge distillation. As validated in experiments, we found that hard samples have detrimental effect on learning the student model. We conjecture that the mismatch between student's and teacher's capacities makes student less capable of learning teacher's knowledge in these hard samples. Thus, we propose that sample weighting should be biased towards these easy samples.

Inspired by previous sample weighting approaches, we first introduce a few baseline weighting methods. They allocate weights based on the pre-defined function of sample's loss contribution. Samples with small loss are given large weights. However, these methods suffer from the sensitive hyper-parameters and the poor ability to distinguish prime samples.

To overcome the drawbacks, we propose a Prime-aware Adaptive Distillation (PAD) method. By modelling knowledge distillation with data uncertainty, each sample is modeled by a Gaussian distribution. The mean of the distribution is the prediction from the student and the variance measures the uncertainty about distilling the knowledge from the teacher. According to the estimated uncertainty from the network, PAD perceives the prime samples corrupted with weak noise in a more feasible and reasonable manner than the baseline methods.

In principle, our approach is fundamentally different from and would complement most (if not all) distillation methods. For this reason, PAD is a versatile method. It is applied in various tasks including classification, metric learning, and detection. It is validated to outperform our baseline weighting methods, and boost the performance of previous distillation methods, achieving new state-of-the-art methods on six datasets.

To summarize, this work makes three contributions.

1. This is the first systematic study on the problem of sample weighting for knowledge distillation. In particular, we point out that previous hard mining approaches are not appropriate for our problem.
2. We propose a simple yet effective distillation method (PAD). PAD helps the student network to perceive the prime samples in distillation by modelling the knowledge distillation with data uncertainty.
3. Comprehensive experiments validate that our approach is effective and establishes the new state-of-the-arts, on a vast range of datasets, baselines and previous distillation methods.

2   Related Work

Knowledge Distillation(KD). Hinton et al. [13] are pioneers in the field of knowledge distillation. They adopted the KL-divergence to penalize the softer probability distribution over classes between the teacher and student. From then on, many seminal studies [6,28,32,39,40] have sprung up. For example, an information-theoretic framework [1] was proposed by maximizing the mutual information between the teacher and the student networks. The correlation between instances was also proved as the valuable knowledge by [24,25].

Besides studies on classification task, DarkRank [5] was proposed to perform distillation in metric learning via cross sample similarities transfer. ROI mimic distillation [21] and fine-grained feature imitation [34] were designed for detection tasks by distilling the regions of interest.

Adaptive Sample Weighting. Adaptive sample weighting by adjusting the contributions of samples for training is a well-studied topic in computer vision. Hard-mining is a typical technique which plays a critical role in one-stage detectors [20,22] and metric learning [12,37]. Hard-mining methods reduce the relative loss for easy samples, putting more focus on hard ones. In contrast, Huber loss and smooth l_1 loss reduce the contribution of hard samples by down-weighting the loss of them. Many researchers [14,41] extended this idea to face recognition for noisy-robust feature learning. Cao et al. [3] paid more attention to prime samples to achieve high detection performance. Our work is the first exploration about adaptive sample weighting in distillation, to our best knowledge.

Uncertainty Estimation. Uncertainty estimation is an effective technique to promote the robustness and interpretability of discriminant deep neural networks [15,16,23]. In deep uncertainty learning, there are mainly two types of uncertainty. Model uncertainty estimates the noise of the parameters in deep neural networks, and data uncertainty measures the noise caused by input data. Predictions of neural networks are unreliable when the input sample is out of the training distribution or corrupted by noise. Uncertainty estimation has attracted much attention in computer vision tasks, *e.g.*, face recognition [30], semantic segmentation [15,16], object detection [7,17] and person re-identification(re-ID) [38]. This paper models knowledge distillation with uncertainty estimation to predict the prime samples in distillation.

3   Introducing Sample Weighting to KD

3.1   A General Formulation of KD

Most of the distillation studies obey a paradigm, whether they are in the task of classification, metric learning or object detection. The paradigm is to make students regress to the knowledge obtained from the teachers. The knowledge can be soft predictions [13], embedding feature [21], feature maps of intermediate layer [28], or activation-based attention maps [40]. Given the input $x_i \in X$, the regression aims to find the approximation function $f_s(\cdot)$ for student, where $f_s(x_i)$ should be close to the knowledge $y_i \in Y$ derived from the teacher.

A typical distillation loss can be formulated as

$$\mathcal{L}_{distill} = \frac{1}{N} \sum_{i=1}^{N} w_i d[f_s(x_i), y_i]. \tag{1}$$

N is the number of samples in a batch. $d[\cdot, \cdot]$ is the distance metric to measure the gap between the student and the teacher. L_2 is in common use as the metric. If there is a mismatch of dimension between $f_s(x_i)$ and y_i, a simple projection function will be added for dimension conversion, following FitNet [28]. For notation convenience, we abbreviate the gap $d[f_s(x_i), y_i]$ between teacher and student for sample x_i to $d(x_i)$. Noted w_i is the weight to measure the importance of x_i to the overall loss. w_i is set to be same for all samples in conventional knowledge distillation methods.

To guide the learning of student network, distillation loss should be combined with the original task-specific loss $\mathcal{L}_{task}$. The overall loss is formulated as

$$\mathcal{L} = \mathcal{L}_{task} + \lambda \mathcal{L}_{distill}, \tag{2}$$

where λ is a hyper-parameter to balance the task loss and distillation loss.

3.2   Sample Weighting and a Few Baselines

Conventional distillation methods treat all samples equally, without considering the difference among them. Hard sample mining is a well-studied sample weighting method in metric learning [37] and object detection [22]. The loss contribution usually reflects the level of sample difficulty [22,37]. The greater the loss is, the more difficult the sample is. Therefore, weighting samples according to their loss contribution is common practice in hard example mining.

Following [37], we also conduct hard sample mining by increasing the weights of samples with large gaps(d) in distillation. Table 1 shows hard-mining is conversely worse than treating samples equally in distillation. Thus, we argue that hard samples are not prime ones in distillation. For further verification, we design a simple weighting scheme, discarding hard samples with the largest distillation gaps(d) in each batch during training. We find that training without the hardest samples slightly improves the baselines. Combining the hard-mining and hard-discarding results, we can come to the conclusion that hard samples have detrimental effect on the training of the student model.

Besides the above simple either-or method, we continue to design better weighting schemes. The weighting function w can be formulated as $w_i = w(d(x_i))$. $w(\cdot)$ is a monotone increasing function instead of a decreasing one in hard example mining. We design two soft weighting schemes, exponential weighting and polynomial weighting [37], to allocate each sample a continuous weight. Exponential weighting is defined as

Table 1. Comparisons of hard-mining (training with large weights for hard samples) and hard-discarding (training without the hardest samples). "↓" means worse than baseline. Experimental settings will be introduced in detail in Sect. 5.

Method	CIFAR100	TinyImageNet	Duke-reID	CUB-200	Pascal VOC07
All samples equally	72.85	63.08	79.5	58.6	45.53
Hard-mining	72.12↓	62.57↓	79.0↓	55.7↓	45.44↓
Hard-discarding	72.91	63.16	79.8	58.3↓	45.94

$$w_{soft\text{-}exp}(d(x_i)) = \frac{e^{-d(x_i)/T}}{\sum_{i=1}^{N} e^{-d(x_i)/T}}, \tag{3}$$

where $T > 0$ controls the power of the suppression against the outliers. And polynomial weighting function can be formulated as

$$w_{soft\text{-}poly}(d(x_i)) = \frac{(1 + d(x_i))^{-\alpha}}{\sum_{i=1}^{N}(1 + d(x_i))^{-\alpha}}, \tag{4}$$

where $\alpha > 0$ is a coefficient for adjusting the weight distribution.

4   Prime-Aware Adaptive Distillation

Besides easy sample mining in distillation, there also exist problems in introducing sample weighting to distillation. The performance of the above baselines is not satisfactory and sensitive to the additional hyper-parameters as shown in Table 6. In light of this, we propose a novel Prime-aware Adaptive Distillation (PAD) method by modeling knowledge distillation with data uncertainty. As data uncertainty can capture the noise inherent in the observations, PAD can perceive the prime samples with little noise and weight them adaptively.

Modelling KD with Data Uncertainty. As discussed in Sect. 3.1, KD can be viewed as a regression task. In most real-world scenarios, paired input-target data contains noise. The target values $\boldsymbol{f}_s(x_i)$ is inevitably corrupted by input-dependent noise $\boldsymbol{n}(x_i)$. The observed data can be modeled by $\boldsymbol{y}_i = \boldsymbol{f}_s(x_i) + \boldsymbol{n}(x_i)$, where the additive noise $\boldsymbol{n}(x_i)$ can be viewed as errors that move the targets away from their true values $\boldsymbol{f}_s(x_i)$ to their observed values $\boldsymbol{y}_i$.

Supposing the noise obeys Gaussian distribution as $\boldsymbol{n}(x_i) \sim N(0, \boldsymbol{\sigma}^2(x_i))$, where σ^2 is the variance of the noise. The target probability distribution $\boldsymbol{y}_i$ for input x_i based on the least-square regression can be formulated as

$$p(\boldsymbol{y}_i|x_i) = \frac{1}{\sqrt{2\pi\sigma_i^2}} \exp\left(-\frac{(\boldsymbol{f}_s(x_i) - \boldsymbol{y}_i)^2}{2\sigma_i^2}\right), \tag{5}$$

where $\boldsymbol{f}_s(x_i)$ corresponds to the mean $\boldsymbol{\mu}_i$ of this distribution and σ_i^2 is the variance to measure the uncertainty of the predicted value $\boldsymbol{f}_s(x_i)$.

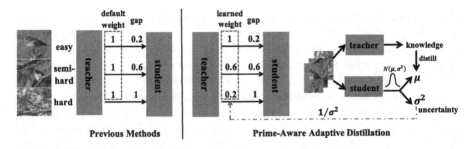

Fig. 1. Previous methods ignore the quality of different samples and allocate the same weight to them. The proposed method perceives the prime samples (usually with small gaps) and enhances them by given large weights, *i.e.*, Prime-aware Adaptive Distillation (PAD). Each sample is modeled by a Gaussian distribution $N(\mu, \sigma^2)$. The mean μ is the prediction of student and the variance σ^2 measures the uncertainty about distilling the knowledge from the teacher. Prime samples are assigned large weights $(1/\sigma^2)$, *i.e.*, small variance (σ^2), indicating that the student is confident about their knowledge.

We should maximize the log likelihood for the input x_i over the observation y_i, so the negative log likelihood is formulated as

$$- \ln p\left(y_i | x_i\right) = \frac{\left(f_s(x_i) - y_i\right)^2}{2\sigma_i^2} + \frac{1}{2} \ln \sigma_i^2 + \frac{1}{2} \ln 2\pi. \tag{6}$$

Based on the above derivation, we can formulate a prime-aware distillation loss to help the student network perceive sample difficulty, as:

$$\mathcal{L}_{PAD} = \sum_{i=1}^{N} \left(\frac{\left(f_s(x_i) - y_i\right)^2}{\sigma_i^2} + \ln \sigma_i^2 \right). \tag{7}$$

Without loss of generality, we take the embedding feature as the distillation target for simplicity. It is easy to generalize to other forms of targets, *e.g.*, by flattening feature map to a vector, we can treat feature map as the feature. Due to the least-square assumption, Eq. (7) can be directly applied to L_2-based methods, *e.g.*, L_2 on the feature, FitNet [28], AT [40], and many detection distillation methods [21,34].

For the application of PAD, the only modification is the addition of a variance branch parallel with $f_s(x)$ to estimate the variance σ. And μ can be viewed as a drop-in replacement of $f_s(x)$ as shown in Fig. 1. Using an auxiliary branch to estimate the variance is a common practice and has been proved to be effective in data uncertainty [15,16,23,38]. The motivation of an auxiliary branch is its provision of the network with the ability to measure the uncertainty. It should also be pointed out that the variance branch only exists in training, thus it will not bring about any extra computational cost for inference. We also find that simple design for the variance branch achieves satisfactory results and the variance branch has almost no effect on training efficiency.

Discussion. In this part, we analyze how uncertainty effects the distillation from the perspective of loss function. First, Eq. (7) indicates the effect from samples with large variances is weakened in network training. And then, a question comes out: what kind of sample will be given a large variance? $ln(\sigma^2)$ can be regarded as a regularization term, which prevents the model predicting large variances for all samples. Simultaneously, model will not produce small variances for all samples, which will make the first term of Eq. (7) increase rapidly. The model therefore allocates large variances to samples with large gaps(d) to reduce the overall loss of Eq. (7). Samples with large gaps(d) are usually difficult for student. That explains why they are termed hard samples. The rationality of the above hypothesis is proved by experimental analysis in Sect. 5.4.

To sum up, $\frac{1}{\sigma^2}$ can be viewed as a weight coefficient. PAD actually provides a mechanism of adaptive weighting different training samples. Easy samples are highlighted and hard samples are restricted under the influence of uncertainty.

Comparison with Sample Weighting Baselines. PAD obtains the weight directly from the network instead of a conversion from the distance by a predefined function. The weights learned from PAD are more accurate in describing sample difficulty than those from baselines, which can be proved by Table 7 and Fig. 3. Besides, PAD introduces no extra hyper-parameters that need to be tuned carefully in those baseline methods. For this reason, PAD exhibits a versatile generalization on various methods and tasks.

Comparison with VID [1]. Though the formula of VID and PAD is similar, the difference is minor but essential. VID is one of the existing distillation works which treats samples equally. As a contrast, PAD is motivated by the"adaptive sample weighting" (*i.e.*, unequal training), which is well-studied in CV community but missing in distillation. Our study is the first work to exploit adaptive sample weighting in distillation and proposes PAD as an effective weighting way. This difference between PAD and VID results in the different derivation of loss and the meaning of variance. PAD is derived from the data uncertainty, while VID is formulated by the information theory. Also, the variance of PAD has a clear meaning, which indicates the strong correlation between variance and sample quality. Last but not least, PAD performs better than VID with a remarkable margin as shown in Table 2.

5   Experiment

In this section, we firstly apply the proposed PAD on three visual tasks: image classification, metric learning, and object detection. Our experiments exhibit two advantages over others. 1) **Stronger baselines**: student baselines in our experiments are obviously higher than those in recent studies [24,32,34], which will be elaborated in the following part. 2) **More extensive experiments on more challenging tasks**: we conduct experiments with ten teacher-student combinations on various tasks, including ImageNet, where it is hard to achieve positive results for distillation [40]. As a comparison, RKD [24] uses five teacher-student combinations and lacks of experiments on large-scale datasets. Also, we compare different methods on detection, whereas almost all the related works [4, 10,21,34] only report their methods without any comparison.

Secondly, comprehensive analysis is given to delve into the learning process of PAD. Finally, we conduct ablation experiments to compare different unequal-learning schemes. All the experiments are conducted on Pytorch. For all the datasets, we follow the train/test splits suggested as popular papers. We carefully tune the weight of distillation loss λ and use the SGD optimizer with a momentum of 0.9 for all the experiments.

5.1   Classification

Firstly, we evaluate PAD on the image classification task where most knowledge distillation methods report their performance.

Dataset Settings. CIFAR100 [18], TinyImageNet [19], and ImageNet [8] are adopted. CIFAR100 contains 50K training images with 500 images per class and 10K test images. TinyImageNet has 200 classes, each with 500 training images and 50 validation images. ImageNet [8] provides 1.2 million images from 1K classes for training and 50K for validation.

Implementation Details. Following original papers or popular implementations, we apply L_2, RKD [24], and CC [25] on the last embedding layer before classification, apply the FitNet [2] on the last two blocks of CNN, and apply AT [40] and VID [1] on the last four blocks. We re-implement the HKD [13], FitNet [2], and L_2 based on the original paper. For RKD, CC, and AT, we use author-provided codes. For VID, we use the author-verified code from [32].

For CIFAR100 and TinyImageNet, we run each model for 200 epochs with a batch size of 128, and the weight decay of 5e−4. We set the initial learning rate to 0.1, dropping 0.2× at 60, 120, 160 epoch. For ImageNet, we run each model for 90 epochs with a batch size of 512, and set the initial learning rate to 0.2, dropping 0.1× at 30, 60 epoch. The weight decay is set to 1e−4. When combined with L_2 and AT, PAD adopts a fully connected(FC) layer, followed by a batch normalization(BN) layer to generate variance. When combined with FitNet, PAD adopts a 1 × 1 convolutional layer followed by a BN layer.

Results on CIFAR100 and TinyImageNet. We adopt the ResNet18 [11] as the teacher network, MobileNetV2 [29] as the student network. We report the top-1 test accuracy on CIFAR100 and TinyImageNet datasets in Table 2.

Results of baseline and compared methods by our implementation are reliable, as they are almost the same as those of [39], and are higher than those of [32]. Weobserve that PAD promotes the performance of three existing classic

Table 2. Top-1 accuracy (%) on CIFAR100 and TinyImageNet

	Teacher	Student	HKD	RKD	CC	VID	AT	PAD-AT	L_2	PAD-L_2	FitNet	PAD-FitNet
CIFAR100	75.86	68.16	70.29	68.34	70.0	68.2	69.06	**69.92**	72.85	**74.06**	71.74	**73.45**
TinyImageNet	63.46	56.16	59.52	55.88	57.14	57.06	58.24	**59.26**	63.08	**65.64**	63.34	**64.20**

knowledge distillation methods(AT [40], L_2, and FitNet [28]) with significant margins. For example, PAD obtains a 1.71% gain for FitNet on CIFAR100 and 2.56% for L_2 on TinyImagenet. PAD combined L_2 outperforms other methods. We also find that relation-level distillation methods (CC [25] and RKD [24]) are not superior to the instance-level methods (HKD [13], FitNet [28], and L_2) on these two classification tasks. VID [1] also performs worse than HKD [13]. Similar observations can be found in [32]. Compared with VID [1], our method obtains significant improvement, which shows the effectiveness of allocating different weights to different samples instead of a same weight.

Results on ImageNet. For fair comparisons with AT [40] and CRD [32], we adopt the models from them, ResNet34 as the teacher and ResNet18 as the student. As shown in Table 3, L_2 performs better than FitNet and AT on ImageNet, so we just apply PAD to L_2. It is worth mentioning that L_2 on the last embedding layer is an effective method for distillation, but we do not find its previous use in classification. The gap of top-1 accuracy between the teacher and student is 3.56%. Our PAD-L_2 method reduces this gap by 1.96%, ahead of the state-of-the-art CRD with a margin of 0.54%. Results on ImageNet indicate that our method is generically applicable in the large-scale classification task.

Table 3. Top-1 accuracy (%) on ImageNet. "*" means the result from the paper.

Teacher	Student	HKD [13]	FitNet [28]	CC [25]	AT [40]	CRD*[32]	L_2	PAD-L_2
73.31	69.75	70.80	70.62	70.74	70.43	71.17	70.90	**71.71**

5.2   Metric Learning

Secondly, we demonstrate the effectiveness of PAD on metric learning.

Dataset Settings. We consider two typical metric learning tasks, *i.e.*, fine-grained image retrieval on CUB-200-2011 [33] and person re-ID on DukeMTMC-reID [27]. CUB-200-2011 contains 200 different classes of birds. We use the first 100 classes with 5,864 images for training and the last 100 classes with 5,924 images for testing. $R@1$ is adopted as the evaluation metric. DukeMTMC-reID is a subset of the DukeMTMC dataset designed for person re-ID. It consists of 36,411 human bounding boxes belonging to 1,404 identities. The training set contains 16,522 images of 702 identities and the rest 702 identities are assigned to the testing set. $R@1$ and mean accuracy precision(mAP) are adopted as metrics.

Implementation Details. Embedding feature is directly used for retrieval in metric learning, thus, we choose the embedding feature as the distillation target layer for all methods. There are few works designed specifically for metric learning. We choose typical L_2, Darkrank [5] and RKD [24] as the compared methods. Two losses are proposed in Darkrank [5], *i.e.*, HardRank and SoftRank loss. We adopt the HardRank loss as it is computationally efficient and also comparable to the SoftRank loss. For RKD [24], we apply both RKD-D and RKD-A with a weight 1:2 on the feature without normalization. The paper [24] suggests that the student should be trained purely by the RKD loss, *i.e.*, removing the task loss. We report results of the student trained with and without task loss.

For CUB-200-2011, we train for 30,000 steps with a batch size of 60 (12 classes and each class 5 samples), weight decay of 4e−5. The initial learning rate is 1e−3, and is divided by 10 every 10,000 steps. For DukeMTMC-reID, the batch size is 36 (12 classes and each class 3 samples) and the initial learning is 0.005 decaying once at 20,000 step. Other settings are same to CUB-200-2011. The variance branch adopts a FC layer followed by BN.

Results on CUB-200-2011. Inspired by RKD, we conduct both compression distillation and self-distillation on CUB-200-2011 with a strong baseline. Compression distillation means distillation to a smaller network and self-distillation means the teacher and student share the same architecture. For the teacher, we adopt the GoogLeNet [31] trained by multi-similarity loss [35], which provides a higher $R@1$ of 64.7 than 61.2 in RKD paper. A strong teacher is beneficial to explore the real performance of self-distillation. For the student in compression distillation, we choose ResNet18 [11] with multi-similarity loss, which also provides a higher $R@1$ of 55.6 than 53.9 in RKD paper.

Table 4 shows the results of different distillation methods on CUB-200-2011. RKD achieves promising results and PAD outperforms the Darkrank and RKD. Self-distillation further improves the performance of the initial teachers. Although our reproduced results (64.7) are inferior to those reported in the paper (65.7) [35], self-distillation by Darkrank, RKD and our PAD outperform the initial teacher and exceeded the reported results of 65.7. The proposed method brings a 1.6% gain. Similarly to RKD, the repeated self-distillation does not provide additional benefits.

Results on DukeMTMC-ReID. For person re-ID, we also choose a strong baseline. The teacher is the ResNet50 trained with both softmax and triplet loss, which gives a gain of 2.1% $R@1$ than only softmax. Multi-similarity loss gives no additional gain than triplet loss in our experiments. Table 4 shows distillation results of different students with different methods. As we see, improvement obtained by distillation is slight when the student baseline is strong. While the improvement becomes remarkable, when the student is trained only by triplet loss. The proposed PAD outperforms RKD and DarkRank based on different baselines. Besides, PAD demonstrates excellent performance in self-distillation compared with other methods.

Table 4. Results on metric learning tasks. w/o task indicates students are trained without task loss, only by RKD. w/ task indicates students are trained with both task loss and RKD.

	DukeMTMC-reID						CUB-200-2011	
	Compression distillation				Self-distillation		Compression distillation	Self-distillation
	Softmax+triplet		Only triplet		Softmax+Triplet		Multi-similarity	Multi-similarity
Method	$R@1$	mAP	$R@1$	mAP	$R@1$	mAP	$R@1$	$R@1$
Teacher	84.9	71.9	84.9	71.9	84.9	71.9	64.7	64.7
Student	79.3	61.1	63.6	43.5	84.9	71.9	55.6	64.7
DarkRank	79.9	62.2	69.9	50.9	85.2	72.2	60.1	65.2
RKD w/ task	68.3	48.9	68.3	48.9	73.1	55.3	60.7	65.8
RKD w/o task	80.3	63.2	70.9	52.3	85.1	73.1	60.7	63.0
L_2	79.5	62.5	72.6	53.7	86.0	72.8	58.6	64.4
PAD-L_2	**81.0**	**63.3**	**77.5**	**60.5**	**87.3**	**74.3**	**61.4**	**66.3**

5.3 Object Detection

Thirdly, we validate the proposed method on object detection which is a fundamental and more challenging task in computer vision.

Dataset Settings. We conduct experiments on Pascal VOC dataset [9] using both two-stage (Faster-RCNN [26]) and one-stage (RetinaNet [22]) frameworks. Following ROI Mimic [21], we use VOC2007 trainval set of 5k images and VOC2012 trainval set of 16k images as training data. And we evaluate our method on VOC2007 test set of 5 K images. Besides $mAP@0.5$ that considers one generous threshold of IoU $\geqslant 0.5$, we adopt the overall $mmAP$ metric, averaging over the 10 IoU thresholds.

Implementation Details. All the detection experiments including baselines are implemented on Detectron2 [36], which provides the strongest baselines for popular object detection frameworks. For example, Detectron2's ResNet50 based Faster R-CNN achieves a $mAP@0.5$ of 80.9 while the fine-grained paper [34] reports that of only 69.1. All the hyper-parameters related to the object detection are consistent with the standard configurations provided by Detectron2. We only tune the parameters of the distillation part.

For Faster R-CNN, the variance branch consists of two 3×3 convolutional layers and two FC layers, generating variance for each ROI extracted by the sampler. For RetinaNet, variance branch consists of five convolutional layers for the whole feature map and then the spatial mask generated in Fine-frained's way [34] filters out the background. Since FPN is adopted in all experiments, distilled features are sampled from all FPN layers.

Results on Pascal VOC07. Following fine-grained [34], we adopt two settings of backbones, *i.e.*, from ResNet101 to ResNet50 and from VGG16 to VGG11.

Table 5 summaries the results of different distillation methods based on different architectures. We have two observations from Table 5. First, PAD is applied to the two most mainstream frameworks and consistently improves the performance of students based on different backbones. Second, the improvement brought by distillation is not as impressive as the original paper [21, 34]. We argue that we should analyze the improvement from a relative rather than absolute perspective when baselines become strong. For example, in first column of Table 5, ROI mimic [21] improves the $mmAP$ of student from 54.00% to 55.52%. This gain covers 68% of the gap between teacher and student. Our PAD not only further narrows the gap but also makes the student exceed the teacher slightly, which is a rare phenomenon in detection distillation. Similarly, Fine-grained method covers 54.40% and 59.25% of the $mmAP$ gaps using two backbones respectively based on RetinaNet. Combined with PAD, the gaps decrease by 90.67% and 93.58% and the performance of students become very close to those of teachers. Results using two typical distillation methods based on Faster-RCNN and RetinaNet show that PAD still performs well on detection.

Table 5. Results on Pascal VOC07 with different backbones. ResNet101-50 refers to the backbone of teacher and student respectively. Results of ROI-mimic based on RetinaNet are missing, as ROI-mimic can only be applied to two-stage frameworks.

| Method | Faster R-CNN | | | | RetinaNet | | | |
| | ResNet101-50 | | VGG16-11 | | ResNet101-50 | | VGG16-11 | |
	$mmAP$	$mAP@0.5$	$mmAP$	$mAP@0.5$	$mmAP$	$mAP@0.5$	$mmAP$	$mAP@0.5$
Teacher	56.22	82.53	46.53	76.86	57.45	82.09	47.18	74.34
Student	54.00	81.98	42.18	72.99	55.52	81.21	43.13	69.57
ROI mimic [21]	55.52	82.25	45.00	75.04	–	–	–	–
PAD-ROI-mimic	**56.41**	**82.46**	**45.62**	**75.79**	–	–	–	–
Fine-grained [34]	54.91	81.93	44.60	74.59	56.57	81.46	45.53	71.99
PAD-Fine-grained	**55.39**	**82.29**	**45.21**	**75.17**	**57.27**	**81.94**	**46.92**	**73.18**

5.4 Analysis

Finally, we give visualization analysis to show the mechanism and effectiveness of PAD. Also, we compare different weighting schemes and conduct ablation experiments. Baselines in this section are students distilled with L_2.

How PAD Affects Distillation? We analyze how PAD affects the student model training in this part. From Fig. 2, we realize that there is a positive correlation between the gap and the variance. From Fig. 3, we observe that the quality of samples decreases with the increase of the learned variance. The above two observations are consistent with our analysis in the method part. With the help of PAD, hard samples are assigned small weights while easy samples are assigned large weights. After adaptive weighting samples by PAD, the effect of

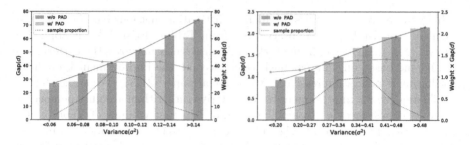

Fig. 2. Relationship between the variance(σ^2) and gap(d) on the training set of Tiny-ImageNet (*left*) and CUB-200-2011 (*right*). Bars refer to the gap(d) between teacher and student for different samples, and x-axis is the corresponding variance bins of these samples. Green dotted lines indicate the sample proportion. Solid lines demonstrate the actual effect (*Weight* × *Gap*) of different samples on distillation. The effect of samples with large variances is obviously weakened. Note that the absolute effect of different methods should not be compared, as we tune the distillation loss weight λ for all methods.

hard samples is obviously weakened, while the effect of easy ones is strengthened as the solid lines in Fig. 2 show. Also, PAD narrows the gaps between teacher and student, which means student trained with PAD achieves a better result in regression to the teacher than the baseline.

Impact of the Hyper-parameters. For sample weighting baselines, extra hyper-parameters are introduced. As shown in Table 6, soft-weighting schemes slightly improve the performance of distillation, and good results rely heavily on the careful selection of parameters.

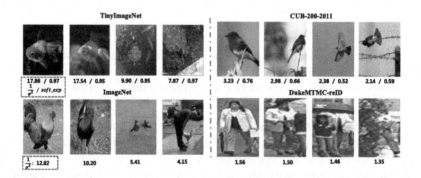

Fig. 3. Examples of the same class or the same person from four datasets. Generally, the larger the variance(σ^2) is, the more difficult the sample is. Thus, PAD assigns large weights $(1/\sigma^2)$ to the prime samples. Weights from soft-exp are not always accurate. For example, soft-exp give large weights to the right hard samples.

Table 6. Effect of hyper-parameters (α and T) in sample weighting baselines. "↑" means better than baselines. Few experiments are better than baselines.

		Baseline	0.1	0.5	1	2	5	10
Soft-exp	TinyImageNet	63.1	61.2	63.2↑	62.6	63.4↑	63.6↑	61.8
	CUB-200-2011	58.6	54.9	58.6	60.1↑	59.2↑	55.8	55.3
Soft-poly	TinyImageNet	63.1	62.6	63.0	62.6	63.5↑	62.3	61.8
	CUB-200-2011	58.6	59.4↑	60.4↑	57.9	57.5	59.5↑	60.3↑

Comparisons of Different Weighting Schemes. We compare different weighting schemes and draw two conclusions from Table 7. First, assigning different weights to different samples is effective in distillation even using a manual way. Soft-weighting schemes perform better than the hard-discarding schemes. Second, the weights learned from the off-the-shelf PAD models can better describe the importance of samples than other schemes. Besides the quantitative indicators in Table 7, we see the difference of PAD and soft-exp from the qualitative results in the first row of Fig. 3.

Distillation Loss Warm Up. We also discover that variances become small at the beginning and then stable during the training process with PAD loss. This leads to an increase of weight for all samples at the beginning. To explore this phenomenon, we design a *distillation loss warm up* experiment, *i.e.*, increasing the weight of distillation loss from 0 to the default weight linearly during the initial epochs. We observe that distillation loss warm up also performs slightly better than the baseline but worse than PAD, which means both increasing the sample weight during training and assigning different samples different weights are effective techniques in distillation. PAD easily combines these two techniques and exhibits as a powerful approach to complement knowledge distillation.

Table 7. Comparisons PAD with other weighting schemes and warm up. Top-1 accuracy on CIFAR100 and TinyImageNet. $R@1$ on DukeMTMC-reID and CUB-200-2011. $mmAP$ on Pascal VOC07.

Method	CIFAR100	TinyImageNet	Duke-reID	CUB-200	Pascal VOC07
All samples equally	72.85	63.08	79.5	58.6	45.53
Soft-exp	73.54	63.64	80.2	60.1	46.23
Soft-poly	73.38	63.50	79.7	60.4	46.25
Weights from PAD	73.72	65.54	80.6	60.2	46.52
Warm up	73.13	63.94	80.4	59.0	46.05
PAD	74.06	65.64	81.0	61.4	46.92

6   Conclusion

This paper explores adaptive sample weighting in knowledge distillation, which is innovative and effective for distillation. With more attention paid to easy samples, simple weighting schemes promote the performance of knowledge distillation. Moreover, Prime-Aware Adaptive Distillation (PAD) is proposed for further improvement. PAD is seamlessly combined with existing methods to refine them by enhancing the perceived prime samples. We hope the new state-of-the-arts established by PAD can serve as a starting point for future research.

Acknowledgements. This work was supported in part by the National Key Research and Development Program of China under Grant 2017YFA0700800. Thanks Xiruo Tang for her help on paper writing.

References

1. Ahn, S., Hu, S.X., Damianou, A., Lawrence, N.D., Dai, Z.: Variational information distillation for knowledge transfer. In: Proceedings of the IEEE Conference on Computer Vision and Pattern Recognition, pp. 9163–9171 (2019)
2. Ba, J., Caruana, R.: Do deep nets really need to be deep? In: Advances in neural information processing systems, pp. 2654–2662 (2014)
3. Cao, Y., Chen, K., Loy, C.C., Lin, D.: Prime sample attention in object detection. arXiv preprint arXiv:1904.04821 (2019)
4. Chen, G., Choi, W., Yu, X., Han, T., Chandraker, M.: Learning efficient object detection models with knowledge distillation. In: Advances in Neural Information Processing Systems, pp. 742–751 (2017)
5. Chen, Y., Wang, N., Zhang, Z.: DarkRank: accelerating deep metric learning via cross sample similarities transfer. In: Thirty-Second AAAI Conference on Artificial Intelligence (2018)
6. Cho, J.H., Hariharan, B.: On the efficacy of knowledge distillation. In: Proceedings of the IEEE International Conference on Computer Vision, pp. 4794–4802 (2019)
7. Choi, J., Chun, D., Kim, H., Lee, H.J.: Gaussian YOLOV3: an accurate and fast object detector using localization uncertainty for autonomous driving. In: Proceedings of the IEEE International Conference on Computer Vision, pp. 502–511 (2019)
8. Deng, J., Dong, W., Socher, R., Li, L.J., Li, K., Fei-Fei, L.: ImageNet: a large-scale hierarchical image database. In: 2009 IEEE Conference on Computer Vision and Pattern Recognition, pp. 248–255. IEEE (2009)
9. Everingham, M., Van Gool, L., Williams, C.K., Winn, J., Zisserman, A.: The Pascal visual object classes (VOC) challenge. Int. J. Comput. Vis. **88**(2), 303–338 (2010)
10. Gao, M., et al.: An embarrassingly simple approach for knowledge distillation. arXiv preprint arXiv:1812.01819 (2018)
11. He, K., Zhang, X., Ren, S., Sun, J.: Deep residual learning for image recognition. In: Proceedings of the IEEE Conference on Computer Vision and Pattern Recognition, pp. 770–778 (2016)
12. Hermans, A., Beyer, L., Leibe, B.: In defense of the triplet loss for person re-identification. arXiv preprint arXiv:1703.07737 (2017)
13. Hinton, G., Vinyals, O., Dean, J.: Distilling the knowledge in a neural network. arXiv preprint arXiv:1503.02531 (2015)

14. Hu, W., Huang, Y., Zhang, F., Li, R.: Noise-tolerant paradigm for training face recognition CNNs. In: Proceedings of the IEEE Conference on Computer Vision and Pattern Recognition, pp. 11887–11896 (2019)
15. Isobe, S., Arai, S.: Deep convolutional encoder-decoder network with model uncertainty for semantic segmentation. In: 2017 IEEE International Conference on INnovations in Intelligent SysTems and Applications (INISTA), pp. 365–370. IEEE (2017)
16. Kendall, A., Gal, Y.: What uncertainties do we need in Bayesian deep learning for computer vision? In: Advances in Neural Information Processing Systems, pp. 5574–5584 (2017)
17. Kraus, F., Dietmayer, K.: Uncertainty estimation in one-stage object detection. In: 2019 IEEE Intelligent Transportation Systems Conference (ITSC), pp. 53–60. IEEE (2019)
18. Krizhevsky, A., Hinton, G., et al.: Learning multiple layers of features from tiny images (2009)
19. Le, Y., Yang, X.: Tiny ImageNet visual recognition challenge. CS 231N (2015)
20. Li, B., Liu, Y., Wang, X.: Gradient harmonized single-stage detector. In: Proceedings of the AAAI Conference on Artificial Intelligence, vol. 33, pp. 8577–8584 (2019)
21. Li, Q., Jin, S., Yan, J.: Mimicking very efficient network for object detection. In: Proceedings of the IEEE Conference on Computer Vision and Pattern Recognition, pp. 6356–6364 (2017)
22. Lin, T.Y., Goyal, P., Girshick, R., He, K., Dollár, P.: Focal loss for dense object detection. In: Proceedings of the IEEE International Conference on Computer Vision, pp. 2980–2988 (2017)
23. Nix, D.A., Weigend, A.S.: Estimating the mean and variance of the target probability distribution. In: Proceedings of 1994 IEEE International Conference on Neural Networks (ICNN 1994), vol. 1, pp. 55–60. IEEE (1994)
24. Park, W., Kim, D., Lu, Y., Cho, M.: Relational knowledge distillation. In: Proceedings of the IEEE Conference on Computer Vision and Pattern Recognition, pp. 3967–3976 (2019)
25. Peng, B., et al.: Correlation congruence for knowledge distillation. In: Proceedings of the IEEE International Conference on Computer Vision, pp. 5007–5016 (2019)
26. Ren, S., He, K., Girshick, R., Sun, J.: Faster R-CNN: towards real-time object detection with region proposal networks. In: Advances in Neural Information Processing Systems, pp. 91–99 (2015)
27. Ristani, E., Solera, F., Zou, R., Cucchiara, R., Tomasi, C.: Performance measures and a data set for multi-target, multi-camera tracking. In: Hua, G., Jégou, H. (eds.) ECCV 2016. LNCS, vol. 9914, pp. 17–35. Springer, Cham (2016). https://doi.org/10.1007/978-3-319-48881-3_2
28. Romero, A., Ballas, N., Kahou, S.E., Chassang, A., Gatta, C., Bengio, Y.: FitNets: hints for thin deep nets. arXiv preprint arXiv:1412.6550 (2014)
29. Sandler, M., Howard, A., Zhu, M., Zhmoginov, A., Chen, L.C.: MobileNetV2: inverted residuals and linear bottlenecks. In: Proceedings of the IEEE Conference on Computer Vision and Pattern Recognition, pp. 4510–4520 (2018)
30. Shi, Y., Jain, A.K.: Probabilistic face embeddings. In: Proceedings of the IEEE International Conference on Computer Vision, pp. 6902–6911 (2019)
31. Szegedy, C., et al.: Going deeper with convolutions. In: Proceedings of the IEEE Conference on Computer Vision and Pattern Recognition, pp. 1–9 (2015)
32. Tian, Y., Krishnan, D., Isola, P.: Contrastive representation distillation. arXiv preprint arXiv:1910.10699 (2019)

33. Wah, C., Branson, S., Welinder, P., Perona, P., Belongie, S.: The Caltech-UCSD birds-200-2011 dataset (2011)
34. Wang, T., Yuan, L., Zhang, X., Feng, J.: Distilling object detectors with fine-grained feature imitation. In: Proceedings of the IEEE Conference on Computer Vision and Pattern Recognition, pp. 4933-4942 (2019)
35. Wang, X., Han, X., Huang, W., Dong, D., Scott, M.R.: Multi-similarity loss with general pair weighting for deep metric learning. In: Proceedings of the IEEE Conference on Computer Vision and Pattern Recognition, pp. 5022-5030 (2019)
36. Wu, Y., Kirillov, A., Massa, F., Lo, W.Y., Girshick, R.: Detectron2 (2019)
37. Yu, R., Dou, Z., Bai, S., Zhang, Z., Xu, Y., Bai, X.: Hard-aware point-to-set deep metric for person re-identification. In: Proceedings of the European Conference on Computer Vision (ECCV), pp. 188-204 (2018)
38. Yu, T., Li, D., Yang, Y., Hospedales, T.M., Xiang, T.: Robust person re-identification by modelling feature uncertainty. In: Proceedings of the IEEE International Conference on Computer Vision, pp. 552-561 (2019)
39. Yuan, L., Tay, F.E., Li, G., Wang, T., Feng, J.: Revisit knowledge distillation: a teacher-free framework. arXiv preprint arXiv:1909.11723 (2019)
40. Zagoruyko, S., Komodakis, N.: Paying more attention to attention: improving the performance of convolutional neural networks via attention transfer. arXiv preprint arXiv:1612.03928 (2016)
41. Zhong, Y., et al.: Unequal-training for deep face recognition with long-tailed noisy data. In: Proceedings of the IEEE Conference on Computer Vision and Pattern Recognition, pp. 7812-7821 (2019)

Meta-learning with Network Pruning

Hongduan Tian[1($\boxtimes$)], Bo Liu[2], Xiao-Tong Yuan[1], and Qingshan Liu[1]

[1] B-DAT Lab, Nanjing University of Information Science and Technology,
Nanjing 210044, China
hongduan.tian@gmail.com, xtyuan1980@gmail.com, qsliu@nuist.edu.cn
[2] JD Finance America Corporation, Mountain View, CA 94043, USA
kfliubo@gmail.com

Abstract. *Meta-learning* is a powerful paradigm for few-shot learning. Although with remarkable success witnessed in many applications, the existing optimization based meta-learning models with over-parameterized neural networks have been evidenced to ovetfit on training tasks. To remedy this deficiency, we propose a network pruning based meta-learning approach for overfitting reduction via explicitly controlling the capacity of network. A uniform concentration analysis reveals the benefit of network capacity constraint for reducing generalization gap of the proposed meta-learner. We have implemented our approach on top of Reptile assembled with two network pruning routines: Dense-Sparse-Dense (DSD) and Iterative Hard Thresholding (IHT). Extensive experimental results on benchmark datasets with different over-parameterized deep networks demonstrate that our method not only effectively alleviates meta-overfitting but also in many cases improves the overall generalization performance when applied to few-shot classification tasks.

Keywords: Meta-learning · Few-shot learning · Network pruning · Sparsity · Generalization analysis

1 Introduction

The ability of adapting to a new task with several trials is essential for artificial agents. The goal of few-shot learning [25] is to build a model which is able to get the knack of a new task with limited training samples. Meta-learning [3,26,30] provides a principled way to cast few-shot learning as the problem of *learning-to-learn*, which typically trains a hypothesis or learning algorithm to memorize the experience from previous tasks for a future task learning with very few samples. The practical importance of meta-learning has been witnessed in many vision and online/reinforcement learning applications including image classification [17,23], multi-arm bandit [29] and 2D navigation [5].

Among others, one particularly simple yet successful meta-learning paradigm is first-order optimization based meta-learning which aims to train hypotheses that can quickly adapt to unseen tasks by performing one or a few steps of (stochastic) gradient descent [5,23]. Reasons for the recent increasing attention

© Springer Nature Switzerland AG 2020
A. Vedaldi et al. (Eds.): ECCV 2020, LNCS 12364, pp. 675–700, 2020.
https://doi.org/10.1007/978-3-030-58529-7_40

to this class of gradient-optimization based methods include their outstanding efficiency and scalability exhibited in practice [21].

Challenge and Motivation. A challenge in the existing meta-learning approaches is their tendency to overfit [20,33]. When training an over-parameterized meta-learner such as very deep and/or wide convolutional neural networks (CNN) which are powerful for representation learning, there are two sources of potential overfitting at play: the inter-task overfitting of meta-learner (or *meta-overfitting*) to the training tasks and the inner-task overfitting of task-specific learner to the task training data. There have been recent efforts put to deal with inner-task overfitting [16,36]. The study on the inter-task meta-overfitting, however, still remains under explored. Since in principle the optimization-based meta-learning is designed to learn fast from small amount of data in new tasks, we expect the meta-overfitting to play a more important role in influencing the overall generalization performance of the trained meta-learner.

Sparsity model is a promising tool for high-dimensional machine learning with guaranteed statistical efficiency and robustness to overfitting [1,19,34]. It has been theoretically and numerically justified by [2] that sparsity benefits considerably the generalization performance of deep neural networks. In the regime of compact deep learning, the so called *network pruning* technique has been widely studied and evidenced to work favorably in generating sparse subnetworks without compromising generalization performance [6,7,11]. Inspired by these remarkable success of sparsity models, it is natural to conjecture that sparsity would also be beneficial for enhancing the robustness of optimization based meta-learning to meta-overfitting.

Our Contribution. In this paper, we present a novel gradient-based meta-learning approach with explicit network capacity constraint for overfitting reduction. The problem is formulated as learning a sparse meta-initialization network from training tasks such that in a new task the learned subnetwork can quickly converge to the optimal solution via gradient descent. The core idea is to reduce meta-overfitting by controlling the counts of the non-zero parameters in the meta-learner during the training phase. Theoretically, we have established a uniform generalization gap bound for the proposed sparse meta-learner showing the benefit of capacity constraint for improving its generalization performance. Practically, we have implemented our approach in a joint algorithmic framework of Reptile [21] with network pruning, along with two instantiations using Dense-Sparse-Dense (DSD) [7] and Iterative Hard Thresholding (IHT) [11] as network pruning subroutines, respectively. The actual performance of our approach has been extensively evaluated on few-shot classification tasks with over-parameterized wide CNNs. The obtained results demonstrate that our method can effectively alleviate overfitting and achieve similar or even superior generalization performance to the conventional dense models.

2 Related Work

Optimization-Based Meta-learning. The family of optimization-based meta-learning approaches usually learn a good hypothesis which can be fast adapted to unseen tasks [5,12,21,23]. Compared to the metric [13,27] and memory [25,32] based meta-learning algorithms, optimization based meta-learning algorithms are gaining increasing attention due to their simplicity, versatility and effectiveness. As a recent leading framework for optimization-based meta-learning, MAML [5] is designed to estimate a meta-initialization network which can be well fine-tuned in an unseen task via only one or few steps of mini-batch gradient descent. Although simple in principle, MAML requires computing Hessian-vector product for back-propagation, which could be computationally expensive when the model is big. The first-order MAML (FOMAML) is therefore proposed to improve the computational efficiency by simply ignoring the second-order derivatives in MAML. Reptile [21] is another approximated first-order algorithm which works favorably since it maximizes the inner product between gradients from the same task yet different minibatches, leading to improved model generalization. Recently, several hypothesis biased regularized meta-learning approaches have been studied in [4,12,35] with provable strong generalization performance guarantees provided for convex problems. In [16], the meta-learner is treated as a feature embedding module of which the output is used as input to train a multi-class kernel support vector machine as base learner. To deal with overfitting, the CAVIA method [36] decomposes the meta-parameters into the so called context parameters and shared parameters. The context parameters are updated for task adaption with limited capacity while the shared parameters are meta-trained for generalization across tasks.

Network Pruning. Early network weight pruning algorithms date back to Optimal Brain Damage [15] and Optimal Brain Surgeon [10]. A dense-to-sparse algorithm was developed by [8] to firstly remove near-zero weights and then fine tune the preserved weights. As a serial work of dense-to-sparse, the dense-sparse-dense (DSD) method [7] was proposed to re-initialize the pruned parameters as zero and retrain the entire network after the dense-to-sparse pruning phase. The iterative hard thresholding (IHT) method [11] shares a similar spirit with DSD to conduct multiple rounds of iteration between pruning and retraining. [28] proposed a data-free method to prune the neurons in a trained network. In [18], an L_0-norm regularized risk minimization framework was proposed to learn sparse networks during training. More recently, [6] introduced and studied the "lottery ticket hypothesis" which assumes that once a network is initialized, there should exist an optimal subnetwork, which can be learned by pruning, that performs as well as the original network or even superior.

Despite the remarkable success achieved by both meta-learning and network pruning, it still remains largely open to investigate the impact of network pruning on alleviating the meta-overfitting of optimization based meta-learning, which is of primal interest to our study in this paper.

3   Method

3.1   Problem Setup

We consider the N-way K-shot problem as defined in [31]. Tasks are sampled from a specific distribution $p(\mathcal{T})$ and will be divided into *meta training set* $\mathcal{S}^{tr}$, *meta validation set* $\mathcal{S}^{val}$, and *meta testing set* $\mathcal{S}^{test}$. Classes in different datasets are disjoint (i.e., the class in $\mathcal{S}^{tr}$ will not appear in $\mathcal{S}^{test}$). During training, each task is made up of support set $\mathcal{D}^{supp}$ and query set $\mathcal{D}^{query}$. Both $\mathcal{D}^{supp}$ and $\mathcal{D}^{query}$ are sampled from the same classes of $\mathcal{S}^{tr}$. $\mathcal{D}^{supp}$ is used for training while $\mathcal{D}^{query}$ is used for evaluation. For a N-way K-shot classification task, we sample N out of the C classes from dataset, and then K samples are sampled from each of these classes to form $\mathcal{D}^{supp}$, namely $\mathcal{D}^{supp} = \{(\boldsymbol{x}_c^k, y_c^k), k = 1, 2, ..., K; c = 1, 2, ..., N\}$. For example, for a 5-way 2-shot task, we sample 2 data-label pairs from each of 5 classes, thus, such a task has 10 samples. Usually, several other samples of the same classes will be sampled to compose $\mathcal{D}^{query}$. For example, $\mathcal{D}^{query}$ is used in Reptile [21] in evaluation steps. We use the loss function $\ell(v, y)$ to measure the discrepancy between the predicted score vector $v \in \mathbb{R}^C$ and the true label $y \in \{1, ..., C\}$.

Notation. For an integer n, we denote $[n]$ as the abbreviation of the index set $\{1, ..., n\}$. We use $\odot$ to denote the element-wise product operator. We say a function $g : \mathbb{R}^p \mapsto \mathbb{R}$ is G-Lipschitz continuous if $|g(\theta) - g(\theta')| \leq G\|\theta - \theta'\|_2$, and g is H-smooth if it obeys $\|\nabla g(\theta) - \nabla g(\theta')\|_2 \leq H\|\theta - \theta'\|_2$.

3.2   Meta-Learning with Model Capacity Constraint

Our ultimate goal is to learn a good initialization of parameters for a convolutional neural network $f_\theta : \mathcal{X} \mapsto \mathcal{Y}$, where θ is the model parameters set, from a set of training tasks such that the learned initialization network generalizes well to future unseen tasks. Inspired by the recent remarkable success of MAML [5] and the strong generalization capability of sparse deep learning models [2,6], during sparse(or network pruning) phase, we propose to learn from previous task experience a sparse subnetwork started from which the future task-specific networks can be efficiently learned using first-order optimization methods. To this end, we introduce the following layer-wise sparsity constrained stochastic first-order meta-learning formulation:

$$\min_\theta \mathcal{R}(\theta) := \mathbb{E}_{T \sim p(\mathcal{T})} \left[\mathcal{L}_{\mathcal{D}_T^{query}} \left(\theta - \eta \nabla_\theta \mathcal{L}_{\mathcal{D}_T^{supp}}(\theta) \right) \right], \text{ s.t. } \|\theta_l\|_0 \leq k_l, \ l \in [L], \quad (1)$$

where $\mathcal{L}_{\mathcal{D}_T^{supp}}(\theta) = \frac{1}{NK} \sum_{(\boldsymbol{x}_c^k, y_c^k) \in \mathcal{D}_T^{supp}} \ell(f_\theta(\boldsymbol{x}_c^k), y_c^k)$ is the empirical risk for task T and $\mathcal{L}_{\mathcal{D}_T^{query}}(\theta)$ is similarly defined as the loss evaluated over the query set and η is the learning rate. In the constraint, $\|\theta_l\|_0$ denotes the number of non-zero entries in the parameters of l-th layer θ_l which is required to be no larger than a user-specified sparsity level k_l, and L is the total number of network layers.

In general, the mathematical formulation of task distribution $p(\mathcal{T})$ is unknown but we usually have access to a set of i.i.d. training tasks $S = \{T_i\}_{i=1}^M$

sampled from $p(\mathcal{T})$. Thus the following empirical version of the population form in Eq. (1) is alternatively considered for training:

$$\min_\theta \mathcal{R}_S(\theta) := \tfrac{1}{M} \sum_{i=1}^M \left[\mathcal{L}_{\mathcal{D}_{T_i}^{query}} \left(\theta - \eta \nabla_\theta \mathcal{L}_{\mathcal{D}_{T_i}^{supp}}(\theta) \right) \right], \text{ s.t. } \|\theta_l\|_0 \le k_l, \ l \in [L]. \quad (2)$$

To compare with MAML, our model shares an identical objective function, but with the layer-wise sparsity constraints $\|\theta_l\|_0 \le k_l$ imposed for the purpose of enhancing learnability of the over-parameterized meta-initialization network. In view of the "lottery ticket hypothesis" [6], the model in Eq. (2) can be interpreted as a first-order meta-learner for estimating a subnetwork, or a *"winning ticket"*, for future task learning. Inspired by the strong statistical efficiency and generalization guarantees of sparsity models [2,34], we will very shortly show that such a subnetwork is able to achieve advantageous generalization performance over the dense initialization networks learned by vanilla MAML.

3.3   Generalization Analysis

We provide in this section a task-level generalization performance analysis for the proposed model in Eq. (2). Let p be the total number of parameters in the over-parameterized network and $\Theta \subseteq \mathbb{R}^p$ be the domain of interest for θ. Let $k = \sum_{l=1}^L k_l$ be the total desired sparsity level of the subnetwork. The following uniform concentration bound is our main result.

Theorem 1. *Assume that the domain of interest Θ is bounded by R and the loss function $\ell(f_\theta(\boldsymbol{x}), y)$ is G-Lipschitz continuous and H-smooth with respect to θ. Suppose that $0 \le \ell(f_\theta(\boldsymbol{x}), y) \le B$ for all pairs $\{f_\theta(\boldsymbol{x}), y\}$. Then for any $\delta \in (0,1)$, with probability at least $1 - \delta$ over the random draw of S, the generalization gap is uniformly upper bounded for all θ satisfying $\|\theta_l\|_0 \le k_l, l \in [L]$ as*

$$|\mathcal{R}(\theta) - \mathcal{R}_S(\theta)| \le \mathcal{O} \left(B \sqrt{\frac{k \log(p\sqrt{M} G R (1 + \eta H)/(Bk)) + \log(1/\delta)}{M}} \right).$$

In comparison to the $\mathcal{O}\left(\sqrt{p/M}\right)$ uniform bound established in Lemma 1 (see Appendix A.1) for dense networks, the uniform bound established in Theorem 1 is substantially stronger when $k \ll p$, which shows the benefit of network capacity constraint for generalization.

Specially for margin-based multiclass classification, let us consider the margin operator $\mathcal{M}(v, y) := \max_j [v]_j - [v]_y$ associated with the score prediction vector $v \in \mathbb{R}^C$ and label $y \in \{1, ..., C\}$. Let $\ell_\gamma(f_\theta(\boldsymbol{x}), y) = h_\gamma(\mathcal{M}(f_\theta(\boldsymbol{x}), y))$ be a *surrogate* loss of the binary loss (i.e., $\mathbb{1}[y \ne \arg\max_j [f_\theta(\boldsymbol{x})]_j]$) defined with respect to proper γ-margin based loss h_γ such as the hinge/ramp losses and their smoothed variants [22]. By definition, we must have $\mathbb{1}[y \ne \arg\max_j [f_\theta(\boldsymbol{x})]_j] \le \ell_\gamma(f_\theta(\boldsymbol{x}), y)$. In this case, we denote $\mathcal{R}_{\gamma,S}$ the meta-training risk with loss function ℓ_γ and $\tilde{\mathcal{R}}_\gamma$ the corresponding population risk in which the task-level query loss $\mathcal{L}_{\mathcal{D}_T^{query}}$ is evaluated using binary loss as classification error. Then as a direct consequence of Theorem 1, we can establish the following result for margin-based prediction.

Corollary 1. *Suppose that the margin-based loss ℓ_γ is used for model training. Then under the conditions in Theorem 1, for any $\delta \in (0, 1)$, with probability at least $1 - \delta$ the following bound holds for all θ satisfying $\|\theta_l\|_0 \leq k_l, l \in [L]$:*

$$
\tilde{\mathcal{R}}_\gamma(\theta) \leq \mathcal{R}_{\gamma,S}(\theta) + \mathcal{O}\left(B\sqrt{\frac{k\log(p\sqrt{M}GR(1 + \eta H)/(Bk)) + \log(1/\delta)}{M}} \right).
$$

Remark 1. We comment that the above $\mathcal{O}(\sqrt{k/M})$ margin bound derived in the context of sparse meta-learning can be readily extended to sparse deep nets training. Also, the bound can be easily generalized for arbitrary convex surrogates (e.g., cross-entropy loss) of binary loss under proper regularity conditions.

4 Algorithm

We have implemented the proposed model in Eq. 2 based on Reptile [21] (see Algorithm 2) which is a scalable method for optimization-based meta-learning in form of Eq. 2 but without layer-wise sparsity constraint. In order to handle the sparsity constraint, we follow the principles behind the widely applied *dense-sparse-dense* (DSD) [7] and *iterative hard thresholding* (IHT) [11] network pruning algorithms to alternate the Reptile iteration between pruning insignificant weights in each layer and retraining the pruned network.

4.1 Main Algorithm: Reptile with Iterative Network Pruning

The algorithm of our network-pruning-based Reptile method is outlined in Algorithm 1. The learning procedure contains a pre-training phase followed by an iterative procedure of network pruning and retraining. We would like to stress that since our ultimate goal is not to do network compression, but to reduce meta-overfitting via controlling the sparsity level of the meta-initialization network, the final output of our algorithm is typically dense after the retraining phase, which has been evidenced in practice to be effective for improving the generalization performance during testing phase. In the following subsections, we describe the key components of our algorithm in details.

Model Pretraining. For model pre-training, we run a few number of Reptile iteration rounds to generate a relatively good initialization. In each loop of the Reptile iteration, we first sample a mini-batch of meta-tasks $\{T_i\}_{i=1}^s$ from the task distribution $p(\mathcal{T})$. Then for each task T_i, we compute the adapted parameters via (stochastic) gradient descent as $\tilde{\theta}_{T_i} = \theta^{(0)} - \eta \nabla_\theta \mathcal{L}_{\mathcal{D}_{T_i}^{supp}}(\theta^{(0)})$, where $\tilde{\theta}_{T_i}$ denotes the task-specific parameters learned from each task T_i, $\theta^{(0)}$ is the current initialization of model parameters, η is the inner-task learning rate, and $\mathcal{D}_{T_i}^{supp}$ denotes the support set of task T_i. When all the task-specific parameters are updated, the initialization parameters will be updated according to

---

Algorithm 1: Reptile with Iterative Network Pruning

Input   : inner loop learning rate η, outer loop learning rate β, layer-wise
          sparsity level $\{k_l\}_{l=1}^{L}$, mini-batch batch size s for meta training.
Output: $\theta^{(t)}$.
Initialization *Randomly initialize* $\theta^{(0)}$.
/* <u>Pre-training with Reptile</u>   */
while *the termination condition is not met* **do**
 | $\theta^{(0)} = Reptile(\theta^{(0)}, \eta, \beta, s)$;
end
for $t = 1, 2, \dots$ **do**
 | /* <u>Pruning phase</u>   */
 | Generate a network zero-one mask $\mathcal{M}^{(t)}$ whose non-zero entries at each
 | layer l are those top k_l entries in $\theta_l^{(t)}$;
 | Compute $\theta_{\mathcal{M}}^{(t)} = \theta^{(t)} \odot \mathcal{M}^{(t)}$;
 | /* <u>Subnetwork fine-tune with Reptile</u>   */
 | **while** *the termination condition is not met* **do**
 | | $\theta^{(t)} = Reptile(\theta_{\mathcal{M}}^{(t)}, \eta, \beta, s)$;
 | **end**
 | /* <u>Retraining phase</u>   */
 | **while** *the termination condition is not met* **do**
 | | $\theta^{(t)} = Reptile(\theta^{(t)}, \eta, \beta, s)$;
 | **end**
end

$\theta^{(0)} = \theta^{(0)} + \beta\left(\frac{1}{s}\sum_{i=1}^{s}\tilde{\theta}_{T_i} - \theta^{(0)}\right)$ with learning rate β. Here we follow Reptile to use $\frac{1}{s}\sum_{i=1}^{s}\tilde{\theta}_{T_i} - \theta^{(0)}$ as an approximation to the negative meta-gradient, which has been evidenced to be effective for scaling up the MAML-type first-order meta-learning models [21].

Iterative Network Pruning and Retraining. After model pre-training, we proceed to the main loop of our Algorithm 1 that carries out iterative network pruning and retraining.

Pruning Phase. In this phase, we first greedily truncate out of the model a portion of near-zero parameters which are unlikely to contribute significantly to the model performance. To do so, we generate a network binary mask $\mathcal{M}^{(t)}$ whose non-zero entries at each layer l are those top k_l (in magnitude) entries in $\theta_l^{(t)}$, and compute $\theta_{\mathcal{M}}^{(t)} = \theta^{(t)} \odot \mathcal{M}^{(t)}$ as the sparsity restriction of $\theta^{(t)}$. Then we fine-tune the subnetwork over the mask $\mathcal{M}^{(t)}$ by applying Reptile restrictively to this subnetwork with initialization $\theta_{\mathcal{M}}^{(t)}$. Our numerical experiment suggests that sufficient steps of subnetwork fine-tuning tends to substantially improve the stability and convergence behavior of the method.

Algorithm 2: Reptile Algorithm [21]

Input   : model parameters ϕ, inner loop learning rate η, outer loop learning
rate β, mini-batch batch size s for meta training.
Output: the updated ϕ.
Sample a mini-batch tasks $\{T_i\}_{i=1}^s$ of size s;
For each task T_i, compute the task-specific adapted parameters using gradient
descent:

$$\tilde{\phi}_{T_i} = \phi - \eta \nabla_\phi \mathcal{L}_{\mathcal{D}_{T_i}^{supp}}(\phi);$$

Update the parameters: $\phi = \phi + \beta \left(\frac{1}{s} \sum_{i=1}^s \tilde{\phi}_{T_i} - \phi \right)$.

The fine-tuned subnetwork $\theta_{\mathcal{M}}^{(t)}$ at the end of the pruning phase is expected
to reduce the chance of overfitting to noisy data. However, it is also believed
that such subnetwork will reduce the capacity of the network, which could in
turn lead to potentially biased learning with higher training loss. To remedy this
issue, inspired by the retraining trick introduced in [7] for network pruning, we
propose to restore the pruned weights that would be beneficial for enhancing the
model representation power to improve the overall generalization performance.

Retraining Phase. In this phase, the layer-wise sparsity constraints are
removed and the pruned parameters are re-activated for fine-tuning. The retraining procedure is almost identical to the pre-training phase, but with the main
difference that the former is initialized with the subnetwork generated by the
pruning phase while the latter uses random initialization. Such a retraining operation restores the representation capacity of the pruned parameters, which tends
to lead to improved generalization performance in practice. For theoretical justification, roughly speaking, since the sparse meta-initialization network obtained
in the pruning phase generalizes well in light of Theorem 1, it is expected to
serve as a good initialization for future retraining via gradient descent. Then
according to the stability theory of gradient descent methods [9], the output
dense network will also generalize well if the retraining phase converges quickly.

4.2   Two Substantialized Implementations

Reptile with DSD Pruning. The DSD method is an effective network pruning approach for preventing the learned model from capturing noise during the
training [7]. By implementing the main loop with $t = 1$, the proposed Algorithm 1 reduces to a DSD-based Reptile method for first-order meta-learning.

Reptile with IHT Pruning. The IHT method [11] is another representative
network pruning approach which shares a similar dense-sparse-dense spirit with
DSD. Different from the one-shot weight pruning and network training by DSD,
IHT is designed to perform multiple rounds of iteration between pruning and

retraining, and hence is expected to have better chance to find an optimal sparse subnetwork than DSD does. By implementing the main loop of Algorithm 1 with $t > 1$, we actually obtain a variant of Reptile with IHT-type network pruning.

5 Experiments

In this section, we carry out a numerical study for algorithm performance evaluation aiming to answer the following three questions empirically: (Q1) Sect. 5.1: *Does our method contribute to improve the generalization performance?* (Q2) Sect. 5.2: *What roles do pre-training phase and retraining phase play in our method?* (Q3) Sect. 5.3: *Can our method work on more complex models, like MetaOptNet [16] and CAVIA [36]?*

5.1 Few-Shot Classification Performances

We first evaluate the prediction performance of our method for few-shot classification tasks on two popular benchmark datasets: MiniImageNet [31] and TieredImageNet [24]. We have also evaluated our method on Omniglot [14] with numerical results relegated to Appendix C.1 due to space limit. The network used in our experiments is consistent with that considered for Reptile [21]. We test with varying channel number $\{32, 64, 128, 256\}$ in each convolution layer to show the robustness of our algorithms to meta-overfitting. See Appendix B for more details about Model, datasets and hyperparameters.

MiniImageNet. The MiniImageNet dataset consists of 64 training classes, 12 validation classes and 24 test classes. For DSD-based Reptile, with 32 channels, we set the iteration numbers for the pre-traning, pruning and retraining phases respectively as 3×10^4, 5×10^4 and 2×10^4, while with $64, 128, 256$ channels, the corresponding number is 3×10^4, 6×10^4 and 10^4 respectively. For IHT-based Reptile model training, we first pre-train the model for 2×10^4 iterations. Then we iterate between the sparse model fine-tuning (with 1.5×10^4 iterations) and dense-model retraining (with 5×10^3 iterations) for $t = 4$ rounds. The setting of other model training related parameters is identical to those in [21].

Results. The experimental results are presented in Table 1 and some additional results are provided in Table 8 in Appendix C. From these results, we can observe that our methods consistently outperform the considered baselines.

In the 32-channel setting in which the model is less prone to overfit, when applying DSD-based Reptile with 40% pruning rate, the accuracy gain is 0.5% on 5-way 1-shot tasks and 1% on 5-way 5-shot tasks. In the 64-channel setting, our IHT-based Reptile approach respectively improves about 1.5% and 1.95% over the baselines on 5-way 1-shot tasks and 5-way 5-shot tasks. In the setting of 128-channel, the accuracy of DSD-based Reptile on 5-way 1-shot tasks is nearly 3% higher than the baseline while on 5-way 5-shot tasks the gain is about 4.47%.

Table 1. Results on MiniImageNet under varying number of channels and pruning rates.

Methods	Backbone	Rate	5-way 1-shot	5-way 5-shot
Reptile baseline	32-32-32-32	–	50.30±0.40%	64.27±0.44%
	64-64-64-64	–	51.08±0.44%	65.46±0.43%
	128-128-128-128	–	49.96±0.45%	64.40±0.43%
	256-256-256-256	–	48.60±0.44%	63.24±0.43%
DSD+Reptile	32-32-32-32	40%	**50.83±0.45%**	**65.24±0.44%**
	64-64-64-64	30%	**51.91±0.45%**	**67.23±0.43%**
	128-128-128-128	50%	**52.08±0.45%**	**68.87±0.42%**
	256-256-256-256	60%	**53.00±0.45%**	**68.04±0.42%**
IHT+Reptile	32-32-32-32	20%	50.26±0.47%	63.63±0.45%
	64-64-64-64	40%	**52.59±0.45%**	**67.41±0.43%**
	128-128-128-128	40%	**52.73±0.45%**	**68.69±0.42%**
	256-256-256-256	60%	49.85±0.44%	66.56±0.42%

Although in 256-channel case the performance of IHT-based approach drops compared with the 128-channel setting, it still achieves ∼1.2% accuracy gain over the baseline on 5-way 1-shot tasks and ∼3.32% on 5-way 5-shot tasks. These results clearly confirm the robustness of our algorithms to the meta-overfitting suffered from the over-parameterization of CNNs.

Figure 1 shows the evolving curves of training and testing accuracy under varying pruning rates from 0% to 40% for DSD and IHT based Reptile. From these curves we can clearly observe that the gap between training accuracy and testing accuracy reduces when the pruning rate increases, which confirms the predictions of Theorem 1 about the impact of network capacity on generalization.

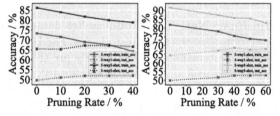

Fig. 1. The generalization performance of DSD-based and IHT-based Reptile on 5-way 1-shot and 5-way 5-shot tasks under 64-channel settings. **Left:** DSD-based Reptile; **Right:** IHT-based Reptile.

Moreover, according to our knowledge, CAVIA [36], which introduces additional context parameters in the model, is also an effective approach for alleviating overfitting. In our experiment, we also compare our method with CAVIA. As shown in Table 8 in Appendix C.2, We can observe that our method can outperform CAVIA in most cases.

TieredImageNet. The TieredImageNet dataset consists of 351 training classes, 97 validation classes and 160 test classes. For TieredImageNet dataset [24], in DSD-based Reptile case, we set iteration numbers for the pre-training, pruning and retraining phase respectively as 3×10^4, 5×10^4 and 2×10^4 for all cases. In IHT-based Reptile, the values of iteration number are the same as those used in the previous experiments for MiniImageNet.

Table 2. Results on TieredImageNet under varying number of channels and pruning rates.

Methods	Backbone	Rate	5-way 1-shot	5-way 5-shot
Reptile baseline	32-32-32-32	–	50.52±0.45%	64.63±0.44%
	64-64-64-64	–	51.98±0.45%	67.70±0.43%
	128-128-128-128	–	53.30±0.45%	69.29±0.42%
	256-256-256-256	–	54.62±0.45%	68.06±0.42%
DSD+Reptile	32-32-32-32	10%	**50.94±0.46%**	64.65±0.44%
	64-64-64-64	10%	**52.62±0.46%**	66.69±0.43%
	128-128-128-128	10%	53.39±0.46%	67.22±0.43%
	256-256-256-256	20%	**54.98±0.45%**	67.98±0.43%
IHT+Reptile	32-32-32-32	10%	50.58±0.46%	63.09±0.45%
	64-64-64-64	20%	**53.22±0.46%**	66.15±0.44%
	128-128-128-128	10%	**53.48±0.45%**	**69.39±0.42%**
	256-256-256-256	10%	**55.06±0.45%**	67.60±0.43%

Results. The experimental results are partly presented in Table 2. More experimental results are available in Table 9 in Appendix C. In 5-way 1-shot classification tasks, both DSD-besed Reptile approach and IHT-based Reptile approach outperform the baselines in all cases. In 32-channel setting, with DSD-based Reptile approach, the improvement of accuracy is 0.42% compared with baseline. In 64-channel setting, the accuracies of DSD-based Reptile and IHT-based Reptile respectively achieve 0.64% and 1.24% improvements. And for 256-channel setting, the best performance is also 0.44% better than baseline.

However, in most 5-way 5-shot classification tasks, the performance of our method drops. We conjecture that the reason is TieredImageNet dataset, compared with MiniImageNet dataset, contains more classes.

5.2   On the Impact of Hyperparameters

We next conduct a set of experiments on MiniImageNet to better understand the impact of pre-training and dense retraining on the task-specific testing performance.

Table 3. Results of ablation study in the 5-way setting. The "±" shows 95% confidence intervals, the "P.T" means "Pre-traning" and the "R.T" means "Retraining".

Methods	P.T	R.T	5-way 1-shot	5-way 5-shot
Reptile baseline(64)	–	–	51.08±0.44%	65.46±0.43%
Reptile baseline(128)	–	–	49.96±0.45%	64.40±0.43%
DSD+Reptile(64, 40%)	√	×	43.92±0.43%	60.09±0.45%
DSD+Reptile(128, 60%)	√	×	47.06±0.44%	55.07±0.44%
IHT+Reptile(64, 40%)	√	×	40.03±0.41%	60.59±0.45%
IHT+Reptile(128, 60%)	√	×	42.01±0.42%	52.71±0.45%
DSD+Reptile(64, 40%)	×	√	50.84±0.45%	66.32±0.44%
DSD+Reptile(128, 60%)	×	√	51.04±0.45%	67.23±0.44%
IHT+Reptile(64, 40%)	×	√	52.07±0.45%	66.90±0.43%
IHT+Reptile(128, 60%)	×	√	52.58±0.45%	67.83±0.42%
DSD+Reptile(64, 40%)	√	√	51.96±0.45%	66.64±0.43%
DSD+Reptile(128, 60%)	√	√	52.27±0.45%	**68.44±0.42%**
IHT+Reptile(64, 40%)	√	√	**52.59±0.45%**	**67.41±0.43%**
IHT+Reptile(128, 60%)	√	√	**52.95±0.45%**	68.04±0.42%

We begin by performing ablation study on pre-training and retraining phases.

Impact of the Retraining Phase. It can be clearly seen from group of results in Table 3 that the retraining phase plays an important role in the accuracy performance of our method. Under the same pruning rate, without the retraining phase, the accuracy of both DSD-based and IHT-based Reptile approach drops dramatically. For an instance, in the 64-channel case with 40% pruning rate, the variant of IHT-based Reptile without retraining phase suffers from a $\sim 11\%$ drop in accuracy compared with the baseline. On the other side, as shown in Fig. 2 that sparsity structure of the network does help to reduce the gap between training accuracy and testing accuracy even without the retraining phase. This confirms the benefit of sparsity for generalization gap reduction as revealed by Theorem 1. Therefore, the retraining phase helps to restore the capacity of the model to further improve the overall generalization performance.

Impact of the Pre-training Phase. From Table 3, we observe that without pre-training phase, the variant algorithms still outperform baselines. Such results demonstrate the importance of pruning and retraining phase from another perspective that merely pruning and retraining the over-parameterized models can achieve similar empirical performance to our method. However, the variant algorithms fail to outperform our method. Since in network pruning, pre-training phase is treated as a necessary phase used to find a set of model parameters which is important [6,7], we conjecture that it is the prematurely pruning before the model being well trained that leads to the drop of the performance.

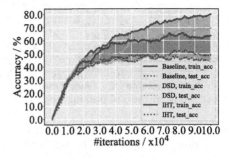

Fig. 2. Ablation study on retraining phase for both DSD-based Reptile and IHT-based Reptile on 64-channel case. The gap between the training accuracy and test accuracy of the variant algorithm of our method becomes smaller than that of baseline.

We now perform experiments to further show how performance varies with different hyperparameters. The tested hyperparameters include (1) The number of pre-training and retraining iterations in DSD-based Reptile; (2) the number of iterations in an IHT pruning-retraining interval; (3) the ratio of pruning iterations in an interval. To be clear, we define $ratio = (Iter_{prune}/Iter_{interval})\%$. In experiments above, we set $Iter_{prune} = 1.5 \times 10^4$ in a 20000-iteration IHT interval, which means the ratio is 75%.

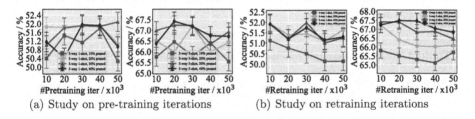

(a) Study on pre-training iterations   (b) Study on retraining iterations

Fig. 3. Study of hyperparameters of DSD-based Reptile. (a). Study on the number of pre-straining iterations. (b). Study on the number of retraining iterations.

DSD-based Reptile. Figure 3 manifests the performance of DSD-based Reptile varying with the two hyperparameters, number of pre-training and retraining iterations. Figure 3(a) reveals that for most cases, too much or too little pre-training will both lead to the deterioration of performance. This is consistent with our ablation study that pre-training helps find a set of robust sparse

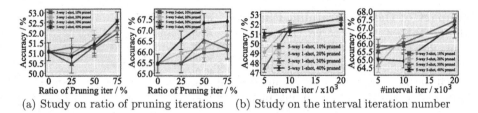

(a) Study on ratio of pruning iterations   (b) Study on the interval iteration number

Fig. 4. Study on hyperparameters of IHT-based Reptile. (a). Study on ratio of pruning iterations. (b). Study on the number of interval iterations.

parameters that is important and excessive pre-training, which reduces the iterations of pruning phase, undermines the generalization performance. Figure 4(a) shows that better performance can be obtained when retraining iterations are smaller than 30K, which indicates that only a small number of retraining steps are required to restore the accuracy without overfitting again.

IHT-based Reptile. Figure 4 shows the hyper-parameter sensitivity results of IHT-based Reptile. Figure 3(b) shows the performance under different ratio of pruning iterations in an IHT interval. It's clear that better performance can be obtained when the ratio is larger than 50%, which means pruning iterations are more than retraining iterations. This reveals that more pruning iterations are required to alleviate overfitting and a small number of retraining steps are enough to help compensate the loss of accuracy. Figure 4(b) shows the performance under varying number of iterations in an IHT interval. We can see that with the interval iterations increasing 5 K to 20 K, the accuracies get improved. This suggests that sufficient steps are required to train a robust model in a loop of pruning-retraining.

Table 4. Results on complex Networks. The "±" shows 95% confidence intervals.

Methods	Backbone	Rate	5-way 1-shot	5-way 5-shot
MetaOptNet(rerun) [16]	ResNet-12	–	61.95±0.60%	77.79±0.45%
DSD-MetaOptNet	ResNet-12	20%	**62.16±0.62%**	77.51±0.48%
CAVIA(rerun) [36]	128-128-128-128	–	48.76±0.99%	62.54±0.78%
DSD-CAVIA	128-128-128-128	10%	**49.53±0.93%**	**63.34±0.79%**
IHT-CAVIA	128-128-128-128	10%	**49.97±0.97%**	**63.48±0.78%**

5.3   Performance on More Complex Networks

We further implement our method on *MetaOptNet* [16] and *CAVIA* [36] to evaluate its the performance on more complex network structures. For MetaOpeNet, we select the ResNet-12 as the network and SVM as the head, and the dropout in the network is replaced by our method. For CAVIA, our methods are applied only on the network parameters. Other settings are the same as those in paper [36]. The dataset used is MiniImageNet. More experimental settings can be referred to Appendix B.3.

As shown in Table 4, for MetaOptNet, our method gains 0.2% improvement on 5-way 1-shot tasks compared with baseline. On 5-way 5-shot tasks, our method can still obtain similar performance. However, there is a trade-off between accuracy and training time. For CAVIA, all cases outperform the baselines, which shows the strong power of our methods in alleviating the overfitting.

6 Conclusion

In this paper, we proposed a cardinality-constrained meta-learning approach for improving generalization performance via explicitly controlling the capacity of over-parameterized neural networks. We have theoretically proved that the generalization gap bounds of the sparse meta-learner have polynomial dependence on the sparsity level rather than the number of parameters. Our approach has been implemented in a scalable meta-learning framework of Reptile with the sparsity level of parameters maintained by network pruning routines including dense-sparse-dense and iterative hard thresholding. Extensive experimental results on benchmark few-shot classification tasks, along with hyperparameter impact study and the study on complex networks, confirm our theoretical predictions and demonstrate the power of network pruning and retraining for improving the generalization performance of gradient-optimization-based meta-learning.

Acknowledgements. Xiao-Tong Yuan is supported in part by National Major Project of China for New Generation of AI under Grant No.2018AAA0100400 and in part by Natural Science Foundation of China (NSFC) under Grant No.61876090 and No.61936005. Qingshan Liu is supported by NSFC under Grant No.61532009 and No.61825601.

A   Proofs of Results

A.1   Proof of Theorem 1

We need the following lemma which guarantees the uniform convergence of $\mathcal{R}_S(\theta)$ towards $\mathcal{R}(\theta)$ for all θ when the loss function is Lipschitz continuous and smooth, and the optimization is limited on a bounded domain.

Lemma 1. *Assume that the domain of interest $\Theta \subseteq \mathbb{R}^p$ is bounded by R and the loss function $\ell(f_\theta(\boldsymbol{x}), y)$ is G-Lipschitz continuous and H-smooth with respect to θ. Also assume that $0 \leq \ell(f_\theta(\boldsymbol{x}), y) \leq B$ for all $\{f_\theta(\boldsymbol{x}), y\}$. Then for any $\delta \in (0, 1)$, the following bound holds with probability at least $1 - \delta$ over the random draw of sample set S for all $\theta \in \Theta$,*

$$|\mathcal{R}(\theta) - \mathcal{R}_S(\theta)| \leq \mathcal{O}\left(B\sqrt{\frac{\log(1/\delta) + p\log(\sqrt{M}GR(1 + \eta H)/B)}{M}}\right).$$

Proof. For any task T, let us denote $\tilde{\ell}(\theta; T) := \mathcal{L}_{\mathcal{D}_T^{query}}\left(\theta - \eta \nabla_\theta \mathcal{L}_{\mathcal{D}_T^{supp}}(\theta)\right)$. Since $\ell(f_\theta(\boldsymbol{x}), y)$ is G-Lipschitz continuous with respect to θ, we can show that

$$
\begin{aligned}
|\tilde{\ell}(\theta; T) - \tilde{\ell}(\theta'; T)| &\leq G \| \theta - \eta \nabla_\theta \mathcal{L}_{\mathcal{D}_T^{supp}}(\theta) - \theta' + \eta \nabla_\theta \mathcal{L}_{\mathcal{D}_T^{supp}}(\theta') \| \\
&\leq G \left(\| \theta - \theta' \| + \eta \| \nabla_\theta \mathcal{L}_{\mathcal{D}_T^{supp}}(\theta) - \nabla_\theta \mathcal{L}_{\mathcal{D}_T^{supp}}(\theta') \| \right) \\
&\leq G(1 + \eta H) \| \theta - \theta' \|,
\end{aligned}
$$

which indicates that $\tilde{\ell}(\theta; T)$ is $G(1 + \eta H)$-Lipschitz continuous for any task T.

As a subset of an L_2-sphere, it is standard that the covering number of Θ with respect to the L_2-distance is upper bounded by

$$
\mathcal{N}(\epsilon, \Theta, L_2) \leq \mathcal{O}\left(\left(1 + \frac{R}{\epsilon}\right)^p \right).
$$

Since the task-level loss function $\tilde{\ell}(\theta; T)$ is $G(1 + \eta H)$-Lipschitz continuous as shown above, it can be verified that the covering number of the class of functions $\tilde{\mathcal{L}} = \left\{ T \mapsto \tilde{\ell}(\theta; T) \mid \theta \in \Theta \right\}$ with respect to L_∞-distance $L_\infty(\tilde{\ell}(\theta_1; \cdot), \tilde{\ell}(\theta_2; \cdot)) := \sup_T |\tilde{\ell}(\theta_1; T) - \tilde{\ell}(\theta_2; T)|$ is given by

$$
\mathcal{N}(\epsilon, \tilde{\mathcal{L}}, L_\infty) \leq \mathcal{N}\left(\frac{\epsilon}{G(1 + \eta H)}, \Theta, L_2 \right) \leq \mathcal{O}\left(\left(1 + \frac{GR(1 + \eta H)}{\epsilon}\right)^p \right).
$$

Therefore, there exists a set of points $\Omega \subseteq \mathbb{R}^p$ with cardinality at most $\mathcal{N}(\epsilon, \tilde{\mathcal{L}}, L_\infty)$ such that the following bound holds for any $\theta \in \Theta$:

$$
\min_{\omega \in \Omega} |\tilde{\ell}(\theta; T) - \tilde{\ell}(\omega; T)| \leq \epsilon, \ \forall T.
$$

For an arbitrary $\omega \in \Omega$, based on Hoeffdings inequality (note that $\ell(\cdot, \cdot) \leq B$ implies $\tilde{\ell}(\cdot, \cdot) \leq B$) we have

$$
\mathbb{P}\left(|\mathcal{R}_S(\omega) - \mathcal{R}(\omega)| > t \right) \leq \exp\left\{ -\frac{Mt^2}{2B^2} \right\}.
$$

For any $\theta \in \Theta$, based on triangle inequality we can show that there exits $\omega_\theta \in \Omega$ such that

$$
\begin{aligned}
|\mathcal{R}_S(\theta) - \mathcal{R}(\theta)| &= |\mathcal{R}_S(\theta) - \mathcal{R}_S(\omega_\theta) + \mathcal{R}_S(\omega_\theta) - \mathcal{R}(\omega_\theta) + \mathcal{R}(\omega_\theta) - \mathcal{R}(\theta)| \\
&\leq 2\epsilon + |\mathcal{R}_S(\omega_\theta) - \mathcal{R}(\omega_\theta)| \leq 2\epsilon + \max_{\omega \in \Omega} |\mathcal{R}_S(\omega) - \mathcal{R}(\omega)|.
\end{aligned}
$$

Applying uniform bound we know that

$$
\begin{aligned}
&\mathbb{P}\left(\sup_{\theta \in \Theta} |\mathcal{R}(\theta) - \mathcal{R}_S(\theta)| \geq 2\epsilon + t \right) \\
&\leq \mathcal{N}(\epsilon, \mathcal{L}, \ell_\infty) \exp\left(-\frac{Mt^2}{2B^2} \right) \leq \mathcal{O}\left(\left(1 + \frac{GR(1 + \eta H)}{\epsilon}\right)^p \exp\left(-\frac{Mt^2}{2B^2} \right) \right).
\end{aligned}
$$

Let us choose $\epsilon = B/\sqrt{M}$ and

$$t = \sqrt{2}B\sqrt{\frac{\log(1/\delta) + p\log(GR(1+\eta H)/\epsilon)}{M}}$$

such that the right hand side of the previous inequality equals δ. Then we obtain that with probability at least $1 - \delta$

$$\sup_{\theta \in \Theta} |\mathcal{R}(\theta) - \mathcal{R}_S(\theta)| \leq \mathcal{O}\left(B\sqrt{\frac{\log(1/\delta) + p\log(\sqrt{M}GR(1+\eta H)/B)}{M}}\right).$$

This proves the desired result.

Based on this lemma, we can readily prove the main result in the theorem.

Proof (Proof of Theorem 1). For any fixed supporting set $J \in \mathcal{J}$, by applying Lemma 1 we obtain that the following uniform convergence bound holds for all θ with $\text{supp}(\theta) \subseteq J$ with probability at least $1 - \delta$ over S:

$$|\mathcal{R}(\theta) - \mathcal{R}_S(\theta)| \leq \mathcal{O}\left(B\sqrt{\frac{\log(1/\delta) + k\log(\sqrt{M}GR(1+\eta H)/B)}{M}}\right).$$

Since by constraint the parameter vector θ is always k-sparse, we thus have $\text{supp}(\theta) \in \mathcal{J}$. Then by union probability we get that with probability at least $1 - \delta$, the following bound holds for all θ with $\|\theta\|_0 \leq k$:

$$|\mathcal{R}(\theta) - \mathcal{R}_S(\theta)| \leq \mathcal{O}\left(B\sqrt{\frac{\log(|\mathcal{J}|) + \log(1/\delta) + k\log(\sqrt{M}GR(1+\eta H)/B)}{M}}\right).$$

It remains to bound the cardinality $|\mathcal{J}|$. From [38, Lemma 2.7] we know $|\mathcal{J}| = \binom{p}{k} \leq \left(\frac{ep}{k}\right)^k$, which then implies the desired generalization gap bound. This completes the proof.

A.2   Proof of Corollary 1

Proof. Let $\mathcal{R}_\gamma$ be a population version of $\mathcal{R}_{\gamma,S}$ with margin-based loss function ℓ_γ used for computing both $\mathcal{L}_{\mathcal{D}_T^{supp}}$ and $\mathcal{L}_{\mathcal{D}_T^{query}}$. Since ℓ_γ is a surrogate of the binary loss as used by $\tilde{\mathcal{R}}$ for query classification error evaluation, we must have $\tilde{\mathcal{R}} \leq \mathcal{R}_\gamma$. Then the desired bound follows directly by invoking Theorem 1 to the considered margin loss.

B   Detailed Experimental Settings

B.1   Model

The model used in our experiments is consistent with that considered for Reptile [21]. The model used throughout the experiment contains 4 sequential modules.

Each module has a convolutional layer with 3×3 kernel, followed by a batch normalization and a ReLU activation. Additionally for the experiments on Mini-ImageNet, a 2 × 2 max-pooling pooling is used on the batch normalization layer output while for Omniglot a stride of 2 is used in convolution. The above network structure design is consistent with those considered for Reptile in [21]. We test with varying channel number {32, 64, 128, 256} in each convolution layer to show the robustness of our algorithms to meta-overfitting.

B.2   Datasets

There are three popular benchmark datasets used in our experiments (Fig. 5).

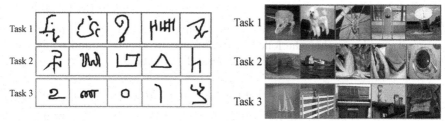

(a) 5-way 1-shot tasks generated from Om-   (b) 5-way 1-shot tasks generated from
niglot   MiniImageNet or TieredImageNet dataset

Fig. 5. Tasks used in our experiments. (a). Tasks generated from Omniglot. (b). Tasks generated from MiniImageNet or TieredImageNet dataset.

Omniglot. The Omniglot dataset has 1623 characters from 50 alphabets. Each character contains 20 instances drawn by different individuals. The size of each image is 28×28. We randomly select 1200 characters for meta training and the rest are used for meta testing. Following [25], we also adopt a data augmentation strategy based on image rotation to enhance performance.

MiniImageNet. The MiniImageNet dataset consists of 100 classes from the ImageNet dataset [37] and each class contains 600 images of size 84 × 84×3. There are 64 classes used for training, 12 classes for validation and 24 classes for testing.

TieredImageNet. The TieredImageNet dataset consists of 608 classes from the ILSVRC-12 dataset [39] and each image is scaled to 84 × 84 × 3. There are 351 classes used for training, 97 classes for validation and 160 classes used for testing.

B.3   Detailed Experimental Settings

The experimental details of DSD-based Reptile and IHT-based Reptile can respectively be seen in Table 5 and Table 6. There are two points of hyper-parameter settings that should be highlighted.

Table 5. Detailed experimental settings for Omniglot, MiniImageNet, TieredImageNet datasets with DSD-based Reptile.

Hyperparameters	Omniglot	MiniImageNet	TieredImageNet
Classes	5	5	5
Shot	1 or 5	1 or 5	1 or 5
Inner batch	10	10	6
Inner iterations	5	8	8
Outer learning rate	1	1	1
Meta batch	5	5	5
Meta iterations	10^4	10^4	10^4
Evaluation batch	5	5	5
Evaluation iterations	50	50	50
Inner learning rate	0.001	0.001	0.001
Pre-train iterations	3×10^4	3×10^4	3×10^4
Pruning iterations(32c)	5×10^4	5×10^4	5×10^4
Retrain iterations(32c)	2×10^4	2×10^4	2×10^4
Pruning iterations(64/128/256c)	5×10^4	6×10^4	5×10^4
Retrain iterations(64/128/256c)	2×10^4	10^4	2×10^4

- The outer learning rate has an initial value 1.0 which will decay with iteration added.
- For MiniImageNet [31] with DSD-based Reptile, the iteration number of pruning phase for 32-channel case is 5×10^4 and for 64/128/256-channel case is 6×10^4. Correspondingly, the iteration number of retraining phase for 32-channel case is 2×10^4 and for 64/128/256-channel case is 10^4.
- For study of complex networks in Sect. 5.3, since our experiments are conducted on 4 RTX 2080Ti GPUs(11GB) while MetaOptNet is trained on 4 Titan X GPUs(12GB), we have to reduce the training shots from 15 to 10 in our experiments. For fair comparison, we rerun the baseline on the same model as in that paper with 10 training shots. We respectively set the number of iterations of pre-training, pruning and retraining as 5 epochs, 20 epochs and 15 epochs. The learning rate is 0.1 in the first 30 epochs, 0.006 in next 5 epochs and 0.0012 in the final 5 epochs.
- For CAVIA, in DSD-based CAVIA case, the numbers of the iterations for pre-training, pruning and retraining phase are respectively 20K, 20K and 20K. In IHT-based CAVIA case, the iteration number of pre-training is 20K, and the iterative phase include 2 sparse-dense processes. Each sparse-dense process 20 K iterations in 16 K iterations are for pruning fine-tuning 4 K iterations are for dense retraining.

C   Additional Experimental Results

This appendix contains complete experimental results for Omniglot, MiniImageNet and TieredImageNet datasets. We performed our methods on 4-layer CNNs with varying channel number $\{32, 64, 128, 256\}$ as mentioned in Sect. B.

C.1   Results on Omniglot dataset

The baselines and all the results of Omniglot dataset are reported in Table 7. For each case, both DSD-based Reptile approach and IHT-based Reptile approach are evaluated on various pruning rates. The settings are the same as proposed in Sect. B.3.

For 32-channel case and 64-channel cases, which is less prone to be overfitting, both DSD-based Reptile approach and IHT-based Reptile approach tend to achieve comparable performance to baselines. When the channel size increases to 128 and 256, slightly improved performance can be observed. This is consistent with our analysis that overfiting is more likely to happen when channel number is relatively large and weight pruning helps alleviate such phenomenon to improve the generalization performance, which then leads to accuracy improvement with retraining operation.

C.2   Results on MiniImageNet dataset

In this section, we report the detailed results of experiments on MiniImageNet dataset.

Table 6. Detailed experimental settings for Omniglot, MiniImageNet, TieredImageNet datasets with IHT-based Reptile.

Hyperparameters	Omniglot	MiniImageNet	TieredImageNet
Classes	5	5	5
Shot	1 or 5	1 or 5	1 or 5
Inner batch	10	10	6
Inner iterations	5	8	8
Outer learning rate	1	1	1
Meta batch	5	5	5
Meta iterations	10^4	10^4	10^4
Evaluation batch	5	5	5
Evaluation iterations	50	50	50
Inner learning rate	0.001	0.001	0.001
Epoch numbers	5	5	5
Iteration numbers per interval	2×10^4	2×10^4	2×10^4
Pruning iterations	1.5×10^4	1.5×10^4	1.5×10^4
Retrain iterations	5×10^3	5×10^3	5×10^3

Table 7. Few Shot Classification results on Omniglot dataset for 4-layer convolutional network with different channels on 5-way 1-shot and 5-way 5-shot tasks. The "±" shows 95% confidence intervals over tasks. The evaluation baselines are run by us.

Methods	Backbone	Rate	5-way 1-shot	5-way 5-shot
Reptile baseline	32-32-32-32	0%	96.63±0.17%	99.31±0.07%
	64-64-64-64	0%	97.68±0.10%	99.48±0.06%
	128-128-128-128	0%	97.99±0.11%	99.60±0.13%
	256-256-256-256	0%	98.05±0.13%	99.65±0.06%
DSD-based Reptile	32-32-32-32	10%	96.42±0.17%	**99.38±0.07**%
		20%	95.98±0.18%	99.33±0.07%
		30%	96.22±0.17%	99.23±0.08%
		40%	96.53±0.17%	99.37±0.07%
	64-64-64-64	10%	**97.64±0.02**%	**99.50±0.05**%
		20%	97.60±0.07%	99.49±0.04%
		30%	97.47±0.05%	99.49±0.05%
		40%	97.43±0.01%	99.45±0.03%
	128-128-128-128	10%	**98.04±0.10**%	99.61±0.10%
		20%	97.99±0.10%	99.62±0.12%
		30%	97.96±0.12%	**99.63±0.12**%
		40%	97.99±0.10%	99.61±0.10%
	256-256-256-256	10%	**98.12±0.12**%	**99.68±0.05**%
		20%	98.02±0.13%	99.66±0.05%
		30%	97.96±0.13%	99.67±0.05%
		40%	97.99±0.10%	99.63±0.06%
IHT-based Reptile	32-32-32-32	10%	**96.65±0.16**%	99.49±0.06%
		20%	96.54±0.17%	**99.57±0.06**%
		30%	96.45±0.17%	99.52±0.06%
		40%	96.21±0.18%	99.48±0.07%
	64-64-64-64	10%	97.63±0.14%	99.49±0.06%
		20%	97.60±0.13%	**99.57±0.06**%
		30%	**97.77±0.15**%	99.52±0.06%
		40%	97.51±0.1%	99.48±0.07%
	128-128-128-128	10%	98.12±0.12%	99.63±0.06%
		20%	**98.22±0.12**%	99.64±0.05%
		30%	98.01±0.13%	**99.65±0.05**%
		40%	98.06±0.12%	99.63±0.06%
	256-256-256-256	10%	**98.16±0.12**%	99.66±0.05%
		20%	98.08±0.13%	**99.69±0.05**%
		30%	98.05±0.13%	99.64±0.05%
		40%	97.90±0.13%	99.65±0.05%

Table 8. Few Shot Classification results on MiniImageNet dataset for 4-layer convolutional network with different channels on 5 way setting. The "±" shows 95% confidence intervals over tasks. The evaluation baselines are run by us.

Methods	Backbone	Rate	5-way 1-shot	5-way 5-shot
Reptile baseline	32-32-32-32	0%	50.30±0.40%	64.27±0.44%
	64-64-64-64	0%	51.08±0.44%	65.46±0.43%
	128-128-128-128	0%	49.96±0.45%	64.40±0.43%
	256-256-256-256	0%	48.60±0.44%	63.24±0.43%
CAVIA baseline	32-32-32-32	0%	47.24±0.65%	59.05±0.54%
	128-128-128-128	0%	49.84±0.68%	64.63±0.54%
	512-512-512-512	0%	51.82±0.65%	65.85±0.55%
DSD-based Reptile	32-32-32-32	10%	**50.65±0.45%**	**65.29±0.44%**
		20%	49.94±0.43%	64.65±0.43%
		30%	50.18±0.43%	**65.78±0.41%**
		40%	**50.83±0.45%**	65.24±0.44%
	64-64-64-64	10%	51.12±0.45%	65.80±0.44%
		20%	**51.91±0.45%**	**67.21±0.43%**
		30%	**51.91±0.45%**	**67.23±0.43%**
		40%	**51.96±0.45%**	**67.17±0.43%**
	128-128-128-128	30%	51.98±0.45%	68.16±0.43%
		40%	52.15±0.45%	68.19±0.43%
		50%	52.08±0.45%	**68.87±0.42%**
		60%	**52.27±0.45%**	68.44±0.42%
	256-256-256-256	60%	**53.00±0.45%**	**68.04±0.42%**
IHT-based Reptile	32-32-32-32	10%	**50.45±0.45%**	63.91±0.46%
		20%	50.26±0.47%	63.63±0.45%
		30%	50.21±0.44%	**65.05±0.45%**
		40%	49.74±0.46%	64.15±0.45%
	64-64-64-64	10%	**52.23±0.45%**	**66.08±0.43%**
		20%	**52.13±0.46%**	**66.78±0.43%**
		30%	51.98±0.45%	66.14±0.43%
		40%	**52.59±0.45%**	**67.41±0.43%**
	128-128-128-128	30%	51.64±0.45%	67.05±0.43%
		40%	52.73±0.45%	**68.69±0.42%**
		50%	52.76±0.45%	67.63±0.43%
		60%	**52.95±0.45%**	68.04±0.42%
	256-256-256-256	60%	**49.85±0.44%**	**66.56±0.42%**

From the table, it can be obviously observed that our method achieves remarkable performance consistently. For one thing, with the number of channels increasing, the accuracies of our methods keep being improved while the baselines perform oppositely. For example, in the 32-channel setting in which the model is less prone to overfit, when applying DSD-based Reptile with 10% and 40% pruning rate, the accuracy gain is 0.35% and 0.5% on 5-way 1-shot tasks and 1.02% and 1% on 5-way 5-shot tasks. In the 64-channel setting, DSD-based Reptile respectively achieves 0.83%, 0.83%, 0.88% improvements over 5-way 1-shot baseline and 1.75%, 1.77%, 1.18% improvements over 5-way 5-shot baseline with pruning rates 20%, 30%, 40%. Meanwhile our IHT-based Reptile approach respectively improves about 1.15%, 1.05%, 1.51% on 5-way 1-shot tasks and 0.62%, 1.32% and 1.95% on 5-way 5-shot tasks with pruning rates 10%, 20%, 40%. In the setting of 128-channel, all the cases of our method outperform the baseline remarkably, and the best accuracy of DSD-based Reptile on 5-way 1-shot tasks is nearly 3% higher than the baseline while on 5-way 5-shot tasks the gain is about 4.47%.

Table 9. Few Shot Classification results on TieredImageNet dataset for 4-layer convolutional network with different channels on 5 way setting. The "$\pm$" shows 95% confidence intervals over tasks. The evaluation baselines are run by us.

Methods	Backbone	Rate	5-way 1-shot	5-way 5-shot
Reptile baseline	32-32-32-32	0%	50.52±0.45%	64.63±0.44%
	64-64-64-64	0%	51.98±0.45%	67.70±0.43%
	128-128-128-128	0%	53.30±0.45%	69.29±0.42%
	256-256-256-256	0%	54.62±0.45%	68.06±0.42%
DSD-based Reptile	32-32-32-32	10%	**50.94±0.46%**	64.65±0.44%
		20%	49.85±0.46%	63.72±0.44%
	64-64-64-64	10%	**52.62±0.46%**	66.69±0.43%
		20%	51.95±0.45%	66.05±0.43%
	128-128-128-128	10%	53.39±0.46%	67.22±0.43%
		20%	52.61±0.46%	66.39±0.43%
	256-256-256-256	10%	54.55±0.45%	**68.60±0.43%**
		20%	**54.98±0.45%**	67.98±0.43%
IHT-based Reptile	32-32-32-32	10%	**50.58±0.46%**	63.09±0.45%
		20%	50.19±0.46%	63.42±0.44%
	64-64-64-64	10%	51.75±0.45%	65.20±0.44%
		20%	**53.22±0.46%**	66.15±0.44%
	128-128-128-128	10%	**53.48±0.45%**	69.36±0.42%
		20%	52.98±0.45%	66.22±0.43%
	256-256-256-256	10%	**55.06±0.45%**	67.60±0.43%
		20%	54.38±0.45%	**69.36±0.42%**

CAVIA [36] is also an effective approach to alleviate overfitting. In CAVIA, additional context parameters are introduced to be updated in task-specific phase while the network parameters are updated during outer loop. In our experiment, we also compare our method with CAVIA. As we can see in Table 8, our method can outperform CAVIA in all cases when the networks have the same number of channels.

C.3   Results on TieredImageNet dataset

In this section, we present the detailed results of experiments on TieredImageNet dataset in Table 9.

From the table, we can observe that our method achieves good performance on 5-way 1-shot classification tasks. For example, in 32-channel settings, the accuracy of DSD-based Reptile with 10% pruning rate is $\sim 0.5\%$ higher than baseline; in 64-channel settings, both DSD-based Reptile and IHT-based Reptile improve the performance evidently, respectively are 0.64% and 1.24%; and in 256-channel settings, the best performance achieves 0.44% improvement over the baseline.

However, in most 5-way 5-shot classification tasks, the performance of our method drops. We conjecture that the reason is TieredImageNet dataset, compared with MiniImageNet dataset, contains more classes.

References

1. Abramovich, F., Grinshtein, V.: High-dimensional classification by sparse logistic regression. IEEE Trans. Inf. Theory **65**(5), 3068–3079 (2019)
2. Arora, S., Ge, R., Neyshabur, B., Zhang, Y.: Stronger generalization bounds for deep nets via a compression approach. In: International Conference on Machine Learning, pp. 254–263 (2018)
3. Bengio, Y., Bengio, S., Cloutier, J.: Learning a synaptic learning rule. In: IJCNN (1990)
4. Denevi, G., Ciliberto, C., Grazzi, R., Pontil, M.: Learning-to-learn stochastic gradient descent with biased regularization. In: International Conference on Machine Learning, pp. 1566–1575 (2019)
5. Finn, C., Abbeel, P., Levine, S.: Model-agnostic meta-learning for fast adaptation of deep networks. In: Proceedings of the 34th International Conference on Machine Learning, vol. 70, pp. 1126–1135. JMLR. org (2017)
6. Frankle, J., Carbin, M.: The lottery ticket hypothesis: finding sparse, trainable neural networks. In: International Conference on Learning Representations (2019)
7. Han, S., et al.: Dsd: Dense-sparse-dense training for deep neural networks. In: International Conference on Learning Representations (2016)
8. Han, S., Pool, J., Tran, J., Dally, W.: Learning both weights and connections for efficient neural network. In: Advances in Neural Information Processing Systems, pp. 1135–1143 (2015)
9. Hardt, M., Recht, B., Singer, Y.: Train faster, generalize better: stability of stochastic gradient descent. In: International Conference on Machine Learning, pp. 1225–1234 (2016)

10. Hassibi, B., Stork, D.G., Wolff, G.J.: Optimal brain surgeon and general network pruning. In: IEEE International Conference on Neural Networks, pp. 293–299. IEEE (1993)

11. Jin, X., Yuan, X., Feng, J., Yan, S.: Training skinny deep neural networks with iterative hard thresholding methods. arXiv preprint arXiv:1607.05423 (2016)

12. Khodak, M., Balcan, M.F., Talwalkar, A.: Provable guarantees for gradient-based meta-learning. In: Advances in Neural Information Processing Systems (2019)

13. Koch, G., Zemel, R., Salakhutdinov, R.: Siamese neural networks for one-shot image recognition. In: ICML deep learning workshop, vol. 2 (2015)

14. Lake, B., Salakhutdinov, R., Gross, J., Tenenbaum, J.: One shot learning of simple visual concepts. In: Proceedings of the Annual Meeting of the Cognitive Science Society, vol. 33 (2011)

15. LeCun, Y., Denker, J.S., Solla, S.A.: Optimal brain damage. In: Advances in Neural Information Processing Systems, pp. 598–605 (1990)

16. Lee, K., Maji, S., Ravichandran, A., Soatto, S.: Meta-learning with differentiable convex optimization. In: Proceedings of the IEEE Conference on Computer Vision and Pattern Recognition, pp. 10657–10665 (2019)

17. Li, Z., Zhou, F., Chen, F., Li, H.: Meta-SGD: learning to learn quickly for few-shot learning. In: Advances in Neural Information Processing Systems (2017)

18. Louizos, C., Welling, M., Kingma, D.P.: Learning sparse neural networks through l_0 regularization. arXiv preprint arXiv:1712.01312 (2017)

19. Maurer, A., Pontil, M.: Structured sparsity and generalization. J. Mach. Learn. Res. **13**(Mar), 671–690 (2012)

20. Mishra, N., Rohaninejad, M., Chen, X., Abbeel, P.: A simple neural attentive meta-learner. In: International Conference on Learning Representations (2018). https://openreview.net/forum?id=B1DmUzWAW

21. Nichol, A., Achiam, J., Schulman, J.: On first-order meta-learning algorithms. arXiv preprint arXiv:1803.02999 (2018)

22. Pillutla, V.K., Roulet, V., Kakade, S.M., Harchaoui, Z.: A smoother way to train structured prediction models. In: Advances in Neural Information Processing Systems, pp. 4766–4778 (2018)

23. Ravi, S., Larochelle, H.: Optimization as a model for few-shot learning. In: International Conference on Learning Representations (2016)

24. Ren, M., et al.: Meta-learning for semi-supervised few-shot classification. arXiv preprint arXiv:1803.00676 (2018)

25. Santoro, A., Bartunov, S., Botvinick, M., Wierstra, D., Lillicrap, T.: Meta-learning with memory-augmented neural networks. In: International Conference on Machine Learning, pp. 1842–1850 (2016)

26. Schmidhuber, J.: Evolutionary principles in self-referential learning. On learning how to learn: The meta-meta-... hook.) Diploma thesis, Institut f. Informatik, Technical University, Munich 1, 2 (1987)

27. Snell, J., Swersky, K., Zemel, R.: Prototypical networks for few-shot learning. In: Advances in Neural Information Processing Systems, pp. 4077–4087 (2017)

28. Srinivas, S., Babu, R.V.: Data-free parameter pruning for deep neural networks. arXiv preprint arXiv:1507.06149 (2015)

29. Sung, F., Zhang, L., Xiang, T., Hospedales, T., Yang, Y.: Learning to learn: meta-critic networks for sample efficient learning. arXiv preprint arXiv:1706.09529 (2017)

30. Thrun, S., Pratt, L.: Learning to Learn. Springer, Heidelberg (2012). https://doi.org/10.1007/978-1-4615-5529-2

31. Vinyals, O., Blundell, C., Lillicrap, T., Wierstra, D., et al.: Matching networks for one shot learning. In: Advances in Neural Information Processing Systems, pp. 3630–3638 (2016)
32. Weston, J., Chopra, S., Bordes, A.: Memory networks. arXiv preprint arXiv:1410.3916 (2014)
33. Yoon, J., Kim, T., Dia, O., Kim, S., Bengio, Y., Ahn, S.: Bayesian model-agnostic meta-learning. In: Advances in Neural Information Processing Systems, pp. 7332–7342 (2018)
34. Yuan, X.T., Li, P., Zhang, T.: Gradient hard thresholding pursuit. J. Mach. Learn. Res. **18**, 1–43 (2018)
35. Zhou, P., Yuan, X., Xu, H., Yan, S., Feng, J.: Efficient meta learning via mini-batch proximal update. In: Advances in Neural Information Processing Systems, pp. 1532–1542 (2019)
36. Zintgraf, L., Shiarli, K., Kurin, V., Hofmann, K., Whiteson, S.: Fast context adaptation via meta-learning. In: International Conference on Machine Learning, pp. 7693–7702 (2019)
37. Krizhevsky, A., Sutskever, I., Hinton, G.E.: Imagenet classification with deep convolutional neural networks. In: Advances in Neural Information Processing Systems, pp. 1097–1105 (2012)
38. Rigollet, P.: 18. s997: High dimensional statistics. Lecture Notes. MIT Open-CourseWare, Cambridge (2015)
39. Russakovsky, O., et al.: Imagenet large scale visual recognition challenge. Int. J. Comput. Vis. **115**(3), 211–252 (2015)

Spiral Generative Network for Image Extrapolation

Dongsheng Guo[1], Hongzhi Liu[1], Haoru Zhao[1], Yunhao Cheng[1],
Qingwei Song[1], Zhaorui Gu[1], Haiyong Zheng[1(✉)],
and Bing Zheng[1,2(✉)]

[1] Underwater Vision Laboratory, Ocean University of China, Qingdao, China
{guodongsheng,liuhongzhi,zhaohaoru,chengyunhao,
songqingyu}@stu.ouc.edu.cn, {guzhaorui,zhenghaiyong,bingzh}@ouc.edu.cn
[2] Sanya Oceanographic Institution, Ocean University of China, Sanya, China
http://ouc.ai

Abstract. In this paper, motivated by human natural ability to perceive unseen surroundings imaginatively, we propose a novel Spiral Generative Network, SpiralNet, to perform image extrapolation in a spiral
manner, which regards extrapolation as an evolution process growing
from an input sub-image along a spiral curve to an expanded full image.
Our SpiralNet, consisting of ImagineGAN and SliceGAN, disentangles
image extrapolation problem into two independent sub-tasks as semantic
structure prediction (via ImagineGAN) and contextual detail generation
(via SliceGAN), making the whole task more tractable. The design of
SliceGAN implicitly harnesses the correlation between generated contents and extrapolating direction, divide-and-conquer while generation-
by-parts. Extensive experiments on datasets covering both objects and
scenes under different cases show that our method achieves state-of-the-
art performance on image extrapolation. We also conduct ablation study
to validate efficacy of our design. Our code is available at https://github.
com/zhenglab/spiralnet.

Keywords: Image extrapolation · GAN · cGAN · SpiralNet

1 Introduction

Suppose that, given a sub-image (*e.g.*, part of a human face), what happens
in your mind when you are asked to draw the entire image (*i.e.*, a whole face)
beyond its boundary? Actually, although the surrounding regions are unseen, we
humans usually first imagine the entire image preliminarily according to the prior

---

D. Guo and H. Liu—Equal contribution.

Electronic supplementary material The online version of this chapter (https://
doi.org/10.1007/978-3-030-58529-7_41) contains supplementary material, which is
available to authorized users.

A. Vedaldi et al. (Eds.): ECCV 2020, LNCS 12364, pp. 701–717, 2020.
https://doi.org/10.1007/978-3-030-58529-7_41

Fig. 1. (a) Our SpiralNet expands a sub-image in four directions evolving along a spiral curve to reach a full image. (b) Exemplar results on different datasets in different cases.

knowledge [21,23], while then draw the details outward from inside progressively based on the sub-image and the imaginary image [36].

Image extrapolation [48] is such a task in computer vision, which aims to fill the surrounding region of a sub-image, *e.g.*, completing an object appearance with part of it or predicting the unseen view from a scene picture. This task is extremely challenging since that: (a) the extrapolated image must be realistic with a reasonable and meaningful context; and (b) the extrapolated region should be consistent in structure and texture with the original sub-image.

Recently, although extrapolating an image is so challenging even for our humans, thanks to the development of Generative Adversarial Network (GAN) [11], a lot of efforts have been made on this task to step forward achieving good performance as well. However, existing GAN-based methods [43,48] for image extrapolation mainly generate a whole image and paste the given part onto it, making the final image look jarring. In addition, due to distant contextual generation problem, directly applying inpainting methods [27,51] tends to generate blurry or repetitive pixels with inconsistent semantics [43].

In this work, motivated by human natural ability to perceive unseen surroundings imaginatively, we propose a novel Spiral Generative Network, **SpiralNet** for short, performing the extrapolation in a spiral fashion. We regard image extrapolation as an evolution process, as illustrated in Fig. 1a, growing from an input sub-image along a spiral curve to an expanded full image. Essentially, SpiralNet is a progressive part-to-whole generation method, "drawing" a full image in four directions slice by slice in a spiral way. In such a way, generation of large surrounding area is divided into turns of easier slice generations, thus yielding results with semantic consistency and vivid details. Figure 1b shows our extrapolating examples in different cases, and we can see that the extrapolating results are all realistic themselves while consistent with original sub-images.

Our **contributions** include: (a) A novel generative framework that extrapolates a sub-image to a full image in a spiral fashion; (b) A SliceGAN that tackles slice-wise image generation and an ImagineGAN that generates imaginary output guiding SliceGAN, equipping a new hue-color loss; (c) State-of-the-art performance on a variety of datasets for image extrapolation in different cases.

2   Related Work

2.1   Generative Adversarial Networks

Starting from the groundbreaking work by Goodfellow et al. [11], GANs have drawn wide attention in computer vision world. Then, many efforts have been made on GANs to improve the generative performance [1,4,12,19,20,29,31,37]. Thereinto conditional GAN (cGAN) [30] is allowed to generate images that have certain conditions or attributes, which can be widely used in many tasks, for instance, image-to-image translation [5,16,17,25,55]. Image extrapolation aims to generate the surrounding regions from the visual content, thus can be considered as an image-conditioned generation task.

Recent cGAN-based models have shown promising results on similar tasks like image inpainting [27,32,50,51], image editing [7,54], and texture synthesis [26,42,49]. But for image extrapolation task, it's really hard for a cGAN to generate semantically consistent content with visually pleasing details, while directly using inpainting methods to image extrapolation is prone to resulting in poor results due to distant contextual generation problem [43,48].

2.2   Image Extrapolation

Image extrapolation fills content outside of visual images. Previous possible solutions can be typically categorized as non-parametric [2,3,9,35,40,45,52] and parametric [43,48] methods. Non-parametric methods mainly formulate the problem into matching and stitching based on a pre-constructed dataset, specifically, they usually retrieve the candidate images by subimage matching, and stitch these wrapped images into the input. Thereby they work in a data-driven manner that is strictly limited by the used dataset, also it's hard to be applied in complex cases like fine texture or sophisticated scene. Recently GAN-based approaches have made great efforts in overcoming weaknesses of non-parametric methods. Particularly, Wang et al. [48] first proposed a cGAN-based approach to address the issues of size expansion and one-side constraints. Teterwak et al. [43] also followed the cGAN framework by introducing semantic conditioning to the discriminator for one-side image extension.

Compared to current cGAN-based extrapolation methods, our method disentangles image extrapolation problem into two relatively independent sub-tasks as semantic structure prediction (via ImagineGAN) and contextual detail generation (via SliceGAN), making the whole task more tractable. The design of SliceGAN implicitly harnesses the correlation between generated contents and extrapolating direction, divide-and-conquer while generation-by-parts.

3   Spiral Generative Network

We regard image extrapolation as an evolution process shown in Fig. 2, growing from an input sub-image along a spiral curve to an expanded full image. Given

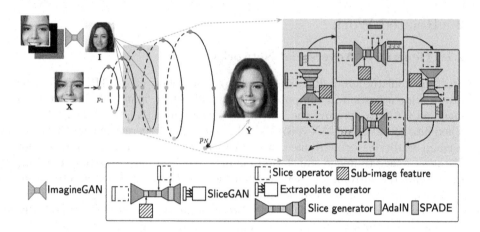

Fig. 2. Our spiral growing evolution for image extrapolation. Refer to text for details.

an input image $\mathbf{X} \in \mathbb{R}^{h \times w \times c}$ and filling margin $m = (m^l, m^t, m^r, m^b)$, where m^l, m^t, m^r, and m^b refer to left, top, right, and bottom filling margin respectively. The goal of image extrapolation is to output an image $\hat{\mathbf{Y}} \in \mathbb{R}^{h' \times w' \times c}$ with a visually pleasing appearance, where $h' = h + m^t + m^b$, $w' = w + m^l + m^r$, and $\mathbf{X}$ is a sub-image of $\hat{\mathbf{Y}}$.

We consider that $\mathbf{X}$ evolves along a series of points $P = \{p_1, p_2, \cdots, p_N\}$ on a spiral curve until it reaches $\hat{\mathbf{Y}}$ after N growth. Each point p on the spiral curve is represented by its turn number and corresponding growing direction (*i.e.*, left, top, right, and bottom). For convenience, we consider that the growing size τ at each point is the same.

According to given margin m and growing size τ, we can figure out total number of points N and total number of turns T for the spiral growing. As to point p on spiral curve, we denote growing function at p as $G_p(\cdot)$. For the k-th point p_k, the input $\mathbf{X}_{p_k}$ grows to $\mathbf{X}_{p_{k+1}}$ by $\mathbf{X}_{p_{k+1}} = G_{p_k}(\mathbf{X}_{p_k})$, where p_{k+1} represents next point on spiral curve. While growing from $\mathbf{X}_{p_k}$ to $\mathbf{X}_{p_{k+1}}$, sizes of input/output and filling margin change accordingly. Finally, $\mathbf{X} \in \mathbb{R}^{h \times w \times c}$ evolves to $\hat{\mathbf{Y}} \in \mathbb{R}^{h' \times w' \times c}$ through growing at N points in T turns, and the evolution can be expressed as:

$$\hat{\mathbf{Y}} = F(\mathbf{X}) = G_{p_N}(G_{p_{N-1}}(\cdots(G_{p_1}(\mathbf{X})))). \tag{1}$$

Meanwhile, h and w change to h' and w' respectively, m_{p_N} becomes $(0, 0, 0, 0)$.

Notably, four total numbers of turns in four directions are not necessarily equal, since sub-image $\mathbf{X}$ may not be located in the center of $\hat{\mathbf{Y}}$, such that the growth in four directions will not stop at the same time.

3.1   ImagineGAN

We present ImagineGAN to "draw" an imaginary result of extrapolation according to given sub-image, regarded as a coarse reference for SliceGAN to refine.

We propose this strategy by mimicking human imagination [21,23] to address the image extrapolation task.

Our ImagineGAN is essentially a cGAN with an encoder-decoder generator G_I, encoding given sub-image $\mathbf{X} \in \mathbb{R}^{h \times w \times c}$ with a margin mask $\mathbf{M}$ and an uniform noise distribution $\mathbf{Z}$, to generate an imaginary output $\mathbf{I} \in \mathbb{R}^{h \times w \times c}$: $\mathbf{I} = G_I(\mathbf{X}, \mathbf{M}, \mathbf{Z})$. Both inputs $\mathbf{X}, \mathbf{M}, \mathbf{Z}$ and output $\mathbf{I}$ have the same small size (e.g., 128×128), taking full advantage of GAN for low-resolution image generation.

Except for adversarial loss, our ImagineGAN is designed with extra losses for better performance. In particular, we propose a novel hue-color loss in this task, to eliminate bright color spots and avoid dark while stabilize the training.

Hue-Color Loss. Hue is the most basic element of a color and what most people think of when they think "color" [10,28]. Thus, it would be helpful to keep consistent hue during extrapolation. However, according to cylindrical HSL/HSV representations of an RGB colorcube [13], same hue may lead to quite different color appearance, which should be avoided for extrapolation. To constrain both hue consistency and color harmony, we formulate a new hue-color loss as:

$$\mathcal{L}_{hue}^{\mathbf{I}} = \frac{1}{h \times w} \sum_{i,j} \left\{ 1 - \min \left[\cos(\mathbf{I}_{ij}, \bar{\mathbf{Y}}_{ij}), \cos(\mathbb{1} - \mathbf{I}_{ij}, \mathbb{1} - \bar{\mathbf{Y}}_{ij}) \right] + \xi \right\}^{\gamma}, \quad (2)$$

where $\bar{\mathbf{Y}} \in \mathbb{R}^{h \times w \times c}$ is the downscaled result of real image $\mathbf{Y}$, ξ is a very small number added to avoid zero, $\gamma < 1$ is used to stretch the difference for better optimization, and we set $\xi = 0.001$ and $\gamma = 0.4$ in our experiments.

Compared to color loss [47] and reconstruction loss [17], our hue-color loss cares about real "color" regardless of gray (please refer to *supplementary file* for mathematical derivation), which is really beneficial to tasks like image extrapolation, which requires both semantic consistency and visual realism. Actually, in our work, we find that synthesized images usually become dark while bright color spots appear on much colorful situations (e.g., Flowers [33]), and our hue-color loss does solve this issue. Furthermore, we surprisingly find that this loss can stabilize the training as well. Please see Sect. 4.5 for ablative experiments.

Perceptual Loss. Following previous works [18,32], we also use perceptual loss $\mathcal{L}_{perc}^{\mathbf{I}}$ to penalize imaginary output $\mathbf{I}$ for that is not perceptually similar to $\bar{\mathbf{Y}}$, by defining a distance measure between activation maps:

$$\mathcal{L}_{perc}^{\mathbf{I}} = \mathbb{E} \left[\sum_u \frac{1}{N_u} \|\sigma_u(\mathbf{I}) - \sigma_u(\bar{\mathbf{Y}})\|_1 \right], \quad (3)$$

where N_u is the number of elements in the u-th activation layer, σ_u is the activation map of the u-th layer of a pretrained network (e.g., VGG-19 [41]).

Adversarial Loss. The adversarial loss $\mathcal{L}_{adv}^{\mathbf{I}}$ of ImagineGAN is:

$$\mathcal{L}_{adv}^{\mathbf{I}}(G_{\mathbf{I}}, D_{\mathbf{I}}) = \mathbb{E}_{(\bar{\mathbf{Y}}, \mathbf{X})}[\log(D_{\mathbf{I}}(\bar{\mathbf{Y}}, \mathbf{X}))] + \mathbb{E}_{(\mathbf{I}, \mathbf{X})}[\log(1 - D_{\mathbf{I}}(\mathbf{I}, \mathbf{X}))], \qquad (4)$$

where the generator $G_{\mathbf{I}}$ is trained to minimize this objective against an adversarial discriminator $D_{\mathbf{I}}$ that tries to maximize it.

Total Loss. The total loss of ImagineGAN is:

$$\mathcal{L}_{total}^{\mathbf{I}} = \lambda_{adv}^{\mathbf{I}}\mathcal{L}_{adv}^{\mathbf{I}} + \lambda_{hue}^{\mathbf{I}}\mathcal{L}_{hue}^{\mathbf{I}} + \lambda_{perc}^{\mathbf{I}}\mathcal{L}_{perc}^{\mathbf{I}}, \qquad (5)$$

where $\lambda_{adv}^{\mathbf{I}}$, $\lambda_{hue}^{\mathbf{I}}$, and $\lambda_{perc}^{\mathbf{I}}$ are weights to balance different losses. We empirically set $\lambda_{adv}^{\mathbf{I}} = 0.1$, $\lambda_{hue}^{\mathbf{I}} = 10$, and $\lambda_{perc}^{\mathbf{I}} = 1$ for our experiments in this work.

3.2   SliceGAN

We devise a novel slice-wise GAN, dubbed SliceGAN, to implement growing function $G_p(\cdot)$ (at point p). As shown in Fig. 2, SliceGAN (at point p) consists of slice operator ψ_p, slice generator G_p^S, extrapolate operator ϕ_p, as well as a spiral discriminator D_S and an extrapolate discriminator D_E (both unshown in Fig. 2).

For the k-th point p_k ($k = 1, 2, \cdots, N$), SliceGAN G_{p_k} takes an extrapolated image $\mathbf{X}_{p_k}$ and an imaginary image $\bar{\mathbf{I}}$ as inputs, and outputs an extrapolated image $\mathbf{X}_{p_{k+1}}$. The imaginary image $\bar{\mathbf{I}}$ has the same size of $\hat{\mathbf{Y}}$, and is upscaled from $\mathbf{I}$ which has the same size of $\mathbf{X}$ and is generated by our ImagineGAN.

Slice Operator. Slice operator aims to cut slice from image. The cutting size of slice operator is equal to growing size at each point, namely τ. For SliceGAN at p_k, there are two slice operators that cut slices $S_{p_k}^{\mathbf{X}}$ and $S_{p_k}^{\bar{\mathbf{I}}}$ from $\mathbf{X}_{p_k}$ and $\bar{\mathbf{I}}$ respectively, $i.e.$, $S_{p_k}^{\mathbf{X}} = \psi_{p_k}(\mathbf{X}_{p_k})$ and $S_{p_k}^{\bar{\mathbf{I}}} = \psi_{p_k}(\bar{\mathbf{I}})$.

Slice Generator. To better use the information from imaginary slice $S_{p_k}^{\bar{\mathbf{I}}}$, original sub-image $\mathbf{X}$, and closest slice $S_{p_k}^{\mathbf{X}}$ for slice-wise extrapolation both semantically and visually, we design a new Encoder-AdaIN-SPADE|Decoder structure for slice-wise generator $G_{p_k}^S$ shown in Fig. 3. The encoder takes in charge of imaginary slice, fusing sub-image style in its latent space by AdaIN [15], and then the decoder combines with semantic information from closest slice via SPADE [34], yielding extrapolated slice: $S_{p_k}^O = G_{p_k}^S(\mathbf{X}, S_{p_k}^{\mathbf{X}}, S_{p_k}^{\bar{\mathbf{I}}})$.

It is worth mentioning that slice $S_{p_k}^{\mathbf{X}}$ in $\mathbf{X}_{p_k}$ is closest to extrapolated slice $S_{p_k}^O$ in $\mathbf{X}_{p_{k+1}}$, while $S_{p_k}^{\bar{\mathbf{I}}}$ in $\bar{\mathbf{I}}$ is corresponding to extrapolated slice $S_{p_k}^O$ in $\mathbf{X}_{p_{k+1}}$. In such a way, we semantically combine meaningful slice information from sub-image and imaginary image for slice-wise extrapolating. Notably, our SliceGAN is designed without independent discriminator, for considering semantic coherence and computational complexity (see Sect. 3.3).

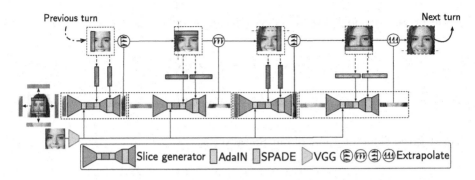

Fig. 3. Four SliceGANs in one spiral turn.

Extrapolate Operator. Extrapolate operator aims to output an extrapolated image $\mathbf{X}_{p_{k+1}}$ by stitching output slice $S_{p_k}^O$ back to input $\mathbf{X}_{p_k}$: $\mathbf{X}_{p_{k+1}} = \phi_{p_k}(S_{p_k}^O, \mathbf{X}_{p_k})$. Now, we complete extrapolation at point p_k using one SliceGAN.

Shared Spiral SliceGAN. Our SpiralNet includes N slice generators for N points on spiral curve, while a complete spiral turn has four slice generators in four directions as shown in Fig. 3. When we need to grow more for extrapolation, we will have more slice generators, and accordingly the number of parameters for the whole SpiralNet will be huge. To tackle this issue, we share the weights of all slice generators. That is, our SpiralNet only has one independent SliceGAN.

3.3 Spiral Loss Design

Adversarial Loss. We devise a spiral discriminator D_S and an extrapolate discriminator D_E to distinguish the whole spiral evolving result $\hat{\mathbf{Y}}$ and the partial extrapolating region $\hat{\mathbf{E}}$ from the corresponding real ones $\mathbf{Y}$ and $\mathbf{E}$, where $\mathbf{E} = \mathbf{Y} \odot (1 - \bar{\mathbf{M}})$ and $\hat{\mathbf{E}} = \hat{\mathbf{Y}} \odot (1 - \bar{\mathbf{M}})$ ($\bar{\mathbf{M}} \in \mathbb{R}^{h' \times w' \times 1}$, $\odot$ represents Hadamard product). Then, the adversarial losses are:

$$\mathcal{L}_{adv}^S(F, D_S) = \mathbb{E}_{\mathbf{Y}}[\log(D_S(\mathbf{Y}))] + \mathbb{E}_{\hat{\mathbf{Y}}}[\log(1 - D_S(\hat{\mathbf{Y}}))], \tag{6}$$

$$\mathcal{L}_{adv}^E(F, D_E) = \mathbb{E}_{\mathbf{E}}[\log(D_E(\mathbf{E}))] + \mathbb{E}_{\hat{\mathbf{E}}}[\log(1 - D_E(\hat{\mathbf{E}}))], \tag{7}$$

where F is evolving function in Eq. 1, which is trained to minimize this objective against D_S and D_E that try to maximize it. The spiral adversarial loss is:

$$\mathcal{L}_{adv} = \left(\mathcal{L}_{adv}^S + \mathcal{L}_{adv}^E\right)/2. \tag{8}$$

Here spiral discriminator takes care of overall consistency, while extrapolate discriminator mainly focuses on stitching continuity.

L1 Loss. We minimize reconstructed differences between $\mathbf{Y}$ and $\hat{\mathbf{Y}}$ by:

$$\mathcal{L}_{L1} = \mathbb{E}_{(\hat{\mathbf{Y}}, \mathbf{Y})}\left[\|\hat{\mathbf{Y}} - \mathbf{Y}\|_1\right]. \tag{9}$$

Style Loss. We adopt style loss [38] to measure differences between covariances of activation maps:

$$\mathcal{L}_{style} = \mathbb{E}_v \left[\|G_v^\sigma(\hat{\mathbf{Y}}) - G_v^\sigma(\mathbf{Y})\|_1 \right], \qquad (10)$$

where G_v^σ is a $G_v \times G_v$ Gram matrix constructed from activation maps σ_v.

Total Loss. The total loss of our SpiralNet is:

$$\mathcal{L}_{total} = \lambda_{adv}\mathcal{L}_{adv} + \lambda_{L1}\mathcal{L}_{L1} + \lambda_{style}\mathcal{L}_{style} + \lambda_{hue}\mathcal{L}_{hue}, \qquad (11)$$

where $\mathcal{L}_{hue}$ is defined the same as Eq. 2, λ_{adv}, λ_{L1}, λ_{style}, and λ_{hue} are weights to balance different losses. We empirically set $\lambda_{adv} = 0.1$, $\lambda_{L1} = 10$, $\lambda_{style} = 250$, and $\lambda_{hue} = 10$ for our experiments in this work.

3.4   Case of Unknown Margin

Suppose that only given input sub-image $\mathbf{X} \in \mathbb{R}^{h \times w \times c}$ and output size $h' \times w' \times c$, it's hard to know the position of $\mathbf{X}$ in $\hat{\mathbf{Y}}$, such that margin m is unknown. In this case, previous approach [48] is unable to work. While, for our approach, thanks to the design of imaginary strategy (without margin mask input), we can match input sub-image $\mathbf{X}$ within upscaled imaginary output $\bar{\mathbf{I}}$ to locate position of $\mathbf{X}$ in $\hat{\mathbf{Y}}$. In such a way, we actually obtain the filling margin indirectly. Meanwhile, this strategy is also helpful to other approaches such as SRN [48]. We adopt normalized cross-correlation template matching method [39] for experiments.

3.5   Implementation Details

Network Architecture. We adopt encoder-decoder structure similar to Cycle-GAN [55] for our ImagineGAN's and slice generators. Differently, for slice generator, we replace eight residual blocks to six in bottleneck, and moreover, we insert one AdaIN layer before bottleneck residual blocks to fuse style information, and two SPADE layers before two transposed convolution layers respectively to combine semantic information, yielding a new Encoder-AdaIN-SPADE|Decoder structure. In addition, we use patch discriminator based on pix2pix [17] for ImagineGAN's and our extrapolate discriminators with replacing batch normalization with spectral normalization [31], and Inspired by MUSICAL [46], we adopt a similar structure to DenseNet [14] as our spiral discriminator. See the details in supplementary file.

Training Details. ImagineGAN is trained independently beforehand, whose generator and discriminator are trained jointly using Adam optimizer [22] with the same parameters of learning rate $\alpha = 0.0002$, $\beta_1 = 0.5$, and $\beta_2 = 0.9$. Then, all SliceGANs and spiral/extrapolate discriminators are trained using the same settings of Adam optimizer as those in ImagineGAN.

Table 1. Training and testing split on eight datasets. The first four are object datasets and the rest are scene datasets.

Dataset	#Train	#Test	#Total
CelebA-HQ [19]	28,000	2,000	30,000
Stanford cars [24]	4,166	1,000	5,166
CUB [44]	4,200	915	5,115
Flowers [33]	7,000	1,189	8,189
Cityscapes [6]	2,975	1,525	4,500
Place365 sky [53]	5,000	100	5,100
Paris street-view [8]	13,000	1,900	14,900
Place365 desert road [53]	5,000	100	5,100

Table 2. User study results. Each entry shows percentage of cases where results by SpiralNet are judged more realistic than Boundless and SRN.

SpiralNet	>Boundless	>SRN
CelebA-HQ	–	88.25%
Stanford cars	–	88.33%
CUB	–	80.00%
Flowers	–	86.67%
Cityscapes	–	77.50%
Place365 sky	–	80.83%
Paris StreetView	93.33%	71.67%
Place365 desert road	63.33%	59.17%

4   Experiments

To evaluate the performance of our proposed method on image extrapolation, we conduct experiments on eight datasets: CelebA-HQ [19], Stanford Cars [24], CUB [44], Flowers [33], Paris StreetView [8], Cityscapes [6], Place365 Desert Road and Sky [53], considering the cases of objects (faces, cars, birds and flowers) as well as scenes (streetview, cityscapes, desert road and sky).

For Stanford Cars and CUB, we crop the objects using given bounding box and then resize them to 256×256, also we drop severely distorted objects for extrapolation task. We list training and testing split on eight datasets in Table 1, where we keep default official split on Cityscapes and Place365 datasets, and select samples randomly on other datasets.

We consider three different cases of image extrapolation task for evaluation: (1) four-side extrapolation for $128 \times 128 \rightarrow 256 \times 256$ on CelebA-HQ, Stanford Cars, CUB and Flowers; (2) two-side extrapolation for $256 \times 256 \rightarrow 512 \times 256$ on Cityscapes and Place365 Sky; and (3) one-side extrapolation for $256 \times 256 \rightarrow 512 \times 256$ on Paris StreetView and Place365 Desert Road.

We compare our method with state-of-the-art Boundless [43] in one-side case and SRN [48] in all three cases. Besides, we deal with the case of unknown margin (see Sect. 3.4, namely SpiralNet-UM) on CelebA-HQ for instance.

4.1   Quantitative Comparison

Following Boundless [43] and SRN [48], we use peak signal-to-noise ratio (PSNR), structural similarity index measure (SSIM) and Frechet Inception Distance (FID) as metrics for evaluating semantic consistency and visual realism (higher is better for PSNR and SSIM, lower is better for FID), and results in Table 3 validate that our SpiralNet outperforms Boundless and SRN in almost all cases. Also note that our ImagineGAN (as a cGAN) performs worse than final Spiral-Net and extremely poor in terms of FID, indicating visually unpleasing results.

To compare photorealism and faithfulness of extrapolated outputs, we also conduct a user study of pairwise A/B tests [17,48]. Our settings are similar to

Table 3. Quantitative comparison results in different cases.

Dataset (case)	Metrics	Boundless	SRN	ImagineGAN	SpiralNet (SpiralNet-UM)
CelebA-HQ (four-side)	PSNR	–	15.17	15.09	**16.05** (15.82)
	SSIM	–	0.6752	0.6361	**0.6815** (0.6350)
	FID	–	32.25	45.92	**21.17** (23.88)
Stanford cars (four-side)	PSNR	–	13.34	13.56	**14.31**
	SSIM	–	0.5479	0.5107	**0.5775**
	FID	–	37.11	53.12	**23.64**
CUB (four-side)	PSNR	–	15.31	15.44	**16.22**
	SSIM	–	0.5112	0.4805	**0.5313**
	FID	–	80.13	97.61	**56.50**
Flowers (four-side)	PSNR	–	13.49	14.98	**15.67**
	SSIM	–	0.4660	0.4681	**0.5078**
	FID	–	66.01	75.11	**52.14**
Cityscapes (two-side)	PSNR	–	20.33	20.12	**20.43**
	SSIM	–	0.6980	0.6642	**0.7125**
	FID	–	28.90	114.00	**22.34**
Place365 sky (two-side)	PSNR	–	21.44	19.90	**21.75**
	SSIM	–	0.7716	0.7479	**0.7834**
	FID	–	52.50	94.41	**51.55**
Paris StreetView (one-side)	PSNR	16.70	16.37	16.39	**17.43**
	SSIM	0.5846	0.5641	0.5377	**0.5970**
	FID	52.02	**30.27**	75.19	35.58
Place365 desert road (one-side)	PSNR	19.04	19.45	19.07	**20.22**
	SSIM	0.6825	0.6877	0.6761	**0.7026**
	FID	86.10	85.59	122.50	**80.66**

SRN [48]. For each dataset, we randomly choose 40 pairwise results extrapolated by SpiralNet vs. Boundless and SpiralNet vs. SRN separately from the same inputs. The users are required to select the more realistic image in each pair, and they are given unlimited time to make the decision. Each pair is judged by at least 3 different users. The results shown in Table 2 validate that our SpiralNet performs better than Boundless and SRN on all available datasets.

4.2 Qualitative Comparison

We also show qualitative comparison of Boundless, SRN and our SpiralNet in Fig. 4. Our method extrapolates more reasonable results with semantic consistency and vivid details avoiding meaningless content and cluttered background. Moreover, Fig. 5 and Table 3 (CelebA-HQ) shows that our SpiralNet-UM also works well. More results are shown in *supplementary file* for further reference.

4.3 Why Spiral Is Necessary

Our spiral architecture is necessary for tasks like image extrapolation conditioned on three aspects below, with various cases of ablation study for validating necessity of each one (results are shown in Table 4 and Fig. 6):

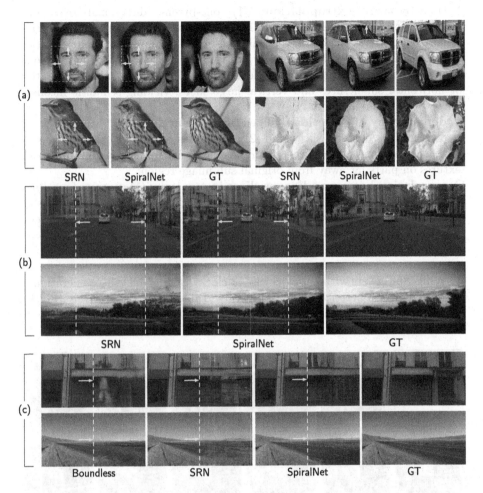

Fig. 4. Qualitative comparison results in different cases. (a) Four-side on CelebA-HQ, Stanford Cars, CUB and Flowers. (b) Two-side on Cityscapes and Place365 Sky. (c) One-side on Paris StreetView and Place365 Desert Road.

Fig. 5. Case of unknown margin on CelebA-HQ.

A. turn-by-turn extrapolation: (1) one-by-one directional extrapolation (A.one-by-one); (2) horizontal-then-vertical directional extrapolation (A.horizontal-vertical); and (3) vertical-then-horizontal directional extrapolation (A.vertical-horizontal). One exemplar in Fig. 6 shows that, destroying the equilibrium of slice growth in four directions, will lead to inharmonious generators for horizontal small slices and vertical large slices, yielding semantic inconsistency with cluttered content.

B. dependency of directional slices in adjacent turns: (1) without closest slice input (B.w/o closest slice); and (2) replace closest slice with sub-image slice (B.w/ sub-image slice). Figures 6d and 6e display blurry details and unrealistic textures on parts far away from original sub-image region.

C. correlation between adjacent slices in one turn: (1) generate four directional slices simultaneously (C.simultaneous); (2) horizontal-then-vertical slice generation (C.horizontal-vertical); and (3) vertical-then-horizontal slice generation (C.vertical-horizontal). Figures 6f, 6g and 6h illustrate that some slice corners are influenced by noncontinuous slice generation in one turn.

While SpiralNets with anticlockwise or clockwise (default) slice generation in one turn, perform better both quantitatively (Table 4) and qualitatively (Fig. 6), indicating that it's effective to do image extrapolation in our spiral way.

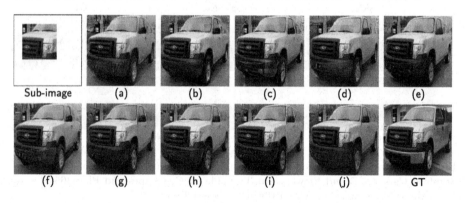

Fig. 6. Qualitative results on why spiral is necessary. (a) A.one-by-one. (b) A.horizontal-vertical. (c) A.vertical-horizontal. (d) B.w/o closest slice. (e) B.w/sub-image slice. (f) c.simultaneous. (g) c.horizontal-vertical. (h) c.vertical-horizontal. (i) SpiralNet.anticlockwise. (j) SpiralNet.clockwise. Please zoom in for better comparison.

4.4 Analysis of SliceGAN

Ternary SliceGAN Inputs. Our SliceGAN (see Sect. 3.2) is designed with a new Encoder-AdaIN-SPADE|Decoder structure, to encode *imaginary slice* (Encoder) into a latent space, and fuse style information from *sub-image* (AdaIN) with the latent code, then combine with semantic information from *closest slice*

Table 4. Quantitative results on ablation study of why spiral is necessary.

Method	PSNR	SSIM	FID
A.one-by-one	14.04	0.5724	23.80
A.horizontal-vertical	14.12	0.5697	24.00
A.vertical-horizontal	14.09	0.5661	26.79
B.w/o closest slice	14.02	0.5652	24.41
B.w/ sub-image slice	14.08	0.5662	22.77
C.simultaneous	14.18	0.5708	**21.96**
C.horizontal-vertical	14.22	0.5741	24.47
C.vertical-horizontal	14.25	0.5756	24.09
SpiralNet.anticlockwise	14.27	0.5753	24.20
SpiralNet.clockwise	**14.31**	**0.5775**	23.64

Table 5. Quantitative results on ablation study of ternary SliceGAN inputs.

Method	PSNR	SSIM	FID
Baseline	13.95	0.5683	26.10
W/sub-image	14.02	0.5652	24.41
W/closest slice	14.18	0.5727	24.64
Exchange imaginary and closest slices	13.98	0.5743	26.86
SpiralNet	**14.31**	**0.5775**	**23.64**

Table 6. Quantitative results on ablation study of different slice sizes for SliceGAN.

τ	4	8	16	32	64
PSNR	13.58	13.70	13.80	**14.31**	14.05
SSIM	0.5486	0.5566	0.5632	**0.5775**	0.5694
FID	27.11	26.14	**20.59**	23.64	21.07

(SPADE) when decode composite latent code back to image space (Decoder), resulting in extrapolated slice with consistency of style, semantic, and context.

We thus conduct ablation study on the ternary SliceGAN inputs: imaginary slice, sub-image, and closest slice, for validating efficacy of them together with corresponding structures. We construct an Encoder-Decoder with the only input of imaginary slice as baseline, then add sub-image and closest slice with Encoder-AdaIN-Decoder and Encoder-SPADE|Decoder respectively for comparison. Besides, we also exchange imaginary slice and closest slice for further analysis.

Table 5 and Fig. 7 show results of ablation study on ternary SliceGAN inputs, which validate strength of our structure. Visually, the style between sub-image and generated slices looks more harmonious with sub-image input (Figs. 7a vs. 7b); and generated slices seems more semantically consistent with sub-image via closest slice input (Figs. 7a vs. 7c); also distorted content with inconsistent semantic appears if we exchange imaginary and closest slices (Fig. 7d); while SpiralNet improves over all the others thanks to our ternary inputs (Fig. 7e).

Different Slice Sizes. We then study the impact of slice size τ, and employ four different sizes of $\tau = \{4, 8, 16, 32, 64\}$ for ablation. Table 6 and Fig. 8 report the results, showing that, small slice size might introduce unclear texture (Fig. 8a), and big slice size may result in a more obvious stitching block effect (Fig. 8d). Considering effectiveness and efficiency, we set $\tau = 32$ for balance.

4.5   Efficacy of Hue-Color Loss

We finally analyze efficacy of hue-color loss. For convenience, we conduct ablative experiments using ImagineGAN on Flowers and Stanford Cars, by removing hue-color loss as baseline and replacing it with color loss [47] and L1 loss [17]

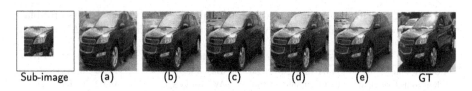

Fig. 7. Qualitative ablation study on ternary SliceGAN inputs. (a) Baseline. (b) w/sub-image. (c) w/closest slice. (d) exchange imaginary and closest slices. (e) SpiralNet.

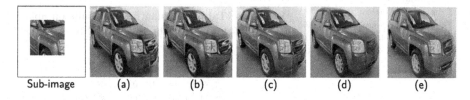

Fig. 8. Qualitative ablation study on different slice sizes. (a) $\tau = 4$. (b) $\tau = 8$. (c) $\tau = 16$. (d) $\tau = 32$. (e) $\tau = 64$.

Table 7. Quantitative results on ablation study of ImagineGAN with different losses.

Model	Flowers			Stanford cars		
	PSNR	SSIM	FID	PSNR	SSIM	FID
Baseline	10.49	0.0832	136.55	10.63	0.1005	120.33
w/ $\mathcal{L}_{color}^{\mathbf{I}}$	9.45	0.1294	250.30	10.75	0.2882	186.46
w/ $\mathcal{L}_{L1}^{\mathbf{I}}$	12.50	0.1266	109.36	11.78	0.2129	104.09
w/ $\mathcal{L}_{hue}^{\mathbf{I}}$	**14.98**	**0.4681**	**75.11**	**13.56**	**0.5107**	**53.12**

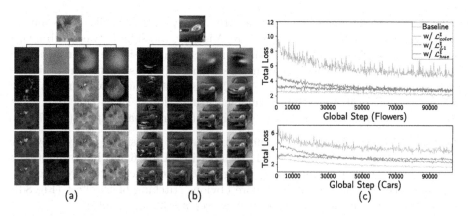

Fig. 9. (a) and (b): Qualitative results on flowers and stanford cars: baseline, with color loss, with L1 loss, and with hue-color loss, from left to right. (c) Corresponding total loss curves on flowers and stanford cars in training by steps.

for comparison. Results in Table 7 indicate that hue-color loss is more helpful in terms of PSNR, SSIM and FID. Figures 9a and 9b illustrate step-by-step extrapolation in training with different losses, from which we observe that it appears dark and bright color spots exist in baseline, L1 loss and color loss may alleviate one of these issues, while our hue-color loss handle both issues very well (Figs. 9a and 9b). Corresponding loss curves in Fig. 9c demonstrate that, by using hue-color loss, total loss descends very quickly at the beginning, thereby the model identifies right color to stabilize training process.

5   Conclusion and Limitations

We propose a novel generative framework, SpiralNet, to extrapolate an image by evolving along a spiral curve, and input image grows a little bit slice in four directions after each spiral turn. With the help of our design, both extensive experiments and ablation study demonstrate the superiority of our method. However, it still has limitation that the results inevitably have trivial block effects. We hope to further explore SpiralNet for this limitation, as well as more extension in general image generation tasks.

Acknowledgements. This work was supported by the National Natural Science Foundation of China under Grants 61771440 and 41776113.

References

1. Arjovsky, M., Chintala, S., Bottou, L.: Wasserstein generative adversarial networks. In: ICML, pp. 214–223 (2017)
2. Avidan, S., Shamir, A.: Seam carving for content-aware image resizing. ACM TOG **26**(3), 10 (2007)
3. Barnes, C., Shechtman, E., Finkelstein, A., Goldman, D.B.: PatchMatch: a randomized correspondence algorithm for structural image editing. ACM TOG **28**(3), 24 (2009)
4. Brock, A., Donahue, J., Simonyan, K.: Large scale GAN training for high fidelity natural image synthesis. arXiv preprint arXiv:1809.11096 (2018)
5. Cho, W., Choi, S., Park, D.K., Shin, I., Choo, J.: Image-to-image translation via group-wise deep whitening-and-coloring transformation. In: CVPR, pp. 10639–10647 (2019)
6. Cordts, M., et al.: The cityscapes dataset for semantic urban scene understanding. In: CVPR, pp. 3213–3223 (2016)
7. Dekel, T., Gan, C., Krishnan, D., Liu, C., Freeman, W.T.: Sparse, smart contours to represent and edit images. In: CVPR, pp. 3511–3520 (2018)
8. Doersch, C., Singh, S., Gupta, A., Sivic, J., Efros, A.A.: What makes Paris look like Paris? ACM TOG **31**(4), 101 (2012)
9. Efros, A.A., Leung, T.K.: Texture synthesis by non-parametric sampling. In: CVPR, pp. 1033–1038 (1999)
10. Fairchild, M.D.: Color Appearance Models. Wiley, Hoboken (2013)
11. Goodfellow, I., et al.: Generative adversarial nets. In: NIPS, pp. 2672–2680 (2014)

12. Gulrajani, I., Ahmed, F., Arjovsky, M., Dumoulin, V., Courville, A.C.: Improved training of Wasserstein GANs. In: NIPS, pp. 5767–5777 (2017)
13. Hanbury, A.: Constructing cylindrical coordinate colour spaces. Pattern Recogn. Lett. **29**(4), 494–500 (2008)
14. Huang, G., Liu, Z., Van Der Maaten, L., Weinberger, K.Q.: Densely connected convolutional networks. In: CVPR, pp. 4700–4708 (2017)
15. Huang, X., Belongie, S.: Arbitrary style transfer in real-time with adaptive instance normalization. In: ICCV, pp. 1501–1510 (2017)
16. Huang, X., Liu, M.Y., Belongie, S., Kautz, J.: Multimodal unsupervised image-to-image translation. In: ECCV, pp. 172–189 (2018)
17. Isola, P., Zhu, J.Y., Zhou, T., Efros, A.A.: Image-to-image translation with conditional adversarial networks. In: CVPR, pp. 1125–1134 (2017)
18. Johnson, J., Alahi, A., Fei-Fei, L.: Perceptual losses for real-time style transfer and super-resolution. In: ECCV, pp. 694–711 (2016)
19. Karras, T., Aila, T., Laine, S., Lehtinen, J.: Progressive growing of GANs for improved quality, stability, and variation. In: ICLR (2018)
20. Karras, T., Laine, S., Aila, T.: A style-based generator architecture for generative adversarial networks. In: CVPR, pp. 4401–4410 (2019)
21. Kihlstrom, J.F.: The cognitive unconscious. Science **237**(4821), 1445–1452 (1987)
22. Kingma, D.P., Ba, J.: Adam: a method for stochastic optimization. In: ICLR (2015)
23. Kosslyn, S.M., Ganis, G., Thompson, W.L.: Neural foundations of imagery. Nat. Rev. Neurosci. **2**(9), 635 (2001)
24. Krause, J., Stark, M., Deng, J., Fei-Fei, L.: 3D object representations for fine-grained categorization. In: ICCVW, pp. 554–561 (2013)
25. Lee, D., Kim, J., Moon, W.J., Ye, J.C.: CollaGAN: collaborative GAN for missing image data imputation. In: CVPR, pp. 2487–2496 (2019)
26. Li, C., Wand, M.: Precomputed real-time texture synthesis with Markovian generative adversarial networks. In: ECCV, pp. 702–716 (2016)
27. Liu, G., Reda, F.A., Shih, K.J., Wang, T.C., Tao, A., Catanzaro, B.: Image inpainting for irregular holes using partial convolutions. In: ECCV, pp. 85–100 (2018)
28. MacEvoy, B.: Color Vision. handprint.com (2010)
29. Mao, X., Li, Q., Xie, H., Lau, R.Y., Wang, Z., Smolley, S.P.: Least squares generative adversarial networks. In: ICCV, pp. 2794–2802 (2017)
30. Mirza, M., Osindero, S.: Conditional generative adversarial nets. arXiv preprint arXiv:1411.1784 (2014)
31. Miyato, T., Kataoka, T., Koyama, M., Yoshida, Y.: Spectral normalization for generative adversarial networks. In: ICLR (2018)
32. Nazeri, K., Ng, E., Joseph, T., Qureshi, F., Ebrahimi, M.: EdgeConnect: generative image inpainting with adversarial edge learning. arXiv preprint arXiv:1901.00212 (2019)
33. Nilsback, M.E., Zisserman, A.: Automated flower classification over a large number of classes. In: ICVGIP, pp. 722–729 (2008)
34. Park, T., Liu, M.Y., Wang, T.C., Zhu, J.Y.: Semantic image synthesis with spatially-adaptive normalization. In: CVPR, pp. 2337–2346 (2019)
35. Pérez, P., Gangnet, M., Blake, A.: Poisson image editing. ACM TOG **22**(3), 313–318 (2003)
36. Pessoa, L., Thompson, E., Noë, A.: Finding out about filling-in: a guide to perceptual completion for visual science and the philosophy of perception. Behav. Brain Sci. **21**(6), 723–748 (1998)
37. Radford, A., Metz, L., Chintala, S.: Unsupervised representation learning with deep convolutional generative adversarial networks. In: ICLR (2016)

38. Sajjadi, M.S., Scholkopf, B., Hirsch, M.: EnhanceNet: single image super-resolution through automated texture synthesis. In: ICCV, pp. 4491–4500 (2017)
39. Sarvaiya, J.N., Patnaik, S., Bombaywala, S.: Image registration by template matching using normalized cross-correlation. In: ICACCTT, pp. 819–822. IEEE (2009)
40. Shan, Q., Curless, B., Furukawa, Y., Hernandez, C., Seitz, S.M.: Photo uncrop. In: Fleet, D., Pajdla, T., Schiele, B., Tuytelaars, T. (eds.) ECCV 2014. LNCS, vol. 8694, pp. 16–31. Springer, Cham (2014). https://doi.org/10.1007/978-3-319-10599-4_2
41. Simonyan, K., Zisserman, A.: Very deep convolutional networks for large-scale image recognition. arXiv preprint arXiv:1409.1556 (2014)
42. Slossberg, R., Shamai, G., Kimmel, R.: High quality facial surface and texture synthesis via generative adversarial networks. In: ECCV, pp. 498–513 (2018)
43. Teterwak, P., et al.: Boundless: generative adversarial networks for image extension. In: ICCV, pp. 10521–10530 (2019)
44. Wah, C., Branson, S., Welinder, P., Perona, P., Belongie, S.: The Caltech-UCSD Birds-200-2011 dataset. Technical report CNS-TR-2011-001, California Institute of Technology (2011)
45. Wang, M., Lai, Y., Liang, Y., Martin, R.R., Hu, S.M.: BiggerPicture: data-driven image extrapolation using graph matching. ACM TOG **33**(6), 173 (2014)
46. Wang, N., Li, J., Zhang, L., Du, B.: MUSICAL: multi-scale image contextual attention learning for inpainting. In: IJCAI, pp. 3748–3754 (2019)
47. Wang, R., Zhang, Q., Fu, C.W., Shen, X., Zheng, W.S., Jia, J.: Underexposed photo enhancement using deep illumination estimation. In: CVPR, pp. 6849–6857 (2019)
48. Wang, Y., Tao, X., Shen, X., Jia, J.: Wide-context semantic image extrapolation. In: CVPR, pp. 1399–1408 (2019)
49. Xian, W., et al.: TextureGAN: controlling deep image synthesis with texture patches. In: CVPR, pp. 8456–8465 (2018)
50. Yu, J., Lin, Z., Yang, J., Shen, X., Lu, X., Huang, T.S.: Generative image inpainting with contextual attention. In: CVPR, pp. 5505–5514 (2018)
51. Yu, J., Lin, Z., Yang, J., Shen, X., Lu, X., Huang, T.S.: Free-form image inpainting with gated convolution. In: ICCV, pp. 4471–4480 (2019)
52. Zhang, Y., Xiao, J., Hays, J., Tan, P.: FrameBreak: dramatic image extrapolation by guided shift-maps. In: CVPR, pp. 1171–1178 (2013)
53. Zhou, B., Lapedriza, A., Khosla, A., Oliva, A., Torralba, A.: Places: a 10 million image database for scene recognition. IEEE TPAMI **40**(6), 1452–1464 (2017)
54. Zhu, J.Y., Krähenbühl, P., Shechtman, E., Efros, A.A.: Generative visual manipulation on the natural image manifold. In: ECCV, pp. 597–613 (2016)
55. Zhu, J.Y., Park, T., Isola, P., Efros, A.A.: Unpaired image-to-image translation using cycle-consistent adversarial networks. In: ICCV, pp. 2223–2232 (2017)

SceneSketcher: Fine-Grained Image Retrieval with Scene Sketches

Fang Liu[1,2], Changqing Zou[3], Xiaoming Deng[1(✉)], Ran Zuo[1,2], Yu-Kun Lai[4],
Cuixia Ma[1,2(✉)], Yong-Jin Liu[5(✉)], and Hongan Wang[1,2]

[1] State Key Laboratory of Computer Science and Beijing Key Lab
of Human-Computer Interaction, Institute of Software,
Chinese Academy of Sciences, Beijing, China
{xiaoming,cuixia}@iscas.ac.cn
[2] University of Chinese Academy of Sciences, Beijing, China
[3] HMI Laboratory, Huawei Technologies, Shenzhen, China
[4] Cardiff University, Cardiff, Wales
[5] Tsinghua University, Beijing, China
liuyongjin@tsinghua.edu.cn

Abstract. Sketch-based image retrieval (*SBIR*) has been a popular
research topic in recent years. Existing works concentrate on mapping
the visual information of sketches and images to a semantic space at the
object level. In this paper, for the first time, we study the fine-grained
scene-level SBIR problem which aims at retrieving *scene* images satisfying the user's specific requirements via a freehand *scene* sketch. We propose a graph embedding based method to learn the similarity measurement between images and scene sketches, which models the multi-modal
information, including the size and appearance of objects as well as their
layout information, in an effective manner. To evaluate our approach,
we collect a dataset based on SketchyCOCO and extend the dataset
using Coco-stuff. Comprehensive experiments demonstrate the significant potential of the proposed approach on the application of fine-grained
scene-level image retrieval.

Keywords: Sketch · Image retrieval · Graph convolutional network

1 Introduction

Sketching is an effective way for humans to express target objects. Using sketches
as a query to retrieve images [25] has drawn increasing interests in the last
decade. Especially with the aid of touch devices, users can easily draw a sketch

---

F. Liu and C. Zou – Equal contributions.

Electronic supplementary material The online version of this chapter (https://
doi.org/10.1007/978-3-030-58529-7_42) contains supplementary material, which is
available to authorized users.

© Springer Nature Switzerland AG 2020
A. Vedaldi et al. (Eds.): ECCV 2020, LNCS 12364, pp. 718–734, 2020.
https://doi.org/10.1007/978-3-030-58529-7_42

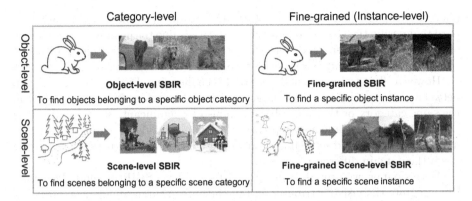

Fig. 1. Illustration of the whole spectrum of SBIR problems. The proposed method, focusing on retrieving the scene-level images satisfying the user's specific requirements via a freehand sketch, is in stark contrast to those of object-level SBIR methods [25,36] and those focusing on retrieving scene-level images of the same scene class [7].

of the desired object, which facilitates the application of sketch-based image retrieval (SBIR). However, it is more desired to retrieve *scene-level* images using an input sketch in applications such as exploring a large number of landscape photos on a phone, or online interior style selection for bedroom design, etc.

Most current SBIR works are limited to retrieving images of the same category, while the shape, pose, and other fine-grained attributes of the retrieved images are often neglected [25]. Researchers presented various global and local descriptors to conduct the SBIR task, in which the key problem is to bridge the domain gap between sketches and images. Recently, the problem of fine-grained sketch-based image retrieval (FG-SBIR) was proposed in [36] (see the upper part of Fig. 1): it still performs the instance-level SBIR task, but allows users to not only query the target image with the same category, but also with the desired instance details. Although existing works conduct inspiring retrieval performance of images with a single object, to the best of our knowledge, sketch-based retrieval of fine-grained scene-level images consisting of multiple objects is still a new problem to explore.

In this paper, we address a new problem of fine-grained scene-level SBIR (see Fig. 1), which aims to conduct scene-level (i.e. with multiple objects and instances) sketch-based image retrieval, and enforces the layout of scenes and objects' visual attributes such as relative sizes and poses. Compared to fine-grained scene-level SBIR, scene-level SBIR [32] overlooks the fine-grained details of scene layout and visual attributes, and only enforces the category of scenes, whereas (fine-grained) object-level SBIR [25,36] only retrieves a single instance and overlooks the scene context of the object. Fine-grained scene-level SBIR can facilitate novel SBIR applications. For example, if a user wants to pick specific photos from the album on his mobile phone, he can first draw a scene sketch on the mobile phone to interpret the query intention, and then retrieve the desired photos. Although text can be an alternative to query scene-level images, it is hard to describe the layout and fine-grained details due to the inherent ambiguity of text. Moreover, users can continuously adjust the shape, size and position of the objects in the input scene sketch to obtain better retrieval results.

However, fine-grained scene-level SBIR is challenging. Firstly, the domain gap between sketches and images is large, and intra-variations between sketches in the same category or the same object can also be significant [33]. Secondly, it is unclear how to simultaneously represent the layout and visual details of instances in the scene sketch and scene image, and design an embedding network to narrow down the domain difference between them.

In this paper, we propose a fine-grained scene-level SBIR method. To explicitly integrate the visual attributes and the layouts of target images, we present a sketch scene graph, which is composed of nodes that represent object entities in a sketch scene and edges that represent node distances and relationships. Then we use a Graph Convolutional Network (GCN) to embed the sketch scene graph into a feature space. To capture the size of instances, we design a category-wise IoU (Intersection over Union) score as the metric to evaluate the similarity between sketches and images. The proposed category-wise IoU can capture the size of object instances better than the IoU used in image segmentation, which is calculated by working out the IoU for each category and then taking the mean. Finally, we design a triplet network using the graph embedding of the layout and the size of object instances.

The main contributions of this work are as follows: 1) To the best of our knowledge, the problem of fine-grained scene-level sketch-based image retrieval is addressed for the first time, which can enable related SBIR research applications; 2) We propose to use a graph-based representation to explicitly model objects and layouts of sketch scenes, and design a category-wise IoU score to evaluate the similarity between sketches and images in terms of objects' relative sizes; 3) We integrate our sketch scene graph embedding and category-wise IoU score via a triplet training process. Experiments show that our method achieves state-of-the-art performance on our scene sketch database.

2   Related Work

Sketch-Based Image Retrieval (SBIR). Sketch-based image retrieval has been extensively studied since 1990s [6], and has attracted more attention recently due to the booming of touch devices. The early SBIR works aim to retrieve images of the same category (category-level), usually using hand-crafted image descriptors (e.g. SIFT, HOG etc.), to conduct shape matching between sketches and edge maps of natural images [3,14,19,20]. Eitz et al. [15] present a benchmark for evaluating the performance of large-scale SBIR systems, and utilize descriptors based on the bag-of-features approach for SBIR. Recently, several deep learning based SBIR methods [4,23,29,34] have been proposed and refresh the performance of the major SBIR benchmarks. Sangkloy et al. [25] present the Sketchy database, the first large-scale dataset of sketch-photo pairs, and use it to train cross-domain neural networks which embed sketches and photos in a common feature space. Furthermore, a few methods of zero-shot sketch-based image retrieval (ZS-SBIR) have been proposed to handle the data deficiency of large-scale sketch-photo pairs. ZS-SBIR is an SBIR task that can conduct the retrieval task on unseen object classes, and it is often treated as a domain adaptation problem [12,38]. Dey et al. [11] construct a dataset named QuickDraw-Extended to simulate ZS-SBIR of the real scenario, and exploit both visual and semantic information to conduct feature embedding.

Fine-Grained Sketch-Based Image Retrieval (FG-SBIR). Compared to object-level SBIR, FG-SBIR requires that the retrieved images contain fine-grained details described in the input scene sketch. Yu et al. [36] introduce a database of sketch-photo pairs with fine-grained annotations, in which only one object exists in each sketch or image, and develop a deep triplet-ranking model for instance-level FG-SBIR. Song et al. [26] propose a fine-grained SBIR model that exploits semantic attributes and deep feature learning in a complementary way. Furthermore, a spatially aware model which combines coarse and fine semantic information is proposed by [27]. Pang et al. [24] identify cross-category generalization for FG-SBIR as a domain generalization problem and propose an unsupervised learning approach to modeling a universal manifold of proto-typical visual sketch traits. Though FG-SBIR research works achieve inspiring progress, they focus on retrieving a single object, which may not fit well to SBIR applications in real scenarios. In this paper, we explore a new scene-level fine-grained SBIR, which utilizes local features such as object instances and their visual detail, and global context such as the scene layout.

Scene Sketch. Existing scene sketch related work includes scene image synthesis via sketches [8], scene image retrieval (not fine-grained) [7], and semantic segmentation of scene sketches [40]. Chen et al. [8] composite a photo-realistic scene image with a hand-drawn sketch and text as input. The key idea is to retrieve initial candidates of object instances via the input text and sketch, and then blend the whole scene's images. Compared to [8], our work aims to retrieve a specific image from an image gallery instead of compositing a syn-thesized image. Similarly, Dey et al. [10] present a multi-object image retrieval system using sketch and text as inputs at a coarse level. Castrejon et al. [7] propose a cross-modal scene representation for multi-modal data, and apply the class-agnostic representation in cross-modal retrieval. Xie et al. [32] introduce an ZS-SBIR framework based on this cross-modal scene dataset. The method mainly utilizes the overall visual features, while the layout and details in the scene are overlooked. Zou et al. [40] present a scalable scene sketch dataset with rich semantic and instance segmentation annotations, named SketchyScene, and conduct a preliminary study of scene-level SBIR using an object-level SBIR method [36].

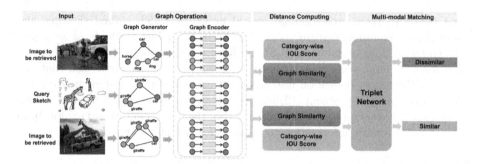

Fig. 2. Overview of our fine-grained scene-level SBIR framework. Our network mainly consists of three phases: graph operations, distance computing and multi-modal matching. We first construct graphs for sketches and images, and then utilize GCNs to encode them. Finally, we integrate the graph information with our proposed category-wise IoU score to conduct retrieval via a triplet training process.

Image Retrieval with Graph Convolutional Networks. Graph convolutional networks (GCNs) [22] are an effective neural network architecture on graphs, which extract features from graphs or nodes in graphs. GCNs have been successfully applied in a variety of applications such as image matching [31], action recognition [17], and text matching [39]. Tripathi et al. [30] adopt scene graphs to model the layouts of images, and apply them to conduct image synthesis. Khan et al. [21] use GCNs to solve the multi-label scene classification problem of very high resolution satellite remote sensing images. Chen et al. [9] develop a multi-label image recognition method, which integrates the dependencies of object labels via a directed graph consisting of the object labels into the extracted image features. Compared to these approaches, our method adopts multi-modal information to construct the node embedding and edge weights, including the size and appearance of objects as well as their layout.

3   Methods

3.1   Overview

In this section, we learn a feature embedding of scene sketches and images to enforce the distance in the feature space to be closely related to the similarities of the layout, appearance and semantic information between scene sketches and images. For fine-grained scene-level SBIR, it is a key issue to model the correlation context between the object instances and capture the fine-grained details of each object instance. In this work, we propose to use graph convolutional networks (GCNs) and category-wise IoU to conduct the feature embedding of scene sketches and images. Figure 2 shows an overview of our method. Our method consists of graph encoders, a graph similarity function, category-wise IoU measures, and a triplet similarity network.

3.2   Scene Graph Generation

We formulate a scene as a weighted, undirected scene graph, which models the visual appearance, size, pose and other fine-grained details of the object instances in a scene sketch or a scene image explicitly. Our scene graph can be represented as $G = (N, E)$, where $N = \{n_i\}$ is the node set and $E = \{e_{i,j}\}$ is the edge set, where $e_{i,j} = (n_i, n_j)$ is the edge connecting nodes n_i and n_j. The category of the node set is denoted as $C = \{c_i\}$, where c_i is the category of node n_i. In this work, the nodes N are defined as the object instances, and E are the edges that link each pair of the nodes. The scene graph generation consists of two steps: node construction and edge construction.

Node Construction. The node set N and the category set C of a scene graph can be obtained by either human annotations, or any pretrained object detectors (e.g. [40]). Each node n_i contains visual features v_i, object category label c_i and its spatial position p_i. In order to get the visual feature of each node, we first adopt a sketch classification task to fine-tune the Inception-V3 [28] pretrained on the ImageNet using the object-level data from the collected dataset illustrated in Fig. 4, and then use this model to extract the 2048-d feature of each object from its bounding box. Category label c_i of each node is encoded to a 300-d vector $\tilde{c}_i$ by Word2Vec [1]. We denote the spatial information of the node by a 4-d vector p_i indicating the top left and bottom right coordinates of the node bounding box. For each node, we get a fusion node feature x_i by concatenating v_i, $\tilde{c}_i$ and p_i. This fusion node feature captures the appearance feature, the semantic feature of each object, as well as the spatial information.

Edge Construction. The object nodes are connected with undirected weighted edges, and the edge weight between a pair of object nodes shows their correlation. Given two object nodes n_i and n_j of the graph, we define the edge weight $A_{i,j} \in (0, 1)$ between them using a normalized Euclidean distance as follows:

$$A_{i,j} = \frac{D_{i,j}}{\sum_{e_{p,q} \in E, p<q} D_{p,q}} \tag{1}$$

where $D_{i,j} = ||x_j - x_i||_2$ is the Euclidean distance of the fusion features of the nodes n_i and n_j.

3.3   Graph Encoder

After we generate the scene graphs for sketches and images, we adopt GCNs to learn node-level representations for our scene graph by updating the node features by propagating information between nodes. A GCN learns a function $f(\cdot, \cdot)$ to extract features on a graph $G = (N, E)$, which takes a feature matrix H^{l-1} and the corresponding adjacency matrix $A = \{A_{ij}\}$ as inputs. The l-th layer of the GCN can be formulated as

$$H^{(0)} = \{x_i\}_{i=1}^n \tag{2}$$

$$H^{(l)} = f(H^{(l-1)}, A), l > 1 \tag{3}$$

Then we adopt the propagation rule introduced in [22], and the function $f(\cdot, \cdot)$ can be written by

$$f(H^{(l)}, A) = \sigma(\hat{D}^{-\frac{1}{2}}\hat{A}\hat{D}^{-\frac{1}{2}}H^{(l)}W^{(l)}) \tag{4}$$

where $\sigma(\cdot)$ is the *leaky_relu* activation function, $\hat{A} = A+I$, and $\hat{D}$ is the diagonal node degree matrix of $\hat{A}$, and $W^{(l)}$ is a weight matrix to be learned.

We denote the outputs of the last layer of graph convolution networks for sketches and images to be two encoded feature graphs $\mathcal{G}_S$ and $\mathcal{G}_I$, respectively, with the encoded node features denoted as $\{\hat{x}_S^i\}$ and $\{\hat{x}_I^j\}$.

3.4   Graph Similarity Function

After we get the encoded feature graphs $\mathcal{G}_S$ and $\mathcal{G}_I$ for a sketch and an image (refer to Sect. 3.3), we utilize a graph matching function to measure the similarity of the two graphs.

Denote N_S and N_I to be the node numbers in $\mathcal{G}_S$ and $\mathcal{G}_I$, respectively. Firstly, we compute a score matrix $\hat{S}$ of the size $N_S \times N_I$ by computing the similarity between all node pairs in $\mathcal{G}_S$ and $\mathcal{G}_I$, where cosine distance is used to calculate the similarity between the features of two nodes. Secondly, we select the maximum score of each row, i.e. for each encoded feature $\hat{x}_S^i$ in $\mathcal{G}_S$, get the most similar node feature $\hat{x}_I^j$ in $\mathcal{G}_I$. Finally, we compute the overall similarity of $\mathcal{G}_S$ and $\mathcal{G}_I$ by averaging the maximum scores of all rows as:

$$\phi_{GM}(\mathcal{G}_S, \mathcal{G}_I) = \frac{1}{N_S}\sum_{p=1}^{N_S} \max_{q \in [1, N_I]} Cosine(\hat{x}_S^p, \hat{x}_I^q). \tag{5}$$

3.5   Category-Wise IoU

To evaluate the similarity of the layout and sizes of object instances between a sketch and an image, we design a category-wise IoU. Denote M_S^i and M_I^i to be the union sets of the object masks for an object category label c_i in a pair of sketch S and image I, respectively. Then we compute the intersection and the union of M_S^i and M_I^i by $M_S^i \cap M_I^i$ and $M_S^i \cup M_I^i$.

Finally, we define the category-wise IoU score ϕ_{IoU} between sketch S and image I as the division of the sum of the intersection masks of all object categories and the sum of the union masks of all object categories:

$$\phi_{IoU}(S, I) = \frac{\sum_{i=1}^{|C|} M_S^i \cap M_I^i}{\sum_{i=1}^{|C|} M_S^i \cup M_I^i} \tag{6}$$

where $|C|$ the number of object categories.

The proposed category-wise IoU can capture the size of object instances better than the IoU used in image segmentation, which is calculated by working out the IoU for each category and then taking the mean (See Sect. 4.4).

Table 1. Comparison of the existing sketch databases and our database.

Dataset	# of sketches	Any images?	Is paired?	Annotation type	Multi-objects?
TU-Berlin [13]	20,000	No	–	Class label	No
QuickDraw [18]	over 50 million	No	–	Class label	No
The sketchy database [25]	75,471	Yes	Yes	Class label	No
Shoes [36]	419	Yes	Yes	Class label	No
Chairs [36]	297	Yes	Yes	Class label	No
SketchyScene [40]	7265	Yes	Yes	Segmentation	Yes
CMPlaces [7]	8694	Yes	No	Class label	Yes
Our scene sketch database	**1225**	**Yes**	**Yes**	**Segmentation**	**Yes**

3.6 Loss Function

Triplet Loss. Inspired by [25,36], we adopt the ranking triple loss that can express the fine-grain relationship better than Siamese loss [25]. The triple loss aims to enforce that the embedding features of two examples with the same label are close and the embedding features of two examples with different labels are far away.

The input of a triplet network is a triplet (S, I^+, I^-), where S is a scene sketch, I^+ is the corresponding image of S, and I^- is an image of a different scene. The triple loss L_{tri} of (S, I^+, I^-) can be computed by

$$L_{tri} = \max(d(S, I^+) - d(S, I^-) + m, 0) \tag{7}$$

where $d(\cdot, \cdot)$ is the distance function in the embedding space, and m is a margin which is set to 0.4.

With three scene graphs G_S, G_{I+} and G_{I-} of the triplet (S, I^+, I^-), we define $d(S, I^+)$ and $d(S, I^-)$ of Eq. (7) by integrating the graph similarity score ϕ_{GM} in Eq.(5) and the category-wise IoU ϕ_{IoU} in Eq.(6) by

$$d(S, I) = 1 - \lambda_1 \phi_{GM}(S, I) - \lambda_2 \phi_{IoU}(S, I) \tag{8}$$

where I is an image (which can be I^+ or I^-), λ_1 and λ_2 are the weights of ϕ_{GM} and ϕ_{IoU}. In our experiments, we set $\lambda_1 = 1$ and $\lambda_2 = 0.8$.

4 Experiments

4.1 Datasets

Although several sketch datasets [7,13,18,25,36,40] are publicly available (shown in Table 1 and Fig. 3), none of them are suitable to evaluate our method. TU-Berlin [13], QuickDraw [18] and The Sketchy Database [25] are all datasets of sketches of single object instances. Sketch me that shoe [36] is the first dataset of fine-grained sketch-photo pairs, and facilitates the fine-grained sketch-related applications. However, each sketch-photo pair in this dataset also contains only

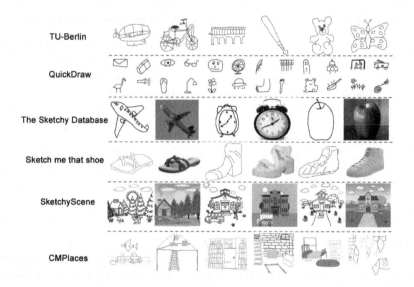

Fig. 3. Examples of the existing sketch databases.

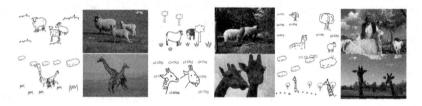

Fig. 4. Examples of our fine-grained scene-level sketch dataset.

one object instance, where all the sketches and images have clean backgrounds. Moreover, there are only a few hundred images in the database, which is insufficient for large-scale SBIR. SketchyScene [40] and CMPlaces [7] are the two available scene-level sketch datasets. SketchyScene cannot be used to train and evaluate our fine-grained scene-level SBIR network, which requires the visual features of object instances, because it does not contain the bounding box or object instance segmentation annotations. The images of SketchyScene are all cartoon clips, while we intend to retrieve natural photos. CMPlaces, in which only scene category labels are available, cannot be used for our problem either. On the one hand, it does not contain paired image and sketch data. On the other hand, it does not contain object instance segmentation annotations such as SketchyScene.

Our Sketch Database. Existing benchmarks for SBIR do not fit our problem, they either just contain a single object in one photo, or no fine-grain annotations of objects are available. Thus, we collect a scene sketch-image database (referred

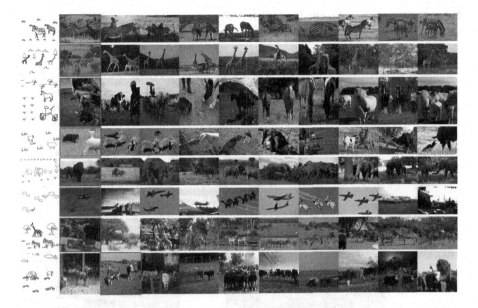

Fig. 5. Top-10 fine-grained scene-level SBIR results with our method. The true matches are highlighted with red rectangles. (Color figure online)

to as our sketch database) based on SketchyCOCO [16], and utilize the Scene SBIR database for our fine-grained scene-level SBIR task. SketchyCOCO contains over 14,000 scene-level sketch-photo pairwise examples, but most of them only contain one foreground instance. We pick up 1,225 scene sketch-photo pairs containing more than one object instance from SketchyCOCO, covering 14 object categories (bicycle, car, motorcycle, airplane, traffic light, fire hydrant, cat, dog, horse, sheep, cow, elephant, zebra, giraffe). Figure 4 shows several examples of our database. In each row, we display three samples with the same object categories, and fine-grained SBIR models are needed to differentiate a specific scene.

4.2   Evaluation Metrics

We split our scene sketch dataset into training and testing sets, containing 1015 and 210 sketch-image pairs, respectively. We adopt a standard evaluation metric for retrieval as [36], recall at rank K (Recall@K), which is computed with the percentage of test queries where the target image is within the top K retrieved images.

4.3   Comparison with Baselines

Fig. 5 shows several fine-grained SBIR examples with our method. For each query sketch, there are typically a handful of visually very similar photos; the lower-rank accuracy, especially at top-1, thus is a better indication on how well the

Table 2. Comparison of scene-level SBIR performance with existing SBIR methods on our database (210 testing images) and our extended database (5210 testing images).

	Our sketch database			Extended database		
	Recall@1	Recall@5	Recall@10	Recall@10	Recall@50	Recall@100
HOG+BoW+RankSVM [20]	0.48	1.43	4.76	0.48	0.48	0.48
Dense HOG+RankSVM [36]	0.48	3.81	5.71	0	0.95	1.91
Sketch-a-Net+RankSVM [37]	0.48	3.33	4.76	0	0.95	2.86
Sketch me that shoe [36]	6.19	17.15	32.86	1.90	6.19	8.57
DSSA [27]	0.48	3.81	7.62	0	0.95	1.90
SketchyScene [40]	1.43	4.76	8.57	0.48	0.95	2.86
Our model	**31.91**	**66.67**	**86.19**	**38.10**	**68.10**	**82.86**

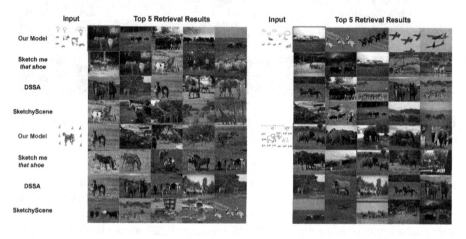

Fig. 6. Comparison of scene-level SBIR results with our method and three state-of-the-art SBIR methods: Sketch me that shoe [36], DSSA [27], SketchyScene [40]. The ground truth matches are highlighted with red rectangles. (Color figure online)

model is capable of distinguishing fine-grained subtle differences between candidate photos. When collecting the dataset, some sketches do not match the photos exactly, thus there are cases that no images in the database can fully match the input sketch. Moreover, we investigate the performance of our fine-grained scene-level SBIR by making images extremely similar in overall layout of sketches, category of objects, and their position and shape, which makes the task more challenging (see supplementary material).

We compare our model with several state-of-the-art (SOTA) object-level SBIR and fine-grained SBIR approaches.

HOG-BoW+RankSVM [20] and **Dense HOG+ RankSVM** [36] are two methods using hand-crafted features. HOG-BoW descriptor is a popular visual feature in SBIR [19,20]. We extract HOG features for each image, and feed them to the BoW (Bag-of-Words) framework for feature encoding. Then, we train a RankSVM model to rank the results as [35]. In the comparison, the used triplet annotations are the same as those we use in our experiment. We also compare with the model [36] by extracting Dense HOG features via concatenating HOG features over a dense grid. We follow the same setting in [36] to extract Dense HOG features.

Sketch-a-Net+RankSVM [37], **Sketch me that shoe** [36], **DSSA** [27], and **SketchyScene** [40] adopt deep features for SBIR. In Sketch-a-Net+RankSVM [37], the deep features are ranked with RankSVM. And Sketch me that shoe [36] presents a deep triplet ranking model for fine-grained SBIR, where free-hand sketches are used as queries for instance-level retrieval of images. We have achieved a better result with our data by loading the pre-trained model and fine-tuning it. DSSA [27] utilizes a deep spatial-semantic attention mechanism for fine-grained SBIR, and it models the fine-grained details and their spatial context instead of only adopting a coarse holistic matching strategy. We also compare our method with SketchyScene, which conducts a scene-level SBIR based on the triplet ranking network similar to the network in [36], using the overall deep features of the scene sketch as input.

Table 2 shows the comparison of the retrieval recalls with our model and the compared methods. Figure 6 compares the qualitative results with our method and most related SOTAs: Sketch me that shoe [36], DSSA [27], and SketchyScene [40]. The results indicate that our model achieves significantly higher recall than the other baselines. Conventional SBIR methods with hand-crafted features designed for SBIR with a single object get poor performance on our scene sketch dataset. Sketch me that shoe [36] is a more related SOTA SBIR model, which is also the first work on fine-grained SBIR task. However, the Recall@1, Recall@5 and Recall@10 with our method are about 25%, 50% and 54% higher than those with Sketch me that shoe. Therefore, our method achieves the best retrieval performance on our database, which demonstrates that our method is effective.

4.4 Ablation Study

Our fine-grained scene-level SBIR method adopts scene sketch graphs to explicitly model the layout and local details of each object in sketches and images, and uses a category-wise IoU score between a pair of sketch and image to enforce the size and position of object instances in sketch and image. In order to demonstrate the contribution of each component, we compare our full model with the following eight stripped-down models:

1. **Visual features as graph only.** When constructing the nodes in the sketch scene graph, we only use visual features extracted by Inception-V3 as the node feature. We use the same category-wise IoU loss as our full model.
2. **Category labels as graph only.** We only use the category label of each object as the node feature, and visual features and spatial positions are not included. The same category-wise IoU loss as our full model is used.
3. **Visual features and category labels as graph.** To show the effect of spatial information, we use the visual features and category label of each

object as the node feature, while no spatial positions of object bounding boxes are included. The category-wise IoU loss as our full model is used.

4. **Graph triplet loss only.** We use the same graph generator and graph encoder as our full model, but category-wise IoU loss is not used.

5. **Category-wise IoU loss only.** We use our category-wise IoU to rank the pairs of sketch and image. The scene sketch graph is not used.

6. $IoU_{category}$ **only.** We replace the category-wise IoU loss in model (5.) by $IoU_{category}$ [2], which is the major evaluation metric in semantic segmentation. $IoU_{category}$ is computed as $\phi_{IoU_{category}}(S, I) = \sum_{i=1}^{|C|} \frac{M_S^i \cap M_I^i}{M_S^i \cup M_I^i}$. The scene sketch graph is not used.

7. **Global IoU only.** We replace the category-wise IoU loss in model (5.) by global IoU [2]. Denote M_S and M_I to be the union sets of all the object masks in sketch and image, respectively. Unlike our category-wise IoU, global IoU ignores category information and is computed as $\phi_{Global\_IoU}(S, I) = \frac{M_S \cap M_I}{M_S \cup M_I}$. The scene sketch graph is not used in this model.

8. $IoU_{category}$ + **Graph feature.** We replace our category-wise IoU with $IoU_{category}$ [2], and combine it with the scene sketch graph via triplet training. The graph feature of our full model is used in this setting.

The performances of our full models and the above eight models on the fine-grained scene-level SBIR are shown in Table 3. 1) Compared to the recalls with scene sketch graphs using different node features (1, 2, 3, 9 in Table 3), we observe that the Recall@1, Recall@5 and Recall@10 using the node features with visual information, category labels and spatial information (our full model) are about 8%, 15% and 9% higher than those using only visual features, about 2%, 4% and 4% higher than those using only category labels, and about 1.5%, 2% and 2% higher than those using visual features and category labels. Thus, visual features, category labels and position information all contribute to enhancing the retrieval performance. 2) By comparing the ranking results using our category-wise IoU only, $IoU_{category}$ only and global IoU, we observe that the recall with our category-wise IoU is better (5, 6, 7 in Table 3). When integrated with graph

Table 3. Effect of each components on the fine-grained scene-level SBIR on our scene sketch database (210 testing images) and our extended database (5210 testing images).

Model settings	Our sketch database			Extended database		
	Recall@1	Recall@5	Recall@10	Recall@1	Recall@5	Recall@10
1. Visual feature as graph only	24.29	51.90	77.14	8.09	18.09	25.23
2. Category label as graph only	29.52	62.86	82.38	8.57	20.95	30.00
3. Visual feature and category label as graph	30.48	64.76	83.81	11.43	23.33	30.95
4. Graph triplet loss only	13.33	30.00	47.62	2.38	6.67	10.00
5. Category-wise IoU only	28.10	61.90	80.0	6.67	19.05	24.29
6. $IoU_{category}$ only	23.82	59.05	76.19	4.76	16.19	23.81
7. Global IoU only	5.24	19.05	28.10	0	0.48	2.38
8. $IoU_{category}$+Graph feature	24.76	59.05	78.57	4.76	16.67	23.81
9. Our model	**31.91**	**66.67**	**86.19**	**12.38**	**26.67**	**38.10**

features (8, 9 in Table 3), category-wise IoU is still superior to $IoU_{category}$. 3) Compared to the recalls with graph features only, our full model gains about 18%, 36% and 39% on Recall@1, Recall@5 and Recall@10 (4, 9 in Table 3). Thus, category-wise IoU is important for our network.

4.5 Results on Our Extended Scene Sketch Database

In order to investigate the performance of our method using a larger image gallery, we extend our scene sketch database with natural images from Coco-stuff [5], named our extended scene sketch database. We select 21,379 natural images, the objects of which are within the 14 categories in our scene sketch database. These natural images do not have corresponding sketches in our scene sketch database. Then, we split these natural images into a test dataset with 5,000 images and a training dataset with 16,379 images, and combine them with the images of the training and test dataset in our scene sketch database.

We compare the scene-level SBIR performance with the existing SOTA methods on our extended database (shown on the right three columns in Table 2). Since Recall@5 of the compared methods is close to zero, we show the Recall@10, Recall@50 and Recall@100 instead. Our method achieves significantly better performance than the compared methods. Existing object-level SBIR methods perform worse due to the fact that these methods directly compare the visual features of sketches and images, but neglect the key scene contexts such as object layout. Figure 7 shows the qualitative results of scene-level SBIR on our extended database. Our model can capture details well and retrieve fine-grained images.

Fig. 7. Examples of scene sketch SBIR results on our extended database.

We also conduct an ablation study of each component of the proposed method on our extended database (shown in Table 3). The results again demonstrate that the scene graph with nodes using visual features, category label and spatial information, and category-wise IoU are both effective.

5   Conclusion

In this work, for the first time, we have addressed and explored the new problem of scene-level fine-grained sketch-based image retrieval. A graph-based framework has been proposed to explicitly model the layout and fine-grained details of sketch scenes at the same time. A category-wise IoU was designed to enhance the SBIR performance in a simple and effective manner. Experiments show that our method is superior to the existing sketch-based image retrieval methods. In the future, we would fuse semantic analysis and scene understanding to promote the method to work on larger datasets.

Acknowledgements. This work was supported by the National Key Research and Development Plan (2016YFB1001200), Natural Science Foundation of China (61872346, 61725204, 61473276), Natural Science Foundation of Beijing (L182052), and Royal Society-Newton Advanced Fellowship (NA150431).

References

1. https://code.google.com/archive/p/word2vec/
2. https://www.cityscapes-dataset.com/benchmarks/
3. Belongie, S., Malik, J., Puzicha, J.: Shape context: a new descriptor for shape matching and object recognition. In: Advances in Neural Information Processing Systems, pp. 831–837 (2001)
4. Bui, T., Ribeiro, L., Ponti, M., Collomosse, J.: Sketching out the details: sketch-based image retrieval using convolutional neural networks with multi-stage regression. Comput. Graph. **71**, 77–87 (2018)
5. Caesar, H., Uijlings, J., Ferrari, V.: Coco-stuff: thing and stuff classes in context. In: Proceedings of the IEEE Conference on Computer Vision and Pattern Recognition, pp. 1209–1218 (2018)
6. Cao, Y., Wang, C., Zhang, L., Zhang, L.: Edgel index for large-scale sketch-based image search. In: Proceedings of the IEEE Conference on Computer Vision and Pattern Recognition, pp. 761–768 (2011)
7. Castrejon, L., Aytar, Y., Vondrick, C., Pirsiavash, H., Torralba, A.: Learning aligned cross-modal representations from weakly aligned data. In: Proceedings of the IEEE Conference on Computer Vision and Pattern Recognition, pp. 2940–2949 (2016)
8. Chen, T., Cheng, M.M., Tan, P., Shamir, A., Hu, S.M.: Sketch2Photo: internet image montage. In: ACM Transactions on Graphics (TOG), vol. 28, p. 124 (2009)
9. Chen, Z.M., Wei, X.S., Wang, P., Guo, Y.: Multi-label image recognition with graph convolutional networks. In: Proceedings of the IEEE Conference on Computer Vision and Pattern Recognition, pp. 5177–5186 (2019)
10. Dey, S., Dutta, A., Ghosh, S.K., Valveny, E., Lladós, J., Pal, U.: Learning cross-modal deep embeddings for multi-object image retrieval using text and sketch. In: 24th International Conference on Pattern Recognition, pp. 916–921 (2018)

11. Dey, S., Riba, P., Dutta, A., Llados, J., Song, Y.Z.: Doodle to search: practical zero-shot sketch-based image retrieval. In: Proceedings of the IEEE Conference on Computer Vision and Pattern Recognition, pp. 2179–2188 (2019)
12. Dutta, A., Akata, Z.: Semantically tied paired cycle consistency for zero-shot sketch-based image retrieval. In: Proceedings of the IEEE Conference on Computer Vision and Pattern Recognition, pp. 5089–5098 (2019)
13. Eitz, M., Hays, J., Alexa, M.: How do humans sketch objects? ACM Trans. Graph. (TOG) 31(4), 1–10 (2012)
14. Eitz, M., Hildebrand, K., Boubekeur, T., Alexa, M.: An evaluation of descriptors for large-scale image retrieval from sketched feature lines. Comput. Graph. 34(5), 482–498 (2010)
15. Eitz, M., Hildebrand, K., Boubekeur, T., Alexa, M.: Sketch-based image retrieval: benchmark and bag-of-features descriptors. IEEE Trans. Visual Comput. Graph. 17(11), 1624–1636 (2010)
16. Gao, C., Liu, Q., Xu, Q., Wang, L., Liu, J., Zou, C.: SketchyCOCO: image generation from freehand scene sketches. In: Proceedings of the European Conference on Computer Vision, pp. 5174–5183 (2020)
17. Guo, M., Chou, E., Huang, D.A., Song, S., Yeung, S., Fei-Fei, L.: Neural graph matching networks for fewshot 3D action recognition. In: Proceedings of the European Conference on Computer Vision, pp. 653–669 (2018)
18. Ha, D., Eck, D.: A neural representation of sketch drawings. arXiv preprint arXiv:1704.03477 (2017)
19. Hu, R., Barnard, M., Collomosse, J.: Gradient field descriptor for sketch based retrieval and localization. In: IEEE International Conference on Image Processing, pp. 1025–1028 (2010)
20. Hu, R., Collomosse, J.: A performance evaluation of gradient field hog descriptor for sketch based image retrieval. Comput. Vis. Image Underst. 117(7), 790–806 (2013)
21. Khan, N., Chaudhuri, U., Banerjee, B., Chaudhuri, S.: Graph convolutional network for multi-label VHR remote sensing scene recognition. Neurocomputing 357, 36–46 (2019)
22. Kipf, T.N., Welling, M.: Semi-supervised classification with graph convolutional networks. arXiv preprint arXiv:1609.02907 (2016)
23. Liu, L., Shen, F., Shen, Y., Liu, X., Shao, L.: Deep sketch hashing: fast free-hand sketch-based image retrieval. In: Proceedings of the IEEE Conference on Computer Vision and Pattern Recognition, pp. 2862–2871 (2017)
24. Pang, K., et al.: Generalising fine-grained sketch-based image retrieval. In: Proceedings of the IEEE Conference on Computer Vision and Pattern Recognition, pp. 677–686 (2019)
25. Sangkloy, P., Burnell, N., Ham, C., Hays, J.: The sketchy database: learning to retrieve badly drawn bunnies. ACM Trans. Graph. (TOG) 35(4), 1–12 (2016)
26. Song, J., Song, Y.Z., Xiang, T., Hospedales, T.M., Ruan, X.: Deep multi-task attribute-driven ranking for fine-grained sketch-based image retrieval. In: BMVC, vol. 1, p. 3 (2016)
27. Song, J., Yu, Q., Song, Y.Z., Xiang, T., Hospedales, T.M.: Deep spatial-semantic attention for fine-grained sketch-based image retrieval. In: Proceedings of the IEEE International Conference on Computer Vision, pp. 5551–5560 (2017)
28. Szegedy, C., Vanhoucke, V., Ioffe, S., Shlens, J., Wojna, Z.: Rethinking the inception architecture for computer vision. In: Proceedings of the IEEE Conference on Computer Vision and Pattern Recognition, pp. 2818–2826 (2016)

29. Tolias, G., Chum, O.: Asymmetric feature maps with application to sketch based retrieval. In: Proceedings of the IEEE Conference on Computer Vision and Pattern Recognition, pp. 2377–2385 (2017)
30. Tripathi, S., Sridhar, S.N., Sundaresan, S., Tang, H.: Compact scene graphs for layout composition and patch retrieval. In: Proceedings of the IEEE Conference on Computer Vision and Pattern Recognition Workshops, pp. 676–683 (2019)
31. Wang, R., Yan, J., Yang, X.: Learning combinatorial embedding networks for deep graph matching. arXiv preprint arXiv:1904.00597 (2019)
32. Xie, Y., Xu, P., Ma, Z.: Deep zero-shot learning for scene sketch. arXiv preprint arXiv:1905.04510 (2019)
33. Xu, P.: Deep learning for free-hand sketch: a survey. arXiv preprint arXiv:2001.02600 (2020)
34. Xu, P., et al.: SketchMate: deep hashing for million-scale human sketch retrieval. In: Proceedings of the IEEE Conference on Computer Vision and Pattern Recognition, pp. 8090–8098 (2018)
35. Yu, A., Grauman, K.: Fine-grained visual comparisons with local learning. In: Proceedings of the IEEE Conference on Computer Vision and Pattern Recognition, pp. 192–199 (2014)
36. Yu, Q., Liu, F., Song, Y.Z., Xiang, T., Hospedales, T.M., Loy, C.C.: Sketch me that shoe. In: Proceedings of the IEEE Conference on Computer Vision and Pattern Recognition, pp. 799–807 (2016)
37. Yu, Q., Yang, Y., Liu, F., Song, Y.Z., Xiang, T., Hospedales, T.M.: Sketch-a-Net: a deep neural network that beats humans. Int. J. Comput. Vis. **122**(3), 411–425 (2017)
38. Zhang, J., et al.: Generative domain-migration hashing for sketch-to-image retrieval. In: Proceedings of the European Conference on Computer Vision, pp. 297–314 (2018)
39. Zhang, T., Liu, B., Niu, D., Lai, K., Xu, Y.: Multiresolution graph attention networks for relevance matching. In: Proceedings of the 27th ACM International Conference on Information and Knowledge Management, pp. 933–942 (2018)
40. Zou, C., et al.: SketchyScene: richly-annotated scene sketches. In: Proceedings of the European Conference on Computer Vision, pp. 421–436 (2018)

Few-Shot Compositional Font Generation with Dual Memory

Junbum Cha$^{(\boxtimes)}$, Sanghyuk Chun, Gayoung Lee, Bado Lee, Seonghyeon Kim, and Hwalsuk Lee

Clova AI Research, NAVER Corp, Seongnam-si, South Korea
{junbum.cha,sanghyuk.c,gayoung.lee,kim.seonghyeon,
hwalsuk.lee}@navercorp.com

Abstract. Generating a new font library is a very labor-intensive and time-consuming job for glyph-rich scripts. Despite the remarkable success of existing font generation methods, they have significant drawbacks; they require a large number of reference images to generate a new font set, or they fail to capture detailed styles with only a few samples. In this paper, we focus on compositional scripts, a widely used letter system in the world, where each glyph can be decomposed by several components. By utilizing the compositionality of compositional scripts, we propose a novel font generation framework, named Dual Memory-Augmented Font Generation Network (DM-Font), which enables us to generate a high-quality font library with only a few samples. We employ memory components and global-context awareness in the generator to take advantage of the compositionality. In the experiments on Korean-handwriting fonts and Thai-printing fonts, we observe that our method generates a significantly better quality of samples with faithful stylization compared to the state-of-the-art generation methods quantitatively and qualitatively. Source code is available at https://github.com/clovaai/dmfont.

1 Introduction

Advances of web technology lead people to consume a massive amount of texts on the web. It makes designing a new font style, *e.g.*, personalized handwriting, critical. However, because traditional methods to make a font library heavily rely on expert designers by manually designing each glyph, creating a font library is extremely expensive and labor-intensive for glyph-rich scripts such as Chinese (more than 50,000 glyphs), Korean (11,172 glyphs), or Thai (11,088 glyphs) [11].

Recently, end-to-end font generation methods [1,4,5,16,17,26] have been proposed to build a font set without human experts. The methods solve image-to-image translation tasks between various font styles based on generative adversarial networks (GANs) [10]. While the methods have shown the remarkable achievement, they still require a large number of samples, *e.g.*, 775 samples [16,17] to

Electronic supplementary material The online version of this chapter (https://doi.org/10.1007/978-3-030-58529-7_43) contains supplementary material, which is available to authorized users.

© Springer Nature Switzerland AG 2020
A. Vedaldi et al. (Eds.): ECCV 2020, LNCS 12364, pp. 735–751, 2020.
https://doi.org/10.1007/978-3-030-58529-7_43

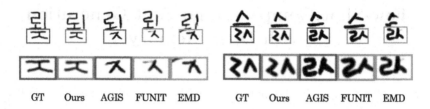

GT   Ours   AGIS   FUNIT   EMD   GT   Ours   AGIS   FUNIT   EMD

Fig. 1. Few-shot font generation results. While previous few-shot font generation methods (AGIS [8], FUNIT [23], and EMD [35]) are failed to generate unseen font, our model successfully transfer the font style and details.

generate a new font set. Moreover, they require additional training to create a new glyph set, *i.e.*, they need to finetune the pretrained model on the given new glyph subset. Thus, these finetune-based methods are rarely practical if collecting the target glyphs is extremely expensive, *e.g.*, human handwriting.

Several recent studies attempt to generate a font set without additional training with a large number of glyphs, but using only a few samples [2,8,30,31,35]. Despite their successful few-shot generation performances on training styles, existing few-shot font generation methods often fail to generate high-quality font library with unseen style few-shot samples as illustrated in Fig. 1. We solve this problem using the inherent glyph characteristics in contrast to most of the previous works handling the problem in the end-to-end data-driven manner without any human prior. A few researchers have considered characteristics of glyphs to improve font generation methods [17,31], but their approaches are either still requiring more than 700 samples [17], or only designed for memory efficiency [31].

In this paper, we focus on a famous family of scripts, called *compositional scripts*, which are composed of a combination of sub-glyphs or components. For example, the Korean script has 11,172 valid glyphs with only 68 components. One can build a full font library by designing only 68 sub-glyphs and combine them by the pre-defined rule. However, this rule-based method has a significant limitation; a sub-glyph changes its shape and position diversely depending on the combination, as shown in Fig. 2. Hence, even if a user has a complete sub-glyphs, generating a full font set is impossible without the combination rule of components. Due to the limitations, compositional scripts have been manually designed for each glyph despite its compositionality [11].

Our framework for the few-shot font generation, Dual Memory-Augmented Font Generation Network (DM-Font), utilizes the compositionality supervision in the weakly-supervised manner, *i.e.*, no component-wise bounding box or mask is required but only component labels are required, resulting on more efficient and effective generation. We employ the dual memory structure (*persistent memory* and *dynamic memory*) to efficiently capture the global glyph structure and the local component-wise styles, respectively. This strategy enables us to generate a new high-quality font library with only a few samples, *e.g.*, 28 samples and 44 samples for Korean and Thai, respectively. In the experiments, the generated

Korean and Thai fonts show both quantitatively better visual quality in various metrics and qualitatively being preferred in the user study.

2   Related Works

2.1   Few-Shot Image-to-Image Translation

Image-to-image (I2I) translation [6,7,15,19,36] aims to learn the mapping between different domains. This mapping preserves the content in the source domain while changing the style as the target domain. Mainstream I2I translation methods assume an abundance of target training samples which is impractical. To deal with more realistic scenarios where the target samples are scarce, few-shot I2I translation works appeared recently [23]. These methods can be directly applied to the font generation task as a translation task between the reference font and target font. We compare our method with FUNIT [23].

As an independent line of research, style transfer methods [9,14,20,21,25,32] have been proposed to transfer styles of an unseen reference while preserving the original content. Unlike I2I translation tasks, style transfer methods cannot be directly transformed to font generation tasks, because they usually define the style as the set of textures and colors. However, in font generation tasks, the style of font is usually defined as discriminative local property of the font. Hence, our work does not concern style transfer methods as our baseline.

2.2   Automatic Font Generation

Automatic font generation task is an I2I translation between different font domains, *i.e.*, styles. We categorize the automatic font generation methods into two classes, which are many-shot and few-shot methods, according to way to generate a new font set. Many-shot methods [1,4,5,16,17,26] directly finetune the model on the target font set with a large number of samples, *e.g.*, 775. It is impractical in many real-world scenarios when collecting new glyphs is costly, *e.g.*, handwriting.

In contrast, few-shot font generation methods [2,8,30,31,35] does not require additional finetuning and a large number of reference images. However, the existing few-shot methods have significant drawbacks. For example, some methods generate a whole font set at single forward path [2,30]. Hence, they require a huge model capacity and cannot be applied to glyph-rich scripts but scripts with only a few glyphs, *e.g.*, Latin alphabet. On the other hand, EMD [35] and AGIS-Net [8] can be applied to any general scripts, but they show worse synthesizing quality to unseen style fonts, as observed in our experimental results. SA-VAE [31], a Chinese-specific method, keeps the model size small by compressing one-hot character-wise embeddings based on compositionality of Chinese script. Compared with SA-VAE, ours handles the features as component-wise, not character-wise. It brings huge advantages in not only reducing feature dimension but also in performances as shown in our experimental results.

Fig. 2. Examples of compositionality of Korean script. Even if we choose the same sub-glyph, *e.g.*, "ㄱ", the shape and position of each sub-glyph are varying depending on the combination, as shown in red boxes. (Color figure online)

3   Preliminary: Complete Compositional Scripts

Compositional script is a widely-used glyph-rich script, where each glyph can be decomposed by several components as shown in Fig. 2. These scripts account for 24 of the top 30 popular scripts, including Chinese, Hindi, Arabic, Korean, Thai. A compositional script is either *complete* or not, where each glyph in *complete compositional scripts* can be decomposed to fixed number sub-glyphs. For example, every Korean glyph can be decomposed by three sub-glyphs (See Fig. 2). Similarly, a Thai character has four components. Furthermore, complete compositional letters have specific sub-glyph sets for each *component type*. For example, the Korean alphabet has three component types where each component type has 19, 21, 28 sub-glyphs. By combining them, Korean letter has $19 \times 21 \times 28 = 11,172$ valid characters. Note that the minimum number of glyphs to get the entire sub-glyph set is 28. Similarly, Thai letter can represent $44 \times 7 \times 9 \times 4 = 11,088$ characters, and 44 characters are required to cover whole sub-glyphs.

Some compositional scripts are not complete. For example, each character of the Chinese letter can be decomposed into a diverse number of sub-glyphs. Although we mainly validate our method on Korean and Thai scripts, our method can be easily extended to other compositional scripts.

4   Dual Memory-Augmented Font Generation Network

In this section, we introduce a novel architecture, Dual Memory-Augmented Font Generation Network (DM-Font), which utilizes the compositionality of a script by the augmented dual memory structure. DM-Font disentangles global composition information and local styles, and writes them into persistent and dynamic memory, respectively. It enables to make a high-quality full glyph library only with very few references, *e.g.*, 28 samples for Korean, 44 samples for Thai.

4.1   Architecture Overview

We illustrate the architecture overview of DM-Font in Fig. 3a. The generation process consists of encoding and decoding stages. In the encoding stage, the reference style glyphs are encoded to the component features and stored into

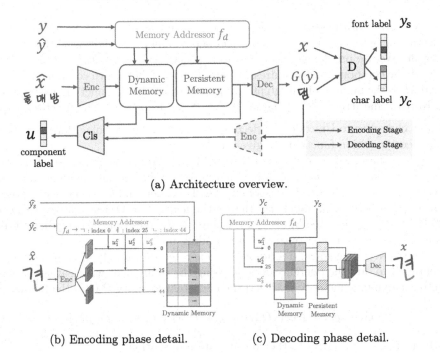

(a) Architecture overview.

(b) Encoding phase detail.   (c) Decoding phase detail.

Fig. 3. DM-Font overview. (a) The model encodes the reference style glyphs and stores the component-wise features into the memory – (b). The decoder generates images with the component-wise features – (c). (b) The encoder extracts the component-wise features and stores them into the dynamic memory using the component label u_i^c and the style label $\hat{y}_s$. (c) The memory addressor loads the component features by the character label y_c and feeds them to the decoder.

the dynamic memory. After the encoding, the decoder fetches the component features and generates the target glyph according to the target character label.

Encoder *Enc* disassembles a source glyph into the several component features using the pre-defined decomposition function. We adopt multi-head structure, one head per one component type. The encoded component-wise features are written into the dynamic memory as shown in Fig. 3b.

We employ two memory modules, where **persistent memory** (PM) is a component-wise learned embedding that represents the intrinsic shape of each component and the global information of the script such as the compositionality, while **dynamic memory** (DM) stores encoded component features of the given reference glyphs. Hence, PM captures the global information of sub-glyphs independent to each font style, while encoded features in DM learn unique local styles depending on each font. Note that DM simply stores and retrieves the encoded features, but PM is learned embedding trained from the data. Therefore, DM is adaptive to the reference input style samples, while PM is fixed after training. We provide detailed analysis of each memory in the experiments.

Memory addressor provides the access address of both dynamic and persistent memory based on the given character label y_c as shown in Fig. 3b and Fig. 3c. We use pre-defined decomposition function $f_d : y_c \mapsto \{u_i^c \mid i = 1 \ldots M_c\}$ to get the component-wise address, where u_i^c is the label of i-th component of y_c, and M_c is the number of sub-glyphs for y_c. For example, the function decomposes a Korean character, "한" by $f_d($"한"$) = \{$"ㅎ", "ㅏ", "ㄴ"$\}$. The function maps input character to Unicode and decomposes it by a simple rule. More details of the decomposition function are given in Appendix.

The component-wise encoded features for the reference $\hat{x}$, whose character label is $\hat{y}_c$ and style label is $\hat{y}_s$, are stored into DM during the encoding stage. In our scenario, the encoder Enc is a multi-head encoder, and $\hat{y}_c$ can be decomposed by $f_d(\hat{y}_c)$ to sub-glyph labels $\hat{u}_i^c$. Hence, the features in DM at address $(\hat{u}_i^c, \hat{y}_s)$, $DM(\hat{u}_i^c, \hat{y}_s)$ is computed by $Enc_i(\hat{x})$, where i is the index of the component type and Enc_i is the encoder output corresponding to i.

In the decoding stage, **decoder** Dec generates a target glyph with the target character y_c and the reference style y_s using the component-wise features stored into the dynamic memory DM and the persistent memory PM as the following:

$$G(y_c, y_s) = Dec\big([DM(u_i^c, y_s), PM(u_i^c) \mid u_i^c \in f_d(y_c)]\big), \tag{1}$$

where $[x_0, \ldots, x_n]$ refers to the concatenation operation.

For the better generation quality, we also employ a discriminator and a component classifier. For **discriminator** D, we use a multitask discriminator [23,27] with the font condition and the character condition. The multitask discriminator has independent branches for each target class and each branch performs binary classification. Considering two types of conditions, we use two multitask discriminator, one for character classes and the other for font classes, with a shared backbone. We further use **component classifier** Cls to ensure the model to fully utilize the compositionality. The component classifier provides additional supervision to the generator that stabilizes the training.

Moreover, we introduce the global-context awareness and local-style preservation to the generator, called **compositional generator**. Specifically, self-attention blocks [3,33] are used in the encoder to facilitate relational reasoning between components, and the hourglass block [22,29] is attached to the decoder to aware global-context while preserving locality. In the experiment section, we analyze the impact of the architectural improvements on the final performance. We provide the architecture and the implementation details in Appendix.

DM-Font learns the compositionality in the weakly-supervised manner; it does not require any exact component location, *e.g.*, component-wise bounding boxes, but only component labels are required. Hence, DM-Font is not restricted to the font generation only, but can be applied to any generation task with compositionality, *e.g.*, attribute conditioned generation tasks. Extending DM-Font to attribute labeled datasets, *e.g.*, CelebA [24], will be an interesting topic.

4.2   Learning

We train DM-Font from font sets $(x, y_c, y_f) \sim \mathcal{D}$, where x is a target glyph image, y_c and y_f is a character and font label, respectively. During the training, we assume that different font labels represent different styles, $i.e.$, we set $y_s = y_f$ in Eq. (1). Also, for the efficiency, we only encode a core component subset to compose the target glyph x into the DM instead of the full component set. For example, the Korean script has the full component set with size 68, but only 3 components are required to construct a single character.

We use **adversarial loss** to let the model generate plausible images.

$$\mathcal{L}_{adv} = \mathbb{E}_{x,y} \left[\log D_y(x)\right] + \mathbb{E}_{x,y} \left[\log(1 - D_y(G(y_c, y_f)))\right], \qquad (2)$$

where G generates an image $G(y_c, y_f)$ from the given image x and target label y by Eq. (1). The discriminator D_y is conditional on the target label y. We employed two types of the discriminator to solve the problem. The font discriminator is a conditional discriminator on the source font index and the character discriminator aims to classify what is the given character.

L₁ loss adds supervision from the ground truth target x as the following:

$$\mathcal{L}_{l1} = \mathbb{E}_{x,y} \left[\|x - G(y_c, y_f)\|_1\right]. \qquad (3)$$

We also use **feature matching loss** to improve the stability of the training. The feature matching loss is constructed using the output from the l-th layer of the L-layered discriminator, $D_f^{(l)}$.

$$\mathcal{L}_{feat} = \mathbb{E}_{x,y} \left[\frac{1}{L} \sum_{l=1}^{L} \|D_f^{(l)}(x) - D_f^{(l)}(G(y_c, y_f))\|_1\right]. \qquad (4)$$

Lastly, to let the model fully utilize the compositionality, we train the model with additional **component-classification loss**. For the given input x, we extract the component-wise features using the encoder Enc, and train them with cross-entropy loss (CE) using component labels $u \in f_d(y_c)$, where f_d is the component decomposition function to the given character label y_c.

$$\mathcal{L}_{cls} = \mathbb{E}_{x,y} \left[\sum_{u_i^c \in f_d(y_c)} CE(Enc_i(x), u_i^c)\right] + \mathbb{E}_y \left[\sum_{u_i^c \in f_d(y_c)} CE(Enc_i(G(y_c, y_f)), u_i^c)\right]. \qquad (5)$$

The final objective function to optimize the generator G, the discriminator D, and the component classifier C is defined as the following:

$$\min_{G,C} \max_{D} \mathcal{L}_{adv(font)} + \mathcal{L}_{adv(char)} + \lambda_{l1}\mathcal{L}_{l1} + \lambda_{feat}\mathcal{L}_{feat} + \lambda_{cls}\mathcal{L}_{cls}, \qquad (6)$$

where $\lambda_{l1}, \lambda_{feat}, \lambda_{cls}$ are control parameters to importance of each loss function. We set $\lambda_{l1} = 0.1, \lambda_{feat} = 1.0, \lambda_{cls} = 0.1$ for all experiments.

5   Experiments

5.1   Datasets

Korean-Handwriting Dataset. Due to its diversity and data sparsity, generating a handwritten font with only a few samples is challenging. We validate the models using 86 Korean-handwriting fonts[1] refined by the expert designer. Each font library contains 2,448 widely-used Korean glyphs. We train the models using 80% fonts and 90% characters, and validate the models on the remaining split. We separately evaluate the models on the seen (90%) and unseen (10%) characters to measure the generalizability to the unseen characters. 30 characters are used for the reference.

Thai-Printing Dataset. Compared with Korean letters, Thai letters have more complex structure; Thai characters are composed of four sub-glyphs while Korean characters have three components. We demonstrate the models on 105 Thai-printing fonts[2]. The train-evaluation split strategy is same as Korean-handwriting experiments, and 44 samples are used for the few-shot generation.

Korean-Unrefined Dataset. We also gather unrefined Korean handwriting dataset from 88 non-experts, letting each applicant write 150 characters. This dataset is extremely diverse and not refined by expert designers different from the Korean-handwriting dataset. We use the Korean-unrefined dataset as the validation of the models trained on the Korean-handwriting dataset, *i.e.*, the Korean-unrefined dataset is not visible during the training, but only a few samples are visible for the evaluation. 30 samples are used for the generation as well as the Korean-handwriting dataset.

5.2   Comparison Methods and Evaluation Metrics

Comparison Methods. We compare our model with state-of-the-art few-shot font generation methods, including EMD [35], AGIS-Net [8], and FUNIT [23]. We exclude the methods which are Chinese-specific [31] or not applicable to glyph-rich scripts [30]. Here, we slightly modified FUNIT, originally designed for unsupervised translation, by changing its reconstruction loss to L_1 loss with ground truths and conditioning the discriminator to both contents and styles.

Evaluation Metrics. Assessing a generative model is difficult because of its non-tractability. Several quantitative evaluation metrics [13,18,28,34] have attempted to measure the performance of the trained generative model with different assumptions, but it is still controversial what is the best evaluation

---

[1] We collect public fonts from http://uhbeefont.com/.
[2] https://github.com/jeffmcneill/thai-font-collection.

Table 1. Quantatitive evaluation on the Korean-handwriting dataset. We evaluate the methods on the seen and unseen character sets. Higher is better, except perceptual distance (PD) and mFID.

	Pixel-level		Content-aware			Style-aware		
	SSIM	MS-SSIM	Acc (%)	PD	mFID	Acc (%)	PD	mFID
Evaluation on the **seen** character set during training								
EMD [35]	0.691	0.361	80.4	0.084	138.2	5.1	0.089	134.4
FUNIT [23]	0.686	0.369	94.5	0.030	42.9	5.1	0.087	146.7
AGIS-Net [8]	0.694	0.399	**98.7**	**0.018**	23.9	8.2	0.088	141.1
DM-Font (ours)	**0.704**	**0.457**	98.1	**0.018**	**22.1**	**64.1**	**0.038**	**34.6**
Evaluation on the **unseen** character set during training								
EMD [35]	0.696	0.362	76.4	0.095	155.3	5.2	0.089	139.6
FUNIT [23]	0.690	0.372	93.3	0.034	48.4	5.6	0.087	149.5
AGIS-Net [8]	0.699	0.398	98.3	0.019	25.9	7.5	0.089	146.1
DM-Font (ours)	**0.707**	**0.455**	**98.5**	**0.018**	**20.8**	**62.6**	**0.039**	**40.5**

methods for generative models. In this paper, we consider three diverse levels of evaluation metrics; pixel-level, perceptual-level and human-level evaluations.

Pixel-level evaluation metrics assess the pixel structural similarity between the ground truth image and the generated image. We employ the structural similarity index (SSIM) and multi-scale structural similarity index (MS-SSIM).

However, pixel-level metrics often disagree with human perceptions. Thus, we also evaluate the models with **perceptual-level evaluation metrics**. We trained four ResNet-50 [12] models on the Korean-handwriting dataset and Thai-printing dataset to classify style and character label. Unlike the generation task, the whole fonts and characters are used for the training. More detailed classifier training settings are in Appendix. We denote a metric is *context-aware* if the metric is performed using the content classifier, and *style-aware* is defined similarly. Note that these classifiers are independent to the font generation models, but only used for the evaluation. We report the top-1 accuracy, perceptual distance (PD) [18,34], and mean FID (mFID) [23] using the classifiers. PD is computed by L_2 distance of the features between generated glyph and GT glyph, and mFID is a conditional FID [13] by averaging FID for each target class.

Finally, we conduct a user study on the Korean-unrefined dataset for measuring **human-level evaluation metric**. We ask users about three types of preference: content preference, style preference, and user preference considering both content and style. The questionnaire is made of 90 questions, 30 for each preference. Each question shows 40 glyphs, consisting of 32 glyphs generated by four models and 8 GT glyphs. The order of choices is shuffled for anonymity. We collect total 3,420 responses from 38 Korean natives. More details of user study are provided in Appendix.

Table 2. Quantatitive evaluation on the Thai-printing dataset. We evaluate the methods on the seen and unseen character sets. Higher is better, except perceptual distance (PD) and mFID.

	Pixel-level		Content-aware			Style-aware		
	SSIM	MS-SSIM	Acc (%)	PD	mFID	Acc (%)	PD	mFID
Evaluation on the **seen** character set during training								
EMD [35]	0.773	0.640	86.3	0.115	215.4	3.2	0.087	172.0
FUNIT [23]	0.712	0.449	45.8	0.566	1133.8	4.6	0.084	167.9
AGIS-Net [8]	0.758	0.624	**87.2**	**0.091**	**165.2**	15.5	0.074	145.2
DM-Font (ours)	**0.776**	**0.697**	87.0	0.103	198.7	**50.3**	**0.037**	**69.4**
Evaluation on the **unseen** character set during training								
EMD [35]	0.770	0.636	85.0	0.123	231.0	3.4	0.087	171.6
FUNIT [23]	0.708	0.442	45.0	0.574	1149.8	4.7	0.084	166.9
AGIS-Net [8]	0.755	0.618	85.4	0.103	**188.4**	15.8	0.074	145.1
DM-Font (ours)	**0.773**	**0.693**	**87.2**	**0.101**	195.9	**50.6**	**0.037**	**69.6**

5.3   Main Results

Quantitative Evaluation. The main results on Korean-handwriting and Thai-printing datasets are reported in Table 1 and Table 2, respectively. We also report the evaluation results on the Korean-unrefined dataset in Appendix. We follow the dataset split introduced in Sect. 5.1. In the experiments, DM-Font remarkably outperforms the comparison methods in most of evaluation metrics, especially on style-aware benchmarks. Baseline methods show slightly worse content-aware performances on unseen characters than seen characters, *e.g.*, AGIS-Net shows worse content-aware accuracy (98.7 → 98.3), PD (0.018 → 0.019), and mFID (23.9 → 25.9) in Table 1. In contrast, DM-Font consistently shows better generalizability to the unobserved characters during the training for both datasets. It is because our model interprets a glyph at the component level, the model easily extrapolates the unseen characters from the learned component-wise features stored in memory modules.

Our method shows significant improvements in style-aware metrics. DM-Font achieves 62.6% and 50.6% accuracy while other methods show much less accuracy, *e.g.*, about 5% for Korean unseen and Thai unseen character sets, respectively. Likewise, the model shows dramatic improvements in perceptual distance and mFID as well as the accuracy measure. In the latter section, we provide more detailed analysis that the baseline methods are overfitted to the training styles and failed to generalize to unseen styles.

Qualitative Comparison. We also provide visual comparisons in Fig. 4 and Fig. 5, which contain various challenging fonts including thin, thick, and curvy fonts. Our method generates glyphs with consistently better visual quality than

(a) Seen character set during training.

(b) Unseen character set during training.

Fig. 4. Qualitative comparison on the Korean-handwriting dataset. Visualization of generated samples with seen and unseen characters. We show insets of baseline results (green box), ours (blue box) and ground truth (red box). Ours successfully transfers the detailed style of the target style, while baselines fail to generate glyphs with the detailed reference style. (Color figure online)

the baseline methods. EMD [35] often erases thin fonts unintentionally, which causes low content scores compared with the other baseline methods. FUNIT [23] and AGIS-Net [8] accurately generate the content of glyphs and capture global styles well including overall thickness and font sizes. However, the detailed styles of the components in their results look different from the ground truths. Moreover, some generated glyphs for unseen Thai style lose the original content (see the difference between green boxes and red boxes in Fig. 4 and Fig. 5 for more details). Compared with the baselines, our method generates the most plausible images in terms of global font styles and detailed component styles. These results show that our model preserves details in the components using the dual memory and reuse them to generate a new glyph.

User Study. We conduct a user study to further evaluate the methods in terms of human preferences using the Korean-unrefined dataset. Example generated

(a) Seen character set during training.

(b) Unseen character set during training.

Fig. 5. Qualitative comparison on the Thai-printing dataset. Visualization of generated samples with seen and unseen characters. We show insets of baseline results (green box), ours (blue box) and ground truth (red box). Overall, ours faithfully transfer the target style, while other methods even often fail to preserve contents in unseen character sets. (Color figure online)

glyphs are illustrated in Fig. 6. Users are asked to choose the most preferred generated samples in terms of content preservation, faithfulness to the reference style, and personal preference. The results are shown in Table 3, which present similar intuitions with Table 1; AGIS-Net and our method are comparable in the content evaluation, and our method is dominant in the style preference.

5.4   More Analysis

Ablation Study. We investigate the impact of our design choices by ablative studies. Table 4a shows that the overall performances are improved by adding proposed components such as dynamic memory, persistent memory, and compositional generator. We report full table in Appendix.

Here, the baseline method is similar to FUNIT whose content and style accuracies are 93.9 and 5.4, respectively. The baseline suffers from the failure of

Table 3. User study results on the Korean-unrefined dataset. Each number is the preferred model output out of $3,420$ responses.

	EMD [35]	FUNIT [23]	AGIS-Net [8]	DM-Font (ours)
Best content preserving	1.33%	9.17%	**48.67%**	40.83%
Best stylization	1.71%	8.14%	17.44%	**72.71%**
Most preferred	1.23%	9.74%	16.40%	**72.63%**

Fig. 6. Samples for the user study. The Korean-unrefined dataset is used.

Table 4. Ablation studies on the Korean-handwriting dataset. Each content and style score is an average of the seen and unseen accuracies. Hmean denotes the harmonic mean of content and style scores.

(a) Impact of the memory modules.

	Content	Style	Hmean
Baseline	96.6	6.5	12.2
+ Dynamic memory	**99.8**	32.0	48.5
+ Persistent memory	97.6	46.2	62.8
+ Compositional G	98.3	**63.3**	**77.0**

(b) Impact of the objective functions.

	Content	Style	Hmean
Full	**98.3**	**63.3**	**77.0**
Full $- \mathcal{L}_{l1}$	97.3	53.8	69.3
Full $- \mathcal{L}_{feat}$	97.8	51.3	67.3
Full $- \mathcal{L}_{cls}$	3.1	16.0	5.2

style generalization as previous methods. We observe that dynamic memory and persistent memory dramatically improves style scores while preserving content scores. Finally, our architectural improvements bring the best performance.

We also explore the performance influence of each objective. As shown in Table 4b, removing L_1 loss and feature matching loss slightly degrades performances. The component-classification loss, which enforces the compositionality to the model, is the most important factor for successful training.

Style Overfitting of Baselines. We analyze the generated glyphs using our style classifier to investigate the style overfitting of the baseline methods. Figure 7 shows the predicted classes for each model output. We observe that the baseline methods often generate samples similar to the training samples. On the other hand, our model avoids the style overfitting by learning the compositionality of glyphs and directly reusing components of inputs. Consequently, as supported

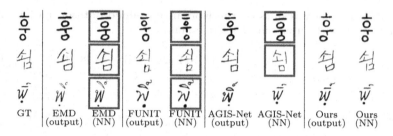

Fig. 7. Nearest neighbor analysis. We report the generated images by each model (output) with the given unseen reference style (GT) and the ground truth samples whose label is predicted by the style classifier (NN). Red boxed samples denote training samples. We can conclude that the baseline methods are overfitted to the training style while ours easily generalizes to unseen style. (Color figure online)

Fig. 8. Component-wise style mixing. We interpolate only one component (marked by blue boxes) between two glyphs (the first column and the last column). The interpolated sub-glyphs are marked by green boxes. Our model successfully interpolates two sub-glyphs, while preserving other local styles. (Color figure online)

by previous quantitative and qualitative evaluations, our model is robust to the out-of-distributed font generation compared to the existing methods. We provide more analysis of the overfitting of comparison methods in the Appendix.

Component-Wise Style Mixing. In Fig. 8, we demonstrate our model can interpolate styles component-wisely. It supports that our model fully utilizes the compositionality to generate a glyph.

6   Conclusions

Previous few-shot font generation methods often fail to generalize to unseen styles. In this paper, we propose a novel few-shot font generation framework for compositional scripts, named Dual Memory-Augmented Font Generation Network (DM-Font). Our method effectively incorporates the prior knowledge of compositional script into the framework via two external memories: the dynamic memory and the persistent memory. DM-Font utilizes the compositionality supervision in the weakly-supervised manner, *i.e.*, neither component-wise bounding box nor mask used during the training. The experimental results showed that the existing methods fail in stylization on unseen fonts, while DM-Font remarkably and consistently outperforms the existing few-shot font generation methods on Korean and Thai letters. Extensive empirical evidence support that our framework lets the model fully utilize the compositionality so that the model can produce high-quality samples with only a few samples.

References

1. zi2zi: Master Chinese calligraphy with conditional adversarial networks. https://github.com/kaonashi-tyc/zi2zi
2. Azadi, S., Fisher, M., Kim, V.G., Wang, Z., Shechtman, E., Darrell, T.: Multi-content GAN for few-shot font style transfer. In: IEEE Conference on Computer Vision and Pattern Recognition (2018)
3. Cao, Y., Xu, J., Lin, S., Wei, F., Hu, H.: GCNet: non-local networks meet squeeze-excitation networks and beyond. In: IEEE International Conference on Computer Vision Workshops (2019)
4. Chang, B., Zhang, Q., Pan, S., Meng, L.: Generating handwritten Chinese characters using cycleGAN. In: IEEE Winter Conference on Applications of Computer Vision (2018)
5. Chang, J., Gu, Y., Zhang, Y., Wang, Y.F.: Chinese handwriting imitation with hierarchical generative adversarial network. In: British Machine Vision Conference (2018)
6. Choi, Y., Choi, M., Kim, M., Ha, J.W., Kim, S., Choo, J.: StarGAN: unified generative adversarial networks for multi-domain image-to-image translation. In: IEEE Conference on Computer Vision and Pattern Recognition (2018)
7. Choi, Y., Uh, Y., Yoo, J., Ha, J.W.: StarGAN v2: diverse image synthesis for multiple domains. In: IEEE Conference on Computer Vision and Pattern Recognition (2020)
8. Gao, Y., Guo, Y., Lian, Z., Tang, Y., Xiao, J.: Artistic glyph image synthesis via one-stage few-shot learning. ACM Trans. Graph. **38**(6), 1–12 (2019)
9. Gatys, L.A., Ecker, A.S., Bethge, M.: Image style transfer using convolutional neural networks. In: IEEE Conference on Computer Vision and Pattern Recognition (2016)
10. Goodfellow, I., et al.: Generative adversarial nets. In: Advances in Neural Information Processing Systems (2014)
11. Han, J., Lee, Y., Ahn, S.: Korean font design textbook. Ahn Graphics (2009)
12. He, K., Zhang, X., Ren, S., Sun, J.: Deep residual learning for image recognition. In: IEEE Conference on Computer Vision and Pattern Recognition (2016)
13. Heusel, M., Ramsauer, H., Unterthiner, T., Nessler, B., Hochreiter, S.: GANs trained by a two time-scale update rule converge to a local Nash equilibrium. In: Advances in Neural Information Processing Systems (2017)
14. Huang, X., Belongie, S.J.: Arbitrary style transfer in real-time with adaptive instance normalization. In: IEEE International Conference on Computer Vision (2017)

15. Isola, P., Zhu, J.Y., Zhou, T., Efros, A.A.: Image-to-image translation with conditional adversarial networks. In: IEEE Conference on Computer Vision and Pattern Recognition (2017)
16. Jiang, Y., Lian, Z., Tang, Y., Xiao, J.: DCFont: an end-to-end deep Chinese font generation system. In: SIGGRAPH Asia (2017)
17. Jiang, Y., Lian, Z., Tang, Y., Xiao, J.: SCFont: structure-guided Chinese font generation via deep stacked networks. In: AAAI Conference on Artificial Intelligence (2019)
18. Johnson, J., Alahi, A., Fei-Fei, L.: Perceptual losses for real-time style transfer and super-resolution. In: Leibe, B., Matas, J., Sebe, N., Welling, M. (eds.) ECCV 2016. LNCS, vol. 9906, pp. 694–711. Springer, Cham (2016). https://doi.org/10.1007/978-3-319-46475-6_43
19. Karras, T., Laine, S., Aila, T.: A style-based generator architecture for generative adversarial networks. In: IEEE Conference on Computer Vision and Pattern Recognition (2019)
20. Li, Y., Fang, C., Yang, J., Wang, Z., Lu, X., Yang, M.H.: Universal style transfer via feature transforms. In: Advances in Neural Information Processing Systems (2017)
21. Li, Y., Liu, M.-Y., Li, X., Yang, M.-H., Kautz, J.: A closed-form solution to photorealistic image stylization. In: Ferrari, V., Hebert, M., Sminchisescu, C., Weiss, Y. (eds.) ECCV 2018. LNCS, vol. 11207, pp. 468–483. Springer, Cham (2018). https://doi.org/10.1007/978-3-030-01219-9_28
22. Lin, T.Y., Dollar, P., Girshick, R., He, K., Hariharan, B., Belongie, S.: Feature pyramid networks for object detection. In: IEEE Conference on Computer Vision and Pattern Recognition (2017)
23. Liu, M.Y., et al.: Few-shot unsupervised image-to-image translation. In: IEEE International Conference on Computer Vision (2019)
24. Liu, Z., Luo, P., Wang, X., Tang, X.: Deep learning face attributes in the wild. In: Proceedings of International Conference on Computer Vision (2015)
25. Luan, F., Paris, S., Shechtman, E., Bala, K.: Deep photo style transfer. In: IEEE Conference on Computer Vision and Pattern Recognition (2017)
26. Lyu, P., Bai, X., Yao, C., Zhu, Z., Huang, T., Liu, W.: Auto-encoder guided GAN for Chinese calligraphy synthesis. In: International Conference on Document Analysis and Recognition (2017)
27. Mescheder, L., Geiger, A., Nowozin, S.: Which training methods for GANs do actually converge? In: International Conference on Machine Learning (2018)
28. Naeem, M.F., Oh, S.J., Uh, Y., Choi, Y., Yoo, J.: Reliable fidelity and diversity metrics for generative models. In: International Conference on Machine Learning (2020)
29. Newell, A., Yang, K., Deng, J.: Stacked hourglass networks for human pose estimation. In: Leibe, B., Matas, J., Sebe, N., Welling, M. (eds.) ECCV 2016. LNCS, vol. 9912, pp. 483–499. Springer, Cham (2016). https://doi.org/10.1007/978-3-319-46484-8_29
30. Srivatsan, N., Barron, J., Klein, D., Berg-Kirkpatrick, T.: A deep factorization of style and structure in fonts. In: Conference on Empirical Methods in Natural Language Processing (2019)
31. Sun, D., Ren, T., Li, C., Su, H., Zhu, J.: Learning to write stylized Chinese characters by reading a handful of examples. In: International Joint Conference on Artificial Intelligence (2018)
32. Yoo, J., Uh, Y., Chun, S., Kang, B., Ha, J.W.: Photorealistic style transfer via wavelet transforms. In: International Conference on Computer Vision (2019)

33. Zhang, H., Goodfellow, I., Metaxas, D., Odena, A.: Self-attention generative adversarial networks. In: International Conference on Machine Learning (2019)
34. Zhang, R., Isola, P., Efros, A.A., Shechtman, E., Wang, O.: The unreasonable effectiveness of deep features as a perceptual metric. In: IEEE Conference on Computer Vision and Pattern Recognition (2018)
35. Zhang, Y., Zhang, Y., Cai, W.: Separating style and content for generalized style transfer. In: IEEE Conference on Computer Vision and Pattern Recognition (2018)
36. Zhu, J.Y., Park, T., Isola, P., Efros, A.A.: Unpaired image-to-image translation using cycle-consistent adversarial networks. In: IEEE International Conference on Computer Vision (2017)

PUGeo-Net: A Geometry-Centric Network for 3D Point Cloud Upsampling

Yue Qian[1], Junhui Hou[1(✉)], Sam Kwong[1], and Ying He[2]

[1] Department of Computer Science, City University of Hong Kong,
Hong Kong, China
yueqian4-c@my.cityu.edu.hk, {jh.hou,cssamk}@cityu.edu.hk
[2] School of Computer Science and Engineering, Nanyang Technological University,
Singapore, Singapore
yhe@ntu.edu.sg

Abstract. In this paper, we propose a novel deep neural network based method, called PUGeo-Net, for upsampling 3D point clouds. PUGeo-Net incorporates discrete differential geometry into deep learning elegantly by learning the first and second fundamental forms that are able to fully represent the local geometry unique up to rigid motion. Specifically, we encode the first fundamental form in a 3×3 linear transformation matrix $\mathbf{T}$ for each input point. Such a matrix approximates the augmented Jacobian matrix of a local parameterization that encodes the intrinsic information and builds a one-to-one correspondence between the 2D parametric domain and the 3D tangent plane, so that we can lift the adaptively distributed 2D samples learned from the input to 3D space. After that, we use the learned second fundamental form to compute a normal displacement for each generated sample and project it to the curved surface. As a by-product, PUGeo-Net can compute normals for the original and generated points, which is highly desired for surface reconstruction algorithms. We evaluate PUGeo-Net on a wide range of 3D models with sharp features and rich geometric details and observe that PUGeo-Net consistently outperforms state-of-the-art methods in terms of both accuracy and efficiency for upsampling factor 4~16. We also verify the geometry-centric nature of PUGeo-Net quantitatively. In addition, PUGeo-Net can handle noisy and non-uniformly distributed inputs well, validating its robustness. The code is publicly available at https://github.com/ninaqy/PUGeo.

Keywords: Point clouds · Deep learning · Discrete differential geometry · Upsampling · Local parameterization · Surface reconstruction

Electronic supplementary material The online version of this chapter (https://doi.org/10.1007/978-3-030-58529-7_44) contains supplementary material, which is available to authorized users.

A. Vedaldi et al. (Eds.): ECCV 2020, LNCS 12364, pp. 752–769, 2020.
https://doi.org/10.1007/978-3-030-58529-7_44

1   Introduction

Three-dimensional (3D) point clouds, as the raw representation of 3D data, are used in a wide range of applications, such as 3D immersive telepresence [34], 3D city reconstruction [24,32], cultural heritage reconstruction [3,47], geophysical information systems [33,35], autonomous driving [6,27], simultaneous localization and mapping [7,10], and virtual/augmented reality [15,41], just to name a few. Though recent years have witnessed great progress on the 3D sensing technology [13,22], it is still costly and time-consuming to obtain dense and highly detailed point clouds, which are beneficial to the subsequent applications. Therefore, amendment is required to speed up the deployment of such data modality. In this paper, instead of relying on the development of hardware, we are interested in the problem of computational based point cloud upsampling: given a sparse, low-resolution point cloud, generate a uniform and dense point cloud with a typical computational method to faithfully represent the underlying surface. Since the problem is the 3D counterpart of image super-resolution [25,53], a typical idea is to borrow the powerful techniques from the image processing community. However, due to the unordered and irregular nature of point clouds, such an extension is far from trivial, especially when the underlying surface has complex geometry.

The existing methods for point cloud upsampling can be roughly classified into two categories: optimization-based methods and deep learning based methods. The optimization methods [2,19,20,30,36] usually fit local geometry and work well for smooth surfaces with less features. However, these methods struggle with multi-scale structure preservation. The deep learning methods can effectively learn structures from data. Representative methods are PU-Net [50], EC-Net [49] and MPU [44]. See Sect. 2 for details. Though these deep learning methods produce better results than the optimization based methods, they are heavily motivated by the techniques in the image domain and takes little consideration of the geometries of the input shape. As a result, various artifacts can be observed in their results. It is also worth noting that all the existing deep learning methods generate points only, none of them is able to estimate the normals of the original and generated points.

In this paper, we propose a novel network, called PUGeo-Net, to overcome the limitations in the existing deep learning methods. Our method learns a local parameterization for each point and its normal direction. In contrast to the existing neural network based methods that generate new points in the abstract feature space and map the samples to the surface using decoder, PUGeo-Net performs the sampling operations in a pure geometric way. Specifically, it first generates the samples in the 2D parametric domain and then lifts them to 3D space using a linear transformation. Finally, it projects the points on the tangent plane onto the curved surface by computing a normal displacement for each generated point via the learned second fundamental form. Through extensive evaluation on commonly used and new metrics, we show that PUGeo-Net consistently outperforms the state-of-the-art in terms of accuracy and efficiency for upsampling factors $4 \sim 16\times$. It is also worth noting that PUGeo-Net is the first neural network that can generate dense point clouds with accurate normals, which are highly desired by the existing surface reconstruction algorithms.

The main contributions of this paper are summarized as follows.

1. We propose PUGeo-Net, a novel geometric-centric neural network, which carries out a sequence of geometric operations, such as computing the first-order approximation of local parameterization, adaptive sampling in the parametric domain, lifting the samples to the tangent plane, and projection to the curved surface.
2. PUGeo-Net is the first upsampling network that can jointly generate coordinates and normals for the densified point clouds. The normals benefit many downstream applications, such as surface reconstruction and shape analysis.
3. We interpret PUGeo-Net using the local theory of surfaces in differential geometry. Quantitative verification confirms our interpretation.
4. We evaluate PUGeo-Net on both synthetic and real-world models and show that PUGeo-Net significantly outperforms the state-of-the-art methods in terms of accuracy and efficiency for all upsampling factors.
5. PUGeo-Net can handle noisy and non-uniformly distributed point clouds as well as the real scanned data by the LiDAR sensor very well, validating its robustness and practicality.

2   Related Work

Optimization Based Methods. Alexa *et al.* [2] interpolated points of Voronoi diagram, which is computed in the local tangent space. Lipman *et al.* developed a method based on locally optimal projection operator (LOP) [30]. It is a parametrization-free method for point resampling and surface reconstruction. Subsequently, the improved weighted LOP and continuous LOP were developed by Huang *et al.* [19] and Preiner *et al.* [36] respectively. These methods assume that points are sampling from smooth surfaces, which degrades upsampling quality towards sharp edges and corners. Huang *et al.* [20] presented an edge-aware (EAR) approach which can effectively preserve the sharp features. With given normal information, EAR algorithm first resamples points away from edges, then progressively upsamples points to approach the edge singularities. However, the performance of EAR heavily depends on the given normal information and parameter tuning. In conclusion, point cloud upsampling methods based on geometric priors either assume insufficient hypotheses or require additional attributes.

Deep Learning Based Methods. The deep learning based upsampling methods first extract point-wise feature via point clouds CNN. The lack of point order and regular structure impede the extension of powerful CNN to point clouds. Instead of converting point clouds to other data representations like volumetric grids [31,39, 46] or graphs [26,43], recently the point-wise 3D CNN [23,29,37,38,42,45] successfully achieved state-of-the-art performance for various tasks. Yu *et al.* pioneered

PU-Net [50], the first deep learning algorithm for point cloud upsampling. It adopts PointNet++ [38] to extract point features and expands features by multi-branch MLPs. It optimizes a joint reconstruction and repulsion loss function to generate point clouds with uniform density. PU-Net surpasses the previous optimization based approaches for point cloud upsampling. However, as it does not consider the spatial relations among the points, there is no guarantee that the generated samples are uniform. The follow-up work, EC-Net [49], adopts a joint loss of point-to-edge distance, which can effectively preserve sharp edges. EC-Net requires labelling the training data with annotated edge and surface information, which is tedious to obtain. Wang *et al.* [44] proposed a patch-based progressive upsampling method (MPU). Their method can successfully apply to large upsampling factor, say 16×. Inspired by the image super-resolution techniques, they trained a cascade of upsampling networks to progressively upsample to the desired factor, with the subnet only deals with 2× case. MPU replicates the point-wise features and separates them by appending a 1D code $\{-1, 1\}$, which does not consider the local geometry. MPU requires a careful step-by-step training, which is not flexible and fails to gain a large upsampling factor model directly. Since each subnet upsizes the model by a factor 2, MPU only works for upsampling factor which is a power of 2. PUGeo-Net distinguishes itself from the other deep learning method from its geometry-centric nature. See Sect. 4 for quantitative comparisons and detailed discussions. Recently, Li *et al.* [28] proposed PU-GAN which introduces an adversarial framework to train the upsampling generator. Again, PU-GAN fails to examine the geometry properties of point clouds. Their ablation studies also verify the performance improvement mainly comes from the introduction of the discriminator.

3 Proposed Method

3.1 Overview

Motivation. In our paper, the input is a point cloud sampled from a 3D surface of arbitrary geometry and topology. Given a sparse point cloud $\mathcal{X} = \{\mathbf{x}_i \in \mathbb{R}^{3 \times 1}\}_{i=1}^{N}$ with N points and the user-specified upsampling factor R, we aim to generate a dense, uniformly distributed point cloud $\mathcal{X}_R = \{\mathbf{x}_i^r \in \mathbb{R}^{3 \times 1}\}_{i,r=1}^{N,R}$, which contains more geometric details and can approximate the underlying surface well. Similar to other patch-based approaches, we first partition the input sparse point cloud into patches via the farthest point sampling algorithm, each of which has M points, and PUGeo-Net processes the patches separately.

As mentioned previously, the existing deep learning based methods are heavily built upon the techniques in 2D image domain, which generate new samples by replicating feature vectors in the abstract feature space, and thus the performance is limited. Moreover, due to little consideration of shape geometry, none of them can compute normals, which play a key role in surface reconstruction. In contrast, our method is motivated by parameterization-based surface resampling.

Local Surface Parameterization. It is known that parameterization techniques depend heavily on the topology of the surface. There are two types of parameterization, namely local parameterization and global parameterization. The former deals with a topological disk (i.e., a genus-0 surface with 1 boundary) [16]. The latter works on surfaces of arbitrary topology by computing canonical homology basis, through which the surface is cutting into a topological disk, which is then mapped to a 2D domain [12]. Global constraints are required in order to ensure the parameters are continuous across the cuts [4]. The Fundamental Theorem of the Local Theory of Surfaces states that the local neighborhood of a point on a regular surface can be completely determined by the first and second fundamental forms, unique up to rigid motion (see [5], Chap. 4). Therefore, instead of computing and learning a *global* parameterization which is expensive, our key idea is to learn a *local* parameterization for each point.

Let us parameterize a local neighborhood of point $\mathbf{x}_i$ to a 2D domain via a differential map $\mathbf{\Phi} : \mathbb{R}^2 \to \mathbb{R}^3$ so that $\mathbf{\Phi}(0,0) = \mathbf{x}_i$ (see Fig. 1). The Jacobian matrix $\mathbf{J}_\mathbf{\Phi} = [\mathbf{\Phi}_u, \mathbf{\Phi}_v]$ provides the best first-order approximation of the map $\mathbf{\Phi}$: $\mathbf{\Phi}(u,v) = \mathbf{\Phi}(0,0) + [\mathbf{\Phi}_u, \mathbf{\Phi}_v] \cdot (u,v)^\mathsf{T} + O(u^2 + v^2)$, where $\mathbf{\Phi}_u$ and $\mathbf{\Phi}_v$ are the tangent vectors, which define the first fundamental form. The normal of point $\mathbf{x}_i$ can be computed by the cross product $\mathbf{n}_i = \mathbf{\Phi}_u(0,0) \times \mathbf{\Phi}_v(0,0)$.

It is easy to verify that the point $\hat{\mathbf{x}} \triangleq \mathbf{x}_i + \mathbf{J}_\mathbf{\Phi} \cdot (u,v)^\mathsf{T}$ is on the tangent plane of $\mathbf{x}_i$, since $(\hat{\mathbf{x}} - \mathbf{x}_i) \cdot \mathbf{n}_i = 0$. In our method, we use the augmented Jacobian matrix $\mathbf{T} = [\mathbf{\Phi}_u, \mathbf{\Phi}_v, \mathbf{\Phi}_u \times \mathbf{\Phi}_v]$ to compute the normal $\mathbf{n}_i = \mathbf{T} \cdot (0,0,1)^\mathsf{T}$ and the point $\hat{\mathbf{x}} = \mathbf{x}_i + \mathbf{T} \cdot (u,v,0)^\mathsf{T}$. Matrix $\mathbf{T}$ is of full rank if the surface is regular at $\mathbf{x}_i$. Furthermore, the distance between $\mathbf{x}$ and $\hat{\mathbf{x}}$ is $\|\mathbf{x} - \hat{\mathbf{x}}\| = \frac{\kappa_1 u^2 + \kappa_2 v^2}{2} + O(u^3 + v^3)$, where κ_1 and κ_2 are the principal curvatures at $\mathbf{\Phi}(0,0)$, which are the eigenvalues of the second fundamental form.

Algorithmic Pipeline. As shown in Fig. 2(a), given an input sparse 3D point cloud, PUGeo-Net proceeds as follows: it first generates new samples $\{(u_i^r, v_i^r)\}_{r=1}^R$ in the 2D parametric domain. Then it computes the normal $\mathbf{n}_i = \mathbf{T}_i \cdot (0,0,1)^\mathsf{T}$. After that, it maps each generated 2D sample (u_i, v_i) to the tangent plane of $\mathbf{x}_i$ by $\hat{\mathbf{x}}_i^r = \mathbf{T}_i \cdot (u_i^r, v_i^r, 0)^\mathsf{T} + \mathbf{x}_i$. Finally, it projects $\hat{\mathbf{x}}_i^r$ to the curved 3D surface by computing a displacement δ_i^r along the normal direction. Figure 2(b) illustrates the network architecture of PUGeo-Net, which consists of hierarchical feature extraction and re-calibration (Sect. 3.2), parameterization-based point expansion (Sect. 3.3) and local shape approximation (Sect. 3.4). We

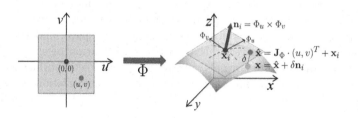

Fig. 1. Surface parameterization and local shape approximation.

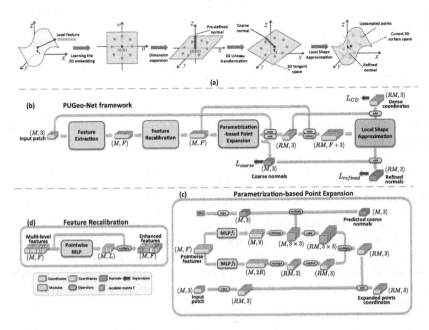

Fig. 2. (a) Illustration the algorithmic pipeline of PUGeo-Net. (b) The end-to-end network structure of PUGeo-Net. The detailed architectures of (c) point expansion and (d) feature recalibration modules

adopt a joint loss function to guide the prediction of vertex coordinates and normals (Sect. 3.5).

3.2 Hierarchical Feature Learning and Recalibration

We apply DGCNN [45] - the widely used point cloud backbone network - to extract hierarchical point-wise features, which are able to encode both local and global intrinsic geometry information of an input patch.

The hierarchical feature learning module extracts features from low- to high-levels. Intuitively speaking, as the receptive fields increase, skip-connection [14, 18, 40], a widely-used technique in 2D vision task for improving the feature quality and the convergence speed, can help preserve details in all levels. To this end, as illustrated in Fig. 2(c), instead of concatenating the obtained features directly, we perform feature re-calibration by a self-gating unit [17,52] to enhance them, which is computationally efficient.

Let $\mathbf{c}_i^l \in \mathbb{R}^{F_l \times 1}$ be the extracted feature for point $\mathbf{x}_i$ at the l-th level ($l = 1, \cdots, L$), where F_l is the feature length. We first concatenate the features of all L layers, i.e., $\widehat{\mathbf{c}}_i = \mathsf{Concat}(\mathbf{c}_i^1, \cdots, \mathbf{c}_i^L) \in \mathbb{R}^F$, where $F = \sum_{l=1}^{L} F_l$ and $\mathsf{Concat}(\cdot)$ stands for the concatenation operator. The direct concatenate feature is passed to a small MLP $h_r(\cdot)$ to obtain the logits $\mathbf{a}_i = (a_i^1, a_i^2, ..., a_i^L)$, i.e.,

$$\mathbf{a}_i = h_r(\widehat{\mathbf{c}}_i), \tag{1}$$

which are futher fed to a softmax layer to produce the recalibration weights $\mathbf{w}_i = (w_i^1, w_i^2, \cdots, w_i^L)$ with

$$w_i^l = e^{a_i^l} / \sum_{k=1}^{L} e^{a_i^k}. \tag{2}$$

Finally, the recalibrated multi-scale features are represented as the weighted concatenation:

$$\mathbf{c}_i = \mathsf{Concat}(w_i^1 \cdot \mathbf{c}_i^1, w_i^2 \cdot \mathbf{c}_i^2, \cdots, \hat{a}_i^L \cdot \mathbf{c}_i^L). \tag{3}$$

3.3   Parameterization-Based Point Expansion

In this module, we expand the input spare point cloud R times to generate a coarse dense point cloud as well as the corresponding coarse normals by regressing the obtained multi-scale features. Specifically, the expansion process is composed of two steps, i.e., learning an adaptive sampling in the 2D parametric domain and then projecting it onto the 3D tangent space by a learned linear transformation.

Adaptive Sampling in the 2D Parametric Domain. For each point $\mathbf{x}_i$, we apply an MLP $f_1(\cdot)$ to its local surface feature $\mathbf{c}_i$ to reconstruct the 2D coordinates (u_i^r, v_i^r) of R sampled points, i.e.,

$$\{(u_i^r, v_i^r)|r = 1, 2, \cdots, R\} = f_1(\mathbf{c}_i). \tag{4}$$

With the aid of its local surface information encoded in $\mathbf{c}_i$, it is expected that the self-adjusted 2D parametric domain maximizes the uniformity over the underlying surface.

Remark. Our sampling strategy is fundamentally different from the existing deep learning methods. PU-Net generates new samples by replicating features in the feature space, and feed the duplicated features into independent multi-branch MLPs. It adopts an additional repulsion loss to regularize uniformity of the generated points. MPU also replicates features in the feature space. It appends additional code $+1$ and -1 to the duplicated feature copies in order to separate them. Neither PU-Net nor MPU considers the spatial correlation among the generated points. In contrast, our method expands points in the 2D parametric domain and then lifts them to the tangent plane, hereby in a more geometric-centric manner. By viewing the problem in the mesh parametrization sense, we can also regard appending 1D code in MPU as a *predefined* 1D parametric domain. Moreover, the predefined 2D regular grid is also adopted by other deep learning based methods for processing 3D point clouds, e.g., FoldingNet [48], PPF-FoldNet [9] and PCN [51]. Although the predefined 2D grid is regularly distributed in 2D domain, it does not imply the transformed points are uniformly distributed on the underlying 3D surface.

Prediction of the Linear Transformation. For each point $\mathbf{x}_i$, we also predict a linear transformation matrix $\mathbf{T}_i \in \mathbb{R}^{3\times3}$ from the local surface feature $\mathbf{c}_i$, i.e.,

$$\mathbf{T}_i = f_2(\mathbf{c}_i), \tag{5}$$

where $f_2(\cdot)$ denotes an MLP. Multiplying $\mathbf{T}_i$ to the previously learned 2D samples $\{(u_i^r, v_i^r)\}_{r=1}^R$ lifts the points to the tangent plane of $\mathbf{x}_i$

$$\widehat{\mathbf{x}}_i^r = (\widehat{x}_i^r, \widehat{y}_i^r, \widehat{z}_i^r)^\mathsf{T} = \mathbf{T}_i \cdot (u_i^r, v_i^r, 0)^\mathsf{T} + \mathbf{x}_i. \tag{6}$$

Prediction of the Coarse Normal. As aforementioned, normals of points play an key role in surface reconstruction. In this module, we first estimate a coarse normal, i.e., the normal $\mathbf{n}_i \in \mathbb{R}^{3\times1}$ of the *tangent plane* of each input point, which are shared by all points on it. Specifically, we multiply the linear transformation matrix $\mathbf{T}_i$ to the predefined normal $(0, 0, 1)$ which is perpendicular to the 2D parametric domain:

$$\mathbf{n}_i = \mathbf{T}_i \cdot (0, 0, 1)^\mathsf{T}. \tag{7}$$

3.4   Updating Samples via Local Shape Approximation

Since the samples $\widehat{\mathcal{X}}_R = \{\widehat{\mathbf{x}}_i^r\}_{i,r=1}^{M,R}$ are on the tangent plane, we need to warp them to the curved surface and update their normals. Specifically, we move each sample $\widehat{\mathbf{x}}_i^r$ along the normal $\mathbf{n}_i$ with a distance $\delta_i^r = \frac{\kappa_1(u_i^r)^2 + \kappa_2(v_i^r)^2}{2}$. As mentioned in Sect. 3.1, this distance provides the second-order approximation of the local geometry of $\mathbf{x}_i$. We compute the distance δ_i^r by regressing the point-wise features concatenated with their coarse coordinates, i.e.,

$$\delta_i^r = f_3(\mathsf{Concat}(\widehat{\mathbf{x}}_i^r, \mathbf{c}_i)), \tag{8}$$

where $f_3(\cdot)$ is for the process of an MLP. Then we compute the sample coordinates as

$$\mathbf{x}_i^r = (x_i^r, y_i^r, z_i^r)^\mathsf{T} = \widehat{\mathbf{x}}_i^r + \mathbf{T}_i \cdot (0, 0, \delta_i^r)^\mathsf{T}. \tag{9}$$

We update the normals in a similar fashion: a normal offset $\Delta\mathbf{n}_i^r \in \mathbb{R}^{3\times1}$ for point $\mathbf{x}_i^r$ is regressed as

$$\Delta\mathbf{n}_i^r = f_4\left(\mathsf{Concat}(\widehat{\mathbf{x}}_i^r, \mathbf{c}_i)\right), \tag{10}$$

which is further added to the corresponding coarse normal, leading to

$$\mathbf{n}_i^r = \Delta\mathbf{n}_i^r + \mathbf{n}_i, \tag{11}$$

where $f_4(\cdot)$ is the process of an MLP.

3.5   Joint Loss Optimization

As PUGeo-Net aims to deal with the regression of both coordinates and unoriented normals of points, we design a joint loss to train it end-to-end. Specifically, let $\mathcal{Y}_R = \{\mathbf{y}_k\}_{k=1}^{RM}$ with RM points be the groundtruth of $\mathcal{X}_R$. During training, we adopt the Chamfer distance (CD) to measure the coordinate error between the $\mathcal{X}_R$ and $\mathcal{Y}_R$, i.e.,

$$L_{CD} = \frac{1}{RM} \left(\sum_{\mathbf{x}_i^r \in \mathcal{X}_R} \|\mathbf{x}_i^r - \phi(\mathbf{x}_i^r)\|_2 + \sum_{\mathbf{y}_k \in \mathcal{Y}_R} \|\mathbf{y}_k - \psi(\mathbf{y}_k)\|_2 \right),$$

where $\phi(\mathbf{x}_i^r) = \arg\min_{\mathbf{y}_k \in \mathcal{Y}_R} \|\mathbf{x}_i^r - \mathbf{y}_k\|_2$, $\psi(\mathbf{y}_k) = \arg\min_{\mathbf{x}_i^r \in \mathcal{X}_R} \|\mathbf{x}_i^r - \mathbf{y}_k\|_2$, and $\|\cdot\|_2$ is the ℓ_2 norm of a vector.

For the normal part, denote $\widetilde{\mathcal{N}} = \{\tilde{\mathbf{n}}_i\}_{i=1}^{M}$ and $\overline{\mathcal{N}}_R = \{\overline{\mathbf{n}}_k\}_{k=1}^{RM}$ the ground truth of the coarse normal $\mathcal{N}$ and the accurate normal $\mathcal{N}_R$, respectively. During training, we consider the errors between $\mathcal{N}$ and $\widetilde{\mathcal{N}}$ and between $\mathcal{N}_R$ and $\overline{\mathcal{N}}_R$ simultaneously, i.e.,

$$L_{coarse}(\mathcal{N}, \widetilde{\mathcal{N}}) = \sum_{i=1}^{M} L(\mathbf{n}_i, \tilde{\mathbf{n}}_i), \; L_{refined}(\mathcal{N}_R, \overline{\mathcal{N}}_R) = \sum_{i=1}^{M} \sum_{r=1}^{R} L(\mathbf{n}_i^r, \overline{\mathbf{n}}_{\phi(\mathbf{x}_i^r)}), \quad (12)$$

where $L(\mathbf{n}_i, \tilde{\mathbf{n}}_i) = \max\left\{ \|\mathbf{n}_i - \tilde{\mathbf{n}}_i\|_2^2, \|\mathbf{n}_i + \tilde{\mathbf{n}}_i\|_2^2 \right\}$ measures the unoriented difference between two normals, and $\phi(\cdot)$ is used to build the unknown correspondence between $\mathcal{N}_R$ and $\overline{\mathcal{N}}_R$. Finally, the joint loss function is written as

$$L_{total} = \alpha L_{CD} + \beta L_{coarse} + \gamma L_{refined}, \quad (13)$$

where α, β, and γ are three positive parameters. It is worth noting that our method does not require repulsion loss which is required by PU-Net and EC-Net, since the module for learning the parametric domain is capable of densifying point clouds with uniform distribution.

4   Experimental Results

4.1   Experiment Settings

Datasets. Following previous works, we selected 90 high-resolution 3D mesh models from Sketchfab [1] to construct the training dataset and 13 for the testing dataset. Specifically, given the 3D meshes, we employed the Poisson disk sampling [8] to generate $\mathcal{X}$, $\mathcal{Y}_R$, $\widetilde{\mathcal{N}}$, and $\overline{\mathcal{N}}$ with $N = 5000$ and $R = 4, 8, 12$ and 16. A point cloud was randomly cropped into patches each of $M = 256$ points. To *fairly* compare different methods, we adopted identical data augmentations settings, including random scaling, rotation and point perturbation. During the testing process, clean test data were used. Also notice that the normals of sparse inputs are not needed during testing.

Table 1. Results of quantitative comparisons. Values are the average of 13 testing models

R	Method	Network size	CD (10^{-2})	HD (10^{-2})	JSD (10^{-2})	P2F mean (10^{-3})	P2F std (10^{-3})	CD$^{\#}$ (10^{-2})	HD$^{\#}$ (10^{-2})	JSD$^{\#}$ (10^{-2})
4×	EAR [20]	–	0.919	5.414	4.047	3.672	5.592	1.022	6.753	7.445
	PU-Net [50]	10.1 MB	0.658	1.003	0.950	1.532	1.215	0.648	5.850	4.264
	MPU [44]	92.5 MB	0.573	1.073	0.614	0.808	0.809	0.647	5.493	4.259
	PUGeo-Net	26.6 MB	**0.558**	**0.934**	**0.444**	**0.617**	**0.714**	**0.639**	**5.471**	**3.928**
8×	EAR [20]	–	–	–	–	–	–	–	–	–
	PU-Net [50]	14.9 MB	0.549	1.314	1.087	1.822	1.427	0.594	5.770	3.847
	MPU [44]	92.5 MB	0.447	1.222	0.511	0.956	0.972	0.593	5.723	3.754
	PUGeo-Net	26.6 MB	**0.419**	**0.998**	**0.354**	**0.647**	**0.752**	**0.549**	**5.232**	**3.465**
12×	EAR [20]	–	–	–	–	–	–	–	–	–
	PU-Net [50]	19.7 MB	0.434	0.960	0.663	1.298	1.139	0.573	6.056	3.811
	MPU [44]	–	–	–	–	–	–	–	–	–
	PUGeo-Net	26.7 MB	**0.362**	**0.978**	**0.325**	**0.663**	**0.744**	**0.533**	**5.255**	**3.322**
16×	EAR [20]	–	–	–	–	–	–	–	–	–
	PU-Net [50]	24.5 MB	0.482	1.457	1.165	2.092	1.659	0.588	6.330	3.744
	MPU [44]	92.5 MB	0.344	1.355	0.478	0.926	1.029	0.573	5.923	3.630
	PUGeo-Net	26.7 MB	**0.323**	**1.011**	**0.357**	**0.694**	**0.808**	**0.524**	**5.267**	**3.279**

CD$^{\#}$, HD$^{\#}$, JSD$^{\#}$: these 3 metrics are used to measure the distance between dense point clouds sampled from reconstructed surfaces and ground truth meshes.

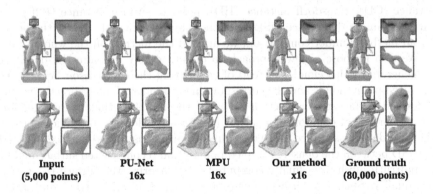

| Input
(5,000 points) | PU-Net
16x | MPU
16x | Our method
x16 | Ground truth
(80,000 points) |

Fig. 3. Visual comparisons for scanned 3D models. Each input sparse 3D point cloud has $N = 5000$ points and upsampled by a factor $R = 16$.

Implementation Details. We empirically set the values of the three parameters α, β, and γ in the joint loss function to 100, 1, and 1, respectively. We used the Adam algorithm with the learning rate equal to 0.001. We trained the network with the mini-batch of size 8 for 800 epochs via the TensorFlow platform. *The code will be publicly available later.*

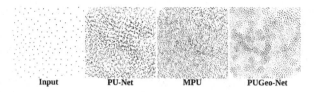

Fig. 4. Visual comparison of the distribution of generated 2D points with upsampling factor $R = 16$

Table 2. Verification of the effectiveness of our normal prediction. Here, the upsampling ratio R is 8. PCA-* indicates the normal prediction by PCA with various numbers of neighborhoods

Methods	$CD^\#$	$HD^\#$	$JSD^\#$	Methods	$CD^\#$	$HD^\#$	$JSD^\#$
PCA-10	0.586	5.837	3.903	PCA-15	0.577	5.893	3.789
PCA-25	0.575	5.823	3.668	PCA-35	0.553	5.457	3.502
PCA-45	0.568	5.746	3.673	PU-Net-M	0.678	6.002	4.139
PUGeo-Net	**0.549**	**5.232**	**3.464**				

Evaluation Metrics. To quantitatively evaluate the performance of different methods, we considered four commonly-used evaluation metrics, i.e., Chamfer distance (CD), Hausdorff distance (HD), point-to-surface distance (P2F), and Jensen-Shannon divergence (JSD). For these four metrics, the lower, the better. For all methods under comparison, we applied the metrics on the whole shape.

We also propose a new approach to quantitatively measure the quality of the generated point clouds. Instead of conducting the comparison between the generated point clouds and the corresponding groundtruth ones directly, we first performed surface reconstruction [21]. For the methods that cannot generate normals principal component analysis (PCA) was adopted to predict normals. Then we densely sampled 200,000 points from reconstructed surface. CD, HD and JSD between the densely sampled points from reconstructed surface and the groundtruth mesh were finally computed for measuring the surface reconstruction quality. Such new measurements are denoted as $CD^\#$, $HD^\#$ and $JSD^\#$. Table 1 shows the average results of 13 testing models, where we can observe that PUGeo-Net can achieve the best performance for *all* upsample factors in terms of *all* metrics.

4.2 Comparison with State-of-the-Art Methods

We compared PUGeo-Net with three methods, i.e., optimization based EAR [20], and two state-of-the-art deep learning based methods, i.e., PU-Net [50] and MPU [44]. For fair comparisons, we retrained PU-Net and MPU with the same dataset as ours. Notice that EAR fails to process the task with R greater than 4, due to the huge memory consumption, and MPU can work only for tasks with R

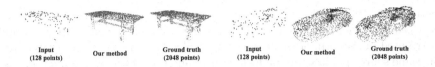

Fig. 5. 16× upsampling results on non-uniformly distributed point clouds.

in the powers of 2, due to its natural cascaded structure. Note that the primary EAR, PU-Net and MPU cannot predict normals.

Visual Comparisons. The superiority of PUGeo-Net is also visually demonstrated. We compared the reconstructed surfaces from the input sparse point clouds and the generated dense point clouds by different methods. Note that the surfaces were reconstructed via the same method as [21], in which the parameters "depth" and "minimum number of samples" were set as 9 and 1, respectively. For PU-Net and MPU which fail to predict normals, we adopted PCA normal estimation with the neighbours equal to 16. Here we took the task with $R = 16$ as an example. Some parts highlighted in red and blue boxes are zoomed in for a close look. From Fig. 3, it can be observed that after performing upsampling the surfaces by PUGeo-Net present more geometric details and the best geometry structures, especially for the highly detailed parts with complex geometry, and they are closest to the groundtruth ones. *See the supplementary material for more visual results.*

Efficiency Comparisons. As shown in Table 1, the network size of PUGeo-Net is fixed and much smaller than that of MPU. Due to the deficiency of the independent multi-branch design, the network size of PU-Net grows linearly with the upsample factor increasing, and is comparable to ours when $R = 16$. Moreover, the running times of PU-Net, MPU and PUGeo-Net are 7.5s, 30.3s and 9.6s for upsampling 1000 patches with $R = 16$ on 2080Ti GPU.

Comparison of the Distribution of Generated Points. In Fig. 4, we visualized a point cloud patch which was upsampled with 16 times by different

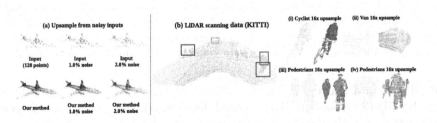

Fig. 6. (a) 16× upsampling results on non-uniform point clouds with various levels of Gaussian noise. (b) 16× upsampling results on real scanned KITTI

methods. As PUGeo-Net captures the local structure of a point cloud elegantly in a geometry-centric manner, such that the upsampled points are uniformly distributed in the form of clusters. Using PUGeo-Net, the points generated from the same source point $\mathbf{x}_i$ are uniformly distributed in the local neighborhood $\mathbf{x}_i$, which justifies our parameterization-based sampling strategy. PU-Net and MPU do not have such a feature. We also observe that our generated points are more uniform than theirs both locally and globally.

4.3 Effectiveness of Normal Prediction

Moreover, we also modified PU-Net, denoted as PU-Net-M, to predict coordinates and normals joinly by changing the neuron number of the last layer to 6 from 3. PU-Net-M was trained with the same training dataset as ours.

The quantitative results are shown in Table 2, where we can see that (1) the surfaces reconstructed with the normals by PUGeo-Net produces the smallest errors for all the three metrics; (2) the number of neighborhoods in PCA based normal prediction is a heuristic parameter and influences the final surface quality seriously; and (3) the PU-Net-M achieves the worst performance, indicating that a naive design without considering the geometry characteristics does not make sense.

4.4 Robustness Analysis

We also evaluated PUGeo-Net with non-uniform, noisy and real scanned data to demonstrate its robustness.

Non-uniform Data. As illustrated in Fig. 5, the data from ShapeNet [46] were adopted for evaluation, where 128 points of each point cloud were randomly sampled without the guarantee of the uniformity. Here we took the upsampling task $R = 16$ as an example. From Fig. 5, it can be observed that PUGeo-Net can successfully upsample such non-uniform data to dense point clouds which are very close to the ground truth ones, such that the robustness of PUGeo-Net against non-uniformity is validated.

Noisy Data. We further added Gaussian noise to the non-uniformly distributed point clouds from ShapeNet, leading to a challenging application scene for evaluation, and various noise levels applying to each dimension in 3D Euclidean space were tested. From Fig. 6, we can observe our proposed algorithm still works very on such challenging data, convincingly validating its robustness against noise.

Real Scanned Data. Finally, we evaluated PUGeo-Net with real scanned data by the LiDAR sensor [11]. Real scanned data contain noise, outliers, and occlusions. Moreover, the density of real scanned point clouds varies with the distance between the object and the sensor. As shown in Fig. 6, we can see our PUGeo-Net can produce dense point clouds with richer geometric details.

Table 3. Ablation study. **Feature recalibration**: concatenate multiscale feature without the recalibration module. **Normal prediction**: only regress coordinates of points. **Learned adaptive 2D sampling**: use a predefined 2D regular grid as the parametric domain. **Linear transformation**: regress coordinates and normals by non-linear MLPs directly. **Coarse to fine**: directly regress coordinates and normals

Networks	CD	HD	JSD	P2F mean	P2F std	CD$^{\#}$	HD$^{\#}$	JSD$^{\#}$
Feature recalibration	0.325	1.016	0.371	0.725	0.802	0.542	5.654	3.425
Normal prediction	0.331	2.232	0.427	0.785	0.973	0.563	5.884	3.565
Learned adaptive 2D sampling	0.326	1.374	0.407	0.701	0.811	0.552	5.758	3.456
Linear transformation	0.394	**1.005**	1.627	0.719	**0.720**	1.855	11.479	9.841
Coarse to fine	0.330	1.087	0.431	0.746	0.748	0.534	**5.241**	3.348
Full model	**0.323**	1.011	**0.357**	**0.694**	0.808	**0.524**	5.267	**3.279**

Fig. 7. Statistical analysis of the predicted transformation matrix $\mathbf{T} = [\mathbf{t}_1, \mathbf{t}_2, \mathbf{t}_3] \in \mathbb{R}^{3\times3}$ and normal displacement δ, which can be used to fully reconstruct the local geometry.

4.5   Ablation Study

We conducted an ablation study towards our model to evaluate the contribution and effectiveness of each module. Table 3 shows the quantitative results for PUGeo-Net with certain module removed. Here we took the task with $R = 8$ as an example, and similar results can be observed for other upsampling factors.

From Table 3, we can conclude that (1) directly regressing the coordinates and normals of points by simply using MLPs instead of the linear transformation decreases the upsampling performance significantly, demonstrating the superiority of our geometry-centric design; (2) the joint regression of normals and coordinates are better than that of only coordinates; and (3) the other novel modules, including feature recalibration, adaptive 2D sampling, and the coarse to fine manner, all contribute to the final performance.

To demonstrate the geometric-centric nature of PUGeo-Net, we examined the accuracy of the linear matrix $\mathbf{T}$ and the normal displacement δ for a unit sphere and a unit cube, where the ground-truths are available. We use angle θ to measure the difference of vectors $\mathbf{t}_3$ and $\mathbf{t}_1 \times \mathbf{t}_2$, where $\mathbf{t}_i \in \mathbb{R}^{3\times1}$ $(i = 1, 2, 3)$ is the i-th column of $\mathbf{T}$. As Fig. 7 shows, the angle θ is small with the majority less than 3 degrees, indicating high similarity between the predicted matrix $\mathbf{T}$ and the analytic Jacobian matrix. For the unit sphere model, we observe that the normal displacements δ spread in a narrow range, since the local neighborhood of $\mathbf{x}_i$ is small and the projected distance from a neighbor to the tangent plane of $\mathbf{x}_i$ is small. For the unit cube model, the majority of the displacements are close to zero, since most of the points lie on the faces of the cube which coincide with their tangent planes. On the other hand, δs spread in a relatively wide range due to the points on the sharp edges, which produce large normal displacement.

5   Conclusion and Future Work

We presented PUGeo-Net, a novel deep learning based framework for 3D point cloud upsampling. As the first deep neural network constructed in a geometry centric manner, PUGeo-Net has 3 features that distinguish itself from the other methods which are largely motivated by image super-resolution techniques. First, PUGeo-Net explicitly learns the first and second fundamental forms to fully recover the local geometry unique up to rigid motion; second, it adaptively generates new samples (also learned from data) and can preserve sharp features and geometric details well; third, as a by-product, it can compute normals of the input points and generated new samples, which make it an ideal pre-processing tool for the existing surface reconstruction algorithms. Extensive evaluation shows PUGeo-Net outperforms the state-of-the-art deep learning methods for 3D point cloud upsampling in terms of accuracy and efficiency.

PUGeo-Net not only brings new perspectives to the well-studied problem, but also links discrete differential geometry and deep learning in a more elegant way. In the near future, we will apply PUGeo-Net to more challenging application scenarios (e.g., incomplete dataset) and develop an end-to-end network for surface reconstruction. Since PUGeo-Net explicitly learns the local geometry via the first and second fundamental forms, we believe it has the potential for a wide range 3D processing tasks that require local geometry computation and analysis, including feature-preserving simplification, denoising, and compression.

Acknowledgement. This work was supported in part by the Natural Science Foundation of China under Grant 61871342, and in part by the Hong Kong Research Grants Council under grants 9048123 (CityU 21211518) and 9042955 (CityU 11202320).

References

1. Sketchfab. https://sketchfab.com
2. Alexa, M., Behr, J., Cohen-Or, D., Fleishman, S., Levin, D., Silva, C.T.: Computing and rendering point set surfaces. IEEE Trans. Visual Comput. Graphics **9**(1), 3–15 (2003)
3. Bolognesi, M., Furini, A., Russo, V., Pellegrinelli, A., Russo, P.: Testing the low-cost RPAS potential in 3D cultural heritage reconstruction. Int. Arch. Photogramm. Remote Sens. Spatial Inf. Sci. **40**, 229–235 (2015)
4. Campen, M., Bommes, D., Kobbelt, L.: Quantized global parametrization. ACM Trans. Graph. (TOG) **34**(6), 192:1–192:12 (2015)
5. do Carmo, M.: Differential Geometry of Curves and Surfaces. Prentice Hall, New Jersey (1976)
6. Chen, X., Ma, H., Wan, J., Li, B., Xia, T.: Multi-view 3D object detection network for autonomous driving. In: Proceedings of the IEEE Conference on Computer Vision and Pattern Recognition, pp. 1907–1915 (2017)

7. Cole, D.M., Newman, P.M.: Using laser range data for 3D SLAM in outdoor environments. In: Proceedings 2006 IEEE International Conference on Robotics and Automation (ICRA), pp. 1556–1563. IEEE (2006)
8. Corsini, M., Cignoni, P., Scopigno, R.: Efficient and flexible sampling with blue noise properties of triangular meshes. IEEE Trans. Visual Comput. Graphics 18(6), 914–924 (2012)
9. Deng, H., Birdal, T., Ilic, S.: PPFNet: global context aware local features for robust 3D point matching. In: Proceedings of the IEEE Conference on Computer Vision and Pattern Recognition, pp. 195–205 (2018)
10. Fioraio, N., Konolige, K.: Realtime visual and point cloud SLAM. In: Proceedings of the RGB-D Workshop on Advanced Reasoning with Depth Cameras at Robotics: Science and Systems Conference (RSS), vol. 27 (2011)
11. Geiger, A., Lenz, P., Stiller, C., Urtasun, R.: Vision meets robotics: the KITTI dataset. Int. J. Robot. Res. (IJRR) 32(11), 1231–1237 (2013)
12. Gu, X., Yau, S.: Global conformal parameterization. In: First Eurographics Symposium on Geometry Processing, 23–25 June 2003, pp. 127–137 (2003)
13. Hakala, T., Suomalainen, J., Kaasalainen, S., Chen, Y.: Full waveform hyperspectral LiDAR for terrestrial laser scanning. Opt. Express 20(7), 7119–7127 (2012)
14. He, K., Zhang, X., Ren, S., Sun, J.: Deep residual learning for image recognition. In: Proceedings of the IEEE Conference on Computer Vision and Pattern Recognition, pp. 770–778 (2016)
15. Held, R., Gupta, A., Curless, B., Agrawala, M.: 3d puppetry: a kinect-based interface for 3D animation. In: UIST, pp. 423–434. Citeseer (2012)
16. Hormann, K., Greiner, G.: MIPS: an efficient global parametrization method. In: Curve and Surface Design: Saint-Malo, vol. 2000, p. 10, November 2012
17. Hu, J., Shen, L., Sun, G.: Squeeze-and-excitation networks. In: Proceedings of the IEEE Conference on Computer Vision and Pattern Recognition, pp. 7132–7141 (2018)
18. Huang, G., Liu, Z., Van Der Maaten, L., Weinberger, K.Q.: Densely connected convolutional networks. In: Proceedings of the IEEE Conference on Computer Vision and Pattern Recognition, pp. 4700–4708 (2017)
19. Huang, H., Li, D., Zhang, H., Ascher, U., Cohen-Or, D.: Consolidation of unorganized point clouds for surface reconstruction. ACM Trans. Graph. (TOG) 28(5), 176 (2009)
20. Huang, H., Wu, S., Gong, M., Cohen-Or, D., Ascher, U., Zhang, H.R.: Edge-aware point set resampling. ACM Trans. Graph. (TOG) 32(1), 9 (2013)
21. Kazhdan, M., Hoppe, H.: Screened poisson surface reconstruction. ACM Trans. Graph. (TOG) 32(3), 29 (2013)
22. Kimoto, K., Asada, N., Mori, T., Hara, Y., Ohya, A., et al.: Development of small size 3D LiDAR. In: 2014 IEEE International Conference on Robotics and Automation (ICRA), pp. 4620–4626. IEEE (2014)
23. Komarichev, A., Zhong, Z., Hua, J.: A-CNN: annularly convolutional neural networks on point clouds. In: Proceedings of the IEEE Conference on Computer Vision and Pattern Recognition, pp. 7421–7430 (2019)
24. Lafarge, F., Mallet, C.: Creating large-scale city models from 3D-point clouds: a robust approach with hybrid representation. Int. J. Comput. Vision 99(1), 69–85 (2012)
25. Lai, W.S., Huang, J.B., Ahuja, N., Yang, M.H.: Deep Laplacian pyramid networks for fast and accurate super-resolution. In: Proceedings of the IEEE Conference on Computer Vision and Pattern Recognition, pp. 624–632 (2017)

26. Landrieu, L., Simonovsky, M.: Large-scale point cloud semantic segmentation with superpoint graphs. In: Proceedings of the IEEE Conference on Computer Vision and Pattern Recognition, pp. 4558–4567 (2018)
27. Li, B.: 3D fully convolutional network for vehicle detection in point cloud. In: 2017 IEEE/RSJ International Conference on Intelligent Robots and Systems (IROS), pp. 1513–1518. IEEE (2017)
28. Li, R., Li, X., Fu, C.W., Cohen-Or, D., Heng, P.A.: PU-GAN: a point cloud upsampling adversarial network. In: Proceedings of the IEEE International Conference on Computer Vision, pp. 7203–7212 (2019)
29. Li, Y., Bu, R., Sun, M., Wu, W., Di, X., Chen, B.: PointCNN: convolution on x-transformed points. In: Advances in Neural Information Processing Systems, pp. 820–830 (2018)
30. Lipman, Y., Cohen-Or, D., Levin, D., Tal-Ezer, H.: arameterization-free projection for geometry reconstruction. ACM Trans. Graph. (TOG) **26**, 22 (2007)
31. Maturana, D., Scherer, S.: VoxNet: a 3D convolutional neural network for real-time object recognition. In: 2015 IEEE/RSJ International Conference on Intelligent Robots and Systems (IROS), pp. 922–928. IEEE (2015)
32. Musialski, P., Wonka, P., Aliaga, D.G., Wimmer, M., Van Gool, L., Purgathofer, W.: A survey of urban reconstruction. In: Computer Graphics Forum, vol. 32, pp. 146–177. Wiley Online Library (2013)
33. Nie, S., Wang, C., Dong, P., Xi, X., Luo, S., Zhou, H.: Estimating leaf area index of maize using airborne discrete-return LiDAR data. IEEE J. Sel. Top. Appl. Earth Obs. Remote Sens. **9**(7), 3259–3266 (2016)
34. Orts-Escolano, S., et al.: Holoportation: virtual 3D teleportation in real-time. In: Proceedings of the 29th Annual Symposium on User Interface Software and Technology, pp. 741–754. ACM (2016)
35. Paine, J.G., Caudle, T.L., Andrews, J.R.: Shoreline and sand storage dynamics from annual airborne LIDAR surveys, Texas Gulf Coast. J. Coastal Res. **33**(3), 487–506 (2016)
36. Preiner, R., Mattausch, O., Arikan, M., Pajarola, R., Wimmer, M.: Continuous projection for fast L1 reconstruction. ACM Trans. Graph. (TOG) **33**(4), 47:1–47:13 (2014)
37. Qi, C.R., Su, H., Mo, K., Guibas, L.J.: PointNet: deep learning on point sets for 3D classification and segmentation. In: Proceedings of the IEEE Conference on Computer Vision and Pattern Recognition, pp. 652–660 (2017)
38. Qi, C.R., Yi, L., Su, H., Guibas, L.J.: PointNet++: deep hierarchical feature learning on point sets in a metric space. In: Advances in Neural Information Processing Systems, pp. 5099–5108 (2017)
39. Riegler, G., Osman Ulusoy, A., Geiger, A.: OctNet: Learning deep 3D representations at high resolutions. In: Proceedings of the IEEE Conference on Computer Vision and Pattern Recognition, pp. 3577–3586 (2017)
40. Ronneberger, O., Fischer, P., Brox, T.: U-Net: convolutional networks for biomedical image segmentation. In: Navab, N., Hornegger, J., Wells, W.M., Frangi, A.F. (eds.) MICCAI 2015. LNCS, vol. 9351, pp. 234–241. Springer, Cham (2015). https://doi.org/10.1007/978-3-319-24574-4_28
41. Santana, J.M., Wendel, J., Trujillo, A., Suárez, J.P., Simons, A., Koch, A.: Multimodal location based services—semantic 3D city data as virtual and augmented reality. In: Gartner, G., Huang, H. (eds.) Progress in Location-Based Services 2016. LNGC, pp. 329–353. Springer, Cham (2017). https://doi.org/10.1007/978-3-319-47289-8_17

42. Tatarchenko, M., Park, J., Koltun, V., Zhou, Q.Y.: Tangent convolutions for dense prediction in 3D. In: Proceedings of the IEEE Conference on Computer Vision and Pattern Recognition, pp. 3887–3896 (2018)
43. Te, G., Hu, W., Zheng, A., Guo, Z.: RGCNN: Regularized graph CNN for point cloud segmentation. In: 2018 ACM Multimedia Conference on Multimedia Conference, pp. 746–754. ACM (2018)
44. Wang, Y., Wu, S., Huang, H., Cohen-Or, D., Sorkine-Hornung, O.: Patch-based progressive 3D point set upsampling. In: Proceedings of the IEEE Conference on Computer Vision and Pattern Recognition, pp. 5958–5967 (2019)
45. Wang, Y., Sun, Y., Liu, Z., Sarma, S.E., Bronstein, M.M., Solomon, J.M.: Dynamic graph CNN for learning on point clouds. ACM Trans. Graph. (TOG) **38**(5), 146 (2019)
46. Wu, Z., et al.: 3D ShapeNets: a deep representation for volumetric shapes. In: Proceedings of the IEEE Conference on Computer Vision and Pattern Recognition, pp. 1912–1920 (2015)
47. Xu, Z., Wu, L., Shen, Y., Li, F., Wang, Q., Wang, R.: Tridimensional reconstruction applied to cultural heritage with the use of camera-equipped UAV and terrestrial laser scanner. Remote Sens. **6**(11), 10413–10434 (2014)
48. Yang, Y., Feng, C., Shen, Y., Tian, D.: FoldingNet: point cloud auto-encoder via deep grid deformation. In: Proceedings of the IEEE Conference on Computer Vision and Pattern Recognition, pp. 206–215 (2018)
49. Yu, L., Li, X., Fu, C.-W., Cohen-Or, D., Heng, P.-A.: EC-Net: an edge-aware point set consolidation network. In: Ferrari, V., Hebert, M., Sminchisescu, C., Weiss, Y. (eds.) ECCV 2018. LNCS, vol. 11211, pp. 398–414. Springer, Cham (2018). https://doi.org/10.1007/978-3-030-01234-2_24
50. Yu, L., Li, X., Fu, C.W., Cohen-Or, D., Heng, P.A.: Pu-Net: point cloud upsampling network. In: Proceedings of the IEEE Conference on Computer Vision and Pattern Recognition, pp. 2790–2799 (2018)
51. Yuan, W., Khot, T., Held, D., Mertz, C., Hebert, M.: PCN: point completion network. In: 2018 International Conference on 3D Vision (3DV), pp. 728–737. IEEE (2018)
52. Zhang, H., Goodfellow, I., Metaxas, D., Odena, A.: Self-attention generative adversarial networks. In: International Conference on Machine Learning, pp. 7354–7363 (2019)
53. Zhang, Y., Tian, Y., Kong, Y., Zhong, B., Fu, Y.: Residual dense network for image super-resolution. In: Proceedings of the IEEE Conference on Computer Vision and Pattern Recognition, pp. 2472–2481 (2018)

Handcrafted Outlier Detection Revisited

Luca Cavalli[1], Viktor Larsson[1(✉)], Martin Ralf Oswald[1], Torsten Sattler[2],
and Marc Pollefeys[1,3]

[1] Department of Computer Science, ETH Zurich, Zürich, Switzerland
{luca.cavalli,vlarsson}@inf.ethz.ch
[2] Chalmers University of Technology, Gothenburg, Sweden
[3] Microsoft Mixed Reality & AI Zurich Lab, Zürich, Switzerland

Abstract. Local feature matching is a critical part of many computer
vision pipelines, including among others Structure-from-Motion, SLAM,
and Visual Localization. However, due to limitations in the descriptors,
raw matches are often contaminated by a majority of outliers. As a result,
outlier detection is a fundamental problem in computer vision and a wide
range of approaches, from simple checks based on descriptor similarity
to geometric verification, have been proposed over the last decades. In
recent years, deep learning-based approaches to outlier detection have
become popular. Unfortunately, the corresponding works rarely compare with strong classical baselines. In this paper we revisit handcrafted
approaches to outlier filtering. Based on best practices, we propose a
hierarchical pipeline for effective outlier detection as well as integrate
novel ideas which in sum lead to an efficient and competitive approach
to outlier rejection. We show that our approach, although not relying on
learning, is more than competitive to both recent learned works as well
as handcrafted approaches, both in terms of efficiency and effectiveness.
The code is available at https://github.com/cavalli1234/AdaLAM.

Keywords: Low-level vision · Matching · Spatial matching · Spatial
consistency · Spatial verification

1 Introduction

Image matching is a key component in any image processing pipeline based
on correspondences between images, such as Structure from Motion (SfM) [15,
41,42,49,52], Simultaneous Localization and Mapping (SLAM) [3,13,29] and
Visual Localization [8,24,36,39]. Classically, the problem is tackled by computing high dimensional descriptors for keypoints which are robust to a set
of transformations, then a keypoint is matched with its most similar counterpart in the other image, i.e. the nearest neighbor in descriptor space. Due

Electronic supplementary material The online version of this chapter (https://
doi.org/10.1007/978-3-030-58529-7_45) contains supplementary material, which is
available to authorized users.

© Springer Nature Switzerland AG 2020
A. Vedaldi et al. (Eds.): ECCV 2020, LNCS 12364, pp. 770–787, 2020.
https://doi.org/10.1007/978-3-030-58529-7_45

Fig. 1. Main steps in our method, from left to right: *1.* we take as input a wide set of putative matches (in yellow), *2.* we select well spread hypotheses of rough region correspondences (blue circles), *3.* for each region we consider the set of all putative matches consistent with the same region correspondence hypothesis, *4.* we only keep the correspondences which are locally consistent with an affine transform with sufficient support (in green). Note that for visualization purposes we do *not* show all the hypotheses *nor* all the matches. (Color figure online)

to limitations in the descriptors, the set of nearest neighbor matches usually contains a great majority of outliers as many features in one image often have no corresponding feature in the other image. Consequently, outlier detection and filtering is an important problem in these applications. Several methods have been proposed for this task, from simple low-level filters based only on descriptors such as the ratio-test [27], to local spatial consistency checks [1,6,8,18,19,22,26,28,31,38,43,47,54,55,58] and global geometric verification methods, either exact [4,5,9–11,14,18,21,31,32,47,48] or approximate [2,17,23,40,53,54]. In the last years, many methods have been proposed to learn either local neighborhood consistency [34,59] or global geometric verification [7,12,30,33,37,57]. Yet, this line of research usually overlooks prior classical methods, and rarely compares with strong classical baselines.

In this paper we revisit handcrafted approaches to outlier filtering. Based on best practices, we propose a hierarchical pipeline for efficient and effective outlier filtering. We show that even though this approach does not involve learning, it achieves competitive performance to learned approaches, greatly outperforming the current state of the art in outdoor scenes and being superior or on par in indoor scenarios. Our results indicate that more research is needed in this area, including properly understanding the performance of learned methods.

Thus, we can summarize our contributions in the following: (**1**) We propose a novel framework that builds up from several past ideas in spatial matching into a coherent, robust, and highly parallel algorithm for fast spatial verification of image correspondences. (**2**) As our framework is based on geometrical assumptions that can have different discriminative power in different scenarios, we propose a novel method that adaptively relaxes our assumptions, to achieve better generalization to different domains while still mining as much information as available from each image region. (**3**) We experimentally show that our adaptive relaxation improves generalization, and that our method can greatly outperform current learned and non-learned state-of-the-art methods on favorable domains, while being on par in unfavorable domains as well. (**4**) We demonstrate that handcrafted methods still have considerable potential and can perform comparably to or better than current state-of-the-art learned methods, showing that there is still much research to be done in this area. (**5**) We provide a publicly available implementation of our method at https://github.com/cavalli1234/AdaLAM.

2   Related Work

Outlier rejection is a long-standing problem which has been studied in many contexts, producing many diverse approaches that act at different levels, with different complexity and different objectives.

Simple Filters. are widely used as a straightforward heuristic that already greatly improves the inlier ratio of available correspondences based on very low-level descriptor checks. In this category we include the classical ratio-test [27] and mutual nearest neighbor check, that filter out ambiguous matches, as well as (Hamming) distance thresholding to prune obvious outliers. These heuristics are extremely efficient and easy to implement, though they are not always sufficient as they can easily leave many outliers or filter out inliers present in the initial putative matches set.

Local Neighborhoods. methods filter correspondences based on the observation that correct matches should be consistent with other correct matches in their vicinity, while wrong matches are normally inconsistent with their neighbors. Consistency can be formulated as a co-neighboring constraint [6,8,28,31, 38,43,47], or enforcing a local transformation between neighboring correspondences [19,26,54,55,58], or as a graph of mutual pairwise agreements of local transformations [1,18,22]. Methods acting at this level can also be very efficient, and represent a more informative selection compared to simple filters.

Geometric Verification. approaches filter matches based on a global transformation on which correct correspondences must agree. This can be achieved by robustly fitting a global transformation (be it similarity, affinity, homography or fundamental) to the set of all the matches, with sampling methods, including RANSAC [14] and its numerous later improvements, either biasing the sampling probabilities towards more likely inliers [9,18,31,47], making iterations more efficient with a sequential probability ratio test [10] or adding local optimization [4,11,21,48], combining all of the previous [32], or marginalizing over the inlier decision threshold [5]. A different line of research in the context of image retrieval uses fast approximate spatial verification to determine whether two images have the same content. They only approximately fit a geometric transformation to efficiently prune the majority of outliers, using the local affine or similarity transformation encoded by each individual match [27]. The space of all transforms is quantized and the set of accepted correspondences is determined by majority voting with a Hough scheme in linear time [2,17,23,40,53,54].

Learned Methods. extract an implicit consistency model directly from data. Several works have been proposed in the last years, acting on different levels, either learning a local neighborhood consistency model [34,59], or a global consistency model [7,12,30,33,37,57]. Many of these target learning epipolar geometry constraints explicitly, formulating the problem either as outlier classification [12,30], or as an iteratively reweighted least-squares problem [33], or biasing RANSAC's sampling distribution towards matches more likely to be correct [7].

The line of research of learned methods in this field, however, usually gives little consideration to the vast literature of classical methods that have been proposed for outlier rejection, and rarely compares against strong classical baselines. As a result, the performance of these methods is not yet well understood. In this paper, we take inspiration from prior work on outlier filtering and compare our classical pipeline with the learning-based ones, showing that we can achieve comparable to superior results on the same datasets they trained on, while offering a comparable runtime on the same hardware.

3   Method

Given the sets of keypoints $\mathcal{K}_1$ and $\mathcal{K}_2$ respectively in images I_1 and I_2, generally the set of all putative matches $\mathcal{M}$ is taken as the set of nearest neighbor matches from $\mathcal{K}_1$ to $\mathcal{K}_2$, where nearest neighbors are defined in descriptor space. In practice, due to limitations in the descriptors, $\mathcal{M}$ is contaminated by a great majority of incorrect correspondences, thus our objective is to produce a subset $\mathcal{M}' \subseteq \mathcal{M}$ that is the nearest possible approximation of the set of all and only correct inlier matches $\mathcal{M}^* \subseteq \mathcal{M}$.

Our method builds on classical spatial matching approaches used both in the field of matching and image retrieval. To keep computational costs down, we limit our search of matches to a subset of a fixed set of initial putative matches $\mathcal{M}$, which we take as the nearest neighbors in descriptor space, and employ classical filters on orientation and scale to efficiently prune confidently wrong matches. The main steps in our algorithm are reported in Fig. 1: (**1**) We select a limited number of confident and well distributed matches, which we call seed points. (**2**) For each seed point we select neighboring compatible correspondences. (**3**) We verify local affine consistency in the neighborhood of each seed point via highly parallel RANSACs [14] with multiple inlier thresholds. For each seed point, we select the best threshold a posteriori, and we accept it if enough inliers agree on the fitted affinity. We output $\mathcal{M}'$ as the union of all the set of inliers of the accepted seed points within the chosen inlier threshold.

3.1   Preliminaries and Core Assumptions

The 3D plane tangent to a point induces an homography between two views, which can be well approximated locally by an affine transformation A in image space [20]. This affine transformation strongly constraints geometrical cross consistency of correct keypoint correspondences, acting as a very reliable filter. However, the underlying assumptions of planarity, locality and correct projections can break in multiple ways in real images: (**1**) The surface on which 3D points lie may not be planar. The offset between the 3D tangent plane at a point and the real surface produces a non-linear deviation in the projections of all the 3D points not lying on the tangent plane, which is more and more significant with the curvature of the surface. (**2**) The detected points may not be near to each other, adding distortion to the affine model which is no longer a good approximation of the induced homography. This error increases with the relative distance of keypoints and with the tilt of the tangent plane. (**3**) Matching keypoints may not represent the projection of exactly the same 3D point. This is a very common problem with wide baseline viewpoint changes, as slight changes in illumination and self occlusions can easily move the peak in saliency for keypoint localization.

To address these problems we propose an adaptive relaxation on our core assumption, that we describe in Sect. 3.4.

3.2   Seed Points Selection

As affine transforms A are a good approximation of local transformations around a 3D point P, we use available nearest neighbor correspondences to guide the search for candidate 3D surface points. More specifically we want to select a restricted set of confident and well spread correspondences to be used as hypotheses for P, around which consistent point correspondences are to be searched, as in [19]. We call such hypotheses *seed points*. As a confidence score we use the classical descriptor ratio test between the nearest neighbor and the second nearest neighbor, while we require a correspondence to have the highest score within its neighborhood with radius R to be selected as a seed point. This way we ensure both distinctiveness and coverage of seed points without causing grid artifacts, while keeping the selection completely parallel for efficient computation on GPU, as each correspondence can be scored and compared to neighbors for seed point selection independently of the final selection of the others.

3.3   Local Neighborhood Selection, Filtering and Validation

The assignment of correspondences to seed points is a crucial step in the algorithm as it builds the search space around each hypothesis of P to find the affine transform A. Wider neighborhoods can more easily include correct correspondences to fit A, while at the same time they implicitly loosen the affine constraints as they violate the assumption on locality.

Let $S_i = (\mathbf{x}_1^{S_i}, \mathbf{x}_2^{S_i})$ be a seed point correspondence, which induces a similarity transformation $(\alpha^{S_i} = \alpha_2^{S_i} - \alpha_1^{S_i}, \sigma^{S_i} = \sigma_2^{S_i}/\sigma_1^{S_i})$ from its local feature frame, decomposed in the orientation component α^{S_i} and scale component σ^{S_i}, and $\mathcal{N}_i \subseteq \mathcal{M}$ be the set of correspondences that are assigned to S_i to verify affine consistence. Let t_α and t_σ be thresholds for orientation and scale agreement between a candidate correspondence and the seed correspondence S_i. In analogy to [38], correspondence $(p_1, p_2) = ((\mathbf{x}_1, \mathbf{d}_1, \sigma_1, \alpha_1), (\mathbf{x}_2, \mathbf{d}_2, \sigma_2, \alpha_2)) \in \mathcal{M}$, which induces a transformation $(\alpha^p = \alpha_2 - \alpha_1, \sigma^p = \sigma_2/\sigma_1)$ is assigned to $\mathcal{N}_i$ if all the following constraints are satisfied:

$$\left\|\mathbf{x}_1^{S_i} - \mathbf{x}_1\right\| \le \lambda R_1, \quad \left\|\mathbf{x}_2^{S_i} - \mathbf{x}_2\right\| \le \lambda R_2, \quad \left|\alpha^{S_i} - \alpha^p\right| \le t_\alpha, \quad \left|\ln\left(\frac{\sigma^{S_i}}{\sigma^p}\right)\right| \le t_\sigma \quad (1)$$

where R_1 and R_2 are the radii used to spread seed points respectively in image I_1 and I_2, and λ is a hyperparameter that regulates the overlap between inclusion neighborhoods. Note that we consider angles α in modulo 2π lying within the interval $(-\pi, \pi]$. Different radii R_1 and R_2 are chosen proportionally to the image area to be invariant to image rescaling.

As from Eq. (1), we include in $\mathcal{N}_i$ all the correspondences in $\mathcal{M}$ that are locally consistent in both images and that induce a similarity transform (α^p, σ^p) which is consistent with $(\alpha^{S_i}, \sigma^{S_i})$ within independent thresholds t_α and t_σ. The independent thresholds encode a confidence over the reliability of the orientation and scale information provided by keypoints. The idea of verification using orientation and scale consistency has been repeatedly proposed for template matching [1,27] and image retrieval [2,17,40,54] as a coarse but powerful indication for outlier pruning.

For each set $\mathcal{N}_i$ corresponding to a seed point S_i, we translate the keypoint coordinates to have their origin in S_i, and we robustly fit an affine transformation A_i using RANSAC with a fixed number m of iterations to run efficiently on highly parallel hardware. At each iteration j, we uniformly sample two correspondences in $\mathcal{N}_i$ and fit the affine transform hypothesis A_i^j centered in S_i with this minimal set of constraints. As the best inlier threshold for RANSAC depends on the amount of noise on the inliers, we score each hypothesis based on multiple thresholds $t_1 \ldots t_n$ and select the best one a posteriori, as explained in the next section (Sect. 3.4). For a correspondence $(\mathbf{x}_1, \mathbf{x}_2)$ we can compute the residuals with respect to A_i^j and the corresponding inlier set $\mathcal{P}$ as follows:

$$R(A_i^j, \mathbf{x}_1, \mathbf{x}_2) = \left\|A_i^j \mathbf{x}_1 - \mathbf{x}_2\right\| \tag{2}$$

$$\mathcal{P}_i^j(t_k) = \left\{ (\mathbf{x}_1, \mathbf{x}_2) \in \mathcal{N}_i \ \middle|\ R(A_i^j, \mathbf{x}_1, \mathbf{x}_2) \le t_k \sqrt{|\det(A_i^j)|} \right\} \tag{3}$$

leading to the hypothesis scoring function C:

$$C(A_i^j, t_k) = \begin{cases} 0 & \text{if } \det(A_i^j) \ge t_\sigma^2 \vee \det(A_i^j) \le \frac{1}{t_\sigma^2} \\ \left|\mathcal{P}_i^j(t_k)\right| & \text{otherwise} \end{cases} \tag{4}$$

where $|.|$ over a set is the count of its elements. Notice that in Eq. (3) we rescale our tolerance threshold t_k with $\sqrt{|\det(A_i^j)|}$, so that t_k is expressed in pixels of error tolerated in image I_1, and it is rescaled in image I_2 according to the scale change encoded in A_i^j. Moreover, we do not accept affine hypotheses with extreme scale changes above t_σ to filter out degenerate cases, as evident in Eq. (4). We do not include any prior from α_i and σ_i from the seed correspondence S_i as they encode the local transformation as a similarity, which may not agree in orientation and scale with the same parameters in the fit affinity when skew is not negligible.

We finally select the affine model that maximizes the score C for each seed point S_i and for each threshold $t_k \in \{t_1 \ldots t_n\}$, we fit A_{i,t_k}^* as the least squares solution that minimizes the residuals on the highest scoring inlier set $\mathcal{P}_i^*(t_k)$.

3.4   Adaptive Assumption Relaxation

Threshold t_k directly determines the tolerance for deviations from the affine model that would hold when all assumptions discussed in Sect. 3.1 are valid. Increasing values for t_k thus relaxes the assumptions, while reducing the reliability of the scoring function C as more outliers pass the checks. The RANSAC inlier count consistently increases in the presence of only outliers with increasing t_k, while it increases strongly for lower thresholds in the presence of noisy inliers. In the following we will make very similar assumptions to [48] about the inlier and outlier distributions.

Let us assume that outlier correspondences $(\mathbf{x}_1^o, \mathbf{x}_2^o)$ are independent and uniformly distributed around S_i within radius λR_1 in I_1, as we only consider correspondences lying within such radius from S_i. Given an affine transform A_i^j then their images in I_2 are uniformly distributed in an area of size $|\det(A_i^j)|\pi\lambda^2 R_1^2$. Given threshold t_k, the acceptance region in I_2 is a circle of radius $t_k\sqrt{|\det(A_i^j)|}$ centered in $A_i^j\mathbf{x}_1^o$, thus having area $\pi t_k^2|\det(A_i^j)|$. The probability of a single outlier correspondence to be counted as inlier in a RANSAC iteration is thus:

$$p_o = \frac{\pi t_k^2|\det(A_i^j)|}{|\det(A_i^j)|\pi\lambda^2 R_1^2} = \frac{t_k^2}{\lambda^2 R_1^2} \ . \tag{5}$$

And the number of positively counted outliers in a single RANSAC iteration follows the distribution $\mathcal{B}(n_o, p_o)$ where $\mathcal{B}$ is binomial and n_o is the number of outliers included in $\mathcal{N}_i$. Let $MAX(n, \mathcal{Y})$ be the distribution obtained by taking the maximum value of n independent random variables following the distribution $\mathcal{Y}$, then the m-iteration RANSAC score $C_{i,k}^*$ of an outlier seed correspondence S_i with all outlier correspondences in $\mathcal{N}_i$ follows the distribution:

$$C_{i,t_k}^* \sim MAX(m, \mathcal{B}(\|\mathcal{N}_i\|, p_o)) \ . \tag{6}$$

Let us now assume that inlier correspondences $(\mathbf{x}_1^i, \mathbf{x}_2^i)$ have dependent distributions of $\mathbf{x}_1^i$ and $\mathbf{x}_2^i$ such that $\mathbf{x}_2^i \sim \mathcal{N}(A_i^*\mathbf{x}_1^i, \sigma^2 I)$. Thus, squared residuals follow

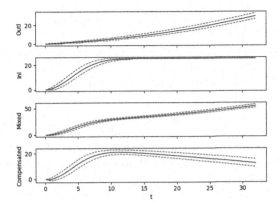

Fig. 2. Simulated inlier count distributions with varying threshold t_k according to our model, with 90% upper and lower confidence intervals (red dashed) and expected value (blue solid). The parameters for this simulation are: $n_i = 25$, $n_o = 80$, $\sigma = 16$, $\lambda R_1 = 60$, $m = 128$. From top to bottom: count component only from outliers, count component only from inliers, overall count distribution, and compensated count. (Color figure online)

a chi-square distribution with two degrees of fredom $R(A_i^*, \mathbf{x}_1^i, \mathbf{x}_2^i)^2 \sim \sigma^2 \chi_2^2$, and the RANSAC score distribution for only n_i inlier correspondences follows the binomial $C_{i,t_k}^* \sim \mathcal{B}(n_i, P_k^i)$ where $P_k^i = P(\sigma^2 \chi_2^2 \leq t_k^2 \det(A_i^*))$ is the probability of an inlier to meet threshold t_k. Considering n_i inlier and n_o outlier correspondences in the same set, assuming independence and assuming that the RANSAC iterations m are enough to find A_i^*, we can approximate the final score distribution as:

$$C_{i,t_k}^* \sim \mathcal{B}(n_i, P_k^i) + MAX\left(\left\lceil m\frac{n_i^2}{(n_o+n_i)^2}\right\rceil, \mathcal{B}(\|\mathcal{N}_i\|, p_o)\right) \ . \tag{7}$$

We correct the number of RANSAC iterations in the outlier counts distribution to consider only the RANSAC iterations that actually sample two inliers.

As we intend to compensate the influence of outliers in RANSAC inlier counts, we subtract from all scores $C_{i,k}^*$ the expected score of the inlier-free case as an upper bound of the actual influence of the outliers. As shown in Fig. 2, this allows to clean the inlier count signal from RANSAC to highlight the threshold range where most inliers are included without exceeding with outlier inclusion.

A perfectly compensated inlier count signal has constant expected value after all inliers are included in the counts. However, outliers still represent a zero-mean noise that can make the optimal threshold unclear. We robustify this approach by overcompensation: the overestimation of the outlier compensation causes their component to have degreasing negative mean. As a result, the best range of thresholds is more robustly highlighted as a peak in the overcompensated inlier counts, as in the last plot of Fig. 2.

Let $\mathbb{E}_o$ be the expectation assuming all outliers, then for each seed correspondence S_i we select the threshold $t_*^i = \text{argmax}_{t_k} \, C_{i,t_k}^* - \mathbb{E}_o \left[C_{i,t_k}^* \right]$ that maximizes the compensated inlier count of the best fit model. We then output all inliers in $\mathcal{N}_i$ included in the set of inliers $\mathcal{P}_i^*(t_*^i)$ for the best threshold, if and only if $C_{i,t_*^i}^* - \mathbb{E}_o \left[C_{i,t_*^i}^* \right] \geq 3$ to ensure that we have a minimal number of inliers and suppress noise from outliers.

As a final robustness step, if only $s < 20$ seed points passed the inlier count test, we also output the top $20 - s$ correspondences in $\mathcal{M}$ based on the ratio-test score. This is to ensure that, when we detect a failure of our procedure, we can still output a set of confident matches. However, in our experiments we observed no significant variation in performance due to this option, which triggers only in extreme cases.

More implementation details and our hyperparameter setup are available in the supplementary material.

4 Experiments

Our experiments aim at comparing our method with existing state-of-the-art methods in Sect. 4.3, and to understand the influence of each component of our method with ablation studies in Sect. 4.4. All experiments measure relative pose estimation performance under the same pipeline and on the same datasets. We evaluate on the same test sets as OA-Net [57], NGRANSAC [7] and GMS [6]: the same four scenes from YFCC100M [46], two from Strecha [44] and fifteen from SUN3D [56] as [7,57], and the same six sequences from TUM [45] as [6].

4.1 Evaluation Pipeline

Our evaluation pipeline aims at measuring relative pose estimation performance within the same settings. More specifically, all methods receive exactly the same keypoints as input and need to output a set of matches that will be used to robustly fit an essential matrix, which is decomposed to rotation and translation. We then measure the rotation and translation errors in degrees and take the maximum of the two, and report the exact Area Under the Curve (AUC) with thresholds of 5, 10, and 20 degrees.

The keypoints are all extracted with OpenCV SIFT [27] with the same parameters as in the code provided by OA-Net [57] and NGRANSAC [7], with a maximum number of 8000 keypoints per image. Keypoints with locations, descriptors, orientation and scale are provided to the matching methods, and matches are produced. For fitting the essential matrix we use the LO-RANSAC [11] implementation in COLMAP [41,42] with minimum 10^3 iterations and maximum 10^4, unless differently specified. The intrinsic camera calibration is assumed to be known and is taken from ground truth.

Table 1. Comparative experiments with the state of the art in indoor and outdoor scenes. All methods fit the essential matrix with LO-RANSAC with maximum 10^4 iterations, except *Ratio test (100k)* that uses 10^5 LO-RANSAC iterations and MAGSAC which runs Ratio test + 100k iterations of MAGSAC. All numbers are in percentages.

Method	TUM [45]			SUN3D [56]			YFCC100M [46]		
	AUC5	AUC10	AUC20	AUC5	AUC10	AUC20	AUC5	AUC10	AUC20
Ours	**24.7**	**37.2**	**48.4**	**7.6**	**18.3**	**33.2**	**57.8**	**71.1**	**81.7**
OA-Net [57]	20.9	32.2	43.3	6.9	16.3	29.4	53.5	66.0	76.7
NGRANSAC [7]	19.4	29.6	38.7	6.2	15.0	27.3	53.8	66.7	77.7
GMS [6]	19.6	30.5	41.3	6.8	15.9	29.1	52.3	65.0	76.0
Ratio test [27] (10k)	16.1	24.8	33.6	5.9	14.1	25.6	51.9	64.9	76.3
Ratio test [27] (100k)	17.3	26.6	36.2	6.1	14.5	26.3	53.2	66.3	77.5
MAGSAC [5]	17.5	27.2	36.5	5.9	14.6	27.0	47.2	58.9	70.6

4.2 Datasets

We evaluate our method on large and diverse indoor and outdoor datasets, using the same scenes as the methods we compare with. For outdoor scenes we use the YFCC100M [46] internet photos, that were later organized into 72 scenes [16] reconstructed with the Structure from Motion software VisualSfM [51,52], providing bundle adjusted camera poses, intrinsics and triangulated point clouds. We select scenes and image couples as to reproduce the test set used by [7,30,57], thus we used the same six scenes, including the two from Strecha [44], with the same sampling procedure. From now on when we refer to YFCC100M, we are referring to the four scenes actually coming from YFCC100M *and* the two coming from Strecha. All images are used with the original resolution.

For indoor scenes we use six sequences from the TUM [45] visual odometry benchmark and the SUN3D [56] dataset, both of which provide ground truth poses together with the RGB images. In particular, for TUM we select the same sequences as the authors of GMS [6], but we use a different subsampling scheme to provide a wider range of image transformations. We take one keyframe every 150 frames, and match it with other 9 images sampled at 15 frames intervals from it. This ensures a sufficient image overlap while gradually increasing the difficulty of the image pair, differentiating the break-down point of the competing alternatives. On SUN3D we use the same fifteen scenes and sampling procedure as [7,30,57]. All images are used with the original resolution.

4.3 Comparison with the State of the Art

We compare our method against sample representatives of the current state of the art. GMS (Grid-based Motion Statistics) [6] is a non-learned method that models the statistics of having locally consistent matches and filters matches based on a statistical significance test over large groups. Designed with the objective of being fast, the authors use 10 000 ORB features [35]. However, we found that with appropriate tuning the performance is higher using our SIFT setup

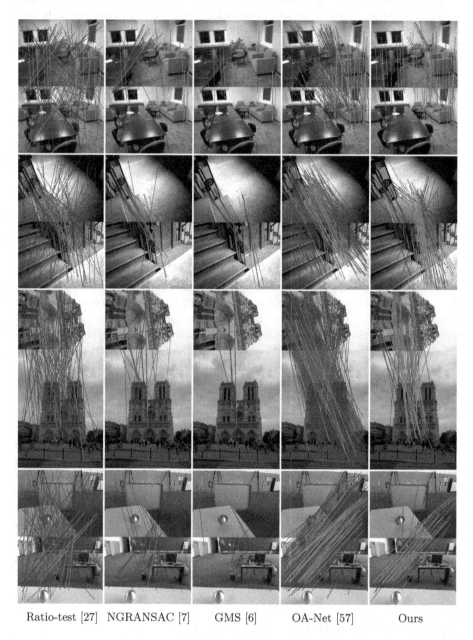

Ratio-test [27]   NGRANSAC [7]   GMS [6]   OA-Net [57]   Ours

Fig. 3. Success cases from our experiments. Matches agreeing with ground truth epipolar geometry are shown in green, others are in red. Examples include cases with very sparse correspondences, local repeated structures, weak texture, strong rotations and perspective deformations. (Color figure online)

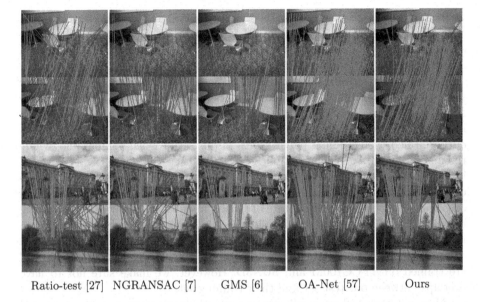

Ratio-test [27]   NGRANSAC [7]   GMS [6]   OA-Net [57]   Ours

Fig. 4. Failure cases from our experiments. Matches agreeing with ground truth epipolar geometry are shown in green, others are in red. The main failure case for our method is wide repeated structures along the image, which can locally mimic the correspondence distribution of the correct region. (Color figure online)

with a ratio-test filtering beforehand, as suggested by the authors. Thus, we report these results using the public OpenCV implementation of the method with rotation and scale invariance. NGRANSAC (Neural Guided RANSAC) [7] uses a neural network to predict sampling probabilities for RANSAC from keypoint locations and ratio-test scores. We use the pre-trained models provided by the authors for essential matrix estimation with SIFT keypoints pre-filtered with a ratio-test of 0.8 (SIFT+Ratio+NG-RANSAC(+SI) label in [7]), which have been trained on both YFCC100M [46] and SUN3D [56]. We experimentally found that, although the method outputs an essential matrix, better performance is achieved by using LO-RANSAC only on the inlier set found by NGRANSAC. Thus, after running both versions we report these results. OA-Net (Order Aware Network) [57] learns to infer confidence scores on nearest neighbor matches looking at the global keypoint spatial consistency. They propose a soft assignment to latent clusters in canonical order, and an order-aware upsampling operation that restores the original size of the input to infer confidences. The authors provide a model pre-trained on both YFCC100M [46] and SUN3D [56]. Our SIFT parameters are taken from the public implementation provided by the authors with the pre-trained model. MAGSAC [5] is a modern RANSAC variant based on the idea of marginalizing over a range of possible inlier thresholds for the purpose of model scoring. In our experiments we run MAGSAC with 100k iterations on correspondences filtered by the ratio-test with a 0.8 threshold. Finally we include a simple baseline using the standard ratio test with a 0.8 threshold, as the default in SiftGPU [50] used in COLMAP [41]. We also try the performance of this simple baseline with ten times more LO-RANSAC iterations, going from the 10^4 used for all methods to 10^5 iterations.

Table 1 reports the results of our experiments on both indoor and outdoor scenes. For comparability and deeper insights we report additional metrics in the supplementary material, including inlier statistics and an upper bound approximation of the AUC used by some of the methods. All the competitor methods outperformed their original paper scores in our setup when comparable, where the main difference is the use of LO-RANSAC rather than OpenCV's RANSAC implementation. We found that local optimization can refine the solution by some degrees, improving the scores for low errors. Results show that our method can drastically outperform current state of the art in outdoor scenarios by exploiting the planarity of most scenes and buildings, while still being very competitive in indoor scenarios where our assumptions are violated more often. While TUM is a completely new dataset for all learned methods, both OA-Net and NGRANSAC are trained on YFCC100M and SUN3D. However, we make sure not to have overlaps between our test set and their training set.

Figures 3 and 4 show qualitative results that represent success cases and failure cases for our method with respect to others. Figure 3 shows how our method captures consistent global motion even when available correct matches are sparse, and is fully invariant to strong rotation and scale changes. As affine coherence in keypoint patterns can give confidence to matches even when descriptors are ambiguous, our method is able to mine correspondences even from almost textureless surfaces or in the presence of locally repeating structures. However, this is not always the case for widely repeating regular structures, as illustrated in Fig. 4. In such cases, there is one or more independent clusters of wrong correspondences that locally mimic the distribution of the correct correspondences. Global approaches in this case have a chance to disambiguate the right cluster, and learned approaches can give priority to the cluster compatible with more likely motions, as OA-Net is doing.

4.4   Ablation Studies

We aim at understanding the contribution of each element we introduce in our method, thus we extensively evaluate different versions of our method subtracting one element at a time. For comparability with other methods, we run the same experiments in the same setting as in Sect. 4.3 on TUM and YFCC100M.

We target three optional steps in our pipeline and re-evaluate removing one or multiple of them. We report as *Full* the complete method, denoted as "Ours" in Sect. 3.1. We remove the filtering with side information in Eq. (1) for the *No-Side* method, we skip refitting the estimated affinities on the final set of inliers for the *No-Refit* method, and we drop adaptive thresholding in the *No-Adaptive* method. We run this last ablation with all the evaluated thresholds of the full method and choose only the one scoring best with respect to ground truth.

Table 2. Ablation tests with varying setups of our method. The numbers are comparable with Table 1. Areas under the curve (AUC) are in percentage; times in milliseconds include nearest neighbor search and outlier rejection. Results and timings for OA-Net [57] are additionally reported for better comparability.

Method	TUM [45]				YFCC100M [46]			
	AUC5	AUC10	AUC20	time	AUC5	AUC10	AUC20	time
Full (Ours)	**24.7**	**37.2**	**48.4**	26ms	**57.8**	71.1	81.7	40ms
No-Side	22.4	33.8	44.2	42ms	54.5	67.4	78.4	64ms
No-Adaptive	22.4	33.7	43.8	17ms	57.5	70.8	81.4	28ms
No-Refit-No-Adaptive	24.4	36.7	47.8	**16ms**	57.8	**71.2**	**81.8**	**26ms**
No-Refit	23.8	35.5	45.5	20ms	57.0	70.25	80.9	33ms
OA-Net [57]	20.9	32.2	43.3	21ms	53.5	66.0	76.7	41ms

We report the results of our ablation in Table 2. On the full method, we measure a runtime of 20–40 ms on image pairs with 4000–8000 extracted keypoints, running on an RTX2080Ti. Since most of the methods we compare with in our experiments provide CPU implementations, or important CPU preprocessing steps, their runtimes are usually higher but not directly comparable with ours; however we found that the public implementation of OA-Net [57] also performs all operations on PyTorch as we do. We measure runtimes of 20–40 ms on the same hardware and keypoint collections. For comparability with the ablations, we also report the performance of OA-Net [57] in Table 2.

The full adaptive method generally outperforms the best fixed threshold, showing that it can make a positive decision on which threshold to use case by case. In general, the adaptive thresholding increases the generalization performance of the method, allowing it to operate effectively in diverse settings without the need to decide for a single fixed threshold. Moreover, as refitting and running multiple thresholds is overall a significant component of our runtime, the ablated versions, particularly the *No-Refit-No-Adaptive*, are straightforward solutions to tune the trade-off between quality and runtime, especially for a fixed domain in which generalization of performance is not a real concern. We finally highlight that smart classical filters can increase both runtime and quality as they reduce the size of the problem by pruning grossly incorrect correspondences at the beginning, and at the same time reduce the number of outliers, providing a more stable inlier count signal.

5   Conclusions

In this paper we proposed a method for outlier rejection of an initial set of putative correspondences inspired by local consistency constraints which have been re-discovered repeatedly in the last years [6,17,19,25–27,38,58]. We show that, by proposing an adaptive relaxation of the underlying assumptions for local consistency, we improve the generalization of this approach to make it competitive in diverse and challenging scenarios. Our method can greatly outperform the current state of the art in favorable settings, where the planarity assumption can be more discriminative, while being on par on unfavorable, less structured ones. At the same time, we formulate our approach as a highly parallel algorithm to be run on modern GPUs in the order of the tens of milliseconds.

Acknowledgements. This work was supported by a Google Focused Research Award, by the Swedish Foundation for Strategic Research (Semantic Mapping and Visual Navigation for Smart Robots), the Chalmers AI Research Centre (CHAIR) (VisLocLearn) and Innosuisse funding (Grant No. 34475.1 IP-ICT). Viktor Larsson was supported by an ETH Zurich Postdoctoral Fellowship.

References

1. Albarelli, A., Rodola, E., Torsello, A.: Robust game-theoretic inlier selection for bundle adjustment. In: International Symposium on 3D Data Processing, Visualization and Transmission (3DPVT2010) (2010)
2. Avrithis, Y., Tolias, G.: Hough pyramid matching: speeded-up geometry re-ranking for large scale image retrieval. Int. J. Comput. Vis. (IJCV) **107**(1), 1–19 (2014). https://doi.org/10.1007/s11263-013-0659-3
3. Bailey, T., Durrant-Whyte, H.: Simultaneous localization and mapping (slam): part ii. IEEE Rob. Autom. Mag. **13**(3), 108–117 (2006)
4. Barath, D., Matas, J.: Graph-cut RANSAC. In: Computer Vision and Pattern Recognition (CVPR) (2018)
5. Barath, D., Matas, J., Noskova, J.: MAGSAC: marginalizing sample consensus. In: Computer Vision and Pattern Recognition (CVPR) (2019)
6. Bian, J., Lin, W.Y., Matsushita, Y., Yeung, S.K., Nguyen, T.D., Cheng, M.M.: GMS: grid-based motion statistics for fast, ultra-robust feature correspondence. In: Computer Vision and Pattern Recognition (CVPR) (2017)
7. Brachmann, E., Rother, C.: Neural-guided RANSAC: learning where to sample model hypotheses. In: International Conference on Computer Vision (ICCV) (2019)
8. Cech, J., Matas, J., Perdoch, M.: Efficient sequential correspondence selection by cosegmentation. Trans. Pattern Anal. Mach. Intell. (PAMI) **32**(9), 1568–1581 (2010)
9. Chum, O., Matas, J.: Matching with PROSAC-progressive sample consensus. In: Computer Vision and Pattern Recognition (CVPR) (2005)
10. Chum, O., Matas, J.: Optimal randomized RANSAC. Trans. Pattern Anal. Mach. Intell. (PAMI) **30**(8), 1472–1482 (2008)
11. Chum, O., Matas, J., Kittler, J.: Locally optimized RANSAC. In: Michaelis, B., Krell, G. (eds.) DAGM 2003. LNCS, vol. 2781, pp. 236–243. Springer, Heidelberg (2003). https://doi.org/10.1007/978-3-540-45243-0_31
12. Dang, Z., Yi, K.M., Hu, Y., Wang, F., Fua, P., Salzmann, M.: Eigendecomposition-free training of deep networks with zero eigenvalue-based losses. In: Ferrari, V., Hebert, M., Sminchisescu, C., Weiss, Y. (eds.) ECCV 2018. LNCS, vol. 11209, pp. 792–807. Springer, Cham (2018). https://doi.org/10.1007/978-3-030-01228-1_47
13. Durrant-Whyte, H., Bailey, T.: Simultaneous localization and mapping: part i. IEEE Rob. Autom. Mag. **13**(2), 99–110 (2006)
14. Fischler, M.A., Bolles, R.C.: Random sample consensus: a paradigm for model fitting with applications to image analysis and automated cartography. Commun. ACM **24**(6), 381–395 (1981)

15. Hartley, R.I., Sturm, P.: Triangulation. Comput. Vis. Image Underst. (CVIU) **68**(2), 146–157 (1997)
16. Heinly, J., Schönberger, J.L., Dunn, E., Frahm, J.M.: Reconstructing the world* in six days *(as captured by the yahoo 100 million image dataset). In: Computer Vision and Pattern Recognition (CVPR) (2015)
17. Jegou, H., Douze, M., Schmid, C.: Hamming embedding and weak geometric consistency for large scale image search. In: Forsyth, D., Torr, P., Zisserman, A. (eds.) ECCV 2008. LNCS, vol. 5302, pp. 304–317. Springer, Heidelberg (2008). https://doi.org/10.1007/978-3-540-88682-2_24
18. Johns, E., Yang, G.Z.: RANSAC with 2D geometric cliques for image retrieval and place recognition. In: Computer Vision and Pattern Recognition Workshops (CVPRW) (2015)
19. Jung, I.K., Lacroix, S.: A robust interest points matching algorithm. In: International Conference on Computer Vision (ICCV) (2001)
20. Köser, K.: Geometric estimation with local affine frames and free-form surfaces. Ph.D. thesis, University of Kiel (2009). http://d-nb.info/994782322
21. Lebeda, K., Matas, J., Chum, O.: Fixing the locally optimized RANSAC-full experimental evaluation. In: British Machine Vision Conference (BMVC) (2012)
22. Leordeanu, M., Hebert, M.: A spectral technique for correspondence problems using pairwise constraints. In: International Conference on Computer Vision (ICCV) (2005)
23. Li, X., Larson, M., Hanjalic, A.: Pairwise geometric matching for large-scale object retrieval. In: Computer Vision and Pattern Recognition (CVPR) (2015)
24. Li, Y., Snavely, N., Huttenlocher, D.P.: Location recognition using prioritized feature matching. In: Daniilidis, K., Maragos, P., Paragios, N. (eds.) ECCV 2010. LNCS, vol. 6312, pp. 791–804. Springer, Heidelberg (2010). https://doi.org/10.1007/978-3-642-15552-9_57
25. Lin, W.-Y., Liu, S., Jiang, N., Do, M.N., Tan, P., Lu, J.: RepMatch: robust feature matching and pose for reconstructing modern cities. In: Leibe, B., Matas, J., Sebe, N., Welling, M. (eds.) ECCV 2016. LNCS, vol. 9905, pp. 562–579. Springer, Cham (2016). https://doi.org/10.1007/978-3-319-46448-0_34
26. Lin, W.Y., et al.: CODE: coherence based decision boundaries for feature correspondence. Trans. Pattern Anal. Mach. Intell. (PAMI) **40**(1), 34–47 (2017)
27. Lowe, D.G.: Distinctive image features from scale-invariant keypoints. Int. J. Comput. Vis. (IJCV) **60**(2), 91–110 (2004). https://doi.org/10.1023/B:VISI.0000029664.99615.94
28. Ma, J., Zhao, J., Jiang, J., Zhou, H., Guo, X.: Locality preserving matching. Int. J. Comput. Vis. (IJCV) **127**(5), 512–531 (2019). https://doi.org/10.1007/s11263-018-1117-z
29. Montemerlo, M., Thrun, S., Koller, D., Wegbreit, B., et al.: FastSLAM: a factored solution to the simultaneous localization and mapping problem. In: Conference on Artificial Intelligence (AAAI) (2002)
30. Yi, K.M., Trulls, E., Ono, Y., Lepetit, V., Salzmann, M., Fua, P.: Learning to find good correspondences. In: Computer Vision and Pattern Recognition (CVPR) (2018)
31. Ni, K., Jin, H., Dellaert, F.: GroupSAC: efficient consensus in the presence of groupings. In: International Conference on Computer Vision (ICCV) (2009)
32. Raguram, R., Chum, O., Pollefeys, M., Matas, J., Frahm, J.M.: USAC: a universal framework for random sample consensus. Trans. Pattern Anal. Mach. Intell. (PAMI) **35**(8), 2022–2038 (2012)

33. Ranftl, R., Koltun, V.: Deep fundamental matrix estimation. In: Ferrari, V., Hebert, M., Sminchisescu, C., Weiss, Y. (eds.) ECCV 2018. LNCS, vol. 11205, pp. 292–309. Springer, Cham (2018). https://doi.org/10.1007/978-3-030-01246-5_18
34. Rocco, I., Cimpoi, M., Arandjelović, R., Torii, A., Pajdla, T., Sivic, J.: Neighbourhood consensus networks. In: Neural Information Processing Systems (NeurIPS) (2018)
35. Rublee, E., Rabaud, V., Konolige, K., Bradski, G.: ORB: an efficient alternative to SIFT or SURF. In: International Conference on Computer Vision (ICCV) (2011)
36. Sarlin, P.E., Cadena, C., Siegwart, R., Dymczyk, M.: From coarse to fine: robust hierarchical localization at large scale. In: Computer Vision and Pattern Recognition (CVPR) (2019)
37. Sarlin, P.E., DeTone, D., Malisiewicz, T., Rabinovich, A.: SuperGlue: learning feature matching with graph neural networks. In: Computer Vision and Pattern Recognition (CVPR), pp. 4938–4947 (2020)
38. Sattler, T., Leibe, B., Kobbelt, L.: SCRAMSAC: improving RANSAC's efficiency with a spatial consistency filter. In: International Conference on Computer Vision (ICCV) (2009)
39. Sattler, T., et al.: Benchmarking 6DOF outdoor visual localization in changing conditions. In: Proceedings of the IEEE Conference on Computer Vision and Pattern Recognition, pp. 8601–8610 (2018)
40. Schönberger, J.L., Price, T., Sattler, T., Frahm, J.-M., Pollefeys, M.: A vote-and-verify strategy for fast spatial verification in image retrieval. In: Lai, S.-H., Lepetit, V., Nishino, K., Sato, Y. (eds.) ACCV 2016. LNCS, vol. 10111, pp. 321–337. Springer, Cham (2017). https://doi.org/10.1007/978-3-319-54181-5_21
41. Schönberger, J.L., Frahm, J.M.: Structure-from-motion revisited. In: Computer Vision and Pattern Recognition (CVPR) (2016)
42. Schönberger, J.L., Zheng, E., Frahm, J.-M., Pollefeys, M.: Pixelwise view selection for unstructured multi-view stereo. In: Leibe, B., Matas, J., Sebe, N., Welling, M. (eds.) ECCV 2016. LNCS, vol. 9907, pp. 501–518. Springer, Cham (2016). https://doi.org/10.1007/978-3-319-46487-9_31
43. Sivic, J., Zisserman, A.: Efficient visual search of videos cast as text retrieval. Trans. Pattern Anal. Mach. Intell. (PAMI) 31(4), 591–606 (2008)
44. Strecha, C., Von Hansen, W., Van Gool, L., Fua, P., Thoennessen, U.: On benchmarking camera calibration and multi-view stereo for high resolution imagery. In: Computer Vision and Pattern Recognition (CVPR) (2008)
45. Sturm, J., Engelhard, N., Endres, F., Burgard, W., Cremers, D.: A benchmark for the evaluation of RGB-D SLAM systems. In: International Conference on Intelligent Robots and Systems (IROS) (2012)
46. Thomee, B., Shamma, D.A., Friedland, G., Elizalde, B., Ni, K., Poland, D., Borth, D., Li, L.J.: YFCC100M: the new data in multimedia research. Commun. ACM 59(2), 64–73 (2016)
47. Torr, P.H., Nasuto, S.J., Bishop, J.M.: NAPSAC: high noise, high dimensional robust estimation-it's in the bag. In: British Machine Vision Conference (BMVC) (2002)
48. Torr, P.H., Zisserman, A.: MLESAC: a new robust estimator with application to estimating image geometry. Comput. Vis. Image Underst. (CVIU) 78(1), 138–156 (2000)
49. Ullman, S.: The interpretation of structure from motion. Proc. R. Soc. Lond. B Biol. Sci. 203(1153), 405–426 (1979)
50. Wu, C.: SiftGPU: a GPU implementation of scale invariant feature transform (SIFT) (2011). http://cs.unc.edu/~ccwu/siftgpu

51. Wu, C., Agarwal, S., Curless, B., Seitz, S.M.: Multicore bundle adjustment. In: Computer Vision and Pattern Recognition (CVPR) (2011)
52. Wu, C., et al.: VisualSFM: a visual structure from motion system (2011)
53. Wu, X., Kashino, K.: Adaptive dither voting for robust spatial verification. In: International Conference on Computer Vision (ICCV) (2015)
54. Wu, X., Kashino, K.: Robust spatial matching as ensemble of weak geometric relations. In: British Machine Vision Conference (BMVC) (2015)
55. Wu, Z., Ke, Q., Isard, M., Sun, J.: Bundling features for large scale partial-duplicate web image search. In: Computer Vision and Pattern Recognition (CVPR) (2009)
56. Xiao, J., Owens, A., Torralba, A.: SUN3D: a database of big spaces reconstructed using SFM and object labels. In: International Conference on Computer Vision (ICCV) (2013)
57. Zhang, J., et al.: Learning two-view correspondences and geometry using order-aware network (2019)
58. Zhang, Z., Deriche, R., Faugeras, O., Luong, Q.T.: A robust technique for matching two uncalibrated images through the recovery of the unknown epipolar geometry. Artif. Intell. 78(1–2), 87–119 (1995)
59. Zhao, C., Cao, Z., Li, C., Li, X., Yang, J.: NM-Net: mining reliable neighbors for robust feature correspondences. In: Computer Vision and Pattern Recognition (CVPR) (2019)

Author Index

Printed in the United States
By Bookmasters